Contents

Business
fc Foundation Degrees
and Higher Awards

Rob Dransfield • Eddie Fox • Philip Guy • Dave Needham • Janice Wilde

www.heinemann.co.uk
✓ Free online support
✓ Useful weblinks
✓ 24 hour online ordering

01865 888058

Heinemann
Inspiring generations

Heinemann Educational Publishers
Halley Court, Jordan Hill, Oxford OX2 8EJ
Part of Harcourt Education

Heinemann is the registered trademark of Harcourt Education Limited

© text Rob Dransfield, Eddie Fox, Philip Guy, Dave Needham, Janice Wilde, 2004
© original illustrations Harcourt Education Limited, 2004
© cover photograph Science Photo Library

First published 2004

09 08 07 06 05 04
10 9 8 7 6 5 4 3 2 1

Illustrations on pages 10, 33, 52, 127, 294–296, 438 and 520 by Keith Richmond
Cover design by Wooden Ark Studio
Project managed, designed, and typeset in Scala Sans and Scala Serif by Bookcraft Ltd, Stroud, Gloucestershire
Printed in the UK by Bath Press Ltd

British Library Cataloguing in Publication Data is available from the British Library on request.

ISBN 0 435 28533 5

Acknowledgements
Every effort has been made to contact copyright holders of material reproduced in this book. Any omissions will be rectified in subsequent printings if notice is given to the publishers.

Websites
Please note that the examples of websites suggested in this book were up to date at the time of writing. It is essential for tutors to preview each site before using it to ensure that the URL is still accurate and the content is appropriate. We suggest that tutors bookmark useful sites and consider enabling students to access them through the school or college intranet.

Introduction

This book is designed to cover the first two years of a degree programme, and comprises the essential content and skills required for Foundation Degrees and Higher Nationals.

The book follows the specifications set out by Edexcel to provide students with a firmly-grounded business degree which can then be topped up with a further year of full-time study leading to a BA or BSc Honours Degree. The book also covers important elements of final year degree studies.

The Foundation Degree in Business is a new development, providing an avenue for many people seeking degree-level qualifications who are currently working for organisations in a range of jobs, including personnel and recruitment, office and administrative work, marketing, leisure and tourism management, advertising and promotion, retail management, financial services, and many other areas. The Foundation Degree helps to complement their work-based development and to give them an important formal qualification in a world in which learning and personal development is highly valued, and in which individuals are seeking accreditation and recognition for their capabilities.

The book covers in detail the core units of the specifications set out for Higher Awards and Foundation Degrees by Edexcel, as well as providing appropriate assessment activities and details of further reading and research.

The book covers the following key areas:

1 **Learning strategies** Introducing students to approaches for undertaking degree-level study, outlining the importance of reading texts and journals, the Internet, and collaborative teamwork.

2 **Professional development** All students following degree courses are expected to keep a portfolio for their own professional development, which is well-organised, reflects on their learning, personal and career development, and can easily be read by an interested third party such as a potential employer.

3 **Work-based learning** This section is designed for students who are already at work, or who carry out work placements as part of their degree course. It identifies ways of making the experience of work meaningful in the context of degree studies, while accrediting the value of work-based learning outcomes.

4 **Research project** Provides a user-friendly outline of approaches to research methods and techniques, and explains how to use a range of appropriate primary and secondary sources.

5 **Essential core business content** Covers the content of the Foundation Degree and Higher Award specification for the core areas of marketing, finance and managing financial decisions, organisations and behaviour, the business environment, business decision making, and business strategy.

6 **Business law (optional unit)** Much of the work included here stems from the business strand of the Business, Information and Communications Technology course at The Nottingham Trent University and similar courses run at New College Nottingham. These have been highly popular courses with outstanding results with many of its students going on to take up important and well-paid positions in the world of business and modern information and communications technology.

The contributors

Formerly at the University of Stirling, **Dave Needham** (Units 8 and 10) has worked both in schools and further education. Many of his articles have appeared in national and international journals. With research interests in cognitive apprenticeship and technological enframing, he has written more than forty curriculum and academic texts, and is editor of *Vocational Education Today*.

Rob Dransfield (Units 1, 2, 3, 7, 9 and 11) is Senior Lecturer in Economics and Business at Nottingham Trent University. With a prolific writing record of more than fifty texts and assorted publications developed for academic markets, and a previous career as the Shell Senior Research Fellow, he is a well-known figure within the field of business education.

Formerly a bank manager, **Philip Guy** (Unit 5) has taught across a range of economic and business courses for more than twelve years. He has contributed to a number of publications, including Heinemann's *Marketing for Higher Awards*. Based at New College Nottingham, he has a number of senior responsibilities for a range of qualification routes.

Eddie Fox (Unit 6) entered teaching after working for a firm of chartered accountants. With nearly thirty years of teaching experience, he makes a valuable contribution to the writing team. He currently co-ordinates AAT qualifications at New College Nottingham.

Janice Wilde (Unit 4) recently graduated from Nottingham Trent University with a first-class honours degree. Having spent many years in insurance and financial services, she brings her valuable experience to this volume. She is currently pursuing a psychology-based career both in teaching and in local services.

Unit 1

Learning strategies

Starting a new degree-level course in business involves developing a range of new skills as well as building on those that you already have. At university you will be able to enjoy going to lectures and discussing new ideas with other students in tutorial sessions. At the same time you will have access to good quality Internet links, and a range of specialist books, periodicals and journals. This unit is designed to introduce you to a range of learning strategies that are typical of business degree courses, and help you start to make the transition from being a learner who depends primarily on lecturers and teachers to a self-managing student, increasingly confident in thinking out and developing your own learning plans.

Summary of learning outcomes

On completion of this unit you will be able to:

♦ identify the learning style that you prefer
♦ know how to prepare for and make effective notes in a lecture
♦ use appropriate reading sources for gathering information
♦ make use of business videos
♦ engage in tutorial discussions
♦ understand the important features of assignment work
♦ reference your work
♦ understand how to write an essay
♦ structure a business report
♦ make a presentation to other students and to other appropriate audiences
♦ understand teamworking and critically appraise your own teamworking skills
♦ appreciate the importance of prioritising in time management
♦ use the Internet for simple searches
♦ convert figures into percentages and calculate a percentage change.

Chapter 1

Introduction to learning strategies

The purpose of this unit is to introduce you to ways of learning on a business degree course. All of us need continually to improve our learning skills.

We can learn from our tutors and lecturers but we can also learn on our own by developing independent learning skills. During your business course you will progress increasingly towards becoming an independent learner.

Dependent learner

Heavily reliant on information and notes from course tutors.

Independent learner

Has developed the research skills to pursue own lines of enquiry and to find out things for themselves.

Figure 1.1   Dependent and independent learners

Independent learners have the confidence to manage their own learning because they have developed an understanding of the sorts of issues that are relevant and important to investigate, and have the necessary investigative techniques, such as searching the Internet, conducting interviews, and finding relevant articles in magazines and specialist journals. Unit 10 focuses on ways of developing research skills.

What type of learner are you?

From the outset it is important to stress that people like to learn in different ways. Psychologists have categorised the way we learn into four broad types. Few people fit neatly into any one type; many have a mixture of two or three styles. As you read through this chapter try to identify the style that most accurately describes the way you learn.

Activitists enjoy *doing*

You are open-minded and enthusiastic about new things. You'll try anything once. Your days are filled with activities. You tackle problems by brainstorming. Once the excitement of one challenge has died down, you look for the next. You are an outgoing person and like to be the centre of attention.

The sorts of learning activities you are most likely to enjoy are:

♦ active/doing sessions
♦ project work
♦ working in groups and brainstorming
♦ trips and visits
♦ role plays.

The areas you are most likely to need help with are:

♦ listening to long lectures
♦ carrying out background reading into a subject
♦ writing up projects
♦ analysing: finding out the meaning of information.

Pragmatists enjoy *trying*

You love new ideas and ways of doing things. You are keen to see whether theories work in practice. You get impatient if people talk too much rather than getting on with the task. You are very practical and down to earth. You see problems as a challenge. You're sure there is always a better way to do things. You believe that if something works then it must be good.

The sorts of learning activities that you are most likely to enjoy are:

♦ examples which show how theory is related to the real world
♦ role play
♦ trips and visits
♦ presenting ideas to others
♦ practical group work
♦ writing up projects
♦ using research findings.

The areas you are most likely to need help with are:

♦ group discussion on abstract ideas
♦ listening to theories
♦ doing background reading.

Reflectors enjoy *thinking*

You like to stand back and think before you act. You enjoy interacting with other people and enjoy watching and listening to others. You are quiet and thoughtful and like harmony. You like to have a good feel for a subject before talking about it. You look at the big picture of any topic and you are very ordered, calm and thorough.

The sorts of learning activities that you are most likely to enjoy are:

♦ thinking about what you have learnt before discussing it
♦ listening to experts
♦ trips and visits
♦ gathering views and opinions
♦ background reading
♦ doing and using your own research.

The areas you are most likely to need help with are:

♦ seeing the big picture before you go into the detail
♦ role play
♦ presenting ideas to a group.

Theorists enjoy *testing*

You are analytical and love detail. You take a logical, structured approach to everything you do. You are hard working and a perfectionist. You enjoy theories and concepts and are quick at pulling odd bits of information together into rational arguments. You do not like uncertainty or anyone being flippant about serious things.

The sorts of learning activities that you are most likely to enjoy are:

♦ lectures with lots of theory
♦ background reading
♦ writing up notes
♦ research
♦ analytical exercises.

ACTIVITY

This test will give you an idea about your preferred style of learning. Tick the statements that apply to you.

❶ In carrying out my work I like to be absolutely correct. ☐

❷ I quite like taking risks. ☐

❸ I don't mind at all if things get out of hand. ☐

❹ I like discussions and meetings to follow a pattern and timetable. ☐

❺ I prefer solving problems step by step rather than randomly. ☐

❻ I prefer simple straightforward things to complex ones. ☐

❼ I like to find out how things work. ☐

❽ I do whatever I need to do, to get the job done. ☐

❾ I often do things just for pleasure rather than thinking about them first. ☐

❿ I rarely take things for granted. I like to check things for myself. ☐

11 It doesn't matter how you do something as long as it works. ☐

12 I can't be bothered with rules and plans. They take all the fun away. ☐

13 The most important thing about what you learn is whether it works in practice. ☐

14 I'm always looking for new things to do. ☐

15 When I hear a new idea, I immediately start thinking how I can work it out. ☐

16 I am keen on fixed routines and timetables. ☐

17 I take great care to work things out. I don't like jumping to conclusions. ☐

18 I make decisions very carefully. I look at all the possibilities first. ☐

19 I don't like 'loose ends', I prefer things to fit into a kind of pattern. ☐

20 I get straight to the point in discussions. ☐

21 I like the challenge of new and direct things. ☐

22 I prefer thinking things through before coming to a conclusion. ☐

23 I don't find it easy to think of wild ideas off the top of my head. ☐

24 I love lots of information. The more I have to sift through the better. ☐

25 I prefer jumping in and doing things than planning in advance. ☐

26 I tend to judge other people's ideas on how well they will work in practice. ☐

27 You can't make a decision just because it feels right. You have to think about all the facts. ☐

28 I am fussy about how I do things: a bit of a perfectionist. ☐

29 I usually come up with lots of unusual ideas in discussions. ☐

30 In discussions, I only put forward ideas that I know will work. ☐

31 I look at problems from as many angles as possible before starting to solve them. ☐

32 Usually I talk more than I listen. ☐

33 Quite often I work out more practical ways of doing things. ☐

34 I believe that careful, logical thinking is the key to getting things done. ☐

35 If I am doing a piece of writing I make out several drafts first. ☐

36 I like to consider all the options before making up my mind. ☐

37 I don't like creative ideas because they are not very practical. ☐

38 Always look before you leap. ☐

39 I usually do more listening than talking. ☐

You can now check your answers to identify which learning style most accurately fits the way you prefer to work. The following responses are represented by:

Activist

2, 3, 9, 11, 12, 14, 21, 25, 29, 32.

Reflector

16, 17, 18, 22, 27, 31, 35, 36, 38, 39.

Theorist

1, 5, 10, 13, 15, 16, 19, 20, 23, 24, 28, 34, 37.

Pragmatist

4, 6, 7, 8, 12, 13, 15, 26, 30, 33.

Into which of the categories do your answers fit most frequently?

The areas you are most likely to need help with are:

♦ group discussion, especially talking about feelings and emotions
♦ presenting ideas to groups.

What to do in lectures

The purpose of lectures is to give an overview of subjects and topics. You will then need to fill in more detail by wider reading. Tutorials provide you with the opportunity to discuss the lectures and to ask questions. Tutorials are carried out in smaller sized groups.

Before the lecture

Find out if there is any background reading to be done before the lecture. Preparatory reading will help you to understand better what is being outlined.

Listening in lectures

Listening is perhaps more important than note taking because it enables you to achieve a better structure to your notes. Sometimes the structure will be given by the lecturer right at the beginning. Quickly take this down because you will then be able to use it as a set of sub-headings under which to write your notes. Listen for the verbal signposts that the lecturer is giving such as 'there are three main areas for discussion', 'the most important factor is' and so on.

Very often the lecturer will hand out a set of key notes for the lecture. If they are giving a PowerPoint presentation, they will often have a handout showing the slides they will use. You can then make notes alongside each of these slides.

Structuring notes

Key aspects of a notes structure include:

♦ breaking your notes down into a series of sub-headings
♦ numbering the points discussed under a given heading, or breaking them down into separate lines
♦ highlighting any examples which illustrate particular points.

If there are any points that you do not understand, highlight them in your notes or put a question mark so that you remember to bring up the topic in a tutorial or ask the lecturer at the end of the session.

Try not to use too many words. If you try to write down everything that the lecturer says you will quickly get left behind. If you do get left behind at any point, leave a gap in your notes so that you can copy up that section from a friend later.

Reading notes after the lecture

After the lecture read any handouts given and check that your notes make sense. Use highlighter pens to outline what you consider to be the most important aspects of the lecture. This will help you to revise the topic quickly at a later date or identify important sections for written assignments.

Storing your notes

Note storage is one of the most important skills required by a university student. The student who files his or her notes in a systematic and ordered way is most likely to feel confident when it comes to revising or assignment writing. The disorganised student is most likely to panic, become stressed and depressed because he or she cannot cope with the chaos of poor structure.

Students need to choose a system of storage which suits them and the available space. Popular methods are:

♦ colour-coded sections in a lever arch file
♦ saving under clearly marked titles on disk or hard drive of a computer, with back-up copies on floppy disk.

Reading for learning

Some people prefer reading more than others. However, for any degree course you will need to read to develop a knowledge base, and business is no exception.

Business is a moving field in which ideas and theories are continually changing. Today's successful business may struggle unless it adapts and changes to be successful in an ever-changing world. It is therefore essential to keep abreast of new ideas and events.

This text is based on up-to-date theory and case study. In addition you will need to use your library to find:

♦ supplementary texts which go into more detail on specific issues (see reading lists at end of each unit or chapter); use the on-line library catalogue to locate relevant texts
♦ newspaper and periodical articles: most libraries keep the most recent newspapers and magazines on a special display shelf; back copies are then usually stored in boxes
♦ journal articles; these are specialist research articles into a particular topic or field, for example research into marketing or human resource management.

Taking notes

Note taking is a very important aspect of student life. If you make notes from books it is helpful to put them in your own words. This helps you to understand what you have read and is also the most useful form of taking down ideas which you may want to include in a written piece of work at a later date.

Before making notes from a book:

♦ make sure that it is recently published: look at the date of publication in the front of the book; there is no point in taking notes about modern business theory from a book that was published five or ten years ago
♦ make sure that the book is relevant to your needs by checking the contents page to see what topics are covered; the introduction to the book will also give you a brief overview
♦ list the name of the author, the title of the work, the date and place of publication, and publisher; you will need this information later on
♦ make a record of the chapter and page number that you take information from.

In taking notes concentrate on relevant points. Break these points down into sub-headings and sections, using different colours to distinguish headings, sub-headings,

lists, and so on. Write the notes in your own words, with the exception of relevant quotes.

Use colour and pictures to give you a strong visual trigger that will help you to understand and remember key points.

Using video materials

Video materials provide an important source of information for students on degree-level Business courses. A number of independent companies have produced excellent specialist business videos on topics ranging from finance and accounts to marketing and business systems.

You will benefit from watching these videos. First take down the title of the video and the name of the company that produced it. As you watch the video list the main theoretical points that are covered. You can then study them in more detail by examining the index of this book to identify the main themes. Videos are particularly useful for giving case examples which can be applied to the theoretical points that you study. These case examples can be used as evidence in assignment work. Note the name of the company and product highlighted in the case example and brief case details.

What to do in tutorials

As well as lectures, students may also be involved in small group discussions and tutorials which may be supervised by an experienced lecturer or a post-graduate student. These sessions are designed to encourage more personal contact and to provide the student with the possibility of discussing ideas and asking questions in a less threatening environment than the lecture hall.

Students may be asked to carry out preparatory work such as reading or the preparation of a brief presentation of ideas for the tutorial. Students may be nervous about doing this, but once you have contributed you will become more confident. Students often worry that they might have got something wrong whereas everyone else knows what they are doing. This is unlikely to be the case.

Remember that you do not have to say something major for it to be worthwhile. Instead, it is often better to help build up discussion by saying something simple that helps the discussion to move along.

A good tutorial member will seek to help others to join in rather than seeking to dominate or leave others out. Joining in a discussion can be done by making a simple opening statement such as 'I agree ...', 'I think ...' , 'That's a good point ...', 'I would just like to add ...', 'I disagree ...', 'How would that work in practice?' and so on.

Listening skills

In order to be able to make an effective contribution you need to listen carefully to what has been said.

When other people are talking show that you are interested by nodding your head, or saying 'yes'. If other members of the group can see that you are interested and value their ideas they are more likely to view your contribution in a positive way.

If you agree with a point, then say so, by saying something like 'That's a good idea'. You can clarify why you agree or disagree by saying something like 'I agree with the statement that businesses are becoming more aware of consumers, for example just recently ...'.

Keep focused on the discussion by listening carefully, for example by showing that the discussion is moving away from its focus by saying 'Haven't we moved away from the point that Pritesh was making about ... ?'.

Presenting a contrasting point of view is extremely useful in helping the learning process, because it enables an idea to be batted around and shaped more thoroughly. Try to explain *why* you disagree with a particular point.

Students can really help discussions to move forward by being heavily involved. Involvement is not just about making contributions, it is also about encouraging other people's contributions.

Remember that in conflict situations it is ideas that you are disagreeing with rather than individuals, although sometimes it is difficult to distinguish between the two. If you feel your anger levels start to rise take a deep breath and keep quiet for a short while.

Think carefully about whether it is the individual or the argument that you disagree with.

Writing an assignment

Assignment work is an important part of a modern degree course. Assignments are designed by course tutors to encourage students to engage fully in the learning process, and are based on clear learning criteria.

When you are given an assignment to carry out, the most important things to find out are:

♦ When is the submission date?
♦ What format must the work be presented in: is it a case study, a written essay, or what?
♦ How many words must the piece of work include?
♦ What are the assessment criteria that must be met?

The assessment criteria set out the areas against which your performance will be judged. It is essential that you understand each of these criteria and what you need to do to show high levels of performance when judged against these criteria. If you are unsure what any of the criteria mean then you should ask your course tutor to explain them to you in plain language.

Bibliography and referencing

In writing an assignment you will make use of books, publications and Internet sources. The books that you read in preparing your assignment and which are relevant to your work should be shown in a bibliography (list of books).

The standard way of setting out this bibliography is in the order: author, title, date, place, publisher. This information can be gleaned from the preliminary pages of the book, for example:

> Dransfield, R. and Dransfield, D. (authors) (2003) (date) *Key Ideas in Economics* (title), Cheltenham (place), Nelson Thornes (publisher).

You should also have a separate section for references. A reference is when you refer to or quote from a particular source as part of your writing.

For example, in the book cited above the authors, Dransfield and Dransfield, argue that many of the ideas of economists are determined by the societies and time they are brought up in. You could therefore set out this information in the following way:

> Dransfield and Dransfield (2003, p. iv) state that: 'Many of the key ideas of economists are shaped by the prevalent concerns of the time they were brought up.'

This would then appear in your references at the back of your work, set out in alphabetical order, as:

> Dransfield, R. and Dransfield, D. (2003) *Key Ideas in Economics*, Cheltenham: Nelson Thornes.

Writing an essay

Typically, an essay will not be broken down into headings and sub-headings. However, it needs to be structured in a logical order which is most likely to consist of:

♦ an introduction
♦ paragraphs
♦ evidence
♦ a conclusion.

The introduction should signpost to the reader the way you propose to tackle the essay. It should immediately show a clear understanding of what is required from the essay, the central issue to be discussed and the essay structure.

There will then follow a series of paragraphs which take the reader through your work step by step. Each paragraph should deal with one major point. The first sentence of the paragraph will introduce the paragraph's point before going on to present and comment on the evidence that is presented in that paragraph. The final sentence of the paragraph should make a link to the next paragraph. The use of evidence in your essay adds authority to what you are saying and makes it believable as well as interesting.

Finally, the conclusion will remind the reader of what has been covered and gives you the opportunity to weigh up the strength of various points and arguments covered in your work.

Writing a report

Sometimes you will be asked to produce a piece of work in 'business report format' because this is common practice in industry.

A report is a written statement from someone who has made a study of something (such as an event, the cause of some occurrence, or the performance of a person or organisation), which is then sent or passed on to someone else to be used for a particular purpose. Often the results of a business report will provide a basis for business decisions. The sequence of preparing for, writing up, and following up a report is shown in Figure 1.2.

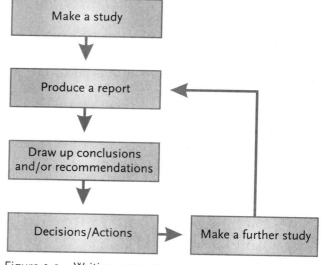

Figure 1.2   Writing a report

A written report is an important form of business communication and a perfectly acceptable and businesslike way of presenting an assignment provided this is appropriate to the criteria.

A suggested form of presentation for a written report is:

1   Title page
2   List of contents
3   Terms of reference

4 Procedure
5 Findings
6 Conclusion
7 Recommendations
8 Signature

The **terms of reference** explain the reasons for the report by referring to the group or persons asking you to produce it. This section should explain why you are writing the report. For example:

> This report has been produced in response to a request from Nestlé to investigate competition within the confectionery market in the UK.

The **procedure** section will refer to the stages that have taken place in the build-up of your report. It describes the research methods that were used: for example, the investigation of relevant market information by using Internet searches of Mintel reports and marketing magazines, as well as interviews with Nestlé managers, and the collection of this evidence in a database which was then analysed so that relevant conclusions could be drawn out.

The **findings** will be the main section of your report and will set out what you have discovered as a result of your investigations.

The **conclusion** will contain a summary of your findings and what they mean.

Recommendations are only necessary where appropriate. For example, you may be asked to suggest ways in which Nestlé should respond to growing competition in the marketplace.

Making a presentation

Students are not able to avoid making a presentation, so the sooner you start practising the better. At university you will be expected to make presentations to other groups of students and you will certainly have to do it at work.

Everybody is nervous when they give a presentation. It is often because they are nervous about whether they are able to give a good presentation. The rules of making a good presentation are very simple:

- Do a lot of preparation.
- Don't use too many visual illustrations.
- Don't speak too quickly.
- Pace your audience, look them in the eye.
- Smile a lot.
- Imagine that you are in the audience: what would you like to see and hear?

You may feel embarrassed, as most people do when giving a presentation, but if you take your time and put over things in an interesting way, then people will feel good about your presentation.

Preparation is the key. You need to know in what order you are going to put over your points, and what messages you are going to put across.

In a 15-minute presentation don't use more than eight slides. If you have too many you will rush through your material and it won't make sense. Having just a few helps you to talk things through in a clear and simple way.

Figure 1.3   Making a good presentation

If you speak too quickly your audience will switch off within two or three minutes: they will start looking bored, and you will find it very difficult to give an interesting presentation. If you find yourself talking too fast, slow down and you will quickly find that your audience switches on again.

People are interested in presenters who look them in the eye. They are not interested in speakers who avoid eye contact. Try to engage as many people in the audience as possible with your eyes. Give them a little smile and they will usually smile back: often they will nod to show that they are interested in what you are saying.

Perhaps the most valuable suggestion is that you imagine that you are sitting in your own audience. What would you like to hear? What would make you sit up and listen?

Try not to talk like a textbook; talk as if you were giving some important information to your friends that you want them to understand.

People tend to think that if they give a PowerPoint presentation using a computer, they are giving a brilliant presentation. Of course PowerPoint is fantastic in the right hands. But remember that the centre of the presentation should always be the presenter, and the way that she or he links together talk, illustration, use of video, visuals and so on.

Here is a checklist to help you prepare your presentation.

Plan and organise the presentation

♦ Set out your objectives.
♦ Set out the main idea and a clear conclusion.
♦ Set out your introduction clearly.
♦ Think about your audience, their interests and their level of knowledge.
♦ Brainstorm some main ideas.
♦ Plan handouts, visuals and use of PowerPoint.
♦ Keep a clear thread linking main points.

Prepare for the presentation

♦ Practise.
♦ Check the equipment.
♦ Set out your notes and handouts in a clear order.

Develop the visual aids

♦ Make them clear and easy to look at.
♦ Choose the correct type of chart.
♦ Have clear titles.
♦ Talk to the audience, not to the visual (don't turn your back).
♦ Place yourself at the centre of the stage.

♦ Use a pointer, but not too often. Often a modern projector will have a laser pointer for use with PowerPoint.

Avoid being nervous

♦ Take deep breaths.
♦ Move during the presentation.
♦ Smile.
♦ Maintain eye contact.

Deliver your presentation

♦ Be aware of what you say and how you say it.
♦ Speak with a strong clear voice, and don't speak too quickly.
♦ Be animated, clear and enthusiastic.
♦ Use eye contact, to make the presentation conversational and personal.

Questions and answers

♦ Prepare for questions and practise the answers.
♦ Ask for questions by stepping forward with hand raised.
♦ Watch the questioner and listen carefully.
♦ Repeat the question to make sure everyone has heard it.
♦ Keep the same bearing as in your presentation.
♦ Use eye contact and look at the whole audience.

Working in a team

It requires skill to work well with other people. Team-working is not just like working with friends; it also involves working with people who may not have quite the same outlook on life as yourself. You may, for example, have to work with people who you consider to be lazy or incompetent.

Working with others therefore requires a lot of maturity and strength of character. In the world of work, people frequently work in teams, and they are expected to share joint responsibility for how the team functions.

Whenever a group works together there will be three strands involved in moving from the start of the decision-making process to the finish. These strands are illustrated in Figure 1.4.

Figure 1.4   Group task work

The **task** is the content of the work. For example, the task of a student meeting may be to choose a student representative. The task of a piece of group work may be to produce an effective assignment. The task is the conversion of the information and opinions from members into recommendations, reports or other outcomes. In general terms, this covers what has to be done and why. Most groups give a lot of attention to the task.

The **action schedule** is concerned with how a group will be organised to do a given task. The schedule will cover such questions as who will fill the necessary roles, how progress will be checked and monitored, and how it will be ensured that the group finishes the task on time. It will also deal with the procedures of decision making: how to ensure that everyone has a say, how conflict will be dealt with, and so on.

In general, the action schedule will cover the 'where' and 'how' of decision making.

An action schedule for a meeting might set down when the meeting will take place, who will attend, who will run the meeting, how decisions will be voted on and other procedural matters.

The **process** is the interaction which takes place between members of a group. It is about how people work together, their relationships and the feelings created by their behaviour within the group. It involves interpersonal skills such as listening to others and helping others to join in a discussion. It involves expressions of feelings and the giving and receiving of feedback. In general it covers 'who does what and when'. Many groups, unfortunately, pay little attention to the process.

If you are going to be an effective team member it is essential that you are aware of these three elements – task, action schedule and process – and help the team to give appropriate priority to blending the three effectively.

Stages of group work

In working as part of a group there are four stages that you need to focus on.

Familiarisation

This involves getting to know other members of the group and familiarising yourself with the task. Everyone needs to be sure about the eventual product of the group, that is, what needs to be done (the task). They also need to be sure about the timescale, and how the group activity is going to be assessed.

Planning

Planning involves agreeing on the various parts of the task and the best ways of achieving them. It helps to draw on the different areas of expertise of group members. An action plan should be constructed to set out:

♦ what actions are needed to achieve the plan
♦ when these actions will be carried out
♦ who is responsible for each action.

Implementation

Implementation involves carrying out the group work to the action plan. Periodic review meetings may be needed to check that the plan is being kept on target.

Completion

The completion is an essential part of the group activity because all loose ends need to be tied up if the task is to be completed successfully. For example, if the outcome of the task is to make a presentation it is essential that all the equipment and materials are there when the presentation takes place and everyone is sure of their own responsibilities.

The profile form shown opposite gives you the opportunity to self-assess your personal and social skills as a member of a team.

As a member of any group are you effective at:

		Experience of			Success at		
		1	2	3	1	2	3
❶	Contributing ideas	☐	☐	☐	☐	☐	☐
❷	Listening to other people's ideas and making use of them	☐	☐	☐	☐	☐	☐
❸	Compromising when your opinion was not shared by others	☐	☐	☐	☐	☐	☐
❹	Taking notes of what went on in the group	☐	☐	☐	☐	☐	☐
❺	Carrying out an agreed task in co-operation with others	☐	☐	☐	☐	☐	☐
❻	Carrying out part of a task assigned to you as an individual	☐	☐	☐	☐	☐	☐
❼	Showing flexibility	☐	☐	☐	☐	☐	☐
❽	Asking for things to be explained even though you could have looked silly	☐	☐	☐	☐	☐	☐
❾	Choosing a person to do a particular task	☐	☐	☐	☐	☐	☐
❿	Keeping a check on how far the group had gone in carrying out a task	☐	☐	☐	☐	☐	☐
⓫	Chairing a meeting	☐	☐	☐	☐	☐	☐
⓬	Giving instructions to others	☐	☐	☐	☐	☐	☐
⓭	Trying to influence others in the group	☐	☐	☐	☐	☐	☐
⓮	Contributing ideas to a group discussion	☐	☐	☐	☐	☐	☐
⓯	Making a formal presentation to a group	☐	☐	☐	☐	☐	☐
⓰	Producing visual material as part of a presentation	☐	☐	☐	☐	☐	☐
⓱	Helping to organise a major event	☐	☐	☐	☐	☐	☐
⓲	Deciding on the best solution and planning a way forward	☐	☐	☐	☐	☐	☐
⓳	Encouraging people to carry on even when they are uninterested	☐	☐	☐	☐	☐	☐
⓴	Getting the group to finish on time	☐	☐	☐	☐	☐	☐
㉑	Sharing any praise	☐	☐	☐	☐	☐	☐

The tick columns are intended to be filled in according to the following pointers:

1 = I am highly experienced at this

2 = I have some experience of this

3 = I have no experience of this

and:

1 = I was very successful at this

2 = I was reasonably successful at this

3 = I was rarely successful at this.

Time management

Using time effectively is a very important skill: it is vital to success that you learn to prioritise activities and tasks. Avoid 'butterflying', where you flit from one task to another without doing anything well. For example, in carrying out a task you should decide:

♦ what the most important elements of the task are
♦ which parts of the task take longest
♦ what sequence the activities need to follow.

It is important that you put most time and effort into those activities which are the key to meeting your objectives. Many people waste a lot of time on minor problems, rather than concentrating upon essential activities.

The 80:20 rule in business states that we waste 80 per cent of our time on doing minor things and spend only 20 per cent of our time on the most important things, which yield 80 per cent of the returns. How can we change our focus from the 20 per cent of less productive activity?

One way of making sure that time is well spent is to undertake a value analysis of the use of time. This is called ABC analysis (Figure 1.5).

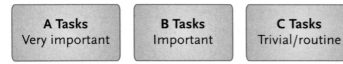

Figure 1.5   ABC analysis of tasks

Time is frequently wasted on trivial problems (C) while the few essential tasks (A) are left undone. Good time management involves ranking activities as A, B or C and then working through them in order of priority:

♦ A tasks are most important and need the most time and resources to be done properly.
♦ B tasks are of less importance and can be delegated.
♦ C tasks are often routine but can command a large share of the work.

Using the Internet

What's good about the net?

♦ The information available: up-to-the-minute information and news stories about business issues and business statistics.
♦ You can find out virtually anything about almost any subject with very little effort.
♦ The net allows people with no other means of doing so, to send their message out to a global audience.

Internet access from home

If you are using the Internet from home you will first need an Internet provider (such as BT, Virgin, Cable & Wireless). The provider will supply you with the software to enable you to connect to their service. Most software can be automatically installed, leaving you very little to configure. If in doubt there are helplines you can access, but watch out for the charges (some cost over £1 a minute).

Internet access from university

Once you have logged on to your university network, click on either the Netscape icon or the Internet Explorer icon and you will be taken to the university home page. From there, type in the address you want in the address bar at the top of the page. If you are not sure of the address you want, then try a search engine (see below). The most popular search engine today is Google. All you need to do is type in the key words of what you are looking for, such as 'Stock Market', and the search engine will reveal whatever sites there are with the most popular at the top. University students are given an individual user name and password which are required for them to be able to log on.

What happens now?

The home page is the first page you see when you are connected to the Internet, at work or in an academic institution (for example, the home page of The Nottingham Trent University is www.ntu.ac.uk). At home it can be any page you like: your favourite page, your own website, whatever you choose. See the user guides in your browser for information on how to choose a home page.

General navigation

Whenever you move the mouse over an area and the cursor looks like a hand, this indicates a link to another part of a document, or a different site entirely. Click on this to follow the link. Also, the area you move the mouse over may change colour, or there may be a different picture entirely.

URLs

A Uniform Resource Location (URL) is the actual address location of websites: you will see them as, for example, http://www.ntu.ac.uk. If you are having difficulty accessing the site double-check the address; if it is a long address try going to the main page first, for example going to www.nestle.co.uk, rather than going to a specific part of the website which will have a longer address.

Remember that the net runs slowly at times and it can take a while to connect to the page you want. If it seems to be taking too long then try pressing the reload/refresh button, depending on your browser.

Information

You will see various extensions at the end of addresses. The main ones are:

.com	commercial organisation
.org	a non-commercial organisation (usually)
.ac	academic institution such as a university
.gov	government
.co.uk	UK site

As the popularity of the web is increasing there are many more extensions available. Check with http://register-names.co.uk which shows the different extensions which are available. This is particularly useful if you want to register your own name.

Downloading at home

You will need some software such as WinZip (which is free of charge for 30 days) for compressed files, and Acrobat (which is free of charge) for files with a .pdf extension. Web addresses for these products can be

found at the end of the unit. Once you have these you should have no problem with downloading, which should then happen automatically. Just remember the name of the file and where it is stored. Always make sure you have an up-to-date virus checker and that you have checked the file and trust the source of the file before you download.

Downloading at university

Do not download any programs. Files which you want to refer to later can be saved by clicking on the **File** menu, choosing **Save As** and then saving to a local hard drive or a floppy disk. As a general rule, pictures are not saved with these files. These can be saved separately by right-clicking on the picture and choosing **Save Picture As**.

Search engines

A search engine is the best way of finding sites on the Internet. The basic principle is that you enter key words in the box at the top of the page, and the engine then searches through the index of Internet pages and the results are returned in a list. There are many different types of engine and they all look for things in different ways. Search engines look for key words, phrases, or the number of times a certain word is used, or a combination of these approaches.

A single search engine such as Lycos will only look through a limited range of pages. A meta-search engine, such as Ask Jeeves, searches several engines at once. You can have UK-specific engines. The best engine to use is the one that suits you.

Sites of interest

Most units in this book identify a number of relevant sites of interest. However, there are a number of general sites which are worth mentioning from the outset that provide general business news. These are:

www.bbc.co.uk
www.economist.com
www.euromoney.com
www.newsunlimited.co.uk
www.independent.co.uk
www.reuters.com

The importance of numerical skills

Being able to work with simple numbers is an important skill for the business student, particularly in the area of finance and accounts and business decision making (Units 6 and 9). Unit 6 introduces a range of useful statistical techniques. However, from the outset of the course it is important to understand how percentages are calculated because they are used so widely as a means of making comparisons.

Percentages

So what is a percentage? The term percentage or per cent means parts out of 100 and is the same as a fraction with a denominator (bottom) of 100. Therefore 10 per cent (10%) means 10 parts out of 100 and is the same as the fraction 10/100; 98 per cent (98%) means 98 parts out of 100 and is the same as the fraction 98/100.

Another way of showing parts out of 100 is using a decimal, so percentages can be expressed as decimals: 10 per cent is the same as 0.10 or 10/100; 98 per cent is the same as 0.98 or 98/100.

There are three main ways in which percentages are frequently used:

♦ to enable data with different sample sizes or totals to be compared
♦ to quantify the amount of change over time
♦ to express an increase or decrease relative to an initial size.

Comparing different sample sizes or totals

When collecting or using sources of data for an assignment you may be faced with the problem that some of your data may have a different sample size or total from another. For example, you may carry out a questionnaire survey in two suburbs of the same town. In 'Redsuburb' you may interview 50 people, and in 'Bluesuburb' your sample size may be 80. How can you then compare the results of your questionnaire?

The answer is to convert your results into percentages. For example, you may be investigating how many people read a tabloid newspaper every day. The results of your survey might be as below.

Those reading a tabloid newspaper every day

Redsuburb	30
Bluesuburb	40

At first glance it appears that people in Bluesuburb are most likely to read a tabloid paper. However, if we convert our figures into percentages we might get a different result.

To convert to a percentage all we need to do is:

1 Work out the figures as a fraction, for example the fraction of people living in the two suburbs who read a tabloid.

2 Convert the fraction to a decimal by dividing the top part of the fraction by the bottom part.

3 Turn the fraction into a percentage by multiplying by 100.

So, for our example, we start with Redsuburb:
The fraction is 30/50
The decimal is 0.60 (30 divided by 50)
The percentage is 60 per cent (0.60 × 100)

Then for Bluesuburb the fraction is 40/80
The decimal is 0.50 (40 divided by 80)
The percentage is 50 per cent (0.50 × 100)

When we look at the percentage figures we can see that according to our survey reading tabloids is more popular in Redsuburb than Bluesuburb.

If our sample figures give us an accurate representation of the total populations of these areas we could then calculate that if:

♦ the population size of Redsuburb is 20,000, then there will be 12,000 daily tabloid readers there (60 per cent).
♦ the population size of Bluesuburb is 20,000, then there will be 10,000 daily tabloid readers there (50 per cent).

Calculating percentage change

Another useful thing that we can do with percentages is to calculate the change that is taking place in various totals. For example, we can compare the change in the sales and profits of two businesses. We can compare the improvements in productivity of different units in a factory, so that we could see which unit was making the most improvement.

Making comparisons in parts per hundred (percentages) is much easier to understand than when we use raw figures. You can see how to measure percentage change by means of using figures in the following table.

Total UK CD sales 1999–2002

Millions of units of CDs sold

1999	180
2000	200
2001	210
2002	212

Using the information in the table the increase in CD sales between 1999 and 2000 can be calculated as a percentage.

You can see that between these two dates sales have increased by 20 million, that is, from 180 to 200.

To express this difference, make a fraction of the starting value (20/180) and multiply by 100.

$$\frac{20}{180} \times 100 = 11.11 \text{ per cent}$$

Now we can look at the difference between the 2000 and 2001 sales:

$$\frac{10}{200} \times 100 = 5.0 \text{ per cent}$$

We can also look at the difference between the 2001 and 2002 sales:

$$\frac{2}{210} \times 100 = 0.95 \text{ per cent}$$

What we are able to see from these figures is that the percentage increase in CD sales has been progressively getting smaller over the period considered. This is as a result of the fact that rather than buying CDs many people today are simply downloading them from the Internet.

Useful websites

Adobe Acrobat Reader   www.acrobat.com
WinZip   www.winzip.com
UltimateZip   www.ultimatezip.com

Unit 2

Professional development

The aim of this unit is to enable learners to assess and develop a range of professional and personal skills in order to promote future personal and career development. Professional development is the process through which individuals identify targets and aspirations for themselves which they seek to work towards at work as well as in their own time. The unit also aims to develop the learner's ability to organise, manage and practise a range of approaches to improve their performance as self-organised learners in preparation for work or further career development. The emphasis is on the needs of the individual but within the context of how the development of self-management corresponds with effective team management in meeting objectives.

Summary of learning outcomes

On completion of this unit you will be able to:
♦ undertake responsibility for your own personal and career development
♦ evaluate progress and achievement of personal development and learning targets
♦ develop a range of interpersonal and transferable skills
♦ demonstrate self-managed learning in a professional context.

Chapter 1

Personal and career development

Today it is widely recognised that we are all involved in a process of lifelong learning and career development. The old days when people went to school, then engaged in a period of training, and then did the same job for the rest of their lives are long gone. Today, most people expect that during their lifetime they may have to make major changes in the type of work they do, and will want to take on more responsibilities within organisations while developing enhanced skills.

It is therefore important at any one time to be aware of:

Figure 2.1   Personal and career development

Portfolio building

All students following courses at university today are expected to develop and maintain a personal portfolio as part of the process of professional, educational and work-related development.

An **individual development portfolio** (IDP) should contain information about all the activities you are undertaking to complete your degree course, as well as your work-related activities and wider development experiences. An IDP helps you to record and reflect on the various learning activities that you carry out during your time in higher education.

At the heart of your portfolio will be your **personal development plan** (see p. 22). Comments from other people who have supported you during your university course, such as course tutors and work mentors, should also be included.

Useful evidence to include in the portfolio will come from:

- skills development areas of your degree
- content development areas of your degree (modules covered, assessment results)
- summaries of projects carried out on work placements
- reports from mentors on work placements
- details of attendance of relevant training programmes
- computer-based training.

You should allocate set periods of time, for example half a day a month, for portfolio building. You should keep a portfolio file which will provide the finished portfolio, and a secondary rough storage file to store information and evidence as you go along.

Individual development portfolio

A useful structure for an individual development portfolio might be:

♦ Front cover
♦ Title page
♦ Acknowledgements
♦ Table of contents
♦ Your profile, work-based experience and learning, degree-based learning (key outcomes)
♦ Personal development plan, including reviews and revisions
♦ Record of a reflection on key development activities during the course and at work
♦ Appropriate indexing and referencing of your work
♦ Appendices, if appropriate.

Do not make the mistake of waiting until near the end of your course to start building your portfolio. By then you are likely to have lost much of the necessary evidence, and will be engaged in other activities such as completing assignment work.

Sometimes an individual development portfolio will be termed a **progress file**. Remember that your individual development portfolio or progress file should be readable in non-academic circles: for example, you will probably want to take it along to a job interview. So think about your external audience. Make sure that the file is:

♦ well structured
♦ easy to navigate around
♦ clear and simple to understand.

The personal development plan (PDP)

The personal development plan, which lies at the heart of your portfolio, is defined as 'a structured and supported process undertaken by an individual to reflect upon their own learning performance and/or achievement and to plan for their personal, educational and career development'.

The PDP involves planning and reflection about:

♦ educational development
♦ personal development
♦ career development.

Self-appraisal

A starting point for developing a PDP is to carry out a frank audit of what you currently do well, and where your weaknesses lie.

Self-appraisal means examining where you are up to and where your strengths and weaknesses lie, before going any further.

You need to be aware that if you stick at something that you identify as an area of weakness, then your confidence will improve. Initially, however, you may lack confidence in your ability to make progress: a bit like when you first learned to walk.

Figure 2.2 on p. 23 illustrates the way in which our confidence increases as we become more capable of doing something, whether it be study or a work-related skill. Work round the diagram from A to B to C to D.

Skills

An important starting point in self-appraisal is to evaluate your self-management, leadership and interpersonal skills. These skills are relevant both to academic study and to work-related activity.

Carry out a self-assessment using the outline provided on p. 24.

As well as ticking the columns that are relevant to your current position in each of the skill areas, you should also write a short statement setting out evidence of your weaknesses and strengths in any of the skills listed. Giving specific evidence of your actions, for example 'I feel embarrassed when expressing my views in front of others in case they don't take me seriously', provides the opportunity to identify ways of taking practical steps to improve your performance, as shown in Figure 2.3.

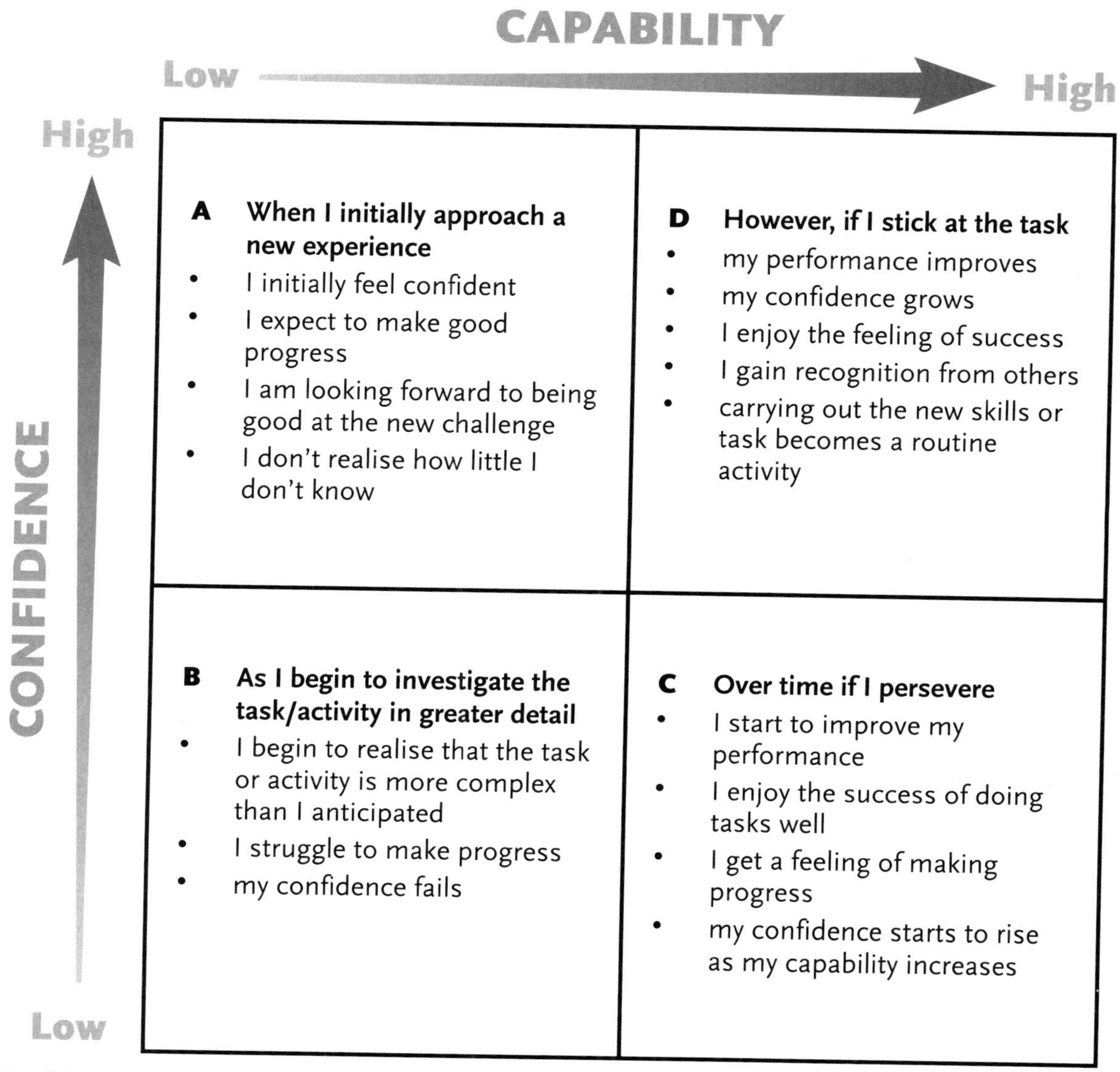

CAPABILITY
Low
High
CONFIDENCE
High
Low
A When I initially approach a new experience
• I initially feel confident
• I expect to make good progress
• I am looking forward to being good at the new challenge
• I don't realise how little I don't know
D However, if I stick at the task
• my performance improves
• my confidence grows
• I enjoy the feeling of success
• I gain recognition from others
• carrying out the new skills or task becomes a routine activity
B As I begin to investigate the task/activity in greater detail
• I begin to realise that the task or activity is more complex than I anticipated
• I struggle to make progress
• my confidence fails
C Over time if I persevere
• I start to improve my performance
• I enjoy the success of doing tasks well
• I get a feeling of making progress
• my confidence starts to rise as my capability increases

Figure 2.2 Confidence and capability

Identifying weaknesses
enables you to
work at reducing these weaknesses
through practical examples
through practical actions

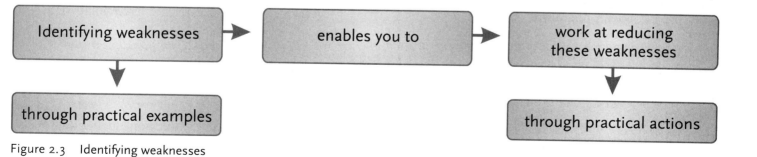

Figure 2.3 Identifying weaknesses

SELF-ASSESSMENT OUTLINE

Skills

Ranking

Skills	1	2	3	4	5
Self-management					
Able to set targets and objectives for own work	☐	☐	☐	☐	☐
Happy working without supervision	☐	☐	☐	☐	☐
Confident in own ability to handle most routine problems when they arise	☐	☐	☐	☐	☐
Confident to ask advice when required	☐	☐	☐	☐	☐
Able to see most projects through from start to finish with minimal assistance	☐	☐	☐	☐	☐
Confident when managing own learning and work-related activity	☐	☐	☐	☐	☐
Leadership					
Confident when taking on responsibility for others	☐	☐	☐	☐	☐
Prepared to make decisions for other people	☐	☐	☐	☐	☐
Prepared to listen to others before making decisions	☐	☐	☐	☐	☐
Willing to take responsibility for leadership actions	☐	☐	☐	☐	☐
Interpersonal skills					
Sensitive to the needs of others	☐	☐	☐	☐	☐
A good listener	☐	☐	☐	☐	☐
Confident when dealing with others	☐	☐	☐	☐	☐
Comfortable in working in team situations	☐	☐	☐	☐	☐
Willing to talk openly in groups	☐	☐	☐	☐	☐
Treats others as equals rather than as superiors or inferiors	☐	☐	☐	☐	☐

Key self-appraisal areas

Key areas for self-appraisal that are relevant to a university degree in business are:

- management of self
- management of learning
- communication
- teamwork
- problem solving
- information and communications technology skills.

Development plan

Remember that your development plan is not only about developing yourself for university and the workplace, it is also about developing yourself for you.

A useful structure for the development plan could be:

- current performance: where you are up to now
- future needs, which can be set out in a framework of aims, objectives, and targets
- review dates: in setting out the plan it is important to set out dates at which progress will be reviewed, for example at the end of each term/semester of a course, at the end of each month
- achievement dates: when particular targets were achieved
- learning programme or activities designed to enable the individual to meet objectives or targets
- an action plan setting out a plan of actions required to meet objectives or targets.

Current performance

Because we are concerned with personal development, as well as career and educational development, it is always important to start by examining yourself. Set out:

- your personal achievements and skills
- your personal qualities, including strengths and weaknesses.

ACTIVITY

A useful way of 'looking in the mirror' is to examine your strengths and weaknesses as other people would see them.

1 List three of what you consider to be your personal strengths.

2 Now ask a friend to make a list of your strengths.

3 Compare the two lists.

4 Now list three areas of weakness that you need to work on.

5 Ask a friend to list three areas for development.

6 Compare the lists.

You should also make a list of your personal achievements, that is, the success areas of your life.

There are all sorts of areas of personal achievement that we tend to overlook. Think carefully about your achievements and list them carefully for your folder. Examples could be looking after an elderly person, decorating a room, repairing an item of equipment, playing for a sports team, solving a difficult problem, helping someone else, doing voluntary work, keeping fit, receiving certificates, passing exams and so on.

There are all sorts of ways of recording information for providing evidence for your individual development portfolio. Here are some examples:

- newspaper cuttings about you
- testimonies, references
- certificates
- awards
- portfolios of work
- photographs
- trophies
- logs and diaries.

Aims, objectives and targets

Aims and objectives are the ends that you are trying to achieve. An aim is a major end that you are trying to achieve, which can typically be broken down into a number of objectives. For example, your aims and objectives might be:

- educational: to get a good degree qualification
- work-related: to develop a career in marketing and eventually to become a marketing director of a major PLC
- personal: to become more confident and sociable.

ACTIVITY

Set out a statement of your main aims for the next two years, and break down the aims into educational, work-related and personal.

Now establish some targets for the next three months. At the end of each three-month period you will need to establish new targets. In the course of time you may also want to adjust your aims.

Make sure that your targets are SMART:

1. Specific: they are easy to understand
2. Measurable if possible (that is, you can attach numbers to them)
3. Achievable
4. Realistic
5. Time-related.

Targets are shorter-term challenges that help you to achieve your aims and objectives. For example, short-term targets may relate to gaining scores of at least 60 per cent on your next three pieces of work.

Review dates and achievement dates

An important part of successful career and personal development is to establish review dates that are adhered to.

As part of the planning process you will establish plans which need to be monitored. For example, if one of your targets is to carry out a confident presentation to a group of fellow students or work colleagues, then you will need to establish dates:

♦ for the presentation
♦ for the preparation of the presentation
♦ to review the effectiveness of the presentation, for example with a course tutor.

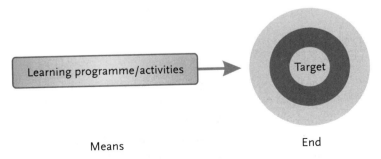

Means   End

Achievement dates are the dates at which you successfully achieve your targets. Setting out achievement dates helps you to build confidence in your portfolio building, because each achievement of a target will provide you with more evidence of successful development.

Learning programme or activities

The learning programme or activities are the means by which you achieve your targets.

Some parts of the learning programme or activities will be designed for you, for example training activities at work and the structure of your Business Higher or Foundation Award. Other activities you may have to design yourself in order to develop the capabilities that you are working towards. Do not expect to receive all the required experiences provided for you 'on a plate'. For example, if part of a research assignment involves collecting primary information, then you will need to take the responsibility to arrange to go and interview relevant individuals yourself. This self-management of learning is an essential part of your development process.

Action plans

Action planning is a crucial part of a degree award. Planning is concerned with providing a structured and organised way of meeting objectives.

There are a number of important reasons why you should plan, including:

♦ to be clear about your objectives
♦ to organise activities into a sequence
♦ to organise the timing of events
♦ to keep a check on progress
♦ to make sure that the important things are not left until last
♦ to plan what resources and materials you need
♦ to save time
♦ to reduce stress
♦ to look at present strengths and how they can be built upon.

A problem for many students is that while they have some idea about the goal or target they are working towards, they are not skilled at planning the steps required to achieve this target. Action planning involves designing a series of sequential steps that will enable you to meet targets.

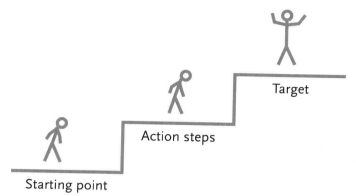

Figure 2.4 Sequential steps

Action plan for an assignment

An important area of action planning on your course will relate to completing assignments on time in order to meet specified criteria:

♦ Be clear about your objective, for example to complete the (named) assignment by the given deadline, covering all of the required critieria.

♦ Organise activities into a sequence. Set out a step-by-step plan of how you will complete this assignment, and how each step is related to the performance criteria.

♦ Organise the timing of events. When will each step in the assignment be completed?

♦ Keep a check on progress. How will you check that you are keeping to deadlines? Will you review your progress with another student, for example?

Development action plan

The importance of action plans is that they help you organise yourself. You should be able to put your plan together quickly with the minimum of paperwork. If an action plan involves a lot of paper and time, then throw it in the bin and start again. Your action plan should be simple and easy to follow.

Write your action plan under these headings:

> **1** Area for development
>
> **2** Name of person responsible for development
>
> **3** Action steps (simple and practical)
>
> i
>
> ii
>
> iii
>
> iv
>
> v
>
> (There may be quite a few of these)
>
> **4** Review of progress (when reviews will occur and who will be involved)
>
> **5** Evaluation of plan (when and how it will take place, how it can be improved).

Area for development

What do you want to plan? Set out your targets.

Person responsible for development

This will be you, or a small group of students. The responsibility lies with you, not with your tutor. Take charge of your own learning.

Action steps

What steps will you need to take to see the plan through? Be specific about the steps that need to be taken. Set out the time when these steps will take place.

Review of progress

When and how will the progress of the action steps and the plan be checked? In writing out your plan you need to set dates for reviewing how successful you have been in carrying out the plan. For example, if you have eight weeks to complete an assignment, you could review your progress after two weeks, four weeks and six weeks. You will need to carry out this review with someone else. Two students can review each other's work, for example.

Evaluation

It is helpful to evaluate the success of your plan in order to help you to action plan in the future.

Make sure that your action steps are clear and practical rather than sketchy and vague. For example, 'reading four journal articles about appraisal processes, and making detailed notes about salient points' is a specific and practical step. 'Doing some reading' is vague. 'Going to computer services, taking out a manual on spreadsheets, setting out a spreadsheet of my research figures' is a detailed description of a practical step. 'Improving my ICT' is not.

A useful layout for your action plan is shown on p. 27.

You can see that the action plan we have outlined does not involve a lot of paperwork. However, it enables you to map out clear steps that you will need to take to meet your targets.

Too often in the past students have found themselves with three or four assignments to do at the same time and have left essential work to the last minute. Action planning helps you to spread out your work over a period of time.

Action planning is used widely in the workplace. If you learn to construct simple action plans now, you will have developed a useful life skill. Finally, never write an action plan after completing an assignment. What a ridiculous waste of time that would be.

Constructing a CV

A *curriculum vitae* (usually called simply a CV) is a summary of your career to date. There are three stages you should follow when setting out your CV:

♦ assemble all the facts about yourself
♦ write a draft CV
♦ edit the document several times.

When writing a CV try to create a favourable impression, but always be truthful. Use positive rather than negative statements about yourself, in other words describe what you can do, not what you cannot

do. Be as specific as you can; vague statements look suspicious.

Choose a font in your word-processing package that is impressive, yet conservative. It should look clear, confident and uncluttered.

Assembling the facts

At this initial stage you are trying to gather together as many relevant facts as possible about your career to date. It does not matter if you put down too many to start with. Make a list of all your educational, work-based and leisure achievements, as well as training activities and courses you have been on. Make brief notes about each of these as well as about projects and assignments in which you have been involved.

Drafting the CV

A CV should be divided under suitable headings and sub-headings.

Curriculum vitae

Sample headings

1. Name
2. Date of birth
3. Address
4. Telephone number
5. Education and training
6. Qualifications
7. Other relevant achievements
8. Interests
9. References

Remember that the key part of the CV is the career history, so the sections that go before should not be too long. For example, when dealing with training, list only the most important and relevant training courses, and then if necessary include some of the others under 'other relevant achievements'.

When you set out your responsibilities and achievements, decide whether it is necessary to put some of them under sub-headings. It is normal practice to start your career history with your most recent job and work backwards in time, because employers are usually more interested in your recent experience.

If some of your experience is of a technical nature, try to present it in a way that can be read easily by the general reader (rather than by the specialist). Avoid jargon.

Try to use dynamic words in your CV. Here are some good examples:

Curriculum vitae

Dynamic words to use

Accomplished	Achieved	Conducted
Completed	Created	Decided
Delivered	Developed	Designed
Directed	Established	Expanded
Finished	Generated	Implemented
Improved	Increased	Introduced
Launched	Performed	Pioneered
Planned	Promoted	Redesigned
Reorganised	Set up	Solved
Succeeded	Trained	Widened
Won	Work	Wrote

Editing the CV

You may need to alter your CV slightly for each job application so that it concentrates as closely as possible on the requirements of that particular job. Look at the details of the job and ask yourself whether your CV suggests that you have the requirements for the post. Imagine yourself in the employer's shoes: what qualities do you think the organisation is looking for?

Here are some useful pointers to constructing a CV:

- Concentrate on your achievements, not just your responsibilities. The reader is looking for someone who can do a job well, not just do a job. If possible quote figures and other evidence.
- Place your most relevant skills and experience in a prominent place to encourage the reader to read on.
- Keep to the point; the quality of your achievements is more important than the quantity.
- Try to keep your CV to a maximum of two pages.
- Ask someone to read through and check your CV with particular reference to grammar, spelling and so on.
- Use good quality white paper.
- List those things that will make you stand out from the competition, that is, things that are relevant but which add value to your application.
- Keep your CV up to date. This should be easy if you store a copy on the hard disk of your computer.

Curriculum vitae

A useful outline for CV construction

Personal contact details

Education (brief summary)

Qualifications + any relevant training experiences

Relevant work experience

Hobbies and interests

Brief summary statement: showing how your capabilities and achievements will help you to fill the required post.

Chapter 2

Personal development and learning targets

Once you have established a **personal development plan** it will be important to evaluate your ongoing performance. The process involved can be illustrated in the form of a cycle, shown in Figure 2.5.

1 Carry out initial audit

2 Establish aims, objectives and targets

3 Create action plan, including review dates

4 Carry out development activities

5 Carry out reviews providing feedback

6 Reset aims, objectives

Figure 2.5   Evaluation cycle

Evaluation of personal development and learning targets needs to be carried out in a systematic way, and a record should be kept of the evaluation.

The review can take place either on a **peer group** basis (with other students), with your **work-based mentor** or with a **course tutor**.

Review meeting

The purpose of the review is really to check that students are managing to combine the sometimes conflicting demands of educational, work and personal development, and that they are working effectively towards achieving goals and targets set out in the personal development plan. Prior to the review meeting you will need to take the following steps:

♦ Check the actions and targets specified in the action plan to be reviewed at the review meeting. Have the actions and targets been completed by you?
♦ Set out on paper your achievements, progress and experiences since the previous review.
♦ Write down some brief reflections on what you have learned and how you have developed since the previous review.
♦ Identify possible improvements and targets to achieve before the next review takes place.
♦ Identify one piece of work that has gone particularly well since the previous review: if possible bring evidence of achievement on this piece.
♦ Identify one piece of work that has gone particularly badly since the previous review. Identify the main problems with this work, so that working with the tutor you may be able to identify ways of progressing the work.

Areas for discussion at a review meeting will include:

♦ punctuality and attendance
♦ attitude to work
♦ ability to manage own learning
♦ ability to work as part of a team
♦ meeting assessment deadline dates
♦ progress with developing important skill areas, such as communication and problem solving.

Review meetings enable students to manage their time and their work in a structured way. It should be fairly obvious if a student is struggling to manage their work commitments and as a result is having difficulty in successfully meeting personal development targets.

At a review meeting the tutor is able to provide constructive feedback to the student, so that together they can reset aims, objectives and targets, as appropriate.

Chapter 3

Interpersonal and transferable skills

There are a number of important interpersonal and transferable skills that are relevant to your personal development. Interpersonal skills are ones that involve the way that you interact with others on your educational course, or in the workplace. Transferable skills are ones that can be transferred between one situation and another. For example, the ability to communicate clearly in making a presentation is transferable across a range of contexts: at university, or in different types of workplace.

The three skills that we examine in this chapter are:

♦ problem solving
♦ verbal communication
♦ time management.

Problem solving

Problem solving is the process of analysing and then seeking solutions to problems. The starting point is to analyse the problem to identify the nature of it.

Types of problem

There are several different types of problem. Here are some of the main types.

A deviation problem

This is where desired results and outcomes are not being achieved. The problem solver therefore has to identify a way of getting back on track, that is, how to remove the deviation.

An improvement problem

This is where something is already working well but it may be possible to make it work better. The problem

therefore is to find ways of improving on current solutions.

Creative problems

This is where problem solving is used as a creative tool to generate new ideas for doing things, starting with a blank sheet of paper.

Clearly, different types of problem solving require different types of thinking: for example, creative problem solving requires a far more flexible approach than solving deviation problems.

Edward de Bono, who is one of the leading exponents of problem-solving techniques in this country, suggests that there are different types of thinking and that we can switch from one to another, particularly if we are aware of these different modes of thinking and can get into the habit of applying whichever is most appropriate to each problem. In one of his books, *Six Thinking Hats*, he proposes a different hat for different types of thinking. So you put on the white hat for dealing with facts and figures, a red hat for emotions and a green hat for creative and lateral thinking, as in Figure 2.6.

The starting point for most types of problem solving is to analyse the problem, that is, to find out what the nature of the problem is. This requires identifying data that is relevant to the problem, and the techniques that can be used to analyse and find solutions to it.

Problem avoidance

Another use of problem solving is to identify ways of dealing with problems should they arise. It may be that at the moment there are no problems, but just in case

Figure 2.6 Different types of thinking

Mind mapping originates from research into the human brain which shows that brain cells have a central body, its nucleus, with lots of 'branches' radiating from it. The branches carry information that is transmitted as electrical energy from one cell to another. At the end of the branches there are chemical messengers which transmit the signal from one brain cell to another. Understood this way, successful thinking can be seen as an efficient system of networks. The pathways that are formed create a memory map: the greater the number of pathways, the more efficient thinking becomes.

A mind map can be used to set out a graphic representation of a problem and its solutions. Every mind map has a central point. This could be a brief description of the problem. The most important themes, the ways of solving the problem, can then be set out as branches emanating from the problem at the centre. This kind of diagram (Figure 2.7) is also called a spider diagram because of its shape.

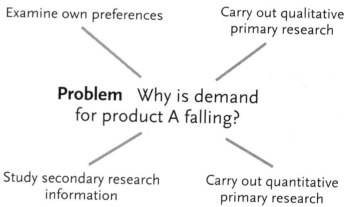

Figure 2.7 Spider diagram

they do arise problem solving can be applied to enable future problem avoidance.

Brainstorming and mind mapping

Alternative approaches to problem solving can be employed, such as brainstorming and mind mapping.

Brainstorming involves generating a lot of ways of dealing with the problem. They can be as crazy as you like because at this stage they are not going to be followed through. Sometimes apparently crazy ideas can be structured into sensible solutions when they have the 'craziness' taken out. In a brainstorming situation participants simply suggest as many ideas as they can without justifying them or having them questioned. The idea is to generate as many solutions as possible.

Generating solutions

The process of generating solutions to problems involves identifying a menu of possible solutions and criteria for evaluating these solutions against, for example feasibility, acceptability to relevant parties, cost and so on.

Having established the menu and the criteria, the next task is to choose the 'best' solution.

33

ACTIVITY

Rank your own problem-solving skills in terms of the profile form below.

Problem-solving skills

Current strength

	Very good				Poor
	1	2	3	4	5
Ability to identify the nature of a problem	☐	☐	☐	☐	☐
Can produce lots of ideas in brainstorming	☐	☐	☐	☐	☐
Can produce useful mind maps	☐	☐	☐	☐	☐
Generate solutions to straightforward problems	☐	☐	☐	☐	☐
Choose an appropriate solution to simple problems	☐	☐	☐	☐	☐
Generate creative solutions to problems	☐	☐	☐	☐	☐
Choose an appropriate creative solution to a problem	☐	☐	☐	☐	☐

Having audited your current problem-solving skills, you should identify ways and opportunities to deal with weaknesses. Where appropriate build them into your personal development plan, and monitor progress in making improvements.

Often problem solving involves creative thinking. We sometimes refer to this as thinking 'out of the box'. Thinking inside the box means coming up with standard 'tried and tested' solutions to problems that do not require a lot of imagination. In contrast, creative thinking involves developing novel solutions and ideas that nobody has thought of before.

Verbal communication

Verbal communication involves aspects of speaking, listening and interacting with others. Some aspects of verbal communication, such as presentation skills, have already been dealt with in Unit 1: Learning strategies.

Effective listening

Listening is not the same as hearing. Effective listening involves really paying full attention to others: his or her words, speech, demeanour and body language. It means asking appropriate questions so as to better understand the meaning of what he or she is trying to communicate.

Effective listening is hard work and requires considerable skill; in social settings individual listeners often fail to listen to the messages that are being expressed because they are distracted by other things, such as the impression that they are making, and a wish to put his or her own point across. To be a 'good listener' requires that sometimes you just sit back and concentrate very hard on the message being put across. You can then prompt the person talking to clarify the meaning of what they say by asking brief questions: 'Can you tell me more about ... ?', 'Do you mean that ... ?' and so on.

Another important communication skill is that of respecting the opinions of others. We can save a lot of time and effort by considering what other people are saying, and forgetting for the time being our own point of view. After all:

♦ we have heard it before
♦ the more views and opinions we listen to the more we are likely to learn.

Respecting the opinions of others is particularly important in team-work situations.

Sometimes you will have to listen to views you do not like, do not understand or to which you cannot relate. A good listener is someone who tries to get a better understanding of views that are different from his or her own in order to see if there is merit in them. The best way of dealing with this is to keep an open mind and ask the speaker, in a non-threatening way, to clarify their ideas. For example, you might say, 'That sounds interesting but could you explain how it will work in practice?' or 'Can you explain to me how that is better than other ideas that have been put forward?' A good listener is constantly seeking to find out the best ideas and solutions even though these may contradict his or her starting position. However, this does not mean that you have to accept someone else's ideas: but you do need to consider them.

Interviewing techniques

If we want to get maximum advantage from our own primary research then it is important to develop interviewing techniques. These are dealt with in greater detail in Unit 10: Carrying out a research project, and market research is covered in Unit 8: Foundations of marketing. A good interviewer will make the interviewees feel comfortable, for example by using non-threatening body language, smiling and encouraging the interviewee. Another important aspect of interviewing is to be well prepared so it is clear you know what you are doing and have visible objectives. If you are using a questionnaire, make sure that it is easily understood and followed; provide a time limit and explain it, so interviewees know how much of his or her time will be involved.

Negotiation

Another important communication skill that is useful in business is that of negotiation. There are many situations where we need to negotiate, such as when needing an extension of the deadline date for completing assignments when we have been ill, the starting dates for work and for pay increases, the terms and conditions of work, and so on. An important aspect of negotiation is to be firm yet flexible rather than being too weak or unbending. A good negotiator will state his or her claim, and rather than getting involved in personalities will concentrate on the main issues and points of contention. Negotiation usually involves being able to make some sacrifices in order to secure a compromise but not to give in on essentials.

Persuasion

Persuasion is another area of communication on which business students will need to work. For example, there would be no point in devising really innovative ideas in the workplace if you could not persuade other people of the strength of them. The key to persuasion is to spell out the benefits accruing to various parties from your proposition or idea, and to show relevant parties, by providing practical examples, how they will benefit. In its simplest terms, explain 'what's in it for them'.

Presentation skills

Effective presentation skills have been described in some detail in Unit 1: Learning strategies. Key elements of a successful presentation are those of thorough preparation, good knowledge of subject, understanding of the needs of the audience, and selection and use of appropriate communications media.

Assertiveness

Being assertive is another important element of good verbal communication. Assertiveness is sometimes confused with aggression, but the two are very different. An assertive individual is someone who will not be taken advantage of or put upon; he or she is prepared to stand up for themselves in a calm, confident and decisive way. Take for example the student busy reproducing material on a photocopier in preparation for a talk. Someone comes along and says, 'You don't mind if I just do these, do you, I'm in a hurry?' An assertive person might say, 'I'm sorry, but I am in a hurry too, and will be finished in five minutes.' An assertive person thinks things through

ACTIVITY

Verbal communication

1 In the table below, look at the categories of communication skill and think of someone you know who performs in each area better than other people. Give an example of what he or she does.

2 Identify actions that you can include in your next action plan for improving on your own skills in terms of some or all of the communication skills outlined below.

Communication skill	Example
Listening effectively	
Showing respect for the opinions of others	
Interviewing	
Negotiating	
Persuading others	
Making presentations	
Being assertive	

in a logical way and presents his or her case clearly and firmly. Being assertive is important in a range of contexts because it is a way of effectively making important contributions, for example to group discussions, without seeking either to hog the limelight or to hide away in a corner. Being assertive enables you to make important contributions while developing a good sense of self-esteem and valuing others at the same time.

Time management

Using time effectively is a very important skill. Students of business need to learn to prioritise activities and tasks as well as workloads. Clear objectives need to be set if time is going to be managed well.

Allocating time

In carrying out a task you should decide:

- what the most important elements of the task are
- which tasks take longer
- what sequence the activities need to follow.

It is important that you put most time and effort into those activities which are the key to meeting your objectives. Many people waste a lot of time on minor problems, rather than concentrating upon essential activities.

Priorities

The nineteenth-century economist Vilfredo Pareto showed that 20 per cent of the population owned 80 per cent of the national wealth. Lothar Seiwart, writing in the 1940s, used this rule to show that 20 per cent of time and effort used well will produce 80 per cent of the results.

ACTIVITY

1 How well do you manage your time? Mark your position on the scale below for the six skills of time management.

2 Identify a project that you have been involved in where you managed time well and one where you managed time badly. What have you learned from these experiences? How could you develop strategies to manage time better? Build these strategies into an action plan for a work-based or education-based activity in which you will shortly be involved. Monitor your progress in meeting the action plan. Carry out an evaluation of your time-management skills as a result of reflecting on the process.

Skill	Strength				Weakness
	1	2	3	4	5
Prioritising workloads	☐	☐	☐	☐	☐
Setting work objectives	☐	☐	☐	☐	☐
Using time effectively	☐	☐	☐	☐	☐
Working steadily	☐	☐	☐	☐	☐
Making and keeping appointments	☐	☐	☐	☐	☐
Estimating task time	☐	☐	☐	☐	☐

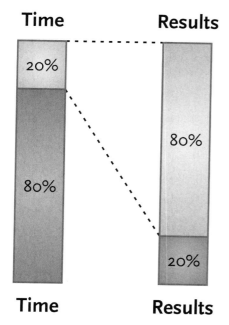

Figure 2.8   The 80:20 rule

Seiwart claims that the 80:20 rule applies in the following situations:

♦ 20 per cent of customers or goods account for 80 per cent of a firm's sales
♦ 20 per cent of meeting time produces 80 per cent of decisions
♦ 20 per cent of desk work makes possible 80 per cent of the success in one's tasks.

By planning our time well we can be more effective. Eight minutes of planning can make sure that we can carry out one hour of effective work. When you have an assignment to complete, think of the 80:20 rule.

One way of making sure that time is well spent is to undertake a value analysis of the use of time. This is called ABC analysis (see Unit 1: Learning strategies).

Appointments

An important aspect of time management is to make sure that you keep appointments. This requires some form of diary or Filofax system, or you could use an electronic organiser on a computer. When organising meetings, arrange not only a start time but also a finishing time. That way the people at the meeting remain focused on their tasks and can arrange their time after the meeting effectively.

Pacing

Try also to work steadily through coursework rather than erratically. It is important to work consistently over a period of time rather than in short, energetic bursts. These bursts can be panic-driven. A sudden burst usually means that you are behind schedule and may rush key elements of your work. On a degree-level course it is essential that you allocate sufficient time for learning and for reflecting on learning processes. It does not have to be done at a desk, but it has to be done.

It is also important to estimate the time that will be taken for certain tasks in order to plan projects and the overall use of your time. Some activities can be broken down into sub-components: we call these **partitionable tasks**. With partitionable tasks it is possible to break up the total time allocated to the project into segments. However, for some activities it is not possible to break the task down into segments, and they must be treated as a whole.

Chapter 4

Self-managed learning in a professional context

It is important for students to become self-managed learners because when they are able to learn for themselves they can achieve far more, are able to produce original work, enjoy their work, have pride in achieving results through their own efforts, and are likely to be highly motivated.

An important goal of personal development therefore is to help individuals to move forward to the point at which they become self-managed learners. This is a valuable skill in the job market. An important recommendation that employers look for on a reference for a potential employee is that they 'can manage their own time effectively', are 'effective self-managed learners', 'can manage projects independently' and so on.

An important outcome of professional development therefore is that individuals can demonstrate self-managed learning either in relation to workplace learning or university/college-based learning. A good opportunity for students to demonstrate that they can self-manage their learning is in their research project (see Unit 10).

Targets

In establishing targets it is important that students are able to establish for themselves the **aims** and **requirements** of the learning that they are undertaking.

Aims and requirements

Students should be able to establish the ends that they are trying to achieve and the requirements that the piece of work will need to fufil in order to achieve the stated aims. For example, if you have decided that you want to use a work-related

spreadsheet application, then you will need to be able to establish an aim, that is, what level of competence in the use of the package will be appropriate if successful learning is to take place? You will then need to set out what is required to learn how to use the package, that is, how you will access the training opportunities, resources, and how you will prioritise the use of time in order to be successful. What will you use the package for, bearing in mind that you are seeking to develop a cross-transferable skill? An important aspect of creating targets relates to **personal preferences** and **personal orientation to the achievement of set goals**.

Independent learning

Learning depends on four key issues:

♦ wanting
♦ doing
♦ feedback
♦ digesting.

To learn independently it is important to start from wanting, that is, the desire to learn. In choosing tasks related to professional development it is therefore sensible to choose tasks which are meaningful to the individual learner so as to maintain interest and motivation. The next step is to develop a fairly clear picture of what has to be learned: in other words, what does it mean to be more knowledgeable or more skilful in the chosen area of self-managed learning? Dates can then be established for the achievement of the learning so as to put the project into a time frame.

Learning styles

In Unit 1 we established that individuals typically show a preference for one or more styles of learning. Honey and Mumford in their book *Using Your Learning Style* argue that there are different learning styles; they maintain that people have their own preference for a particular learning style, which can change over time.

♦ Some people are **activists**. They respond immediately to concrete experiences without spending too much time on the reflection process. They may be seen as being impulsive and action orientated.

♦ **Reflectors** want to spend a considerable amount of time reflecting on the implications of concrete experiences. They also want to spend time on observation and mulling over their reflections. They will be less action orientated.

♦ **Theorists** want to take things a step further. They are concerned with creating ideas and generalisations based on their reflections.

They will try to order and construct new theories. Again, they will not be action orientated.

♦ **Pragmatists** are concerned with putting new theories into practice. They will want to test out the implications of new ideas and to see how they work. They thus have an action orientation.

None of these learning styles is necessarily better than the others.

The learning process

Kolb's learning cycle (Figure 2.9) is a useful starting point for examining the learning process.

For example, a **concrete experience** for a student may be that he always arrives late for lectures in the first two weeks of term. His **observations** indicate that there is a lot of traffic on the road at the time he is going to the college. He begins to develop theories (**concepts and generalisations**) that it is the time he is setting out to work that is causing the difficulties because so many others are on the road at the same time. Perhaps he would benefit from setting off a quarter of an hour earlier? The next day he **tests the implications** of his new theory by starting out fifteen minutes earlier, and, lo and behold, he arrives well in advance of his lecturer. His **concrete experience** is now that he arrives with plenty of time to prepare for his lecture. He feels more calm and relaxed. He reflects that this is a desirable state of affairs.

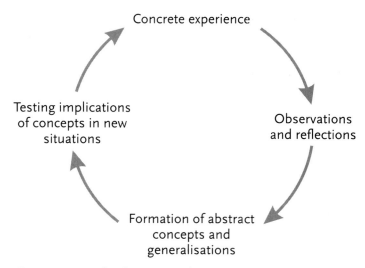

Figure 2.9 Kolb's learning cycle

ACTIVITY

Use the following template to assess a self-managed learning activity that you have devised.

What was the learning activity?

What were the learning objectives?

Describe what was involved in the learning activity, such as resources, structure, timing.

What skills were you able to work on as part of the learning activity? What sort of skill improvements were you hoping to achieve?

What were the main learning achievements?

What were the main disappointments?

Describe what you have found out about yourself during the learning experience in the following areas.

What role, such as organiser or leader, do you like to play in learning?

What do you work best with: people, ideas, information, physical things ... ?

What sort of learning tools do you prefer to work with: books, manuals, newspapers, the Internet, newsgroups, a mentor, training events, instruction manuals ... ?

What sort of help do you find most useful: friends, work colleagues, a mentor, a skilled specialist ... ?

Where do you most like to work from?

Learning can start from any point of the cycle, but according to Kolb it must involve all four points:

♦ Concrete experience is about responding to what happens, to events and direct experiences.
♦ Reflective observation involves having the ability to reflect on these concrete experiences, taking into account a number of views and perspectives.
♦ Forming abstract concepts involves integrating experiences and reflections into theories.
♦ Testing out implications involves putting theories into practice through experimentation.

Effective learning

By carrying out a self-managed learning project you should be able to gain an idea of the sorts of experiences that create effective learning. We have already outlined the importance of the process shown below:

Wanting ⇒ Doing ⇒ Feedback ⇒ Learning.

Skills of personal assessment are important as part of the learning process. You need to be able to honestly evaluate your own learning. You need to be able to answer the question: After carrying out the learning activity, what do I know? What am I able to do that I didn't know or have the skill to do before?

For effective learning to take place it is essential that activities are well planned with clear objectives, time schedules, and so on. Activities need to be well organised in a clear structure designed to achieve learning objectives. Finally, the learning that takes place needs to be evaluated. What have you learned? What have you learned about yourself? For example, what is your preferred learning style? Are you a good planner, a good organiser? What improvements could you make to your planning and organising?

On-line research methods

An important part of modern independent learning is the ability to use the Internet. The Internet provides access to up-to-the-minute data from a range of sources and is an invaluable source of research information. Using the Internet is introduced in Unit 1 and is also covered in Unit 10 and elsewhere in this book. In the context of independent learning, students should be able to access and navigate the Internet to search for relevant sources.

A useful way of sharing information and finding out information from others is through **newsgroups.** The term 'news' refers to messages stored in about 100,000 discussion groups. A newsgroup is dedicated to the discussion of a particular topic or issue. **Usenet news** is the Internet's main discussion area.

Newsgroups

A Usenet newsgroup operates rather like a free public notice board. If you post an item on the 'notice board' everyone who uses that particular newsgroup can read it. They can post a reply or email you personally. You can't tell who reads your messages unless they post a reply. The amount of time an item stays on the notice board depends on your news provider's system. However, it does give you access to lots of up-to-date research information.

You will also find discussion groups which are referred to by a number of names such as bulletin boards, egroups and forums. Like newsgroups they allow you to post notices for others to read. Thousands of these are indexed at www.tile.net/lists/

Using newsgroups and bulletin boards which relate to a piece of work you are carrying out means you can ask other people for information which might help you. It is also a way of sharing your ideas and findings with others working in the same field.

Assessment of learning

Having engaged in learning activities it is possible to assess the learning that has taken place. By engaging in self-managed learning activities you should become more confident in your ability to undertake further personal learning.

Students should be able to identify and produce evidence that shows improvement in levels of certain skills, such as time management, problem solving, communication skills, and so on. So in planning learning experiences you must be careful to establish targets and reviews for the skills that you are seeking to develop as part of the learning experience.

On completion of the learning activity you should also be able to reflect on the learning achievement and any disappointments, and use these reflections as a means of improving further learning.

End of unit assignment

In order to meet the learning outcomes for this unit you will need to build up a portfolio to include the following three items.

1 A personal development plan, for career and personal development. It should include a skills audit, aims, targets, review dates, achievement dates, learning activities and action plans. Include also an up-to-date curriculum vitae. Make an evaluation of progress and achievement of personal development and learning targets.

2 An audit of your problem-solving, verbal communication, and time-management skills coupled with an action plan for improvements and a review of improvements made.

3 An example of a self-managed learning project that you have done setting out:

- targets and why they were chosen
- a time schedule for achieving targets
- an assessment of your preferred learning style
- a personal evaluation of how effective the learning was, and how you could have organised it better
- an assessment of the learning achievements and disappointments.

Further reading

Arnold, J. (2003) *Managing Careers into the 21st Century*, London: Pearson Books.

Corfield, R. (2003) *Preparing Your Own CV*, London: The Times.

Eales, R. (2004) *The Effective Leader*, London: Kogan Page.

Jay, R. (2004) *The Successful Candidate: How to be the Person They Want to Employ*, London: Financial Times.

Kay, F. (2003) *Time Your Management*, Oxford: Capstone Publishing.

Megginson, D. and Whitaker, V. (2003) *Continuing Professional Development*, London: Chartered Institute of Personnel and Development.

Pareto, V. (1896) *Cours d'économie à l'Université de Lausanne*, Lausanne: Rouge.

Pettinger, R. (2002) *Mastering Employee Development*, Palgrave Master Series, Basingstoke: Palgrave.

Seiwart, L. (1987) *Master Your Own Time*, Munich: Gabal.

Yale, M. (2003) *The Ultimate CV Book*, London: Kogan Page.

Unit 3

Employability skills

This unit provides an opportunity for the learner to improve their own learning styles and develop an understanding of their own and others' responsibilities and performance. It considers the skills required and the dynamics of working with others in teams or groups. It also deals with the everyday working requirement to solve problems. This includes identifying the problem, specifying approaches to its solution, and evaluating the results of the solution through reflective practices. The unit provides an opportunity to consider and develop communication skills. These include handling, processing and communicating information, and again critical reflection on the effectiveness of the methods chosen.

Students may like to keep a portfolio of employability skills based on the activities outlined in this unit.

Summary of learning outcomes

On completion of this unit you will be able to:
♦ identify, describe and evaluate your own and others' responsibilities and performance
♦ investigate and describe the dynamics of working with others
♦ develop, present and evaluate a strategy for solving a problem
♦ develop, present and evaluate a strategy for handling, processing and communicating information.

Chapter 1

Responsibilities and performance

Business is a subject which is applied to real world experience in the workplace. Most, if not all, students following a business degree will have experience of the world of work:

♦ some will have full-time jobs
♦ some will have part-time jobs
♦ nearly all will have some experience of the workplace
♦ many will have a work placement integrated into their degree studies.

It is important for employees to have a clear picture of how they fit into the organisation that they work for; their rights and responsibilities, and the sorts of factors that determine individual motivation and performance.

Job descriptions and job specifications

A **job description** describes what a person carrying out a post is expected to do. They can be defined as 'a broad statement of the purpose, scope, responsibilities and tasks which make up a certain job'. Job descriptions are very important for the organisation and the individual because they make it clear who does what in the organisation, and the responsibility and accountability attached to a position.

A job description consists of:

♦ a job title
♦ the department in which the job holder works
♦ a statement outlining how the job fits into the overall strategy of the organisation
♦ an outline of the purpose of the job
♦ details of the job's content, such as the tasks which must be performed and the responsibilities involved

♦ if appropriate, a brief description of any resources which the job holder will be responsible for
♦ in a large organisation, the hours and precise place of work may be included as this can provide useful information in determining availability and suitability for proposed training programmes.

A **job specification** goes beyond a simple description by highlighting the knowledge and the mental and physical attributes required of the job holder and the environment in which the job is performed. These activities are normally classified under the heading of 'knowledge and skills' and sometimes a heading of 'attitudes' is used. In the case of an administrator's job, two of the tasks in the job description might be word-processing documents and answering the telephone. Two of the associated 'physical and mental activities' might be knowledge of relevant information technology packages and interpersonal skills required in dealing with customers on the telephone.

ACTIVITY

1   Place a copy of your job description and job specification from work in your employability skills folder. Describe the main work roles and/or tasks and responsibilities that you perform in the workplace.

2   Analyse these roles, tasks and responsibilities in terms of how demanding they are, how important they are to the organisation, and how important they are in supporting other people at work. Explain why it is important to have a clear job description. At what times might you need to refer to the job description?

Reward systems

Another important aspect of work is the reward system that operates, that is, the system of rewarding employees for their efforts. **Pay scales** are typically related to aspects such as experience and seniority, as well as the qualifications required to carry out particular jobs. Pay is also frequently related to performance, so the measurement of performance is an important aspect of the reward system.

Rating systems are frequently used in determining pay. A standard rate is established for meeting required standards. Higher rates can then be earned for superior performance. **Bonus** and **incentive schemes** are often used to encourage employees to meet superior performance targets. For example, commission on sales is a form of incentive scheme encouraging those job holders who meet higher sales targets.

Flexibility in working relationships is also related to reward systems. Increasingly employees are asked to work non-standard hours, or non-standard contracts. For example, the number of hours they work each week may be related to the number of orders that a company receives. As a result there will be considerable flexibility in the associated reward system: some days or weeks an individual will work longer hours and receive higher rewards, other days they will work shorter hours.

ACTIVITY

This is another piece of work for your employability skills portfolio.

1   Describe the reward system that is associated with your job description, or terms and conditions of work. How are pay and other rewards determined?

2   Evaluate the effectiveness of the reward system in the company you work for in terms of gaining the commitment of the employees and helping the organisation to meet its objectives.

Responsibilities

Within your job role you will normally be held accountable for your actions and be responsible to a line manager. In return you will have a number of responsibilities: for example, responsibility for resources, responsibility to meet given deadlines, and sometimes responsibility for other people.

ACTIVITY

Set out a table with the following information to include in your employability skills folder.

1   Title of your job

2   Responsible to:
    (who do you have to report to?)

3   Responsibility for:
    ◆ Resources
    ◆ Time management
    ◆ People.

Some of the relationships you have at work will be direct and others will be indirect. For example, if you work in the customer services section of a store, then you will have a direct relationship with customers. However, if you are unpacking boxes in the storeroom your relationship with customers will be indirect. In a similar way you will have a direct relationship with other members of your team, and an indirect relationship with senior managers of the store. In developing relationships with people at work it is important to be adaptable because in the fast-changing world of modern workplaces you cannot expect to carry out the same routine operations day after day and year after year.

It is therefore important to develop the ability to learn and develop within your work role. Individuals who want to progress in the workplace therefore need to develop attitudes that welcome change and opportunities to learn new skills.

Decision making

Decision-making processes and skills are another important aspect of your relationships with others in the workplace. Decision making involves making a choice between alternative courses of action, for example in managing resources in the workplace, managing time in the workplace, or managing relationships with others.

Decision-making skills involve being able to assemble relevant evidence about alternative choices, weighing up the alternatives, and making and carrying out a decision.

Employees also have an important responsibility in terms of health and safety legislation. All organisations that employ five or more people must have a written health and safety policy, which sets out:

♦ who is responsible for workplace health and safety
♦ arrangements that have to be made for health and safety.

This policy must be communicated to all employees. Employees must comply with company procedures and arrangements for health and safety. All employees must be trained and provided with clear information about risks at work and the steps to take in dealing with them.

The Control of Substances Hazardous to Health Regulations sets out clear rules for the handling, storage, and recording of the use of dangerous chemicals. The Health and Safety (Display Screen Equipment) Regulations set out clear directions and requirements for the use of display screens on word processors, as a measure to prevent illnesses and headaches resulting from the use of such equipment.

The Employment Relations Acts of 1999 and 2003 provide a range of contractual rights for employees, including:

♦ entitlement to an itemised pay statement
♦ entitlement to the National Minimum Wage
♦ the terms and conditions of work being set out in writing
♦ protection against unfair dismissal at work.

The Sex Discrimination Act protects employees against discrimination on the grounds of gender, while the Race Relations Act provides similar protection against discrimination on grounds of race. The Equal Pay Act sets out that women and men should receive the same pay for doing the same type of work or work ranked as being of the same value. The Disability Discrimination Act requires employers to accommodate the needs of the disabled. The Working Time Directive 1999 guarantees all employees a maximum 48-hour working week and a four-week holiday, although employees can choose to opt out.

Performance targets

It is important to have targets so that you have something tangible to aim for and against which to evaluate your performance.

Personal targets

These targets are ones that you set yourself, and will be related to work and study. Some of these targets will be short term, for example to master a particular IT package or to complete a work- or study-based assignment. Other personal targets will be longer term, such as to develop the work-based competences required for you to move up another grade at work.

Financial targets

These targets are ones that can be measured by financial indicators. For example, targets for a business will relate to the value of sales, profit and other financial indicators. An individual's financial targets relate to income, saving, and other personal balances.

Work-rate targets

These relate to meeting certain standards, for example the number of customers served, number of units produced, number of calls answered, and so on.

Outcome targets

These relate to previously planned outcomes, such as to finish a project on time, to reach a given level of competence in performing a task.

Some of these performance targets may be written into your job description; for example, you may be expected to perform to a given targeted standard, or be expected to produce work of a certain quality.

All organisations set and monitor performance targets because this gives direction to organisational activity. At an organisation-wide level there will be performance targets which then translate down into unit-level targets, team targets and individual targets. For example, the organisation that sets itself the target of reducing consumer complaints by 10 per cent will

drill this target down to individual targets of reducing consumer complaints by 10 per cent. By setting these targets it is then possible to assess the performance of individual employees.

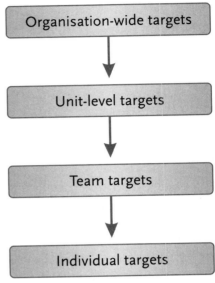

Figure 3.1   Targets

Individual appraisal and development systems

Development is concerned with the needs of individuals who work for organisations. Most people are motivated by being given personal development opportunities in the workplace. Many people want to develop greater levels of knowledge, skill and capability at work. They know that this sort of development will enable them to perform their jobs better, enable them to take on promotion opportunities and to gain more fulfilment at work. Individuals also want to develop themselves because they have a life outside work, and because they may want eventually to work for other organisations and to take on more responsibility.

Performance appraisal

The most important way of identifying individual development needs is **performance appraisal**. Appraisal is a formal assessment of the performance of an employee.

Appraisal involves establishing clear objectives for each employee and evaluating actual performance in the light of the achievement of targets.

The most important part of an appraisal system is usually a one-to-one discussion between an individual and his or her line manager. This can be held frequently, but usually takes place once a year. There are two key parts to this process:

♦ assessment of performance against expectations or targets
♦ identification of the strengths and weaknesses that lie behind the performance.

If appraisal is to be successfully related to training and development, then:

♦ the appraiser and the appraisee need to have a shared understanding of the purpose and value of the appraisal process, and a common commitment to its objectives
♦ both of the parties involved must see the appraisal as a learning process, not just the appraisee
♦ the appraisal process needs to be focused on shared objectives relating to work and development rather than being focused on criticism and blame
♦ appraisal needs to be seen as part of an overall development process rather than a 'bolt-on extra'.

The appraisal discussion may consider specific performance measures such as individual output or involve a more general review of the contribution that the employee makes to the smooth running of the business.

Reasons for using performance appraisal

These include:

♦ to improve the performance of the employee
♦ to provide feedback to the individual about his or her performance
♦ to recognise the future training needs of the individual
♦ to consider the development of the individual's career
♦ to identify employees in the organisation who have potential for advancement.

Outcomes of the appraisal process

The outcomes of performance appraisal should always contain the following elements:

♦ motivation, to sustain the ongoing motivation of the appraisee
♦ an increased understanding by both parties of issues related to the appraisee's performance
♦ accurate diagnosis of the learner's learning needs
♦ a development step for the appraisee outlined with the appraisal discussion.

For development purposes, some form of 'multi-input' appraisal process has great benefit. The form of appraisal called **360-degree appraisal** involves some form of feedback about performance from superiors, peers and subordinates within the organisation and enables an individual to identify their strengths and weaknesses through a number of eyes.

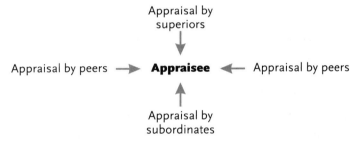

Figure 3.2   360-degree appraisal

Performance appraisal is invaluable for identifying **training needs**, because it involves an input both from the organisation (to meet business development needs) and the individual (to meet personal development needs).

Figure 3.3 is an example of a typical appraisal form.

Work performance rating

Appraisal that is linked to performance typically involves some method of **rating** the work performance of individuals. For example, one method is to set out a checklist of competencies that need to be achieved. Today many organisations use a competency-based checklist. **Competency** is defined as 'an underlying characteristic of an individual which is related to effective or superior performance in a job'.

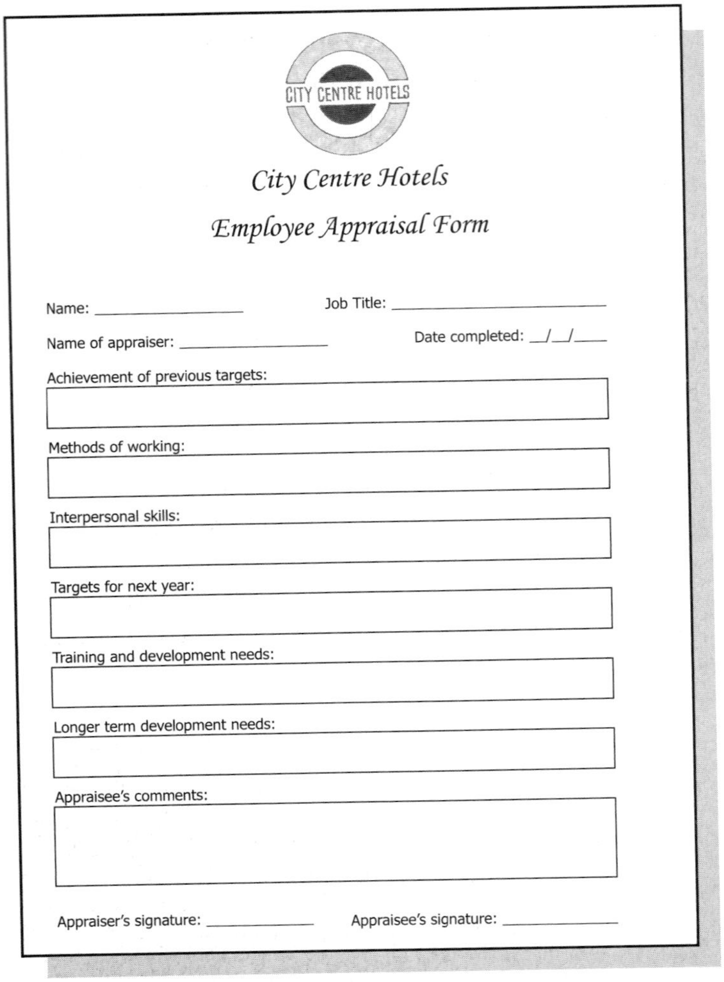
CITY CENTRE HOTELS

City Centre Hotels

Employee Appraisal Form

Name: ______________ Job Title: ______________

Name of appraiser: ______________ Date completed: __/__/__

Achievement of previous targets:

Methods of working:

Interpersonal skills:

Targets for next year:

Training and development needs:

Longer term development needs:

Appraisee's comments:

Appraiser's signature: ____________ Appraisee's signature: ____________

Figure 3.3 Typical appraisal form

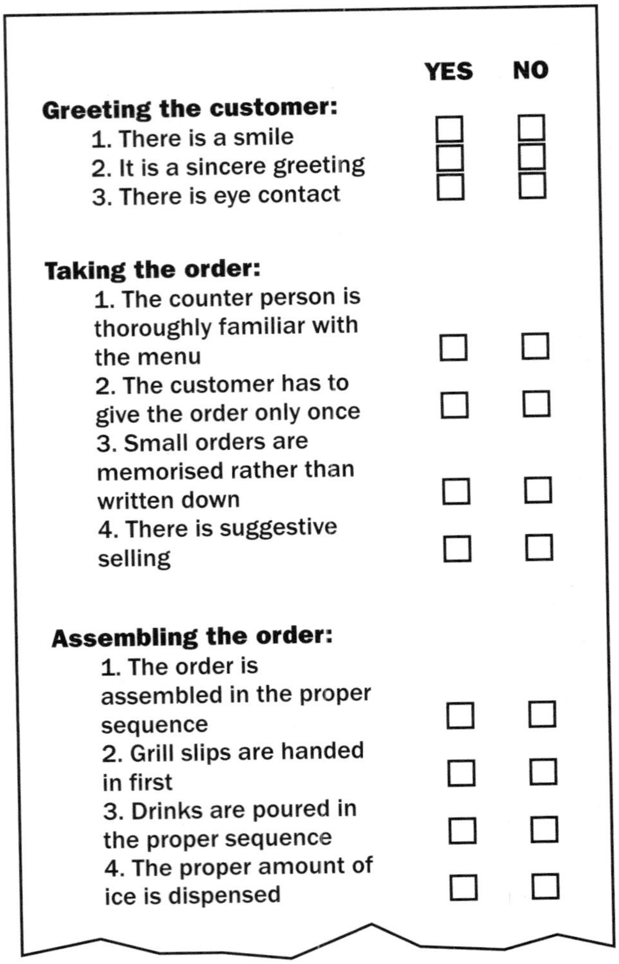
	YES	NO
Greeting the customer:		
1. There is a smile	☐	☐
2. It is a sincere greeting	☐	☐
3. There is eye contact	☐	☐
Taking the order:		
1. The counter person is thoroughly familiar with the menu	☐	☐
2. The customer has to give the order only once	☐	☐
3. Small orders are memorised rather than written down	☐	☐
4. There is suggestive selling	☐	☐
Assembling the order:		
1. The order is assembled in the proper sequence	☐	☐
2. Grill slips are handed in first	☐	☐
3. Drinks are poured in the proper sequence	☐	☐
4. The proper amount of ice is dispensed	☐	☐

Figure 3.4 Competency list in a fast food restaurant

Figure 3.4 illustrates a competency list used by managers to evaluate counter staff performance in a fast food restaurant.

Behaviour scales

Many appraisal schemes include a **behaviour scale** because it is felt that behaviour rather than personality should be appraised and rewarded.

Behaviour scales describe a range of behaviours that contribute to a greater or lesser degree to the successful achievement of the cluster of tasks which make up a job. Supervisors carrying out appraisal are asked to indicate which statements on the specially designated form most accurately describe a subordinate's behaviour. A detailed version of this is the Behaviourally Anchored Rating Scales (BARS).

Statements about work behaviour are used to create scales, which must then be tested to confirm their relevance and accuracy.

Some form of **paired comparison** may be used to compare one job in relation to another, or one employee's performance of a job in comparison to that of another. Alternatively, individual performance may be ranked, that is, evaluated in terms of an order of performance, with the most successful performance receiving the highest rewards and benefits. Management by objectives involves establishing objectives for many areas of work and then assessing performance in terms of whether these objectives are achieved. Individual objectives can be related to departmental and organisational objectives.

Performance and employee potential

Performance appraisal from the organisation's point of view therefore is a very useful way of matching organisational needs with employee potential. For example, the results of appraisal can be used to identify those employees who are most suitable for specialist training, such as management training. As we saw in Unit 2: Professional development, a personal development plan can be created for every employee in the workplace. A **personal development plan** (PDP) is a document setting out personal targets for development of individual employees usually informed by the appraisal system.

ACTIVITY

Obtain a copy of your latest appraisal form for your employability skills portfolio. Produce a written commentary to accompany it, setting out:

♦ how appraisal is used in the organisation that you work for
♦ how you see appraisal helping your own personal development
♦ what your main short- and long-term targets are
♦ what rating methods are used in relation to your own job.

Motivation and performance

Workplace experience helps you to apply and appraise **motivational theories**. The work of key motivational theorists is covered in Unit 4: Foundations of organisations and behaviour. One of the broad findings of modern motivational theory is that for individual employees to be truly motivated they need to be given opportunities to fulfil their own needs through their work. Motivation is thus determined by intrinsic rather than extrinsic factors. Committed employees enjoy their work, enjoy being given responsibility and the opportunity to express themselves through their work.

Of course, rewards and incentives play an important part in encouraging people to work hard, but rewards do not create commitment to an organisation.

Motivation and management

Motivation is an important aspect of the manager's role. An important aspect of management is that of making sure that tasks are carried out by other people. A motivating manager will succeed in making subordinates or team members work *with* them, rather than work *for* them. A motivating manager will find out about the needs and aspirations of the people who they work with, and identify ways of helping those individuals to develop in the workplace.

ACTIVITY

This task is for your employability skills portfolio. Read Unit 4, pp 125–7, which examines approaches to motivational theory. To what extent does your experience of working, and working with others, support the views put forward by motivational theorists such as Herzberg and Maslow? How important are monetary and non-monetary rewards and incentives in determining commitment and effort in your workplace? How is the context in which work takes place likely to determine motivation?

ACTIVITY

This task is for your employability skills portfolio. Identify the attributes of two contrasting managers: one who is good at motivating and one who is poor at motivating others.

In the workplace it is also important to consider self-motivational factors, that is, the drives and other influences that encourage you to work hard both for yourself and the organisation. Important factors are your levels of self-esteem that lead you to have a pride in what you are doing and a sense of personal worth, as well as your desire for advancement and promotion.

Chapter 2
The dynamics of working with others

This chapter examines the nature and importance of team-working. It should therefore be read before carrying out the tasks and activities that are outlined in this part of the unit.

Working in teams

The nature of modern workplaces is that a lot of work activities are organised in teams. This means that as an employee you will be expected to work with others as a normal part of work activity. It is important to develop an understanding of how teams interact, that is, **team dynamics**. A distinction is sometimes made between a group, which is just a collection of individuals who are loosely bound together, and a team, in which individuals have a collective sense of responsibility to each other and work hard for the team.

Another important distinction is between a **formal** and an **informal** group or team. An informal team is simply one that comes together to achieve a particular purpose but does not have a formal structure. For example, motorists coming together to deal with a road traffic accident may work as an informal group or team. The structure may then become more formalised when members of the emergency services arrive on the scene, with their more formalised structures for working together.

As an individual you will belong to both formal and informal teams. The formal team will be the one that is officially set up by the organisation for a specific purpose, for example a project team. At the same time you may frequently work in informal teams with other work colleagues to share responsibility for achieving certain tasks.

Purposes of team-work

Teams and groups are set up in the workplace to achieve a range of different purposes, for example:

♦ Teams are just one component of the organisational structure designed to enable the organisation to meet its objectives and strategies. For example, a training team may be assembled to educate employees about a new piece of software, which will enable the organisation to develop a better communication system.
♦ Teams are frequently brought together for problem-solving purposes. For example, quality circles are small teams of employees who come together on a regular basis to discuss and find ways of tackling work-related problems and issues.
♦ Teams are frequently created for short-term development projects. Once the project is complete the team members will be re-assembled into other work teams.

ACTIVITY

This task is for your employability skills portfolio.

1   Identify one formal and one informal team or group of which you are a member at work. What is the purpose of the group or team?

2   Describe the structure and dynamics of the team, that is, what are the main types of relationships and communication systems within the team?

Teams and team building

Some teams involve an element of leadership while others are self-managing with a more democratic structure. However, it is important that if there is no formal leader that there is a structure to team activity: for example, in clarifying objectives, deadlines, expected outcomes, and so on. In this sense a team will always have an element of leadership because in some situations the team itself will take on the leadership role.

Selection of team members

The selection of team members depends on the mix of personalities and the purpose of the team. Sometimes a team is selected on the basis of the different skills that are required: for example, a book-publishing team may require people with skills in project planning, editorial, picture research and production. On other occasions team selection may be based on the different approaches that team members will employ: for example, creative types who come up with exciting new ideas, pragmatists who focus the team on practical solutions, resource investigators who will find ways of providing the resources required for the project, and so on. Some members of the team will be full-time members, whereas others, such as specialist outside consultants, may be pulled in and work part time.

Team roles

In carrying out a project it is important to identify team or group roles to make sure that the team employs an appropriate range of approaches for the task in hand.

ACTIVITY

This task is for your employability skills portfolio. Carry out an analysis of one or more teams of which you have recently been a member. Analyse the team or group roles using the following headings:

1 Purpose of the team

2 Members of team
(Identify full-time and part-time members.)

3 Leadership of the team
(How was the team led? How effective was the leadership?)

4 Role of each member

5 Effectiveness of the team
(Could the team have been made more effective by including members with different skills or approaches?)

6 Evaluation of team performance
(How could team-working and team performance have been improved?)

Team development

There are a number of stages involved in team development. Team building is an important part of getting everybody working together to achieve common goals. There are a number of ways of building teams:

◆ Team building can take place by taking group members away from their normal group setting and carrying out a range of (teamwork) activities in which the team thinks about how it can work better together, where problems arise in teamworking etc. The purpose of such an initiative is to help the group to think more as a team.

◆ Team building can take place through continuous improvement processes. The team leader and team members take responsibility for team building activities, usually involving a series of ongoing team meetings.

◆ Another approach is through some form of outdoor experience where groups have to work together to meet a set of challenges related to outdoor pursuits. By working together in a new setting in which members are forced to rely on each other it is possible to build up new bonds and real teamwork.

Team building

An important part of team building for the organisation is to try and create a shared set of values which represent what the organisation is trying to achieve. When groups and teams share the same values as the organisation the best results will be achieved.

There are a number of aspects of team building, including:

♦ helping team members to identify shared beliefs, objectives and purposes
♦ developing interpersonal skills within team members, such as listening skills
♦ developing team rewards for supporting behavior
♦ developing collective problem-solving skills
♦ building up a store of personal goodwill to overcome problems
♦ developing team confidence and competence
♦ recognising personal strengths and weaknesses – technical and personal
♦ all of the above will help to create team loyalty, identity and motivation.

Stages of team building

The typical stages of team building are:

♦ identifying a problem in terms of existing team relationships or an opportunity to build a new team structure
♦ group members work together to gather data relating to the problem or opportunity
♦ group members collaboratively analyse the data and create a plan for improvement; targets are set for improving team performance
♦ group members collaboratively create action plans for improvement
♦ the action plan is implemented by the team
♦ the team collaboratively evaluates the impact the new plans are having; this involves monitoring progress and using feedback for ongoing improvement
♦ ongoing improvement of the process.

Frequently teams will be organised on multi-disciplinary lines, that is, using the skills of individuals from a range of different functions and specialisms within the organisation. This enables a combination of knowledge and skills which can then be applied to project management and problem solving.

Two useful tools to use in planning effective teamwork are:

♦ skills analysis
♦ team health evaluation.

A **skills analysis** is simply an audit of the various skills of team members, used to check that team members have the required skills necessary for effective team functioning. If the team lacks the appropriate skills then it may be necessary to bring in other specialists, or for existing team members to undertake relevant training.

ACTIVITY

This task is for your employability skills portfolio. Produce a short written log identifying the processes involved in building teamwork in a team that you have recently been a member of or a team that you created. This should answer such questions as:

♦ What activities were used to develop teamworking?
♦ What processes were employed to create motivation, identity, loyalty and commitment to shared beliefs within the team?
♦ How were target setting, action planning, and monitoring and feedback used to maintain and improve team performance?
♦ Could any of the above have been improved on? How?

In addition, set out a questionnaire survey that could be used with team members to assess the level of team health over time.

A **team health evaluation** is a tool that is used to check on how the team is working together, and will typically involve an analysis of relationships within the team, the motivation of team members, team members' understanding of objectives, and team members' commitment.

Coaching and mentoring

Coaching and mentoring are other important ways in which you might be asked to work with others in the workplace. Both **mentoring** and **coaching** involve an experienced hand helping a learner to become more effective in their role. However, there are four key differences between mentoring and coaching:

♦ mentoring is a long, if intermittent, relationship; while coaching can cover a long time span, it can also be limited to a single session

♦ coaching is a valuable skill for line managers; the mentoring role, by contrast, is separate from that of line manager and the same person should not carry out both

♦ the mentoring relationship is more about context than content: it is less concerned with day-to-day work than with longer-term issues such as working relationships and career paths

♦ coaching can be public: groups of people can be coached; mentoring is conducted in confidence on a one-to-one basis.

ACTIVITY

This task is for your employability skills portfolio. Identify one individual who has worked with you in a coaching or mentoring role at work. What aspects of the way they worked with you were particularly effective? How can you use the experience that you have had of being coached or mentored to become a coach or mentor to someone else in the future?

Chapter 3
Solving problems

There are many ways of solving problems, and which one is used depends on the nature of the problem, the time frame in which to solve the problem, whether the problem requires conventional or creative thinking, who is solving it, and other factors. A number of different types of problem solving were described in Unit 2, chapter 3.

This chapter focuses on providing one type of framework for tackling a problem at work, and therefore follows a fairly standard approach to problem solving, which is illustrated in Figure 3.5.

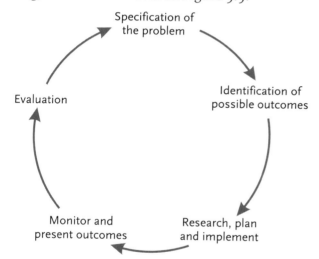

Figure 3.5   Solving problems

Try using this approach to manage systematically a problem-solving activity at work, either as an individual or working with others in a team.

Specify the problem

The first action in problem solving is to try and **specify what the problem is**. For example, the problem might be that an individual or team is failing to meet its targets, or although it is meeting targets it may be felt that improvements can be made. Alternatively, a problem might be in finding a new way of managing work, or of promoting a new product.

Try to specify what the problem is in as few words as possible, and to set out the likely causes of the problem. Data may need to be collected and analysed to give a better understanding of the problem and its causes. For example, if customer satisfaction targets are not being met it will make sense to keep a record of customer complaints, and then to analyse them to find out where the major problems lie.

Presentation techniques

It is helpful to present the problem using a range of techniques such as written reports, and diagrammatic means such as charts, graphs and diagrams. For example, a pie chart might be used to show a breakdown of the main sources of consumer complaints and a line graph to show trends over time in customer satisfaction. You may also need to produce an oral report supported by

ACTIVITY

This task is for your employability skills portfolio. Identify a problem at work that is suitable for investigation using problem-solving techniques. You will need to present the problem by producing an illustrated report. In your report:

♦ specify the nature of the problem
♦ outline the causes of the problem
♦ produce and analyse data relevant to the specification of the problem and identification of its causes.

Present the problem using charts and diagrams generated using computer software.

a PowerPoint presentation to explain the problem to an audience. You can also specify the nature of the problem using computer-based methods, including presentation software, spreadsheets and graphics.

Identify possible outcomes

When you identify a problem it is impractical to conduct a full analysis every time. A starting point therefore might be to 'brainstorm' with your team the possible benefits of changing an existing system: perhaps there are no benefits at all.

There are a number of possible outcomes that will result from implementing problem-solving strategies. Some of these outcomes will be desirable and others undesirable, as illustrated in Figure 3.6.

Desired outcomes	Undesired outcomes
The solution leads to greater satisfaction among relevant parties, such as customers, employees.	The solution leads to dissatisfaction among all or some of the parties.
The solution creates an improvement by creating more desired outcomes.	The solution has undesired effects, such as shifting the problem elsewhere in the organisation.
The solution creates better products and processes.	The solution leads to less desirable products and processes.
The solution leads to greater sales, profits etc.	The solution increases costs.

Figure 3.6　Desired and undesired outcomes

ACTIVITY

This task is for your employability skills portfolio. With reference to the work-based problem that you are seeking to solve, outline a range of desired possible outcomes and undesired outcomes to possible solutions.

Research, plan and implement

Now it is time to investigate ways of solving your problem. A useful starting point is to carry out some research into what other similar organisations or groups are doing to solve problems of a similar nature to your own.

Research

Research into methods of problem solving might involve examining websites or visiting other companies that are facing similar problems: you may even find good ideas within your own organisation.

You need to examine a range of methods that can be used to solve the problem. Some of the methods that can be used include brainstorming ideas or setting out spider diagrams to build links between ideas. You may want to use some quantitative techniques such as calculating probabilities of possible outcomes (see Unit 9).

Analysis of the problem might come under a number of headings:

♦ needs of the organisation
♦ needs of individuals working for the organisation
♦ performance: including what is wrong with current performance
♦ the current system for handling the problem.

On the basis of this analysis it should be possible to outline possible alternative systems or solutions that can be introduced to deliver improved outcomes for relevant parties and the system as a whole. An important consideration will be the costs involved in introducing a new system or solution.

Planning and implementation

Planning involves identifying objectives and targets to work towards in introducing new systems or solutions. Once the objectives and targets have been established then the new systems or solutions can be worked out.

Having planned how the solution to the problem will be delivered, implementation can start to take place. The solution will need to be explained to all concerned. Some say that you need to get all those involved to agree to the solution: in particular, that they can meet the targets set out in the solution. The solution should include the following elements:

♦ a timescale: often this will involve setting out short-term (definite) solutions, medium-term goals, and long-term projections of outcomes
♦ stages: breaking down the achievement of the solution into relevant components where appropriate
♦ resources: those required to achieve the solution
♦ finance: that required to implement the solution
♦ critical path analysis: when it is possible to quantify the time required to carry out a project and the sequence of steps in which the project will be carried out, it is then possible to set out diagrammatically what is referred to as a **critical path**, for example if there are two sets of processes required to complete a project.

Critical path analysis

C takes 3 days and follows B.
B takes 3 days and follows A.
A takes 2 days.
E takes 4 days and follows D.
D takes 4 days and follows A.
F follows C and E, and takes 2 days.
F completes the project.

There are thus two routes to the completion of the project:

♦ route 1: A ⇒ B ⇒ C ⇒ F ⇒ completion
♦ route 2: A ⇒ D ⇒ E ⇒ F ⇒ completion.

Route 1 takes 10 days: 2 + 3 + 3 + 2
Route 2 takes 12 days: 2 + 4 + 4 + 2.

We call route 2 shown above the **critical path** because if this sequence of activities is not completed on time, then the project will fall behind 12 days. We therefore put the emphasis in our project-management skills and resources into making sure that route 2 is

completed on time. In contrast, we can allow the sequence in route 1 to fall a little behind time, because it will only take 10 days, and we have 12 days 'to play with'.

ACTIVITY

This task is for your employability skills folder.

1 What sources of information will you use to research your solution to your problem? Outline the main information that you gained from this research. How did you analyse this information?

2 Set out the timescale, stages, resources, and finance required for your plan.

3 Set out a critical path diagram to illustrate the stages in your plan and how they will be implemented.

Monitor and present outcomes

Once you have reached the stage of implementing your solution to the problem, you will need to **monitor the outcomes** and **present progress** in an appropriate form so it can be understood by a relevant audience.

Having done the background research to inform problem solving, you will be able to create a **menu of possible solutions** to a problem. From this menu you can select the most suitable options.

The chosen option can then be broken down into a number of stages (as, for example, in critical path planning), and then results can be monitored to check progress.

It is important to establish criteria and feedback tools to check on progress in implementing solutions. These feedback tools should be designed before the chosen solution is implemented. Progress can then be appraised and **feedback** provided on progress and ways of improving solutions to make better progress.

Presentation techniques

Once again results attained in implementing a problem-solving solution can be presented in a variety of ways, for example written reports, diagrams such as charts and graphs, and oral reports. Computer-based methods can be used; for example, progress in achieving the critical path can be illustrated using dedicated computer packages. Line graphs are a useful technique for presenting performance over time, while pie charts help to show the breakdown of totals into sub-components.

Five-minute management

Modern car plants, such as Jaguar at Castle Bromwich, use a 'five-minute management' approach for **visual problem solving**. The workforce is organised into teams who have their own work and recreation areas alongside the production line. A certain amount of time is set aside each week for the team to discuss work-related activities using problem-solving approaches. In a typical session, the team:

♦ identifies a current work-based problem
♦ brainstorms ideas for solutions to the problem
♦ discusses these solutions to see which are the most practical
♦ chooses a solution
♦ illustrates the solution graphically on a display board using simple pictures.

The idea is that anyone visiting the work area and examining the display board should be able to understand the problem and its solution within five minutes.

Evaluation

You have now reached the end of the problem-solving cycle. You specified the problem, identified possible outcomes, researched, planned and implemented your solution, and monitored and presented the outcomes. In order to move the process forward you need to evaluate your problem-solving activities in a critical and honest way.

ACTIVITY

This task is for your employability skills folder. Either on your own or working as a team, identify the most appropriate solution for a work-based problem that you have researched, and develop a plan for its solution. Set out a log to monitor and record progress in implementing the solution. Set out the stages, progress and results in implementing the solution. Describe the appraisal and feedback approaches that will be used to monitor ongoing progress. Present the results using appropriate graphical techniques. Set out a visual display of how the problem has been tackled and the results using a 'five-minute management' approach.

A starting point is an analysis of strengths and weaknesses. This can be done using the following headings:

1 Solution to the problem
2 Strengths of the solution
3 Weaknesses of the solution

Factors to consider in completing this analysis are:

♦ Was the solution appropriate to the problem?
♦ Did the solution simply transfer the problem somewhere else?
♦ Was the solution time and resource efficient?
♦ In retrospect, was there a better solution?
♦ Has the solution satisfied the relevant stakeholders in the problem?

Critical reflection

This type of reflection typically involves setting out in writing a thoughtful analysis of the solution chosen and how it could be improved upon. Critical reflection is often aided by the use of 'critical friends' who

ACTIVITY

This task is for your employability skills portfolio.

1 Set out a strengths and weaknesses analysis of your solution to the problem.

2 Set out a critical account of your solution, with a comment from a critical friend.

3 In the light of the above, suggest possible adaptations to the solution.

4 Measure the effectiveness of the solution against the original specification and desired outcomes.

provide honest feedback. The feedback should focus on the solution to the problem, rather than the personalities concerned.

In the light of the strengths and weaknesses analysis and critical evaluation, it is often helpful to outline **possible further adaptations** to the solution and its implementation.

A final way of evaluating the solution is to measure the solution against the specification and desired outcomes. Providing the specification and desired outcomes are the most appropriate ones for solving the problem, then a high level of fit with the solution will give high levels of satisfaction.

Chapter 4

Handling, processing and communicating information

Good communication is an important skill that is required in a range of business situations, from making a presentation to interacting with colleagues and customers. In this final chapter of the employability skills unit, we look at ways that you can develop, present and evaluate a strategy for handling, processing and communicating information. It should help you to improve your communication skills at work.

Your communications plan, and its delivery, will need to be based on the cycle shown in Figure 3.7.

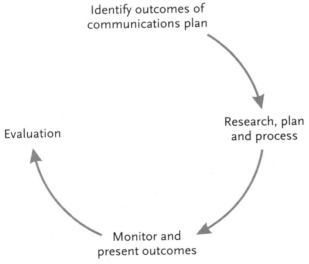

Figure 3.7 Delivering a communications plan

Identify outcomes

An important starting point is to identify the outcomes that you are trying to achieve through your communications plan. The objective is to improve communication. However, there are many ways in which you can improve communication, so the outline given below relates to a range of contexts.

Examples of situations where you may want to improve communication include:

- customer service, dealing with people face to face, or other forms of communication with customers, for example by phone or electronic media
- producing a report
- making a presentation to a selected audience, often aided by PowerPoint images
- discussion or written presentation about a complex subject
- trying to influence people, or to persuade other people at work.

The choice of communication methods will need to suit the task and the audience. For example, in introducing a complex subject orally it makes sense to provide the audience with written summaries of the presentation, setting out key points. The justification for using a particular communication method (such as oral, written, electronic) should be that it is the most suitable method, employing the most suitable medium to transmit the message to the targeted audience.

ACTIVITY

This task is for your employability skills folder. Identify the outcomes of your communications plan.

- Who is the audience?
- What is the type of communication that you are trying to improve?
- What communication methods will you be using?
- Why have you chosen these communication methods?

Research, plan and process

Having decided the outcomes that you are working towards in your project, you can then begin to research, plan and process relevant information.

The information sources that you use will need to be relevant to the information that you need to research and communicate. Examples of relevant information sources will include:

♦ manuals, such as training manuals, product usage manuals and so on
♦ abstracts, that is, summaries of relevant articles
♦ customers: for example, views of customers in relation to current levels of satisfaction, opinions about products and/or services, and so on
♦ colleagues: their views and opinions about new company initiatives, efficiency within the organisation, processes, and so on
♦ the Internet, which will provide a wealth of information on nearly every subject, though be careful to verify the accuracy of information provided
♦ intranet: stores of information kept within an organisation's own internal network of resources and information
♦ references: there are all sorts of sources that you will want to refer to, such as text, journals, magazines, newspapers, on-line sources, and so on
♦ summaries: of articles, ideas and initiatives that appear in the press, in press releases and other sources.

Make sure when you are researching information that you will want to communicate at a later stage that you record the source of the information, so that you can refer back to it, find out more information from the same source, or seek permission to quote a source.

You will need to plan how you are going to research information, that is, what sources you are going to use and when. In addition, you need to plan the methodologies that you will use to access, structure or make sense of the information, such as:

♦ by making structured notes
♦ keeping records on a database

♦ using flow charts to illustrate the relationships between processes or related activities
♦ by taking photographs to illustrate important points, for example what a new product looks like, the layout of a store
♦ creating mind maps to show the links between various activities and processes (see p. 33)
♦ recording audio tapes, such as taped conversations, and using video footage.

You also need to decide how you are going to handle and process the wealth of information that you collect so that you can structure it in an intelligible form for your audience. Processing information involves separating the relevant from the irrelevant, and those bits of information which are particularly effective in clearly communicating targeted messages.

Once you have decided what you are going to do, you need to proceed to producing communications which are interesting and relevant to your targeted audience.

ACTIVITY

This task is for your employability skills portfolio.

1   Produce a brief summary setting out how you intend to research, plan and process information for your communication exercise. Then carry out the research, choosing relevant methodologies for making sense of the information, and presenting it in a structured way.

2   Using the information that you have organised and structured you will need to create an effective communication exercise for the targeted audience. This may take the form of a report, oral presentation, customer relations activity, or other form of communication exercise that is relevant to work-based learning.

Monitor and present outcomes

The next stage is to refine the information that you have recorded and gathered so that you can present the finished piece of work. You will need to monitor and present the outcomes of your work. The information that you have gathered and recorded will need to be organised for the presentation. Select the information that is most relevant and suitable for a presentation to the chosen target audience and then synthesise (rearrange) it so that it fits into a well-organised structure.

You will then be ready to present or otherwise communicate the information to your audience. The format you choose might be a written or oral report, an extended essay, or business document. Use computer-based methods where these are relevant, for example word, image and data processing, PowerPoint, or a graphics package. However, it is always important to remember that it is you who is delivering the presentation, and you cannot rely on PowerPoint or the graphics to do the work for you. An attractive PowerPoint presentation can be deadly dull if the presenter does not also project their personality and ideas to the audience.

Before making a presentation ask a critical friend to listen to or read your work. Take on board the constructive criticisms they make.

ACTIVITY

This task is for your employability skills folder. Present your communication activity, making sure that it is set at the level of the targeted audience. Make sure that your communication activity is clearly structured, and where appropriate that you use relevant computer-based methods.

Evaluation

Having completed the communications plan and executed it in a communication exercise it is time to evaluate the process in order to learn for the future.

As with your problem-solving strategy (pp. 32–3) you will need to use a range of evaluation tools:

♦ an analysis of the strengths and weaknesses of the communications plan and communication activity
♦ critical reflection on the process, including critical support from a critical friend
♦ identification of ways to improve or adapt the process
♦ measurement of the effectiveness of the chosen methods compared with the original objectives and expected outcomes.

ACTIVITY

This task is for your employability skills portfolio.

Evaluate your communications plan and communication activity by means of:

♦ strengths and weaknesses analysis
♦ critical reflection
♦ suggestions for improvement
♦ measurement of the effectiveness of the communication.

Assessment

In order to achieve the outcomes for the Employability Skills module you will need to produce an employability skills folder, substantially based on the tasks set out in this chapter.

Further reading

Dransfield, R. (2001) *Human Resource Management*, Oxford: Heinemann.

Mumford, A. (2000) *Management Development*, London: Institute of Personnel Development.

Pearn, M. (2000) *Empowering Team Learning*, London: Chartered Institute of Personnel and Development.

Seely, J. (2002) *One Step Ahead: Writing Reports*, Milton Keynes: Open University Press.

Smith, D. (1998) *Delivering People and Organising*, London: Kogan Page.

Thompson, L. (2004) *Making the Team: a Guide for Managers*, New Jersey: Prentice Hall.

Also titles in the Essential Managers series, London: Dorling Kindersley
    Communicate Clearly
    Making Presentation
    Managing your Time
    Managing Teams
    Motivating People

Unit 4

Foundations of organisations and behaviour

This unit introduces you to the nature of organisations and their management practices. We will look at organisations using both theory and practical approaches, to understand the behaviour of people within organisations and recognise the importance of organisational design, leadership styles and motivational factors. This unit provides a good foundation for more specialised business study.

Summary of learning outcomes

On completion of this unit you will be able to:
♦ explore organisational structure and culture
♦ examine different approaches to management and leadership, and theories of organisation
♦ examine the relationship between motivational theories
♦ demonstrate an understanding of working with others, teamwork, groups and group dynamics
♦ describe different leadership styles and the effectiveness of these leadership approaches
♦ analyse how organisational theory underpins principles and practices of organising and management
♦ compare the different approaches to management and theories of organisation used by two organisations
♦ explain the different motivational theories and their application within the workplace
♦ assess the relationship between motivation theory and the practice of management
♦ describe the nature of groups and group behaviour within organisations
♦ investigate the factors that lead to effective teamwork and the influences that threaten success
♦ evaluate the impact of technology on team functioning within a given organisation.

Chapter 1

Organisational structure and culture

This chapter aims to help students demonstrate an ability to:

♦ compare and contrast different organisational structures and culture
♦ analyse the relationship between an organisation's structure and culture and the effects on business performance
♦ analyse the factors which influence individual behaviour at work.

Organisational structure

For the purpose of looking at organisational structure, we are assuming that an **organisation** is an established body, with a clear structure and deliberate planning process, within which people work, co-ordinating activities and co-operating to achieve a common goal or goals.

ACTIVITY

1 What are the key features of an 'organisation'?

2 In the above assumption of what an organisation is, which words are important when considering business organisations?

Every organisation has **goals** and **objectives**. To achieve those, the organisation needs to divide the work required between its members. To divide the work up and to monitor and co-ordinate the workers, the organisation's structure is developed.

The **structure** is the framework of management and employee relationships, which operate at different levels within the organisation. This structure determines how responsibilities are allocated, how decisions are made and how processes are linked and co-ordinated. It deploys and delegates power, and shares wisdom and expertise to form a productive working structure.

However large or small an organisation is, it needs a clear structure effectively to distribute tasks and define who is responsible and accountable for what. Structure depends very much on the history and ownership of the company, its size, its environment, goals and objectives, its technology and its people culture.

Most organisations are not designed, they evolve. For example, if you start up a business selling books your prime concern will be making a profit and surviving. As time passes and you gain more customers, you may need to take on an employee to help to absorb some of the workload. Once you start to employ more staff, things become more complicated and roles need to be defined, authority and accountability made clear, and this is usually where organisational structures begin to develop.

One exception to this 'evolutionary process' is Richard Branson's Virgin Atlantic Airlines, which Branson designed from scratch, as a plan on paper, before appointing employees to the positions he had created.

The larger the organisation is, the more formal the structure tends to become, in order to co-ordinate larger numbers of workers, departments, and/or diversity of products or services. **Differentiation** establishes individual tasks and jobs, whilst **integration** links and co-ordinates all these individual tasks and jobs.

Without an effective structure, a number of problems can arise:

- different disciplines are managed by the 'wrong' managers
- individuals suffer through lack of clearly defined responsibilities and job descriptions
- resources are wasted: money and people's talents are misdirected or not used
- roles become overloaded or under-utilised
- conflict of ideas and decision making occurs
- the organisation is not responsive to market opportunities and changing trends.

Benefits of structure

Structures enable:

- co-ordination of different areas of business (so 'the left hand knows what the right hand is doing')
- efficient use of resources
- monitoring of production processes
- monitoring of employee satisfaction
- efficient performance in all areas and at all levels.

CASE STUDY

Two organisations in the making

SMITH & SON FARRIERS

Bert Smith is a farrier, or blacksmith. He learned the trade from his father, who kept horses for farm work and shoed horses for the neighbouring farm and riding stable. Bert now continues to shoe horses for the neighbouring farm and stables, but he also travels and services a number of equestrian centres in his locality. He has enough work to keep him busy most of the time and earn a modest living.

1 Does Bert's business need a formal structure?

2 If Bert wished to expand and take on apprentices and other staff, will he be able to continue to work as he does at the moment?

VIRGIN ATLANTIC AIRWAYS

In the early 1980s, Virgin Records (an innovation of Richard Branson) had grown to be one of six top record companies in the world. In 1984, Branson received a phone call suggesting he set up an airline passenger service between London and New York. Branson thought this was an excellent idea, even though his fellow directors thought he must be mad.

Not to be put off by them, Branson announced to the world that 'Virgin Atlantic Airways' would begin operating within three months!

3 How was the 'birth' of Virgin Atlantic Airways different to the establishment and expansion of Smith & Son Farriers?

4 What sort of structure would Branson have needed in place and what sort of 'help' would he need, before he could even start to do business?

5 Would Bert Smith need the same kind of help to get started?

Importantly, structures are **flexible**. They need to self-monitor constantly, to ensure they are responding and adapting to the constantly changing demands of modern markets and business practices.

Organisational architecture

The term **organisational architecture** refers to the general way in which an organisation is structured and the way in which traditional departments and more informal project teams can fit together, and how teams operate.

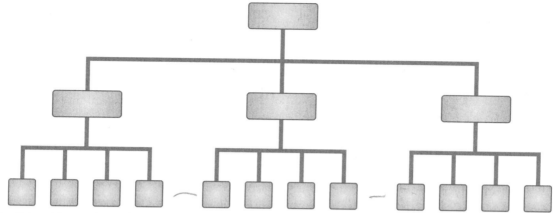

Figure 4.1   Traditional hierarchical structure

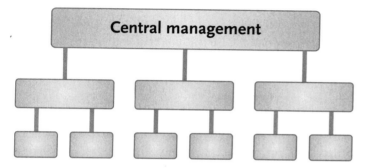

Figure 4.2   The modern way of organising teams

Much emphasis is placed on work teams in modern business, the idea being that a large number of people can carry out a variety of activities working in small groups and using skills which complement those of the others. This moves businesses away from the traditional hierarchical structures which featured a bureaucracy of clearly defined departments such as marketing or finance, ruled by a top-down flow of authority. The late 1900s and early 2000s have seen a move away from the 'telling the workers what to do' method of management, towards a more democratic work process, and today more businesses have a flattened structure, with groups of employees focusing on complete processes, designed to meet customer demand. A traditional hierarchical structure is shown in Figure 4.1. Decisions are made at the top of the hierarchy but implementation happens low down. The modern way of organising is shown in Figure 4.2.

Formal and informal structures

Within the formal structure will be seen the informal accepted behavioural norms and social interactions of the employees, which enable communication and co-operation between individuals and departments. (For more information on this see the section on Organisational charts on p. 92.) Various different methods of dividing the work to achieve the desired objectives can be used.

Types of organisation and associated structures

As the American J. Stoner (1982) said, 'Early management writers attempted to find the "one best way" or the "universal" approach to designing organisations. They tried to establish a set of principles that would yield an organisational structure efficient and effective in most situations ... Today, management writers have moved from [this] approach to a contingency approach. They argue that an organisation is highly interdependent with its environment and that different situations require different structures. Managers, then, must identify the variables that affect their organisation so that they can design it appropriately.'

Functional

Perhaps the most common way of grouping workers, the functional approach groups different specialisations or functions, the general idea being that staff in the different groups share expertise and support each other, as in Figure 4.3.

Figure 4.3   A functional grouping

Shared resources, or shared staff, produce the goods. **Task** staff produce the product or service, whilst **element** staff support the task process. The support staff would probably consist of personnel, PR, planning and administrative staff: the 'behind the scenes' workers.

There are a number of advantages with this system:

◆ each department can concentrate on its own function and thereby contribute effectively to the overall corporate objectives
◆ there is no duplication of work; for example, the finance department controls budgets and invoices customers for all departments
◆ experts in specific fields work together to share similar knowledge and skills.

One drawback of this structure is that it tends to be very hierarchical, with one manager asserting authority over all areas, and can lead to functional rivalry between different groups or departments. Other disadvantages may be:

◆ there is little opportunity to move between departments, thus limiting career progression
◆ specialist departments do not necessarily get a good overview of the whole operation or corporate activities, thus isolating them within their specialism.

The larger an organisation becomes, the more exaggerated these problems may become, and communication channels become slow and unreliable.

Product based

Each product (for example, wheels, engines or body parts) has its own team of workers. This team will be replicated for each product, and consists of, for example, researchers, marketing staff, planning and finance staff. In an insurance company, each specialised service department – household claims, life insurance, sales and marketing, car insurance, and so on – has its own team of manager, team leader, inspectors and assessors or underwriters and administration staff. Pirelli, a world leader in tyre manufacturing, is divided into two divisions. One works on production of tyres, one on cables.

This arrangement ensures different specialisms have their own specialised and expert staff and uses the contributions of different specialists in each different area of work and/or product. It also means different divisions can be monitored for their individual performance ratings and profitability: insurance credit controllers can be measured in terms of credit limits adhered to (providing profitable cash flow) and claims departments can be monitored in terms of the time taken to settle claims. This means that in large multi-product organisations, effective and profitable departments or lines can be expanded and developed, whilst unprofitable lines can be run down or disposed of. The strengths are developed; the weaknesses eliminated, as in Figure 4.4.

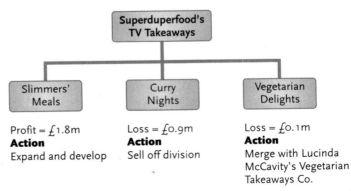

Figure 4.4   A product-based grouping

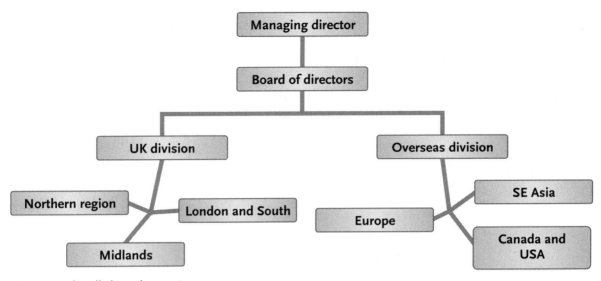

Figure 4.5   A geographically based grouping

Product-based structures can, however, lead to departmental isolation or independence from the main organisation as a whole, which again can bring about interdepartmental disagreements or competition, and make co-ordination difficult, whilst at the same time making it difficult to adapt to customer demand quickly and effectively.

Geographically based

Different parts of a group provide different services or goods, dependent on their geographical location and local demand. For example, urban and rural communities often have different requirements, and local authorities use local knowledge and resources to accommodate these.

Many large organisations have branches spread all over the country or overseas. Good examples are high street branches of banks, or shops belonging to chain stores like Marks & Spencer or House of Fraser.

An international retailing organisation might have a structure like the one in Figure 4.5.

Different regions have responsibility for regional management, training and so on, so regions are able to respond quickly to local requirements, customer demand and local labour availability and trends. Also, local requirements such as language and legal requirements can easily be met. There are, unsurprisingly, disadvantages too:

♦ too many regional divisions can bring about duplication of roles and facilities
♦ too few divisions can lead to gaps in communication and co-ordination
♦ regional rivalry can become evident as regions become competitive and lose sight of the corporate goals
♦ disagreements can occur as local conditions could be very different from those at head office.

Modern Information and Communications Technology (ICT) has, to a degree, lessened the importance of location, because information is accessible long-distance and communication can be instant from almost anywhere in the world. Some aspects of businesses require geographical accessibility, for example for raw materials such as coal, stone, or slate. Even with these requirements, though, the administrative, sales and support staff can operate from different locations to the actual site or factory location.

Service organisations (insurance, telecommunications, and so on) are increasingly relocating call centres and service centres to locations as far away as Delhi where labour is cheap. Clothing companies can also, through technological advances in recent years, take advantage of cheap labour and resources from abroad. Not all Marks & Spencer clothes are made in Britain any more, and Nike sports goods are no longer produced in America: both are far more likely to have travelled here from Taiwan, China, or other Asian countries. When you place your summer wardrobe order from a mail order catalogue on the Internet, it will more likely be routed to, and delivered from, an Indonesian factory than from a factory in Britain.

The effect of technology on business in the UK and worldwide has been phenomenal in many respects. The effects of technology are discussed further under Impact of technology on p. 192.

ACTIVITY

1   Identify three organisations with product-based structures. What are their main product divisions?

2   Identify three organisations with geographically based structures. Where do they operate? What are their main products? Why is it necessary for them to have regional control?

CASE STUDY

Geographical outsourcing of labour

Nike's methods of outsourcing manufacturing processes to overseas locations have spread to many other transnational companies. The Vans running shoe company, Adidas and Levis are all now outsourcing production. This means that their goods are produced in overseas locations where labour and raw materials are cheapest. For the managers and shareholders this can mean cheaper production and higher profits. For local workers, though, it means shutting UK or USA factories and moving production to Indonesia,

---

China, and other Asian countries where labour is cheaper.

British Telecommunications said in 2002 that it was keeping operations entirely in the UK, but in 2003 announced it will be moving some operations to Delhi. Even if current employees are not made redundant, the next succession of those UK jobs is lost. Big finance and insurance companies like Aviva and HSBC are also moving to cheaper labour call centres in India; again they attract criticism here because of the exploitation of cheaper labour and loss of UK jobs.

♦ What are the advantages of running a business in this way?
♦ What are the disadvantages?

Multifunctional and multidivisional structures

Some organisations are small and will be seen to operate largely within one of the types of structure already described. However, most organisations use a mix of types to co-ordinate the different areas of the organisation's operations.

Matrix structures

These structures co-ordinate expertise in project-orientated work groups. Businesses may operate two or more types of organisation in a matrix structure. For example, they might mix functional and geographical lines of control. Developed in the 1960s in the USA, individual project or product managers are responsible for meeting objectives, be they delivery deadlines or budgeting targets, and these teams are also divided by function (such as sales or production). The system is useful where staff and resources of different departments need to be shared, or where there is more than one type of business or goods being produced. More than one mind is applied to each process being carried out. In Figure 4.6, note how the lines of authority go across as well as down.

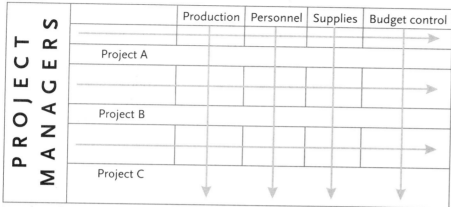

Note how the lines of authority go across as well as down

Figure 4.6   A matrix structure

Matrix structures:

♦ combine functional departments which specialise in a permanent location
♦ integrate different activities and departments using projects, geographical and product bases.

In many modern organisations communication structures tend to be less formal, and responsibility tends to be horizontal between individuals and departments, rather than hierarchically upwards or downwards. One advantage is that it is cross-functional yet retains the specialisations of individuals and departments. It also allows freedom for change and encourages commitment to the overall strategy of the organisation. Significantly, it also cuts out lengthy and complex communications up and down the traditional hierarchical structure.

Teams of experts from each function, and staff from different departments, are allocated to different projects, to work on new projects for as long as necessary, or use one project manager on each project with authority over all other functions.

Projects may be based on products, geographical area, type of customer, or other specific criteria. This system features several disadvantages:

♦ too many staff may be needed; for example, each project requires a secretary and a design engineer, instead of the same secretary and design engineer working on several projects

♦ many multi-skilled roles need to be filled, and individuals have to be multi-skilled and fill several roles
♦ job descriptions and responsibilities can become ambiguous and confused
♦ lines of authority and accountability may be unclear or confused
♦ co-ordination of many roles can be difficult
♦ the complex structure can be confusing and hard to clarify. The structure will undoubtedly be complicated, and must be well laid out.

There are, of course, advantages:

♦ it is possible to use groups from specific departments in the required numbers for each project
♦ flexibility within both the structure and the roles of individuals can lead to more staff development and career progress
♦ the matrix design is useful where internationalisation of organisations occurs, as cross-country co-ordination needs localised expertise and knowledge of legal barriers and customer requirements in different countries
♦ new product development can be speedier and cross-functional roles can aid sharing of experience and innovative ideas
♦ it is useful in companies with several distinct lines of business, where a two-way flow of authority is required, for example in insurance companies, as in Figure 4.7.

Again, note how lines of authority go down as well as across.

Matrix structures are becoming increasingly popular because of the need to respond quickly to ever-changing work environments. Project managers can be allowed authority over all required activities to achieve the overall objective, which means rapid decision making and progress are possible.

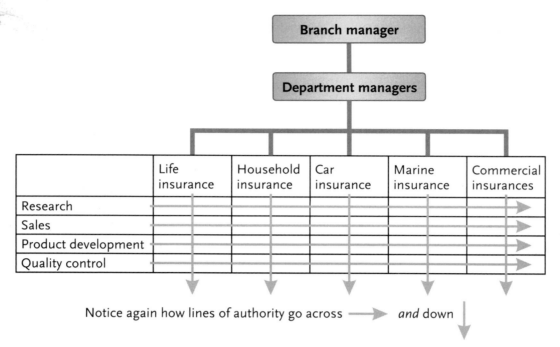

Figure 4.7   Matrix structure of an insurance company

Choosing a structure

In deciding on a structure to be used for an organisation, a number of issues must be considered.

Size

When it comes to organisations, size is important. If there are only three employees, it is unlikely you will build several project teams. Three people cannot cover a large geographical area or run a number of regional offices.

Technology

Where different technologies are used, there will be functional separations. If different products use different technology, product division will occur.

The market environment

The product needs to respond to consumer demand and be competitive in relation to other organisations' available products.

Expertise and skills

The level of expertise and range of skills that are required, and their availability, will have a bearing on choice of structure. If many specific areas of expertise are needed, teamworking may suit best.

Centralisation and decentralisation

Centralised and decentralised are terms used to illustrate the relationship between a company's corporate centre and its organisational divisions.

Centralisation exists where the main responsibilities and running of the business are carried out within departments at a central headquarters (HQ).

Decentralisation occurs where responsibilities are delegated to different branches or satellite offices away from the central HQ.

Centralisation can strengthen management control, to improve co-ordination, reduce costs and monitor quality. Strong competition can lead to greater centralisation as management attempts to increase its control over the production process.

Decentralisation occurs mainly in larger organisations. Some decentralisation is necessary in many organisations to extend the availability of services or goods over a larger area or to obtain raw materials from other locations. Decentralisation should consider the nature of the product, the day-to-day company management, terms of employment and the need for standardisation or specialisation of products. There are four kinds of decentralisation.

Federal decentralisation features independent units operating under their own control, contributing to the parent body's achievement of objectives.

Functional decentralisation features individual products within the organisation.

Vertical decentralisation happens when authority is handed down through the layers of management.

Horizontal decentralisation happens when authority moves sideways across the organisation, perhaps giving power to the technocracy as well as to management.

Some organisations centralise certain functions such as strategic planning and finance, but decentralise other functions such as sales and recruitment; in other words, the local branches decide how best to market their products locally, or how to recruit staff. Passing on this type of decision making to local management is decentralising. Each has its advantages and disadvantages, as shown in Figure 4.8.

As with any structure, there is no one 'ideal' level of centralisation or decentralisation. Organisations need to find the most efficient method of allocation of responsibility and resources to achieve corporate goals.

Centralisation

ADVANTAGES
One management structure
= Quick decision making
= Consistent strategy throughout organisation
Easy to control and monitor one policy for the whole organisation
Departments/teams don't become isolated or competitive
Easy to co-ordinate
Reduced overheads – *One* location = *One* set of premises etc. costs
Can afford advanced and sophisticated equipment, if supplying for one location only.

DISADVANTAGES
Inflexibility
Need to monitor subordinates
More impersonal for staff. They become 'just a number' in a big office.
Fewer managers means fewer prospects for promotion/career progression
Staff are remote from 'point of sale' contact with customer
Not special to local requirements
Impersonal to customers *and* staff.

Decentralisation

ADVANTAGES
Flexibility
Allows a swift response to local needs or conditions
Local staff have responsibility and so feel involved in decision making
Scope for individual initiative
Supervision of subordinates shared among regional managers
More personal environment. Staff feel valued in small numbers
More career and self-development opportunities
More personalised service for customers

DISADVANTAGES
More difficult to monitor and control
Increased overheads with multiple locations to support
Different locations/teams can become competitive or lose sight of corporate goals.

Figure 4.8   Centralisation and decentralisation

CASE STUDY

Centralisation and decentralisation at Shell UK

For any company, but particularly one with a wide geographical spread and a huge range of product types, decentralisation of one kind or another is essential. Most decisions, especially tactical ones, cannot be taken effectively at the centre, which may be miles or continents away, because they have to be taken quickly, on the spot, by people who know all the circumstances. There is often no time for a referral back to central office, even if it has a complete understanding of that particular problem.

One way of encouraging centralisation that involves changing the structure of the company is to 'flatten' the organisational hierarchy by removing one or more of its layers, so that each divisional head reports directly to the Managing Director rather than to other directors who themselves report to the top person.

Another way is to create separate profit centres: sections of the overall business that are given the responsibility and resources (and guidance where necessary) to operate as if they were independent. For instance, Shell's bitumen business is now run by Shell Bitumen UK, a separate profit centre within Shell Oil UK. Emstar Ltd is responsible for Shell's energy management business in the UK, and Synthetic Chemicals Ltd, a subsidiary of Shell Chemicals UK, specialises in the fine chemicals. Strategic decisions, with long-term implications for all parts of the company, are still taken centrally. Even so, many different people will be required to contribute to them, simply because the amount of input needed when a major decision has to be made can be immense.

Of course all decisions, at whatever level, are made in the context of the company's specific business objectives. These are determined by central management, but have to be in line with the general directions, capacities and culture of the company.

ACTIVITY

We can see from the structures previously described that the structure and management or authority patterns determine how a business operates.

- How can a good or bad structure affect productivity?
- How does structure affect morale of the workforce?
- How could structure affect the motivation of individuals?
- Name three advantages and three disadvantages of each of the structures previously described.

Choose an organisation that is familiar to you.

- Which structure does it operate under?
- What other structures might also work for it?
- What structures would *not* work for it? Why wouldn't they work?

Administrative systems and economic spaces

JOURNAL ARTICLE

This article looks at the relationship between administrative reforms and economic change. Bennett argues that **decentralisation and centralisation** are happening in response to economic change. Such areas as fiscal reforms, territorial boundary reforms and changes in tiers and responsibilities are examined. The types of changes that are happening and current trends are looked at in terms of urban and rural settings and across decentralised government systems and decentralised market systems. The impacts of institutional activities on economic development are also examined.

Bennett, R. J. 'Administrative systems and economic spaces', *Journal of the Regional Studies Association*, 1997, Vol. 31, No.3, May, pp 323–36.

Standardisation, centralisation and marketing

JOURNAL ARTICLE

A survey of 200 Australian subsidiaries of multinational companies was conducted to investigate whether, when a company is centralised, it also implements standardised marketing strategies, as much literature on MNCs seems to suggest. In other words, the literature assumes that *centralisation* usually results in marketing *standardisation*. The researchers concluded that standardisation is usually consistent across services and products within any one organisation although, surprisingly, standardisation and centralisation are *not* correlated at the organisational level. They suggest that further reviews of this issue are needed, because many fundamental

assumptions are made in some literature on multinational companies. Obviously if assumptions are persistently made, research will not be valid, so further, unbiased research may be a good idea.

Quester, P. J. and Conduit, J. 'Standardisation, centralisation and marketing in multinational companies', *International Business Review*, 1996, Vol. 5, No. 4, August, pp 395–421.

Indigenous knowledge as intellectual property

JOURNAL ARTICLE

This article looks at the Onge people of the Indian Nicobar and Andaman Islands in the Bay of Bengal. These native people possess important indigenous local knowledge and so have attracted the interest of many northern MNCs. Indigenous knowledge incorporates ecology, medicine, biology, and is a huge potential source of money making. The interest in accessing indigenous knowledge, especially for pharmaceutical products, is vast. Public policies have been devised to protect the Onge social organisation, and protect the Onge's rights by ensuring control of use of that knowledge remains with *them*. Cultural and customary law are important issues examined here.

Norchi, C. H. 'Indigenous knowledge as intellectual property', *Policy Sciences*, Vol. 33, No.3, May, pp 387–98.

Also have a look at Khandwalla, P. 'Effect of competition on the structure of top management control', *Academy of Management Journal*, 1973, No.16, pp 285–95.

Organisational networks and linkages

Organisations operate on a foundation of interactions between individuals and a network of interdependent activities. Networking involves managers and staff interacting with others, both inside and outside the organisation, building a network of *inter*dependent units and co-operative relationships, which help the organisation to function effectively and use all the available resources, skills and links.

Networks of interdependent groups, personnel and/or departments work together and these interactions affect both individuals and the group performance as a whole.

Internal and external network structures

Building networks require managers and staff interacting with other people and organisations to build up a framework of co-operative relationships. These networks often operate essentially outside of the formal organisational structure.

Internal networks

Staff within any organisation need to communicate and interact so that different personnel and departments can co-operate with each other and reciprocate to achieve the organisation's goals.

Likert's (1961) 'linking pin' structure shows how the boss of one group is subordinate in the next group, thereby acting as the 'link-pin' – a kind of piggy-in-the-middle – between the two departments. A link-pin is therefore anyone who belongs to two groups within the organisation, normally as a superior in one group and as a subordinate in the other. This increases two-way communication and aids co-ordination and co-operation between groups.

External networks

Organisations usually depend on resources and supplies controlled by other organisations. Building contractors need to buy materials from building merchants; office managers buy computers from computer manufacturers. Every company's success is dependent to a degree on a wider web of other organisations or individuals. Interactions between organisations as well as within organisations therefore need to be co-ordinated.

A 'network' is defined by Cook and Emerson (1984) as 'sets of connected exchange relationships between actors controlling business activities'.

When businesses interact with each other they exchange products and services. They influence the way each other's organisation works. If the builder usually buys his materials on the day he wants them, but the builders' merchant wants a month's notice to supply bricks, then the builder has to adapt his way of working to fit in with his supplier, or find a different supplier. The builder's merchant, in his turn, is reliant on, say, the brick manufacturer to supply the bricks on time. Networks develop and evolve from interactions between individuals and organisations. They are often influenced in this way by relationships with third parties: the builder's materials supplier, the competition, the transporters, and so on.

Cook and Emerson (1984) look at how social exchange theory explains the '... emergence of various forms of social structure, including networks and corporate groups.'

Social exchange theory essentially explores the process of communication and the operation of networks. When people or organisations interact and exchange ideas, resources or supplies, then the relationship between them is also dependent on their relationship with *other* interdependent contacts they may have.

Most organisations use internal and external networks. A good example of one which uses external networks extensively might be Social Services. It has the usual internal organisation and interaction of departments and it also has contact with many outside agencies such as the health service, police and educational establishments.

Business operations overseas have led national markets to become linked with international ones. The new 'network economy', developed with the advent of the Internet, increases business relationships and connections many-fold (see Kelly, 1998). The Internet multiplies business connections rapidly, enlarging the company 'web' hugely.

Anderson *et al.* (2002) examined the importance of 'external networks as a strategic resource for performance and competence development in multinational corporations'.

As business networks grow, so the competition grows and companies need to respond.

All organisations operating internationally have to consider that local employment laws, minimum wage restrictions, the WTO and GATT directives, and tariffs and taxes all influence how operations are run.

Formal and informal interactions will exist both in internal networks and in external networking and communications. This may have negative points. For example, internally favouritism can be practised at an informal level. Even if the established system says that person A should see the manager before person B, if the secretary likes B better, she may make the boss available to person B first. The power of the secretary to allow – or not allow – access to the manager can be an influential phenomenon.

The evolution of firm networks

JOURNAL ARTICLE

This article considers whether networks of 'socially embedded ties' or sparser networks are more likely to influence the success rate of new organisations. The authors consider that networks of new firms evolve in order to adapt to changing challenges and changing needs for resources. As firms develop, their networks grow from socially 'tied' connections with similar identities. As they grow, their networks move towards network connections based more on economic benefits. This shift from identity-based to more calculative networks moves from 'path-dependent' to a more intentionally managed network. The authors suggest then, that both cohesive and sparse networks are useful for organisational success when they address the firms' changing resource requirements.

Hite, J. and Hesterly, W. S. 'The evolution of firm networks: from emergence to early growth of the firm', *Strategic Management Journal*, 2001, Vol. 22, Issue 3, March, pp 275–286.

Intercultural relationships

JOURNAL ARTICLE

As global competition increases, organisations are finding it increasingly necessary to develop cross- and inter-cultural relationships with a diverse range of partners, customers and employees. They need to understand and develop intercultural communications and this requires complex management understanding. Communication with many partners, all with unique national and organisational cultures, is not easy. This article proposes a process for developing effective communication strategies and examines what is needed to manage a wide mix of different cultural relationships.

Harvey, M. G. and Griffith, D. A. 'Developing effective intercultural relationships: the importance of communication strategies', *Thunderbird International Business Review*, 2002, Vol. 44, Issue 4, July/August, pp 455–76.

Knowledge-sharing networks

JOURNAL ARTICLE

Previous research has suggested that diffusion of knowledge happens faster within Toyota's production network than it does among other vehicle manufacturing networks. The authors here look at Toyota's black box of knowledge sharing and show how Toyota's ability to create and manage 'network-level knowledge-sharing processes' helps to explain the productivity advantages which Toyota enjoys. Toyota motivates its members to openly share knowledge and reduces the costs of finding valuable knowledge by creating a *network identity* with rules for participation and entry into the network. Toyota's strong network has established a variety of routines that enable multidirectional knowledge flow among its suppliers. This appears to create competitive advantage by creating and recombining knowledge, thereby creating a diversity of knowledge within the network, which other automotive manufacturers lack.

Dyer, J. H. and Nobeoka, K. 'Creating and managing a high-performance knowledge-sharing network: the Toyota case', *Strategic Management Journal*, 2000, Vol. 21, Issue 3, March, pp 345–67.

Environmental management and sustainable development   JOURNAL ARTICLE

This is a special issue of *Business Strategy and the Environment*, which examines the role of networks in environmental management and sustainable development. The paper examines the role of networks from a number of theoretical and empirical perspectives and looks at networks and their contribution to environmental management and sustainable development. The author anticipates that the current interest in networks will continue, as attention moves from environmental issues to sustainable development. The author also looks at links between sustainable development and global change. The paper suggests a number of research themes that need attention in the future.

Roome, R. 'Conceptualising and studying the contribution of networks in environmental management and sustainable development', *Business Strategy and the Environment*, 2001, Vol. 10, Issue 2, March/April, pp 69–76 .

Network effects on innovation   JOURNAL ARTICLE

Love and Roper say 'Developments in economic geography and regional innovation systems have emphasised the potentially important role of networking'. Their analysis in this study does not necessarily support the idea that firms in the UK,

Ireland or Germany develop 'greater innovation intensity' if they have strong external networks. However, they conclude that inter-organisational links *are* important for achieving commercial success.

Love, J. and Roper, S. 'Location and network effects on innovation success: evidence for UK, German and Irish manufacturing plants', October 1999, Northern Ireland Economic Research Centre, Queen's University of Belfast, Belfast.

The organisation of innovation   JOURNAL ARTICLE

The same researchers (Love and Roper) examined again the way in which UK and German organisations use inter-plant collaboration, co-operation and multifunctional working. Based on a large-scale survey of manufacturing plants in the UK and Germany, they explore the reasons for differences in the two countries' patterns of involvement.

In Germany, organisational and social norms encourage collaboration, but German skills training and industrial relations makes it difficult for them to use flexible internal systems.

In the UK though, the competitive nature of organisational relationships makes it difficult to establish external networking based on mutual trust. Fewer restrictions in the UK labour market structure though, make it easier for UK plants to use multifunctional working.

Love, J. and Roper, S. 'The organisation of innovation: collaboration, co-operation and multifunctional groups in UK and German manufacturing', September 2001, Northern Ireland Economic Research Centre, Queen's University of Belfast, Belfast.

Flexible working

There is no single type of structure that is the best; the right structure for any one organisation depends on its nature, products, size, and so on. The structure needs flexibility so that it can adapt to modern business pressures, such as economic pressure and competition, often on a global scale. Organisations need to adapt quickly to constantly changing trends. Competition and advances in IT and communications systems necessitate even greater, and faster, flexibility.

Atkinson's (1984) 'flexible firm' suggested that firms need:

◆ functional flexibility: to redeploy or multi-skill employees quickly in response to new needs
◆ numerical flexibility: so employee numbers can increase or decrease with demand
◆ financial flexibility: so costs (pay, pensions and raw materials) match availability or demand of labour; also to enable new pay systems to be incorporated quickly where necessary.

Flexible working takes many forms. Often it can be viewed as in Figure 4.9.

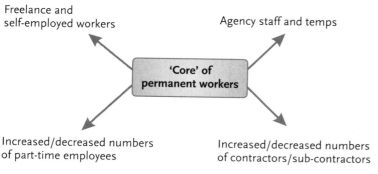

Figure 4.9   Flexible working

The main core of staff is permanent and consists of management and the essential, full-time permanent employees. The remainder of employees are taken from the different types of workers shown. They may be directly employed on a part-time basis, to suit work demands, or they may be self-employed, agency or contractual workers, who are paid as they are needed.

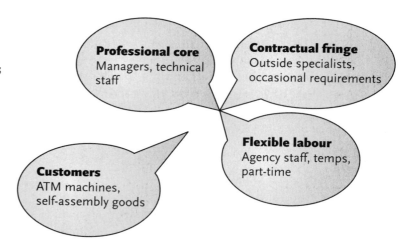

Figure 4.10   Shamrock organisation

Handy's (1989) **shamrock organisation** illustrates a flexible system with the different departments fitting together as the leaves of a shamrock (see Figure 4.10). There is the core of permanent employees who keep the company operating; the 'contractual fringe', employed as needed and paid by results; and the flexible labour force, casual and/or part-timers who are taken on as and when needed.

A fourth 'leaf' has been suggested, which in modern times consists of the customer contributing to the labour process, such as in building self-assembly furniture, or using automated cash points and Internet ordering, all of which reduce labour costs for the product provider and thus reduce costs.

Because of its differing nature, each different 'leaf' or sector needs a different type of management and system of control.

The 'flexible labour' leaf is probably the fastest-growing employment pattern today. Short-term, part-time and freelance contracts abound, and fee-paying work is on the increase. This means there is less commitment from the employer, who can use outside staff and expertise, which is readily available without the need for expensive training. Organisations gain a competitive advantage by reducing core staff costs (National Insurance, pensions, sick-pay schemes) and being able rapidly to increase or decrease staff numbers employed at any one time, to suit demand.

Individuals can benefit by being able to tailor the hours they work to fit in with home and family commitments. Many part-time workers may actually be working full time; they work for several different employers at the same time: what is known as **portfolio working**.

Annual hours contracts

These are becoming increasingly popular. Workers contract to work a set number of hours per year, and the hours worked alter to suit business demand daily, weekly, monthly or seasonally. Examples are harvesting on farms and tourism in the season.

Flexi-time working

Flexi-time working involves employees working **core hours**, probably between 10 a.m. and 4 p.m., and outside of those hours they work an agreed number of extra hours, at a time that suits them best. Instead of working 9 a.m. to 5 p.m., they may prefer to work 8 a.m. to 4 p.m., or 10 a.m. to 6 p.m., to suit their domestic and/or travel arrangements.

Home teleworking

This system is also increasing. Computer and telephone networks enable people to work from home. Answering services can field phone calls for business people, or inquiries for a number of different businesses at once, without the need for a secretary in the office.

Both flexi time and home teleworking systems can increase an individual's control over their leisure time and therefore increase motivation, though many criticise this type of working because it isolates workers from the main body of the organisation.

Telework research | JOURNAL ARTICLE

The authors say, 'Telework has inspired research in disciplines ranging from transportation and urban planning to ethics, law, sociology, and organisational studies.' The authors investigate who does telework, why, and what happens when they do. Research suggests that it is mostly male professionals and female clerical workers who do telework, but the researchers found that commonly perceived reasons for doing it, such as reducing commuting time or family obligations, do not appear important. There is little evidence to suggest that telework aids job satisfaction or productivity, either. Bailey and Kurland suggest future research should consider group and organisational level impacts and should reconsider *why* people telework.

Bailey, D. E. and Kurland, N. B. 'A review of telework research: findings, new directions, and lessons for the study of modern work', *Journal of Organisational Behavior*, 2002, Vol. 23, Issue 4, June, pp 383–400.

Flexibility management | JOURNAL ARTICLE

Flexibility means organisations can respond effectively to the ever-changing needs of the customer and these authors propose that flexibility needs to be built into the 'total chain of acquisition, processing, and distribution stages'. Although a lot of flexible mechanisms can be examined, flexibility remains, they claim, 'poorly understood and utilised in practice'.

These authors look at organisational structure flexibility, technology flexibility, Information system flexibility, and human resource flexibility. The impact on human factors are investigated, and many flexibility 'mechanisms' are identified.

Kara, S., Kayis, B. and O'Kane, S. 'The role of human factors in flexibility management: a survey', *Human Factors and Ergonomics in Manufacturing*, 2002, Vol. 12, Issue 1, pp 75–119.

Many changes to work processes such as these flexible ways of working are altering the way organisations operate. The very culture of the organisation begins to alter over time. Many people are resistant to change, and cultural change especially takes time; 'eight to ten years', according to Mullins (1999, p. 657).

Organisational culture

Culture is the social organisation, or way of life for a particular group or society; the norms, beliefs and values of that group, and the social heritage that has resulted in it being what it is. Cultures are created by the society we grow up in or live in. We learn values from parents, school and religion, or from the environment we live and/or work in. Culture is what distinguishes the way a group of people live or work; their 'blueprint' for living. The way we live guides our responses and behaviours and we generally adapt these behaviours to 'fit in' with our immediate environment.

In a working organisation, the culture is about the 'personality' of the company, the way it is run: the typical way the staff actually do things, its rules, values and the 'norms' that operate. The structure may be hierarchical or democratic, but its values underlie that structure regardless. In any dealings you have with an organisation, you will get the feel of its nature. How is it run? Is it well organised or is it unprofessional and lax? Is it welcoming, friendly and helpful, or do you get the impression they don't really want you there, or that you're interrupting their leisure time? You can usually find someone to help you shop and pack your bags in the supermarket, but how long do you have to wait for assistance in a big DIY store on a Saturday afternoon?

The culture of an organisation puts pressure on employees to behave in certain ways which fit in with the culture of the organisation. **Formal cultures** have written rules, regulations and ethical procedures. These rules are clearly defined and enforced. **Informal cultures** operate along unwritten rules, with subgroups operating within unspoken, flexible guidelines that are mutually understood and respected.

Classification of organisational culture

The culture of an organisation dictates how it operates, so the culture must be understood if managers are to understand how to help their employees to contribute to the success of its operations.

Different cultural styles usually require different styles of management and leadership (which is examined in the next chapter).

Handy (1991) cites **power cultures** as having central powers which control all decision making, whereas **role cultures** follow a more bureaucratic framework. **Task cultures** distribute power by ability and expertise – a network of teams – whilst **person cultures** centre on the individual as being important.

Power culture

Power is usually centralised in this type of culture. Small businesses and entrepreneurial set-ups are often controlled by a powerful person or small group of people. Power cultures are often illustrated similarly to a spider's web (see below), with the central area of power radiating outwards to influence and control the workers further away from the power centre.

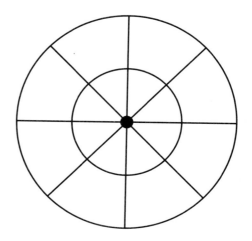

Power not only radiates out from this centre but makes sideways links across the organisation. The dominant influence of the centre results in a structure that is able to move quickly and respond to change and outside threats. One advantage is that decisions can be made quickly and with little need for consultation, but over time employees may feel limited by their inability to be innovative or put forward their own suggestions and develop themselves as well as the business. Also, as the organisation grows in size, the web becomes weaker and unable to sustain the weight put upon it. One, or a few people, can only oversee so much activity before more help and a different structure is required.

Role culture

The role culture is possibly the most common and easily recognised of all the cultural types. It is based around the job or role rather than the individual performing it and is often seen represented in the traditional hierarchical structure. Imagine it as a pyramid of boxes, each box containing a job, or role. The pyramid remains stable and intact, even if the people performing the jobs in the boxes change.

Relationships between the different roles depend on job descriptions and prescribed communication channels. Rules and procedures are the main influence on how things are done and power comes from an individual's position within the hierarchy.

One advantage is predictability and stability while disadvantages may be seen as inflexibility and the difficulty in responding quickly to change.

Because of the focus on the role rather than the person, this culture can be impersonal, and is sometimes seen as preventing individuals from innovative suggestions for improvements. They must fulfil their role. But that is all they must do. There is little scope for individual self-development and employees can feel limited by this. Change tends to happen relatively slowly.

Task culture

In a task culture, management is basically concerned with the continual successful solution to problems. The main emphasis is placed on tasks (or jobs) and projects, so it is a team culture. Handy (and other theorists) describe it as a net, where the power lies at the junctions or interstices, and some lines or strands of the net are stronger than others (see below).

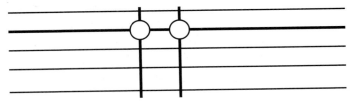

Performance is judged on results and problems solved. The structure is flexible and capable of being reformed depending upon the task or project required. Work teams are formed for specific projects and success depends on the united power of the group to complete the project. Power comes from individual knowledge rather than position, power being designated among various positions, depending upon the current task.

This culture is very flexible and will need to have procedures which reflect this, but it allows employees freedom and can be a rewarding working environment for individuals. Lack of formal authority can, however, make management and control difficult.

Modern task cultures are popular, as self-managed teams are created and develop **quality circles**, in which the people actually performing the project monitor its quality and progress.

Person culture

Individual talent is the key ingredient here, and this talent is used within a structure which co-ordinates the talents of educated and articulate employees: specialists with a common interest such as solicitors or academic researchers. Individuals with specialised skills have high status and the structure exists purely to serve the individuals within it. Management within these cultures tends to be through persuasion or influence, rather than by command. This could well be the only acceptable structure for particular groups such as workers' co-operatives or on a kibbutz, or in small partnerships such as solicitors or architects.

Hierarchies only exist by mutual consent, and individuals operate at the same level of power. Charles Handy, in his video 'The Gods of Management', describes attempting to control this type of organisation as 'like trying to herd a group of tom cats'. The larger an organisation grows, the less likely it is that it can survive as a person-centred culture, although this is probably the culture most people would choose to work within if they could.

Culture change

Modern organisations have much flatter structures than previously, with less 'top' managers and more responsibility and power being distributed among the lower levels of the structure. Organisations allow employees to use their initiative and make more decisions themselves instead of awaiting authority from above. Cultures grow from their history of traditions, the industry they operate within and it's policies and procedures. As outside companies change their methods of working and as competition changes, organisations must adapt and alter their own culture to remain competitive.

There are many constraints to these changes. Written documentation and regulations have to be amended; management-initiated change is often resisted by employees, and indeed by managers who fear loss of power. The industries within which organisations operate, and legislation, can also be barriers to change. It is necessary for any change to be incorporated with the minimum of conflict and with the organisation's objectives always in mind.

Unitarist perspective

Within an organisation, a unitarist approach assumes that all of those within the organisation have the same objectives as one another. A unitarist organisation will normally be seen to be management-led and adopt a managerial perspective: the management assumes that all employees and stakeholders have one common objective. Employees need to be committed to their work to be able to perform satisfactorily within this rather dictatorial setting.

Pluralist perspective

This approach, in contrast, acknowledges that different stakeholders will have different objectives. Shareholders and investors will have different objectives to, say, the customers or perhaps the local community. All interests need to be considered and conflicts need to be addressed and reconciled. Ways of working have to be established which suit all the parties concerned and achieve all the required objectives.

Corporate culture, as described by Turner in *Organisational Symbolism* (1990), is 'used largely to describe a set of cultural values, norms and their symbolic manifestations, devised by management and transmitted, both formally and informally, to the rest of the workforce'.

Cultural norms and symbols

While culture may be viewed as the personality of the organisation, or 'the way we do things around here', it is essentially more complicated than that. Some organisations have clear identities, but with many it is less clear just what they do or how they operate.

Culture is difficult to define, but a business's culture is essential to its success. Goffee and Jones, in *The Character of a Corporation: How Your Company's Culture can Make or Break Your Business*, identify four main cultures: fragmented, networked, mercenary and communal. The idea is not that any of these is ideal, but that some are more appropriate to certain types of organisation, and often a mix of more than one type can work well. Handy (1985) claims that mixed cultures can work well if used in a controlled manner. For example, some organisations exhibit a mixed power and task culture. Handy suggests organisations are best served if different functional specialities have different cultures depending on the nature of the organisation.

Cultural norms are simply what is seen as normal behaviour within an organisation. This varies between organisations, even within the same industry. Employees are usually under a great deal of pressure to conform to the norms of the organisation, be they guided by attitudes to other staff and customers, by dress code, or by relationships between members. A high-street bank employee would be under great pressure to conform to the 'collar and tie' dress code, rather than greeting bank customers at the counter wearing jeans and an army camouflage T-shirt. Call-centre employees are expected to be polite and tolerant to customers (however rude a customer may be).

Cultural symbols reflect the nature of an organisation. These symbols may take the form of buildings: extravagant and large, or small and insignificant; of logos: the Nike 'swoosh' or the Coca-Cola bottle. Advertising methods can be symbols of the culture and nature of the organisation. Coca-Cola spent millions on an advertising campaign with Michael Jackson; Nike signed star athletes, such as basketball player Michael Jordan (1985), in their advertising campaign, and entered huge sponsorship programmes to advertise their new air-pocket trainers. A local tree surgeon is more likely to be symbolised by a flyer distributed locally, or an ad in the local free paper.

Organisations also have their own technical terms and jargon, used to describe their competitors, or their personnel. New employees readily slip into usage of these terms to fit in to the culture that is new to them.

Values and beliefs

Over time, people within an organisation will come to share values and beliefs about the way things should operate, both within the organisation and externally.

Values and beliefs are things that motivate you: the things you believe in. Organisations need to build on their core beliefs and values to set clear goals for business activity.

When we make decisions we make value judgements, influenced by our personally held beliefs as well as by the immediate situation we are in. Within many organisations, decisions will be made collectively and the differing values of all the individual decision makers will influence those decisions. People have different ideals and values, so there are different ideas about how things should be run, or what are acceptable methods or goals. 'Acceptable' is whatever each individual, group or organisation *thinks* it should be.

As Roberts and Dowling (2002) say, 'Good corporate reputations are critical because of their potential for value creation, but also because their intangible character makes replication by competing firms considerably more difficult. Existing empirical research confirms that there is a positive relationship between reputation and financial performance ... firms with relatively good reputations are better able to sustain superior profit outcomes over time.'

Peters and Austin (1985) also say that 'shared company values affect individual performance', because shared values mean employees work within a framework which can flexibly and quickly respond to new situations, whereas rules and procedures can be 'a strait-jacket'.

Development of organisational culture

Much emphasis is placed on the culture of an organisation today. Managers continually strive to better the organisation's culture, and ensure an appropriate culture is helping them move towards a better way of producing. An appropriate mission, objectives and set of values is important for successful companies and a number of issues influence the development of an organisational culture.

In developing values and beliefs, employees pay regard to the origins of the company and what its original purpose was. How did the founder operate it? How the organisation first formed will usually influence that organisation for many years. Was the founder a former musician, now content to supply his local neighbourhood with CDs, tapes and popular music goods from his little corner shop, or did he want to build a worldwide entrepreneurial empire, like Richard Branson's Virgin Records?

Cultures may change as new management moves in, but the origins of the organisation, the culture, will continue to be an important determinant of 'the way we do things round here'.

Cultural integration   **JOURNAL ARTICLE**

Bondebjerg claims that although 'the American threat' has been an issue for European cultural and political elites for almost a century, 'the mass audience doesn't care'. Bondebjerg believes people simply accept the American culture as fundamental and familiar. If this is the case, then for

European cultural and political elites, this means that European integration and European culture is 'a living paradox: we live in a local and national culture with global dimensions and we inhabit an American global culture as a natural part of our national and local culture'. This article presents an interesting angle on cultural differences and cultural integration. After all, if cultures are to be integrated on a global scale, how can they also remain as differentiated cultural entities?

Bondebjerg, I. 'European media, cultural integration and globalisation. Reflections on the ESF-programme Changing Media–Changing Europe', *Nordicom Review*, 2001, Vol. 22, No.1, June.

Authority and power

Every manager's job involves exercising authority to some degree, and leading others. People 'obey' those with expertise and authority.

A somewhat controversial study of obedience was carried out by Stanley Milgram in 1963. Milgram found that participants repeatedly gave potentially fatal electric shocks to another person, simply because they were told that the experiment required that they must do so. Indeed, against all expectations and predictions, 65 per cent of participants administered shocks (or thought they did) to a fellow human being.

Managers can get the job done these days without reverting to such extreme levels of ordering others what to do and can find other means of exercising their authority.

Signs of *having* authority include job title, position, consent to make decisions, sign cheques, and so on, whilst signs of *being an* authority might include formal qualifications as well as the ability to display and share knowledge and technical expertise in a particular area. People take more notice of experts in their field if they think they really know what they are talking about: if they can display expertise.

Organisational structures are, in the simplest sense, concerned with allocation of authority and power. Importantly, that power and authority needs to

be allocated appropriately and effectively. As we have seen, in traditional hierarchical structures, the power tends to be at the top of the structure, and command moves in a downward direction to the lower levels. Senior managers (at the top of the hierarchy) make the important decisions, as they have the appropriate powers delegated to them. In more modern, flatter organisations, there are still big differences in levels of power delegated to different individuals, but power tends to be more evenly distributed.

Today, more individuals tend to have authority to make their own decisions and act on their own initiative, and giving them accountability means they are responsible for the consequences of those decisions and actions. Most people are happy to be able to work very much under their own direction, but organisations can only hold them accountable if they are given appropriate recognition for that extra responsibility. Placing trust in employees to perform their job well is fine, but in return the employees trust the employer to recognise that responsibility. (See 'Rewards and incentives' on p. 160.)

Formal patterns of authority have traditionally been established using organisational charts. Clear organisational charts lessen the likelihood of confusion and help plan for future changes and development of both the organisation and the individuals within it.

Again though, managers must be aware of the need for flexibility. Inflexible charts will be difficult to adapt to any changes required in the future. Business environments change constantly, and this must be recognised when developing organisational charts.

As Randall (1962) commented, 'Now, obviously, to know who is to do what and to establish authority within an institution are the basic first principles of a good administration, but this is a far cry from handing down immutable tablets of stone from the mountain top. Not even the Ten Commandments undertook to do more than establish general guidelines of conduct. They contained no fine print and no explanatory notes. Even the Almighty expected us to use our own good judgement in carrying them out.'

Organisational charts

Just as with organisational structures and cultural structures, we will be more likely to find organisational charts operating in larger sized organisations than in very small businesses. The more employees there are, the more likely a formal organisational chart is needed, to illustrate channels of authority and hierarchical divisions.

What is an organisational chart?

An organisational chart identifies clearly the characteristics of an organisation, and helps both employees and outside agents (suppliers, customers, and so on) to identify the way the organisation is made up. It shows how many people work for the company, what the company aims to achieve (its goals and objectives) and its pattern of command. It will make clear:

♦ who is responsible for what areas of the business or particular projects
♦ how different departments and areas of business link together
♦ principal areas and lines of authority
♦ levels of responsibility
♦ who deals with problems which arise in different areas
♦ the company's 'reason for being' and what it aims to achieve
♦ who reports to whom.

Organisational charts usually make clear the different levels within the organisation that have roughly equal amounts of authority or responsibility (see Figure 4.11). Top level may be the managing director, who manages upper middle managers, who are responsible for, say, marketing and production. Below these come middle management, usually responsible for their own particular field or functions, followed by supervisors at the lower middle level, who in turn supervise the lower level – comprised usually of the operatives – the shop floor workers, the office clerical staff, the shop sales assistants, and so on.

Organisational charts do have disadvantages:

♦ people low down the chart may abdicate responsibility, saying some tasks are others' responsibility
♦ charts only illustrate the formal structure. Most organisations rely heavily on informal structures

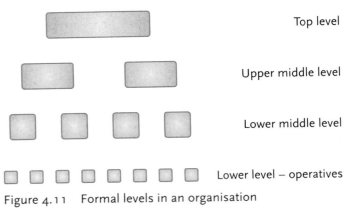

Figure 4.11   Formal levels in an organisation

and procedures, which cannot be illustrated in a formal chart.

Formal and informal structures

As mentioned previously, many organisations rely heavily on informal procedures and channels of communication. The formal structure would almost always be viewed in the sense of a straightforward organisational chart, but the informal structure, which most employees realise exists, will not be obvious.

Argyris, as far back as 1964, criticised formal, bureaucratic structures because they can limit individual growth and development and cause frustration for employees who have innovative ideas and ambition.

Decisions are not always made in formal meetings, but often ideas are discussed and decisions arrived at in the informal meetings at the golf club, on the squash court, or in the pub. The informal groups become more apparent to people the longer they work within an organisation. Effective communication channels are a major issue in many establishments.

The informal culture of the staff-room or perhaps the office canteen, as a means of support, communication and advice, can be an invaluable prop for many individuals, especially those new to the company. Often the more experienced staff only have the *time* to chat about who can authorise that, or who is the best person to ask about this, while they are relaxing over a cup of coffee or a pint.

Another example of formal and informal processes can be seen in looking at student assessment. Student assessment is seen at the formal level in official tests and paper assessments, in exams and course work and

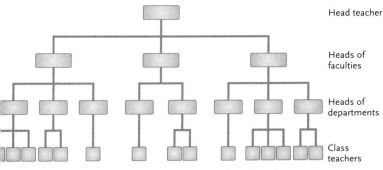

Figure 4.12   The formal structure of a school

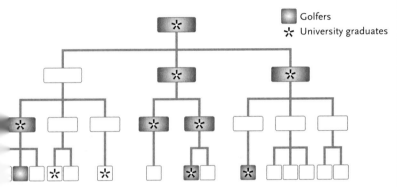

Figure 4.13   Hidden influences in an organisational structure

in internal and external moderation, for and by the examining bodies. At an informal level, student assessment is a continual and ever-present process in the classroom. Tutors assess student progress continually through observation, informal discussion and questioning, and through simply getting to know students. They note constantly who is paying attention, who is looking bored, and should be constantly assessing who understands what they are doing and, most importantly, whether they are learning. Informal assessment and sympathetic explanations can be as important to some students or employees as having the right books or equipment and being in the right room.

Spans of control

An individual's 'span of control' is the number of people he or she manages directly. Only so many people can be managed at any one time by one person, depending on the type of work involved. The best 'spans of control' balance control with trust. Employees need to be trusted to get on with their work, but at the same time there needs to be a sufficient level

CASE STUDY
The office mafia

At Midtown Secondary School the senior management team is made up of a head teacher, two deputy head teachers and three senior teachers. They meet fortnightly to discuss developments and policies. There is no set agenda: items to be discussed are decided by the head teacher and one of the deputies.

Other members of staff are consulted once a week at a 20-minute meeting before school on Monday. The briefing involves the head teacher introducing policy issues and allowing staff to present feedback to the senior management team who give announcements.

A number of major decisions are made by the school governors. The head teacher and senior deputy are governors.

The head and deputies rely heavily on the secretarial staff for day-to-day administration. They also handle the day-to-day accounts of the school and staff expenditures. The head and deputies spend a lot of the day in the school office and build up particularly close relationships with secretarial staff.

ACTIVITY

1 Which groups within Midtown School are most likely to be involved in major decision-making processes about policy?

2 Is the informal structure of the school likely to be much different from the formal structure?

3 Which groups may feel that they are not playing an appropriate part in the decision-making process?

4 What suggestions do you have for improving the management of this school?

of supervision to ensure the work is being carried out properly and effectively. A *narrow* span of control, where an individual only controls a few subordinates, enables close supervision and easy communication. *Wide* spans need higher levels of trust, as supervisors are responsible for much larger numbers of employees, on whom they cannot keep an eye all the time. Spans are usually wider when work is routine and straightforward or repetitive, or where workers are experienced and competent in their work.

Factors which influence spans of control:

♦ nature of the organisation: complexity of the work and range of responsibilities
♦ ability and personal qualities of managers and operatives
♦ time available to spend in supervision and monitoring
♦ ability and competence of operatives
♦ effectiveness of co-ordination, communication and production systems
♦ physical location of all members of the organisation.

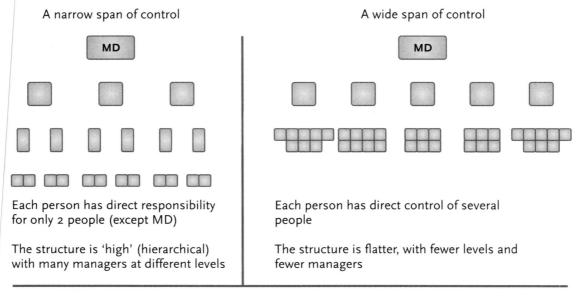

A narrow span of control

A wide span of control

MD

MD

Each person has direct responsibility for only 2 people (except MD)

Each person has direct control of several people

The structure is 'high' (hierarchical) with many managers at different levels

The structure is flatter, with fewer levels and fewer managers

Figure 4.14   Narrow and wide spans of control

Narrow span of control	Wide span of control
Greater number of specialists and managers at middle and lower levels	Fewer specialists/managers, distributed mostly at upper levels
Incompetent and/or untrained managers	Thorough and effective training
Ineffective communications and interactions between levels	Effective communications and proper structure, with effective interaction and delegation between levels
Unclear instructions or job descriptions	Clear instructions and understanding of job requirements
Rapid changes in external/internal environments	Slow changes in environment – internal or external
Unclear objectives and quality standards	Clear objectives and quality standards
Unclear or inappropriate delegation of authority	Clear lines of communication and effective interaction within them
Inadequate training	Competently and appropriately trained managers
Non-productive meetings	Effective, productive meetings
Complex procedures and tasks	Simple tasks and procedures

Figure 4.15   Typical features and influences on span of control

Controlling operations

The following are factors to consider when deciding the best way to control operations:

♦ the business environment in which the organisation operates: whether the industry is dynamic and constantly changing, or a long-established, static type of environment
♦ the cultural environment and background: different countries, regions, religions, and so on all operate in different ways
♦ the organisation's own culture and history
♦ the technology it uses and how many people use it.

Successful strategies maximise the strengths of the organisation and eliminate weaknesses; objectives need to have flexibility, and so do the productive processes, so that they can improve the efficiency of operations over time.

As proposed by Lawrence (1967) a 'close fit' is needed between the structure of the company and its strategic plans, so that the structure is capable of providing the means by which the organisation can achieve its objectives.

Greene (1982) said that maintaining a 'fit' between the organisation and its external and internal environments is crucial. He identified the external environment as comprising:

♦ the natural, or physical environment
♦ the technological environment
♦ human resources
♦ political environment
♦ social or socio-economic factors
♦ the market.

He identified the important internal environmental features as:

♦ productivity
♦ value and attitudes
♦ new organisational goals
♦ motivational dynamics
♦ new technology and its effect
♦ use and misuse of power by employees.

An efficient organisation with appropriate spans of control will be productive, efficient and profitable. Less efficient or inefficient systems will lead to many negative effects such as low morale, dissatisfaction, ineffective decision making and conflict, which lessen productivity and profit.

The human resource function

According to Graham and Bennett, in the *Human Resource Management Journal* (1992, p. 176), 'Human Resource Management concerns the human side of the management of enterprises and employees' relations with the firms.'

The following criteria are extracts from a variety of job vacancy advertisements published in national newspapers and on Internet sites. All the posts advertised were for human resources officers, managers or personnel. These should give you an idea of what human resources staff are actually required to do in modern organisations.

... provide support and advice to the management team ... create a working environment that supports organisation and brand values.

... to maintain our competitive edge, our Human Resources function has to apply its energy and expertise to build an environment where the best people do the best work, thereby creating sustainable benefit for our customers, shareholders and employees ...

... our HR team works in partnership with the Group's businesses, enabling them to achieve their strategic goals and add value to all people related business decisions ...

... Our HR expertise supports the delivery of our Group Strategy and People Strategy, embedding our vision of becoming ...

... Human Resources Manager is responsible for all aspects of the human resources function, including operational management and strategic planning ...

... management of change, staff involvement and education, training and development.

... Think about how large our operations are – the varied locations around the world, the vast numbers of people employed – and you begin to realise the size of the task.

... you will need to be able to work across the entire business to ensure its success through people ... The need for companies to recruit and retain the best possible people is vital for success. You will be focused on motivation, training and development. You will work with all functions to encourage and enable creativity, dynamism and innovation – this is the culture you will need to help foster.

If businesses are to achieve their objectives, they must indeed plan their human resources function so they have the right number of employees with the right qualifications and the right training to meet the needs of the business.

Human resources management (HRM) incorporates the personnel department functions and develops them. The role of HRM is to develop workers who can contribute their maximum efficiency towards the business objectives. HRM is no longer just about 'people management', controlled by the 'personnel manager'. It involves managers across the whole organisation in selecting, motivating, developing and evaluating their staff.

Employees were once seen as cost items. Today they are viewed as assets. Those companies with the best employees are the ones that are in the lead today and management teams have increasingly realised that money is not the most important asset of a company; its people are.

Torrington and Hall (1998) suggest several reasons for the change from 'personnel' to 'human resources':

- the phrases 'manpower' and 'manpower planning' are sexist
- a facelift was needed in the modern, popular atmosphere where personal relationships are more important than just giving orders

- personnel managers wanted to be viewed in a more favourable light and have their status increased.

The term 'personnel' was seen by many to be just that – about 'persons' – and the main function of the personnel department was to monitor the workforce. The people in this workforce, though, have feelings, aspirations and ideas, and should be able to express their views. Those views and ideas can indeed be valuable to the company. So it was recognised that personnel managers need to understand the aspirations and ambitions of their workers and utilise their enthusiasm to the full, for the good of the organisation. The human resource (as opposed to financial or material resources) is a less flexible resource, because it concerns people, who want to express their views and feel valued and valuable at work.

Personnel managers are therefore company managers, who are concerned with the company's success as a whole, and, importantly, with how the workforce can contribute to that success.

The personnel function can be viewed therefore as a mediating force between management and employees rather than a distinct and separate unit of the company. This encourages two-way communication and feedback, which can be used to develop and improve procedures, channels of communications, and ultimately productivity. It can be seen as a beneficial, cyclic feedback process, rather than simply a line of command, as shown in Figure 4.16.

Employees can help an organisation to create a competitive advantage by using their ideas, creativity and initiative. Being recognised and acknowledged can also increasingly motivate workers, leading to improved performance and better customer care, which in turn leads to greater productivity and profitability.

Personnel managers often spend much of their time working with the lower level workers, or operatives, than they do with the higher levels of management. This means they are more in touch with what is needed at the lower levels and they adopt many cultural and assumed values of this level of the organisation. They can often see what the operating problems and their possible solutions really are. These can then be conveyed to the managers.

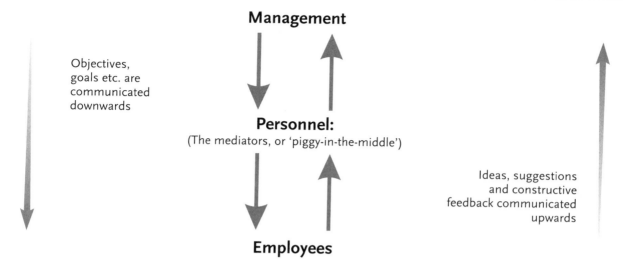

Figure 4.16   Personnel function as mediator

Workers doing the job can often come up with money-saving or more effective ways of working. If HR managers can support and encourage these people and

---

ACTIVITY

Before you read further, try and write down several comparisons between personnel management and human resource management.

Now compare your answers with those suggested in Figure 4.17, by Torrington and Hall (1998).

---

their ideas, then we can see that HRM plays an important overall strategic role, in just the same way as the marketing or finance departments do. There is no point in advertising and financing a product if the employees are unable or unwilling to deliver the service or level of quality that has been promised.

The important distinction as to whether an organisation focuses on personnel or human resources is probably best identified at the strategic level. At a strategic level, the organisation identifies its core values and objectives, and these are the important factors in deciding how human resources are deployed.

Personnel Management

People have a right to be treated as human beings at work

People will only be motivated and effective if their personal job-related needs are met

Interventions are needed by personnel to ensure that job-related personal needs are attended to

Other managers may neglect personnel work as they see themselves as other kinds of specialists – not 'people' specialists – so specialist 'people' managers *are* needed

Human Resources Management

People have a right to be treated as human beings at work

Management of *human* resources is the same as management of any other resource

HRM should be shared across the organisation, rather than separated off to people specialists

Efficient management, with a focus on human needs, is required throughout the whole organisation

HR managers need to support other managers and ensure that HRM is a corporate, strategic issue for everybody

HR managers need to ensure there are enough of the right people working in the right place at the right time

Figure 4.17   Personnel and human resources management

Those who focus on human resources are concerned with stressing to managers across the whole organisation the importance of using human resources effectively, rather than expecting the personnel manager to do it. After all, each manager knows his or her own function and its staffing requirements better than anyone else in the organisation.

The HRM emphasis is on the organisation *as a whole* being human resource managers and on the organisation *as a whole* being marketing managers and on the organisation *as a whole* being finance managers, and so on. It emphasises how everybody in the organisation has an indirect responsibility for its success.

You could have an efficiently planned domestic appliance repair service, with the right people in the right jobs, in the right numbers. That is no good however if the engineer sent out to repair the Smith's washing machine is not committed to the success of the company and its image, is rude to the customer and has no respect for the customer as an important stakeholder in his organisation and therefore in his employment. The Smiths will not use your company again, or recommend it to friends, so opportunities are lost. Just as employees can create a competitive advantage, they can easily destroy it.

Managers today need to be able to take a holistic view of their organisation as well as being experts in their own field; they need to be aware of the issues that affect the whole business. This generalism is concerned with working relationships, so HRM can be viewed as a strategic function. The tactics and methods employed by HRM – recruitment, staff training and development, equal opportunities, and so on – are therefore the concern of managers across the board, not just the responsibility of one specialist department.

The government-implemented strategy *Partnerships with People* emphasises the importance of its 'five paths to success'. These are:

- shared goals
- shared culture
- shared learning
- shared effort
- shared information.

This emphasis on shared input and results means all staff pull together towards achieving their shared goals.

CASE STUDY

The National Health Service plan *More Staff, Working Differently* published in July 2002 brought together a range of national initiatives, designed by the government to help the NHS deliver the larger workforce required to deliver the NHS plan's promises to its consumers. Nottingham City Hospital Trust said the following of their Human Resource Function in response to the plan.

HUMAN RESOURCE IMPLICATIONS IN THE NATIONAL CONTEXT

The Trust's HR Strategy must address the initiatives specified [in the NHS plan] and should be developed within the framework defined by the national strategy. This incorporates four main pillars as follows:

- Making the NHS a model employer.
- Ensuring the NHS provides a model career.
- Improving staff morale.
- Building people management skills.

The Nottingham City Hospital Trust HR team have to work, therefore, not just to the goals and objectives of the Nottingham NHS, but to the national goals and objectives set by the government. Remember that national and legal guidelines impact on any organisation's HR department.

(Section 1.3.4 of their HR strategy plan)

ACTIVITY

What difficulties might Nottingham NHS have in achieving their own objectives within the national plan?

- Who controls and specifies local objectives?
- Who controls national objectives?
- How might this impact on Nottingham's objectives and service delivery?

CASE STUDY

Central Bank: Change to an HRM perspective – an imaginary case

In the early 1990s Central Bank – one of the UK's major high street banks – felt that it needed to change the way in which it treated its people. Increasingly banks were operating in a competitive environment driven by information technology. Gone were the days of the top-down hierarchical bank with the bank manager handling all key lending decisions from his inner sanctum, the manager's office. Information technology made it possible to give responsibilities to junior members of the organisation who would be able to make key decisions supported by centrally created information systems. Information technology also made it possible to reduce staffing levels, and a number of branches were closed down in urban areas as telephone banking began to take off.

Up to the 1990s, the personnel department had played a key part in the bank, taking responsibility for recruitment and selection of staff, training, wages and salaries, and so on. It was now felt that many of these tasks could be carried out at a branch level, supported by a central HRM department. Managing and looking after people was to become a branch rather than Head Office responsibility. For example, training courses and appraisal could be carried out largely within the branch. Key initiatives included empowerment of employees, the development of self-managing teams, quality circles, a greater harmonisation of terms and conditions of employment, team briefings, and so on. In effect there was a whole raft of initiatives which were representative of the changed perspective. These changes were a key part of the organisation's strategic plan for the millennium and great emphasis was placed on HRM in the corporate mission statement and objectives.

ACTIVITY

1   What were the chief catalysts for the change in approach?

2   To what extent would you argue that Central Bank has moved from a personnel management approach to an HRM approach?

A stakeholder perspective

Organisations are made up of a number of different interested parties, or **stakeholders**. For each of these groups of stakeholders, the organisation serves a different purpose. Just as a woman may have many roles, as a mother, wife, daughter, sister, friend, employee, manager, tennis partner, and so on, and she means something different to all these people, so different stakeholders in an organisation want something different from that organisation.

Companies have to consider accountability to their stakeholders. Stakeholders include:

◆ employees, who want a secure job, good wages and prospects
◆ governments, who impose taxes and laws
◆ communities, who want a safe environment and provision of jobs
◆ consumers, who have choices, so expect value for money and high quality products
◆ shareholders, who want a good return on their investment.

Internal and external stakeholders

The internal stakeholders in an organisation include:

◆ owners
◆ managers
◆ employees.

The external stakeholders in an organisation include:

♦ customers
♦ government
♦ community
♦ suppliers.

HR managers need to ensure they operate an effective stakeholder approach, and stress the importance of employees as stakeholders. They should also stress to the employees the important part they, as individuals, play in the overall success of the organisation.

All stakeholders want worthwhile rewards for their investment. Shareholders particularly want more money back than they put in, and employees as stakeholders want rewards for their effort and commitment too. Recognising and rewarding commitment usually produces motivated employees,

ACTIVITY

1 To what extent are each of the companies mentioned using a stakeholder perspective that includes employees?

2 What organisations are you familiar with that operate a very strong stakeholder approach to HRM? Explain your answer.

Human capital   **JOURNAL ARTICLE**

This article states, 'We live in a world where share price is king and where it seems that some directors and boards will go to any length to protect it. It is against this backdrop that shareholders are increasingly seeking more transparency and accountability.'

As we have said, human capital is now regarded as any company's main asset. This article argues that shareholders are denied information on human capital. (The Accounting Standards Board recently recommended that data on human capital should be incorporated into annual reports and accounts.) Human capital and effective leadership are what lead to competitive advantage and this paper examines how recent government reports, such as the White Paper on Company Law Reform and the Kingsmill Enquiry on women's pay, recommend including data regarding human capital in annual reports and accounts so that shareholders have a clearer picture.

'Measuring human capital: the key to organizational success?', *Development and Learning in Organizations*, 2003, Vol. 17, No. 3, pp 7–9.

CASE STUDY

Taking a stakeholder approach

Company X had building work going on during the summer of 1998. As a sweetener, they put water coolers in each of their offices. When the building work was finished, they took out the coolers. The response from employees was intense: people felt very resentful. They felt that their company didn't care about them.

Spedan Lewis, the son of the founder of the John Lewis Partnership, drew up a futuristic constitution which contained mission statements such as 'The Partnership's ultimate aim shall be the happiness in every way of its members' and 'The Partnership shall recognise that only fools put business too far before pleasure, especially health and happiness, and that there is almost infinite scope for imagination and energy in the promotion of happiness in the more important sense of that word'.

notable by their enthusiastic approach and in their positive efforts to ensure customer satisfaction. Acknowledging and praising these efforts means employees feel their efforts are worthwhile not only for the customer, but for themselves as well.

Personnel management roles

Personnel managers need to know when they appoint other managers what authority and leadership qualities these managers are going to need, and how they will develop the required qualities in those new recruits. Personnel managers can influence promotions, pay and benefits and they need to maintain technical personnel expertise to continue to be effective personnel managers.

Legge (1978) describes four models of personnel management. These can provide fuel for the debate about what 'personnel' does and the purpose of the managerial function.

Normative model of personnel management

The usual expectations are that personnel recruit, train, reward and develop employees in ways that reward them with job satisfaction and enable them to perform to their full potential. The normative view is that if managers do this, the organisation will achieve its goals.

Descriptive-functional model

This is the systems-oriented approach, which emphasises the policies, processes, roles and structures of the organisation.

Personnel management is concerned with job descriptions, organisational structuring, recruitment and selection, training, appraisal, benefits and rewards, and discipline, ensuring that all adhere to the requirements of external regulators such as legal bodies and trade unions.

Critical-evaluative model

Legge (1978) claims there is a credibility gap between the image of human relations and normative aspirations. Watson (1986) also took a critical view of personnel management and its functions. He questioned the 'justificatory overtones and mystifications' of the normative approach, as he claimed the interaction between employer and employee is not on an equal basis, so the personnel manager is needed as a go-between to balance the equation. This critical view suggests that personnel practice is exploitative and dictatorial, and secondary to what should be the prime concerns: profitability, growth, market share, and so on. The modern concern for total quality emphasises the investment needed to develop team commitment and improve communications. Team managers should be responsible for the personnel management requirements of their own team, within the policies of the organisation as a whole.

Descriptive-behavioural model

This approach focuses on actual behaviours of personnel teams: what they really *do*, and, importantly, others' perceptions of what they do. Many employees' perceptions of the personnel role are ambiguous.

Ask any employed person you know what their personnel department does, and you will probably get answers ranging from 'give out the pay slips', through 'use lots of psychological testing and fancy buzz words' to 'reserve car park spaces and send out the company newsletter'. Many see the personnel function as simply acting as referee between line managers, who know too little employment law to resolve staffing problems.

It *is* difficult clearly to identify the role of the personnel department, because it does cover a wide range of activities. These include:

- strategy and policy making, with an emphasis on development of the human resources
- negotiating: acting as piggy-in-the-middle between different departments and interests
- administration: paying wages, monitoring health and safety, ensuring legal requirements are observed
- welfare: looking after employees and their needs
- supporting: helping managers develop their staff
- education and training: educating and providing appropriate training for employees to develop their careers and their contribution to the company.

This multi-role function demands tact and diplomacy on the part of the personnel manager, who has the interests of individuals as well as the organisation to consider and mediate between. This becomes particularly difficult at times such as during pay-rise disputes and restructuring processes, or where redundancies are required. The personnel manager may, on a personal level, want to give everybody a 6 per cent pay rise, but on an organisational level, has to acknowledge that anything more than a 2 per cent increase might jeopardise the organisation's financial security.

Storey (1992) in the early 1990s collected data from personnel managers and line managers involved with those personnel managers, and identified four main types of personnel worker:

- Handmaidens, who are personnel managers subservient to line managers. The role is ambiguous and not very well co-ordinated.
- Regulators, who have a hands-on role: setting up and monitoring the organisation's employment rules. These may range from writing personnel procedure manuals to making agreements with trade unions. Many see these as the firefighters brought in to extinguish the fire at turbulent times, rather than setting up a long-term strategy for effective human relations, which would prevent the fires in the first place.
- Advisors, who leave the day-to-day running of the organisation to line managers, but are familiar with current developments and step in to advise when asked to do so.
- Changemakers, who attempt to empower individuals, and create teamworking for the benefit of both individuals and the organisation, by changing the work environment to one which encourages employee commitment and effective human relations.

Storey found that managers are taking responsibility for HRM more and more, at the operative working level. He argues that this has come about because of organisational delayering, and the devolution of responsibility to regional offices and managers rather than at the centralised head office. He says managers now take on a more direct role in briefing employees and talks of more 'devolved management accountability' and of 'deproceduralising'.

Again, as with organisational structure, cultural structure, and so on, the role of the personnel function will depend on a range of factors such as history and ownership of the company, its size, environment, goals and objectives, and its technology and people culture: is it people-intensive or capital-intensive?

Senior management in many companies today are changing their views, and do see HRM as a strategic issue. Traditionally, personnel were concerned mainly with the 'employment procession': what you may

recognise as the 'hiring and firing' function. In modern organisations, though, personnel is responsible for many more areas of the business: for appraisal, the monitoring and career development of individuals; for equal opportunities; for developing and supervising pay structures and negotiation with trade unions; for administering disciplinary procedures and for supervising health and safety, and other employment-related issues.

Personnel policies

A **policy** is a general statement used to guide decision making and the general thinking which is employed in deciding future actions. Most organisations will, for example, have policies on health and safety, equal opportunities, customer service, and so on. The government has policies on education and employment which declare their intentions as to how they will develop and govern these areas. Torrington and Hall (1991, p. 33) describe policy as a 'declared mode of action for the future'.

Business policies concern decisions about whether to expand and diversify or retrench; whether to go international or global; whether to, and how to, reduce staffing levels. They are all concerned with a plan for the future. The policy is a framework for future action and this policy is communicated to all employees so they can all work within the same overall picture.

Miller (1989, p. 49) states that 'Strategy is a market-oriented concept. It is fundamentally concerned with products and competitive advantage.'

Business environments change so rapidly today, that companies need to consider long-term policies which they can sustain – and which sustain the company – rather than setting up 'quick-fix' short-term repairs.

Personnel strategy usually refers to planning the objectives and desired achievements, whereas **personnel policy** is the framework within which the plans will be implemented.

Why bother with policy statements?

One reason is that they stabilise and standardise management behaviours. All managers should behave consistently, without constantly changing direction and confusing each other and their employees.

Another reason is that they reduce the dependence on individuals in the framework: a strong, flexible framework shares knowledge better and reduces the need for specific individuals who are the *only* ones who know how to carry out a particular part of the overall process. Whilst it is important to treat important individuals well to retain the human capital, it is also important for the organisation that nobody is indispensable.

There are other good reasons to have policy statements:

- they clarify policies: they explain why, for instance, a manager wants ten more staff, what those people will achieve and how this benefits the organisation
- they empower the specialists: if a manager can develop a sound and workable policy to implement his or her ideas, then people are more likely to listen
- everybody in the organisation knows where they stand: policies inform employees of future intentions and likelihood of security, and allow managers to re-evaluate and adapt their own policies to fit in with others that may be changing
- they enable response to legal, external or market pressures: altered legal procedures are communicated by government policies, for example the 1984 Data Protection Act for which every organisation had to form procedural policies to comply with its provisions.

ACTIVITY

If policy is badly communicated or not communicated to all staff, what is likely to happen? Write down three or four ideas.

CASE STUDY

The Ferret and Fiddle is an imaginary nationwide pub–restaurant chain. They are introducing a new policy for staff appraisals. This is how they promote it to their managers and staff:

'An appraisal regularly records an assessment of an employee's performance, potential and development needs. The appraisal is an opportunity to take an overall view of work content, loads and volume, to look back at what has been achieved during the reporting period and agree objectives for the next.' (ACAS)

'The Ferret and Fiddle's new staff appraisal policy demonstrates how committed we are to the development and support of our staff. The new appraisal policy and procedures are part of our drive to continually improve the quality and service to our customers and to have the highest regard for the welfare of our employees. The system is designed to encourage staff at all levels to become involved in the daily operations of our pubs and restaurants, to become active and valued participants in our organisation, and to help us focus on our other most important asset – our customers.'

Any member of staff, as Charles Handy (1975) states, 'needs to see his work in context, have some ideas of what is expected of him, how he will be judged, and where his goals are in that job'. The Ferret and Fiddle's new appraisal system policy sets out how this will happen for all staff. The new system will enable them to:

- identify training and development needs and thus influence training policy
- assess current performance and recognise talent and potential
- set clear goals and give staff ownership of their individual targets
- increase motivation in the individual
- promote and improve teamwork

- improve future performance of individuals *and* the establishment
- provide a foundation for future career progression
- provide regular feedback, to monitor progress and ensure targets can be met.

'In the Ferret and Fiddle establishments, motivated employees will be notable by their enthusiastic, cheerful approach and in their positive efforts to ensure customer satisfaction. They will be smiling, happy, helpful people for whom nothing appears too much trouble.'

ACTIVITY

1 How might personnel promote the new system initially, to persuade managers and staff to implement it successfully?

2 Who do you think should be responsible for assessing current performance and setting goals?

3 How might progress be recorded?

4 What methods might managers use to give staff ownership of their targets?

It may sound a little idyllic, yet an effective appraisal policy, properly communicated, can promote this kind of motivation by acknowledging and praising these efforts and formally recording them, so that the employee feels his or her efforts are worthwhile not only to the customer, but to him or herself as well. A good appraisal system will map out clear 'smart' goals and follow them up to ensure appropriate training and development opportunities are available. This means employees are all involved in the organisation and the way it operates. Teamwork is crucial to keeping customers happy, and **total quality management** works from the bottom of the company up: those working with the public know how best to keep that public happy and solve their own working problems.

Employees are empowered and everyone is committed to customer satisfaction. Appraisal policies can encourage initiative and innovation and provide the customers with top quality service, in the most efficient and economical way possible.

Effective policies involve all levels of staff: in the Ferret and Fiddle's case, from part-time bar staff right up to the top management levels. At the first contact level, bar staff need to take orders correctly. These orders must be communicated correctly to the chef and waiters or waitresses. All must play their part in the chain of events which leads to happy customers. Reorganising operational policies and processes and in some areas delayering of management hierarchies has led to increased responsibilities at the 'lower' levels and increasingly calls for multi-skilling, which can in itself lead to a greater appreciation of the part others play in the overall sequence.

Strategies and operating plans

Corporate strategy concerns the long-term plans of an organisation. It is about the whole organisation (the corporation), formulating, implementing, understanding and monitoring the long-term plans (the strategy), which will ensure the organisation runs smoothly and profitably. Strategic planning is done in stages: see the **strategic planning steps** advocated by J. Thompson (1995). The company identifies its past achievements and looks at how it sits within its industry's environment. It monitors the changes taking place there. Building on its strengths, it will form the foundations of the strategic plan and the objectives which will implement it, to take it successfully into the future.

The basics of managing people lies in who does the work and how it gets done. So the thinking behind why we should decide on one particular plan or course of action over another is fundamental to the personnel manager.

Strategic goals for personnel

Human resource management needs to be closely interlinked with business strategy and distinguished from traditional personnel management by being concerned with achieving business objectives through the way it manages its human resources. Corporate strategies provide a framework for human resource requirements over a defined period and it is now widely recognised that an organisation's success depends on the competencies of its employees. This suggests that people management should perhaps lead, rather than follow, business strategy, and build employee competence through effective selection, development and reward. In other words, the human resource strategy needs to be an integral part of the corporate strategy, so recruitment, selection, training and pay, and so on, all need to be included in the overall corporate strategy.

Some organisations try hard to achieve strategic HRM, whereas others use the term but fail to put people at the centre of their operations. All organisations can be placed somewhere along the continuum shown below.

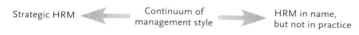

Strategic HRM ← Continuum of management style → HRM in name, but not in practice

At the strategic end of the continuum, we can consider the two types of strategic approach: so-called soft and hard HRM.

Hard and soft HRM

To be successful and effective, HRM must be a two-way process. It has to take account of individual employees' goals as well as the objectives of the organisation. If employees are to show loyalty to the company they need to gain personal satisfaction in their work and feel that they are developing personally, as well as producing results for the employer.

The notion of hard and soft HRM was originally put forward by Storey (1987). A soft HRM approach puts the employees' interests on an equal basis with the organisational aims and encourages intrinsic motivation through valued rewards. Soft HRM takes a human approach: people are developed for themselves as well as to suit the organisation. The company will have its organisational objectives: a 'vision' of where it wants to be in four or five years' time, and will know what or whom it needs to get there. It will recognise that its employees will also have visions and goals and will actively seek to find out what these goals are.

These individuals will then be offered the training and development they need to reach their own goals, in conjunction with serving the organisational needs. The company will identify training requirements and use its own staff (rather than outside recruits) to develop towards a mutually beneficial end. They will tie in their own objectives and performance with personal development and reward.

Expectations

One thing that will affect soft HRM is the way in which expectations of their staff will change over time, and changes in their own industry: what are other similar organisations offering in terms of staff benefits that may tempt their own staff to move to other employers? If staff are leaving, *why* are they leaving and what can be done to reduce staff turnover and retain loyal staff? A hard HRM approach, conversely, would be more concerned in this scenario with looking at where to find more staff to replace those dispensable people who have gone.

Flexibility

The soft HRM approach is concerned with flexibility for the workers as well as to benefit the organisation. If more flexible working hours, or childcare facilities will encourage loyalty, then they will be introduced as further incentives to persuade people to stay. Employees are empowered by being given more responsibility and more involvement in decision making. Profit-share initiatives can make them feel that they are rewarded for their contribution and belong more, and independent teams, who plan their own ways of working, feel their views are really being acknowledged and acted upon. This empowerment leads to increased production and is cost-effective, yet still offers its workers a feeling of fulfilment, job satisfaction and security.

Hard HRM, on the other hand, applies the concept that if staff are treated well, then the organisation will get what it wants from them. Hard HRM aims to maximise production, sales and profits, with little concern for the development of the individual. This is a business-oriented approach to strategic management. A hard HRM company will have a long-term view of where it wants to be, but it will look more at the *numbers* of people it will need, rather than *who* it will need. Past trends will predict future needs, without looking at what internal or external changes brought about those trends. It employs a *workforce* rather than *separate people*.

Appraisal

Often, companies adopting hard HRM will use appraisal as a punitive rather than a developmental tool. Personal development and self-evaluation are not always considered or recognised, as organisational objectives are paramount over personal ambitions. The hard HRM approach displays a unitary style, assuming that all employees want the same outcomes as the management perspective desires. There is little room for plurality in the hard approach. In the hard HRM environment, managers may be distant, off-hand and negative. Their values and practices may be exploitative.

Hard HRM might be seen in an environment that:

♦ employs casual or short-term contract staff only
♦ keeps wages and benefits to a minimum
♦ behaves insensitively towards employees
♦ supervises employees closely and does not develop their trust
♦ is not interested in the personal development of employees.

Hard HRM is concerned with the questions, 'What is needed?' and 'How can it be provided?' and uses information to:

♦ formulate goals
♦ identify problems
♦ evaluate options
♦ select and implement a plan to achieve the desired (organisational) outcome.

Soft HRM might be seen in an environment that:

♦ responds to the aspirations of individuals in the organisation
♦ encourages people to be part of a team
♦ develops policies which reflect personal needs for fairness and equality

♦ optimises the use of human resources by putting the right people in the right jobs and giving them fair rewards (tangible and non-tangible)
♦ matches people appropriately to jobs, to achieve the organisation's goals
♦ gets results by securing the commitment, loyalty and trust of employees.

Management strategy | JOURNAL ARTICLE

Looking at power and domination in the workplace, Knights and Morgan say that management strategy is all about power and domination. They say that managers claim strategies, 'Provide a rational and scientific impetus to the development of management techniques and processes' and point out that 'strategists are reluctant to admit failure; instead, they reconstitute the goals and end results of strategy so that it can be defined as success.'

This implies that managers develop strategies to achieve their aims, but if these don't work, they then redefine their original goal, so that they can say their strategy *did* work. Controversial perhaps, but many workers in large organisations might agree with the idea from their personal experiences.

Knights, D. and Morgan, G. 'The concept of strategy in sociology: a note of dissent', *Sociology*, 1990, No. 24, pp 475–83.

Soft systems methodology | JOURNAL ARTICLE

Brocklesby looks at research conducted in a New Zealand market research company, and shows how soft systems methodology (SSM) can be used for developing 'competence profiles' in HRM.

The study was carried out because a particular company was having trouble recruiting and retaining suitable staff as project managers. Traditionally, teamworking abilities and technical knowledge were the main criteria used for recruitment and for evaluating performance. Although these criteria were still considered relevant, a review was carried out to try and point to why recent recruitment exercises had failed, and to examine what other key skills were becoming increasingly needed because of technological, market and business advances happening in the industry. The research was concluded with a look at how SSM can be used to gain information more useful than that obtained through more conventional methods.

'Competence profiles' were developed to increase managers' ability to identify the corporate mission and objectives; identify the competences needed to achieve these objectives; develop these competences through recruitment and selection or training and development strategies (all the domain of 'personnel'); and implement these strategies to reinforce desired behaviours.

The article argues that a lot of data which organisations use to provide the basis for HRM decisions is now useless because it comes from old-fashioned methods and the social context from which it evolved, rather than paying attention to modern-day technology and management thinking.

Brocklesby, J. 'Using soft systems methodology to identify competence requirements in HRM', *International Journal of Manpower* 1995, Vol. 16, No. 5/6, pp 70–84.

Managing change   JOURNAL ARTICLE

Burnes opens by saying, 'In an age where effective leaders are at a premium and where continuous change appears to be the order of the day, this article argues that organisations need to align organisational change and management development strategically and operationally in order to maintain and increase their competitiveness.' Burnes examines two organisations that made huge organisational changes, and looks at the benefits of viewing managerial development as parallel and equal to organisational change.

Burnes, B. 'Managing change and changing managers from ABC to XYZ', *Journal of Management Development*, 2003, Vol. 22, No. 7, pp 627–42.

HM and the Internet   JOURNAL ARTICLE

Kumar says, 'The past decade has witnessed dramatic changes in the types and composition of the workforce.' This report examines the impact of the Internet on human resources management. It looks at this from employers' and workers' perspectives, examining, for example, how a large number of people now work from home and how there is greater accessibility to available jobs. It also looks at how employers have better access to potential recruits. Human resource 'initiatives' are examined to see how to seek a 'technologically adept workforce'.

Kumar, S. 'Managing human capital supply chain in the Internet era', *Industrial Management and Data System*, 2003, Vol. 103, No. 4, pp 227–237.

Diagnosing behavioural problems

Psychology is the study of human and animal behaviour. Psychologists study behaviour in all areas of life: at work, school and within the family, looking, for example, at cognitive development, interpersonal skills, emotions, abilities, and social and genetic influences.

Business organisations are interested in psychology to seek answers to two key questions about human behaviour at work:

- Why do people behave as they do?
- How can organisations get people to behave as they want them to?

Psychologists can play an important part in solving 'man-management' problems in an organisation and offer insight into areas such as:

- absenteeism
- levels of motivation and levels of effort
- intelligence and learning; how to train for the best results
- group interaction
- aggressive behaviour
- stress management
- resistance to change
- over-conformity (sticking to the rules).

Concepts, principles and perspectives

Different approaches in psychology – behaviourist, cognitive or psychoanalytical – assume different methods of research, depending on their area of study. The main psychological approaches used in organisational psychology are psychoanalytic, behavioural psychology, cognitive psychology, social psychology and the phenomenological approach. We shall look briefly at each of these in turn.

The psychoanalytic approach

Most people have heard the name Freud, or of 'a Freudian slip', where we say something quite unlike what we intended to say (but maybe what our subconscious really *wanted* us to say). Sigmund Freud (1856–1939) was the founder of psychoanalysis. Educated at the University of Vienna Medical School, he specialised in neurology. He has been one of the most influential scientists of the last century.

Freud believed that people are mostly guided in their behaviour by forces in their unconscious. He likened the human mind to an iceberg: the bit exposed above the water is our conscious mind, while that much larger part, invisible beneath the surface, is our unconscious mind. As many of our instinctive urges are repressed during our early childhood, these repressed parts of our character remain with us in our subconscious, and in later years manifest themselves in our behaviours, our fears and

Figure 4.18   Sigmund Freud

neuroses and sometimes in obsessive behaviours or psychoses. This implies that we don't always understand our own motives and behaviours, but that we are 'controlled' by our subconscious. Freud's notions may seem extreme, but then how often have you caught yourself saying to yourself or to friends 'I don't know *why* I did that, it's not like me at all'?

An important aspect of a psychologist's work is to understand what motivates and influences individuals in their behaviour, and psychoanalytical psychologists seek many of their explanations through methods such as interviews, word association, dream analysis and how people complete sentences and phrases, or how they might interpret a picture.

Since Freud's studies, new theories continue to evolve, still concerned with the way that each of us has parts of our personality which affect the way we act, according to the situation and circumstance we find ourselves in.

Eric Berne, author of *Games People Play* and *What Do You Say After You Say Hello?* proposed the notion that our personality consists of three 'ego states': parent, child and adult. In any 'transaction' or interaction with others, one of these ego states will dominate us. Associated with each of these ego states are distinctive communicative behaviours, as described below. They are not necessarily associated with age-related stages of psychological development; adults can display child-like behaviour and children can just as easily exhibit adult-like behaviour.

The parent

This is our learned conditioning, learned from the attitudes and examples set when we were young by our parents, teachers, neighbours, and, increasingly, from television and other influential media. The parent in us is formed by external events and influences as we grow through childhood. We can change these attitudes if we wish, but it is difficult to lose the attitudes that are 'bred' into us as we grow up. They affect our relationships with others and how we behave in relation to others, in response to our own values and beliefs. As part of our growing up, we need constantly to re-evaluate our values and beliefs and make sure they are up to date and in touch with modern thinking. Your values today may be far different from those that your parents or grandparents accepted.

The child

Our reactions to external events and our personal feelings form the 'child'. We see, hear and feel all manner of experiences and emotions every day, and when anger or disappointment take over from rational reasoning, the child in us is evident. Feelings can be triggered that link to past events, and affect how we react to current events. Shouting, crying and 'stamping your feet' can all be related to the child inside you.

The adult

The 'adult' enables us to think, to reason and determine how to behave for ourselves, based on past experience and the current situation. We can gather and process information and decide on the best course of action. The 'adult' in us starts to develop as early as ten months old, and helps us to balance the parent and the child inside us.

Each of these elements of our personality is with us at all times and when we communicate we are doing so from any one of these ego states. How we feel at the time determines which one emerges, and almost anything can cause a switch from one state to another.

Berne's theory is that successful transactions, or effective communications, need the receiving ego state to correspond to the sending ego state; so if the parent is to speak to the child, the response needs to be child to parent. So if the communication is 'boss' to 'subordinate', but the response elicited is boss to boss, then conflict and ineffective communication is likely.

Critics of psychoanalysis claim there is no scientific proof of the causes of human behaviour, and particularly that Freud's theory is so open-ended it can be twisted to 'prove' itself under any given circumstances.

Behaviourism

The psychologist John Watson first presented his ideas on behaviourism in 1908, and by 1912 use of the term 'behaviourist' was his trademark. He published an article, 'Psychology as the Behaviourist Views It', that introduced behaviourism as an 'objective experimental branch of natural science'. Behaviourism came to be a widely accepted approach among psychologists from the 1920s through to the 1960s. Behaviourism, with its potential for the possibility of producing behavioural change, gained huge popularity in the USA. It also moved psychological experiments to a more 'scientific' level, which left no room for conjecture about unobservable mental processes such as thoughts and dreams, but sought to 'prove' scientifically how hypotheses of cause and effect in relation to behaviour could be proved or disproved.

Burrhus Frederic (B. F.) Skinner (1904–1990), a former writer who studied psychology at Harvard University, became immersed in behaviourism. In the laboratory of an experimental biologist, he worked on behavioural studies with rats, designing boxes to reward behaviour, such as pressing a lever to gain food, or pushing a button for rewards.

Gaining recognition for his designs, known as Skinner boxes, he began development of a controversial 'baby box'. His second daughter spent much of her babyhood in one of these: a controlled-environment chamber, which ethical guidelines would prohibit today.

Figure 4.19   B. F. Skinner

Skinner, a strict behaviourist, believed everything we do is shaped by punishment or reward. Behaviourists today believe that the main influence on people and their behaviour is their environment and that experiences from infancy through to adulthood shape the way we behave. Positive and negative reinforcements of our behaviour will guide how we behave, just as punishment is meant to deter us from undesirable behaviour.

Positive reinforcement

This is where something pleasant happens to reward us for a particular behaviour. It may be praise from a parent or teacher or money given for completing a particular task; it may be a pat on the head for the dog for obediently sitting at the kerbside.

Negative reinforcement

This is where the removal of something unpleasant follows the correct behaviour. Early psychologists tried electric-shock tactics and the removal of them, to encourage desired behaviours in animals. An example in the workplace might be where someone is rewarded for completing an unpleasant task by removing that unpleasant task from their list of duties.

Punishment

This is where an unpleasant consequence follows undesired behaviour. Examples might be criticism or reprimands, withdrawal of pay for not performing as required, or even formal disciplinary warnings or dismissal.

Both negative and positive reinforcements have been shown to improve behaviour, though punishment is usually only effective if it is immediate and delivered every time the unwanted behaviour is practised. If a thief gets away with theft again and again, then one short spell in prison will probably not deter him from thieving again. However if he expects to get caught and punished every time he steals, it is unlikely that he will continue to offend.

Using behaviourism

Skinner (1973) set out five rules for positive reinforcement:

♦ be specific: give as much information as possible; specify desirable achievements, not a general 'you've done well this week'
♦ be immediate: praise needs to be in prompt response to the act, not ten months later at appraisal
♦ ensure targets are achievable: small and frequent successes are encouraging
♦ remember the intangible: sometimes the boss's thanks can be more important than a pay-packet bonus
♦ keep it unpredictable: unexpected praise or reward is always welcome, so don't always buy cream cakes every time you hit credit control targets, it can get a little boring and uninspiring.

ACTIVITY

How effective is behaviourism?

Think of a workplace with which you are familiar. Try to give some practical examples of when these principles have been:

♦ applied
♦ not applied when they should have been
♦ wrongly applied.

Criticisms of behaviourism

Behaviourism focuses on simple, basic learning only. It leaves no room for examining how perception, thinking, language and problem solving affect behaviours. It misses out many areas of human behaviour because it tends to exclude reports and experiences of individuals, which it cannot easily explain.

The stimulus–response and reinforcement concepts are difficult to observe and/or measure outside of a laboratory setting. Just because a rat in a maze, or a pigeon in a box, learns by reinforcement, it is not realistic to extrapolate these actions to all human behaviour, even though many of the observations noted can be observed to a degree in humans.

Cognitive psychology

Cognitive psychology is a discipline that examines the role of internal mental processes in behaviour. Individuals differ from one another for infinite reasons and the way individuals interpret information and react to it – how they respond to a stimulus – is governed by the brain and the nervous system and the complex processes which operate them. Mental processes and individual reactions are affected by many things: genetics, whether you are male or female, physique, personality, intelligence and social influences, as well as memory of past experiences and other mental and evaluative skills.

The study of all these cognitive processes impacts on organisations, because intelligence, memory, verbal ability, reaction times, motor co-ordination and spatial skills, as well as computer literacy, numerical ability and problem-solving skills are all relevant to selection of personnel and to job design. Changes over recent years have had a huge impact on individuals at work. Globalisation through technology and communications, stronger job competition, and the increased speed of the world of work through email and Internet links mean more immediacy of action is required from workers. Individuals and organisations need to respond more quickly than ever, to keep up with the competition.

Social psychology

This is the study of how social, individual and group influences shape our social behaviour. Interactions between individuals are significant in the daily operations of any organisation, and social psychology fields of study can be applied in many contexts of organisational operations. For example:

- how teams and immediate work groups affect individuals' behaviour
- how different leadership and management styles affect behaviour
- how behaviour in negotiations affects the outcome of the negotiations
- how individuals respond to conflict: passive, assertive and aggressive behaviours
- stress: what causes it, people's responses to it, how to reduce it
- how non-verbal communication operates in the workplace.

Many of us are unaware of the influences we are under from the day we are born, from our environment and the people – or groups of people – within it. Our society, class, religion, family, friends, school, teachers, work associates and personal experiences all shape the way we develop our values and beliefs, and how we behave.

ACTIVITY

Do you 'know your place?'

1 Imagine yourself at an interview. What behaviour is expected of you? And do you conform?

2 What is likely to happen if you don't 'know your place'?

3 What if *you* ask all the questions and tell them nothing about yourself?

Skilled interactions require us to know our role in the interaction, and fitting in with the group we are with takes learning and experience. We learn what's expected of us in different situations and how we learn to be socialised and conform is of interest to social psychologists.

The phenomenological approach

Phenomenology started as a school of philosophy and looks mainly at subjective experience, to examine how consciousness and memory 'distort' reality, to 'arrive at a more adequate approximation of what is' (Spinelli, 1989).

The emphasis for psychologists here is on human experience rather than behaviour. Behaviour results from an interaction between an individual and the environment. This behaviour will depend on that individual's values and beliefs, attitudes, needs and expectations, as well as their personal interpretations of the situation and their practised behavioural strategies. Behaviour is not simply a passive reaction.

At meetings, for example, people put forward different ideas and those ideas are reacted to in different ways by other members of the group. All this will depend on a number of things:

- their attitudes to the topic being discussed: they may not welcome ideas about change
- their motives and their interpretation of others' motives
- relationships and seniority within the group: managers and supervisors may feel more confident expressing their views than lower level employees
- they will have different interests and personal objectives to others in the group: the sales manager may want to spend more on advertising to increase sales, while the finance department may be trying to cut back on spending.

Personal construct theory

This theory, devised by Kelly (1955), looks at the phenomenological basis of personality: an individual's perceived world and experiences, as opposed to objective reality. Managers need to remember that not everybody sees a situation in the same way.

Methodology

Psychologists use a range of methods and different types of data to research human behaviour, emotions and thought processes in the workplace.

Research methods relate to the procedures used to gather information, while **research design** is the overall strategy used to carry out the research.

The design depends on what the researcher is studying and what kind of data they need to obtain.

Research methods

There are six main research methods.

Interviews

These can be carried out on a one-to-one basis or in groups. Data can be gathered from answers to structured formats where the same questions are asked of all interviewees, or from unstructured formats where the interviewee is left to talk freely about their views and/or experiences about a given topic.

Observation

Non-participant observation occurs where the researcher wants simply to watch what is happening in a given situation without intervening or guiding the behaviour, such as finding out which employees are actively contributing to a meeting and which ones just sit quietly and say nothing. **Participant observation** occurs when the researcher is part of the group being researched. As a participant, the researcher is engaged with the group and environment, to gain first-hand experience. **Structured observation** involves the use of clear sets of data to observe, such as how many times did Fred speak in the meeting? How many words did Jane speak? How many times did Sue object to Fred's ideas? How many of his ideas did she agree with?

Questionnaires and psychometric tests

Questionnaires can be designed to investigate detailed survey work and can reach large numbers of people at one time. Psychometric tests are often used to assess a person's suitability for a job, or to explore aspects of their personality, such as whether they are introverts or extroverts.

Diaries

These are used to record key events, feelings and experiences of individuals. They can take the form of written diaries or video diaries.

Psychological assessment

This involves measuring biological, neurological and physiological states, as they relate to a person's psychological functioning. Stress levels can be recorded through blood pressure, heart rate, and so on, in different work situations, or levels of cortisol (the 'stress hormone') in the bloodstream can be monitored.

Primary archives

Existing records can be researched for information in such areas as past absenteeism rates, and so on.

Research design

Experimental design

Researchers carry out experiments in the workplace in order to try and develop inferences about cause and effect. If a workplace procedure is changed, for example, researchers can look at the effect that change has had and decide whether the results are worthwhile or not. For example, working hours may be altered to incorporate shorter days, or more breaks, or to shorten shifts, to see what effect these different combinations may have on, for example, productivity or absenteeism. Do workers produce more in a different environment?

It is standard practice in experiments to use *control* groups – those for which nothing is altered – compared with the experimental group, in which certain conditions are changed, to measure the effect of those changes.

Survey design

Surveys are important tools for social research. Surveys conducted using questionnaires, for example, can cover a large portion of the population, and can elicit from wide samples large amounts of quantitative data for measuring, for example, attitudes and reactions to changes or events.

Care has to be taken in designing questionnaires, to ensure the responses give the true information required. One problem with questionnaires is bias in interpretation, both of the respondents' interpretation of the questions (and their interpretation of why the researchers asked them in the first place) and in researchers' interpretation of the answers.

Whether **quantitative** data, which consists of hard, clear figures and calculations, is required, or whether **qualitative** research methods are used, depends on the type of investigation to be conducted. Do researchers need control of statistics, for example, or do they need more in-depth 'feelings' and opinions in their results?

Qualitative research

Qualitative research gives information on individuals' feelings and how they interpret situations, in keeping with the phenomenological approach mentioned earlier. Qualitative research can begin from a very general concept for investigation ('staff morale is really low') and give generalised information and opinions, which can then be used to direct more detailed research into more specific problems. Psychological and organisational theory often tends to emerge from qualitative inquiry.

Qualitative research, through observation, interview and case studies, produces detailed information of a subjective kind, which can give a great insight into and explanation of behaviour. A case study, for example, 'allows an investigation to retain the holistic and meaningful characteristics of real-life events' (Yin, 1989) and participant observation can report on behaviour 'from the point of view of those being studied' (Bryman, 1996).

Quantitative research

Quantitative research, through experiments, surveys, or tests and questionnaires, gives hard, numerical, quantifiable data, which can be counted and analysed numerically and objectively. Quantitative research is structured whereas qualitative is not necessarily so.

One problem with qualitative research is that it is that it is subjective and can take on the researchers' interpretations or biases as well as those of the participants.

There are advantages and disadvantages to both methods. Positivists argue that only scientific (quantitative) methods and observable phenomena are valid for 'knowledge', yet attitudes and employees' opinions are important in research and cannot always be accurately ascertained from more controlled methods of inquiry. It must always be remembered though, that conclusions drawn from any kind of experimental data cannot always be reliably used for accurately predicting behaviours; participants may behave differently in the 'false' laboratory or observational settings to how they would in a natural or organisational setting.

Case studies cannot usually be used to generalise to the whole population as they concern only one individual or a small, non-representative group. Interviews can be difficult to control, and a balance is needed to obtain a relaxed and informative, yet objective, response. Body language and verbal intonation infer a lot during interviews, which can be difficult to include in results, and in analysis interpretation by the researcher can bias reporting of these factors. On the other hand, such qualitative research offers much useful detail and explanation of human behaviour that could not be gained from many experimental settings.

As Walker (1985) said, 'Certain questions cannot be answered by quantitative methods, whereas others cannot be answered by qualitative methods.'

Action research

Often researchers will use their own organisations to look at areas for development and potential change. Action research has a long history and has been used in areas where an understanding of prevailing social situations has been examined, to try and improve conditions in areas such as industry, the health service, community and work settings.

In organisations, the action researchers are involved with doing the job, as well as looking at ways of trying to improve how it is done. They work with people in the organisation to develop a generalised knowledge of the areas requiring investigation.

Perception

Perception is important in organisational behaviour for several reasons, but particularly because:

♦ people make judgements based on their perceptions of a given circumstance or situation
♦ decision making and behaviour is guided by those perceptions
♦ misconceptions or misperceptions cause a lot of confusion and conflict in the workplace.

What is 'perception'?

How an individual interprets a situation will guide how they respond to it. An individual's **perception** of what is happening to them is critical to the mental process they will use to decide how to react to that stimulus and what their response will be.

Definition

For the purpose of looking at individuals' behaviour in a work situation, we can view perception as a process which individuals use to interpret and organise sensory impressions in their mind, to give meaning to their environment and their actions.

Perception is the psychological process by which stimuli are received and organised into meaningful patterns, it is how we receive, organise and interpret information.

There are three elements of the process of perception to remember.

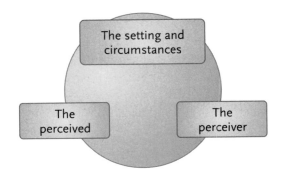

All three interact to produce the understanding the perceiver has of the actual situation.

The **perceiver** is the one receiving the message or the one trying to understand the situation. The way they interpret the situation depends a lot on what they want out of it: their motives, what their past experiences of similar situations have been, their attitudes, values and personality or temperament. Stereotypes and prejudices are almost inevitably going to be part of this process.

The **perceived** is determined more by contrast, size, intensity and motion or novelty. Something that stands out from the crowd is more noticeable than something run of the mill.

The **setting**, the physical, social or organisational context is crucial. If you are waiting in a queue, you accept it as part of the normal way to behave. If you are in the crush to get near the front at an open-air rock concert, you won't be expecting people to wait for you to go first. Situation is all-important.

Things are not always as they seem. How often have you misjudged a situation or a person? Arnold *et al.* (1998) defines **person perception** as 'how we perceive and interpret the behaviour and characteristics of other people, and the causes of events involving them'. They consider person perception at three levels:

♦ perceiving the behaviour of other people
♦ perceiving the personality of other people
♦ perceiving the causes of events involving other people.

It is claimed that interviewers decide in the first 20 seconds of an interview whether a candidate is suitable or not. This first impression is based on their stereotyped understanding of the 'look and feel' of the person (are they smart or scruffy, are they clean, are they polite?) as well as their initial interaction with the person as a whole. How can you understand the whole of a person in just 20 seconds? People who have been married for 50 years still don't know the *whole* other person.

Managers need to be aware that many distortions and biases can affect their perception of people and events. They need to be able to do the above three things accurately, and not be misdirected by things such as:

♦ interpreting the situation wrongly: you may have a clear idea of who was there and what has happened, but you may not have the insight or enough information to work out *why* it happened

♦ unconscious personal biases: you may think you are being objective and impartial in your decision making, but are you subconsciously protecting yourself or others, or being swayed by innate prejudices against certain people or procedures?

Perceptual selection

This is a process we use to filter out those bits of information we don't need. We usually use only a small amount of the information presented to us at any one time, because we either subconsciously choose what we want to perceive, or because we can't take all the information in at once. You may have heard of 'selective deafness', referring to those who only hear what they want to hear.

In making sense of a situation, or deciding how to react to it, we collect the data presented to us, categorise the information to make it easier to process, and then make predictions.

Social judgement theory

Muzafer Sherif, a psychologist at the University of Oklahoma, claimed (1961, 1965) that how an individual processes information is determined by their level of involvement. Highly involved individuals will interpret a message that coincides with their view of a situation, more positively than it actually is: the **assimilation effect**. A message that does not agree with their view will be judged as more negative: the **contrast effect**. The assimilation and contrast effects are particularly important for managers and group leaders. Involved individuals are usually thought more likely to be loyal.

Repetition also makes messages more likely to be perceived and remembered. Advertisers who show the same commercial on television many times use this concept.

While perception is very much in the mind, perception is nonetheless reality, for that individual. Individuals see what they expect to see. Objects that do not fit with their surroundings, or are unexpected, are more likely to be noticed and remembered. Figure 4.20 is a good example.

Figure 4.20   An object that does not fit with its surroundings is more likely to be remembered

Having formed a perception, a person will interpret that perception; they will decide what it means. There are common mistakes made in attributing behaviour, both in oneself and in others. One is called the **fundamental attribution error**; this means the way that people underestimate the influence of the situation and overestimate the effect of individual characteristics.

A second attribution error is the **actor–observer effect.** People tend to see their own behaviour as due to, and in keeping with, the situation, but they see others' behaviour as due to temperament or personality. The third attribution error is the **self-serving bias**. People tend to give themselves the benefit of the doubt. They are ready to take credit for success, but make excuses for failure.

One important aspect of perception which you will probably have come across is the notion of stereotyping.

Stereotyping

Stereotyping is about the way in which we assign certain traits or qualities and characteristics to a person based on that person's appearance, or membership of a group, for example. If you are involved in an accident and see somebody dressed as a nurse coming to your aid, you are comforted by the thought that you are about to get help from a medical professional. Actually, it could be a teacher or shop assistant *en route* to a fancy dress party. What image sprang to your mind when you read 'nurse': a woman in a blue dress? Lots of nurses are men. We stereotype people almost immediately because of their age ('unruly teenagers', 'old fogies'), sex ('typical of a bloke'), socio-economic status ('rich, arrogant snobs'), occupation, dress, even the cars they drive.

To categorise people in this way, we take the information we have about them and allocate it according to our experience – our schemas – of similar types of people. **Schemas** are cognitive pictures we build in our mind, dependent on our experience. A child going to a party for the first time will have no picture in mind of what a 'party' is. After the party he may come home with the image of party games, and a cake with candles. Next time he goes to a party he knows what to expect because he has his 'party schema' all worked out. When he arrives for his second party at the swimming pool, and has an inflatables swim session before the jelly and cake stage, he expands this schema to cover a broader idea of what a party is. By the time he's adolescent or adult, he'll probably be expecting music, alcohol and dancing to take priority over the jelly-and-cakes stage.

Self-schemas are how we organise information about our own dress, personality and behaviour.

Person schemas are used to categorise people into certain groups or 'types'. Prior information guides us in judging even before we've met or seen someone. We may be told: he's a punk; she's really pretty; he's a barrister. The person may be a punk, pretty, *and* a barrister, but it's easier to imagine the three separate stereotypes, because they are the schemas you are used to.

Role signs are very important here. When people wear the dress of a particular occupation, we immediately make assumptions about them. A fireman, a policeman or a barrister in courtroom robes are all easily identifiable. Or so we think. A woman dressed in a white coat was found to have abducted a baby from a maternity hospital, because people assumed she was a doctor.

Perception and work behaviour

As you can see, people don't always behave in a way that is appropriate to reality, but in a way that is appropriate to what they *perceive* is reality.

Perception is important when looking at the behaviour of individuals in organisations. Managers and workers need to be aware of how individuals' perceptions can differ, to overcome the problems related to these differences and to understand individuals' behaviour. A manager's perception of his or her workforce will influence how he or she deals with them and successful, influential managers are those with a good understanding of individual differences and perceptual processes.

CASE STUDY

Selective perception in the social services

In the middle of January 1999, a couple who disappeared with their two foster daughters after they were refused permission to adopt wrote an emotional letter pleading to be allowed to keep them. Jeff and Jennifer Bramley disappeared from their Cambridgeshire home in September 1998 with the two girls, aged five and three. In the letter the couple said:

'We Jeff, Jenny [and our two girls] write this letter to tell the plight of a family that love each other and wishes to stay together. [The girls] were told about us and told we would be their forever Mummy and Daddy. After we had met the girls several times in their foster home, they came to live with us. They soon grew to love us as their Mummy and Daddy, as we grew to love them as our daughters. [They were both] looking forward to their new lives with us.'

The Bramleys said they were good, honest, caring people who were willing to give up their home, friends and jobs to keep the girls 'with the parents they love and desperately want to share their lives with':

'We were approved to be [their] new Mummy and Daddy, they were placed with us for us to adopt. It is misleading to call us foster parents. Social services seemed pleased with us and told us everything was fine until one day they said we were too safety conscious by saying 'no' and 'don't' too often.'

Police were not able to track down the family for several months and there were few sightings. In early 1999 they were allegedly 'seen' by a retired clergyman on the North Yorkshire Moors Railway (subsequently it was proved to have been a false sighting, because the family was in Ireland at the time).

He described the children as 'out of control' and said that the Bramleys, and particularly Jenny, looked depressed, worn-out and beaten.

Social services denied ever saying that the Bramleys were 'too strict', and totally dismissed rumours that they were considered too religious. There was also absolutely no suggestion of any kind of abuse. Quite simply, a spokesperson said, it was concluded 'after working with the couple for six months' that they seemed to lack the special parenting skills needed. When asked why the children had been placed with the Bramleys, the social service replied that placement 'is not a perfect science'.

ACTIVITY

1   What does the case study tell us about selective perception?

2   How in this case has selective perception led to difficulties?

3   What lessons can be learnt from the case by social service managers?

CASE STUDY

Perception of availability

You work in a company whose employees are spread out across the country. Your boss is based in London. You don't want to commute to London but feel you're being overlooked when it comes to promotion and work on new projects. Your boss would prefer you to work in London but your partner has a good job too where you live now, and you want to spend time at home and with the children, as well as be seen to be doing a good job.

If you are being passed over for opportunities, it may be because of your boss's perception that you are unavailable. How can you change that perception?

Put yourself in the boss's shoes; if working from your current location really *is* impractical, how can you change your employee's perception of being 'passed over' and help them towards promotion or new fields of work?

Attitudes

Attitudes have been an important dimension of psychology since research into them began in the 1920s and 1930s (for example, LaPiere, 1934). Some psychologists (Allport, 1954; Fiske and Taylor, 1984) claim attitudes are the key concept in psychological study. In business situations people's actions, reactions and individual behaviour will depend as much on their attitude as on their perception of the situation.

Definition of attitude

We are all familiar with the phrase, 'He's got attitude'. Indeed, all of us have attitudes, lots of them. But what *is* an attitude? Bem (2002) claims, 'Attitudes are likes and dislikes: favourable or unfavourable reactions to objects, people, situations, or any other aspects of the world.' Mednick *et al.* (1975) define attitude as, 'A predisposition to act in a certain way towards some aspect of one's environment, including other people.'

People develop attitudes through learning and direct experience. Attitudes are the schemas mentioned previously, used to organise one's perceptions of the world, or unconscious thoughts, related to personal values. Attitudes help us belong and adjust to our community or social group, be that because of religion, or allegiance to friends and family, or work environment. People working in the same organisation or profession are likely to share many values and attitudes and as such find it easy to interact

and relate to one another. Shared attitudes give a stable frame of reference to behave in accordance with any given situation. Bem (2002) claims people do not 'simply subscribe to a random collection of beliefs and attitudes but have internally consistent belief systems'. These belief systems are what we understand in layman's terms to be our values or principles.

Attitude and behaviour

Rokeach (1973) differentiates between values, beliefs and attitudes. 'Attitudes are "groups" of several beliefs, but a value is a single belief about a desired state or way of behaviour.'

Attitudes, values and beliefs are all internal constructs that can't be directly observed. They are inferred through verbal expression and behaviour, though behaviour is not always consistent with the attitude expressed verbally (see LaPiere, 1934, below). How consistent our behaviour is will be dependent on the attitude, how strongly we feel about it, and the consequences of not behaving in accordance with it.

Positive and negative attitudes

If we hold a positive attitude towards Tony Blair, we might say good things about him, or vote for him. If we hold a negative attitude towards a colleague, we may make derogatory comments about them, and probably wouldn't go out socially with them. If you have a positive attitude to your work, you will probably view problems as a challenge and an opportunity to improve, but if you have a negative attitude, you might just view problems as a threat or obstruction.

When managers propose changes at work, each employee will receive the news differently in their own mind. Their reactions will depend on their attitude to the speaker and to the proposed changes. Some may trust the manager's claim that he is trying to improve productivity and profitability; others may judge him to be deviously trying to add to people's workloads or 'push people out'. We use our attitudes to filter the information we receive.

It might be concluded, then, that behaviour is determined by the social situation as well as by prejudices and attitude. For example, in the LaPiere study, faced with polite, pleasant customers,

Do we mean what we say?

A classic study by LaPiere (1934) showed that behaviour and attitudes are not necessarily consistent. He travelled across the USA with a Chinese couple and stayed at numerous hotels and dined in many restaurants on the way. In one establishment they were refused service; racial prejudice was commonplace and openly displayed at that time.

When the trio had returned home, LaPiere wrote to the 250 establishments they had visited during their travels and asked them if they would accept Chinese people in their restaurant or hotel. A staggering 92 per cent of these establishments replied that they would *not* allow Chinese people in.

So they let them in when they arrived at the door, yet they said they would not when asked in advance. Thus their behaviour towards the Chinese, in serving them when they arrived, was inconsistent with their declared prejudiced attitude.

proprietors found it difficult to act in accordance with their prejudice, and refuse to serve the Chinese.

Measurement of attitudes and public opinion is not easy or straightforward, yet is important in the workplace for gauging the feelings of employees.

Price (1992) said, 'Public opinion is one of the most vital and enduring concepts in the social sciences.' Opinion polls are a popular and frequently used tool for research, particularly in marketing and political fields, yet they can't always predict behaviour. After the re-election of the Conservative government in 1992, public opinion polls lost considerable credibility, because all predictions were that Labour would win. This shows again how people may say one thing, yet act in a contradictory manner. Managers must remember, then, that even where attitudes can be judged from what people say, subsequent behaviours will not necessarily be in keeping with what was said.

Changing attitudes

Significant life events can change people's attitudes. Unemployment, illness and disability, or the death of a family member may cause us to view life differently. We may *say* 'life's too short to worry about it', yet we still worry that we haven't finished the decorating. If somebody close to us dies at a young age, we may actually stop worrying about wallpapering and get on with the attitude 'live for today', because we adopt the attitude that life really *is* too short to worry about the decorating.

Attitudes are usually deeply ingrained into us and are therefore difficult to change. Managers sometimes need to persuade people to change their attitudes though, and skill is required in persuading people to think – or at least behave – in different ways. People change their attitudes for numerous reasons. McKenna (1987) cites three possible reasons:

◆ compliance: people may adopt another's attitude in anticipation of extrinsic reward; for example they may adopt the boss's attitude if it will get them a pay rise
◆ identification: attitudes can be adopted to help us to fit in; we act differently, and display different attitudes, dependent on who we are with and the situation we are in
◆ internalisation: this happens when somebody adopts an attitude because it suits their personal values; a racist's attitude to new arguments about ethnic minorities will most probably fit the pattern of their other racist attitudes.

Leon Festinger (1954) developed the **social comparison theory**, according to which we evaluate ourselves in comparison to others, and our behaviour as a result changes, and shifts towards the social norms of those around us. At home we might agree with our mum how important it is to complete any homework before going to the pub, while at university we agree with our mates that going to the pub takes priority over writing that essay on 'attitude'. Festinger says when we're not sure how to behave we take our cue from the actions of those around us. At work people may display positive attitudes to please those around them whom they respect.

Ability and aptitude

Aptitude describes the capability of a person to learn something. Most of us find we have an aptitude to learn in some areas but not in others. We may be brilliant at maths, but hopeless at spelling. **Ability** describes the capacity of someone to carry out the specific tasks needed to perform a particular job. This ability to carry out different jobs is dependent upon our natural aptitude, our education and training, and our experience. Intelligence is one component of natural aptitude.

So we can say that aptitudes are potential abilities, while abilities are the knowledge and skills that individuals already possess.

Employers are interested in aptitude and ability for many reasons, and numerous tests have been devised to measure mental and physical aptitudes and abilities. Intelligence Quotient (IQ) tests are well known, but employers also use various other measures of ability to test such areas as numerical and verbal ability, spatial ability and manual dexterity or mechanical ability.

Other tests of aptitude and ability commonly used by employers include:

♦ personality questionnaires
♦ work samples, where a candidate produces a sample of work to display their ability
♦ in-tray exercises
♦ on-the-job tests
♦ interviews
♦ handwriting analysis.

How reliable these approaches are is open to much dispute, and organisations generally use the types of tests which seem to get the best results for their particular organisation's field of work. Companies want to employ people who fit in with their values and attitudes, and who have the aptitude to work in a manner appropriate to achieving that organisation's goals.

Intelligence

The nature of the human intellect has fascinated academics, researchers and managers for centuries. Around 335BC, Aristotle, and as long ago as 387BC, Plato, asked the sort of questions that led to modern explorations of intelligence. Current trends in intelligence theory involve the formation of complex multiple intelligence theories and criticise the validity of standardised testing to measure intelligence. After all, before something can be measured, we have to define what it is we are measuring.

ACTIVITY

What is intelligence?

Before you read further, write down a short definition of what you believe 'intelligence' is. See how it fits in with what follows.

There are many definitions of intelligence, though none is universally accepted, as intelligence isn't necessarily a definable entity. There is much academic debate surrounding the layperson's belief that levels of intelligence can be accurately measured by IQ testing. Many different theories examine the levels of cognitive processing that are needed when one is interpreting information or problem solving and when one is actively using intelligent reasoning abilities. Wechsler (1944) called intelligence, 'the capacity of an individual to act purposefully and think rationally and to deal effectively with the environment'.

Research into intelligence has covered biological, racial, cultural and sexual differences, as well as the different 'components' of intelligence itself. As Shaffer (1985, p. 382) states, 'Although few topics in psychology have generated as much research as intelligence and intelligence testing, even today there is little consensus about what intelligence is.'

Spearman (1923) proposed a 'two-factor theory of intelligence' which defined general (g) and specialist factors of intelligence, and Cattell (1963) broke this 'g factor' down into 'fluid' intelligence: the ability to reason or utilise available information, and 'crystallised' intelligence: that gained from experience and learned knowledge. These probably relate most closely to what managers may be concerned with when they consider aptitude in employees. How much can they learn and remember, and how good are they at using that knowledge in a constructive way?

Generally, we recognise that 'human beings exhibit, somewhat independently of the amount of education to which they have been exposed, grades of intelligence ranging from idiocy or feeble mindedness, through average, up to genius' (Sternberg, 1990, p. 35).

Intelligence tests

As mentioned, organisations use a variety of tests which they believe measure intelligence or aptitude, if they feel these tests help in selecting employees for posts which require specific qualities. These might include:

- verbal comprehension: these may involve rearranging sentences, or filling in missing words
- word fluency: solving anagrams, identifying rhyming words, and so on
- number: mental and written arithmetic tests
- space: rearranging shapes into sequences or identifying relationships between shapes
- associative memory: memorising associated words
- perceptual speed: rapid visualisation of similarities and differences in figures, shapes and text
- induction and general reasoning: this may be tested by working out the formula or rule in a sequence of numbers or patterns.

You can get an idea of the type of tests mentioned above by visiting Mensa's website (see Useful websites). Mensa is the internationally renowned 'high IQ' society, to which members can only gain entry if they can prove their IQ is among the top 2 per cent of the population. Test yourself with some of their quizzes.

As Mensa says, many people are surprised to find their IQ is above average. Remember that just as many people will have a below average IQ. After all, that is how an average is arrived at. If you try any 'intelligence' test and don't do well at it, remember that practice in these types of tests is a key element to success.

Intelligence and aptitude obviously affect how an individual tackles work problems.

CASE STUDY

The 'practice effect' was a strong argument put forward in respect of the 11+ examination. This exam was used to decide whether 11-year-olds would go to grammar or secondary modern or technical schools after leaving primary education, under the old 'tripartite' education system before the introduction of comprehensive schools in the 1970s. Those primary schools which gave pupils training and practice in 11+ exams got much better results, and sent more of their pupils to grammar schools, than those schools who did not have the time or opportunity to let pupils practise like this. They didn't necessarily have more intelligent pupils; they just gave better training for the task in hand.

ACTIVITY

Have a look at the BBC Test the Nation website (see Useful websites). *Test the Nation* was an ambitious nationwide intelligence quiz show, first televised by the BBC in 2003.

Nature versus nurture

Gardner (1999) proposed seven types of intelligence: linguistic, spatial, interpersonal, intrapersonal, musical, bodily-kinesthetic and logical/mathematical. These different talents can be evident to some degree in all of us: which are *you* good at? Probably not all of them. Each of these abilities would be useful for solving different types of problems. Gardner claims, quite logically, that early training, heredity, and learning opportunities all contribute to the development of intelligence in the individual. Indeed the debate as to whether intelligence is the product of 'nature' (genetics and heredity) or 'nurture' (education, upbringing, social environment, and so on) plods on alongside the never-answered debate about what intelligence actually is.

Whether intelligence can be learned has been researched extensively. Environment and peer pressure can certainly affect achievement, but can they affect actual intelligence? How much is innate and how much is learned? Knowledge is obviously an important feature of intelligence. Knowledge can be learned, but the individual's ability to interpret and utilise learned knowledge varies from person to person. Managers can train people every day or provide them with endless information, but if an individual is not able to process this information and use it productively, it's not worth much to the employer or the employee. You could read dozens of business studies books, but if you can't then assimilate that information and use it in a constructive manner – to write an informative essay, or to solve problems in the workplace – it isn't really much use to you or your employer.

Types of thinking

People solve problems in different ways. Some see the whole picture and tackle the overall problem in a holistic way. Pask (1961) in his book *An Approach to Cybernetics* describes them as holists. Alternatively, some people prefer to approach every little part of the problem separately. As each part of the problem is resolved, the overall problem becomes sorted as well. Pask calls these the serialists.

Another division can be made between divergent thinkers and convergent thinkers.

In **convergent** thinking, the person brings material from several sources and uses it to solve a problem. This kind of thinking works well in science, maths and technology. Because of the need for consistency and reliability, some have argued that this is really the only form of thinking that can be measured. It has therefore been the only type of thinking traditionally tested in IQ tests and academic examinations.

With **divergent** thinking, a person's skill is centred more in creative development of ideas prompted by a stimulus. The divergent thinker sees all sorts of ways

---

ACTIVITY

Uses of objects test

Below are five objects. Think of as many different uses as you can for each. The more you can think of, the more divergent is your way of thinking. Take about 15 minutes.

- A barrel
- A paper clip
- A tin of boot polish
- A brick
- A blanket

(Source: Hudson, 1967)

---

to tackle a problem and can think up many different views of a situation or, say, uses for a tool. As far back as 1967, Hudson devised his 'uses of objects' test to measure creative thinking.

Many modern-day management training courses support the idea of thinking 'out of the box' or 'outside the box'. Consultants run courses explaining what 'out of the box thinking' is, but maybe it is just 'thinking up an idea'.

Convergent thinkers would be thinking inside the box, that is, solving problems using previous experience. Divergent thinkers would be thinking outside the box, or 'getting ideas'.

Lateral thinking is also a commonly used concept. This is a way of solving problems by using unorthodox and sometimes seemingly illogical methods. Lateral thinkers see a wide view of something and are prepared to risk different methods to solve the problem.

Different jobs require different abilities and different ways of thinking and the interpretation of intelligence, and how it should be used, varies greatly. One person may see being able to build a shed as clever, whereas another might consider managing company finances as cleverer. It is in this vein that diversity and individual differences can reciprocate and complement each other in society. Most communities – and many businesses – need a mix of abilities to function adequately. A construction company needs the brains to plan and manage, and the muscle to build and maintain. As Sternberg (1990, p. 801) says, 'A complex society requires variation in intelligence for optimal adaptation.'

The divide between vocational and academic ability and qualifications also seems to be merging. Learning for its own sake is being overtaken by learning that can be applied in a practical, or work, context. NVQs were designed to develop workplace competences, whilst GNVQs aimed to develop broader, general competences, which individuals could employ in the constantly changing modern world of work.

Sex differences

Beloff, in her 1992 study *Mother, father and me: our IQ*, noted correlations with IQ and occupation; more men occupied those jobs judged to be correlated with a higher IQ. Men have tended traditionally to dominate the high-powered jobs and therefore be perceived as more intelligent, as those types of jobs are for intelligent people. This sort of old-fashioned stereotyping is thankfully dying out as more women filter into the high-powered jobs, but this stereotyping, where it remains, can influence behaviour and attitudes.

An interesting social angle on this gender stereotyping was noted by Furnham (2000), who found most people believe that spatial and mathematical abilities (where men are usually estimated higher) are considered the most 'important' components of intelligence. He said, 'what people believe really contributes to a high overall IQ score is logical, then spatial, then verbal intelligence ... those abilities that men tend to do better at are those that most people consider to be the essence of intelligence' (p. 512).

Managers need to be aware of this long-standing type of stereotyping when it comes to recruitment and appraisal or promotions.

Beloff's research is referred to and discussed in a more recent, and particularly thought-provoking, journal article by Adrian Furnham.

Original thinking — JOURNAL ARTICLE

This paper discusses the requirements of information retrieval systems, used to support creative and convergent thinkers. Creative thinking is explored, as well as a variety of current information systems. The development of IR systems which are able to provide direct support for creative thinking depends on integrating high-order knowledge with flexible applications. Systems may help information-seekers to access a range of diverse information to aid the development of divergent – or indeed convergent – ideas.

Ford, N. 'Information retrieval and creativity: towards support for the original thinker' *Journal of Documentation*, 1999, Vol. 55, No. 5.

Sex differences and IQ — JOURNAL ARTICLE

Beloff examines the traditional gender-stereotyped image of males as being more 'intelligent' than women. She links 'intelligence', and individuals' *perception* of intelligence, with occupations, sexes and social structures (family particularly). Some of the findings are indeed disturbing if we consider the modern approach to sex discrimination and how it should not influence judgements in the workplace.

Beloff, H. 'Mother, father and me: our IQ', *The Psychologist*, 1992, No.5, pp 309–11.

IQ and stereotypes — JOURNAL ARTICLE

Furnham examines here the concept of intelligence as it is understood by psychologists and laypeople, and discusses in a interesting and very readable way a number of interesting social angles on intelligence. Furnham found that people believe spatial and mathematical elements (where men are usually estimated 'more intelligent') are considered the most 'important' components of intelligence. He said, 'what people believe really contributes to a high overall IQ score is logical, then spatial, then verbal intelligence ... those abilities that men tend to do better at are those that most people consider to be the essence of intelligence' (p. 512).

He cites many studies which repeatedly found that participants perceive men's IQ to be higher than women's, and women consistently perceive their own IQ to be lower than men's. In one of his studies, he said, 'there are clear generational effects in IQ. They [relatives] tend to believe they are a little brighter than their mothers ...' and 'parents also tend to believe their children are brighter than they are themselves'. And other studies have found '... some direct evidence for the assumption that estimates of intelligence are susceptible to gender stereotypes'.

About this stereotyping in general, Furnham says, 'For some researchers this remains a shocking finding explicable only by sociological processes' (p. 514). Indeed it is a shocking finding in today's world of non-discrimination and equal status employment environment.

Furnham, A. 'Thinking about intelligence', *The Psychologist*, 2000, Vol. 13, Part 10, October, pp 510–15.

Significance and nature of individual differences

As we all know, no two people are the same. It may be assumed then that individuals differ in their approach to work; how they perform at work and interact with others, why they work, their readiness to take risks, and so on. Many individual differences are observable and, some would argue, measurable. 'Success' can be measured by sales targets, salary level, or

qualifications, but can you really measure how extrovert or intelligent somebody is?

Physical differences are easily observable but different physical qualities may be important in different work situations. Sensory capability may be important: smell and taste for the wine merchant or food sampler; good hand–eye co-ordination for the machine operator. Physical ability is closely linked to other abilities such as thinking (cognitive skills) and affective skills: the ability to make friends and form relationships.

Self and self-image

Knowing oneself is an important part of any individual's psychological make-up. People who know and *like* themselves usually regard others more positively than do those people who have a poor self-image. Self-image is built up over many years and is directed by sociological and psychological experiences. Individuals who receive good feedback about themselves and their work gain self-confidence and develop a sense of worth and positive self-image. Positive feedback in the workplace is important to encourage good performance, self-confidence and initiative. Formal feedback, in the form of honest appraisal in the workplace, works well in letting individuals know how they are progressing. As such, formal appraisal should be an open and constructive exercise, not a blaming, or punishing process.

Different types of self-image include:

♦ ideal self-image: how people would like to perceive themselves
♦ actual self-image: how they actually perceive themselves
♦ expected self-image: how they would like to see themselves in the future
♦ social self-image: how people think others see them
♦ ideal social self-image: how they would like others to see them.

The creation of self-image

The biological, psychological, social, cultural and educational interactions which influence an individual mean that personality, self-image and individual behaviours are very complex constructs.

Types of self

Locus of control

This approach concerns the extent to which an individual feels able to affect, or control, events in their life. Rotter (1966) first proposed the concept of locus of control, claiming that some individuals believe they have control over events: they have internal control; whereas others feel they are controlled by forces beyond their control: an external locus of control. 'Internals' attribute cause for events mainly to themselves, for example they believe they did well because they worked hard. 'Externals' attribute causes of events to outside influences: they believe they did badly because the tutor dislikes them. (Have a go at the activity on p. 126.)

Authoritarianism

This approach to the self is concerned with the extent to which individuals adhere strictly to patterns, rules and chains of command. The authoritarian individual wants everything done 'by the book'.

Self-monitoring

Self-monitoring is about the ability of the individual to adjust their behaviour to suit environmental or external factors. Some people are very aware of what is going on around them, whereas others seem to 'walk round with their eyes shut'.

Machiavellianism

This approach is derived from the politician, Count Niccolo Machiavelli, who explained in his book *The Prince* how any individual can use power and influence for their own interests. Psychologists have developed a series of instruments called **Mach scales** to measure a person's Machiavellian orientation: how much they use power for their own gain.

Personality and work behaviour

Personality is widely regarded as possibly the most important factor in predicting how successful a person will be working with others in an organisation.

Personality could be defined as the sum total of all the behavioural and mental characteristics which make an individual unique. Personality is what gives each of us our distinctive social character. The Oxford English Dictionary describes personality as 'distinctive personal character'.

Eysenck's 1953 definition of personality is, 'the more or less stable and enduring organisation of a person's character, temperament, intellect and physique which determines his unique adjustment to the environment'.

There are several different psychological approaches to studying personality. Humanists (for example, Carl Rogers) look at the whole person aspiring towards self-fulfilment; the psychoanalysts (Freud and his followers) see personality as intuitive and dependent upon past experiences in the early years of life.

There is a general acceptance that our behaviour reflects our personality differences and that we all behave differently because of the person we are. Our personality is a relatively stable and enduring aspect of us: it does not change from day to day.

Research has shown that we are not particularly good judges of others' personalities, as we usually meet people in a specific role relationship, such as student and lecturer, doctor and patient, and assess personality in terms of that role. We **stereotype** people into the role we expect of them. We often say that we see 'a different side' to a person under different circumstances. The doctor we view as confident and knowledgeable, may seem like a different person when looking helpless at the side of the road with a punctured tyre.

Personality has an important impact on how people behave at work and upon what type of work or career they choose. A quiet, shy, introverted person is more likely to be happiest working alone with a computer screen, rather than delivering lectures to a room full of people, or getting up on stage and performing in public. People who are perfectionists may find it impossible to work with others who are disorganised and muddled in their approach to work.

ACTIVITY

Who or what controls your life?

Please read the following statements and indicate in the spaces provided whether you agree more with choice **A** or choice **B**.

A

❶ My achievements in education and training are due more to luck than my own efforts. ☐

❷ Promotions at work are mainly earned through hard work and ability. ☐

❸ If I make an effort in education and training I can improve myself. ☐

❹ The best way to deal with problems is to avoid thinking about them. ☐

❺ Finding a good job is a matter of luck. ☐

❻ If someone is really determined to master a skill or subject, they will usually succeed. ☐

❼ I can influence what might happen to me tomorrow by what I do today. ☐

❽ Getting along with people is a skill that must be practised. ☐

❾ Planning is often a waste of time. ☐

❿ What happens to me in life is mostly of my own making. ☐

B

❶ My achievements in education and training are due to my own efforts. Luck has little or nothing to do with it. ☐

❷ Promotions at work are really a matter of being a little luckier than the next person. ☐

❸ I feel its almost useless to make an effort in education because most people are brighter than me. ☐

❹ If I work hard at tackling a problem, I can usually solve it. ☐

❺ If I work hard to improve my skills and qualifications I will be more likely to get a good job. ☐

❻ Many people will never master particular skills and subjects, no matter how hard they try. ☐

❼ What happens to me tomorrow will be mainly due to the course of fate. ☐

❽ It is almost impossible to get along with some people. ☐

❾ It usually pays to plan ahead. ☐

❿ What happens to me in life is mostly a matter of fate, luck or chance. ☐

Score 1 point for each of the following selections and 0 for other selections:
1B 2A 3A 4B 5B 6A 7A 8A 9B 10A.
Total score:

Scores can be interpreted as follows:
8–10:   High internal control
6–7:   Moderate internal control
5:     Mixed
3–4:   Moderate external control
1–2:   High external control

The higher the score, the more you believe that you control your own destiny.
The lower your score, the more you believe that what happens to you in your life is due to luck or chance.
This exercise uses sample items adapted from a selection of locus of control scales. It is not a standardised test.

(Source: Rotter, 1966)

Drives

Different individuals are 'driven' for different reasons. Individuals develop drives in keeping with their upbringing and environment. People who share similar backgrounds and socialisation processes often share similar drives. McClelland (1960) in *The Achieving Society* identified four main drives.

Achievement motivation

Individuals may have to achieve different goals to arrive at where they want to be in, say, their careers or social status. Achieving these separate goals becomes important and individuals with strong achievement drives work hard as they believe they will gain personal credit for their input. (This is indicative of an internal locus of control.) Managers who have high levels of achievement motivation often expect the same of their employees, and expect the same achievement-oriented goals to motivate them.

Affiliation motivation

This is the need to associate with people on a social basis. Affiliation-driven individuals 'like to be liked'. They enjoy friendship and the social aspects of work, and like to be complimented for their friendly and co-operative attitude. Some theorists claim that women are more likely to be affiliation-driven than men, as they enjoy group friendship and empathising with friends. Managers with strong affiliation drives can sometimes, therefore, find it hard to make tough decisions: they don't like to upset anybody or become unpopular.

Competence motivation

This is about people who need to be good at something. A job well done is a reward in itself. Competence-driven people like to master the skills of the job and seek solutions to problems. A competence-motivated individual is more likely to ask how well they have done a job whereas an achievement-driven person is more likely to ask how many they can do.

Power motivation

These people want to influence and motivate others and change things for the better. They like to control people and events and don't mind taking risks to do so. They can of course use the power ineffectively or unfairly. Power-motivated managers often get the job done fast, but are not necessarily very well liked. If they seek power for personal gain, they can become disliked and ineffective as managers. If they seek power for the good of the organisation they are more likely to gain support and be successful.

Personality and the self are looked at again under the heading 'individual behaviour at work' on p. 130.

Conflict

Figure 4.21 A poor way to resolve conflict

Conflict at work can be worrying and costly not only to an organisation, but also to the individuals involved.

Conflict can arise because of assumptions that people make, sometimes wrongly, about situations or the actions of others. Opinions can be formed, or rumours started, even though they may be inaccurate. Organisations, and most individuals, do not usually welcome conflict, because their effectiveness depends on teamwork and people working together.

Conflict is not necessarily good or bad; every new idea will probably conflict with a long-established way of operating. It is how we perceive conflict individually, and respond to it, that makes it good or bad. Conflict can be productive as well as destructive. It is an inevitable aspect of social life, and can lead to beneficial change.

Conflict isn't bad. Unresolved conflict is bad.

What causes conflict?

Conflicts emerge as the interests of different parties conflict, or when a relationship becomes unbalanced or oppressive. Divergence of interests occurs where, for example, managers in an organisation want productivity, efficiency and economy, whereas non-managers are seeking high pay, independence and responsibility, or scope for self-development. These interests will invariably conflict to a certain degree. Different departments within an organisation may have conflicting interests too. Sales departments want money to market new products; finance departments want to cut spending.

Conflicting sides then develop hostile attitudes and conflict starts to grow. It may spread and draw in other individuals or departments. Outsiders become involved and this can make it difficult to identify the origin of the conflict.

Potential benefits of conflict

Clearing the air: people get a chance to have their say and air their views.

Introducing new rules: changing the rules can improve conditions and increase effectiveness.

Repositioning the goalposts: unpopular goals can be redefined and the goalposts moved by agreement between both parties.

Increased understanding of others' role: when parties have to put their case forward, this serves to clarify to people outside of specific roles exactly what these people do and how best they can do it. It may make managers more aware of what happens on the shop floor, or it may help different divisions within an organisation better to understand their role in relation to each other's.

Potential drawbacks to conflict

Wasting time and energy: much personal energy can be put into arguing and being directed away from the actual work in hand. Strikes and negotiations cost money and time. Individuals can become engrossed more in the conflict itself than its original cause.

Stress: individuals react differently to conflict. Some find it very stressful, whereas others enjoy the stimulation a dispute can bring. Organisational stress can be costly in diverting energies of employees and in absenteeism.

Risk: any disagreement carries a certain risk. If it can be resolved quickly, all well and good. If not, unfavourable situations can escalate and when badly handled, can make situations far worse than they need to be.

Decline in communications: communication can become difficult between the warring factions. They stop listening to each other. Each side wants to put their own view forward over the other's and causes of conflict can become blurred. Stereotyping of behaviours can occur and distort the picture further. When attitudes underpinning the communications become personalised and inappropriate to the problem, hostility develops and effective negotiation becomes more difficult.

Resolving conflict

Resolving a conflict might involve a shift in attitudes, or a change in relationships and structures. Leaders of nations are expected to defend the national interest, and defeat the interests of opposing parties to do so. The possible outcomes could be win–lose (one wins, the other loses) or compromise (they split the difference). Ideally a win–win situation can be arrived at, where both parties are happy with the outcome. In a business environment this is usually the favourable way to resolve a dispute. 'Win–lose' may provide a temporary resolution, but usually the loser returns at a later date, wanting a better deal and the conflict re-emerges. Roy J. Lewicki (2002) has identified five major strategies for approaching conflict.

Accommodation: a resolution is reached where differences of opinion, or conflict of interests, are allowed to continue, but a way of living with the differences of opinion are agreed upon. Mum does not think it's right for you to keep a python in your bedroom, but as long as it stays in there and she does not have to feed it, it can stay. You think the python should have the run of the house, but you agree with Mum, so that you can keep the python.

Avoidance: this is the 'ignore it and it'll go away' attitude. It might work by keeping the peace for a while, but when conflict does erupt it may be more difficult to deal with. If managers organise their business so there is no outlet channel for conflict of ideas, they will be suppressed and individuals will become frustrated and de-motivated. Where employee representation is obvious and easily accessed, where people can easily air conflicting ideas without fear of retribution, problems can be identified and resolved more easily.

Competition: this is a win–lose approach. As stated above, it may be the only strategy available at the time which will achieve the necessary changes. In an emergency, such as in a lifeboat team when a life is at stake, there is no time to negotiate and resolve disagreements between the team members. When other strategies have failed, someone has to lead the team without wasting time on heated discussions.

Collaboration: collaboration with other individuals, departments or companies can often work to the mutual benefit of the parties involved, instead of the parties wasting time and energy arguing about issues. In the fields of research and development, for example, or production, quality assurance, or distribution, input from more than one department or individual can share knowledge and expertise which will in turn benefit others. Collaboration between departments or functions can optimise the use of internal and external inter-firm co-operations.

Compromise: 'splitting the difference' can work where neither party can agree, and a middle ground may be agreed upon. If employees want a 10 per cent pay rise and management only offer 5 per cent, they may reach a compromise and pay 7½ per cent. The problem with this is that neither party actually wins. Both gain a little, but both lose a little as well.

ACTIVITY

The handshake

This game needs two people. Stand opposite each other and join hands, as if shaking hands. There are two rules:

1 Win as many points as you can.

2 Score yourself one point every time the joined hands touch your hip.

Play the game for two minutes; keep a note of your score. Afterwards, ask yourself these questions:

♦ What strategy did I use to win points?
♦ Did I use a competitive approach? Why?
♦ Did we find a 'win–win' method, whereby both of us scored lots of points by co-operating?

Share your results, strategies and thoughts with your colleagues. What can you learn about real life conflict from this exercise? Think of examples of conflicts you have been involved in.

♦ Which had win–win outcomes?
♦ Which had lose–lose outcomes? How could you have dealt with this better?

The manager's role and functional HRM policies are important where there are groups with different interests and objectives and therefore a potential for conflict. Managers must manage conflict professionally by:

♦ taking the initiative: accept that there is conflict and look for ways to resolve it
♦ developing organisational relationships that anticipate problems and minimise the likelihood of conflict
♦ consulting and negotiating
♦ responding constructively to complaints or challenges to authority.

Individual behaviour at work

This section looks at issues relating to how individuals behave at work, concentrating particularly on personality and trait theories.

Personality

We have already looked at personality, but will now consider how it affects the way an individual behaves at work. Kagan and Havemann (1976) define personality as, 'the total of characteristic ways of thinking, feeling and behaving that constitute the individual's distinctive method of relating to the environment'.

In using the term personality to describe the characteristics of an individual, which make them different or unique from every other person, we tend to generalise their character by using terms such as 'bubbly personality', or 'boring', or even 'he's had a personality bypass'.

We usually judge personality to be made up of the stable and consistent elements of a person's behaviour: the things that make us comment 'she's always so cheerful', or 'that was really out of character for her'.

Stable characteristics are those which we recognise as being present all the time. **Distinctive characteristics** are those which set somebody apart from the crowd. A group of people may share similar traits of reliability and thoroughness in their work, but Fred stands out because at times of crisis he always has an answer to the problem or he can always calm a situation down.

Nomothetic and ideographic approaches to personality

Nomothetic describes the scientific and empirical collection of data about people. It concerns the study or formulation of general and universal laws (like the law of gravity). It uses studies of large numbers of participants to find out what is average for a particular group, and to distinguish individuals from the established norms. The terms normal and average are used in a statistical sense, so talking of people who deviate from the norm does not necessarily label them as weird, or social outcasts.

The nomothetic approach builds on the assumption that personality is mainly inherited; you are born 'you' and environmental influences and experiences don't affect your personality much. This approach acknowledges the difficulties in *measuring* personality, but maintains that it is possible to predict expected behaviours in certain personality types, under certain circumstances.

Ideographic approaches are just about the opposite and are concerned with understanding the uniqueness of individuals and the development of 'self'. It considers that personality development is a gradual process, influenced by upbringing and environment, and as such is dynamic and open to change. Interactions of people with their environment and those around them is more important than 'what they were born with'.

Traits and types

Recall Eysenck's (1953) definition of personality from p. 125. In the mid-1980s, H. J. and M. J. Eysenck developed an approach to personality based on scientific and statistical evidence: a quantitative rather than qualitative research approach. They set out to identify underlying traits of personality which might explain human behaviour in a range of situational and circumstantial settings. **Traits** are a person's relatively stable dispositions to behave in a certain way. Traits are part of the person, not the environment. They fit closely with everyday descriptions of personality such as 'shy', 'introvert', 'bubbly' and the like.

Factor analysis is used to build a picture of the structure of human personality. Psychologists use personality questionnaires on large numbers of people to see how they behave and feel in various situations.

Extroverts and introverts

Two key factors identified from factor analysis were what Eysenck described as introversion versus extroversion, which relate to a person's tendency to seek stimulation and excitement in the external environment. **Extroverts** are sociable, vociferous and adventurous, whilst **introverts** are less sociable, introspective, and quiet. Eysenck also identified neuroticism versus stability: a person's tendency to be anxious and tense or easily upset, rather than being calm and relaxed.

Eysenck claimed introverson and extroversion were the product of both nature and nurture. We are born with some of the traits innate in us, whilst others develop with experience. Freud maintained that our pre-school experiences are our most important and these are what shape us as adults. Freud's theory does not, however, allow for any flexibility or adaptability of the adult human to new situations and experiences in adulthood. In looking at personality, and particularly when using the notions of extroversion and introversion, it is generally accepted firstly that most people are actually **ambiverts**. That is, they will be seen to be somewhere along the continuum between extrovert and introvert, rather than at either extreme.

Those who are more extrovert enjoy working in a busy, sociable environment. They enjoy challenges and are quick to make suggestions and put forward new ideas. They work well with other people, though can be domineering with those who are more withdrawn, or introvert. Extroverts need environments where lots is happening and they can't concentrate for long with mundane or repetitive work. On the other hand, introverts can usually concentrate for longer on given tasks and can be focused on intricate or repetitive tasks for long periods. Managers therefore need to identify the extroverts and introverts in the workplace and provide suitable and appropriate work patterns and environments to allow all personality types to work to their optimum ability and potential.

Similarly they must be able to recognise neuroticism and organise work so that individuals do not get overstressed or feel threatened by certain events or situations.

Tools for measurement

The most widely recognised tools used by psychologists to 'measure' personality traits are questionnaires. The Eysenck Personality Inventory (EPI) is a questionnaire which measures degrees of extroversion and neuroticism. It is completed by the individuals being studied and therefore relies on self-report. The Eysenck Personality Questionnaire (EPQ) measures extroversion and introversion, and psychoticism.

Research by the Eysencks and other psychology trait theorists claims to have identified five key areas of personality, commonly referred to as the **big five**.

Key personality areas

All personalities are made up of a combination of these five factors, in varying degrees. They are:

◆ extroversion–introversion
◆ neuroticism
◆ conscientiousness: an individual's orientation towards the organisation, objectives and targets
◆ agreeableness: how co-operative a person is and how eager to get on with others
◆ openness to experience: how one is prepared to change views in the light of experience, rather than have a closed, fixed view.

We must remember that psychometric definitions of personality *are* based almost entirely on research from questionnaires. This means that the validity of the theory is questionable, as it is highly dependent upon the validity of the questionnaires. Are they reliable? Is a Yes/No answer accurate enough?

An individual's answers to many of the questions used in these questionnaires would really depend on situation, mood, the company they are in, etc., so we must remember that situation and circumstance can have a strong bearing on how people will behave on different occasions.

The questionnaire on p. 132 purports to measure Type A Behaviour Pattern (TABP), which is another dimension of personality and behaviour. Type A Behaviour Pattern was first identified by cardiologists Friedman and Rosenman (1959, 1974). They called TABP a, 'chronic, incessant struggle to achieve more and more in less and less time, and if required to do so, against the opposing efforts of other things or other persons' (1974, p. 84). Monat and Lazarus (1991) conducted further studies and described Type A as, 'A competitive, multiphasic, achievement-oriented person who possesses a sense of urgency and impatience and who is both easily aroused and hostile or angry.'

A significant discovery by Friedman and Rosenman was that Type A people had an increased risk of coronary heart disease.

ACTIVITY

Look at the questionnaire below. Consider how, with each question, your mood, or the situation you imagine yourself in when you answer the question, could well affect your answers.

For example, take the question, 'How competitive are you?' At work you may be unambitious and content in your present role, so don't feel the need to compete with others. On the other hand, if you are playing in an important football match, you may be aggressively competitive through your desire to help your team win the league. It depends a lot on circumstance.

Questionnaire Type A/B

Please circle the number which best describes you, on a scale of 1–5

Between one extreme ...	I rate myself					... and the other
Casual about appointments	1	2	3	4	5	Never late
Not competitive	1	2	3	4	5	Very competitive
Patient while waiting	1	2	3	4	5	Impatient while waiting
Never feel rushed	1	2	3	4	5	Always in a hurry
Slow deliberate talker	1	2	3	4	5	Fast, forceful, emphatic talker
Care about self-satisfaction, no matter what others think	1	2	3	4	5	Want a good job recognised by others
Slow doing things, e.g. eating, walking	1	2	3	4	5	Fast doing things, e.g. eating, walking
Express feelings	1	2	3	4	5	Hide feelings
Satisfied with job	1	2	3	4	5	Ambitious
Many outside interests	1	2	3	4	5	Few interests outside home/work
Take things one at a time	1	2	3	4	5	Juggle many things
Laid back	1	2	3	4	5	Eager to get things done
Good listener	1	2	3	4	5	Anticipate what's coming, nod, interrupt, finish sentences
Easygoing	1	2	3	4	5	Push self and others

Type As are the type constantly 'on the go'. They are never satisfied with what they have achieved; they are always trying to do better; they are probably usually trying to 'do three things at once' (*multiphasic*).

Friedman and Rosenman also identified a 'Type B'; the opposite to A; relaxed, unhurried, and calm. You could probably name several people in your own workplace who exhibit these traits.

Modern lifestyles can mean that busy schedules can make relaxation or 'switching off' difficult.

In these days of mobile phones, Internet and emails, communication is instant and expects immediate responses. This can lead to high stress levels and increased TABP. As West (2000) claims, 'it appears that the Type A Behavior Pattern has reached epidemic proportions' (p. 3). Kirkcaldy *et al.* (2002) comment, 'Type A personality characteristics and an external locus of control appear to induce high levels of stress, with negative consequences for job satisfaction and physical and mental health.'

Personality and its relevance in understanding self and others

Mead (1934) suggested two components of the self:

♦ The 'I' is made up of the unique, individual, conscious and impulsive aspects of the behaviour of the individual.
♦ The 'Me' takes in a broader range of norms and values of the society that each of us learns and internalises.

Mead used the term 'generalised other' to refer to the expectations we think society has of us. The 'Me' is simply a process we use that helps us reflect objectively on our own behaviour. The 'I' is an impulsive component of the self. While we have external pressure to conform to the 'norms', we can also be creative and impose elements of 'I' on our wider environment; we can influence it, just as it influences us.

When we discussed earlier (p. 124) self and self-image, we described five types of self-image. Personality is not necessarily stable, because we change our values, attitudes and outlook in response to new experiences and what we learn. Our perceptions and what motivates us change over time, and, similarly, so can our behaviour change. In this way, our 'self' changes over time. The term **personality change** is used to describe this process.

If someone becomes unemployed or a partner leaves them, their self-esteem gets a bit of a beating. On the other hand, if someone is promoted or does well in exams, this can give a boost to their self-esteem and confidence, and thus increase their performance and productivity. In this way empowerment in the workplace helps individuals to gain confidence in themselves and their organisation.

Personality can develop in a conscious and organised way, giving a perception of oneself that matches reality. Conversely, some people feel threatened by experiences and feelings which don't match their perceived self-image. Often described as **maladjusted**, they feel threatened if they are not in control of a situation, or can be easily made to feel inferior by others. Carl Rogers' view is that all people aspire towards 'self-actualisation', wanting to fulfil their potential. This requires a positive and encouraging social environment and 'unconditional positive regard' from those around them. This has strong implications for the workplace as it suggests people need an atmosphere where they are respected and trusted and feel valued. In return for this opportunity for self-development, employees are expected to be trustworthy and flexible and contribute to the overall development of the organisation.

Chapter 2

Approaches to management and leadership

Development of management thought

The main objective of managers is usually to secure maximum profitability and prosperity for the organisation and maximum pay and job satisfaction for the employees. The way this is done has moved from hierarchical top-down management to empowerment of employees to manage themselves. So in giving responsibility and accountability to the workers lower down the organisations, managers work more as consultants and mentors. The trend at the beginning of the twentieth century was for scientific managers.

Scientific management

The founder of scientific management was F. W. ('Speedy') Taylor (1856–1915). Although he was a law school dropout, he was also a perfectionist, always looking for the one best way to do things. At the time he began imposing his ideas on American industry, **systematic soldiering** was a term used for the informal agreement that workforces established as their view of a fair day's work: they did what was necessary, but nothing more. They could implement this in practice by slowing down the rate at which they worked and taking long tea breaks. But 'Speedy' Taylor preferred that everybody should work as hard and as fast as possible, to enable maximum productivity. He introduced several means of making this happen, believing workers to be motivated by money and thereby assuming that higher pay would bring higher output.

His methods, now widely known as Taylorism, introduced:

- A time-study pay-rate system: he would find the fastest worker in the organisation, then observe that worker on the job, and use that as the 'benchmark' for other employees to work to.
- Functional foremen: they supervised not workers but work processes; if an assembly line had eight steps to the end product, Taylor used a span of control of eight supervisors.
- Cost accounting: 'clocking on and off', not into and out of work, but at the start and end of a specific task so different lengths of time taken for the same job could be examined.
- Paying the person, not the job: those who got the best results in their job (on paper) were paid more than others.

His most impressive improvement to production came when he worked at Bethlehem Steel, where in two years he achieved a 200 per cent increase in productivity with only a 50 per cent increase in wages.

'Taylorism' is now used to mean perfectionist or efficiency expert.

One important aspect of this method of management was that the knowledge was retained within management circles. Managers told people what to do, not how or why they were doing it, or even sometimes what the end result would be. They gave out the tools to use, the materials to use the tools on, and that was that. Workers didn't need to think, or have any responsibility.

Several characteristics were common:

- authority came 'from the top'
- structure was a formal hierarchical one
- specialisation was evident in labour processes, machinery and departments

♦ co-ordination was carried out by management, to link the many specialised areas.

This was typical in many businesses until as late as the 1960s. This mechanistic view of how to use humans most effectively from an organisational point of view moved on in later years to a system of **classical administration**.

ACTIVITY

What examples of modern scientific management can you think of? Is this system still in use?

Which organisations do you think use it? Is it effective? Why?

Classical administration

Again, this is a 'top-down' system with a hierarchical structure and clear chains of command.

Managers are responsible for functions within the organisation and have particular responsibility for specified personnel. Division of labour operates according to the specialised functions carried out by different departments. Each supervisor usually has responsibility for several subordinates.

The whole organisation is set up to serve the needs of the organisations, rather than the individuals within it. The jobs are put in place, then people are recruited to perform these specified jobs.

Bureaucracy

Max Weber (1846–1920) was a German sociologist and the first to observe and comment critically on bureaucracies which were evident in Germany during the nineteenth century. He said that bureaucracies were efficient and rational. Weber believed that bureaucratic co-ordination of human behaviours was a distinctive feature of modern social structures. Weber's ideal bureaucracy consisted of:

♦ a hierarchical authority system
♦ impersonality to individuals
♦ written rules

♦ promotion based on individual achievement
♦ specialised divisions of labour
♦ organisational efficiency.

According to Weber, bureaucracies are goal-oriented organisations within which information flows up the chain of command whilst directives flow downwards, as shown in Figure 4.22.

Capitalism came about through industrialisation; capitalists owned the means of production, while the workers made the money for them: a highly unbalanced interdependence. Braverman (1974) and Weber claimed that capitalism is about getting the most from the workers, for the least.

Operations of bureaucratic organisations are characterised by explicit rules and standardised procedures. Supervisors are highly specialised and the organisation has one goal; to achieve the organisation's goals.

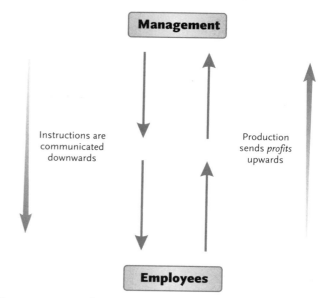

Figure 4.22 Weber's bureaucracy

Advantages of bureaucratic organisations

Specialisations in labour, combined with modern technological advances, have increased production levels dramatically.

Bureaucratic frameworks are clear and predictable. People know where they are and what is expected of them.

It can be considered a 'fair' system. Officials are appointed on the basis of their qualifications to do the job, and promotions come about through clearly-defined criteria: there is no room for nepotism, favouritism or the 'old boy network' offering favours.

Negative aspects of bureaucratic organisations

Bureaucratic organisations can be a bit 'old-fashioned' and/or reluctant to change their ways of doing things.

Decision making can be slow because ideas have to be directed through the right channels for a decision to be made.

Procedures and methodology can get in the way of, or obscure, goals and objectives.

Bureaucratic organisations can be impersonal and take no account of individuals' aspirations and needs. This can result in wasted ideas and talents, or in high staff turnover.

ACTIVITY

Weber said, 'No machinery in the world functions so precisely as this apparatus of men and, moreover, so cheaply ... Rational calculation ... reduces every worker to a cog in this bureaucratic machine and, seeing himself in this light, he will merely ask how to transform himself into a somewhat bigger cog ... The passion for bureaucratisation drives us to despair.'

1   Does Weber sound as though he supported bureaucratic organisation in making this comment?

2   Do you agree with the statement about no other apparatus functioning 'as cheaply as man'?

3   Would you be happy to be elevated to being a bigger cog?

4   What alternatives to bureaucracy might be preferable?

Human relations approach

Between the First and Second World Wars, modern management thinkers began to realise that more could be gained by respecting the value of human input into organisations than in 'flogging' them to produce. Give them some respect and incentive, motivate them, and they'll do more in return, was the idea. The HR approach arose largely from the work of humanistic psychologists, who stressed the importance of self-development and realising individual potential. They advocated that individuals should be given the opportunity to develop and flourish in their work by 'rising to the challenge' and gaining a sense of personal achievement. In return, they would help the organisation to develop and flourish through their skills, talents and innovative thought processes. See The human resource function on p. 95.

The HR approach looks at the importance of the people aspects of how an organisation is run, and places great emphasis on individual development. It regards informal structures and informal channels of communication to be just as important as the formal ones.

Systems approach

Webster's *New 20th Century Dictionary* defines a system as, 'a regularly interacting or interdependent group of items forming a unified whole', which 'is in, or tends to be in, equilibrium'.

Systems theory examines organisations as open systems, which are affected and influenced by factors such as openness to the environment and interdependence on others within the organisation and on the processes used to achieve the organisational aims. Basically, it explores the process of inputs, processes, outputs, and the various environments in which groups of employees work.

Any system has an input area, a processing area (in the middle), and an output area.

Input ⟶ **Process** ⟶ Output

The human body can be viewed as a system; we eat food (input), our digestive system processes it (process), and we produce energy, tissue repair and growth (output). We also produce waste, as do most production processes, which from an organisational (and an environmental) point of view needs to be kept to a minimum.

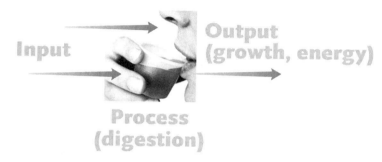

Figure 4.23   The human body as a system

System theory is concerned fundamentally with the interaction of relationships, of interdependence and with the structures within which the interdependent parts work. As Katz and Kahn (1964) said, 'systems theory is concerned basically with problems of relationship, of structure and of interdependence'.

All systems have general observable characteristics and tend to follow basic rules. They generally consist of subsystems which are interdependent within their specific environments. (The human digestive system is interdependent on many organs and processes such as the liver, pancreas, intestines, enzyme production.) If organisational systems can be mapped and the processes and interdependent parts identified, managers can learn a lot about how the system operates and thereby find ways of improving it.

Organisational systems have **goals**, that is, they work towards goal achievement. Systems tend to be **open** or **closed**. Closed systems receive no input from their environments, but environmental input is usually necessary if the system is to survive. Open systems are 'accessible' to the environmental factors that will influence how well they work. In an organisation, environmental factors might include competition from rival groups, or changes in the industry itself. If a system is closed to these

influences, it will soon fall behind and diminish its chances of survival.

All systems depend on the subsystems producing effectively. The stomach won't digest food if there is no production of digestive acids to be pumped into it. Organisational subsystems (different departments, divisions, or processes on the production line) have to co-operate for the good of the overall organisational system. It is about teamwork.

Closed systems have also been described as **rational systems**, or natural systems, which tend to view the organisation as closed to, or separate from, the environment, unlike open systems, which are open to and dependent upon the environment.

The subsystems within the organisation ensure appropriate input (production) and effective use (sales) of the output; and maintain good relationships between the subsystems, the organisation and its environment.

Maintenance subsystems might include personnel, for effective recruiting, training, motivating and disciplining, or purchasing, for effective buying of raw materials and requisite resources.

All systems need to ensure that the organisation can respond to the changing needs of the environment (research, development, and so on).

Advantages and disadvantages of systems theory

Applying systems theory can:

♦ increase clarity of goals
♦ increase understanding of the interdependency between departments and people
♦ increase awareness of the need to consider economic, social and environmental factors
♦ show how the component parts contribute to the whole.

However, there can be problems with systems theory:

♦ managers need to understand the needs of the whole system and its subsystems
♦ managers need to understand the interactions of the people and departments

- managers need to understand how the system operates within its environment
- it needs a shared vision, so that everybody involved knows what they are trying to achieve
- it needs a reciprocal effort from all those involved.

ACTIVITY

Discuss the following questions with your colleagues or cohort.

1 What environmental factors might influence how a system works?

2 If a system is closed, what effect could this have on its efficiency?

Contingency approach

Contingent means dependent, so it follows that the contingency theorists considered there was no single best way to manage, but depended on a number of factors. They studied a range of organisations, systems, environments and people, concluding that the best way to manage depended on situation, circumstance and the nature of the organisation. As Scott (1998) said, 'the best way to organise depends on the nature of the environment to which the organisations relate' (p. 96).

Steinmann and Schreyögg (2000) cited four important factors in organisations:

- Environment: that which affects organisations through legal and governmental regulations, culture, competition, and so on.
- People: those who have a huge influence on success because of their behaviours and skills, which shape how the organisation functions; in return, organisations have a responsibility to meet the different needs and expectations of its people.
- Technology: the technology employed and its interdependence with the environment has to be

taken into account when looking at organisational systems.
- Lifecycle: it will make a huge difference to the way the company is run, if the company has just been set up, or if it is many years old.

The lifecycle view accepts that the organisation must have the ability to adapt to changes. Organisational lifecycles don't necessarily determine the management approach, but there is a relationship between the two. Managers need to consider the 'evolutionary' progress of the organisation in terms of its size, complexity, stability, and so on.

Paul Lawrence and Jay Lorsch (1976) were two Harvard researchers and contingency theorists. They defined organisation as, 'the process of co-ordinating different activities to perform planned transactions within the environment'. The environment, they maintain, comprises three components: market, technology, and research and development. They examined **differentiation** and **integration** as key requirements for adapting effectively to environmental change.

Differentiation and integration

Integration is the required collaboration among departments and specialists to achieve a common goal. This unifies and co-ordinates the organisation. Differentiation refers to the tendency of different departments and specialists to think and act in limited ways. This can 'separate' the different parts of the organisation.

If an organisation is set up in different departments, or divisions, there is a natural tendency for those groups to stay as separate groups rather than work as a cohesive team (differentiation). With formal management, good communication and standard policies, the group tends more to be brought together and work as a team (integration).

Lawrence and Lorsch claim that every organisation needs a dynamic balance between differentiation and integration and the more unstable or changing the environment is, the more flexible and adaptable the management structures need to be.

Categorisation of organisations

Tom Burns and George Stalker, two British psychological behaviourists, looked at categorisation of organisations by their structural design. All organisations tend to fall somewhere along a continuum, within the following extremes.

Mechanistic organisations are rigid and inflexible and have strong bureaucratic and hierarchical characteristics.

Organic organisations are more flexible and can adapt easily and effectively to change.

In a stable environment, mechanistic structures, with clearly defined structures and functions, and clear roles and routines, tend to develop.

In a dynamic environment, Burns and Stalker argue that structure needs to be less clear-cut, with responsibilities and decisions being shared and responding to the particular prevailing conditions present at any one time.

Modern contingency approaches take the view that organisations have many tasks that need to be carried out and many people who perform those tasks. Within the organisational environment, the people designing the structures need to take account of the best-fit approach, and use the structure that is most appropriate for the current situation, circumstances and people concerned. It follows then, that different management styles and organisational patterns might be appropriate even within the same organisations, or at different times of development, or depending on market and environmental circumstances.

CASE STUDY

AT&T, the American Telephone and Telegraph Company

AT&T has been established for over a century and has seen major organisational changes in this time. AT&T began in 1875 when Alexander Graham Bell invented the telephone. In 1877 the Bell Telephone Company (BTC) was formed, which in 1885 was renamed

AT&T. Until the mid-1970s AT&T had the monopoly on the telecommunications business in the USA and therefore operated in a stable environment because of government regulation. This monopoly also allowed AT&T control of any technological advances and with no competition from other companies, made growth and development of a nationwide telecommunications company easy for the managers to operate.

The organisation therefore stuck with its vast, decentralised system for many years, becoming gradually entrenched in traditional ways of operating. This meant, though, that AT&T lost touch with the dynamic environment of the 1960s and having been protected from any competition for so long, was not ready for the necessary changes when they lost the monopoly.

Technological developments and changes in government regulations meant that in 1996, the Telecommunications Act, signed by President Clinton, allowed local phone companies to be deregulated and freed them to enter a new, competitive telecommunications market. At the same time AT&T sold operations that no longer fitted their organisational goals (such as AT&T Submarine Systems and Skynet Satellite). The AT&T that survived the 1990s is different again in the new millennium. It has successfully reorganised and reincarnated its business many times over, reorganising structures and planning new strategic goals again and again.

To develop the 'new' AT&T, its managers have responded to internal, external and governmental pressures and changed to suit customer demands. It has entered into new, competitive markets and its new divisional structure now puts pressure on its competitors to follow suit. AT&T now covers a wide range of communications services: it's no longer just a telephone company.

(See *AT&T: A Brief History*, under Useful websites.)

Functions of management

Managers are the people who get things done by using other people. Organisational management involves deciding on how the agreed objectives are to be met, using the people and other resources available to them. To do this they have to plan, organise, command and co-ordinate activities and ensure that all the various operations involved are brought together in a way which leads activities to the achievement of the agreed objectives. The whole operation has to be controlled, to see that the plan is being adhered to – and is working – and that objectives are being met.

Perhaps more importantly than anything else, managers have to manage *people* and ensure they are committed to meeting the set objectives and that they are happy in the way they are doing this.

Theories of management function

Fayol's theory

Henri Fayol said the main functions of management were:

- planning
- organising
- leading
- controlling.

Drucker: management by objectives

Peter Drucker created the idea of **management by objectives** and cited five main operations carried out by managers.

Setting objectives

Managers decide what the goals and objectives will be. They decide what needs to be done to achieve these objectives. Managers then communicate them to the people who will perform them so that everybody is clear about his or her role.

Organising

Managers analyse the objectives and resources available, then divide the work into manageable pieces. These pieces are divided into individual, manageable jobs. These jobs are incorporated into an organisational structure and the jobs delegated to the relevant responsible parties.

Motivating and communicating

The manager in charge of his or her particular team will take up the responsibility of motivating and rewarding those workers. Constant two-way communication between employee and manager is crucial to this process being carried out effectively. It's no good offering rewards if they are not the sort of rewards the employees want.

Job measurement

The manager establishes standards to which employees are required to work and ensures these are measurable by standard benchmarks. The measurements focus on the performance of individuals and at the same time on the work of the whole organisation. The manager analyses individual and team performances against these benchmarks and appraises and interprets progress.

Developing people

The manager directs (or misdirects) his staff. He should aim to bring out the best in them. Managers who are good or bad at doing this, can respectively strengthen and develop individuals, or weaken and limit them.

Mintzberg on management

Mintzberg (1989) categorises the functions of management into three categories which are then expanded into subgroups, or **roles**. His three categories and their subgroup roles are:

- Interpersonal roles: figurehead, leader, liaison (inside and outside).
- Informational roles: monitor (of internal and external information), disseminator (of information), spokesperson.
- Decisional roles: entrepreneur or innovator (change agent), disturbance handler, resource delegator, negotiator.

Managers need to be flexible yet still establish clarity of purpose and aims in what can be a difficult, dynamic and challenging environment.

Planning

Management plans need to be convertible into achievable aims, objectives and tasks. Organisational objectives have to be divided into achievable separate tasks and allocated to appropriate workers or teams. Planning makes it possible to measure, evaluate and control performance against clear performance standards. Figure 4.24 shows how activities and objectives interrelate with each other. Many individual operational tasks, activities and objectives are amalgamated at different stages, to all arrive at the one main organisational objective and mission.

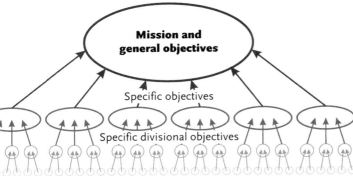

Figure 4.24   Providing direction through planning

Top managers need to ensure that their plans can translate down into the lower levels as achievable aims or activities. Different levels of management are involved with planning at many levels in an organisation. All these plans need to co-ordinate with and complement each other if they are to work.

Here are some of the plans which arise from top management:

- mission statement
- objectives
- strategic plans
- policies
- rules and procedures
- programmes
- budgets.

Mission statement

Once the mission statement of the organisation is established, all the other strategic plans and activities need to be formulated and slotted in, to move the organisation towards that mission (see personnel policies, strategies and operating plans under Authority and power on p. 102).

When the mission statement is decided upon, managers translate this mission into workable activities which will form the strategic plan and the objectives which will implement it. Who does the work and how they do it will dictate which particular course of action will be used, so it is fundamental to the managers to get it right.

According to Thompson (2000), 'Ideally the mission will state the basic purpose of the business, together with a summary of appropriate activities, how progress towards achievement of the purpose might be managed and monitored and how the company might create competitive advantage.'

Objectives

Corporate strategies provide the framework within which aims and objectives are agreed. Managers must carefully put together a set of objectives which will be carried out at each level of the organisation. If a company decides one objective is to be the market leader within 12 months, then it needs to translate this into specific objectives for, say, sales objectives, and perhaps budget objectives. Objectives need to have flexibility and be able to improve the efficiency of organisational operations over time.

Policies

A policy is a general statement which guides decision making and the general thinking that is employed in deciding future actions. Most organisations will, for example, have policies on health and safety, equal opportunities, customer service etc. The government has policies on education and employment; schools have policies on assessment and bullying. These policies state the intentions of the organisation and say how they will develop and monitor these areas.

Business policies concern decisions about whether to expand, whether to introduce new products, whether to alter staffing levels. Policies form a framework for future action and all employees work within the same overall plans.

Miller (1989) states that, 'Strategy is a market-oriented concept. It is fundamentally concerned with products and competitive advantage' (p. 49).

A policy on the other hand is a general decision-making guide which serves to focus all employees' attention on the objectives to fulfil. Policy statements can stabilise and standardise behaviours and reduce the dependence on individuals. They inform employees and the public of future intentions.

Rules and procedures

Rules and procedures set out the way particular activities will be done. Rules are far more specific than procedures. The rules must be adhered to, whereas procedures are more flexible guidelines to help jobs to get done. The rules might say 'do not run in the corridors'; the procedures to be followed might say 'conduct yourself in an orderly fashion in public or common areas'. Rules are for not breaking; procedures are for guidance.

Programmes

Programmes are sets of policies, procedures, rules and regulations, and tasks which comprise a particular course of action to be carried out: setting up a youth job-seekers' programme, say, or planning an environmental improvement programme.

Budgets

Budgets are the financial (or other) resources to be used to implement a particular programme or plan of action. Budgets can be compiled of resources such as machinery, labour force, raw components or time. You may come across budgets being referred to as profit plans. The profits will be communicated in numerical form: of product units, labour or machine hours available, or units of money.

Organising

Managers are expected to organise. They organise themselves, they organise their work and their workers; they organise the organisation. Organising means setting up systems and procedures or structures which will achieve the aims and objectives in a logical and efficient manner. Organising means making the most of the available resources and ensuring effective structures are in place to do this.

Organising involves giving priority to the essential aspects and ensuring processes are carried out in a logical order. What are the most important activities, what can take second place, and what is even less important? Resources and energies can then be directed to the most important tasks in hand.

Organising requires managers to:

- determine how the business will operate
- choose tasks to be completed
- choose who will do them
- determine the different sources of input
- assign tasks to individuals or teams
- delegate authority and responsibility
- make sure they are all co-ordinated correctly to achieve the objectives.

Commanding

Scientific management is one approach which places the manager in command of operations. Scientific managers made decisions at the top and commanded those lower down the organisational structure. They communicated information through the required channels and only the people at the top were able to tell others what to do. So good managers were those who were well organised and gave out the right commands to subordinates.

Modern managers still command whenever necessary, but are more likely to get things done by empowering employees to get on with the job their way, or develop supportive and trusting relationships with employees so that commanding isn't required. Effective managers encourage people to use their initiative, their ideas and their talents so that they can gain a sense of self-satisfaction in their work, whilst contributing to the organisational objectives at the same time.

Co-ordinating

Large organisations, as we have seen, can have many divisions, departments and separate objectives or work processes within them. The manager's job is to co-ordinate the activities of all these different aspects, so that they all work together for the organisational good. It is no good having an excellent sales staff and an excellent production factory, if the sales team don't know what the production team are making. It is no good having a wonderful plan if nobody can co-ordinate the departments to work together within that plan.

Effective co-ordination requires managers to:

- know the plan
- know the objectives
- know what other departments can or can't do
- know who is doing what, and why, and when
- know how to fit all the pieces together.

Co-ordinating isn't the same as commanding. Co-ordinating puts all the bits of the jigsaw together and shares responsibility for making sure all the pieces of the jigsaw are in the box to start with. Managers today often use computerised systems to aid the co-ordination process and employ such tools as critical path analysis and decision trees.

Controlling

Control is about measuring performance and progress, then correcting the parts that are not working well. We have already established that organisations must have a plan in force and objectives to be met within that plan. Performance and successful achievement need to be measured against agreed criteria or standards, to measure how well those objectives are really being met.

Measurement of performance

Measurement of performance shows how well the organisation is meeting its stated goals. Businesses often measure performance by indicators like sales figures, net profit, or units of production. The most important aspect to remember is that to control effectively managers need to be able to accurately measure progress and results. To do this they need to follow a basic three-step process:

- set the required standards

- measure performance and production against those standards
- correct any areas that are not 'measuring up' to the required standards.

Using the plan and objectives already set up, standards have to be established so that performance against them can be measured. Clear, measurable standards are needed in order to measure performance. 'Produce 500 portable 12-inch TV sets this week' is a clear standard, 'make lots of television sets this week' is not.

There are numerous different types of standards. The example above is one. Clear goals and specific targets are one type of standard. Another specific goal might be for a team to install and have fully operational a new computer system by a certain date. **Benchmarking** is often used to compare one organisation against others, especially those which are operating particularly efficiently and profitably. Benchmarking can have two advantages here: first, the organisation can see how it compares with those whose performance it wishes to equal or improve upon; second, it helps organisations to get ideas about how to reach optimum performance, whether that be in profit, production, or managerial practices. Benchmarking against established standards, such as ISO 14000, might be useful, for example, for those organisations with environmental issues to attend to.

Standards and goals

Standards and goals need to be clear if they are to be measurable and a growing trend in modern business practice is to use performance indicators to verify goals.

The measurement of performance against standards is generally considered best used as an improvement tool. Managers need to anticipate deviations from the standard (and understand why they are happening) to be able to verify realistic standards to be set. Routine tasks should be quite easy to measure against a standard, but non-routine or one-off activities will obviously be much more difficult to standardise. Manual production standards are also usually easier to set than, say, academic or intellectual tasks. The less routine a task is, the more difficult it is to set a standard for it.

ACTIVITY

Consider the following tasks, and set measurable targets for each one. Say how you will measure whether or not they have been achieved.

Which ones are easy to measure and which ones are not? Why is this?

1 Build a small retaining wall in a garden.

2 Teach a class of students how to make garlic bread.

3 Install and make 'operational' a new computer system for your department.

4 Work as the GP for a day in the local medical centre.

5 Design and make a wedding dress for a royal wedding.

6 Put together components of electrical goods on an assembly line.

7 Paint a family portrait for an important family christening.

Performance of organisational goals and individual standards in comparison to the required standards can be accomplished through periodic audits or other assessment activities, but it must be remembered that standards set must be realistic, clear and measurable. 'Minimum acceptable standards' have been used in the past, but it is possible that these may slow down production, particularly among enthusiastic highly motivated individuals. If there is no 'maximum' acceptable standard for them to aspire to, they could become apathetic. If there is no recognition for exceeding expectations, there is little motivation to do so.

So it is the manager's job to not just see themselves as controllers or measurers, but as motivational influencers who encourage employees to work to their maximum potential and be committed to the success of the organisation.

Continuous improvement can be achieved not only through performance measurement but also through employee involvement programmes that provide the opportunity to learn from past performance and offer innovative and constructive suggestions for future improvements.

Managerial roles

What are the recognised roles of the 'average' manager? Henry Mintzberg suggests three broad managerial roles which can be divided into sub-roles. These are interpersonal, informational and decisional.

Interpersonal roles

These include:

- figurehead role
- leader role
- liaison role.

Interpersonal roles are important for all managers, as they need to be able to work with other people and to encourage other people to work together as well. A lot of modern organisations are now in the service sector, so customer service is the prime concern of the organisation at all times. This increasing emphasis on customer care heightens the need for interpersonal skills. Like the staff at the point of sale, the manager needs to lead by example and that example has to be permanently enthusiastic, if he or she is to expect enthusiasm in return.

Coaching

Coaching is becoming increasingly popular as a way for managers to encourage development of interpersonal and job-related skills among employees on a one-to-one basis. This continual process usually works well where somebody with experience and expertise works alongside less experienced employees to help them develop the necessary skills and knowledge for the job.

Informational roles

These include:

- disseminator: acting as a channel of information
- monitor
- spokesperson.

Informational roles involve communicating information to employees in an effective and useful way. Managers have the information required to get the job done, but that is no good to them if they can't communicate that information to the employees responsible for carrying out the required tasks. Communication skills required by managers are not purely informative skills; they include listening and taking in any appropriate information they may read. They need to be able to use all the information they gather to motivate, guide and organise people into an effective working team.

Decision-making roles

These include:

♦ innovator and entrepreneur
♦ mediator or disturbance handler
♦ decisional allocation of resources
♦ negotiator.

Decisions have to be made constantly. This means managers have to gather all the available information, consider all the available options, and then decide which option is best. Most decision-making classifications are based on predictability of what those decisions will achieve. Simon (1957) in *Models of Man* differentiated between **programmed decisions** and **non-programmed decisions**.

Programmed decisions are those which are frequently made, routine, and straightforward: such as whether to order more fabric or photocopier paper.

Non-programmed decisions are one-off, unusual or unstructured decisions to be made. A new situation may have arisen; a new method may have been suggested; new machinery may be available.

Gilligan *et al.* (1990) also classify different types of decision making. They cite:

♦ strategic decisions
♦ periodic control decisions
♦ short-term operating control decisions.

Strategic decisions are ones that are made at a corporate strategic level, and affect the whole organisation. They need lots of informational input in order to assess what course of action will be best.

Periodic control decisions are ones made on a periodic basis to monitor progress and ascertain what changes, if any, need to be made. It may concern pricing of products to ensure they remain competitive, or re-allocating money or other resources to improve progress in certain areas.

Short-term operating control decisions are those that need to be made frequently and cover short-term requirements: whether the manager of the corner shop should order additional stock to cover the bank holiday weekend.

Charles Handy argued that attempting to define management in any one sense was too broad an aim to be able to do accurately. As you have indeed seen so far, the manager's role is wide and varied in nature and requires skill in many different areas.

The nature of managerial authority

Power

Power gives the ability to influence people and modify events. Power is gained by people or groups through their position, their activities and through their individual personality. Four main types of power that individuals can acquire are shown in Figure 4.25.

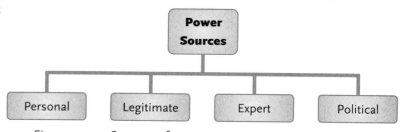

Figure 4.25   Sources of power

Personal power

Some people have 'charismatic' or 'referent' power: it seems to come to them naturally – they have charisma and easily influence other people. Charismatic leaders draw people along with them and naturally take the leading role. These types of leader are often sensitive to their followers' needs and focus on meeting those needs. Many will have heard of incidences of religious cults forming as people follow one influential leader or group of leaders in their chosen activities or paths. This can be a supportive and constructive leadership, or at times a negative and hazardous one.

CASE STUDY

David Koresh and the Branch Davidians

Figure 4.26   The Waco compound, home of the Branch Davidians

What follows is part of a BBC news report. David Koresh, leader of the Branch Davidians, a religious group in Waco, Texas, considered himself to be an 'agent of God'. Koresh was born in Texas in 1959, and was raised by his grandparents. The government knew him as a trigger-happy criminal, guilty of the physical and sexual abuse of several children he fathered himself, with his followers. He died, along with almost eighty of his followers, in the fire which followed an FBI assault on their Waco compound, raising questions about the raid and questioning the intentions of the charismatic religious leader.

Figure 4.27   David Koresh, whose charismatic leadership ended in disaster

Koresh suffered from dyslexia and bullying at school, and left school before the ninth grade [Year 9]. He was interested in the Bible and memorised large chunks of it as an adolescent. He joined the Branch Davidians in 1981 and soon became entangled in a power struggle for leadership of the religious group. He left, taking a group of followers with him, then returned in 1987 with seven of his 'disciples'. Armed with five semi-automatic rifles, two .22 calibre rifles, two shotguns and 400 rounds of ammunition, they laid siege to the Waco compound. George Roden, then the leader of the group, was wounded in the attack and Koresh and his seven followers were tried for attempted murder. His seven followers were acquitted, but for Koresh, a mistrial was declared.

In 1990, he became the head of the Branch Davidians at Waco, where on 28 February, 1993, agents with the Bureau of Alcohol, Tobacco and Firearms tried to arrest him on illegal firearms and explosives charges, and gunfire broke out. Four ATF agents were killed and 16 were wounded. An undetermined number of Davidians were killed and many, including Koresh, were wounded. President Clinton endorsed a negotiated settlement and negotiations began the next day, when ten children were released. Koresh refused to surrender and made rambling religious statements and threats of violence.

On Sunday 18 April, as armoured vehicles moved in, the Davidians held children up in windows with a sign saying, 'Flames await'. The FBI were concerned that the Davidians were about to commit mass suicide and on Monday 19 April, the FBI told the Davidians they were about to commence a tear gas assault. The Davidians began shooting when the gas attack began. The gas attack continued for several hours, whilst armoured vehicles began smashing holes in the buildings. At noon, several fires started within the compound, which the FBI maintain were started by members of the cult. Despite fire-fighting efforts, wooden structures quickly became engulfed in flames and Koresh and 76 followers, including more than 20 children, died. Charismatic leadership obviously drew Koresh's followers in, but what 'charisma' is necessary – or able – to get people to actually commit suicide to please a leader? Hopefully charismatic managers will more often guide their followers along a more positive and constructive path.

Legitimate power

This concerns the power of people who are positioned within a legitimate framework or organisational structure. In particular cultures, power is designated to the chosen positions or people and the rest of the group accept this as a 'legitimate' state. It is usually accepted in large organisations that the managers have power to pass instructions down to their subordinates and the lower level workers.

Expert power

This requires specialist or expert knowledge. If our car breaks down we trust the expertise and specialist knowledge of a mechanical engineer to get it going again. We bestow power upon them through our trust in their expertise.

Political power

To gain political power, other people need to trust that your policies will be to their benefit and politicians have to both earn trust and appease various groups in order to gain power. Politics within organisations works in much the same way, and gaining political power can be time-consuming.

Tactic	Example
Alliance	A group of department heads join together to exert pressure for improved health and safety standards in the organisation
Association with those with more power	An individual has social contact with someone in a senior position in his or her organisation (for example, membership of the same social club); the power then 'rubs off' on the junior, increasing the latter's power base
Tradeoffs	One department head supports another in return for reciprocal favours
Control of information	The market research department has first insights into customer needs and preferences which determines new products
Power plays	One manager increases the size of his or her sphere of influence by creating new subdivisions, departments, and so on
Selective service	Favouritism is shown to certain individuals, groups and departments in an organisation (for example, their work is processed more quickly by another department)
Networks	Individuals can develop formal and informal contacts within an organisation to enhance their power base

Figure 4.28   Tactics when seeking political power

Control over critical resources such as money gives the financiers power in an organisation. Parents withholding pocket money are exercising power over their children by limiting their resources. Managers can limit resources, be it money, manpower or raw materials, to get things done their way. Control over critical resources can therefore be seen as an important organisational power source.

Power through dependence comes about when others depend on you for a particular resource or function. The teenager is dependent on the parent for money and it therefore follows that that parent has power through that dependence. In an organisation, if department Y is dependent on the produce of department X, then X gains power over department Y.

Power sharing is probably the most sensible solution to ensuring the organisational goals are met. Managers who share power with employees increase job satisfaction, motivation and productivity. Managers who empower their employees and give them responsibility for their own work are likely to get good results from those employees.

Figure 4.29   John D. Rockefeller

CASE STUDY

John D. Rockefeller

Today we might describe someone as being 'a real Rockefeller', but many people are unaware of the origin of the term. For many years John D. Rockefeller was associated with the capitalist dream. He was the man who created Standard Oil in the USA in 1880. The company went from strength to strength until it was broken up by the US Supreme Court in 1911. At an early age Rockefeller stumbled upon a resource that was to revolutionise society: oil. Rockefeller quickly developed a knowledge of the oil industry which was to be the envy of many others in the field. Not only did he know the ins and outs of oil extraction and refining, but more importantly he had a detailed understanding of all of the business aspects of running a successful operation. He was a strong-willed character who was able to stamp his ideas on his associates and subordinates. Within a short period he was able to gain a stranglehold on the market for kerosene in the USA, with 90 per cent of the market.

He was able to win this share by a ruthless policy. He crushed almost all of his refining rivals by a combination of undercutting on price, industrial espionage, the secret ownership of companies that pretended to be rivals and, above all, the securing of hidden rebates from railway companies for every barrel they shipped, not just of his oil but of oil produced by his competitors too. A good example of this ruthlessness occurred when grocery stores offered kerosene from independent refiners; they found that, suddenly, a competing store would open across the street in which everything, not just kerosene, would be suspiciously cheap.

In 1872 he perpetrated the 'Cleveland Massacre', in one stroke buying out 22 of his 26 rivals in the city. The result of the Rockefeller strategy of buy-out or crush was the virtual monopoly that Standard Oil quickly became. Standard Oil was referred to as 'the octopus'.

On a personal level, Rockefeller believed that his achievements were all for the greater good of society. Indeed he managed to bring the price of refined oil down from 23 cents to 7 cents per gallon.

Rockefeller believed that it was in the public interest to have large firms controlling industries, rather than the chaotic conditions of free competition in which new enterprises would enter the industry and then collapse owing to unregulated competition. Rockefeller was a devout Baptist and he believed that the system he supported was based on co-operation between the big railway companies, steel companies, oil companies, and so on. He believed that everyone would benefit from the actions of powerful individuals like himself who could dominate the market in the general interest of mankind. He expected people to listen to what he said, and to have confidence in his wisdom and trust in his abilities. He once referred to Standard Oil as 'the Moses who delivered them [the refiners] from their folly which had wrought such havoc in their fortunes'. He went on: 'It was not a process of destruction and waste: it was a process of upbuilding and conservation of all the interests ... in our efforts most heroic, well meant – and I would say, reverently, Godlike – to pull this broken-down industry out of the Slough of Despond.'

Rockefeller stated that: 'I believe it is my duty to make money, and still more money. And to use the money I make for the good of my fellow man according to the dictates of my conscience.' He was one of the greatest philanthropists the world has ever seen.

ACTIVITY

1   What do you think were the major sources of Rockefeller's power: individual, legitimate, expert or political? How would these sources of power be important in different situations?

2   Contrast Rockefeller's sources of power with those of a more recent prominent business leader.

3   List five other charismatic leaders, living or historical. What do these leaders have in common?

4   What tactics might a political leader employ to maintain his or her power base?

5   Why is the use of power, and an understanding of the nature of power, of importance to a manager?

Authority

Authority is not the same as power. It can be viewed as a type of legitimate power in that authority can be delegated to individuals by those in powerful positions within an organisation. That authority will be supported by a contract of employment or by the rules and regulations of the organisation. Police have the authority to stop vehicles in the street; teachers have the authority to tell students to be silent during examinations. The finance director has the authority to sign cheques.

If a manager chooses to 'exercise his authority' this means he is acting in accordance with the authority bestowed upon him. A teacher might exercise his authority by placing a pupil in detention for bad behaviour. A detective might exercise his authority to search premises, that authority having been granted through the issue of a search warrant.

Responsibility

Anyone who has been trusted with authority will be held accountable for decisions they make using that authority. If the finance director signs a cheque for purchase of goods that were not required, he or she can be held accountable for the waste of money caused. Modern organisations work on trust and individuals therefore have to show themselves worthy of that trust by using their authority in an appropriate and profitable way.

Managers need to be clear about what their responsibilities and accountabilities are, so that they can act accordingly.

Delegation

Delegation is about giving your work to someone else to do. Managers delegate for two main reasons:

♦ they do not have the time, skill or resources to perform the task effectively
♦ they want to give a subordinate more responsibility.

Reasons that managers might avoid delegating could include:

♦ lack of trust: the feeling that 'if you want a job doing properly, do it yourself'
♦ they still have responsibility for the task, so need to ensure it is done properly and promptly
♦ it would take too long to show someone else how to do it
♦ because the person delegated to do the job will complain about having to do it.

If someone is delegated to perform an **assignment**, they are asked to do a one-off specific job or task, such as write a report, or take a parcel to somebody.

If they are delegated a **project**, there will be more work involved because projects consist of sets of interlinked tasks but are usually also one-off individual projects which are unlikely to be repeated.

If someone is delegated an **area of work**, they are likely to be doing this over a longer term. An area of work may be something like receiving visitors, filing reports or checking health and safety requirements are being met around the working environment.

Some managers will delegate certain tasks simply because they don't want to do them themselves. This may buy them a little extra time, but will not necessarily gain them the respect and trust of their employees.

Conflict

Managers are responsible for ensuring the smooth running of their part of the organisation and as such, will be the ones who have to defuse difficult situations and resolve conflicts in the workplace. Have a look again at 'Conflict' on p. 127 for a more detailed view of why conflicts arise and how managers can resolve conflict.

Managers need to manage conflict effectively, by taking the initiative and accepting that there will be conflict and that they can look at ways to resolve it. They can develop relationships that anticipate conflict and minimise both the likelihood of it happening and the damage it might do. They can even use it to the organisation's benefit.

Frames of reference for leadership activities

Leaders are the people responsible for generating a sense of meaning in the daily work tasks, which acts as the driver of superior performance from individuals.

In the 1960s and 1970s Jane Loevinger (1976) proposed a developmental theory to monitor adult development. This was revised by Bill Torbert (1991), concentrating on professional and management issues, leading to the creation of the 'Leadership Development Framework', a management 'tool' now widely used and researched.

This framework is concerned with the process of our ability to make meaning of experiences and, ultimately, with how we behave in response to those experiences. The Leadership Development Framework describes progressive developments in individuals' abilities as they mature and can be utilised in organisational developments too, in that the Framework examines the stages of development of a leader and classifies different styles of leadership.

The opportunist

This leader looks at immediate needs and opportunities. She seeks short-term advantage for herself. She has very short time outlooks and blames others rather than accepting the blame may lie with herself.

The diplomat

This leader displays what might be considered socially expected behaviour. The diplomat seeks conformity, belonging and loyalty. He provides the cohesion for a group, and likes belonging and wants low stress relationships. The diplomat fears breaking rules and dislikes conflict.

The technician

The technician seeks expertise and perfection within a consistent framework or logic. This type of leader will identify strongly with what they know and what they are perfecting. She seeks efficiency and decisions based on unarguable facts. She strives for continuous improvement and believes in the 'right way' to do things. The technician develops her own skills and expertise to become a 'master'. She likes efficiency, consistency, logical, stage-by-stage improvement and perfection.

The achiever

This leader wants results! He seeks effectiveness and results through application of strategies, plans and actions. The achiever works towards given goals, breaking the rules if necessary. He feels like an initiator, but is more likely to take on laid-down goals than create his own. He sets high standards for self and others and feels guilt if these standards are not met. The achiever seeks constant feedback to confirm achievements.

The strategist

The strategist enjoys the complexity which comes from people's differing views and abilities. She sees the world as a dynamic mix of inter-related relationships. This leader works for the moment but holds long time outlooks and sees the big picture. She seeks to harness diversity and is guided by principles. Playing many roles, she values integrity and principles; she also values freedom to create positive change.

The magician

The focus here is on transformation of society, th organisation and the self. This leader seeks the common good. He enjoys the interplay of purposes, actions and results. The magician is illusive, chameleon-like and may be powerful, and often dislikes inevitability of paradox in human affairs.

The pluralist

This leader sees the views of all individuals in the organisation, whereas the individualist increasingly focuses on self and subjective experience rather than goals. She understands herself to be just one player in a complex game and recognises that the needs of all individuals and functions need to be considered.

Transformational leaders

Transformational leaders develop a personal and social identity among organisational members, using the organisational mission and goals. They raise the level of awareness about the importance of desired outcomes, and ways of achieving them.

Transformational leaders leave behind their own self-interest for the sake of the team and the organisation. They can alter individuals' needs levels (see Maslow p. 154) and widen our range of wants and expectations by explaining the rewards to be gained.

Leadership style and situation

Hersey and Blanchard (1977) identified four leadership styles that could be used to deal with different situations.

Telling
(high task/low relationship behaviour)

This style features a leader giving direction to subordinates by paying a lot of attention to defining roles and goals. The style has been recommended for dealing with new staff, or in menial and repetitive

e limits need to be adhered to.
 as being unable to do a good

;hip behaviour)

... most of the direction comes from the leader,
but there is an attempt to encourage people to accept
responsibility for, or to own, the task. Sometimes
described as coaching, it is useful when people are
motivated but don't have the necessary skill or ability.

Participating
(high relationship/low task behaviour)

Decision making here is shared between the leaders
and their followers. The main role of the leader is to
facilitate and communicate. It needs high support
combined with little directing and is used when people
are able, but may be unwilling or insecure.

Delegating
(low relationship/low task behaviour)

The leader still identifies the problem or task, but the
responsibility for carrying out the work is that of the
followers. It needs a high degree of competence and
maturity in the workers, that is, people know what to
do, and want to do it.

Change

The business world of today is a highly competitive
and dynamic environment. To survive, organisations
need to adapt constantly to the needs of a rapidly
changing environment and, indeed, world. Resistance
to change does not work today: organisations have to
change to keep up with the competition. Customers
expect and demand excellent quality and service, and
they want it faster. If organisations don't respond to
these expectations, their competitors will.
Organisations have to reshape themselves quickly, to
meet their customers' needs and expectations. The
organisation's leaders are the ones who have to head
this process so that success is the end result.

In support of leadership theory, Peter Drucker
points out that management's truly new frontier, the
non-profit social sector, is where 'systematic,
principled, theory-based management can yield the
greatest results the fastest'.

Chapter 3
Motivational theories

Much research has been carried out to ascertain why some people seem motivated to work hard, and also to discover how to encourage people to perform to the best of their ability, particularly in work environments. Motivational and psychological research is used consistently today in industry and business organisation. Motivation concerns why people do the things they do; why they behave in a certain way, such as revise hard for exams or sit back and hope for the best.

Managers need to know what motivates people to work hard, in order to get the best from their employees. Some people view work merely as a means to an end, usually money, whereas others gain – and seek – intrinsic satisfaction from their work as well as financial reward. Higher pay may mean people work harder, but it cannot make them actually take pleasure in the work process itself.

Brian Baxter (2003) says, 'the meaning of work has shifted from either a necessary evil or the primary source of their self-identity, to simply one of a number of very important places where their personal values, expectations, beliefs and assumptions are affirmed, challenged and re-built on a daily basis'.

Handy (1994) says, 'The individual is not so much interested in the work itself as in the results which that work will produce for himself or herself", and 'the work is a means to an end, not an end in itself".

Work can be more fulfilling when people have some involvement in decision making, some control over their work processes, and responsibility in their daily activities. Conversely, it can be alienating if work is boring and repetitive and does not fully utilise an individual's skills and abilities. A manager needs to know what motivates workers, then provide the right environment and conditions to enable workers to be *self*-motivated.

Motivation, from the Latin word for move, has many textbook definitions. Torrington and Hall (1991) state that, 'Motivation is a psychological concept related to strength and direction of behaviour', whilst Buchanan and Huczynski (1997) claim, 'Motivation is the internal process of initiating, energising, directing and maintaining goal-directed behaviour.'

G. A. Miller (1967) said, 'The study of motivation is the study of all those pushes and prods – biological, social and psychological – that defeat our laziness and move us, either eagerly or reluctantly, to action.'

Korman (1933) claimed, 'The psychology of motivation concerns itself with attempting to understand (and predict) the arousal, direction, and persistence of behaviour, given the characteristics of the behaving subject at the time and the characteristics of the environment (both real and perceived) at the time.'

All these definitions have implications of one sort or another for organisational managers.

Motivation is born through biological needs for food, water and air (see Maslow, 1954), and from psychological needs for personal achievement, power and the approval of others. There are several theoretical approaches to studying motivation and we will look at some of these.

Satisfaction theorists (such as Herzberg) believe that satisfied workers stick with one employer for longer and 'happy' workers have higher morale, better mental health, higher levels of self-motivation and are consequently more productive.

Incentive theorists maintain that higher production is brought about through higher rewards, using the psychological principle of reinforcement.

Intrinsic theorists (such as Maslow) believe the greatest motivator is self-satisfaction and belief in one's own worth.

Maslow's hierarchy of needs

A good place to begin is with what motivates any living creature to do anything. Maslow's (1954) hierarchy of needs claimed our motivation begins at a very basic level: the motivation to survive. At the bottom of the **needs hierarchy** are the needs for food, water, warmth, clothing and sex. Once these basic instinctive needs are met, we can move on to higher order needs such as security and self-esteem, as demonstrated below.

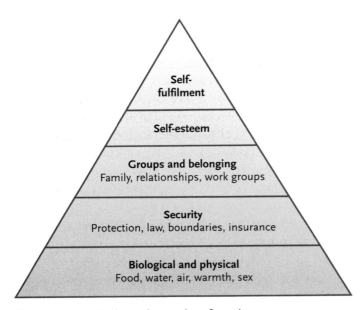

Figure 4.30   Maslow's hierarchy of needs

Behaviour pathways are established to achieve various goals, and these satisfy increasingly psychological needs, rather than biological.

If the lower needs are not met, we lose interest temporarily in the higher order needs, until the lower needs are again satisfied. For example, we won't be interested in finishing an essay until we have satisfied our biological need for food. As long as the foundations remain stable, however, we can concentrate on satisfying our more cerebral, or intellectual, needs higher up the pyramid.

In the workplace, basic physical needs are usually met with money (a wage or salary) and comfortable working conditions.

Security at work demands, again, physical safety through safe working practices, appropriate resources and regard for health and safety regulations, as well as through financial security from employment laws, pension schemes and job security or trade union protection.

Belonging is important to most people. They want to feel they are part of a relationship, family, or work group. The more employees an organisation has, the more the workers might come to feel they are 'just a number'. Smaller organisations, or smaller working groups and teams within an organisation, can benefit individuals by helping them feel they are more part of the team, whilst retaining their individual identity.

Self-esteem concerns the individual's accomplishment of becoming what, or whom, they want to be, through utilising their skills and talents to their best advantage, working to their full potential and using their creative talents and initiative to the full. This is what Carl Rogers (1961) called **self-actualisation**.

If we have made the effort to complete a degree course and expand our skills and specialist knowledge, then we will want to use that new-found expertise in a constructive way. Employees who gain job satisfaction in this way are usually highly self-motivated, have clear personal objectives in mind and work hard to achieve those goals. Whilst monetary reward is important to them, satisfaction from the work process itself is also rewarding, and, in turn, motivating.

We must remember, though, that not every individual strives for such high levels of self-fulfilment, and a 'life in the fast lane'. Some people are content with little responsibility and purely monetary reward. Some can also reach the higher levels of Maslow's hierarchy without all the interim stages being satisfied first; Harry might need to feel a sense of belonging in his team, before he can enjoy self-esteem, but Harriet may be perfectly happy to work alone and apart from company, without that affecting her self-esteem or path to self-actualisation.

Even Maslow acknowledged his hierarchy to be rather inflexible, unlike people. Each of us has different needs and priorities and good managers acknowledge and respond to that diversity.

Maslow's level	Individual	Organisational
Physiological	Food, water, warmth	Pay, environment, lunch allowance
Security	Shelter	Employment law. Name at least three others
Groups and belonging	Family	Work teams. Name three other aspects
Self-esteem	What works for you?	Feeling valued. Add some more
Self-fulfilment	Passing exams	Promotion, more responsibility

Figure 4.31   Maslow's levels interpreted

Herzberg's hygiene theory

Frederick Herzberg (1968) also believed that people have needs that must be satisfied, and claimed that

Figure 4.32   F. Herzberg

satisfied employees will be productive employees. He maintained that in order to motivate people they need to have their working life enriched, and receive constructive and complimentary feedback, perhaps, for example, through structured training. He acknowledged that even if a large number of people are satisfied or dissatisfied in the same workplace, this will not necessarily be for the same reasons.

Herzberg claims we have two sets of needs:

♦ an instinctive need to avoid pain
♦ to develop psychologically as a person (again, similar to Rogers' self-actualisation).

He believed some factors – motivators – really do spur people to action voluntarily, whereas other factors have the opposite effect and can lead to dissatisfaction simply by *not* being present: the **hygiene factors**.

Motivators (or 'satisfiers') in the workplace would be things such as personal development, achievement, recognition, promotion, responsibility and the actual nature of the work itself. These satisfy and motivate people to work.

Hygiene factors (or 'dissatisfiers') would be such things as effective company policy and management practices, good work conditions and relationships, salary, prestige, personal life and job security. People strive to have them because they are dissatisfied without them. However, the satisfaction of gaining them can be a transitory feeling. The novelty soon wears off and satisfaction with hygiene factors is a temporary state.

Hygiene factors and motivators are equally important and are not opposites of each other. Managers need to attend to the motivating factors and personal development aspects to increase productivity or performance and at the same time ensure hygiene factors are met, to avoid dissatisfaction.

Herzberg advocates that satisfaction from work processes will increase motivation, but his theory does not consider how to make work processes, or job design itself, a vehicle to increase job satisfaction.

It must also be borne in mind that not all satisfaction of a person's needs are met through work. Some needs can only be met through home or social situations, so do not need to be, and cannot be, met through working processes or conditions.

Herzberg's research indicates that whilst satisfaction at work can lead to lower staff turnover rates, it does not necessarily lead to increased production. High production levels and good performance, however, can lead to increased satisfaction for an individual, which may in turn increase self-motivation. But remember, each of us is different.

ACTIVITY

Think of two people who do very different jobs. Can Maslow's or Herzberg's theories be easily applied to all aspects of these people's work? Why is that?

Under ideal work conditions, could all their:

♦ physiological
♦ psychological

needs be met at work?

An individual's *perception* of how they will or can achieve the satisfaction they want is crucial. If a person believes that hard work leads to promotion, and promotion would satisfy them, then that person will probably work hard. If they believe – or expect – that continued years of service is the only way to gain promotion, they will probably stay with the organisation, but not work so hard. If they believe it does not matter what they do, they'll never get promoted, they may lose motivation and/or make excuses for why they are not so successful as others.

Expectancy theory proposes a cyclic progression, as shown in Figure 4.33.

Figure 4.33   Expectancy theory

Vroom's expectancy theory

Vroom (1964) first developed **valence–expectancy theory**, which supposes that motivation results from the expectancy that a satisfying reward will be gained from the input of hard work, or effort, by the worker. A worker needs to believe that if he tries, he will succeed in achieving a particular goal. Valence refers to the level of satisfaction an individual will gain from a particular outcome. Some may prefer praise and recognition to monetary reward for a particular task. Hence a person's level of motivation depends on what they expect to gain in return for their efforts. If the rewards for their efforts are, in their eyes, worthwhile, then motivation is likely to be high. The higher, or more satisfying, the level of reward, the higher the level of motivation is likely to be.

Vroom believed four factors are involved in what motivates an individual:

♦ people have differing feelings about whether an available outcome is worth striving for
♦ people expect that a particular effort will produce a particular outcome
♦ people expect specific behaviours to produce favourable outcomes
♦ the amount of effort input depends on the amount they expect to receive in return.

Extrinsic and intrinsic rewards

In considering the levels of satisfaction one might expect to gain, we can look at intrinsic and extrinsic rewards.

Extrinsic rewards can be closely related to Herzberg's hygiene factors and Maslow's physiological needs. **Intrinsic rewards** can be likened to Herzberg's motivators, or to Maslow's self-esteem and self-fulfilment levels.

Changes in needs

Again, we need to remember that each individual is motivated by different rewards. Vroom accepts individuality in the worker and accepts that different workers want different outcomes and rewards. Needs also alter over time. In the 1950s, essentials for everyday living were food, clothes, warmth (a coal fire) and money. Today most people believe essential items include central heating, a car, a washing machine, a mobile phone and TV/DVD player. People work for personal, social and material satisfaction. The importance of each of these changes along the continuum of intrinsic versus extrinsic satisfaction with age, experience and personal circumstances. Individual circumstances alter over time. Someone saving today for a sports car, in five or ten years' time might be concentrating on finding money for a deposit on a house, a wedding reception, or school fees. Today you want cash, tomorrow you may want financial security.

Intrinsic rewards (self-fulfilment, motivators)	Extrinsic rewards (physiological, hygiene factors)
Self-respect	Wage/salary
Praise	Financial package
Feeling valued for work produced	Company car
	Pension,
Better career prospects	profit-sharing
Good relationships	Work environment
Sense of achievement	

Figure 4.34   Intrinsic and extrinsic rewards

Different countries and cultures also have different goals. For example, Spain and the UK rate comfort at work as very important, but Belgium and the Netherlands rate it as a very low priority. The Netherlands rates relationships at work as very important, yet UK and US managers give them a low priority (Hunt, 1992).

Different educational systems (within Europe as well as worldwide) also disagree on the best type of education – vocational versus academic – for training people for work (Mercado *et al.*, 2001).

The implications for employers and managers are many. Employers have to examine how their pay systems and benefits packages appropriately reward the workers' efforts. They also need to ensure employees see the link between high performance and reward (their perception of fair rewards and

conditions) and have clear methods of measuring performance and production, so that rewards can be appropriate to these measures and enable profit and career progression for people who want it. As Charles Handy (1975) said, any worker will, 'from time to time appreciate friendly counselling, in difficulties, in career decisions, in planning his own development, in working to improve his talents and modify his shortcomings'.

Maccoby, McCrae and Costa: personality dimensions

Recall from the discussion of personality traits and types (p. 130) the big five key areas of personality identified by the Eysencks and many other psychology trait theorists.

Growing consensus among psychologists claims that the five broad dimensions validly represent individual differences and that these personality traits influence whether managers are suited to different positions in different types of organisations because of their personality traits.

ACTIVITY

How do Vroom's expectancy theory and Maslow's needs theory contribute to your understanding of what motivates people at work?

How can managers use these theories?
Are they applicable to all work situations?
Discuss the following with your fellow workers and students:

♦ 'Motivating employees within a multicultural workforce is more difficult than in a single-culture environment.'

How might managers in multicultural settings deal with this? Draw up some guidelines for your own hypothetical multicultural work setting.

Michael Maccoby is an American anthropologist, psychoanalyst and management consultant. In *The Productive Narcissist* (2003) he links leadership styles to the four major personality types identified by the psychoanalyst Sigmund Freud and his successors.

Obsessive types

These are the kind that make executives. They are conscientious, independent and organised. They promote self-development programmes and have strong consciences, so can prove to be good leaders. Maccoby claims that, 'the best obsessives set high standards and communicate very effectively' but they can be quite blinkered specialists, who fail to take a holistic view of things.

Erotic types

This category refers to those who need to be liked and loved. Maccoby claims they make ineffective managers and can be seen largely represented in the leadership stakes, among the likes of most politicians.

Marketing personality types

People of this type (originally proposed by Erich Fromm) are 'motivated by a radar-like anxiety that permeates everything they do', according to Maccoby. He continues, 'because they are so eager to please and to alleviate this anxiety, marketing personalities excel at selling themselves to others'. But 'marketing types generally make poor leaders in times of crisis'. He says they are not innovative and are too responsive to current trends, rather than pro-active about future expectations or demands.

Narcissistic types

These are the 'productive narcissists' who make it to the top and constantly try to change the rules. Maccoby says that narcissists 'come closest to our collective image of great leaders'. Narcissists, he explains, can be wonderful visionaries. They can envisage how things could be or ought to be, and work to make those visions a reality. He describes them, though, as 'isolated, paranoid, and grandiose'. Not necessarily the type of person you might feel a lot of respect for all of the time. However, with the modern trend of perpetual change, organisations are increasingly selecting leaders who display this personality type. They are adventurous and ambitious and prone to high risk-taking. They are, Maccoby says, the people who 'have the audacity to push through the massive transformations that society periodically undertakes'. They don't 'play well' with others, and they are thin-skinned and arrogant or grandiose; they hate opposition, and can react aggressively when challenged.

ACTIVITY

Have you witnessed this type of behaviour at work? How did it make you feel?

Maccoby believes that in today's rapidly changing high-tech and information-rich environments it is best to have a narcissist as the leader to follow.

Managers do need to be aware of how personality can be very important in management issues. Conventional leadership theories emphasise empathy, listening skills and sensitivity to be key. These may create a pleasant working environment, but won't always guarantee corporate success. What might is a mix of narcissism and strategic intelligence: skills which managers employ to keep the more aggressive elements of narcissism to a minimum. Maccoby says, 'If you're like most people, you think a narcissist is a vain, self-centered egomaniac. But this is a description of behavior – and most likely, bad behavior – rather than a portrait of a personality type.'

McCrae and Costa (1988), in researching personality traits, claimed that agreeableness and conscientiousness are independent factors, both comparable to extroversion and neuroticism. As for openness, Eysenck (1985) claims that it should not be considered a personality factor at all.

Costa and McCrae's (1992) Neuroticism-Extroversion-Openness Personality Inventory (NEO-PI) was a questionnaire specifically designed to measure the big five factors, the aim being to improve diagnosis of personality disorders and determine appropriate treatment. Two points worthy of note for managers are that:

- high neuroticism has been closely linked with stress
- low extroversion has been linked with low social support.

The NEO-PI claims to be a precise measure of the big five major areas of personality, but delves deeper, citing six facets within each of the domains, as shown in Figure 4.35.

1 Conscientiousness facets	2 Openness facets	3 Agreeability facets
Competence	Fantasy	Trust
Order	Aesthetics	Straight-forwardness
Dutifulness	Feeling	Altruism
Self-discipline	Action	Compliance
Deliberation	Ideas	Modesty
Achievement-striving	Values	Tender-mindedness

4 Neuroticism facets	5 Extroversion facets
Anxiety	Warmth
Angry hostility	Gregariousness
Depression	Assertiveness
Self-consciousness	Activity
Impulsiveness	Excitement-seeking
Vulnerability	Positive emotions

Figure 4.35   Personality facets

The idea of the inventory is to get a detailed assessment of 'normal' personality, for use in human resource development and organisational settings, as well as for job-related counselling and guidance. It consists of 240 items and three validity items with an administration time of 35–45 minutes. Whilst it may prove a useful management tool to some, it must be ascertained first whether the cost (time, as well as professional psychological interpretation) is worth the result. What is the result for the organisation? Can personality traits be measured? And if they can, can that information be put to real practical and developmental use in a specific area? It may be useful in some areas or divisions, but not so in others.

Motivation and performance

So what makes people want to work? What is their real motivation for getting on with the job? Research has shown that workers respond to HRM practices and the evidence would suggest that the 'soft' approach to HRM is more productive in terms of intrinsic motivation and employee loyalty. Whilst the hard approach to HRM might be more conducive to higher profits, as more and more managers realise and acknowledge that their biggest asset is their employees, more employers want to maintain a low staff turnover and high morale.

Leadership style   JOURNAL ARTICLE

Maccoby examines two types of leader in two recent books: Jack Welch and John A. Byrne (2002) *Jack, Straight from the Gut*, New York: Warner Business Books; and Jim Collins (2001) *Good to Great*, New York: Harper Business. Maccoby poses the question 'for which kind of company would you rather work? One led by a charismatic CEO who makes constant changes, introduces big programs and demands constant high performance; or one led by a determined yet self-effacing CEO who uses basic strategy, moves logically, and balances high standards with personal and family values?'

Welch describes how he managed for twenty years to make General Electric the most valuable company in the world. As one reads, his powerful personality is evident. Collins looks at leadership styles and practices, used in companies that did well for their shareholders over a 15-year period.

The main message from both of these books is that people are the most important resource to a company's success and the company must have the right leader. Who is the right leader?

Good to Great gives the message that the best leaders are humble but determined and put the company in front of their egos. They don't like extravagant perks, and tend to lead a modest lifestyle.

Collins says (p.127), 'Throughout our research, we were struck by the continual use of words like disciplined, rigorous, dogged, determined, consistent, focused, accountable, and responsible ... people in the good-to-great companies became somewhat extreme in the fulfilment of their responsibilities, bordering in some cases on fanaticism.' Innovation, vision or risk taking are not mentioned. Psychoanalysts would view this manager as an obsessive; the kind of person you need on your team, but who might need a little man-management training.

Maccoby, M. 'What we can learn from Jack', *Research Technology Management*, 2002, Vol. 46, No. 2, March–April, pp 57–9.

Five factor model of personality

JOURNAL ARTICLE

The five factor model is widely considered as a comprehensive model of personality traits. The claim that these five factors represent basic dimensions of personality is based on four lines of reasoning and evidence. In this article, the relation between openness and psychometric intelligence is described, and problems in rotation of the factors are discussed.

Costa, P. T. and McCrae, R. R. 'Four ways five factors are basic', *Personality and Individual Differences*, 1992, Vol. 13, pp 653–65.

Rewards and incentives

Every successful organisation needs a good remuneration system, which ensures that individuals receive appropriate recognition for their efforts in the workplace.

Traditionally, organisations rewarded staff with pay increases, often based on seniority, length of service or inflation rates, but more often these days the trend is towards performance-related pay: people are paid for how well they perform, alongside other benefits packages.

Financial and non-financial recognition can be used to acknowledge the personal contribution that individuals make to the overall value and productivity of the organisation.

Motivation and managers

Much psychological and sociological research has been carried out in respect of workers' motivation and the effect of different reward systems. Daniel (1973) suggested that every employee 'is likely to have different priorities at different times and in different contexts'. Grint (1998, p. 24–25) claims that, 'workers with heavy family responsibilities tend to be more concerned with extrinsic rewards (money and security) than those without'. This is very probably the case and managers need to be aware that work can have different meanings and a different purpose for different people.

As we have discussed, the organisations people work for have changed radically over time, as have the pay and rewards systems. As Smart (1992) says, we have seen 'major transformations in social relations and forces of production', partly due to multinational extensions of corporate operations and a growing global labour market. Grint points out, 'attitudes to work are not stable, they change as individuals change their status, their family situation, their age and their interpretation of the discourses imbricated around such categories' (1998, p. 26).

Evidently, managers need to understand what motivates their employees, and ascertain what type of reward is likely to improve their performance and maintain their commitment and motivation.

Goldthorpe *et al.* (1968) examined workers' instrumental, bureaucratic or solidaristic orientations to work. Those with an **instrumental orientation** saw work as the means to an end (an end disconnected from work) such as money, for family responsibilities. The main relationship between employer and employee here is money and there is no particular expressive or self-fulfilling satisfaction in the work itself.

The **bureaucratic worker** saw work as service to the organisation as well as to himself: work and non-work fit together from a 'working hours' point of view and from a social aspect. He had commitment and loyalty to the organisation as well as just earning money.

For **solidaristic workers**, work is a group, or community activity almost (as in mining), and features moral involvement with the employer and the work-orientated community.

Daniel (1973) spoke of a bargaining context, whereby workers are there simply for the money and see management as the opposite side. Conversely he suggested a work context, in which work also brings social rewards of contact and communication with others, so work itself has interest; there is intrinsic satisfaction to be gained.

At one time the world of work was very male-orientated but today more women work, and gone are the days when it was thought that secretaries should 'have an aptitude for thoroughness and application, but are not perhaps particularly extrovert personalities' (ASTMS, 1980, p. 43), suggesting that women were really at work to be seen but not heard. Tepperman described the old-fashioned view of women at work only to perform 'menial' tasks, as 'labelling of female clerical labour as mindless and unimportant' (1976, p. 7). Those days appear to be behind us and one would not expect to encounter those kinds of attitudes today. Indeed it is now illegal overtly to display such attitudes in the UK workplace, thanks to modern opinion, and just a little help from legislation. Women are now entitled to equal pay and equal opportunities, but they, as well as the male working population, may not be in work 'just for the money'.

Reward schemes

Any organisation, in creating and developing reward schemes, needs to:

◆ maintain a structure and organisational culture that 'fits' both employee and organisational interests
◆ recognise and reward individuals as well as team performances, in a way appropriate to the contribution they make and to what motivates them
◆ ensure fair treatment and recognition of all employees, regardless of seniority, sex, and so on.

Employees need the rewards that will motivate them to produce. An effective appraisal system (see p. 106) can promote this kind of motivation by acknowledging and praising these efforts and formally recording them, so that the employee feels his or her efforts are worthwhile not only to the customer, but to him or herself as well.

Not many performance appraisal systems will work unless they operate within a system that employees trust and believe really works for *them*. Even after the appraisal has confirmed their entitlement to 'reward', it has to decide what kind of reward is going to work best, because rewards come in all shapes, sizes and packages. They can be in monetary or non-monetary forms.

Rewards: monetary and non-monetary

Monetary rewards come in financial form. Wages, private health insurance, bonus payment schemes, pay awards for achieving professional qualifications and enhanced pay for specific skills all represent monetary reward.

Non-monetary rewards can often be overlooked as a method of reinforcing and encouraging better performance in many employees. Think about the voluntary sector: volunteers are not paid for working, so what do they get out of it? Why make the effort?

Non-monetary rewards might include compliments, a face-to-face 'thank you', training programmes, flexible work schedules or the granting of unpaid leave.

They may come in the form of an achievement certificate or career development opportunity, or as gifts such as mugs, T-shirts, and golf umbrellas. Extra time off may be granted or simply on-the-spot thanks or a 'pat on the back' when an employee is doing an especially good job. All of these can reinforce good performance, provide recognition of the employee when peers are present, and encourage everyone present to strive for their best performance. These types of remuneration are often described as internal (or intrinsic) rewards, because they serve the employee's internal needs such as self-esteem, recognition and personal fulfilment. These are some of the key factors employees use when evaluating their satisfaction with a job, and they can really influence motivation levels. Non-monetary rewards can be used frequently, and often have a longer lasting effect than money.

Advantages of non-monetary rewards

Jerry McAdams, co-author of the American Compensation Association's report, *Organizational Performance and Rewards*, observed that non-monetary awards can have four major advantages over monetary awards.

Memory value

The value of informal recognition, whether it's a mug, a certificate, or a pat on the back, is longer lasting than money, because money gets spent and is gone, whereas tangible items remain.

Trophy value

Non-monetary rewards can be shown off to friends and family as a trophy for hard work, unlike pay cheques and bank statements.

Flexibility

There are an infinite number of ways that non-monetary recognition can be given. Team trophies can be given; individuals can be told 'thank you, you did really well there' and often a well-placed compliment can mean much more than just another pay slip.

Cash awards cost money

Employers can spend a lot less money on non-monetary awards. Some are even free. How often have you heard someone say 'good manners cost nothing'? Well a 'thank you' costs nothing either. Employers have repeatedly reported, in numerous research projects, that practically the same level of performance improvement can be produced from non-monetary awards and that employees often credit them with an equal value to monetary rewards.

CASE STUDY

Thanks – you made a difference!

One example of an organisation utilising non-monetary awards is the Naval Aviation Supply Office (ASO) in Philadelphia, Pennsylvania (USA). ASO's programme upholds *corporate* strategies of employee empowerment.

As an example, they have an award called 'Thanks – you made a difference!' The winner of the award is chosen by colleagues and peers, who recognise group or individual efforts that have exceeded expectation: people who have 'gone the extra mile' to help others, or get the job done. Individual employees receiving recognition get a standing ovation from peers, a certificate congratulating them on their performance, some balloons, a photographic record, and other small tokens displaying the company logo. There is also a 'grand draw' in which previously recognised employees can receive other non-monetary awards, such as a reserved parking spot for six months (which would be worth a fortune if you work in inner London) or having a work area named after them.

Whilst some individuals might cringe at the thought of such public attention, such schemes have been shown to have, in some cases, quite dramatic results.

Motivation and emotional wellbeing

JOURNAL ARTICLE

The whole issue of this journal concentrates solely on motivation and emotional wellbeing in the workplace. People experience the whole range of human emotions in the workplace and it is the job of managers to try and provide a happy and contented emotional atmosphere in the working environment.

Different papers in this journal volume look at issues such as performance monitoring, organisational change and its effect, role conflict, and so on.

Motivation and Emotion, 2002, Vol. 26, No.1. March.

Intrinsic motivation

JOURNAL ARTICLE

These two studies looked at measures of intrinsic motivation and examined the effect of performance-contingent rewards on individual autonomy and perceptions of competence.

Extrinsic rewards and motivators (such as money or deadlines) are often used to encourage people in uninteresting or monotonous activities. The second study attempted to encourage *intrinsic* satisfaction (and thereby motivation) in the task, by demanding participants' personal justification of the value of completing the task.

Houlfort, N., Koestner, R., Joussemot, M., Nantel-Viveur, A. and Leke, N. 'The impact of performance-contingent rewards on perceived autonomy and competence', *Motivation and Emotion*, 2002 Vol. 26, No. 4, December, p 279.

Reeve, J., Jang, H., Hardere, P. and Omura, M. 'Providing a rationale in an autonomy-supportive way as a strategy to motivate others during an uninteresting activity', *Motivation and Emotion*, 2002, Vol. 26, No.3, September.

Leadership

Leadership is a human skill and a vital constituent of any group or organisation. Some people are natural leaders, displaying signs of leadership ability from an early age. The captain of the school football team is probably chosen or elected for his natural ability to persuade and influence, though it is possible to develop leadership qualities in some individuals, with the right training and education. To develop these qualities in people though, it must be made clear what leadership *is*, in order to look at how it can be developed.

Leadership is difficult to define and there are many different perspectives from which it can be viewed. We generally accept the idea that leaders are people who gain commitment from members of a group, and establish a direction for those members to move in, to achieve a common goal. Leaders motivate group members and use management skills to gain the commitment of people. They influence others to work towards the common mission of the group.

Leadership in organisations

Whilst we have discussed how modern management methods now lean towards autonomy and responsibility among the workers, and self-managing groups, those groups and the organisations that employ them still need leaders.

Leadership is not a one-off solution to human or organisational problems, but rather a cyclic process that requires commitment over the long term. Effective leadership requires trust between the leader and followers and is about developing ways to lead those followers better every day. We will focus on leadership in organisations, which to be effective in the long term needs to concentrate on persuading the members of the group towards achieving the organisational mission and objectives. Leadership isn't about commanding and ordering people but about influencing them.

Leadership skills

Hersey and Blanchard (1988) claimed that, 'leadership occurs when one attempts to influence the behaviour of an individual or group'. They identify three main skills required of a leader.

Diagnosing

This is a cognitive skill required by leaders. They need the ability to understand the current situation and how that situation may change in the future. The problem the manager then needs to resolve is the **performance gap**; that is, the gap between what is the situation now, and what changes will be needed for the future expectations of the situation. Closing that gap is the task of the leader.

Adapting

This is a behavioural skill. Leaders need to change their behaviour and adapt resources in order to close the performance gap.

Communicating

This is a process skill: it is no good diagnosing a problem and adapting resources to resolve it, if the solution is not communicated effectively to those who will implement it.

Roles for leaders

So two key roles for leaders are to:

♦ ensure the goal or task is achieved
♦ maintain good relations within the organisation by maintaining a good leader–follower relationship, in order to achieve the goal.

In leading others in an organisational context, the leader will be concerned with:

♦ the task: leaders need to clarify the objectives; they look for ways to organise people and activities in order to meet those objectives
♦ the group and its constituent individuals: leaders need to hold the group together and see their followers as people. At the same time as achieving the objectives, they attend to individual needs, interests, problems and development.

Organisational structures need to be developed and maintained in a way that enables the leaders to lead effectively, and provides the support they need to do so.

Recall the four leadership styles identified by Hersey and Blanchard (see p. 151) that could be used to deal with different situations.

Managers and leaders

Bennis and Nanus (1985) claim that, 'Managers are people who do things right and leaders are people who do the right thing.' In a study of 90 leaders in various organisations, they concluded that leaders were concerned with the objectives and direction of the organisation, rather than with the 'nuts and bolts' which hold it together. The mission of an organisation, then, is what leaders are eager to work towards to achieve organisational aims.

Bennis and Nanus cite four requisite attributes for leaders:

♦ vision: encouraging other members to share this vision and believe in the purpose of the organisation
♦ communication: communicating the vision clearly and acting accordingly, leading by example
♦ trust: being reliable and delivering on promises, to gain the trust of followers
♦ self-knowledge: recognising their weaknesses and being able to build on their strengths.

Leaders' goals need to fit the goals of the organisation; to achieve those goals, the leader needs to be able to manage as well. Sometimes organisational influence (such as structure) will affect how well a leader operates in different circumstances, but leadership is still viewed as a personal, or characteristic, attribute of certain individuals. John Gardner (1989), in studies of North American organisations and leaders, concluded that there are a number of qualities or attributes that indicate that a leader in one situation, could also lead in another. These included:

♦ physical vitality and stamina
♦ skills in dealing with people
♦ understanding people's needs and the ability to motivate them
♦ self-confidence, assertiveness and decisiveness
♦ courage and resolution and the willingness to accept responsibility
♦ the need for achievement
♦ competence related to the task
♦ intelligent judgement
♦ trustworthiness.

ACTIVITY

Examine all the points listed above, and think about how or why they might be relevant in a variety of organisational settings.

ACTIVITY

Discuss the question in small groups, then as a larger group.

Figure 4.36
Condoleezza Rice

Figure 4.37
Bill Gates

Figure 4.38
Clare Short

Figure 4.39
Richard Branson

♦ What traits do the people shown have in common that make them good leaders?

Leadership traits

As we saw earlier, 'traits' are our relatively stable personality dispositions which make us behave in a certain way and distinguish us as individuals.

Trait theories are built on the idea that people are born with certain characteristics or traits that help them to be natural leaders. As we have seen, the traits required by leaders have conventionally been thought of as self-confidence, intelligence, determination, decisiveness and the desire for achievement.

Modern organisations, though, which rely heavily on teamwork, may require different leadership approaches. You can probably think of many people who are decisive and ambitious, but can they also be sensitive to the needs of others and recognise the importance of interpersonal relationships? Margaret Thatcher claimed in a speech in 1976, after the Kremlin dubbed her 'the iron lady', 'I stand before you tonight in my green chiffon evening gown, my face softly made up, my fair hair gently waved. The iron lady of the western world? Me? A Cold War warrior? Well, yes: if that is how they wish to interpret my defence of values and freedoms fundamental to our way of life.'

Obviously different opinions exist about whether she was a sensitive leader or an 'iron lady'. In respect of the notion that her leadership abilities may have been something she was born with, she claimed to be a good leader because, 'I've got a woman's ability to stick to a job and get on with it when everyone else walks off and leaves it' (government speech, 1975).

Bennis claims that leaders are people who are able to express themselves fully. He says, 'They also know what they want, why they want it, and how to communicate what they want to others, in order to gain their co-operation and support.' Lastly, 'they know how to achieve their goals' (Bennis, 1998, p. 3).

Strong versus teamwork leadership

Modern organisations, then, and their leaders, need to consider what is an appropriate style with which to approach leadership today. The modern method of teamwork requires a more involved approach than simply 'ordering' or dominating proceedings. A **strong leadership approach** needs:

♦ self-confidence
♦ dominance over others
♦ intelligence

- determination
- decisiveness
- desire for personal achievement.

A **teamwork approach** needs:

- self-confidence
- sensitivity to others
- intelligence and interpersonal skills
- perseverance
- wish to create and work towards team goals
- desire for co-operation and team success.

CASE STUDY

Heroes defy the mould

In an article in the *Independent on Sunday* on 19 June 1994, Tom Peters discussed twelve of his heroes. He argued that they share, more or less, 13 traits that add up to a fair guide to success in general. The traits were described by Peters as follows:

1 Self-invented. 'I am an American, Chicago-born,' begins Saul Bellow's novel *The Adventures of Augie March*, 'and go at things as I have taught myself, free-style, and will make the record in my own way.' All my Mount Rushmore nominees have chiselled their masterpieces from the granite of life in a distinct, unusual fashion. Standard career path? Forget it. One company, one job? Not even close.

2 Ever changing. I don't think any of my dandy dozen has a split personality in the clinical sense of the term; but surely all are chameleons, not bound by consistency they have tried a plethora of outfits while remaining desperately and passionately committed to whatever it is they are pursuing at the moment.

3 Battered and bruised. My heroes have screwed up things at least as often as they have gotten them right. Their collective motto could be: 'A road without potholes not a road worth travelling.' Failure does not seem to faze them. If anything, setbacks amuse them and motivate them.

4 Inquisitive. No question goes unasked for this squad of achievers. Sometimes I think there is literally nothing that does not interest them. They are determined to get to the bottom of any topic they touch – on or off the job. (Job? They are what they do. Job is not part of their vocabulary.)

5 Childlike. This naive crew – who refuse to grow up – are not afraid to ask dumb (even very dumb) questions if they are not getting the message. Their appetite for knowledge and exploration is far greater than any fear they have of looking idiotic.

6 Free from the past. Gravity has no meaning for this group. They are not weighed down by history. In a flash they will thumb their noses at what only yesterday they were fervently espousing.

7 Comfortable, even cocky. My Hall of Famers are at ease with themselves, unperturbed by the idea of life as an elusive moving target – an adventure to be relished, mostly for its detours.

8 Jolly. These people laugh a lot. They marvel at human intrigues, and their appreciation of the absurd stokes their marvellous sense of humour. All of them have wrinkles – you know the kind ... those that can only be attributed to smiles and laughter.

9 Audacious and a bit nuts. They will try anything – from learning a language to starting a new career – with barely a moment's hesitation. Moreover, by the standards of the majority, they view the world through decidedly cockeyed glasses.

10 Iconoclastic. Conventional wisdom, to my pilgrims, is like a red cape to a bull. I sometimes think they're only happy when they're on the 'wrong' side of an issue or truism.

11 Multidimensional. We're not dealing with saints. All members of this tribe have flaws, often as pronounced as their strengths. But, then, when was the last time you observed an insipid soul accomplishing much of anything?

12 Honest. It's not that they always tell the truth or are above pettiness. Hey, we're all human. It's just that this set is attuned to reality and especially to their own foibles. They are consummate and often quixotic truth-seekers, with little time for those who aren't as confused as they are.

13 Larger than life. Our Gang of Twelve are all heroic. That is, they paint the canvasses, large and small, with bold strokes. They are fearless in their own fashion. They embrace the circus of life, rather than shrink from it.

Management style

Management style refers to the pattern of behaviour one adopts over time, in carrying out a management or leadership role. There are three main types of management style.

Autocratic

This style could also be described as tightly controlled. Here the leader makes decisions alone and then conveys these to the staff who will work with those decisions.

Democratic

This style predominates where decisions are made after consideration of the ideas of all those involved. **Persuasive democratic management** usually means that the leader makes the decisions anyway, and persuades the followers that it is the right decision. **Consultative democratic** management means the group will heavily influence the final decision, even if the leader still has the final word.

Laissez-faire

From the French, and meaning 'let well alone', this is a loose management style with no real formal decision-making pattern. The leader's opinions are not pushed on to people.

Do these management styles all work? Usually, different approaches will work best in different situations.

ACTIVITY

1 Do you think the traits outlined would 'add up to a fair guide to success'?

2 Is there anything you think should be removed from the list?

3 Is there anything you would like to add to the list?

4 Try to establish your own list of traits that you think would contribute to success based on your experience of working with 'leaders'.

5 Identify your own list of people who have some or all of these traits.

ACTIVITY

Discuss the following questions in your group.

1 Select five current leaders. To what extent do your chosen five appear to have the traits of leadership that have been mentioned?

2 Now focus on leaders with whom you work quite closely to consider their traits. To what extent does the leadership trait theory seem to be valid for them?

Blake and Mouton's (1978) **management grid** shows a matrix management model which looks at this concern for people, or production, in the organisation. You will see that only the management style that would fit into section 9:9 on the grid shows a high concern for both people *and* production.

Whilst the 9:9 management style is the 'ideal' team approach, it will not necessarily work in all situations. Leaders need to be able to gauge situations and circumstances on a day to day, or even hour to hour, basis sometimes, to see which management style is needed on different occasions, in different situations and with different types of employees.

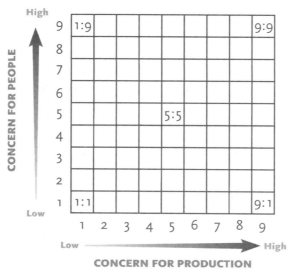

Figure 4.40   A management grid

Contingency approach

Contingency theories recognise that different variables affect what management style may be appropriate in particular situations. What decision is to be made, who is involved, and current trends or situational factors all affect appropriateness of style.

Managers need to consider:

♦ the task
♦ the nature of the group
♦ the leader's position in relation to that group
♦ the environment and nature of the organisation.

Fiedler (1967) suggested that whether an authoritarian or a democratic approach might be best

	Advantages and	Disadvantages
Autocratic	Rapid decision making. Good for armed forces, fire services, for example	Can lead to dissatisfaction. Motivation can drop
Democratic	Encourages 'consulted' decision making. Makes use of many ideas	Not always as 'democratic' as it claims to be. Can slow decision making
Laissez-faire	Employees have freedom. Few limits on employees due to unclear goals	Poor motivation and productivity

Figure 4.41   Management styles

depends on whether management face a favourable or unfavourable situation. A favourable situation would be when the leader is well liked and trusted by the group; when the task for completion is well defined and clear to all; when the power granted to the leader is high.

Fielder supported the idea that an authoritarian approach is best if the task is well defined and the leader is highly respected, because subordinates will respect and support their leader. He also advocated an authoritarian approach if the task is vague and ambiguous and the leader is not well respected by the group, because in this situation the leader needs to assert authority and clarify the objectives, to get the task completed.

On the other hand, if a task is ambiguous but the leader is well respected, the leader can afford to invite opinion from all members of the group, yet still retain authority.

In looking at the four considerations listed above, the leader will need to choose the **'best-fit' approach** and use whatever strategy and style is best suited to the task in hand. The best-fit approach supports the notion that there is no best way to lead, but that different styles are appropriate to different situations and circumstances.

CASE STUDY

Qualities of leadership

In his book *Understanding Organisations*, Charles Handy wrote that individuals need to learn to do the following:

♦ develop and communicate a clear vision of the task, so that a sense of purpose develops in the group
♦ allow others to influence the vision, so that they are committed to it
♦ build up the trust and respect of their group so that they have the essential conditions to allow them to adapt their style to the contingency requirements
♦ remember that successful performance of their ambassadorial role is essential if they are to have freedom to behave as they think best within their group
♦ remember that they represent the organisation to their subordinates and should practice all the precepts enjoined on the senior managers.

Individuals and organisations should bear in mind that the individual who meets these requirements will tend to:

♦ have high tolerance for ambiguity and be good at handling open-ended problems
♦ be good at differentiating between people and situations
♦ have a clear self-concept which will tend to go with self-confidence
♦ have a high reservoir of energy
♦ be prepared to set moderately high standards for himself or herself and co-workers and to give and receive feedback on performance.

ACTIVITY

1 What form of management do you think Handy is advocating: autocratic, participative or free-rein?

2 To what extent does Handy advocate a 'contingent' approach to management?

3 What do you perceive to be the benefits of the approach outlined by Handy?

Handy argued that faced with a lack of fit, leaders need to adjust some of the factors involved to make a good fit. It would probably be difficult to alter the environment, or the workers, or the task, so it would most likely be easiest for the leader to alter the leadership style instead.

Leadership and organisational culture

If you take all the elements of the best-fit approach that need to be considered, it becomes clear that the leadership style of an organisation's managers contributes greatly to the culture of that organisation. Leaders who have a vision of what is their desirable and achievable state for the organisation in the future will be able to give that organisation a sense of direction.

If employees within an organisation have a clear picture of what the organisation hopes to achieve, what their role within the organisation is and what the organisation's role within its environment and society is, they are likely to feel they fit in, and be motivated to work towards the organisational goals. A sense of pride in the organisation generates a sense of pride, enthusiasm and loyalty in the employees and this is apparent to those people dealing with the organisation from outside.

Edwin Baker (1980) lists ten techniques which he claims leaders of organisations use to build corporate culture:

- role modelling: the manager leads by example, acting in exactly the same way he expects his employees to act
- face-to-face communication: the manager talks personally to all employees, at whatever level in the organisation they are
- written communication: newsletters, posters and booklets are used regularly to communicate relevant issues
- positive reinforcement: reward and recognition are given for appropriate and desired behaviour
- recruitment policy: only people who fit the desired look and feel of the organisation will be recruited
- promotion and transfers: those who personify the desired company image are promoted into the key positions
- training: training and particularly induction instil company philosophy and attitudes
- personnel policies: these do not favour any particular employees above others
- physical factors: quality of facilities, open-plan offices, customer reception facilities, and so on, all give an instant overall impression of the company's image
- showmanship and symbolism: slogans, logos, roadshows, advertising campaigns all portray the desired image.

Leadership and successful change in organisations

Organisational change can be brought about for reasons arising from within the company, or be required in response to, or be forced by, external factors such as increased competition, legal changes, or technological advances. One sign of a successful company is that it can respond to pressures with the ability to change. External changes will affect the internal culture of an organisation and to change successfully organisations need proactive, knowledgeable leaders to introduce and oversee necessary changes.

The success of these leaders in implementing change will depend on their ability to nurture and maintain positive relationships between employees throughout the organisation and in successfully communicating the need for, and process of, change to those employees. Whilst any external changes could affect the internal culture of an organisation, the existing culture will quite probably determine the way change is introduced and just how extensive that change will be. **Homeostatic** cultures (resistant to change) see change as a threat and tend to be resistant to change, whereas **morphogenetic** (dynamic and constantly evolving) cultures regard change more as an opportunity and a desirable process for its own sake.

According to Lewin (1951) in Mullins (1999) successful change involves three stages:

- unfreezing the existing situation: this involves reducing habitual behaviours and recognising the need for change
- movement, or changing: this means developing new attitudes, implementing changes and adapting to the new organisational culture
- refreezing: this requires the new form to be stabilised and accepted, so that it becomes the new predominant culture.

Barriers to change

There are many obstacles to change, such as structural inertia, where the culture of the organisation resists change, or the existing power structure, within which current managers or leaders may feel threatened by the prospect of change. Resistance from work groups is one of the greatest barriers to change, as individuals (including leaders) feel threatened by proposed changes.

So resistance to change occurs at organisational levels as well as at the individual level. Reasons for resistance to change might include:

- for individuals: habit, inconvenience, fear of loss of security
- for the organisation: culture, investment in resources, existing contracts, threats to influence or market position
- other reasons: self-interest, misunderstanding or lack of communication and lack of trust.

If an organisation is to survive and incorporate change smoothly, leaders have to tackle internal problems whilst responding to the requirements of the external environment. Where managers are trying to alter the whole culture of an organisation, they concurrently attempt to change the behaviour of the people within it to 'become' the culture. The process of change can be introduced smoothly and with minimum disruption or it can leave employees and the organisation confused, alarmed and lacking in efficiency.

The process of change

Change is inevitable. How it is handled is of the utmost importance. Leaders need to recognise the stages in any change process:

♦ the vision stage: how we would like things to be
♦ the analysis stage: how are things at the moment?
♦ the unfreezing stage: identifying what needs to change and the processes that will implement those improvements
♦ setting achievable goals
♦ implementing: putting the ideas and processes into practice, introducing transactional changes, and so on
♦ review and monitoring.

The change process is simple in itself but many organisational change strategies fail to make a smooth transition, and can leave a bad taste in the mouths of employees.

A pluralistic approach

As discussed earlier under Organisational culture (p. 87), the pluralist approach, in contrast to the unitarist approach, acknowledges that different stakeholders have different interests. Shareholders and investors will have profit in mind, whereas the local community will have job availability or perhaps environmental issues in mind. The interests of all parties involved in change need to be considered and conflicts addressed and reconciled, by the leaders responsible for implementing changes. Ways of changing that suit all the parties involved need to be established, and the desired objectives of all parties should be achieved as far as possible.

Transformational leaders

James Burns (1978) defined transformational leaders as those who 'shift the beliefs, needs and values of followers'. If a leader can inspire and support employees emotionally and intellectually, then she or he can develop organisational structures that will manipulate the existing culture (Bass, 1985, 1990).

Transactional changes

Transactional changes involve changes to systems and processes, whereas transformational changes delve deeper, examining strategic objectives, the organisational culture, leadership styles and the like.

Transformational change involves almost a change in identity, and it emphasises individual change and transformation as well as organisational change.

CASE STUDY

Incorporation in the further education system, April 1993

Following the 1992 Education Act came 'incorporation'. Under incorporation, colleges became responsible for their own finances and funding, which previously had been controlled by local education authorities. Colleges had to pay their own staff and fund their own courses. New colleges were set up and new funding methods adopted which led to aggressive competition between colleges. New employment contracts were drawn up either according to post-incorporation design, or continued on the old regime if staff opted for this. Many faced redundancy or early retirement against their wishes, and department closures left many staff facing an unknown future.

FENTO (Further Education National Training Organisation) standards were introduced, which set new 'ideals' that teachers were expected to adopt and believe in. Thus it would follow that the whole college institution would also believe in it and a whole new value system, or culture, would be born. Many claimed that teachers were being brainwashed into taking on the new system and its values and beliefs. Coombe Lodge training centre was accused of 'programming' college principals and senior lecturers into their own beliefs, 'in search of excellence'. New rules and methods were introduced to shape the way of thinking or behaving. Some behaviours were promoted and rewarded, and others were actively discouraged, so as to develop a whole new way of working. Whilst the quest for excellence is usually commendable, the very same methods are not necessarily suited to every situation.

Dr Bridge (1994) of the South Thames College Corporation advocated that teachers needed to be persuaded to 'embrace new ways' instead of 'persistently moaning' and reacting to outside 'faults'. He also claimed, 'Inappropriate cultural values are usually held by people who have been too long, rather than not long enough, in the organisation. Therefore I have concluded that over the years it is almost impossible to have too much selective early retirement and targeted voluntary redundancy within an FE college.'

ACTIVITY

1　Does this seem to have been a 'fair' comment, or way of introducing change?

2　How might a consultation process have helped to smooth the way?

Transformational change will normally involve the following aims as important issues for the individuals involved.

Security

A sense of security needs to be developed so that employees feel at ease even in the face of major changes. Increased security reduces dissatisfaction and unease and fosters loyalty.

Health

The aim here is less stress, and thereby less illness and fewer accidents, which means less absenteeism.

Meritocracy

A meritocracy develops: people with objectivity are appointed to the appropriate roles and assume responsibility.

Collaboration

People become clearer, more objective, and with less internal conflict, collaboration is much easier. There is less conflict and more unity.

Leadership

Leadership is based on expertise rather than power, or force or historical habits.

Interaction

Interaction both within and outside the organisation becomes more meaningful and co-operative, based on trust and mutual respect.

Pluralistic structures　**JOURNAL ARTICLE**

Larry Greiner and Virginia Schein claim that trust, co-operation, and collaboration can only exist within a pluralistic structure or culture. They accept the 'fact of life' that organisations have self-interested individuals who seek their own goals, but believe that hierarchical power can be used constructively and responsibly.

Greiner, L.E. and Schein, V.E. *Power and Organizational Development Mobilizing Power to Implement Change*, Reading, Mass: Addison-Wesley, 1989.

Transactional and transformational leadership

Transactional leaders:	*Transformational leaders:*
Recognise what it is that workers want to get from work and try to ensure that they get it if their performance deserves it.	Raise levels of awareness and consciousness about the significance and value of required outcomes, and ways of reaching them.
Exchange rewards and promises for effort.	Persuade workers to give up their self-interest for the sake of the team, or organisation.

Figure 4.42   Transactional and transformational leadership

Leadership is closely linked to the organisation's mission and objectives. Transformational leadership involves creative direction-setting and creating a shared vision that is clear and inspiring to employees. So leaders may need to transform a corporate strategic objective into a personally involved vision to motivate and persuade reluctant employees of its worth. Well-communicated visions and aspirations are an important element encouraging new behaviours and a new direction for an organisation and its employees.

Because individuals are so affected by transformational change, people can feel insecure or threatened and react by resisting the change. It is therefore the responsibility of a good leader to 'smooth the water' throughout the change, whilst achieving corporate goals as well.

Transactional and transformational leadership

JOURNAL ARTICLE

Researchers Bruce Avolio and Bernard Bass and colleagues examined how transactional and transformational leadership by military platoon leaders and sergeants predicted their unit's cohesion and performance. The ratings were done four to six weeks before each platoon participated in a two-week combat simulation. A total of 1,594 'soldiers' participated and rated their platoon leaders and sergeants.

Examples of transactional leadership statements and beliefs are, 'Reward us when we do what we are supposed to do'; 'Directs attention toward failure to meet standards'. Examples of transformational leadership include, 'Talks about the importance of the Army ethics and values'; 'Emphasises the importance of having a collective sense of mission', and 'Helps platoon members develop their strengths'. Cohesion of the platoon was determined by three measures that assessed how well the platoon pulled together to get the job done.

Both forms of leadership brought cohesion in the platoons and success in the simulated training exercises, said the authors, and they both appear to be necessary for good performance. The authors claim that transactional contingent reward leadership 'establishes clear standards and expectations of performance, which builds the basis for trust in a leader'. Transformational leadership can then build on these initial levels of trust.

Bass, B. M. *et al.* 'Predicting unit performance by assessing transformational and transactional leadership', *Journal of Applied Psychology* 2003, Vol. 88, No. 2, March.

Communications

Communication becomes even more crucial at times of organisational change. Employees who are not well informed make assumptions, worry unnecessarily about what is going on, and are susceptible to rumour. Morale can take a dive, motivation decreases and people become suspicious and wary of other employees and their motives. Effective leaders keep their employees informed of what's happening – and why – so that they do not feel alienated from the change process, or feel secrets are being kept from them. Internal communications are critical from the start. Selling the vision and sharing success, supports those responsible for implementing change and involves people at all levels. Change can only work if the workforce makes it work, and to do this they need to be told what is happening.

Conflict at times of change

Many images which we associate with leadership have their origins in conflict. Envisage Hitler, or Blair, Gandhi or Napoleon, and the image of conflict immediately springs to mind. It is the job of politicians to convince and direct groups into action; it is the job of national or army leaders to take control of a crisis and outwit their opponents to protect their own people. In times of crisis the actions of one person can be crucial in determining what happens next. The quality of leadership is therefore central to the survival and success of the organisation and it is rarely that one will find a situation where everybody agrees, or where everybody has identical interests. As mentioned under Personality and work behaviour (p. 130), every new idea could conflict with one or another long-established way of operating. **Divergence of interests** can interfere in the decision-making process and effective leaders need to recognise these issues to be able to deal with them.

Avoiding conflict

Effective ways of incorporating change with the minimum of conflict include:

- involving people in the changes
- keeping people well informed
- letting experienced people implement the changes: people who can give time to their current responsibilities as well as managing the change programme.

Organisational cultures can be changed, but it requires effective leadership and a well-managed process. Attention must be paid throughout changes to maintaining current performance and improving it to work towards the organisation's future potential. Effective leaders will celebrate success and acknowledge what has been achieved; this is an often neglected area in change processes, yet can make an enormous difference to the individuals concerned.

Perceptions of leadership behaviour | JOURNAL ARTICLE

The article describes a study which focused on how a leader's gender, self-monitoring ability and the organisational context related to differences in the leader's self-perceptions and the perceptions of group members of how the leader worked. They used 49 male and 49 female leaders from educational and industrial settings, along with members of their work teams.

Results indicated that women leaders in industrial settings, such as banking, accounting, or manufacturing, experienced greater differences in self- and subordinate perception, than did female leaders in education, or male leaders in industry. Differences were also bigger for high self-monitoring female leaders in industry. The writers claim this research has 'important implications for understanding issues involving the effectiveness of female leaders ... The fact that the greatest discrepancies were found for women in non-traditional leadership roles, especially high self-monitoring women, is very significant for understanding the barriers faced by women in leadership' (p. 240).

These discrepancies might then result in reduced perceptions of the leader's effectiveness, which might suggest that 'female leaders working in non-traditional roles ... may also be perceived as less effective'. To counter this problem, the authors suggest that upward feedback 'may help reduce discrepant perceptions by redirecting [the female leader's] focus of attention to their subordinates' perceptions and expectations' [rather than their own], which could 'improve the leader's effectiveness'. They conclude, 'When training women in some leadership behaviours, it may also be advantageous for the trainer to advise those in non-traditional settings of the possible side-effects of their behaviour'(p. 241).

Becker, J., Ayman, R. and Korabik, K. 'Discrepancies in self/subordinates' perceptions of leadership behavior: leader's gender, organizational context, and leader's self-monitoring', *Group and Organization Management*, 2002, Vol. 27, No. 2, June, pp 226–44.

The equality rule   JOURNAL ARTICLE

This research looks at how the role of leader or follower influences a group, in particular looking at the use of the equality rule (dividing resources equally). Different positions in the hierarchy seem to bring about different role expectations of how individuals ought to behave. Leaders believe they should act responsibly, yet think they deserve certain privileges from the allocation situation. The researcher predicted that leaders would allocate more resources to themselves than to followers. Three studies showed that leaders did allocate more than their fair share to themselves. The results are discussed in terms of leadership and some practical implications are suggested.

DeCremer, D. 'How self-conception may lead to inequality: effect of hierarchical roles on the equality rule in organizational resource-sharing tasks', *Group and Organization Management*, 2003, Vol. 28, No. 2, June, pp 282–302.

Conflict management   JOURNAL ARTICLE

This article claims, 'In today's workplace communication is key, collaboration crucial and teamwork a top management buzzword. And rightly so, for these facets encourage knowledge sharing, co-operation and a joint sense of purpose. However, such an increase in interpersonal relationships all too often creates an unwanted and often unmanaged side-effect: conflict.'

The article states that 65 per cent of performance problems result from tense relationships. Managers who used to just 'tolerate' peers are now required to co-operate and co-ordinate with other departments, which can lead to differences of opinion, which, unless dealt with promptly, can become destructive.

The leadership models proposed and examined in this article are quite straightforward and give 'tips for managers', who have to intervene when conflict occurs. Whilst this article can be difficult to read, it is well researched with important implications for managers.

'Conflict management: keep disagreements healthy and productive', *Development and Learning in Organizations*, 2003, Volume 17, No. 3, pp 23–26.

Chapter 4

Working with others: teamwork, groups and group dynamics

The nature of groups

Earlier (p. 98) we looked at the government-implemented strategy Partnerships with People which named 'five paths to success': shared goals, culture, learning, effort and information. Evidently the emphasis is on *shared* input and results, which means all members of the group pull together towards their shared goals. Teamworking motivates employees and multi-skilling involves everybody in all aspects of the business.

Groups and teams

Charles Handy (1993) defines a group as any collection of people who perceive themselves to be a group. Handy therefore uses the subjective feeling of belonging to define the group. Banyard and Grayson (2000) support this notion in saying, 'To belong to a group means to adjust to other people and to conform to at least some of the social norms of the group.'

When people feel they are part of a group they begin to share characteristics of that group, such as the name of the group, the dress of the group, or the shared values and language. Aronson (1999) states, 'if we find a person or group attractive or appealing in some way, we will be inclined to accept influence from that person or group and adopt similar values and attitudes ... simply to be like that person or group'.

Groups obviously perform important functions for both organisations and for individuals, but when we talk about groups we need to define whether we are referring to formal groups, those, for example, set up by the organisation to carry out specific tasks, or to informal groups, which arise out of chance or spontaneous interactions.

Informal and formal groups

Formal groups

Formal groups are those created for a specific purpose: a work group, a project team, a football team. Formal groups will have specific responsibilities. In an organisation they might be responsible for implementing a new production process or producing a specific report. Temporary work groups may be set up, then disbanded once their project is complete; permanent work groups tend to be present in most organisations or establishments: the finance department or the personnel department. Some groups are enjoyed by their members, whilst some are intensely disliked. An employee might enjoy being part of the firm's football team, but hate being part of his current project group at work, as he does not particularly like the people or the task he's currently working with.

Formal groups tend to have clear structures, aims and distinct rules or schedules.

Likerts (1961) 'link-pin' role (see Internal networks, p. 82) joins the different groups together. A link-pin is someone who belongs to two groups within the organisation and performs a role which links the groups together.

Informal groups

Informal groups come into being by chance, rather than being planned or specifically created. Most formal groups will contain many informal groups. The company you work for or the college you attend are both formal groups, set up to produce, or educate that group of people recruited to it. Within those formal groups though, will be groups of friends, who usually sit in the staff room together, or who met in the pub, or in the dinner queue, or who share common interests outside of work or college. Informal groups can provide invaluable support for formal groups. Groups of friends within a larger, workplace group can support each other emotionally and socially, and informal groups strengthen the feeling of belonging and cohesiveness.

Purpose of teams

What is the point of having a 'team'? We have all heard the phrase 'two heads are better than one', or 'a problem shared is a problem halved'. Teams give an opportunity to share ideas, strengths, and a variety of viewpoints or experiences.

A team is much more than just a group. A team will share a common purpose and goal. Team members will share an identity or name as well as having common values and beliefs. A team is a group of people who will work together to achieve that common goal or aim. Teams, unlike groups, share a mutual responsibility (to get the ball in the opponent's net), a common commitment ('let's beat them!') and reciprocity ('quick, pass it to me'). Team leaders seek to develop a group of individuals so they become a cohesive and productive unit which relies on contributions from all members of the team.

Dumaine (1994) identified five types of team:

Management teams

These are teams of managers who represent different functions such as production or sales. They co-ordinate the work of other teams within the organisation.

Problem-solving teams

Employees who form a team to work together to solve specific problems. They are temporary teams who disband once their project is complete.

Work teams

Increasing in popularity, these teams carry out the day-to-day activities of the organisation, working under their own authority and direction. When given this level of power or authority they are known as self-managed teams.

Quality circles

These are groups of workers and supervisory staff who work together to discuss workplace problems and propose solutions.

Virtual teams

These are composed of groups of workers who participate in group activity and discussion, but instead of doing this as a face-to-face group, they communicate via computer.

Dumaine proposes that one of the most common misuses of teams is where the wrong teams are used for the wrong job, or where teams are used in situations which might be more effectively dealt with by just one or two individuals.

Delayering and downsizing in recent years has led to many employees being involved more and more in decision-making teams that used to be the responsibility of middle managers. The essence of effective teamworking lies in the assumption that a group of people will perform better than would all the individuals independently. The idea is a good one, but for it to work in practice the team needs to operate effectively and cohesively. We will look therefore at the processes involved in teamworking and at the characteristics of an effective team.

Teams and team building

Team building is the process used to enable a group of people to learn to work together to reach their goal. The main areas necessary for team building are:

♦ to clarify the goals
♦ to identify barriers to those goals
♦ to address those problems, remove the barriers and enable the goals to be achieved.

Organisational team building is team building on a grand scale. It is difficult for individuals other than senior managers to make a real impact on the corporate culture, but an effective team can have a huge impact. In the process of team building individuals' behaviour and attitudes tend to be 'moulded' to fit in with those of the organisation.

There are several aspects to consider in the process of team building. Team members need to be helped to:

♦ identify their purpose and shared objectives
♦ develop team confidence and competence
♦ develop interpersonal skills to enable this: listening, supporting and encouraging skills
♦ develop collective problem-solving skills
♦ develop appropriate team rewards
♦ build goodwill and trust between members
♦ recognise personal strengths and weaknesses, both technical and personal, and help individuals to develop their strengths for the good of themselves and the team.

Many approaches can be taken to team building: meetings to discuss objectives and methods, or outdoor activities weekends to build team collaboration, which are becoming increasingly popular. Typical stages in the team-building process are shown in Figure 4.43.

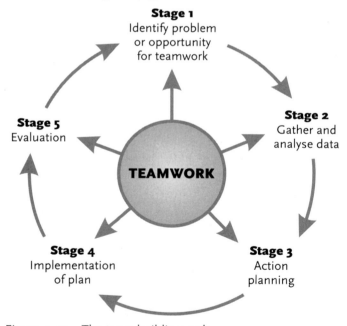

Figure 4.43   The team-building cycle

✳ Selecting team members

The process of team selection involves identifying what contributions can be made to the team by potential team members and which members would pull together and work as a team. Choosing individuals

CASE STUDY

Why bother with teamwork?

Staff at the PeachyTin fruit canning plant have worked for years under a traditional hierarchical structure. The managers decided corporate goals, decided how to achieve them and told employees how they wanted it done. Employees got on with the job. Employees got paid and went home. The managers achieved their goals. Everyone was happy.

Over the years, fruit canning has changed. New laws have been introduced and new standards have to be adhered to. New technology has resulted in the canning process becoming mainly computerised. The assembly line is operated by computers and robots, not people. Because all the control of machinery and equipment is done at the shop floor level, the ground-level employees have the responsibility for making it all work. Employees are finding more and more that they need to share their knowledge: of systems, of technology, of standards, and so on. To do this they need teams of people to share knowledge and rely on each other to 'keep the wheels turning'. The managers still know what they want to achieve, but lack the technical know-how to keep the machinery running smoothly.

ACTIVITY

1   Why does the hierarchical top-down approach not work so well any more?

2   How can PeachyTin managers help their employees develop the new skills required to deal with the new technology?

3   What skills will the PeachyTin employees need to develop to work together and deal with the responsibility of keeping the wheels turning?

178

with expert technology skills, or skill in the required task, or with the highest level of intelligence, would not necessarily constitute a successful team. It would merely constitute a group of individuals with different skills. To make a team, leaders need to choose individuals who can be relied on to listen to each other's ideas, to motivate and encourage others, to share their own ideas and knowledge and to contribute to decision making.

The aim of all team development activity is to achieve a functional and effective team, whose members concentrate on the task, how to achieve it, and how to maintain the full and effective participation of all of the team members. In this way the group achieve synergy, which can be defined as 'the action of two or more substances or organisms, which achieves a result greater than the sum of the effects of individual substances or organisms effects'.

This simply means that individuals working in teams can achieve more than they would as individuals. It is this result that makes working in teams beneficial to the individuals involved.

Team roles

People working together will adopt particular roles within the group. For example, one may step in as leader and one may act as timekeeper. Social psychologists have suggested that roles form when recurring behaviours prove useful to the team. An individual might act spontaneously in a particular way which proves helpful and which can be employed by other individuals to gain similar results. This behaviour then becomes standardised as a role.

Imposed and emergent roles

Imposed roles are those where somebody is appointed – by management or by election – to a particular role. Role allocation might be based on particular criteria such as technical expertise or formal qualifications. Emergent roles come about more by chance or they just happen. Informal leadership, for example, can occur spontaneously in a project team. How many times have you been in a group where one or more people have taken on the role of leader? Others in the group will follow these informal leaders if they appear to fit the role.

Task and maintenance functions

Usually some members of a team will take on task functions and others will take on maintenance functions.

Task functions help the group get things done efficiently. Task functions are those such as:

♦ clarifying goals and suggesting objectives
♦ seeking information and other's opinions
♦ summarising ideas and suggesting ways to progress
♦ keeping the group on target
♦ evaluating ideas and suggestions.

Maintenance functions are those which:

♦ monitor the group
♦ support other members
♦ reconcile disagreements
♦ reduce tension, perhaps by making others laugh
♦ suggest compromises.

How effective a team will be depends on an appropriate mix of roles, and individuals with the requisite skills and personal qualities.

Belbin's theory

Dr R. Meredith Belbin's *Management Teams: Why They Succeed or Fail* (Heinemann, 1981) is claimed to be one of the most imaginative and influential books in management research. Belbin studied the way people behaved when put into groups, or syndicates, at Henley Management College. Their various projects were scored, enabling the success of different teams to be measured. He identified eight different roles that members could fill and found that the winning teams were those whose members covered all these different roles.

♦ The chair: co-ordinates the team efforts and ensures all resources are used effectively in achieving goals.
♦ The shaper: sets the objectives and priorities and guides the team towards completion of the task.
♦ The plant: the creative, 'ideas' person.
♦ The monitor evaluator: is shrewd and analytical and analyses problems and evaluates progress.

- The resource investigator: is extrovert and good at making outside contacts and reporting on developments outside the organisation.
- The company worker: practical, loyal and task orientated.
- The teamworker: caring and very person orientated. Keeps the team together and improves communications within the team.
- The finisher: maintains momentum and ensures completion of the task.

These roles are not personality types, just people's preferences for the way they like to operate when they are doing a shared task. You choose your role, depending on the way you like to work and the group's need, or the demands of the particular project.

ACTIVITY

Gather together a group of people, for example at college, in the pub or at home, and give them a task to complete in, say, 20 minutes. If you cannot get a group together, think about a group you have been in recently. Observe the members of the group as they complete the task.

1 Can you identify these particular roles being acted out?

2 Which role comes most naturally to you?

3 Were leaders or other roles allocated or elected?

4 Did a leader (or other roles) emerge?

5 Why do you think this was?

The purpose of roles in team building

Using roles to build teams has a number of merits:

- it gives members the tools they need for better performance
- it helps them respect people with different aptitudes and skills

- if members understand each other, they usually communicate more effectively
- effective communication means they make less errors
- achievement usually increases motivation.

Belbin's work has provided a clearer insight into team relationships and the need for clarification of roles. Following from Belbin's work, Charles Margerison and Dick McCann (2000) developed the **team management wheel** in 1984 (see Figure 4.44). The idea of this is that at the centre of all management teams is the fundamental fact that people like to work in different ways. In 1985 they came up with nine possible team roles instead of the original eight featured in the wheel. Some are natural roles and some are roles that a person can learn to use if necessary. Some roles may be very hard for a particular person to adopt.

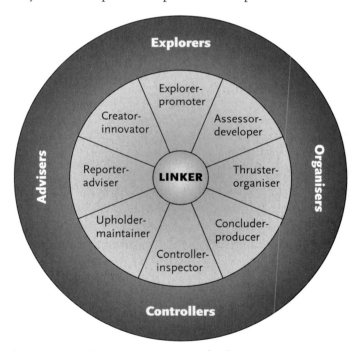

Figure 4.44 Team management wheel

They try to explain what the different preferred styles are and how they relate to one another. McCann's ideas, which derive from neurolinguistic programming, do not relate, as some think, to a theory of personality types, but to people's working preferences. The roles they identified are as shown in the wheel.

Reporter-adviser

This person gathers and gives out information. These people enjoy gathering all sorts of information and giving it back to others in ways which they can understand. Often it can be a start for launching a new product or service, where information is sought about competition. These people are valuable support members of a team. They are not particularly good organisers, but they will make sure the job gets done, and gets done properly.

Creator-innovator

Innovation is about new ideas and thinking up new ways of doing things. Innovators tend to be independent people who enjoy experimenting and persisting with their ideas, no matter how diverse they may be from current methods. Research and development units often house these people and innovation is an important element of most organisations. Failure to think of new ideas or new ways of working usually lead eventually to organisational failure.

Explorer-promoter

The explorer-promoter is involved in promotion and marketing new ideas. These people will look at what the competition is doing and compare ideas. They enjoy looking for new opportunities and persuading others that these are worthwhile. Information about new market possibilities might be gathered and it is the promoter's job to sell the idea to management and to gather all the resources needed to get the project started. They are capable of promoting ideas, even if they are not very good at organising the work processes.

Assessor-developer

When an idea has been sold to management, development needs to take place. These people are the ones who will find out whether the market needs this new product. The new product is subjected to analytical processes and developed to the stage where it is likely to sell. Creativity is needed here but the developer also needs to have respect for the realities of the marketplace. Once they have set the wheels in motion, they will leave it to somebody else to produce, and move on to another development project.

Thruster-organiser

This involves getting the job done. Deadlines are established and benchmarks set, then the organiser gets the team moving to achieve the goals of the team and the organisation. These people set up a structure and allocate resources so that the product or scheme will work. The 'cut and thrust' that is often associated with this role requires tough, go-getting people whom others may find it difficult to deal with on occasions because of the hard decisions and pushing that are often required.

Concluder-producer

Actually produces the goods and feels fulfilled if quotas and targets are met. Producing is usually at the centre of most organisations. The regular production of the goods or services brings in the profits. People working in production may spend most of their time in repetitive working but gain pride in a job well done and don't mind the repetition. The important thing for them is to use their skills to the full.

Controller-inspector

Likes to ensure that the goods being produced on a regular basis are of the required standard or quality. Maintaining high quality and accurate records is essential. This is the inspecting type of work characteristically carried out by accountants and quality controllers. Procedures are set out and monitored and have to comply with safety, legal and other regulatory guidelines.

Upholder-maintainer

Maintains the social and physical aspects of the organisation. They ensure that a sound structure is maintained so that the team can work to maximum efficiency. This role is associated with the support staff and background work which ensure that organisational requirements can be met quickly and efficiently. The emphasis is on standards, quality and codes of behaviour at work.

Linker

This role is central to the success of all teams. Someone has to co-ordinate all the other team members to ensure that there is appropriate co-operation and interaction between members. Managers should always be able to perform well as linkers, as the linking function can mean the difference between effective and ineffective teamwork. Teams may have members who are highly skilled and individually capable but if the linker is not co-ordinating their activities, the team as a whole is likely to fail.

Most managers find the wheel a useful representation of a high-performing team, whether these teams are whole organisations, or smaller project groups.

Stages in team development

Katzenbach and Smith (1993) define a team as, 'a small number of people with complementary skills who are committed to a common purpose, performance goals and an approach for which they hold themselves accountable'. They say that a group is not a team until it satisfies certain requirements, and make the point that managers need to be able to understand the ingredients of a team if they are to be successful in managing their organisation. They used a team performance curve to demonstrate the development stages of a team (see Figure 4.45).

The **loose working group** is a collection of individuals who have no real need to be part of a team. These individuals all produce something which helps the team effort, but they do this independently of the group. They perform no better and no worse whether they are members of the team or not.

The **pseudo team** consists of individuals who work better alone than as part of a team. They have no common sense of purpose in their tasks, so confusion arises as to what each should be doing as part of a team effort. This is a frustrating way of working as team members feel very much in the dark as to what they are doing and why.

The **potential team** share a clear performance requirement. They are looking to impact on the group achievements through individual efforts. They realise they can improve their performance as a team and they wish to do so. They tend to lack the focus and discipline required, though, to be an effective team. They still need to establish who is accountable for what, so that the team effort has all the necessary ingredients input. This is a management challenge present in many organisations; the manpower is available, the team has great potential; they just need organising properly.

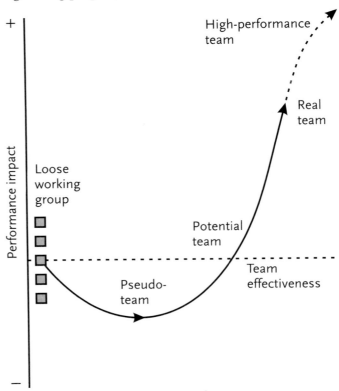

Figure 4.45   A team performance curve

The **real team** is the people actually working together and functioning effectively as a team.

The **high-performance team**, as well as meeting all the requirements to be a real team, also shares a goal to aim for team growth and development, which brings personal development and success for its individual members as well. The commitment of the members to achieving this growth means they can outperform other teams consistently.

Another approach to team development stages was taken by Tuckman and Jensen (1997), who described four phases of team development (see Figure 4.46).

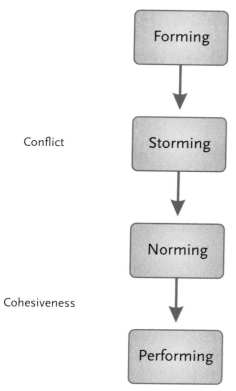

Conflict

Cohesiveness

Figure 4.46   Four phases of team development

Forming

A group of individuals come together and attempt to establish a purpose for their group. How is it going to operate? How long will it need to operate? Who will do what and when? They look at how others operate and what contribution each will make.

Storming

The group's members exchange ideas and try to agree objectives and a strategy for achieving them. This tends to be the conflict stage, at which consensus of opinions is challenged. Hostility can develop as individuals disagree on the best way forward. Different sub-groups may form and there can be resistance to leadership.

Norming

Norms and standards are established as the group begins to share and agree on ideas. There is reconciliation of conflict and members start to co-operate.

Performing

The group becomes a team, working effectively and productively together. Efforts are directed to task and objectives rather than social relations, and a pattern of working is established.

Changes to the nature or purpose of the group will bring about repeats of these development stages. This means a group can pass through these stages many times during its existence. Early stages tend to be dominated by several individuals (emergent leaders, perhaps) until leadership is established. Care must be taken at this stage not to ignore the voices and ideas of the less forceful members of the team. Very task-oriented groups may make good initial progress, but toleration of conflict and social relations within the group need to be developed to build a team spirit which will hold the team together at difficult times. Conflict behaviours can actually assist the process of group development and, in the long term, improve the group's cohesion and performance.

In addition to the identified stages of team development, there are two types of process involved in any group dynamic: the task and maintenance processes (see p. 179). Within an effective group, leadership in task and maintenance processes will be shared throughout the group, though often groups may choose one member as the task leader. A description is given in Figure 4.47 of some leadership activities associated with task and maintenance activities which can aid group development.

New contacts and the influence of others will broaden a person's views and possibly change certain aspects of how they behave: the way they dress, talk, or join in. We all conform to some degree to our situation and surroundings to try and fit in.

Aronson (1999) defines conformity as, 'a change in a person's behaviour or opinions as a result of real or imagined pressure from a person or group of people'.

Task leadership	Maintenance leadership
1 Giving or seeking information or opinions. This starts up the meeting for the task in hand.	1 Encouraging. Showing interest or agreeing; listening and drawing speakers out.
2 Elaborating on other people's arguments; giving examples, suggesting how an idea might work in practice.	2 Harmonising and conciliating. Tactfully resolving conflicts.
3 Co-ordinating contributions: 'I think Fred and Sue are trying to say that ...'	3 Soothing members. When ideas are rejected or criticised, 'soothing' can help prevent withdrawal.
4 Co-ordinating the meeting. Frequently summarising progress and restating objectives.	4 Accepting people's ideas. Showing they have value and are worthy of discussion.

Figure 4.47   Task and maintenance leadership

Team building

Training people in teamworking can be done using two basic approaches; experiential learning and counselling.

Experiential learning

This is learning by doing; it may be by actually carrying out team tasks, or by role play and case studies. Usually it will involve carrying out a number of tasks, which can only be completed if all those involved use the necessary team skills. After each task has been performed, the trainer, or leader, will help the group analyse how well they did to achieve (or not) the required task. The tasks need to be taken seriously by members if experiential

learning is to work. If there are no real consequences to failure or success, then members of the team may not involve themselves at a committed enough level to really learn from the experience. This is one reason why managers are increasingly using the services of outdoor activities courses to build team cohesion. Building a raft to carry the team and their lunch packs down an icy river is more real than building one of paper in a classroom. If the consequences of failure are real, they are more likely to be remembered.

CASE STUDY

Core Solutions

Core Solutions is a national partnership of counselling and development organisations based in the Scottish Highlands. It uses consultancy counselling and outdoor activities to provide an individually tailored service to develop boards of directors. Building trust within the team is central to its activities. It argues that trust is the basis of open and collaborative relationships. It holds teams together and reduces resistance to change. Transferable team skills are now essential if one wants to get things done. Bonding people together into teams is no longer a luxury but a necessity.

ACTIVITY

1 Why do people who normally work in teams need to engage also in team-building activities?

2 What do you think the advantages are of developing experiential teamworking in outdoor activities as opposed to simulated games in indoor workshop sessions?

Counselling approach

This is used more often where senior management teams rely on a trainer to act as consultant and mentor to the team, working with the team at the same time as training them.

Team identity

Creating a team identity is an important part of giving the team members a feeling of belonging and in developing cohesiveness within the group. Teams gain an identity when they are distinctive. Many argue that premier league football teams have a distinctive identity not only because of their team colours, but also because of their obvious loyalty to the team and their pride in a good team effort. Some organisations have initiation ceremonies and tests to incorporate new members.

Team cohesion tends to be more obvious and work better when:

♦ members have similar interests, attitudes and backgrounds
♦ members have the same aims or objectives for their group
♦ they acknowledge and respect other's worth to the team
♦ the team is not too big to lose the camaraderie it has developed
♦ they are a group which needs to stick together against the opposition
♦ they can rise above temporary problems and occasional failures and use them for improving performance in the future
♦ they can share every success as a team result, even if one person helped more than others on any particular occasion.

Team cohesiveness is built further if the team is effectively rewarded for success and the air of rivalry against other teams is maintained. Teams that stick together for a long time are often more loyal to each other and more cohesive as a group, than new or relatively new teams.

CASE STUDY

Hartson joins 'The Crazy Gang'

The Wimbledon football team is famous for its initiation ceremonies in order to become a member of 'The Crazy Gang'. When John Hartson joined Wimbledon from West Ham in January 1999 he was given a typical welcome. First his new team mates hung his designer tracksuit out of the changing room window at the club's training ground and set it ablaze. Next he was thrown into a puddle of water. It was not the sort of treatment most £7.5 million strikers would have expected, but Hartson took it in good heart. 'I am up for a laugh and maybe if a new player signs next week I will be getting involved,' he said.

ACTIVITY

1 What are the benefits of building team identity?

2 What characteristics do team players need to survive?

3 What is the function of initiation ceremonies? Describe any initiation ceremonies of which you are personally aware.

4 What would you ask new members of *your* team or group to do, if you had one? How would this help them become part of the team?

Team loyalty

Loyal team members value and enjoy the privilege of being a part of that team. The more team members show loyalty to each other and conform to team norms, the more likely they are to be a successful unit. Failures can often result in individual team members being blamed for problems and this can lead to disloyalty and a lack of direction for the group. If members of the team accept that nobody can get it right all the time, and show support and tolerance as well as unity, then the team is more likely to survive occasional hitches in performance. Strong support for others and a sense of togetherness leads to strong group norms of behaviour and a keen sense of bonding between individuals.

Individuals who have to work hard to get into a team are usually more committed and loyal to it. Rivalry for a place on the team, as well as rivalry against other teams, is a strong foundation for group loyalty.

Rivalry with other teams is probably the strongest bonding agent for a team. In their desire to beat the opponents no matter what, individuals will work hard together to overcome the competition and take great pride in a positive result.

Team spirit develops and strengthens over time, so the longer a team is together, the more close-knit it tends to become. The more successes the team shares, the more close they are likely to become too, as winning is their reward for hard work. The more they win, the more cohesive the team becomes. The more cohesive the team, the more likely it is to succeed. Success breeds success.

Commitment to shared beliefs

The longer individuals are members of a team, the more likely they are to adopt the norms of behaviour of that team, and the more likely they are to adopt team values and beliefs. As Banyard and Grayson (2000) said, 'To belong to a group means to adjust to other people and to conform to at least some of the social norms of the group.'

People begin to think in a similar way to other members of the team, they may dress like them and use common language, idiosyncrasies or 'jargon'. Some people talk of **tribal features** to describe the way members take on the cultural values of a particular group of people. They become increasingly needy of

the company of their own tribe or cultural group, and feel more and more hostile towards members of opposing groups or tribes.

Teams rely heavily on each other to arrive at their goal or objective. The team helps them to achieve what they cannot achieve alone. This interdependence on each other means mutually beneficial behaviour is vital for a successful team. Modern organisations place great importance on **employee involvement** (EI) to foster this attitude of shared beliefs and aims. EI groups have been developed in many companies to discuss work problems and how to address them, in a similar way that 'quality circles' meet and plan actions *as* a team, *for* the team. This involvement of employees not only enables teams to look at problems at production level, but also gives team members a feeling of belonging to and contributing to the organisation as a whole. These types of approach tend to work particularly well when employees have direct reward for success, in the form of, say, shares in the profits. If they know they will get a share of the success, they will feel motivated to work hard towards that success.

Self-managing teams

Self-managing teams are often a part of the EI organisation's way of doing things. Self-managed teams have the authority to manage themselves and thereby achieve their objectives through their own ideas and efforts. In self-managed teams, members usually:

◆ decide for themselves who does what
◆ can multi-skill and take on more than one role at once
◆ work out their own time plans and deadlines
◆ help and train each other to become proficient at all aspects of the team's responsibilities
◆ evaluate and suggest improvements for their own, each other's and the team's performance
◆ are jointly responsible and accountable for the performance of the whole team.

If team members have played a large part in deciding the objectives, they can usually more easily clarify them to each other: clarification of objectives being an essential element of successful team working. With no clear aim, there can be no clear result.

Multi-disciplinary teams

Colin Hastings together with Peter Bixby and Rani Chaudhry-Lawton (1994) look at teamworking, in particular at 'new ways of using old teams and new ways of using new kinds of teams'. They discuss 'superteams' which need a strong relationship between the team and the organisational vision. They say the vision is all-important as, 'a powerful and vivid picture of a desired state of affairs that is widely shared and understood and which acts like a magnet to draw people towards it'.

Multi-disciplinary teams, as the name suggests, do not concentrate on just one area: they look at all aspects of the organisation's work and produce innovative ideas and suggestions for improvements. Operational problems are examined across the board; different departments are all involved in looking at the same operational problems. Different work groups look at policy and organisational practices as a whole, rather than just from the point of view of one department. The aim of these teams is to resolve issues such as what new areas the organisation might look to diversify into to enable future growth plans, and what structures would be needed to carry out those objectives. They would be concerned, for example, with improving customer service and increasing productivity and growth at the same time.

Team decision making   **JOURNAL ARTICLE**

This article looks at how managers make decisions and formulate strategies, using cognitive models of decision making. It examines individual levels of information processing and how this is applied to team decision making. The authors suggest that, 'cognitive schemas and team-decision-making structure will focus decision-maker attention on different types of information for different categories of decisions.' The conclusions drawn suggest similarities and differences in the circumstances which bring about tactical or strategic decisions.

Lant, T. and Hewlin, P. 'Information cues and decision making: the effects of learning, momentum, and social comparison in competing teams', *Group and Organization Management*, 2002, Vol. 27, No. 3, September, pp 374–407.

Team dynamics

Building a cohesive and supportive team means the organisation can enjoy higher productivity and have good morale, leading to better results. Many team-building exercises have been used to form the ideal team. Behind any approach should be the desire to understand individuals and their reasons for behaving as they do, and their motivation to be involved in a team. Understanding individuals in a team will help managers to organise the team and build on its strengths.

Edgar Schein (1988) describes how new recruits to a group will have various concerns:

♦ How will they interact with other members of the group?
♦ Will they be allowed to participate very much?
♦ Will they have any control over the team?
♦ Will they have the same goals and expectations as other team members?
♦ Will they be able to work with the current processes?

Schein recommends that team leaders ensure clarity of individual roles and overall objectives, as without these ambiguity in requirements of any individual in the team can lead to problems, especially where team members are new to the group. He identifies three types of reactions which people might display which will lead to *ineffective* contributions to the team effort.

The **tough battler** is so anxious to make an early impression on the team that she or he is forthright and aggressive from the start, trying to establish their place and get noticed in the team. This approach can upset the harmony of the group. It can make other people feel that they, too, have to become aggressive and forceful to be heard.

Objective thinkers try to link their personal aims and objectives with the team aims and objectives in a way that 'matches' them to the team goals. This may not be as straightforward as they hope and until they can match themselves in with the team purpose, they will not contribute as well as they might to the group effort.

Friendly helpers want to be liked and will do anything necessary to achieve this. They concentrate on making friends and getting involved in friendly groups. They put so much effort into this initially that they miss the point of the team objectives and push their energies elsewhere, rather than on the task in hand.

Even when teams are long established, role ambiguity can occur and confuse the various members of the team who are unsure of quite what is expected of them. New products, new systems, new management, can always produce role ambiguity and create anxiety, leading to the responses mentioned above, even among well-established teams. Role negotiation is therefore an important part of managing ongoing team dynamics, in order to clarify, or re-clarify, roles within the team. Individuals need to establish what their role is and how this fits in with other team members' roles, to work towards the team objectives and goals.

Group norms

People who live in Western societies such as the USA and the UK have traditionally tended to define themselves as independent entities with individual, personal aims and goals. Eastern Asian societies such as Japan and China have a tendency as individuals to view themselves more in the context of their interdependence with others, such as family and social groups. Recent psychological research, however, has suggested that how we tend to define ourselves – whether we think of ourselves as an individual or a part of the family, society, or the workplace – is due to the way we identify with particular social groups.

Jetten *et al.* (2002) researched group identity and individualism in both Eastern and Western cultures and interestingly found that even though some people do show more individualist behaviour, this may actually be because of their level of conformity with their group (rather than 'real' individualism). Often members of a group do not realise how much they take on the identity of the group, because conformity to the group becomes a natural, unconscious acceptance of a particular way of behaving. Sometimes the most fundamental foundations of a group are the informal, unwritten rules that people abide by without necessarily realising it: the group norms. These norms can include such things as going to the pub on a Friday lunchtime with colleagues, having a collection for a colleague who is leaving, or working extra hard together to get a project finished on time. There are two types of group norm to consider.

Proscriptive norms are the accepted rules of the workplace: you do not sit in the boss's chair when she's out of her office; you do not hug your lecturer when you walk into your first lecture; you would not normally arrive to work at a bank in shorts and T-shirt.

Prescriptive norms are the things most group members should or will do. Be polite to each other and customers, keep their desk tidy, make proper use of resources and limit personal phone calls to the absolutely necessary or emergency.

These norms develop in organisations and groups over time and just become the accepted way of doing things. They may develop over time as just the way things are: we call the boss Mr Smith but the lady who brings sandwiches round is called Gladys. These norms may come from 'outside' the group – a new recruit will probably still do things pretty much the way he was used to doing it in his last organisation, unless other members of the group give explicit instructions.

Sometimes particular events or actions will become the norm in future: 'ever since we bought a wedding present for Sue, we have a collection for everybody getting married now'. Reporting of a particular event in the press may mean that a group in the public eye will not perform that particular act in the future to avoid adverse publicity. If the local rugby team is noted for bad behaviour after a match, it may confine its drinking and celebratory activities to private areas not accessible to the public or press, and this will become the norm for the future.

The way the majority behave will be picked up by other members of the team and they will usually behave in like fashion. If everybody is staying late to finish a job, it is unlikely that one member will feel comfortable leaving early. They will usually conform to the behaviour of the other members.

These norms reflect the formal culture of the organisation and form an important part of the cultural framework of the company. Formal rules and behavioural guidelines will be an integral part of this informal framework and formal disciplinary actions will be brought upon those who fail to comply with regulations.

Decision-making behaviour

Vroom and Yetton (1973) examined how leaders can behave in certain circumstances, depending on the level of involvement of the other team members in the decision-making process. With the development of self-directed teams, decision making often happens in a different context to that which has traditionally been the way. Self-directed teams have responsibility for managing themselves and as such make decisions for themselves rather than waiting for instructions from management. Decision making at a team level needs to be realistic and economical: could the decision be made as easily by an individual? Does it need a team effort?

Vroom and Yetton cited three main criteria for measuring how effective decision making is:

♦ the quality of the ultimate decision
♦ how long it took to reach the decision
♦ how acceptable the decision is to those who will be implementing it.

Decisions taken by a team can have a higher level of acceptance and commitment to make it work, because the members made the decisions themselves. It can, however, take a team longer than an individual to reach a decision. Schein (1988) identified six methods that teams use to make decisions:

♦ Unanimity: every member of the group agrees on the same course of action.
♦ Consensus: not everyone agrees initially on a particular course of action, but everybody agrees to try it.
♦ Majority rule: a vote is taken and the majority vote wins.
♦ Minority rule: a small group decides the course of action to be taken by all members, via domineering decision-making behaviour.
♦ Authority rule: the boss or one in charge of the group makes the decision.
♦ Lack of response: a particular course of action is chosen simply because nobody else will discuss it or suggest any other course of action.

ACTIVITY

Assemble a group of people, the larger the better, and show them an envelope which contains a certain sum of money, say £10. If, as a group, they can decide unanimously on a suitable charity to receive the money, you will give the money to that charity. They have five minutes.

Observe and make notes on the group in action.

Some groups will probably decide quickly and take the money. Other groups, especially those of large numbers or conflicting personal interests, are likely to argue more and take much longer. This is not just about decision making, it is also about where individual roles within a group become important. If nobody adopts the role of timekeeper, the group may well run out of time and lose the chance of getting the money at all. If nobody takes charge and forces a quick decision, it may be too late. What if some members disagree with the final decision? Are there grumblings about unfairness, or do all members accept the overall decision and commit to it?

Obviously some methods will be far better than others. Authority decisions might be made quickly, but fail to involve everybody in the decision-making process, so may not carry the same weight of commitment to the task than a unanimous decision. On the other hand, the more people that are involved in making a decision, the longer it may take to make. It may even be too late to use it if it takes too long to agree.

If decisions are made purely through lack of response or interest there will be little commitment from other members to the decision.

The same could be argued for a minority rule or an authority rule, where the decision is quick and easy, but leaves out many participants in the process. A majority rule, whilst more fair, still excludes some people and where conflict arises votes can be cast in favour of a person rather than an idea. Decisions made by consensus can be better for commitment from the group, and they do at least get other members of the team to accept and try out others' ideas. It can be argued that an unanimous decision is the best option whenever possible, as everyone is involved, everyone accepts it and everyone can work with it in a committed way.

Schermerhorn *et al.* (1997) posited the following ideas for achieving group consensus:

♦ Present the case clearly and logically and listen to other group members' responses and observe their reactions.
♦ Don't change your mind just to keep others happy or get to a quick decision.
♦ Don't try to reach a quick decision just to reduce conflict, for example by tossing a coin or taking the majority vote.
♦ Get everybody involved. Ask for, and respect, all contributions. Different ideas, or arguments for and against those ideas, can bring valuable experience into the equation and draw attention to important facts.
♦ Don't assume there must be losers in the decision-making process. Persist until there is a general agreement with one way of doing things.

Dysfunctional teams

A dysfunctional team is one in which the team members fail to work effectively together. That may be because they have not yet arrived at an agreed common goal, or because they are simply not working well together to achieve a goal. Often it can be seen that one or more team members are not:

♦ contributing towards achieving the goal
♦ supporting other team members
♦ building any sense of commitment to one another
♦ developing a feeling of interdependence.

Possibly they lack a clear objective, or are confused about the task or the processes required, either of themselves or of the group. Clashes in personality, or the inability of some members to cope well with change, can also upset the balance and prohibit proper contributions from all members.

Dysfunctional teams inevitably lead to wasted resources and time, and to demotivation of team members. Investing time initially in helping teams get off to a good start is an obvious way to try and prevent dysfunctional teams.

Rescuing a dysfunctional team

What happens if a team is falling apart? Team building can be reintroduced to try and put the team back together, or managers could adopt the following approaches:

♦ Help team members recognise and anticipate dysfunctional behaviours and agree as a team how to deal with such events.
♦ Provide training for effective team working and devise a system for managing conflict.
♦ Ensure teams are appropriately put together and ensure they have clear goals and everyone understands his or her role.
♦ Let team members have responsibility for successfully developing their team.
♦ Monitor progress and identify problems in time to deal with them.
♦ Encourage team feedback.

Team members themselves could also help rescue the situation, by following these procedures:

♦ Agree common goals.
♦ Get to know each other well and establish a team identity.
♦ Establish the ground rules; what is acceptable and what is not.

- Clarify each member's role.
- Give feedback and encouragement to one another.
- Ask for help when they need it. Too often this does not happen and problems go unrealised, and therefore unresolved.
- Work together to build a group cohesiveness.

Cohesiveness

Cohesiveness refers to the degree to which team members are attracted to the group: their willingness to co-operate and co-ordinate efforts to a team result, and how resistant they might be to leaving the group. Cohesive groups display a team spirit; they *want* to go to meetings, they enjoy being with the group. They are friendly and willing to help each other; they are effective in achieving their goals. Groups which are not cohesive are often recognisable by their levels of absenteeism, or their antagonism and argumentative ways, as well as their lack of achievement.

ACTIVITY

To find out whether your team is a cohesive group or not, think about the following questions:

- How happy are members with the group and with being part of it?
- Do they enjoy each other's company?
- Do they show a sense of shared purpose?
- Do subgroups or gossips dominate?
- Do members say 'we', or 'I'? Do they say 'we did' or do they say 'you should'?
- Do individuals try to take the credit for successes?
- Do individuals have a similar perception of themselves as other team members have of them?

Johari windows

The 'Johari window' is named after the first names of its founders, Joseph Luft and Harry Ingham. It is a useful model for describing the process of human interactions.

A four-paned 'window', as illustrated in Figure 4.48, divides our personal awareness into four types, as shown in the four quadrants: Open, Hidden, Blind, and Unknown. The lines between the four panes can move as an interaction progresses or changes.
Look at the chart below and see how each 'pane' of the window represents a different aspect of you, as seen by yourself and as seen by others.

	Known to self	*Unknown to self*
Known to others	Open area	Blind area
Unknown to others	Hidden area	Unknown area: the potential 'discovery' area

Figure 4.48   Johari windows

The **open area** is known to you and to others, the things we know about ourselves and that other people know about us, and we are happy for them to know: he's married, she likes cycling, he enjoys his work.

The **blind area** is the bit of you that others recognise in you, but you do not necessarily realise yourself: you are good at calming situations, thinking up solutions to problems.

The **hidden area** is what only you know about you. This might just be your private thoughts and feelings about a person or situation, or it might be your 'skeletons in the closet' that you want to keep to yourself.

The **unknown area** is the part of you which you do not know yourself and neither do others; it might affect how you would react to new situations and experiences, or how you would deal with problems you have never encountered.

Successful teams rely on high levels of trust, so the Johari window ideal is to make the open area bigger and decrease the other areas. Building the potential discovery area not only helps individuals build their confidence and competence, but also helps the team identify your hidden qualities that can be used to the team's advantage.

The impact of technology on team functioning

Technology

Information technology (IT) or ICT (Information and Communications Technology) or ILT (Information Learning Technology) are all familiar phrases. The rapid growth of technology has brought us electronic data transfer, robotic production plants, expansion of computer network information systems and an abundance of personal computers producing information and entertainment in the home, office and factory.

Small companies can compete with big companies on the Internet because of advances in information networks. For example, obtaining a quotation for car insurance used to be a laborious process requiring a visit to a broker, listing details handwritten on a form, and waiting several days for a response. Today, insurance company quotation systems allow rapid comparisons of the premiums charged by different insurance companies and immediate insurance cover should you so request it.

Some critics claim that technology is dissolving national cultures and economies through economic globalisation, and that national strategies of economic management are becoming ineffective (see Hirst and Thompson, 2000).

Certainly technology has had a huge impact on the way organisations operate and on the individuals within those organisations. Technology replaces human skills and indeed jobs. Whether this is deskilling, as Braverman claimed, or development of different skills, is debatable. But, just as with Fordism, increased output leads to increased income, even though the work may be boring.

Technological advances can interfere with human interactions. Communications technology can remove the spatial and interpersonal aspects of communication, as Zuboff (1988) found. 'Before I was able to get up and hand things to people without having someone say, what are you doing? Now, I feel like I am with my head down, doing my work' (p. 146).

Human contact and interaction can be reduced, and many employees find this an uncomfortable aspect of working life. Some people find it difficult to interact with others and where computerisation enables them to retain that distance from co-workers, interpersonal and social skills are unlikely to be

---

Information technology and knowledge

JOURNAL ARTICLE

The authors remind the reader that, 'during the past three decades, corporations, governments, and educational institutions in industrialised nations have adopted information technology to run their daily operations' (p. 29). Information technology certainly does seem to be the epicentre of knowledge-based economies today. Knowledge is a valuable commodity in the economy of industrialised countries, and this article examines 'knowledge' and attempts to explain 'knowledge management' from a technological point of view. It also highlights some important issues and challenges to IT 'knowledge management'. IT may have turned business organisations upside-down, but as the authors conclude, 'After all, it takes humans to capture knowledge, humans to ask questions, and humans to answer them.'

Kim, Won and Park, Seung-Soo, 'Knowledge management: a careful look', *Journal of Object Technology*, 2003, Vol. 2, No. 1, January–February, pp 29–38.

Information technology and business

JOURNAL ARTICLE

Ward and Peppard examine how the relationship between the IT organisation and the rest of the business has been difficult to co-ordinate. This gap between the two has been explained by the cultural differences, but beyond the centralisation–decentralisation debate not much else has been investigated until now. Some organisations opt for outsourcing to resolve differences, but the 'long-term consequences of short-term decisions' appear to be a hindrance here. These researchers try to interpret problems, explain gaps in relationships, and offer advice. A framework for further research is also discussed.

Ward, J. and Peppard, J. 'Reconciling the IT/business relationship: a troubled marriage in need of guidance', *Journal of Strategic Information Systems*, 1996, Vol. 5, No. 1, March, pp 37–65.

Figure 4.49   Sometimes technology can make workplaces a little too cosy

developed. Computerisation has advantages though, argues Zuboff, in the quick spread of information and in encouraging creativity. How technology affects an individual depends largely on their perception of it and their consequent approach to it. Some reject and try to avoid technology completely, so workers' interpretation of technology, as well as organisational and social pressures, will both impact on work processes and the team effort.

Communication

Many companies today are **centralised**: they concentrate their operations in one or a few carefully selected locations, whilst others are **decentralised**, and

maintain small sales and servicing outlets to cater for local markets. Communication is still a vital element of any working relationship, but is very often carried out in a different way these days because of technology. Computers and video links enable meetings and conferences to take place on screen instead of in the office, or in an office abroad. Obviously the savings to the organisation are great: instead of paying for flights, hotels and expenses, the organisation just pays the phone bill.

The cost to human interaction can be great though. Many people believe that personality is vital in business relations and negotiations, but modern communications systems negate the need for that personal interaction a lot of the time.

Change

The nature of work and attitudes towards it vary between generations and cultures. In pre-industrial society in the UK, agriculture and domestic textiles were the most common form of work. This work was located close to home because of limited transportation. Following the Industrial Revolution, machinery changed the traditional approaches to work. Factories sprang up and time-based work patterns were established, so people used to task orientation were indoctrinated into time-regulated working patterns: the morning to evening factory shift, or the 9 to 5 office shift today. But if progress is to be made, things have to change.

As Olson (1982) argued, the longer an organisational system survives, the more sclerotic it becomes. Sometimes companies are shocked into reorganisation and they then change radically.

Modern organisations have to change constantly to keep up with competitors' advances and, inevitably, people and their communications networks can get entangled – or fall apart – at times of change.

Networks and virtual teams

We are all familiar with the concept of computer networks. They can enhance and assist organisational and personal networks.

Communications networks such as the Internet, telephone and email have no respect for the geographical and territorial boundaries that once used to limit business transactions, so organisations operate and compete in a market which covers the entire planet. As a result of business strategies expanding to operate in this global market, we have what we now recognise as globalisation, 'a shift in organisational interactions, from a local or national level to an international level', according to Held *et al.* (1999).

The new 'network economy', developed with the advent of the Internet, increases the network of business relationships and connections. The Internet multiplies business connections rapidly, thus enlarging the company 'web'. Shared information systems and business databases enable more interaction between organisations in, for example, accessing supplies more quickly or in sharing information to mutual benefit.

The manager who has just left the (virtual, video-link) meeting in Japan can immediately contact his suppliers and order the materials he needs, without even speaking to them. This 'team' of managers, customers and suppliers can all interact without any personal human contact whatsoever. This makes virtual teamworking via modern technology quick, easy and convenient and undoubtedly more profitable. Some might argue that the loss of the human element of interaction is a loss in itself and creates more problems than a real team faces. Virtual teams have been created all over the globe, with members geographically spread out, but electronically joined. In *Reaching across Space, Time and Organisations with Technology*, Lipnack and Stamps (1997) argued the case for focusing on the teamwork requirement rather than the technology requirement when considering the managing of virtual teams.

Local and Wide Area Networks

Networking by computer is done via Local Area Networks (LANs) or Wide Area Networks (WANs). LANs link together a series of computers, workstations, printers, scanners and other technological equipment in one building or locality. This linking is done by cables, along which data travels between the various pieces of equipment or workstations – or nodes as they are known. Computers are linked to a cable interface, which links it to the LAN.

The physical layout of a LAN is called its topology. There are three major types of topology.

A **star network** links all of the machines in the LAN to a central computer. The computer then serves as the host or the file server. The file server controls the LAN as well as all of the messages through it.

A **ring network** connects all of the nodes in the LAN in a circular framework. With this type of network there is no host machine. Messages simply flow around the network until they reach their destination. This simply involves linking the microcomputers within an office.

A **bus configuration** is sometimes called a broadcast network. This uses a single cable known as a bus, and directs messages by identifying codes. With this system each computer carries out some management task. The failure of one node would not put the whole network out of operation.

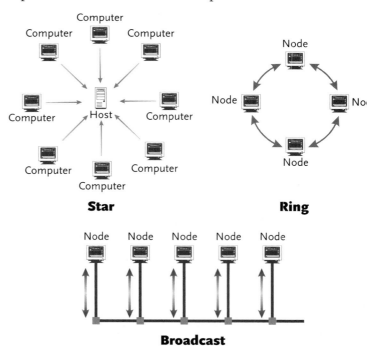

Figure 4.50   Star, ring and broadcast networks

There is an increasing usage of in-house Intranet systems within large organisations, enabling staff to view numerous applications and 'pages' of, say, job vacancies or sales results and performance figures.

Wide Area Networks link communications equipment between companies or separate divisions of a company. Computers can communicate with each other wherever they are located, and they can also communicate with other networks and systems outside of their own. This makes sharing of data and information on a global scale easy, but carries drawbacks such as different holiday periods or time zones. Language and currency barriers can interrupt the smooth running of international systems and whilst many companies and countries use standardised equipment and systems, not all countries use the same standardisations.

Have a look at the website http://www.cybergeography.org/atlas/atlas.html, which provides maps and graphic representations of Internet networks and the World Wide Web. Created by cyber-explorers from various disciplines, these will help you visualise digital landscapes and global communications networks.

A useful book is *Virtual Teams: People Working Across Boundaries with Technology* by Jessica Lipnack and Jeffrey Stamps (1997), which looks at global technology in the workplace, examines virtual teamworking, and provides numerous case studies as illustrations of technology in use.

Global and cross-cultural teams

Cross-cultural teams are, today, a necessary commodity when you consider local markets and the need for local knowledge within them. Different cultures, different languages and different legal systems all need their respective expert managers to handle business at a local level. 'Local' probably means which country or continent they are operating in today, rather than whether they are serving rural or metropolitan England.

We need technology for corporations to survive modern competition. Customer expectations have changed too. People expect fast, efficient service, but many dislike the impersonal technology and call centre ethos. However, we accept the new values and systems, often because there is no alternative, and so progress continues. Further development of communications technology is most probably inevitable and this will continue to 'modernise' the future of work, for better or worse. Braverman (1974) claimed that, 'The more science is incorporated into the labour process, the less the worker understands of this process' (p. 425), inferring that the technological aspects of modern business organisation is not a complete success, and perhaps turns the workers – or the teams – into robots. But the more that science is incorporated into the labour process, the more people, especially the younger generations, seem to accept it as the way forward. What effect this lack of personal interaction may have on individuals, teams and organisations in the long term really has yet to be seen.

Globalisation and business **JOURNAL ARTICLE**

This article examines the trend to globalisation, triggers for change, changing structures and business process 're-engineering'. Areas such as organisational strategy, people performance, and IT were examined. The authors concluded that, 'globalisation was a real and significant force for change affecting organisation strategy, operations, and characteristics' and that 'evolution (rapid or slow) to a virtual enterprise' is feasible for most modern organisations.

Wright, D. T. and Burns, N. D. 'New organisation structures for global business: an empirical study', *International Journal of Operations and Production Management*, 1998, Vol. 18, No. 9, pp 896–923.

References

Allport, G.W. (1954) 'The historical background of modern social psychology', in G. Lindzey (ed.) (1998) *Handbook of Social Psychology* (4th edn), Cambridge: Addison Wesley.

Anderson, U., Forsgren, M. and Holm, U. (2002) 'The strategic impact of external networks: subsidiary performance and competence development in the multinational corporation', *Strategic Management Journal*, Vol. 23, (11), pp 979–96.

Argyris, C. (1964) *Integrating the Individual and the Organisation*, London: Wiley.

Arnold, J., Cooper, C. and Robertson, I. (1998) *Work Psychology*, 3rd edn, London: Pitman.

Aronsom, E. (1999) *The Social Animal* (8th edn), New York: Worth.

ASTMS (1980) 'Technological change and collective bargaining', Discussion paper, London: ASTMS.

AT&T: A Brief History available at AT&T Online. http://www.att.com

Baker, E. (1980), in *McKinsey Quarterly*, Autumn.

Banyard, P. and Grayson, A. (2000) *Introducing Psychological Research*, 2nd edn, Basingstoke: Palgrave.

Bass, B. M. (1985) *Leadership and Performance Beyond Expectations*, New York: Free Press.

Baxter, B. (2003) Available at www.theabp.org/artBB01.html.

Belbin, R. M. (1981) *Management Teams: Why They Succeed or Fail*, Oxford: Heinemann.

Beloff, H. (1992) 'Mother, father and me: our IQ', *The Psychologist*, Vol. 5 pp 309–11.

Bem, D. J. (2002) *Introduction to Beliefs, Attitudes and Ideologies*, Crow Resources; also available at www.psych.cornell.edu/courses/Psych489/Introduction_to_Beliefs_%26_.html.

Bem, D. J. (1970) *Beliefs, Attitudes and Human Affairs*, Belmont, CA: Brooks/Cole Publishing.

Bennis, W. and Nanus, B. (1985) *Leaders: The Strategies for Taking Charge*, Harper & Row.

Blake, R. and Mouton, J. (1978) *The New Managerial Grid*, Houston.

Braverman, H. (1974) *Labor and Monopoly Capital*, New York: Monthly Review Press.

Brewerton, P. and Millward, L. (2001) *Organisational Research Methods*, London: Sage.

Bryman, A. (1996) *Quantity and Quality in Social Research*, London: Routledge.

Buchanan, D. and Huczynski, A. (1997) *Organizational Behaviour: An Introductory Text*, 3rd edn, Essex: Prentice Hall Europe.

Buchanan, D. and Huczynski, A. (2000) *Organisational Behaviour*, London: Prentice Hall.

Burns, J. M. (1978) *Leadership*, New York: Harper & Row.

Burns, T. and Stalker, G. M. (1994) *The Management of Innovation*, London: Oxford University Press.

Cattell, R. B. (1963) 'Theory of fluid and crystallised intelligence: a critical experiment', *Journal of Educational Psychology*, Vol. 54, pp 1–22.

Christie, R. and F. L. (1970) *Mach scales: Machiavellianism Scales*, GeisACAS.

Cook, K. S. and Emerson, R. (1984) 'Exchange networks and the analysis of complex organisations', *Research in the Sociology of Organisations*, Vol. 3, pp 1–30.

Cooper, C. (2003) Review of Nancy Foy's *Empowering People at Work* (Aldershot: Gower Press) Avaliable at: http://www.apmforum.com/review/fr10.htm [accessed 29.06.04].

Costa, P. T. and McCrae, R. R. (1990) 'The five-factor model of personality', *Journal of Personality Disorders*, Vol. 4, pp 362–71.

Costa, P. T., and McCrae, R. R. (1992) *The Revised NEO Personality Inventory (NEO-PI-R) and NEO Five-Factor Inventory (NEO-FFI) Professional manual*, Odessa, Fl: Psychological Assessment Resources.

Costa, P. T. and McCrae, R. R. (1992) 'Four ways five factors are basic', *Personality and Individual Differences*, Vol. 13, pp 653–65.

Daniel, W. W. (1973) 'Understanding employee behaviour in its context', in J. Child, (ed.) *Man and Organisation*, London: Allen & Unwin.

Fielder, F. (1967) *Theory of Effective Leadership*, New York: McGraw-Hill.

Deutsch, M. (1990) in B. H. Sheppard, H., Bazerman, and R. J. Lewicki, (eds) *Research on Negotiation in Organizations*, Vol. 2, London: JAI Press.

Dumaine, R. (1994) *Team Structures*, London: Penguin.

Eysenck, H. J. (1953) *The Structure of Human Personality*, London: Methuen.

Eysenck, H. J. and Eysenck, M. J. (1985) *Personality and Individual Differences: A Natural Science Approach*, London: Plenum.

Eysenck, H. J. and Eysenck, S. B. G. (1969) *Personality Structure and Measurement*, London: Routledge & Kegan Paul.

Eysenck, M. (1985) *A Handbook of Cognitive Psychology*, London: Erlbaum.

Fayol, H. (1916) *General and Industrial Management*, London: Pitman.

Filstead, W. J. (1979) 'Qualitative methods: a needed perspective in evaluation research', in T. D. Cook and S. L. Reichardt (eds) *Qualitative and Quantitative Methods in Evaluation Research*, Beverly Hills, Ca: Sage.

Fiske, S. T. and Taylor, S. E. (1984) *Social Cognition*, Wokingham: Addison Wesley.

Foy, N. (2003) *Empowering People at Work*, Aldershot: Gower Press.

Friedman, M. and Rosenman, R. H. (1974) *Type A Behaviour and Your Heart*, New York: Knopf.

Furnham, A. (2000) ' Thinking about intelligence', *The Psychologist*, Vol. 13, Part 10, pp 510–15.

Gardner, H. (1999) *Intelligence Reframed*, New York: Basic Books.

Gardner, J. (1989) *On Leadership*, New York: Free Press.

Gilligan, C., Neale, B. and Murray, D. (1990) *Business Decision Making*, Philip Allen.

Goldthorpe, J. H., Lockwood, D., Bechofer, F. and Platt, J. (1968) *The Affluent Worker: Industrial Attitudes and Behaviour*, Cambridge: Cambridge University Press.

Graham, H. T. and Bennet, R. (1992) *Human Resource Management*, 7th edn, London: M&E.

Greene, K. (1982) *The Adaptive Organisation*, London: Wiley.

Grint, K. (1998) *The Sociology of Work: An Introduction*, 2nd edn, Cambridge: Polity Press.

Handy, C. (1975) 'Organisational influences on appraisal', *Industrial and Commercial Training*, Vol. 7, No. 8, pp 326–7.

Handy, C. (1989) *The Age of Unreason*, London: Hutchinson Business Books.

Handy, C. (1991) *Gods of Management: The Changing Work of Organisations*, 3rd edn, London: Arrow Business Books.

Handy, C. (1993) *Understanding Organisations*, London: Penguin.

Handy, C. (1994) *The Empty Raincoat: Making Sense of the Future*, London: Hutchinson.

Hastings, C., Bixby, P. and Chaudhry-Lawton, R. (1994) *Superteams: Building Organizational Success Through High-Performing Teams*, London: HarperCollins.

Held, D., Mcgrew, A., Goldblatt, D. and Perraton, J. (1999) *Global Transformation: Politics, Economics, Culture*, Cambridge: Polity Press.

Hersey, P. and Blanchard, K. H. (1977) *The Management of Organizational Behaviour*, New Jersey: Prentice Hall.

Hersey, P. and Blanchard, K. H. (1988) *The Management of Organizational Behaviour*, New Jersey: Prentice Hall.

Herzberg, F. (1968) 'One more time: how do you motivate employees?', *Harvard Business Review*, Vol. 46, pp 53–62.

Herzberg, F. (1968) *The Motivation to Work*, London: John Wiley & Sons.

Hudson, L. (1967) *Contrary Imaginations; a Psychological Study of the English Schoolboy*, Harmondsworth: Penguin.

Hunt, J. W. (1992) *Managing People at Work*, 3rd edn, New York: McGraw Hill.

IRS (annual), Industrial Relations Service Trends, London: IRS.

Jetten, J., Postmes, T. and McAullife, B. J. (2002) 'We are all individuals: group norms of individualism and collectivism, levels of identification and identity threat', *European Journal of Social Psychology*, Vol. 32, pp 189–207.

Kagan, J. and Havemann, E. (1976) *Psychology: An Introduction*, Harcourt Brace Jovanovich.

Katz, D. and Kahn, R. (1964) *The Social Psychology of Organisations*, London: John Wiley.

Katzenbach, J. and Smith, D. (1993) *The Wisdom of Teams*, Harvard Business School Press.

Kelly, G. (1955) *The Theory of Personal Constructs*, New York: Norton.

Kelly, K. (1998) *New Rules for the New Economy: 10 Ways the Network Economy is Changing Everything*, London: Fourth Estate.

Kirkcaldy, B. D., Shephard, R. and Furnham, A. (2002) 'The influence of Type A behaviour and locus of control upon job satisfaction and occupational health', *Personality and Individual Differences*, Vol. 33, No. 8, pp 1361–71.

LaPiere R. T. (1934) 'Attitudes versus actions', *Social Forces*, Vol. 13, pp 230–7.

Lawrence, P. R. and Lorsch, J.W. (1967) *Organisation and Environment*, Boston: Harvard University Press.

Legge, K. (1978) *Power, Innovation and Problem-solving in Personnel Management*, New York: McGraw Hill.

Lewicki, R., Saunders, D. M., *et al.* (2002) *Negotiation: Readings, Exercises, and Cases*, Boston: McGraw-Hill / Irwin.

Likert, R. (1961) *New Patterns of Management*, New York: McGraw-Hill.

Lipnack, J. and Stamps, J. (1997) *Reaching across Space, Time and Organisations with Technology*, London: Prentice Hall.

Loevinger, J. (1976) *Ego Development*, San Francisco: Jossey-Bass, Inc.

Luft, J. and Ingham, H. (1955) *The Johari Window, a Graphic Model for Interpersonal Relations*, University of California Western Training Laboratory.

Maccoby, M. (1976) *The Gamesman: the New Corporate Leaders*, London: Secker & Warburg

Maccoby, M. (2003) *The Productive Narcissist: The Promise and Peril of Visionary Leadership*, New York: Broadway Books.

Margerison, C. J. and McCann, D. (2000) *Team Management*, Mercury.

Maslow, A. H. (1954) *Motivation and Personality*, London: Harper.

Maslow, R. H. (1968) *Toward a Psychology of Being*, New York: Van Norstrand Rinehold.

McClelland, D. (1960) *The Achieving Society*, New York: Free Press.

McCrae, R. R. and Costa, P. T. (1990) *Personality in Adulthood*, Guilford Press.

McCrae, R. R. and Costa, P. T. (1988) 'Personality in adulthood: a six-year longitudinal study of self-reports and spouse ratings on the NEO personality inventory', *Journal of Personality and Social Psychology*, Vol. 54, pp 853–63.

McKenna, E. (1987) *Psychology in Business*, Laurence Erlbaum.

Mead, G. H. (1934) *Mind, Self and Society*, Chicago: University of Chicago Press.

Mednick, A. S., Higgins, J., and Kirschenbaum, J. (1975) *Psychology: Explorations in Behaviour and Experience*, London: Wiley.

Mercado, S. *et al.* (2001) *European Business* (4th edn), London: Pearson Education and Prentice Hall.

Milgram, S. (1963) 'Behavioural study of obedience', *Journal of Abnormal and Social Psychology*, No. 67, pp 371–78.

Miller, G. A., in R. Gross (ed.) (1967) *The Science of Mind and Behaviour*, London: Hodder & Stoughton.

Minzberg, H. (1973) *The Nature of Managerial Work*, Henry Mintzberg.

Monat, A. and Lazarus, R. (eds) (1991) *Stress and Coping*, 3rd edn, New York: Columbia University Press.

Mullins, L. (1999) *Management and Organisational Behaviour* (5th edn), Harlow: Prentice Hall.

Olson, M. (1982) *The Rise and Decline of the Nations: Economic Growth, Stagflation, and Social Rigidities*, Connecticut: Yale Universtiy Press.

Pask, G. (1961) *An Approach to Cybernetics*, London: Hutchinson.

Peters, T. and Austin, N. (1985) *A Passion for Excellence: The Leadership Difference*, London: Collins.

Porter, L. and Lawler, E. (1968) *Managerial Attitudes and Performance*, New York: Irwin.

Price, V. (1992) *Public Opinion*, London: Sage.

Randall, C. (1962) *The Folklore of Management*, Boston: Little, Brown.

Roberts, P. and Dowling, G. (2002) 'Corporate reputation and sustained superior financial performance', *Strategic Management Journal*, Vol. 23, Issue 12. pp 1077–93.

Rogers, C. (1961) *On Becoming a Person: a Therapist's View of Psychotherapy*, London: Constable.

Rokeach, M. (1973) *The Nature of Human Values*, New York: Free Press.

Rotter, J. B. (1966) 'Generalised expectancies for internal vs external control of reinforcement', *Psychological Monographs* Vol. 80 (1), pp 1–26.

Schein, E. (1988) *Process Consultation*, New York: Addison-Wesley.

Schermerhorn, J., Hunt, J. and Osborn, R. (1997) *Managing Organisational Behaviour*, London: John Wiley.

Scott, R. W. (1998) *Organizations: Rational, Natural, and Open Systems*, Upper Saddle River, NJ: Prentice-Hall.

Shaffer, D. R. (1985) *Developmental Psychology: Theory, Research and Applications*, California: Brooks/Cole Publishing.

Sherif, C., Sherif, M. and Nebergall, R. (1965) *Attitude and Attitude Change: The Social Judgment-Involvement Approach*, Philadelphia: Saunders.

Sherif, M. and Hovland, C. I. (1961) *Social Judgement*, New Haven, Connecticut: Yale University Press.

Simon, H. (1957) *Models of Man*, London: John Wiley.

Skinner, B.F. (1973) *Beyond Freedom and Dignity*.

Smart, B. (1992) *Modern Conditions, Postmodern Controversies*, London: Routledge.

Spearman, C. (1923) *The Nature of 'Intelligence' and the Principles of Cognition*, London: Macmillan.

Spearman, C. (1927) 'The doctrine of two factors', in S. Wiseman (ed.) (1973) *Intelligence and Ability* (2nd edn), Harmondsworth: Penguin

Spinelli, E. (1989) *The Interpreted World: An Introduction to Phenomenological Psychology*, London: Sage.

Steinmann, H. and Schreyögg, G. (2000) *Management: 'Grundlagen der Unternehmens-führung'*, Germany: Gabler.

Sternberg, R. J. (1990) *Handbook of Human Intelligence*, Cambridge: Cambridge University Press.

Storey, J. (1992) *The Management of Human Resources*.

Storey, J. (1987) 'Developments in the management of human resources: an interim report', Warwick Papers in Industrial Relations, Coventry: Warwick University SIBS.

Tepperman, J. (1976) 'Organising office workers', *Radical America* Vol. 10, No. 1, pp 10–17.

Thompson, G. H. and Hirst, P. (2000) *Globalisation in Question*, 2nd edn, Oxford: Blackwell.

Torbert, W. R. (1991) *The Power of Balance: Transforming Self, Society and Scientific Enquiry*, Newbury Park, California: Sage.

Torrington, D. and Hall, L. (1991) *Personnel Management: A New Approach*.

Torrington, D. and Hall, L. (1998) *Personnel Management*, London: Prentice Hall.

Tuckman, B. and Jensen, M. (1977) 'Stages in small group development', *Group and Organisational Studies*, Vol. 2, pp 419–427.

Turner, B. (1990) *Organisational Symbolism*, Berlin: de Gruyter.

Vroom, V. H. (1964) *Work and Motivation*, London: Wiley.

Vroom, V. H. and Yetton, P. W. (1973) *Leadership and Decision-making*, Pittsburgh, Pa: University of Pittsburgh Press.

Walker, R. (1985) 'An introduction to applied qualitative research', in R. Walker (ed.) *Applied Qualitative Research*, Aldershot: Gower.

Watson, T. (1986) *Management, Organisation and Employment Strategy*, London: Routledge.

Wechsler, D. (1944) *The Measurement of Adult Intelligence*, 3rd edn, Baltimore: Williams and Wilkins.

West, C. (2000) 'Social accessibility and involvement: challenges of the twenty-first century', *Contemporary Sociology* Vol. 4, pp 584–90.

Yin, R. K. (1989) *Case Study Research: Design and Methods*, London: Sage.

Zimbalist, A. (1979) *Case Studies on the Labour Process*, New York and London: Monthly Review Press.

Zuboff, S. (1988) *In the Age of the Smart Machine*, New York: Basic Books.

Further reading
CHAPTER 1

Bem D. J. (1970) *Beliefs, Attitudes and Human Affairs*, Belmont, Ca: Brooks/Cole Publishing.

Ajzen, I. and Fishbein, M. (1980) *Understanding Attitudes and Predicting Social Behaviour*, Englewood Cliffs: Prentice Hall.

Checkland, P. (1984) *Systems Thinking, Systems Practice*, London: John Wiley & Sons.

Cornelius, H. and Faire, S. (1989) *Everyone Can Win: How to Resolve Conflict*, Australia: Simon and Schuster

Eysenck, H. J and Eysenck, M. J. (1985) *Personality and Individual Differences: A Natural Science Approach*, London: Plenum.

Eysenck, H. J. (1953) *The Structure of Human Personality*, London: Methuen.

Fisher, R., Kopelman, E. and Kupfer-Schneider, A. (1994) *Beyond Machiavelli: Tools for Coping with Conflict*, Harvard: Harvard University Press.

Friedman, M. and Rosenman, R. H. (1974) *Type A Behaviour and Your Heart*, New York: Knopf.

Handy, C. (1993) *Understanding Organisations*, Harmondsworth: Penguin.

Hardy C. and Clegg, S. (1996) 'Some dare call it Power', in C. Hardy *et al.*, *Handbook of Organisation Studies*, London: Sage.

Harvard Business Review on Negotiation and Conflict Resolution, http://www.psych.cornell.edu/courses/Psych489/Introduction_to_Beliefs_%26_.html

Kagan, J. and Havemann, E. (1976) *Psychology: An Introduction*, Harcourt Brace Jovanovich.

Kirkcaldy, B.D., Shephard, R. and Furnham, A. (2002) 'The influence of Type A behaviour and locus of control upon job satisfaction and occupational health', *Personality and Individual Differences*, Vol. 33, No. 8, pp 1361–71.

Kowalski, R. (1993) *Discovering Yourself: Breaking Walls, Building Bridges*, London: Routledge

Lewicki, R., Saunders, D. M. *et al.* (2002) *Negotiation: Readings, Exercises, and Cases*, Mayfield.

Likert, R. (1932) 'A technique for the measurement of attitudes', *Archives*.

McEwant, T. (2001) *Managing Values and Beliefs in Organisations*, Financial Times/Pearson Education.

Mead, G.H. (1934) *Mind, Self and Society*, Chicago: University of Chicago Press.

Monat, A. and Lazarus, R. (eds) (1991) *Stress and Coping* (3rd edn), New York: Columbia University Press.

Oppeneheim, A.N. (1986) *Questionnaire Design and Attitude Measurement*, Aldershot: Gower.

Price, A (2003). *Human Resource Management in a Business Context*, 2nd edn, Thomson Learning.

Rogers, C. (1961) *On Becoming a Person: a Therapist's View of Psychotherapy*, London: Constable.

Schein, E. (1985) *Organisational Culture and Leadership*, San Francisco: Jossey-Bass.

Tjosvold, D., and Tjosvold, M. M. (2002) *Psychology for Leaders: Using Motivation, Conflict, and Power to Manage More Effectively*, Wiley Europe.

Tuckman, A. (1994) 'The yellow brick road: total quality management and the restructuring of organisational culture', *Organisation Studies*, Vol. 5, No. 15, pp 27–51.

Turner, (2001) 'Organisational symbolism', in P. Hancock and M. Tyler, *Work, Postmodernism and Organisation: A Critical Introduction*, London: Sage.

West, C. (2000) 'Social accessibility and involvement: challenges of the twenty-first century', *Contemporary Sociolology*, Vol. 4, No.29, pp 584–90.

Wilmott, H. (1999) 'Strength is ignorance, slavery is freedom: managing culture in modern organisations', *Journal of Management Studies*, Vol. 4, No. 30, pp 515–52.

Zimbardo, P., Ebbesen, E. and Maslach, C. (1977) *Influencing Attitudes and Changing Behaviour*, 2nd edn, London: Addison-Wesley.

CHAPTER 2

Baxter, B. (2003) Available at www.theabp.org/artBB01.html.

Buchanan, D. and Huczynski, A. (1997) *Organizational Behaviour: An Introductory Text*, 3rd edn, Essex: Prentice Hall Europe.

Costa, P.T. and McCrae, R.R. (1992) 'Four ways five factors are basic', *Personality and Individual Differences*, Vol. 13, pp 653–65.

Costa, P.T. and McCrae, R.R. (1990) 'The five-factor model of personality', *Journal of Personality Disorders*, Vol. 4, pp 362–71.

Costa, P.T. and McCrae, R.R. (1992) *The Revised NEO Personality Inventory (NEO-PI-R) and NEO Five-Factor Inventory (NEO-FFI) Professional manual*, Odessa, Fl: Psychological Assessment Resources.

Eysenck, H. J. and Eysenck, S. B. G. (1969) *Personality Structure and Measurement*, London: Routledge & Kegan Paul.

Eysenck, M. (1985) *A Handbook of Cognitive Psychology*, London: Erlbaum.

Handy, C. (1993) *Understanding Organisations*, London: Penguin.

Handy, C. (1975) 'Organisational influences on appraisal', *Industrial and Commercial Training*, Vol. 7 No. 8, pp 326–7.

Handy, C. (1994) *The Empty Raincoat: Making Sense of the Future*, London: Hutchinson.

Herzberg, F. (1968) 'One more time: how do you motivate employees?', *Harvard Business Review* Vol. 46, pp 53–62.

Herzberg, F. (1968) *The Motivation to Work*, London: John Wiley & Sons.

Hunt, J. W. (1992) *Managing People at Work*, 3rd edn, McGraw Hill.

Maccoby, M. (1976) *The Gamesman: the New Corporate Leaders*, London: Secker and Warburg.

Maccoby, M. (2003) *The Productive Narcissist: The Promise and Peril of Visionary Leadership*, Broadway Books.

Maslow, A. H. (1954) *Motivation and Personality*, London: Harper.

McCrae, R. R. and Costa, P. T. (1988) 'Personality in adulthood: A six-year longitudinal study of self-reports and spouse ratings on the NEO personality inventory', *Journal of Personality and Social Psychology*, No. 54, pp 853–63.

McCrae, R. R. and Costa, P. T. (1990) *Personality in Adulthood*, Guilford Press.

Mercado, S. *et al.* (2001) *European Business*, 4th edn, Pearson Education & Prentice Hall.

Miller, G. A. in R. Gross (ed.) (2000) *The Science of Mind and Behaviour*, London: Hodder & Stoughton.

Porter, L. and Lawler, E. (1968) *Managerial Attitudes and Performance*, New York: Irwin.

Rogers, C. (1961) *On Becoming a Person*, Boston: Houghton Mifflin.

Torrington, D. and Hall, L. L. (1991) *Personnel Management: A New Approach*, London: Prentice Hall.

Vroom, V. (1964) *Work and Motivation*, London: Wiley.

CHAPTER 3

Bass, B. M. (1985) *Leadership and Performance Beyond Expectations*, New York: Free Press.

Burns, J. M. (1978) *Leadership*, New York: Harper & Row.

CHAPTER 4

Mackay, L. and Torrington, D. (1986) *The Changing Nature of Personnel Management*, London: Institute of Personnel Management.

Bryman, A. (1996) *Quantity and Quality in Social Research*, London: Routledge.

Unit 5

Foundations of the business environment

The aim of the unit is to encourage you to identify the objectives of organisations and the influence of stakeholders. You will also be investigating the operation of organisations in relation to the local, national and global environment.

Summary of learning outcomes

On completion of this unit you will be able to:
♦ identify and analyse the mission, objectives and responsibilities of an organisation within its environment
♦ discuss the impact of the economic, social and global environment in which organisations operate
♦ analyse the behaviour of organisations and the market environment
♦ explore the significance of international trade and the European dimension for UK businesses.

Chapter 1

Objectives and responsibilities of organisations

Categories of organisation

Categorising by size

A question new students regularly ask is 'What's the biggest company in the world?' This sounds like a simple question, but is it?

How do we define 'big' when we are describing a company? If you ask several people to classify a person, they might do it in different ways, according to their perspectives. One might say 'He's tall', another might say 'He's kind to animals', another 'He's loaded!' They might all be true, and they are all useful in different contexts.

Businesses are not unlike people in that there are an endless number of variations on the same basic theme, and many ways to classify them. So how would you define 'the biggest company'? The one with the biggest revenues, the most profits, the most valuable? The one with the most employees, or the most factories, branches or outlets? We could use all of these, and each would probably give different results. The tables below shows some of the world's

biggest businesses. Do the firms you expect to be there appear?

World's biggest businesses based on revenues (2002)

	Company	Origin	Revenues
1	Wal-Mart Stores (including ASDA)	USA	$219.8 billion
2	Exxon Mobil	USA	$191.6 billion
3	General Motors	USA	$177.3 billion
4	BP	Britain	$174.2 billion
5	Ford Motor	USA	$162.4 billion
6	Enron	USA	$138.7 billion
7	Daimler Chrysler	Germany	$136.9 billion
8	Royal Dutch Shell	Netherlands/ Britain	$135.2 billion
9	General Electric	USA	$125.9 billion
10	Toyota Motor	Japan	$120.8 billion

Source: Fortune Magazine

World's biggest businesses based on market value (2003)

1	General Electric	$286.1 billion
2	Microsoft	$263.9 billion
3	Exxon Mobil	$244.9 billion
4	Pfizer	$244.8 billion
5	Wal-Mart Stores	$232.2 billion
6	Citigroup	$210.8 billion
7	Johnson & Johnson	$161.4 billion
8	Royal Dutch Shell	$158.5 billion
9	BP	$153.2 billion
10	AIG	$150.9 billion

Source: Morgan Stanley Capital International

ACTIVITY

There is a salutary message in the figures shown in the tables. Find out where the firm that appears in sixth place on the first table would appear today. Search using the company name on one of the broadsheet newspaper websites (such as www.telegraph.co.uk) and see what happened to them in 2002. Many firms aim to grow so as to ensure their long-term survival, but such a strategy does not always work.

World's biggest businesses based on highest profits (2003)

1	Citigroup	$15.3 billion
2	General Electric	$15.1 billion
3	Altria Group	$11.1 billion
4	Exxon Mobil	$11.0 billion
5	Royal Dutch/Shell	$9.4 billion
6	Bank of America	$9.3 billion
7	Pfizer	$9.1 billion
8	Wal-Mart Stores	$8.0 billion
9	Toyota Motor	$7.9 billion
10	Microsoft	$7.8 billion

Source: Morgan Stanley Capital International

By far the **biggest employer** in the world is Wal-Mart Stores, which employs 1,240,000 people worldwide; the next closest is General Motors which employs a mere 386,000, so Wal-Mart appears to be comfortably first in that league. Of course, biggest is not always best. Wal-Mart has come in for considerable criticism in the USA for its employment policies, which tend to pay workers relatively low wages.

ACTIVITY

Which is the biggest company in the world? Use the information above to make your judgement.

To confuse matters further, there are a number of definitions concerning the size of companies given in law or by government.

The UK **Department of Trade and Industry** uses the definitions in the following table:

	Employees
Micro firm	0–9
Small firm	10–49
Medium firm	50–249
Large firm	250+

The **European Commission**, on the other hand, uses a different definition:

	Micro firm	Small firm	Medium firm
Turnover	Not defined	Max. 7m euros	Max. 40m euros
Balance sheet	Not defined	Max. 5m euros	Max. 27m euros
Employees	Max. 10	Max. 50	Max. 250

Finally, the **Companies Act** uses yet another definition:

	Small company	Medium company
Turnover	Max. £2.8 million	Max. £11.2 million
Balance sheet	Max. £1.4 million	Max. £5.6 million
Employees	Max. 50	Max. 250

Categorising by sector

Business is a wide and varied area encompassing many different types of organisation, from a small sole trader selling newspapers in the street to huge global organisations offering services to an international customer base. Because the output of industry is so varied it is helpful to group similar types of business together and refer to them collectively. We therefore talk about the three different **sectors of business**.

The primary sector

Any firm that produces a natural raw material is in the primary sector. Coal mines, farms, oil producers, logging companies and fishermen all therefore fall into this category.

The secondary sector

Any firm that makes something is in this sector. Firms such as clothes manufacturers, furniture makers, CD manufacturers and potters all fall into this category.

The tertiary sector

Any firm that provides a service is in this sector. Companies such as banks, insurance companies, travel agents, shops, logistics firms and airlines all fall into this category. Entertainment falls into this sector, so football teams, theatres and cinemas also qualify.

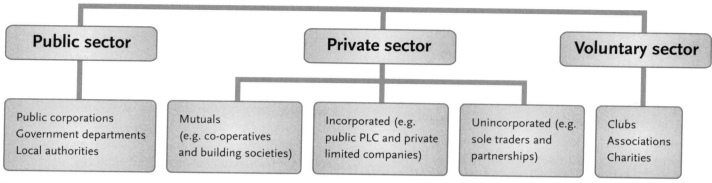

Figure 5.1   Types of UK firms

Categorising by type

It can also be helpful to categorise firms by ownership, as this often sheds light on the organisation's objectives and motives. There are three basic types of organisational structure: the **public**, **private** and **voluntary** sectors, but these can be further subdivided as shown in Figure 5.1.

The public sector

Any organisation that is owned and run by the government is in this sector. The Post Office, for example, provides a service and so appears in the tertiary sector, but it is also owned by the government and so is part of the public sector.

The number of public sector companies was reduced during the 1980s and 1990s as the UK government sold off companies that it controlled into private hands. There was a lot of criticism of publicly run businesses in the 1960s and 1970s. They were seen as being inefficient, absorbing large amounts of public money, employing excessive numbers of people and generally providing poor services. Whilst not all of the criticisms were fair, some undoubtedly were, and by the late 1970s it was generally accepted that something needed to be done to make these organisations more efficient. When a Conservative government was elected in 1979 under Margaret Thatcher one of its major policy ambitions was to privatise as many of these industries as possible in order to gain efficiencies. The process began in 1979 with the part privatisation of British Petroleum (BP) and many others followed during the next decade, including British Aerospace, BritOil, Jaguar, British

Telecom, British Gas, British Airways, British Airports Authority, Rover, British Steel, the water authorities, the electricity generators and distributors, British Rail and British Coal. You may be surprised to realise that some of these businesses used to be nationalised, that is, owned by the government.

The main reason for the inefficiency of nationalised industries, the argument went, was that they faced no competition. Companies such as British Gas, the Electricity Board and British Telecom were the sole providers of their services in the country. It was understood by the managers and workers alike in these industries that the government would keep them afloat however much money they lost, so there was no incentive for them to become efficient and turn in surpluses or profits. Similarly, since they had no competitors, it did not matter if the service that they offered was poor, as customers had no choice but to buy from them. The government believed that the best way to eliminate this wastage was to introduce competition into these markets, the idea being that this would force them to be efficient. Selling the companies to private shareholders would make it imperative for the firms to turn in profits, as shareholders would expect returns on their investments. If they did not improve, the fact that they were now facing competition from other firms would force them out of business. Thus inefficient industries would be forced to become efficient, or they would die, beaten by better competitors. The government saw that privatisation should not only save them from paying out large subsidies to these firms, but should also improve service to customers.

The benefits of privatisation

◆ Increased efficiency.
◆ Exposing firms to the discipline of the market, thus promoting greater competition.
◆ Improved levels of service to customers.
◆ Raising revenue for the government (privatisation proved to be a big source of revenue for the government for a number of years).
◆ Raising investment capital through the introduction of share capital.
◆ Promoting wider share ownership (it was hoped that selling the industries off to the general public would make us a nation of share owners, each with a stake in the efficiency of British companies).

The process of privatisation is simply to sell the firm or industry to new shareholders, and can be achieved in several ways.

Methods of privatisation

Selling the entire company to the public

Shares are offered to the general public who bid to buy the shares. Such offers were often over-subscribed and prospective shareholders were consequently allocated a proportion of the shares bid for. This method was adopted with the privatisation of the energy providers in the UK, such as British Gas and the electricity boards. Shares were sold to a very large number of individuals, although a large percentage of these shares were later sold by those individuals and many are now held by institutional investors such as pension funds and unit trusts.

Partial sale of the company to the public

Sometimes the government chooses to keep some shares, thereby maintaining a limited degree of control over the company. The government sells off some of its holding in the firm but keeps some back, perhaps for sale at a later date. For example, when British Petroleum was privatised in 1977 the government reduced its ownership share from 66 to 51 per cent, reducing gradually to zero by 1995.

Private placing

Instead of selling direct to the public, sometimes the government arranges to sell the shares directly to institutional investors or private buyers who agree a price. When British Coal was privatised it was sold directly to new owners such as RJB Mining.

The privatisation controversy

Privatisation has remained a controversial policy, and has not met with unanimous approval. Workers in the industries concerned have found the going tough at times, as the privatised companies have often had to reduce staff numbers significantly in the chase for efficiency. The government has also been criticised for selling firms that were contributing profits to the public purse into the hands of a privileged few shareholders. It has been alarming to see how a number of the privatised industries have found their way into the hands of foreign companies. A number of the electricity distributors, for example, have been bought out by foreign electricity companies. In a famous speech, Harold Macmillan, the former Prime Minister, accused the government of 'selling off the family silver', in other words, selling our national assets for short-term financial benefit.

Despite its critics, the privatisation programme has undoubtedly achieved some of its aims. The introduction of competition in the telecommunications market, for example, has led to vastly improved levels of service and to lower bills than they would have been. Similarly, levels of service offered by the energy producers have improved considerably, and much wastage has been eliminated. The government no longer has to 'prop up' these industries financially, so it has saved considerable sums of money. At the same time, the levels of investment in these industries has improved substantially.

Airport privatisation

JOURNAL ARTICLE

Traditionally airports were publicly owned enterprises; they were operated and subsidised by the UK government because they were seen to be providing significant economic benefits to the country. However, the forecasted growth in air traffic has given the UK government and other governments around the world cause to think again about the financing and control of airports. Many airports around the world are now congested and the burden on the public purse to increase the capability of airports to cope with the increases in traffic appears to be too great. Consequently the UK government, along with more than 80 other governments around the world, have looked to privatising their airports in order to attract private sector investment.

You should investigate this topic further by referring to the original article which tells the story further.

Adapted from 'Airport privatisation', Ian Humphries and Graham Francis, *British Economy Survey*, Volume 31, Number 2, Spring 2002, Section 13.

ACTIVITY

1   Examine a company or industry that has been privatised over the period since 1980. You might choose the gas or electricity industries, British Telecom, BP or any of the other privatised companies. Examine the extent to which you think they are now more efficient and provide better choice, quality and service to customers.

2   As a result of your investigations, do you think privatisation has worked? Give evidence for your answer.

The private sector

Any organisation that is owned and run by individuals is in this sector whether they be sole traders, partnerships or shareholders. Private sector businesses will also be in one of the primary, secondary or tertiary sectors. Boots PLC, for example, is in the private sector as the firm is owned by shareholders, but is also in the secondary sector as it manufactures products, and in the tertiary sector as it owns a chain of shops.

As Figure 5.1 on p. 207 shows, the private sector can also be further subdivided.

Unincorporated organisations

These are firms whose owners have **unlimited liability**. This means that the owners are personally responsible for the debts of the firm and could have their assets seized to pay company debts. This includes sole traders and partnerships.

Incorporated organisations

These firms carry **limited liability**, meaning that the firm and the owners are separate legal entities, so a shareholder can only lose his or her shareholding in the firm and no more. This includes Private Limited Companies (Ltds) and Public Limited Companies (PLCs).

Mutuals

These organisations are technically not-for-profit organisations and they do not have shareholders; instead they distribute surpluses to members, who are also the owners of the organisations. Therefore mutuals are set up for the benefit of members, not shareholders. Some building societies are mutuals (all account holders are members) and any organisation set up as a co-operative is also similar in its outlook. Mutuals are good for members as no dividends have to be paid to shareholders so they receive more benefit, but they are limited in their development possibilities as they have no shareholders to inject capital to fund expansion. Consequently, many mutuals have 'demutualised' in recent years and become PLCs.

CASE STUDY

The Daily News –
Comment on demutualisation

For a number of years now, investors have debated over which type of organisation produces better returns: PLCs or mutual organisations.

Proponents of PLCs argue that they are leaner, more cost efficient and are in a better position to raise the capital required for expanding the company. As a result they would argue that demutualising a mutual company offers benefits to policyholders, staff and people who become shareholders.

In 2002, however, the International Cooperative and Mutual Insurance Federation released a report that indicated that average returns on investments in mutual companies were 20 per cent higher than for PLCs. The analysis over the four years prior to the report showed that whilst PLCs had cut their payouts each year as the stock market slumped, the mutuals had maintained the levels of their payouts to investors.

ACTIVITY

1 Explain the following sentence: 'demutualising a company offers benefits to policyholders, staff and people who become shareholders'. Outline the benefits that each of these stakeholders might expect from a demutualised company.

2 What additional pressures on PLCs do you think have resulted in them cutting their payments during a period of turmoil in the stock market?

The voluntary sector

A voluntary organisation is an alternative to the 'for profit organisation'. It is a 'not-for-profit organisation'. It is set up, organised, staffed and run by people who are working purely on a voluntary basis, usually for a 'good cause'. However, just because an organisation is run as a voluntary activity does not mean that it should not operate in a professional way. Voluntary organisations like any others use scarce resources – these need to be used to optimal effect, or else money and time will be wasted. Examples of voluntary organisations are the Women's Royal Voluntary Service (WRVS) and Voluntary Service Overseas (VSO).

People who work for these organisations will receive no more than is required for living, travel and other forms of expenses. However, the voluntary organisation needs to establish clear objectives, and then create structures, policies and practices that best enable the organisation to meet these objectives.

Charities

A charity is an organisation set up to raise funds and support other people or a cause. The objectives of charities are to raise a surplus to use for helping others. A surplus is a positive balance from the income of a charity after all costs have been paid. This contrasts with the profit-based objective of a private sector organisation. The management of charity work is overseen by a group of trustees, who are volunteers with a reputation as responsible citizens. Many will have a variety of experience in both charity and business activities. Charities have to register as such and must produce annual accounts that are available for anyone to see.

Most charity organisations start out when someone recognises the need for such an organisation and acts accordingly. For example, the charity Shelter was set up in 1966 to help the many homeless people on the streets. The Toybox Charity was founded in 1991, by the Dyason family, who were horrified by a television documentary showing the plight of some of the 250,000 children orphaned by civil war in Guatemala. The charity grew into a comprehensive rescue strategy for children who live on the streets of Guatemala City.

CASE STUDY

War Child

War Child was founded in 1993 by film makers Bill Leeson and David Wilson as an emotional response to the plight of children caught up in the war in former Yugoslavia. Initially raising money through entertainment events and public appeals, War Child set out to bring immediate material help to children of all ages and ethnic backgrounds. With a few old trucks and the help of a handful of unpaid volunteers, War Child began delivering food, clothing and medical equipment to wherever it was needed most. It also supplied musical instruments and CDs to young people and radio stations, and initiated a diabetes programme supplying insulin and blood-testing equipment throughout Bosnia. In all, thanks to significant financial support from the general public and the music and entertainment industries, War Child provided millions of pounds worth of aid to the former Yugoslavia. War Child has grown from a two-man organisation working from a sitting room in North London, into an international aid agency with offices in half a dozen countries. Now, the charity is also involved in development initiatives, such as the rehabilitation of war-traumatised children and 'education for peace' programmes. At the heart of War Child's philosophy is the realisation that the war-scarred younger generation is the key to a peaceful future.

Charities employ paid managers and workers (unlike voluntary organisations, which rely on the goodwill of their staff). Many large charities employ resources on a large scale in the same way as private business organisations. These resources need to be managed effectively and efficiently to ensure that they are used in the optimum way to meet the needs of various stakeholder groupings. Today, therefore, charities employ professional business managers who are accountable for using resources in the best possible way to meet the objectives of the charity.

Mission, objectives and values of organisations

The concept of corporate mission or vision

The business strategy

Business strategy is concerned with developing a clear picture of the direction an organisation needs to go in, coupled with a well thought-out plan of how to steer the organisation in the chosen direction. In the words of Peter Drucker, 'strategy converts what you want to do into an accomplishment'. Strategy therefore involves setting long-term goals and short-term objectives to achieve those goals. It also requires the firm to take decisions and develop the ability to achieve the ends. The overarching aims of the organisation are referred to as the firm's 'mission'.

Mission

Before an organisation can devise a strategy it must know where it is going: it needs to define the direction that the strategy will be devised to pursue. In other words, all organisations need an aim which they seek to work towards. Today it is common practice for organisations to set out their aim in a 'mission statement' and/or a 'vision statement' for the organisation.

J. Thompson (1990) defines mission as 'The essential purpose of the organisation ... the nature of the business(es) it is in and the customers it seeks to serve and satisfy.'

Corporate mission statements

Pfizer (the largest pharmaceutical company in the UK)

Pfizer's corporate mission is to become the world's most valued company to patients, customers, colleagues, investors, business partners and the communities where we work and live.

Kingston upon Hull City Council

The Council will strive to secure a positive and sustainable future for the city. This will be achieved through decisive leadership, consultation, the development of inclusive and meaningful partnerships and the support of active and empowered communities.

Mission statements set standards for the company to strive for, and all of the activities of the firm should relate to the mission statement. Many firms will have the mission on the wall for employees to see; they may ask employees to think what they are doing and how it serves the mission. This may encourage workers who are unclear about their roles and it may persuade workers to stop doing things that are not contributing to the mission.

Ben & Jerry's, the ice cream manufacturers and retailers, have a mission that breaks down into three sections.

Ben & Jerry's statement of mission

Ben & Jerry's is founded on and dedicated to a sustainable corporate concept of linked prosperity. Our mission consists of three interrelated parts.

1 *Product mission*

To make, distribute and sell the finest quality all-natural ice cream and euphoric concoctions with a continued commitment to incorporating wholesome, natural ingredients and promoting business practices that respect the earth and the environment.

2 *Economic mission*

To operate the company on a sustainable financial basis of profitable growth, increasing value for our stakeholders and expanding opportunities for development and career growth for our employees.

3 *Social mission*

To operate the company in a way that actively recognises the central role that business plays in society by initiating innovative ways to improve the quality of life locally, nationally and internationally.

Central to the mission of Ben & Jerry's is the belief that all three parts must thrive equally in a manner that commands deep respect for individuals in and outside the company and supports the communities of which they are a part.

Newcastle United PLC sets out its mission in the following way:

The business of Newcastle United is football – our aim is to play attractive football, to win trophies to satisfy our supporters and shareholders and to continually improve our position as a top European club.

Having established this mission (aim), it becomes possible to devise a strategy. Figure 5.2 illustrates how this might be achieved.

The mission for the organisation needs to be realistic given the organisation's existing resources and

Aspect of mission	Supporting strategy
Play attractive football	Appoint a management team capable of delivering attractive football
Win trophies	Build the team and support structures that will ensure competitive success
Satisfy supporters	Success and value for money
Satisfy shareholders	Strategies that will keep crowds paying at turnstiles and for merchandise
Improve European position	Generate the success that will support a European strategy, such as purchase of world-class players

Figure 5.2　From mission to strategy

capabilities, and to provide a clear focus for organisational activity. Having a 'sense of mission' is not the same thing as having a mission statement. It is possible for an organisation to have a mission statement but only a poor sense of mission. A mission statement may simply be propaganda or wishful thinking on the part of management.

The Ashridge Mission Model (created by the Ashridge Management School) sets out that a mission should consist of four key elements (see Figure 5.3):

♦ purpose
♦ values
♦ strategy
♦ behaviour standards.

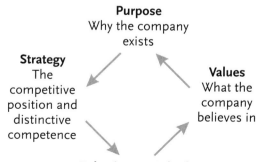

Purpose
Why the company exists

Strategy
The competitive position and distinctive competence

Values
What the company believes in

Behaviour standards
The policies and behaviour patterns that underpin the distinctive competence and the value system

Figure 5.3　Ashridge Mission Model

CASE STUDY

Here is the mission statement of the computer game software writers Eidos (creators of Lara Croft), taken from their website:

Mission Statement
Committed to the Gameplay Experience

ACTIVITY

1　Compare this with what you have read about the content of mission statements. How effective do you think this statement is?

2　What would you include in the mission statement if you were managing Eidos?

3　Write a mission statement for your college or university.

Vision

A vision is something more than a mission. The vision tends to be more futuristic and idealistic. The vision sets out what the organisation can become. You will often hear business and political leaders state, 'I want to share my vision with you'. The vision sets out an ideal future for an organisation which it is to be hoped can be grounded in reality.

Richard Koch (1997) defines vision as, 'An inspiring view of what a company could become, a dream about its future shape and success, a picture of a potential future for a firm, a glimpse into its Promised Land. A vision is a long-term aspiration of a leader for his or her firm, that can be described to colleagues and that will urge them on through the desert.'

Koch makes a useful distinction between mission and vision in the following way: mission is why a firm

213

exists, its role in life; vision is a view of what the firm could become, imagining a desired future.

Aims of organisations

Organisations need to have aims and objectives to be able to focus on the clear direction needed for success in the modern business world. The aim is the overarching goal for the organisation, which can then be broken down into a subset of objectives to achieve the aim. To take a military parallel, the aim may be 'to win the war' and the objectives will be the subset of major requirements which must be met in order to achieve that. Business organisations' aims usually relate to profit, market share, return on capital employed, sales, growth, levels of service and customer and/or user perceptions.

Establishing objectives may be done in a number of ways, such as by looking at what is 'normal' in the industry, or previous years' figures. A third element, which is a popular one, is growth in earnings per share. Clearly, shareholders are major stakeholders in the organisation and this is an objective they can relate to. Of course, a danger of focusing on earnings per share is that the company may begin to borrow more money in order to maintain the level of earnings per share.

Once the organisation has established corporate objectives in financial terms, then these objectives need to be segmented into divisional objectives and profit-centre objectives. The expected rate of return from each division may well depend on the amount of risk taken and on market conditions.

Management by objectives

In his book *The Practice of Management* (originally published in 1954, latest edition 1995), Peter Drucker set out the concept of management by objectives (MbO), in which managers set specific objectives for each area of business performance, including the work and progress of subordinates, and set attainable targets at each level of the organisation, agreed by consultation. These objectives need to be co-ordinated with the strategic objectives of the whole organisation. MbO is now a widely used business practice which can be used to upgrade targets in the light of experience.

Most managers use MbO either explicitly or implicitly in their actions. The MbO approach is closely associated with organisations which have detailed planning structures focused on a clear mission.

Peter Drucker wanted to find out how best to manage a business to make sure that profits are made and that the enterprise is successful over time. He felt that business objectives help management to explain, predict and control activities. The business should establish a number of objectives in a small number of general statements. These statements can then be tested in the light of business experience, and it becomes possible to predict performance. The soundness of decisions can be examined while they are being made, rather than by looking back on what has happened. Performance in the future can be improved in the light of previous and current experience.

Figure 5.4 shows that specific objectives can act as a standard to measure performance.

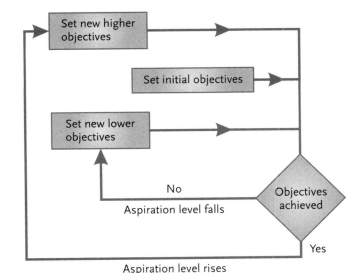

Figure 5.4   Management by objectives

If objectives are not met, they may need to be readjusted or processes and activities altered. Alternatively, if they are met, new and higher objectives can be set. Such objectives force the business to plan its aims in detail and to work out ways of achieving them. Management is the job of organising resources to achieve satisfactory performance.

Drucker listed eight areas in which performance objectives need to be set out:

- market standing
- innovation
- productivity
- physical and financial resources
- profitability
- manager performance and development
- worker performance and attitude
- public responsibility.

Managers need information which enables them to measure their own performance and that of their organisation. MbO provides an excellent link between aims and performance, and aims and measurement of performance.

Profit as an aim

Business organisations need to make profits if they are to move forward and grow. A company has responsibilities that extend well beyond its purely commercial ambitions. However, it should organise itself in such a way that it can meet all its responsibilities and still make a profit. According to Drucker, 'It is the first duty of a business to survive. The guiding principle of business economics, in other words, is not the maximisation of profits; it is the avoidance of loss. Business enterprise must produce the premium to cover the risks inevitably involved in its operation. And there is only one source for this risk premium: profits.'

Unless a business makes a profit it cannot afford to modernise itself, install new technologies, or take commercial risks with, say, new product ranges. It cannot continue to fulfil its social responsibilities. Nor can it justify the investment of its owners – private individuals or institutions such as pension funds and insurance companies – who need to seek the best possible long-term return on their resources.

In a free competitive market, and in all but the shortest term, profit is the measure of how good a business is, how well run and how effectively it meets its responsibilities to all its stakeholders. However, according to Drucker, 'Profit is not a cause. It is the

result – the result of the performance of the business in marketing, innovation and productivity. It is at the same time the test of this performance – the only possible test, as the Communists in Russia soon found out when they tried to abolish it in the early twenties. Indeed, profit is a beautiful example of what today's scientists and engineers mean when they talk of the feedback that underlies all systems of automatic production: the self-regulation of a process by its own product.'

Note that there is a key difference between profit maximisation and making a profit. Profit maximisation is concerned with making as much profit as you can over a period. Profit maximisation occurs when there is the maximum difference between the total revenue coming into a business and the total cost being paid out. If we measured profit simply in money terms, then it would seem logical to assume that in the long term the rational business will seek to maximise the difference between its total revenue and its total cost. Accountants, for example, claim to be able quickly to weigh up the success of a business in terms of 'the bottom line'.

Profit is, of course, a major driving force. For example, at the end of the twentieth century many business writers recognised Coca-Cola as an object lesson in how to conduct a business well. Coca-Cola ploughs 60 per cent of its profits back into the business, into product development and opening up new markets. Coca-Cola is able to make high profits on a very high sales figure. It then puts these profits back into research and development, promotion and advertising, market research, opening up new distribution channels, and so on. It is thus able to out-compete all its rivals. Profits yield higher sales and still higher profits.

Setting profitability as the key aim for an organisation should then determine the way the organisation runs. In the past this often led to a very mechanistic approach in tightly controlled top-down organisations in which a strong emphasis was placed on driving down costs. Today, many business writers see the route to profit as creating priorities which are focused on enabling the organisation to develop its full potential, for example by identifying and meeting the needs of customers (a marketing orientation) and bringing the best out of staff (a human resource orientation).

In his book *Emotional Capital*, Kevin Thomson argues that very few companies know how to capitalise on the power of an asset they glibly describe as their 'most valuable'. He says that they seek instead to value and capture 'know-how', or 'intellectual capital', as the measure that truly defines the effectiveness of a workforce in any company. However, Thomson argues that this is a fallacy. 'Harnessing and managing knowledge is one thing, but organisations need to manage the emotions, feelings and beliefs that motivate people to apply that knowledge constructively. Then, and only then, can a company's lifeblood – emotional capital – make an impact on financial performance.'

Organisations therefore not only need to clarify their aims (for example, profitability), they also need to develop a clear picture of how best to achieve those aims.

Profitability is the chief spur to business activity. However, in a study carried out by Shipley in 1981 (*Journal of Industrial Economics*), the author concluded that only 15.9 per cent of a sample of 728 UK firms could be regarded as 'true' profit-maximisers. This conclusion was reached by cross-tabulating replies to two questions shown in Figure 5.5. Shipley considered as true maximisers only those firms that claimed both to maximise profits and to regard profits to be of overriding importance. Of course, there are a number of criticisms that can be levelled at any form of statistical analysis of motivations. However, there would appear to be a clear case for arguing that profit is only part of a set of business objectives.

ACTIVITY

1   Try out the questions outlined in Figure 5.5 on a group of managers to whom you have access. You might try the managers in your college or university, or alternatively those you work with.

2   To what extent do your results reveal them to be 'profit maximisers'?

Questions	Percentage of all respondents
1 Does your firm try to achieve:	
(a) maximum profits?	47.7
(b) satisfactory profits?	52.3
2 Compared with your firm's leading objectives, is the achievement of a target profit regarded as being:	
(a) of little importance?	2.1
(b) fairly important?	12.9
(c) very important?	58.9
(d) of overriding importance?	26.1
Those responding both 1(a) and 2(d)	15.9

Responses from a sample of 728 firms

Figure 5.5   Part of Shipley's questionnaire

Market share as an aim

Many firms seek to be market leaders, others aim to improve their market share. Those going for leadership may want to sell more products than all rival brands combined, or simply to sell more than the next best-selling brand. The most reliable indicator of market share is relative to other brands: that is, the ratio of a company's market share to that of its largest competitor.

Relative market share =

$$\frac{\text{Market share of the company}}{\text{Market share of the nearest competitor}}$$

A well-known study by the Boston Consultancy Group argued, on the basis of statistical information, that a ratio of 2:1 would give a 20 per cent cost advantage (that is, a company would be able to operate with costs 20 per cent lower than its nearest rival). If a company dominates the market it can produce on a larger scale than its rivals. It can therefore spread its costs over a larger output, and can then produce more cheaply than rivals. Profits can then be ploughed back into research, advertising and further expansion to maintain market leadership.

We can illustrate the relationship between market share and cost leadership by means of a simple graph (see Figure 5.6). Whereas the market leader produces at point A, market followers at points B and C are faced by higher costs at lower outputs.

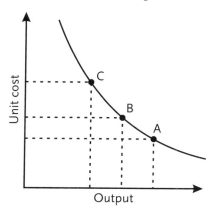

Figure 5.6   Market share and cost leadership

Market share and cost advantage

Case examples from the real world demonstrate clearly why firms seek market leadership. For example, supermarkets fight hard for market share. In recent years Tesco and Asda have substantially increased their market shares whilst Sainsbury's, the former market leader, have seen their market share consistently eroded. This has undoubtedly caused the managers of Sainsbury's some sleepless nights.

Many of the products that each of the supermarkets sell are standard items, such as Andrex toilet paper, Heinz baked beans, Walkers crisps. If you have the largest market share then you are able to spread your costs over a larger output (for example, the costs of distributing toilet paper, beans and crisps). Lose market share and your unit costs relative to those of rivals are likely to rise. Firms become progressively more or less competitive over time. A deteriorating performance is likely to have an on-going effect, unless drastic actions are taken. Business people work to a simple maxim: gain the lion's share of the market and the profits will follow.

If an organisation has the aim of being the market leader this will impact on its objectives and the way it carries out its business. For example, the organisation may focus on providing extra value for money compared with rivals to win increasing market share.

A supermarket will offer discounted petrol and 'loss leaders', more variety, better service, additional extras, longer opening hours, and so on, in order to win increasing market share. An organisation that strives for market share will often sacrifice short-term profits in order to win a bigger share of the market.

CASE STUDY

Taking advantage of market leadership

In a recent statement to shareholders, the chairperson of a company producing the leading name in branded nappies made the following points.

Over the last few years we have sought to drive our advantage home. Our product is recognised as being the most reliable, convenient and useful on the market. We currently have three times the sales of our nearest rival producer, and this has enabled us to pass the advantage of scale production on to consumers. We firmly believe that the road to success is to 'gain the lion's share of the market and then watch the profits flow in'. We will continue to find out what our consumers require in an ever-changing marketplace in order to better meet their needs.

ACTIVITY

1   How will the company benefit from making three times as many sales as the nearest rival?

2   How will consumers benefit?

3   Explain how gaining the lion's share of the market will lead to a flow of profits.

4   How can competitive advantage today lead to further competitive advantage tomorrow?

Sales as an aim

In some companies the salaries earned by managers depend on the size of the business. Their aim therefore may be to make the business as large as possible. Controlling a large business concern might also give an individual satisfaction derived from the power at their command. Increased sales might also mean reduced sales for competitors, which in the long term can be seen as consistent with a policy of profit maximisation.

In a college or school, a head teacher's or principal's salary may increase when the number of students goes over a certain threshold. This is of particular significance for senior managers who are relatively close to retirement age, as their pensions will be determined by their final few years' salary. Such managers have a big incentive to increase the number of students in their colleges, especially since any problems arising from over-expansion will have to be dealt with by someone else.

Peter Drucker points out that a number of business people argue that 'we don't care what share of the market we have, as long as our sales go up'. Drucker says that this view sounds plausible enough but it does not stand up under analysis.

'By its self, volume of sales tells little about performance, results or the future of the business. A company's sales may go up and the company may actually be headed for rapid collapse. A company's sales may go down – and the reason may not be that its marketing is poor, but that it is in a dying field and had better change fast.'

Absolute sales figures are meaningless on their own. They need to be projected against actual and potential market trends. It is also important to look at sales as a percentage of the market. A business that supplies less than a certain share of the market is a marginal supplier and may be squeezed out.

A big incentive to increase sales is that the cost of making additional sales will often fall as sales rise. As a general rule, therefore, companies will be happier with higher sales figures. Study any company report and you will immediately notice the high prominence given to turnover as a financial highlight. This may be because turnover is the figure which is most likely to show improvement year on year. Of course it is important to examine sales in relation to other figures which appear in the accounts.

ROCE as an aim

Return on Capital Employed (ROCE) is frequently used as an aim for a business. The idea behind ROCE is that the capital invested in a business could be invested in alternatives. The next-best alternative is termed the opportunity cost (that is, the sacrifice, what is given up).

ROCE is a measure of an organisation's return on capital invested. In simple terms, if a company invests one million pounds on a particular project and gets a 10 per cent return, then this is its ROCE. When deciding whether to put £100 in the Best Building Society or the Second Best Building Society (SBBS), you will be influenced by the fact that the Best Building Society offers you 10 per cent interest compared with SBBS's 8 per cent.

In establishing the required ROCE for a particular organisation, a key consideration will be what the return would be on the capital invested in its next-best use. After all, shareholders will not be keen to keep their shareholding in a public limited company like Shell if they could make a better return on BP shares, or in oil industry shares at all if they could make a better return by investing in entertainment.

Setting an aim based on ROCE means that an organisation must create sets of tight objectives and operational standards to ensure that it meets the financial requirements. Clearly ROCE as an aim will help the organisation to focus on providing shareholder value. In recent years ROCE has also been used as an aim in public sector organisations (such as, to achieve a return on capital invested equivalent to what the investment could have earned in the private sector). In the privatised industries, regulators also often set targets for ROCE, although the intention here may be related to controlling profiteering and to stop the exploitation of consumers.

Growth as an aim

A firm that grows quickly may find it easier to attract investors and thus be able to produce on a larger scale. However, one of the biggest mistakes that business people make in the early days is that of overtrading. If that happens, there can be problems: not enough cash to pay bills in the short term, managing a large staff, and so on. It is surprising how many people fall into this trap. Often someone will set up a new business and, because of its early success, decide to expand, only to find it difficult to manage a larger business, or to bring in the extra customers that are needed. A fairly common pattern is for an entrepreneur to start with one business interest, expand to two or three interests, and then end up with no viable business interest.

Businesses that aim for growth are ones with a higher propensity to accept risks. Such organisations may be more willing to borrow, and to consider joining or taking over other existing concerns. An organisation with a growth focus will need fairly dynamic structures because people in the organisation have to learn to live with regular change.

One form of growth is to move into a number of markets. This makes it possible to spread risks. If one market fails, another may support the loss. However, opening into new markets also exposes a business to fresh risks.

Level of service as an aim

Customer service is a term describing the overall activity of identifying and satisfying customer needs, and keeping them satisfied. The term 'service' is used in three distinct ways:

♦ To contrast an intangible 'product' from tangible ones. Services are intangible things like a train journey, a haircut, or advice on investment.
♦ As an extra you get when you buy a product. You buy a TV set and the shop will 'service' it for you: that is, it will make sure the TV will continue to work.
♦ As an overall description of the desired relationship between a supplier and a customer. 'Service' in this sense is based on the premise that every commercial transaction is a service.

For example, if an oil company assumed that the function of its retail network was simply to sell petrol and lubricants it would quickly lose business to competitors. Its real function is to supply a 'customer service': in its case the service of enjoyable, trouble-free motoring. Petrol and lubricants are only part of that. The provision of somewhere to rest and refresh, to eat and drink, to buy gifts and groceries, to make a phone call and buy a newspaper, and all in a clean, friendly environment, is an equally important part.

In an age of competitiveness, it is not surprising that service is given a high priority in many organisations. In a range of surveys of the importance of elements in the marketing mix, service has come out as being the third most important ingredient behind product and price, but ahead of advertising, promotion and sales effort. More importantly, with each passing year customer service has been ranked higher as an important ingredient in the marketing mix. In their book *Relationship Marketing*, Christopher, Payne and Ballantyne argue that customer service has become so important for two main reasons:

♦ Changing customer expectations. In almost every market the customer is now more demanding and more sophisticated than, say, 30 years ago. With changing customer expectations, competitors are seeing customer service as a competitive weapon with which to differentiate their sales.
♦ The need for a relationship strategy. To ensure that a customer service strategy which will create a value proposition for customers is formulated, implemented and controlled, it is necessary to establish it as having a central role and not one that is subsumed in various elements of the marketing mix.

Customer or user perceptions

What do customers and users think and feel about an organisation? Most modern organisations want to be seen in a favourable light. It is perception that drives purchases and customer loyalty. If you think that 'You can be sure of Shell', then you may become a lifelong Shell user. If you believe that 'Coca-Cola is the real thing' then you may drink little else.

CASE STUDY

Service at John Lewis

The following relates to service at the John Lewis Partnership, as described by the organisation.

Here are some examples of the myriad services we offer:

♦ We install and balance long-case clocks.
♦ We make rugs to most shapes, sizes or designs.
♦ We make curtains, pelmets and blinds to measure, for any window, whether it be in a palace, a wendy house or your home.
♦ We make club ties to order.
♦ We have a full re-upholstery and loose-cover service for all traditional or modern suites, armchairs and sofas.
♦ We sell extra-small baby clothes for premature babies.
♦ We make pillows, pillowcases, sheets and quilts to any shape or size.

Our selling assistants are ready to offer help when you need it. All receive extensive training and most are full-time, permanent staff, so whoever you speak to will know what they are talking about. If they cannot answer your question themselves, they will do their best to find out. Examples of the high level of service on offer include the following:

♦ Our children's shoe-fitters are professionally trained in measuring children's feet.
♦ We offer an expert bra-fitting service, our assistants being trained to fit junior and maternity bras, and bras for special needs like sport or mastectomy.
♦ It is not our policy to persuade you to buy something, we only help and advise.

ACTIVITY

1 What does the information above tell you about the aims and objectives of the John Lewis Partnership?

2 Why do you think it focuses on these aims and objectives?

Positive perceptions take a long time to build, and can be destroyed in just a few minutes. When Gerald Ratner told the world (through the media) at a business dinner that most of his jewellery was 'crap', his business folded within months. Today, organisations continually seek improvements in their product and service to make sure that they are well thought of: that they are 'the world's favourite airline', 'the team you can trust', 'the customer's first choice', and so on.

The best way to create customer belief in a product is to ensure total quality systems at every stage at which the product, the brand and the company comes into contact with its many publics.

Stakeholders

Identification of stakeholders

The traditional view of business in the UK has been that there are only two parties who are interested in the success of a company: the owners and the workers. Whilst the owners were keen to make as much profit as possible from the resources available to the business, the workers had a different agenda, looking for fair working conditions, security of employment and good wages. Today, however, we recognise that there are a number of other groups who also have legitimate interests in the success of the company. The people and businesses in the local community benefit from the success of the firm, society is keen to see that environmental damage by the company is kept to a minimum, the suppliers to the firm hope that the firm does well so that their custom may increase. All of these (and others) have an interest in the success of the firm, and this makes each of them stakeholders in the company. Therefore, any person or group of persons that are affected by the success or failure of a company are considered to be stakeholders in that firm.

Who are the stakeholders in a business?

Shareholders

The shareholders have invested their wealth in the business. They receive two benefits from the firm doing well: the shares may rise in value if the firm is successful and also the dividends that they receive will increase if profits improve. Conversely they could lose all of the value of their investment should the business fail.

Directors

Their jobs will depend upon the success of the firm, as may the level of their remuneration. This may vary according to bonuses related to the financial success of the firm.

Employees

Their jobs also depend on the success of the firm, but also the nature of the work that they are required to do may change according to its success. A firm in a competitive environment may experience regular change and the nature of work and the levels of responsibility that workers may be required to undertake may change. Firms that are struggling may 'release' some staff, remaining staff may then have to take on more responsibility than they would choose. A solid firm, however, provides the employees with job security which lends security to their personal lives.

Customers

If a company works in a competitive market, customers may benefit through lower prices, but too much competition could leave them looking for a new company to buy from.

Suppliers

Companies that supply goods or services to a firm will want the firm to do well so that they have a regular customer.

Creditors

Creditors are people or organisations that are owed money by the firm, such as the firm's bankers who have lent it money. They would like to see the firm succeed so that they get their money back and make a profit from the deal. If the company fails, the bank could be left with a bad debt, but if it is successful the relationship could be mutually profitable.

Government

Every firm pays Corporation Tax from profits and most raise VAT through sales, so all firms are of some interest to the government. Some firms are more significant, however. The government would not like to see a company that is a major employer in a town struggling. If it should fail that would leave the government with a substantial problem in terms of the number of newly unemployed people.

Society

Society would like to see the firm trading in a responsible manner so that danger to the public is minimised along with damage to the environment. If the firm is struggling, cost cutting may compromise these objectives. Pressure groups may be formed to put pressure on the firm to conform.

Local community

There are many local businesses that will depend on the success of a firm. A number of businesses will spring up to service the needs of a large local company and to provide for the needs of the people who work there. Newsagents, public houses, restaurants, sandwich shops, and so on will all rely on the business continuing to succeed. If it fails, they may go down with it.

2000 jobs to go at coalfield that lost millions

The Selby Coalfield in North Yorkshire is to close following losses of £107 million over the last 42 months. The field is the major employer in the town.

UK Coal who own the coalfield said that there seemed to be little prospect of it ever making profits and therefore all 2100 jobs would be phased out over the next two years. Skilled face workers can earn up to £1000 per week. Analysts suggest that a further 3000 people along with local companies will be affected by this decision. The government announced today that it will contribute £10 million towards redundancy payments and will set up a task force to help regenerate the area.

Conflict of stakeholder expectations

The power that goes with stakeholding will depend on many factors, but generally speaking the most important will be the extent to which the organisation is dependent on the stakeholder.

Stakeholders can make organisations dependent on them in a number of ways, such as by supplying key resources or key skills. A supplier of a major component can exert a lot of pressure on an organisation, as can a key knowledge worker, and as can suppliers of finance. Also, of course, all businesses are dependent on their customers.

Stakeholders can also exert power through their ability to make demands on the organisation (for example, in the case of a powerful trade union, or a strong pressure group which has the ear of the media).

Although the objectives of organisations usually reflect a general agreement between stakeholders about values and aims, it frequently happens that policies adopted tend to favour some groups of stakeholders over others. Such policy clashes might include how much of the company's profits should be distributed to shareholders, or whether employees should be given more of a say in decision making, or whether an organisation should be allowed to expand its operations in an area of natural beauty.

The following list describes further situations in which stakeholder conflicts may occur:

♦ Interpretations of who the organisation should serve. One of the strongest arguments put forward against building societies converting to public limited companies was that they would no longer serve their members' (for example, savers' and borrowers') interests but instead would primarily serve the needs of shareholders. In a similar way, conflicts can arise over the interpretation of business objectives (for example, where a new managing director introduces policies which seem to fly in the face of existing practice).

♦ Deliberate misinterpretations of objectives. At any time it is possible for stakeholders with the responsibility for making key decisions to deliberately misinterpret objectives, often to increase their own power and prestige. Individual managers may start to create their own policies and practices which further the interests of their own departments.

♦ Changes in strategies and policies. Dynamic organisations adjust their direction according to changes in circumstances. Unless these changes are communicated to and agreed by all key stakeholders, some people may continue working using old approaches while others adopt the new ones. This may result from deliberate sabotage or genuine lack of understanding.

- Internal politics. Different segments of an organisation may be allied with different stakeholders (for example, employees and shareholders). This is likely to lead to clashes within the organisation and between the organisation and its external stakeholders.
- Bad management. Poor management allied with poor communication can create an atmosphere in which stakeholder conflicts arise.
- Inevitable differences in objectives, policies and procedures. There is a certain inevitability in the way conflict may arise in organisations through a lack of shared priorities. Organisations are made up of people rather than machine parts, so differing aspirations and understandings are almost certain to lead to conflict.

Coalitions between stakeholders

It makes sense to forge a coalition between stakeholders who share similar interests. The coalition may be developed over a long period or may be created to fight on a common front over a specific issue.

In terms of marketing, the most significant alliance is that forged with the end consumers. However, it is also possible to see all of a firm's stakeholders as consumers. After all, each and every stakeholder group is 'buying' from an organisation, so it must strive to win their loyalty and commitment.

Marketing orientation thus involves treating all stakeholders as customers and seeking to satisfy their aspirations and needs. This is most likely to occur by creating open communication channels, and using sophisticated research techniques to find out what exactly each and every stakeholder seeks from the organisation.

Achieving stakeholder satisfaction

Identification of aspirations

The starting point in achieving stakeholder satisfaction is to find out exactly what it is that the stakeholder

CASE STUDY

GM crops

Monsanto is a research company in the UK that is investigating the potential of genetically modified crops. Monsanto's website says:

'We're excited about the potential for genetically modified food to contribute to a better environment and a sustainable, plentiful, and healthy food supply. We recognise, however, that many consumers have genuine concerns about food biotechnology and its impact on their families.'

Field trials suggest that genetically modified crops can produce increases in crop yields of up to 80 per cent, compared with non-GM counterparts. Other trials show no difference.

While many groups have opposed GM crops, others argue there is a moral case for introducing GM technology to developing countries, to help tackle poverty and hunger. Results in 2004 from Africa, however, suggest GM crops do not save costs.

ACTIVITY

1. Identify the stakeholders in Monsanto and the work that they are doing in developing GM crops.

2. Identify the conflicts in stakeholder interest that exist.

3. Divide your group into two and debate the case for and against the development of GM crops.

aspires to. For example, do employees want to have more say and influence in decision making? This can be found out by using techniques such as employee appraisal.

Do customers want products which are more environmentally friendly? This can be found out by market research. Do creditors want to be paid more quickly? This can be found out by creditor surveys. What do citizens who come into contact with the company want to see happening? This can be found out by holding open forums and public meetings. Each of the above examples highlights the importance of open communications.

Satisfaction and dissatisfaction cycles

Modern organisations use the expression 'growing more contented customers'. The implication is that you can create satisfaction cycles as an on-going process: a satisfied customer will want to build a stronger relationship with an organisation, a stronger relationship builds customer satisfaction, and so on. This is a 'virtuous circle'. In contrast, dissatisfied customers will want to loosen their relationships with an organisation, leading to a downward spiral.

The concept of a customer can be extended to include stakeholders and of course includes the 'internal customer' (stakeholders within the organisation). 'Internal customers' are people inside the company receiving products (usually unfinished) or services from their colleagues also in the company.

This extended concept is useful for several reasons. It enables people inside the company to realise the importance of what they are doing. It makes the point that the quality of the products and services sold to the external customer depends on the quality of products (perhaps only half-finished products) and services provided to colleagues within the company. Perhaps most usefully, it helps people to realise their own significance: each person is an expert with something unique and essential to contribute.

Power–influence matrix

Managing organisations effectively involves a considerable amount of politics and alliance brokering. It is important to have an idea of the relative strengths and influence of stakeholders within an organisation.

Woe betide the company that misjudges the power of influential stakeholders such as the media!

Johnson and Scholes, in their widely read and influential book *Exploring Corporate Strategy*, have identified a number of matrices which serve as useful tools to those who seek to make changes in business policy and need to examine the implications of their actions for the various stakeholders within the organisation.

The power–dynamism matrix

This matrix helps assess, in the early stages of developing a new strategy, where 'political effort' might be needed to influence key stakeholders.

The power–dynamism matrix (Figure 5.7) focuses on the amount of power (high or low) that groups of stakeholders have and the predictability of their views (high or low) in relation to a key change in business policy.

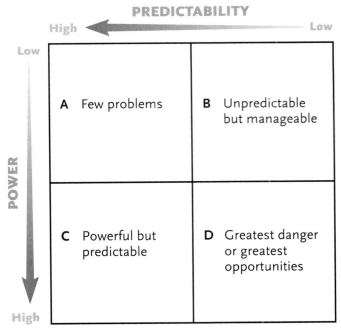

Figure 5.7   The power–dynamism matrix

♦ Stakeholders in the A and B groups have low power. However, this does not mean that they are unimportant, because their views may influence other stakeholders.

- Stakeholders in the C group have high power but their views are predictable. There should be no surprises.
- Stakeholders in the D group are the most difficult to influence or persuade and their views may also be the most difficult to predict. In managing change or in developing policy, therefore, it is important to pay considerable attention to this group in order to seek their support for change.

The power–interest matrix

This matrix (Figure 5.8) examines stakeholders in relation to the power they hold and the degree of interest they show in the organisation.

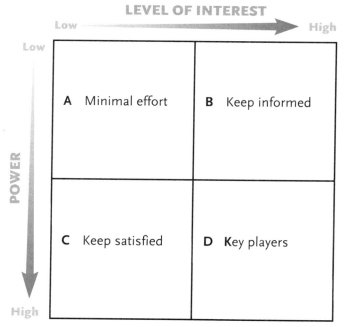

Figure 5.8   The power–interest matrix

Satisfying stakeholder objectives: bargaining options

Successful management therefore involves a careful assessment of the aspirations of its stakeholders, an understanding of their sources of power, and the mapping of the levels of predictability, interest and power of these groupings.

There are a number of bargaining options available to managers seeking to win the support of stakeholders. One option is to ignore a stakeholder's interest completely, but clearly this is a risky strategy as the stakeholder may be able to gain considerable support for their case. Frequently we come across stories in the press where individuals have been unfairly dismissed at work, where customer complaints have been ignored, or where a company has ridden roughshod over the local community. When these cases come to light they lead to the loss of goodwill for the company, and internal dissension.

Another negative option is to fight the stakeholder, perhaps by taking the stakeholder to court (for example, where a company takes a libel action against someone who it feels to be defaming the name of the organisation). Again, this is a high-risk strategy because it brings the dispute out into the public arena.

A third option is to set out to appease the stakeholder, perhaps by making some concessions (for example, by offering compensation to individuals and groups who suffer because of the company's actions).

A more positive approach is to try to win the stakeholder over by some form of persuasion. This involves opening up a dialogue with opposing stakeholders (for example, by the use of newsletters or public meetings). When Shell UK was accused of being unfriendly to the environment in its intention to place derelict oil rigs at the bottom of the sea, it arranged a series of public meetings in an effort to convince detractors that this was the Best Possible Environmental Option (BPEO).

Another option is to form a coalition (a special relationship) with the stakeholder based on shared interests. Again this will involve the opening up of communication channels on a wide front.

The organisation can also take on board the stakeholder's feelings by offering pride of place in developing on-going strategy. This could take place if the stakeholder is able to put forward a convincing case.

Finally, the organisation might take the path of transforming itself into a new pattern which is determined by the stakeholder (for example, when one company is taken over by another which previously had been the junior partner in the relationship). In a similar way a vocal group of shareholders might take over control of a company and refashion it in the way they see fit.

Responsibilities of organisations

Of course all companies have responsibilities to their stakeholders, and this has been discussed at length previously. Let us go on to look at other responsibilities companies have.

Legal responsibilities to consumers

Although most businesses trade in an honest and ethical way, not all firms are to be trusted. Some will sell defective goods and inadequate services if they can get away with it, and it is on these occasions that government finds it necessary to intervene to protect vulnerable consumers. This is done by means of law, and the main legislation is summarised here.

Trade Descriptions Acts 1968 and 1972

It is a criminal offence to give a false or misleading description to goods, services, accommodation or facilities, and firms may be prosecuted for not abiding by this. With regard to sale prices, the Act insists that goods must have been sold at the higher price for at least 28 consecutive days during the previous 6 months if they are to be labelled as sale items.

Sale of Goods Act 1979

This Act imposes five key conditions:

♦ the seller must have the right to sell the goods (for example, goods were not stolen by the seller)
♦ the goods will correspond with any description given when selling them (the seller does not have to describe goods for sale, but if description is given the goods delivered must fit that description)
♦ the goods should be of satisfactory quality
♦ the goods should be fit for the buyer's purpose (so a new piece of furniture should not break when used)
♦ where goods are sold by sample, the bulk delivered must correspond with the sample.

There are various remedies open to customers who feel that they have not been treated fairly, including claims for damages.

Supply of Goods and Services Act 1982

This implies three terms when services are supplied:

♦ the supplier will carry out the service with reasonable care and skill
♦ the service will be performed within a reasonable time, and a reasonable price will be charged.

Food Safety Act 1990

This requires those businesses that handle food to take all reasonable precautions when manufacturing, transporting, storing, preparing and selling food items to ensure that food sold is perfectly safe. In early 1999 the UK government announced the launch of the Food Standards Agency to monitor such processes and to give the consumer confidence when buying such products. This followed some high-profile news items suggesting that food items were not safe, such as the BSE beef crisis and outbreaks of *E. coli* bacterial poisoning.

Consumer Protection Act 1987

This covers safety regulations for dangerous products such as flammable items and poisonous products such as chemicals and bleach. Warnings should be placed on such items and damages can be claimed against manufacturers of defective products which cause death or injury.

Consumer Credit Act 1974

All businesses offering credit (for example, banks, retailers) must be licensed through the Office of Fair Trading (OFT) which sets out strict requirements when offering and selling credit. This is to protect consumers against unscrupulous lenders charging very high interest rates and making it difficult for customers to amend or cancel agreements.

Weights and Measures Act 1985

It is an offence for traders to give short weights of items bought or short measure on fluids. Inspectors will check shops, restaurants and garages to ensure that the pumps, dispensers or scales used are accurate.

Environmental Protection Act 1990

This controls pollution, noise (when it might affect health), and waste disposal where this might damage the environment

Sunday Trading Act 1994

The Act was to regulate the activities of shops opening on Sundays. Whilst allowing them to open, it restricted large businesses to opening for six hours only, between 10 a.m. and 6 p.m., although small businesses may ignore these rules, as may chemists, service stations and petrol stations.

Legal responsibilities in employment

Common law protection

The common law recognises that employers have certain implied responsibilities towards their employees, it also recognises certain implied rights for employers.

Major responsibilities of an employer

Pay

The employer has a duty to pay the employee an agreed remuneration for being ready and willing to work. There is a statutory minimum wage which applies in the UK, which was £4.60 per hour in 2003.

A limited duty to provide work

Only in exceptional cases is an employer compelled to provide an employee with work. The duty exists, for instance, where lack of work would mean a wage reduction or where the work is on commission or piecework. The duty also exists where lack of work may have a damaging effect on the employee's reputation. Two obvious examples would be actors or television presenters, but more recently the courts have shown some sympathy towards senior executives or employees with a high level of technical skill who need to work to maintain their skills at a particular level.

Expenses

There is the duty to indemnify the employee if he or she has necessarily incurred expenses in the course of employment.

The duty of mutual trust or confidence

This could also be called the duty to provide reasonable management. The old legal terminology of 'master' and 'servant' has been replaced with 'employer' and 'employee'. This has signalled a change in the courts' view of the employment relationship and what could be considered to be reasonable behaviour by both parties. For examples of the breakdown of such a relationship, see the discussion later of unfair dismissal.

Contractual rights

The employer has a duty to provide proper information to an employee about his or her rights under the contract. This is a relatively new area and has arisen from a House of Lords decision in Scally *v* Southern Health & Social Services Board (1991) ICR 771. New employees were not informed of their rights to enhance their years of pension entitlement, but the Lords held there to be an implied term that they should have been provided with this information.

The duty to ensure safety

Most of the legislation relating to the employer's responsibility for health and safety is now covered by the Health and Safety at Work Act and several EU Directives. However, the extent of the employer's responsibility in this respect can be illustrated by two cases reflecting modern attitudes towards health, and in particular towards stress at work and smoking at work.

In Walker *v* Northumberland County Council (1995) IRLR 35, a social work manager suffered a nervous breakdown and was off work for five months. On his return he was not given the support promised and his workload was increased. He suffered a second nervous breakdown and was dismissed on the grounds of ill health. The court found there to be no reason why psychiatric damages should be excluded from the scope of duty of care of the council provided it could have been foreseen that the employee was at risk. The first breakdown may not have been foreseen. The second should have been.

In Waltons & Morse *v* Dorrington (1997) IRLR 488, Ms Dorrington was a legal secretary and non-smoker who had worked for a firm since 1984. In 1992, she was moved to another office which was at the end of a corridor and close to the room occupied by three heavy-smoking solicitors. She complained. Although some modifications were made in the workplace that did not resolve the problem. As a result she left the firm and claimed constructive dismissal. The Employment Appeal Tribunal upheld her claim on the following grounds.

> It is an implied term of every contract of employment that the employer will provide and monitor for employees, so far as is reasonably practicable, a working environment which is reasonably suitable for the performance by them of their contractual duties.

Statutory protection

The Employment Rights Act 1996 (ERA 96) and its predecessors were introduced for the same reasons as were other forms of protective legislation. Although the common law does give the employee some protection, it is rarely able to develop sufficiently quickly to meet the needs of the modern business world. One of the major provisions of ERA 96 is the requirement that an employer should provide an employee with certain written terms and conditions of employment. This means that, for most employees, their rights and obligations are clearer because the law normally allows express terms in a contract to take precedence over implied terms.

Terms and conditions

A contract need not be in written form, but ERA 96 requires that certain terms and conditions must be in writing. They are:

- the names of the employer and employee
- the date when employment began
- whether the employment counts as a period of continuous employment with a previous employer, and the date of commencement of the previous employment where this is the case
- the scale or rate of pay and the method of calculating pay where the employee is paid by commission or bonus
- when payment is made (that is, weekly or monthly), and the day or date of payment
- the hours to be worked, including any compulsory overtime
- holiday entitlement and holiday pay
- sick pay and injury arrangements
- entitlement to a pension scheme
- the length of notice of termination an employee must receive or give
- the job title
- the duration of temporary contracts
- the work location or locations
- any collective agreements affecting the job
- when the job requires work outside the UK for more than one month, the period of such work, the currency in which the employee will be paid and any other pay or benefits
- grievance procedures
- disciplinary procedures.

Certain of these particulars can be given by reference to a common document, such as a collective agreement or a staff handbook, but such information must be readily accessible to the employee at all times.

Additional statutory rights of employees

Not only are employees entitled to a written statement, they are also statutorily entitled to certain other rights.

Time off work

For public duties

Under certain circumstances, employees have a right to time off work, sometimes with pay. These include:

- trade union activities, both as a trade union member and as an official
- public duties, for work as a magistrate, member of an employment tribunal, and so on
- a redundancy situation, to allow time off to look for another job or to make arrangements for training for future employment
- lay-off, to allow employees with four weeks or more of continuous service a guaranteed payment up to a maximum sum if they are not provided with work on a normal working day
- occupational pension schemes, for nominated trustees of occupational pension schemes
- antenatal care.

Holidays

Under the Working Time Regulations 1998, workers who have been employed for at least 13 weeks have a right to three weeks' paid annual leave. This right applies to both full-time and part-time workers and means that a part-timer working two days a week, for example, has a statutory right to six days' paid annual leave. Where a part-timer's working time is set in terms of hours, then the leave may also be expressed in terms of hours.

For sickness

Employers are required to provide statutory sick pay (SSP) on behalf of the government. SSP is currently paid by them for up to 28 weeks of incapacity for work during a three-year period. The first three days of sickness are 'waiting days' and no SSP is payable. However, during subsequent periods of sickness, if the employee has not been back at work following the first period of sickness for eight weeks or more, the periods are linked and there are no statutory waiting days. Under the SSP Percentage Threshold Order 1995, employers will recover on a percentage threshold scheme; that is, the employers will take the National Insurance contribution (employer's and employee's) paid in any given tax month. They will then ascertain the SSP paid in the same month. If this is more than 13 per cent of the NIC figure, they will recover the excess.

Payment details

Itemised pay statement

Before the introduction of employment protection legislation, there was no obligation upon employers to provide their employees with itemised pay statements. Provided payment was made, that was all the law required. However, ERA 96 now requires that employees must receive a statement before or at the time of receiving their pay, showing:

- gross pay and take-home pay together with the variable deductions which make up the difference between the two figures
- details of how it is to be paid.

Fixed deductions need not be itemised every pay day, provided the employer gives the employee a separate statement containing details of them every month.

Deductions from pay

Part 11 of the Employment Rights Act 1996 removed the right of employees to be paid in cash. Deductions from pay are unlawful unless:
- they are authorised by statute (in the case, for instance, of NI and tax deductions) or
- they are included in a written contract of employment, or
- the employee has put in writing beforehand his or her agreement to the deductions.

Notice of termination

Prior to statutory legislation, the question of the length of notice of termination of employment was a contractual issue between the employer and employee. The ERA, however, now lays down certain minimum

ACTIVITY

Rules relating to deductions from pay occur most frequently in the service industries, and normally arise through cash shortages or stock deficiencies. Deductions from workers' pay in the retail trades are limited to 10 per cent of the gross wages and may be made only within the period of 12 months from the date when the employee knew or ought to have known about them.

1 Why do you think the service industries are the most frequent users of the right to make deductions from employees' pay?

2 Why are more stringent limitations imposed upon employers in those industries?

ACTIVITY

Discuss the following questions in your group.

1 Why should employees on monthly fixed-term contracts be given the right to notice after three consecutive months?

2 Why should the law require that employees give only one week's notice no matter how long they have worked for the organisation? What possible problems can you foresee in enforcing that provision?

notice requirements. If a person has been continuously employed for at least one month, he or she must be given:

◆ not less than one week's notice if the period of continuous employment is less than two years
◆ not less than one week's notice for each year of continuous employment if the period of continuous employment is two years or more but less than 12 years
◆ not less than 12 weeks' notice if the period of continuous employment is 12 years or more.

It is not necessary to give notice to any employee at the expiry of a fixed term as notice has been given at the start of the contract that it will end at a certain date. However, those employed on fixed-term contracts of one month or less and who have been continuously employed by the employer for at least three months have the same notice rights as other employees.

Employees must give their employers at least one week's notice if they have been continuously employed for one month or more. The period does not increase with longer service.

Working time

Recent legislation has concentrated on the hours employees can be expected to work. Of relevance here are the Working Time Regulations 1998 (implementing the EU Working Time Directive 93/104/EC) and the Young Worker's Directive (EU Directive 93/33/EC). These working time regulations now provide that a person's average weekly working time (including overtime) should not have to exceed 48 hours, averaged over a reference period of 17 weeks. Individuals can agree to be excluded from the maximum working week requirement on a voluntary basis.

Night working should not have to exceed eight hours in each 24-hour period, over a reference period of 17 weeks. Provided compensatory rest is permitted or appropriate protection given, the rules on night working are excluded for 'special case' workers, and they can be modified or excluded for other workers by a collective or workplace agreement.

Adult workers must be permitted to take a rest period of not less than 11 consecutive hours in each 24-hour period, and a weekly rest period of not less than 24 hours in each seven-day period. Young workers are entitled to a daily rest period of 12 consecutive hours, except in unexpected and unpredictable occurrences where compensatory rest may be permitted within three weeks.

Adult workers whose daily working time exceeds six hours are entitled to a rest break in accordance with the terms of a collective or workplace agreement. Where there is no such agreement a minimum break of 20 minutes is laid down. Young workers are entitled to a rest break of at least 30 minutes after 4½ hours' work.

Actual dismissal

The first step a dismissed employee must take, if he or she does not accept the position, is to prove that dismissal has actually occurred. In most cases this is relatively simple, but there can be problems arising from the wording of the dismissal. If, for instance,

ACTIVITY

Discuss the following questions in your group.

1. Since an employee can opt out of the agreement, does that not defeat the protective purpose of the legislation?

2. Why should young workers have more protection than older workers? Is not an 18-year-old likely to be fitter than a 50-year-old?

3. 'For many employers, the introduction of the regulations will provoke major changes in the organisation of work.' Discuss.

there is an argument between a supervisor and employee and words such as 'get lost' or 'there's the door' are used, they could be construed as words of dismissal. Much depends on the circumstances. Is the working environment such that arguments of this sort occur frequently without any real intent to dismiss? Is there a marked difference in the status of both parties?

Constructive dismissal

Of equal importance is the concept of constructive dismissal. This is in some respects the reverse of actual dismissal, in that the employee leaves without having been dismissed because he or she feels that the employer has been in fundamental breach of contract and has forced its termination. Obviously this links closely with the employer's implied obligation to manage reasonably. Examples include:

◆ unilaterally changing the terms of the contract to the employee's disadvantage (for example, increasing the hours, reducing the pay)
◆ an unreasonable accusation of theft against an employee of good character and many years' standing
◆ an arbitrary refusal of a pay rise to one employee when everyone else receives one
◆ very abusive language on a number of occasions
◆ publicly criticising an employee, particularly in front of his or her own staff
◆ demotion.

Employment Act 2002

The Employment Act 2002 came into force on 6 April 2003 and made some significant changes to the rights of employees. The Act was said by the government to be 'a balanced package of support for working parents, while reducing red tape for employers'. The provisions of the Act were to be introduced in stages, but by the time you read this it should all be in force. The Act covers a number of key areas.

Statutory disciplinary and dismissal procedure

These conditions are to be implied into every contract of employment. From 2003 all employers must follow the following stages in any disciplinary or dismissal cases. If these stages are not followed and an employee is dismissed, this will be automatically considered to be an unfair dismissal.

Stage 1 The employer must provide a written statement of the grounds for disciplinary action to the employee. An invitation will be sent to the employee to attend a meeting to discuss the matter further.

Stage 2 The meeting must take place before any disciplinary action is taken, although the employee can be suspended on full pay whilst waiting for the meeting if this option is stated in the contract of employment.

At the meeting both the employer and employee will explain their cases. After the meeting the employee must be informed of the decision and given the option to appeal against the decision.

Stage 3 If the employee wishes to appeal against the decision, then he or she must inform the employer and the employer must invite the employee to attend a further meeting.

The employee must take all reasonable steps to attend that meeting.

After the meeting, the employer must inform the employee of the decision.

Instant dismissal for gross misconduct

The employer is required to produce the statement of grounds for action and outline the employee's right to appeal. However, there is no requirement to hold a meeting prior to an instant dismissal. Such a step would be highly unusual, however, and to be safe the company should always follow the stages outlined above. Breach of these disciplinary procedures may be considered by the courts to be a fundamental breach of contract. In such a case, the employee would be allowed to resign and claim constructive dismissal.

Statutory grievance procedures

If an employee has a grievance against their employer, the following stages should be followed in pursuing that grievance:

Stage 1 The employee must explain their grievance in writing to the employer.

Stage 2 The employer must invite the employee to at least one meeting to discuss the matter and the employee must take all reasonable steps to attend. After the meeting the employee must be informed of the decision.

Stage 3 If the employee is unhappy with the decision, he must inform the employer that he wishes to appeal.

The employee must then be invited to attend a second meeting and the employee must take all reasonable steps to attend.

After the meeting the employee must be informed of the decision.

Maternity provisions

Statutory maternity leave has been improved significantly. Prior to the Act, an employee had to be employed for a year before she was entitled to maternity leave; this has been reduced to 26 weeks. Leave used to last up to 18 weeks, but it is now available for up to 26 weeks. The amounts to be paid have been increased. The first 6 weeks of maternity payment should now be at 90 per cent of her average weekly earnings. The following 20 weeks is paid at £100 per week or 90 per cent of average weekly earnings (whichever is less).

Adoption leave

This is a new benefit for people who adopt a new child. If an employee has been continuously employed for 26 weeks by the week in which an approved match with the child is made, the employee is eligible to 26 weeks paid leave followed by 26 weeks unpaid leave.

Parental leave

An employee who has a relationship with a new or adoptive mother is entitled to up to two weeks paternity leave which must be taken within 56 days of the birth of the child. The employee must have been continuously employed for 26 weeks by the 14th week before the child is born, or by the week in which a match is made with the adopted child, to qualify for this leave. Partners under this Act also include people in same-sex relationships, so a woman could request parental leave to be with her female partner.

Flexible working

These conditions apply to all parents with children under the age of 6 (or 18 where the child is disabled) and who have over 6 months of continuous service. An employee wishing to adopt flexible working practices should outline their proposals in writing to the employer. The employer is required to consider this request and meet with the employee to discuss the proposals within four weeks. Within two weeks of the meeting the employer should write to the employee either accepting or rejecting the request. If the request is to be rejected, the employer must give good reasons for the rejection. Acceptable reasons might be that it would impede customer service or place an unreasonable financial burden on the company.

Fixed-term work

The new regulations are intended to prevent the less favourable treatment of fixed-term employees compared with their permanently employed colleagues. A statutory maximum of four years will be placed on the use of successive fixed-term contracts after which time the employee must be made permanent, unless there is an objectively justifiable reason not to. Fixed-term employees are also given the same employment rights upon termination of a contract as an employee

Time off for trade union learning representatives

Employees who are training to be trade union officials are entitled to take paid time off.

CASE STUDY

Flexible working arrangements

Many employers have taken 'flexible working' to mean letting employees have some time off when they need it for personal reasons, but the requirements of the Act actually go much deeper than that.

Employees who are parents of young or disabled children now have a legal right to request an actual change to the terms and conditions of their employment so that they can look after their children.

Employees may request to vary:

♦ the hours they work
♦ the times they work, and/or
♦ their place of work.

Some employees may only request small changes, such as beginning work a little late so that a child can be dropped off at school, but employers can also expect requests for more major changes, such as requests for workers to go part-time, to work from home via teleworking, to look for job-sharing arrangements, or even to work only in school term-times. All such requests must be given serious consideration, and if approved they will constitute permanent changes to the employees terms and conditions of employment.

Legal responsibilities in disability discrimination

The Disability Discrimination Act 1995 was introduced to remove the discrimination faced by many disabled people. It provides rights in a number of areas, but one of the key ones is in employment. It applies to those employers employing more than 15 people and it requires employers to consider making changes to their premises in order to help access for disabled people. The law identifies two ways by which an employer might unlawfully discriminate against a disabled employee or job applicant:

♦ By treating the person less favourably than other employees or applicants as a result of the disability.
♦ By not making reasonable adjustments to working practices or premises to accommodate disabled people (unless there is reasonable justification for this). Adjustments could involve wheelchair ramps or flexitime to allow for treatment. The company can apply for help from the government scheme Access to Work. From October 2004 all provisions also cover businesses with fewer than 15 employees.

Firms must therefore look carefully at their procedures and premises to ensure that no disabled person is disadvantaged. Particular attention should be paid to those procedures used in recruiting new staff. The word 'reasonable' is important here. The law does not require employers to go to every conceivable length to provide for a disabled person's needs, only that they make reasonable efforts.

In the case Kenny v Hampshire Constabulary 1998 a man who suffered from cerebral palsy and who needed assistance when going to the toilet, was not unlawfully discriminated against when an offer of employment was withdrawn because the necessary assistance could not be provided. The respondents asked for volunteers from the department but no one was available. It was suggested that the applicant could work from home but this was rejected for security reasons. An application to the Access to Work scheme for funding for a part-time carer proved to be too time-consuming so the offer was withdrawn. The court found that the Hampshire Constabulary had made reasonable efforts to accommodate Mr Kenny and so had not acted unlawfully.

The law also specifies what constitutes a disability, and this definition is wider than you might think. In 1999 a saleswoman won £7000 compensation when she became the first person in Britain found to have been discriminated against for suffering from agoraphobia.

Natasha Jeary was terrified of travelling by train or alone by car and she had a number of panic attacks whilst at work. She was asked to attend a sales meeting, she drove to the meeting to avoid going by coach but suffered a further attack on the way there and had to return home. That same day she was summoned to see her manager and was sacked for gross misconduct. The court ruled that the company had breached the Disability Discrimination Act and Miss Jeary received £7216 compensation.

CASE STUDY
What have you got to offer?

On 16 October 2000, the Disability Unit in the Department for Work and Pensions launched the 'What have you got to offer?' campaign. The aim was to encourage small to medium sized businesses to make reasonable adjustments to the way they deliver their services so that disabled people can access them. The campaign included press and website ads, posters, articles in national, regional and specialist press.

The posters in Figure 5.9 are some of those that ran during the campaign.

Examine a local business. What simple, practical ideas could be implemented to make life easier for disabled customers of that business?

Figure 5.9   Posters in the DfEE's 'What have you got to offer?' campaign

Legal responsibilities in health and safety

Clearly businesses today also have a responsibility to make their workplaces as safe for their employees as possible. The British health and safety law is rooted in the Health and Safety at Work Act (HASAWA) 1974, and the Management of Health and Safety at Work Regulations 1999 (the Management Regulations). These Acts outline the duties which employers have towards employees and members of the public, and which employees have to themselves and to each other. There are numerous other Acts specific to certain workplaces. It is necessary, therefore, for a particular employer to acquaint themselves with any laws specific to their industry.

The responsibilities imposed by the HASAWA are not just upon employers, it also imposed obligations on the employee with regard to responsibility for health and safety. Section 7(a) requires all employees to take reasonable care for their own health and safety at work and that of others who may be affected by their acts or omissions. Section 7(b) requires all employees to co-operate with their employer in the discharge of health and safety responsibilities. Section 8 requires all employees not to interfere intentionally or recklessly with, or misuse, anything provided in the interests of health, safety and welfare.

What employers are required to do under the Health and Safety at Work Act 1974 is to look at what the risks are in their particular workplace and take sensible measures to tackle them, 'so far as is reasonably practicable', taking account of the degree of risk in a particular job or workplace.

The key requirement of employers is to carry out a **risk assessment** in their workplace and record the significant findings of the risk assessment. Following this assessment, the employer should then:

- appoint nominated employees to implement the health and safety measures identified as necessary by the risk assessment
- set up emergency procedures, and
- provide clear information and training to employees.

The Management of Health and Safety at Work Regulations 1999 covers standards of care in a number of areas:

- the maintenance of the workplace and of equipment, devices and systems
- ventilation, temperature in indoor workplaces, and lighting
- cleanliness and the handling of waste materials
- room dimensions and space
- floors and organisation of traffic routes
- windows and transparent doors, gates and walls
- ability to clean windows safely
- escalators and moving walkways
- sanitary conveniences
- drinking water
- accommodation for clothing and facilities for changing clothes
- facilities for rest and to eat meals.

The safety adviser

The regulations suggest that one of the company directors should be appointed Health and Safety Director to oversee these matters for the company. They also make it clear that a safety officer or adviser should be appointed, but it gives no further details on his or her role. It is the employer's responsibility, therefore, to formulate a suitable job description for the needs of the establishment. In general the adviser will be expected to:

- be the company adviser on all health and safety matters
- give advance warning to senior management of any changes in health and safety legislation
- advise on health and safety training
- carry out safety inspections, investigate accidents and incidents, and ensure compliance with statutory reporting requirements
- liaise with external safety bodies
- maintain and update the company safety policy
- organise the safety committee (see below).

In many cases, too, the safety adviser may be expected to advise on and draft a code of practice for the company which the senior management team can then implement. The safety adviser should, of course, be aware of any industry-wide codes of practice.

The safety committee and safety representatives

Article 11 of the EC Framework Directive places emphasis on worker consultation and collaboration over health and safety. The Safety Representatives and Safety Committees Regulations 1977 (SRSCR 77) and the Health and Safety (Consultation with Employees) Regulations 1996 (HSCER 96) attempt to comply with this requirement by:

♦ allowing recognised trade unions to appoint safety representatives from among the employer's workforce (SRSCR)

♦ requiring employers to consult all employees not already represented by trade union safety representatives (HSCER).

Safety representative functions

The major functions of a safety representative are:

♦ to investigate potential hazards and dangerous occurrences at the workplace
♦ to examine the causes of accidents at the workplace
♦ to investigate employee complaints about health, safety or welfare
♦ to make representations to the employer about health, safety and welfare matters
♦ to carry out inspections to represent employees when consulting inspectors of the Health and Safety Executive (HSE)
♦ to attend meetings of the safety committee.

CASE STUDY

Health and safety at work

The following graphs are taken from the Health and Safety Statistics Highlights 2001/02 produced by the Health and Safety Commission on behalf of the UK government.

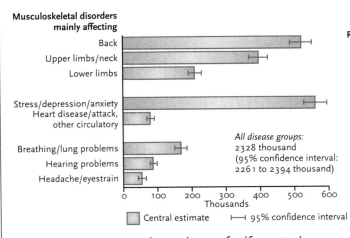

Figure 5.10   Estimated prevalence of self-reported work-related illness, 2001/02

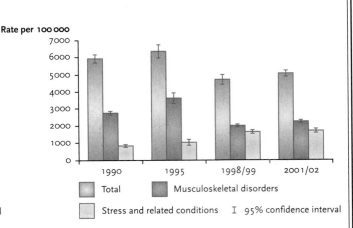

Figure 5.11   Estimated prevalence of self-reported work-related illness, restricted to people who worked in the last 12 months in England and Wales

Safety committee terms of reference

A safety committee must be given terms of reference, which will usually include the following:

♦ to investigate and report on accidents or incidents
♦ to examine national health and safety reports and statistics
♦ to review health and safety audit reports
♦ to draw up work rules and instructions on safe systems of work
♦ to oversee health and safety training
♦ to promote and advise on relevant publicity campaigns
♦ to maintain links with external health and safety bodies
♦ to recommend updates to the company safety policy
♦ to consider and advise on impending legislation.

The UK government has set up the Health and Safety Commission and Executive (HSC/E) in order to help firms implement the requirements of health and safety law. The HSC/E has published extensive guidelines for employers and if this guidance is followed it will normally be sufficient to comply with the law. There is extensive help available on the HSC/E website.

Legal responsibilities in equal opportunities

In an ideal world legislation to counter discriminatory behaviour would not be necessary, but unfortunately people do harbour prejudices and sometimes these affect their decision making to the detriment of employees or job applicants. It is necessary therefore to protect the interests of these people. There has been a substantial shift in attitudes in the UK over the last 40 years; not long ago it was not unusual or even unacceptable to view people different to ourselves in a stereotypical way, nor to expect the roles of men and women to be quite different, but today we try to take a more enlightened view. The basic principle is to treat people as individuals and to respect differences. There are currently four main pieces of legislation that are applicable in this area, although this is developing rapidly. The main Acts are:

♦ The Sex Discrimination Act 1975
♦ The Race Relations Act 1976
♦ The Equal Pay Act 1970
♦ The Disability Discrimination Act 1995.

The last of these was discussed at length earlier, so let us examine the other three.

Sex and marital discrimination

The Sex Discrimination Act 1975 intends to make sure that both sexes are treated equally in the workplace. It is illegal for employers to discriminate in the following key areas:

♦ selection procedures
♦ terms on which employment is offered
♦ opportunities for training and development
♦ fringe benefits
♦ choice of who will be made redundant.

Unlawful discrimination means giving less favourable treatment to someone because of their sex or because they are married or single.

Under the Act, discrimination can be either direct or indirect. Direct sex discrimination occurs when someone is treated less favourably than a person of the opposite sex would be in the same circumstances. For example, if only men are made managers, and sex is the criterion for appointment, this counts as direct discrimination.

Indirect sex discrimination is less easy to pinpoint. It means introducing a requirement which on the face of it applies equally to both men and women, but which in practice can be met by a much smaller proportion of one sex than the other. For example, when an organisation requires applicants to be a certain height. Since on average men are taller than women, this could be construed as indirect sex discrimination.

Direct marriage discrimination means treating a married person less favourably than an unmarried person of the same sex. For example, a policy not to recruit married people for a job that involved being away from home would be classed as discrimination.

Sex discrimination legislation covers recruitment, during employment and when employment ceases. It is therefore unlawful to discriminate against someone during the recruitment process, when selecting for promotion or when selecting people for redundancy or dealing with dismissals.

The Sex Discrimination Act 1985 also covers victimisation. Victimisation means treating someone less favourably than others because 'in good faith' they have made allegations about discrimination or unfair treatment.

CASE STUDY

Mrs X had worked for a solicitor as a small claims manager in Sheffield for three years. In March 2002 she informed her employers that she was expecting her first child. A month later she was suspended from her job; the grounds given for her suspension were that she had not carried out her work properly and had failed to supervise her team. Mrs X said that she firmly

believed that had she not been pregnant the errors made by her and members of her team would not have resulted in her suspension and then dismissal for gross misconduct.

She claimed that she was not made aware of any problems with her work before the suspension and believed that the pregnancy was the trigger for the disciplinary action. She accused the firm of giving her inadequate training with defendant work while increasing the burden of defendant files. She claimed stress and anxiety through her workload in a busy office had brought about a life-threatening illness which ultimately led to a premature birth and directly to the death of her son.

An employment tribunal in Sheffield decided unanimously that she had been sexually discriminated against and unfairly dismissed. Mrs X made a claim for damages which could run into six figures.

ACTIVITY

Discuss the following question in your group. What lessons are to be learned from this case? Think of this from the point of view of both employers and employees.

Race discrimination

The Race Relations Act 1976 aims to protect members of ethnic minorities from discrimination and unfair treatment.

The Act was introduced in order to address discrimination against ethnic minorities, but it can be used by people from any background as the following case study shows.

Race relations became a very prominent issue following the case of the death of Stephen Lawrence, a black youth who was killed by a group of white youths in 1993. No one has ever been convicted of the crime, and the case brought by the police collapsed through

CASE STUDY

In 2001 Mrs R (a white woman) was working as a petrol station cashier in Hartlepool. A new Asian manager was appointed who then proceeded to replace the eight employees with people of Asian origin. Mrs R was given little work to do whilst two of the Asian men were given 12-hour shifts 7 days a week. Mrs R was told she was no longer needed, but after she left she was replaced by one of the new manager's friends.

Mrs R made a claim for racial discrimination and was awarded £5000 in compensation. A spokesman for the Campaign for Racial Equality said: 'This is an example that racial discrimination legislation applies to everyone and that everybody is entitled to be treated equally on the grounds of race.'

lack of evidence. An inquiry followed in 1998, headed by Sir William Macpherson, and this was very critical of the police investigation, and in particular the racist attitudes within the police force. He concluded that the Metropolitan Police suffered from 'institutional racism'. The result of this report was that race relations became very prominent in the public consciousness, and the government decided that the current laws needed reinforcing.

The new laws came into force in December 2001 and now public bodies have extensive new statutory duties to deliver racial equality. All public organisations, such as councils, schools and the armed forces, are under a legal obligation to publish race equality schemes and carry out ethnic monitoring of their workforces. The Commission for Racial Equality now has the power to take court action against any public body deemed to have failed to fulfil its duties. Organisations are required to prepare written policies on race equality and conduct regular assessments of

their impact. They must also keep figures on the racial balance of employees and monitor the numbers who are promoted, receive training or are subject to disciplinary proceedings. Similar policies should also be adopted by private organisations.

Equal pay

The Equal Pay Act 1970 states that employers must pay equal amounts to men and women if they are doing the same work, or work which rates as being equivalent, or if they are doing work of equal value. Under the Act, anyone making a claim for equal pay must be able to compare themselves with a person of the opposite sex doing the same or equivalent work.

The Act has done much to address some of the inequities between the sexes, however there is still considerable work to be done. In February 2000, a cabinet office report entitled *The Cost of being a Woman* revealed that major differences in pay still exist. The report showed that a woman with school qualifications but no degree will have lifetime earnings £241,000 less than a man with equivalent skills. The difference in the lifetime earnings of a woman graduate with two children and a male graduate will be an estimated £162,000 as a result of lower salaries and pay forfeited as a result of being a mother. Lady Jay, Minister for Women, said, 'We should celebrate the fact that women have made great progress in the labour market over the last 20 years, but the analysis starkly underlines there are still many barriers that need to be overcome.'

The report indicated that the earnings gap with men differs according to the level of a woman's education. Female graduates may earn up to one-eighth less in their lifetime than an equivalent man, while low or medium-skilled women may lose more than one-third of their salary. The 2003 report *Facts About Women and Men in Great Britain* produced by the Equal Opportunities Commission reported that:

♦ female employees working full-time earn on average 18.8 per cent less than the average hourly earnings of male full-time employees
♦ women's gross individual income, including income from employment, pensions, benefits, investments, and so on, is on average 51 per cent less than men's.

The Equal Opportunities Commission has been running a 'Valuing Women' campaign since 1999 to bring these issues to the attention of people, employers and government.

The main requirement for businesses is to ensure that the rules are not breached, not just because it could lead to damages claims, but because it is wrong to treat people differently. Firms should therefore review their pay, bonus and promotion systems carefully and eliminate any sex bias.

The government is keen to keep up the momentum for equal pay, and so the Employment Act, which became law in July 2002, gives complainants the right to ask employers for comparative information about pay levels. Women will therefore have the right to ask for and be given information about how much their male colleagues are paid. It is hoped that this new 'transparency' will encourage employers to ensure that there is no sexual bias within their systems.

Figure 5.12 Poster in the Equal Opportunities Commission's 'Valuing Women' campaign

CASE STUDY

The City analyst

In January 2002 a female City analyst won her case for unfair dismissal and sex discrimination. In 2001 when she was working for Schroder Securities, she was awarded a bonus of £25,000, while two of her male colleagues received £650,000 and £440,000. The tribunal decided that the bonus award had been 'picked from the air' and was part of a strategy to drive her out. The tribunal ruled that she would not have been treated as she was by her boss 'but for the fact that she was a woman'. It also agreed that the figure she received was not the market rate for an analyst and did not reflect a genuine valuation of her performance.

She was awarded £1.5 million in compensation by the tribunal.

CASE STUDY

Diversity: The Equal Treatment Directive

The Equal Treatment Directive makes it unlawful to discriminate not only on existing grounds of sex, race and disability but also on grounds of sexual orientation and religion or other belief. Beliefs are defined as 'any religion, religious belief or similar philosophical belief', a very wide-ranging definition indeed.

♦ By December 2006, age discrimination will also be unlawful. These changes clearly have significant implications for companies. For example, employers who ask job applicants questions about their marital status could face prosecution, as this could be interpreted as discrimination against homosexuals, lesbians or bisexuals. The regulations do, however, contain exemptions when discrimination is a 'genuine occupational requirement'.

Unusually, the onus will also be on the employer to prove that he or she did not commit the alleged act of discrimination or harassment. A tribunal can order unlimited compensation against the firm if a case against it is proven.

ACTIVITY

1   List the implications you think there will be for firms when the full directive is in force covering discrimination for sexual orientation, religion and age. What changes might firms have to make to their procedures?

2   What possible problems do you envisage arising from the new directive?

Legal responsibilities in stakeholder pensions

It is a sad fact that many people in employment are relatively ignorant about their pension arrangements. Most are aware of the state pension provided by the government and many seem to think that this will be sufficient to maintain their current lifestyle. They are in for a big shock. Many pensioners on benefit live on the minimum income guarantee, which in 2003 was £102.10 per week, which is insufficient to provide a decent standard of living. In July 2003 the Department for Work and Pensions published a report showing that 50 per cent of adults have unrealistic expectations of their likely future pension, and that many have not heard of stakeholder pensions.

Stakeholder pensions are aimed at those who are on low incomes and who do not have personal or occupational pensions. The government has reluctantly admitted that the state pension will be insufficient in the future and it therefore wants people who can save for retirement to do so. The stakeholder pension scheme was set up by the government for people without access to employer-sponsored pension arrangements. They are intended to be secure and to provide the opportunity for many more people to save for retirement.

The government has been so worried about the problem of pensions that it decided to make it a legal requirement for firms to offer some form of pension scheme to employees. The legal requirements for stakeholder pensions are included in the Welfare Reform and Pensions Act 1999 and the Stakeholder Pension Schemes Regulations 2000.

Employers who are not exempt must offer access to a stakeholder pension scheme and if any employees join the designated scheme, the employer must offer a payroll deduction facility to those who want it. The company will only be exempt if it employs fewer than five people or where an alternative personal pension scheme arranged through an insurance company is provided.

The legislation requires employers to:

♦ consult with the company employees in choosing a stakeholder pension scheme offered by a pension provider. The government has set up the Occupational Pensions Regulatory Authority (OPRA) to assist companies with this decision. The scheme chosen should be one that is registered with OPRA as an acceptable scheme
♦ provide employees and trade unions with information about the scheme
♦ offer payroll deductions from an employee's earnings
♦ maintain records of employee deductions and payments to the scheme.

CASE STUDY

In August 2003 a report by the Association of British Insurers outlined a number of problems following the launch of stakeholder pensions:

♦ by August 2003 only 1.5 million had been sold

- of the 350,000 schemes set up by employers, 82 per cent had not received any contributions and had no members
- sales in 2003 were 10 per cent down on the previous year
- the average contribution in 2003 was £155 per month, which suggests that the target customers (those on salaries of less that £20,000 per year) are not buying the plans.

The ABI Director-General Mary Francis said 'We need more action now to ensure people use them to start saving for a decent retirement. Active employer involvement in pensions works. That is why we're recommending employer action to boost take-up.'

ACTIVITY

1 Why do you think the take-up on stakeholder pensions has been so low?

2 What steps do you think should be taken to encourage more sales of stakeholder pensions? What could or should employers do?

3 What role should the government play in this?

4 What alternatives are there to pension schemes when saving for retirement? What are the advantages and disadvantages of these methods compared with saving in a pension scheme like a stakeholder pension?

Environmental responsibilities

Increasingly today, firms are becoming aware of, and doing something about, their responsibilities to the environment, but it has taken many years for industry to take this area seriously, because it can cost significant sums to be environmentally friendly.

Business activity gives rise to costs, some of which we term private costs and some external costs. Private costs involve the monetary costs that businesses incur, such as buying raw materials, paying labour and other bills. Clearly firms will attempt to minimise such costs because they reduce profits. However there is no such drive on firms to reduce their external costs as these are costs borne by society around them. They might consist of pollution, loss of green land, harm to the environment and congestion of towns and cities. These problems are referred to as **negative externalities** and it is often governments, central and local, that have to bear the costs of dealing with them. Indeed, market forces actually encourage firms to disregard the costs of negative externalities; firms attempting to minimise their negative effects on the environment will incur additional private costs as a result (due to the introduction of cleaner air filters or different working practices) and this may make their products uncompetitive when compared with a firm that does not attempt to do the same. governments are exploring ways of 'internalising' these costs, by charging producers for the damage they cause by the use of financial penalties for companies that damage the environment, but satisfactory methods for this have yet to be devised.

It is common to think of business operations in terms of social costs and benefits. Social benefits are benefits to the community or positive externalities, whilst social costs are not monetary costs, they are opportunity costs, that is, what communities have had to give up to allow business to operate in the ways it does. They are negative externalities.

Social costs

Depletion of natural resources and destruction of the environment

Industry is clearly using up the natural resources available to the world, and this is happening at an increasingly alarming rate. The *Living Planet Report* by the World Wide Fund for Nature published in October 1998 estimated that one-third of the Earth's natural resources had been lost in the past 25 years. The report claimed that freshwater ecosystems declined by 50 per cent between 1970 and 1995 and the world's natural forest cover declined by about 10 per cent. The report measured the impact of modern living and industry on the health of the world's forest, freshwater and marine ecosystems, and its findings showed that the Earth has lost more than 30 per cent of its natural wealth over the period of the report.

Much, but not all, of this destruction has been caused by the activities of businesses around the world and it is the responsibility of governments, industry, businesses and consumers worldwide to help to reduce this tremendous pressure on the environment.

Pollution

Industry creates pollution, by-products of industrial activity that dirty our environment. Industrial sites release millions of tonnes of chemicals each year into the environment through chimneys, outfall pipes, sewers, accidental leaks or produced as solid waste. Pollution comes in various types.

Water-quality pollution This is caused by emissions into rivers, lakes, canals and seas, either deliberately, as in the case of treated sewage, or accidentally, when oil tankers spill crude oil into the sea producing oil slicks. All of these have tremendously harmful effects on the ecosystems that they enter.

Air-quality pollution Chimneys, cars and aerosols (to name but a few) pump a variety of chemicals into the air, many of which are depleting the quality of the air we breathe. One particularly problematic form of air pollution is acid rain created by coal-fired power stations and road traffic emissions. Acid rain has led to the death of forests and also numerous fish, plants and animals.

Other types of air-quality pollution include:

◆ Dust, which has led to the steep increase in the incidence of bronchitis and asthma.
◆ Ozone in the lower atmosphere, which reduces crop yields, reduces forest growth, damages buildings, and is harmful to people and animals.

◆ Depletion of the ozone layer, which exists in the stratosphere. Ultraviolet radiation from the sun naturally forms ozone directly from the oxygen in the air. The ozone layer protects plants and animals against dangerous levels of ultraviolet radiation. Some modern chemicals, such as the synthetic CFCs, break down ozone more quickly than it forms naturally. Scientists have shown that this has thinned the ozone layer to such an extent that an 'ozone hole' has formed above the Antarctic threatening life there.
◆ The greenhouse effect. We depend on the Earth's natural greenhouse effect, which maintains an average temperature of about 15°C across the world. Without this the temperature would be much lower and the oceans would freeze. Water vapour, carbon dioxide (CO_2), methane and nitrous oxide are all natural gases that contribute to the greenhouse effect. Our use of coal, oil and natural gas has led to large amounts of CO_2 being released, and scientists now believe that these emissions are creating an imbalance in the carbon cycle. This may intensify the greenhouse effect and cause global climate change. This would raise global temperatures and perhaps lead to changes in rainfall patterns and a rise in sea level.

Noise pollution Certain sounds produced by business activity can be harmful to people's health as well as causing mental stress and it may contribute to mental illness. It can cause hearing loss, lack of sleep, irritability, ulcers, and high blood pressure. Noise-induced stress can create severe tension in daily living. As a result, the European Commission has produced a number of directives which seek to draw a balance between reducing noise whilst not unduly harming business interests. There are directives relating to noise from motor vehicles, motorcycles, aircraft, lawnmowers and machinery.

Waste

Industry creates waste, much of which is distinctly undesirable. One form of waste that causes considerable public concern is nuclear waste. Nuclear waste is very dangerous to humans and animals. If not stored properly nuclear waste may seep into the ground and the water table. If it contaminates water and is drunk it may result in extreme sickness and death.

Other forms of undesirable waste are chemical by-products (which pose health risks), slag heaps (which are unsightly and pose the danger of slipping), non-biodegradable plastics (that pose serious health risks to animals who eat them or get trapped in them) and waste paper (which fills landfill sites if it is not recycled).

CASE STUDY

The Newbury Bypass

In 1995 the Highways Agency in the UK highlighted a problem of severe and increasing traffic congestion in Newbury. At the time the A334 inner relief road in Newbury was becoming increasingly busy, with over 50,000 vehicles travelling through Newbury daily, and the predictions in the table were made for traffic growth in the area.

Traffic in Newbury

Year	Without bypass		With bypass	
	Low growth	High growth	Low growth	High growth
2000	57,000	63,000	35,000	39,000
2005	61,000	70,000	38,000	43,000
2010	65,000	78,000	40,000	48,000

A solution was proposed: the A34 Newbury Bypass. The bypass would ease the situation by allowing through traffic to avoid the town. Vodaphone, one of the biggest employers in Newbury, was a big supporter of the new scheme. When planning permission was given, there ensued the biggest environmental campaign against a development ever seen in the UK, before or since.

The protests were many and various, and Friends of the Earth, who put up many arguments against the proposed road development, co-ordinated many of them. They stated that the bypass would damage

- three Sites of Special Scientific Interest (SSSIs) and a number of local nature reserves, including Snelsmore Common, one of the best remaining heathlands in Berkshire and the nature reserve of Rack Marsh, a habitat for protected wildlife
- a registered battlefield (the Civil War 'First Battle of Newbury' of 1643)
- an area of outstanding natural beauty (the North Wessex Downs)
- Reddings Copse, which harboured protected bats and dormice
- twelve sites of archeological importance including the Lambourn Valley Mesolithic site (of national importance), and a Romano-British Villa
- the idyllic rural atmosphere in the picturesque village of Bagnor

Despite the many protests, which saw environmental supporters camping out in trees to stop building work, the project went ahead and was completed. By the time the road was opened in November 1998, more than 1000 people had been arrested for protesting. Subsequent reports have suggested that the amount of traffic passing through Newbury has gone down, but not nearly as much as was predicted.

ACTIVITY

The project was intended to help ease both commuter and commercial traffic through the Newbury area. To what extent do the commercial benefits to industry and new job opportunities outweigh the environmental interests in cases such as this?

Environmental audit

An environmental audit is an evaluation of a company's performance, carried out regularly, systematically and objectively. The procedure began in the USA as an assessment of a company's compliance with official regulations on the environment. Now its role has been extended. Today, environmental auditing is a management tool used to improve practices as well as ensuring that the company's and the government's policies on the environment are fulfilled. The audit should be carried out by personnel who are expert in the technologies used at the sites to be inspected, and they should have the enthusiastic backing of top management.

A typical environmental audit in the oil industry consists of a visit by the audit team to the site: which could be a refinery, a factory, an offshore oil production platform, a laboratory or a distribution depot. During the visit, the team interviews staff and inspects records, facilities, equipment and the immediate surroundings of the site according to a systematic testing procedure. As a result of the visit, the team prepares a detailed report. Following discussion an action plan is agreed. This in turn becomes a regular agenda item at management meetings to ensure that the action plan is effectively monitored. The audit is repeated at regular intervals.

The benefits of auditing include:

♦ more effective compliance with company environmental goals and official regulations
♦ increased employee awareness of environmental requirements
♦ improved environmental training
♦ reduction of waste
♦ better environmental reporting to government and public.

Role of Environment Agency

The Environment Agency was set up by the UK government to help businesses to meet their environmental responsibilities, and to oversee and enforce the laws regarding protection of the environment. It is concerned with:

♦ improvements in the quality of air, land and water
♦ encouraging the conservation of natural resources, animals and plants
♦ pollution control
♦ providing defence and warning systems to protect people and property against flooding from rivers and the sea
♦ reducing waste
♦ encouraging recycling
♦ improving waste disposal
♦ informing and educating people about environmental issues.

You can find out more about the activities of the Environment Agency at their website (see end of unit).

Aviation and the environment

JOURNAL ARTICLE

Air transportation has increased significantly in recent years; traffic at UK airports has increased from 1,120,000 landings and take-offs in 1990 to 1,674,000 in 2000, an increase of almost 50 per cent in just 10 years. Clearly this has had significant positive effects in terms of employment in the UK, both directly in the air transport industry and also indirectly in cargo handling and the holiday industries. However, there are many negative environmental effects that have come along with this growth.

You should investigate this topic further by referring to the *British Economy Survey*, Volume 31, Number 2, Spring 2002, Section 11. The article 'Aviation and the environment' by Stephen Ison outlines the problem in detail and also suggests government policy options for dealing with the problem. He takes up this theme again in Volume 32, Number 1, Autumn 2002, Section 11.

CASE STUDY

Friends of the Earth Factory Watch

Friends of the Earth is a pressure group which aims at persuading industry and governments to act in a more environmentally friendly way. In 1995 they set up a new website called 'Factory Watch'.

Figure 5.13   FoE Factory Watch's website identified factories which were the biggest polluters.

The objective of the site was to make information more readily available to the general public about which factories were the biggest polluters and where they were located. Visitors could investigate their local area to see how polluting their local firms were, the aim being to put local pressure on local firms to mend their ways.

The site was very successful in bringing these issues to the public, and Friends of the Earth believe that it has contributed to a 40 per cent reduction in releases of cancer-causing chemicals across England and Wales between 1998 and 2001. The site caused such a stir that the UK government's Environment Agency now has included similar information and monitors on its site. The site has now been closed down. It has done its job and new campaigns are beginning.

Ethical practice

Ethics are moral principles or rules of conduct which are generally accepted by most members of a society. They involve what individuals and groups believe to be right and what is considered to be wrong. An 'ethic' is therefore a guide as to what should be done or what should not be done.

From an early age, parents, schools, religious teaching and society in general provide moral guidelines to help us to learn and form our ethical beliefs. Many ethics are reinforced in our legal system and thus provide a constraint to business activities, while others are not. In areas covered by law, there may well be social pressure to conform to a particular standard. Pressure groups often set out to force individuals and organisations to operate in an 'acceptable' way.

Through the media we hear about questionable business activities: issues such as insider dealing, animal rights protesters involved in disputes with organisations producing cosmetic and pharmaceutical products, protests about tobacco sponsorship, and trading links with countries with poor human rights records. As a result, consumers have become more aware of the ethical and moral values underlying business decisions.

Today's consumer is more concerned than ever before with what an organisation stands for, who it trades with, what it does, whether it supports any political party, whether it is an equal opportunities employer and how it behaves in the community as a whole. When *Which?* magazine carried out a survey, 63 per cent of those who responded were concerned about the activities of companies they might invest in.

Chapter 2

Economic, social and global environment

Resource issues and types of economic system

Have you noticed how house prices have been rising so rapidly in recent times? One of the main reasons for this is that we have an ever-increasing demand for housing, but we cannot seem to build new properties quickly enough. There is an insatiable demand for housing in the UK, yet our stock of housing is seriously limited.

The basic economic problem: scarcity and choice

Recently the government has been debating where to build new houses, whether on greenfield sites, out of town or on derelict brownfield sites closer to town centres. Although it seems that many houses are being built all of the time, we never seem to reach a point where we have enough; there are always more people wanting houses than there are houses available.

As environmentalists remind us, the world's resources are strictly limited. That is only a problem because our needs and wants appear to be infinite. We never reach a point at which we are satisfied: once we satisfy one desire we go on to the next. We save up and buy whatever we most want, or buy on credit, but are we then satisfied? No, we simply start saving for the next. It seems to be part of the human condition that we must strive continually to acquire more. Unfortunately the fact that the resources of the world are limited means that we can never satisfy all of the desires of everybody. We therefore have to make difficult choices about how we allocate our limited or scarce resources so that we can satisfy as many people as possible.

This is the basic economic problem, and the principles of scarcity and choice underpin all economic decisions.

Opportunity cost

Let us assume that you would like to buy a CD costing £14 and a book costing £10; however, you only have £16. You decide to buy the CD. What does it cost you? You would probably reply that the cost was £14, but is that the true cost? The real cost of anything that we choose is what we have to give up in order to obtain it, so the true cost of buying the CD is not really £14, it is actually the book that we must give up to allow us to buy the CD. The real cost of any decision is therefore the opportunity cost, that is, the next best alternative that we give up. Because of the basic economic problem, that of scarce resources, we have to decide what we will buy and at the same time what we will give up.

Imagine that you are the government and you have £4250 million to spend; what might you spend it on? The following are some alternatives:

- new defence equipment
- new hospitals
- improved social security payments to the old, sick and unemployed.

Whichever you choose to spend the money on, when you pick one you are at the same time choosing not to have another; if you choose the aircraft you are also choosing not to have the hospitals or the social security improvements. The true cost of choosing the aircraft is not, therefore, £4250 million, it is the hospitals or the benefits that you have given up. This is the opportunity cost.

Types of economic system

Until the late 1980s it was common practice to classify world economic issues into:

- the First World: the richer, developed, market-based economies including West Germany, the USA, Japan and the UK
- the Second World: the socialist and communist states such as East Germany, the Soviet Union, North Korea and China
- the Third World: developing countries such as Rwanda, Ethiopia and Bangladesh.

In the late 1980s this classification became redundant as a number of communist regimes collapsed and as a number of former Third World countries experienced dramatic increases in growth rates.

Since 1989 the success of market economies has led some to assume that a certain type of free market economic structure has become the basis for economic activity across the globe. However, it is relevant to ask whether the type of economic system we see in the UK and the USA is to be found in other economies in the European Union, Japan, China, Burma and in the remainder of the world's nation states. The organisation of economic activity differs remarkably across these economies, so there are important differences that will be of significance for companies and managers trading abroad.

All societies must develop a system for dealing with three interrelated issues:

- What will be produced?
- How will it be produced?
- For whom will it be produced?

We can illustrate the wide differences in possible systems by looking at two imaginary island communities which are dependent on fishing and farming. Call these two communities Sealand and Skyland.

In Sealand all decisions are made by a small group of chieftains. The chieftains decide who will do the fishing and who will do the farming. They decide how many hours are to be put into each activity and how the necessary equipment will be made (for example, the fishing boats, agricultural implements). They have also decided that everyone will receive an equal share of the produce – except for the chieftains, who will have a double portion of everything.

In Skyland there is no organising group. Individuals are left to their own devices. They decide individually what to make and they trade or store their surpluses. They decide how to produce their equipment, and how long to spend at particular activities. They consume the bulk of their own produce, except for what they can exchange.

ACTIVITY

1   Make a list of eight strengths and eight weaknesses of each of the economic systems described.

2   Devise a third system which you would regard as preferable to those of Sealand and Skyland. In what ways do you think that your system is preferable?

3   Why might other people disagree with you? What would be the reasoning behind these objections?

In the past, the basic economic problems were solved by custom and tradition; for example, the way crops were grown and shared out was decided by folk tradition. In many parts of the world traditional economies have given way to three major systems:
- the planned system
- the free market system
- the mixed system.

Within these three basic models, there will be a wide range of variations and differences.

Any society must decide how to use the resources that are available to it. Choices have to be made which involve sacrifices. The challenge facing each country is how this should be done. Should it be left to individuals and organisations to bid for resources, on the basis that they can produce what people need as long as it is profitable for them? If they fail to produce what is required, then they cease to trade, and the resources that they were using can be purchased and used by others to produce profitable items. We know this as the free market solution, which involves solving the problem of scarcity by providing a rationing mechanism based on price and profit.

A major challenge for the free market approach is whether it can build a long-term future, with the requirement to undertake investment that may not be profitable for some considerable time. Will the market be able, for example, to provide for skills in the workforce that may be needed ten years (or further) into the future?

ACTIVITY

One of the major problems facing the UK economy in the last half of the twentieth century was a skills gap between the nation and its major competitors. This skills gap existed in a wide range of occupational areas. Do you think that the free market is likely to lead to a solution to the skills gap in this country, or should the government intervene to provide the sort of educational and training opportunities that would close this gap?

What is true for education and training can also be the case for health, social security policing and defence, which then introduces a high-profile role for government. This mixed-economy regime also incorporates anti-competitive measures to deal with the rise of monopolies and monopolistic practices that free markets have a tendency to create.

Likewise, the problem of externalities – such as air and land pollution – can create a role for government. It can try to measure the pollution costs borne by the general community, and reach a decision as to the most effective way to deal with this.

The planned economies of eastern Europe and the old USSR took the role of government to be of paramount importance. Under the label of 'democratic socialism', the state owned the means of production in the name of the people, arguing that a market system exploited the masses, by building up profits that benefited the minority at the expense of the majority. A market solution was divisive and degrading for the population, so the state had to organise production and distribution, in order to resolve the problem of scarcity without the exploitation normally associated with capitalism.

These three broad-based classifications of the free market, mixed and planned, are useful devices for seeing the basic differences that exist between them in trying to resolve the problem of scarcity. A degree of caution is required when using this approach. It is clear that many countries do not conform to the classification allotted to them, so even under the old Soviet-style planned economics immense differences could be found between Hungary, East Germany and the USSR. Likewise, the mixed economies of France, Germany and the UK show clear preferences in respect to government intervention that goes some way to explaining their problems over European integration. Moving further afield, where would the Islamic countries of Iran and Syria be placed?

Many approaches to internal business focus on the degree of risk associated with business opportunities in overseas countries. One aspect that has not been mentioned so far is the degree of political and legal control exerted by government and the regulatory agencies. From the brief description of the three economic systems, it is clear that legal and regulatory control in a planned economy would be high, with individuals given few opportunities to own property or to have ownership rights when it comes to natural resources or the assets of an enterprise. Free- and mixed-market approaches would create opportunities for individuals and groups to have ownership rights, as private companies provide a high proportion of the output that a society requires.

Planned systems

Planning involves some form of official co-ordination of activities. This can take place at either a local or a centralised level. Planning authorities will be responsible in some way for the creation of targets, systems and procedures. The process of organised planning is most commonly associated with countries in the former communist bloc.

It is worth examining some of the common features associated with centrally planned economies. However, it must be stressed that in recent years many communist countries have experienced substantial phases of economic reform, such as *perestroika* in Russia. Such changes have involved a relaxation of price controls and of production control from the centre and a greater freedom to set up private enterprises.

Countries with centrally planned economic systems (including Kampuchea, North Korea, Cuba and China) represent a large proportion of the world's population and industrial output. It is interesting to note that in recent times increasingly large parts of the Chinese and Cuban economies have been liberalised. However, central authorities still play a major role. We should not underestimate the importance of the Chinese economy which is expected to take over shortly as the world's major economic superpower.

Although there are wide differences in the economic organisation of centrally planned economies and their respective stages of development, there are also a number of important similarities:

♦ The means of production are publicly owned. This takes the form of state, collective or co-operative ownership. However, decisions about their use can be made in a variety of ways, ranging from collective decision making to decision making by a small committee of people.
♦ Planning is centralised and strategies to increase the quantity and/or quality of overall output are laid down by the planning authority.
♦ There is a market for consumer goods (although consumers will not necessarily have the freedom to spend money in the way they would wish) and a

market for labour. Wages are paid, and a large proportion of consumer goods are exchanged in the market, in transactions using some form of money.
♦ Prices for all goods sold by the state are decided by planning authorities. They are not able to change spontaneously.
♦ Nearly all decisions relating to capital formation will be made and controlled by planning authorities. Capital formation is the production of those goods and equipment that go into further production, such as that of factory machinery.

The key feature of a planned, or command, economy is that it is planning committees who decide what will be produced, how it will be produced and how products will be distributed. Smaller groups such as factories and other business units submit their plans to a local committee, which decides which resources will be made available to each local area, which in turn will allocate resources to each factory, farm or other productive unit.

Productive units are often set production targets, and are then given a quantity of resources and a time constraint to meet the targets.

Advantages of a planned economy

♦ Effective long-term strategies can be developed taking into account the needs of the total system.
♦ Planning can be carried out according to the collective needs and wants of each of the individual parts of a system.
♦ Duplication of resources can be eliminated.
♦ Resources and products can be shared out more equitably according to the dominant value system prevailing in that society.
♦ Planning decisions can be made in a consistent manner.
♦ The system can be shaped in such a way as to reflect the social and political wishes of a group of people.

Disadvantages of a planned economy

♦ Heavy-handed planning and control may stifle individual enterprise.

- The process of planning itself uses up scarce resources for administration and supervision.
- The absence of the profit motive removes the spur to individual effort and enterprise. It is argued by some that people are more inclined to work harder and to make personal sacrifices if they can profit from doing so.
- The process of communication between consumers and producers can become distorted so that the goods that are produced fall far short of consumer requirements. If planning decisions are made well in advance of consumption decisions, then by the time goods appear in the marketplace tastes and fashions may have changed.
- Where price controls are established, unofficial black markets may develop, leading to bribery and corruption.

CASE STUDY

Changes in economic systems

In the period 1945 until the end of the 1980s it looked as if the world economic system would continue to be divided between two sets of economic ideologies and principles: state planning and the market economies. In the socialist economies decisions were made by central planners working to models of how resources should be utilised. At one stage, for example, planners in the Soviet Union had created a huge model of their system which they housed in an aircraft hangar. They used markers to represent flows of goods between industries. It was not surprising that while the model was effective in the confines of the hangar, it led to glaring inefficiencies in the real world. The Third World of the developing countries, as they were called at the time, was a battleground between the two ideologies.

Then, suddenly at the end of the 1980s the whole house of cards came tumbling down,

first with *perestroika* bringing an end to the Soviet Union and the Cold War, and other movements such as Solidarity in Poland. The reunification of Germany saw an end to the old Cold War frontier between the Western and Eastern powers.

At first there was a rush by countries like the Czech Republic, Hungary, East Germany and Poland to embrace market systems. However, these solutions have not always been successful, and it was not surprising that a few years later countries like Poland took a few steps back towards the protection of socialism. Poland has joined the European Union and recognises the importance of opening up freer markets if it is to be accepted. However, at times of extreme hardship, such as international recession and stagnation in the world economy, Poland has sought to create key aspects of social welfare protection while advancing some way towards capitalism. The free market solution is not an easy option for economies that have been struggling to use their resources effectively for a number of years.

ACTIVITY

1   What do you see as being the five major points of difference between a centrally planned economy and a free market one? Set out your answer in the form of a table.

2   Why do you think that at the end of the 1980s citizens of eastern European countries were so keen to embrace the market system?

3   Why was accommodating to the free market not an easy transition?

4   Why have some countries taken some steps back towards socialism?

The free market system

In a free market, the production decisions about 'what?', 'how?' and 'for whom?' are made by consumers and producers; the government does not intervene. Consumers in effect 'vote' for a certain pattern of output by the way in which they distribute their spending between the alternatives on offer. How much they are prepared to pay is thus a reflection of the strength of consumer preferences. Another view is that it does not always work quite like this; producers often decide what they would like to make and then persuade consumers to follow their wishes through advertising.

The prices at which producers offer their goods for sale will depend on their production costs. The prices charged will thus reflect the relative scarcity of the various resources needed in order to produce that good for the market. If a product sells well firms will be inclined to produce it; if no one buys the product firms will stop making it, since under the market system firms seek to make profits from all the goods they sell. Producers are thus forced to pay attention to the wishes of consumers in order to survive.

The interests of consumers and producers conflict. Consumers want to pay low prices while producers would like to charge higher prices. The market serves to strike a balance, with profits settling at just those levels that match the strength of consumer preferences with the scarcity of resources. When prices change this acts as a signal for the pattern of production and consumption to alter. For example, when a new fashion style becomes popular, the producers are able to charge a higher price and to put more resources into producing more such garments, while for clothes that are no longer fashionable manufacturers may be forced to lower their price, put less resources into their production and eventually stop making them altogether.

Advantages of the free market system

♦ Production reflects the wishes of the consumer.
♦ The system is flexible in the way it can respond to different conditions of demand and supply.
♦ Individuals have greater freedom to make their own demand and supply decisions.
♦ Scarce resources do not have to be wasted on administering and running (planning) the system.
♦ It is argued that the free market will lead to larger, better-quality outputs at lower unit costs.

These arguments are succinct but extremely powerful. Their power is reflected in the way in which most economies in the world have moved towards freer market systems in recent years.

Disadvantages of the free market system

♦ The free market system does not guarantee everyone what many would regard to be the minimum acceptable standard of living in a healthy society. The price mechanism, when it is freely operating, fails to provide a 'safety net' for citizens less able to compete, including the sick and elderly.
♦ There are some goods which by their very nature include elements of what is known as 'non-excludability'. For example, all ships using a particular seaway benefit from its lighthouse; all citizens (except perhaps for pacifists) could be seen to benefit from a national system of defence. If we take the example of bridges, it is immediately apparent why the price system could not always be effective as a means of provision. If people were made to stop and pay to go over all bridges the traffic system would rapidly snarl up. Chaos would arise if London's bridges all operated on a toll payment system.
♦ The free market can lead to great inequalities. Those with the means to purchase large quantities of goods can use their money to ensure that the goods and services they want are produced (hence taking away resources from other products). One way of looking at the opportunity cost to society of producing luxury goods (speedboats, expensive clothes) is to consider the inability of society to meet the needs of the less fortunate.
♦ Resources may not be able to move as freely as a pure market theory would suggest. Regarding human resources (labour), people may be resistant to moving to new areas and away from their

established roots. They may be reluctant to learn new skills which offer high pay packets if they feel that the job does not meet their needs for such factors as self-respect, pride in the job or the ability to work at one's own pace.

♦ Many buying decisions are made by consumers with an imperfect knowledge of the market. Producers frequently change the details of their products, including price, shape, size and packaging. This makes it very difficult for consumers to weigh up alternative purchases, and many buying decisions may be based on impressions rather than hard evidence. For example, a recent survey conducted by the authors reveals that, out of a sample of 400 shoppers, fewer than 10 per cent of them could remember the prices of five randomly selected commonly used items in their shopping basket.

♦ In a free market many resources can be wasted through the high failure rate of new businesses. A lot of time and money is spent on setting up a new business. When it closes down after a few months, many of its resources may end up as little more than scrap.

The mixed economy

In the real world no economy relies exclusively on the free market, nor can we find examples of purely planned economies. A mixed economy combines elements of both the free market and planned systems; some decisions are made solely through the private sector while others are made by the government.

The UK is a good example of a mixed economy. Some parts of industry are owned and operated by the government but large chunks of the business world remain in private hands. The public sector is that part of the economy that is government-owned; the private sector is that part of the economy that is owned by private citizens.

Throughout much of the twentieth century, government spending in the UK has made up a significant percentage of all spending. Then, during the 1980s and until 1997, steps were taken by Conservative administrations to reduce the relative size of government spending. A major aim of the

Conservatives since coming into office in May 1979 was the restoration of market forces throughout the economy.

With the return of a Labour administration in 1997, the emphasis has moved towards the creation of a social market in which the government plays a role in helping the market to work more efficiently, making sure that large organisations do not take advantage of less powerful individual organisations, and ensuring a measure of social justice.

In a mixed economy, one of the central issues of debate will be about the nature of the mix between the private and public sectors.

The role of the state

Much of the political debate in recent centuries, and particularly in the twentieth century, has concerned the role of the state in the life of the nation, in fashioning relationships between nations, and in the relationships between individuals and organisations.

The spectrum of political philosophy

The mainstream spectrum of political philosophy in relation to business in the economy runs from pure communism at one extreme to completely free markets at the other. Ideological battles have been waged in the twentieth century between the communists (adherents of Marx, Lenin, Trotsky and Stalin) and the followers of the free market (adherents of Adam Smith, Friedrich Hayek, Milton Friedman, and so on).

The communists see the state as representing the interests of the community, and hence of individuals. Communists contrast this view with a philosophy of individualism based on self-interest. For example, in *The German Ideology* (1939) Karl Marx and Friedrich Engels wrote, 'All history is the history of man's enslavement to an alien power, the world market. After the communist revolution, with the abolition of private property, this power will be dissolved. Then genuine spiritual riches will be available to each individual. He will be free of national and local limitations, be enabled to enjoy the "all-sided production of the whole earth". The natural co-operation of men hitherto forced by the rule of the market system, will arise spontaneously in the wake of the communist revolution.'

Communists therefore placed a strong emphasis on the role of the state and the planned economy as representing the people's interests. This view is in clear contrast with that of neo-liberal thinkers (supporters of the free market), one of whom summed up free-enterprise ideology with the phrase 'least government is best government'.

One of the most important contributions that economists can make is to shed some light on how the economy can best serve the interests of each and every person in a society. Joseph Schumpeter, the great Austrian economist, wrote the following in 1942:

'Queen Elizabeth [the First] owned silk stockings. The capitalist achievement does not typically consist in providing more silk stockings for queens, but in bringing them within the reach of factory girls in return for steadily decreasing amounts of effort.'

Schumpeter was arguing that the 'market' serves to meet the needs of the consumer, while at the same time providing the employment that enables people to become consumers. Since Schumpeter's time, technological progress has continued to erode privilege. The Green Revolution has helped to bring to tens of millions in Asia and elsewhere the food security previously familiar only in wealthy nations. And, of course, the multimedia PCs currently being snapped up by many families in this country offer computing power comparable to that used only by rocket scientists three decades ago.

Schumpeter's vision describes how the long sweep of capitalist development reduces inequality, eventually. Yet when innovations first appear, they can make life worse for poorer people, sometimes for decades. Some three centuries ago, the development of high-yield crops to feed livestock paved the way for massive increases in agricultural output, and this led to the population boom that accompanied the Industrial Revolution. Ultimately, this led to an increase in living standards beyond anyone's dreams, but the short-term impact was misery as peasants could no longer graze their animals on common or fallow land. Naturally, such changes are bitterly resisted.

Adam Smith, the famous British economist, provided a strong case for capitalism. In his book *The Wealth of Nations* (1776), he argued the case that producers of goods will supply to the market what consumers wanted in order to make profits. The driving force behind this process was personal greed: but the effect of this greed was the betterment of society.

Economic perspectives

Over the course of time various groups of economists have presented differing theories as to how the economy works.

The classical economists

The classical economists follow in the line of Adam Smith, arguing that the market is the best way of deciding how resources should be used in society (the allocation of resources). They argue that the market leads to the best solutions because the forces of demand reflect people's preferences for what goods and services should be supplied. Interfere with this market at your peril. Anyone who artificially tries to set prices at 'non-market rates' will create inefficiency, leading to waste and unemployment. We use the term neo-classical economist to denote a modern-day adherent of the principles of the free market.

Marxist economists

Marxist economists would argue that there is no such thing as a free market. The market is a 'smokescreen' for the exploitation of the proletariat (those who do not own capital) by the capitalist class. Once the proletariat fully realise the extent of this exploitation they will rise up and destroy the system to replace it with 'advanced communism'. Modern-day Marxists are described as neo-Marxists.

Keynesian economists

Keynesian economists are supporters of the ideas of the English economist John Maynard Keynes, and they provide another challenge to the classical school. They argue that the market provides no guarantee of efficiency. We can never be sure that the supply of goods in the economy (national output) will be purchased in its entirety by consumers. Should total demand fall short of total supply then producers will want to cut back on their level of output, rather than carry the cost of unsold stocks. Once output starts to decrease, then people will have less money in their pockets as some of them start to lose their jobs. A fall in income leads to a fresh fall in spending and a downward spiral in the economy. Keynes provided a strong case for government interference in the economy to manage the level of demand in order to encourage producers to produce enough goods to guarantee full employment.

The ideas of Keynes gained popularity in the period from 1945, after the Second World War. Between 1945 and 1979 all the major political parties committed themselves to the creation of full employment.

The classical revival, 1979–97

In the late 1970s, classical economics became popular once again; indeed it became the new orthodoxy. In the 1950s and 1960s, Keynesian policies had seemed to work and unemployment had been low. However, in the 1970s many economies experienced rising levels of unemployment coupled with rising inflation. Inflation was now seen as the evil that was more likely to destroy economies rather than unemployment.

The neo-classical economists argued that it was government interference (expenditure and resource waste) that had created an inefficient economy. The emphasis was then on reducing the role of the state (for example, through the privatisation of industry) and on using the interest rate as a way of taking inflation out of the system. Higher interest rates encouraged saving and hence cut back on expenditures.

The UK's mixed economy

In the nineteenth century the UK government played only a small part in the control of the economy. Today, the proper role of the government is open to debate, but most people accept that it should at least try to influence economic activity. Why has this change in attitude taken place over time?

In some towns in the 1920s, over half of the potential labour force were unemployed. Many people felt, in the light of the terrible suffering and waste

during this period, that the government should play a central role in creating and sustaining employment. Most of the politicians who made the key decisions in this country from the Second World War onwards had vivid memories of this period. Politicians of all parties were therefore prepared to give high priority to curing unemployment.

The 1970s was a period of rapid increases in prices. People felt the effects of inflation in different ways depending, amongst other things, on how much power they had to raise their own incomes to cope with price rises.

The general effect of price rises is to distort the working of the price system. Trading ideally needs to take place in settled conditions. If you expected to be paid £100 in three months' time you would be very disappointed if you found that when you received payment you could purchase only half of the goods you would have been able to obtain today.

If people become reluctant to trade, then fewer goods will be produced for sale. If fewer goods are made, fewer people are employed in production. Price disturbances can therefore cause the whole economy to stagnate.

After 1979, with the election of Margaret Thatcher's first administration, economic policy in this country changed dramatically. The emphasis was very much on resurrecting a liberal model of the economy based on competition and free enterprise. Many industries previously owned by the state, such as telecommunications, fuel and power, rail and air transport, were privatised (sold to shareholders). Services such as health and education were increasingly placed in a competitive environment in which individual units became self-managing and responsible for handling their own budgets. Of course, there is a strong emphasis on public accountability. Local managers need to be able to show how they are spending their funds. They need to manage their budgets wisely. Citizens have far more access to complaints and appeals procedures. In addition, privatised industries are subject to the controls of 'regulators' who are there to ensure fair competition and to ensure that the rights of all stakeholders are effectively maintained.

The 'Third Way'

In 1997, Britain elected a Labour government with alternative views about how the economy should be run. This they labelled the 'third way'. In particular, in the autumn of 1997 the Chancellor of the Exchequer, Gordon Brown, emphasised that the prime target for economic policy should be that of abolishing unemployment.

However, many argue that the government has failed to articulate fully the nature of its third way. What is clear is that Labour's emphasis on modernisation is based on a belief that the market must play a key part in macro- and microeconomic decision making. Firms need to operate in a competitive environment in which the state does not grant unfair subsidies to 'lame duck' industries.

The third way seems to be concerned with unleashing enterprise and market forces in the economy while at the same time ensuring key social provision to support social policies, including the protection of weaker members of society. So, for example, Labour turned round the previous Conservative government's policy of Care in the Community for the elderly and people with mental problems. Some individuals were to be given greater provision and care both to protect themselves and society in general.

A new paradigm?

A further way of thinking about the economy has recently arisen in the United States. According to this view, recent developments in the world have created a situation in which both unemployment and inflation can be kept at low levels. This optimistic view is based on the belief that underlying productivity growth has been greatly boosted by the revolution in information technology and other spin-offs from the microchip. This, it is claimed, has greatly boosted the potential output of the services sector, but the official GDP statistics have not correctly accounted for this change. Hence policymakers have not fully appreciated just how much productivity has actually risen.

A second assertion is that wage inflation has been held down by the opening of a new global labour market, in which competition from the developing world has depressed the wages of unskilled workers in the West.

If these assertions prove correct then there is scope for optimism about economic growth. We might see the possibility of more and more goods becoming available to the ordinary person.

Public and private sector initiatives

Private finance initiatives

Private finance initiatives (also called public private partnerships) were first used in the UK in the early 1990s. The UK government was faced with a major problem of how to finance major public capital expenditure. The 'public purse' is clearly limited and increasing taxes to pay for additional expenditure was expected to be very unpopular, so a new way was sought. In addition, it was commonly believed that management in the private sector was superior to that in the public sector, so a way of including private expertise in capital project management was also seen as preferable. Hence the private finance initiative (PFI) scheme was born.

The PFI enlists the skills and expertise of the private sector in providing public services and facilities. The scheme encourages private companies to be involved in the building and running of public services, such as hospitals, colleges, railways and schools. The idea is that private companies, 'in partnership' with either national or local government, provide these services, with the government providing part of the money and the rest paid by the private company. However it is not only about finding additional money for capital investments, but also about exploiting the full range of private sector management, commercial and creative skills. There are benefits for both sides to the partnership; the public sector has access to the private sector's expertise, innovation and management, whilst the private sector gains a new business opportunity and a funding stream that should provide a good return on its investment.

Many PFI schemes are what is called DBFO (design, build, finance and operate). This means that the private sector partner is responsible for

- designing the facilities, although the requirements will initially be specified by the public partner, that is, the school, college or hospital
- building the facilities
- financing the capital cost (the private partner will then make a profit by taking an income from the public partner for providing the facility), and
- operating the facilities, providing facilities management and support services.

The public partner will define their capital needs and invite private sector bidders to present their plans for meeting those needs. For large schemes the private sector partner will often be a consortium of companies providing different skills and experiences.

The volume of PFI contracts that the UK government has awarded has steadily increased. By mid-2003 over 550 contracts, worth £35 billion, had been signed, including 200 schools and 34 hospitals; analysts were expecting a further £12 billion worth of PFI contracts to be awarded by the government before 2006. However, although the government seems to be very committed to the use of PFI to finance public projects, they have not been met with universal approval. Trade unions in particular have been critical of them; Unison and the Transport and General Workers Union (TGWU), for example, have publicly stated that they do not believe that PFI offers the taxpayer value for money. They also claim that the system can create 'two-tier' workforces, with employees taken on after a service is contracted out not being offered the same terms as those who started when the work was in the public sector.

Another criticism that has been levelled at PFI schemes has been inaccurate estimates of project costs, which have led to a number of projects going over budget, requiring the tax payer (via the government) to find increased sums of money. For example, in 1997 it was decided that GCHQ, the government's intelligence gathering organisation,

should relocate and that this should be financed using a PFI. The initial estimate was £1.07 billion, but by 2003 this had risen to £1.62 billion. As a result the government was faced with a £315m shortfall that would have to come from taxes. The rise in costs was blamed primarily on the cost of installing its new computer systems which increased from an initial £40m to £450m. However, the Treasury in a recent report said that 89 per cent of projects had been completed on time and within budget.

CASE STUDY

Private finance initiatives

Carillion is the former construction services arm of Tarmac. It used to be a traditional commercial construction business, but in recent years it has reinvented itself, and now 25 per cent of its business comes from private finance initiative projects, such as building and running hospitals. PFI work certainly carries a lot of risk; it takes a long time, for example, to achieve preferred bidder status, and the financial penalties for missing delivery dates can be severe. However, the management of Carillion believe that the returns are potentially much better than from traditional building contracts.

ACTIVITY

What do you think are the major advantages and disadvantages to making PFI work such a major part of your business?

Government policy

Government has two key weapons when controlling the economy, these being fiscal policy and monetary policy:

♦ **Fiscal policy** refers to changing government spending and taxation levels.
♦ **Monetary policy** refers to changes in money supply and levels of interest rates.

Both tactics may be used to regulate levels of demand in the economy, and both can therefore be used to either stimulate the economy to help businesses and jobs, or to slow it down to reduce inflation.

Fiscal policy in the UK

Fiscal policy aims to alter levels of demand by using taxation and government spending changes.

Some types of UK taxes

Taxes can be split into two major types, **direct taxes**, which are paid according to a person's income or wealth, and **indirect taxes**, which are added to the prices of goods and services sold. Whilst you do not need to know how each of these works in detail, you should know a little about them.

Direct taxes

Income tax is charged on earned income. The more you earn the more you pay, and this is known as a progressive tax.

Corporation tax is a tax on business profits; this is proportional to the size of those profits and is therefore another example of a progressive tax.

National Insurance is a direct tax deducted from wages to contribute towards the NHS, social security and state pensions.

Capital gains tax is a tax on investments that have gained in value; however you only pay this tax when you sell or realise the assets.

Inheritance tax is paid on large inheritances.

Council tax is paid to local government to pay for local services. The amount that you pay is relative to the value of your home, the higher the value the more you pay. In theory this is also a progressive tax aimed at charging those with greater wealth more, however some elderly people have found themselves in houses that have grown substantially in value and have found themselves facing high council tax bills even though their incomes are relatively low.

Indirect taxes

Value added tax is charged on goods bought; the tax is added to the price paid. At the moment VAT is charged at 17.5 per cent on most items, although some such as food and drugs are zero-rated. VAT is known as a regressive tax, meaning that you will pay the same amount however much you earn. Thus someone who buys a new camera will pay the same amount of VAT amount on the purchase whether they earn £20 or £20,000 per week.

Excise duty is an additional sales tax levied on certain goods such as alcohol, cigarettes and fuel; this is also a regressive tax.

Customs duties are paid on all goods imported from outside the EU; again this is regressive.

Other types of tax

Stamp duty is a 1 per cent fee charged on property sales.

Insurance tax is an additional tax payment built into the premiums of all motor and home insurance.

Air travel tax is a flat rate payment charged on all airline tickets.

Licence duties are such things as TV licences and driving licences. These are set fees and are therefore regressive taxes.

These are by no means the only taxes used, but they are a number of the more important ones. Government can alter demand levels in the economy by altering the rates of tax charged, as shown in Figure 5.14.

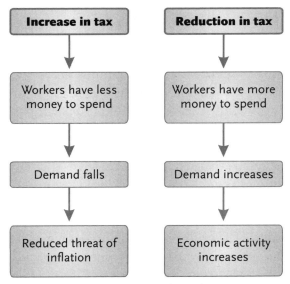

Figure 5.14   Altering demand levels in the economy

Since government is the major spender in the economy, it is in a unique position to influence levels of demand. Government spends on a multitude of areas, such as health, education, road building, social security, defence, regional policy and the arts. If it increases spending in these areas this will automatically create demand, and this should aid business profits and jobs. If, however, it reduces spending, business profit earning is threatened and firms may have to cut costs, possibly shedding jobs.

The budget

Fiscal decisions are made annually by the Chancellor of the Exchequer in the budget which is delivered each March or April. The budget is a statement of the

The government's fiscal rules   JOURNAL ARTICLE

Dissatisfied with the previous system for allocating fiscal spending, in 1998 the UK government introduced two 'fiscal rules' to help achieve high and stable economic growth. The rules were:

1   The Golden Rule: the government would only borrow to invest and not to fund current spending.

2   The Sustainable Investment Rule: net public debt would be held at 40 per cent of GDP.

Gordon Brown has used these in trying to set his budgets ever since.
In the *British Economy Survey*, Volume 31, Number 1, Autumn 2001, Section 5, Alan Griffiths' article 'The government's fiscal rules' examines the need for these rules, how effective they have been and the problems that they have set the government in trying to stick to them. You should read this article to gain a greater understanding of this area.

CASE STUDY
Fiscal policy and National Insurance

When we think of fiscal policy and changes in tax we normally consider the most visible taxes, income tax and VAT; however one of the UK government's biggest tax earners is National Insurance. Increases in income tax are always considered bad news by most of the population, so in his 2002 budget, Gordon Brown opted to increase NI contributions instead, which did not have such a frosty reception from the general public. It was, however, a big blow for UK industry.

Many people are unaware that when they pay National Insurance from their wage packets, their employer also pays too on their behalf, and the employer actually pays more than the employee does. Businesses therefore generally regard National Insurance as a tax on employing people as the companies that employ the most people pay the most National Insurance, and increases in NI rates are therefore generally unwelcome.

In April 2003, a 1 per cent rise in NI contributions came into effect. The rise hit both public and private sector businesses. The NHS is the biggest employer in the UK, and it estimated that its additional NI bill would be approximately £240 million, a huge additional cost to the organisation. BT employs over 100,000 people and it expected its additional bill to run to about £23 million. Ruth Lea, the head of policy at the Institute of Directors, said: 'This couldn't come at a worse time. It's bad for the consumer when confidence is crumbling and it's bad for business as it is yet more cost.'

ACTIVITY

1   In groups consider the merits and problems associated with increased NI payments. Do you feel that rises in income tax or NI are fairer? Explain the reasons for your answers.

2   What do such increases do for the competitiveness of UK industry? In what ways would you expect companies to respond to this increase in NI? What effects may these responses have to the UK economy?

estimated revenue and expenditure of the government for the coming year; it states how the money will be spent and how it will be raised, including any changes to tax rates or allowances. The budget has twin aims:

◆ to regulate the economy by manipulating levels of demand through fiscal measures
◆ to redistribute income and wealth fairly across the country.

Monetary policy in the UK

Monetary policies have been used extensively in the UK since 1979 when Margaret Thatcher came to power. She decided a new approach was required and the methods she adopted were very successful in controlling inflation, so much so that they are still used actively today.

Monetarist policies are based on the assumption that the economy can be regulated by measuring and manipulating the levels of money supply in the economy. The money supply is simply the total amount of money available for spending within a country. You might like to think of the money supply as being the total amount of **purchasing power** within the country. The government expends much effort in attempting to calculate the money supply accurately, and several definitions have been proposed in recent years. All of the definitions are prefixed with the letter M, thus the definition Mo covers the actual notes and coins in circulation, whereas later definitions such as M4 and M5 include bank and building society accounts as well as a variety of accounts with other financial institutions. The most commonly used definitions are Mo and M4, which do seem to give a clear picture of how purchasing power is changing, and that is sufficient to guide the government in its inflation policy.

Monetary policy is the government's main tool for controlling inflation in the UK, and it assumes that inflation is created by excess aggregate demand in the economy.

Demand pull inflation

If resources are being used efficiently in the economy this may lead to increases in demand in the country. Excessive demand, over and above our ability to expand production, can lead to prices rising, as shown in Figure 5.15.

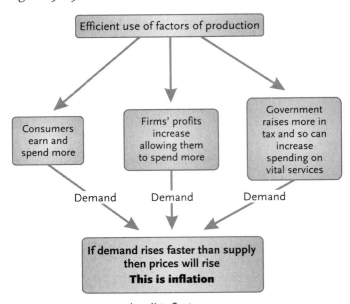

Figure 5.15   Demand pull inflation

This explanation of the roots of inflation has become increasingly important as the government's strategy for controlling inflation for the last 20 years has been largely based on tackling this cause.

The monetarist theory on inflation assumes that there is a direct link between bank lending, the money supply and ultimately inflation, and it works as in Figure 5.16.

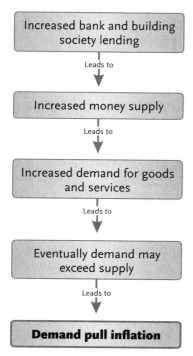

Figure 5.16   Monetarist view of demand pull inflation

This theory therefore draws a direct link between bank lending and the rate of inflation. If there is indeed a causal relationship between these two then controlling bank lending should control levels of inflation. If we reduce bank lending this should reduce purchasing power (money supply), this in turn should reduce demand and that will reduce or eliminate demand pull inflation. Monetarists assume that the key factor determining the amount of bank lending taking place is the rate of interest charged; if rates are high this discourages lending (as the repayments are so high) and if rates are low lending is likely to increase. The government can therefore regulate the economy by altering interest rates to suit their objectives at the time. Interest rate policy can be used

in two main ways, to reduce inflation or to stimulate the economy, as shown in Figures 5.17 and 5.18.

Figure 5.17   Using interest rates to reduce inflation

Figure 5.18   Using interest rates to stimulate the economy

The two policies may be used at different times when priorities change.

In 1979, when the main priority was to reduce inflation, interest rates were increased in order to reduce inflation, and this tactic did have the desired effect. However, there is a price to pay for this success. Inflation is reduced in this way by suppressing demand in the economy. Unfortunately industry needs demand to enable it to develop, so a regime of high interest rates can be very difficult for industry. Not only is business borrowing more expensive, increasing operating costs and preventing expansion, but demand is also low. High costs and low demand is a bad recipe for business, not surprising then that many businesses found it difficult to survive under high interest rates. However it did achieve its objective and inflation did fall dramatically.

As we attempted to come out of the deep recession of the early 1990s the government was aware that industry needed help to get it moving again, and this was provided by using interest rate policy in the opposite way; to stimulate the economy. Interest rates were reduced, thus reducing business costs and stimulating demand; a fine recipe for business success. This was one of the key factors that helped the UK out of the recessionary problems of the early 1990s. There may be a price to pay however, as increased demand may ultimately lead to further inflation, so the government treads cautiously when changing interest rates, often choosing to change them by small amounts of 0.25 or 0.5 per cent. The government is treading a tightrope all the time, wanting interest rates to be high enough to discourage inflation, but also low enough to stimulate industry.

The effectiveness of interest rate changes

JOURNAL ARTICLE

Interest rates are now the main tool of short-term economic management around the world, and in the 1990s changes in the rate were definitely a powerful tool for influencing aggregate demand; however doubts have begun to creep in in recent years. In 2001 the UK, Europe, Japan and the USA all cut interest rates in the hope of stimulating demand in their economies, but they have met with varying success.

Susan Grant examines this recent trend in detail in the *British Economy Survey*, Volume 31, Number 1, Autumn 2001, Section 1. Her article 'The effectiveness of interest rate changes' examines recent experiences and looks at whether interest rate changes are as potent as they used to be.

The effects of interest rate policy

Interest rates, therefore, may be raised in order to control inflation, but what are the other effects of such a policy? High interest rates affect many players in the economy, as Figure 5.19 illustrates.

Interest rate changes, therefore, have a variety of effects, not all of which are positive for the economy.

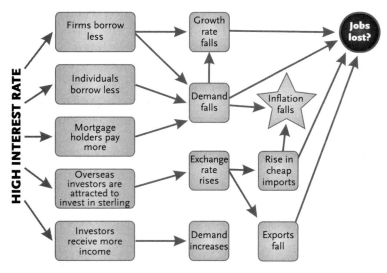

Figure 5.19   The effects of a high interest rate

The monetary policy committee

Until May 1997 all UK monetary policy decisions were taken by the UK government through the Chancellor of the Exchequer, who made the decisions and announced any changes. In May 1997 the new Labour government decided to alter this. There had been accusations that some interest rate changes were made not at times that suited the economy best, but at times that suited the government best. So interest rates might be reduced just before an election to make the government more popular and give them a greater chance of re-election. To avoid this possibility of bias in the future, the Chancellor of the Exchequer, Gordon Brown, announced that in the future all interest rate decisions will be made by the Bank of England. He appointed a monetary policy committee (MPC), chaired by the Governor of the Bank of England and instructed them to meet monthly to decide on interest rates for the next month, with the specific objective of achieving the government's underlying inflation target of no higher than 2.5 per cent. Whilst the Chancellor retained the right to overrule the committee's decisions in 'extreme economic circumstances', the committee is now free to independently make decisions that it believes are right for the country, without fear of bias. The process has been operating for some time now and appears to be working smoothly. Although not everyone agrees with all of the decisions taken, we can be sure that they were made without the influence of political pressures.

You can obtain more detail on the role of the MPC at the Bank of England MPC website.

ACTIVITY

Visit the Bank of England website at www.bankofengland.co.uk and check the latest decisions on interest rate changes that have taken place.

1   What do you think were the reasons behind the latest decisions taken by the MPC?

2   What effects will those decisions have had on the following groups?

- ◆ Mortgage payers
- ◆ Businesses
- ◆ Exporters
- ◆ Investors
- ◆ Companies looking to expand
- ◆ Consumers.

Monetary policy, inflation targeting and asset prices

JOURNAL ARTICLE

The UK government has spoken proudly in recent years of its change in the operation of monetary policy in the UK by giving the Bank of England control over interest rates, the so-called policy of 'independence' for the central bank. However, this independence only extends to the setting of the interest rate, the actual objective of the policy, keeping inflation within 1 per cent of 2.5 per cent per annum, is still set by the UK government. We can contrast this 'operational independence' with the 'full independence' enjoyed by other central banks, such as the US Federal Reserve and the European Central Bank. Those banks are able to set policy as well as decide how to achieve it.

In the *British Economy Survey*, Volume 32, Number 1, Autumn 2002, Section 14, Peter Howell's article 'Monetary policy, inflation targeting and asset prices' examines monetary policy and inflation targeting in detail and looks at the effect of the MPC in the UK.

Industrial policy in the UK

Despite the large share of GDP that is still accounted for by public expenditure, the privatisation of nationalised industries has reduced direct state intervention in industry. The main policy initiatives are summarised as follows.

Enterprise culture

There have been initiatives to help create small businesses and to reduce their tax burden. In 1999 the government gave more freedom to the Post Office to operate in a competitive environment and in a more market-orientated fashion. The Labour government has followed its Conservative predecessor in emphasising the role of enterprise.

Reduction of subsidies

The aim of both Conservative and Labour governments has been, where possible, to reduce subsidies or phase them out altogether. Whether it be in steel production or shipbuilding, running the railways or the operation of the BBC, the market has been asked to work without the distortion of subsidies. However, the current Labour government has created some new subsidies, for example in creating employment under the New Deal Scheme.

Privatisation

Many things, from council houses to public utilities, were sold off from 1979 onwards. However, the Labour government has found it increasingly difficult to privatise further because nearly all of the enterprises that private investors see as being a worthwhile investment have already been sold.

Privatisation does not on its own create competition, so regulations and the gradual introduction of competition have been seen as the way to reduce the monopoly power of water, electricity, gas and other utilities.

In October 1998, Tony Blair tried to explain his 'third way' to senior civil servants by giving examples. These included his government's use of a public–private partnership, rather than outright privatisation, to modernise the London Underground; government co-operation with the Wellcome Foundation, a charity to invest in public research laboratories; and an invitation to private firms to help raise school standards in designated 'education action zones'.

Deregulation

Sometimes referred to as 'reducing red tape', the purpose of deregulation is to eradicate as many restrictions as possible. Progressively governments have sought to remove unnecessary regulation while creating new regulatory powers where they are necessary to ensure fair competition in the marketplace.

Incorporation

From trust hospitals to further education colleges, incorporation allows an organisation to make more decisions on its own, and crucially to be free of local authority control. Funding becomes more centrally controlled and the organisation is rewarded (or not) on its success in meeting nationally determined performance criteria.

Mergers and business practice

There are various regulating agencies that review mergers, monopoly power and unfair trading. New Labour has followed the line of maintaining a competitive industrial framework while at the same time providing funds to attract employment-creating initiatives in the UK.

Social welfare policy in the UK

Social welfare is a key aspect of government policy, and social security, health and education are three major components of government expenditure in this country. Indeed, it is difficult to disentangle the connections between economic and social and welfare policies. When Tony Blair stated that his government's priority policy was 'Education, Education, and Education', he was not only promising a basic entitlement for all citizens to have a high standard of education, he was also making a connection between a well-educated workforce and international competitiveness in a world in which the 'knowledge worker' is the greatest asset of the modern economy.

The earlier Conservative governments placed an emphasis on creating an enterprise culture in which people would have the incentive to go out to work: 'to get on their bikes to seek work', as Norman Tebbit (a Conservative minister) described it. The Conservatives sought to reduce the role of the 'nanny state', which not only protected those genuinely in need, but also enabled people to avoid work and social responsibilities. The Conservatives reduced income taxes and decreased some state benefits, which was intended to give people more of an incentive to work. Critics of the Conservatives pointed out that they failed to differentiate between the 'shirker' and the 'needy', and that they failed to introduce effective programmes to create real opportunities for those seeking work.

The Conservatives also sought, through the policy of 'Care in the Community', to reduce the number of elderly people, and those with physical or mental difficulties, occupying hospital beds and places in state accommodation. Many such people were placed back in the community, often in sheltered accommodation. However, this led to a series of difficulties because of a failure to provide adequate care. (For example, a number of people with mental health problems failed to carry on taking their medicines.) A number of highly publicised cases led to a rethink of this policy, which was partially reversed by the Labour government.

Labour's 'third way' involves differentiating between those economic policies which are best left to market forces, and key social policies involving the protection of individuals and the community which need to be steered by a paternalistic state. A major emphasis has been on creating new opportunities for people to make a go of things in society: 'Instead of welfare there should be work'. Labour believes that work provides dignity and opportunity for individuals; they can stand on their own feet rather than feel that they are receiving handouts from the state, and so are less than complete citizens.

Labour's 'New Deal' for young people includes the options of a subsidised job with an employer, a subsidised job in voluntary-sector employment, a subsidised job with the Environmental Task Force, or a subsidised period of full-time education leading to a recognised qualification.

Labour's 'Welfare to Work' programme is not without its critics, particularly those who see the reduction of state benefits as a threat to the genuine needs of specific groups of people such as the disabled. Such critics argue that benefits should not be cut off from those who have no realistic opportunity to hold down a job. However, the government would contend that everyone should have the opportunity to have a decent job. This involves creating the opportunities and the belief that everyone can move from welfare to some type of work, paid or unpaid.

Examples of Labour's welfare-to-work policies include:

♦ a lone-parents initiative offering practical help in returning to work; specially trained personal advisers help participants to overcome barriers to employment and encourage them actively to seek work
♦ the provision of childcare for pre-school and school-age children.

Labour has also introduced a national minimum wage to make sure that all employees receive a wage which prevents them from being exploited in the labour market.

Economic growth

Economic growth occurs when a country increases its ability to produce goods and services. Economic growth is important as it provides a measurement of how standards of living in the country are changing. Steady growth leads to substantial improvements in standards of living. Increased growth provides additional earned income, improved employment prospects, additional business profits, further government spending on vital services and therefore improvements in standards of living for all citizens.

The value of the output produced within the boundaries of a particular nation is known as the Gross Domestic Product or GDP.

Economic growth is measured by calculating the percentage changes in GDP and/or GNP from one year to the next. For example, examine the following GDP figures for the UK:

	GDP (£ billion)
2000	829
2001	847
2002	863

The economic growth for 2001 is $\frac{847 - 829}{829} \times 100$

$= 2.17\%$

The economic growth for 2002 is $\frac{863 - 847}{847} \times 100$

$= 1.89\%$

We always describe economic growth in terms of percentages, and the above figures are fairly respectable, although they may not seem it. Growth rates of 4 or 5 per cent are exceptional, and if they can be maintained for a number of years they can lead to substantial rises in living standards for a country. Typically, in the UK over the last 40 years we have achieved between 2 and 3 per cent per year, which is respectable but not nearly as great as those experienced by some of our trading partners such as Germany and Japan, which regularly achieve growth rates in excess of 4 per cent. Whilst these differences may not seem great, taken over a period of years they can lead to widening gaps in standards of living, gaps that are very difficult to reduce. It is therefore important for governments to achieve growth, and as a minimum this should be as good as our trading partners, and ideally higher than them. Otherwise their standards of living will outstrip ours.

Figure 5.20 shows how the UK economy grew over the period 1985 to 1995 in comparison with other trading nations.

Policies to encourage growth

Given that this is an important objective, governments may use the following tactics to encourage economic growth.

265

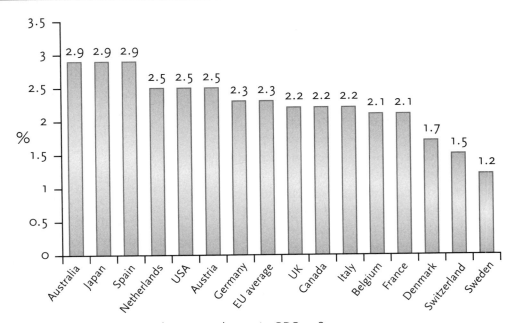

GDP growth

Australia	2.9
Japan	2.9
Spain	2.9
Netherlands	2.5
USA	2.5
Austria	2.5
Germany	2.3
EU average	2.3
UK	2.2
Canada	2.2
Italy	2.2
Belgium	2.1
France	2.1
Denmark	1.7
Switzerland	1.5
Sweden	1.2

Figure 5.20   Average annual per cent change in GDP 1985–95

Promote savings In order for businesses to develop they need a steady flow of investment capital. In the UK we do not have a tradition of investing in our industry, but it is no coincidence that some of the more successful economic nations do have this culture. To encourage flows of investment into industry, the government can encourage savings through a variety of financial service providers. Savings into pension funds and insurance policies are often reinvested in stocks and shares, some increased savings of this type will benefit industry. The UK government has encouraged direct investment into industry in recent years through the PEP (Personal Equity Plan) scheme and also with the new ISA (Individual Savings Account). Promoting a culture of

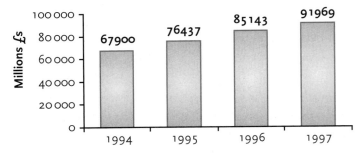

Figure 5.21   Business investment in the UK

thrift will ensure a ready supply of investment into industry and that can be used to improve our productivity and generate growth. Figures for investment in UK industry in recent years are shown in Figure 5.21. As you can see, growth has been steady but not spectacular, and certainly not as much as industry would like.

Promote mobility Geographical and occupational mobility (discussed in detail earlier in this chapter) can be encouraged by offering grant aid. These should help us to use our factors of production more efficiently and thereby increase productivity and growth.

Promote education and training An educated workforce is a more productive workforce, so funding academic and vocational training effectively and promoting new ways of encouraging individuals to become more skilled should make the country more efficient and promote growth. Hence the introduction of schemes in the UK such as Youth Training, Modern Apprenticeships and new qualifications such as NVQs and AVCEs.

Promote research and development For industry to develop new ideas and processes that will be wealth generators for the nation, much money must be spent on R&D to discover these new ideas. This is a very costly process and the investment required can be prohibitive for some firms. In these circumstances governments might consider offering grants to firms for use in R&D, or they might enter into jointly funded projects with industry. In 2002 the UK government introduced tax credits for firms involved in R&D in order to encourage more development activity.

CASE STUDY

Economic growth: compound rates of growth

It is easy to underestimate the power of compound growth; even relatively small rates of growth sustained for lengthy periods can have huge effects in the national income of a country.

It is quite simple to work out how long it would take income in a country to double. Simply divide the growth rate into the number 72. Growth in the UK, for example, has averaged about 2 per cent over the past few years; if this were to continue, national income would double every 36 years (72/2 = 36). In little over 100 years, income would increase eightfold. This is the reason why governments are so concerned over relatively small rates of growth.

ACTIVITY

China is currently experiencing growth rates of 8 per cent per annum. How quickly is income *per capita* doubling in China?

Economic performance in the UK

Although the UK is not the most successful economy in the world, it remains very robust and contains more strengths than weaknesses. Indeed, recent economic performance has been very good in comparison to many other countries.

Growth

Economic growth has slowed in the UK since 2000 but not as much as in many of the other major economies. Growth was certainly hampered by this slowdown in other countries as demand from overseas for UK products and services has slowed somewhat. Growth in the UK was 1.8 per cent in 2003.

Industry

The tertiary sector of industry continues to strengthen as does construction, whilst manufacturing continues to decline, especially some of the high-tech industries that have been badly affected by the global downturn. Manufacturing has continued to suffer from the fact that sterling has remained strong relative to the US$ and the euro, hampering our ability to exploit foreign markets. The strong pound has encouraged increased import penetration and consequently our balance of payments trade deficit has continued to widen.

Public spending

In the early 1990s, the UK government decided to try and address the lack of investment in public services in the UK, and consequently spending was stepped up considerably in key public service areas, notably public transport, health and education. The government's success will undoubtedly be judged by the improvements that are made in these areas. To pay for these changes the government has increased the tax burden on UK citizens (although it has avoided increasing income tax rates), so if the public does not perceive significant improvements in these areas, there may be some form of backlash against the government.

Employment

The UK continues to perform well in the jobs market. Despite the continued job losses in manufacturing industry, overall unemployment continues to fall. The UK has had a comparatively good record on unemployment for a number of years, and this trend has continued in recent years. The rate of unemployment in the UK (Figure 5.22) was around 5 per cent in 2003 and has remained at about this level for some time.

Unemployment rates 2001

UK	5.5%
France	8.8%
Germany	7.9%
USA	4.8%
Spain	10.5%
Italy	9.5%
Japan	5%
Australia	6.6%
Belgium	7%

Source: United Nations

Figure 5.22   Unemployment rates

However, productivity in the UK remains low compared to many other advanced economies. The government believes that this is partly due to education standards, so efforts are being made to improve literacy and numeracy standards in the country.

Saving and borrowing

People in the UK are saving less as a proportion of their income today than they did in the 1990s and previously. Falling interest rates and rapidly rising house prices have boosted the confidence of consumers to the extent that more prefer spending to saving. Mortgage, loan and credit card lending has increased to unprecedented levels (a record £9.93 billion was lent in June 2003). This has led some observers to fear that the UK economy is becoming over-dependent on lending. Should interest rates have to rise again in the future, we could see many people struggling to meet their debt repayments.

Wages and inflation

Wages have only risen by modest amounts for a number of years, and price inflation has been exceptionally low. Using the new harmonised measure for inflation (HICP), the period 2000–2003 was the UK's lowest sustained inflationary period for many decades, averaging about 1 per cent since February 2000. This compares very favourably with the rest of the EU, which averaged about 2.5 per cent. Using the underlying inflation rate measurement (Retail Price Index minus mortgage interest payments) which the UK government the average rate has been closer to 2.5 per cent, but this is still within the government's target.

The UK government has used a number of measurements for inflation over the years, and the situation has recently changed again. The Retail Price Index (RPI) takes a range of goods and services and values them each year. The average change in price gives us our measure of inflation. This was later refined to give us the Underlying Rate of Inflation (RPIX). This measurement is the RPI with the effect of changes in mortgage interest payments deducted. This has been the government's preferred measurement of inflation for a number of years.

In the 2003 budget, however, Gordon Brown announced that the UK would adopt the HICP: the harmonised index for inflation used for international comparisons across the EU. Ultimately the government may benefit from this change, as the HICP formula is apparently less susceptible to an upward bias in measured inflation. Whilst the RPI uses an arithmetic mean (the total divided by the number of items), the HICP uses a 'geometric mean' to calculate an inflation figure. That means it multiplies the rises together and takes the nth root. Consequently, the geometric average tends to provide a lower inflation figure, but it is considered to be a better estimate of the impact of inflation on consumers, as it assumes that we tend to switch our spending away from items with big price rises, towards those with lower price rises. Currently the UK government is still producing figures for RPI and RPIX, but is now moving towards using the HICP. Under the new measure, the government has revised its target for inflation down from 2.5 per cent under RPIX to 2 per cent under HICP.

The Confederation of British Industry

The CBI was founded in 1965 as a non-profit-making, non-party political organisation with the objective of creating and sustaining the conditions in which business in the UK can compete and prosper. On the CBI website, www.cbi.org.uk, they describe their role thus, 'It exists to ensure that the government of the day, the European Commission and the wider community understand both the needs of British business and the contribution it makes to the well-being of UK society.'

Organisations and companies become members of the CBI and together they form a voice for UK industry. The CBI is the advocate of policies that will most benefit businesses, and as a result it lobbies and advises both the UK and EU governments, trying to influence public policy in the interests of UK companies. Sometimes the CBI will concentrate on using the national and regional press to put pressure on government; at other times radio and television interviews will be used to put across their views.

The CBI also acts as a source of advice and information for companies and a forum for exchanging views and making business contacts. Many UK companies, big and small, are members of the CBI, and consequently its voice is influential.

The CBI influences government in many fields of interest to its members. In mid-2003, for example, some of the areas they were involved with were as follows.

Basic skills

The CBI criticised the government, saying that many school leavers do not have the basic skills needed for employment. As a result, it said, employers called for the government to 'make eradicating this scandalous weakness its top priority'.

Export credits

The CBI told the government that UK business needs the same level of help on export credit as firms in Germany, France and the USA. A letter was sent to the Trade Secretary, Patricia Hewitt, urging review of the Export Credits Guarantee Department (ECGD), warning that without export support, business, jobs and skills would go overseas.

Attitudes to the UK

The CBI released a detailed assessment of business attitudes to the UK as an investment location. The survey suggested that while the majority of respondents still found the UK an attractive business climate, it had certainly deteriorated.

Retail sales (August 2003)

A CBI report said that official retail sales figures showed the public continued to spend, boosting the economy, while industry continued to have problems. Retail had an exceptional month in June 2003, when sales rose 1.9 per cent when they were expected to fall.

Pensions

As a result of the increasing worry over company pension schemes, the CBI was actively involved in advising government on ways to improve pension provision without adding unnecessary burdens to UK industry.

The Trades Union Congress

The Trades Union Congress (TUC) was formed in 1868 and is the national organisation representing trade unions in Britain. It is made up of 74 unions and it aims to promote the rights and welfare of people at work and campaign for policies which help the unemployed find jobs. Its roles are:

- bringing Britain's unions together to draw up common policies
- lobbying the government to implement policies that will benefit people at work
- campaigning on economic and social issues
- representing British workers in international bodies, in the European Union and at the UN employment body, the International Labour Organisation
- researching into employment-related issues.

Therefore, whereas the CBI tends to represent the views and interests of employers, the TUC will represent the interests of employees. In mid-2003, for example, some of the areas they were involved with were as follows.

Health and safety at work

The TUC publishes regular bulletins in this area; in 2003 they were looking at teleworking and site safety.

269

Directors' notice periods

The TUC was lobbying the government through the DTI to change the law to limit directors' notice periods so that they are the same as those for the majority of other employees in the firm. They were also demanding that severance packages awarded to departing executives should contain no elements of performance-related pay or bonuses.

Working hours

The TUC's 'It's about time' campaign was aimed at tackling Britain's culture of working long hours, and persuading the European Commission to end the UK opt-out from the Working Time Directive when it was due for review. Research undertaken by the TUC suggested that one in four people in the UK who had signed an opt-out from working time rules were given no choice about opting out and that only one employee in three even knew that there is a 48-hour limit on the average working week.

CASE STUDY

TUC and pensions

In recent years, one of the major areas in which the TUC has been active is in the area of company pension schemes. The collapse in share prices in 2001–2002, following heavy speculative buying in the late 1990s, hit company pension schemes very hard, as many were very exposed to equity investment. As a result, in 2003 many companies began to downgrade pension provision for members of staff, or even to close company schemes to new entrants.

The TUC has seen this as a matter of great concern as it is disadvantaging many employees who are not in a position to do anything about it. The TUC has been further alarmed by the fact that many companies have not downgraded directors' pensions, only

those of their employees. In 2002 the TUC launched Pensionwatch to monitor pension provision in the UK. They are currently pressing for new legislation to compel employers to provide more for their employees, possibly involving increasing contributions over a person's working life.

ACTIVITY

1   Visit the TUC website at www.tuc.org.uk and view their latest findings in the pensions problem in the UK. The TUC is obviously a voice for the workers, so to what extent do you feel their coverage of the problem is balanced?

2   Look at recent newspaper articles on this subject and examine the TUC proposals on the issue. What do you feel would be the best and fairest approach to solving this problem?

3   To what extent do you think that employers and government have an obligation to solve this problem?

The global economy and UK industry

The ability to sell to the rest of the world is vital to the economic success of the UK and also to the industrial success of many individual companies. The UK's biggest exported products are petroleum, cars, telecom equipment and power-generating machinery, and we also sell large amounts of services including banking, shipping, insurance and tourism. The UK is still one of the top five exporters and importers in the world (although it seems likely that the UK will soon be overtaken by China), and so international trade is very significant to our economic well-being. The UK has a number of multinational companies, that is, firms that trade within more than one nation, including BP, British Nuclear Fuels, The National Grid and North West Water. The trend has been for the UK continually to increase the value of exports sold; unfortunately the import bill has also increased at an even faster rate than our increase in exports. For more details see Chapter 4, International trade and the European dimension.

International trading

One of the main problems with international trading, and one of the factors that prevents many firms from breaking into world markets, is that of uncertainty. Trading with another firm in the UK raises several potential problems:

♦ Will I be paid?
♦ How quickly will I receive my money?
♦ Will the goods I ordered be delivered on time?
♦ Will I receive them at all?
♦ Will they be of the correct quality?

These problems are magnified when dealing with a firm located in another country. When the company we are selling to or buying from is based thousands of miles away, how do we trade with confidence?

The UK government is well aware of these doubts but is keen to allay such fears so that more firms will trade internationally and thereby boost the wealth of the country. The DTI has set up an organisation called Trade Partners UK (www.tradepartners.gov.uk) to help in this area. The Trade Partners UK Information Centre is a free information resource for potential exporters. It contains data on over 200 countries and export sectors, much of which is supplied by contacts in High Commissions, Consulates and Embassies throughout the world. It gives access to:

♦ market information on all overseas countries trading with the UK
♦ an extensive collection of statistical, marketing and contact information

♦ information on business opportunities.

The organisation can also help:

♦ prepare firms for trading
♦ make contacts with firms that are already trading in the target countries
♦ help firms to visit target countries (including organising trade fairs and exhibitions)
♦ advise and help with promoting products and services abroad.

The UK government has also set up the Export Credit Guarantee Department (ECGD) to help remove some of the financial risk involved in international trade. This is essentially an insurance scheme that insures importers and exporters against financial loss as a result of specific trading deals. The ECGD offer the following services.

Providing insurance Insuring exporters against the risk of non-payment by overseas buyers for reasons such as buyer default or insolvency, war or lack of foreign exchange.

Loan guarantees The ECGD guarantees loans provided by banks to overseas borrowers who want to buy from the UK. This ensures that UK exporters are paid on delivery, while the buyer has time to pay. Export Finance Schemes can be arranged in a number of currencies to suit the foreign buyer.

Exchange rate risks The ECGD can enable a firm to fix contract prices in a foreign currency when tendering for a contract and offer protection against exchange rate fluctuations.

Both of these organisations help to reduce the uncertainty associated with international trade and boost the UK's competitiveness abroad.

World Bank

The World Bank is the popular name for the International Bank for Reconstruction and Development (IBRD) and the International Development Association (IDA). These organisations provide low-interest loans, interest-free credit, and grants to developing countries. Low-income countries normally cannot borrow money in international markets or can only do so at high interest rates. The World Bank will provide grants, interest-free loans, and technical assistance to enable these countries to provide basic services. In the case of the loans, countries have 35–40 years to repay, with a 10-year grace period.

The World Bank works to bridge the divide between the very rich countries of the world and the poorer developing nations. The aim is to turn rich country resources into poor country growth. The World Bank helps developing country governments to build schools and health centres, provide water and electricity, fight disease, and protect the environment.

Chapter 3

Behaviour of organisations in their market environment

When assessing potential markets to move into, the nature and relative strength of competition within the market should be considered. Moving into a well-established market with a small number of very strong players can be hazardous. If we can identify other markets where there is freer competition, we may have more success establishing our new brand.

Types of market

The variety of different types of market are represented by considering the following continuum.

At the two extremes of the market continuum are the **monopoly**, where there is only one supplier of a particular good or service, and the **perfect market**, where there are a large number of suppliers of any one good or service. Whilst the perfect market is seen as an ideal situation, the monopoly may exhibit many of the worst excesses of anti-competitive behaviour.

The perfect market

These are the features of a perfect market:

♦ It contains a large number of buyers and sellers of the good or service, so that no one person can affect the market price through his or her own actions.
♦ There is freedom of entry and exit to the market for both buyers and sellers, therefore any new company may trade freely within the market and any firm is free to withdraw when it wishes.

♦ Products are homogenous, that is, all goods sold are identical in quality, so we would never buy a product and then wish we had bought it elsewhere as the quality was inferior.
♦ There is perfect knowledge of the market on the part of both the buyers and sellers, therefore no buyer need ever pay more than they needed to and all sellers know exactly what their competitors are doing.
♦ It must be possible to buy or sell any amount of the commodity at the market price.
♦ Buyers must be perfectly mobile. This ensures that buyers can travel to a bargain rather than having to remain close to home and pay higher prices.
♦ The **factors of production** must also be perfectly mobile. They can therefore be moved to the production of those products or services that are in heavy demand relatively easily.

You may be thinking by now that the perfect market could never exist, and you would be right. It is a theoretical concept that has never and probably will never exist, containing all that is best about markets. In that case why do we analyse it and include it in textbooks on business? The answer is simple; if we ever hope to aspire to improvement we have to have a firm idea of what standard we are aspiring to. The perfect market is therefore a set of standards by which we may judge all other markets. The fact that it does not exist is therefore irrelevant; its importance lies in the fact that it may be used as a yardstick by which all other markets may be judged. The degree to which they meet the standards set by the perfect market will indicate to us how desirable that particular market is; it will highlight any excesses that are being practised so that we can identify which aspects of the market could be improved.

ACTIVITY

Having said that the perfect market does not exist, the advent of e-commerce is helping to make markets more perfect. Choose a product or service, refer to the features of a perfect market listed above and then answer the following questions:

1 To what extent has Internet trading made the market for your product more perfect? Answer by referring to the features listed above.

2 What might need to happen to make it even more perfect?

3 Give examples of markets that are being made more perfect by e-commerce and some which you consider may not be affected by this change. Give reasons for your suggestions.

Let us look now at the other end of the market continuum.

Monopoly

A monopoly, strictly speaking, exists where there is only one supplier of a particular good or service; however UK law recognises that any firm that has more than 25 per cent of the market is acting in a position of monopoly power.

A **duopoly** exists where there are only two suppliers of a good or service, and an **oligopoly** where there are only a small number of suppliers of a good or service.

All of these types of market contain firms that carry considerable power, power that they may wield if it consolidates their market dominance. Entering a market that is currently monopolistic can be especially difficult, as the current dominant players will do their best to prevent new firms from stealing their market share, and indeed they may even go to such lengths as forcing competitors out. Such firms may engage in

what are known as anti-competitive practices, and a quick look at these should convince you of how difficult entering such a market could be.

Competitive advantage

In order to maintain competitive advantage, firms behave in certain ways or adopt certain strategies.

Anti-competitive practices

Many firms would like to be able to dictate to us as consumers. They would like to ensure that we always buy their products and that we pay prices that yield high profits for them. Consequently when firms find themselves in strong positions within markets, they often do whatever they can to influence our buying behaviour. Whilst there is nothing basically wrong with firms trying to encourage us to buy from them, some firms become over-vigorous in their tactics and may engage in activities that restrict our freedom of choice to such an extent that consumers get a raw deal. Anti-competitive practices, those that attempt to remove competition from markets to benefit specific, often large, firms, are therefore frowned upon by both consumers and governments alike.

Restrictive practices

These are tactics used by large influential firms to strengthen their hold over the markets in which they operate, to increase their market share, to eradicate competition, to restrict consumer choice and therefore allow the firm to charge prices well above those that would be established in a competitive market. Restrictive practices are anti-competitive and penalise consumers, so governments go to some lengths to try and stamp out such practices when they are spotted.

In 1948 the Monopolies and Restrictive Practices Act was passed establishing the **Monopolies Commission** with powers to investigate any accusations of firms engaging in restrictive practices. By 1956 it was decided that the Commission lacked power and that it was not right that the burden of proof should lie with the Commission, that is to say that it was up to the Commission to prove that a firm was guilty. The Restrictive Practices Act 1956 therefore passed the burden of proof onto business, and it is now up to the firm accused to prove to the Commission that the practices it is engaging in are not against the best interests of the public. A restrictive practice is now illegal unless the firm is able to justify it under one of the following criteria:

- the removal of the restriction would lead to a substantial increase in unemployment
- the removal of the practice would deny the public certain advantages, for example that the high prices were required in order to fund research into new products that would benefit the public
- the agreement was necessary to counteract the existing market power of other businesses
- it was necessary to prevent the consumer from injury
- it made the industry more competitive abroad.

Restrictive practices take a number of forms, the following are the most common types.

Price fixing

Firms in monopolistic positions are often accused of setting prices that are well above what they would be if the market were competitive. In other words they abuse the dominant position that they have by charging excessive prices to boost profits knowing that the customer has no one else to buy from. As a result, both consumers and the government would agree that competition would have a healthy downward push on prices from which we would all benefit, so one would think that entering such a market would be generally beneficial. However, the monopolist will go to extreme lengths on occasions to prevent this from happening.

Predatory pricing

Unfortunately firms in monopolistic positions are often very large, and consequently when competition tries to move in they have the financial muscle to do something about it. **Predatory pricing** involves the monopolist reducing their prices to such an extent that the new competitor cannot compete. This may involve the monopolist selling the items at less than the cost of production, and whilst this will clearly lead to operating losses in the short term, the monopolist may consider it worthwhile if it forces the competition out

of the market. Once the competitor has withdrawn, the monopolist will increase prices again, often back up to excessively high levels to maximise profits. Whilst the Office of Fair Trading (OFT) would disapprove of such a pricing regime by a monopolist, by the time they took action it may be too late for the new competitor.

In 1985 the OFT investigated the case of Grey-Green Coaches in London. They ran coaches along the Isle of Grain–London route, and when a new competitor moved in, Grey-Green offered free travel on its coaches on the route. The OFT considered this to be anti-competitive and in this case they insisted that Grey-Green withdraw the offer.

When they launched the budget airline Go!, British Airways were accused by easyJet and DanAir of engaging in predatory pricing when they announced their intention to enter the budget flights market. Whilst BA staunchly claimed that it was entering the market simply to promote competition between firms and give customers a better deal, the small budget firms claimed that they were trying to force the smaller firms out of the skies. Why else, they asked, would BA be prepared to launch a new company that would run at a loss for probably the first three years of operation? In the end, Go! was not as successful as BA hoped, so the potential threat was never fully realised, and indeed Go! has since been sold by BA.

Vertical restraints

Another way the monopolist may seek to exclude new competitors from becoming established in their market is by applying pressure on the retailers through which the products will be sold. There are a number of these and they are known collectively as vertical restraints.

Retail price maintenance This is the situation in which the monopolist insists that their products are sold at specific prices, with the threat that a retailer who does not comply will not be allowed to stock the monopolist's products in future. Clearly if the line is one that makes significant profits for the retailer, he or she will have to comply or lose profits.

A few years ago, the Office of Fair Trading investigated two sportswear manufacturers, Puma and Asics, who supplied replica Leeds United team strips.

A retailer in Leeds was selling the strips at £25 instead of the usual £40. Puma and Asics had told the retailer that if he continued to do so they would not continue to supply him. Fortunately in this case, the OFT investigated and the firms were made to promise that they would not carry out such threats, allowing the retailer to continue to discount the price of the shirts.

Exclusive dealing The monopolist puts pressure on the retailer only to stock their brand of product and not those of rivals. Again the threat is that the monopolist will cease supplying if the retailer does not comply.

Exclusive supply arrangements The supplier only supplies to one dealer in a specific geographical area, and in return the dealer agrees to stock its products exclusively. This has the effect of both restricting outlets to new firms and maintaining high prices.

Tie-in sales The supplier requires the retailer to take all of that firm's product range, thereby discouraging new market entrants. This practice is also known as **full-line forcing**.

In October 1997 Microsoft was fined a record sum by the US Justice Department for requiring personal computer manufacturers who wanted to license its Windows 95 operating system also to license and distribute its Internet browser, Microsoft Internet Explorer.

Quantity discounts The retailer receives discounts that get progressively larger the more they buy. This encourages retailers to stock predominantly one brand, again discouraging competition by restricting the outlets they may sell through.

In 1991 British Coal were employing a discount scheme that only provided discounts to those customers who bought exclusively from British Coal. The OFT decided that this was anti-competitive.

Long-term supply contracts These tie the retailer in to one supplier and often carry hefty penalties for termination.

More details of examples of restrictive practices can be found on the Office of Fair Trading website: www.oft.gov.uk

CASE STUDY

Hasbro

Hasbro is Britain's biggest toy maker, producing some of the UK's biggest selling toys such as Sindy, Monopoly, Pictionary, My Little Pony and Cluedo. In November 2002, Hasbro was fined £4.95 million for price fixing; however this could have been a great deal more.

Hasbro entered into agreements with Argos and Littlewoods to fix the prices of Hasbro toys between 1999 and 2001. Hasbro also persuaded ten other distributors also to fix prices. Following an OFT investigation, Argos was fined £17.28 million and Littlewoods £5.4 million. The initial decision was that Hasbro should be fined £15.59 million; however this fine was reduced because Hasbro had provided vital evidence in the OFT investigation and had co-operated fully with investigators.

The OFT operates a 'whistleblowing' scheme, where members of price-fixing agreements can reduce or even eliminate their liability for fines if they inform on their fellow agreement members and provide evidence to support convictions. Hasbro were dealt with very favourably in this case because they had informed on their fellow companies.

Following the judgement, a spokesperson from the Consumers Association said, 'Price fixing is theft. It rips off consumers. Parents everywhere will thank the OFT for boosting competition in the run-up to Christmas.'

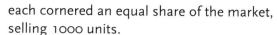

Cartels

Sometimes price competition breaks out in oligopoly markets. Whilst this is usually good news for customers, the same is not always true of the oligopoly companies themselves. When price wars begin, the company that starts the war will normally make initial increases in revenue, however this will not often last.

CASE STUDY

Chips with everything!

On 1 April 1994 a notable inventor, Boris Bogle, produced a revolutionary new combined CD player and chip fryer. He sold the patent rights to three companies: Sound Bites Ltd, CD Chip Ltd, and Unique Electronics Ltd. In 1995 the three companies started selling the new units, each at the same price of £125. Each had total production costs of £100,000 and

each cornered an equal share of the market, selling 1000 units.

The revenue for each firm was therefore £125 (price) ×1000 (quantity sold) = £125,000. Each company therefore made profits of £125,000 (revenue) minus £100,000 (costs) = £25,000.

We can therefore set out the situation at the end of 1995 like this:

1995	Costs	Price	Sales	Revenue	Profit
Sound Bites Ltd	£100,000	£125	1000	£125,000	£25,000
CD Chip Ltd	£100,000	£125	1000	£125,000	£25,000
Unique Electronics Ltd	£100,000	£125	1000	£125,000	£25,000

In 1996 Sound Bites decided to attract more customers and therefore reduced its price to £115. As a result its sales increased at the expense of its competitors. The 1996 results are as follows. For simplicity of calculation, the costs of each firm stay the same, although clearly they would change.

1996	Costs	Price	Sales	Revenue	Profit
Sound Bites Ltd	£100,000	£115	1200	£138,000	£38,000
CD Chip Ltd	£100,000	£125	900	£112,500	£12,500
Unique Electronics Ltd	£100,000	£125	900	£112,500	£12,500

In 1997 the price war broke out in earnest. CD Chip Ltd also dropped its price to £115, but Unique Electronics decided to outdo both and reduce the price to £105. 1997 results look like this:

1997	Costs	Price	Sales	Revenue	Profit
Sound Bites Ltd	£100,000	£115	900	£103,500	£3,500
CD Chip Ltd	£100,000	£115	900	£103,500	£3,500
Unique Electronics Ltd	£100,000	£105	1200	£126,000	£26,000

Finally in 1998 Sound Bites Ltd and CD Chip Ltd also had to drop their prices to match Unique Electronics, and the last year ended like this:

1998	Costs	Price	Sales	Revenue	Profit
Sound Bites Ltd	£100,000	£105	1000	£105,000	£5,000
CD Chip Ltd	£100,000	£105	1000	£105,000	£5,000
Unique Electronics Ltd	£100,000	£105	1000	£105,000	£5,000

What you will no doubt notice is that the price war ended with all the firms still selling to the same number of customers, but at a lower price, so that profits were reduced. It is interesting to work out the cumulative profits for each of the firms, that is, the total amount of profit made by each firm over the four-year period. The results are as follows:

	Sound Bites Ltd	CD Chip Ltd	Unique Electronics Ltd
1995	£25,000	£25,000	£25,000
1996	£38,000	£12,500	£12,500
1997	£3,500	£3,500	£26,000
1998	£5,000	£5,000	£5,000
Totals	£71,500	£46,000	£68,500

The price war clearly created winners and losers, Sound Bites having done best and CD Chip having come off worst. But in a very real sense, all the firms are losers. Imagine what would have happened if the price war had never taken place, if all the firms had continued to sell at the starting price of £125, each selling to 1000 customers per year. In this case the profit of £25,000 that each firm made in 1995 would be repeated for each of the subsequent years, and the total profit for each of the firms would be 4 × £25,000 = £100,000. This is significantly higher than the profits made by any of the firms, so it is true to say that all four firms would have benefited significantly had the price war never taken place. Whilst the firms that reduced their prices made gains in the short term, over the longer period they all lost out.

The imaginary case study shows us that although price wars do break out sometimes in oligopoly markets, their effect will be to increase revenues for some firms in the short term, but they will always lead to a long-term reduction in profits for all firms in the market. Oligopolists are well aware of these facts and consequently they will go to some lengths to avoid price wars breaking out. They are also well aware that if they each ensure that they all sell at similar prices, all the firms will benefit. This leads to oligopolists sometimes forming informal agreements not to engage in price competition and to ensure that price rises are always done together so that all firms benefit. These agreements are known as **cartels**. Cartels are clearly bad news for consumers as we do not benefit from price competition, and if all the oligopolists raise their prices in unison, they could set prices that are unrealistically high and we would still have to pay them as no cheap alternatives exist. Cartels are therefore illegal, and the government takes a very dim view of firms that engage in cartels as they simply abuse the customers by limiting choice and keeping prices high. If it can be proved that firms are operating a cartel, the Office of Fair Trading will take rigorous steps to ensure that the practice is stopped. The problem, of course, is proving that a cartel exists. Firms are not foolish enough to write anything down; cartels will be formed by verbal agreements and this makes them very difficult to identify.

CASE STUDY

Public school cartel?

During 2003, the Office of Fair Trading commenced an investigation into alleged price fixing among four leading public schools, including Eton and Winchester. This was quickly widened to include 700 fee-paying schools across Britain. The schools were accused of consulting each other before setting their fees. The maximum penalty for price fixing is five years in prison for individuals convicted and a maximum fine of 10 per cent of three-year turnover for the businesses, which could come to around £10 million for some of the wealthier schools.

The investigation followed record fee increases in 2003 averaging more than 9 per cent, which was about four times the rate of inflation at the time. Emails apparently circulated between the bursars of the schools containing spreadsheets comparing the proposed fee increases at their schools. For example, the bursar of one leading school informed his governors of the fee increases at 20 leading schools and suggested that they should therefore increase fees by 9 per cent. It is difficult to believe that he was unaware that he might be transgressing competition law when he added, 'Confidential, please, so we aren't accused of being in a cartel.'

The schools co-operated fully with the OFT inquiries, but parents were said to be considering suing schools found to have fixed their fees with others. It was also alleged that some schools had asked parents to sign contracts preventing them from applying for places at other schools.

Commentators were expressing concern over the fact that there was very little diversity in prices across the public school sector. Whilst some top-class schools might be able to justify such high prices, it was curious that there were no schools offering a cheaper option.

ACTIVITY

1. On what basis might the public schools be able to form a defence against these allegations?

2. It is probably true that many of the bursars involved had no idea that they were transgressing competition law. In such circumstances, would it be fair to prosecute them if they are found to have been acting illegally? Explain your reasoning.

Fair Trading much increased powers for investigating and prosecuting anti-competitive behaviour, in particular cartel activities. The OFT now has the power to make unannounced visits to the premises of companies under investigation, to seize any documents therein, to restrict correspondence in and out of the firm and to restrict the movements and activities of the staff and directors of the firm whilst the investigation continues. Ultimately firms can be fined up to 10 per cent of turnover if the case against them is proved, which is a substantial deterrent to anti-competitive behaviour.

Competition policy

The UK government has set up a range of measures to regulate competition issues, including both laws and organisations, and they are collectively known as UK Competition Policy.

The Competition Act 1998 was the most significant piece of legislation in recent years as it gave the Office of

Figure 5.23   Regulatory bodies

Apart from legislation, there are also a number of organisations in place to regulate competition matters. Figure 5.23 outlines the organisations that are in place.

European Commission

The European Commission (EC) is the ultimate authority in the UK, although most competition matters will be resolved by the UK government. Competition cases will be considered by the EC if the firms or industries involved are sufficiently large and the case crosses national boundaries within the EU.

In 2002 the EC investigated the car industry in the UK, on account of the fact that car prices were so much higher in the UK than other EU countries, and they found fault with the dealership arrangements operated in the UK. Car makers were allowed to limit their sales outlets to single-brand dealerships on the grounds that cars were so complex a product that sales could legitimately be restricted to specialist exclusive distributors. The Commission decided that this was no longer true and has made it easier for dealers to sell several brands and sell in several countries. In addition, dealers can just sell cars and leave repair and maintenance to other firms, or *vice versa*. The Commission expects the extra competition to narrow price differentials between national markets in the EU, and the new rules should make it easier for consumers to buy at the best price.

Secretary of State for Trade and Industry

This official has overall responsibility for UK competition policy and is the ultimate decision maker in such cases. The trade and industry secretary will also be responsible for deciding whether or not mergers should be referred to the Competition Commission.

Office of Fair Trading

This government office is headed by the Director General of Fair Trading (DGFT). Its functions are as follows:

♦ investigating cases of unfair contract terms and misleading advertising
♦ investigating the fitness of consumer credit licence applicants

CASE STUDY

The Office of Fair Trading

Under the Competition Act 1998, the powers of the OFT were considerably increased. They now undertake a wide range of inquiries, all aimed at improving competition and making things better for consumers and companies. In summer 2003 they were involved in the following cases:

♦ Liaising with Catalan competition authorities to shut down a Spanish company that had misled UK businesses into paying for adverts in its European City Directory. The adverts gave the impression that inclusion would be free, the small print required firms to pay up to £1455 for three entries in the directory.
♦ Persuading Exmouth-based holiday voucher redemption company Travel Quest Group Limited to stop publishing misleading advertisements and to honour consumer contracts for free flights and/or accommodation.
♦ Conducting an informal fact-finding review into store cards looking at marketing, sales practices and interest rates.
♦ Refusing Liverpool-based motor dealer Elite Fleet Ltd a consumer credit licence as they had contravened a provision of the Consumer Credit Act 1974 in providing false information on its credit application form.
♦ Insisting that tour operators include Aviation Security Charges (ASC) in basic holiday prices. Companies were warned that misleading customers by failing to advertise brochure prices fairly would result in enforcement action.

- investigating cases where the OFT has reasonable grounds to suspect a breach of the Competition Act
- with the Serious Fraud Office (and the Crown Office in Scotland) investigating potential criminal cartel cases
- considering public mergers and referring more complex cases to the Competition Commission
- a consumer education programme.

ACTIVITY

Visit the OFT website at www.oft.gov.uk and see what recent cases the OFT has been involved in. Prepare a short presentation to the rest of your group on the benefits of having the OFT in place.

Competition Commission

The Competition Commission was established by the Competition Act 1998 and replaced the Monopolies and Mergers Commission in 1999. The Commission conducts in-depth inquiries into mergers, markets and the regulation of the major regulated industries. Every inquiry is undertaken in response to a reference made to it by another authority: usually by the OFT but in certain circumstances the Secretary of State, or by the regulators.

The Commission is responsible for making decisions on the competition questions and for making and implementing decisions on appropriate remedies. The Commission has to determine whether cases are against the public interest.

Specialised regulatory bodies

These organisations are often concerned with public utilities or organisations that occupy central roles in the economy. It is very much in the interest of the general public that they act as efficiently as possible, so they keep a constant watch on their particular industries to ensure that they maintain good standards of service and charge realistic prices. The regulator can order changes to service levels and pricing structures, which the

companies must obey, although they always have recourse of appeal to the Competition Commission if they feel that they have been dealt with unfairly.

The following table gives a list of the current regulators and their websites. You might like to visit them and find out more about their activities.

Regulators

Communications and media

Office of Communications
http://www.ofcom.org.uk

Finance

Financial Services Authority
http://www.fsa.gov.uk
Securities and Futures' Authority
http://www.fsa.gov.uk/sfa/
Takeover Panel
http://www.thetakeoverpanel.org.uk

Transport

Civil Aviation Authority (CAA)
http://www.caa.co.uk
Office of the Rail Regulator
http://www.rail-reg.gov.uk
Strategic Rail Authority
http://www.sra.gov.uk

Utility

Office of Gas and Electricity Markets (OFGEM)
http://www.ofgem.gov.uk
Office for the Regulation of Electricity and Gas (OFREG)
http://ofreg.nics.gov.uk
Office of Water Services (OFWAT)
http://www.ofwat.gov.uk

Regulatory bodies

Most of the industries that were privatised during the 1980s and 1990s, including the telecommunications, power supply and water supply industries, amongst others, are monitored by these regulators, and part of their remit has been to encourage competition in these markets and not allow the big players such as British Telecom to dominate the markets to the exclusion of new competitors. This regulation has created opportunities for new competitors that would not have existed had they not been appointed.

BT, for example, has been severely restricted in the nature of the services that it may offer, in order to allow smaller competitors to get a foothold in the market. Many cable and satellite companies now provide packages allowing the consumer to receive TV, telephone and video on demand all via one link and for one monthly payment that is somewhat less than that for each service separately. BT, however, was prevented from doing likewise so that the new companies could get established. OFTEL also dictates to BT prices that it may charge, again in order to help new competitors. These types of restrictions are common in all of the similarly regulated markets, and this has clearly created significant opportunities for new suppliers.

CASE STUDY

OFCOM, a new regulator

In January 2003, Stephen Carter, the former head of telecoms group NTL, was appointed as the first chief executive of OFCOM, the new regulator responsible for TV, radio and telecommunications. His first job was to meld together five existing regulators: the Broadcasting Standards Commission, the Independent Television Commission, OFTEL, The Radiocommunications Agency and the Radio Authority.

However, by mid-2003 doubts were already being expressed about the new regulator's ability to monitor all aspects of these industries. Patricia Hodgson, the final chief executive of the Independent Television Commission, expressed her fears that OFCOM may become too involved in competition and takeover issues rather than in the quality of public service broadcasting. She was worried that OFCOM would not be alert to the dangers of broadcasters neglecting expensive documentaries and dramas in favour of cheap to produce, crowd-pleasing soaps and reality TV. In her view, quality of programming should always come before economics, but she was worried that OFCOM would be unable to deliver.

David Edmonds, the outgoing OFTEL director-general, also offered advice to his successor, recommending 'proportionate regulation'. 'Proportionate regulation', he said, 'means being ready to intervene wherever necessary – without fear or favour – to protect consumers or to ensure increased competition; but doing so in a way which is not so heavy-handed as to deter companies from investment in new services or products.'

ACTIVITY

1 What do you think the UK government saw as the main advantages to combining the five regulators into one?

2 What do you feel are the main issues facing the new regulator?

3 From a consumer's point of view, what would you like to see OFCOM doing?

Market forces and organisational responses

Supply and demand

The strength of demand for a particular item has an influence on the price that will be charged for it. For example, every year at about Christmas time there is a new toy that every child seems to want, so much so that the shops sell out very quickly. A few years ago the Thunderbirds Tracy Island model sold out as fast as the shops could stock them. In recent years Buzz Lightyear and Tellytubby dolls have been virtually impossible to find in the shops. As a result people end up paying inflated prices for these items when they become available. In December 1996, for example, a man paid £94.10 at auction for a Buzz Lightyear doll because he could not get one anywhere else; in 1997 people were reportedly paying up to £200 for secondhand sets of Tellytubby dolls retailing at less than £50. The more people want an item, therefore, the more the price tends to rise.

In economic terms we describe this situation as an **excess of demand over supply**, that is, when lots of people want to buy but not enough is being supplied to meet that demand. Such a situation always leads to prices rising, as we shall see later.

Phil's Foods

MEGASAVE

With up to

50%

OFF

Final reductions now
with additional savings
off MegaSales prices

Figure 5.24   Big price reductions

Contrast that situation with the poster. Here we have a very different situation. Phil's Foods (Figure 5.24) clearly wants to sell more food; there are probably large stocks in store that they need to sell

quickly as idle stock is costly for a business. To attract more customers the firm has reduced its prices. Here, therefore, we have a shortage of customers and the result has been that prices have had to fall to attract some more. In economic terms we would describe this as an **excess of supply over demand**: Phil's Foods wants to supply a lot but few customers are willing to buy, and this situation will invariably lead to a fall in price.

Demand curves

If we were to survey the general public and ask them how much of an item they were prepared to buy at different prices, we could tabulate this information and this table would be known as a **demand schedule**. If you were to interview your friends about how many Star Burgers they would buy at different prices you might tabulate the results and draw up a demand curve like this:

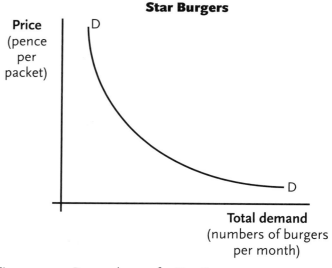

Figure 5.25   Demand curve for Star Burgers

Almost all demand curves look like Figure 5.25, that is, they slope downwards from left to right, although the gradients of the curves vary greatly. Whenever you draw up a demand curve you should always remember the following rules:

♦ the graph is always titled using the name of the product
♦ prices always go on the vertical axis
♦ total demand always goes on the horizontal axis

- always state the units on your axes ('pence per burger')
- the curve is always labelled D, customarily at both ends.

Drawing and using a demand curve

As prices rise we expect fewer people to buy a product, and conversely as the price falls we expect more people to buy that product. A demand curve illustrates this relationship and enables us to quantify how much demand rises or falls when the price changes. A demand curve illustrates the relationship between the price of a product and the demand for that product. We can read off the curve at different price levels to see how much demand changes. Look at Figure 5.26. We can establish the demand at a price by reading horizontally across from that price until we hit the demand curve and then dropping vertically down and reading the level of demand off the horizontal axis. Therefore the demand at a price of 250p per packet is: about 14,000 packets per week.

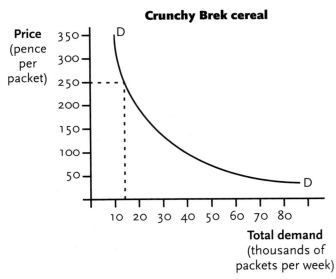

Figure 5.26   Demand curve for Crunchy Brek cereal

Figure 5.27 shows what would happen to demand if we drop the price to 100p per packet.

Demand has now gone up to about 40,000 packets per week. The first important rule with regard to demand curves, therefore, is that we can identify the

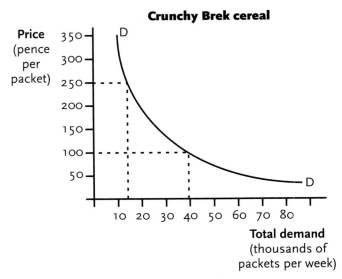

Figure 5.27   Demand at 100p per packet

impact on demand of any change in price by simply reading off at different points on the demand curve. With falls in price we are sliding down the slope of the curve and with rises in price we are sliding up the slope of the curve.

Profit motive and the choice of product

Clearly most businesses require profits in order to survive and consequently a key factor to take into account when deciding exactly what to make will be which goods or services will maximise profits. Profits are important because:

- they provide resources to pay shareholders dividends (shareholders must be paid in order to maintain confidence in the company)
- they allow the firm to invest in further factors of production
- they provide reserves that the firm can draw upon in the future when required.

Maximising profit depends upon the price that may be charged for the product, and, in general terms, as the price of product rises, producers will be inclined to produce more of that item. There is therefore a direct relationship between price and supply: the higher the price, the more the supply. We can represent this relationship graphically using a **supply curve** as in Figure 5.28.

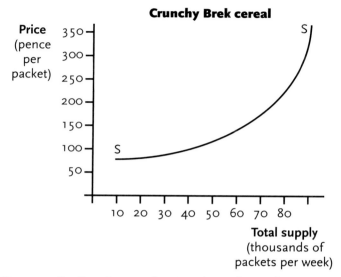

Figure 5.28　Supply curve for Crunchy Brek cereal

Demand and supply interaction

Who decides the price for a particular product or service? The customer? The manufacturer? The government?

Some countries, specifically those run by communist governments such as China, believe that prices should be determined by the government. In such countries the government uses statisticians to calculate how much of each item needs to be produced to make sure that everyone who needs an item can get one, and also what the optimum price will be to ensure that everyone can afford to buy what they need. There are problems with such a system, of course, in that such calculations are subject to error. As accurate as we try to be, there are bound to be mistakes leading to insufficient or excess production, or prices that are either too low leading to high demand or too high leading to low demand. As a result communist economies often suffer from either excess production and wastage or insufficient production and shortages. In capitalist economies, however, such as the UK and the USA, a very different system is adopted, allowing market forces to determine prices and supply.

A market for a particular product or service is made up of two key forces, those of **demand** and

supply. If we allow these forces to interact without interference they will automatically produce prices for items and they will also determine how much producers should make of the items. If we take our demand and supply curves for Crunchy Brek cereal and put them together on one graph we get a new graph, Figure 5.29.

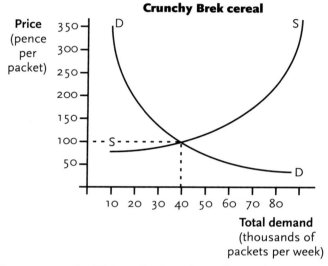

Figure 5.29　Equilibrium for Crunchy Brek cereal

The point at which the two curves cross is particularly significant as it is this point that establishes the price and quantity supplied of the product. This point is known as the **equilibrium point** and we can read horizontally left from this point to identify the equilibrium price and vertically down from this point to establish the equilibrium quantity. What our graph above shows us is that if free market forces (of demand and supply) are allowed to dictate conditions in the market for Crunchy Brek cereal, 40,000 packets per week will be produced and they will be sold at a price of £1.00 per packet. Free market forces therefore avoid the need for statisticians to determine how much of an item needs to be made and what price they will be sold at; demand and supply will answer these questions for us.

Not only will the market mechanism make these decisions for us, it will also correct any errors that occur, if we set prices wrongly or produce the wrong amount. For example, Figure 5.30 shows what would

285

happen if the price for Crunchy Brek cereal was set at £2.50, above the equilibrium position.

Crunchy Brek cereal

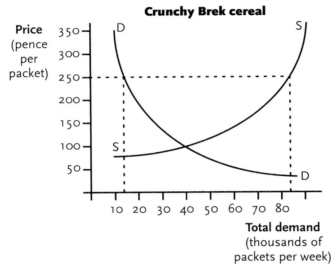

Figure 5.30   Demand and supply curve at £2.50 per packet

Reading across from the price of £2.50 the first curve we meet is the demand curve. If we drop down at this point we find that demand at this price is 14,000 packets per week. Carrying on across from the price of £2.50 we eventually meet the supply curve and if we drop down from this point we find that the supply at this price is 84,000 packets per week. Therefore at a price of £2.50 the manufacturer would like to sell a lot of the product but customers feel that the price is too high. We therefore get an excess of supply over demand, the excess being 84,000 – 14,000 = 70,000 packets per week. This situation is just like that Phil's Foods faced earlier. Faced with this situation, Phil's Foods had to reduce its prices and this is exactly what will happen to Crunchy Brek cereal: the price will fall until the equilibrium is established. In this way the extra production will be eliminated and the price will fall to a level that is acceptable to both producers and consumers. As a general rule, therefore, if the price is set too high in a free market it will always fall until the equilibrium is established.

A similar thing is true if the price is set too low. In this case the level of demand will end up being higher than the level of supply, a case of excess of demand over supply, and the price will rise to meet the equilibrium, as in Figure 5.31.

Crunchy Brek cereal

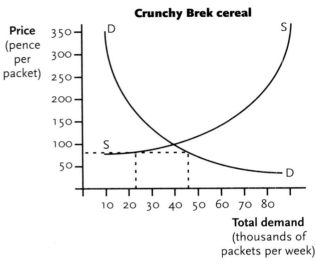

Figure 5.31   Demand and supply curve at 80p per packet

If we set the price at 80p per packet, supply would be only 24,000 packets per week whilst demand would be 46,000 packets per week, a shortage of 22,000 packets per week. This is similar to the situation with the Buzz Lightyear dolls where the shortage of supply forced up the price of the dolls. The price of Crunchy Brek cereal will rise until the equilibrium price of £1.00 is re-established.

The determinants of demand

Clearly one of the key factors that determines the level of demand for a product or service is the price at which it is sold, but as we all know this is not the only consideration. What was the last CD that you bought? Did you buy it specifically because it was cheap? You may have done, of course, but the chances are that you bought it because you like that particular band or artist. Why do many people choose to buy branded goods such as Calvin Klein clothing? It is certainly not because it is cheap; so presumably they do so for other reasons such as style or quality. The total demand for a product or service therefore is determined by a combination of a variety of factors other than price, and these are known as the **determinants of demand**. The determinants of demand affect our equilibrium in a way we have not seen yet; they actually move the demand curve itself. It is moved to the left for a reduction in demand and to the right for an increase in demand. For example, suppose Crunchy Brek cereal was reviewed in a national newspaper and came out as the most popular breakfast cereal, that would be likely to increase demand. Since this is a factor that is influencing demand *other than the price of the product* it must be a determinant of demand, and determinants of demand always shift demand curves. Since it will increase demand it will shift the curve to the right, as in Figure 5.32.

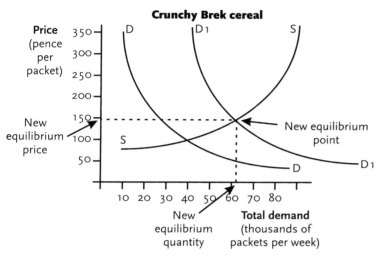

Figure 5.32   Determinant of demand

Note that the shift of the curve has produced a new equilibrium and this should always be shown on any diagrams that you draw. The new curve should also be labelled D1. Further demand curves would be labelled D2, D3 and so on. The extra demand has prompted an increase in supply and the manufacturers have taken the opportunity of this new-found popularity of their product to raise the price, as we would expect.

The rule of demand curves

If we are simply changing the *price* of our product then the curve will not move, we simply move up or down the existing curve as the curve shows us the relationship between demand and price. However, if *anything else* that will affect the level of demand changes, this must be a determinant of demand and this will shift the curve, to the left for a reduction in demand and to the right for an increase in demand.

The determinants of demand are as follows; all of these will shift the demand curve.

The price of substitute goods and services The classic example of this is butter and margarine. Since each is potentially a substitute for the other, if the price of one rises some consumers may switch to buying the alternative. A rise in the price of margarine, for example, might cause more people to buy butter thus shifting the demand curve for butter to the right and simultaneously shifting the demand curve for margarine to the left.

The price of complementary products Complementary products are those that we have to buy together, such as DVDs and DVD players, where one is no use without the other. As the price of DVD players has dropped the demand for DVDs has increased, thus the demand curve for DVDs has shifted to the right.

Fashion That is, the tastes and preferences of the customer. People's taste changes and demand curves shift as a result.

Population changes These affect demand in two ways:

♦ The *size* of the population affects demand; the larger the population the more people are likely to want to buy and the more demand curves shift to the right.
♦ The *structure* of the population has an effect. We have an ageing population in the UK, meaning that we have more old people in society today, and this has increased demand for those products that old people use, especially some types of medicines or nursing care. The demand curve for nursing homes has shifted well over to the right in recent years.

Quality We can create higher demand by improving the quality of our product, but we can equally shift our demand curves to the left if we allow quality to decline.

Income levels When income levels in the country rise people have more money to spend and consequently they buy more. This shifts demand curves to the right.

The state of the economy During the recession in the early 1990s many consumers were worried about their jobs and demand for all products went down, shifting demand curves to the left. When we go through better times and consumer confidence is high they move to the right.

Availability of credit You can increase demand for your products by making loans easily available to your potential customers. This will encourage more people to buy and shift your curve to the right.

The expected price of a product If people expect the price of a product to rise then they will buy immediately, thus shifting demand curves to the right. This happens on Budget Day if the Chancellor announces that petrol prices are to rise that evening; everyone fills up their cars with fuel before they do. Similarly, if customers foresee that the price will fall they may delay their purchase until later.

Government policy If the government is taxing the country heavily demand will reduce and shift curves to the left, if they reduce taxes, however, curves will move to the right as demand increases.

The determinants of supply

Just as factors that influence demand (other than price) shift the demand curve, so factors that affect levels of supply (other than price) will shift the supply curve, and the rule of thumb is exactly the same as that for demand curves. They will move the supply curve right for an increase in supply and left for a reduction in supply.

Home improvements: the new rock 'n' roll?

JOURNAL ARTICLE

As we have just discussed, tastes and fashions are big factors in influencing levels of demand for a product. Recent years have shown an interesting trend, that of the media (in particular TV programmes) creating demand for certain products and services. The supermarket Sainsbury's was inundated with requests for specific ingredients for particular recipes being shown on cooking shows by Delia Smith and Jamie Oliver, to the extent where stores ran out of food items that were previously only moderate sellers. Another industry that has benefited significantly from TV coverage has been the home improvements and DIY industries, boosted by lifestyle programmes.

You should investigate this topic of trends in the market for home improvements and the factors affecting those trends further by referring to the *British Economy Survey*, Volume 31, Number 2, Spring 2002, Section 2. The article 'Home improvements' by Robert Paisley tells the story further.

The rule of supply curves

If we are simply changing the *price* of our product then the curve will not move, we simply move up or down the existing curve as the curve shows us the relationship between supply and price. However, if *anything else* that will affect the level of supply changes this must be a determinant of supply and this will shift the curve, to the left for a reduction in supply and to the right for an increase in supply.

The determinants of supply are as follows; all of these will shift the supply curve.

The cost of production If costs fall more profit can be made, and therefore more firms are keen to produce that product; supply increases, shifting the supply curve to the right. If costs increase, this would have the opposite effect.

Technology As our methods of production improve we are able to make more, thus shifting our supply curves to the right. In the case of the mining or extraction industries, for example, 100 years ago the level of technology employed was probably limited to a shovel and a bucket, whereas today grinding machinery means that one man can produce far more than before.

Crop yields A high yield will shift agricultural supply curves to the right; a poor harvest will shift them to the left.

Discoveries Finding new sources of supply, such as new coal reserves, will shift curves to the right.

Subsidies These are payments made by governments to producers to help them with the costs of production. Firms often choose to make those items that attract subsidies and this will shift those supply curves to the right.

Productivity deals These are designed to encourage workers to produce more in return for increased pay or improved conditions of service. They can enable the firm to shift supply curves to the right.

Economies of scale The more a firm produces of a particular item the cheaper each becomes to produce. There is a strong drive, therefore, for firms to increase the scale of production, and the more economies of scale that are available, the more supply curves will shift to the right. For more detail on economies of scale, see later in the chapter.

Artificial restrictions Sometimes producers will artificially restrict supply in order to shift supply curves to the left and thereby increase the selling price. In March 1998, for example, the world's oil producers were concerned because the price of crude oil had fallen to a particularly low level of $13 per barrel, jeopardising their revenues. The OPEC (the

Oil Producing and Exporting Countries) countries agreed to cut production by 1.2 billion barrels and the result was that on 23 March the price of crude oil went up by $2 to $15.35. This effect is illustrated in Figure 5.33.

> ### ACTIVITY
>
> 1 Draw a demand and supply chart for sales of UK beef.
>
> 2 Show additional curves on the chart to illustrate the effect of the 1990s foot and mouth outbreak in the UK.
>
> 3 What happens to the price and quantity of beef sold as a result?

Price elasticity

What is your favourite magazine? If it is your favourite, presumably you buy it regularly and you find the price charged acceptable. What if the price rose by 10 per cent, would you still buy it? What if it doubled? Quadrupled? You might say that you would still buy it whatever the price because you really enjoy it, or you might decide not to buy it even if there were only a relatively modest increase because there may be alternatives you could buy, or maybe you would do without rather than be exploited. Your answer will be dictated by what you see as the degree of **price elasticity** of the magazine.

When British Rail existed it was continually criticised by customers and the media alike for its policy on fares. At one time BR had a policy of increasing fares every six months, not a popular move with travellers, particularly those who used trains regularly and for whom there was no viable alternative, such as commuters into London. Why did BR do it? Because it was trying to increase the revenue of the company and reduce the losses that it was making. Whenever a company raises prices it is usually trying to increase revenue, but is this always what will happen? It is not hard to imagine a situation where a price rise annoys so many customers that they seek

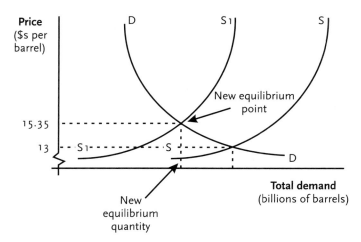

Figure 5.33   Artificial restrictions

and find alternatives, and consequently the firm's revenue goes down. There is also a third possibility, that it may lose some customers but the extra revenue generated from those that stay just balances out the loss of custom. **Price elasticity of demand** attempts to calculate and thereby anticipate the strength of customer reaction to changes in prices. There are three types of situation that can be found.

Price elastic demand

A rise in price reduces total revenue and a fall in price raises total revenue. This is because if demand is **price elastic**, any change in price will cause a large change in the number of customers wanting to buy. This is good news, from a revenue point of view, if you are looking to reduce prices as you will attract lots of new customers and revenue will rise, but it is bad news if you put prices up as you will lose a large proportion of your customers and revenue will consequently fall.

Price inelastic demand

A rise in price raises total revenue and a fall in price reduces total revenue, because if demand is **price inelastic**, the customer base will not change much when prices are changed. If we drop prices we will gain some customers, but not many, consequently our total revenue will fall, but if we increase prices we will not lose many customers and consequently our total revenue will increase. This is why the Chancellor of the Exchequer always adds duty onto the same products each budget day, that is, alcohol, cigarettes and petrol, because he knows demand for these is relatively inelastic and consequently we will still buy them even at the higher price.

Price unit elastic demand

A change in price leaves total revenue unchanged, as the changes in price and number of customers balance each other out in revenue terms.

To calculate which of these situations we find ourselves in, we use the following formula:

$$PED = \frac{\text{Percentage change in quantity demanded}}{\text{Percentage change in price}}$$

This can be written another way:

$$PED = \frac{\Delta Dx / Dx}{\Delta Px / Px}$$

where:

ΔDx = the change in quantity demanded of good X
Dx = the original demand for good X
ΔPx = the change in price of good X
Px = the original price of good X

Let us do some calculations to see how this works. We will base it upon the following simple demand schedule:

Demand schedule

Price (£s)	Demand
1	600
2	500
3	400
4	300
5	200
6	100

Firstly let us consider the price elasticity should we reduce the price from £5 to £4.

ΔDx = the difference between the demand at £5 and that at £4 (300 − 200 = 100)

Dx = the original demand, that is, at £5 (200)

ΔPx = the difference between the original and new prices (£5 − £4 = £1)

Px = the original price, £5

$$PED = \frac{100 / 200}{1 / 5} = \frac{0.5}{0.2} = 2.5 \text{ this is the coefficient of}$$

elasticity.

To see what the coefficient tells us, let us see how the change would have affected revenue:

Revenue = Price × Quantity
Revenue at £5 = £5 × 200 = £1000
Revenue at £4 = £4 × 300 = £1200

So the price has fallen but revenue has increased. If you compare this with the three definitions given above you will find that this is **price elastic demand.**

The rule of thumb with coefficients of elasticity, therefore, is as follows:

- if coefficient is more than 1, demand is price elastic
- if coefficient is less than 1, demand is price inelastic
- if coefficient equals 1, demand is price unit elastic.

An important point to note, however, is that demand can have different degrees of elasticity at different points on the demand curve, therefore we should always quote the range of prices we are considering when stating degrees of elasticity. For the above example, therefore, we would state that 'Demand is price elastic over the range £5 to £4'.

ACTIVITY

To illustrate how elasticity can change along the curve, now use the same demand schedule above and calculate the price elasticity assuming a reduction in price from £2 to £1. Calculate the coefficient of elasticity, state what this tells you and confirm the degree of elasticity by calculating the change in revenue over the same range.

The answer is below, so please cover it up while you attempt the task.

If all went according to plan, you should have a coefficient of 0.4, indicating that demand is price inelastic over the range £2 to £1. The revenue will have changed from £1000 (£2 × 500) to £600 (£1 × 600), confirming our coefficient calculation, as here we have a fall in price leading to a fall in total revenue; our definitions given before confirm this as a price inelastic situation.

Clearly the extent to which prices affect levels of demand in the market are going to have a bearing on our decision when selecting a target segment. In price elastic situations price cuts will be beneficial whilst price rises will lose us revenue, and vice versa for inelastic situations. Comparing elasticity positions across different segments should help to inform our choice of segment.

Growth of organisations

Industrial concentration

If we were to examine the changes in industry over the past century and more we would obviously notice many significant changes. Many industries with a history are almost unrecognisable today compared to what they were like 50 to 100 years ago. One of the biggest changes we would observe when looking at industry as a whole, however, would concern the size of businesses today. Historically industry was made up of a large number of relatively small firms, many of which would serve small, possibly localised markets. A coal pit would employ local people and sell to the immediate locality with coal only being transported as far as villages close by. Shops all served small communities and there were no chains of shops, each shop being owned by local families and serving principally friends and neighbours. Today many firms are countrywide and increasingly they are global concerns, selling worldwide. The biggest companies in the world today are vast concerns worth many billions of dollars. Wal-Mart Stores was the biggest earning firm in 2002, and their total revenue of $219.8 billion was more than the entire GDP of Israel and Ireland combined, so there are now firms that are more economically significant than whole countries.

Industry today is dominated by smaller numbers of very large firms, and this movement is known as industrial concentration.

INDUSTRIAL CONCENTRATION

Industry dominated by large numbers of small firms

↓

Industry dominated by small numbers of large firms

This change in the structure of industry has been achieved not only through natural, organic growth of firms but also through mergers (where firms combine together) and takeovers (where one firm buys another out). What has prompted firms to go for such growth are the benefits to be gained from large-scale production, or the **economies of scale**.

Economies of scale

The basic principle on which economies of scale are based is that it is cheaper and more efficient to produce on a large scale than a small one. It is not dissimilar to the principle of bulk-buying. If you buy a single can of Coca-Cola you will probably pay around 45p but if you buy a 12-pack of Coca-Cola each individual can would probably cost only 25p–30p. When we buy in bulk we normally get each individual item cheaper, and consequently buying is better and more efficient if done on a large scale. Businesses find a similar situation where production costs fall as the scale of the organisation increases. This is because the fixed costs per unit fall as production rises, and firms too are able to benefit from discounts for bulk purchase when buying raw materials or components. Thus larger production is more efficient than smaller production, and this has been a great spur encouraging business leaders to expand the size of their operations.

Economies of scale are not simply limited to reduced unit costs, however. There are a number of other areas that can become more efficient on a large scale than a smaller one, and these too come under the heading of economies of scale.

Marketing economies

Larger firms have more financial resources available to them and they can therefore use more costly but more effective advertising media such as TV. Large firms may also employ their own distribution vehicles thus saving on distribution costs. Larger organisations can also employ specialised marketing staff and management who are skilled in those areas, whereas smaller firms may rely on a small group of individuals to perform various tasks, including marketing. Employing specialists should produce better results.

Managerial economies

Just as large firms can employ specialist marketing staff, they may also employ specialists in other technical and managerial areas, such as accountants, production managers and sales managers, all of which should improve company performance.

Financial economies

If you or I ask a bank for a loan and we are accepted, we are unlikely to have much room for negotiation with regard to the interest rate charged. That is because although the loan may seem large to us, to a bank it is small change. If a large firm approaches a bank for a large sum of money, however, banks will attempt to offer the most attractive deal. Firms can consequently negotiate with a number of banks to get the most attractive loan deals possible, and the larger the firm is the more muscle it has in its negotiations, as it will have substantial assets to offer as security.

Also, since large firms have such substantial assets, they are in a better position to raise finance by means of share issues. The number and value of shares that a firm may issue depends to a large extent on the value of the firm, and large firms are more valuable than small ones. Consequently a large firm is able to raise money more easily through issues of shares, and this is an ideal way of borrowing for a firm as it does not have to make repayments, only to provide dividends to shareholders.

Large firms, therefore, can raise finance more cheaply and easily than small firms.

Technical economies

Large firms are better able to employ division of labour and specialisation amongst their workforces and consequently they can produce more efficiently. Since they also have substantial monies at their disposal, they are also in a better position to develop or buy in and use new technology and new productive processes at an early stage, enabling them to get ahead of their competitors.

Indivisibility economies

Some production processes are not possible or are not financially viable on a small scale, such as the production of aircraft or railway carriages, and therefore firms have to become large to contemplate moving into such areas.

Risk-bearing economies

Although this is not strictly an economy, it is a substantial spur encouraging firms to become larger. The basic principle is that a small firm relying on a limited range of products and serving a small market is vulnerable. Taken to its extreme, a one-product firm whose demand for that product falls dramatically will not survive. Similarly, a firm selling to a small community will struggle if the fortunes change for that community. The villages that sprang up around coal mines are good examples of this; businesses in villages such as Cotgrave in Nottinghamshire have suffered terribly since the local pit closed down in recent years. Because many of the local people relied on employment from the pit for their livelihoods, when it closed all the local shops and places of entertainment suffered too, and many have closed altogether.

Businesses can try to avoid this risk by **diversifying**. This simply means doing a wider range of things, producing a wider range of products and selling to a wider spread of customers. If we produce thirty different products and one fails, the firm will be kept alive by the other twenty-nine, and if we sell across the whole country and one area suffers we will be supported by the others that are still going strong. Firms are therefore keen to spread the risk of failure by diversifying both their ranges and their markets, and one good way of doing this is to expand the firm.

Merger as a method of growth

A great way to expand your firm quickly, to get into new markets, to diversify your product range almost overnight and to make substantial cost savings into the bargain is to **merge** with another firm. Mergers seem to be in the news almost daily.

Direct Line and Churchill Insurance to combine forces

Tesco, Sainsbury, ASDA and Morrisons fight over Safeway Takeover

British Airways and Iberia Airline to merge

Express Dairies and ARLA merger proposals referred to Competition Commission

During 2003 Barclays Bank was looking for major European banks to merge with. It started with a £1.1bn acquisition of Banco Zaragozano of Spain, but late in the summer it was still reported to be seeking another merger with a major European bank. Such mergers have three advantages to Barclays:

♦ Barclays had been a takeover target themselves from American banks, but the bigger the Barclays Group becomes, the harder it is for a hostile takeover bid to succeed
♦ considerable economies of scale are possible
♦ it allows Barclays access to the European markets much more easily than if it was forced to set up a string of branches of its own in Europe.

Merging in this way would immediately give Barclays access to a large existing customer base with outlets already well established in Europe. This would give a new ready market for Barclays products and services, as well as combining the technical expertise of the two firms, thus producing one bigger, more efficient and innovative whole.

Generally mergers are done for reasons of efficiency and cost saving and sharing of expertise, but there are other key reasons that prompt firms to look for merger partners.

Vertical mergers

If a firm chooses to merge with another that is involved in the same chain of production but is operating at a different stage in that chain, then it is involved in a **vertical merger**. Take, for example, the chain of production shown in Figure 5.34.

Each of these firms is in the beer industry, the first making the raw materials, the second making the product and the third selling that product to the public. If these firms should choose to merge together then we would describe this as a vertical merger. If the public house decides to merge with the brewer, that, from the public house's point of view, would be a vertically backward merger, because it is finding a partner further back in the chain of production. If the farmer decided to merge with the brewer, then from the farmer's point of view this would be a vertically forward merger, as he is merging with a firm later on

293

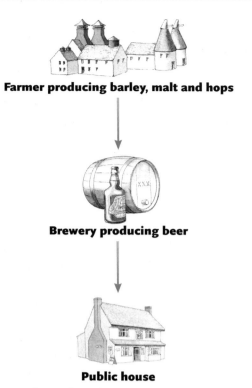

Figure 5.34   Chain of production

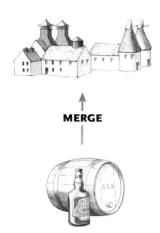

Figure 5.35   Vertically backward merger

in the same chain of production. What might encourage such mergers to take place? Clearly economies of scale will play a part, but what other advantages might these firms experience?

Motives for vertically backward mergers

If we think first about a vertically backward merger, what might encourage the brewer to merge with the farmer? One of the motivations might be that the brewer wishes to ensure that it always has a ready supply of high-quality raw materials available. If the ingredients are in short supply, or if a particular farmer is producing a strain of hops, for example, that gives the brewer's beer a distinctive flavour, then the brewer might wish to ensure that the farmer always supplies to it and is not tempted by offers from other brewers. What better way to ensure that the farmer will always supply you, will never supply your competitors without your knowledge, and will supply the ingredients at a price that is acceptable to you, than to merge together? Once you are one you then have complete control over your supply, and you can

guarantee the continued availability of that supply. Merging vertically backward, therefore, enables you to control your sources of supply.

Motives for vertically forward mergers

What might encourage the brewer to merge with the public house, or better still a chain of public houses? Just as the vertically backward merger might be done for reasons of control, so might the vertically forward merger. If the public houses remain free houses then they have complete freedom of choice concerning which brewers' products they will stock. If they decide not to stock your beer, then you have lost valuable custom. Manufacturers are, by and large, absolutely dependent upon retail outlets to sell their products for them. It is very rare for the general public to buy direct from the manufacturers, we normally buy from shops,

Figure 5.36   Vertically forward merger

so the manufacturer has to ensure that it always has retailers willing to stock their products, or the manufacturer will not survive. The best way to ensure this is for the companies to become one. If the brewer owns the public houses then it will always stock that brewers products, and not only that, the brewer can insist which, if any, competitors' products are stocked in those pubs and, to a certain extent, what prices are to be charged for the products. The manufacturer now has total control over its outlets and so there will always be a ready market for its beers.

A key word, therefore, when we are considering mergers, is **control**. Always consider what extra control the merger gives the participants, and this will undoubtedly be a strong motivating factor in the deal. The brewing industry is a highly vertically integrated one with companies owning and therefore controlling all of the stages in the above chain of production. In that way they are effectively ensuring ready markets, continued supplies and therefore long-term survival for all the firms involved.

Horizontal mergers

A horizontal merger involves two firms that are at the same stage in the same chain of production merging together.

Figure 5.37   Horizontal merger

The two firms are producing items that compete against each other in the same market, so the above example shows two breweries merging together. They both produce similar items, in this case they both brew different brands of beer, and they are therefore in direct competition with each other. What might be the motivations behind a merger of this type?

Motives for horizontal mergers

Economies of scale will clearly be a key motivating factor, and the economies to be gained in a horizontal merger can be particularly beneficial. Since the two

firms are engaged in almost exactly the same productive processes, it is not hard to imagine where savings might be made. In our example, perhaps one of the brewers has some spare capacity in one or more of its factories, perhaps some employees are under-used or machinery is lying idle at certain points in the day or week, maybe delivery vans go out only half full, and so on. In these instances the new combined firm can make more efficient use of these under-used factors of production. It is possible of course that the new firm may not need all of the combined factors of production, and maybe some can be sold off, or in the case of staff, laid off. In addition each firm will have its own marketing, administration and finance departments, to name but a few, both of which will be doing similar tasks. Will the new firm need both? It is unlikely.

Horizontal mergers therefore present many opportunities for economies and more efficient use of resources, making the combined firm more efficient and profitable than the two separate ones. Such mergers take place very regularly. In November 1997, two cross-channel ferry companies, P&O and Stena Line, decided to merge. It was speculated at the time in the press that this would lead to a loss of 1000 out of the 5000 jobs that existed prior to the merger, a substantial saving for the combined company. In February 1998, Somerfield and Kwik Save, two discount supermarket chains, decided to merge, with the potential loss of 850 jobs nationwide. In the same month two of the UK's largest insurance companies, Commercial Union and General Accident, planned to merge, threatening a further 3000 jobs. Clearly there are considerable savings to be made through horizontal mergers.

Competition is another key motivator to this type of merger. As we discussed earlier, whilst we as consumers like competition, businesses hate it. What better way to eliminate a competitor than to merge with that company. Once the firms are combined there will be no further need to compete on price or in any other way. This will put the larger firm in a substantially stronger position in the market, much more in control of the conditions in which it sells.

Such a merger could clearly act against the interests of the general public, keeping prices high by restricting choice. Consequently the government may look into such a merger to make sure, as far as possible, that this does not happen. See later how the government goes about this, under the previous section entitled 'competition policy'.

Market share A horizontal merger is also a quick way of increasing your firm's market share and widening your potential customer base.

Lateral mergers

Lateral mergers are the combining together of two companies that produce products that are linked or connected in some way, but that do not compete directly with one another.

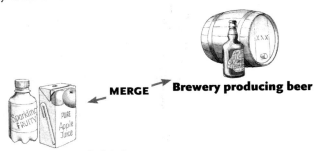

Company producing soft drinks

Figure 5.38 Lateral merger

In the above example, therefore, the brewer is merging with the soft drinks manufacturer. Both are producing beverages, each of which are likely to be found in the same outlets, such as public houses, restaurants, supermarkets, grocers, and so on, but they do not attempt to lure customers from each other. Each has a distinct target market to supply, one to the drinkers of alcoholic beverages, one to those people preferring a non-alcoholic drink. Thus the products are linked but are not the same. The reasons for this type of merger are similar to those for horizontal mergers: there are likely to be economies of scale, the target market becomes larger, the market share is increased and the firms can offer a wider range of products to their customers. To this end lateral mergers will often take place between firms that complement each other in the things that they produce. A firm will look for another firm to merge with that produces a range that

does not duplicate what they make, but rather fills the gaps in their product range.

Conglomerate mergers

A conglomerate merger takes place when two firms whose products have nothing in common join together, as the example shows. The two products do not compete with each other, nor do they complement each other's product range.

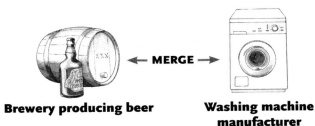

Brewery producing beer   **Washing machine manufacturer**

Figure 5.39   Conglomerate merger

Consequently, whilst there may be some economies of scale with such a merger, these will be limited. The major reason for this type of merger is the desire for risk-bearing economies; the prospect of diversification means that the company is spreading the risk of failure over an even wider product range. Today there are some very large conglomerate firms that supply a very wide range of products and services, many of which are vast global concerns trading across many countries.

CASE STUDY

Mergers: Carlton and Granada

In 2003, Carlton and Granada TV companies announced their intention to merge and form a firm worth around £4.1 billion. It was estimated that the new company would control about 50 per cent of the television advertising market. Advertisers and media agencies both expressed their fears over the potential creation of a single airtime sales house if the two existing sales houses owned by the two companies were to combine. The Competition Commission decided that an investigation was in order, and they produced a 456-page report into the proposed merger. Trade Secretary Patricia Hewitt made her announcement over the conditions for the merger in October 2003.

ACTIVITY

1 Outline the benefits to the two companies of the proposed merger.

2 Outline the reasons why you think the Competition Commission was concerned over the proposed merger.

3 On the Internet, look up the result of Patricia Hewitt's deliberations and her decision over the merger. To what extent do you agree with her judgements?

Multinational corporations

An inevitable result of industrial concentration and the benefits of the economies of scale has been the development of multinational corporations or MNCs, also known as transnational corporations (TNCs). In their desire to get bigger, firms have not been content to operate solely within the shores of their parent nation; today they have extended beyond their original national boundaries and operate in many countries around the world.

Many of these firms now also produce around the world. Sometimes they will base production abroad in order to produce close to the consumer market to avoid transport costs. On other occasions production is based abroad to take advantage of lower labour and production costs in order to reduce company costs and boost profitability. Many of these firms have become household names throughout the world, employing people and selling products globally.

Growth of multinationals

The number of transnational corporations in the world has increased very rapidly, from 7000 in 1970 to 40,000 in 1995. Ninety per cent of all these transnationals are based in the northern industrialised countries, more than half from just five nations: France, Germany, the Netherlands, Japan and the United States.

Operating globally has allowed many of these companies to expand dramatically, so dramatically in fact that they are now more economically significant than many countries. The biggest TNC in the world is currently Exxon, and it is comparable in economic size to the economies of Chile or Pakistan, while the economy of Nigeria is only slightly bigger than General Electric. The trend is a growing one. In 1990, just 24 TNCs appeared in the top 100 economic entities in the world, while in 2000 this had grown to 29. The highest placed British-owned company is BP in 68th position, above nations such as Cuba, Uruguay and Croatia.

Concerns about multinationals

The growth of these transnational companies has caused considerable concern for many people. Because they are so big and powerful, they are able to exert influence over national governments. They also have control over many of the world's natural resources, such as oil, coal and gas. They are involved in the production of many of the world's medicines, chemicals and communication links. TNCs are also regularly accused of exploiting cheap labour in low-cost, low-wage countries, and even employing children and paying them a pittance. Clearly the firms refute these claims and go to great lengths these days to persuade the general public that they trade responsibly and ethically, but there are many people around the world who are highly suspicious of the motives and activities of these massive international players.

ACTIVITY

'While multinational corporations would prefer to comply through voluntary initiatives, the public interest can only be fully served through stronger regulation and monitoring.' (Peter Utting, research co-ordinator at the UN Research Institute for Social Development.)

Split your study group in two. Using the Internet and textbooks in your library, one group should identify the main benefits that transnational corporations have given to the world, whilst the other should look up the worries and potential problems that TNCs present.

Prepare a debate over whether you agree with Peter Utting's statement. Does the public interest require that the TNCs have more regulation, and if so, what form should that regulation take? Or do you believe that TNCs are a force for good and should be left to develop and bring more prosperity to the world?

Financing growth

Finding the money to allow a firm to grow can be done through the traditional route of bank loan, but the firm could also raise money through **rights issues** (in the case of limited liability companies) or through **venture capital.**

Rights issues

A rights issue gives existing shareholders the right to buy new shares in the company in proportion to their original holding, usually at a favourable price. Shareholders can be informed of the expansion plans of the company and asked to support the venture by buying some additional shares. This will be attractive to them as the venture, if successful, should enhance company profits and their dividends; since rights issues will often be sold at a discount, the investment should also be seen as a bargain and a reward for their loyalty as shareholders. There is a big bonus to the firm of raising money through this route, and that is

that money raised via share issue does not have to be repaid (unlike a bank loan). If a shareholder wishes to realise their investment, they sell their shares to a broker, the firm can retain the original investment.

Venture capital

Venture capital firms will invest money into rapidly expanding firms that would perhaps struggle to raise finance from traditional routes. Venture capitalists look for firms with the potential to develop into significant firms, which may be new or existing companies; their aim is to help them grow and develop. They will provide finance to such companies and will also assist in the management of company development, often by taking a seat or seats on the board of directors. This can be very useful to the company as venture capitalists have wide experience in helping similar firms to grow and develop their businesses. A number of the world's biggest names have used venture capital to help them develop, including Microsoft, Intel and Federal Express.

Venture capitalists will invest in companies at various stages in their business lives:

- **seed investing** is providing finance before a real product or service has been decided
- **early stage investing** is helping a company to start up and guiding it through the first tricky stages
- **expansion and later stage financing** is helping a more mature company to expand and develop to become a more significant firm
- **turnaround financing** will enable failing firms to survive and rediscover success.

Joint ventures

Sometimes companies decide that they would like some of the benefits of merging without having the managerial and organisational problems that a full merger would bring about; in these circumstances they may choose to pursue a joint venture instead. This is where two or more companies set up a separate division or company that is financed jointly and run by a combination of people from each of the involved companies. This is a good way of breaking into foreign markets.

Setting up in another country is a time-consuming and costly process, but engaging in a joint venture is a quick way of establishing yourself abroad. It also enables firms to share expertise, particularly useful in technological industries. For example, there have been a number of 'strategic alliances' between firms in the motor industry in recent years so that they can share design and engineering skills.

Outsourcing

Outsourcing has become increasingly popular in recent years as a way of reducing company costs and/or improving service levels of the organisation. It can also offer a way for the firm to finance growth, and if a company cannot afford to employ staff itself to do a certain role, outsourcing may provide the answer.

Outsourcing means finding a person or company from outside the firm to carry out certain tasks for the firm. For example, a firm may choose to employ a contract cleaning firm to do office cleaning for them, rather than employing their own staff. Many firms also outsource maintenance contracts. This presents the firm with a number of benefits:

◆ The firm does not have to spend money or use up time training staff for those jobs.
◆ There are no recruitment costs involved.
◆ There are no problems with sackings or redundancies for the firm if work is found to be unsatisfactory. The contract with the outsourcing firm can simply be terminated and a new supplier found.
◆ The firm can start a new service very quickly by outsourcing the work.
◆ It is easy to get specialists doing the work.
◆ The outsourcing firm will have the problem of covering staff absences rather than your company.
◆ The company does not incur any additional costs associated with staff, such as National Insurance contributions, pension administration, sick pay, and so on.

When a firm is looking to grow, it can be deterred by the problems associated with employing more people and arranging additional training. Outsourcing, however, gives a quick and easy solution and encourages firms to grow. Management consultants and specialists can also be employed on a short-term basis to advise managers on the best ways to grow the company to supplement the skills of the existing company management.

When the UK government wished to expand the number of prisons available in the country, they turned to outsourcing by contracting security companies such as Group 4 to run some prisons. Recently they have also turned to private companies in trying to expand the number of routine operations being performed by the NHS. Private clinics are to be set up, employing staff from other countries, to perform many of the routine operations that the NHS has been struggling to fit in. Outsourcing has been seen as the quickest way of expanding and providing the service that is urgently needed.

Technology and innovation

One of the best ways of growing and moving ahead of your competitors is to design new and better products, but there is a problem here. **Research and development** (R&D) is a very expensive and time-consuming process, and so only larger firms are in a position to afford the time and money to engage in R&D effectively. As a result innovation often needs the resources of a big company. There is a vicious circle here: we must innovate to grow, but we must also be big to afford to innovate.

R&D is a risky business as there is no guarantee that it will yield anything saleable, and in truth a lot of R&D expenditure is wasted as researchers pursue new ideas that ultimately do not make it to the production line. The risk can be very worthwhile, however, as a market leading new idea can yield massive profits for a company. Large firms are better able to afford this risk, and so today a lot of the R&D that takes place is concentrated amongst the large firms of the world. The top 11 R&D companies in 2002 are shown in Figure 5.40.

As you can see, these are all very large firms, indeed many of them are transnational companies. Notice that only one of these, GlaxoSmithKline, is a UK firm.

299

Top 11 Research and Development companies

2002

1 Ford
2 General Motors
3 Siemens
4 Daimler Chrysler
5 Pfizer
6 IBM
7 Ericsson
8 Motorola
9 Matsushita Electric
10 Cisco
11 GlaxoSmithKline

Source: The Times 14 October 2002

Figure 5.40   Top 11 R&D companies

	All	Men	Women
Degree or equivalent	48%	55%	39%
Higher education	38%	44%	33%
GCE A-level or equivalent	23%	25%	18%
GCSE grade A–C or equivalent	17%	22%	13%
Other qualification	15%	17%	12%
No qualification	8%	10%	7%
All employees	25%	30%	20%

Source: Labour Force Survey

Figure 5.41   Proportion of working-age UK employees that were managers by highest qualification, Winter 2002/03

Labour market trends

The state of the labour market will have a significant impact on a firm's ability to grow. Recruiting the right staff will be crucial to this, and so the availability of people with the correct skills and experiences will either help or hinder the firm's plans.

In the UK we have seen a continued fall in the pool of unemployed people since 1993. In May 2003 the unemployment rate in the UK stood at 5 per cent, equating to about 1.47 million people, which is significantly below the EU average of just over 8 per cent. On the face of it this could be considered bad news for human resource executives as they seek to fill the jobs they have available: the smaller the pool of workers, the less choice we have in filling those posts. Equally significant, though, is the quality of worker available, that is, how educated and experienced those people are.

The UK government is making significant strides in boosting levels of education in the country in order to prepare people to take on challenging jobs and help companies develop. Figure 5.41 shows how significant qualifications can be in preparing workers for responsible positions in employment.

The table clearly suggests that higher level qualifications are necessary for managerial positions.

Economic inactivity in the labour market   **JOURNAL ARTICLE**

When we consider the labour market, we usually consider three classes of person: the employed, the unemployed and the economically inactive (these last being the 'unemployable' people in society). Effort is normally put into trying to move people from the ranks of the unemployed to the employed, but with a falling number of unemployed in the UK, attention is now switching to the economically inactive. The reason for that is that we now recognise that some of the economically inactive people are potentially capable of being introduced to the labour force.

You should investigate this topic further by referring to the *British Economy Survey*, Volume 32, Number 1, Autumn 2002, Section 6. The article 'Economic inactivity in the labour market' by David Pierce examines the makeup of the stock of economically inactive people and their potential for the working population of the UK.

This is the reason behind the UK government's plan for more people to enter further and higher education in the UK. If the labour market is going to have sufficient well-qualified people to meet the needs of industry in the future, we need more people with HNDs and degrees. Tony Blair has expressed his desire to get 50 per cent of young people studying in higher education, and the numbers are indeed rising.

In addition, with those people who choose not to go on to higher education, much effort is being put into encouraging young people to go into work-based training. By October 2002, approximately 284,000 young people were involved in such training, including Modern Apprenticeships.

Sometimes firms have found that the UK labour market has not been able to supply the skills needed, and have been forced to look abroad for those skills. In a world of rapidly improving communications technology, it is easy to interview staff via video conferencing, and employ people remotely in offices based abroad, call centres in foreign countries or through teleworking from anywhere in the world. BT, for example, now employs call centre workers in India, allowing it to tap into the skills of the people in that country, and also to incur lower costs than it would by employing people in the UK.

Understandably, not everyone sees this as a step forward for the UK economy.

Chapter 4

International trade and the European dimension

Global markets and the UK economy

International trade has been one of the big drivers for economic growth for all industrial nations over the past 150 years. GDP has increased very rapidly during that time, and it is not a coincidence that at the same time many nations were promoting international trade within their industries. Since 1950, trade has increased by 1700 per cent and GDP has increased by 600 per cent.

Advantages of international trade

There are many advantages in trading globally; some of them are advantages to consumers, some for producers and most are benefits to the economy as a whole.

Choice

If you go to buy a product today there is plenty of choice. Take hi-fi systems, for example. The amount of choice is bewildering. Whilst the number of products to decide between is large, the variety of choice enables a buyer to get a system that was just right for his or her particular requirements: not too big, with plenty of inputs into the amplifier, read MP3 discs, and so on. One can choose from the products of many different firms from many different countries.

Quality

Why do people in Britain like buying BMW cars? Or Japanese hi-fi systems? Trade not only gives us lots of choice, but also gives us quality that is not available from British manufacturers. It is trade that has given us these opportunities.

Price

Some countries can produce products more cheaply than we can in the UK, so buying them in from abroad means that our consumers can get those items more cheaply. This not only benefits them, but it also helps to keep inflation down.

We can buy things we cannot produce at home

Why do we buy bananas from the West Indies? Because it's difficult to grow bananas in the rain. Trade allows us to buy things that are uneconomical to produce at home because of natural disadvantages we may have in producing them.

Wider markets

There is a limit to how much we can sell in the British market. With a limit of roughly 60 million people to sell to, a company can only expand to a certain extent. However, if it trades globally, sales expansion potential is almost limitless. Trade therefore allows firms to grow and earn more wealth.

Less unemployment

Because firms can grow more easily, output expands and therefore more employees are needed. More employment injects money into the economy through wages which helps to increase growth in the economy.

Wealth earned for the nation

When we sell abroad there is a flow of foreign currency into the country. This earns wealth for the nation and the economy grows.

Trade therefore helps the economy to grow and as a result contributes to higher standards of living for all of the citizens in our country. Good international trade relations actually boost all the economies of all of the countries taking part.

Comparative and absolute advantage

David Ricardo, writing nearly 200 years ago, devised a theory about trade, called the **theory of comparative and absolute advantage**. He identified the key role international trade has to play in creating economic growth and boosting living standards. The basis of his theory is actually very simple: if each nation specialises in what it is good at producing, more will be produced globally. We probably could grow bananas in the UK if we invested enough resources into capital equipment to produce an artificial environment, but we could not produce many and it would be terribly wasteful of our factors of production. So specialisation increases global output. If we then trade with each other, all countries can get the products that they need and more needs and wants can be satisfied around the world. Thus international trade can contribute to solving that basic economic problem of scarcity.

The following simple example illustrates this principle. Here we have two countries, the UK and Kenya, both producing machines and food. We will assume that each country has 10 workers divided equally between production of machines and food.

	Production	
	Machines	Food
UK	40	40
Kenya	5	250
Totals	45	290

We can see from the table that five workers in the UK can make 40 machines (eight per worker) whereas Kenya can only make five machines (one per worker). The UK therefore has an absolute advantage in the production of machines and Ricardo's theory suggests that it should specialise on the production of machines. Kenya, however, has an absolute advantage in the production of food, it should therefore specialise in food production. Total production should therefore increase:

	Production	
	Machines	Food
UK	80	0
Kenya	0	500
Totals	80	500

As long as the UK sells machines to Kenya and Kenya sells food to the UK, more needs and wants will be satisfied in both countries.

This concept is fairly straightforward. However, Ricardo went on to say that trade could still be advantageous when one country has an absolute advantage in both products, as long as there is a difference in their relative efficiencies. The following example illustrates the **principle of comparative advantage**.

Once again there are 10 workers per country divided equally amongst the two products.

	Production	
	Machines	Food
UK	50	350
Kenya	10	250
Totals	60	600

It can be seen that the UK has an absolute advantage in both machines and food. However we could say that the UK has a comparative advantage in producing machines as it can produce five times as many cars per worker as Kenya, whereas with food it can only produce 40 per cent more. Total production can still be increased if Kenya concentrates on food production (in which it has a comparative advantage) and the UK uses most of its resources to produce machines.

	Production	
	Machines	Food
UK	80	140
Kenya	0	500
Totals	80	640

The UK as an exporting nation

We are quick to put down the UK when we comment on industrial performance, but we should not be too negative. The UK is still one of the top five exporters for merchandise in the world, beaten only by the USA, Germany, Japan and France (although we will soon be overtaken by China), and we are comfortably the second biggest exporter of services, beaten only by the USA. In 2001 the UK exported $273.1 billion worth of merchandise and $108.4 billion worth of commercial services. The UK is therefore one of the biggest players in world trade, although our share of the trade market has been reducing for a number of years. Trade is therefore vitally important to the well-being of our industry and our nation, offering new markets and expansion potential to many of our companies.

Balance of payments

Exports are those goods we sell abroad, imports are those that we buy from abroad. The **balance of payments** is, in its simplest terms, an account showing the difference between the total exports and the total imports for a country. Any individual or business will wish to ensure that they have more income than outgoings, and countries are no different, except that they hope to encourage more exports than imports and thereby earn wealth for the country. A situation where we sell more abroad than we buy from abroad is known as a **surplus** situation, and this is what governments regard as a sound balance of payments.

Construction of the balance of payments

The balance of payments is made up of two major sections, the **current account** and the **capital account**. It is constructed as shown in the table on p. 305.

Patterns and trends in international trade

In the UK we have been traditionally weak in our performance in visible trade but much stronger in our invisible trade. We regularly run visible trade deficits

---

The UK balance of payments

In each issue of the *British Economy Survey*, Section 7 includes an article on the current state of the UK balance of payments. These are very useful for keeping up to date with changes in the UK trade position. They also update you on changes to accounting procedures, and discuss future prospects for the UK.

The structure of the balance of payments is very clearly explained, and recent trends are examined in some detail in the *British Economy Survey*, Volume 31, Number 2, Spring 2002, Section 7 with the article 'UK balance of payments' by Michael Morris.

---

but our invisible balances are usually in surplus, although not always enough to put the whole current account balance into surplus. The following table shows the situation in the UK in recent years.

	Current account balance	Trade in goods	Trade in services
1990	−14370	−18707	4337
1991	−6121	−10223	4102
1992	−7568	−13050	5482
1993	−6485	−13066	6581
1994	−4747	−11126	6379
1995	−3542	−12023	8481
1996	−4125	−13722	9597
1997	186	−12342	12528
1998	−9147	−21813	12666
1999	−17257	−29051	11794
2000	−21282	−33120	11838
2001	−29270	−40570	11300
2002	−32128	−46287	14159

Figure 5.42 Current account figures for the UK (in millions of pounds)

When we imagine imports and exports we typically think of goods moving between countries, such as food items and machines such as cars. Any physical items such as these are known as items of **visible trade.** If we add up the value of all of our visible exports and deduct from this the total value of our visible imports we have calculated our visible trade balance. If this is a positive figure it is called a surplus, if it is negative we term this a deficit.

Total Visible Exports
minus
Total Visible Imports
= Visible Trade Balance

Countries do not just sell visible items, they also sell services such as insurance, banking and shipping services. Trade in these services is known as **invisible trade.** If we add up the value of all of our invisible exports and deduct from this the total value of our invisible imports we have calculated our invisible trade balance. Once again, if this is a positive figure it is called a surplus, if it is negative we term this a deficit.

Total Invisible Exports
minus
Total Invisible Imports
= Invisible Trade Balance

We now take our visible and invisible trade balances and add them together. This gives us the current account balance. This is the figure that is generally quoted in the newspapers and on TV when they comment on our balance of payments performance.

Visible Trade Balance
Plus
Invisible Trade Balance
= Current Account Balance

The second part of the balance of payments is known as the **capital transfers account** and this consists of flows of capital into and out of the country. These are often referred to as **official capital transfers**, and these occur when one government lends to another.

Total Capital Inflows
minus
Total Capital Outflows
= Capital Transfers Balance

Thirdly we have financial transactions (private capital flows) and these occur when individuals or companies choose to invest money abroad either in a financial institution or by setting up a factory or outlet in a foreign country. The total capital inflows minus the total capital outflows gives us our **capital account balance.**

Total Financial Transaction Inflows
minus
Total Financial Transaction Outflows
= Net Financial Transactions

To balance the balance of payments we finally introduce the **balancing item** to cover transfers not covered by the other sections in the balance.

Current Account Balance
minus
Capital Transfers Balance
minus
Net Financial Transactions
minus
Balancing Item
= 0

Figure 5.43   Balance of payments

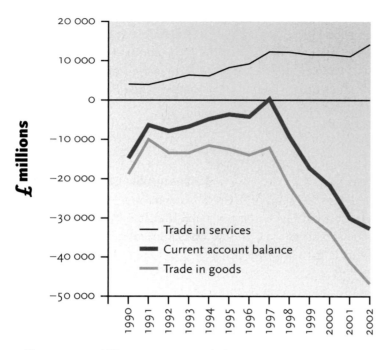

Figure 5.44   UK current account balances 1990–2002

		(£ million)
1	USA	28401.1
2	Germany	21635.3
3	France	18507.1
4	Irish Republic	15698.1
5	Netherlands	13758.5
6	Belgium	9989.9
7	Italy	8410.2
8	Spain	8349.6
9	Sweden	3838.2
10	Japan	3303.9

Source: UK Trade Trends June 2003, HM Customs and Excise

Figure 5.45   UK exports and dispatches 2002

As you can see, over the years since 1990 only once have we in the UK enjoyed a current account surplus. Whilst our performance in selling services to the world continues to improve, our trade deficit in primary and secondary products is declining rapidly.

UK trade with the EU, USA and other countries

Export partners

Although many people consider the US market to be most important to the UK, it is true to say that the EU is by far our largest trading partner. Approximately 58 per cent of all of our export trade heads for the EU, hence our need for close ties and trading links with mainland Europe. The USA is undoubtedly important, and is the single biggest buyer of UK goods and services, but it still only accounts for about 15 per cent of our sales abroad.

Our main exports in the UK are in financial services, tourism, manufactured goods, fuels, chemicals, food, beverages and tobacco. Figure 5.45 breaks down our export performance further.

Import partners

There is a similar picture when we consider the UK's import position. The EU is our biggest supplier, accounting for about 51 per cent of the goods and services we buy, whereas approximately 13 per cent of our imports come from the USA. Our principal imports are manufactured goods, machinery, fuels and foodstuffs. Figure 5.46 gives some more detail on our import figures.

		(£ million)
1	Germany	30530.1
2	USA	26042.2
3	France	18857.6
4	Netherlands	15182.7
5	Belgium	11668.2
6	Italy	10760.3
7	Irish Republic	9454.9
8	Japan	8491.0
9	Spain	8170.2
10	China	6973.6

Source: UK Trade Trends June 2003, HM Customs and Excise

Figure 5.46   UK imports and arrivals 2002

ACTIVITY

1   Examine the two tables. You should be able to see that we have trade surpluses with some countries and deficits with others. Work out which countries we earn foreign currency from and those who drain our currency reserves.

2   Knowing what you do of developments in world economics, in what ways do you anticipate these tables changing over the next 10–20 years?

Protectionism

As we have seen, free trade brings multiple advantages to nations, but it also brings problems too. Much manufacturing industry in the UK has found it very difficult to survive in the face of fierce foreign competition. Many companies have died as a result, and those that have survived have only done so thanks to severe cost cutting or redesigning of products. Consequently governments around the world are lobbied by representatives of industry to protect their livelihoods by reducing the quantity of imports allowed in. Sometimes governments have sympathy with these lobbies, and in those cases the governments may resort to protectionist measures, steps to reduce the volume of imports. These can take a number of forms; these are some of the most popular methods.

Tariffs

Taxes are placed on all goods entering the country. These have the effect of increasing the selling price of these items when in the shops and making home-produced products more competitive. Thus sales of home-produced products rise (because they are now relatively cheaper) and import sales fall.

Quotas

A limit to the number of imported items is set. Once this is reached, no more are allowed to enter the country.

Subsidies

These work like tariffs except that the government gives money to the home producer so that they can make the products more cheaply and therefore be more competitive.

Administrative barriers

These are sneaky. The government does not prohibit imports at all, but does insist that imports must meet very stringent quality standards or makes the paperwork required very onerous. The hope is that importers will not be able to reach these standards, so imports are reduced.

All of the above methods prevent free trade and therefore distort world markets. All of them potentially hinder growth prospects for the world economy, so all are generally frowned upon by governments. The World Trade Organisation (WTO) is an organisation that comprises most of the industrialised nations of the world, and their goal is to eliminate all protectionist measures and thus promote world trade and prosperity.

Trading blocs of the world

Sometimes countries that have strong economic and trading ties decide that there would be many mutual benefits if they were to strengthen those links by creating a **trading bloc**. Countries in a bloc will normally share some common cultural background and will be located close together. The bloc is simply an agreement that enables the members to co-ordinate their foreign trade policies for the benefit of all bloc members. Although there are a great many trading blocs around the world, there are three major trading blocs that you should be aware of, in North America, Europe, and Asia. The North American bloc (NAFTA) comprises USA, Canada and Mexico. The European bloc contains most of Western Europe with leading roles played by Germany, Britain, and France. The Asian bloc includes Japan, Korea, Taiwan, Hong Kong, Malaysia and others.

Maastricht Treaty

This is an agreement among the 12 EU nations signed in 1992 and it was designed to form a more economically and politically integrated European economy, including the reduction or elimination of tariffs and non-tariff barriers and the creation of a monetary unit (the euro).

North American Free Trade Agreement (NAFTA)

This treaty between the USA, Canada and Mexico was launched in 1994, probably in response to the threat posed by the Maastricht Treaty two years earlier, to also eliminate trade barriers between the member nations, including the reduction or elimination of many tariff and non-tariff barriers. The USA is currently engaged in negotiations for a new bloc to be called Free Trade for the Americas (FTAA) covering both North and South America and including over 30 countries.

Although the trading blocs eliminate tariffs between members, tariffs may be, and often are, imposed on imports coming from outside the bloc. In the EU, for example, we use the **common external tariff** (CET) that imposes tariffs on goods and services entering the EU from non-EU countries. This has the effect of encouraging trade within the bloc and hampering potential imports from elsewhere.

In the last 10 years there has been a large number of new blocs created, and today about 43 per cent of all trade in the world takes place within trading blocs.

New protectionism and the North American Free Trade Agreement
JOURNAL ARTICLE

Most nations of the world agree that free trade is the best way to promote economic growth for nations, but achieving free trade has not proved easy. Many governments do not seek complete free trade, rather they seek free trade 'on their terms', that is, with strings attached that benefit them. NAFTA is a good example of this; tariffs have certainly been reduced through NAFTA, but the NAFTA agreement actually endorses other

forms of protectionism, such as administrative barriers. It is clear that the agreement has been set up to protect the interests of the dominant power in NAFTA, the USA.

The motivations behind NAFTA and the protectionist rules enshrined therein are examined in detail in Kieron Toner's article 'New protectionism and the North American Free Trade Agreement'. You will find this in the *British Economy Survey*, Volume 30, Number 2, Spring 2001, Section 14.

Is international trade a barrier to development?
JOURNAL ARTICLE

As we have seen, classical economic theory insists that international trade increases economic welfare and that barriers to trade circumvent this benefit and are a problem for all. However, not all economists still think this is a flawless theory. Developing nations are always encouraged through the WTO to drop any protectionist measures protecting their infant industries, but there are examples where this has actually reduced the developing nations' ability to develop their GDP. Ironically, the countries that insist on this requirement to drop protectionist measures (including the USA and the UK) built their wealth with the use of protectionism in the first place. There could be a strong economic argument for allowing developing nations to protect their infant industries if they are ever to develop their economies.

You should investigate this topic further by referring to the journal *Economics Today*, Volume 11, Number 1. The article 'Is international trade a barrier to development?' by Richard Pratt tells the story further.

UK membership of the EU

The UK's membership of the European Union (EU) is undoubtedly one of the major influences on the UK economy today, and as European integration continues it will become an increasingly important influence. The development of ever-closer links with the EU has been accelerating since the 1980s, and there are two major threads to this union: greater economic ties, and greater political ties.

The business world is concerned mainly with the economic ties. A number of large companies in the UK want to have even greater economic ties within the EU. In particular they would like to be part of the single European currency (the euro) because this, they claim, would mean greater simplicity and security in doing business with our European neighbours. For example, there would not be the uncertainty of changes in the value of currencies against each other. There would not be the costs incurred in changing money from one currency to another. Moreover, business has been one of the major drivers behind the enlargement of the EU that took place in 2004. This major change to the makeup of the Union saw ten new countries joining, these being:

- Cyprus
- Malta
- Slovenia
- Hungary
- Lithuania
- Slovakia
- Poland
- Czech Republic
- Estonia
- Latvia.

These are now joined with the original members: UK, France, Germany, Italy, Spain, Belgium, Austria, Denmark, Germany, Finland, Ireland, Luxembourg, the Netherlands, Portugal and Sweden. More economies put together like this provide a bigger single market to sell into, which is always attractive to business.

However, there is no consensus about greater political ties. The main worry about greater political union relates to policies and rules being determined outside the UK. Rather than decisions being made by parliaments in the UK, increasingly decision making is being carried out by EU institutions. There is the fear of losing autonomy and lack of regional focus.

There is also a fear of losing control over internal economic policy. When the UK government is in charge of controlling the UK economy it can take measures which are UK-focused: for example, lowering interest rates to encourage spending in the economy when there is a recession. If decisions about interest rates were taken by the European Central Bank, then the Bank would be pursuing European-wide objectives which may exclude an immediate concern for what is happening in the UK. This could harm business. Instead of UK business people being able to lobby the government in Westminster for change, they would have to turn to Brussels and Strasbourg, far more remote centres of government.

A further problem is the potential for waste that is inherent in a very large 'superstate' like the European Union may become. In 1999, for example, there was widespread concern in the EU about corruption that had led to waste in a number of EU areas of administration, such as subsidies to farmers. The danger is that if you have such a large and bureaucratic system then it becomes very difficult to identify waste and inefficiency.

The European Union

Throughout the course of history, attempts have been made to bring the European nations together into a single system: the Roman and Napoleonic Empires are examples of this. Although the European Union is the only example of a democratic attempt to unite (politically and economically) the European nations, unity is not a new idea.

Origins of the EU

The 'rebirth' of the European idea was taken up by European and US leaders at the end of the Second World War in an attempt to bring lasting stability,

309

security and prosperity. They aimed to achieve this by means of economic co-operation and integration. It was hoped that European economic integration would accomplish two political objectives.

The founders of the Union intended to make further wars amongst the European neighbours a practical impossibility. They set out to do this through increased co-operation and understanding between the nations, and by integrating their economies so closely together that war would become economic suicide.

By the end of the Second World War, the balance of world power had shifted; the United States and the Soviet Union were the new superpowers. It was hoped that a strengthened bloc of economically united and democratic western European nations would halt the spread of communism from the east.

Main steps to unification

The European Coal and Steel Community

The first step towards European unification was the creation of the European Coal and Steel Community (ECSC) in 1951. The ECSC aimed to 'pool' German and French coal and steel resources. The French and Germans were to give up their sovereignty on policy issues relating to their respective coal and steel operations to an independent High Authority which would manage and co-ordinate policies in this field, thus linking two of their essential resources. Italy, Belgium, Luxembourg and the Netherlands also joined in the venture. The ECSC was hailed by its drafter Jean Monnet as, 'The first expression of the Europe that is being born.'

The European Economic Community

The next step towards unification came in 1956 when the six countries of the ECSC agreed plans to form a European Economic Community (EEC). For a number of years after the Second World War, the countries of western Europe had debated the benefits of adopting a **free trade** area; it was thought that this would promote trade, increase prosperity and help the countries' economies in the processes of reconstruction and redevelopment. However, the

European countries were divided on how this was to be achieved.

The six members of the ECSC felt that a free trade area would not be sufficiently binding to deliver the security and economic benefits to which they aspired. They favoured a supranational model of organisation, in which countries would give up a portion of their decision-making powers to a higher authority (as in the ECSC). This was to be reinforced by the adoption of a common customs union and tariffs barrier.

Britain and another group of European countries (Denmark, Portugal, Switzerland, Norway, Austria and Sweden) preferred a free trade area based on intergovernmental co-operation. They objected to the idea of giving up a portion of their sovereignty: their ability as separate nations to control policy making in every policy area.

In 1957, the ECSC six signed the Treaty of Rome. This effectively created both the EEC and EURATOM (the European Atomic Community). Together with the ECSC, these three organisations became known as the 'three communities'. Because of the objections outlined above, the other western European countries declined to join the organisation, although most of them eventually became members.

The Single European Act

The Single European Act was eventually signed by twelve members of the EEC in 1986. Its aim was to kick-start the flagging process of European unification, and with this purpose in mind a deadline was set for the completion of a 'Single Market' by 1992.

The Single Market

The Single European Act created a European common market protected by a customs union and an external tariffs barrier. A common market involves the free movement of goods, trade, labour, services and capital between a group of countries. For member countries the single market area now became their 'home market'. One problem was that although the Treaty and Act had removed the most obvious barriers to trade (customs duties and tariff barriers) the member states found other ways of protecting their true home markets against their 'internal' trading partners.

Although they had promised to remove all barriers to trade, in practice they used non-tariff barriers to give their markets at home an unfair advantage. Examples of non-tariff barriers include state aid such as production subsidies, market-sharing cartels, use of different technical rules and standards (such as different specifications on packaging design or composition), a refusal to recognise other states' professional or educational qualifications, and so on. Non-tariff barriers are generally hard to detect, and the EEC's practice of unanimous voting to make decisions meant that removing them was a slow process.

To summarise, the intention of the Single European Market Act was to create an internal European trading space, free from any national trading barriers. The aim of the Act was to remove the hidden, non-tariff barriers to trade which might otherwise prevent member states from trading with each other on an equal basis.

The Cecchini Report (1992) identified four main consequences of a well-organised single market which would be of benefit to business:

♦ Cost reductions. Because companies would produce on a larger scale in a new mass market, this should lead to falling costs for each unit of production.
♦ Improved efficiency. Industries would need to reorganise to serve mass markets. This reorganisation, coupled with competition, should increase efficiency.
♦ New patterns of competition. Those industries and areas with the most effective resources would make the biggest gains.
♦ New innovations, processes and products. These would flow from the larger, more competitive, market.

The Maastricht Treaty on European Union

Over the years, members of the EEC have massively increased the scope for action at European level. Swathes of policies have been added. Recent additions include a common fisheries policy limiting the size of catches, the types of nets that can be used, and so on, and an environmental policy governing such things as water quality standards and regulations relating to air pollution.

After much debate, the Maastricht Treaty was ratified in November 1993. The Treaty significantly altered the shape of the European Community. Many of the new policies have been placed within the existing EEC treaties. This means that they operate within the normal framework of Community decision making. They are given a supranational character, that is, the member states' governments no longer have direct control over what happens in those fields of policy.

However, in addition to revising the existing European Community treaties, the new treaty incorporated two new areas of policy co-operation: the Common Foreign and Security Policy (CFSP) and Justice and Home Affairs. The member states have promised to 'co-operate' on issues arising in these new areas, and decisions will be made on 'intergovernmental' rather than on 'supranational' lines. This means that normal community decision-making procedures will not apply in these two areas; the European Court of Justice will have no powers of jurisdiction, the European Commission and the European Parliament will have only limited roles to play, and the main sources of power will come from the Council and the European Council, both of which are accountable to national parliaments.

The Maastricht Treaty increased the part played by the European Parliament, allowing it to block laws in some areas and giving it the power to approve or reject the European budget. The Parliament also has the power to censure (and remove if necessary) European Commissioners. The Commission is now accountable to the Parliament.

Maastricht enables the European Court of Justice to take action against those who do not implement agreed EU rules. It also defines the scope for EU activity in such areas as education and training and health by setting out the sort of action the EU should take. Maastricht also enabled EU action in other areas, such as protecting the environment.

Because the scope of European co-operation has been extended to include policies made on intergovernmental as well as supranational lines, the new structure of the EU has been likened to a Greek temple. The overall 'building'(the EU) is now supported by three 'pillars':

- the revised EEC treaties (supranational)
- the Common Foreign and Security Policy (intergovernmental)
- Justice and Home Affairs (intergovernmental).

New features of the revised treaty

- Any national of a member state of the EU is now an EU citizen and may live, reside and move freely anywhere in the EU.
- The Treaty includes new provisions in European monetary policy and set 1999 as the deadline for the final stage of monetary union: the replacement of existing currencies by a common European currency, the euro.
- The Social Chapter (see below) aims to give the Union a 'human face' and prevent unfair competition in the Single Market.

Co-operation in justice and home affairs

The member states will designate for joint action areas of common interest and concern, such as crime, law and order, and immigration. 'Joint action' means that the member states will decide upon common courses of action for the designated areas and will subsequently promise to respect the agreements and act together in those areas. Areas already designated for joint action include customs co-operation, international fraud, drug addiction, and Europol, an organisation set up to help cross-border police co-operation in the fight against international crimes such as terrorism, fraud or drug trafficking.

Co-operation in common foreign and security policy (CFSP)

The CFSP works on the same principle as Justice and Home Affairs, in that the member states designate areas of common concern for joint action. Alternatively, and depending upon the particular circumstances, they might choose to react to a particular event by 'adopting a common position' or by issuing a 'joint statement'. For example, the members of the EU might collectively issue a statement condemning a particular country for its poor record in human rights, or for its persecution of a particular

section of its population. Under the CFSP, the member states have been able to deal with issues such as the Yugoslav war, the Middle East peace process and stability in central and eastern Europe. Action in the field of the CFSP does not yet include defence, although it does allow for the possibility of a common defence policy.

The Social Chapter

The Social Chapter was created with two main purposes in mind.

- It is part of an attempt to give the European Union a 'human face'. Those involved in shaping the EU realised that it appeared bureaucratic and detached from ordinary people. They took account of the fact that European unification was not just an economic venture and that it needed the understanding and support of the people in order to succeed.
- In order to guard against 'social dumping'. As part of the attempt to run a fair single market, the member states wanted to prevent countries with poorer social standards from reaping benefits over those with more stringent standards. By maintaining differences in social standards – particularly with regard to employment (minimum pay, annual holiday entitlement, maternity leave, health and safety at work, and so on) – one country could maintain an advantage over the others in attracting employment opportunities created by foreign investment.

The Social Chapter is not actually part of the Treaty on European Union; it is a protocol (an agreement) attached to the Treaty. It was initially signed by eleven member states, not including Britain: France, Germany, Italy, Belgium, the Netherlands, Luxembourg, Spain, Portugal, Greece, Ireland and Denmark.

The eleven signatories wanted to increase their joint co-operation in the field of social policy, using the aims set out in the Social Charter as their basis for doing so. The Social Charter is a non-binding agreement which was adopted at the Strasbourg summit in December 1989. It laid down certain social policy aims and objectives for the member states:

- freedom of movement
- employment and remuneration
- living and working conditions
- social protection
- freedom of association and collective bargaining
- vocational training
- equal opportunities
- information, consultation and participation for workers
- health and safety in the workplace
- protection for children, elderly and disabled persons.

All of the above have important implications for UK firms. In the 1990s, enlightened UK companies introduced the new requirements voluntarily in anticipation of being obliged to make the changes at a later date.

Originally the eleven wanted to incorporate the Chapter into the Treaty. Britain, however, objected to this and consequently the eleven made a separate agreement on social policy: a protocol, which is attached to the Treaty but not a part of it. Other social policy provisions that were included in the original EEC treaty and extended by the Single European Act still apply to Britain, but Britain was exempt from any decisions made under the Social Chapter protocol. This has changed now that Labour has signed up to this protocol (as have other new members of the union).

Even though the protocol is not part of the Treaty and therefore not subject to normal Community decision-making processes, it allows the signatories to 'borrow' the use of the Community institutions in order to make decisions legally and communally binding.

Article 1 of the Social Chapter outlines the Community's main aims in implementing a social policy.

> The Community and the member states shall have as their objectives the promotion of employment, improved living and working conditions, proper social protection, dialogue between management and labour, the development of human resources with a view to lasting employment, and the combating of exclusion.

An example of regulations resulting from EU social policy are the **working time regulations** (part of EU health and social requirements rather than a direct part of the Social Chapter). Under the previous Conservative government the UK had tried to avoid having to comply with the EU's working time directive which stemmed from the Social Chapter. The British government referred the matter to the European Court of Justice which, in the autumn of 1996, ruled that Britain should adopt the 48-hour week legislation.

CASE STUDY

Working Time Regulations 1998

In November 1993, members of the Council of Ministers decided by majority vote to introduce a directive on working time, under Health and Safety Article 118A. This enabled Council members to introduce a 48-hour maximum working week. This directive then was implemented in the Working Time Regulations 1998.

The Regulations give rise to wholly new rights and obligations relating to work and rest. The principal provisions are for:

- a limit on average weekly working time to 48 hours (though individuals can choose to work longer)
- a limit on night workers' average normal daily working time to 8 hours
- a requirement to offer health assessments to night workers
- minimum daily and weekly rest periods
- rest breaks at work
- paid annual leave.

The Regulations also implement provisions of the Young Workers Directive which relates to the working time of adolescents (those over the minimum school leaving age but under 18). Adolescents are given rights that differ from those of adult workers. These relate to health assessments for night work, minimum daily and weekly rest periods, and rest breaks at work.

The Regulations define a worker as someone to whom an employer has a duty to provide work, who controls when and how it is done, supplies the tools and other equipment and pays tax and National Insurance contributions. However, these are indicators rather than exhaustive or exclusive criteria. The majority of agency workers and freelancers are likely to be workers in the context of the Regulations.

The Regulations do not apply to certain classes of workers (apart from juveniles) in a number of sectors, including: air transport, rail, road transport, sea transport, inland waterways and lake transport, sea fishing and 'other work at sea' (essentially offshore work in the oil and gas industries).

Some of the measures can be adapted through agreements between workers and employers, so as to allow flexibility to take account of the specific needs of local working arrangements.

ACTIVITY

1   From a business point of view, what do you consider to be the main arguments for and against the adoption of a 48-hour maximum working week?

2   From a social point of view, what do you consider to be the main arguments for and against the adoption of a 48-hour week?

3   Can you think of any organisational or procedural problems that might arise through the implementation of the 48-hour week ruling?

4   Which kinds of business organisations will benefit from the 48-hour week ruling, and which will not?

Enlargement of the European Union

The European Union is currently preparing for its biggest enlargement. Thirteen countries have applied to become new members: ten of these countries (Cyprus, the Czech Republic, Estonia, Hungary, Latvia, Lithuania, Malta, Poland, the Slovak Republic and Slovenia) joined on 1 May 2004. Bulgaria and Romania plan to become members by 2007. Turkey has also applied for membership but their application is currently on hold.

The EU has gradually evolved since its inception in 1951 and it has already been enlarged successfully on four previous occasions. The Treaty of Rome was signed in 1957 establishing the European Economic Community (EEC). This was drawn up by the six original founding members, these being Belgium, France, Germany, Italy, Luxembourg and the Netherlands. Enlargement has happened as follows:

1973   Denmark, Ireland and the UK
1981   Greece
1986   Portugal and Spain
1995   Austria, Finland and Sweden

The current enlargement, however, is the biggest yet, both in terms of the number of countries involved (ten), the geographical area (an increase of 34 per cent) and population (an increase of 105 million).

In order to become members each of the countries has had to supply evidence that they can fulfil the economic and political conditions known as the Copenhagen Criteria. These state that each new member must:

◆ be a stable democracy, respecting human rights, the rule of law, and the protection of minorities
◆ have a functioning market economy
◆ adopt the common rules, standards and policies that make up the body of EU law.

It is anticipated that there will be a number of benefits from this enlargement. All countries should benefit from a wider zone of peace, stability and prosperity in Europe; it should help to boost economic growth and create jobs in both existing and new member states; there should be a better quality of life for citizens of the new members, and enlargement will also strengthen the position of the EU in world affairs. The more people the EU represents, the more influential it becomes in areas of global policy.

Enlargement will give existing EU members increased access to these new markets. Some progress has already been made in developing these markets, the enlargement will significantly increase this. There are clearly many benefits which are likely to arise for UK-based companies stemming from an enlargement of the EU. The Czech Republic and Hungary have already made large steps towards developing market economies. UK companies have already set up a number of joint ventures and taken over business concerns in these markets.

Many Polish, Czech and Hungarian consumers are already taking on board patterns of consumer spending and a taste for consumer goods at much higher levels than before. They have developed a taste for Western goods. As these economies have been reconstructed they have sought to replace their existing capital goods industries with newer technologies and methods imported from the West. On the consumer goods side, for example, we have seen Cadbury setting up chocolate and confectionery

manufacturing plant in Poland, and in the capital goods industry Ready Mixed Concrete (RMS) and other building companies such as Costain have set up joint ventures in the former East Germany, Poland and elsewhere. Shell is building new pipelines for the transportation of gas and oil in some of these countries. We are able to benefit from purchasing raw materials, foodstuffs and some finished manufactured goods from these countries while selling them more sophisticated goods.

The benefits of the enlargement are greater for the new members, since they are currently less economically developed, but there are benefits to the existing members too, particularly in terms of new markets to sell to. A study in 1997 by the Centre for Economic Policy Research estimated that the enlargement would bring an economic gain for the existing members of €10 billion, and for the new members of €23 billion. This was backed up by a further study in 2001 by the European Commission which estimated that enlargement could increase the growth of GDP of the new members by between 1.3 per cent and 2.1 per cent annually, and for the existing members by 0.7 per cent.

Question: Generally speaking, do you think that (COUNTRY)'s membership of the European Union would be ... ?

CC EB 2002.2	CC13 Average	2004 Countries	Bulgaria	Cyprus	Czech Republic	Estonia	Hungary	Latvia
a good thing	64	58	70	72	47	32	63	37
a bad thing	8	8	3	4	13	16	7	15
neither good nor bad	20	26	17	21	32	42	23	40
DK – no opinion (spontaneous)	8	8	10	3	9	10	8	8
Total	**100**	**100**	**100**	**100**	**101**	**100**	**101**	**100**

	Lithuania	Malta	Poland	Romania	Slovakia	Slovenia	Turkey
a good thing	65	51	61	74	59	58	67
a bad thing	9	19	7	2	5	7	11
neither good nor bad	23	24	23	15	30	33	14
DK – no opinion (spontaneous)	3	6	9	9	6	3	8
Total	**100**	**100**	**100**	**100**	**100**	**101**	**100**

Figure 5.47   Support for EU membership

CASE STUDY

Enlargement of the EU

The Eurobarometer Report produced by the European Commission and published in June 2003 said:

'Citizens in the 2004 member states (those about to join in 2004) are increasingly optimistic about the EU membership of their country, and are now much more supportive to each other's membership as well. But they have growing concerns if current member states are welcoming them in the Union.'

ACTIVITY

1 What reasons do you think are behind the increasing popularity of EU entry amongst the 2004 countries?

2 Why do you think the citizens of these countries might 'have growing concerns if current member states are welcoming them in the Union.' For what reasons might some EU members be unwelcoming of these new members?

Emerging markets

In recent years a number of countries have become more important in the area of world trade. These countries have made moves to becoming more market oriented and are expanding their manufacturing output significantly and quickly. The improved economies provide these nations with higher income levels, better health and social services, and more stable political structures. Examples of emerging market nations are China, Hong Kong and India, but there are many others. In Eastern Europe, Poland and Hungary have developed recently, in Latin America, Brazil and Mexico are

emerging whilst Africa contains a number of emerging nations such as Tanzania and Nigeria. As these nations become members of the World Trade Organisation, their activity in trading internationally begins to grow.

Emerging countries often receive a range of international financial support to help them to improve their economies, including loans from the International Monetary Fund and the World Bank or foreign aid from the richer nations. Special trading status and reduced tariffs may be offered to more advanced countries. A number of trading blocs have also been created, such as MERCOSUR, including Argentina, Brazil, Paraguay and Uruguay.

The emerging nations have seen significant increases in their trade in recent years. In 2003, the WTO World Trade Report reported the increases shown in Figures 5.48 and 5.49 in trade for 2002.

World average	4%
USA	−5%
Mexico	1%
MERCOSUR	1%
European Union	5%
Central/Eastern Europe	12%
Russian Federation	4%
Africa	1%
Japan	3%
Developing Asia	10%
China	22%

Figure 5.48   Percentage change in merchandise exports 2002

World average	5%
USA	3%
Mexico	0%
MERCOSUR	−13%
European Union	8%
Central/Eastern Europe	3%
Russian Federation	18%
Africa	−6%
Japan	2%
Developing Asia	6%
China	13%

Figure 5.49   Percentage change in service exports 2002

CASE STUDY

The *Daily Paper* – 4 November 2001

This week China became the latest nation to join the World Trade Organisation after fifteen years of trying to gain entry. The Chinese government yesterday predicted an average 5 per cent growth rate for China over the next five years, despite that fact that the world is going through a recession at the moment. Beijing now hopes to encourage Western businesses to invest billions of pounds into China. Whilst joining the 'WTO Club' gives the 140 members easier access to Chinese markets, it also brings with it the promise of increased export trade and investment for China. Some caution would be appropriate, however, as the economies of the emerging nations are volatile, and they therefore present both challenges and opportunities to global investors. Emerging markets are changing, and therefore they are subject to volatility in politics, industry, currency and share prices.

ACTIVITY

1 What sort of investment is the writer talking about when he says 'Beijing now hopes to encourage Western businesses to invest billions of pounds into China'?

2 To what extent do you consider this to be an opportunity for UK industry?

3 In what ways might it be a threat?

4 Draw up a strategy for a UK manufacturer to exploit the opportunities and limit the threats from this change.

This development presents a number of opportunities for companies, but also a number of threats as new trade competitors emerge. Nigeria, for example, needs to import items such as machinery, chemicals, transport equipment, food and manufactured goods. This represents a significant opportunity for exporters from the UK, although a number of other countries have also joined in,

notably France, Germany, China and the USA. At the same time, Nigeria is expanding its exports of petroleum, cocoa and rubber, and although these do not directly threaten exports from the UK, for other producers of similar products, the competition may not be so welcome. For UK importers the introduction of a new supplier in the market may enable them to obtain cheaper raw materials.

Cultural diversity and clusters

The economies of Europe

The economies of Europe are many and varied. Here are brief details of the European countries that are currently members of the European Union, followed by those that joined in 2004. Figures for 2002 are shown in Figure 5.50.

GDP	Growth	Inflation	Unemployment	Exports	Imports	Main export partners	Main import partners
Austria A well-developed market economy, a high standard of living, a high reliance on service industry (65 per cent), attractive to foreign investors.							
$226 billion	0.6%	1.8%	4.8%	$70 billion	$74 billion	EU 63%, Switzerland 5%, US 5%	EU 68%, US 6%, Switzerland 3%

Figure 5.50   Economic details of EU countries

GDP	Growth	Inflation	Unemployment	Exports	Imports	Main export partners	Main import partners
Belgium A modern private enterprise economy with a well-developed transport network. Belgium has few natural resources so imports many raw materials. Very dependent on service industry (74.3 per cent).							
$297.6 billion	0.6%	1.7%	7.2%	$162 billion	$152 billion	EU 73.3%, US 7.7%	EU 71.4%, US 6.3%
Denmark A modern market economy with high-tech agriculture, extensive government welfare measures and good living standards. Very dependent on service industry (71 per cent).							
$155.5 billion	1.8%	2.3%	5.1%	$56.3 billion	$47.9 billion	EU 64.7%, US 6.9%, Norway 5.5%	EU 69.9%, US 4.2%
Finland A highly industrialised, free-market economy. Very dependent on manufacturing especially engineering, telecommunications, and electronics industries.							
$136.2 billion	1.1%	1.9%	8.5%	$40.1 billion	$31.8 billion	Germany 12.4%, US 9.7%, UK 9.6%	Germany 14.5%, Sweden 10.2%, Russia 9.4%
France A modern economy that features extensive government ownership. High tax burden but excellent public health and welfare. Very dependent on service industry (71 per cent).							
$1.54 trillion	1.0%	1.8%	9.1%	$307.8 billion	$303.7 billion	EU 61.3%, US 8.7%	EU 58.6%, US 8.9%
Germany An affluent and technologically powerful economy for whom the modernisation and integration of the eastern German economy has been a costly long-term problem. Unemployment is a continuing problem. A 68 per cent dependence on service industry.							
$2.184 trillion	0.4%	1.3%	9.8%	$608 billion	$487.3 billion	France 11.1%, US 10.6%, UK 8.4%	France 9.4%, Netherlands 8.4%, US 8.3%
Greece A mixed capitalist economy with a strong public sector. Heavily dependent on tourism and agriculture, but has been growing faster than most EU economies thanks to EU aid.							
$201.1 billion	3.5%	3.6%	10.3%	$12.6 billion	$31.4 billion	EU 51.6%, US 5.7%	EU 66.2%
Ireland A small but modern economy with excellent growth rates in recent years. Agriculture and industry are very important sectors.							
$118.5 billion	5.2%	4.6%	4.3%	$86.6 billion	$48.6 billion	UK 23.9%, US 18.1%, Germany 7.2%	UK 35.9%, US 15.8%, Belgium 14.4%
Italy A capitalist economy that is industrial in the north and agricultural in the south. Unemployment is high but evenly spread. Most raw materials are imported.							
$1.438 trillion	0.4%	2.4%	9.1%	$259.2 billion	$238.2 billion	EU 53.8%, US 9.7%	EU 56.5%, US 4.9%

Figure 5.50   Economic details of EU countries (continued)

GDP	Growth	Inflation	Unemployment	Exports	Imports	Main export partners	Main import partners
Luxembourg A stable economy which enjoys high income levels and good growth. An important industrial sector and a growing financial sector.							
$20 billion	2.3%	1.6%	4.1%	$10.1 billion	$13.25 billion	EU 85.6%, US 2.6%	EU 78.6%, US 3.9%
Portugal Increasingly dependent upon services, but a poor educational system and poor productivity have hampered its growth.							
$182 billion	0.8%	3.7%	4.7%	$25.9 billion	$39 billion	EU 79.7%, US 5.8%	EU 74.2%, US 3.8%
Spain A mixed capitalist economy with high but falling unemployment. Strong tourist industry and agriculture.							
$828 billion	2.0%	3.0%	11.3%	$122.2 billion	$156.6 billion	EU 71.3%, Latin America 6.1%, US 4.4%	EU 63.9%, OPEC 7.3%, US 4.6%
Sweden Excellent standards of living with extensive welfare benefits. It has modern communications, and a skilled labour force. Low agricultural output, dependent on service industry.							
$227.4 billion	1.8%	2.2%	4.0%	$80.6 billion	$68.6 billion	EU 54.6% US 10.5%, Norway 8.6%	EU 66.3%, Norway 8.5%, US 6.7%
The Netherlands A prosperous economy, important for its transport links. A very productive agricultural sector, the country is very attractive to foreign investment.							
$434 billion	0.3%	3.4%	3.0%	$243.3 billion	$201.1 billion	EU 77.1%	EU 53.1%, US 8.7%
UK One of the four biggest economies of Western Europe, with an efficient agricultural sector producing about 60 per cent of food needs with only 1 per cent of the labour force. Heavily dependent on services, particularly financial services.							
$1.52 trillion	1.6%	2.1%	5.2%	$286.3 billion	$330.1 billion	EU 58.1%; US 15.4%	EU 51.7%; US 13.2%
Cyprus A wealthy nation but with varied growth rates as a result of political instability in the region and resultant fluctuations in tourist visitor numbers. Water shortages create regular problems and the economy is very dependent on agriculture and government services.							
Greek Cypriot area: $9.4 billion; Turkish Cypriot area: $787 million	Greek Cypriot area: 1.7%; Turkish Cypriot area: 2.6%	Greek Cypriot area: 2.8%; Turkish Cypriot area: 24.5%	Greek Cypriot area: 3.3%; Turkish Cypriot area: 5.6%	Greek Cypriot area: $1.03 billion; Turkish Cypriot area: $46 million	Greek Cypriot area: $3.9 billion; Turkish Cypriot area: $301 million	Greek Cypriot area: EU 36%; Russia 10%, Syria 7%; Turkish Cypriot area: Turkey 36.3%, UK 26.5%, Middle East 7.0%	Greek Cypriot area: EU 52%, US 10%; Turkish Cypriot area: Turkey 65.1%, UK 10.4%, other EU 13.4%

Figure 5.50   Economic details of EU countries (continued)

GDP	Growth	Inflation	Unemployment	Exports	Imports	Main Export Partners	Main Import Partners
Czech Republic A stable and prosperous state with good growth rates and an economy that is becoming attractive to foreign investment. Domestic demand is increasing, strong manufacturing and developing service industry.							
$155.9 billion	1.5%	0.6%	9.8%	$40.8 billion	$43.2 billion	Germany 35.4%, Slovakia 7.3%, UK 5.5%	Germany 32.9%, Slovakia 6.4%, Russia 6.0%
Estonia A newer country that is developing a modern market economy that is greatly influenced by the economies of its major trading partners, Finland, Sweden and Germany.							
$15.2 billion	4.4%	3.7%	12.4%	$3.4 billion	$4.4 billion	Finland 33.8%, Sweden 14%, Latvia 6.9%, Germany 6.9%	Finland 18%, Germany 11%, Sweden 9%, China 9%
Hungary A developing services sector has contributed to strong growth; the economy has a high degree of foreign ownership and investment.							
$134.7 billion	3.2%	5.3%	5.8%	$31.4 billion	$33.9 billion	Germany 34.9%, Austria 8.7%, Italy 5.9%, US 5.6%	Germany 26.4%, Italy 8.3%, Austria 7.9%, Russia 6.8%
Latvia A transitional economy that was heavily dependent on Russia. Many companies are now privatised, although the state still controls several large industries.							
$20 billion	4.5%	2.0%	7.6%	$2.3 billion	$3.9 billion	Germany 17%, UK 16%, Sweden 10%	Germany 17%, Russia 9%, Lithuania 8%
Lithuania Was very dependent on trade with Russia, high but improving unemployment. Domestic demand and investment are increasing and trade is gradually moving towards western Europe.							
$29.2 billion	6.7%	0.8%	12.5%	$5.4 billion	$6.8 billion	UK 13.8%, Latvia 12.6%, Germany 12.6%, Russia 11%	Russia 25.3%, Germany 17.2%, Poland 4.9%
Malta A developing economy that is dependent on foreign trade, manufacturing and tourism.							
$7 billion	2.2%	2.4%	7.0%	$2 billion	$2.8 billion	US 20.2%, Germany 14.1%, France 10.2%, UK 8.8%	Italy 19.9%, France 15.0%, US 11.6%, UK 10.0%

Figure 5.50   Economic details of EU countries (continued)

GDP	Growth	Inflation	Unemployment	Exports	Imports	Main Export Partners	Main Import Partners
Poland A large but inefficient agricultural sector, the country is going through extensive privatisation in preparation for EU membership.							
$368.1 billion	1.3%	1.9%	18.1%	$32.4 billion	$43.4 billion	Germany 34.3%, Italy 5.4%, France 5.4%	Germany 23.9%, Russia 8.8%, Italy 8.2%
Slovakia The country has been going through extensive privatisation and the banking sector is now almost completely in foreign hands. Foreign investment is expanding.							
$66 billion	4.0%	3.3%	17.2%	$12.9 billion	$15.4 billion	EU 59.9%, Czech Republic 16.6%	EU 49.8%, Czech Republic 15.1%, Russia 14.8%
Slovenia One of the more successful transition economies, privatisation has moved quickly and growth is accelerating, although inflation and unemployment remain problems.							
$36 billion	3.0%	7.4%	11.0%	$10.3 billion	$11.1 billion	Germany 26.0%, Italy 12.4%, Croatia 8.6%	Germany 19.6%, Italy 18.0%, France 10.8%

Source: CIA World Factbook 2003 www.cia.gov/cia/publications/factbook

Figure 5.50   Economic details of EU countries (continued)

ACTIVITY

Examine the facts presented about the major European economies above. Working with a partner and using Internet and library resources, expand on the detail given to get a wider picture of the economies.

We are moving towards greater European integration, but how similar are the economies of the EU?

1   Compare and contrast the economies. How similar are they? What are the major differences?

2   If there were ever to be a central European government, what problems might it face in setting policies suitable for all the EU nations?

3   Compare and contrast the existing EU economies with those joining in 2004. What challenges does this enlargement present for the economy of the EU?

European Monetary Union (EMU)

EMU refers to that section of the Maastricht Treaty which provides for the creation of a 'monetary union' between EU members. It was decided that individual currencies such as the pound, or the franc, the mark and the lira would, in effect, cease to exist and would be replaced by a single currency, known as the euro.

The single European currency

For the individual UK citizen this would mean that they could spend the domestic currency, the euro, in any other country in the EMU. In principle, it would therefore mean that people could move their personal assets – bank balances or other financial assets – much more easily from any part of the EMU to any other part (as they are, at present, able to do in the UK). Were Britain to join, from the monetary point of view transactions with citizens of other members of the EMU would be little different from transactions at present with other citizens of the UK. We do not think

321

of transactions across the borders of England, Scotland, Wales or Northern Ireland as in any way problematic. This would also be true of transactions with other European countries.

Trade and the SEC

For companies, such a development could be even more significant. International trade does not consist of large numbers of 'one-off' transactions. By and large it consists of well-established trading relationships between companies and individuals who know each other well and who have a substantial track record of mutually beneficial commercial transactions. Some of these take place between different sections of the same international organisation: Ford Motors in the UK trading with Ford Motors in Belgium, for instance. Very many of these relationships are enshrined in contracts which specify products, prices and conditions of supply months, and sometimes years, ahead. Such arrangements offer security of service and a guarantee of essential components some way into the future. The production process is planned some time in advance of intended delivery dates. Clearly it is advantageous to companies if prices are also negotiated in advance, in order to secure future supplies of components or finished goods at pre-determined prices.

Where the trade is conducted within a single country with a single currency, this presents little problem in principle. An agricultural co-operative in the Paris basin would not think twice about agreeing to purchase a Renault tractor from a local supplier in three months' time at a fixed price. They may, however, have cause to ponder about importing a tractor from a supplier in the UK at a fixed price in three months' time. For instance, between late August and late November in 1996, the value of the franc fell by over 15 per cent against the pound sterling. If the price had been agreed in advance in sterling the French co-operative would have paid in November at least 15 per cent more francs in exchange for the sterling required to purchase their British-made vehicle than they expected when they signed the contract in August 1996. Such movements were undoubtly significant in influencing France to join the euro.

In these circumstances, then, the exchange rate between currencies can play havoc with perfectly sound commercial calculations and can make international trading a hazardous business. Of course, companies try to build into their contracts safeguards against currency fluctuations, but no safeguard is foolproof or free of cost. Such fluctuations discourage medium- and long-term trading relationships and make longer-term commitments, such as major investment decisions across international boundaries, riskier than domestic investment. It is clear, therefore, that for individuals, firms and investors, currency fluctuations add uncertainty and cost to cross-border trade.

It is possible to reduce some of the uncertainty by establishing a fixed-parity exchange level between two or more currencies. In 1944, the Bretton Woods Agreement sought to establish a postwar system of fixed international rates of exchange in which currencies were permitted to float against each other only within narrow bands. The disadvantage of this scheme was that it could operate only if trade patterns were relatively stable and if international speculation in currencies was made extremely difficult. This was achieved by limiting capital transactions between currencies. In turn, this had the undesirable effect of restricting opportunities for real capital investment abroad.

The Exchange Rate Mechanism

The Community next attempted to create a similar system in the form of the ERM, the **Exchange Rate Mechanism**. This mechanism was designed to restrict currency fluctuations between European currencies by establishing large gold and foreign-currency reserves which the central banks of Europe could use collaboratively to stem a 'run' on any currency: in effect preventing speculators from causing large short-term swings in the value of any particular currency. However, the events leading to the departure of the pound sterling from the mechanism (when Chancellor Norman Lamont took the pound out of the ERM after failing to stem speculation by changing the bank rate several times in the course of one afternoon) make it clear that, even with substantial resources, substantial inter-bank co-operation and the willingness to take drastic action, speculators will not be discouraged if they feel that they have a 'killing' to make by continuing to sell any particular currency.

The advantage of a common currency across Europe, as opposed simply to an exchange rate mechanism, is that if one currency prevails there is no opportunity for international speculation against those member states which share the same currency. This would produce as much medium- or long-term certainty regarding impending price fluctuations as would be true of domestic trade. Thus an important element of risk would be eliminated from cross-border trade. Moreover, costs of international financial transactions should be substantially reduced, since all would be conducted in a single currency, obviating exchange commission charges by banks.

However, there are disadvantages to a single currency, which are highlighted in the case study below.

Arguments for the euro

- A fixed exchange rate will end currency instability in Europe.
- It will make it much easier for firms to trade across Europe, opening up new markets for UK firms.
- It will be substantially easier for travellers from the UK to Europe, there would be no need to exchange currencies prior to travelling.
- Firms would avoid the costs of exchanging currencies when buying and selling with Europe. This could encourage additional trade.
- The exchange risk would be eliminated. Sometimes a firm agrees a deal, but by the time payment for the sale is made the exchange rate changes making the deal much less profitable. This danger would be eliminated under the euro and therefore more trade should take place. Exchange risk is one of the main deterrents to trade with Europe.
- It will create price transparency, that is, it will be simple to compare prices for the same products from different countries. This should increase competition and improve prices for consumers.
- Joining the ERM will mean that the UK would adopt the same interest rate as the rest of Europe.

This lower rate would reduce mortgage and loan prices encouraging more borrowing and growth in sales.

CASE STUDY

The Referendum Party manifesto

The following are edited extracts from the general election manifesto of the former Referendum Party, set up by the late Sir James Goldsmith, a prominent businessman with extensive European financial interests.

'Britain could be on the brink of surrendering all its powers to determine interest rates, the rate of inflation, levels of unemployment and the rate of growth. That is what will happen if the government of the day commits the country to monetary union. The European Central Bank [ECB] would take over these responsibilities in 1999.

'Sterling would be irrevocably fixed to the euro, and Europe's new synthetic currency would take over from national currencies ... The Treasury and the Bank of England will lose virtually all their powers over monetary policy. The Bank will be a sort of agent – an errand boy – for the ECB ... The ECB will control interest rates and credit throughout all participating countries. The same for all. It does not matter whether one country is suffering from a long slump and another is feeling the heat of incipient inflation; all and every one must be given the same medicine under the ECB.

'Monetary union is seen as the lynchpin of this greater union centred around Germany. The concentration of monetary power spawns the concentration of budgetary and political power, and ultimately of security and foreign policy.'

ACTIVITY

1   What do you see as being the main points of criticism of the single currency by the Referendum Party?

2   How valid are these criticisms?

- Unstable markets have caused economic crises in the past, forcing governments to choose between high interest rates (leading to unemployment) and currency devaluation (leading to high inflation).
- Low interest rates and a fixed exchange rate will encourage more progressive and long-term government domestic policies, and boost trade and investment.
- No one member of the EU will be able to dictate monetary policy.
- The euro should be strong enough to compete against the dollar and the yen on world markets.
- The extra trade encouraged by the euro should create new jobs in the UK as more workers are required to meet the extra demand.
- It will improve relationships with the rest of Europe.

Arguments against the euro

- National governments will have less control over monetary policy. Effectively the UK would lose the ability to alter interest rates to affect monetary policy to the benefit of the UK economy. It has taken 20 years of tight monetary policy to deliver a UK economy with low inflation and steady growth. Do we really want to lose the control that has been instrumental in delivering those sound economic conditions?
- The European Central Bank would set an interest rate to cover the whole of Europe. It is difficult to imagine a rate that would deliver the right economic conditions for the variety of different economies in the UK. What might be right for Germany could be a major problem for Greece. Ireland have found this very problem; since joining the euro their inflation has risen but they are

powerless to control this using interest rates. This problem would be exacerbated if some of the 2004 new members eventually join the euro.

- Losing the pound is a loss of heritage for the UK.
- If we join when the exchange rate for the pound is high, we will be locked into a situation of expensive imports and cheap exports. It would take a long period of cost reductions to make up for such a trap.
- The cost of converting computer systems and cash registers is enormous, and this cost would have to be borne by industry. Marks & Spencer estimated the cost to be over £100 million for their company alone.
- Global economic shocks are likely to affect member states in different ways.
- Unemployment could increase, at least in the short term, if a government comes under pressure to cut public expenditure owing to restrictions relating to the requirement to limit its deficit.
- Critics fear that the German central bank (the Bundesbank) will dominate proceedings.
- The European Monetary Institute and European Central Bank might not look beyond the issue of price stability and might ignore the knock-on social and political effects of monetary policy.

The birth of the euro

On 1 January 1999, eleven sovereign nations finally handed over control of their currencies to a committee of bankers. The meeting took less than 30 minutes. Five hundred blue balloons were released into the sky over Brussels. The euro, the world's newest, least visible and second-most important currency was born (weighing in at slightly more than a dollar or just over 70 pence). Britain was the only EU member declining to join.

It took a little time for the notes and coins to appear, and many of the countries ran parallel systems for a short while, but now the old European currencies have gone; the franc, the lira, the mark, and so on are all relics of the past. All decisions affecting the euro, on interest rates or monetary flows, are now taken by the European Central Bank in Frankfurt. Jacques Santer, the European Commission President at the birth of the euro, stated, 'Europe can speak with a single voice. It is now up to us to proceed. We embark on the next stage leading to political unity, which I think is a direct consequence of economic unity, so Europe can play a leading role on the international stage, even including a common defence policy.'

This goes well beyond the introduction merely of the euro; it heralds a new departure for Europe. The creation of the single European currency will progressively demand more co-operation on the big economic and political decisions affecting everything from public spending to unemployment and, up to a point, taxes. In turn, this will demand more direct democratic control of decision making in Brussels, which would itself be a federalising influence: another step towards some form of 'European government', however loosely drawn.

The EEC/EC/EU has always proceeded in this way. It sets ambitious but abstract economic targets: the common market, the single market, now the single currency. The often unseemly struggle to achieve these targets, and make them stick, forces member states to draw closer and closer together politically.

The performance of the euro

The European Central Bank had (and still has) high hopes for the performance of the euro. It was hoped that it would quickly establish itself as a **reserve currency**. A reserve currency is a national currency used by many countries to settle debit balances in their international accounts. Central banks generally hold a large portion of their monetary reserves in reserve currencies as they are generally regarded as safe stores of value because they are in demand. The US dollar and pound sterling are two of the oldest and most trusted reserve currencies. It was hoped that the euro would strengthen in value and take its place amongst the group of reserve currencies.

On the day of launch the euro was valued at about 71p or US$1.2. Within days it was falling in value, and the fall became a rapid one. In little over a year it lost 20 per cent of its value against sterling and over 30 per cent of its value against the US dollar. Panic began to set in. For companies in countries such as Germany and France which had been used to trading using

Figure 5.51   Currency values, euro vs sterling

Figure 5.52   Currency values, euro vs US dollar
Images from www.timesonline.co.uk

strong currencies, this was a real blow. Imports from the USA were costing 30 per cent more, and from the UK they were 20 per cent more expensive. The problem was simply a lack of demand; people and companies were not using the euro in the quantities expected, and investors did not have sufficient faith in it to buy it as a store of value. The launch of the euro also coincided with a downturn in economic growth in Europe and improved prospects for the US economy, which also helped to reduce demand for the euro.

By autumn 2000, the European Central Bank felt that it could no longer allow the euro to continue its slide in value, fearing real economic turmoil induced by the deflating currency. It decided to act in two ways:

♦ By buying euros to stimulate demand for them and push up the value (this was done in conjunction with the other central banks in the G7 countries). Whilst this did bring about a temporary recovery in the value of the euro, when the Central Bank buying stopped, so did the climb in value, so the cure was very short term indeed.

♦ By increasing interest rates for the Eurozone countries. High interest rates tend to attract foreign investment, and this in turn should create a demand for the currency used in that country. An investor from Japan, say, who wished to invest in Europe would need to sell Japanese yen and buy euros, thus creating a demand for euros. If there is sufficient demand for euros from investors, the value of the currency should rise. Between 5 November 1999 and 6 October 2000, the ECB raised interest rates seven times. Whilst this did go some way to stopping the slide in the value of the euro, it did not increase its value significantly, and the euro remained at a value of between 60p and 64p until the end of 2002.

However, during 2003, the euro finally began to gain some value against both the US dollar and sterling. By summer 2003 it was exchanging for about 73p sterling and nearly US $1.2 as the performance of the Euroland economies has improved. So, perhaps now, four years after its inception, the euro is finally establishing itself as a good store of value and a currency of choice in international trading.

Today the UK remains on the sidelines with regard to euro membership; the government seems to be quite divided over the merits of the euro, whilst the general public in the UK seems to be basically sceptical over the benefits to be had. As more UK citizens travel to the continent and use the euro, we may see a softening of this scepticism, particularly amongst those who travel between European countries and experience the convenience of not having to change currencies. The UK government has promised a referendum on the subject before we ever join, but even that does not seem to be imminent. The latest predictions were that it would be unlikely to happen before 2005.

The pro-euro lobby was given a substantial blow in September 2003 when Sweden had a referendum over joining the euro. The result was a surprising 56 per cent against joining the euro, which was a major setback to the Swedish government which had been keen to join. It seems unlikely that Sweden will join now for at least the next ten years.

2002: Year of the euro?

JOURNAL ARTICLE

Since January 2002 the single currency has been operating in the EU, so we now are in a position to make some judgements about how successful this period has been and to draw some lessons from our first two years of exposure to this new currency. How has it affected the different members of the Eurozone?

You should investigate this topic further by referring to the *British Economy Survey*, Volume 31, Number 2, Spring 2002, Section 4. The article '2002: Year of the euro' by Peter Howells provides more information.

The EU budget

The budget of the European Union is relatively small at around 93 billion euros, which is only approximately 1.1 per cent of the combined GDPs of the member countries. The largest share of the budget goes on the **Common Agricultural Policy** (CAP), followed by regional and restructuring policies. The Germans are the largest contributors to the budget of the EU (in recent years they have wanted to see this burden reduced).

The budget must, year on year, be substantially in balance. In 1985–86 the budget was in substantial deficit, which led to reform, particularly of the common agricultural policy which was limited to 75 per cent of the growth of the overall budget, and the setting of four-yearly targets with annual reviews.

In the mid-1980s Margaret Thatcher argued very aggressively the case for reducing the UK's contribution to the budget. It was argued that the UK contributed a disproportionate amount compared with, for example, France which, despite being an 'industrialised nation', was a net beneficiary of the CAP. This was the source of an on-going rebate won by the Conservatives. However, the rebate has been called into question.

The biggest difficulty over the budget is that it is a 'zerosum' game: if one country pays less, another must pay more. Any attempt to increase the budget of the EU will therefore inevitably lead to increased bickering between nations.

Import duties and levies

The development of an economic community can be seen as involving a number of steps with each step leading to closer co-operation. The early stages of creating the EEC (European Economic Community) were in large measure concerned with breaking down import duties and levies, which were concerned with cross-border trade within the EU, and the creation of a common external tariff between the EU and the rest of the world.

Free trade

Developing a free trade area involved getting rid of some of the barriers to free trade. In particular, it involved the removal of quotas and tariffs between members of the trading community.

Customs union

In 1986, the Community created a customs union with moves towards positive integration of economies. In addition to the free trade area, member states operated a common external tariff. This meant that an import from a non-member country (such as Canada) would carry the same tariff whether it entered France, Germany, Italy or any other member state. Within the customs union the member states developed common trading policies and moved towards equal conditions for individuals, firms and groupings operating within the union.

Common market

The creation of a common market took the integration process a step further. A common market involves the

free movement of factors of production (land, labour, capital and enterprise) and the free movement of goods. Over the years we have seen a harmonisation of policies designed to create freedom of movement. The Single European Act 1986 highlighted what are known as the four freedoms:

- Freedom of movement of services
- Freedom of movement of capital
- Freedom of movement of goods
- Freedom of movement of people.

Economic and monetary union

As we have seen earlier in this chapter, economic and monetary union is becoming a reality with the creation of a single European currency and a Central European Bank in Frankfurt. To create EMU the participating countries progressively brought their economies into line, reducing their inflation rates and interest rates below a given figure, limiting the size of central government budget deficits and so on. Once these were in line (the theory ran) then the economies could be run more or less as a single entity through a central banking institution.

Full integration

Full integration still remains for the future and will depend on greater political cohesion. Economic policies on, for example, taxation and spending would be determined by EU institutions. We will see whether this will happen, but probably not for quite a long time.

Agricultural import levies

The Treaty of Rome and ensuing legislation and policies from the EU guaranteed incomes to farmers by setting prices for agricultural products. These minimum prices set out to ensure that farmers earn enough to keep farming. The price that the Common Agricultural Policy (CAP) guarantees will normally be higher than the free market price. The CAP is discussed further later.

EU producers are also protected from cheaper imported foodstuffs from the non-EU countries (such as American cereals). Imported non-EU foodstuffs can be sold only at a threshold price. Import taxes (tariffs) are placed on these imports to bring them up to this threshold price. The effect of this important policy is to make EU foodstuffs more competitive within the internal market.

The result of guaranteeing farmers minimum prices is that more goods are provided than can be sold as supply exceeds demand. This is a very wasteful policy as the surplus has to be stored, at an additional cost.

In recent years some of the worst excesses of these protectionist policies have been cut back, particularly as a result of greater co-operation in the world resulting from the creation of the World Trade Organisation which seeks to cut back on international restrictions on trade through co-operative actions between countries.

Value-added tax (VAT)

In order to come into line with the European Community, the UK had to abandon its former expenditure tax ('purchase tax') to introduce a system of value-added tax. VAT, as the name suggests, is levied on the value added in the production process by a firm. Typically a firm buys in inputs from another firm, adds value to these inputs, and then sells on its final products (either to another producer or an end consumer). For example, in a given month a jeans manufacturer may buy in £100,000 worth of material for processing into jeans. At the end of the month the firm may be able to sell the jeans on to retailers for £250,000. The firm has therefore added £150,000 of value, a sum that is taxed at the current rate. Today most products that consumers buy have a VAT element, although there are some exceptions such as children's clothes and other necessary items (strictly, they carry a VAT rate of zero per cent).

Tax harmonisation

In recent years increasing pressure has built up for the greater equality of tax systems within the European Union in order to create a level playing field for competition between firms, as well as helping to harmonise social policies. As long ago as July 1987 when the Single European Act was passed, reference

was made to tax harmonisation. Five priorities were listed:

♦ to create a uniform VAT basis
♦ to bring excise rates closer together
♦ harmonisation of taxation which directly affects capital movements
♦ harmonisation of company taxation
♦ extending duty-free concessions throughout the EU (this has now been abolished).

In 1999, Oscar Lafontaine, the newly appointed German finance minister, thrust tax harmonisation to the top of the agenda, supported by the new German premier, Gerhard Schroeder. He called for the rapid harmonisation of tax rates throughout the EU. However, Lafontaine resigned his position later owing to differing opinions on policy.

In recent times tax harmonisation has taken a back seat within the European Union. There appears to be a recognition now that full harmonisation is not necessary. In 2000 the European Commission produced a paper called 'Tax Policy in the European Union' which stated, 'The European Union plays only a subsidiary role on taxes and social security contributions. Its aim is not to standardise the national systems of compulsory taxes and contributions but simply to ensure that they are compatible not only with each other but also with the aims of the Treaty establishing the European Community.'

Therefore fairness in taxation appears to be the new goal, rather than all countries charging precisely the same rates.

The Common Agricultural Policy (CAP)

The main purpose of the Common Agricultural Policy has been to guarantee future supplies of food in Europe. The experience of rural decay during the inter-war period, and food shortages during the Second World War (caused by the strategic interruption of food imports to Europe), prompted the European leaders in the postwar era to make plans for the revival and modernisation of the agricultural industry. The intention of the CAP was therefore to make Europe self-sufficient in the production of its own food and non-reliant on the importation of food from countries outside the EU. The CAP was adopted by the Community in the 1960s in order to realise those intentions.

The main objectives of the policy were:

- to keep people on the land to ensure a viable agricultural sector
- to prevent rural decay
- to ensure reasonable incomes for farmers
- to modernise the agricultural industry and make it more efficient.

In simple terms, the policy was intended to work on the two-fold principle of:

- subsidising farmers, and
- protecting the price of their produce within the common market from directly competitive exposure to lower 'world prices', such as those maintained outside of the common market.

Protecting the farmers

The CAP enabled farmers to keep the price of their produce in the single market artificially higher than the price outside (that is, the flat price paid in the rest of the world: the 'world price'). This was achieved by placing an import tax on all cheaper foodstuffs entering the common market. This created a 'threshold price': the import tax effectively raises the price of cheaper imports up to the same level as that of the common market (and often higher).

Subsidising farmers

The farmers have been subsidised by EU citizens and consumers who pay an artificially high price for their food products. They are also subsidised by the member states, who pay large sums of money to the community budget so that the EU can guarantee a market for their produce. When farmers produce too many goods for the market, the EU buys up the surplus and stores it (hence the notorious 'wine lakes' and 'butter mountains' that used to be in the news so often). This ensured a stable price for foodstuffs and a good income for farmers.

Many people have felt that the CAP has been ripe for reform for some time. In 1999 it still took 50 per cent of all EU spending. In 1997, Agenda 2000 was presented by the European Commission.

This included proposals for reforming the CAP, bearing in mind past experiences, international trends, enlargement of the EU and the budgetary controls affecting member states. Agenda 2000 comprised essentially the farm and financial reforms needed to prepare for the EU's eastward enlargement.

Although there have been criticisms of the CAP over the years, the EU has been working hard to reform the policy to make it more workable. These reforms will need to continue as the EU prepares for enlargement in 2004 when ten new member states will be joining the policy. The World Trade Organisation has also put pressure on the EU to reform the policy in order to tackle the distortions to world trade caused by the policy's restrictions and export subsidies.

The emphasis of the policy is shifting somewhat, so that rural development is becoming a major priority in order to achieve sustainable agriculture and preserve the environment. The CAP no longer aims just to support farmers financially, it now focuses on food quality, preserving the environment and animal welfare, landscapes, cultural heritage and social balance and fairness.

Reform of the CAP began in 1992 and since then guaranteed prices of beef, dairy and cereals have been cut and by 2006 the cost of supporting arable crops, beef and dairy production will have fallen from €34 billion in 2000 to €14 billion. The 'mountains' of surplus products that brought the CAP into such disrepute have become much less of a problem, and imports from developing countries have been substantially increased. Export subsidies have also been severely reduced.

The CAP is one of the key benefits for the countries planning to join the EU in 2004. It will benefit their farmers in several ways:

- they will have access to an EU market of 500 million consumers
- they should receive better prices for their products and access to the CAP support mechanisms
- they will be supported with their rural development policies.

CASE STUDY

Update on the Common Agricultural Policy

In June 2003 European agriculture ministers finally agreed reforms to the CAP that would guarantee farmers' subsidies until at least 2013, as long as they work to produce better food quality and provide greater environmental care. This means that farmers will no longer qualify for subsidies according to the quantity of food that they produce, and Margaret Beckett, the Agriculture Secretary, said she would decouple all English farmers' subsidies from January 2004. The agreement will require farmers to keep their land in 'agricultural order', for which they will be paid a fixed, single farm payment no matter how much or how little food they produce.

Farms that continue to produce food will have to meet 18 'cross-compliance' requirements on environmental, animal welfare and food quality standards to receive their payment. Mrs Beckett said that by removing the link between farm subsidies and quantity of food production, farmers would be able to 'produce for the market, not the subsidy'. The new agreement should also satisfy the World Trade Organisation as they have demanded that the EU end its trade-distorting subsidies.

Countries will be able to retain 25 per cent of cereal production subsidies and the new agreement also gives some limited control over subsidies for the production of cattle and sheep. Up to 10 per cent of CAP payments will also be used to encourage farming in less favoured areas.

Not everyone was happy about the new agreement though. French farmers, the largest beneficiaries of CAP payments, were very concerned about their futures.

ACTIVITY

1 Explain the phrase 'farmers would be able to "produce for the market, not the subsidy"'.

2 Explain the phrase 'The new agreement should also satisfy the World Trade Organisation as they have demanded that the EU end its trade-distorting subsidies.'

3 What do you think is the logic behind subsidising farms that no longer produce food?

Regional policy

Jacques Delors, who was a major figure as EU president until 1994, set out the Delors proposals covering the period 1987–97. These have since been extended by Jacques Santer to the year 2007.

The emphasis in these proposals was on moving the union towards economic and social cohesion. The Delors proposals recognised that the growth of free trade in the internal market of the union would not lead to benefits for all regions. Therefore it was essential to provide assistance and support for economically backward and declining regions. Economic and social cohesion policies set out to make sure that the less-favoured regions also benefit from the advantages of free trade among the member states. The Delors package therefore set out to double the money available for restructuring policies.

Between 1987 and 1992 the proportion of the EU budget allocated to structural funds increased from 17 to 27 per cent, and today this is nearer 30 per cent. Europe certainly has plenty of poor regions, from the eastern Lander of Germany to southern Italy to the Scottish Highlands, and it acquired more with the enlargement that happened in 2004. There seems to be evidence that the EU's regional policy is having a positive effect on the less prosperous regions of the Union. Between 1988 and 1998 the average GDP in the least prosperous member states rose from 67.6 per cent of the EU average to 78.8 per cent. Ireland has done particularly well. In 1973 when it joined the EU, its GDP was 63.8 per cent of the EU average, but by 2002 it had increased to around 107 per cent.

Disadvantaged regions

The EU is made up of an advantaged 'core' and a disadvantaged 'periphery'. The 'depressed south' is the most serious regional problem facing the EU at present. The European Commission identifies a number of types of 'disadvantaged' regions. These are as follows.

Lagging regions

These have never really started to develop. There are a number of such regions in the Mediterranean zone with poor communications, low-output agriculture and very low incomes for many people.

Declining industrial regions

These are areas in which industry was once important but has now gone into decline, such as the north-west of England and parts of South Wales.

Peripheral regions

These are areas far from the centre of large markets (such as the Highlands and Islands of Scotland, Ireland and Sicily).

Border regions

In the past a number of border regions were favoured because of the services they offered (such as warehousing for goods being traded between countries). With the lifting of border restrictions these areas now require assistance.

Urban problem areas

The big cities of Europe, such as Paris, Lyons and London, have particular social problems associated with crime, congestion, drugs, pollution, and so on.

Rural problem areas

Some areas with poor climates for farming have particular problems. These areas have been adversely affected by reductions in subsidies to agriculture. The EU has a number of structural funds which provide help and support to these areas; for example, there are projects in declining coal and steel communities, helping with assistance and training schemes to deal with long-term unemployed, the promotion of development schemes in rural and lagging areas, and increased employment help for young people.

Social policy funding

Funds are channelled to the poorer nations of the community: Ireland, Portugal, Greece and Spain particularly for developing infrastructure such as transport and communications systems, and for training projects. The Delors proposals have been behind the on-going increase in the proportion of money spent on regional support.

Policy is built on the following **structural funds**:

♦ the European Regional Development Fund
♦ the European Social Fund
♦ the Guidance Section of the Common Agricultural Policy's Guidance and Guarantee Fund
♦ the Financial Instrument for Fisheries Guidance
♦ the Cohesion Fund (finances transport and environment infrastructure in member states with a GDP less than 90 per cent of the Union average, that is, Greece, Ireland, Spain and Portugal).

The funds concentrate on three **objectives**:

♦ Objective 1: Seventy per cent of funding goes to improving basic infrastructure and encouraging business investment in the bottom 50 regions of the EU.
♦ Objective 2: To assist economic and social conversion in areas experiencing structural difficulties, such as transport or telecommunications.
♦ Objective 3: Funding also goes towards the modernisation of education and training systems.

There are also four **community initiatives** spending money on:

♦ cross-border and inter-regional co-operation
♦ sustainable development of cities and declining urban areas
♦ rural development
♦ combating inequalities and discrimination in access to the labour market.

Enlargement of the Union poses particular problems for the EU regional policy since the countries joining live in regions of low GDP. Therefore the Union has created specific schemes for the period 2000–2006 to help the new countries prepare for EU membership.

End of unit assignment

You will need to investigate a company, ideally in your local area so that you can visit and interview staff members. Alternatively it could be a company that can supply you with plenty of information by post or perhaps via their website. The company should not be a multinational but may already have some involvement in selling abroad. For the purposes of this assignment, you are to assume that you work in the marketing department of your chosen company, and the Marketing Director is Ms Diana Dooley.

Outcome 1

Ms Dooley has asked you to prepare some notes for inclusion in the next Annual Report and Accounts of your company. Your notes should be detailed, in a suitable format for an Annual Report and Accounts (you may need to look at some to give you ideas for presenting this information), and should cover the following areas:

♦ Identify the mission, values and objectives of your selected organisation.
♦ Identify the stakeholders for your chosen business. Explain what makes them stakeholders and analyse any potential conflicts between those stakeholders.
♦ Evaluate the extent to which your chosen organisation achieves the objectives of each of the stakeholders that you have identified.

♦ Explain the responsibilities of your organisation and the strategies it employs to meet them.

Outcome 2

The directors are pleased with your notes for inclusion in the Annual Report and Accounts and consequently Ms Dooley has asked you to help her prepare for a speech that she needs to give at the next annual conference. She has been asked to talk about the influence of the macro-economic environment on your company and she asks you to prepare a set of notes that she can use to prepare that speech.

You should examine the following policy measures, explain the major changes in each in the last five years and examine the effects these changes have had on your chosen company and each of the stakeholders in your company:

♦ fiscal policy
♦ monetary policy
♦ industrial policy
♦ social welfare policy
♦ policies to encourage economic growth
♦ private finance initiatives.

Explain how different economic systems attempt to allocate and make effective use of resources. Outline the economic system in the UK and contrast this with at least one other nation.

Outcome 3

The Marketing Department is preparing for its annual team conference and you are helping the Marketing Director to prepare for sessions to be run during the day. She has asked you to write a formal business report to her.

1 Explain what perfect competition is and how and why real markets tend to deviate from this ideal. Give examples of the different competitive market types and describe the market in which your chosen company operates. Illustrate the degree of competition in your chosen company's market.

2 Using market statistics, examine how demand for the products or services produced by your chosen

company have changed in recent years. Use a series of demand and supply graphs to illustrate these changes. Ensure that these are fully annotated with accurate descriptions and explanations of the shifts of curves and changes in equilibrium shown. You should illustrate changes in both demand and supply curves in your answer.

3   Give a detailed description of the price and non-price competition strategies used by your chosen company. Analyse the successfulness of these strategies and make your own recommendations for possible future strategies. You should justify in detail your chosen methods.

4   Evaluate the role of the Competition Commission and the other regulatory bodies. Explain what they do and why they are necessary. Illustrate your evaluation by using real examples. Outline steps your chosen company will need to take to ensure that it does not infringe competition rules and law.

Outcome 4

Your chosen company is planning to expand into new foreign markets. Ms Dooley has asked you to prepare and deliver a presentation to the Board of Directors of the firm outlining the following points:

♦   The importance of international trade, economic integration and global markets to UK business organisations and to your chosen business in particular.
♦   An analysis of the impact of two recent policies of the European Union on your chosen organisation.
♦   An analysis of the economic implications for the UK and for your chosen company in particular of entry into EMU. Explain whether you feel this would be beneficial to your company when selling abroad.

References

Koch, R. (1995) *The Financial Times Guide to Strategy,* London: Financial Times/Pitman.

Ricardo, D. (1817) *On The Principles of Political Economy and Taxation.*

Thompson, J. (1990) *Strategic Management,* Norwell MA: Chapman and Hall.

Further reading

Economics Today, Economics Today Ltd, published Quarterly

Dransfield, R. and Dransfield, D. (2002) *Economics Made Easy,* Cheltenham: Nelson Thornes.

Hill, B. (1991) *The European Community, Studies in the UK Economy,* Oxford: Heinemann.

Grant, S. (1999) *Economic Growth and Business Cycles, Studies in the UK Economy,* Oxford: Heinemann.

Smith, D. (1999) *UK Current Economic Policy,* 4th edn, *Studies in the UK Economy,* Oxford: Heinemann.

Russell, M. and Heathfield, D. F. (1999) *Inflation and UK Monetary Policy,* 3rd edn, *Studies in the UK Economy,* Oxford: Heinemann.

Maunder, P., Myers, D., Wall, N. and Miller, R.L. (2000) *Economics Explained,* 3rd edn, London: Collins.

Sloman, J. (2002) *Economics,* New Jersey: Prentice Hall.

Useful websites

www.ukonline.gov.uk
This is the UK government's main website. It has links to all of the government departments and organisations. A very comprehensive and up-to-date resource.

www.telegraph.co.uk
In the author's opinion, this is the best on-line newspaper, simply because of the extremely powerful search facility which allows you to search 5 years of back issues free. A fantastic source of up-to-date news material.

www.statistics.gov.uk
One of this author's most visited sites. All the latest statistics affecting people and businesses in the UK.

http://www.europa.eu.int/index_en.htm
This is the main website for the European Union and contains links to all EU organisations and activities.

www.economist.com
This is a site requiring the payment of a subscription, but it is well worth it. If you are lucky, your college or university will have paid already and you will be able to access it from the library.

www.bized.ac.uk/
A useful set of resources written by academics concerning many business topics. There is a very interesting UK economy simulation on this site.

www.bized.ac.uk/stafsup/options/aec/resource.htm
You can search back issues of *Economic Review and Economics Today* at this address. Part of the Biz Ed site.

www.bankofengland.co.uk/geninfo1.htm
The Bank of England's explanations of monetary policy. A very readable summary.

www.tradepartners.gov.uk
A UK government site offering free information to potential exporters.

www.oft.gov.uk/
The latest news from the Office of Fair Trading. A good way of keeping up to date on competition matters.

www.cia.gov/cia/publications/factbook
A mine of statistics and information about every country in the world.

www.objectivetwo.co.uk
This site allows you to check to see whether a postcode is in an eligible or transitional ERDF Objective 2 ward area.

www.disability.gov.uk
A UK government site focusing on the rights of and issues surrounding disabled people.

www.hse.gov.uk
The Health and Safety Executive. Comprehensive information about health and safety matters in the workplace.

www.environment-agency.gov.uk
Full details of the activities of the Environment Agency and the responsibilities of companies for environmental protection.

www.cbi.org.uk
The main site for the Confederation of British Industry.

www.tuc.org.uk
The main site for the Trades Union Congress.

Unit 6

Foundations of finance and managing financial decisions

This unit introduces the major sources of finance available to new and existing businesses in the UK, and considers the implications of finance as a resource within a business. It explains the purpose of the main financial statements and describes their composition, showing how the information they contain is used to evaluate and analyse the financial performance of business. Finally, it examines the role of financial information in management decision making.

Summary of learning outcomes

On completion of this unit you will be able to:

♦ identify the major sources of finance available to business
♦ select appropriate sources of finance for a business project
♦ assess the implications of different sources of finance
♦ assess and compare the costs of different sources of finance
♦ explain the importance of financial planning and the flow of financial resources
♦ explain the importance and use of financial information for decision-making purposes and identify the information needs of different decision makers
♦ describe the impact of finance on the financial statements with reference to assets, liabilities and ownership capital
♦ explain the main financial statements, their purpose and use
♦ analyse financial performance using relevant accounting ratios
♦ make comparisons between two different businesses and compare their results to industry standards
♦ make appropriate pricing decisions for businesses
♦ use investment and project appraisal techniques to assess the viability of a project.

Chapter 1

Sources of finance

New and established businesses

A lot of people are interested in working for themselves, where they have control over their working environment and can determine their own destiny. The attractions of being a business owner include the motivation and self-fulfilment of being successful as well as the financial rewards of the profits going to the owners. However, one of the difficulties of starting a new business is to raise the necessary finance to fund the essential assets. All new businesses need **capital** to fund **fixed assets** such as vehicles, equipment, premises, and stock if the business is selling goods. However, financial institutions are often reluctant to lend to new businesses because of the high risks of such borrowers not being able to repay.

Once a business is well established and successful, obtaining further funds becomes easier as this successful track record means potential investors and lenders will be keen to support the growth and development of such entities. Dysons PLC is a company which is one of the leaders in the vacuum-cleaner market. It has also branched out into other products. The founder of this company is an inventor who revolutionised the domestic cleaner with bagless technology which led to improved suction and cleaning power. The developments made by Dyson PLC have now been copied by the big competitors in this field, such as Hoover and Electrolux. However, the founder of Dyson PLC could not obtain financial support for his venture which has now proved to be a phenomenal success and made him a multi-millionaire.

It is not a difficult process to find out the sources of a business's funds. The balance sheet of a PLC, for example, will show a section titled 'Capital and Reserves' which will indicate the extent of owner capital and the section titled 'Creditors: amounts due after more than one year' will give details of long-term lenders.

Financial institutions

Financial markets provide the link between those people and organisations which have spare funds and those that require funds. The financial institutions, such as banks, finance houses and discount houses, are the financial intermediaries which provide the link between the borrowers and lenders. They are effectively selling the public financial products such as pension plans, saving schemes, assurance policies and unit trusts to attract the funds which will then be invested to accommodate the appropriate levels of financial return, risk and liquidity.

The **financial return** is the compensation for giving up the use of money and it could be in the form of interest, dividends, discounts on short-term securities or even an increase in the value of the investment. The **risk** refers to the degree of uncertainty of the income being paid and the capital figure being repaid.

Liquidity refers to the extent to which an investment can be turned back into cash. The investor wants to achieve a high return with low risk and high levels of liquidity, but these attributes of an investment are not compatible. For example, a high return could be obtained by investing in the ordinary shares of a quoted company such as Microsoft or EasyJet. However, there is also high risk as the company may perform badly and not pay any dividends, or worse, fail altogether and the capital invested will be lost, as happened with Marconi and Enron. By investing in a quoted company the investment is highly liquid because it can quickly be turned back into cash. Depositing money in a bank on a term deposit is relatively risk free but will have a lower return and less liquidity. Having a bank deposit with immediate access has high liquidity but will command a lower rate of interest.

Main sources of finance

Funds for financing a business come in many forms and guises. A sensible way to differentiate between such sources is by the length of time such funds are available and the terms and conditions for repayment if relevant. Figure 6.1 summarises this approach.

Permanent capital

This is capital which will remain in a business as long as it remains in operation and thus never has to be repaid if the business is a 'going concern'. A **going concern** means the business has a long-term future and will be able to meet its commitments as they become due. It is illegal for a business to continue trading if it is not a going concern. This type of capital will cease to exist if a business is unable to repay its debts because the business will be placed into either liquidation as a company or into bankruptcy as an incorporated business. When this occurs all the assets of the business will be sold and as many debts as possible repaid. It is unlikely that the owner's capital will ever be repaid unless the business voluntarily ceases to trade.

The owners of a business are the ultimate risk-takers as they provide the business with capital and obtain a return only if the business is profitable. Relative to other investors, providers of ownership capital benefit most when the business is successful but will lose most if it fails. The different legal status of

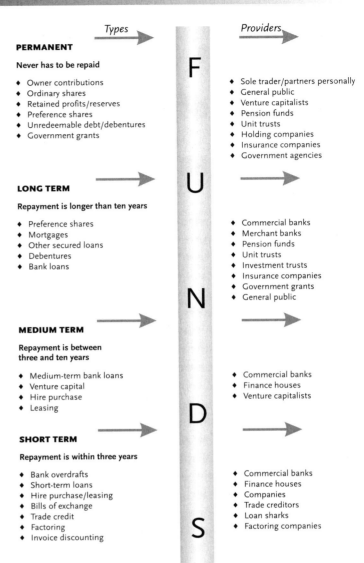

Figure 6.1   Sources of finance

the business also has a bearing on the descriptions of the ownership funds.

Unincorporated businesses: sole traders, partnerships

In this type of businesses the capital is provided by either an individual or by a group of individuals acting collectively, that is, a partnership. Establishing unincorporated businesses is relatively easy as such businesses do not need to be registered and are not separate from their owners. There is a danger here for the owners as the businesses have **unlimited liabilities** which means that the owners personal property is vulnerable if the business is unable to settle its debts and bankruptcy occurs. Another major problem of these types of business organisation is the difficulty of raising more capital. Often partnerships are created for this reason as additional owners will bring more capital into the business. However, if partners leave a partnership they have to be paid off and this can cause problems as much of the capital is tied up in essential assets.

Incorporated businesses: limited companies and co-operatives

These types of business are more difficult to establish and have to comply with a variety of legal requirements. Incorporated businesses have to be registered before they officially come into existence. Companies have to register with the Registrar of Companies by filing a number of documents (the Memorandum and Articles of Association and a statutory declaration by the founding members who agree to serve the company) which detail the constitution of the organisation. The Registrar of Companies will then issue a **certificate of incorporation** which gives the company an official legal existence. Incorporated businesses have their own legal personality which is separate from the shareholders who are the owners of the business. Each year the company has to file an **annual return** which gives details of shareholder movements and an **annual report and accounts** which can be viewed by any member of the public. Therefore the affairs of a limited company are no longer private and confidential. Co-operatives also have to be registered in a similar way but this is with the Registrar of Friendly Societies.

The capital contributed by the owners is divided into shares with a nominal or face value, for example £1. Each of these shares is a tradable security which means it can be bought and sold without the business being affected directly. Unless it is a new issue of shares, the sale proceeds pass between the buyer and the seller of the shares without cash implications for the company. The company can continue its trading operations when investors decide to withdraw their funds because they will be replaced by another investor.

Shareholders in a company enjoy the benefits of **limited liability**. This is where the maximum amount that an investor can lose is the amount they paid for

their shares. If the company fails the maximum loss of the shareholders is their investment, unlike the investors in sole traders or partnership organisations where the personal possessions of the owners are endangered as they can be acquired to settle the debts of the business. Shareholders do take risks but for the rewards of dividends being paid from the profits earned and the increase in the value of the shares.

Limited companies can be of two types:

♦ private limited companies and
♦ public limited companies (PLCs).

To become a PLC a company must have at least £50,000 of issued and paid-up share capital and also have PLC after its name. The Registrar of Companies will then approve them to operate as a PLC. All companies that are not PLCs are private limited companies. Generally PLCs are larger organisations that can offer their shares to the public whereas the issue of shares for private limited companies are more restricted. Some private limited companies are very large, for example Littlewoods Ltd, but these are controlled by a relatively small number of shareholders and are often family concerns. The big advantage of limited companies is the amount of capital that can be raised because it is provided by a large number of investors. The disadvantage is of course that the original owners will potentially lose their control over the business. PLCs can obtain a listing on the **Stock Exchange** which means that there will be an official market for the company's shares with the general public being able to buy or sell the shares at the prevailing market price. The share price will provide an indication of the success of a company. A rising share price will reflect good performance and future potential whereas a falling share price will reflect disappointing results and a questionable future.

Companies are managed on behalf of shareholders by the Board of Directors who are elected by the shareholders at the Annual General Meeting (AGM). Each share owned entitles the owner to one vote so the control of a company is by the shareholders who own the most shares. If a shareholder owns more than 50 per cent of the shares in a company then they have ultimate control and can effectively make all the decisions. In large PLCs there will be millions of shareholders but the major influence will come from the large institutional investors, such as the pension funds, insurance companies and unit trusts, which are entrusted to look after the funds of millions of private savers.

When companies obtain a full stock exchange listing they have access to far greater sources of funds but do have to comply with more onerous and costly reporting requirements. All shares must be freely traded and at least 25 per cent of the shares must be held by the general public. Some well-known entrepreneurs, such as Richard Branson with Virgin, have bought all the shares and taken the company back to a private limited company because they are frustrated by the controls placed on themselves by being a PLC.

Co-operatives

Co-operatives are a different sort of corporate body. They still have limited liability but are established for the specific benefit of the participating members who could be consumers or employees.

In being recruited by a worker co-operative an employee would have to buy a share in the organisation and would thus become a member. There is a restriction on the number of shares that can be bought by individuals and each member will have one vote in the decision-making process irrespective of how many shares are owned. This type of business is more democratic in its approach and prevents a few individuals gaining control over a business by acquiring a majority of the shares in the business. However, co-operatives will never have a quoted share price. This is because when members leave the co-operative they can withdraw their funds but it will only be what they originally invested. They will have benefited from membership by receiving a share of the profits made in the form of **dividends**. The John Lewis Partnership is managed on a co-operative basis.

Alternative Investment Market

The Alternative Investment Market (AIM) provides a market for smaller PLCs which are growing and want access to further funds as well as a price for the shares. It was launched in June 1995 and is supervised by the London Stock Exchange. It is an alternative to raising capital from venture capitalists and has grown significantly since its inception. It has many of the advantages of having a full listing on the Stock Exchange but there is no minimum capitalisation figure or a need for a three-year trading history. Also there is no requirement for at least 25 per cent of the shares being available to the general public. There are, however, significant costs to floating on AIM which may be higher than other sources of finance, but it does provide greater long-term flexibility. In addition to the cost there are obligations as with a full listing to publish annual and interim accounts, observe restrictions on share dealings and make announcements that affect the progress and future of a company.

Types of shares

Limited companies are restricted on the amount of shares they can issue by their Memorandums of Association. The maximum amount of share capital permitted is referred to as the **authorised share capital**. It can only be increased if the existing shareholders approve a motion put forward in a general meeting. This ensures that the share issues are properly made in line with shareholders' wishes and with regard to the company objectives and shareholder interests, protecting their ownership proportion of the company. Approval to increase the authorised share capital usually occurs because the Board of Directors wants to fund the growth of the business or reduce the debt position of the company.

The **issued share capital** is the nominal or face value of the shares actually issued. On issuing shares the company will receive cash in exchange for a part ownership of a company. Shares can be sold for a **share premium** which means that the price is above the nominal values of the shares, as for example when a £1 share is sold for £2. The share capital of a company will always be recorded at the nominal value in the accounting records. Not all shares carry the same rights within a company in respect of voting at AGMs, receiving dividends and capital repayment. The type of shares issued and the rules governing them are determined by the company founders and are contained in the Articles of Association. They can be divided into two types:

♦ ordinary shares
♦ preference shares.

Preference shares can be broken down into cumulative and non-cumulative preference shares. Figure 6.2 gives details about the various aspects of these share types.

Methods of issuing shares

For a private limited company the founders will agree on the number of shares to be issued and bought. For a PLC, however, there are several different ways of raising funds via a share issue.

Issue by prospectus

This method invites offers from the public via a prospectus which gives detailed information about the company and its future prospects and potential. In the prospectus there will be an application form which has to be completed with the number of shares required accompanied by a cheque covering the amount. Such offers are managed by a merchant or investment bank which will underwrite the issue for a set price to remove the risk and uncertainty.

The problem with such a method is fixing a price; it could be too high and the required number of shares will not be sold, or too low when the amount of money that is raised is less than it could have been.

A placing

This involves shares being sold directly to a select number of interested investors again by a merchant

Types of share capital	Security or voting rights	Income	Amount of capital
Ordinary shares or equity	Usually have voting rights in general meetings of the company. Rank after all creditors and preference shares in rights to assets on liquidation.	Dividends payable at the discretion of directors (subject to approval by the shareholders) out of undistributed profits remaining after senior claims have been met. Amounts available for dividends but not paid out are retained profits in the company which belong to the ordinary shareholders.	The right to all surplus funds after prior claims have been met.
Cumulative preference shares	Right to vote at a general meeting when the dividend payment is in arrears or when it is proposed to change the legal rights of the shares. They rank after creditors but before ordinary shareholders in liquidation.	Dividends payable at the discretion of the directors (subject to approval by the shareholders) out of undistributed profits remaining after senior claims have been met.	A fixed amount per share.
Non-cumulative preference shares	Likely to have some voting rights at all times rather than in specified circumstances as in the case of cumulative preference shares because they carry more risk. They rank as cumulative in a liquidation.	A fixed amount per year, as for cumulative preference shares, but arrears do not accumulate. If there is insufficient profits to pay dividends in a particular year then the dividends are lost forever.	A fixed amount per share.

Figure 6.2   Types of shares

or investment bank. The types of investors could be pension funds, unit trusts, investment trusts, insurance companies and even personal investors.

A rights issue

This is where a PLC offers to sell further shares to existing shareholders at a discounted price. This approach will be a cheaper and more certain option of raising the necessary share capital.

Share buyback

A limited company may, in certain specified conditions, be able to buy back its own shares. This can only be done if it increases shareholder value and this would occur if the management perceived that the shares in the company provide a better financial return than further investment in the activities of the business or investment in other companies' shares. By reducing the number of shares that have been issued the company can benefit the remaining shareholders by saving on future dividends and also by having a positive influence on the share price.

For a company to purchase its own shares there are a number of formalities that have to be addressed to protect the interests of creditors:

◆ the company has to seek the approval of its shareholders in a special resolution
◆ the company has to seek confirmation by a court that it may proceed: the court will want to be assured that the creditors' interests are not being compromised by the withdrawal of capital from the business; this may take the form of insisting that creditors give formal approval, although for a company that is able to demonstrate that it clearly possesses funds in excess of its trading needs, the court may forego such a requirement.

Retained profits and reserves

A major source of finance for many businesses is the retention of profits in the business. Instead of distributing all the profits to the owners, that is, in dividends to shareholders, some of the profits are invested in further assets enabling the business to expand and thus to increase potential future earnings as well as the value of the business. If you examine the balance sheets of PLCs you will usually see the retained profits and reserves forming the most significant part of the 'financed by' aspect.

Benefits of using retained profits

Using this as a way of financing expansion has the following benefits:

◆ the company is not vulnerable to external lenders
◆ this finance does not have to be serviced in the same way that borrowing has to be.

The shareholders will of course want to see that the company is using their funds effectively and efficiently and if this is not occurring then they will sell the shares and find alternative investments for the funds. The directors of a company are accountable in their stewardship role to protect the interests of the shareholders and this would not be happening if the retained profits could be better invested elsewhere.

The reserves of a company could be the share premium figure, any revaluations of fixed assets which have occurred, such as land and buildings, or capital redemption funds set up for the repayment of long-term loans.

Sometimes companies can tap into funds from the government, for example government grants available for the purchase of specific assets or for being located in a particular area. Also tax relief is available in specific circumstances.

CASE STUDY

Boots pledges to return £700m to shareholders

At the end of May 2004 Boots set out plans to return £700m to shareholders over the next two years at the same time as it announced a 5 per cent increase in underlying sales.

The health and beauty retailer announced that it would increase its share buyback programme from £250m to £350m a year after identifying 'surplus share capital'. However, when the news of this was announced, the credit ratings agency Standard & Poor cut Boots' rating by two notches, noting that the group would have less cash to pay off its debt. Boots' net debt in the year ending 31 March rose £97m to £149m. Shares in Boots nevertheless rose 7 per cent to 675.5p as investors welcomed the buyback.

ACTIVITY

1   Why do you think that Boots decided to increase its share buyback programme?

2   Why do you think that investors responded to this move positively?

3   Why have Standard & Poor reduced the credit rating of Boots?

4   Why might a company want to increase its share issue?

5   Why might a company decide to buy back shares?

CASE STUDY

Umbro scales share issue price back

Also at the end of May 2004, Umbro, the maker of England football shirts, was forced to slash the price of its flotation by one-third after institutional investors baulked at the initial share price range being offered by the company's bankers, Cazenove.

When the shares were floated on 3 June they were priced at 100p, valuing the 84-year-

old company at about £110m. That was a significant discount to the 150p to 170p that the company was initially aiming for.

The reduced price hit Umbro's chief executive, the former footballer Peter McGuigan, personally. Initially, his 8.4 per cent stake was set to be worth in the region of £10m.

Because of uncertainty in the market it was thought that the company might hold back from going for a full Stock Exchange listing. However, it was decided to go ahead because of the belief that there was considerable appetite in the City for the sports company's equity. The cut in the price reflected wider turbulence in the market.

The uncertainty spelled bad news for other companies that chose to sell shares in themselves at the same time, including Halfords, the car and bicycle accessories maker, and Admiral, the motor insurer.

Umbro had timed the sale of shares to make the most of Euro 2004 football fever, in the lead up to the tournament in Portugal. However, there was pessimism about buying shares in the wider market resulting from rises in petrol prices and instability in the Middle East, and worries about a downturn in the world economy.

ACTIVITY

1   Why might a company like Umbro want to sell shares which would be traded on the Stock Exchange?

2   Why is the timing of the sale so important?

3   Why would the company have chosen the time that it did?

4   What went wrong with the sale?

5   How would this have affected the company and its financing?

Long-term capital

This is funding which does not have to be repaid until at least ten years have elapsed. For unincorporated businesses the opportunity to arrange such long-term loans is usually confined to land and buildings under a mortgage where the asset provides security to the loan or if personal guarantees are made by the owner.

Debentures

For a company, long-term loans are more accessible either from financial institutions or through the issue of **debentures**. A debenture is essentially an IOU but is a marketable security because it is issued as a certificate under the company's seal and can be bought or sold in the capital markets. These securities are sometimes called **company bond** or **loan stock**. The certificate will give details of the loan, including the interest rate that will be paid, the date of redemption if it is not an irredeemable debenture and any security attached to the loan.

Advantages of debentures

The advantages of issuing such securities are:

- the company will not be vulnerable to just one lender
- more funds can be raised when required, by issuing more securities
- from the lender's viewpoint, there will always be accessibility to the funds if required but for a reasonable rate of return.

Secured and unsecured debentures

Debentures can be classed as either **secured** or **unsecured** depending on whether a trust deed is in force to protect the debenture holders in the event of the company infringing the terms of the debt agreement. The rights of the secured debenture holders can be strengthened by a charge made in their favour over either specified assets of the company or a floating charge over all of the assets of the company.

Where the security is a specified asset the debenture is known as a **mortgage debenture**. In the case of a floating charge the assets of the business will be continually changing, but at the point the company defaults on the debt the charge becomes fixed.

Secured debentures can place restrictions on the use of an asset, particularly in the case of mortgage debentures that are secured by specific assets. For example, changing the use of property from offices to factory space may be prohibited because of a perceived adverse effect on the asset's value.

Fixed charges on assets will prevent them being sold unless the permission is given by the relevant debenture holders.

The trust deed of a secured debenture will also describe such things as the rights of the debenture holders to hold meetings, to enforce contracts and to appoint a new manager (a receiver) to run the business until the obligations have been fulfilled. An unsecured debenture has no trust deed, so the lender has to rely on the courts in the same way as other unsecured creditors.

Redeemable and irredeemable debentures

In addition, debentures can be either **redeemable** or **irredeemable**. The company has to repurchase redeemable debentures on a fixed date or during a range of dates, whereas it has no such obligation for irredeemable debentures. For example, a 6 per cent irredeemable unsecured debenture of £1000 will pay the debenture holder £60 per annum in perpetuity. There would be no obligation for the company to pay back the capital sum, although of course it may negotiate a buyback if it had the available cash. If such a debenture was traded on the Stock Exchange then the company could buy it back at the prevailing price and cancel it.

Convertible debentures

Convertible debentures are debentures that can be converted from loan stock into shares at some future date. For example, a 5 per cent convertible debenture at a predetermined price between 2007 and 2009 of £100 will pay annual interest of £5, and then in accordance with the terms of the debenture will become convertible into ordinary shares at a predetermined price. In this example the debenture holder will normally exercise the option only if the market price for an ordinary share is higher than the option price. The attraction for the lender is the possibility of future capital growth if converted into equity but with a certain fixed return in the meantime. For the company the debenture interest will be lower than on non-convertible debentures and this will save on interest in the short term. The other advantage of converting debt into equity is that it reduces financial gearing and makes the company less vulnerable to its long-term creditors.

CASE STUDY

Tamaris

Tamaris PLC is a fast-expanding nursing home operator that uses sale and leaseback as a strategy towards its objective of increasing shareholder value. The company buys nursing homes, sells the buildings to a finance house and then leases them back. Tamaris can in this way expand the number of beds it has under management without having to ask shareholders for more funds. Return on capital is 35 per cent, compared with 20 per cent if it were to use normal bank borrowing.

ACTIVITY

1   What is it about the nature of Tamaris' business that makes sale and leaseback such a viable source of finance?

2   What are the possible drawbacks of the company's strategy in the long run?

Bank finance

The clearing banks (Barclays, HSBC, RBS Nat West, Lloyds TSB) and the merchant banks (Schroders, Rothschild, Merrill Lynch) all provide financial products for businesses. However, banks in the UK do tend to have a more cautious approach to lending and require detailed business plans and financial information to show how the funds will be repaid and thus reduce the risk element of lending.

Medium-term finance

Medium-term finance ranges from three to ten years for repayment. It could be bank loans from commercial banks of similar types to long-term loans but with shorter repayment terms. Alternatively, funds might be provided by specialist venture capital companies which provide high-risk finance for businesses either experiencing financial difficulties or which are seeking growth by exploiting new products.

Venture capital companies will provide the funds and have representation on the board, but only have the intention of remaining with the borrower until it is back on its feet or has achieved the growth. Sometimes the venture capital company will take an equity stake in the company it is supporting with the intention of seeing the enterprise float on the Stock Exchange and thus recouping the investment made.

Hire purchase or leasing

Alternatively, some **instalment finance** may be sought to fund specific fixed assets that are required either by hire purchase (HP) or leasing. HP allows a business to use an asset without having to find the money to pay for it immediately. A finance house buys the asset from the seller and retains ownership of it during the period of the agreement. The business pays a deposit on the asset and further regular equal payments to the finance house over the term of the agreement. At the end of the HP agreement the ownership of the asset will be passed from the finance house to the business. If the purchaser defaults on the payments the finance house has the right to repossess the asset and sell it to recoup the amount owed. However, even though the asset is legally owned by the finance house it will be included in the fixed assets of the purchasing company and depreciated in the normal way with the amount owed under the HP agreement being shown under 'creditors'.

Leasing an asset provides similar benefits to HP. A leasing agreement with a finance house (the lessor) allows the purchasing business (the lessee) to use an asset without buying it outright. There are two types of lease arrangement.

Operating lease

An **operating lease** is a rental agreement for a short period of time relative to the asset's useful life, for example the hire of a specialist piece of equipment like a van, lorry or JCB digger for a month would be typical of this type of lease. The company hiring the equipment would buy the equipment with the intention of hiring it out on a regular but short-term basis.

Finance lease

A finance lease involves the lease running over the useful life of the asset. A finance house will buy the asset for the customer who will lease it over its expected life. The lease payments will therefore consist of a recovery of the original price plus the financing costs of the funds used. As the asset will have a negligible value at the end of the lease, it will contain a clause which allows the lessee to continue leasing the asset for a nominal rent or buy it at a nominal price.

The difference between the two types of lease is reflected in other terms to the agreement.

Under an **operating lease** the lessor will be responsible for the maintenance and insurance of the asset whereas under a finance lease the risk of ownership is largely transferred to the lessee who has to maintain and insure the asset. One consequence of assets being acquired under HP or finance lease agreements will be the restrictions on modifications and alteration because high residual values need to be maintained as the asset is security for the finance outstanding and the value of the asset could be impaired by anything that alters its standard specification.

For many businesses there is little difference in cost between leasing an asset and taking out a bank loan to purchase the asset outright. One of the biggest advantages of leasing is the relative convenience because of the willingness of financial institutions to provide finance against a specific asset. The finance houses which provide the funds for HP and leasing arrangements are usually subsidiary companies of the commercial banks, for example Lombard Tricity Finance. These finance houses will want to be assured on the creditworthiness of the lessor and check also on their past repayment record.

Short-term finance

Banks

Short-term finance ranges from less than a year to three years for repayment. It is often needed to overcome temporary cash flow shortages although some HP and leasing agreements may be within this time limit. Commercial banks may provide short-term loans of similar types to those described previously. However, they will also provide **overdraft facilities** for businesses. This is the most flexible form of finance, in that interest is only charged on the outstanding overdrawn current account balance. The major problem is that an overdraft is repayable on demand although in practice the bank will usually provide such a facility for a definite period of time after which it will be subject to regular reviews.

Trade debtors and factoring

Another way of solving short-term funding problems is to use some of the short-term assets of a business, that is, the trade debtors. Businesses that sell on credit may have to wait between 30 and 90 days before payment is received and sometimes even longer. These debts are valuable assets and businesses can use these to acquire funds from **factoring companies**; for example, Alex Lawrie Ltd Factoring Companies provide two factoring services:

♦ factoring trade debts
♦ invoice discounting.

The factoring function is passing the role of credit control and debt collection to the factor for a fee of usually between 2 and 4 per cent of the value of the debts. In addition the factoring company will advance up to 80 per cent of the value of the debts outstanding. The additional 20 per cent will be received when it is collected. For an additional fee the factoring company may offer a **non-recourse agreement** whereby they will cover any bad debts that arise but at a higher charge. **Invoice discounting** is where a business sells some of its invoices at a lower value to the factoring company for immediate funds. The factoring company will collect the full value of the debt at the end of the credit period allowed. The factoring company will choose the best invoices to discount, these being the largest and the ones to the most reliable and creditworthy customers.

Creditors

Creditors are another valuable short-term source of finance. The suppliers to a business will provide goods and services on credit terms. If the credit terms can be improved by increasing the credit limit and/or extending the length of the repayment period, for example from 30 to 40 days, this will provide the equivalent of additional funds and, more importantly, at no cost. The situation can of course be reversed where a business's credit customers seek the same sort of arrangements or even deliberately pay late. This means that a business becomes an unconscious supplier of funds. Businesses should operate an efficient credit control system to ensure that customers do pay on time. Of course, collecting debts in more quickly is a source of funds as visualised by using a factoring company.

Late payment and credit terms

Late payment has become a very sensitive issue, especially where large companies use their market power to force smaller firms to accept longer periods of credit and deliberately delaying payment knowing that there will be no repercussions. Businesses may trade profitably but still fail through cash flow problems because credit customers do not keep within their credit terms.

The UK government has attempted to tackle this problem by issuing a statutory instrument requiring all trading companies to disclose in their annual report and accounts the number of days credit taken from suppliers. In addition, in November 1998 new legislation came into force to give greater protection to smaller businesses with fewer than 50 employees. These small firms can now charge large businesses interest on debts that are outside the credit terms but unfortunately smaller businesses rarely use this opportunity because it will adversely affect their business relationship. Such businesses cannot afford to lose their major customers whereas the major customers have numerous opportunities to replace one of their small suppliers. A change of attitude is needed and the CBI now has a Code of Good Practice on the prompt payment of suppliers which will hopefully make larger firms aware of their responsibilities.

Other creditors

There are other creditors within businesses but these are usually priority creditors that have to be paid on time, for example Inland Revenue, Customs and Excise. However, funds can be created by companies by declaring lower dividends and therefore increasing the level of retained profits. Here of course the Board of Directors will have to persuade the shareholders to accept such a policy which may prove difficult if the company is very profitable.

Bills of exchange

Finally, large companies can use bills of exchange to obtain immediate payment from credit customers. Bills of exchange are short-term securities that overcome the problem of the supplier wanting immediate access to the debt whereas the customer wants more time to settle the debt. A bill of exchange provides the solution. It will be prepared by the seller requesting the debtor, by signing the bill, to accept an obligation to settle the debt at some future date, for example in 90 days time. The bill of exchange can then be held for 90 days and then presented for payment or sold for cash in the money markets at a discount. When 90 days have elapsed the holder of the bill will present it to the debtor for payment. The bill may have changed hands many times over that 90-day period. This is a very flexible way of accessing funds when needed. If the bill of exchange is countersigned by a bank then it gains additional status and marketability because the bank is guaranteeing payment if the payee defaults on the bill.

Loan sharks do exist to accommodate companies that have extreme financial problems but these companies lend at very high interest rates with very stringent and onerous repayment terms. Using loan sharks should be avoided.

Choosing a source of finance

For any given business proposal there are likely to be a number of sources of finance that may be suitable. It is important to be aware of some of the basic principles and the relative advantages and disadvantages of each alternative. Financing strategy should take account of the following considerations and implications:

♦ the duration for which the finance is required
♦ the available funding options for particular purposes
♦ the cost of alternative sources of finance
♦ the flexibility of the financial source chosen
♦ gearing and interest cover: the financial implications of debt finance
♦ the stage of development of the business
♦ security that is required by the lender
♦ financial support offered by the government and other institutions such as grants and interest-free or low-interest loans.

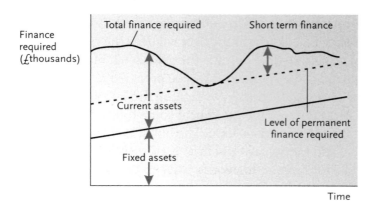

Figure 6.3   Duration of finance

ACTIVITY

1   Consider what kind of finance would be suitable for a business purchasing fixed assets that are expected to last for five years, and needs to arrange affordable finance that could at least be repaid within five years.
   ♦ Would an overdraft be advisable? If not, why not?

2   Consider what kind of finance would be suitable for a business that needs some funds to overcome a short-term requirement and would not take on a long-term loan because it would be incurring the interest costs when the funds are no longer needed.
   ♦ Would some short-term finance be appropriate? If so, what kind?

Duration of finance

It is important to arrange the finance requirements in line with the needs of the business from a time perspective.

All businesses do need working capital and this needs to be a part of the permanent or long-term finance that is required. In the planning process a business can identify the minimum level of long-term finance required and then ensure that it is properly funded. The short-term fluctuations could be accommodated as they arise using appropriate short-term finance options such as a bank overdraft or factoring the debtors. This is illustrated in Figure 6.3.

In the UK the banks have a different attitude to their European counterparts. They tend to be very cautious in their approach and are less likely to provide medium- and long-term finance because of the higher risks involved and the lower flexibility levels. This approach does present real difficulties for smaller businesses which find it difficult to fund growth and innovation.

Available funding options for particular purposes

Businesses need to consider the available options to deal with a particular funding problem and choose the best one in terms of cost and appropriateness. For example, a business may be about to invest in a new fleet of vehicles. It would have to consider the range of options available to it which could include a bank loan, a leasing arrangement or an HP scheme. It is only after the consideration of a range of possible finance methods that the optimum option can be determined.

Cost of alternative sources

In making a funding choice it is necessary to consider the costs involved. Clearly businesses should opt for the cheapest option provided it meets the other necessary requirements. Therefore businesses need to weigh up the costs of different options and compare the other aspects that are inclusive in a funding transaction. For example, one provider may provide a lower interest option but it does not allow a loan to be extended beyond its set term. If a business needs more flexibility then it may consider the higher service costs for a loan to be worthwhile.

Flexibility of the finance source chosen

Cash budgeting is difficult to do with accuracy and therefore some contingencies are needed to deal with unexpected fluctuations. Some businesses may always maintain a healthy bank balance or some short-term investments that can be quickly turned into cash, for example government bonds or treasury bills. Alternatively a bank overdraft facility could provide the necessary flexibility.

Gearing and interest cover

Gearing is the relationship between equity and debt finance. It is important to have a balance between the two. The gearing ratio indicates the level of risk and vulnerability of a business to its lenders.

If a business has a high gearing ratio it means that it has high long-term debt relative to equity, that is, ordinary share capital and reserves. Long-term debt has to be serviced: interest has to be paid for the use of

the funds. With high amounts of long-term debt a business will have to pay high interest charges and will be vulnerable to rises in interest rates and also a downturn in sales in an economic recession. A business has the option of not paying dividends to shareholders but the interest on loans has to be paid irrespective of the performance of the business. There are variations on how the gearing ratio is calculated but the following will achieve the objective of measuring the vulnerability of a business.

$$\frac{\text{Long-term debt + Preference shares}}{\text{Ordinary shares + Reserves + Long-term debt + preference shares}} \times \frac{100}{1} = \text{Gearing ratio}$$

High and low gearing in companies

Preference share capital is included as part of the long-term debt figure. These shares are classed as the equivalent of debt because there is a fixed rate of return, that is, a fixed dividend if profits are earned. If the gearing ratio is over 50 per cent then a business will be very highly geared and be in a vulnerable position. Financial institutions would be reluctant or completely unwilling to lend to a company with a gearing ratio above 50 per cent where £0.50 of long-term debt is matched by £1 of equity and long-term debt. The following example will illustrate the importance of the capital structure of a business and thus the gearing ratio.

Company A	Equity capital	£100,000
	Long-term loans	£20,000

$$\frac{20,000}{100,000 + 20,000} \times 100 = \mathbf{17\%}$$

Company B	Equity capital	£40,000
	Long-term loans	£80,000

$$\frac{80,000}{40,000 + 80,000} \times 100 = \mathbf{67\%}$$

Company A is a relatively low geared company whereas Company B is a high geared company. Both companies have the same amount of long-term capital employed but Company A's is mainly equity capital while Company B's is mainly long-term debt. If both companies are making profits before interest of £10,000 and paying a 10 per cent interest rate on long-term debt then the following results would occur.

	Company A	Company B
Profits before interest	10,000	10,000
less interest on loans	(2000)	(8000)
Profit after interest	8000	2000

Company A is less weighted down by long-term debt and can easily service its long-term loans. If the interest rate went up by 50 per cent Company A could still service its debt comfortably because the interest charge would only rise to £3000 and profits of £7000 would be attributable to the ordinary shareholders. However, for Company B the interest charge would rise to £12,000 and the company would move to a loss of £2000 for the year. A similar result would occur if profits halved because of poor trading conditions. Company A would still make a profit of £3000 but Company B would move into a loss of £3000. Company B is much more vulnerable to its long-term lenders than Company A and it would be much less financially adaptable because it would have difficulty in raising further funds. In addition long-term loans will have to be repaid in the future whereas equity capital is permanent and will never have to be repaid. Clearly companies do need to look after their equity shareholders, and paying them regular dividends is essential to maintaining their support, but there is much more flexibility for companies that are not burdened with heavy long-term debt. Companies with higher gearing ratios are in a much more risky position than companies with low gearing ratios.

Interest cover measure

The above analysis can be complemented by the use of the **interest cover measure**. This examines the relationship between interest payments and the profits generated by a business. It is calculated by the following formula:

$$\frac{\text{Profit before interest and tax}}{\text{Interest paid}} = \text{Interest cover multiple}$$

Using the example of Company A and Company B from the gearing exercise, the interest cover is as follows:

Company A $\quad \dfrac{10,000}{2000} = 5 \text{ times}$

Company B $\quad \dfrac{10,000}{8000} = 1.25 \text{ times}$

It is clear that Company A can comfortably afford to meet its interest payments whereas Company B is struggling to cope with them. If the same changes occurred in respect of interest rises and profit falls the following would occur:

Interest rise

Company A $\quad \dfrac{10,000}{3000} = 3.3 \text{ times}$

Company B $\quad \dfrac{10,000}{12,000} = (1.2) \text{ times}$

Profits fall

Company A $\quad \dfrac{5000}{2000} = 2.5 \text{ times}$

Company B $\quad \dfrac{5000}{8000} = (1.6) \text{ times}$

In both of the above situations, Company A can manage the adverse changes but Company B cannot because it is weighed down by the excessive external debt which has to be serviced. Businesses should therefore be careful about the way they raise further funds for expansion. In examining their capital structure businesses may consider it more appropriate to raise further funds by the issue of equity capital rather than increased borrowing.

Stages of business development

The ability of a business to access the various sources of finance available will depend on its trading history. Many providers of finance are looking for established, expanding and profitable businesses that offer good returns and relatively low risk. However, new businesses

without a proven record still need to raise funds but this will not be forthcoming from the traditional sources. This gap is now filled by venture capital companies.

Venture capital

These companies will provide loans or take an equity stake in an enterprise knowing that there is high risk because, for example, the commercial banks would not support such businesses. The venture capital company would of course examine the business plan thoroughly before committing their support to a business but knowing that it is carrying high risk.

Venture capitalists work on the premise that some projects will be successful and these will more than compensate for those that fail. Venture capitalists are represented by the British Venture Capital Association (BVCA) and this organisation provides links and communication between seekers of finance and its members. These companies specialise in start-up companies, expansions, management buy-outs and rescues of failing operations. In all cases the venture capitalist will be helping to direct an enterprise towards future success which would often result in a Stock Exchange flotation and thus yield high returns for the venture capitalist, who would usually provide a mix of equity and debt finance.

Security requirements

Lenders often require **security** for loans. This means that in the event of a default in the payment of interest or the repayment of capital the lender can call on the security of the loan. The security could be assets that are attached to the loan which would have to be sold to settle the debt, or personal guarantees from the directors of a company. Companies seeking funds must be careful about the terms and conditions attached to loans as they may reduce the flexibility of its operations. For example, there might be a clause in the loan agreement which prevents the assets securing the loan from being modified.

Governmental and other financial support

Businesses should research all possible sources of finance and this includes options that might be provided by central government, local authorities and other agencies. There might be grants and low-interest loan options available.

ACTIVITY

Gearing and interest cover

The following companies are from the same industry:

	Red	Green	Orange
Profits before interest	£120,000	£120,000	£120,000
Capital structure:			
Ordinary share capital	£800,000	£600,000	£400,000
Debentures @ 10%	£200,000	£400,000	£600,000

Forecasts indicated profits may fall by 50 per cent for all three companies during the next year.

1 Calculate the current year's gearing ratio for each company.

2 Calculate the current year's interest cover for each company.

3 Repeat the interest cover calculations for the forthcoming year.

4 Evaluate the companies' financial structures on the basis of the ratios calculated.

ACTIVITY

For each of the following investment proposals, identify the most relevant sources of finance as requested, stating also when each would be most appropriate. Where the issue of share capital is recommended, also state the method of issue.

1 Pritesh Pancholi needs a new computer system costing £5000 for his business. Identify three ways of financing the purchase.

2 Harwood and Sons Ltd wants to expand its factory building. The cost will be £500,000. Identify three ways of financing the expansion.

3 Sahota and Scarrat Ltd is having temporary problems with its cash flow. Identify two ways of financing its working capital shortfall.

4 Pantheon International PLC needs to raise £5 million for a new office complex. It currently has a gearing ratio of 2. Identify two ways of raising the finance.

5 EuroTunnel suffered trading losses in its first few years of operation. If the company wanted to maintain its gearing ratio at the same level as in previous years, what type of finance would it have to raise?

6 Carlton Holdings PLC has a long-term strategy to increase the number of companies it owns. Identify three ways of financing this growth.

7 Connors and Moore Ltd has experienced poor sales in the last few years and this has resulted in substantial losses. The business needs to develop and launch a new product if it is to be saved. It could take up to four years for the new product to generate profits. The company's gearing ratio is currently just under 1. Identify two ways of financing this project.

ACTIVITY

Joyce and Gary Redfern wish to start up in business with £100,000 of personal capital to be invested in ordinary shares. The business requires total finance of £500,000 and this will be provided by a mixture of debt and equity finance. Debt finance is available in the form of 8 per cent loan stock for amounts of £100,000 and £200,000. However, if this were raised to £400,000 the outside investors would require interest at 10 per cent to cover what they perceive as higher risk. The remaining finance required would be in the form of shares issued to the external parties. Annual business profits are forecast to be £120,000, but with a chance they could be as low as £70,000 and as high as £150,000.

1 Calculate the gearing ratio for each level of debt.

2 Calculate the amount of interest payable and the residue available to the company's shareholders for each combination of profit level and gearing.

3 Calculate interest cover for each combination of profit level and gearing.

4 Calculate the percentage return on capital for ordinary shareholders for each combination of profit and gearing.

5 Produce a narrative addressed to Joyce and Gary to accompany your calculations, highlighting relevant points to help them decide on an appropriate financing mix.

CASE STUDY

Encouraging signs of public offerings in 2004

Research carried out by the accountancy group Ernst and Young in June 2004 showed that company flotations around the globe could be back up to levels not seen since the days of the dot-com bubble burst. It stated that 1000 companies worldwide will seek to float in 2004.

Ernst and Young say that 639 companies listed between September 2003 and March 2004 compared with less than half that number the year before.

However, this still contrasts unfavourably with the millennium year when 2000 companies listed on stock exchanges.

The next market likely to pick up is the United States following on from Asia. However, in Europe market confidence is not so strong. In 2000 Europe accounted for almost half of all flotations. In 2003 the figure was only 12 per cent. However, there is more optimism in Britain where up to 60 firms might list in 2004.

ACTIVITY

1 Why do firms seek to list on the Stock Exchange?

2 What are the financial benefits to companies of raising finance in this way?

3 Why is the level of business optimism so important when arranging to raise finance through Stock Exchange listing?

Summary

The sources of finance used by a business should reflect the need for which the funds are required, having regard for the duration, purpose and cost. In addition, consideration should be given to the nature of the business and its existing financial structure, in particular its level of gearing and interest cover.

It is also important to appreciate that finance for business is viewed from two perspectives: the business has its objectives but so do the external investors. External parties include insurance companies, pension funds and banks which are looking for investment opportunities for periods of months to many years. Their willingness to invest will depend on the likely risk and financial return for their investment. They will also be interested in how easy it is to liquidate their funds to discharge their own financial commitments.

Some investors may wish to participate in the profits of the business and so will become equity stakeholders. This will be a more attractive proposition to investors if the shares are listed on the Stock Exchange.

Some providers may require safe fixed returns but with the possibility of long-term capital growth. This could be met by preference shareholders and debenture holders being offered the opportunity to convert these securities into ordinary shares. For all investment it must be remembered that there is always a risk element and the higher returns are the compensation for the higher risks taken.

Chapter 2

Finance as a resource

The cost of finance

All organisations require resources in order to provide a product or a service and the acquisition of these resources incurs **costs**. These costs could be paying wages to employees or the rent of premises or the depreciation on fixed assets. One of the resources required is finance and this in turn has a cost.

All businesses are indebted to their investors, that is, equity holders and lenders, for the finance provided and it is therefore the responsibility of the management to provide a financial return on it. This financial return is referred to as the **cost of capital**.

Risk and accessibility

The cost of capital will depend on the terms and conditions on which the funds were provided. All investors expect a return on their investment and the level of return will depend on:

♦ the level of risk being taken
♦ the accessibility of the funds.

For example, some investments such as bank deposits carry very low risk and will therefore earn a low rate of return. Other investments may lose the investor the use of the funds for a long period of time, for example pension funds and savings schemes, and the return needs to be high to compensate for the loss of accessibility to these funds. Some investments are secured by personal guarantees or property and will have lower returns because the level of risk is lower. Different investors have different priorities, with some wanting a fixed regular return, such as a fixed rate debenture loan, whereas others are prepared to accept uncertainty in the quest for higher returns, such as ordinary shareholders.

Ordinary share capital

The cost of using ordinary share capital or equity, including retained profits, can be considered from the shareholders' perspective. Returns to the ordinary shareholder come in two forms:

♦ the receipt of regular dividends each year
♦ the appreciation in the value of the ordinary shares as the business grows.

The **appreciation** of the investment can be measured in the movement of the share price of a company's shares for quoted companies, with the share price theoretically reflecting the underlying value of the company. This is not always the case because investors do speculate and the market forces can then lead to a quoted company being overvalued, with the share price too high, or undervalued, with the share price too low. Where the share price is too low then such companies are prime targets for a takeover bid.

Annual return on investment

The annual return on the investment in ordinary shares can be expressed as a percentage as follows:

$$\frac{\text{Dividends received } + \text{ Increase in share value}}{\text{Value of shares at the start of the year}} \times \frac{100}{1}$$

$$= \text{Annual return on ordinary shares}$$

For example, an investor could buy ordinary shares in a company at £5.00 each now. In a year the price increases to £5.50 and dividends of £0.50 are paid. The return on investment is:

$$\frac{£0.50 + £0.50}{£5.00} \times \frac{100}{1} = 20\%$$

For quoted PLCs dividends are typically paid twice a year. Firstly there would be an **interim dividend** paid after the half-yearly results and then a **final dividend** being proposed at the Annual General Meeting after the directors have laid before the meeting the financial results for the year. The payments of the dividends would be made to the persons who were registered as shareholders in the Share Register of the PLC. However, in quoted companies the shares are continually bought and sold and it is important to ensure that the dividend is paid to the right person. Clearly a share that has a dividend attached to it is more valuable than a share immediately after the right to the dividend has passed. Quoted share prices are expressed as being either **cum-dividend** which means it includes entitlement to the forthcoming dividend, or **ex-dividend** after the dividend has been paid. When a share becomes ex-dividend its price will naturally fall. Figure 6.4 shows a typical PLC annual calender of events.

31 March 2002	5 June 2002	16 June 2002	24 July 2002
Accounting year-end	Announce-ment of results	Ex-dividend date	Annual general meeting
15 August 2002	29 October 2002	February 2003	31 March 2003
Dividend payment date	Announce-ment of interim results to 30/9/03	Interim dividend payment date	Accounting year-end

Figure 6.4   A typical PLC calendar of events

In the case shown in Figure 6.4, shares bought on 15 June 2002 entitled the buyer to the dividend paid from the profits earned up to 31 March 2002. For share trades after this date the share seller retained the rights to receive the dividend even though it was not paid until 31 August 2002.

Cost of shareholder funds

To sustain continuing growth in a company's share price it is necessary to make on-going investment in fixed and current assets with some of these investments being funded by retained profits. The management of companies must of course maintain the support of the shareholders and this means providing them with satisfactory dividends which at least cover the opportunity cost cash returns of alternative forms of investment.

It should be evident that establishing the cost of shareholder funds is not a simple task. It requires forecasts of shareholders' expectations in respect of future dividends and share price appreciations. Especially problematic is putting a figure on a future share price, particularly when some shareholders hope merely for speculative gains.

Despite the widely held view that short-term share price changes are dictated by changes in sentiment for the economy as a whole, it is of more academic interest that the company should be aware of its costs of finance. For investment in new projects, such as developing new products, the financial benefits should outweigh the cost of the capital involved. If the benefits do not exceed the costs then the company is not increasing shareholder value which is of course one of the primary responsibilities of the directors in their stewardship role.

Shareholder funds and the Stock Exchange

The share price for a company should reflect its current position and also its future growth potential but this can only be achieved through the availability of timely and accurate information on the profits and progress made. For a company whose share price is quoted on the Stock Exchange, the management has the responsibility to inform the Stock Exchange if the actual performance is not in line with market expectations: hence the periodic issue of **profit warnings** by companies failing to meet those expectations.

All stock exchanges strive to be efficient markets for the securities traded there. This requires prompt communication when financial performance and share price levels are inconsistent. By ensuring that the current share price is a fair reflection of at least the short-term profit level, there can be informed discussions at investor briefings and annual general meetings that can attempt to resolve apparent differences between expectations and actual investment returns. In this way, and using other companies in the same industrial sector as a benchmark, it should be possible to discern the long-term cost of equity finance.

In addition to the on-going costs of using shareholder funds, a quoted PLC will also incur significant costs in the issuing of shares: up to 10 per cent of the sums raised. This is because there are onerous obligations set down by the Stock Exchange to ensure that a fair and efficient market exists for a company's shares. There are numerous expensive activities involved in issuing new shares including:

♦ gathering all the information needed for the published prospectus
♦ the printing and postage costs in communicating to existing and potential new shareholders
♦ underwriting premiums to insure against a failed flotation
♦ professional fees for legal and financial advisors.

ACTIVITY

1 An investor buys shares in Manchester United Football Club at the start of the year for £3.00 each and during the year receives 15p in dividends on each share. At the end of the year the share is worth £3.85. Calculate the annual return on the shares for the investor.

2 An investor buys Marks & Spencer shares for £4.00 each at the start of the year. The company pays an interim dividend of 10 pence and a final dividend of 15 pence for each share. At the end of the year the shares are still only being traded at £4.00 each. What is the annual return on the share for the investor?

3 Explain how an investor might make a negative return on holding shares in a company.

Cost of fixed-return finance

Preference shares

The cost of using debt finance or preference shares is explicit with a stated interest rate or fixed dividend per share. Preference shares usually give a fixed rate of return; for example, 8 per cent £1 preference shares entitle shareholders to an 8p dividend per year for each share held to be paid before the dividends to ordinary shareholders. Preference shares that are convertible into ordinary shares at some future date will potentially dilute further gains through an increase in ordinary shareholders, and this is an added cost which needs to be considered. In addition, some preference shares are redeemable so the company must prepare itself for repaying the capital when it becomes due. Often this is achieved by issuing more shares.

As with ordinary shares there may also be issuing costs for a company. The major advantage for a company of this type of fixed-cost finance is that the dividends only have to be paid when the company is profitable and if losses are incurred then the preference shareholders will receive no return.

Debentures

Debentures, like preference shares, carry a fixed rate of return. This is, however, an interest charge and has to be paid even when a company is in a loss-making situation. For example, a 6 per cent unsecured loan stock issued in units of £100 would entail a cost of £6 per year for every unit of stock outstanding. There will be issuing costs for stocks, as with other sorts of marketable stock, that are listed on the Stock Exchange.

The cost of fixed-return finance will depend on the financial risk being taken by the lenders and the prevailing interest rates that exist in the market for long-term funds. Commercial companies will have to pay higher rates of interest than government stocks (or gilts) because the latter would be considered a lower risk. The rate of interest will be higher if the risk being taken is higher.

Rates of interest and fixed-rate loan stock

Changes in market rates of interest will have a direct effect on the price of fixed-rate debentures being traded on the Stock Exchange. For example, if a company issues 5 per cent irredeemable debentures in £10 units, this would mean that each year a £10 investor would receive £0.50 per return. The funds would be lent if this was a competitive return compared with other similar types of lending option. If the rates of interest were to fall, then the price of these debentures would rise because this loan stock would represent a better return than other comparable investments. There would be a higher demand for this stock which would drive the price up. If on the other hand rates of interest were to rise, then this investment would provide a lower return than other investments and so with the demand falling the price of these debentures would also fall. There is thus an **inverse relationship** between the rate of interest and the price of fixed-rate loan stock. Using the irredeemable £10 debenture stock paying a 5 per cent rate as an example, this stock will always pay a £0.50 return annually. The following examples will demonstrate how the change in interest rates will affect the value of the debenture because the return is fixed at £0.50.

◆ If the rate of interest rises to 6%

$$\text{Value of debenture} = £0.50 \times \frac{100}{6} = £8.33$$

◆ If the rate of interest falls to 4%

$$\text{Value of debenture} = £0.50 \times \frac{100}{4} = £12.50$$

In both these cases the fixed annual return of £0.50 as a percentage of the new price of the debenture will give a yield equivalent of the new rate of interest. For redeemable stock which has a specified repayment date the market price will reflect an appropriate yield for loan stock of that duration with the price being nearer to the redemption value as it nears that date. The price of redeemable loan stock will be less sensitive to interest rate changes.

Trade credit

Trade credit does not normally incur an explicit cost. However, in cases where a cash discount is offered for payment within a certain period, failure to take up the discount can prove to be expensive in annual terms. For example, if the credit terms are full payment within 30 days but a 2 per cent discount for payment within 7 days, then conceding the discount can prove very costly. In effect by not claiming the cash discount a company is obtaining an extra 20 days credit at a cost of 2 per cent, which annually would be a rate of 2 per cent × 365/20 = 36.5 per cent.

Bank loans, overdrafts and commercial mortgages

These are usually charged interest at an agreed premium over the bank base rates. The premium will vary according to the type of customer. A low-risk customer may be charged 1.5 to 2 per cent above base rate whereas a high-risk customer may be charged 4 to 6 per cent above base rate. In addition there might be additional fees to pay, such as arrangement fees or security fees, and these can be very expensive on small loans.

The commercial banks do have heavy penalty charges for unauthorised overdrafts with a one-off charge and very high interest charges on top. Clearly the cost of an overdraft is based on the amount outstanding on the current account, and the cost is therefore related to the usage of the funds, whereas the interest on a loan is at the full outstanding value of the loan even if it is not being utilised.

Hire purchase and finance lease agreement

These include a charge that is made explicit in the terms of the contract. These arrangements are rarely cheap, but they are often convenient and costs are comparable with those of alternative sources of finance. A business is getting the use of an asset without having to tie up large amounts of funds but before making such an agreement it would always be sensible to see if alternative ways are more economical. Sometimes interest-free loans are available for buying certain assets as companies try to boost their sales.

Debt factoring

This typically involves charges of 2 to 4 per cent to manage a company's sales ledger and be responsible for collecting the debts. In addition the company will charge an interest rate of between 1 and 3 per cent for advancing the funds, but in evaluating the service it is necessary to consider the cost savings involved in not having to administrate the sales ledger.

Sale and lease back arrangements

These release funds which will either reduce the cost of borrowing or for the investment needed to expand a business. However, the cost of such an arrangement will be the on-going lease payments and the potential loss of property value appreciation.

Weighted costs of finance

Different investors have different expectations in respect of the required rate of return on their investment. This means that the lenders may expect lower returns than shareholders but there will be a **weighted average cost of capital** which is the average needed to satisfy all investors who contribute funds to a business.

For example, a company has:

♦ total shareholder value of £200,000 (share capital of £100,000 and retained profits of £100,000)
♦ £50,000 of 10 per cent debentures
♦ trade credit of £30,000.

The shareholders require a rate of return of 15 per cent. What is the required rate of return from the average business activity, that is, the weighted average cost of capital as it weights to the various expectations?

$$\frac{\text{Total returns required}}{\text{Total finance employed}} \times \frac{100}{1}$$

$$= \text{Weighted average cost of capital}$$

$$\frac{\text{Returns to shareholders + Returns to debentures}}{\text{Shareholder funds + Debentures + Trade credit}} \times \frac{100}{1}$$

$$= \text{Weighted average cost of capital}$$

$$\frac{(200,000 \times 15\%) + (50,000 \times 10\%)}{£200,000 + £50,000 + £30,000} \times \frac{100}{1}$$

$$= 12.5\%$$

This example shows that the company needs on average to earn a 12.5 per cent return on capital employed to satisfy the requirements of all the providers of finance, one of which, the trade creditors, has a zero requirement. Therefore all activities and projects should be targeting a 12.5 per cent return for them to be viable.

In practice there could be some refinement on this approach because activities and projects might be separated and analysed individually. In these cases the evaluation of a project would relate the relevant costs of capital to the project which would be the marginal increase in capital needed. For example, the acquisition of a new piece of equipment on a finance lease could be appraised using the finance charges associated with that lease to determine its viability. When it is not possible to separate activities and projects then using the weighted average cost of capital as a target is the most appropriate methodology.

However, there will inevitably come a time, after continuing to finance expansion on an *ad hoc* basis, when the whole capital structure has to be reviewed. When this occurs a company could issue more share capital or raise further loans or adjust its dividend strategy to equity holders.

Whilst individual finance agreements will each reflect short-term interest rates in the marketplace, the business must actually meet the expectations of many investors over the longer term. Despite market variations in short-term interest rates, the returns expected by shareholders vary very little: the annual rate of 5 per cent in addition to inflation is typical. Investors may expect greater returns when the economy and stock markets are booming, and less at times of recession, but in the longer term the large institutional investors, such as pension funds and insurance companies, have to be assured of funding their own long-term obligations. It follows that a business should consider a long-term return that will meet investors' expectations and also reflect the long-term capital structure of the business. Therefore an individual activity or project should earn sufficient return to satisfy the business's long-term average cost of capital.

The rate required will vary over time, following movements in long-term market rates and changes in the perceived riskiness of the business.

ACTIVITY

1　A company has shareholder funds of £500,000 and debentures of £100,000 at 10 per cent. If the shareholders require a return of 20 per cent, what is the required return from the average business activity?

2　A company has shareholder funds of £1m and debentures of £200,000 at 8 per cent. If the shareholders require a 10 per cent return, what is the required return from the average business activity?

Risks and rates of return

Risk is the uncertainty of predicting a particular outcome. Statistically it may be referred to in terms of the range of possible outcomes, or the deviation around some average value. Risk refers to the possibility of a result that can be better than, as well as worse than, expected. In general, certainty is something that most investors would make some sacrifice to achieve, in terms of potential financial returns. Risk can have two components.

Operational risk

This depends on the technical and commercial viability of the business proposal, with special consideration given to the ability of the management and the inherent competitive advantage that the business has.

Financial risk

This will depend on the financial terms and conditions (such as the duration of the investment) and the security provided in case the business defaults, and on the likely rate of return for the investor. The financial risk will also be affected by the terms given to other investors in the business. For example, a large new long-term loan will increase the gearing ratios and increase the risk for investors including equity holders.

The trade-off between rate of return and risk is illustrated by the long-term returns on **gilts**, that is, government stocks and on ordinary shares. Gilts give a modest rate of return but are very low risk investments. In contrast, ordinary shares in a relatively new and growing business may promise high returns but are accompanied by high risk and the chance of complete failure when the investment will be lost. It follows that the cost of capital of a company cannot be stated without reference to the risk it poses for investors.

Risk and portfolio theory

However, when evaluating an activity or project, it may not be adequate to view the project in isolation from the other aspects of the business. **Portfolio theory** suggests that, unless the returns on individual projects are perfectly and positively interrelated, the risk of one project may to some extent offset the risk of another. This means that the riskiness of a company may be less than the combined risk of its individual activities and projects.

As an example, consider an engineering company that operates one factory supplying tooling to food manufacturers and another factory supplying components for construction equipment. Demand from construction plant customers will swing markedly with the economic trade cycle, whereas other factors, such as changing customer tastes, will affect demand from food manufacturers. Thus, while the expected return from the company as a whole will be the weighted average returns from the two parts of the business, total risk will be less than the weighted average return because the financial results of the two parts of the business are not perfectly and positively correlated.

Individual project risk

Understanding how the risk of an individual project affects the cost of capital for the whole company is not easy. In practice, often the best that can be expected is at least some allowance, perhaps in the form of an ABC risk classification system, where A is low risk and C is high risk. Taking the risk-free rate as a benchmark, increasingly risky projects will be required to generate higher expected rates of return. So, for example, class C projects, perceived as high risk, will have a correspondingly large risk premium added to the risk-free rate as seen in Figure 6.5.

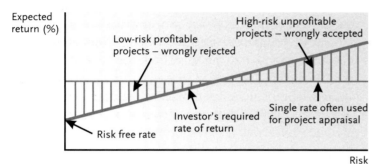

Figure 6.5 Risks and returns

It is clear that businesses which choose a single rate of return in project appraisal are in danger of selecting high-risk unprofitable projects at the expense of low-risk profitable ones. Investors will accept lower returns for low risk but will not want the businesses to enter into riskier projects without expecting a higher return.

Tax considerations

The British tax system affects the relative costs of different sources of finance, and has been instrumental in the growth of debt finance over preference shares. Put simply, interest charges are tax-deductible but dividends are not. This means that in terms of net cost to the company, the percentage rates attached to preference shares and debentures are not directly comparable.

Imagine two companies, X and Y, which:

♦ have both made annual profits of £500,000 before finance charges and taxation
♦ both have capital employed of £2 million
♦ both have ordinary share capital of £1.5 million.

However, Company X is funded by £0.5 million of 10 per cent debentures whereas Company Y is funded by £0.5 million of 10 per cent preference shares. For the providers of the finance both preference shares and debentures give a gross return of 10 per cent and are subject to the same rates of income or corporation tax. It is the ordinary shareholders who are affected by the different financing arrangements. As shown in the results below the ordinary shareholders in Company X have gained to the extent of the tax relief on the debenture interest, that is, 20 per cent of £50,000, which is £10,000.

	Company X (£000s)	Company Y (£000s)
Profit before interest and tax	500	500
Interest	(50)	0
Profit after interest and before tax	450	500
Corporation tax at, say, 20%	(90)	(100)
Profit after tax	360	400
less preference dividends	0	(50)
Profit attributable to ordinary shareholders	360	350

The earlier calculation of the weighted average cost of capital (WACC) can now be refined, having regard to the tax position, by the formula below. In this formula:

♦ I = interest rate
♦ T = the corporation tax rate.

$$\frac{\text{Returns to shareholders} + \{\text{Debt finance} \times I \times (I - T)\}}{\text{Shareholder funds} + \text{Debt finance}} \times \frac{100}{I}$$

= Weighted average cost of capital

The following example will illustrate the effect of tax on the WACC. A company is funded by:

♦ £1 million of ordinary share capital
♦ £0.5 million of 8 per cent preference share capital
♦ £0.5 million of 7 per cent debentures.

Ordinary shareholders receive a dividend of 3 per cent and expect long-term capital growth of 7 per cent per year, that is, an expected return on investment of 10 per cent. Corporation tax is 40 per cent. The WACC can be calculated as follows:

$$\text{WACC} =$$

$$\frac{(£0.5m \times 7\%) + (£0.5m \times 8\%) + (£1.0m \times 10\%)}{£0.5m + £0.5m + £1.0m} \times \frac{100}{1}$$

$$= 8.05\%$$

Note that the relative cost after tax for loan stock is 4.2 per cent, that is, 7 per cent multiplied by 0.6 and for preference shares it is the full 8 per cent.

ACTIVITY

A company is funded by ordinary share capital of £200,000, 8 per cent preference shares of £50,000, 9 per cent loan stock of £70,000, and a bank loan of £30,000 with interest at 10 per cent. Ordinary shareholders enjoy a dividend yield of 5 per cent and expect long-term capital growth of 10 per cent. Corporation tax is 25 per cent. Calculate the weighted average cost of capital (WACC).

Flow of finance

The flow (or cycle) of financial resources is similar to the water cycle in nature. Funds are transformed from a liquid resource into other resources or assets such as property, equipment or stocks. These resources are then used to generate income from customers, which is eventually received in the form of cash ready to continue the cycle. As with the life-giving qualities of water, the flow of cash is essential to the survival of a business. The faster the flow the more financially efficient is the business. It is vital, therefore, that the receipts and payments of cash are properly understood, monitored and controlled.

Cash flow forecast

The **cash flow forecast** or **cash budget** is an invaluable tool in the financial management of a business. It is used to estimate the sources of cash and how it is predicted to be spent. By predicting the amounts that are to be received and spent, and when it is likely to take place, the management of a business can identify when additional finance is likely to be required and make appropriate arrangements. It can also enable the management of a business to earn income for the business by investing surplus funds which are not needed immediately.

Cash flow forecasting is essential for all organisations because their survival and thus ultimate success is dependent on meeting their obligations. Businesses can be profitable but fail because they are not controlling their cash effectively. An example of a cash flow forecast is shown in Figure 6.6. It shows that the process involved is to:

♦ estimate and record the amount of receipts and when they are likely actually to be received
♦ estimate the amount of payments and when they need to be met
♦ calculate the total receipts and the total payments and then the net cash flow that occurs for each time period
♦ adjust the cash/bank balance for the net cash flow for the period to arrive at the estimated new closing balance.

The format of the cash flow forecast should convey a clear and accurate message to its user. The receipts and payments descriptions should be linked and appropriate to the business's accounting system, as should the time divisions. Some businesses may

Example Ltd

Cash flow forecast for the six months ending 30 December 2004

	July	August	Sept	Oct	Nov	Dec	TOTAL
Receipts schedule							
Capital introduced					5000		5000
Cash sales	2400	2400	2400	2700	2700	2700	15300
Credit sales	600	600	800	800	800	800	4400
Computer sales	2960	2220	4440	5180	5920	8880	29600
TOTAL	**5960**	**5220**	**7640**	**13,680**	**9420**	**12,380**	**54,300**
Payments schedule							
Motor vehicle	13,800						13,800
Shop fittings		1000	5000				6000
Equipment							0
Rent, rates, insurance	380	380	380	380	380	380	2280
Purchases	1000	1200	1200	1200	1200	1200	7000
Computer purchases		3520	2640	2640	2200	4840	15,840
Services	80	80	80	80	80	80	480
Advertising, print	50	50	50	50	50	50	300
Sundries	35	35	35	35	35	35	210
Drawings	600	600	600	600	600	600	3600
Interest		78	92	112	41	1	324
TOTAL	**15,945**	**6943**	**10,077**	**5097**	**4586**	**7186**	**49,834**
NET CASH FLOW	**(9985)**	**(1723)**	**(2437)**	**8583**	**4834**	**5194**	**4466**
Balance brought forward	655	(9330)	(11,053)	(13,490)	(4907)	(73)	**655**
Balance carried forward	(9330)	(11,053)	(13,490)	(4907)	(73)	5121	**5121**

Figure 6.6   Cash flow forecast for Example Ltd

prepare cash flow forecasts based on weeks whereas others may do it monthly or quarterly.

Positive carried forward balances indicate cash in hand whereas negative carried forward balances, shown in parentheses, indicate an overdraft position. Once the estimated cash flow forecast has been completed, the management will be able to identify any future problems that are likely to arise and then take measures to deal with them. If there are cash shortfalls predicted then a number of possible actions could be taken, such as:

♦ raising more capital
♦ arranging an overdraft or even a loan
♦ collecting in the debts from credit customers more quickly
♦ delaying payments to credit suppliers and try to negotiate longer payment terms
♦ selling some assets that will not hinder a business's operation, for example manage with less stock or sell some fixed assets.

It is only when the cash flow forecast has been prepared that a business will be able to manage its financial resources effectively and efficiently. For larger enterprises the cash flow forecast will split cash flows up into various categories, these being:

♦ the operating cash flows
♦ capital expenditure flows
♦ other flows.

The operating or cash cycle

The operating cycle or cash cycle refers to cash flows from regular trading activities. This will vary from a manufacturing business compared to a retail business but the principles involved will be similar. For a manufacturing business the operating cycle (see Figure 6.7) will begin with the purchase of raw materials which will then be processed into finished goods which will then be stored as stock until finally sold to customers. If the sale is on credit then the business will only be paid when the customer actually settles his or her account, probably at the end of the agreed credit period.

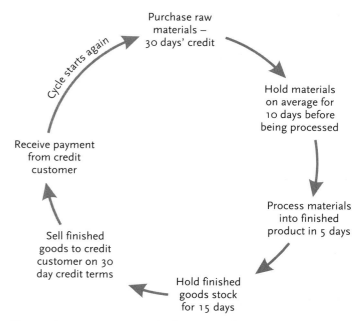

Figure 6.7   Operating cycle for a manufacturing company

The purpose of considering the operating cycle is to identify the level of funds that are tied up in working capital which are not actually earning anything for the business. **Working capital** refers to the funds that are needed by businesses to manage their daily trading activities.

In this example, the manufacturing business needs to pay for a number of costs before receiving any payment from its customers. The business buys raw materials but does not have to pay for them for 30 days. However, it takes 10 stock days before the raw materials are used and then 5 days of manufacturing costs which raises the value of the product and therefore the level of working capital. When the product is completed and ready for sale it is estimated that it will be warehoused for 15 days after which it will be sold, but the payment will not be received for 30 days. This means that the operating or cash cycle in days is:

Stock days	30
+	+
Debtor days	30
−	−
Creditor days	30
=	=
Operating cycle in days	**30**

This means that the business has to fund all sales it makes for at least 30 days before receiving payment. Now if the total costs of the product was £1000 then the business would need to have working capital of £1000 for 30 days. This process will be continuous because every day additional sales will be occurring and additional new production will be going ahead. If the business's sales and production remained at a constant level then a fixed amount of working capital would be required. However, if the business doubled its activity levels then it would need a lot more working capital to finance the additional stock and debtors.

All businesses need sufficient financial resources to meet all their commitments. If a business does not have enough resources then it is **overtrading**. This does not mean that it is trading unprofitably but that it does not have enough funds to finance its operations. When businesses expand they need to increase the levels of working capital available.

In preparing a cash flow forecast the operating cash flows must be included at the point of being paid, for example trade creditors, wages and other expenses, or received, for example debtor receipts.

Capital expenditure

Capital expenditure predictions need to be included in the cash flow forecast. This is expenditure on fixed assets such as premises, vehicles and machinery. Sometimes fixed assets are expected to be sold and then the predicted receipts will need to be included.

Other flows

These could include such payments as taxation, interest on loans and dividends to shareholders. Alternatively a business may predict tax rebates, interest receivable from deposit accounts or dividends receivable from investments in other companies.

The cash flow forecast is a vital component in managing the financial resources of a business and is an essential tool for management to ensure that the business can meet its commitments when they become due but is not using the funds inefficiently.

Finance and the financial statements

All businesses need to prepare financial statements which will detail:

♦ the performance of the business: the **profit and loss account**
♦ the financial position of a business: the **balance sheet**.

Each of these statements will provide the vital and essential information for a wide variety of the users of final accounts, including potential investors, suppliers, lenders and the management. It is therefore necessary to be familiar with these statements to identify where the different sources of finance and their costs can be located.

ACTIVITY

Haroon Malik is planning to set up in business from March as a renovator and retail outlet for antique pine furniture imported from eastern Europe. Before receiving sales income he requires property, a van and stock, which he will collect from the importer's premises. He has found a suitable building on a three-year let, £3000 payable each quarter in advance. He has the opportunity of a second-hand van costing £3700, which he intends to pay for out of the £7000 capital he has paid into the business bank account.

He estimates that his first six months of stock purchases will be £5000, £3000, £2000, £2500, £3000 and £3000. Fortunately the importer is a former business acquaintance of Haroon's and so he has been able to negotiate payment in the month following purchase. Other items of expenditure are estimated to be: vehicle running costs: £500 in the first month and £200 per month thereafter; property-related running costs: £100 per month; occasional help in the shop: £300 per month, and consumable materials for renovation at 10 per cent of each month's stock purchases. Sales will be for cash only and are forecast to start from April, his second month in business. The first monthly sales are forecast to be £2000, £3000, £4000, £5000 and £5000. Haroon has decided to draw up to £700 out of the business each month, assuming there are adequate funds available at the bank.

1   Prepare a cash flow forecast for Haroon for his first six months of trading.

2   What are the significant features of the cash flow?

3   If additional finance is required, suggest three suitable sources with a description of the relevant advantages and disadvantages.

Businesses are started with various objectives in mind. From a purely economic perspective the main goal is to maximise the profitability of an enterprise. Entrepreneurs develop ideas and start up businesses to exploit these ideas. The business might be joining an already existing market where the product or service is delivered to customers by some already established enterprises. In this case the entrepreneur would be confident of being more efficient than existing suppliers and capturing some of their customers. It could be somebody starting a fast food outlet, a fashion shop or providing electrician or plumber services. On the other hand, the business may be started to offer a completely new product or service, such as soft contact lenses, large-headed tennis rackets, laser treatment for eyes or satellite TV. In both types of case the business needs funds, which means acquiring the necessary resources to make and deliver the product or service.

The funding of a business is therefore a means to an end and without the funding in a modern developed society a business will never develop and prosper. All the financial flows of a business are reflected somewhere in the final accounting statements.

Before examining the location of finance in the final accounting statements it is therefore worth briefly considering the accounting equation which underpins all accounting processes and recording. It is built on the premises that:

Assets = Capital + Liabilities

This can then be arranged as:

Assets − Liabilities = Capital

This simple view of accounting means that all businesses need to have funds to buy resources either to make products or to deliver services to customers. The initial finance may be provided by the founder of a business. As soon as the funds are provided to the business a bank account will be opened and the business will possess an asset (money) but have an obligation to the owner. These funds can then be used to buy or hire fixed assets, such as vehicles, premises and machinery, and other resources such as labour, electricity and materials in order to make the product or undertake the service for a customer, who will in turn pay for it.

The final accounts of a business are therefore a summation of how the funds under the stewardship of the management have been spent. For example, if some new equipment is purchased by cheque then one asset (the bank balance) is replaced by another (the equipment). If materials are bought on credit then the business acquires an asset but has an obligation to the supplier, that is, to settle the liability. If the customer buys goods on credit then an asset will disappear: the stock figure will fall but an asset will be acquired, which is the debtor who will eventually pay for the goods. These simple descriptions of a range of transactions demonstrate how businesses are dynamic, changing organisations whose final accounts show the ways in which the finances have been utilised.

367

The balance sheet

This statement is a more complicated version of the accounting equation. An example is shown in Figure 6.8 for a limited company, Pick Ltd. This statement presents the value of all assets, liabilities and capital in a particular way.

Firstly the fixed assets (those that last for a long time) are listed in particular categories. This is followed by the current assets (those which are continually changing) which are netted off against the current liabilities, that is, creditors who have to be paid within one year, to arrive at a figure called **net current assets**.

Then the long-term liabilities (the creditors who do not have to be paid until after at least one year) are listed before being deducted from the total assets less current liabilities figure. Finally any provisions for liabilities and charges (liabilities that are uncertain in amount and time of settlement) are deducted to arrive at the value of the company, its net worth. This is financed by the capital and reserves which means the owner's contribution to the company. This statement therefore identifies where the external funding comes from. In the case of Pick Ltd the external funding has come from:

♦ shareholders contributing capital in exchange for an ownership stake
♦ the retained profits of the company when the shareholders' dividends are less than the attributable profits
♦ long-term lenders found under the heading of 'creditors: amounts due after more than one year'
♦ short-term providers found under 'creditors: amounts due within one year', which could be overdrafts and loans or trade creditors.

The balance sheet provides the source of information to show how the assets of a company have been financed and the make up of the capital structure of the company.

Pick Ltd

Balance sheet as at 31 March 2004

FIXED ASSETS	£s	£s	£s
Tangible assets			
Land and buildings	407		
Plant and machinery	105	512	
Investments			
Other fixed asset investments		100	612
CURRENT ASSETS			
Stocks			
Finished goods		340	
Debtors			
Trade debtors	328		
Prepayments and accrued income	52	380	
Cash at bank and in hand		10	
		730	
CREDITORS: AMOUNTS FALLING DUE WITHIN ONE YEAR			
Bank loans and overdrafts	(28)		
Trade creditors	(94)		
Other creditors including taxation and social security	(145)		
Accruals and deferred income	(72)	(339)	
NET CURRENT ASSETS (LIABILITIES)			391
TOTAL ASSETS LESS CURRENT LIABILITIES			1003
CREDITORS: AMOUNTS FALLING DUE AFTER MORE THAN ONE YEAR			
Debenture loans			(100)
			903
PROVISIONS FOR LIABILITIES AND CHARGES			
Taxation including deferred taxation			(70)
			833
CAPITAL AND RESERVES			
Share capital			400
Share premium			50
Profit and loss account			383
			833

Figure 6.8   Balance sheet for Pick Ltd

Profit and loss account

This statement also identifies where finance comes from and how it is spent but concentrates more on the regular flow of funds. The **profit and loss account** shows the sales or turnover and other income that flows into a business and the costs and expenses that are paid out, for example the cost of sales, administration expenses, interest charges and taxation. These financial flows are continuously taking place but comprise one-off transactions that are usually completed quickly. To undertake trading activities a business needs the long-term investments from the owners and lenders which are found in the balance sheet, with these funds being essential for the support of the trading activities. However, the profit and loss account does show how the long-term investors are serviced with interest being paid to lenders and dividends to shareholders. After the appropriations of dividends to shareholders is a line entitled 'retained profit for the year' and this figure indicates the profits that are not distributed and therefore build up the shareholder value in the company. This is added onto the previous retained profit figure to arrive at a profit and loss account balance which appears in the balance sheet. This figure is a part of ordinary shareholder value and if it keeps on increasing, a long-term source of finance.

Pick Ltd
Profit and loss account for the year ended 31 March 2004

	£s	£s
Turnover		
Continuing operations		1040
Cost of sales		(385)
Gross profit (or loss)		655
Distribution costs	(234)	
Administration expenses	(190)	(424)
Operating profit		
Continuing operations		231
Income from other fixed asset assessment investments		25
		256
Interest payable and similar charges		(13)
Profit (or loss) on ordinary activities before taxation		243
Tax on profit (or loss) on ordinary activities		(90)
Profit or loss on ordinary activities after taxation		153
Appropriations		
Dividends		
Interim dividend	(40)	
Proposed dividend	(80)	(120)
Retained profit (or loss) for the financial year		33
Balance brought forward		350
Balance carried forward		383
EPS = 38.3p per share		

Figure 6.9   Profit and loss account for Pick Ltd

In the **annual report and accounts** of limited companies the financial statements will be supported by notes to the accounts which will provide detail and clarification for the various figures found in these financial statements.

Financial information for decision making

Effective decision making is about making informed choice. The decision maker requires information in order to evaluate the implications of a particular alternative. For example, the decision about whether to buy a component from a supplier or to make it in-house should be based on a whole range of information, including the relative costs involved. Because business is about utilising financial resources in the quest for wealth creation, a substantial amount of information for decision making is inevitably of a financial nature.

The use of financial information means that operational issues can be appreciated from a strategic perspective. Money is used to measure the relevant costs and benefits that would otherwise be difficult to compare. Examples of such issues include:

♦ whether it is worthwhile investing in a new machine to shorten production times
♦ whether quality control be strengthened to reduce product failure rates
♦ whether components should be ordered in bigger batches to take advantage of quantity discounts.

Management decision making requires information that is relevant to future conditions. This requires forecasts based on a set of assumptions, often with regard to historical information, from which valid conclusions can be drawn about future circumstances. For example, if customers are habitually paying their debts late, the implication is that this will continue unless credit control policies are changed.

Decisions requiring financial information can be categorised as relating to either planning or control.

Business planning

Business planning aims to formulate appropriate strategies and policies to achieve the goals of the business. The implementation of business plans gives leadership and motivation to employees and co-ordinates the various activities of the organisation towards a common objective. Planning includes:

♦ allocation of resources between alternative activities or projects, such as whether to proceed with product A or B
♦ evaluation of alternative strategies and/or policies, such as whether to sell through agents or a dedicated sales team
♦ sources of finance for funding a business, for example whether to lease or to buy from retained funds.

Control of activities

This is necessary to ensure that performance is acceptable and is in accordance with the plan. Criteria

are formulated so that performance can be measured and compared against the relevant benchmarks, which may include **costs per unit** and **average selling prices achieved**. Features of a financial control system include:

♦ individuals being held accountable for a specific area, which may be locations such as branch offices, business processes such as credit control or products
♦ a process for performance measurement being established: recording data, collating data and reporting information
♦ performance being compared against a benchmark, such as a planned amount or the value from a previous period
♦ appropriate feedback being given to the managers responsible
♦ deviations from acceptable performance resulting in remedial action being instigated.

Changes in management accounting

Before the 1960s the finance function was primarily charged with fulfilling regulatory requirements for financial reporting and taxation purposes, and as a by-product of this activity it was possible to prepare financial accounts on a monthly basis for internal use. In the past few decades these **management accounts** have been augmented with budgetary information and operational statistics primarily to facilitate the control of the business's activities. In addition to showing progress towards an annual target, they have provided benchmarks to facilitate **management by exception**. For any particular item, for example travel costs, the current spend can be compared with a predetermined budget or a previous period's actual result. Exceptions, highlighted by the calculation of a variance to the benchmark, have been the trigger for management action.

In more recent years, with information technology speeding up basic bookkeeping and report writing, the finance function has been able to turn to the specific demands of the operational management. There has been a call for information to be more accessible and more relevant to the decision-making process. Whilst the finance team has always reported progress towards enhancing shareholder value, it is now required to contribute towards the goal itself. This has required finance managers to sit in on the decision-making process and to enhance the value of the financial information provided.

A primary requirement has been to relate the financial statements presented to the senior management, like the profit and loss account and the balance sheet, to the concerns further down the organisation structure. This requires financial variables to be expressed in terms understood by operational managers. For example, a wage budget represents so many weeks available to complete a specified task.

A top-level concern for any business, whether to grow or merely to survive, is the volume of business (**throughput**). It is not enough to know about the conditions at a point in time, such as the bank balance. There must be information about business activity relating to a period of time, such as sales per week or units per hour.

What financial information is needed?

Financial information must have the properties that distinguish information from mere data. It should be relevant, timely, accurate and give an appropriate level of detail.

Information technology and financial information

Recent innovations in information technology have helped managers to access good-quality financial information. When specific details are required, on-line reporting systems now allow users to investigate high-level summary figures, such as the running costs of the distribution network, by 'drilling down' to the level required. This means obtaining information on the whole distribution operation and then breaking it down into different components such as salaries, transport, administration or premises. These components can in turn be broken down if required, such as the salaries

component into salaries of drivers, warehouse staff or administration. Access to such information in various levels of detail is important because managers tend to have specific needs depending on their function and level within the organisation. By relaying the relevant information operational problems could be identified and decisions made to solve such problems and cut costs. If, for example, driver salaries in the distribution area are higher than expected then investigations can be undertaken to establish the cause and remedy the problem. Without the availability of the detailed information the high costs of driver salaries in the distribution area may never have been discovered.

Long-term planning

Some managers, with long-term planning horizons and wide areas of responsibility, require reports that underpin the primary financial performance indicator, often **return on capital employed**. From a strategic perspective, managers will want to know how financial resources are deployed in the business. This requires an analysis of fixed assets and working capital between the business's various divisions, whether these are factory sites, business functions or product groups. Together with information concerning income and costs, this information can identify how different areas of the business contribute towards financial goals. This information clearly has value for the control of existing activities, but also indicates areas for future expansion and contraction. A decision concerning a new investment or a change in business strategy requires evaluation of its financial implications.

Medium-term planning

Middle managers with functional responsibilities such as marketing, production, finance, and so on are concerned with medium-term planning and historical performance for a particular part of the business. Most of the financial information they receive is for control purposes and tends to involve the highlighting of **variances against an approved budget**. Factory management will be informed of production costs against production volumes. Sales management will be informed of sales costs and revenues for each sales team and individual. There will often be participation in forward planning, although perhaps restricted to annual budgets that relate to their area of responsibility.

Day-to-day management

The day-to day management of financial resources is often the preserve of middle managers in the finance department. To fulfil their responsibilities, they rely heavily on financial information generated by accounting staff.

Financial management is required to ensure the efficient deployment of financial resources and the raising of appropriate new finance when needed. Without active management, financial resources may be tied up unnecessarily in a form that generates more costs than benefits. For example, poor credit control is unlikely to improve customer relationships significantly, but the business will incur charges on the funds invested in trade debtors. Even more importantly, if cash flows cannot satisfy financial obligations to employees and suppliers, there is a threat to the business's very survival.

Stock control

Stocks often represent a significant investment, and at each stage from raw materials to finished goods there is the potential for hold-ups whether systematic or as a result of unplanned events. Good stock control minimises the risk of both too much and too little stock. Adequate stock needs to be held in order to satisfy customer demand in terms of range and delivery times. A stock-out situation may mean gross margin is irreversibly lost, and can even lead to lost future custom. On the other hand, storing materials also incurs significant cost; there are the financial costs of tying up funds that could have been deployed elsewhere, and there are the costs associated with storage, including handling, insurance and clerical costs. In addition, there is the risk of obsolescence, deterioration or theft.

The general rule is to minimise stocks within the context of operational needs. A business should aim for high stock turnover with systematic ordering in line with economic batch quantities. In order to make

appropriate decisions, it is important to have information concerning future demands, lead times and the costs of storage. A significant amount of this information is financial.

Credit control

Like stocks, debtors need to be minimised, with tight control maintained on the credit allowed to customers. Old debts become more difficult to collect, but in addition there is the danger of compounding bad debts with continuing supplies to a debtor.

It is necessary to develop a **credit policy** that addresses each stage from sale through to final payment.

Terms of trade

The first step is to decide on the terms of trade, for example payment at the end of the month following delivery.

Creditworthiness

Then the creditworthiness of the potential customers should be evaluated; this may require references from their bank and other businesses with which they trade. It may also be necessary to make enquiries with credit-rating agencies and obtain the customer's last set of final accounts. The problems with many of these procedures is that they rely on information that soon becomes dated, and in the case of references these may not be representative of how other creditors have been serviced.

Credit limit

More information and confidence will be gained after trading with the customer for a period of time, so it may be appropriate to apply an initial credit limit that is reviewed at a later date.

Invoicing

Once a supply has been made, customers should be invoiced promptly and those customers who persistently extend the credit period afforded to them should be pursued. This requires information that is in sufficient detail for the credit controller to deal with customer queries. Information needs include:

- an age analysis of each customer's debt, with a facility to 'drill down' to specific invoices and delivery details
- a customer's payment record will also be an important consideration when deciding on whether to accept future sales orders.

Fixed assets

Whilst investment in working capital causes most liquidity problems, funds can also be unnecessarily tied up in fixed assets. Any purchase of fixed assets must be the best use of the funds available, and should be the subject of formal capital expenditure authorisation procedures. Unlike investment in working capital, fixed asset expenditure is often discretionary and its authorisation is usually the sole prerogative of senior management.

The purpose of investment in fixed assets may be to:

- replace existing fixed assets that are no longer economical to use, or are technologically obsolete
- comply with health and safety regulations
- expand capacity.

When cash is scarce, decisions have to be made either to defer certain items of expenditure, or consider alternatives, such as short-term hire in the case of assets used infrequently. If some assets are to be hired and some purchased, risk is reduced and flexibility maintained if business funds are tied up in general purpose assets rather than specialist ones. A decision requires financial information about each alternative.

Reporting timetables

Once it has been established what information individual managers require to carry out their decision-making responsibilities, this information must be delivered in a timely and appropriate way. In keeping with other business processes, reporting timetables are continually getting shorter. At one time it was acceptable for management accounts to be issued two weeks after the month end. Now, many firms are aiming for a lead time of just a few days for

formal accounts, and immediate access to key performance indicators such as turnover and committed expenditure. This has been made possible by the advance of information technology. Many firms have replaced the traditional printed financial report with an electronic copy that can be accessed in the office or off-site, using **business intranets** based on Internet technology. Financial reports are now either emailed directly to recipients, or made available in designated areas of the firm's computer network.

Internal financial reports

Internal financial reports typically display the following characteristics:

- **reporting period**: prepared on a monthly basis (either calender month or a discrete number of weeks) with figures for the month and year to date
- **timeliness**: prepared to strict timetables, often within one week
- **detail**: far greater analysis than accounts for publication, including a break-down by department and cost centre
- **format**: an emphasis on clear presentation with a structure of accounts relevant to the activities of the business (unlike published accounts which comply with standard formats); different versions may be issued to different managers depending on their area and level of responsibility
- **comparisons**: actual performance compared with budget and possibly with the same period of the previous year
- **performance measures**: financial and non-financial measures may be included.

Summary

Financial resources have a cost, although the amount is not always explicit in the financing agreement. Cost of finance may be expressed as a fixed rate of return, but for risk capital its valuation will be more subjective, such as the returns expected by ordinary shareholders. The **weighted average cost of capital** attempts to determine the business's overall cost of capital, having regard to the business taxation system that tends to favour debts finance over shareholder finance.

When evaluating business investments, projects must promise a greater return than the cost of capital.

Financial resources are required to fund working capital and to acquire fixed assets. The flow of funds is demonstrated by the various categories of cash flow, such as the operating cash flow cycle.

Good financial management aims to minimise hold-ups in the flow of funds by controlling the amounts invested in the various assets of the business. Efficient flow minimises risk and the amount of funds required, hence reducing financial costs.

The financial statements, the profit and loss account and balance sheet provide valuable information identifying the sources of funds. They can also give indicators of the soundness of the capital structure of a business.

To make decisions that will benefit the financial position of the business, management must be properly informed. The needs of different managers are diverse so financial information should be appropriately designed and delivered to management's requirements wherever possible.

ACTIVITY

Downy Brothers is a department store, selling a range of products from clothing to kitchenware. Each department is a profit centre and department managers are held directly responsible for the contribution they make towards general overheads and profits. General overheads comprise the running costs of the building, general management and central administration.

It is your job to ensure that managers receive financial information that is appropriate to their needs and responsibilities, and that monitors actual performance against budgeted figures.

1   Prepare a list of:

   ♦ ten retail departments within Downy Brothers
   ♦ the type of costs incurred by each department
   ♦ the type of costs incurred in general overheads.

2   Prepare a monthly report for sales and costs using illustrative figures for:

   ♦ a departmental manager
   ♦ the store's general manager.

3   Explain the main features of the reports and how the reports would aid decision making.

Chapter 3

Financial performance

Background to financial performance

It has become a normal practice in the current economic climate for all organisations, whether they are businesses, not-for-profit bodies or public sector organisations, to have their performance evaluated. This involves comparing their actual performance against preset targets or alternatively against their own historic performance or against competitors.

The targets against which performance can be assessed are often referred to as **performance indicators**. They can cover a broad spectrum of activity which can be as diverse as profitability ratios in business, examination success rates in educational institutions, crime detection rates in the police force and success in curing illnesses and injuries in hospital. All these examples focus on different issues but are all concerned with the effective and efficient use of resources.

To be able to carry out objective performance appraisal, organisations need to process and gather relevant information which in turn needs to be both accurate and reliable. Therefore all organisations need to have **recording and reporting systems** in place to ensure that the information collected is appropriate and accurate. The emphasis in this chapter is on business organisations and the way that their annual financial statements can be interpreted for the wide variety of interested parties involved.

All business organisations need to prepare **financial statements** but there are varying requirements for different types of business. For example, unincorporated business, such as sole proprietors and partnerships, do not have legally to prepare financial statements but the Inland Revenue does provide an effective enforcement process in respect of its tax assessment and collection duties.

Companies, however, do have to comply with the statutory requirements set out in the Companies Acts which compel companies to prepare annual financial statements in a standardised format. All financial statements should also conform with accounting standards which in the UK are established by the Accounting Standards Board (ASB).

The financial statements

The emphasis in this section is on the financial statements which by law have to be prepared by limited companies. Unincorporated businesses will prepare similar types of **statements to companies** but they do not have to be in a standardised format. For limited companies the **annual report and accounts** document is sent to the shareholders and then presented at the Annual General Meeting. This procedure enables the senior management team, the Board of Directors, to meet their stewardship responsibilities of accounting for the financial resources entrusted in them by the shareholders. The annual report and accounts document, which must be presented to the shareholders within ten months for a private limited company and seven months for a PLC, consists of the following statements.

Legally required statements

- Profit and loss account
- Balance sheet
- Directors' report
- Notes to the accounts
- Cash flow statement
- Auditor's report (unless the company is exempted from having an annual audit)

Optional statements

- Chairperson's statement or review

The annual report and accounts for PLCs can be obtained without charge from the Company Secretary's Department and it would be worthwhile asking for copies of these for a number of companies which interest you.

Profit and loss account

This is the performance statement for a business for a year's operations. Large companies will report to the shareholders twice a year, these being the **Interim report** after six months' trading and then the **Final report** after a full year's trading. In between these the finance department would usually prepare monthly management accounts so that a company's performance can be continually monitored and decisions made to overcome problems that may arise.

This statement details a company's revenues and costs to determine how profitable a company has been and also shows how any profits have been distributed. The profit and loss account for management purposes will be prepared in an established format but will nevertheless be designed to meet the information requirements of the management. The published profit and loss account, however, has to be in a prescribed format. This is advantageous for all external users because they will be familiar with the presentation and as all limited company accounts will be prepared on the same basis, they can be much more easily used for comparison purposes. Examples of a published profit and loss account and a profit and loss account for management are shown in Figures 6.10 and 6.11.

Published accounts
Pickers PLC

Profit and loss account for the year ended 31 March 2003

	£000s	£000s
Turnover		20,300
Cost of sales		(13,850)
Gross profit (or loss)		6450
Distribution costs	(2314)	
Administration expenses	(1424)	(3738)

Operating profit		2712
Income from other fixed asset assessment investments		125
		2837
Interest payable and similar charges		(813)
Profit (or loss) on ordinary activities before taxation		2024
Tax on profit (or loss) on ordinary activities		(690)
Profit or loss on ordinary activities after taxation		1334

Appropriations

Dividends		
Interim dividend	(240)	
Proposed dividend	(480)	(720)
Retained profit (or loss) for the financial year		614
Balance brought forward		23,350
Balance carried forward		23,964

EPS = 38.3p per share

Figure 6.10   Published profit and loss account

Management accounts
Pickers PLC

Profit and loss account for the year ended 31 March 2003

	£000s	£000s	£000s
Sales			20,300
less Cost of goods sold			
Opening stock		4500	
add Purchases		14,543	
		19,043	
less Closing stock		5193	(13,850)
GROSS PROFIT			6450
Add income			
Income from other fixed asset assessment investments			125
			6575

	£000s	£000s	£000s
less Expenses			
Administration			
Rent and rates	41		
Wages and salaries	1226		
Telephone and postage	32		
Motor expenses	48		
Sundry expenses	37		
Depreciation			
Buildings	10		
Equipment	12		
Motor vehicles	28	1424	
Distribution			
Rent and rates	168		
Wages and salaries	1350		
Telephone and postage	88		
Motor expenses	176		
Advertising	134		
Depreciation			
Buildings	30		
Plant and machinery	112		
Motor vehicles	256	2314	
Financial expenses			
Interest on loans and overdraft		813	4551
Profit (or loss) on ordinary activities before taxation			2024
Tax on profit (or loss) on ordinary activities			(690)
Profit or loss on ordinary activities after taxation			1334
Appropriations			
Dividends			
Interim dividend		(240)	
Proposed dividend		(480)	(720)
Retained profit (or loss) for the financial year			614
Balance brought forward			23,350
Balance carried forward			23,904

Figure 6.11 Management profit and loss account

There are a number of terms that are included in this statement which need to be explained and fully understood.

Profit and loss account financial terms

Turnover: this refers to sales and represents the value of goods and services sold to customers excluding VAT.

Cost of sales: this refers to the cost value of the goods sold to the customers. For a trading organisation like Pickers PLC this is calculated by adding opening stock to any purchases before deducting closing stock. For a manufacturing business this figure will be comprised of the costs of manufacturing finished goods before they are actually sold. These manufacturing costs could be raw materials, direct factory labour, as well as overheads such as production management salaries, factory expenses and the depreciation of plant and machinery. For published accounts all the expenses are classified into the two categories of distribution costs and administration expenses.

Distribution costs: these refer to the costs of distributing the goods to the customers and will include the costs of retail outlets, warehousing, advertising and marketing, transport and delivery.

Administration expenses: these refer to the costs of general administration such as general management salaries, office costs, general insurance, accounting costs, administrative overhead costs, and so on.

Operating profit: this is the profit from operating activities and excludes investment income and the costs of external funding.

Income from investments: this refers to the dividends from ordinary shares that have been bought by a company as an investment. It is classed as unearned income. When investing surplus funds the expectation is that the shares will earn a return as well as increasing in value. Another sort of unearned income could be interest received on bank deposits.

Interest paid or payable: this refers to the costs of borrowing funds to finance a business. It has to be shown separately and is useful in that it can show how vulnerable a business is to external lenders.

Taxation: this refers to taxation that companies, which are separate legal entities, have to pay on profits. It primarily refers to corporation tax.

Dividends: these are the rewards to shareholders for their investments in a company's shares. The shareholders of large PLCs are likely to receive an interim dividend halfway through a company's accounting year and will also be the recipient of a final dividend which will be proposed by the directors at the AGM and which needs to be approved by a majority of the shareholders. Dividends will usually only be paid if a company is making profits although the directors can call on past profits to pay dividends if they are insufficient in the current year.

Retained profits for the year: these are the profits earned in a particular year that are not distributed to shareholders as dividends but are kept by the company to finance its growth and development. These retained profits will represent increased shareholder value because they do belong to the ordinary or equity shareholders.

Balance brought forward: these are the retained profits over the whole life of a company up to the beginning of the current accounting year. This figure will generally be the largest figure for funding companies that have had a relatively long existence. This can be confirmed by examining the annual report and accounts of some PLCs.

Balance carried forward: this represents the current year's retained profits added to the retained profits over the previous life of the company.

Earnings per share (EPS): this is a very important indicator which is calculated by dividing the profit on ordinary activities after taxation less preference dividends by the average number of ordinary shares in existence at the year end. It is a quick measure of the value created during the year for one ordinary share.

The management accounts show more detail and will allow the senior managers to examine costs and expenses more closely to identify specific problems and consider the actions needed to resolve such problems.

Depreciation

One item in the management accounts that needs further explanation is depreciation. This is the cost of the fixed assets shared out over the number of years expected to benefit from its use. It can be calculated by a number of methods but the two most commonly used are the **straight line method** and the **reducing balance method**. A company is permitted to choose the method used but this must be stated in the first note to the accounts titled 'accounting policies'. Whichever method is used the effect will be the same over the life of the fixed asset, but the costs will be distributed differently over the various accounting years.

Straight line method

The straight line method shares the cost of the fixed asset equally over its expected life by dividing the cost of the fixed asset by the number of years of expected use.

Reducing balance method

The reducing balance method on the other hand uses a fixed percentage figure on the net book value of the fixed asset. In the first year this will be the cost but in subsequent years it will be the cost less the accumulated depreciation, that is, the total depreciation over the life of the fixed asset to date.

This means that the depreciation figure in the early years of a fixed asset's life carries more depreciation than the later years. It must be realised that depreciation is an expense to a business, which is why it appears in the profit and loss account, but in total it is set against the cost of the fixed asset in the balance sheet. It is not directly shown in the published accounts because it is a part of the costs included in either the cost of sales or distribution costs or administrative expenses. However, a note will always be attached to the published accounts called a **movement of fixed assets schedule**. This will disclose:

♦ the amount of depreciation set aside for the year
♦ the costs of the various categories of fixed asset
♦ the accumulated depreciation on these fixed assets
♦ the net book value of each category of fixed asset.

Although a business will estimate the expected life of a fixed asset it may be disposed of earlier than this date, which will lead to either a profit or loss being made on it.

ACTIVITY

The figures below set out an extract from a profit and loss account. Work out the missing figures for:

♦ gross profit
♦ operating profit
♦ profit before taxation
♦ profit for the financial year (after tax)
♦ profit retained.

Profit and Loss Account for Exclusive Hotels for the year ended 31 December, 2005

	£m
Turnover	700
Cost of sales	400
Gross profit	?
Administrative expenses	100
Operating profit	?

	£m
Interest payable	(20)
Profit before taxation	?
Taxation	(30)
Profit for the financial year (after tax)	?
Dividends	50
Profit retained	?

CASE STUDY

Profits dip at Ryanair

Ryanair, the low-cost Irish airline, warned of a 'bloodbath' among European carriers as it reported its first quarterly loss since flotation (1997) when it published its results in June 2004.

Losses in the final quarter from January to March were 3.5m euros. The three-month loss helped contribute to Ryanair's first fall in annual profits for 15 years, after a year in which the airline's average fares fell 14 per cent and the industry as a whole was riven by surging fuel costs, the war in Iraq and threat of terrorist attacks.

Pre-tax profits for the year fell 14 per cent to 228.5m euros, although on an after-tax basis the decline was smaller than expected, at 5 per cent. Michael O'Leary, Ryanair's chief executive, predicted that Ryanair's own fares would fall by another 5–8 per cent in 2004. 'It's a bloodbath out there and it's going to continue,' he said. 'It's a very shitty marketpace with fare wars breaking out all over the place. But we look forward to that because we remain convinced that the lowest cost operator will win.'

1 Which item in the profit and loss account are rising fuel costs most likely to affect?

2 Which item in the profit and loss account are lowering prices of fares most likely to affect?

3 Explain how these changes will have led to the fall in annual profits.

4 How might lowering prices help to increase profitability at Ryanair in the longer term?

Balance sheet

This is the **positional statement** of a business which shows its value at a particular point in time. This can be visualised by the value of the net assets, that is, the total assets less total liabilities, or the amount of shareholders funds. The example in Figure 6.12 shows the composition of a balance sheet. The management accounting balance sheet will not be significantly different from a published accounts balance sheet.

As with the profit and loss account there are a number of terms that are included in this statement which need to be explained and fully understood.

Balance sheet financial terms

Assets: these are either physical or intangible items which a business owns or the amounts owed to a business.

Fixed assets: these are assets that are purchased to help a business be more efficient, productive and successful. They are usually higher value items that will last a number of years. They are either:

♦ **Intangible assets**: assets that can be purchased or built up over time but are difficult to value, such as patents on a new invention, copyright on publications, goodwill (which is where the value of a company is higher than the value of its net assets because of such things as a loyal workforce, an exceptional reputation, a loyal customer base, a high-quality management team).

♦ **Tangible assets**: physical assets that can seen and touched. They include such things as plant and machinery, land and buildings, motor vehicles, fixtures and fittings, equipment.

♦ **Investments**: the ownership of shares in another company or securities which will yield some income and will hopefully retain or increase their value. There is always the risk that they may fall in value. Companies undertake such investment because they have surplus funds which cannot be utilised in a better way or because they want to build up a stake in a company with the intention of launching a takeover. They are classed as fixed asset investments purely because the company through the directors intends to keep them for a long period of time.

Current assets: these are short-term assets which do not remain with the business for long. They are continually changing. They include:

♦ **Stocks**: raw materials waiting to be processed into finished goods or services, work in progress which are goods which have not been fully manufactured, finished goods which are waiting to be sold to customers.

♦ **Debtors**: amounts owed to a company; could be credit customers who are owing for the goods or services purchased, services that have been prepaid by a company. They change continually because customers are always settling their debts and purchasing new supplies.

♦ **Investments**: these could feature under this heading because a company may intend to keep them for a short period of time, usually less than a year.

♦ **Bank/Cash**: the amount of money held at the bank or in the tills or office safe. It will again continuously change because customers will be settling their accounts and a company will be paying its suppliers.

Liabilities: these are amounts owing to suppliers or to lenders. They can be put into two broad categories:

♦ **Creditors: amounts falling due within one year**: these are often referred to as current liabilities, that is, those amounts that are owed that have a short settlement period. They could be trade creditors, bank overdrafts, accruals (expense creditors). Other examples are corporation tax liabilities at the end of an accounting year and proposed dividends.

♦ **Creditors: amounts falling due after more than one year**: these are often referred to as long-term liabilities and refer to those debts that do not have to be settled for at least a year. They could be bank loans, debentures or mortgages.

Net current assets/liabilities: calculated by deducting from current assets all the creditors' amounts due within one year. It is an important figure because it gives an indicator of the immediate vulnerability of a company and whether it can meet all of its commitments as they become due. It is sometimes referred to as working capital.

Provisions for liabilities and charges: these are special amounts that are transferred from the profit and loss account to deal with special situations which are uncertain in amount and time. One example is a company's commitments to pay its employees' pensions. If the pension is a defined benefit pension, in other words one based on an employee's final salary, then it is a liability, which is difficult to evaluate. The company will not know what the employee is going to be earning when they return or when they retire or for how long they are going to live after retirement.

Capital and reserves: these refer to how the net assets of a company are financed. Capital is the amount of share capital contributed by the owners and reserves refers to the other ways that assets are funded other than by money being received from share capital contributors.

Share capital: the shareholders are the owners of a company. They become shareholders by paying for shares offered by the company. It is a way of raising large amounts of total capital because a large number of subscribers can each contribute a small amount of the share capital.

Share premium: a share premium occurs when a company sells its shares for a higher price than their nominal or face value. Companies are able to sell shares at higher prices because the market recognises that this is their true worth. This higher value could be because of the future potential of the company or because of the reserves of a company which belong to the shareholders and raise the value of each share. In the case of Pickers PLC there are 5 million shares of £1.00 each which according to the balance sheet are worth 34,824,000 divided by 5,000,000 which equals £6.97 per share. If further shares were issued at this price the share premium would be £5.97 per share.

Other reserves: these occur where value is transferred from the profit and loss account to another reserve such as a general reserve.

Revaluation reserve: this occurs when assets which had been bought a number of years ago are revalued. This will mean that the asset, for example land or buildings, will rise in value and increase the shareholder value as per the balance sheet; it must be reflected in the 'financed by' section.

Profit and loss account: the value in this account is the result of past profits that have not been distributed to the shareholders, that is, the retained profits.

**Published accounts
Pickers PLC**

Balance sheet as at 31 March 2004

FIXED ASSETS	£s	£s	£s
Intangible assets		970	
Tangible assets		27,605	
Investments		2100	30,765

CURRENT ASSETS			
Stocks		5193	
Debtors		3480	
Cash at bank and in hand		130	
		8803	

CREDITORS: AMOUNTS FALLING DUE WITHIN ONE YEAR (3914)

NET CURRENT ASSETS (LIABILITIES) 4889

TOTAL ASSETS LESS CURRENT LIABILITIES 35,654

CREDITORS: AMOUNTS FALLING DUE AFTER MORE THAN ONE YEAR (650)

35,004

PROVISIONS FOR LIABILITIES AND CHARGES (180)

34,824

CAPITAL AND RESERVES		
Called up share capital (£1.00 ordinary shares)		5000
Share premium		1000
Other reserves		2860
Revaluation reserve		2000
Profit and loss account		23,964
		34,824

Figure 6.12   Published balance sheet

Notes to the accounts

The notes to the accounts have to be attached to the financial statements and are a statutory requirement. They provide further explanations and clarification of the data found in the financial statements. The notes to the accounts therefore need to be closely examined when reviewing and analysing the performance of a company. The notes will deal with items in both the profit and loss account and the balance sheet.

It is worth looking at some examples of areas that require notes to the accounts.

General

The first note to the accounts will always be about the accounting policies adopted by the company. This is an important disclosure requirement for anybody using the financial data within the financial statements. This is because different companies may adopt different methods of dealing with items in the financial statements. Examples of the accounting policies which have to be disclosed are:

♦ the way in which the depreciation of fixed assets is dealt with: this involves stating the method of depreciation, for example the straight line method as opposed to the reducing balance method and the rates used, which will need to be taken into account when comparing the performances of two companies (although the profitability in the profit and loss account might be the same the depreciation costs that are included as expenses may be different because of the different methods and rates used)
♦ the way in which stocks are valued
♦ the approach to dealing with bad debts and potential bad debts.

Profit and loss account

There will always be a note on the average number of staff employed and the staff costs.

Details of certain costs included in the calculation of operating profit are given, such as depreciation, auditor's remuneration, hire of plant and equipment and directors' salaries.

Segmental reporting occurs where there is a breakdown of turnover and operating profit into:

♦ different operating activities, such as brewing and distilling alcoholic drinks and managing a chain of pubs and hotels
♦ different geographical areas, such as the UK, USA, Europe.

This will allow the analyser of the final accounts to see how different sections of the company are performing.

Balance sheet

A **movement of fixed asset schedule** has to be prepared which provides details of each category of fixed asset in respect of costs, additions, sales/disposals and depreciation.

There will be an analysis of the type of stocks in existence between raw materials, work in progress and finished goods.

There will be a breakdown of debtors into different types, such as trade debtors (amounts owed by credit customers), prepayments, other debtors such as loans to subsidiary companies.

Also included is a breakdown of both 'creditors amounts due within one year', for example trade creditors, taxation, proposed dividends, accruals, and 'creditors due after more than one year', such as bank loans, mortgages, debentures.

A note will be included on the movements of share capital and reserves, for example new share capital subscribed during the year, transfers into reserves, revaluations of fixed assets.

All of the above will enable the analysis of both the performance and the position of a company to be improved.

Cash flow statement

The cash flow statement is another statutory document that must be prepared by companies and is controlled by Financial Reporting Standard 1: Cash flow Statements (FRS 1). Accounting standards are set in the UK by the Accounting Standards Board (ASB) which investigates a current accounting issue and then produces a discussion document called a Financial Reporting Exposure Draft (FRED). Once feedback has been received and further modifications have occurred, such standards become part of a set of rules which have to be adhered to when recording information in the books of account and preparing financial statements.

Cash flow statements are statements which focus on activities during a particular accounting period, usually a year, but with the emphasis being on cash generation and usage. It must be understood that businesses can make profits and still fail, that is, become **insolvent** because they cannot meet their commitments to suppliers and lenders. Alternatively businesses may make losses but still be able to survive because they have sufficient cash generation and cash resources to meet their commitments. Cash flow statements examine the cash generated by a company and how it is used. FRS 1 sets out the way that cash flow statements must be presented and what information they are to contain. An example is shown in Figure 6.13, in respect of Pickers PLC. The various headings and terms need further explanation.

Cash flow statement financial terms

Reconciliation of operating profit with cash flow from operating activities: this reconciliation is to move from the operating profit, that is, the profit from day-to-day trading activities, to the cash generated from such activities. This reconciliation is necessary because profit is not the same as cash. Within the reconciliation there are items that:

♦ have affected profit but do not affect cash, such as depreciation which is an expense but does not involve cash being paid out so it is added back

♦ items that do not affect profit but do affect cash, such as changes in working capital. For example, if creditors are reduced then cash is being used up but profit remains unchanged, or if debtors are being reduced then cash is being received but again profit remains unchanged. This analysis can be applied to all the items contained in the reconciliation.

The final figure that appears in the reconciliation is the first figure that appears in the actual cash flow statement. All items in this statement will affect the cash/bank balance directly.

Returns on investment and servicing of finance: this part examines the effects on cash of interest paid for the use of funds, that is, loans and also the income that flows in from investing surplus funds in, for example, ordinary shares or deposits at a bank.

Taxation: again the focus is on cash flow and in this case one has to be careful. The taxation figure in the profit and loss account is an estimate for the current year and becomes a year-end creditor which will not be paid until nine months after the year end. However, last year's taxation figure will be paid in the current year and so this is the figure which needs to be included in the cash flow statement.

Capital expenditure and financial investment: this refers to expenditure on fixed assets which will lead to outflows of cash, and sales of fixed assets which will result in inflows of cash. In addition a company may sell investments, such as ordinary shares, with cash flowing into the business or it may purchase more investments in which case cash will flow out of the business.

Equity dividends: these are dividends paid out on ordinary shares. They could be interim dividends or final proposed dividends which are approved by the shareholders at the AGM. As with taxation, the final proposed dividends will not be paid until the next accounting year but last year's proposed dividend will be paid in the current year along with any interim dividends.

Management of financial resources: this refers to assets that are almost the equivalent of cash and thus carry very low levels of risk in holding them. Alternatively they might be called marketable securities because they can be bought and sold very quickly, for example treasury bills issued by the government, or bills of exchange.

Financing: this refers to any changes in the way that the company is financed. For example, more share capital being ssued will result in inflows of cash whereas repayments of long-term loans will lead to outflows of cash.

Pickers PLC

Cash flow statement for the year ended 31 March 2003

	£000s	£000s
Reconciliation of operating profit with cash flow from operating activities		
Operating profit		2712
Depreciation for the year		448
Profit from the sale of fixed asset invesments		0
Increase in stocks		(242)
Increase in debtors		(168)
Decrease in creditors		(136)
		2614
Net cash inflow from operating activities		2614
Returns on investment and servicing of finance		
Interest paid	(813)	
Dividends received	125	(688)
Taxation		(586)
Capital expenditure and financial investment		
Purchase of tangible fixed assets	(1426)	
Sale of fixed asset investments	40	(1386)
Equity dividends		(600)
Management of liquid resources		0
Financing		
Share capital issued	200	
Share premium	1200	
Bank loans repaid	(300)	1100
Increase in cash		454

Figure 6.13   Cash flow statement for Pickers PLC

The final figure in the cash flow statement shows how the cash figure has either increased or decreased during the year. This figure will match the difference in the cash/bank figure from last year's balance sheet to the figure in the current balance sheet. Cash flow statements can only be prepared when last year's and this year's balance sheets are available and preferably with this year's profit and loss account.

ACTIVITY

1   What is typically the main source of cash inflow to a hotel chain?

2   Give two other possible sources of cash inflows.

3   Explain three typical sources of cash outflows from the hotel chain.

Auditor's report

The accounts of a limited company, with a turnover of more than £5.5 million, are required by law to be audited by a firm of independent accountants who are approved to undertake audits. The audit report is included in the annual report and accounts.

The **auditors** are required to verify the accuracy of the underpinning records and to ensure that the final accounts are consistent with those records. The accounting treatment of all material items should be confirmed as being in accordance with the relevant legislation and complying with accounting standards where appropriate.

Responsibilities of auditors

The overriding responsibility of the auditors is to protect the interests of the shareholders and confirm that the final accounts show a 'true and fair view' of the performance of the company in respect of the profit and loss account and the valuation of the company as per the balance sheet. This is an important function and any interested party should examine the auditor's report to see whether the final accounts do show a 'true and fair view' of the company.

Qualification of report

If the auditors are able to confirm the accuracy of the final accounts then an **unqualified report** will be given. However, if there is some uncertainty about the results then the auditors will have to give a **qualified report**. These qualified reports could be of two types:

An exception report

This means that the auditors do not agree with the accounting treatment of one particular aspect of the business but apart from this the financial statements do show a true and fair view of the performance and position of the company.

A disagreement report

This means that there are fundamental disagreements with the management on the underlying accuracy of the records and/or the accounting treatment and therefore the financial statements do not show a true and fair view of the performance and position of the company.

The qualification of an audit report will have implications for the users of that information. If the information is subject to doubt and unreliability then the interested parties who are analysing the financial statements will probably take little credence of the results.

Financial information: the users and interpretation

By having access to the financial statements of a business (the profit and loss account and balance sheet), the various stakeholders are able to use these results to interpret the performance and position of the business. This function of interpretation is to convert the information in the financial statements into a simpler form to evaluate the management's stewardship of the business. This is achieved by **ratio analysis** which can be defined as, 'the process of converting the information in the financial statements into an easier interpretive form which will reveal the strengths and weaknesses of a business and identify the causes which have contributed to these strengths and weaknesses to enable corrective action to be undertaken if appropriate'.

In calculating **accounting ratios** or **performance indicators** it is important to put them into context, as users could be easily submerged by too much data which will lose its meaning and purpose. It is sensible to calculate a range of accounting ratios but it is then vital to focus on those that are exceptional. In identifying exceptional ratios there is a need to compare the ratios calculated from reference points or standards, that is, benchmarks. These standards or benchmarks can be established by examining business performance:

♦ over time to establish trends; this could be done over months, quarters or more commonly years
♦ against other businesses of a similar type where trade averages can be used; other businesses of a similar size; businesses in different industries, that is, analysis could be against competitors, different types of business; different sizes of business
♦ against objectives which need to be met, which are set by the management in terms of profitability, sales or asset growth; alternatively standards be established by interested parties such as suppliers or lenders.

What is a trade average?

A trade average is where a trade association for a particular type of business, such as the Society of Motor Manufacturers and Traders, obtains the financial statements for all its members and calculates average ratios for the trade.

The ratios can be calculated for any type of business organisation, such as a sole proprietor, partnership, limited company or co-operative, although the presentation of the accounts will be slightly different in each case. The focus of this analysis will be on limited companies.

Users of accounting information or accounting ratios

The interpretation and analysis of financial statements is an important function in evaluating the performance and position of an organisation whatever its objectives might be. The interested parties, that is, the stakeholders who review the financial statements, will have different perspectives on the results which will be dependent on their relationship or potential relationship with the organisation. Some of these perspectives are now considered.

Focus of interest for different user groups

Investors and owners

The investors and owners of a business are interested in two aspects:

♦ return on investment
♦ the increasing value of the investment.

   The focus will thus be on the profitability and growth of a business.

Employees and trade unions

The employees and/or trade unions are interested in improving their working conditions, including higher pay and sustaining jobs. Improving profitability and growth will put employees in a stronger negotiating position to obtain better working conditions and more secure employment.

Lenders and financial institutions

Lenders and financial institutions are interested in ensuring that loans that are approved will be repaid. This involves examining the **stability and liquidity** of a business as opposed to its profitability.

Suppliers and trade creditors

Suppliers and trade creditors are interested in when debts are likely to be settled or if there are dangers that they will not be settled at all.

Credit customers

Credit customers are interested in continuous supplies from suppliers, as their own business would be affected by any disruption in supply arising from a lack of stability in the supplying organisation.

Government and tax authorities

The government and tax authorities are interested in the profits and sales of businesses to ensure that tax has been accurately assessed.

Management

The management use the financial statements to identify problems which need solving so that a strategy can be implemented to remedy such problems.

General public

The general public may be interested in companies' financial statements because of excessive profits being made, or low wage costs or a poor environment record.

Calculating key ratios

The range of ratios to be calculated can be very broad but will be confined to those falling into the following categories:

♦ profitability
♦ liquidity and short-term solvency
♦ stability and long-term solvency
♦ efficiency/asset utilisation
♦ company/investment ratios
♦ other ratios.

   All of these ratios can be calculated using information that can be extracted directly from the final accounting statements. Also consider the **operating or cash cycle** described on pp. 365–7.

Profitability ratios

All businesses have an objective of making profit and the profitability ratios examine the relationship between profit against sales, assets and capital employed.

Gross profit percentage (or gross margin)

$$\frac{\text{Gross profit}}{\text{Sales (or turnover)}} \times \frac{100}{1} = \text{Gross profit \%}$$

This ratio expresses the gross profit (GP) in relation to sales, that is, gross profit per pound of sales, and this would usually be expected to remain reasonably constant for a business. However, this percentage figure will be different for different types of business; food retailing will have a low GP percentage but jewellery retailing GP percentages will be very high. If there is a significant change in the figure or the figure is markedly different from that of competitors, then an investigation needs to be undertaken to establish the causes which can be attributed to either a change in the selling price or the purchasing price or manufacturing cost. It is also important to realise that a higher figure is not always a better figure because it may be due to higher prices being charged which could lead to lower volumes being sold and less overall gross profit.

Net profit percentage (or net margin)

$$\frac{\text{Net profit}}{\text{Sales (or turnover)}} \times \frac{100}{1} = \text{Net profit \%}$$

N.B. For a company 'net profit' refers to 'profit on ordinary activities before taxation'

This ratio expresses the net profit (NP) in relation to sales, that is, net profit per pound of sales. As the net profit is calculated after expenses (overhead costs) this ratio is essentially measuring the efficiency of the use of these expenses. If the NP percentage decreases then an investigation into the various expenses will isolate the cause of the change and enable corrective action to be implemented. Many businesses facing difficult trading conditions consider a range of cost-cutting options in the expenses area.

Return on capital employed (ROCE)

$$\frac{\text{Profit on ordinary activities before interest and tax}}{\text{Capital employed (share capital and long-term liabilities)}} \times \frac{100}{1}$$

$$= \text{ROCE \%}$$

This ratio shows how effectively the capital employed, and thus the assets, are being used in the business. The result can thus be compared with alternative ways of investing the capital, such as the return offered by a building society, bank or another business.

With this ratio the higher the percentage the better the performance. One problem involved with the calculation is determining the 'capital employed' figure which leads to many possible ways of calculating the ratio. In the formula identified above, share capital and reserves and long-term liabilities have been used. The use of the 'return on equity' formula below does help to overcome the problem of identifying a relevant 'capital employed' figure. An additional problem, having determined the components of the 'capital employed' figure, is to decide whether to use opening balance or the average balance or the closing balance, although usually the closing balance will be used.

Return on equity (ROE)

$$\frac{\text{Profit on ordinary activities after tax and pref. dividends}}{\text{Ordinary share capital and reserves}} \times \frac{100}{1} = \text{ROE \%}$$

This ratio examines the performance of just equity capital but is based on similar principles and techniques. The higher the ratio the better the performance.

Liquidity and short-term solvency ratios

All businesses have an objective of survival which means that all commitments (creditors) must be met at the right time. Many businesses fail because they have liquidity problems rather than a lack of profitability. Liquidity problems relate to insufficient assets that will be turned into cash to meet such regular commitments. Creditors who become impatient can take civil action because of a breach of contract which could lead to business failure. These ratios are therefore focusing on the financial stability of a business.

Current ratio (or working capital ratio)

$$\frac{\text{Current assets}}{\text{Current liabilities}} = \text{Current ratio}$$

Working capital is needed by all businesses in order to finance day-to-day trading activities. The current ratio measures the relationship between current assets and current liabilities, that is, those assets which will become perfectly liquid within 12 months against those liabilities that will have to be paid within 12 months.

Although there is no ideal current ratio a well-established benchmark of 2:1, that is, two pounds of current assets covering one pound of current liabilities, is recognised as being safe although many businesses, especially those in the retail trade, can operate well below this figure. It should also be acknowledged that the current ratio could be too high when too much value is held in working capital – for example, too much stock is held or trade debtors are too high – which in itself does not generate revenue. It is therefore necessary to balance the ratio between safety and return.

Acid test ratio (or quick asset ratio)

$$\frac{\text{Current assets} - \text{Stock}}{\text{Current liabilities}} = \text{Acid test ratio}$$

This ratio measures current assets minus stock against current liabilities, and thus examines whether a business has sufficient cash or very liquid resources to meet its immediate commitments. Again there is no ideal ratio but a well-recognised benchmark for

safety is 1:1 even though many businesses may operate well below this figure. Also, as with the current ratio, this figure could be too high which means that financial resources are not being effectively used as too much capital is tied up in non-income creating assets. This particular ratio will provide evidence of a stock control problem when both the current and acid test ratios are considered together. If the current ratio is satisfactory but the acid test ratio is dangerously low it indicates that too much stock is being held.

Stability and long-term solvency ratios

Capital gearing ratio

$$\frac{\text{Prior charge capital}}{\text{Total capital}} \times \frac{100}{1}$$

$$= \text{Capital gearing ratio}$$

The liquidity ratios (current and acid test ratios) focus on a business's ability to meet short-term commitments whereas the gearing ratios are concerned with the long-term financial stability of the business. The capital gearing ratio relates 'total capital' (ordinary share capital, preference share capital and loan capital) with 'prior charge capital' (preference share capital and loan capital) to highlight the vulnerability of a business to its external financiers. The higher the ratio the more vulnerable the business will be. As with liquidity ratios, although there are no ideal standards it is generally acknowledged that a ratio above 50 per cent is unacceptable and places a company in a critical position. When the percentage figure is rising a company is becoming more highly geared, and less stable. This is because the interest on the long-term debt has to be repaid reguarly and also the loan capital has to be eventually repaid. With equity capital there is more flexibility because dividends will be paid when they can be afforded and the ordinary share capital will never have to be repaid. For the purposes of the calculation, preference shares are classed as loan capital. It is necessary to be watchful when reviewing ratio results as there are alternative ways of calculating this ratio.

Debt:equity ratio

$$\frac{\text{Prior charge capital}}{\text{Ordinary share capital and reserves}} \times \frac{100}{1}$$

$$= \text{Debt:equity ratio}$$

This is a similar ratio to the capital gearing ratio but using a slightly different formula. With this ratio a company is highly geared if the ratio is more than 100 per cent. It is considered to be in the safety zone if the ratio is less than 100 per cent, that is, when one pound of equity capital is covering one pound of long-term loan capital.

Cash flow ratio

$$\frac{\text{Net cash inflow}}{\text{Total debts}} = \text{Cash flow ratio}$$

This ratio measures the 'net cash inflow' against 'short-term and long-term creditors' and gives an indicator of whether a company is generating sufficient cash from operations to meet its foreseeable debts and commitments.

Interest cover

$$\frac{\text{Profit before interest and tax}}{\text{Interest charges}}$$

$$= \text{Interest cover mulitple}$$

This relates the interest charges to the profitability of a company to see how easily these charges can be met, and how vulnerable the company would be to changes in interest rates and/or profitability. The higher the multiple the lower the risk involved.

Efficiency and asset utilisation ratios

These ratios measure the management efficiency of various current assets and liabilities and the efficiency in the use of fixed assets.

Stock turnover

$$\frac{\text{Cost of goods sold}}{\text{Average stock}}$$

$$= \text{Stock turnover in a year}$$

$$\frac{\text{Average stock}}{\text{Cost of goods sold}} \times 365$$

$$= \text{Stock days}$$

This ratio relates the 'cost of goods sold' to average stock levels over a specific period of time, usually a year. Business will be seeking to increase the stock turnover per year or reduce the stock days. Different types of business will have different stock turnover rates, but increasing the rate or reducing stock days will reflect improving efficiency and more effective stock control. This can arise by either reducing the level of stock but maintaining sales levels or increasing sales levels without having to increase stock levels by the same relative amount. As with other ratios, performance can be judged against previous years' and against other businesses. This ratio cannot of course be used for a business that only provides a service.

Debtors' collection period

$$\frac{\text{Trade debtors}}{\text{Credit sales}} \times \frac{365}{1} = \text{Average debtor days}$$

This ratio shows how many days, on average, trade debtors take to settle their accounts. This figure can be compared with the usual credit terms and conditions that are granted and also against previous years' results and those from similar businesses. If the collection time is increasing it is an indication of ineffective credit control within a business.

Creditors' settlement period

$$\frac{\text{Trade creditors}}{\text{Credit purchases}} \times \frac{365}{1} = \text{Average creditor days}$$

This calculation is the opposite aspect to that of the debtors' collection period. The ratio measures how many days, on average, it takes a business to pay its trade creditors. Again this figure can be compared with the average credit terms provided by suppliers and also against previous years' results and those from similar businesses. Increasing the creditor settlement period can be a useful source of finance but problems can arise if payments are made after the date allowed, such as deteriorating relationships with suppliers, the possibility of discontinued supply and a poorer reputation within the trade.

Fixed asset and sales ratios

$$\frac{\text{Sales (turnover)}}{\text{Fixed assets}} = \text{Asset and sales ratio}$$

This ratio measures the efficiency of the use of fixed assets in generating sales. An increasing ratio will indicate improved efficiency that will be the result of either rising sales or the sale of fixed assets that were being under-utilised. As with the other ratios, different businesses will have different fixed asset to sales ratios. Also comparisons can be made against previous years' results and those of similar businesses for a more comprehensive evaluation. The ratio could be modified to include all assets, that is, including current assets as well as fixed assets.

Company and investment ratios

These ratios are used by business people and investors who intend to buy either a whole business or holdings of shares in limited companies. The ratios will help to assess the performance of the company in which they wish to invest.

Earnings per share (EPS)

$$\frac{\begin{array}{c}\text{Profit on ordinary activities after tax adjusted} \\ \text{for preference dividends and extraordinary items}\end{array}}{\text{Number of issued ordinary shares}}$$

$$= \text{Earnings per share (EPS)}$$

Earnings per share (EPS) measures the amount of profit earned by each share after tax and preference dividends have been deducted. It is a very common statistic used for assessing company performance. It needs to be noted that the profits earned by each share include those that are paid out in dividends and those that are retained for further investment.

Dividend yield

$$\frac{\text{Dividend per ordinary share}}{\text{Market price of ordinary shares}} = \text{Dividend yield}$$

If a company has a quoted share price then the dividend yield can be calculated. It gives the investor the annual percentage return paid based on the price of the share. It is not an adequate measure as it ignores the profits or earnings that are retained by the company which should boost the share price.

Price:earnings ratio

$$\frac{\text{Market price of ordinary shares}}{\text{Earnings per share}}$$

$$= \text{Price:earnings ratio}$$

The price:earnings ratio (often abbreviated to P:E ratio) compares the current market price of a share with the earnings per share. For example, if a particular share was priced at £4, and the last EPS figure was 20p, then the P:E ratio would be 20. It means that it would take 20 years of the current earnings to pay for the cost of the share. This statistic is often used by investors to assess whether a share is good value. Two viewpoints are possible when appraising P:E ratios.

Some investors would consider a high P:E ratio as a good sign as it indicates expected improvements in the future performance of a company and thus excellent potential, for example Internet companies. Other investors may look at a low P:E ratio which will give good value for money; the share is very cheap. However, this may be due to predictions of weak future performance for the company and limited potential. It is therefore necessary to use P:E ratios carefully and in conjunction with other information that is gathered.

Dividend cover

$$\frac{\text{Profit after tax and pref. dividends}}{\text{Interim and final dividends}}$$

$$= \text{Dividend cover multiple}$$

This relates the dividends for the year to the profitability of a company after tax and preference dividends to see how easily these can be met from profits. The higher the multiple the lower the risk involved but the lower the multiple the larger will be the distribution of profits.

Other ratios

There are a range of other ratios that are used to assess business performance. The following are some that could be encountered.

Expense:sales ratios

$$\frac{\text{Specific expenses}}{\text{Sales}} \times \frac{100}{1} = \text{Expenses:sales ratio}$$

This ratio could compare a number of different expenses, such as wages, advertising or administration to sales, to examine how effectively the expense costs are being used. The lower the percentage figure the better the performance. If the percentage figure is rising then some managerial investigation could be carried out to establish the causes and implement some corrective action.

Sales (or turnover) per square metre

$$\frac{\text{Sales}}{\text{Space in square metres}} = \text{Sales per square metre}$$

This ratio examines how efficiently a business is using space. The higher the sales per square metre the more effectively the business is using the space. The figure can be compared with other similar businesses to evaluate efficiency in the use of space as a resource.

Sales (or turnover) per employee

$$\frac{\text{Sales}}{\text{Number of employees}} = \text{Sales per employee}$$

This ratio examines how efficiently a business is using its workforce. The higher the figure the more effectively the business is using its employees. If it is falling it may indicate an overstaffing problem which needs to be tackled. The figure can of course be compared with that of other businesses of a similar type.

Occupancy rate

$$\frac{\text{Number of rooms used}}{\text{Number of rooms available}} \times \frac{100}{1} = \text{Occupancy rate}$$

This ratio applies specifically to the hotel trade and measures how effectively hotels use the accommodation resources available. Higher efficiency is reflected by a higher occupancy rate. Again the results can be compared over time or against hotels within the same business or against competitors.

These are just a selection of other ratios that may be encountered. It is necessary to have a flexible approach to examining ratios because a great variety exist to evaluate the specific performance of businesses. In today's world performance indicators are an important instrument used in assessing performance and identifying problems and weaknesses.

Limitations in the interpretation of financial statements

Accounting ratios are an important part of assessing the financial strengths and weaknesses of a business. However, there are some limitations that must be taken into consideration when using ratio analysis.

Retrospective nature of accounting ratios

Accounting ratios are inevitably based on past rather than current performance and so the results may be out of date. This could therefore give a misleading impression of the strengths and weaknesses of the business as further events could have occurred since the preparation of the financial statements used. For example, a debtor may have gone into liquidation leading to bad debts and falls in future sales or additional large orders could have been obtained from new customers.

Difference in accounting policies

When the accounts of a business are compared, either with previous years' figures, or with figures from similar businesses, there is a danger that the accounts are not drawn up on the same basis as those currently being worked on.

The results will not allow consistent and objective comparisons if the accounting policies, in respect for example depreciation and stock valuation, are different.

Availability of comparable data

Ratio analysis only becomes useful if comparisons can be made, and sometimes available and comparable information either historically or against competitors is not available.

Inflation

Inflation may also cause a problem for comparing financial statements as such statements are prepared on an historic cost basis. For example, improvements in ratios, such as return on capital employed or sales to fixed assets, may be the result of rising sales values when fixed assets were bought some time in the past.

Reliance on standards

Often benchmarks are given for ratios but these are likely to vary for different types of businesses so it is unwise to rely too heavily on such standards. Other factors should also be considered. For example, a business with high cash sales will be able to operate on lower liquidity ratios.

Different ratio formulae may be used

There are no standardised ratio formulae that have to be used so different organisations may adopt different approaches.

Ratios can be subject to manipulation

Financial statements may be prepared to present the best ratio picture or the ratio formulae may be chosen to give the best performance review.

Other considerations

Other factors should also be considered in evaluating financial performance. The general economic climate should be taken into account as well as the actual state of the business. These factors could affect future performance that would not be revealed by ratios calculated from existing financial statements. For example, the launch of new products would not affect the existing ratios but will have a bearing on future results. This has resulted in other ways of measuring company performance such as the **balance scorecard** or **most admired companies analysis**.

Overall, ratio analysis is subjective rather than definitive and therefore has to be used with care and caution. However, it is still probably the best method of evaluating financial performance and stability.

When interpreting and using the results of ratio calculations it is essential that it is done objectively. One of the mistakes that can be made is to consider and analyse all of the ratios calculated. This will probably confuse the reader and hide the important aspects of the analysis. It is therefore best to take an overview of the results highlighting the exceptional ratios and then providing explanations for these ratios being either very weak or very good. Some recommendations can then be made to remedy the problems or exploit the strengths. This will generally be asked for in a report format.

CASE STUDY

Home Furnishings PLC is an (imaginary) company which sells the full range of household furnishing both in the retail trade (85 per cent for cash) and wholesale trade (15 per cent on credit). It is based in the Midlands and operates a chain of shops and warehouses. The company experienced rapid growth during the 1990s and went public in 2000. The finance department always calculates a range of ratios each year to evaluate the financial performance of the company. In addition to the results of the company the company accountant receives data on the average performance of the sector from the Wholesale and Retail Home Furnishing Federation (WRHFF).

ACTIVITY

As the assistant accountant, you should calculate a range of ratios and prepare a written report on the performance and solvency of Home Furnishings PLC using the information shown in the figures (Extracts A to E) which follow.

Extract A

Home Furnishings PLC Y/E 30 June	2002	2003
Total retail space in square metres	17,400	17,400
Number of employees	148	156

Extract B

WRHFF (Wholesale and Retail Home Furnishing Federation) — 2002 (Averages)

Profitability

Gross profit	45%
Net profit	12%
Return on capital employed	16%
Return on equity	16%

Liquidity and short-term solvency

Current ratio (or working capital ratio)	2.1:1
Acid test ratio	1.0:1

Stability and long-term solvency

Capital gearing ratio	50.0%
Debt to equity ratio	50.0%
Interest cover	6 times

Efficiency and asset utilisation ratios

Creditor payment period (based on 365 days)	34 days
Debtor collection period (based on 365 days)	32 days
Stock turnover (based on 365 days)	8 times
Fixed asset and sales ratio	2.0:1

Company and investment ratios

Earnings per share	45p
Dividend yield	10%
Price:earnings ratio	10.0
Dividend cover	10%

Other ratios

Sales per employee	£65,000
Sales per square metre	£600

Extract C

**Trading and profit and loss accounts
for the years ended 30 June**

	2002		2003	
	£000s		£000s	
Sales (15% on credit)		10,400		11,222
less Cost of goods sold				
Opening stock	587		520	
add Purchases	4910		6005	
Goods available for sales	5497		6525	
less Closing stock	520	4977	685	5840
GROSS PROFIT		5423		5382
Profit from the sale of fixed assets		0		0
		5423		5382
less Expenses				
Overheads				
Wages and salaries	990		1040	
Rent and rates	485		512	
Heating and lighting	407		416	
Advertising	300		280	
Telephone, printing, stationery	218		204	
Interest and bank charges	105		115	

	2002		2003	
	£000s		£000s	
Other overhead expenses	945		1046	
Depreciation				
Premises	110		110	
Fixtures and fittings	320		350	
Motor vehicles	280	4160	380	4453
Profit on ordinary activities before tax		1263		929
Tax on profit on ordinary activities		150		160
Profit or loss on ordinary activities after tax		1113		769
Appropriations				
Preference dividends (paid before year end)	70		70	
Ordinary dividends				
Interim paid	–		–	
Proposed	340	410	340	410
Retained profit for the year		703		359
Balance brought forward		2223		3306
Balance carried forward		2926		3665
Share price		210p		180p

Extract D

Balance sheet as at 30 June

| | 2002 | | | 2003 | | |
| | £000s | | | £000s | | |
FIXED ASSETS	**Cost**	**Acc. Dep.**	**Net**	**Cost**	**Acc. Dep.**	**Net**
Premises	5500	550	4950	5500	660	4840
Fixtures and fittings	3500	894	2606	3854	1244	2610
Motor vehicles	1890	770	1120	2836	1150	1686
	10891	2214	8676	12190	9136	

CURRENT ASSETS						
Stocks		520			685	
Trade debtors		160			208	
Prepayments		70			73	
Bank		457			598	
Cash		33			40	
		1240			1604	

less

CREDITORS: AMOUNTS DUE WITHIN ONE YEAR

Trade creditors	457			526		
Accruals	43			49		
Bank	–			–		
Taxation	150			160		
Dividends	340	990		340	1075	

NET CURRENT ASSETS			250			529

TOTAL ASSETS LESS CURRENT LIABILITIES			8926			9665

less

CREDITORS: AMOUNTS DUE AFTER MORE THAN ONE YEAR

15% debenture stock			1000			1000
			7926			8665

Financed by

CAPITAL AND RESERVES

Ordinary share capital (£1 shares)			4000			4000
7% preference share capital			1000			1000
Profit and loss account			2926			3665
			7926			8665

Extract E

Home Furnishings PLC
Ratio results for the period 2002–2003

	2002	2003	WRHFF 1999
Profitability			
Gross profit	52.1%	48.0%	45.0%
Net profit	12.1%	8.3%	12.0%
Return on capital employed	14.7%	10.8%	16.0%
Return on equity	18.2%	12.1%	16.0%
Liquidity and short-term solvency			
Current ratio (or working capital ratio)	1.25:1	1.49:1	2.1:1
Acid test ratio	0.73:1	0.86:1	1.0:1
Stability and long-term solvency			
Capital gearing ratio	22.4%	20.7%	50.0%
Debt to equity ratio	28.9%	26.1%	50.0%
Interest cover	13 times	9.1 times	6 times
Efficiency and asset utilisation ratios			
Stock turnover	8.99 times	9.69 times	8 times
Debtor collection period	37.4 days	45.1 days	32 days
Creditor settlement period	34.0 days	32.0 days	34.5 days
Fixed asset and sales ratio	1.20:1	1.23:1	2.1:1
Company and investment ratios			
Earnings per share	26p	17.4p	45p
Dividend yield	4.1%	4.7%	10.0%
Price:earnings ratio	8.1:1	10.4:1	10.0:1
Dividend cover	3.3	2.7	5
Other ratios			
Sales per square metre	£598	£645	£600
Sales per employee	£70,270	£71,295	£65,000

Comments and interpretation in report format

The following informal report (Figure 6.14) is an analysis of the accounting ratio results with recommendations for further courses of action. It should be noted that some general comments have been made with the significant aspects being examined in greater depth.

The report does not go into detail on all the ratios calculated but highlights significant weaknesses and strengths and considers ways to tackle the problems identified.

To: Chief Accountant   31 August 2003
From: Assistant Accountant

Introduction

You asked me to examine the financial statements for Home Furnishings PLC and calculate a range of accounting ratios for the years ending 30 June 2002 and 2003 as well as analysing the results. I have enclosed a table of the ratio results (Extract E) along with this report.

Findings

The profitability of the company has deteriorated over the last two years with the Net Profit % and Return On Capital Employed ratios being lower than the trade association average. The Gross Profit % figure did fall but it is still higher than the trade association average (52% to 48% compared with the trade association average of 45%). A more competitive pricing strategy would explain this trend and account for the rising sales levels. The more concerning trend, however, is the downward movement of the Net Profit % and Return On Capital Employed figures (the Net Profit % declined from 12.1% to 8.3% compared with the trade association average of 12% while the Return On Capital Employed declined from 14.7% to 10.8% compared with the trade association average of 16%). These disappointing results can be attributed to the decline in Net Profit arising from the rising expenses that occurred over the two years with the other expenses category being especially significant.

The liquidity ratios showed an improvement over the two years but are still below the trade association average (the current ratio moved from 1.25:1 to 1.49:1 compared with the trade average of 2.1:1 and the the acid test ratio moved from 0.73:1 to 0.86:1 compared with the trade average of 1:1). This trend reflects the improvement in the company's management of working capital. The company is in a strong position in respect of gearing with debt to equity ratio being stable at well below the trade association average.

The efficiency and asset utilisation ratios were generally sound with the stock turnover and creditor settlement period being stable and comparing favourably with the trade association average. However, the weaker aspects were the debtor collection period which deteriorated from 37 days to 45 days compared with the trade association average of 32 days. Also the sales to fixed asset ratio was lower than the trade association average (1.2:1 compared with 2.1:1) which indicates that the fixed assets could be used more efficiently.

In respect of the other ratios the price:earnings ratio improved over the two years although the Earnings Per Share was weak compared to the trade association average. The company was using the space effectively as reflected by the sales per square metre figures and the sales per employee results increased and remain above the trade average.

Conclusions and recommendations

Summarising the results, the weak areas of financial performance were in:

♦ the Net Profit % and Return On Capital Employed % figures
♦ Debtor Collection Period and Fixed Assets:Sales Ratio.

The company should investigate the expense figures and consider ways of making economies without impacting on sales and the service provided to customers. Also the credit control system should be examined to establish why the debtor collection period is rising and to consider improvements in the system to prevent an increase in bad debts and improve the company's cash flow.

Figure 6.14   Report on financial position

An alternative look at balance sheet analysis   **JOURNAL ARTICLE**

In this lengthy article, Peter Anderson claims that analysing a set of accounts is an area which is sadly misunderstood and is usually approached with a total lack of confidence. He blames the use of ratios for this state of affairs. These figures are supposed to enlighten the analyst: in reality they do no such thing. They are at best dangerous and at worst utterly misleading. Much of Anderson's argument is contained in the section which follows.

Anderson, P. 'Balance sheet analysis'.

An alternative to using ratios

In the article mentioned above, the objections raised to ratios are:

♦ ratios are psychological props which hinder a proper understanding of the business in question
♦ a ratio converts two figures which are not understood into one figure which is not understood; this figure is then compared with a benchmark and a conclusion drawn
♦ ratios are based on out-of-date, static information.

Businesses are not static, they are dynamic. The figures are invariably six months out of date, possibly twelve months. The conclusions that can be drawn from the information are surely limited.

Anderson goes on to look in detail at two ratios: the current ratio and the gearing ratio.

Current ratio

This is also referred to as the liquidity ratio and is supposedly of prime importance. It expresses current assets as a percentage of current liabilities and so measures the extent to which the business could satisfy its current liabilities out of current assets. Frequently a norm of 150 per cent (1.5:1) is quoted although some authorities prefer to see a 2:1 ratio.

Anderson's objections are:

♦ It is not in touch with reality. In a going concern liabilities do not all fall due together and ratios are essentially used as an aid to going concern analysis as debts fall due consecutively.

♦ Even if all liabilities were to fall due for payment on the same day it is quite wrong to imagine that they could be met with current assets. Liabilities are met with cash: nobody has yet devised a way of paying his creditors with debtors or stock. A current ratio of 3:1 will be of little use if there is no cash available and the current assets comprised bad debts and unsaleable stock.

The same objections apply to the acid test ratio which purports to compare 'liquid' current assets with current liabilities. Although stock is taken out of the equation, the assets include debtors. One cannot pay debts with one's debtors!

To conclude that a business is weak because it has a current ratio of less than, say, 1:1 is dangerously misleading.

What about the trend in this ratio? This is often considered a useful guide to the progress of the business in liquidity terms. This is fine in theory but can be very misleading in practice. Look at these examples:

Current assets	Current liabilities	Current ratio	Current surplus
£200,000	£100,000	2:1	£100,000
£270,000	£150,000	1.8:1	£120,000
£450,000	£300,000	1.5:1	£150,000

The current ratio has distinctly worsened. In actual fact the business has made progress as illustrated by the continuing improvement in net current assets. Because the figures are expressed as a ratio, however, the position appears to worsen.

The following example will reinforce the point:

Current assets	Current liabilities	Current ratio	Current deficit
£100,000	£200,000	0.5:1	£100,000
£150,000	£260,000	0.6:1	£110,000
£300,000	£420,000	0.7:1	£120,000

The danger here is obvious. The current ratio is showing steady improvement. The liquidity of the business is becoming more satisfactory. Except that it isn't. The current deficit is continually worsening but a ratio doesn't show it as such.

The moral? Look behind the figures. To check trends in liquidity the best tool is simply the net current asset position. It is easier to calculate than a ratio, easier to understand and less prone to mislead. Stick with that.

Gearing ratio

This key ratio compares borrowings (bank loans, HP) with capital resources. In principle this seems logical enough. Remember, however, that 'resources' are based on book values and may not reflect accurate underlying values. Suppose a business is borrowing £100,000 against resources of £50,000. The gearing ratio is an unacceptable 2:1. Suppose that the business assets include freehold property in the books at £50,000 but with a true value of £250,000. There is a capital reserve here of £200,000. This gives a true gearing ratio of £100,000 + £250,000 = 40 per cent or 0.4:1 which appears very acceptable. In reality, however, nothing has changed. Gearing tells you nothing about repayment ability and thus the acceptability of the proposition.

The real danger here is the benchmark. The traditional view is that the ratio should not exceed 100 per cent. Above this the business is overgeared, below it the business is sound. This is nonsense! Why do we happily grant 95 per cent mortgages to first-time buyers? Here we gear people up perhaps by nearly 2000 per cent, nearly 20:1, without any real worries.

You may say that these are different circumstances, our mortgage customers are in employment which ensures a steady (not fluctuating) and regular flow of income with which to meet the repayments. This surely proves the point, according to Anderson. We have not looked at the gearing ratio and said that the mortgage could not be granted because the customer would then be too highly geared. We have rather looked at the income flow and said that the customer can meet the repayments and thus his or her high gearing ratio is no reason to decline the advance.

This is a crucial point. We need to pay attention to income flows when looking at gearing. The important question is: Can this customer repay? We lent to our mortgage customer because of her regular and steady income flow. So it should be with a business. The higher the borrowing, the more important a steady and regular income becomes. Fluctuations in income are dangerous. For a mortgage customer we do not wish to see successive annual income figures of, say, £20,000, £2000, £20,000 and £2000. The good years are fine, but how does she meet the repayments during the bad times? The gearing ratio is misleading.

The contention here is that the use of these three ratios – current, acid test and gearing – is a major cause of difficulty in interpreting accounts. A business may work well and be profitable. If its gearing ratio is 150 per cent and its current ratio 80 per cent then confusion results.

An alternative approach

So if ratios are to be largely discounted, how are we to analyse accounts? The answer, surely, is that the accounts should not be understood as an end in itself, but rather the accounts should be used as an aid to understanding:

♦ how the business actually works
♦ how this will be changed by the lending proposals under consideration.

The following procedure is suggested.

Look at net worth

This must be the starting point. What is the quoted net worth? Perhaps more importantly, what is happening to it? We need to look at the dynamics of the business. An increasing net worth is a good sign, a falling net worth is a bad sign.

Always account for the change in net worth. Usually it will be as a result of retained profits. This is good; those profits will be available to make loan repayments if such a facility is requested. Compare this with increases in resources due to asset revaluations. Loans cannot be repaid with a property revaluation.

Look at profits

Profits are important. Loan repayments are made with cash, but the source of this cash has to be retained profits otherwise the structure of the business will be weakened.

Compare the retained annual profit figure with loan repayments. Alternatively add back any book entries to profits and compare this with loan repayments. The usual book entry is, of course, depreciation. If loan repayments exceed annual profits plus depreciation then the proposition is a dead duck unless you can be convinced that profits will increase by sufficient to cover loan repayments in the near future.

Conversely, of course, should retained profits exceed potential loan repayments then this is a very encouraging sign and the analysis can certainly continue to investigate whether cash will be available to meet the repayments.

Remember to look at the past profit record. Is it liable to severe fluctuations? If so, future loan repayments could be threatened.

Confirm that net worth and profits are accurately stated

Are there any hidden reserves in property or other assets which will increase net worth? This may do nothing in itself to help repayments but it will give us a better idea of the risks we take and will show the value of any potential security.

Is there any evidence of overvalued stock? Look at the stock turnover figure and in particular the trend.

The calculation is:

$$\text{Stock} \times 365 + (\text{sales} + \text{gross profit})$$

The resulting figure is the average period that stocks are held expressed in days. A significant increase (above, say, 15 per cent) in the days stock held figure needs investigation. You must be satisfied that it is not due to unsaleable stock. If it is, then you will need to adjust both the net worth figure and past profit figures to reflect the true position. In each case the adjustment will be downwards.

Is there any evidence of bad and doubtful debt? Look at the credit given figure. The calculation is:

$$\text{Debtors} \times 365 + \text{sales}$$

Rather than worry about whether the figure is 'acceptable for the industry' it is much more meaningful to look at the trend. A significant increase in the average period of credit granted needs investigation. You need to be sure that it is not due to bad debts that have not yet been written off. Again, an overstated figure for debtors results in both net worth and past profits being overstated. Make any necessary adjustments.

How has the structure of the business changed over the last few years?

This entails the preparation of a **funds flow statement** which will show the following:

♦ Whether the business is putting its continued existence at risk by pouring cash into fixed assets at the expense of payments to creditors. This financing of long-term assets with short-term monies is dangerous.

♦ Whether there is any cash available to meet loan repayments. Profits may well cover these but if all the profit is tied up in increased debtors then cash will not be available to meet the repayments. In these circumstances a working capital overdraft may also have to be granted to free some profits.

Look at the cash operating cycle

This will show how the business actually works. Does it receive cash from its customers before it has to pay its suppliers. This implies no need for a working capital overdraft.

If suppliers have to be paid before cash is received from debtors then an overdraft facility may well be needed. This is particularly important with increases in turnover which may well be the result of a bank loan to increase productive capacity, such as buying a new machine. In these circumstances it may not be enough to finance the new machine, increased debtors and stock may also need financing.

Summary

The balance sheet is a snapshot, probably at least six months old. There is a limit to the amount of information that can be obtained and the conclusions that can be drawn. The monthly balances schedule is useful in showing the up-to-date position. It will certainly show liquidity problems more graphically than a balance sheet ratio ever will.

Businesses are not static, they are dynamic; they change. Anderson's approach concentrates on understanding the business by focusing on these changes. How has the structure of the business changed? How does the business actually work?

This is surely a sounder technique than one based solely on ratios.

Chapter 4

Financial decisions

Management accounting

In the previous chapter the focus was on financial accounting which is recording transactions that have actually taken place. These historic results are used to evaluate past performance and do provide a basis for identifying weaknesses in a business. However, another branch of accounting, management accounting, needs to be examined.

What is management accounting?

It is defined by the Chartered Institute of Management Accountants (CIMA) as follows:

'Management accounting is the application of the principles of accounting and financial management to create, protect, preserve and increase value so as to deliver that value to the stakeholders of profit and not-for-profit enterprises both public and private.'

This is a typical wide-ranging and official definition but it does get to the heart of management accounting. It refers to the fundamental roles of management accounting which involve gathering and presenting information for:

♦ budgeting: planning future activities
♦ cost analysis: controlling and monitoring activities to improve efficiency
♦ enabling calculated decision making, that is, how growth can be achieved and performance enhanced.

The role of the management accountant does not only involve an analysis of the whole business, but also of different aspects of a business to measure the performance of products and its different sections. For example, Tesco PLC, the leading supermarket in the UK, will need to review the performance of different stores within the group. If some are under-performing then some detailed analysis is required to discover the causes. The analysis will in turn lead to decisions being made which could include changes in the management or even the closure of an outlet. It focuses on such activities as costing products and services, valuing stocks and evaluating investment projects.

Analysis of costs

Costs are the money values involved in acquiring resources. Such expenditure could be classified as either capital or revenue expenditure.

Capital expenditure

This is generally large expenditure to buy fixed assets, such as land and buildings, or motor vehicles, which will be in use within a business over a long period of time. This is not continuous regular expenditure.

Revenue expenditure

This is continuous regular expenditure which involves buying goods for resale, materials for manufacturing products and services such as electricity, insurance, and so on. This type of expenditure is ongoing for a business.

Both kinds of cost can be applied to a variety of different enterprises such as manufacturing, retail or service-based companies.

For example, a manufacturing company will buy in raw materials to convert into a finished product by processing the raw material through the use of machinery and labour. Such companies will still have expenses to pay. The machinery is a capital expenditure item but all the other costs are revenue expenditures.

For a retail business, finished goods are purchased for resale and these along with labour costs and expenses are again examples of revenue expenditure. The fixtures and fittings in the shop and the shop itself would be capital expenditure if the shop was purchased outright.

For a service sector company, although the final product is a service, materials might be needed to complete the service but labour costs and expenses would certainly be incurred. Operating a restaurant is a service sector activity where meals are the service provided. To deliver this service food and drink will be needed along with labour inputs, for example the chef, waiting staff, and expenses, for example the rent of the premises, telephone, and so on.

Cost information

All organisations need to collect cost information in order to manage and control costs. There is a need to understand how this may be undertaken and therefore some key terms need to be defined.

Definition of terms

Cost units: these are units of output to which costs can be charged; outputs are the end product of business activity and a cost unit could be viewed in a variety of ways, such as:

♦ a physical unit of output which is manufactured, for example cars, televisions, shirts
♦ a unit of service, for example passenger miles in a taxi, treatments in a hospital, number of meals in a restaurant, hours of accountancy service.

Care must be taken when choosing a cost unit because several different types could be chosen. For example, in a college either a course or a student may be used as a cost unit.

Cost centres: These are sections of a business which incur costs in order to be operational. In a company there might be a variety of cost centres such as the personnel department and the finance department which are support services and do not sell products, to a manufacturing department which makes a physical product which is sold for revenue.

Collecting costs by cost centres assists the control function of a company because the manager of a cost centre will be accountable for its costs and meeting the targets set.

Classification of costs

Costs can be classified in three main ways.

Classification by element

This is when the costs are divided up into three cost categories that are needed to make a product or deliver a service. These three elements are **materials** which are included in the product, for example fabric and buttons in a coat; **labour** costs in the actual manufacturing process where an employee's time is identified in the product; **expenses** which are the essential support services, such as insurance, administration, telephone, and so on.

Classification by function

This is focusing on costs in different sections of an organisation according to their function, or the kind of work being done. The divisions could be production which is involved with the manufacture of products; marketing and selling, personnel, finance, research and development, and so on. These costs are all incurred, whichever classification system is used, but are organised differently.

Classification by nature

This is examining the nature of costs and in particular how they behave with changes in the levels of output or activity. Costs classified by nature can be further divided.

Fixed costs

These are costs that do not change when output changes, for example rent and rates, depreciation, managerial salaries.

Semi-variable costs (or semi-fixed)

These are costs which have some fixed element and some variable element to them, for example telephone costs where there is a fixed line rental but the costs of calls is dependent on usage.

Variable costs

These are costs which vary directly with output, for example more materials and direct labour are needed to produce more volume.

By classifying costs in several different ways the management will see three different viewpoints on the business which should assist them in running the business more efficiently and effectively. If the costs are viewed by:

♦ element, the management could discover that some cost elements are too high and identify a strategy for economising that could be employed
♦ function, the management could see which departments or functions are high spending ones and thus identify sources of cost savings
♦ nature, a business will be able to see if the resources obtained from the fixed cost expenditure are being optimally used. If, for example, the premises are too large for the current level of activity then either more output needs to occur or cheaper premises found.

Other cost definitions

Direct costs: these are costs which are identified specifically with a unit of output, that is, they can be actually seen in the finished product. For example, the direct materials in a new front door are the wood, the metal letter box and the door handle, whereas the direct labour is the time specific workers spent on its manufacture. Direct expenses can occur, such as royalty payments on each unit or the cost of specialist sub-contractors or consultants.

All the direct costs added together are often referred to as **prime costs**.

Indirect costs: these are the costs that cannot be identified and seen in a particular product and are sometimes described as **overheads**. These costs include such items as telephone, insurance, administration wages, motor expenses and depreciation.

It needs to be understood that variable costs are similar to direct costs, and fixed costs to indirect costs. The difference between these two types is the extent to which the costs can be seen in the product. For example, the transport costs cannot be linked directly

to a unit of output but this cost may change with volume: more transport cost will be incurred as more output is produced.

All the costs described fit somewhere into a businesses profit and loss account and so the total profit can be calculated. However, this will not tell the management what each product or service is contributing towards this profit. The management accountant collects cost and revenue information to identify which products or sections of a business are doing well and which are doing badly. This is the sort of information that is needed for the management to make positive and objective decisions, such as discontinuing a product or activity.

Unit cost calculations: product and job costing

All organisations need to be able to calculate the unit costs of a product or a job. This means identifying all the costs that go into making up a product or a specific job. It is important to do this for planning and scheduling production, for pricing and for controlling costs.

ACTIVITY

Technology Ltd assembles computers and makes one model, called the Plum. The following information applies to the forthcoming year of operation, ending 31 March 2005.

Using the figures supplied, complete the cost per unit section of the costing statement shown in Figure 6.15.

Direct materials	Monitors	£800,000
	Components	£1,900,000
	Packaging	£80,000
Direct labour	Assembling	£600,000
	Packaging	£200,000
Overheads	Production	£400,000
	Distribution	£200,000
	Administration	£150,000

Forecast cost statement for the year ending 31 March 2005
'Plum' Computer

Volume 20,000	**Total**		**Unit**	
	£000s	£000s	£s	£s
Direct costs				
Materials				
Monitors	800		40.00	
Components	1900			
Packaging	80		4.00	
		2780		
Labour				
Assembling	650		32.50	
Packaging	195		9.75	
		845		42.25
Prime costs		3625		
Overheads				
Production	550		27.50	
Distribution	250			
Administration	200		10.00	
		1000		
TOTAL		4625		

Figure 6.15   Forecast cost statement for the Plum computer

Costing statement

The costing statement provides a lot of useful information for the management. For example, the direct cost of labour is predicted by looking at the number of hours needed to complete the year's scheduled production multiplied by the rate per hour. This information will indicate the number of employees needed to meet the target. Also it can enable the management to evaluate the make-up of the various cost elements and consider whether some cost aspects are too high. In addition, the management can compare these forecasts with what actually occurs, and explain why there is a difference. This is the control process.

Control process

This is a relatively easy process when there is only one product being produced. If a range of products are being produced, the process becomes more difficult because some costs (fixed costs) do not change when volume changes. The management have to solve the problem of how to deal with overheads over a range of products. It can be achieved by sharing the overheads over the range of products, that is, **absorption costing**, or dealing with them after the contribution towards fixed costs and profit has been calculated, that is, marginal costing.

Absorption costing

This is a method of ensuring that overheads can be included in a finished product or service. It is widely used throughout the world. It involves three processes that have to be undertaken to absorb the overheads into a product, job or service, these being:

1 Allocation

This is where there are specific costs which are sent or allocated directly to the cost centre that has actually incurred them and which is getting benefit from them. It could, for example, be the production manager's salary or the repairs to some plant and machinery. These are clearly production costs but are overheads because they cannot be identified with a specific unit of output. Another example could be the advertising for new staff which would be allocated to the personnel cost centre.

2 Apportionment

This is where there are general overhead costs which cover a number of different cost centres.

These costs have to be shared or apportioned on a fair basis between the cost centres that are getting benefit from them. For example, the rent of the premises is paid for the whole business and all the cost centres will be receiving some benefit but not an equal one. In this case the costs could be apportioned on the basis of space or area used by each of the cost centres. Using Technology Ltd as an example, there are three cost centres:

♦ production: 1500 square metres
♦ distribution: 400 square metres
♦ administration: 100 square metres.

Production should bear the largest cost of the rent, followed by distribution, with administration incurring the least cost. If the rent had been £10,000 per annum then the apportionment would be:

♦ production: £7500 (£10,000 × 1500/2000)
♦ distribution: £2000 (£10,000 × 400/2000)
♦ administration: £500 (£10,000 × 100/2000).

Other costs could be apportioned on different bases but applying the same technique such as:

♦ indirect wages: number of staff
♦ insurance of equipment: value of equipment
♦ building maintenance: space or area.

Secondary apportionment

Having apportioned the overhead costs to cost centres it must then be realised that some cost centres are service centres, which do not generate revenue. Businesses could not operate without such cost centres but the costs of these cost centres need to be apportioned, again on a fair basis, to the cost centres which do sell products or services. This is called secondary apportionment.

For example, Technology Ltd has a canteen which provides a free service for all employees as a part of their terms and conditions of employment. The canteen is a cost centre which has specific costs allocated: the cooks, the food and drink; and apportioned costs: rent, depreciation. The total costs of this cost centre now need to be secondary apportioned to the three departments getting benefit from it, production, distribution and administration, on a fair basis, with this usually being the number of employees in each of these cost centres.

3 Absorption

All the overhead costs of a business have now been placed into revenue-creating cost centres. It is now necessary to get these overheads into the product, job or service. This is achieved by the absorption process. It involves absorbing the overhead costs using an overhead absorption rate (OAR) which is based on an activity level of the cost centre. The activity levels chosen are referred to as **bases for absorption**. The most common bases used for the OAR are cost:

♦ per direct labour hour
♦ per machine hour
♦ per unit of output.

The base chosen should reflect the importance of that base to the business. Using a 'per unit' base is sensible for a company with just one product, but if the company is capital intensive then using 'machine hours' would be most appropriate; for a labour-intensive company 'direct labour hours' would probably be best. The outcome of the process is that each unit – job or service – will carry or recover an element of overheads.

The OAR would be calculated by dividing the predicted overheads by the activity level chosen, for example:

£100,000 of overheads divided by 20,000 direct labour hours means that every direct labour hour will recover £5.00 of overheads.

ACTIVITY

Reconsider the Technology Ltd plan for the forthcoming year ending 31 March 2005. The company has the opportunity of assembling a laser printer as well which could be sold with the Plum computer. The company would split the production up into two cost centres, one for the computers (C1) and one for the laser printers (L1). The following additional information is available from the plans in respect of the bases that can be used for apportioning overheads:

	Total	C1	L1
Floor space (square metres)	6000	4500	1500
Number of employees	100	80	20
Value of machinery (£000s)	300,000	275,000	75,000
Number of units	30,000	20,000	10,000
Admin hours	9000	6750	2250

The predicted total overhead costs for Technology Ltd are shown in Figure 6.16, which then deals with the allocation and apportionment to the two cost centres C1 and L1.

Apportionment workings

For 'premises costs' it is shared as follows:

Premises	Total (£s)	Apport (£s)
C1	320,000 ×4500/60,000 =	240,000
L1	320,000 ×1500/6000 =	80,000

Check the calculations in respect of the other apportionments of the overheads.

Technology Ltd has chosen to use 'direct labour hours' to absorb the overheads into the two different products. The estimated direct labour time for assembling and packaging the two products per unit is as follows:

'Plum' computer	Assembling hours	5.0 hours per computer
	Packaging hours	1.5 hours per computer
Laser printer	Assembling hours	1.5 hours per printer
	Packaging hours	0.25 hours per printer

The total direct labour hours predicted for each product would be as follows:

Total direct labour hours

	Hrs per unit	No of units	Total hrs
C1			
Assembling	5.0 ×	20,000 =	100,000
Packaging	1.5 ×	20,000 =	30,000
L1			
Assembling	1.5 ×	10,000 =	15,000
Packaging	0.25 ×	10,000 =	2500

Now the overhead costs can be absorbed into each of the two products on a reasonably fair basis so that a full product cost can be established.

Overhead costs for allocation and apportionment

Apportionment

		Total (£000s)	C1 (£000s)	L1 (£000s)
Production	**Basis**			
Allocated		150	110	40
Premises costs	Floor space	320	240	80
Supervisory/canteen costs	Number of employees	100	80	20
Plant and machinery costs	Value of P and M	80	60	20
		650	490	160
Distribution	Number of units	300	200	100
Administration	Admin hours	200	150	50

Figure 6.16   Overhead costs for allocation and apportionment

The **absorption rates per direct labour hour** are calculated as follows:

	Production	OAR (£s)	Distribution	OAR (£s)	Administration	OAR (£s)
C1	490,000/130,000 = 3.77		200,000/130,000 = 1.54		150,000/130,000 = 1.15	
L1	160,000/17,500 = 9.14		100,000/17,500 = 5.71		50,000/17,500 = 2.86	

Forecast cost statement for the year ending 31 March 2005

	Computer		Laser printer			Computer		Laser printer	
	£s	£s	£s	£s		£s	£s	£s	£s
					Labour				
					Assembling	32.50		9.75	
Direct costs					Packaging	9.75		3.25	
Materials							42.25		13.00
Monitors/ container	40.00		12.00				181.25		53.00
Components	95.00		26.00		**Prime costs**				
Packaging	4.00		2.00		*Overheads*				
					Production	24.50		16.00	
		139.00		40.00	Distribution	10.01		9.99	
					Administration	7.47	41.99	5.01	31.00
					TOTAL		223.24		84.00

Figure 6.17   Unit forecast cost statement

Concluding analysis

The previous considerations have examined how business organisations analyse and manage the costs of production. The main difficulty is dealing with overhead or indirect costs because they cannot be attached specifically to a product. The absorption costing method is one way of tackling the problem of dividing shared costs over different products, jobs and services.

In the Technology Ltd example, the overheads would be absorbed into the products being made. However, it appears that the overheads to be absorbed by the L1 product are relatively higher than in the C1 product. This was because the L1 product had a much smaller expected volume as it was a new product being considered and hence there was less spreading of the overheads. The statements show that for the C1 the overheads absorbed per unit were reduced when a new product was to be introduced because these were shared over more activity. If the volume of L1 were to double, then there would be a significant impact on the overheads per unit for this product because the number of direct labour hours would double but the overheads may not change much at all.

Absorption costing does not provide a perfect solution for dealing with overheads but it is widely practised because it allows businesses to cost products, jobs and services fully for pricing purposes.

Marginal costing

An alternative way of dealing with overheads and their recovery is to adopt a marginal costing approach. This focuses on how costs change when activity levels (cost behaviour) change. This approach is built on variable costs (those that change directly in line with volume) and their relationship with fixed costs (those that do not change with volume). Also costs could be semi-variable, where some variable and some fixed costs are included in one cost category, such as motor expenses. Finally there could be stepped costs which are fixed costs which jump up another level when a capacity level is reached and further output is only possible by acquiring additional machinery or supervisory staff.

This approach to costing is widely used for decision making as it can provide predictions on profitability and break-even points for particular products and activities. Before examining the approach a few key terms need to be defined.

More definitions

Marginal cost: the extra costs incurred for producing an extra unit or batch of units. In practice, from an accounting viewpoint the marginal cost is the same as the variable cost because the only costs which change when output changes are variable costs.

Break-even point: this is the point where neither a profit nor a loss occurs and is therefore where costs exactly match sales revenue. It can be calculated by:

$$\frac{\text{Fixed costs}}{\text{Contribution per unit}} = \text{Break-even point in volume}$$

Contribution: this is the amount of sales revenue from each unit or activity that contributes to the fixed cost and the profit of an enterprise. It is calculated by:

Sales revenue − Variable cost = Total contribution

ACTIVITY

Use the costing information for Technology Ltd (pp 407–8) when both the Plum computer and the laser printer are to be assembled. Assume that the prices are fixed as follows:

- Plum computer   £260.00
- Laser printer   £100.00

The break-even point and profit prediction for the Plum computer are calculated as follows:

Contribution per unit $= 260.00 - 181.25 = £78.75$

Break-even point $= \dfrac{490,000 + 200,000 + 150,000}{£78.75}$

$= \textbf{10,667 computers}$

Profit at 20,000 sales $= 20,000 - 10,667 \times £78.75$
$= \textbf{£734,974 profit}$

Alternatively $= 260,000 - 223.24 \times 20,000$ units
$= \textbf{£735,200 profit}$

The difference in profit is due to rounding to the nearest penny for the absorption rates and is not material in respect of the turnover and total profit made. The profit calculation works because beyond the break-even point all contribution goes to profit as the fixed costs have already been recovered.

Now for the laser printers calculate:

♦ contribution per unit
♦ break-even point in volume
♦ profit at 10,000 units.

The calculations are very useful for calculating alternative situations. For example, you can very quickly deal with the following type of questions:

♦ What would be the effect of a price rise? The break-even point would be lower as there would be greater contribution from each unit.
♦ What would be the effect of a rise in direct labour costs? The break-even point would be higher as there would be less contribution from each unit.
♦ What would be the effect if fixed costs rose? The break-even point would be higher as more contribution would be needed to cover these higher fixed costs.

These questions can be posed by the decision makers who need to consider the alternative possibilities. These are 'what if? ' questions and are an example of **sensitivity analysis**. This is described as, 'a risk assessment procedure in which changes are made to significant variables in order to determine the effect of these changes on the expected outcome'.

Margin of safety

This risk procedure can be emphasised in break-even analysis by calculating the **margin of safety**. This is the difference between the planned output and the break-even point and is usually expressed as a percentage figure of the planned output. It can be calculated as follows:

$$\dfrac{\text{Planned volume} - \text{Break-even volume}}{\text{Planned volume}} \times 100\%$$

$=$ Margin of safety

Continuing the Technology Ltd case, the margin of safety for the Plum computer would be as follows:

$$\dfrac{20,000 - 10,667}{20,000} \times 100$$

$= 9333$ computers or 46.7%

It provides some useful guidelines on the vulnerability of a product or activity to a change in circumstance, for example a fall in sales demand.

ACTIVITY

Now calculate the margin of safety for the Technology Ltd laser printers.

Break-even and volume/profit analysis can be solved by a graphic approach. This means drawing a graph showing a total revenue curve and a total cost curve and reading off the break-even point or the profit at various levels of output. This can be demonstrated using the Technology Ltd case (see Figure 6.18).

ACTIVITY

Now draw a break-even chart for the Technology Ltd laser printer and match the results with those that were calculated numerically.

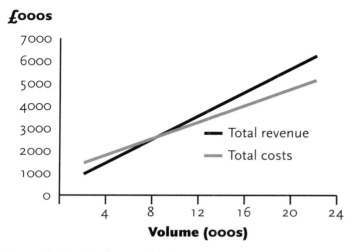

£ooos

Figure 6.18   Break-even chart

The use of marginal costing, break-even and volume/ profit analysis are important tools for the decision maker. It can solve a variety of questions such as:

♦ Should an order be accepted or not?
♦ Should a company make a product or buy it in?
♦ Should a company terminate an activity or continue it?
♦ What would be an appropriate selling price?
♦ What is the target profit which is being sought?

In each of the above cases the key issue will be does the activity 'make a contribution'? If it does then accept the order or continue with an activity. For example, if Technology Ltd receive an offer for 500 Plum computers at a price of £210 should it be accepted? On purely financial grounds it should, if there was enough capacity. This is because these additional sales would 'make a contribution' of £14,375.00 ((£210.00 – £181.25) × 500) and increase profits by this figure. In making this decision the management would need to consider the effects of the:

♦ lower price level on its existing markets and customers
♦ additional volume on its workforce.

Relevant costs

These are costs that need to be accounted for in the decision-making process. However, when evaluating different courses of action **relevant costs** are those costs which will change as a result of any decision made. If some costs have already occurred then they are not relevant but are **sunk costs** and therefore should be ignored. **Unavoidable costs** are also irrelevant because they will have to be paid whatever the decision made. These are fixed costs. **Opportunity costs** are relevant costs because they are the value of a benefit foregone as a result of a particular course of action.

CASE STUDY

Relevant costs for Jill's bananas

Consider the case of Jill who is a market trader and has come to the end of a day selling fruit and vegetables. She had purchased 100 kg of bananas for £50 and had sold 90 kg for £90. The remainder will not keep for the following week but a local trader offers to buy them for 25p a kg. Jill has hired a trolley for £2 to move any unsold stock. She has to decide what price to charge in the final few minutes of trading for the remaining 10 kg of bananas.

In analysing Jill's costs the relevant ones need to be identified:

♦ The price originally paid is not relevant because it is a sunk cost.
♦ The price offered by the local trader is an opportunity cost and is a relevant cost.
♦ The trolley hire is unavoidable and is not a relevant cost.

In this case the only relevant cost is the opportunity cost of 25p per kg offered by the local trader.

The minimum price Jill should charge is 25p per kg. In this case the contribution made by accepting the offer would be £2.50, so any increase in contribution would improve Jill's profits. Only relevant costs must be included when undertaking marginal cost analysis.

The pricing decision

The pricing of products and services is a major policy decision for any business entity. There are several approaches to tackling this problem which are now outlined.

Full cost pricing

This approach is to calculate the costs of the product or service and add a mark-up on to it. This means taking the full cost of a product and adding a percentage on to this cost to arrive at a selling price. If the subsequent price is too high then a supplier may be left with unsold stock or a service provider with not enough work.

Included in the cost of the product or service would be the direct material and labour costs and also an element of overheads which would probably have been calculated using an absorption costing approach.

For the Technology Ltd case the full cost of the laser printer was £84.00 and adding a 19 per cent mark-up leads to a rounded price of £100.00.

Demand pricing

This is where the market determines a price for a product and the supplier accepts the price and then decides whether to supply to that particular market. It is at this point that marginal costs are relevant because where the price exceeds the marginal cost then a contribution will be made and it is a worthwhile venture.

Marginal cost pricing

This is where the marginal costs are calculated and a mark-up is applied to these marginal or variable costs. There is an expectation that in the future the contribution will lead to the fixed costs being covered and a profit being made. Many retailers adopt a strategy of marking up on the buying in price.

Pricing products is a very uncertain strategy in a dynamic and highly competitive business environment, so although certain principles may be followed, there is likely to be flexibility in the system. Many enterprises practise different pricing strategies for the same services. This is demonstrated by the off-peak pricing of leisure activities and the different prices charged for train and air travel dependent on when a passenger actually travels.

Absorption costing or marginal costing?

Absorption costing absorbs all costs (direct and overhead costs) into each unit. It means that the value of the stock will include overheads and thus for this method not all the overhead costs will be written off in the accounting period in which they arise. Any closing stock will contain overheads as well as direct costs so the higher closing stock figure will reduce the 'cost of goods sold' and raise the profits for a period. This will be balanced out because the higher closing stock in one accounting period will be higher opening stock in the subsequent accounting period. This method is predominantly used for preparing the financial statements for businesses.

Marginal costing focuses on variable or marginal costs in recognising that fixed costs vary with time rather than activity. Therefore all the fixed costs are written off in a particular accounting period and the stock would be valued on a marginal basis: only the direct costs would be included in the product. The effect, of course, is a lower closing stock valuation and thus a higher 'cost of goods sold' figure and therefore lower profitability.

The total profitability of an enterprise over a number of years would be the same for both costing approaches but within those years the profitability would vary according to which approach was used.

Budgets and budgetary control

All organisations need to plan for the future. It is through a budgeting system that this can take place. A **budget** is a formal co-ordinated financial plan of what is expected to happen in the future. It is constructed by the managers of organisations in line with the objectives and goals of the organisation which are filtered down to its different sections.

Benefits of budgets

There are five specific purposes and benefits of using budgets.

Planning

The budget compels planning. By formalising the agreed objectives of an organisation through a budget preparation system, an organisation can ensure that its plans are achievable. This will also provide the organisation with the opportunity to ensure that the appropriate resources are in place at the right time in order to achieve the objectives set.

Communication

The budget communicates and co-ordinates. As organisation objectives and also budgets are agreed, all the employees will be working towards the same end. A communication and co-ordination process therefore occurs between the various departments to ensure that all parts of the organisation are working collectively towards the same objectives. The budgeting process should enable any potential problems to be resolved and areas of confusion over responsibilities to be clarified.

Authorisation

The budget can be used to authorise. For organisations where control of activities is deemed to be a high priority the budget can be used as a primary tool to ensure conformity to agreed plans. Once the budget has been agreed it can effectively become the authority to follow a particular course of action or to spend a certain amount of money.

Monitoring

The budget can be used to monitor and control. An important reason for preparing a budget is so that management can monitor the actual results against the budget. This is so that action can be taken to modify the operation of the organisation as time passes or to change the budget if it becomes unachievable. A controlling function is therefore imposed on the budgeting process.

Motivation

The budget can be used to motivate. A budget can be a part of an organisation's techniques for motivating managers and other staff to achieve the organisational objectives. The extent to which this happens will depend on how the budget is agreed and set and whether it is seen as fair and achievable. However, keeping within a budget can be constraining on staff and cause them to be less creative and innovative.

Operational and strategic budgets

Budgets could be prepared over the medium and long term, such as a five-year plan, or be **operational budgets** which means they are prepared for months, quarters or a whole year. The long-term budgeting is often referred to as **strategic budgeting** with the aims and objectives being less specific and also more difficult to prepare with accuracy. Operational budgets are short term and need to have the relevant resources available to meet targets and are therefore easier to monitor and control.

The budgeting process

The budgeting process in larger expanding businesses will probably be undertaken quite formally and regularly. There will be an established system in place with committees and a budget officer or co-ordinator in place. The committees will allow the managers, who will be responsible for individual budgets, to play a role in setting budgets and requesting resources for their own department or function. The budget co-ordinator has a responsibility for collecting the information for the business-wide budget, which will include integrating budgets of the different departments and functions of a business.

Limiting factors

For all budget preparation it is essential to establish what are the limiting factors involved. For commercial organisations the key budget factor is often the **predicted level of sales** which will then lead to the other budgets being prepared. Sometimes the limiting factor is the **productive capacity** of a business because it is never able to meet all its sales demands in its present position. In this case the strategic approach would be to plan or budget for increasing the productive capacity of the business. The budget process will then result in separate budgets for each area of business activity, which will ultimately lead to the master budget which is the forecasted profit and loss account, balance sheet and cash budget for the business. This process is shown in Figure 6.19, for a manufacturing firm with sales as the limiting budget factor.

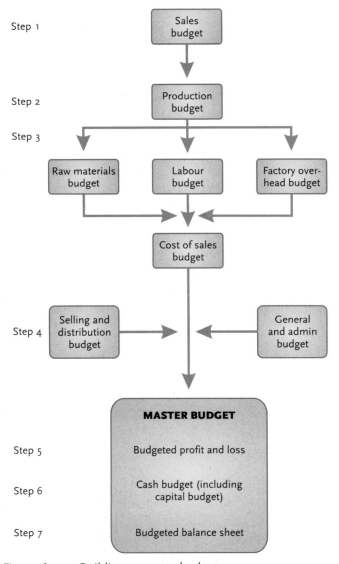

Figure 6.19   Building a master budget

The numbered steps shown in Figure 6.19 are the stages which have to be passed through to get to the next stage; for example, the labour budget is dependent on the production budget. A lot of the functional budgets will be included within the general headings, for example the factory overhead will include quality control, maintenance and servicing, and so on. In reality all the budgets will be prepared by the departmental and functional managers simultaneously to meet deadlines. Clearly these managers will be liaising with each other for essential information; for example, the human resources department will liaise with other departments to determine the staffing levels and thus the training and development budget.

Quantity measurements

Within each area the money values used in these budgets will usually be underpinned by other quantity measurements, such as weights, units or hours to ensure consistency across the various functions. They also provide some relevance to operational activity and so facilitate subsequent monitoring of a function's performance.

The exact nature of functional or subsidiary budgets will depend on the organisation's structure and the operational processes of the business. It is, however, usual for each budget to be analysed over a set time period such as a week, month and eventually a year. The government's budget is one with which we are most familiar, because it occurs in March or April of each year, the budget co-ordinator being the Chancellor of the Exchequer.

Targets and predictions

The processes are the same as any other budget: targets and predictions are made with the various departments or ministries (health, education, defence, and so on) making claims on public funds in order to achieve these targets. Although the out-turns will almost certainly be different from the targets or aims, the process provides the necessary framework to work towards particular goals.

Accountability

For control purposes, it is important for each manager to be held accountable for the specific parts of the budget applicable to his or her area. However, it must be recognised that the ability to control financial transactions will depend on the amount of discretion delegated to the various levels of the organisational structure. Can a particular manager, for example, control the incidence of a specific cost such as wages paid within the department being managed? It is unlikely that the manager will be able to control the wage and salary levels because they will be determined by other departments, such as human resources, or at a much higher level. Some control could be exercised over the amount of hours worked but even this would be restricted for permanent staff. It is wrong and demotivating for individuals to be held responsible for costs over which they have no control. Therefore in budgets costs would be divided up into **controllable costs** and **uncontrollable costs** when monitoring and review occurs.

Using the budget tool

It must be emphasised that budgets are a planning tool and not a straightjacket. Budgets can be harmful in achieving goals if managers perceive them in this way. For example, a production manager may turn down requests for overtime to meet a deadline because the budgeted overtime hours have been reached, with this decision resulting in the delivery being late and a financial penalty occurring along with the potential loss of good customer relationships and reputation. Alternatively a manager who has not spent all the budget allocation will launch into a spending spree with unnecessary items being bought. Sometimes very difficult decisions have to be made and this is evident in, for example, Hospital Trusts which may have their budgets 'capped' and find themselves unable to fulfil their obligations, such as performing operations.

Budget models are usually constructed using spreadsheets or specialist modelling programs which provide decision makers with valuable 'what if?' tools which allow several courses of action to be tracked. When such facilitates are available then changing

some variables will allow the decision makers to see the effects of such decisions on the various areas of a business and how these are interrelated.

CASE STUDY

A mug's game

A manufacturer of souvenir mugs has a production capacity of 2000 mugs per month and aims to maintain a minimum stock of 500 mugs at any time. Sales of mugs are forecast to be:

♦ 1000 in both March and April
♦ 1500 in May
♦ 2000 in June
♦ 3000 in July.

A production budget is needed to cover the five-month period. The problem is that July will experience sales that are 1000 mugs in excess of production capacity. By working back from July it is possible to find the nearest months that will have sufficient capacity to build up stocks in readiness for July sales.

	March	April	May	June	July
Stock b/f	500	500	1000	1500	1500
Production	1000	1500	2000	2000	2000
Sales	1000	1000	1500	2000	3000
Stock c/f	500	1000	1500	1500	500

Figure 6.20   Sales figures

In June, maximum production is matched by sales, so April and May are the latest months available that can contribute towards a build-up in stocks before the July peak period. To increase stocks in March would increase unnecessarily the period of investment in higher stocks.

ACTIVITY

A manufacturer of T-shirts has a production capacity of 5000 per month and aims to maintain a minimum stock of 1000 at any time. Sales of T-shirts are forecast to be 2000 in both March and April, 4000 in May, 6000 in June and 8000 in July. Prepare the production budget to cover the five-month period.

Flexible budgeting

For control purposes the original budget may need some adjustments in the light of the actual business performance. This is because the original budget estimates are made on particular volume or activity levels. If the actual activity levels are very different from the budgeted ones then it would no longer be useful and effective to make comparisons and calculate variances. The adjusted volume or activity levels would have effects on the costs which would be outside the control of particular managers. For example, the production manager may have a budget to produce 100,000 units of a product. If the actual output was 120,000 units then clearly the production manager would be substantially exceeding the materials and direct labour budget but this would not necessarily be a reflection of inefficiency and lack of control. These costs would be expected to rise and so calculating a variance for these costs would have little use or value. Therefore it is necessary to **flex** the budget in line with the different levels of volume or activity.

When flexing the budget it is necessary to analyse the cost behaviour of the various inputs as some costs will change with different levels of activity and some will not. For example, variable costs will need to be changed directly in line with different activity levels whereas fixed costs will not change at all. Some costs will be semi-variable and therefore change will occur but it will not be in line with the changing levels of activity.

The table shows some details of the annual budget for a bus company (the original budget). The bus company's actual activity level was twice that of the budget.

Bus company details

Details of cost	*Type of cost*	*Original budget (£)*	*Flexed budget (£)*	*Actual costs (£)*
Depreciation of vehicles	Fixed	100,000	100,000	110,000
Maintenance of vehicles	Semi-variable (50:50)	50,000	75,000	70,000
Diesel	Variable	100,000	200,000	210,000

Figure 6.21 Bus company details

If the performance of the bus company was based on the original budget, then it would be heavily criticised for exceeding its budget, especially in respect of maintenance (40 per cent above budget) and fuel usage (110 per cent above budget). However, when the budget is flexed to the actual activity level, that is, double the budget, then it shows that:

- 8 per cent lower costs for maintenance have been achieved compared to the budget, that is, £70,000 compared to £75,000
- 5 per cent higher costs have occurred in respect of diesel compared to the budget, that is, £210,000 compared to £200,000.

If the budget had not been flexed the results based on the original budget would be distorted, and this information would not be useful or relevant for making management decisions. For depreciation there would be no difference because it is a fixed cost and in this case it is 10 per cent above the budget whether it be the original or the flexed budget.

ACTIVITY

The following budget data (Figure 6.22) for April 2004 relates to Brampton Tools Ltd, a manufacturer of machine tools.

	Budget (% of capacity)			Actual
	At 80% (£)	At 90% (£)	At 100% (£)	(£)
Direct materials	28,000	31,500	35,000	24,250
Direct labour	39,200	44,100	49,000	35,400
Rent	10,000	10,000	10,000	10,000
Electricity	3400	3650	3900	3450
Factory supervision	18,000	19,000	20,000	17,500
Administration	37,000	40,000	43,000	35,400

Figure 6.22   Budget data for Brampton Tools Ltd

The original budget was constructed on the assumption that business activity would be 90 per cent of factory capacity. This equated to 12,600 standard units of work and would produce a 20 per cent margin. An analysis of costs was undertaken at the time the budget was prepared and this was used to produce indicative amounts if output deviated by 10 per cent of total capacity. Actual production at 70 per cent capacity fell outside the expected range but budget selling price was achieved.

1 Produce a profit statement with columns for actual performance, original budget, flexed budget, and variance from flexed budget.

2 Comment on the results.

Contents of the budget

The budget, as we have seen, will consist of subsidiary budgets leading to the master budget. The supporting schedules will provide analysis in volume and money terms of sales, production and stock levels. In addition there will be detailed statements of the make-up of debtor and creditor balances and of individual department expense budgets.

The following case study will help your understanding of the processes and outcomes involved with a cash flow forecast.

CASE STUDY
The builder's books

Jack Stanton owns a small building firm, working mainly on house extensions and repair. He employs four workers, each paid an average £6.00 per hour. They work for a basic 162.5-hour calender month which equates to 7.5 hours a day. Where necessary Jack pays overtime at time and a half. Jack estimates that work measured in labour hours for the next 12 months together with material costs will be:

Year 2004	July	Aug	Sept	Oct	Nov	Dec
Hours	900	850	900	800	600	301
Materials (£)	4000	4000	4000	3500	2500	1001

Year 2005	Jan	Feb	Mar	April	May	June
Hours	250	300	400	500	600	801
Materials (£)	1000	1500	2000	2500	2500	4011

Jack has agreed the following number of holidays with his workers including his own:

Year 2004	July	Aug	Sept	Oct	Nov	Dec
Holidays	10	10	10	15	5	35

Year 2005	Jan	Feb	Mar	April	May	June
Hours	12	5	5	8	5	5

Jack takes £2000 out of the business each month and works a basic 37.5 hours a week productive work. Running costs every month amount to £900 for his yard, and £500 for a van and various items of small plant. Hire of specialist equipment will cost him £1 of charges for every productive labour hour.

Building jobs are quoted at £15 per man-hour plus materials cost. There are no partly completed jobs at the end of the month in which they are incurred. On 30 June 2004 there was £251 in the business bank account and customers owed £16,000 for work completed in June 2004.

In February 2005 Jack plans to purchase a new van for £10,000 and a concrete mixer for £1800 in May 2005.

ACTIVITY

1   Prepare a twelve-month cash flow budget for Stanton & Co from 1 July 2004 to 30 June 2005 (round all figures to whole pounds).

2   Comment on the pattern of cash flows for the firm and establish reasons for it.

3   Recommend ways in which the cash deficit could be financed, assuming similar trading activity in future years.

4   How could the firm's cash position be improved without resorting to additional finance being sought?

Investment and project appraisal

Management accounting is about evaluating the potential performance of different aspects of businesses and different courses of action. It is therefore necessary to provide the management of a

company with relevant and appropriate information for decision-making purposes. Investment usually involves large initial expenditure and from a business perspective means either capital expenditure or increases in working capital.

Capital expenditure

This is expenditure on fixed assets. Such expenditure could arise for a number of reasons such as:

♦ the purchase of new plant and equipment to improve the operating efficiency of a business
♦ the purchase of the essential specialist plant and equipment required for the production and delivery of new products and services to customers
♦ a particular project which is being considered.

Increases in working capital

This is essential expenditure for companies experiencing rapid growth. If a company grows very quickly then apart from needing additional productive capacity it will also need to fund increases in stocks, debtors and creditors.

Capital investment project

In simple terms a **capital investment project** is the spending of money now in order to receive benefits (which could be revenues or reduced costs) in future years. It can be illustrated by Figure 6.23.

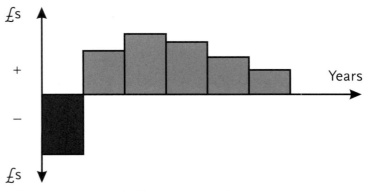

Figure 6.23   A capital investment project

Appraisal

All investment needs to be appraised to ensure that it is commercially viable. This means that the investment will improve the efficiency and profitability of a company. An appraisal of such expenditure is needed to ensure that the limited funds available to a company are used in the most efficient and productive way. However, some of the costs and benefits might be difficult to quantify and have more qualitative outcomes. For example, when building a new factory the appraisal should not just

Investment Ltd has three investment opportunities which are detailed below. The company has a strict policy on investment decisions, these being:

1 the investment must have a return on capital (ARR) which exceeds 10%
2 to obtain internal funding the investment must be a better investment than other competing investment opportunities
3 the return on capital must be higher than the cost of capital (the cost of borowing) if additional external funding is to be sought.

Year	Project 1 cash flow (£)	Project 2 cash flow (£)	Project 3 cash flow (£)
Initial costs 0 (present)	(50,000)	(50,000)	(30,000)
1	19,000	14,000	12,000
2	19,000	14,000	10,000
3	18,000	14,000	7000
4	9,000	14,000	4250
5		14,000	4250

At the end of the life of each of the projects the fixed assets purchased, that is, the initial costs, will have a zero residual value.

Only 50,000 of internal funds are available for these three projects and the cost of capital is 10%.

Figure 6.24   Predicted information by Investment Ltd

be confined to profits of the company and effects on the local economy, but also the scenic effects on the locality. Wherever possible the assumptions used in justifying a project should be measurable so that as the project progresses the management can review the value of the estimates to establish whether the expectations are actually met in the ways that were outlined in the planning process. The feedback and monitoring of investment outcomes is helpful in improving the accuracy of the investment appraisal process.

Businesses will often adopt different methods for appraising investment which will involve preset targets or benchmarks that have to be met. There are several ways by which the worthwhileness of investment can be judged, these being:

♦ accounting rate of return method (ARR)
♦ payback method
♦ discounted cash flow (DCF) method or net present value (NPV) method
♦ internal rate of return method.

These investment appraisal techniques will be considered in turn using the predicted information (Figure 6.24) on three projects being considered by a company, Investment Ltd, with limited internal funds available for investment.

Accounting rate of return

Business performance is often measured by its **return on capital employed** so it is a reasonable strategy to appraise investment expenditure on the same basis. The **accounting rate of return** (ARR) compares the net profits earned from an investment with the capital actually invested. This can be achieved by applying the following formula to any investment project.

$$ARR = \frac{\text{Average annual profits}}{\text{Average capital employed}} \times 100$$

Once the ARR has been calculated the management of a company will have to make a decision on the viability of this investment within their own particular circumstances. This will involve several considerations:

♦ comparing the ARR of all the investment projects available
♦ comparing the ARR with the company benchmark which all investment projects must achieve
♦ comparing the ARR with the cost of borrowing additional funds.

In using the ARR method it is necessary to calculate the average profits that are earned from the investment. It will therefore require the depreciation of the fixed assets to be calculated in order to adjust the cash flows to obtain the net profits earned.

Once the ARR for several competing investment projects have been calculated, then the investment projects can be placed in order of ARR. The funds will subsequently be applied to each investment project until the funds run out. The final consideration is whether to seek additional external funds for the funding of the investment projects which have a high ARR and which would cover the cost of further borrowing.

ARR assessment of Project 1

$$\text{Depreciation for Project 1} = \frac{\text{Cost of fixed assets}}{\text{Life of asset (years)}}$$

$$= \frac{£50,000}{4 \text{ years}} = £12,500 \text{ per annum}$$

Average profits per annum
= Total cash flows – Total depreciation/Number of years

$$= (£19,000 + £19,000 + £18,000 + £9000) - £50,000/4$$

$$= £3000$$

The average capital employed is calculated by taking a simple average between the capital invested at the start of the project and the balance at the end of the project, that is, the expected sale price of the fixed assets purchased. In this case the value at the end of the project is zero.

Average capital employed = $(50000 + £0)/2 = £25,000$

$$\text{ARR} = \frac{£3750}{£25,000} \times 100 = 15\% \text{ per annum}$$

ACTIVITY

1 Calculate the ARR for Projects 2 and 3.

2 Using the results obtained for each of the three projects:

♦ choose the project which should use the £50,000 of internally available funds based on ARR
♦ decide whether further external funds should be sought to finance any of the other projects.

Payback method

The rationale behind the payback method of investment appraisal is to select the investment which pays back the initial outlay in the quickest time. The theory is that the quicker the money is repaid the quicker those funds can be used for other investment projects. This method concentrates on **cash flows** and not net profits. The **payback period** is the time required for a project to repay the initial investment. It can be calculated by aggregating the negative and positive cash flows for each year until the cumulative cash flow reaches zero.

The final analysis, as with ARR, is to place the investment projects in payback order. The available funds will subsequently be applied to each investment project until the funds run out, that is, the project with the fastest payback period will be started first, then the second fastest, and so on.

Payback method assessment of Project 1

The table (Appendix A) shows the results of aggregating the cash flows over the expected life of the investment project (Project 1). These results show that the payback period falls somewhere between the end of year 2 which has a negative aggregate cash flow, and the end of year 3 which has a positive cash flow. It is now necessary to determine where between these two dates the payback period ends. This can be achieved by the following formula, assuming that the cash flows do occur evenly during year 3.

$$\frac{\text{Years of negative aggregate}}{\text{cash flow}} + \frac{\text{Deficit remaining}}{\text{Cash flow in relevant year}}$$

= Payback period in years

APPENDIX A

Project 1

Year	Cash flow (£s)	Aggregate cash flow
0 (present)	(50,000)	(50,000)
1	19,000	(31,000)
2	19,000	(12,000)
3	18,000	6000
4	9000	15,000
5		

$$2 \text{ years} + \frac{£12,000}{£18,000} = 2.66 \text{ years}$$

This could be converted into months by:

2 years + (0.66 × 12) months = 2 years 7.9 months

ACTIVITY

1 Calculate the payback period for Projects 2 and 3.

2 Using the results obtained for each of the three projects, choose the project which should use the £50,000 of internally available funds based on the payback method only.

The investment project with the shortest payback period is the one which would be preferred, as the longer the life of the investment project the higher the risk of unforeseen circumstances occurring which would affect the original estimates.

It is especially good for high technology and fashion projects as they have a high level of uncertainty where earlier cash flows are likely to be more accurate estimates. The drawbacks to this method are:

◆ The payback period does not consider the pattern of payback within the payback period. For example, one investment project (A) may have very high cash flows at the start of the project which then fall very rapidly, whereas another investment project (B) may have low cash flows at the start which then increase rapidly. The decision on which investment project to opt for would be based on when payback is achieved and this might be project B even though project A had almost reached the payback point long before project B.
◆ More importantly, the payback calculations ignore the cash flows that arise after the payback period and so do not provide data on the profitability of an investment project.

Despite these shortcomings, this method is widely used to appraise investment. This is because it is the simplest technique to apply. Often, with large organisations, it is used as a support or secondary measure to one of the other techniques.

Discounted cash flow (DCF) method

The two methods examined so far are the most simple to understand and apply. However, they lack the sophistication to be comprehensively objective in appraising an investment project. The discounted cash flow (DCF) method, also called the net present value (NPV) method, applies more rigour and objectivity to the process which is why it is used extensively in large organisations.

The NPV method introduces the notion of the **time value of money** and integrates the cost of capital into the appraisal mechanism.

The time value of money means that the money now, at its present value, is worth less than it would be in the future. This can be demonstrated in the following case study.

CASE STUDY

What is the time value of money?

The time value of money can be demonstrated by asking yourself the question: Would you give up £100 now for £100 in a year's time?

The answer to this question is, of course, No, because if you give up £100 now you would expect more than £100 in a year's time. This is because you can deposit it in a bank and earn interest on the £100. Therefore the interest represents the time value of money.

However, if you were asked to give up the £100 for two years, you would expect two years' interest on the concession but after the first year you would also benefit from interest on the interest earned in the first year. This is **compound interest**. The following example of £100 deposited at a bank using an annual rate of interest of 10% will illustrate the process. It means that £100 now is worth £146.41 in four years time at an interest rate of 10%.

Original deposit	£100.00
Interest for year 1 at 10%	£10.00
Value at the end of year 1	£110.00
Interest for year 2 at 10%	£11.00
Value at the end of year 2	£121.00
Interest for year 3 at 10%	£12.10
Value at the end of year 3	£133.10
Interest for year 4 at 10%	£13.31
Value at the end of year 4	£146.41

The figure can be calculated more quickly by applying the following formula which calculates compound interest, with r being the rate of interest.

$$\text{Deposit} \times \frac{(1 + r)^n}{1} = \text{Value in } n \text{ years}$$

Here it is applied to the example of a deposit of £100 at 10 per cent compound interest.

$$£100 \times \frac{1.1}{1} \text{ (that is, } 1.1) = £110.00$$

$$£100 \times \frac{1.1 \times 1.1}{1} \text{ (that is, } 1.21) = £121.00$$

$$£100 \times \frac{1.1 \times 1.1 \times 1.1}{1} \text{ (that is, } 1.311) = £131.10$$

$$£100 \times \frac{1.1 \times 1.1 \times 1.1 \times 1.1}{1} \text{ (that is, } 1.4641) = £146.41$$

The process can be worked from a different perspective. What, for example, would £110 have been worth a year previously at an annual 10 per cent rate of interest, or £146.41 four years previously? In both cases the figure would be £100. This is discounting the future values back to the present value. It can be calculated by adjusting the compound interest formula to the discounting formula.

$$\text{Value in } n \text{ years} \times \frac{1}{(1 + r)^n} = \text{Net present value (NPV)}$$

$$£110.00 \times \frac{1}{1.1} \text{ (that is, } 0.9091) = £100$$

$$£121.00 \times \frac{1}{1.1 \times 1.1} \text{ (that is, } 0.8624) = £100$$

$$£131.10 \times \frac{1}{1.1 \times 1.1 \times 1.1} \text{ (that is, } 0.7513) = £100$$

$$£146.41 \times \frac{1}{1.1 \times 1.1 \times 1.1 \times 1.1} \text{ (that is, } 0.6830) = £100$$

The results obtained from the above calculations are the same but are viewed from a different perspective. A DCF approach is a valuable technique for valuing receipts and payments that occur at different times over the life of an investment project as it reduces these future cash flows to a common measure, the NPV. This technique will enable managers directly to compare investment projects on the same bases with the **cost of capital** being included directly into the process.

Unlike the ARR method the DCF method is based on actual cash flows rather than net profits. These cash flows will include **inflows**:

♦ actual receipts from sales
♦ sales proceeds from the disposal of fixed assets
♦ government grants

and **outflows**:

♦ investment in fixed assets
♦ the increase in working capital (stocks, debtors)
♦ operating costs (materials, labour, expenses)
♦ tax payments.

The technique is easy to apply because it involves multiplying the future cash flows by the discount factor. The **discount factor** for a 10 per cent rate is

Years			Rates of interest			
	5%	6%	7%	8%	9%	10%
1	0.9524	0.9434	0.9346	0.9259	0.9174	0.9091
2	0.9070	0.8900	0.8734	0.8573	0.8417	0.8264
3	0.8636	0.8396	0.8163	0.7938	0.7722	0.7513
4	0.8227	0.7921	0.7629	0.7350	0.7084	0.6830
5	0.7835	0.7473	0.7130	0.6806	0.6499	0.6209
6	0.7462	0.7050	0.6663	0.6302	0.5963	0.5645
7	0.7104	0.6651	0.6227	0.5835	0.5470	0.5132
8	0.6768	0.6274	0.5820	0.5403	0.5019	0.4665
9	0.6446	0.5919	0.5439	0.5002	0.4604	0.4241
10	0.6139	0.5584	0.5084	0.4632	0.4224	0.3855

Figure 6.25   NPV table

shown in the previous example in brackets (0.9091 for year 1; 0.8264 for year 2, and so on). These discount factors do not need to be calculated as they can be looked up on an NPV table, as in Figure 6.25.

The outcome of the DCF method will show that:

♦ the NPV of future cash flows will be lower as the length of time into the future increases
♦ the NPV of future cash flows will be lower when the cost of capital (discount rate) rises.

DCF method assessment of Project 1

The net cash flows over the life of the investment project were detailed in Figure 6.24. It is now necessary to discount these cash flows to NPVs using the appropriate rate which in this case is 10 per cent. This is achieved by multiplying the estimated cash flows by the discount factors.

Year	Project 1 cash flow (£)		Discount factor (10%)	NPV (£)
0 (present)	(50,000)	×	1	(50,000)
1	19,000	×	0.9091	17,273
2	19,000	×	0.8264	15,702
3	18,000	×	0.7513	13,523
4	9000	×	0.6830	6147
			Positive NPV	2645

These results show that the NPV of the future cash flows is a positive figure of £2645 after accounting for the cost of capital, a 10 per cent interest rate. This means that the cost of the investment project will be profitable because the NPV of the cash flows exceeds the cost of the investment by £2645. If the NPV was a negative figure then the investment project would make a loss and would thus be rejected.

By applying the technique to a number of possible investment projects the results can be directly compared. The investment projects with the highest positive NPV figure would be the most profitable and the ones to opt for.

423

ACTIVITY

1   Use the DCF method of investment appraisal to evaluate Projects 2 and 3.

2   Using the results obtained for each of the three projects:

   ◆ choose the project which should use the £50,000 of internally available funds based on the DCF method only
   ◆ advise the management whether additional funds should be sought in order to implement Projects 2 and 3.

Using the DCF method of investment appraisal has some advantages:

◆ all cash flows are used
◆ the timing of cash flows is taken into account
◆ it is easy to implement by using the table for discount factors.

However, there are some drawbacks to using this method:

◆ changing interest rates makes it difficult to determine the cost of capital over the life of a project
◆ the meaning of NPV is not always clear to the users of the information
◆ the investment project with the highest positive NPV does not always represent the best option for businesses because other factors may need to be taken into account which cannot be costed into the estimates, for example the effect on the morale and motivation of the workforce if new equipment is purchased.

	Project 1	Project 2	Project 3
ARR method	15%	16%	10%
Payback method	2.66 years	3.57 years	3.24 years
DCF method	£2645 NPV	£1485 NPV	(£26) NPV

Results of the analysis

Three methods have been used to appraise Investment Ltd's three investment projects. The results are as follows.

Businesses are likely to consider more than one method of appraising investment projects but the results show that although the decision is easy to reach for each different method it is not easy when evaluating the overall merits. In the case of Investment Ltd's Project 1, this has a slightly lower ARR compared to Project 2 but has a shorter payback period and a higher NPV figure. Project 3 is clearly the weakest investment project but it does have a quicker payback period than Project 2. It would be discarded, however, on the basis of a negative NPV figure.

Overall the best investment project is Project 1 with Project 2 also having good potential; but Project 3 would be rejected. However, in each of the three methods considered, no account is taken of the amount of capital expenditure required. In this instance Projects 1 and 2 have the same initial costs but it could have been that Project 1 required double the amount of capital investment than Project 2. These methods do not discriminate by this aspect. An alternative way of examining investment projects would be to extend the DCF method and calculate what is called the internal rate of return (IRR).

Internal rate of return method

This method is sometimes called the DCF yield method.

Internal rate of return (IRR) is equal to the rate of cost of capital, that is, the discount rate at which the present value of net cash inflows exactly balances the initial investment. It means that the net cash flows after being discounted give a nil value.

This can be calculated by using a spreadsheet with a built-in function for calculating the IRR. However, it can also be estimated mathematically or graphically.

Mathematical calculation of IRR

This is achieved by calculating the NPV at two different discount rates, ensuring that one is positive and one is negative. The closer they are to a zero NPV the more accurate will be the result. The assumption is that there is a straight line relationship between the discount rates and the NPV figures. The following formula will lead to the IRR for a project.

$$LDR + \left(\frac{HNPV \; DR}{HNPV + LNPV} \times (HDR - LDR) \right)$$

LDR = Lower discount rate
HDR = Higher discount rate
HNPV = Higher net present value (positive)
LNPV = Lower net present value (negative)

Using Investment Ltd's Project 1 to demonstrate the process, the formula would be applied as follows. The NPV already calculated was £2645 at a 10 per cent discount rate. By taking a discount rate of 14 per cent the NPV would be £1234.

ACTIVITY

Calculate the IRR for Project 2. The NPV at 10 per cent was £1485 and taking a discount rate of 14 per cent the NPV was £1935.

$$10\% + \left(\frac{2645}{2645 + 1234} \times (14\% - 10\%) \right) = 12.7\%$$

Graphical calculation of IRR

The IRR can be found by drawing a graph with the horizontal axis measuring the **cost of capital percentage** and the vertical axis the NPV values, both positive and negative amounts. The process involves plotting the two co-ordinates of:

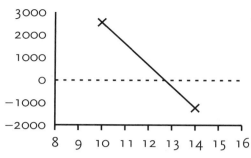

Figure 6.26   Graph showing the IRR for Project 1

♦ cost of capital percentage and positive NPV
♦ cost of capital percentage and negative NPV on the axes.

Then draw a line (see Figure 6.26) connecting the two co-ordinates and the IRR will be where this crosses the horizontal axis.

Other considerations

A range of methods have been examined for appraising capital expenditure, each with different slants to the problem and varying levels of sophistication. They are all, however, focused on numerical techniques. It is important not to be constricted by this numerical analysis as other factors also need to be considered before reaching a final decision.

Total implications

An investment project could have wide-ranging effects on a business, including:

♦ the effects on sales of increases in output
♦ the effects on output with changing manufacturing techniques leading to more staff training but fewer employees
♦ more working capital required as business activity increases
♦ the effects of increased needs for resources such as premises, materials and transport.

Cost of finance

The cost of capital may change during the life of an investment project and sometimes this risk cannot be overcome by having a fixed rate of interest on

425

borrowing. The economic climate may change and lead to higher rates of interest which will affect the viability of an investment project.

Tax considerations

All investment projects will be affected by any changes in tax relief and tax rates which again could affect project viability.

Forecasting techniques

These techniques can be used for the estimating of sales figures and corresponding cost implications. This can help to assess the effects of price falls or cost increase.

End of unit assignment

Part 1

You are employed as an assistant accountant in the Finance Department of Perfect Brew PLC, a quoted company which operates in the brewing, pubs and restaurants sector. The financial director, Fiona Tippler, often employs you to carry out special projects for her. The company has been progressing well over a number of years, experiencing encouraging growth in sales, profitability and capitalisation value. Fiona has been asked by the board of directors to examine the possible direction that the company can go in the future. She has decided to undertake a thorough review of the performance of the company over the past two years and compare this with other companies in the same line of business and of a similar size. She is also considering ways of continuing the expansion programme of the company and wants to investigate the possibilities of a takeover of a rival company.

You have a meeting with Fiona in which she outlines a number of tasks she wants you to do.

Task 1

I need to have a detailed analysis of the performance of our company over the past two years. It is necessary to investigate changes over time and against our main market rivals. Could you therefore use the copies of the annual accounts (Appendix 1) of Perfect Brew PLC for the past two years and analyse the performance by calculating a range of accounting ratios and performance indicators.

For ONE of our major rivals obtain a copy of their latest annual report and accounts and calculate similar ratios and/or performance indicators, in order to compare their performance with our own. You can obtain copies of the annual report and accounts by contacting the company secretary at the registered office. You will be able to find the addresses/telephone numbers on the Internet or from sources in the library. Choose one of these companies:

- Burtonwood PLC
- Belhaven PLC
- Eldridge Pope and Co PLC

I have also enclosed (Appendix 2) a copy of our trade association (Brewers and Pub Retailers Federation) average results for the latest available year.

Tabulate the results of the ratios calculated and attach copies of the source documents and a 'workings sheet' giving details of the formulae used and the actual calculations. It would be advisable to include the trade association average figures in your table.

Task 2

Write a brief confidential report addressed to me personally which covers the following:

- an evaluation of the company's financial performance over the past two years, identifying the strengths and weaknesses of the company
- some recommendations to solve the problems and/or exploit the strengths which have been identified.

Task 3

Prepare a document for me using the information from Tasks 1 and 2 (Perfect Brew PLC's annual accounts and the annual report and accounts of the rival company) to explain and compare the way the two companies are being financed and how it has changed over the last two years of results. This will involve a thorough examination of the financial statements to identify and explain the following sources of finance:

♦ What types of long-term finance are being used and in what proportions and at what cost?
♦ What types of short-term finance are being utilised and in what proportions and at what cost?
♦ Explain the different sources of long- and short-term finance and identify the disadvantages and advantages of using these different types of long- and short-term finance.

♦ From the analysis above briefly evaluate the ways the companies are being funded and make recommendations, where appropriate, to improve the financial structure to solve any problems identified.

Task 4

I would also like to have your views on whether the rival company that you have investigated would be a worthwhile takeover target for Perfect Brew PLC. Please prepare a memo which outlines your thoughts with supporting analysis.

APPENDIX 1

Perfect Brew PLC

Trading and profit and loss accounts for the years ended 30 September

	2003 £000s		2004 £000s	
Sales		59,800		65,562
less Cost of goods sold				
Opening stock	1790		1860	
add Purchases (all on credit)	31,200		33,696	
Goods available for sales	32,990		35,556	
less Closing stock	1860	31130	1980	33,576
GROSS PROFIT		28,670		31,986
less Expenses				
Overheads				
Wages and salaries	8790		9240	
Rent and rates	1980		2050	
Heating and lighting	1100		1198	
Advertising	950		1127	
Telephone, printing, stationery	789		897	
Interest and bank charges	391		512	
Other overhead expenses	3054		3576	

	2003 £000s		2004 £000s	
Depreciation				
Premises	790		856	
Fixtures and fittings	1700		1830	
Motor vehicles	1492	21,036	1582	22,868
Profit on ordinary activities before tax		7634		9118
Tax on profit on ordinary activities		1680		1984
Profit or loss on ordinary activities after tax		5954		7134
Appropriations				
Preference dividends (paid before year end)		300		300
Ordinary dividends				
Interim paid	500		500	
Proposed	2300	3100	2500	3300
Retained profit for the year		2854		3834
Balance brought forward		12606		15460
Balance carried forward		15,460		19,294
Share price		210p		225p

APPENDIX 1 (continued)
Perfect Brew PLC
Balance sheet as at 30 September

FIXED ASSETS		2003 £000s			2004 £000s		
	Cost	Acc. Dep.	Net	Cost	Acc. Dep.	Net	
Premises	39,260	5352	33,908	46,604	6208	40,396	
Plant, equipment, fixtures and fittings	21,268	4982	16,286	22,879	5140	17,739	
Motor vehicles	10,543	3480	7063	13,690	3762	9928	
CURRENT ASSETS							
Stocks		1860			1980		
Trade debtors		5478			5896		
Prepayments		160			190		
Bank		–			820		
Cash		15			19		
		7513			8905		
less							
CREDITORS: AMOUNTS DUE WITHIN ONE YEAR							
Trade creditors	4860			5010			
Other creditors and accruals	6380			7180			
Bank	90			–			
Taxation	1680			1984			
Dividends	2300	15,310		2500	16,674		
NET CURRENT LIABILITIES			(7797)			(7769)	
TOTAL ASSETS LESS CURRENT LIABILITIES			49,460			60,294	
less							
CREDITORS: AMOUNTS DUE AFTER MORE THAN ONE YEAR							
8% debenture stock			4000			6000	
			45,460			54,294	
Financed by							
CAPITAL AND RESERVES							
Ordinary share capital (£1 shares)			20000			22000	
Share premium account			5000			8000	
6% preference share capital			5000			5000	
Profit and loss account			15,460			19,294	
			45,460			54,294	

APPENDIX 2

BPRF (Brewers and Pub Retailers Federation)	2003 (Averages)
Gross profit	45%
Net profit	10%
Return on capital employed	15%
Current ratio (or work capital ratio)	0.8:1
Acid test ratio	0.4:1
Creditor payment period (based on 365 days)	40 days
Debtor collection period (based on the sales figures of 365 days)	25 days
Stock turnover	15 times
Gearing ratio (i.e. debt:equity ratio)	20%
Sales:fixed assets ratio	1.2:1
Earnings per share	25p per share
Dividend yield	4%
Price:earnings ratio	10
Dividend cover	3.5 times
Interest cover	4 times

Part 2

You work as an accounts clerk in the Finance Department of Superplay Limited. This company is the manufacturer of a specially designed squash racket called the Hammerhead. It was invented and developed by the company founder, Don Reval. It has already obtained a high reputation amongst both professional and ordinary club players and sales have been very promising. Don has assembled the following cost information for the year ending 31 March 2005.

Cost estimates for year ending 31 March 2005

Raw materials	fibreglass/boron	£12.50 per racket
	strings	£2.10 per racket
Direct labour	moulding and finishing	£14.75 per racket
	stringing and packing	£2.65 per racket
Indirect factory costs		£220,000
Selling and distribution costs		£66,000
Administration expenses		£88,000
Finance expenses		£22,000

Don asks you to complete the following tasks for him.

Task 1

1 Calculate the 'variable costs per racket' for manufacturing the Hammerhead squash racket and establish the two possible prices using:

 ◆ a mark-up of 80 per cent (19,000 rackets could be sold)
 ◆ a mark-up of 110 per cent (14,000 rackets could be sold).

2 Provide a brief explanation with examples of the difference between variable costs and fixed costs.

Task 2

1 Prepare two 'forecasted profit statements' for the two different prices (as calculated above) for the year ended 31 March 2005 which will disclose:

- the total contribution and contribution per unit
- the total profit or loss for the year.

2 Write some brief notes analysing the profit statements prepared in order to assess:

- the most appropriate price to charge for the rackets
- the future prospects of the company.

Task 3

1 Calculate the break-even points for the company in both sales volume and sales value at each of the proposed price levels.

2 Calculate the margin of safety for the product at each of the two price levels.

3 Briefly explain what is meant by 'break-even point' and 'margin of safety' and why it is useful to calculate them.

Task 4

Superplay has also received an offer to supply an overseas sporting goods company with 1000 rackets at a price of £35.00 per racket. This offer could be easily satisfied and without Superplay affecting their fixed costs. You are required to write a brief report to Don advising him on whether to accept or reject the offer, giving justification for your recommendations.

Task 5

The company has the opportunity to purchase new machinery, which is currently being developed, in March 2005 at a cost of £250,000, which would have a projected life of six years after which it could be sold for £5000. The new machinery would improve the efficiency of the manufacturing process leading to the following if the new machinery was purchased:

- the raw material costs of the fibreglass/boron would fall from £12.50 per racket to £10.00
- the direct labour costs of moulding and finishing would fall from £14.75 per racket to £12.50. It is necessary to evaluate the purchase of the machinery using the various methods of investment appraisal (payback, accounting rate of return, net present

value). It is expected that the following production and sales will take place over the six-year life of the new machinery.

Production and sales forecasts for the six years to 31 March 2011

Year	Production	Sales
2006	16,000	16,000
2007	18,000	18,000
2008	19,000	19,000
2009	14,000	14,000
2010	11,500	11,500
2011	10,000	10,000

Write a brief report to Don, using the information above, appraising the investment option in the new machinery. In doing this it is important to consider all of the three investment appraisal methods and also to advise Don on whether to go ahead with the investment in the new machinery. Note that Superplay Limited is seeking the following performance requirements on any new investment:

- the acceptable payback period for the investment is under three years
- the accounting return is on average between 10 and 15 per cent
- the NPV approach can be calculated using an 11 per cent discount rate with this being the equivalent interest rate for borrowing.

Task 6

- Prepare a 'cash budget' from the information provided below, for the year ended 31 March 2005.
- Analyse the statement prepared to identify any problems that the company may face in the next year, bearing in mind that the overdraft facility has been set at £100,000 after recent negotiations with the bank. Write a memo to Don explaining these problems and make some recommendations on how to avoid them.

Additional information

- It is expected that the new machinery will be purchased in March 2005 ready for production in the new financial year ending 31 March 2006. The costs will be £250,000.
- Interest on any overdraft that arises will be at an annual interest rate of 8 per cent.
- The rackets are to be sold at the price determined in Task 1 with 20 per cent being sold for cash and 80 per cent on one month's credit. Debtors at the end of March 2004 were £42,000.

- The estimated direct materials costs and direct labour costs per racket are on p. 429.
  Suppliers of the raw materials provide one month's credit and the creditor at the end of March 2004 was £15,500.
  All other payments are itemised in the table below.
  The bank balance as at 31 March 2004 was an overdraft of £44,000.

Production and sales of the 'Hammerhead' in volume

Year ending 31 March 2005

	April	May	June	July	August	Sept	Oct	Nov	Dec	Jan	Feb	March
Sales	800	600	400	400	300	2850	2450	1400	1800	1050	950	1000
Production	1000	1000	1000	1000	2000	2000	1000	1000	1000	1000	1000	1000

Fixed costs (£s)

Year ending 31 March 2005

	April	May	June	July	August	Sept	Oct	Nov	Dec	Jan	Feb	March
Factory indirect costs	30,000	15,000	15,000	15,000	25,000	25,000	15,000	15,000	16,000	19,000	15,000	15,000
Selling and distribution costs	4500	4500	4500	6000	8000	8000	5000	8000	4000	4500	4500	4500
Administration expenses	8000	7000	7000	7000	7500	7500	7500	7500	7000	7000	7000	8000
Finance expenses	8000			3000			8000			3000		

It would be sensible to do the cash budget using a spreadsheet. If you opt to tackle it in this way keep a hard copy of the formulae used.

Further reading

Books

Atrill, P. and McLaney, E. (2004) *Accounting and Finance for Non-specialists*, 6th edn, London: Financial Times/Prentice Hall.

Brett, M. (2002) *How to Read the Financial Pages*, 5th edn, London: Financial Times Books.

Dransfield, R. and Coles, M. (2002) *Accounts Made Easy*, 2nd edn, Cheltenham: Nelson Thornes.

Dransfield, R. (2003) *Financial Information Made Easy*, Cheltenham: Nelson Thornes.

Dyson, J. (2004) *Accounting for Non-accounting Students*, 6th edn, London: Financial Times Books.

McLaney, E. (2003) *Business Finance*, 6th edn, Prentice Hall.

Thomas, A. (2003) *Introduction to Financial Accounting*, 4th edn, Maidenhead: McGraw-Hill.

Journals

The most useful journal for students to read is *Student Accountant*, which is specifically designed to cater for ACCA students. The following also include interesting articles:

Journal of Accountancy
Accountancy Age

The Accountant

Unit 7

Foundations of business strategy

The aim of this unit is to develop the learner's ability to evaluate and select strategies appropriate to business organisations. This will involve an analysis of the impacts of the external operating environment and the need to plan organisational strategies to ensure effective business performance.

Summary of learning outcomes

On completion of this unit you will be able to:

♦ analyse how the business environment is considered in strategy formulation
♦ understand the process of strategic planning
♦ examine approaches to strategy evaluation and selection
♦ analyse how strategy implementation is realised.

Chapter 1

Strategy formulation

Strategic contexts and terminology

Business strategies are well thought-out plans which enable the whole organisation to be successful in a changing business environment. Planning strategies for the whole organisation involves developing a clear understanding of the environment in which the organisation works and then seeking to match the organisation and its capabilities to this environment in such a way as to gain the greatest competitive advantage over rivals.

In order to see how this works in practice you first need to understand some of the basic terminology.

The role of strategy

Strategies are the means through which organisations are able to achieve the **objectives** that they set for themselves. Objectives are the desired results that the organisation seeks to achieve. Some strategies will be successful while others will fail to deliver the desired results. For example, an organisation like Ryanair that sets out to be the number one low-cost airline in the world has a strategy of expansion, with investment in new planes and the takeover of other airlines. An organisation like Manchester United which seeks to be the number one football club in the world has a strategy of buying the best players, developing its own talent and building links between the Manchester United brand and other leading brands such as Vodafone.

Strategies are major decisions, such as what products and markets a company should focus on and how the company should be structured, rather than the day-to-day operational decisions.

Objective	Strategy

To be the world's number one football brand	Buy the best players, build the brand, link the brand with other brands, and so on

To be the world's number one low-cost airline	Develop more routes, buy new planes, take over other airlines

Figure 7.1   Objectives and strategies

Objective	The end to be achieved
Strategy	The means to achieve the end

Strategic management

Strategic management is therefore a very important part of organisational life because in large international companies decisions will involve many millions of pounds, vast resources, and the livelihoods of large numbers of people.

Strategic management decisions made by managers at the top of the organisation trigger dozens or even hundreds of other decisions of lesser magnitude made by lower level managers in the organisation. If the strategies created by senior managers are inappropriate then this will lead to ineffective choices being made at all levels within the organisation.

Strategic management involves four essential processes, as shown in Figure 7.2.

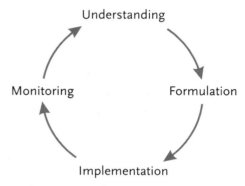

Figure 7.2   The process of strategic management

Understanding

The first process is understanding the strategic situation in which the organisation is placed. This involves carrying out a strategic audit: a process of researching and understanding the total business environment. Understanding also involves finding out about the marketplace, and about competitors.

Formulation

This is about choosing suitable strategies for the organisation. The first stage here is to decide on the future direction of the organisation. This involves defining the aim of the organisation which is termed the mission. It is also important to agree on the values of the organisation, that is, what it stands for and the way in which the organisation and its people should behave. With the mission and values in place it is possible to decide on the strategies to be pursued to achieve the chosen aims.

Implementation

This is about making the chosen strategies happen. This involves putting into practice the chosen strategies at all the various levels within the organisation.

Monitoring

This process is about checking and evaluating the success of the chosen strategies, in order to make adjustments where necessary.

Developing corporate strategy is an ongoing rather than a one-off process. Managers would rarely develop a strategy from scratch (except in the case of a start-up business). At any one time an organisation will be working with a set of strategies: some of which are more successful than others. Devising strategy usually involves deciding whether to continue with existing strategies, or to devise a series of new strategies to take the organisation into the future.

There are thus three levels of strategic management – business strategy, competitive strategy and functional strategy.

> Business strategy: The organisation-wide plan (dealing with the long-term health of the whole organisation).
>
> Competitive strategy: Concerned with seeking and gaining a competitive advantage over rivals.
>
> Functional or departmental strategy: Identifying and applying competitive strategies in functions or departments.

CASE STUDY

The nature of competitive strategy

Michael Porter (1998) argues that competitive strategy involves being different. 'It means deliberately choosing a different set of activities to deliver a unique mix of values.' He states that in recent years many companies have mistaken operational efficiency for strategy. They have set out to carry out their activities in a highly efficient way often by following the best practice of their rivals. However, this does not translate into high levels of profitability: because competitors are doing exactly the same thing. Competitive strategy therefore involves being excellent at everything you do while at the same time concentrating on being different from rivals. John L. Thompson (1995) defines competitive strategy as being 'concerned with creating and maintaining a competitive advantage (superiority over rivals) in each and every area of the business'. For each function part of a business (for example, marketing, finance and accounts, and so on) there will need to be a strategy, but these strategies will be part of a co-ordinated whole (functional strategies).

ACTIVITY

1   Can you identify an organisation with a clear competitive strategy which involves setting itself apart and beyond its rivals as suggested by Porter? How successful is this organisation?

2   Can you identify other organisations which appear simply to be following the excellent lead of their rivals rather than seeking to be better? How successful are they?

3   How important is it to make sure that every part of the business is better than rivals as suggested by John L. Thompson?

Missions

All organisations should have a purpose which they seek to work towards. We call this purpose the **mission**. One of the best-known examples of a mission was that set out by the US President John F. Kennedy for the country's space agency NASA in 1962; this was to 'Land a man on the moon and return him safely to earth'. (By the end of the decade the mission was achieved.) Today, it is common practice for organisations to set out this

purpose in a mission for the organisation. A simple definition of a mission is 'The essential purpose of the organisation … the nature of the business(es) it is in and the customers it seeks to serve and satisfy.'

Mission is also discussed in some detail in Unit 5: Foundations of the business environment, p. 203.

Mission statement

A good **mission statement** will define the fundamental, unique purpose that sets the company apart from other firms of its type and identifies the scope of the company's operations in terms of the goods and services offered and markets served. It might also include the firm's philosophy about how it does business and treats its employees. For example, the charity Oxfam sets out its mission as follows.

> Oxfam works with others to overcome poverty and suffering.

The mission needs to be realistic given the organisation's existing resources and capabilities and to provide a clear focus for organisational activity.

Having a 'sense of mission' is not the same thing as having a 'mission statement' (a written statement outlining the mission). It is possible for an organisation to have a mission statement but only a poor sense of mission. A mission statement may simply be propaganda or wishful thinking on the part of the management.

Figure 7.3   Elements of an effective mission

Andrew Campbell and Sally Young of the Ashridge Management School have set out a model for an effective mission for an organisation based on four key elements, shown in Figure 7.3.

Visions

Whereas the mission sets out the purpose of the organisation, that is, why it exists, a **vision** sets out what a firm can become: it presents a picture of a desired future.

Some organisations place a strong emphasis on their mission, while others place more emphasis on the vision of an organisation. This is because the vision seeks to inspire and take the organisation into the future.

However, it is important that in creating a vision, the chief executive or group of strategy planners that formulate it are not carried away: the vision needs to be possible to achieve, rather than being 'pie in the sky'.

There are a number of important characteristics therefore for an effective vision, including that the vision should:

♦ inspire organisation members to achieve it
♦ be realistic and achievable
♦ be easy to understand.

Business (and political) leaders frequently say that they want to share their vision with others. If this is the case it needs to be easy to communicate. For example, in the food industry, two rival companies Nestlé and Kraft have the following vision statements.

> Nestlé: To be the world's number one food company.

> Kraft: To be recognised as the undisputed leader in the global market for foods.

Clearly these visions are achievable for these huge organisations with the vast resources that they have (although clearly they cannot both be the leader). The vision is easy to understand and provides company employees with something to inspire them.

ACTIVITY

1   Examine vision statements of major business corporations by carrying out an Internet search putting in the name of the company and the word vision. How effective do these visions appear to be given the criteria outlined above?

2   Create a vision statement for an organisation of your choice, justifying it in terms of it being inspirational, achievable, and easy to understand.

A useful way of thinking about a vision to see it as a bridge (Figure 7.4) that forms a link between the past, present and future of the organisation.

Present

♦ How did we get here?
♦ What are we good at?
♦ What are our success factors?
♦ What kind of people are we?

Future

♦ Where do we want to go?
♦ What do we want to become?
♦ What do we need to do to make it happen?

Figure 7.4   The vision as a bridge

CASE STUDY

A car for the great multitude

Henry Ford created the modern mass production car industry in the early days of the twentieth century. He was a farm boy who walked the eight miles to a Detroit machine shop at the age of 16 and began to work in manufacturing. He quickly realised the appeal of the motor car.

Figure 7.5   Henry Ford

He built the famous River Rouge motor plant in Detroit. His backers wanted him to build a car for the rich. But Ford's vision was significantly different. 'I will build a car for the great multitude,' he said in 1907, a year before the famous Model T was created, 'so low in price that not many will be unable to own one.' He told a potential investor: 'The way to make automobiles is to make one automobile like another, to make them all alike, to make them come through the factory alike, just as one pin is like another pin when it comes from a pin factory.' His vision quickly materialised and by 1913 Ford was the richest man in America.

ACTIVITY

1 What was Henry Ford's vision?

2 What was required to put the vision into practice?

Strategic intent

The **strategic intent** of an organisation is the desired future state that it is working towards. For example, in the case of Nestlé the strategic intent is to become 'The World Food Company', and for Coca-Cola to place its product 'within an arm's reach of desire' (the notion that consumers will have worldwide access to Coca-Cola).

Figure 7.6   The strategic intent of these two companies is to continue to expand their global presence

Every organisation needs to be clear about its strategic intent if it is to plan ahead rather than simply to react to changes as and when they occur. A truly successful strategy is one that matches what the organisation is able to achieve within its environment. Nestlé and Coca-Cola are able to meet the increasing demands from global consumers because their profits and capital base enable ongoing expansion.

Hamel and Prahalad (1989) argue that, 'companies that have risen to global leadership over the past 20 years invariably began with ambitions that were out of all proportion to their resources and capabilities. But they created an obsession with winning at all levels of the organisation and then sustained that obsession over the 10–20 year quest for global leadership. We term this obsession "strategic intent".'

Hamel and Prahalad give examples of strategic intent, including Canon's intent to 'beat Xerox', Honda striving to 'become a second Ford', and Komatsu to 'encircle Caterpillar'.

Strategic intent, they say, is more than just an ambition, it also includes an active management process which focuses 'the organisation's attention on the essence of winning; motivating people by communicating the value of the target; leaving room for individual and team contributions; sustaining enthusiasm by providing new operational definitions as circumstances change; and using intent consistently to guide resource allocations'.

Goals and objectives

It is helpful at this stage to draw a distinction between the terms **goals** and **objectives** because a number of writers use these terms interchangeably. Johnson and Scholes (2000) suggest that 'if the word goal is used it usually means a general aim in line with mission. It may well be qualitative in nature. On the other hand, an objective is more likely to be quantified, or at least to be a more precise aim in line with the goal.'

Whilst the mission provides a generalised purpose for the organisation it is also essential to establish objectives to work towards.

Business (organisational) objectives provide the direction for strategic management, and relate to the performance of the total organisation. Business objectives can then be further broken down into **operational objectives** for day-to-day decision making.

Corporate strategy needs to be based on clear and decisive objectives. Efforts need to be directed towards clearly understood, decisive, and attainable overall goals. The overriding goals of the strategy for all units must remain clear enough to provide continuity and cohesion for tactical choices during the time horizon of the strategy.

Long- and short-term objectives

A distinction can be made between long-term objectives and short-term objectives.

Long-term objectives focus on the desired performance and results of the organisation on an on-going basis. Short-term objectives are concerned with short-term performance targets that the organisation is working towards in pursuing its strategies.

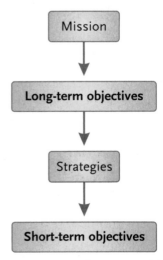

Figure 7.7   From purpose to short-term objectives

Open and closed objectives

A further distinction can be made between open and closed objectives. Closed objectives are clearly measurable and are often finance based; for example, to achieve a rate of return on capital employed in the business of 18 per cent over the next twelve months. In 2001 Ryanair set itself some closed objectives in terms of expanding its capacity to 9 million passengers in 2001 and 14 million passengers by 2004.

Open objectives are less specific and set continuing goals for the organisation, for example 'to ensure continued customer satisfaction' or 'to achieve a competitive return on capital employed'.

CASE STUDY

Management by Objectives

In the 1960s Peter Drucker popularised the idea of Management by Objectives (MbO) and this approach is still popular with some managers today. Management by objectives enables managers:

◆ to focus the management task on a specific outcome (for example, a 5 per cent increase in sales)
◆ to provide a means of assessing whether the outcome has been achieved after the event (did sales increase by 5 per cent?)
◆ to set ongoing objectives (if the 5 per cent sales target was achieved should a new 6 per cent outcome be set for the next period?).

The great thing about objectives is that they can be 'drilled down' through the various levels within the organisation, enabling all organisation activities to be geared towards achieving corporate mission, as shown in Figure 7.8.

Drucker identifies a number of key result areas for which it is possible to establish organisation objectives:

♦ market standing
♦ innovation
♦ productivity
♦ physical and financial resources
♦ profitability
♦ manager performance and development
♦ employee performance and attitude
♦ public responsibility.

In the modern business world it is important that these objectives are flexible.

ACTIVITY

1 What do you understand by the term Management by Objectives?

2 What do you see as being the advantages and disadvantages of this approach in the modern business world?

3 Examine the mission of a well-known organisation. Explain how this mission can be drilled down to individual objectives affecting a specific employee of that organisation.

Business objectives

Business mission

Strategic business unit objectives (SBUs)
(for example, in a food company
the SBUs will be different food
categories)

Departmental/operational objectives

Subunit objectives

Individual objectives
(for members of the organisation)

Figure 7.8 Drilling down goals and objectives

Effective objectives

There are a number of characteristics that objectives need to have if they are to be effective.

Understandable

They should be easily understood. The managers who create objectives may only play a small part in implementing the actions required to achieve these objectives. The objectives therefore need to be presented in clear and easy to understand language so that there is no ambiguity.

Widely communicated

Organisational objectives affect many people. Problems will occur if key objectives are not communicated widely to everyone concerned.

Challenging

They should not be too easy to achieve. They should stretch the organisation, its business units and people in a rewarding way.

Attainable

When objectives are unattainable this will lead to frustration and lack of motivation and loss of shareholder confidence.

Quantifiable

If relevant and possible, objectives should be expressed in terms of numbers. Quantification enables target setting and effective measurement of results.

Core competences

The **core competences** of an organisation are the things that the organisation is particularly good at, that is, the resources, processes and skills which give it a competitive advantage.

It is very important to identify and build on these core competences because they are what enables the organisation to stand out from the crowd. For example, core competences of Manchester United would include:

♦ its star players
♦ the interaction between team members

- the Manchester United brand
- the distinctive red and white shirt
- the links between the club and other businesses
- the building up of a global fan base
- the Manchester United website.

It is important to identify the core competences, and then to invest further in them, and to make them more distinctive. An important part of strategy is to build on core competences.

Strategic architecture

We use the term **strategic architecture** to refer to the process of building sets of interlinking competences that will enable the organisation to develop competitive advantage. Organisations need to identify the main sources of competitive advantage in the sector or market segment that they are operating in, for example having the fastest and most reliable distribution links, the most rapid response to consumer requirements, the most reliable components, and so on. They then need to design and build the core competence which enables them to win and maintain competitive advantage: the strategic architecture.

For example, the strategic architecture for a low-cost airline might include:

- developing links and contracts with aircraft suppliers
- developing preferential links with airports
- building a reputation for reliability and concern for customers
- developing the skilled pilots and airline crews to develop a quality service

- making sure that all of the processes involved in running the airline fit in with the concept of high quality at low cost.

The strategic architecture is thus concerned with enabling the organisation to combine processes, resources and competences to put the strategy into effect. Specific actions and tasks are then implemented in order to put the strategy into effect.

Strategic control

Having implemented a strategy by means of appropriate actions and tasks it is important to monitor the extent to which the strategy is effective in meeting the objectives of the organisation.

Strategic control is concerned with monitoring the performance of the strategy, and then taking appropriate actions to make sure that the strategy is effective. Control is concerned with identifying what is going well and what is going badly and then taking appropriate actions to remedy any problems.

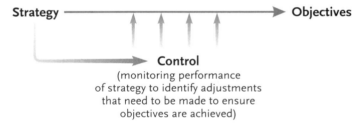

Figure 7.9 Control to make sure strategy meets objectives

Stakeholder analysis

To be successful a firm needs to control the forces that influence its activities as far as possible. In particular the organisation needs to be in tune with its stakeholders.

The range of stakeholders is shown in Figure 7.10.

Stakeholders are those individuals and groups who depend on an organisation to achieve some of their goals and on whom in turn the organisation depends for the full realisation of its goals.

Stakeholders are individuals and groups which are involved with the organisation in some way and include shareholders, suppliers, governments,

Figure 7.10   Stakeholder environment

employees/trade unions, special interest groups, competitors, customers, creditors, trade associations and communities. In creating a strategy it is important to take into account the wishes of these stakeholders and the coalitions that exist between these stakeholder groupings.

Shareholders are often the most important stakeholder. Their prime interest will be in receiving a good return on their investment, and they may therefore seek to block strategies which threaten the dividends that they expect to receive. However, in given situations other stakeholders may be more significant: for example, the government may block a business strategy to merge with another company because of the resulting monopoly that might arise. Employees and trade unions may resist strategies which threaten employment. Customers are always an important stakeholder interest and no company can afford to alienate its customers.

Stakeholder significance grid and stakeholder mapping

In planning strategies it is important to develop an understanding of the significance of particular stakeholders and stakeholder groupings and to appreciate how much power they are likely to exert in given situations. Such processes make it possible to determine:

♦ the extent to which stakeholders are likely to seek to put pressure on strategy formulation
♦ how much power they will have in doing so.

Stakeholders should be categorised in terms of their power and interest. This can be set out on a four-quadrant grid as shown in Figure 7.11. Stakeholders are categorised according to their power and their interest.

Clearly those with power must be satisfied, especially if they have high interest in the activities of the organisation. At the same time those with less power but high interest need to be kept informed.

STRENGTH OF ACTIVE INTEREST IN THE ORGANISATION

	Low →	High
High	Need to be satisfied even though little interest	Top priority – essential that they be kept informed and satisfied
Low	Shouldn't be given priority at expense of others	Must be kept fully informed of events and progress

RELATIVE POWER

Figure 7.11   Stakeholder significance grid

The power–interest matrix provides a useful way of mapping and evaluating the effects of stakeholders and of drawing conclusions about the way they should be treated.

ACTIVITY

Identify a current change of strategy involving a major organisation, or another organisation with which you are familiar with (based on your own experience or reading in the press). What is the change of strategy? Set out a stakeholder significance grid identifying the various stakeholders that will be affected by the change and what actions need to be carried out to keep these stakeholders behind the strategy. Locate each grouping in the right part of the quadrant.

Environmental auditing

Businesses are decision-making units which develop strategies within an environment of change. The term 'environment' is used to describe the general conditions that surround an organisation. For example, a competitive environment is one in which there is a lot of rivalry between firms, a dynamic environment is one in which there is rapid change, and so on. In relation to the study of business strategy, the term 'the environment' is used to describe everything and everyone outside the organisation. Business strategies regard the environment as uncertain. The **business environment** is made up of a number of change elements as shown in Figure 7.12.

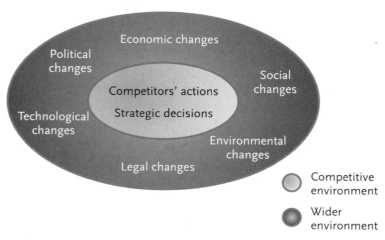

Figure 7.12   The competitive and wider environments

Organisations need to be in tune with their environment. They therefore need to audit this environment regularly to identify changes, in order to make appropriate strategic responses to these changes.

Environmental auditing enables the organisation to be proactive (to shape change) rather than reactive (to respond to change). The effective organisation will put a lot of effort into the process of environmental auditing.

There are three key steps in analysing the environment in which the organisation operates.

Audit environmental influences

This involves identifying those environmental influences which have affected the organisation's development and performance in the past and seeking to identify those that will be significant in the future.

Stability

It is important to have a view of how stable or unstable is the environment in which the organisation is operating. In a stable environment a historical and present analysis will be very useful. In an unstable environment a future analysis will be more relevant.

Specific influences

This is the carrying out of an analysis of specific environmental influences. A structural analysis (that is, an analysis of the major factors and how these factors work together) will help to identify the key forces at work.

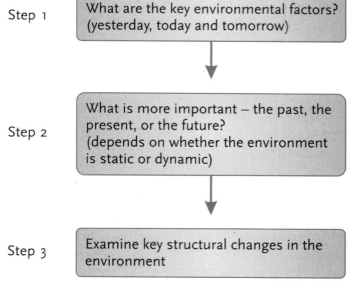

The PESTEL analysis

The PESTEL analysis looks at political, economic, social, technological, environmental and legal changes which are likely to affect the business. A

PESTEL analysis is a very detailed study of these changes using a range of published sources such as government surveys, statistics about the state of the economy, social trend surveys, as well as some primary analysis.

It is important to remember that there will be considerable overlap between PESTEL factors so it is not necessary to neatly categorise them into a separate box.

Political changes

A shift in political thinking associated with a change in government can have a major impact on business. For example, the Conservative government of 1979–97 emphasised the importance of individuals in society looking after themselves and promoted an enterprise culture which encouraged business initiative. While the current Labour government is still very concerned with the development of enterprise and partnership with business, it is also concerned with creating an 'inclusive society' in which the state seeks to include everyone rather than to exclude: for example, through job creation schemes so that everyone is included in work in the economy. Under Labour, taxes on business have increased and measures such as the adoption of the minimum wage are seen by some businesses as harmful because it may raise their costs. Other political changes of significance are different parties' views on the European Union. For example, Labour is far more committed to the UK adopting the euro than is the Conservative Party.

Economic changes

The economy goes through a cycle of periods of increasing economic activity followed by periods of recession. Business needs to be aware of where the economy stands in relation to this cycle. Boom periods encourage business strategies of expansion and growth while recessions create a hostile environment.

Other economic factors that business needs to take into account are changes in interest rates and changes in exchange rates. A rise in interest rates discourages business growth, while reductions in interest rates have the reverse effect. A rise in the price of the pound against competing currencies may have a negative impact on businesses that export because this raises UK prices relative to those of competing firms. A reduction in the pound makes UK goods more competitive.

Other key economic indicators that need to be considered in a PESTEL analysis include inflation, consumer expenditure and disposable income, and various costs (transport, energy, communication and raw material costs).

Social changes

Over time many changes take place in society which are relevant to business. Key changes include those in population, in tastes and buying patterns, in employment patterns, and so on. Trends and tastes are constantly changing leading to regular changes in buying patterns. Employment patterns also need to be studied: for example, the growing numbers of women in the workplace have led to an increased demand for convenience food, and so on. Other important social changes are shifts in values and culture, education and health, and distribution of income.

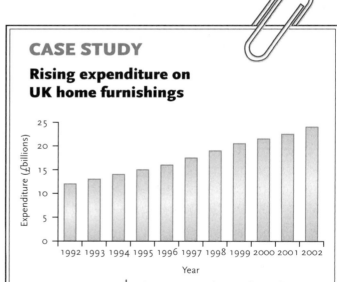

CASE STUDY

Rising expenditure on UK home furnishings

Figure 7.13   Expenditure on UK home furnishings

The home furnishings market was estimated to be worth £24 billion in 2002 and is one of the fastest growing parts of the retail sector. Driven by low interest rates, low unemployment, a strong housing market and a large capacity for debt, the market for homeware is buoyant. Add in the growing number of single households and the fashionability of home furnishings helped by television makeover programmes, it is not surprising that more and more retailers are moving into this market as part of a strategy of growth.

The market is currently split between a number of players with the largest, Argos, only having 5.5 per cent of the market followed by IKEA 4.8 per cent, and MFI 4.3 per cent. However, it is a very competitive market, that is split into a number of specialist segments, so that although many companies are attracted by the growth figures there are considerable dangers involved in moving into this market.

ACTIVITY

1 What social and economic factors might encourage a new retailer to move into this market?

2 Why might such a strategy be dangerous unless a much more detailed analysis of social and economic trends is carried out?

Technological changes

The application of information and communication technologies in the first decade of the twenty-first century is having a dramatic impact on business. More people than ever before are buying on-line, forcing most large businesses to develop strategies involving e-commerce. Other technological changes involve the product of new research initiatives, levels of expenditure on research and development, and government support of new technologies.

Environmental changes

Increasingly, organisations have had to develop environmental strategies. Today there are international and British standards for environmental quality procedures. Organisations need to be in the forefront of making these changes rather than come from a catch-up position. In addition, organisations need to respond to 'green issues' being voiced by customers and community groups.

Legal changes

Organisations need to anticipate and prepare themselves for changes in the law. For example, recently the European Union has created new legislation making airlines responsible for paying compensation for delayed and cancelled flights, leading to substantial increases in costs for airlines.

A good PESTEL analysis is not simply a list of changes in the environment that may affect the business, rather it involves identifying the key structural changes in the business environment that are relevant to a specific business, and the links that exist between these changes. The PESTEL analysis enables the organisation to create the strategies that prepare it for change in advance of the changes occurring.

Porter's five forces analysis

There are two contrasting views about how best to deal with competitors. One view is that an understanding of your competitors, their actions, and how to beat them is at the heart of competitive advantage. The other view is that you focus on your own business, identify your own core competences, concentrate on doing them really well, cut down your costs, identify and satisfy your customers and forget about the competition.

The best way forward probably lies somewhere between these two views. There is no point in studying competitors just because it seems like the right thing to do. In studying competitors you need to have some fairly focused questions which are of use to your own development. Michael Porter (*Competitive Advantage*, 1985) argues that effective strategic management is the positioning of an organisation, relative to its competitors, in such a way that it outperforms them. Organsations therefore need to know something about the competitors that they wish to outperform.

Porter argues that five forces determine the profitability of an industry, as shown in Figure 7.14.

Figure 7.14   Porter's five forces

At the centre of the industry are rivals and their competitive strategies linked to, for example, pricing or promotional activity. However, it is also important to look beyond one's immediate competitors as there are other determinants of profitability in the industry.

In particular, there might be competition from **substitute products** or services; these alternatives may be seen as substitutes by buyers even though they are part of a different industry. An example would be plastic bottles, cans and foil for packaging soup. Or, there may also be a potential threat of **new entrants**, for example new firms might move into producing packaging materials if the profits are sufficiently attractive.

Finally, it is important to appreciate that companies purchase from suppliers and sell to buyers. If these forces are powerful they are in a position to bargain profits away through reduced margins, by forcing either cost increases or price decreases. For example, for many years Marks & Spencer has had considerable power in forging supply contracts with suppliers of textiles and foodstuffs because it is such a large buyer.

Any company must seek to understand the nature of its competitive environment if it is to be successful in achieving its objectives and in establishing

appropriate strategies. If a company fully understands the nature of the five forces, and particularly appreciates which ones are the most important, it will be in a stronger position to defend itself against any threats, and to influence the forces with its strategy. The situation, of course, is subject to continual change, resulting in the need to monitor and stay aware, which is continuous. Hence the importance of auditing the environment.

Strategic positioning

Igor Ansoff (1984) defined strategy in terms of the relationship between the organisation and its environment. 'The positioning and relating of the firm or organisation to its environment in a way which will assure its continued success and make it secure from surprises' (Ansoff, 1984).

This section therefore sets out to outline the sorts of general positioning that an organisation can take to create an appropriate fit between strategy and the organisational environment. It starts off by examining some of Ansoff's ideas about choosing a growth strategy that takes account of the product and market influences.

In developing its portfolio strategy (that is, a portfolio of products and services on which to focus), an organisation can choose a number of alternatives to generate ongoing growth. Figure 7.15 illustrates the possibilities open to the organisation.

	Current products	New products
Current markets	Product market penetration	Product market development
New markets	Market development	Diversification

Figure 7.15   Ansoff's product–market expansion grid

Key positioning strategies

There are four key strategies open to the firm.

Market penetration

This involves selling more of the same product to the same types of people. This is possible either by increasing market share at the expense of others, by developing a competitive advantage, or by growing the total market size.

Product development

This involves a company exploiting the strength of its relationship with customers and using its creative ability to develop new products suited to their needs. Supermarkets are a good example of this. They have gradually moved away from simply selling groceries to selling a wide range of other products including household goods, clothes, petrol, computers and even cars.

Market development

New customers can be more difficult to develop than products, but where an organisation has significant product strengths this can be a good opportunity for growth. Examples can include selling to export markets, or a different customer type. Lucozade, a high-energy drink, was originally sold to speed recovery from illness, but the company developed a new market among sports people.

Diversification

This involves developing new expertise both in terms of product and markets and is the highest risk alternative. Often companies, rather than develop their own expertise, will buy another company to achieve their objectives. For example, Ford Motor Company acquired the Kwik-Fit replacement car tyre and exhaust fitting company.

Matching the strategy with the environment

Ansoff's matrix outlines a range of ways in which organisations can seek to position their strategy in relation to their environment. There are a number of strategies available to create an appropriate position. They are briefly described here.

Growth

The Ansoff matrix is essentially concerned with growth strategies. Growth is one of the most frequent strategies that an organisation considers. In thinking about growth it needs to examine the external environment: for example, is there going to be enough growth in the market to warrant expansion? Will the organisation be able to outcompete the competition?

The Coca-Cola Corporation is an example of an organisation that has successfully engaged in a process of growth in recent years. It has ploughed back its profits into supporting its existing products in more and more markets, while at the same time developing new soft drinks, such as Diet Coke and Fruitopia. It has used the very large sums earned from its major cash cow to support the growth of the business.

Stability

Stability is always an important strategy for an organisation. There are times when it will need to consolidate on its existing position. Stability makes sense when an organisation has experienced previous periods of rapid growth. The organisation then needs to establish clear systems and procedures that enable it to consolidate its position. For example, although the Virgin group is seen as a dynamic organisation which frequently moves into new areas, it also believes in consolidating new businesses once they are established. Virgin believes that once it has gone through a period of rapid expansion, for example moving into contraceptives, or into Virgin Cola, it needs to establish these lines before moving on to new things. This would involve ensuring that all systems within a new business venture are customer driven and based on quality performance.

Many organisations will seek stability at times when the environment becomes a bit rocky. A useful analogy can be drawn with the piloting of an aeroplane. When the pilot hits a patch of bad weather, then all efforts will be focused on stabilising the aeroplane.

448

Profitability

Seeking profit is always an important ingredient of strategy, particularly in organisations in which shareholders are the key stakeholders and where the stakeholders' perception of the organisation is influenced by the profit. Although organisations like to take a longer-term view on profits, where shareholders are influential (and where shareholders can switch their shareholding easily) organisations are also forced to consider the shorter and medium term. Market share is often an important driver of profitability.

Efficiency

Johnson and Scholes (2002) identify efficiency as being an organisational strategy which is of critical importance 'for those organisations which either choose or are required to compete on the basis of cost competitiveness'. They cite the example of public services. Efficiency is concerned with how 'well' resources have been put to use, irrespective of the purpose for which they were deployed. There are all sorts of ways of assessing efficiency. For example, profitability is a broad measure of efficiency particularly in looking at profit in terms of the amount of capital utilised in the business (such measures as ROCE). Other measures of efficiency include labour productivity, yield, capacity fill, working capital utilisation and the efficiency of production systems.

Market leadership

Many companies will pursue a strategy designed to give them market leadership because they know that should they win the lion's share of the market then the profits will follow. The market leader is best able to manage the external environment because profits can be channelled into securing ongoing competitive advantage.

We see market leadership strategies being pursued in many areas of business, for example:

♦ the lead of BSkyB in digital television
♦ Manchester United's lead in football

Figure 7.16 Tesco and ASDA Wal-Mart both have a strategy of market leadership in the supermarket industry

♦ the struggle between Tesco and ASDA Wal-Mart to win market leadership in the UK supermarket industry.

Market leadership is both a short-, medium- and long-term strategy. By winning market leadership, an organisation's rivals will always be coming from a catch-up position and will be hampered by disadvantages, particularly in areas related to technology (economies of scale, research and development) and marketing (depth of consumer research, advertising spend, promotional activity, and so on).

CASE STUDY

ASDA Wal-Mart poised to win market leadership in UK supermarket industry

ASDA Wal-Mart is poised to win market leadership in the UK supermarket industry at the expense of Tesco and Sainsbury's, the traditional market leaders.

Wal-Mart is a giant US-based company that saw the opportunity to expand into the UK market using existing successful formulae, including heavy discounting of prices, massive economies of scale of bulk buying, American-style high standards of consumer service, and well-organised and consumer-friendly stores.

Previously ASDA had modelled itself on the Wal-Mart way of working so it was only natural for the American company to take over ASDA and engage in an aggressive series of new store building in key locations.

The result has been a rapid rise in the fortunes of ASDA Wal-Mart in the UK.

449

ACTIVITY

1 What aspects of the external environment has ASDA Wal-Mart been so in tune with in the UK?

2 Why does ASDA Wal-Mart have the resource base and competences required to be successful in the supermarket industry in the UK?

3 What benefits will ASDA Wal-Mart gain from becoming the market leader?

Survival

Peter Drucker (1995) wrote that, 'It is the first duty of a business to survive. The guiding principle of business economics, in other words, is not the maximisation of profits; it is the avoidance of loss. Business enterprise must produce the premium to cover the risks inevitably involved in its operation. And there is only one source for this risk premium: profits.'

Drucker referred to the 'required minimum profit' as representing for the business enterprise 'at the very least the profit required to cover its own future risks, the profit required to enable it to stay in business and to maintain intact the wealth-producing capacity of its resources'. He sees businesses as being there fundamentally to serve customers and to innovate in order to progress and develop. The business will therefore be seeking a strategy which enables it to survive in the long term. Taking this view, the organisation will be seeking a safe path through a turbulent environment, powered by its resources and dynamic core competences, and steered by the intelligence of its strategists. We are all too aware of this survival imperative when we see the results of organisations which for a number of years have been tremendously successful, experience a downturn, run into difficulty, reshape and reposition, ride another wave, and so on. Of course, some organisations go under, but the intent is there: the strategic intent to survive.

Mergers and acquisitions

Mergers and acquisitions are another key strategic route for the organisation, enabling a change in positioning in an existing marketplace or movement into new marketplaces. The organisation needs to look at its environment, its core competences and its resources, and match its strategy to these factors. Merging with another organisation often provides the best and most logical way to build on its core competences or to acquire new competences.

A traditional retailer recognises that it doesn't have the Internet and web page competences required to survive in the changing world of e-tailing

Acquires a small .com e-tailing business with the competences required

RESULT

Successful strategic positioning enabling ongoing success

Expansion into the global marketplace

Globalisation can be defined as the increasing integration of markets for goods, services and capital. Globalisation involves an acceleration in the expansion of international production, distribution and selling of goods into more worldwide geographical locations in response to changing demands in the marketplace. Much of this pressure for changes comes from consumers: today we expect our local supermarket to supply us with exotic food products from all over the world throughout the year, and we accept it as the norm to buy consumer durables such as cars, televisions, DVD players, and so on which may have been produced in Brazil or South-East Asia.

UK companies respond to this globalisation process by developing global strategies based on sensitivity to events and forces that are reshaping the business environment. An organisation must respond to its external environment and adjust its corporate strategy accordingly. For example, technological advances are opening up world markets to an organisation's competitors. If the organisation does not respond to this challenge then its own business will get left behind.

As businesses become more involved with the global economy, they will need to constantly review the appropriateness of their current mission and objectives. Long-term planning has to be adjusted to take into account the changes involved in the global economy. Mission, objectives and strategies need to be adjusted to build in a global dimension.

The organisational audit

The notion of environment–values–resources (EVR) congruence (Figure 7.17) is a useful one to demonstrate the underlying concept of strategic management.

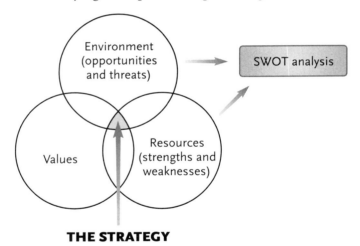

THE STRATEGY

Figure 7.17   EVR congruence to form strategy

Strategies are being managed effectively when the organisation's resources are used in such a way that the business meets the demands and expectations of its stakeholders, and responds and adapts to changes in the environment. In other words, it has strengths which take advantage of the opportunities and deal with potential threats in an environment of change.

The three elements in EVR are:

♦ E: Managers would need to fully understand the dynamics, opportunities and threats present in their competitive **environment**, and that they are paying full regard to this environment.
♦ V: The values of the organisation would need to match the needs of the environment and the key success factors. These values would need to be shared and followed throughout the organisation.
♦ R: The resources of the organisation would need to be managed strategically taking into account the strengths, weaknesses and opportunities for the organisation.

In order to create this match between the organisation and its environment it is essential to audit key aspects of the organisation.

The internal audit will be concerned with outlining the key resources of the organisation, the key competences, strengths and weaknesses.

Benchmarking

Benchmarking is a procedure for weighing up the existing performance of the organisation in comparison with what 'can be achieved'. The process of benchmarking serves as a first-class internal auditing process which can be used to diagnose organisational weaknesses and identify ways of turning them into strengths.

Benchmarking is the process of identifying best practice in the areas of a business which are 'critical success factors' in terms of providing customer satisfaction. Benchmarking studies involve making comparisons with competitors' practices, the practices of business in other sectors, best practice within the organisation itself, best practice internationally or a mixture of all of these approaches.

The first western company to employ benchmarking was the Xerox Corporation which adopted the procedure from their Japanese subsidiary, Fuji-Xerox.

Philip Sadler (1994) describes the process of benchmarking as involving six stages:

- decide which processes to benchmark; this involves deciding what the critical success factors are that create and maintain customer satisfaction
- develop accurate, objective descriptions of the existing processes affecting the critical success factors
- decide what to measure and how to measure it
- choose companies (or units) against which to benchmark
- measure the 'competitive gap', the measured difference between the current internal process effectiveness and the effectiveness of the best practice identified elsewhere
- implement the findings so as to close the gap.

Benchmarking is an essential part of developing a competitive strategy because it identifies the extent of a weakness (or a strength) and indicates what needs to be done to close a competitive gap.

It must be remembered that the purpose of benchmarking is not just about making a comparison with existing best practice, rather it is an attempt to identify best practice and then to restructure the organisation to become the best. As a result the typical benchmarking sequence will be as follows:

1   explore the results of benchmarking investigations

2   redefine performance targets within your own organisation in line with learning from benchmarking

3   restructure and upgrade the assets and systems of your organisation

4   develop new performance objectives for individuals and groups which raise the bar (that is, raise expectations).

SWOT analysis

This is the simplest and perhaps most effective way of assessing the relationship between an organisation and its external environment. SWOT is an acronym used to describe the particular Strengths, Weaknesses,

Opportunities and Threats that are strategic factors for a specific business. It has been suggested that this could be called a WOTS-UP analysis (Figure 7.18).

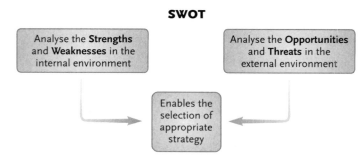

Figure 7.18   Elements of a WOTS-UP analysis

The student is likely to come across the SWOT analysis in studying marketing in relation to the preparation of marketing strategies. Here we are concerned with a whole business strategy.

Strengths and weaknesses are internal to the organisation and often relate to resources: for example, the organisation does not have people with the right skills (a weakness), the organisation is generating a healthy profit (a strength), and so on.

Opportunities and threats relate to the external environment, for example the threat of a downturn in the economy, or the opportunity of new markets abroad. Opportunities often relate to the development of new customers and new markets, and threats often relate to the actions of competitors.

Carrying out an effective SWOT analysis enables an organisation to develop strategies for the future. Having carried out a detailed SWOT the following questions should be asked:

- How can we reduce or neutralise critical weaknesses or turn them into strengths?
- How can we reduce or neutralise critical threats or even turn them into opportunities?
- How can we best exploit our strengths in relation to our opportunities?
- What new markets and market segments might be suitable for out existing strengths and capabilities?
- Given the changes that are taking place in our existing markets, what changes do we need to make to products, services and processes?

For example, the organisation that recognises that it has a weakness in terms of not having the right people with the right skills can engage in a training programme to make sure that its people are ahead of the field, or recruit new people with the right skills. The organisation that recognises the threat that its competitors are gaining an edge by employing sophisticated e-commerce techniques can develop its own websites and e-commerce presence.

In addition to the benchmarking process and SWOT analysis it is helpful for the organisation to assess what is known as the strategic gap.

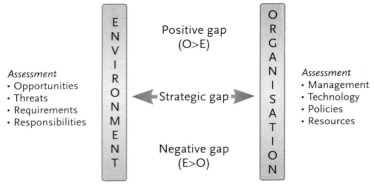

Figure 7.19   Illustrating the strategic gap

The **strategic gap** is the difference which exists at any one time between the capabilities of the organisation and the most significant environmental factors, as shown in Figure 7.19.

The strategic gap reflects the imbalance between the current strategic position of the organisation and its desired strategic position. The gap is measured by comparing the organisation's capabilities with the opportunities and threats in its external environment.

A **capability profile** establishes the principal capabilities of the organisation. The four main areas of weakness and strength include:

♦ management: the extent to which existing management has a good decision-making track record

♦ technology: the extent to which the organisation keeps up with state-of-the-art developments in its field

♦ policies: the extent to which there are clear and well-focused policies covering all aspects of the organisation's activities

♦ resources: the extent to which the organisation has the right balance of relevant resources.

The **environmental assessment** examines:

♦ opportunities: situations with a potential to enhance the competitive position of the organisation; clearly, opportunities need to be matched with capabilities

♦ threats: there are a range of threats but the most common are competition and technological obsolescence

♦ requirements: include statutory requirements, legal codes and other government-related restrictions on strategic choices

♦ responsibilities: consist of expectations on the part of the stakeholder groupings including social responsibilities.

A positive strategic gap exists when the organisation is greater than its environment (O>E). In this situation the organisation is well placed to exploit opportunities, cope with threats, or meet requirements and responsibilities in the external environment.

A negative strategic gap exists when the organisation is less than its environment (O<E). This requires management actions to reverse the gap because the organisation is unable to take up opportunities, respond to threats, or its responsibilities and requirements in the external environment.

Perhaps, the best state of affairs for an organisation is one in which O=E because the organisation is in tune with its environment and is taking up appropriate opportunities, responding to threats as and when they arise, and dealing effectively with its requirements and responsibilities.

CASE STUDY
WOTS-UP at easyCinema

Figure 7.20   Stelios Haji-Ioannou

Stelios Haji-Ioannou is the well-known flamboyant entrepreneur who set up the highly successful low-cost airline easyJet. In 2003 he sold up his shares in the company to concentrate on other business ventures.

For example, in the summer of 2003 he cashed in £17.4 million of shares in easyJet to fund a cut-price film venture easyCinema.

A major problem for the new business was that of securing the rights to show first-run Hollywood films at a discount. Initially easyCinema consisted of a ten-screen multiplex in Milton Keynes which was limited by being able to show Hollywood blockbusters only several months after their release or art-house films.

The cinema opened in May 2003 and was initially able to attract 2500–3000 customers a week with many tickets selling for as little as 20p.

Most of the big Hollywood studios resisted supplying film to Stelios, but he has had some limited success, for example when Colombia Tristar, part of the Sony Group, agreed to let him screen *Charlie's Angels*.

EasyCinema showed this film for a ticket price of £2, half the amount a big cinema chain would charge.

Stelios has other 'low-cost' plans: including a cut-price inter-city bus service, a pizza chain, a low-cost hotel business, and a cheap cruise line.

ACTIVITY

1   Draw a box and divide it into four. In the four boxes briefly identify the internal strengths and weaknesses of the easyCinema company, and the external opportunities and threats.

2   Identify a low-cost opportunity of your own for the formation of a new business for which you think you would be able to receive financial backing from investors. Set out a brief SWOT analysis for this company.

The following advice is useful in creating a SWOT analysis for an organisation to examine the match between its internal and external environments:

- keep it brief
- relate strengths and weaknesses to critical success factors
- identify strengths and weaknesses in relation to the competition: it is important to be better than the competition
- statements should be clear
- identification of strengths and weaknesses should be realistic.

Product positions

The position of a product consists of a number of elements which are important in assessing its strengths and weaknesses:

- The position of the product in relation to its lifecycle: is it fresh and vital or tired and jaded?

♦ The position of the product in relation to competition: is it ahead of the competition or behind?

♦ The position of the product in relation to market perceptions: for example, is it an up-market or down-market product, and what are the implications for profitability?

Michael Porter argues strongly that organisations need clearly to identify the position of a product in terms of this last element. Is it seeking to create competitive advantage from being seen as a low-cost product, for example a no-frills low-cost airline such as Ryanair, or is it seeking a competitive edge through differentiation, for example by offering a more exclusive service which is differentiated in a number of ways, such as that offered by British Airways?

ACTIVITY

Identify businesses that have sought product positions primarily based on differentiation and those chiefly based on low-cost from:

♦ the supermarket industry
♦ the airline industry
♦ local hairdressing
♦ another industry of your choice.

An important part of the internal analysis of a business is to examine the **product portfolio**. This involves looking at each of the products in the portfolio and assessing where they stand in relation to:

♦ stage of maturity
♦ competitiveness against rival products.

This is illustrated in Figure 7. 21.

By carrying out such an analysis of all of a company's products it is possible to assess which areas need most support, which need cutting out, and which products are likely to generate profits to support those that are in most need.

COMPETITIVENESS OF PRODUCTS

	Strong	Industry average	Weak
Introduction			
Growth			
Maturity			
Decline			

(STAGE OF MATURITY)

Figure 7.21   Competitiveness of products

This can be related to the Boston Consultancy Group Matrix (see p. 464). This matrix indicates how surplus profits from cash 'cows' can be channelled into building the stars and question marks while the 'dogs' can be eliminated, as shown in Figure 7.22.

MARKET SHARE

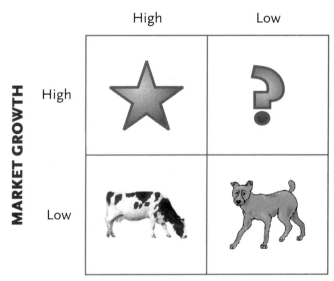

Figure 7.22   Analysing and building an appropriate portfolio

455

Value-chain analysis

Michael Porter (1985) sees the creation of a value chain as being of fundamental importance in organising the organisation and its relationship with other organisations. An audit of the existing value chain is therefore essential in identifying the internal strengths and weaknesses of the organisation.

The **value chain** can be defined as an organisation's co-ordinated set of activities undertaken to satisfy the customer, beginning with relationships with suppliers and procurement, and going through production, selling and marketing and delivery to the customer.

Each link in the value chain must seek competitive advantage, either by creating lower cost, or differentiation.

The value which consumers place on goods and services is determined by the way in which the activities required to design, produce, market, deliver and support the product are performed.

The organisation therefore needs to build a value chain with strong and effective linkages with suppliers and customers, as shown in Figure 7.23.

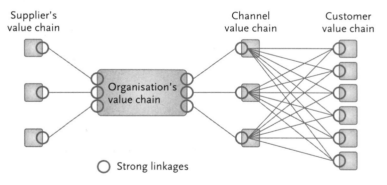

Figure 7.23   Building a strong value chain

Porter identified five main primary activities and four support activities which are key to the success of the value chain. The five primary activities are:

♦ inbound logistics: receiving, storing and distributing the inputs to the goods
♦ operations: transforming the various inputs into the final good
♦ outbound logistics: collecting, storing and distributing the goods to consumers

♦ marketing and sales
♦ service: the activities involved in enhancing the product, for example installation, repair.

The four support activities are:
♦ procurement: getting hold of the various resource inputs required for the primary activities
♦ technology development
♦ human resource management
♦ management systems.

Human resource audit/demographic influences

An important part of the internal audit is that of the **human resources audit**. In most organisations today people are the most important resource. The knowledge and skills of individuals are essential in creating competitive advantage.

A human resource audit therefore takes into account basic **demographic factors** such as the number of employees, employee turnover, ages of employees, make up in terms of gender, race, and so on.

In addition it is also important to audit:

♦ the structure of the organisation: is it appropriate, for example, in creating the right sort of motivation and interface with consumers
♦ organisation control structures: are they effective in implementing strategic decision
♦ teamworking skills
♦ levels of skills and capabilities required now and in the future
♦ morale and rewards
♦ selection, training and development.

The structure of an organisation must be capable of implementing the strategies, and in this way can be seen as the means by which an organisation seeks to achieve its strategic objectives. The structure is the configuration of the people within the organisations and must be capable of formulating and implementing strategy.

The structure of the organisation can thus be designed to break down the operations that are required to implement strategies. The organisation will be structured into a series of divisions, business units or functions.

Culture and values

An organisation's culture is its personality and its values are what it stands for. The culture is the typical way of working in an organisation that develops over time.

The culture and values need to be such that they are appropriate to the organisation's chosen strategy. For example, if the organisation is seeking to develop a customer-focused strategy it needs to have people who know how to value customers' needs, feelings and requirements. If the organisation is seeking to be innovative then it needs to have employees who are prepared to take risks, rather than simply wait to be told what to do.

Many modern organisations have a 'values statement' which sets out the values the company believes in. These values will lie at the heart of organisational culture.

It is therefore important in auditing the organisation to assess the culture and values to check that these are in line with the company's mission and strategies.

ACTIVITY

Carry out an Internet search to find the values statement of a well-known organisation. Also carry out a search for the current strategy of that organisation. Evaluate how effectively the values statement matches the chosen strategy.

Scenario analysis

Another useful approach that enables an organisation to cope with a changing environment and to develop plans to deal with these changes is scenario analysis.

This approach was pioneered by the oil company Shell in the 1970s. At the time, Shell was all too aware of how its industry could rapidly change as the result of oil producers joining together to push up the price of oil.

What Shell did was to devise a series of scenarios. A **scenario** is a model of a future environment for the organisation. The organisation can then plan strategies to deal with a range of scenarios. For example, Shell could plan scenarios for a rise in the price of oil by 50

per cent over the next ten years, or a 10 per cent rise, and so on. Scenarios could involve wars in significant parts of the world, or the complete banning of private cars on the roads as a result of 'green pressure'. The aim of scenario planning is not to predict the future but to explore a set of possibilities and then to prepare appropriate responses.

The following guidance is helpful in building scenarios:

♦ Start from an unusual viewpoint. Examples might include the stance of a major competitor, a radical change of government or the outbreak of war.
♦ Develop a qualitative description of a group of possible events or a narrative that shows how events will unfold.
♦ Explore the outcomes of this description or narrative of events by building two or three scenarios of what might happen. Two scenarios will lend themselves to a 'most optimistic outcome' and a 'worst possible outcome'.
♦ Include the inevitable uncertainty in each scenario and explore the consequences of this uncertainty to the organisation concerned. PESTEL factors should provide some clues here.
♦ Test the usefulness of the scenario by the extent to which it leads to new strategic thinking rather than merely the continuance of existing strategy.

Synergy

Synergy is a factor that is often overlooked in auditing an organisation and its resources. Synergy occurs in situations where two or more activities or processes complement each other, so that their combined effect is greater than the sum of their parts. For example, a production and marketing team in an organisation may be able to bounce ideas off each other to create outcomes which would not occur if these components were kept separate. Synergy may be created within a team. Breaking up these teams and alliances in a corporate restructure may destroy such synergy.

Similarly, synergies can be created by intelligent linking of processes and teams. Auditing to identify these synergies is therefore a very important part of organisational analysis.

Research and topical articles

A useful source of information when studying business strategy is to examine the mission statements, values statements, and other objectives of companies which appear on their websites, as well as outlines of their current strategies in company reports and critical reviews of these in the national press.

Another excellent source is the *Journal of Business Strategy,* an article from which is outlined below.

Mission statements JOURNAL ARTICLE

The article starts out by highlighting a report in *Business Week* showing that firms with well-crafted mission statements make a 30 per cent higher return on some financial measures than those without. The authors also point to academic studies which indicate a close relationship between high performance and effective mission statements.

David and David studied 95 mission statements from across the banking, food and computer industries and analysed them in terms of nine main components. They found that many statements were strikingly lacking.

The authors see the features of a good mission statement as including:

♦ being longer than a phrase or sentence, but not a two-page document
♦ not being overly specific (there is no need to get down to amounts in pounds and dollars)
♦ being inspiring (after reading it the reader should want to be part of that organisation
♦ the projection of a sense of worth, intent and shared expectations.

The document should include the following:

1   Customers (the target market)
2   Products/services (offerings and value provided to consumers)
3   Geographic markets (where the firm seeks customers)
4   Technology (the technology used to produce and market products)
5   Concern for survival/growth/profits (the firm's concern for financial soundness)
6   Philosophy (the firm's values, ethics, beliefs)
7   Public image (contributions the firm makes to communities)
8   Employees (the importance of managers and employees)
9   Distinctive competence (how the firm is different or better than competitors).

A total of 95 statements were collected from the Internet: 27 from firms in the computer industry, 36 from the food industry, and 32 from the banking industry. Three raters were asked independently to examine each document and assign values to each statement, where:

1 = statement does not include the component
2 = statement includes the component in vague terms
3 = statement includes the component in specific terms.

The results of the rating of PepsiCo's mission statement is shown in Figure 7.24.

PepsiCo's mission statement

PepsiCo's mission is to increase the value of our shareholder's investment. We do this through sales growth, cost controls and wise investment of resources. We believe our commercial success depends on offering quality and value to our consumers and customers, providing products that are safe, wholesome, economically efficient, and environmentally sound, and providing a fair return to our investors while adhering to the highest standards of integrity.

Rating

Component	PepsiCo's statement
1 Customers	2
2 Products/services	2
3 Geographic markets	1
4 Technology	1
5 Survival/growth	3
6 Philosophy	3
7 Public image	3
8 Employees	1
9 Distinctive competence	1

Figure 7.24 Rating of PepsiCo's mission statement

The authors conclude their investigation by stating that when it comes to company mission statements there is a great deal of room for improvement. The sample firms in their study 'generally did not include needed components in their mission statements'.

They suggest that if business leaders spend more time in creating effective mission documents this will have a rewarding payoff.

David, F. R. and David, F. R. 'Its time to redraft your mission statement', *Journal of Business Strategy*, 2003, January/February, pp 11–14.

ACTIVITY

Discuss in your group the following questions.

1 Is it possible to put the amount of detail into mission statements that is suggested by David and David while meeting the criteria of producing a brief statement?

2 Collect a sample of mission statements from an Internet search. Evaluate these statements in the light of criteria suggested by David and David.

3 Is it possible to evaluate these statements in an objective way?

4 Do you agree with the authors that there will be a substantial payoff from producing an effective mission statement?

Chapter 2
Strategic planning

Strategic planning is the process of creating a formal planning system for the development and implementation of an organisation's strategies. It is an ongoing process responding to changing circumstances.

Strategic plans should integrate the activities of the whole organisation and set out a timetable for the completion of relevant parts of the plan.

Strategic thinking

Strategic thinking involves thinking ahead so that you can shape the future of the organisation and its relationship with the environment, rather than simply reacting to environmental change. Strategic thinking involves taking an overview of the relationship between the organisation and its environment and making informed strategic decisions for the whole organisation. This involves a number of important threads, illustrated in Figure 7.25.

Figure 7.25   Strategic thinking

John L. Thompson (2001) states that companies that are adept at strategic thinking adopt the following practices:

♦ Identify more adeptly than rivals the key success factors involved in their line of business.
♦ Segment their markets to identify those segments where they are most likely to achieve competitive advantage.

♦ Base their strategies on the analysis and measurement of competitive advantage.
♦ Anticipate their customers' responses.
♦ Look for new competitive opportunities.
♦ Give investment priority to businesses or areas that promise a competitive advantage.

The future direction of competition

An approach known as **strategic group analysis** involves identifying organisations that are following similar strategies or competing in similar ways. Such groups can be identified because they have two or three sets of key characteristics which form the basis of competition. For example, in the European food-marketing industry it is possible to identify a number of strategic groups, for example multinational companies such as Nestlé, Heinz, Kraft and Unilever. These multinational major branders share common characteristics of having a wide geographical coverage in nearly every country in the European Union, and at the same time having a very high marketing intensity (measured by costs as a percentage of sales). In the same industry there are other strategic groups, for example national major branders (for example, UK manufacturers focusing on the UK market alone with a high marketing intensity), and minor national branders (for example, UK manufacturers focusing on the UK market alone with a low marketing intensity).

Strategic group analysis is helpful to an organisation in identifying direct competitors, and also in identifying gaps in the market. Identifying the future direction of what your competitors are likely to do involves:

♦ examining what they are doing now, particularly new initiatives
♦ examining possible changes that your competitors may adopt, for example new technologies

◆ competitor research, for example by studying competitor reports, websites, in-house journals and so on; this may involve directly 'spying' on organisations, for example by pretending to be a customer.

Many industries in the UK are highly competitive. Actions by one competitor lead to reactions by another, which trigger further actions and reactions. The resulting situation is often described as **competitive chaos**.

John L. Thompson suggests that there are three main skills required by organisations in such an environment:

◆ the ability to discern patterns in this dynamic environment and competitive chaos, and spot opportunities ahead of their rivals
◆ the ability to anticipate competitor actions and reactions
◆ the ability to use this intelligence and insight to lead customer opinion and outperform competitors.

CASE STUDY

McDonald's responds to the competition

Figure 7.26   McDonald's well-known trademark

For businesses to understand adequately the nature of the competition they face, they must define their market accurately. This involves recognising a broad base of competitors. McDonald's has thousands of competitors, each seeking a share of the market. McDonald's recognises that it is up against not only other large burger and chicken chains

but also independently owned fish and chip shops and other eat-in or take-out establishments.

A company like McDonald's, therefore, has to develop competitive strategies that differentiate it from its rivals.

All organisations need to be in touch with their business environment in order to make sure that what they do fits with customer expectations. These expectations change over time. Moreover the IEO (informal eating out) market in which McDonald's operates is becoming increasingly competitive, as Figure 7.27 illustrates. This market is defined as, 'Casual places where consumers buy a quick, inexpensive prepared meal or snack that they eat there, take with them, eat in the car or have delivered.'

Fast food outlets	Pizza/pasta	Fish and chips	Pub food	Coffee shops
Store/ supermarket	Ethnic including takeaway	Sandwich bars	Cafés	Petrol station forecourts

Figure 7.27   The market of IEO

Recently, in this crowded marketplace, McDonald's competitive lead came under pressure, largely because many fast-food outlets have either:

◆ copied the trail-blazing ideas that previously set McDonald's apart and put it ahead of the field
◆ promoted new ideas of their own, for example urban supermarkets and petrol stations that sell convenient, portable mealtime replacements.

McDonald's recognises the need to respond. It is looking to increase the competitive gap by:

◆ adding greater value through innovation
◆ making the process of visiting a McDonald's less routine and controlled
◆ enhancing the overall in-house experience.

461

For example, part of McDonald's response to give it a competitive edge has been a McCafé concept targeted at customers who appreciate quality coffee and who want an excellent product in an attractive, undaunting environment. The concept was initially trialled in Australia and New Zealand before being rolled out in this country. McCafé's are targeted primarily at females in the age group 25–39, many of whom have young families. McCafé's are designed to offer them a place to meet friends and enjoy a quality coffee experience as well as keep the children fed and entertained.

ACTIVITY

1 How is the development of McCafé's a response to growing competition?

2 Why does McDonald's need to outcompete the competition?

3 What other examples can you think of where organisations have developed new strategies designed to outsmart the competition?

Needs of customers

At the heart of strategic planning lies the anticipation and fulfilment of customer requirements and needs. Incisive strategic thinking involves recognising the importance of the customer.

In the case study above we identified ways in which McDonald's is responding to its competitors. Strategic planning at McDonald's is equally concerned with a customer orientation. In terms of the product lifecycle, quick-service restaurants have reached maturity in the UK and need an injection of fresh life through innovative ideas if their lifespan is to be prolonged.

Market research reveals that snacking is an increasingly important trend and is particularly popular amongst teenagers and young people. However, the total number of meals eaten in the non-quick-service restaurant sector has risen, while meals eaten in the quick-service restaurant sector has fallen in total. Rising incomes allow people more opportunities to turn eating out into a more individualised experience rather than a routine 'quick fix'. At the same time, when it comes to informal eating out, people may be moving away from burgers and fries towards other meals that are promoted as the healthy option, for example sandwiches and salads. At the same time organic food is rising in importance.

McDonald's strategic thinking and planning has involved providing appropriate solutions to these changing trends. In particular:

♦ consumers are seeking more food variety and healthier eating: McDonald's is providing a more balanced offering that includes fruit, sugar-free fruit drinks for children and more chicken products

♦ price is becoming more critical to decision making: McDonald's has created an Extra Value Meal and a McChoice menu offering a flexible combination of drinks, sandwiches and so on in addition to the meal, thereby providing what they regard as excellent value for money.

Gaining and maintaining competitive advantage

Michael Porter (1985) suggests that effective strategic management involves positioning an organisation relative to its rivals in such a way that it maintains and sustains competitive advantage. The McDonald's example above indicates how McDonald's has responded to losing some of its competitive advantage by developing new strategies.

Porter focused on two main aspects of an organisation's position relative to competitors:

♦ The number of firms in the relevant market segments, their size, relative power, rate of growth and ways in which they compete: organisations need to be in the right industries and market segments given their competitive capabilities.

♦ The size and market share of the firm are important in creating competitive advantage, and whether it has an appeal to particular segments of its markets.

In short, competitive advantage will be gained by being in the right industry and in the right position within that industry.

Successful competitors will:

♦ create value by giving customers what they want, and by developing clear advantages at every stage of the value chain
♦ develop competitive advantage in creating this value
♦ run their businesses well: meeting their objectives and using resources efficiently.

Clearly, therefore, to gain competitive advantage you need to plan and organise your business and to do these things better than your rivals.

Porter (1980) argued that given similar abilities to supply goods, the customer will choose to buy from one supplier rather than another, because:

♦ the price of the product or service is lower than that offered by rivals
♦ the product or service is seen by the customer to offer better 'value added' than that offered by a rival.

ACTIVITY

Compare firms in the following industries in terms of whether they are seeking competitive advantage through lower price, or through more value added.

♦ Cosmetics industry
♦ Newspaper industry
♦ Book publishing
♦ Computers
♦ Tinned food.

Porter showed that the best way to gain and maintain competitive advantage is not to be average. The low-cost firm can make higher than average profits by selling a lot more than its rivals and employing economies of scale. The differentiating firm can gain competitive advantage by giving its customers more value added.

Competitive strategies

Porter identified four possible favourable competitive strategies:

Broad differentiation strategy

This strategy involves selling a differentiated product to the mass market. Coca-Cola does this: its product is differentiated through advertising and marketing as well as the product itself.

Focused differentiation strategy

This strategy involves selling a differentiated product to a narrow market segment or niche market, rather than to a total market, for example a speciality high-quality magazine.

Broad low-cost strategy

This strategy involves selling a largely undifferentiated product to a mass market using low cost to drive sales, for example bags of sugar with simple packaging.

Focused low-cost strategy

This strategy involves selling an undifferentiated product or service to a smaller market segment, for example selling unbranded biscuits and sweets in a local market.

Typically, modern businesses will seek a differentiation strategy based on building in more value added than rivals, for example through:

♦ offering a more personalised service
♦ building relationships with customers
♦ built-in extra features
♦ speed and reliability of service
♦ superior design
♦ more sophisticated technology.

Ansoff's growth-vector matrix

We have already seen Ansoff's product–market expansion matrix (Figure 7.15). Ansoff maintained that in developing its portfolio strategy an organisation can choose a number of alternatives to generate intensive growth.

Product market penetration

The firm tries to increase its product's share in the markets it currently services. It can achieve this in various ways:

Product-line stretching The firm adds new items to its existing product line in a market segment which it has already penetrated. The aim is to attract more customers from rivals and current non-users of the firm's products (to reach a broader market). For example, Coca-Cola has added new items to its basic product and now offers Diet Coke and Cherry Coke in some of its world markets. The Japanese car manufacturers first penetrated the European car market with medium-sized cars; this product line then stretched to small cars, and now they have extended their product lines to target the luxury segments of the car market.

Product proliferation This involves offering many different product types. For example, Seiko offers a variety of watches with different features, functions, and so on.

Product improvement This involves updating and augmenting the existing product. It entails application of the latest technology to improve the product's capabilities, improving customer services, and so on.

Market development

This strategy involves developing new markets for the firm's current product lines. Expansion of this type is most suitable:

- where minimum product modification is required
- where profit margins are diminishing because of intense price competition in the firm's existing markets
- if the product's lifecycle is similar in various markets.

Product market development

This strategy involves the firm maintaining its existing markets but developing new product markets within them. For example, a firm selling software to the industrial segment in market X might go after the consumer segment in the same market.

Diversification

Diversification strategies involve the firm entering new product markets outside its present business. The firm may wish to pursue this line of expansion:

- when opportunities in the new product market are highly attractive
- when the firm wishes to reduce the impact of a negative environmental trend in its existing industry, for example to reduce the economic impact of a decline in cigarette smoking or the ageing of the UK population.

Portfolio analysis

Portfolio analysis is a key part of strategic thinking and involves assessing whether the organisation is running with an appropriate balance of business units and hence products. The Boston Consultancy Group's matrix (Figure 7.22), splitting products into cash cows, dogs, question marks and stars, is a good example of this. It showed the importance of having cash cows to provide investment capital for other business units, while at the same time it is important to develop stars and perhaps question marks which can become the cash cows of the future.

Portfolio analysis needs to be based on a long-term view of the organisation and asks questions not just about the current mix of business units, but also what this will look like next year, in five years' time and in the long term.

Planning systems

Kerry Napuk (1996) has defined strategic planning as, 'a total concept of the whole business involving a framework and a process that guides its future'. You can see from this definition that strategic planning involves considering the organisation as a whole in order to come up with 'holistic' plans. These plans are then put into action. They are not plans that are simply filed away in company records: they are plans which provide an on-going direction to practical actions. The strategy needs to be shared among all members of the organisation so that they are all pulling in the same direction.

It is possible (though dangerous) to think of strategic planning as a structured process which can be set out in a neat way, as illustrated in Figure 7.28.

Step	Tools associated with process
Identify your past achievements	
Identify the nature of the environment in which you operate and changes that are taking place in this environment	PESTEL
Outline your current strengths and weaknesses, identify opportunities and threats	SWOT
Identify a chosen direction	Mission, objectives
Choose a strategic plan to take the organisation into the future	Strategy
Monitor the progress of that strategy	Control and performance analysis
Make adjustments as and when necessary	

Figure 7.28   Outline of a prescriptive view of strategic planning

In an extreme form it is possible to see the centre of the organisation as having the responsibility for orchestrating and controlling the activities of its various parts in seeing that the plan is effectively delivered. We shall see in the sections below that there are alternative, more democratic views of strategic planning.

Top-down, bottom-up and integrated planning

Typically, there have been three main approaches to formal strategic planning.

A **top-down approach** occurs where plans are created, developed and managed by the centre of the organisation, for example from Head Office. As a result these plans can be seen as being created at the top of the organisation by senior executives and then passed down. These plans may also be created by professional planners who report directly to the strategic leader.

A **bottom-up approach** is where the sub-components of an organisation, for example strategic business units such as divisions, take responsibility for strategic planning. The role of the centre is to provide guidance, and to judge the performance of these strategies. Functional and business unit managers evaluate the performance of their particular area and identify the sorts of resources and requirements of their part of the organisation in relation to future plans.

The third way is an **integrated approach** involving ongoing dialogue and feedback between the top (centre) and the strategic business units (bottom) of the organisation.

It is important to see strategic planning as an ongoing process involving lots of input, and modification, resulting from informed input from the various components of the organisation.

Richard Lynch provides a useful outline of this ongoing planning process. He shows that a starting point is to identify the background assumptions on which a business is based, including the key success factors. The company can then outline a vision and overall strategic direction – which is likely to be developed over a number of years and will include the development of new technologies and ideas. With this background work established it is then possible to develop a medium-term plan for two or three years (assuming a relatively stable environment). It is then possible to establish short-term plans and budgets, as shown in Figure 7.29.

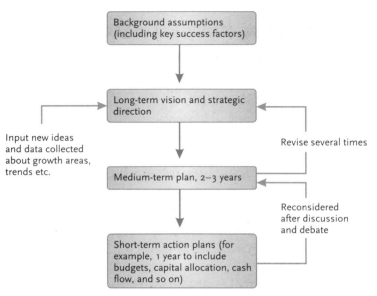

Figure 7.29   The basic strategic planning process

Behavioural approaches

There are a number of types of behavioural approach but typically this involves managers working together to discuss the future opportunities and threats in areas in which the organisation might develop. Managers are encouraged freely to discuss objectives and problems in order to reach an agreement about future priorities. This approach involves considerable involvement with strategic planning and a commitment to it because so many people have had an input. Of course, although different views are aired not all conflicts will be resolved but at least they will have been discussed. It is argued that such an approach will lead to the greatest dedication to implementing a strategic plan.

Informal planning

Informal planning typically takes place in individual managers' and strategists' heads rather than being part of a formalised document or written plan. This approach is most likely to be successful in small entrepreneurial organisations by managers with a flair for executing these informal plans. It is least likely to be successful in large organisations by individuals with little creative flair and with limited ability to communicate their plans to others.

CASE STUDY

Changing culture at Cummins

Cummins Inc. is one of the world's leading manufacturers of high-performance, low-emission diesel engines and power generation systems. In the early part of the new millennium the organisation engaged in a culture change process so that it would retain its existing strengths while at the same time embracing new ways of doing things that are essential to drive the business forward. In particular it wanted to create a shared vision of the organisation.

In preparing for change, Cummins arranged a series of focus workshops across the company. These were designed to be 'inclusive': they encouraged and took account of the ideas and views of a full range of people from across the company's different locations worldwide. Individuals and groups were encouraged to identify aspects of their existing ways of working that they valued and wished to retain. These were referred to as the organisation's 'sacred bundles'.

This part of the process was essential in enabling the organisation to build on the bedrock of existing values and practice, while at the same time recognising the need to move forward. Participants' preferred values often included aspects such as 'respect for each other and for the customer' and the need for 'a sense of community'.

At the same time as seeking to re-energise current values, Cummins realised the importance of creating a new, clear vision that would bring about consistency and cohesion across the global organisation. A set of common values, beliefs and goals was agreed and adopted.

The focus group process revealed a high degree of pride in the ability of the company, its products and its employees to improve the lives of people: helping customers to succeed, improving local communities and generating new solutions to reduce emissions and benefit the wider environment. When linked to the core business of providing power, the new vision proclaimed a strong statement with which employees could identify:

'Making people's lives better by unleashing the Power of Cummins.'

The vision is supported by a mission statement showing how it will be achieved:

'We unleash the Power of Cummins by':

♦ motivating people to act like owners working together

♦ exceeding customer expectations by always being first to market with the best products

♦ partnering with our customers to make sure they succeed

♦ demanding that everything we do leads to a cleaner, healthier, safer environment

♦ creating wealth for all stakeholders.

ACTIVITY

1 How would you characterise the planning approach used at Cummins: top-down, bottom-up, integrated, behavioural or informal?

2 What do you see as being the advantages of the planning approach that was used?

3 Compare this planning approach with two other approaches that could have been employed. In your view which is the most effective?

Strategic planning issues

We now need to examine the actual processes and issues involved in effective planning, in particular examining such detail as when to plan and who should be involved in this process.

Impact on managers

Involvement in the planning process is very important to the organisation and its members. Through this process individual managers are able to take part in the identification and discussion of organisational (and personal) priorities, and in identifying and providing solutions to problems.

The **strategic planning process** should improve communications within the organisation, whatever the model chosen for the process (for example, top-down or bottom-up). Involvement in the process should lead to high levels of motivation and commitment to organisational objectives.

A particular advantage of the planning process will be the co-ordination of organisational activities around the plan so that each manager will be able to see how their contribution fits into the overall planning structure.

The corporate (or total business) plan will feed down into plans for strategic business units and departments. Individual managers will therefore be able to see how their departmental plan fits into the overall planning structure and enable the setting of departmental priorities, plans and objectives.

Targets

Henry Mintzberg, in his 1994 book *The Rise and Fall of Strategic Planning*, suggested that the main role of strategic planning is 'to make plans operational'. In other words, after the plan has been conceived and set out it needs to be put into practice. He therefore argued that planning should be carried out by line managers rather than by a separate planning department because he felt that line managers were best qualified to understand how the organisation works in practice. He backed this up by saying that only line managers have the commitment and detailed knowledge to carry out the strategy decisions.

Line managers are best placed to establish **appropriate targets** for the various parts of the organisation which will enable the delivery of organisational objectives.

> Essentially a target is a stated level of future performance that a manager or other member of an organisation aims to achieve within a given time frame.

Targets can be set out in general or specific terms but it should be clear what the level of performance is that is required to achieve the target.

Target setting enables managers to operationalise the broad strategy of the organisation, and to identify whether or not targets are being achieved. Targets can be applied to a wide range of organisational activities, for example sales, production, financial performance indicators, and so on. In the following section we identify the importance of target setting as part of the strategic plan, showing how targets can be set both centrally and from management lower down the organisation.

When to plan

It is important to understand that business planning is an ongoing process. In the modern world in which businesses are dealing with a continually changing environment, it would be foolish to think that the plan can be designed and delivered in neatly created boxes with no need for adjustment.

Gary Hamel (1996) states, however, that 'In the vast majority of companies, strategic planning is a calendar-driven ritual ... (which assumes) that the future will be more or less like the present.'

From the observations which Grant made during the research mentioned above, he drew out a generic planning cycle which is illustrated in Figure 7.30.

Strategic planning in oil companies

Robert M. Grant (2003) carried out research into corporate strategy in a sample of the world's major oil companies (including Shell, Elf, Mobil and Amoco) which he identified as having increasingly to develop strategies in a turbulent business world. He noted that all of the companies in his sample carried out a formal, strategic planning process based on an annual cycle.

Grant, R. M. 'Strategic planning in a turbulent environment: evidence from the oil majors', *Strategic Management Journal*, 2003, No. 24, pp 491–517.

Key stages in the planning process

Grant identified the following key stages.

Planning guidelines

The yearly cycle started with the announcement by corporate headquarters of guidelines and assumptions to be used by the businesses in preparing business-level strategic plans. These were based on a view of the external environment (for example, changes in the

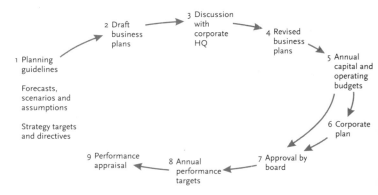

Figure 7.30   Generic planning cycle

energy market in the period ahead: demand, supply prices, and so on), and overall direction to the planning process through a statement of priorities, guidelines and expectations. A key aspect of this direction was setting company-wide performance targets (for example, 'raise return on capital employed to 12 per cent', 'reduce costs per barrel by 10 per cent', and so on.

Draft business plans

Strategic plans were formulated bottom up, that is, individual businesses took the initiative in formulating their strategic plans.

Discussion with corporate HQ

Draft plans were submitted by businesses to corporate headquarters. These were analysed and then a discussion took place between planners from head office and managers from the business units.

Revision of plans

The above process enables the revision of the plans.

Annual capital and operating budgets

The whole process was closely allied to budget setting. The first year of the strategic plan typically provided the basis for the next year's capital expenditure and operating budgets.

Corporate plan

The corporate plan is the result of building up a picture of the individual business plans.

Approval

The next stage is approval by the Board of Directors, in this case of the oil companies.

Performance targets

It was then possible to establish a broad range of performance targets involving financial and strategic targets.

Performance appraisal

The performance plans and targets then provided the basis for performance appraisal.

For companies whose financial years corresponded to calendar years, the planning cycle started in the spring, with corporate and business plans finally approved in November or December, and performance reviews occurring around the start of the following year.

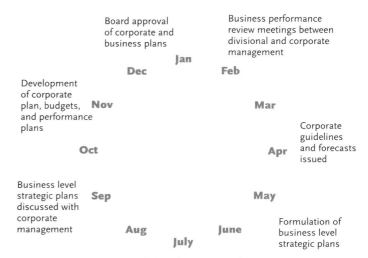

Figure 7.31   Timing of the planning cycle in oil majors (based on Grant, 2003)

ACTIVITY

1   To what extent is it important to establish a planning cycle like the one in Figure 7.31?

2   Why might it be important to develop ongoing mechanisms for adjusting the plan?

3   Compare the planning cycle outlined in Figure 7.31 with that of another organisation, for example the university or college where you are studying.

Intended and realised strategy

It would be convenient if an organisation had complete mastery of the development of its strategies. The reality is far removed from this (see Figure 7.32).

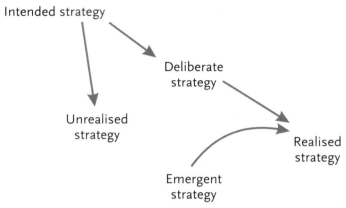

Figure 7.32   Intended and realised strategy

The strategic planning process enables an organisation to choose a strategy which can be regarded as its **intended strategy**. However, in the course of time, unforeseen events take place which force the organisation to abandon some of its original intentions (**unrealised strategies**) and to take on board new elements of strategy (**emergent strategies**) which are not what the organisation originally intended. The strategy which materialises in the real world is thus a combination of realised strategies and emergent strategies: that is, a combination of elements of intended strategy which work in practice, and new elements of strategy which emerge along the way.

For example, in the early part of the new millennium the football club Leeds United developed a strategy of seeking to be one of the top four clubs in Britain by investing heavily in its youth team, and by attracting a squad of expensive players. Part of the strategy was to move to a new stadium. However, targets and results failed to live up to expectations and the club was forced to develop a survival strategy which meant stripping out some of its best players and putting on hold plans to move to a new stadium. The strategy that emerged and was realised was thus radically different from the original intended strategy.

There are a number of views on the extent to which strategy can be tightly planned. A number of writers on strategy, such as Ansoff, are seen to belong to a 'design school of strategic management', suggesting that strategy can be deliberately managed in a logical sequence of steps.

In contrast, Mintzberg and others see strategy as 'emerging' over time, involving an element of trial and error. Strategy emerges, adapting to human needs and continuing to develop over time. Managers are not fully able to prescribe strategy because:

♦ they are only capable of handling a selected number of strategic options at a time
♦ they perceive data in a biased way
♦ they are more likely to seek satisfactory solutions rather than maximise the objectives of the organisation
♦ organisations consist of coalitions of people formed into power blocks; strategy formulation is likely to come from compromises between different power blocks rather than being made by a single managerial group seeking to achieve a common set of objectives
♦ decision making relies on the culture, routines, and politics of an organisation as much as on rational decision making.

Who should be involved?

In terms of the creation of strategies, the stakeholders of organisations seek some sort of directive leadership from senior managers, and from the centre of a large organisation. The responsibility of the directors and senior managers within an organisation is to create strategy (after consultation) and then to set out the structures for implementing that strategy.

Ideally, strategy should be created by a consultation with all stakeholders in the organisation. Typically, the final creation of an organisational strategy document and plan will be in the hands of a small group of senior planners with a good understanding of the issues involved. However, through the process or consultation with stakeholders, they should create a commitment to the strategy.

Dangers of centralised strategy making

Richard Koch (1995) warns of the dangers of centralised strategy making in the large corporation. He argues that the confidence of those who believe corporate strategists can come up with the right ways to lead a company to success is often unfounded. He believes that the corporate centre in large, or multi-business companies should wherever possible leave much of the strategic decision making to individual business units within the company. He states that 'managers at the centre, however competent, are natural value destroyers'.

Koch's criticisms are as follows:

- corporate centres are usually large and expensive to run; a lot of the profits made by operating businesses are swallowed up by the centre
- corporate centres do not add enough value to a business to justify their costs
- most corporate centres destroy more value than they add.

Where corporate strategy is formulated by a centralised planning team, then it is essential that they arrange meetings and feedback sessions to take in the views of members of the organisation from right across the business. A two-way communication process is essential in the creation of business unit level strategies.

The role of planning

This section should have made it clear that planning lies at the heart of effective corporate strategy. Clear planning mechanisms are required so that the structure of the strategy is easy to follow and monitor. Planning involves setting out step-by-step sequences of actions that are required to achieve key objectives.

A centralised planning department can take a major role in creating the structure of the planning framework. However, it is clear that the input of ideas into this structure should come from those with most knowledge about the operation of the organisation, which will typically be managers 'on the ground'.

Kerry Napuk provides a simple and useful outline of the steps required to prepare strategic plans.

Steps to making a strategic plan

1 How did we get here?
   1.1 Successful factors.
2 Where do we want to go?
   2.1 Vision
   2.2 Objectives
      i internal evaluation of strengths and weaknesses
3 How do we get there?
   3.1 Strategies
      i External evaluation: opportunities and threats
4 How do we make it work?
   4.1 Structure
   4.2 Implementation
      i Action programme
   4.3 Review

Planning is essentially concerned with the question, 'how do we make the strategy work'? This involves creating an outline of the structure of the organisation that will deliver the plans, and a plan of implementation, involving an action programme which is the plan itself.

Planning can be carried out centrally or by unit level managers, and preferably by a combination of the two.

Action plans can be set out as a series of targets and achievement of the plan depends on these targets being successfully met.

It should be clear from this chapter that considerable flexibility needs to be built into planning to cater for a highly volatile external environment.

Robert M. Grant's research into strategic planning in the oil majors showed that typically corporate planners are drawn from line management positions within businesses and in some cases from staff functions such as finance and IT. Planners typically spend three to five years in corporate planning posts before returning to line management. A number of the oil companies explained their staffing of corporate planning departments in terms of the intent to combine analytic skills of younger staff with the experience of long-serving managers.

Grant's research also indicates that in a turbulent world the planning process is becoming increasingly informal, with the balance of meetings shifting from presentations towards discussion of issues. The balance of responsibility for strategic planning has also shifted away from the centre to increasing emphasis on individual business unit development of plans.

Strategic planning techniques

Strategic planning techniques that involve the collection and use of quantitative data can be very useful in supporting the planning process. In particular they can:

♦ help to reduce the risks involved in decision making
♦ help in establishing priorities particularly when companies operate in many locations and produce many different products
♦ indicate the likelihood and influence of particular threats
♦ help to establish the likely results of particular strategies.

However, it is important to recognise the limitation of data used in a particular technique and the validity of the assumptions that are made. Techniques therefore are a support to decision making.

BCO: growth–share matrix

We have already mentioned the Boston Consulting Group's growth–share matrix (see p. 464, and Figure 7.22). This is a useful technique in positioning products relative to their stage in the product lifecycle. The matrix gives an indicator as to the cash needs of particular products. Of course, it is important to remember that managers involved directly with the products concerned are most likely to understand the nature of competition and market potential for the profits under consideration rather than planners at a distance.

A multi-product firm will have some products that are profitable and some that are not. Profits from products in mature markets can be re-invested in new growth areas, rather than in areas which are likely to experience decline.

It is suggested that the following strategies can be employed with products and business units:

♦ cash cows can be milked so that the cash flow from them can be used elsewhere
♦ dogs can be closed down, so that the freed resources can be channelled elsewhere
♦ stars require injections so that their competitive position can be enhanced in growth industries
♦ question marks may need investment if it is felt that this will be appropriate to profitable growth.

Directional policy matrices

Directional policy matrices have been employed since the 1970s by large businesses such as Shell to help with investment and divestment strategy making.

The illustration (Figure 7.33) shows a typical direction policy matrix as developed by Shell. You can easily see similarities with the BCO growth–share matrix.

In Figure 7.33 the horizontal axis shows the prospects for profitable operation in the relevant sector. The vertical axis represents the competitive position of the business in relation to rivals. (New prospects can be evaluated first along the vertical axis by examining the prospects for developing competitive advantage.) Each factor is given a weighting according to its importance.

In outlining the matrix it is necessary to assume that resources are limited so you cannot invest in everything; choices have to be made about priorities. Strategic planning therefore involves analysing existing businesses and possible business opportunities in order to make appropriate choices.

INDUSTRY ATTRACTIVENESS

		Unattractive	Average	Attractive
COMPETITIVE POSITION	Weak	Divest		Invest for market share or withdraw
		Phased withdrawal		
	Average	Invest selectively to maximise cash generation	Invest to retain market share as industry grows	
	Strong			Priority products and services

Figure 7.33   A directional policy matrix

The overall attractiveness of products in the matrix is reduced as we move from the bottom right-hand side of the matrix to the top left. The priority for resource allocation should be given to products shown in the bottom right of the matrix.

Strategic Position and Action Evaluation (SPACE)

This is a model focusing on four variables, the extremes of which are shown in brackets:

♦ the stability or turbulence of the business environment (turbulent/stable)
♦ the attractiveness of the industry (high/low)
♦ the extent of competitive advantage (high/low)
♦ the financial strength of business as measured by such indicators as profitability and liquidity positions (high/low).

Scores are given to each of these four factors and this is represented in Figure 7.34.

The type of strategy that is appropriate depends on the pattern that emerges from this analysis. Four major types of strategy are identified that are pertinent to given situations, and these are shown in Figure 7.34.

For example, Figure 7.35 illustrates a business unit with low financial strength, in a very attractive industry, which is strongly competitive, and where the environment is unstable. The appropriate strategy to select is therefore a competitive one. Features of competitive strategies would include securing finance

Variables	Type of strategy			
	Aggressive	Competitive	Conservative	Defensive
Financial strength	High	Low	High	Low
Industry attractiveness	High	High	Low	Low
Environment	Stable	Unstable	Stable	Unstable
Competitiveness	High	High	Low	Low

Figure 7.34   SPACE analysis

to pursue opportunities, while seeking to improve productivity and hence lower costs to secure an even more competitive position.

A **defensive strategy** would involve cutting back on and closing down activities.

A **conservative strategy** too might include cost reductions and cutting back on non-core activities.

An **aggressive strategy** would involve some form of growth perhaps by taking over other businesses, and taking advantage of opportunities.

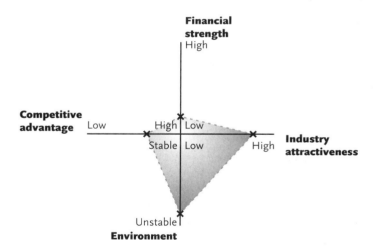

Figure 7.35   A SPACE that would suggest a competitive strategy

Profit Impact of Market Strategy (PIMS)

In recent years there has been a lot of interest in the impact of strategy on company performance, chiefly measured by profitability. The Strategic Planning

Institute (SPI) which is based in the USA has been gathering data on about 3000 companies, over 600 of which are based in Europe.

This information fits into three main types:

♦ the results of strategies in terms of indicators such as profit and market share
♦ the inputs (for example, investment into plant, productivity levels, and so on) by companies into their strategies
♦ the industry conditions in which the business operates (for example, the growth of the market, the power of customers, and so on).

This information is stored in a databank termed the PIMS databank which stands for Profit Impact of Market Strategy.

Analysis of this data involves statistical work to identify correlations between the various inputs and outputs of strategies, for example the relationship between investment in physical plant and market share, the relationship between spending on marketing activities and profits, and so on.

One of the findings of this ongoing research is that the most important determinant of a business unit's performance is the quality of its products and services compared to that of competitors.

ACTIVITY

Study the data below based on research carried out using the PIMS database. (The figures shown are percentage return on investment.)

Relative quality	Relative market share		
	Low (below 25 per cent)	Medium	High (above 60 per cent)
Inferior	7	14	21
Roughly equal	13	20	27
Superior	20	29	38

Chapter 3

Strategy evaluation and selection

In this chapter we examine a number of strategies available to organisations before going on to look at how to select from the strategies available by evaluating their relative merits.

The four major types of strategy examined are:

♦ market entry strategies
♦ substantive growth strategies
♦ limited growth strategies
♦ disinvestment strategies.

It is important to create a menu of strategic options rather than to limit choice. The most obvious choice is not necessarily the best.

Market entry strategies

In recent years we have heard a lot about 'first mover advantage', that is, the advantage to be gained from being the first into an industry. This has been particularly relevant in relation to new .com businesses such as lastminute.com, the Internet trader offering a range of deals to last minute purchasers, including theatre tickets and holidays.

lastminute.com

Figure 7.36   lastminute.com, an increasingly well-known brand

It is suggested that if you get in to the market first and establish relationships with customers and suppliers then you can gain a considerable competitive advantage. The process of expanding into new markets can be illustrated in a systematic way by setting out what is known as an **expansion method matrix** showing the various ways of expanding either geographically or in terms of inside or outside the company.

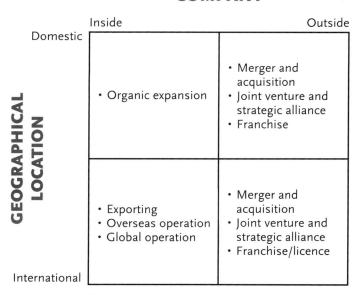

Figure 7.37   The expansion method matrix

Where an industry continues to grow quickly then new firms will be encouraged to enter the industry.

Organic growth

A common way of entering an industry is through **organic growth**, that is, where a firm finances entry and expansion through ploughing back profits into market entry. This is particularly suitable for existing businesses that want to develop a new product or business in a growing industry: they can channel funds into a new business unit through existing cash cows. Virgin is particularly associated with this strategy. Richard Branson's company has financed market entry into a number of new business lines through milking funds from existing Virgin businesses: for example, he has moved from airlines into railways, cola drinks, insurance and contraceptives.

Merger or acquisition

Another important way of entering a market is through **merger or acquisition**. This enables either geographic market entry (for example, the takeover of a South-East Asian company by a European one) or market entry within an organisation's existing sphere of operations. Merging with another organisation often provides the best and most logical way for an organisation to build on its core competencies. There will often be clear synergies to be built in this way. The organisation will not only be able to build market share to drive competitive advantage, but will also be able to build on its existing strengths or reduce existing weaknesses. This is a relatively quick method of expansion which may have the benefit of cutting out competitors. Costs are saved through economies of scale. However, this may be an expensive way of expanding and unless synergies are quickly achieved may lead to a reduction in efficiency.

Strategic alliances or joint ventures

This is where a company's shares are jointly owned by two companies. This approach has become particularly popular in international links between European and American companies and partners in former communist countries. This may be the case where there are differences in business cultures and practice so that it makes sense to work with a partner when working in a market with which you are not familiar. These approaches enable an organisation to spread its business quickly and is cheaper than outright acquisition. However, it involves some loss of control, as well as the sharing out of profits.

Licensing and franchising

A licence to produce, or to employ a certain type of technology, is granted by licence and a royalty fee is paid. This is a relatively simple arrangement but may suffer from difficulties in ensuring the quality of work carried out by the licensee.

Franchising is a form of licensing where the franchisee is given the right to trade under a well-known business name in a particular geographical area. The franchisee is also supplied with other benefits such as equipment, training and marketing know-how. Franchising involves a lower investment by the franchiser because the franchisee commits their own capital. However, it involves sharing profits and the success of the venture depends on how much the franchisee is willing to put into the marriage.

CASE STUDY

Going for growth

Dixons Group PLC is the UK's leading retailer of electrical and electronic products for the home. Its core products include audio, television and photographic equipment, home computers, phones, faxes and pagers and other domestic electrical goods.

Dixons' objective is constant: profitable growth. By acquiring the 'best players' in a range of European locations, the group has sought to gain the ability to increase not only in absolute scale, but also geographical spread. The businesses acquired in Europe were already either the number one or number two players in their respective countries and their core operations were aligned with those of the Dixons Group.

A key advantage in operating across markets is to obtain expertise and apply new and best business practices across markets, while maintaining and recognising the cultural differences. By learning from best practice – sharing ideas from different markets and business cultures – synergies are brought to the group. Consolidation also strengthens buying power on a global scale. The group now has a portfolio of products and markets.

In 1997 Dixons Group acquired the retail assets of Harry Moore Ltd, Ireland, which was relaunched as Dixons.

In December 1999, Dixons Group PLC purchased Elkjøp which already had 154 stores across the Nordic region selling electrical goods.

Early in 2000, the Group purchased Ei system, the leading PC retailer in Spain and Portugal. The Group has also bought into a leading electrical retailer in Greece and is seeking further European expansion opportunities.

ACTIVITY

1 Why do you think that Dixons is expanding in Europe?

2 What would be the dangers of not doing so?

3 What are the benefits of this expansion?

Substantive growth strategies

Substantive growth strategies (that is, growth strategies involving substantial changes in resources and often markets) usually involve acquisition, merger or the establishment of a joint venture rather than the internal growth of a business. The business may also decide to expand in a major way by franchising, as for example Coca-Cola has done with its bottling plants.

Horizontal and vertical integration

Vertical integration involves moving forward and/or backwards in the operating chain, and horizontal integration involves joining with parallel businesses. Integration is also discussed in Unit 5: Foundations of the business environment, p. 203.

Vertical integration seeks to improve business performance by taking ownership of more parts of the value system, so that linkages become internal to the organisation. However, there are potential drawbacks if co-ordination is poor. An example of backward vertical integration would be a car manufacturer taking over a supplier of car tyres to ensure quality, regular supply and control over the profit margin on the product. Forward vertical integration might involve the car manufacturer taking over car showrooms to gain better control over marketing efforts and presentation of the end product.

Horizontal integration (taking over a firm at the same stage of production) makes it possible to reduce competition and to benefit from economies of scale. By bringing together two parallel companies it is also possible to rationalise and cut out less efficient units.

CASE STUDY

Integration at Rolls-Royce

Rolls-Royce still makes aero engines, but no longer manufactures cars. Instead, the company has transferred its core strengths and expertise into other markets in which it has the greatest competitive strengths. These are the civil aerospace, defence aerospace, marine and energy markets.

Rolls-Royce's strategy is to secure and retain the leading position in its key markets. The company recognises that an increasing number of customers want to deal with as few suppliers as possible in order to reduce purchasing and search costs. Therefore, customers look for suppliers who are able to meet the full range of their needs with the highest level of service.

This case study focuses on acquisitions made by Rolls-Royce in the marine market. In 1999, Rolls-Royce acquired Vickers PLC. Vickers was already a key player in the marine market, providing leading-edge marine equipment. The takeover demonstrated Rolls-Royce's strategic intent to become the dominant player in the marine market. This acquisition gave the company a range of leading-edge businesses.

The faster the growth of a particular market, the greater is the amount of expenditure required in order to maintain position in that market. In a dynamic market, considerable expenditure is required on investment in product lines. Intelligent organisations identify those areas of a market that are experiencing the highest levels of growth and then seek to increase their share of these market sectors.

Marine activity accounts for about 15 per cent of Rolls-Royce's turnover and this figure is growing.

Given the high level of global competition, a company like Rolls-Royce can survive and prosper only in those markets in which it is a dominant force. The marine market has proved to be an outstanding opportunity for expansion for two main reasons:

♦ The marine industry is looking to increase the engine power associated with movement of passengers and freight by sea.
♦ The marine industry is under pressure from governments to produce engines that meet more demanding regulations on emissions.

Meet these requirements and you are best placed to win the largest share of the market.

Rolls-Royce has developed a world-leading marine business that services customers in global commercial and naval markets. Today, more than 20,000 commercial and naval vessels use Rolls-Royce equipment, and the company's engines power 400 ships in 30 navies. In the marine market, Rolls-Royce provides high capital-value products, services and systems and develops long-term relationships with customers.

The acquisition of Vickers in 1999 added a range of complementary products and services and expanded the Rolls-Royce route to market.

The products acquired as a result of the Vickers takeover are market-leading brands in the commercial and naval marine business and include Ulstein, Bird-Johnson, Aquamaster, Kamewa and Brown Brothers.

The effect of adding Vickers Ulstein Marine Systems to the existing capabilities of Rolls-Royce was to:

♦ make Rolls-Royce a world leader in marine systems
♦ broaden routes to market
♦ create new business opportunities
♦ broaden the product range and allow integrated systems to be developed and/or offered
♦ build a strong global support network.

Today Rolls-Royce provides the widest range of marine products because a range of key brands are now part of the Rolls-Royce portfolio.

ACTIVITY

1   How would you categorise the form of integration in which Rolls-Royce has engaged in the marine market?

2   What do you see as being the principal benefits of such integration?

3   What dangers might there be for Rolls-Royce in engaging in such a strategy?

Related and unrelated diversification

Related diversification, also called concentric diversification, involves some form of move away from existing products and markets but where there is some link with what has gone before. On the other hand, in unrelated diversification, also called conglomerate diversification, there is no apparent link with previous products and markets.

In **related diversification** the relationship may be in the types of technology employed or in similarities in marketing. For example, a manufacturer of standard chocolate bars might move into Easter eggs to boost profits at Easter time. A producer of wedding dresses may diversify into producing ball gowns using the same equipment and technology, and so on. The organisation is seeking to build on its existing core competencies by moving into new value-added lines.

In pursuing related diversification a firm will seek out other firms and opportunities where there are similar:

- products
- technologies
- resource requirements.

For example, Mars's strategy of moving on from chocolate bars to Mars ice cream can be seen as substantive related diversification involving similar ingredients and distribution channels although the technology employed was a new innovation.

Unrelated diversification takes place where there is no clear link between existing and new products, services and markets. The purpose of the diversification is to seize opportunities for additional profits. Of course, this is usually a higher risk strategy because it involves moving away from existing core competencies to employ new technologies, and new markets for new products and services. Typically, a firm engaging in such diversification will quickly seek to acquire additional resources: for example, skilled technologists, managers, and plant which are suitable to the new areas covered.

Typically, a strategy of unrelated diversification is part of a process of developing a broad portfolio of different products and markets, and is seen as a way of spreading risks.

Limited growth strategies

Companies may want to engage in a limited growth strategy, rather than engage in the higher risk, higher involvement substantive growth strategy.

There are a number of options available, including:

- do nothing
- market penetration
- market development
- product development
- innovation.

Do nothing

An option favoured by risk-averse organisations or ones operating in an uncertain environment is simply to carry on with existing business and competitive strategies: hence 'do nothing'. This makes sense when the organisation is 'bedding in' an existing strategy the results of which are still uncertain, or because the company is unsure about how the market is developing.

A company may actually be developing new ideas and products but be reluctant to risk putting them to the market until they have a clearer idea about changes in the business environment.

Market penetration

Market penetration is all about doing better what you already do by building on your existing distinctive competences. This strategy is employed when the company knows that it has a good product that it makes well using the 'right' technology. It therefore seeks to build the brand in order to penetrate the market still further.

The rationale behind this strategy is:

- to increase market share
- to prevent competitors from stealing market share
- to take market share away from rivals.

An obvious way of building market penetration is through advertising products and brands.

Market penetration strategies have a good chance of success because they simply build on existing competences, and if the product is a good one, then it can be built through value-adding activities such as improved promotion and more effective distribution channels.

Market development

Again, this strategy involves building on what the company already does well and therefore is a relatively low-risk strategy.

Markets can be developed by:

♦ modifying an existing product so that it appeals to wider segments of the market
♦ identifying new uses for the product
♦ identifying new geographical areas in which to sell the product.

For example, in the confectionery market in recent years we have seen the modification of many products, for example:

We have seen Smarties being extended into Giant Smarties, new coloured Smarties such as the Blue Smartie, new flavours of Smarties, and so on.

New flavours with new wrappings being added to the Quality Street Collection.

New varieties of Polos, including being sold the holes from the middle of the mints.

Product development

Product development involves a more substantial alteration in a product to make it, effectively, a different product, so that market penetration is increased. This strategy is often carried out when a product is nearing the end of its lifecycle. For example, this textbook is a complete rewriting of two earlier editions because:

♦ the subject matter of degree-level business study has altered
♦ the case studies needed to be updated
♦ degree-level specifications have altered
♦ the wider audience of foundation degree-level students need to be catered for.

This book is broken up into units that are different from those in previous editions, is made up of different chapters, has different case studies, has a different team of authors, has modifications such as the references to research literature, a new cover and a new title.

The strategy is driven by a need to cater for the changing needs of customers.

This strategy is more expensive to pursue than 'do nothing' and 'market penetration', and potentially more risky although the potential rewards are much greater because if the research for the product has been done accurately customers will be delighted with the results.

ACTIVITY

Identify situations in which products with which you are familiar have been developed:

♦ through modification
♦ with new uses
♦ through sale to new geographical locations.

CASE STUDY

The relaunch of Mars

In 2002, the Mars bar was relaunched. The major elements of the relaunch were:

♦ **Recipe change** There was a change in the production process which resulted in the nougat being whipped more to increase the feeling of lightness.

◆ **Packaging** The wrapper design was modified to deliver a more classy yet friendly brand image as well as improved eye-catching visibility in-store.

◆ **Advertising message** The new strapline for the Mars bar is 'Pleasure you can't measure' which reflects the taste and immeasurable everyday enjoyment that consumers get from the Mars bar.

Mars created its strapline 'Work, Rest and Play' in 1959. It became one of the most famous slogans of all time. In early 2002, almost seventy years after its introduction, the Mars bar was still the UK's best-selling chocolate bar with 7.2 per cent of market sales. However, in the all-important chocolate confectionery market, Mars bar sales began to decline faster than the market segment as a whole.

Particular factors that hit the sales of Mars bars were the aggressive marketing campaigns of rivals, the proliferation in the number of confectionery products to choose from, and an increased emphasis on healthy eating. While some rival products have gone for market penetration strategies like the Yorkie bar which carried out an advertising campaign stating (tongue in cheek) that it is 'not for girls', Mars has opted for product development. The lighter Mars bar and the more feminine tones of its advertising campaign suggest that it is seeking to win the support of more health-conscious individuals and to win increasing support from a female as well as the core male audience.

ACTIVITY

1 Why do you think that Mars chose a strategy of product development?

2 What are the risks associated with this strategy?

3 What are the potential benefits?

Innovation

Innovation is the process of turning new ideas into realistic affordable solutions that consumers want. As such an innovation strategy goes beyond product development to creating new products which are substantially different from what has gone on before (although there is a fine and not always distinct line between product development and innovation).

Innovations are developed by entrepreneurial individuals and organisations who are prepared to 'think outside the box'. A good example of an innovation was the Post-It note introduced by 3M or the Mars ice cream introduced by Mars.

The danger of innovation as a strategy is that this can be expensive, as for example an innovation in motor car engine technology which can involve a multi-million pound investment if it is going to be transferred into a new production line system. Another disadvantage of innovation is that the market may not be ready for new ideas, and by the time it is someone else might have copied the new idea.

James Dyson's innovatory new twin cyclone is a good example of a successful innovation, but he had to fight off in the law courts rivals who tried to copy his idea.

Disinvestment strategies

So far we have concentrated on strategies related to growth. However, given that an important business objective is that of survival we also need to outline disinvestment strategies which involve organisations reducing the size of their operations. There are a number of reasons for disinvestment, including:

◆ falling profits
◆ falling market share
◆ variations in the performance of items in the organisation's product portfolio
◆ a failed business marriage, for example a merger where the expected synergies have not materialised
◆ a weak competitive position in certain markets.

Typical disinvestment strategies include:

- retrenchment
- turnaround strategies
- divestment
- liquidation.

Retrenchment

Retrenchment involves cutting back activities away from niche or peripheral markets. The purpose here is to enable an organisation better to concentrate on its core activities as a focus for its energies.

Retrenchment is most likely to occur during a period of economic downturn and/or when company profits fall significantly. At such times it is necessary to do a detailed financial analysis of where weaknesses lie, coupled with a detailed market analysis to identify long-term market trends. This analysis may reveal areas where the greatest losses are being sustained and how extensive a drain this will be on company resources.

The process of retrenchment will then be concerned with:

- selling off inefficient business units
- cutting back surplus assets
- cost reductions, for example by laying off staff, changing the nature of contracts, for example leasing rather than buying equipment, and so on
- seeking ways of generating revenue to balance the books.

CASE STUDY

Retrenchment to focus on most profitable lines

Although it makes sense to expand into more and more overseas markets, in an era of global competition it also makes sense to retrench and focus on your best lines to avoid the pitfalls of overstretching. By selling off less profitable lines, resources can be channelled into the most profitable ones.

In June 2001, Stagecoach, the train and bus group, announced the sale of its troubled Portuguese operations as a further step in its recovery. The company struck a deal to sell the loss-making business to another European transport group for £14m.

At the time Stagecoach Portugal ran 135 buses on a network of services to the north and west of Lisbon. The company moved into Portugal in 1995 when it acquired the business, then called Rodoviaria Lisbon. The move to sell off Stagecoach Portugal was part of a strategy, to focus the business on its main operations in Britain and on Coach USA, its American bus business. This followed the recent disposal of Prestwick airport.

Strategists working for Stagecoach felt that the Portuguese business was consuming too much management time and would never produce adequate results from the resources it needed.

ACTIVITY

1   Did it make sense to sell off Stagecoach Portugal?

2   What could the resources acquired from the sell-off be used for?

3   Why do organisations seek to focus their strategies?

4   Study the national press to identify another retrenchment strategy. What was the justification for the strategy?

Turnaround strategies

This can be seen as the follow-up to retrenchment. The process of retrenchment frees up resources which can then be diverted into the turnaround strategy: for example, existing managers can be redeployed elsewhere.

Strategists will need to consider how they can turn the business around, and this involves a lot of discussion of ideas as to how to generate increased revenue streams. This may mean refocusing advertising and promotional budgets on what are seen as the areas of the business most likely to be successful, concentration on better lines and products, and some discounting of the prices of some products.

Successful retrenchment and turnaround involves accurately identifying which areas of the business to cut back on and which to focus on. In the previous case study we saw that Stagecoach cut out Prestwick airport and Stagecoach Portugal so that it could focus on the British and American markets.

In a similar way in the early part of this decade Marks & Spencer developed a turnaround strategy which involved retrenching by cutting back (closing) its continental European and American businesses to focus on the UK where it was rolling out a series of 'new concept stores'.

Divestment

Divestment is the process of selling off a business unit to another company. In the modern world businesses expand by internal growth and by integrating with other businesses that are seen as useful to the process of business growth. The purpose of expansion is to achieve economies of scale, synergies and other benefits. Where these benefits are limited it often makes sense to sell off (divest) poorer performing units and ones that take up too many resources.

Poorly performing business units can lead to a rapid leakage of resources, and will often need to be sold quickly, often at knock-down prices which fail to reflect the true worth of the business. A major problem is that in periods of economic downturn business units are likely to be the greatest sap on a company's resources, and it is during the downturn that businesses are most difficult to sell.

ACTIVITY

Identify from the business press a company that is currently selling off one or more of its businesses. What is the rationale for this move?

Liquidation

Liquidation involves selling off a complete business either in its entirety or as separate pieces. The financial press typically sees this as the sign of failure of a business strategy, but it may simply be that the business has outlived its usefulness, rather like an old car.

Strategy selection

In this chapter we have examined a number of strategies that will be relevant in different circumstances. These strategic options need to be weighed up against each other.

There are three important criteria for evaluating options:

♦ suitability
♦ acceptability
♦ feasibility.

Suitability concerns whether the strategies fit the situation. For example, tools such as PESTEL, SWOT and competitor analysis provide a good view of the relationship between the internal organisation and the external environment. The organisation then needs to look at whether their strategic options provide a suitable use of resources in a given environment; for example, whether a strategy:

♦ fits with internal weaknesses or external threats facing an organisation
♦ builds on an organisation's existing strengths and environmental opportunities
♦ matches the organisation's stated objectives.

Acceptability is concerned with whether a strategy will be acceptable to the organisation and those with a significant interest in it. For example, is the level of risk acceptable and are shareholders and other stakeholders prepared to agree to the plans? They may have reservations based on what they consider to be ethical, fair and reasonable. For example, strategies involving high financial returns in a developing market may have to be shelved if influential stakeholders see the environmental costs as being too high a price to pay.

Feasibility is concerned with whether strategic plans can work in practice and primarily whether the organisation has adequate resources to carry out particular plans, for example whether:

♦ the funds are available
♦ the organisation will be able to sustain the required level of output

♦ the organisation will be able to deal with the competition that it generates
♦ it will be able to meet the required market share.

Choosing an appropriate corporate strategy therefore involves a range of considerations, in order to make sure that the option selected will work in practice.

Chapter 4
Strategy implementation

The realisation of strategic plans to operational reality

Business strategies are made at the level of the whole organisation. They are then translated into a series of generic and competitive strategies for each business unit, product and/or market. **Functional strategies** (if the organisation is organised on a functional basis) are designed to carry out the competitive strategies and these will be translated into a series of action plans. To complement this process the structure of the organisation is designed to break down the work and other tasks to be completed. The organisation will be structured into a series of divisions, business units or functions. The people that comprise these substructures will be working to objectives, targets, plans, programmes, policies and procedures which give them a direction for their activities, as indicated in Figure 7.38.

Figure 7.38 The translation of corporate strategy into individual action plans

Of course, the translation of corporate strategy into individual action plans is not and should not be seen as a simple, static and one-way process. Rather it is a complex, dynamic and multi-directional process. As we have seen earlier, **strategy formulation** is an adaptive process responding to changes within and outside the organisation. Changes at lower levels within the organisation will lead to emergent functional, competitive and in turn corporate strategies.

Communication: selling the concepts

Effective communication is a two-way process. Not only do managers need to communicate the nature of strategy to their team members, but individual implementers of strategies need to understand what is being communicated to them. Hence the importance of feedback in the communication of strategies. Multi-channel flows (in which ideas and information flow in all directions) of communication are helpful in creating a shared sense of ownership of corporate strategy.

Some writers argue that in communicating strategies it is best to focus on a small number of core themes rather than getting bogged down in trying to explain the fine details. The choice of communication media is pertinent to the message to be conveyed. Complex messages are best communicated in face-to-face interactions, whereas a broad outline can be set out in a company magazine or bulletin board. Personal memoing and email communication can be used for routine communications of routine changes.

Organisations are described as **transformational** when they have the ability to simultaneously manage structural and strategic changes. We use the term 'learning organisation' to describe organisations which 'encourage continuous learning and knowledge generation at all levels, have processes which can move knowledge around the organisation easily to where it is needed, and can translate that knowledge quickly into changes in the way the organisation acts, both internally and externally' (Senge, 1991).

The **learning organisation** is based on effective communication channels enabling strategies to be quickly adopted and adapted in response to ongoing feedback.

CASE STUDY

Creating a key strategic change at Blue Circle Cement

Like many companies in the UK in the late 1980s Blue Circle Cement was desperately in need of change. Blue Circle is the UK's largest cement producer, supplying about half of the country's needs. In the mid-1980s it was decided to make a major investment in new highly automated, computer-controlled plant in a small number of cement works. It was decided that cement works which developed the new technology would also pioneer new modern work practices involving greater empowerment of employees.

The UK cement industry at the time was characterised by high manning levels of both salaried staff and hourly paid workers, relatively low wages and high overtime levels. A working week in excess of 60 hours was common. Restrictive working practices were the norm with strict demarcation between crafts and between process and craft workers. Productivity was very low and the amount of supervision was high. Morale was poor and conflict was common. Management and employee relationships were characterised by low levels of trust and an adversarial culture which talked of 'them and us'. All change was regarded with extreme suspicion.

Compounding the situation was the lack of international competitiveness, in particular in Europe. In the 1980s the UK cement market was in steep decline and under increasing threat from lower-priced imports.

It was obvious that the organisation could not continue this way. Radical changes were needed to ways of working and to the culture of the organisation. A new vision was needed for the organisation as well as a radical change in working practice. Trade unions representing employees of Blue Circle agreed to support the change initiative, subject to negotiation with the view to creating a shared vision.

First it was decided to identify best practice (that is, the benchmarks in other companies). Visits were made by a joint group of management and shopfloor representatives to encourage growth of a new team spirit. The result of this research, fact finding, analysis and discussion was the creation of a new vision of how the business units could run. The shared vision for the future was to have a highly skilled and flexible workforce, working as an integrated team which, together with the new technology, would be able to compete with the best in the world.

Key elements of the new strategy were:

♦ enhanced skills for individuals with a reduction in the number of job grades, leading to greater flexibility
♦ introduction of a simple pay structure with the elimination of paid overtime and bonuses and increased basic wage levels
♦ significantly reduced manning levels and a reduction in total labour costs
♦ new ways of working based on increasing teamwork and shared decision making.

Team training was seen as being essential to build the new organisational structure on which the strategy depended. It included everyone in the workplace and consisted of four main elements.

♦ A senior managers workshop. This looked at all aspects of team building, leadership and teamwork, including the nature of high-performance teams and how they could be structured.

- ◆ Staff team training. This was given to all middle managers and supervisors. It focused on how to put teamwork into operation.
- ◆ Team leader briefings. These prepared the team leaders for the workshops with their teams.
- ◆ Team building workshops. The workshop was the key element of the change process. During the workshop, an important part of the leader's job was to make the team comfortable with new ways of working. The emphasis was on participatory and co-operative approaches that represented the new way of working in the organisation.

The new strategy involved a major shift in the use of new technologies at Blue Circle and changes to the structure of the organisation. It took two-and-a-half years to implement the new strategy but by the early 1990s the plant which pioneered the change had become among the most productive in Europe.

ACTIVITY

1   How substantial was the change in strategy at Blue Circle?

2   What was the relationship between the new strategy and the structure of the organisation?

3   What were the main processes of communication involved in the change?

4   How important was effective communication to making the changes work well?

5   What part did the creation of teams have in ensuring an effective communication process?

Project teams

A useful way of delivering strategy is through project teams. **Project teams** work towards achieving given objectives tied to the overall strategy. In a learning organisation the work of these teams is likely to lead to changes in the organisation's strategy over a period of time.

In terms of strategy implementation it is important to establish project teams with a responsibility for ensuring that different components are delivered. For example, at board level in a major company there will be a project team with overarching responsibility for strategic implementation. The team will need to work with clearly defined objectives in line with the mission of the organisation. Its job will be to oversee the various stages of strategy implementation. Where changes of strategic direction are taking place, a key part of the remit of the team will be the management of change and the development of new working practices in the organisation (as illustrated by the Blue Circle case study).

The central project team will then need to establish a range of project teams responsible for the implementation of strategy at other levels within the organisation, for example in specific business units, plants, and so on. This cascade process for strategic implementation will only be effective if objectives are clearly delineated, and there is a clear sense of where responsibility lies in terms of strategy development and the management of change.

Identification of team and individual roles

Kerry Napuk (1996) suggests that implementation of corporate strategy will be most effective where the organisation appoints teams to solve problems and implement the strategies. 'Every implementation team should have an identifiable leader. The importance of action teams cannot be ignored. The most effective way to get anything done in an organisation is to create a highly motivated team, provide a clear but tight brief, give the team authority and then monitor progress.'

For project teams to be successful they need to have clear, agreed, shared objectives, coupled with an effective communication system. Team roles and individual roles need to be clearly identified if clashes and confusion are to be avoided.

In completing a project successfully there needs to be a framework of guidelines within which to work and often a given timespan for completion of the project. Different individuals have different skills and it is therefore helpful to allocate team roles on the basis of individual skills and aptitudes.

Meredith Belbin (1981) identified a number of characteristics that different individuals can contribute to teams. Individuals will contribute in a number of areas but their particular strengths lie in specific areas. The contributions that individuals can make to teams relate to leadership, providing ideas, resolving conflicts, gathering and analysing information, developing relationships within the team, and carrying out detailed procedural work. It can be seen that a balance will be required if a team is to successfully manage tasks allocated to it.

For example, we can relate this to the development of departmental strategy. It is to be hoped that there will be people who can:

♦ come up with innovative and creative ideas
♦ draw out the contributions of quieter but intelligent thinkers
♦ make sure that the fine detail of the strategy is carried out, and so on.

Temporary project teams can play an important part in helping to manage strategic change in an organisation. Peters and Waterman (1982) show that such a team is often in evidence in the most successful large companies. Teams of managers are brought together from across the organisation to work on a particular project for a period of time before returning to their normal jobs. Because these teams may be short-lived, there needs to be a particular clarity about roles and responsibilities in the team: the objectives of the team and the individual objectives within it. Temporary project teams are particularly effective in bringing about change, particularly where the managers concerned have developed experience of managing the change process.

Responsibilities and targets

Within a team structure it is essential to set out a clear definition of an individual's role. Performance can then be measured against agreed targets. In this way, individual and team targets can be set and progress monitored.

Within individual teams clear accountability needs to be set out in relation to assignments; in other words, who does what and who is responsible for what? **Accountability** is a key ingredient of management delegation and performance measurement.

We have already examined the way in which an organisation establishes objectives in order to pursue its general aim, or mission. It is helpful to establish objectives at each level within an organisation so the individuals know what is expected of them. Responsibility for achieving these objectives will then rest with the relevant individual and with his or her supervisors in a hierarchical organisation.

Budgets

Budgets are another approach used to translate strategic plans into concrete activities. Budgets can be planned for all sorts of organisational activities, for example to set production targets, sales targets, use of materials targets, and so on. Responsibility can be allocated to ensuring that budgets are met, and this can then be used as a measure of performance and to outline possibilities for improvement.

Milestones

Milestones are very effective in establishing defined points to measure progress and hold team managers accountable. Each milestone must be defined clearly and be achievable. Milestones need to be tied to strategies to have meaning, and they have to be clearly communicated and accepted by the teams and individuals who are to reach them.

CASE STUDY

Tight or loose?

H. E. Wrapp in the *Harvard Business Review* (1967) argues the case for imprecision in creating targets and objectives in organisations. He asks, 'Why does the good manager shy away from precise statement of his objectives for the organisation? The main reason is that he finds it impossible to set down specific objectives which will be relevant for any reasonable period into the future. Conditions in business change continually and rapidly, and corporate strategy must be revised to take the changes into account. The more explicit the statement of strategy, the more difficult it becomes to persuade the organisation to turn to different goals when needs and conditions shift.'

Wrapp suggests that in creating responsibilities and targets in organisations it is healthy to rely on a certain degree of looseness. The tighter you wrap things up the less capable will individuals be of meeting challenges and responding to change. This provides a salutary lesson to those who see corporate strategy as a tight and scientific approach to achieving results.

ACTIVITY

1   What do you think: should managers set targets which are tight or loose?

2   Give specific examples of objective setting to illustrate your points.

Programme of activities

A programme is a statement of the activities or steps needed to accomplish a single-use plan. It makes the strategy action-oriented. For example, a pharmaceutical company may establish a specific programme of research activities for its cancer-treating drugs. A training programme might be devised to develop an understanding among employees of how to use a particular Information and Communications Technology package.

In implementing a strategy, a number of programmes will need to be implemented to secure the effectiveness of the strategy; for example, there may be programmes associated with retrenchment, such as a closure programme, or a programme associated with the launch of a new product.

Programmes can be differentiated from Standard Operating Procedures (SOPs) which are systems of sequential steps or techniques that describe in detail how a particular task or job is to be done. They typically detail the various activities that must be carried out in order to complete processes in an appropriate way.

Benchmark targets at different levels of the organisation

A benchmark is a selected measure for comparison. By establishing benchmarks an organisation is able to identify the best possible standard within the organisation and within the organisational environment in order to establish targets that enable the organisation to lead the field.

Benchmarking seeks to compare the competence of an organisation and parts of that organisation with the 'best in the field'. By making this comparison it becomes possible to identify the size of the gap between what you are currently doing and what can be achieved. The aim is then to close the gap.

A number of organisations circulate managers with information about their current performance (or the performance of the unit they manage), and comparison figures for other units within the organisation (and in the industry). Managers of underperforming units can then get in touch with better performers to try and identify where they are going wrong.

In establishing targets at different levels of the organisation, it is helpful to use benchmarking as a framework for continual improvement of the organisation. Rather than simply asking 'how can we improve?', it makes more sense to ask 'what targets do we need to achieve to keep up with the best?'

Resource allocation

An important part of strategic implementation is that of allocating resources in order to support strategies.

The key resources of any organisation are:

◆ finance
◆ human resources
◆ materials
◆ time.

Finance

Budgeting is an important aspect of strategy implication. The various components of a business organisation need to put in bids for financial resources. Financial resources are not infinite and therefore central strategic planners will need to decide how to allocate finance in such a way as best to meet the mission and objectives of the organisation.

The strategic planning process will identify priorities for the future. For example, an organisation that is focusing on product development will want to see resources being channelled towards new products and to the departments responsible for product development. At the same time finance will be channelled away from 'dogs'.

In deciding on the allocation of finance, a number of factors will be considered using projected financial ratios, for example return on capital invested, projected profit percentage figures, and so on.

The emphasis on finance found in most organisations stems from the profit objective. An organisation that concentrates on primary profit

targets is able to establish a clear pattern of objectives, all directed towards the bottom line. For example, Figure 7.39 shows that at every level in the organisation the primary objective is profit. However, this is a simplistic view because most organisations work to meet a number of criteria apart from short-term profits.

Figure 7.39   Drilling down profit objectives

Human resources

Planning for **human resources** is one of the most important resourcing areas. Human resource planning can only be effective if personnel are regarded as a key factor by management. The human resource director should play a central role in top-level corporate planning, and human resource managers should have a key input to business unit and operational plans.

From the organisation's point of view the purpose of human resource planning is to identify and meet future labour and staff requirements. This involves employing the right people, at the right time, with the right skills and commitment.

Human resource planning needs to be considered in the same way as investment in products, that is, strategically.

Creating a human resource plan involves:

◆ forecasting likely future demand for labour and the future supply of labour in order to estimate and then fill any gap

♦ analysing and improving the present use of the existing resource; a human resource management approach recognises people as the most vital resource and tries to create genuine job satisfaction and commitment in the workplace.

Materials

An organisation will only be able to deliver an effective strategy if it can deliver the materials in the right places and at the right times: this is the function of **logistics**. In recent years we have learnt a great deal from the Japanese about Just-In-Time (JIT) approaches to stock control and inventory levels.

Johnson and Scholes (2002) alert us to the importance of effectively managing each of the key ingredients of the value chain and the links in this chain. Three of Porter's primary activities in the value chain – inbound logistics, operations and outbound logistics – are all directly concerned with the handling and processing of materials. If the organisation is going to meet customer requirements in the marketplace, then it is necessary to make sure that all materials conform with requirements (the quality hallmark). An appreciation of the importance of resources such as materials reinforces the understanding that strategy is as dependent on effective operations as operations are on effective strategy: what is required is a top-to-bottom integrated emphasis on total quality standards within the organisation.

Time

Another strategic resource that is often overlooked is that of time. There is never enough time to achieve everything that an organisation would like to achieve. It is therefore a matter of prioritising the use of this scarce resource so that strategies can be implemented on time.

CASE STUDY

The .com boom

At the turn of the new millennium everyone heralded the .com boom that was expected to transform the economy. The shares of new high-tech companies soared while those in what was referred to as the old economy slumped.

A range of new Internet businesses sprung up – clothing retailers, on-line information services, and many more. Most of these ventures were based on exciting new ideas, and it seemed as though massive fortunes would be made overnight. Share prices soared in the high-tech sector and with them the fortunes of the .com entrepreneurs.

Unfortunately, however, what many people had overlooked was the importance of timing and the development of a long-term plan. While these businesses were able to attract large (sometimes very large) sums of investment capital, the businesses would take a long time to form into viable organisations. Starting a business from scratch means that not many people know about its products and services. As a result a lot of money is needed to advertise the websites and the new brands.

We all know what happened next. Many of these organisations ran out of time. The pot of investment capital ran out before they were able to make the sorts of sales required to break even and then prosper. Given more time many of these businesses would have thrived; instead it was parts of the 'old economy' that really benefited. Existing firms that already had established reputations and brand names followed the .com entrepreneurs into e-tailing, and website selling. Indeed they were able to take on skilled employees that were shaken out by the .com collapse.

The .com boom and bust provides an important lesson in timing. Time is a scarce resource. If you are not careful you will run out of time before your strategy starts to take effect. As a result you need carefully to plan the use of your time to concentrate on the essential aspects of the strategy.

ACTIVITY

1 Can you think of businesses that went under during the .com boom and bust? What do you think that these businesses did wrong?

2 Can you name others that have survived? Why do you think that these others survived?

An important way to manage time as a strategic resource and to make sure that tasks are completed within their deadlines is 'ABC' analysis, which is a value analysis on the use of time. This analysis is described in Unit 1, on p. 14.

Review and evaluation

It is essential to evaluate the benchmarked outcomes in given time periods in relation to corporate operational and individual targets.

A control tool is a mechanism for controlling a plan or activity. If performance does not meet the required standard then actions are put in place to rectify the situation.

Control needs to take place at four levels within the organisation:

♦ strategic level control
♦ management level control
♦ operational level control
♦ individual level control.

Control processes make it possible to check that objectives have been met, and to make adjustments to strategy as and when appropriate. In order to be able to control performance, managers need to be clear about targets and must be able to measure performance against benchmarked targets. Managers therefore need clear and common measurements in all areas of business. These measurements need not be rigidly quantitative, nor need they be exact. But they have to be clear, simple and rational. They have to be relevant and direct attention and efforts where they should go.

The sorts of analysis that an organisation will need for control purposes would include the items in Figure 7.40.

Analysis of	Used to control
Financial analysis	
Ratio analysis	Aspects of solvency, liquidity, profitability
Variance analysis	Costs and revenues
Cash budgeting	Cash flows
Capital budgeting	Investment
Market analysis	
Market share analysis	Competitive position
Market research information	Types of goods and services offered
Sales analysis	
Sales budgets	Effectiveness of selling
Human resource analysis	
Labour turnover	Workforce stability
Work/output measurement	Productivity
Physical resource analysis	
Product inspection	Quality

Figure 7.40   Analysis necessary for an organisation to evaluate performance and to take control

Managers need to have the information that is required to measure performance against benchmarks. By evaluating performance in this way it then becomes possible to work towards meeting targets and hence organisational objectives at all levels within the organisation.

Gap analysis is a useful evaluative tool. It is used to determine the gap between what a company, unit, team or individual's performance is and what it could be. We can illustrate gap analysis with reference to the 'profit gap', which outlines the gap between what a company's profits might be and what they are likely to be if it carries on operating as it is at the current time. The benchmark can be both the organisation's potential and the industry's current performance.

The gap provides a useful warning: 'If we don't do something to change the way we are working we will start going backwards.' The starting point is to set out the desired profit target on a graph (see Figure 7.41 where for simplicity's sake this is shown as a straight line). The profit target is set out over the next few years. The second stage is to draw a profit forecast based on the assumption that the organisation makes no changes in its range of operations.

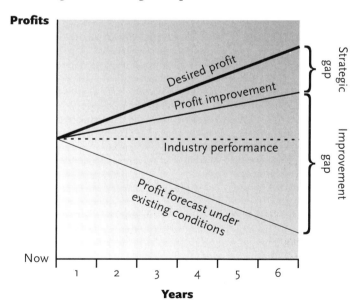

Figure 7.41   Gap analysis

There are three main ways of making the projections for this line:

- the sum of the profit targets for individual operating divisions (probably the simplest method)
- a model of the organisation's profits given certain assumptions
- total up the results of the operating plans of all managers.

Whichever method is chosen, a line can be drawn showing the expected profit. Very often this line will move down, simply because by standing still in a competitive environment profits are likely to fall; divisional and line managers know this only too well.

Two more lines can be drawn on the graph:

- The industry performance line, which shows the return on an equivalent investment made within the industry in which the organisation is operating, for example by looking at figures for other companies. This will be easier if there is a similar organisation operating in the same industry.
- The profit improvement line, which shows the improvements that could be made to profits by altering strategies in the existing sectors of the company.

The **improvement gap** identifies the scope for improvement by altering strategies in the existing sectors of the company. The **strategic gap** shows the scope for improvement by invigorating the organisation, by implementing new strategies, including movement into new sectors and activities.

Gap analysis identifies the importance of continued transformation of an organisation in dynamic markets. It is often complicated and time-consuming to prepare and requires detailed forecasts and information. It may require more than just financial information.

Research and assessment

There are many useful articles about current strategies of leading businesses that regularly feature in the national business press, for example business supplements to national newspapers. *The Times 100 Online* outlines a range of interesting and up-to-date strategy case studies. The *Journal of Business Strategy*, and *Strategic Management Journal* both feature a range of up-to-date articles about corporate strategy coupled with detailed analysis of this field.

Strategy in action **JOURNAL ARTICLE**

The article starts out by outlining the story of how chief executives of Coca-Cola famously scoured the back streets of major cities as well as small rural villages to find places where Coca-Cola was not readily at hand, and shortly after the local representative who accompanied them would make sure that it was there. This was all part of a strategy of making sure that the product was everywhere to win global dominance. Coca-Cola has an unrivalled record of global success in an industry that is mature in the United States.

However, in addition to this growth story what is frequently missed out is that the company's success is also a result of the way in which business design was altered so that Coca-Cola has become responsible for the provision of the syrup and the advertising while Coca-Cola bottlers are responsible for the manufacture of the product and its distribution across the globe. In effect Coca-Cola has become the 'value-chain manager'.

Rick Wise then goes on to examine a number of other major companies and their success and failures before going on to show that in the modern fast-changing world there are new factors driving the success of a business strategy. In the past companies could rely on such strategies as differentiation, growth, and economies of scale.

Rick Wise suggests that other companies can follow the Coca-Cola lead to reap the benefits of new business design leading to clear financial benefits, as well as creating a common understanding of business strategy development with partners and all members of the organisation.

Wise, R. 'Why things got better at Coke', *Journal of Business Strategy* 1999, Jan/Feb, pp 15–19.

Today's key elements of successful strategy are based on having a consumer-focused strategy, an emphasis on what the future market environment will look like, and most important 'an emphasis on the strategic dimensions that drive shareholder growth'.

While in the past strategies focused on a small number of product-centred elements, today business design needs to focus on five elements which create shareholder value:

- customer selection: choosing which group of customers offers the most potential for growth
- value capture: how the organisation gets rewarded for the value it creates for customers: it is not just about selling a product or service, it is about earning revenue from all of the other things that go with the sale, for example providing finance for customers, selling an ancillary product, and so on
- strategic control: the company's ability to retain customers and profits – for example by having a product which is well ahead in time of rivals, having a trusted brand, and so on
- scope: choosing the range of products and service offerings that customers will continue to find relevant to them
- organisational systems: having the organisation organised in the most suitable way to meet the other four dimensions.

In his article, Rick Wise explains how Coca-Cola has achieved each of the five design dimensions outlined above. The key was in developing new relationships with bottlers (to win superiority over rival Pepsi).

Coca-Cola broadened its definition of 'consumers' from consumers of soft drinks to consumers of liquids. As a result it changed its strategy in relation to distribution. Instead of focusing on supermarkets it examined how it could increase distribution in vending machines and restaurants, for example setting up a division to help restaurant chains expand internationally.

Coca-Cola changed the scope of its business: for example, by 'forward integration' into soft drink bottling, acquiring some bottlers and purchasing controlling positions in others. Coca-Cola provided bottlers with capital to invest in vending machines.

Coca-Cola focused bottlers on higher profit market segments.

Coca-Cola established strategic control through its strong position in the high profit vending and cooler segment, and through a low-cost distribution system, when it aligned the interests of its previously fragmented independent bottling network.

Coca-Cola changed its organisational system, emphasising skills critical to bottling management, such as plant operations and regional marketing and distribution.

ACTIVITY

Discuss the following questions in your group.

1 What do you see as being the prime elements of Coca-Cola's effectiveness in developing a global brand and a global market?

2 What aspects of customer focus highlighted in the case study do you see as being particularly relevant to this success?

3 How has Coca-Cola been able to generate shareholder value?

4 Why is the 'value chain' so important to Coca-Cola's success?

5 Apply the key points relevant to Coca-Cola's success to another organisation with which you are familiar.

Competitive analysis

JOURNAL ARTICLE

This article starts off by outlining how recently a leading technical provider in the life sciences area was taken unawares by the competitive actions of a rival. The rival had appeared to be lacking in resources, and only had a limited market share. However, the company had overlooked its rival's technical and business relationships.

The author, Darrell Mockus, therefore suggests that it is important to identify, map and analyse what your competitors are doing, because failure to do so might mean that they suddenly steal a march on you.

In particular study the relationships that your competitors are developing, and how they structure their products and services to build such relationships. By uncovering these relationships you are better placed to find out additional information about your rival.

Mockus, D. 'Competitive analysis: do you REALLY know what the competition is doing?', *Journal of Business Strategy*, 2003, Jan/Feb, pp 8–10.

The relationships Mockus described in his article can be mapped in a diagram which gives you a much better picture of your rival. The diagram can look something like Figure 7.42.

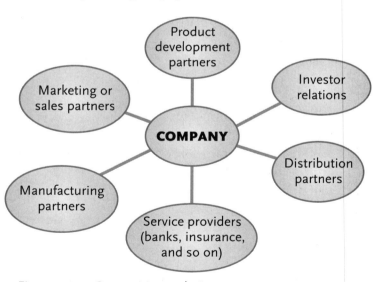

Figure 7.42   Competitive analysis

By analysing these relationships it is possible to develop a much clearer picture of your rival's strategy and its strengths and weaknesses, as well as your own strengths and weaknesses.

ACTIVITY

1 Carry out a competitor analysis for the rival to a firm with which you are familiar.

2 What does the competitor analysis tell you about the strengths and weaknesses of the rival, and the strengths and weaknesses of your company?

End of unit assignment

This assignment can be researched by using company websites, journals, newspapers and magazines, and interviewing key personnel in a targeted organisation.

Completing the assignment will show that you can successfully meet the outcomes for this unit.

Outcome 1
Analyse how the business environment is considered in strategy formulation

1 Describe the mission (and/or vision), strategic intent, objectives, goals and core competencies of a chosen organisation.

2 Explain how stakeholder analysis is useful in gaining an understanding of the chosen organisation's strategy.

3 Conduct an environmental and organisational audit of that organisation.

4 Identify the strategic position of the chosen organisation.

Outcome 2
Understand the process of strategic planning

1 Demonstrate an ability to think strategically in planning and organising your business planning assignment (cite evidence of your strategic thinking).

2 Prepare a strategic plan for the organisation that you are investigating based on your background research for Outcome 1.

Outcome 3
Examine approaches to strategy evaluation and selection

1 Evaluate possible alternative strategies: substantive growth, limited growth or retrenchment in relation to strategies currently being undertaken by well-known organisations (use articles from the press).

2 Identify and evaluate resource requirements to implement a new strategy for a given organisation. This could be the organisation studied for Outcome 1, or it could be for another organisation with which you are familiar (examine key resources, finance, human resources, materials and time).

Outcome 4
Analyse how strategy implementation is realised

1 Compare the roles and responsibilities for strategy implementation in two different organisations (this task is best carried out by groups of students focusing on separate organisations and then comparing results).

2 Identify and evaluate resource requirements to implement a new strategy for a given organisation (as above).

3 Propose targets and timescales for achievement in a given organisation to monitor a given strategy.

References

Belbin, M. (1981) *Management Teams: Why they Fail or Succeed*, Oxford: Heinemann.

Drucker, P. (1989) *The Practice of Management*, Oxford: Heinemann.

Mintzberg, H. (1994) *The Rise and Fall of Strategic Planning*, London: Prentice Hall.

Peters, T. and Waterman, R. (1982) *In Search of Excellence*, London: Harper and Row.

Porter, M. (1980) *Competitive Advantage*, London: Collier Macmillan.

Porter, M. (1985) *Competitive Advantage: Creating and Sustaining Superior Performance*, London: Collier Macmillan.

Porter, M. (1998) 'What is strategy?' in *The Strategy Reader*, Oxford: Blackwell Business.

Sadler, P. (1994) *Designing Organisations*, Stroud: Mercury.

Senge, P. (1991) *The Fifth Discipline: The Art and Practice of the Learning Organisation*, New York: Doubleday.

Thompson, J. L. (1995) *Strategy in Action*, London: Chapman and Hall.

Thompson, J. L. (2001) *Strategic Management*, 4th edn, London: Chapman and Hall.

Further reading

Coulter, M. (2001) *Strategic Management*, 2nd edn, London: Prentice Hall.

Dransfield, R. (2001) *Corporate Strategy*, Oxford: Heinemann.

Johnson, G. and Scholes, K. (2002) *Exploring Corporate Strategy*, London: Prentice Hall.

Lynch, R. (2000) *Corporate Strategy,* London: Prentice Hall.

Thompson, J. L. (2001) *Understanding Corporate Strategy*, Stamford: Thomson Learning.

Journals and newspapers

Financial Times (London)

Videos

'John Harvey Jones: Trouble-shooter' series
'Blood on the carpet' series
'The Business'
'Trouble at the Top' series
Other business series, often from BBC2

Useful websites

www.hemscott.net/
www.Bloomberg.com
www.emerald-library.com/EMR/
www.ft.com
www.tt100.biz

Unit 8

Foundations of marketing

Marketing is about understanding the customer and ensuring that products and services match the existing and potential needs of the customer. Marketing is also about looking at ways of influencing the behaviour of customers.

In this unit you find out about the marketing process by looking at the evolution of the marketing concept, before looking at how marketers use segmentation, targeting and positioning to provide a distinct edge for their organisation. You will also look at marketing strategies by focusing on the marketing mix and learn to appreciate the different types of markets and contexts served through effective marketing.

Summary of learning outcomes

On completion of this unit you will be able to:
♦ investigate the concept and process of marketing
♦ explore the concepts of segmentation, targeting and positioning
♦ identify and analyse the individual elements of the extended marketing mix
♦ apply the extended marketing mix to different marketing segments and contexts.

Chapter 1

Concept and process of marketing

How easy it is to take all that we have for granted! Wherever we look there are advertising messages bombarding us with images of goods or services designed to provide us with more choices and a better lifestyle. Shops, mail order services and even the Internet provide us with the opportunity to buy almost anything we want, as long as we have the money, or credit. It was only in 1942 that Joseph Schumpeter, the great Austrian economist, wrote, 'Queen Elizabeth I owned silk stockings. The capitalist achievement does not typically consist in providing more silk stockings for queens, but in bringing them within the reach of factory girls in return for steadily decreasing amounts of effort.'

Today we live in a **market economy**, in which many consumers have been able to enjoy the range of goods and services that were previously afforded only by kings and queens. The existence of a market makes it possible for consumers to express their preferences for the goods and services they would like, and prices act as signals to suppliers informing them which goods are most in demand.

Figure 8.2   Modern shoppers can have virtually anything they want

In this marketplace today's consumer indicates to suppliers through their purchases what should or should not be produced for the market. In effect they have become like royalty.

This sounds dramatic, and it is. We live in a consumer world, full of messages relating to our lifestyle. From the moment we are born we use a huge range of products and services associated with living in the western world in a new millennium. Even only forty years ago, life for our parents and grandparents was ostensibly very different. It is easy to take all of this for granted. We may think of marketing only as an academic discipline, but it is a tangible link between organisations and their commercialisation, and their success or otherwise, which simply affects how we live through the products and services we enjoy.

Figure 8.1   Modern royalty: historically, monarchs could have whatever they wanted

CASE STUDY

What sort of life do you want?

Recently a reporter travelling around the world said that she thought that the 'peoples of the world's poorer nations only think they want to emulate America ... They want what we have – but they don't realise how ugly it is,' she said.

Her argument was based upon how Americans simply take their wealth for granted. She implored her fellow Americans to 'stop using so much ... stop driving everywhere or carpool, stop wearing clothes that have brand names on them, stop using paper napkins for everything, stop using paper cups, carry your own travel mug, read Julia Hill's book, *One Makes a Difference*.'

It could be argued that in the developing world products have more meaning, simply because there are fewer. As a result people look after them and think about how best to use and conserve their resources. A CNN news reporter recently said, 'I think the developing world has a lot of lessons for us as Americans in terms of limiting our consumption and reducing our waste.'

ACTIVITY

1 How do the sort of goods and services required by individuals from poorer nations differ from those taken for granted in the West?

2 What are the problems and issues with having too much (such as obesity, pollution) and how might these be damaging western society?

3 What can the West learn from the developing world?

4 Who are the winners, the 'have-nots' or the 'haves'? Discuss your answer.

Definitions of marketing

There are a number of definitions and interpretations of marketing and practices related to marketing. As a result, if you ask a number of different people what marketing is, you may well receive a number of different responses, all of which might be right, each in their own particular way. Here are some examples.

> The Chartered Institute of Marketing (CIM) defines marketing as, 'The management process responsible for identifying, anticipating and satisfying customer requirements profitably.'

This definition provides an important starting point to gaining a clear picture of the major issues facing a market-focused organisation.

There are a number of key words in that definition:

◆ **Management process**: this indicates the level of importance of marketing decisions. Successful marketing requires managerial input because it requires constant information gathering, as well as analysis of data in order to make decisions.

◆ **Identifying**: this involves answering questions such as 'How do we find out what the consumer's requirements are?' and 'How do we keep in touch with their thoughts and perceptions about our goods or service?'

◆ **Anticipating**: this takes into account that consumer requirements change all the time. For example, as people become richer they may seek a greater variety of goods and services. Anticipation involves looking at the future as well as at the present. What will be the Next Best Thing that people will require tomorrow?

◆ **Satisfying**: this involves meeting consumer requirements. Customers seek particular benefits. They want the right goods, at the right price, at the right time and in the right place.

◆ **Profitability**: the margin of profit motivates organisations to supply goods to consumers in a market. Of course, profit may be simply one motive for supplying goods to a market. Others may include market share or market leadership. A recent major study of some 1700 companies showed that marketing-orientated firms have enhanced profitability. Good marketing therefore helps managers to improve the performance of their part of the business and meet the most basic of business objectives, profit.

One of the key components of marketing therefore is anticipating market needs and opportunities.

The American Marketing Association (AMA) defines marketing thus. 'Marketing is the process of planning and executing the conception, pricing, promotion, and distribution of ideas, goods, and services to create exchanges that satisfy individual and organisational goals.'

The key element within the context of this definition is that they emphasise the planning and strategic elements of marketing. In other words it is about using information, presumably from market research, to plan and then take action to provide goods and services that satisfy both individuals and organisations. The link between the consumer or the receiver of the goods or services and the organisation are the actions that an organisation takes in providing the good or service, such as pricing, promotion and distribution.

Marketing is therefore the process through which Jaguar is able to identify the kinds of cars that people will want to buy in the near future, and the features that should be built into those cars; it helps Reebok anticipate changes in consumers' preferences for trainers and Sky Television to identify the types of channels that viewers will want to watch in the future.

Every organisation needs to have clear goals, and the major route to achieving organisational goals will depend upon **strategy**. It is important, therefore, to be clear about the difference between strategy and tactics. These terms originate from military use (military strategy before and during a battle is the general policy overview of how to defeat an enemy). Developing a strategy involves looking at the whole of an organisation and trying to understand how it meets its goals. Tactics are more specific actions taken as part of that strategy that help it to meet its objectives.

It could therefore be argued that marketing can be seen as the process of developing and implementing a strategy to plan and co-ordinate ways of identifying, anticipating and satisfying consumer demands, in such a way as to help an organisation to meet its objectives, and that it is this strategic process that is at the heart of marketing.

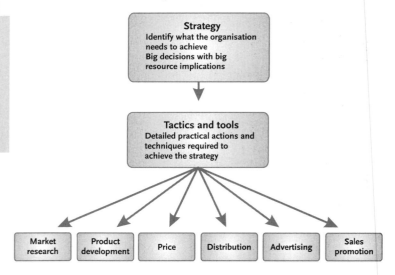

Figure 8.3 Marketing strategy and tactics

Marketing within business strategy

Business strategy is concerned with the big decisions that organisations make. This may involve substantial implications for the whole organisation that influence the future of a business for a long time to come. For example, a strategic decision for a car manufacturer may be to produce a new model of a car. This may involve channelling resources into building a new factory, re-financing the business as well as employing new workers and developing the awareness of this new model.

An organisation with a strategy knows where it is going, because it is planning ahead. Marketing strategy is concerned with successfully identifying and meeting the requirements of customers so that the organisation can meet a range of objectives (see Figure 8.4).

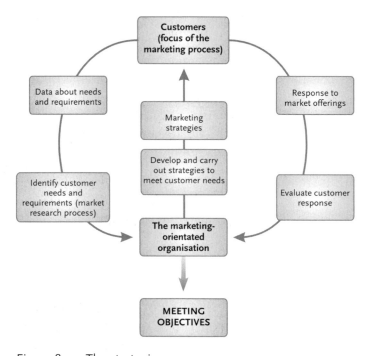

Figure 8.4   The strategic process

Because modern organisations focus so much attention on the customer, marketing today has come to be seen as a strategic discipline. Marketing strategies are the means by which organisations attempt to find out exactly what their customers want and then to influence customers in a way that is favourable to the organisation.

Marketing strategies require detailed research to find out:

♦ about the customers' requirements
♦ the right products to develop to meet customer needs
♦ how to position the product or service in relation to other products and services
♦ the right marketing mix.

It has also been said, again using military parlance, by the Chartered Institute of Marketing itself, that 'marketing is the generalship of business'. Certainly, marketing has increasingly become a key area within all types of organisations, in both the public and private sectors. It helps them not only to compete, but also to function. Marketing is also being increasingly viewed as a total business concept, with an acceptance that everybody within an organisation, no matter what their role, has something to do with marketing. For example, as I, a university lecturer, sit here in my office writing this, the quality of the dialogue that I produce for you will help determine how palatable this book is. Similarly as I, later in the morning, go into a classroom to teach my students, the quality of my teaching is a product provided by my institution that will have an impact upon how they, as customers of the university, perceive the service they are receiving.

ACTIVITY

Think about your role at work, whether you work full time or part time. Describe how the activities you perform, in one way or another, contribute to providing some element of customer satisfaction.

Satisfying customers' needs and wants

Philip Kotler (1996) provides a much more practical definition of marketing when he describes it as 'the performance of business activities that direct the flow of goods and services from producers to consumers'.

Customers, being human, are all different. But only a few companies can provide products specifically for each individual customer. Most marketing activities are designed to meet the needs of groups of customers within a market.

A market is made up of actual or potential buyers of a product and the sellers who offer goods to meet buyers' needs. The market for computers is composed of existing owners and prospective buyers of computers, and manufacturers such as Dell or Acer who make them available for the public. A market requires a process of exchange between buyers and sellers.

The first challenge is to find a set of customers and identify their needs so that appropriate goods and services can be developed. Once organisations have a product, then marketing processes are used both to communicate with customers and also to distribute the goods or services to them.

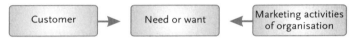

Figure 8.5   Satisfying customers' needs or wants

In recent years we have seen increasing efforts to meet the individual wants and needs of customers. Where the individual needs of each customer are met in a particular way, this is known as **customisation**. This has been particularly noticeable in service industries, where services like delivering parcels, guarding property or maintaining equipment can be developed to meet the need of each individual customer.

ACTIVITY

The chances are that if you asked a group of teenagers what is 'hot' right now they would identify a series of brand names you have never heard of. From music to footwear, jeans to phones, the emerging generation plugs into new ideas at a phenomenal rate. They do not want what everyone else has. They take huge comfort from the fact that what they know and like is unknown. In your group, discuss the implications of this for marketers of large brands.

Exchange relationships

The exchange process lies at the heart of modern marketing. Henry Assael (1993) defines the exchange process as, 'a dynamic process in which a seller

requires payment to satisfy a buyer's need for a valued object or service'. There are four main parts to this process:

- two or more groups participate
- each party must possess something of value that the other party desires
- each party must give up something of value for something of value: the satisfaction of both parties is dependent on the excess return over investment
- the parties must communicate, so that they generally know about the product of value becoming available.

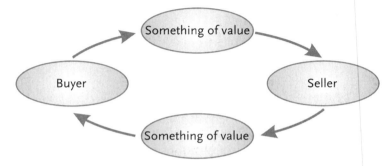

Figure 8.6   The exchange process

The key component of exchange in all advanced economies is a **price mechanism** that reflects the value of the good to the buyer. I may be willing to pay £7000 for a Ford Ka, but if it rises to £8000 I might buy some other type of motor car.

Another key ingredient of exchange is **communication** from seller to buyer, to inform buyers about product characteristics, price and availability. Increasingly, such communication takes place through sophisticated forms of advertising as well as through face-to-face interactions.

Delivery of value is the other important ingredient of exchange. Marketing has been described as 'selling goods that don't come back to people who do'. If you do not give value for money, goods may be returned, and your customers are likely to abandon you.

In the long term, the success of an organisation may depend on its ability to provide customers with value for money through the exchange process.

Changing emphasis of marketing

One of the key factors in any market is the existence and strength of competition. In a competitive environment organisations are forced to be on their toes. They cannot allow rivals to gain advantage by offering lower prices or goods that customers perceive to be substantially better.

In order to be successful, organisations will gear their activities to being better than their competitors, and to keeping up with any improvements that competitors make. For example, in the UK newspaper industry we find that newspapers in a similar market segment, such as tabloids, tend to have similar prices. They also have similar stories, offers and promotions such as scratch-card games. In fact the tabloid press is known for the 'spoil up': a process whereby one newspaper tries to spoil another's exclusive by creating a similar story of its own.

You only have to walk down the aisle of a local supermarket to appreciate the large number of competing brands of products. From time to time a new product will arrive which is subtly different from existing brands. If the new product is successful this will lead to a flurry of business activity as existing producers try to produce rival versions. For example, the introduction of 'I Can't Believe It's Not Butter' by Van der Bergh Foods, led to the development of numerous products that not only looked the same but also had similar brand names. Marketing in any organisation must constantly seek to enable the organisation to manage the effects of change and competition. In other words, marketing today is about constantly changing and refining an organisation to meet the needs of its customers better than its competitors, in whatever way it can. This used not to be the case.

ACTIVITY

What is the purpose of marketing?

In your groups, discuss the statement: 'Marketing, therefore, is concerned with attempting to reduce risk by applying formal techniques systematically to assess the situation and develop the company's response to it.'

The marketing concept

The evolution of marketing

In a relatively short period of time organisations have moved forward from **production orientation** to **sales orientation** and more recently to **marketing orientation**.

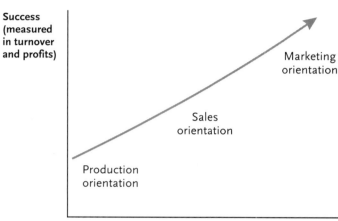

Figure 8.7   The rise of market orientation in business

In a market dominated by production orientation, manufacturers feel that they know what is best for customers. When there is little competition, for example where there is only one supplier of telecommunications services in a particular geographical area or where there is only one producer of motor vehicles, organisations may not have to pay close attention to customer needs.

As consumer incomes began to rise after the Second World War, standards of living began to improve. It was over this period that:

♦ rising disposable incomes meant that consumers could choose from a broader range of goods
♦ consumers started to shop around
♦ increasing amounts of information became available for consumers
♦ there was an increased number of sellers
♦ the increased scale of production led to longer production runs and falling unit costs of production
♦ there was more choice for consumers.

During the 1950s and 1960s emphasis was therefore upon sales orientation. Harold Macmillan claimed that 'You've never had it so good!' and the focus was upon trying to persuade customers that they needed the goods, rather than attempting to find out about the needs of the buyers. This was the time of 'piling it high and selling it cheap'.

Marketing orientation is all about focusing the activities of organisations on meeting the needs of consumers. It means that the consumer is the driving force behind everything that an organisation does. No longer is marketing something that is simply added on to a number of company functions. Today, the customer drives all of the activities of a market-focused organisation.

Few organisations today operate in a static world. Today we live in a global marketplace for many goods and services in which technology, purchasing power, tastes and many other factors are changing at the same time. In adapting to many of these changes, good marketing is a key factor.

Unfortunately, over the course of time, many organisations develop a product orientation rather than a market orientation. Marketing orientation is based on the belief that if organisations do not satisfy the needs of customers they will not survive. It is therefore essential to match the production and development of goods and services with the identification and anticipation of customers' desires and requirements.

It is important then for organisations not just to look at their competitors' products, but also at how they deal with their customers. Customer needs and requirements are identified in every area of organisational activity, from the original idea and then design right up until the final sale and then after-sales support.

Marketing orientation can be contrasted with production and sales orientation. A production-orientated company holds the view that products will tend to find their own markets if they can be produced cheaply and be of good quality. Such companies spend relatively little time investigating consumers' wishes. As a result they often come to grief because, although their products are good in a technical sense, they do not provide the benefits that consumers require.

A sales-orientated company holds the view that success depends on effective advertising, selling and promotion rather than on achieving a real difference between the product it is selling and those offered by its competitors. This philosophy will fail if consumers shop around.

The real distinction between a marketing orientation and a sales orientation is that selling tries to make the customer want what the company has; marketing on the other hand tries to make the company produce what the consumer wants.

ACTIVITY

Use an example of an organisation known to you to describe how it anticipates market needs and opportunities. Show how the development of products or services it provides has been market led. How do you think that consumer opinion was researched?

Societal issues and emergent philosophies

Some critics of marketing see it as a selfish discipline that supports societies focused on self-interest. By seeking to meet the individual needs and wants of consumers it may be overlooking the greater social good. For example, a rich consumer in Western society may be enchanted by the complicated packaging and charm of a throwaway modern product. However, in terms of environmental and ethical standards the product may have many negative features.

Phil Kotler (1991) suggests that we ought to take a wider view of the marketing concept. 'The societal marketing concept holds that the organisation's task is to determine the needs, wants, and interests of target markets and to deliver the desired satisfactions more effectively and efficiently than competitors in a way that preserves or enhances the consumer's and the society's well being.'

This broader definition requires marketers to balance the interests of consumers who have wants and needs to be met, and business organisations who need to make profits, with the wider goals and aspirations of society.

> Societal marketing = Balance of interests of consumers, the organisation and wider society.

A good example of an organisation that has firmly opted for societal marketing in recent years is the Co-operative Retail Society. The values expressed by the organisation include, 'honesty, openness, social responsibility and caring for others'. The Co-op is putting its declared values into practice via its Responsible Retailing Strategy (RRS), and a campaign for honest labelling.

The American Marketing Association (AMA) has established a code of ethics to provide guidelines for ethical conduct, which states that, 'Marketers shall uphold and advance the integrity, honour and dignity of the marketing profession by being honest in serving consumers, clients, employees, suppliers, distributors and the public.'

CASE STUDY

Can we trust food labels?

How far do we believe what we read on food labels? Manufacturers in the UK were criticised by the National Consumer Council (NCC) over misleading food labels when the findings of a new report suggested that labels are more likely to confuse and mislead consumers than inform them.

The report prepared by the NCC claims that the sheer number of labelling schemes has caused confusion among consumers who do not know what the labels mean. NCC chairman Deirdre Hutton said, 'Our research shows that consumers do not understand what the majority of logos mean. What is needed are credible labelling schemes which have great potential to inform consumers and offer them real choices.'

Findings suggest that consumer confusion is caused by the fragmented approach to the way that food labelling schemes are developed and the sheer number of schemes. One consumer is quoted in the report as saying, 'We want honesty, to be told the truth in black and white. A clear definition of what it stands for, up front, enabling consumers to make their own choice based on thinking and their pocket.'

The issue of food labelling is one which simply refuses to go away, and is in fact gaining in momentum. The UK Consumer Association, voicing its concern over misleading logos, launched the 'Honest Labelling' campaign, but the issue was already a cause for concern as far back as 1993, when Sustain (the alliance for better farming and food) launched the Food Advertising Project to ensure that food advertising encourages healthy eating to help improve the health of future generations.

Undeniably, manufacturers and retailers need to find routes to gain the advantage in an ever more competitive market. But it is undoubtedly in the interest of both the consumer and the food industry that the issue of food labelling is tackled once and for all. Enough talking, it's time for action!

ACTIVITY

1 What responsibilities do food manufacturers have when they promote their products?

2 To what extent and in what circumstances might food labels be unethical?

3 Identify other promotional practices that could be cited as being unethical.

4 To what extent are your own values associated with the word 'unethical' and how might those values relate to your work within an employment context?

Customer and competitor orientation

In addition to customer focus, many organisations orientate their marketing activities towards finding out what the competition is doing. Competitor activity provides one of the biggest threats to a business organisation.

Henry Assael (1993) argues that, in general, before 1975 business firms were not adequately evaluating competition when developing marketing strategies. He says that most companies would 'embark on a certain course of action and then react to competitors' responses'. Today, businesses are far more competitor orientated than in the past. They carry out an **environmental analysi**s, which involves looking at their own strengths and weaknesses as well as external threats and opportunities. Business organisations are now very much concerned with ways in which they can cut costs, while at the same time increasing productivity and the value they are able to add to products for consumers.

Competitor orientation sits alongside customer orientation: they are the driving forces which constantly encourage organisations to make sure that their offerings provide more value for money than those of rivals. Indeed, competitor orientation is in many ways another form of customer orientation. Your rivals will provide a threat if they have a better understanding of customer wants and needs than you have.

Efficiency and effectiveness

The prime cost of marketing activities is in the use of scarce resources such as time, money and people. It can be argued that the more an organisation spends on marketing activities, the less would be available for other key functions within an organisation. Marketing is an expensive function which involves either running a marketing team and paying for a range of activities or the contracting out of marketing services.

For marketing to be cost effective it needs to be built into every aspect of what an organisation does, rather than being a 'bolt-on extra' competing for resources against other parts of the organisation. Real marketing encourages product and technology developments rather than trying to mislead consumers about products. From a societal point of view some people see marketing as bordering on the unethical when tools such as advertising are used to create 'false needs' in gullible consumers. Marketing should be about finding out consumer wants and needs in order better to serve these needs, and should involve the optimal use of resources in an organisation to serve the customer with quality products.

ACTIVITY

In your group, discuss how you would justify increases in expenditure in a marketing department of an organisation, when budgets for other parts of the organisation are being cut.

Limitations of the marketing concept

Do not believe that marketing-orientated organisations are always good. They may have good products and appear to be well positioned in the minds of their consumers, but do their customers really need their products? It could be argued that if we focused more upon our basic needs, fashion or cosmetic industries could be construed as unnecessary. There are a number of arguments that put marketing activities into context. For example, it could be claimed that:

♦ expenditure on marketing is wasteful and could be used for other purposes
♦ marketing activities may serve to distort the marketplace, with those providing the strongest messages taking the lion's share of the market
♦ consumers may be confused by the messages
♦ a market that is dependent upon promotional activities may be distorted by the largest advertisers
♦ consumers simply view the product and the marketing surround and do not think about all that has gone into delivering it to them.

Consumer protection

It is often argued that marketing creates needs in consumers that many did not realise they had, and certainly could do without. For this and other reasons, such as consumer protection, consumers need to be better protected as and when organisations use persuasive messages and actions. For example, they may need to be protected against:

- poor quality services or damaged goods
- goods or services which failed to match the descriptions applied to them
- manufacturer's or supplier's negligence affecting the safety of the product or service
- breach of contract
- misleading offers, information, advertising or labelling
- unfair terms in contracts
- monopoly control or lack of competition limiting the quantity and/or quality of a product and resulting in artificially high prices.

Greater equality, freedom of speech, improved educational standards, increased government regulation, and vastly improved communications are all factors which have encouraged greater consumer power. Consumers today expect a product to be safe and to perform and function well. They also feel that it is important to be protected against questionable products and practices. Marketers are expected to behave in a socially responsible manner. The newspapers and the consumer organisations are there to bring wrongdoers to the public attention, and the law courts are there to punish offenders when necessary.

Voluntary and statutory controls as well as the formation of active pressure groups, which often gain popular support from the media, have helped to develop a changing climate for marketing activity.

Organisations today can no longer disregard groups of consumers, or wider issues in which they should be involved, and have to show increased sensitivity to their many publics.

Advertising Standards Authority

The Advertising Standards Authority (ASA) was set up in 1962. It is an independent body that exercises control over all advertising except that on radio and television. This includes:

- the press: national and regional magazines and newspapers
- outdoor advertising: posters, transport and aerial announcements
- direct marketing: including direct mail, leaflets, brochures, catalogues, circulars, inserts and facsimiles
- screen promotions: including cinema commercials and advertisements in electronic media such as computer games, video, CD-ROM and the Internet
- sales promotions: such as on-pack promotions, front-page promotions, reader offers, competitions and prize draws.

The Authority draws up its own codes which it uses to ensure that advertisements are 'legal, decent, honest and truthful'. Advertisements should be prepared with a sense of responsibility both to consumers and society and conform to the principles of fair competition. The ASA has no statutory powers to force companies to comply with its rulings but relies on consensus, persuasion and an effective network of sanctions which stem from its own authorship of the codes.

The ASA identifies a number of advantages of self-regulation over a legislative process. The ASA process is accessible – with complainants needing only to write a letter to initiate action – and fast, with no complex legal procedures to undergo. This means the ASA can secure the withdrawal of misleading or offensive advertisements within a very short time. The process is free, with complaints investigated at no cost to complainants and incurring no legal fees.

It is argued that in many instances the ASA's codes go further than the law requires, and while the ASA does not enforce the law, it will refer complaints which fall directly under legislation to the appropriate law enforcement body. Should an advertiser refuse to remove an advertisement the ASA could use a number of sanctions to enforce its decisions, such as:

♦ adverse publicity generated by monthly reports of adjudications
♦ refusal of media space
♦ withdrawal of privileges such as discounts and incentives resulting from membership of advertising bodies
♦ legal proceedings against persistent offenders.

British Code of Advertising Practice

Advertisers, agencies and the media whose representatives make up the **Code of Advertising Practice Committee** support the British Code of Advertising Practice. This code sets out rules which those in the advertising industry agree to follow. It also indicates to those outside advertising that there are regulations designed to ensure that advertisements can be trusted.

Chartered Institute of Marketing

The Chartered Institute of Marketing has its own code of practice to which members are required to adhere. The code refers to professional standards of behaviour in securing and developing business, and demands honesty and integrity of conduct.

British Standards Institution

Voluntary subscriptions and government grants finance the British Standards Institution. Its primary concern is with setting up standards that are acceptable to both manufacturers and consumers. Goods of a certain standard are allowed to bear the BSI kitemark, showing consumers that the product has passed the appropriate tests.

Professional and trade associations

Professional and trade associations promote the interests of their members as well as the development of a particular product or service area. In order to protect consumers, their members will often set up funds to safeguard consumers' money. For example, the Association of British Travel Agents (ABTA) will refund money to holidaymakers should a member company fail.

Business ethics

Ethics are moral principles or rules of conduct generally accepted by most members of society. Most organisations today believe it is necessary to take up a stance that shows the public they operate in an ethical manner. Emphasis on the interests of the consumer is a key aspect of many organisations.

Some ethics are reinforced through the legal system and thus provide a mandatory constraint upon business activities, while others are as a result of social pressure to conform to a particular standard.

Potential areas of concern for organisations include product ethics, where issues such as genetically modified foodstuffs or contaminated food may seriously and quickly affect short-term demand. For example, criticism of marketing various baby milk products in developing countries resulted in widespread criticism and boycotts of powdered milk manufacturers.

Another area of concern relates to business practices, where restrictive practices and poor treatment of employees have been highlighted in the media and businesses have faced criticism from the public. Trading policies of companies who buy cheap imports from overseas organisations involved in 'sweat-shop labour', or who trade with businesses employing young children in unacceptable conditions, have also faced critical scrutiny from both the media and the public.

Environmental performance

With many companies' environmental performance becoming central to their competitiveness and survival, a range of new tools of environmental management have been developed. They include **environmental impact assessments**, which assess the likely impact of major projects, and **environmental audits** or eco-audits, which involve carrying out an audit of current activities to measure their environmental impact. Alternatively, by looking at the environmental impact of a product through its lifecycle, from the sourcing of raw materials to the final disposal of waste products, a **product lifecycle analysis** can be established.

Organisations face many potential dangers with regard to ethics and public opinion. No organisation is capable of satisfying all stakeholders, but by becoming good corporate citizens and being socially responsible they can generate considerable goodwill. This strategy can be developed as a marketing advantage.

Marketing process overview

All businesses operate within an environment of change. Some of these may be relatively slow, for example a steady change in the population that may be predicted. Other changes may be rapid and dramatic, such as the sudden development of new technological processes, the entry of new competitors into a market or simply the fickleness of consumer demand.

If a business wants to succeed, it needs to be able to anticipate and be ready for all types of change. The key is to build a flexible organisation that can adjust quickly to new changes.

ACTIVITY

Make a list of five rapid changes and five relatively slow changes which are taking place in the environment of a business with which you are familiar. What can an organisation do to anticipate and respond to these changes?

In this world of change it is imperative that organisations think and plan ahead. In order to do this they need to understand the environment in which they operate and be able to make strategic decisions based upon their own capabilities. This is at the core of the process of marketing planning. According to Henry Assael (1993) a marketing plan is 'a corporate game plan that will map out where the

ACTIVITY

In your group, discuss the truth of the statement that, 'A business is only as good as its next product'.

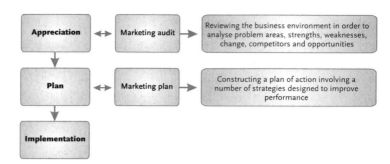

Figure 8.8   Creating a marketing plan

company should be going over the next five years and how to get there'.

Marketing is therefore used both as a means of assessing past performance (its traditional function), for analysing its business environment and for evaluating future courses of action.

It is argued that good marketing involves:

♦ looking outwards in order to respond to changes in markets, business conditions and competition
♦ looking inwards in order to develop the organisation so that it can meet all of those consumer needs which have been identified by the marketing process.

Figure 8.9   Ensuring a good fit between the external environment and the resources of an organisation

A widely used model for strategic marketing is based upon the three elements of strategic analysis, strategic choice and strategic implementation. The auditing process is primarily concerned with the first stage, that is, strategic analysis (see Figure 8.10).

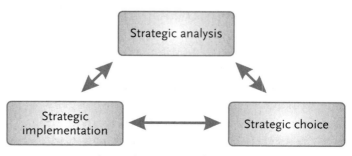

Figure 8.10   A three-phase model for marketing activity

Strategic analysis

Strategic analysis is concerned with understanding the strategic position of an organisation. For example, in what sort of environment are we operating? What is the scope of our operations? How can we match our activities to our environment and our resource capability? Do we have marketing systems, policies and activities that will enable us to meet our objectives?

These questions are really about matching what an organisation intends to do with the reality of the marketing environment. The strategic reality for the organisation is shaped by the nature of the environment in which it operates. Strategic intentions are concerned with plans and proposals for the future. These intentions must be based upon a thorough knowledge of the environment if they are to be realistic.

Strategic choice involves:

♦ setting out a menu of strategic options
♦ comparing the options provided by the menu
♦ choosing the best option from the menu.

Strategic implementation involves putting the chosen marketing strategy into action.

Remember that this model should be viewed by an organisation as an ongoing process based upon continuous analysis of the business environment through which information and data filter through to help to evaluate performance and influence business strategies.

Marketing audit

The word 'audit' means a review or appraisal of a business function or activity. A marketing audit is therefore a review that includes the strategic thinking behind marketing plans as well as a review of the detail of marketing operations. It can be defined as a systematic and critical review and appraisal of the total marketing operation, which includes the basic objectives and policies of the operation and the assumptions that underlie them, as well as of the methods, procedures, personnel, and organisation employed to implement the policies and achieve the objectives.

Marketing audits are used to assess past and present performance as well as to evaluate possible future courses of action. Today, the audit is no longer seen as a process that is carried out only to deal with problems, but as a systematic, ongoing check on organisational performance.

The audit should concern itself with every aspect of marketing activity, and should take place at regular intervals because the marketing environment is constantly changing. Also, it should be carried out independently, by a team of marketing auditors.

Integrated marketing

A company structured in a traditional way will have individual departments dedicated to a specific discipline, such as sales, marketing, market research, customer service, advertising, promotion, public relations, trade shows, events, information technology, manufacturing, and distribution. The problem is that these departments may operate as separately run units within their own little worlds. For example, instead of working together, each department may have their own agenda.

Integrated marketing brings together all of an organisation's marketing strategies under a single vision. This means that instead of working in opposite or complementary directions departments are working in harmony, pursuing the same goals by sharing strategies.

Figure 8.11   Integrated marketing

CASE STUDY
Nielsen McNally's Online Marketing Audit

The following extract appears on Nielsen McNally's website.

♦ Improve your marketing
♦ Develop a marketing Action Plan
♦ Increase your profits

With the online Marketing Audit!

The Marketing Audit provides an easy and cost-effective access to professional marketing advice, in the form of an interactive questionnaire.

By completing this questionnaire, you can discover hidden weaknesses in your strategy, and learn how to correct them. You can also use the questionnaire to adjust your marketing priorities, giving most effort to those activities that work best for you.

The questionnaire generates a priority list for you automatically. It also helps you to schedule the activities in your priority list, using a built-in Gantt chart.

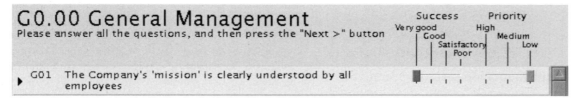

Figure 8.12   Simply answer the multiple choice questions

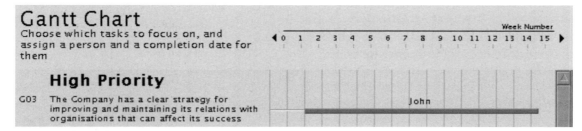

Figure 8.13   Use the built-in Gantt chart to create your Action Plan

ACTIVITY

1   Why might customers want to use a marketing audit?

2   What sort of issues might it highlight?

3   Use an example to describe the extent to which these issues might be dealt with through using some form of marketing audit.

Within the integrated marketing model, the enterprise becomes a cohesive unit with a single overall goal based on maximising awareness among the target audience and making sure that consistent policies are distributed across all marketing-related departments so that everyone is working together towards the common goal.

Marketing integration provides organisations with a competitive edge by focusing all of the sales, marketing, and other resources on pursuing the same direction and promoting the same message. At the same time, it stops parts of an organisation from working in isolation.

Environmental analysis

The student of marketing needs to bear in mind that the key feature of markets is change. Indeed Charles Handy, the UK's foremost business guru, has stated that, 'in today's marketplace the only constant is change' (Handy, 1994). The marketing environment includes the influences and trends outside the organisation which affect its ability to meet customer needs. Generally, the two most important external influences on an organisation are its customers and its competitors. It is necessary to develop a strategy that will establish an advantage over competitors while meeting customer needs.

Business organisations need to scan the market environment to identify likely changes and their implications for the organisation. Organisations need to understand the key changes that currently face them, as well as likely future changes, if they are able to plan for change, and react to changes effectively.

SWOT analysis

A particularly useful approach to examining the relationship between an organisation and its marketing environment is to carry out a SWOT analysis. A market environment analysis should start by identifying those influences that have been particularly important in the past, then looking at those that are prominent today, before trying to identify those that are likely to be most significant in the future.

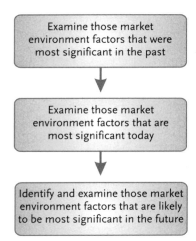

A SWOT analysis sets out to focus upon the Strengths, Weaknesses, Opportunities and Threats facing a business or its products at a given moment. It includes both an internal and an external element. The internal element looks at current strengths and weaknesses of the organisation. The external element looks at the opportunities and threats present in the environment in which an organisation operates.

Within the organisation (internal)	In the external environment (external)
Strengths + positive	Opportunities + positive
Weaknesses – negative	Threats – negative

Figure 8.14 SWOT analysis

Carrying out a SWOT analysis requires research into an organisation's current and future position. The analysis is used to match an organisation's strengths and weaknesses with the external market forces in the business environment.

As a result of carrying out a SWOT analysis an organisation should go on to develop policies and practices that will enable it to build upon its strengths, minimise its weaknesses, seize its opportunities and take measures that will cancel out or minimise threats. The SWOT is thus sometimes called 'the planning balance sheet'.

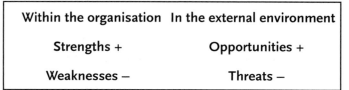

Within the organisation	In the external environment
Strengths +	Opportunities +
Weaknesses −	Threats −

Figure 8.15   The planning balance sheet

A simplified SWOT analysis of a business organisation might show, for example, that it has the following:

Strengths

♦ good product
♦ good relationship with customers
♦ good management team

Weaknesses

♦ operates on a small scale
♦ regular cash-flow problems
♦ deals in a limited market

Opportunities

♦ new and rapidly growing markets
♦ changing tastes of consumers
♦ could diversity into a number of product lines

Threats

♦ growing competition from rivals
♦ recession leading to poor demand in the economy
♦ development of foreign competitors

Marketing objectives

Marketing objectives are an essential part of the marketing plan as they provide direction for activities to follow. Without clear objectives it is difficult to evaluate what a marketing plan is trying to achieve or whether a plan has been successful. It is usual to translate marketing objectives into quantifiable 'result areas', such as market share, market penetration or growth rate

of sales. Some of these may be further broken down into specific sales volumes, value goals or geographical targets. Marketing objectives may have a time frame and direction. They also provide a basis for evaluation. Marketing must ensure that organisational activities are co-ordinated in a way that marketing objectives are met.

Marketing objectives should therefore be:

♦ **achievable**: they should be based upon a practical analysis of an organisation's capabilities
♦ **understandable**: they need to be clear so that everyone knows what they are trying to achieve
♦ **challenging**: they should be something for which everyone has to strive
♦ **measurable**: quantification makes it possible to record progress and to make adjustments if marketing objectives are not being met.

For example, if market research indicates that people who visit multiplex cinemas are unwilling to stand in the rain queuing for an hour for the last seat to be sold just in front of them, then it is essential for the organisation to find solutions. In Manchester the UCI multiplex has a bank of 90 telephone operators at the end of a Freephone number taking nationwide bookings. Consumers can say where they want to sit. The transaction takes on average 64 seconds. Marketing thus has a responsibility to ensure that all aspects of the way in which an organisation operates are geared to meeting consumer requirements.

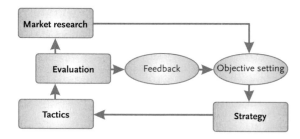

Figure 8.16   A cycle of marketing activities

It is important that marketing objectives provide a direction for activities to follow and make sense in terms of the marketplace and the SWOT analysis. The logical approach is to start with broader objectives which can then be translated into quantifiable results areas such as market share, market penetration or growth.

Constraints on marketing activities

Every organisation involved in marketing activity is faced with a number of constraints that may limit their activity. They then need to work within these constraints.

Internal constraints

Internal constraints relate to the resource capabilities of an organisation. For example, an organisation might identify potential customers but how capable is it in meeting their needs? It might not have the resources to follow the direction that it wants to adopt.

When a company wants to develop new products or services it needs the resources to finance expansion. The bigger the scale of the development projects, the more resources are required. Sometimes companies finance expansion by selling off existing assets; for example, ICI has moved into higher value-added chemical products, such as components for lip glosses and eye shadow. To finance this move it sold off a number of its existing heavy chemical plants which had low long-term profit potential.

In addition to financial resources, business organisations need the skills and know-how for a range of marketing activities. Increasingly, companies rely on buying in expertise from outside the organisation.

External constraints

External constraints involve a series of factors within the business environment in which an organisation operates that limit in one way or another their activities.

Consumers

If an organisation is not market-focused or if consumers are not interested in a product, then it will be difficult to market.

Competitors

It may be difficult to market a product for which a competitor already has an advantage.

Economy

In a period of economic recession when consumers have falling incomes, it may be difficult to market a luxury product.

The law

There may be a number of laws constraining the activities of a business and making it difficult for it to do well.

The market-focused company will fully research all of these constraints and try to find solutions that enable it to turn weaknesses into strengths and threats into opportunities.

Options

In carrying out marketing activities a range of options will always be available to the organisation. This is why the process of marketing audit, environmental analysis, SWOT analysis, setting objectives and understanding constraints is so important. The sections described within the marketing process stress the depth of research that is necessary for making successful marketing decisions. Armed with a series of reports and sets of information, marketers must make a choice between a number of options.

The best choice will depend on the nature of the organisation, the type of market and competitive environment in which it competes, the customer groups it serves and whether the organisation is a risk taker or is risk averse. It will depend on estimations of the size of opportunities in the marketplace and the uncertainty of the environment in which the organisation is operating.

CASE STUDY

Becoming millionaires

Dan and his younger brother Ron are experienced market traders, flitting from one market to another across south-east London. They are self-motivated entrepreneurs whose main aim in life is to become millionaires. As small businessmen, they do not always find life easy.

Dan was recently offered the opportunity to buy some of the latest videos, which were claimed to be 'above board'. This was a big opportunity to expand the business, with an up-to-date consumer product that will bring in the punters. The great benefit is that if customers are interested in the videos, Dan knows that he can do a deal with some quick-boiling kettles he bought a few weeks ago that he has had trouble selling. The kettles look smart but actually take 15 minutes to boil.

Dan's real problem is that he has not got the ready cash to buy the videos. Ron never has any money and cannot help. He is wondering about whether to sell off the van to provide him with the capital. The problem then would be that they would have to buy an alternative form of transport such as company mopeds, however this may have the added benefit of allowing them to start some courier work.

Another idea Dan has to expand the business is to use Ron's expertise in information technology to set up training courses. Though Ron was very good with computers, he has not used one for five years, and feels that if Dan is going to do this, they need to buy in help from another person.

ACTIVITY

1 Identify two internal and two external constraints upon Dan and Ron's business.

2 Describe how these constraints limit their activities.

3 Explain how they could or should deal with these constraints.

Planning target markets and marketing mix

Once the organisation has decided on the route it wants to take, through its strategic marketing plans and its product plans, it will need to set out clearly the target market at which it is aiming. Having established this target market it will be best placed to select an appropriate marketing mix. The **marketing mix** includes the range of strategies used to serve its customers. In its simplest form it is sometimes known for learning purposes as 'the four Ps'.

The first element in what is known as the marketing mix is the **product**. Once organisations have a product, then all of the other elements in this marketing mix can be engaged in order to meet customer needs. These may include developing the **pricing** for the product or service provided, working out how to **distribute** (place) goods to the customers as well as how to **promote** them.

Figure 8.17   The marketing mix

ACTIVITY

The purpose of this activity is to undertake a competitive audit.

Identify two market-leading products. These may be in markets such as tomato sauce, chilled ready meals, packet soups, pet food or sectors of confectionery. Use a matrix like the one in Figure 8.18 to make comparisons.

	Product A	Product B
Product	Features Benefits Design Brand Other elements	Features Benefits Design Brand Other elements
Price	High price Market price Low price	High price Market price Low price
Place/ distribution	Availability Types of outlet	Availability Types of outlet
Promotion	Advertising Sales promotions Publicity and image	Advertising Sales promotions Publicity and image

Figure 8.18   Competitive audit

Scope of marketing

According to Sally Dibb *et al.* (1994), 'It is important to study marketing because it permeates society. Marketing activities are performed in both business and non-business organisations. Moreover, marketing activities help business organisations to generate profits and income, the life-blood of an economy. The study of marketing enhances consumer awareness. Finally, marketing costs absorb about half of what the consumer spends.'

This simple interpretation of marketing activities emphasises that marketing affects everybody in one way or another. Because we are bombarded with marketing messages as consumers, we need to understand what is happening to us, and how we are being influenced. These activities are not just from private sector organisations but also from public sector businesses, such as a university which has relentlessly in recent years pursued strategies that have earned it a unique market position. Although Dibb *et al.* talk about profits, the cost element of marketing is simply related to the achievement of marketing objectives, to provide a sound financial base for an organisation.

Simplistically, it could be said that marketing has an influence upon our lives in two ways:

♦ As employees we all, in one way or other, represent our organisation. How well we perform our task will in some way influence how others feel about the quality of service or product they receive. We are, therefore, within the context of a total business concept, involved in some way in marketing.
♦ As consumers, we have to make discerning decisions every day of our lives, based upon our limited incomes. To make the best use of our resources and to make the better decisions we need to understand marketing practices and principles.

Costs and benefits

As with any activity there are both costs and benefits that have to be weighed up against each other. Although the marketing process will always affect everybody in one way or another within the organisation, the amount of emphasis that is placed upon it as an area, at both strategic and tactical level, will depend upon the rewards that good marketing is expected to generate.

Providing customer satisfaction

Peter Drucker (1970) wrote, 'there is only one valid definition of a business purpose: to create a customer'.

519

Having created customers, the next step is to satisfy them; 'customer satisfaction' has become the watchword of business in the early twenty-first century. A key reason for this change is **oversupply**. With the globalisation of markets, abundance has become chronic with the supply of everything from motor cars to microchips. At the same time, today's customers are active participants in the world of change. They are also more demanding, reflected by the rise in disposable incomes fuelled by economic growth. Rising affluence and education have bred a race of highly active consumers who increasingly want what is available in the marketplace to be tied to what they want.

According to Sally Dibb *et al.* (1994), 'Customer satisfaction with a purchase depends on the product's performance relative to a buyer's expectations.' This emphasises that, depending upon the product or service being offered, customer satisfaction will vary, with the product either meeting and exceeding expectations providing them with 'delight' or falling short of expectations and providing dissatisfaction and disappointment.

Figure 8.19   Customer dissatisfaction and customer delight

Customer expectations are complex interpretations of what is offered within a marketplace. Sometimes they are based upon past experiences or the recommendations of a friend. For example, if you have been really happy with a meal from a restaurant, when you go back there again, you expect the same level of cuisine or service. Contented and happy customers will also be prepared to pay more when they are happy with a product.

CASE STUDY
A new customer experience

For the motor industry, Lexus is a relatively young company designed to provide up-market motor cars from a Toyota background. The following is taken from the Lexus website.

'At Lexus we believe what makes owning a Lexus special, unique even, is the way we treat our customers. Which is why, from the company's US launch in 1989, we have put customers at the very centre of our thinking.

'For the first ever model, the LS400, the engineering challenge was for it to drive as well at 80,000 miles as it did at new, recognising the demand for greater quality and reliability. It also offered complete specification, from leather interior to climate control and hi-fi quality audio, making extras obsolete and great value standard.

'We also realised that customer satisfaction was about having the right people as well as the right cars.

'Since 1998 we have been building a totally new network of Lexus Centres across the country, run by teams committed to improving and redefining the luxury car experience.

'Our growing network of showrooms has been designed from the customers' viewpoint – in look and feel, convenience and ease of access. The result is a contemporary luxury environment that encourages customers to feel at home, to relax, browse and enjoy themselves.'

ACTIVITY

1 How important was it for Lexus to establish an up-market image?

2 To what extent does customer service become a product itself when providing high-value motor cars?

3 In what way does the provision of customer service provide Lexus with a strategic opportunity to position itself within the motor marketplace?

Desired quality and customer care

Organisations are finding it more and more difficult to demonstrate product superiority or even product differentiation over competitors, though they are constantly trying and often succeed. Customer service is an area that offers almost endless opportunities for developing product superiority.

The ideal relationship is one where the customer feels that he or she is receiving the **desired quality** and good **customer care**.

Consumers know what they mean by desired quality and the marketer needs to find this out and translate the concept into required goods and services. Desired quality does not necessarily mean the most expensive: it means that the solution best meets a customer's need. For example, in Japan a chain of 'capsule hotels' has been set up for business people in major cities. Each room is only just large enough for a person to lie down and watch TV. However, they are popular because they are 'fit for purpose' in that they meet the needs of busy business people. In contrast, other people prefer to hire a spacious penthouse suite in large hotels. The job of marketing is to identify how different market segments perceive quality and then to deliver a marketing mix that provides it.

It can be argued that initially consumers become aware of products rather than service. However, as competition arrives, companies have to differentiate to maintain their market position through added features and branding. As markets develop, products become technically much more similar. As this happens customer service becomes more important. Initially this involves keeping the product working or providing customers with support, but eventually it moves into customer care, the aim of which is to make sure that the benefits the customer derives are

delivered reliably from the time the customer approaches the supplier.

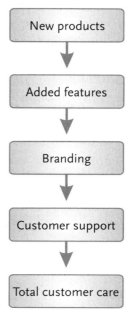

Figure 8.20 The movement towards customer care

Relationship marketing

Building a one-to-one relationship with customers is always ideal. Organisations selling products that must be mass produced tend to use two main techniques to help and build relationships with specific groups of customers.

Market segmentation

This involves producing and presenting different products to suit different groups of customers. For example, a multiplex cinema shows a wide range of films for many different customer groups or segments, such as those for younger children, teenagers, families, twenty-somethings, and older people, all of them comprising different groups of customers, although some may enjoy more than one type of film.

Customer service

The second technique used by organisations aiming to achieve a one-to-one relationship with customers is through the provision of customer service. In one sense, customer service is the overall objective of all that a company does, but the term can be used more precisely to describe a personal relationship between the customer and the organisation and more particularly between the customer and the people who represent the organisation. For example, it would include how the customer is treated by sales staff on the telephone and in the shop, the way in which complaints and queries are handled, and the use of ICT to communicate issues through mailshots and others forms of communication.

In her influential 1992 book *The Popcorn Report*, the American guru Faith Popcorn charts the rise of **consumer bonding** or relationship marketing. The principles that she identifies are encapsulated in the following sentence: 'We do need to build relationships with our consumers, to create a dialogue, expose them to our corporate values, establish a bond based on something more deep-seated that product quality, brand image, or even simply meeting consumer needs.'

The American writers Don Peppers and Martha Rogers (2000) urge organisations to form impregnable relationships with individual customers, and they provide a range of examples of ways in which even mass marketers can strike up relationships. This involves gathering as much information as possible about individual customers and then developing the organisation to meet individual needs. They refer to this as **customer segmentation**.

Peppers and Rogers give the following example of gift order catalogues to highlight their point:

- The customer may order gifts for friends and relatives many months in advance.
- The supplier then schedules the delivery of gifts on the right days.
- The customer would be charged for each gift two days before delivery.
- The customer would receive a reminder postcard ten days before each gift is sent.
- When the annual catalogue is sent to the customer, they would receive a reminder of last year's gifts and addresses.

Although the authors acknowledge that the product must remain important, they identify the change in focus from high quality products towards high quality relationships.

Customer retention

Customers are the most important people for any organisation. They are simply the natural resource upon which the success of any organisation depends. When thinking about the importance of customers it is useful to remember the following points:

- Repeat business is at the backbone of selling. It helps to provide security and certainty.
- Organisations are dependent upon their customers. If they do not develop customer loyalty and satisfaction they could lose their customers.
- Without customers the organisation would simply not exist.
- The purpose of the organisation is to fulfil the needs of customers.
- The customer makes it possible to achieve everything for which the business aims.

Many argue that all organisations have both **internal** and **external customers** (see Figure 8.21). The belief is that the quality of customer service provided outside the organisation is dependent upon how well employees within the organisation treat each other. For example, if an employee makes an enquiry to personnel or writes out a requisition for some stationery, he or she should expect to be treated with the same respect as a customer outside the organisation. This approach helps to encourage the teamwork and customer care which lead towards total quality management.

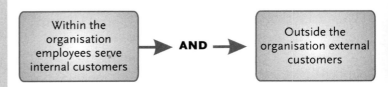

Figure 8.21 Internal and external customers

Many UK companies try to explain the concept of the internal and external customer by referring to the link which starts with the needs of external customers and then includes all of the people involved in bringing together resources to satisfy such needs. Everyone has a role in satisfying customers. This process helps to emphasise that all employees within an organisation are part of a quality chain which is improved with better teamwork, training, employee care and communications procedures.

Though the concept of the internal and external customer is widely used, it has been criticised for focusing an organisation's efforts internally upon itself instead of spending more time and attention upon using resources to satisfy the needs and expectations of external customers.

Customer satisfaction is at the heart of the selling process. One estimate is that it costs five times as much to attract new customers as it does to keep an existing one. The relationship between the customer and the organisation is, therefore, an important one.

According to Sarah Cook's *Customer Care Excellence* (2002) customer relationships can be depicted in terms of a loyalty ladder. The willingness of individual customers to ascend the loyalty ladder will depend upon how they are treated when doing business with the organisation. Well-targeted sales methods and efficient personal service will help to convert one-off purchasers to occasional users, then to regular customers and advocates.

In developing a relationship with its customers an organisation must concentrate on both the selling process and how the relationship between the buyer and seller is managed. This is part of what is widely known as **relationship marketing**, where an organisation has to develop all of its activities in ways which take into account how their activities may affect their relationships with customers. Examples are order times, reputation, the changing of goods or providing of refunds, dealing with faults, correctly addressed letters and the overall efficiency of operations.

In developing suitable ways of meeting the needs of their customers, organisations have to balance their own objectives against the needs of customers. In order to be able to do this they need to understand how customers view their organisation as well as what their customers want from it.

ACTIVITY

On the basis of your own experiences, provide two examples of:

◆ good customer service
◆ poor customer service.

In each instance, explain how these affected your repeat-purchasing patterns.

Roderick M. McNealy, in his book *Making Quality Happen* (1993), refers to the 'making customer satisfaction happen' model (Figure 8.22). This, he claims, is a continuous circular process that provides an equation for satisfying customer needs which can then be used as part of an organisation's strategic approach to business.

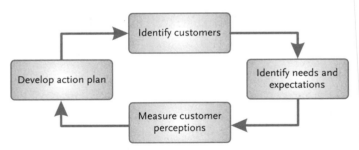

Figure 8.22   The 'making customer satisfaction happen' model

Avis, the car hire company, has a customer care balance sheet which shows the annual sales lost from both customers who complain and from those who are dissatisfied but do not bother to complain. This notion is quite important as it recognises that not dealing properly with customers incurs a significant cost.

Customer requirements

So, what do customers want and how can their expectations be satisfied by the different services and selling methods provided by an organisation? Customers may require any or all of the following:

Quick and easy purchasing procedures

For example, it is important that they understand purchasing procedures. At the same time they may wish to sample products, see how they function or ask for specialist help.

Clear and accurate information

This may refer to products or purchasing procedures and may influence the final decision. In particular, consumers may wish for advice which helps them to weigh up a range of alternatives.

Clear refund procedure

Consumers are much happier to commit themselves to a purchase when they know that if the product does not match up to expectations, is damaged or does not perform to its advertised functions, they can bring it back easily for a refund. Many supermarkets have a refund desk at their entrance, and some large organisations such as Marks & Spencer have a good reputation for dealing with returns.

Easy exchange of goods

Similarly, exchanging goods if they are not suitable helps to provide a service which closely meets the needs of customers.

Complaints procedure

There is nothing worse than customers having their complaints passed around from person to person and department to department. This creates a bad impression of the organisation, wastes time and may cause a lot of personal anguish. An efficient customer complaints procedure may help to retain business that might otherwise be lost.

Special services to meet special needs

Different groups of customers may have different needs. For example, how many stores can deal with wheelchair access or access for mothers with young children in buggies? Similarly, will organisations provide specialist help or a wide range of services for their customers? Does free delivery extend outside the boundaries of a local town? What credit facilities will an organisation provide? Do the opening hours meet the needs of all customers? Does the product range stock provide enough specialist products for all types of consumers? It there a customer helpline, and do customers know about it? Is the organisation willing to order products on behalf of customers?

Customer profitability

Some customers are worth more to an organisation than others. If an important well-established customer decides to shop elsewhere this can have a dire result upon an organisation. For example, when Marks & Spencer decided to source more products from overseas, companies like Courtaulds within the UK were badly affected, and this in a number of instances led to the closing down of factories. A key element therefore within marketing relationships is to appreciate the profitability attached to each customer. If employees understand how much each relationship helps to contribute to an organisation, then they can link their actions to keep customers delighted with products and services in a way that further develops and builds other profitable relationships.

Costs of too narrow a marketing focus

Heavy focusing on marketing within the organisation and product marketing in particular do not come without costs. The prime cost of marketing activities is in the use of scarce resources: time, money, people, and so on. The more you spend on marketing the less you have for other key functions within the organisation. Marketing is an expensive business which involves either running your own marketing team or contracting out marketing services.

Too narrow a focus

A number of factors may encourage too narrow a marketing focus within an organisation:

Design-based products

While many goods and services are designed to meet the needs of consumers, others are created by designers who then need to find a market for their product. Some designers create brilliant products but are then not prepared to compromise design principles in order to best meet customer requirements.

Consumers may then be frustrated by a company that fails to tailor new products to meet customer needs: this is a throwback to product orientation.

Domination of markets by monopoly producers

A pure monopoly exists where there is only one firm in a market, where it can dictate price and supply conditions. The consumer cannot turn to rival products because there are none. This situation can be frustrating. In many areas markets have become more competitive in recent years: examples include telecommunications and opticians. However, this is not always the case. Satellite TV producers often gain exclusive rights to many sporting events, providing the consumer with no choice at all.

Too much choice

Some commentators argue that modern consumers are bombarded by too much choice. There are so many varieties and types of products available to consumers that it is no longer possible to make rational decisions. This is particularly a problem in markets where goods are continually changing, such as home computers.

Total quality marketing

Total quality management (TQM) is a philosophy that shapes relationships between suppliers and customers. Three principles guide the relationship:

♦ The customer is an important stakeholder in a business: quality should be judged by the customer, and all products and services contribute value to the customer and lead to customer satisfaction.
♦ The most productive relationships are the ones where all parties benefit from an activity: there are no winners or losers, but rather everybody wins.
♦ The underpinning basis of any relationship is trust.

Within the context of sales this means that a salesperson must be constantly gathering information on customer needs, informing management of their requirements and contributing to the design of the company's products and the services that support the sale of the products. Within the wider marketing context, total quality marketing involves energising and engaging everybody within an organisation upon the needs of the customer so that they can each appreciate the value of the contribution they make towards customer satisfaction.

The ultimate consumer's perspective

JOURNAL ARTICLE

In academic terms the whole area of marketing can, at the very least, be described as a young and evolving discipline. In a rapidly changing business environment, there is no doubt that marketing will continue to evolve in a variety of ways in years to come.

Svensson argues that, 'the marketer's understanding of the customer's perspective must be extended to including the ultimate consumer's perspective. Therefore, the original significance of the marketing concept is proposed to be extended to comprise the customer's customer and eventually the ultimate consumer's perspective.' He goes on to argue that organisations should not just think of the customer but look beyond the customer to the distribution channel they serve to think of the final consumer. He says that, 'The marketing channel is therefore proposed as having the final consumer market as its starting point, rather than the final one. In consequence, the underlying principle of the marketing concept has to be extended to comprise the customer's customer and eventually the ultimate consumer.' Svensson summarises by arguing that, 'The point of departure for any theory building, modeling, or development of conceptual frameworks must emphasise the customer's perspective and eventually the ultimate consumer's perspective. Subsequently, let us begin the new millennium with an extension of the marketing concept!'

Svensson, G. (2001), 'Re-evaluating the market concept', *European Business Review*, Vol. 13, No. 2, pp 95–101.

Marketing in politics

JOURNAL ARTICLE

Do politicians use marketing and if they do, how well do they market themselves? Does this mean that we simply vote for politicians who provide a political diet closest to our needs? Apparently not so in some research undertaken in Australia by Aran O'Cass.

Aran O'Cass argues that, 'examining political and electoral processes from a marketing perspective offers new insights into the behaviour of political parties. However, research into the marketing activities of political parties is still growing at this stage, and very few papers address the marketing orientation of political parties, while none address the marketing concept.' He presents 'the findings of an exploratory research project carried out in Queensland. The results indicate that key political marketing decision makers within the party examined often have a limited understanding of the marketing concept.'

O'Cass's 'redefinition of the marketing concept into political terms received a high level of acceptance from certain groups of respondents within the study'. His research showed 'that the marketing concept with its customer-centred orientation created a major concern from the perspective of the state executive decision-making category interviewed in this study. This was so primarily because this key decision-making category indicated the role and significance of the voter (customer) in developing the political product is negligible.'

O'Cass, A. (1996), 'Political marketing and the marketing concept', *European Journal of Marketing*, Vol. 30, No. 10, pp 37–53.

Chapter 2

Segmentation, targeting and positioning

Business activities, by their very nature, are competitive. Within a dynamic business environment producers may be constantly entering and leaving the market. At the same time, changing consumer preferences may provide signals for them to develop new strategies with different products and services. Whereas some organisations will succeed and achieve or surpass their marketing objectives, others will inevitably not perform as well.

Market research

In the last chapter we learnt about how market orientation was about 'identifying, anticipating and satisfying customer requirements'. The key issue is, how do organisations do this? Market research is that vital link in the chain between buyers and suppliers. It does this by enabling those who provide goods and services to keep in touch with the needs and wants of those who buy the services.

The American Market Research Association defines market research as, 'The systematic gathering, recording and analysis of data about problems related to the marketing of goods and services.'

We can break this definition down into its various ingredients:

- **systematic**: in other words using an organised and clear method or system
- **gathering**: knowing what you are looking for, and collecting appropriate information
- **recording**: keeping clear and organised records of what you find out
- **analysing**: ordering and making sense of your information in order to draw out relevant trends and conclusions

- **problems related to marketing**: finding out the answers to questions which will help you to understand better your customers and other details about the marketplace.

> ## ACTIVITY
>
> It has been said that 'a problem well defined is a problem half solved'. How might this relate to the context of market research?

Risk

All organisational activities take place in an environment where there is some element of risk. For example, last year a firm might have sold 40,000 fridges to a market in Italy. Who is to say that they will sell the 50,000 they planned to sell this year? They may suddenly find new competitors in this market with a much better product, being sold at a lower price. Italy may go through a cold spell. There may be problems in the economy that reduces the likelihood of people buying a new fridge. To reduce risk, market research provides an invaluable source of information to help organisations to make decisions and develop strategies for products. For example, it could help them to:

- identify their competitors
- improve their knowledge of consumers and competitors so that changing trends can be identified
- use trends to forecast activities
- monitor their market position and develop plans and strategies
- improve their competitive advantage.

Decision making

All organisations require answers to key questions. Answers help decision makers to understand the nature of the decisions they have to make about the products they provide and the markets in which they operate.

   Questions may include:

♦ How do we define the market? What are its features such as size and character, and what is the nature of the competition?
♦ What do customers require? At the heart of marketing should be the ongoing activities of satisfying the needs and aspirations of customers.
♦ Who are the target groups and how do we reach them? The market may be made up of different groups and segments. Different distribution channels may be used to reach different groups of customers.
♦ What strategies are used by our competitors? It is important to know and understand how the actions of competitors might influence the market.
♦ How do we measure our performance? Market performance may be measured according to a number of key criteria, such as the value or volume of sales as well as brand or market share.
♦ Where is our competitive position? An important feature of marketing analysis is an ongoing review of where the organisation is within the market, its competitive advantage and how changes in its actions might influence market shape and market share.

> In short, the purpose of market research is to make the process of business scientific, by cutting out unsubstantiated guesswork and hunches.

CASE STUDY

US government export advice: step-by-step approach to market research

STEP 1 FIND POTENTIAL MARKETS

Obtain trade statistics that indicate which countries import your type(s) of products.

   Perform a thorough review of the available market research reports in the country(ies) and industries in question to determine market openness, common practices, tariffs and taxes, distribution channels, and other important considerations.

   Identify five to ten large and fast-growing markets for the firm's product(s). Analyse them over the past three to five years for market growth in good and bad times.

   Identify some smaller but fast-emerging markets where there may be fewer competitors.

   Target three to five of the most statistically promising markets for further assessment.

STEP 2 ASSESS TARGETED MARKETS

Examine consumption and production of competitive products, as well as overall demographic and economic trends in the target country.

   Ascertain the sources of competition, including the extent of domestic industry production and the major foreign countries the firm would compete against.

   Analyse factors affecting marketing and use of the product in each market, such as end-user sectors, channels of distribution, cultural idiosyncrasies, and business practices.

   Identify any foreign barriers (tariff or non-tariff) for the product being imported into the country and identify any US export controls.

STEP 3   DRAW CONCLUSIONS

If the company is new to exporting, it is probably a good idea to target two or three markets initially.

STEP 4   TEST DEMAND

There are a number of low-cost on-line and off-line services that can help new exporters gauge foreign market interest and collect overseas inquiries.

One	Research brief	Define the problem to be investigated
Two	Plan of work	Specify the data to be collected, the method of collection and the timings
Three	Collection of data	The efficiency of each stage should be checked
Four	Analysis and evaluation of data	Data storage and retrieval using a marketing information system
Five	Presentation of findings	This should be made to management groups and decision makers, together with conclusions and recommendations

Figure 8.23   The five phases of a market research programme

ACTIVITY

1 How difficult might it be for exporters to understand the business environment they will be serving?

2 How might exporters find out about targeted markets?

3 What sort of research is this case study encouraging?

4 Evaluate how an organisation could combat some of the risks associated with exporting.

Stages in market research

The process of market research should not be a 'one-off' activity which takes place as part of new product development. It should be ongoing, so marketers should constantly be collecting and analysing information and feeding it through for planning and decision-making purposes. There are five identifiable stages in the setting up of a market research programme. These are shown in Figure 8.23.

Reactive and proactive approaches

Some organisations are creative in their outlook to planning and research. These businesses may anticipate developments in markets and introduce new ideas and new methods to exploit opportunities or minimise problems. In doing this they may take risks to develop new ideas. In contrast other businesses will wait to see what their competitors do before reacting.

Some businesses therefore use market research to move ahead of the competition while others simply see it as a way of keeping up with their competitors. The first type of firm we would describe as being proactive, while the second we would describe as reactive.

The **proactive** business will be the first to come up with new ideas, and consequently will be well placed to exploit their ideas in meeting adventurous marketing objectives such as brand leadership in a new market. Sony are famous for breaking new ground and taking risks through proactive planning and research.

529

The **reactive** business does not put itself at the mercy of such risk and can never be in a position to make the same sort of impact as a proactive firm. Equally, it does not fall foul of the mistakes made by proactive firms.

Types of research

One of the most important things to remember is that what comes out of market research is only as good as what goes in. Identifying the information required, successfully choosing the most suitable research method and then the type and nature of questioning should all be carefully considered before any project proceeds.

The information gathered through market research may be described as being either qualitative or quantitative in nature. **Qualitative** information informs the organisation about the opinions and preferences of individuals and cannot always be interpreted statistically. For example, in response to a qualitative interview about cakes one person might feel that the cake is too moist and rich, while another might think that it has a rich taste. Qualitative research is therefore about descriptions. This type of information is difficult to categorise and measure because it is based upon personal views deemed to be subjective.

Figure 8.24   Qualitative information

On the other hand, **quantitative** information is research that produces figures that can be examined statistically. For example, 15 out of 20 people might prefer one brand to another. As this is considered to be based upon hard facts, it is considered to be objective.

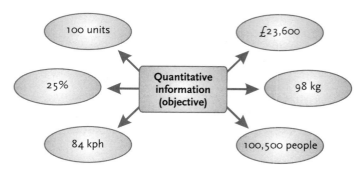

Figure 8.25   Quantitative information

Many research methods supply both qualitative and quantitative information, and the two are closely interlinked. Qualitative information provides the context within which quantitative facts operate. The 'What do you think about … ?' approach gives people the opportunity to offer a variety of opinions, reasons, motivations and influencing factors. A group discussion, for example, allows different opinions to be offered, which will frequently lead to a consensus, giving an idea of the popular view. People enjoy offering their opinions on subjects as diverse as the current political climate and the taste of a particular margarine, and what this gives the researcher is an overall view of that particular audience's reaction to a proposition.

Quantitative data helps to produce an idea of the size and overall shape of markets and the effects of strategies on the demand for goods and services. Qualitative data helps to take this process further to show how goods and services have met the needs of current and potential customers, as shown in Figure 8.26.

Figure 8.26   Supporting quantitative data by qualitative information

There are two broad areas in which market research can take place (see Figure 8.27). If information does not already exist in an identifiable form it will have to be collected first-hand. This is known as **primary research**. Any information that is already published outside an organisation is known as **secondary research** data.

Figure 8.27   Sources of research data

Macro-environment

Organisations need constantly to analyse what is happening within the business environment as it is this that influences whether or not organisations can go on to fulfil consumer needs. According to Kotler (1988), a business marketing environment includes, 'the actors and forces external to the marketing management function of the firm that impinge on the marketing management's ability to develop and maintain successful transactions with customers'.

What this emphasises is that the marketing environment is the outside world faced daily by organisations as and when they attempt to meet customer needs. In order to change and adapt to this constantly changing environment, organisations have to look outwardly at what is happening and adapt inwardly to meet such changes.

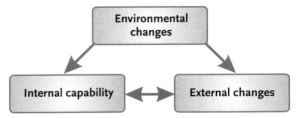

Figure 8.28   Matching the changes within the organisation to changes in the business environment

This all sounds very easy. The real problem is that examining the marketing environment is a difficult thing to do. Gerry Johnson and Kevan Scholes (1997) identify two elements that have to be taken into account when analysing the environment. Firstly, they point to the diversity of influences and issues within the business environment that could affect the organisation. They even emphasise that it is just not possible to 'list all conceivable environmental influences'. Secondly, they refer to the issue of uncertainty. Although many people emphasise that the pace of change is faster than ever before, the real problem is that if you have a large number of uncertain variables in the business environment today, predicting how these variables will change in the future is very difficult indeed.

Environmental scanning

The process of 'knowing the other' is often referred to as 'scanning the environment'. A key part of this is understanding the nature of rivalry in the field and the threat of new entrants. The scanning process may highlight changes an organisation needs to take. For example, J Sainsbury acquired Texas in order to gain a major share of the DIY market. Coca-Cola and McDonald's moved into Russia in order to spread control over market shares in new markets ahead of opposition.

Examining the business environment helps an organisation to develop appropriate marketing strategies including the marketing mix. Important external forces that influence the marketing strategy might include:

♦ the customer: buying behaviour of customers including why they buy, their buying habits and the size of the market
♦ the industry: the behaviour of organisations within the industry, such as retailers and wholesalers, their motivations, structure and performance
♦ competitors: their position and behaviour
♦ the government and regulatory bodies: their influence over marketing and competitive policies.

Selection of an appropriate marketing mix involves creating the best possible match between the external environment and the internal capabilities of the organisation. Though the elements of the marketing mix are largely controllable by marketing managers

531

within an organisation, many of the changes and forces within the business environment are not. The success of the marketing programme therefore depends upon how well an organisation can match its marketing strategies and marketing mix to the external business environment in which it is operating. Developing an appropriate marketing strategy involves creating the best possible match between the external environment and the internal capabilities of the organisation.

PEST model of external forces

One useful way of analysing an organisation's external environment is by grouping external forces neatly into four areas by using a PEST analysis. PEST stands for Political, Economic, Social and Technological influences, all of which are external.

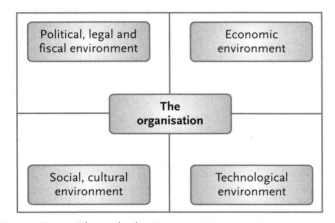

Figure 8.29   The wider business environment

Carrying out a PEST analysis involves identifying the key factors external to an organisation which are in a state of flux and are likely to have an influence on the organisation in the coming months and years.

Whereas identifying these factors is relatively easy, assessing their ongoing impact and effect is more difficult. An effective PEST analysis will be based on detailed research using all of the latest journals and publications. For example, if certain taxes are likely to be lowered, by how much are they likely to be lowered? What will be the impact on the sales of each product? Figures need to be as accurate as possible: if interest rates are expected to go up, by how much will they go up? For how long will they be raised? What will be their impact upon sales and costs?

Political, legal and fiscal factors

Business decisions are influenced by political, fiscal (taxation) and legal decisions. For example, although in recent years many people have been encouraged to become self-employed, there has been a feeling by many of these people that they are over-regulated. These influences might include:

- ♦ changes in the tax structure
- ♦ privatisation
- ♦ the influence of unions
- ♦ changes in the availability of raw materials
- ♦ duties and levies
- ♦ regulatory constraints such as labelling, quality, safety.

The political environment is created by governments and powerful decision makers who are able to create laws, regulations and codes as well as decide on tax levels. For example, the UK government has the power to make anti-pollution laws softer or stronger. The EU has the power to pass laws and regulations affecting all member states.

The way in which business is treated by governments will vary from nation to nation. However, while 20 years ago only about 40 per cent of the world's population lived in a fully functioning market economy, it is now nearer 95 per cent, though some of the new market economies are only rough versions of the genre.

In marketing it is very important to have an understanding of likely changes in the political environment both within the UK and in an international context. It is important to be aware of the way in which the government hopes to reform the macro-market as well as of specific changes that affect individual product markets. In recent years we have seen an increasing consensus in this country that governments need to work to support the smooth running of the marketplace.

Economic factors

Though the economic environment is influenced by domestic economic policies, it is also dependent upon world economic trends. Rates of economic growth, inflation, consumption patterns, income distribution and many other economic trends determine the nature of products and services required by consumers, as well as how difficult it becomes to supply them. Influences might include:

♦ inflation
♦ unemployment
♦ energy prices
♦ price volatility.

Changes in the wider economy usually have a key impact on business fortunes generally. The economy tends to experience a cyclical pattern of rises and falls in economic activity. A boom generates optimism, rising incomes, rising employment, and increases in expenditure: this is a period of well-being for a large number of organisations. In contrast, a downturn in economic activity leads to a fall in incomes, expenditures and sales.

As well as understanding the level of economic activity in the economy, organisations also need to know about the implications of changes in important economic variables such as interest rates, taxation, credit arrangements and the exchange rate. When interest rates rise, this puts a dampener on economic activity because it becomes more expensive to borrow money, and consumers are likely to spend less. A rise in expenditure taxes such as VAT puts up the price of goods, leading to a fall in purchases. If changes in credit regulations make it harder for people to buy goods on credit, this will again lead to a fall in spending.

The exchange rate is particularly significant for organisations that export. A rise in the value of the pound sterling makes UK goods more expensive in international markets, and thus can cause export orders to fall away.

Economic variables cannot be separated; they tend to interact. For example, in a period in which inflation (the general level of prices) is rising, the Bank of England will raise interest rates to cut consumer spending. The rise in the interest rate will tend to lead to an increase in the value of the pound sterling (because overseas investors will get a higher interest rate from holding their money in the UK than elsewhere, and will therefore demand sterling). The economy is usually the main external actor influencing the general level of demand in the marketplace.

Periods of increasing economic activity	Periods of declining economic activity
♦ rising expenditure	♦ falling expenditure
♦ a good time to introduce new products	♦ a risky time to launch new products
♦ a period in which consumers are more inclined to try out new products	♦ a period in which consumers are likely to be conservative
♦ a period in which consumers are more inclined to borrow money, and buy on credit	♦ a period in which consumers put off spending and borrowing
♦ a period in which there may be more spending on luxury items	♦ a period in which consumers may focus more on necessary expenditures

Figure 8.30   Features of increasing and declining economic activity

Social and cultural factors

To understand the social and cultural environment involves close analysis of society. Demographic changes such as population growth, movements and age distribution will be important, as will changes in cultural values and social trends such as family size and social behaviour. Factors might include:

♦ consumer lifestyles
♦ environmental issues
♦ demographic issues
♦ education
♦ immigration and emigration
♦ religion.

Social trends are very important in influencing marketing decisions. Indeed, any serious student of the marketing environment should examine the government publication *Social Trends*, which provides up-to-date information on trends and patterns in UK society. Social trends are concerned with changes in four factors. These include:

- demographics: population size, structure and distribution
- lifestyles: the range of consumer activities, interests, opinions that we associate with a particular group
- cultural values: beliefs shared by a large number of people in society leading to common patterns of behaviour (consumerism, for example, became embedded in the attitudes of large sections of the population in the late twentieth century)
- sub-cultural influences: the values and behaviours that characterise the thinking, beliefs and actions of particular groups within the wider society.

In examining social trends it is important to keep an eye on all the latest information and surveys about spending patterns, about the household and family make-up, about attitudes and beliefs, and so on.

CASE STUDY

New product trends

Boiling eggs for specific entrées or meal options has become a thing of the past in Canada, with the launch of Hard Boiled Eggs from Burnbrae Farms. The eggs are high in omega-3 polyunsaturates and are an excellent source of vitamin E and protein. Produced by flax-fed hens, they are packed in a container. The company suggests rinsing the eggs before use.

Coca-Cola in Japan has launched a new line of canned, ready-to-drink coffees, under the Georgia Area Blend brand. The four varieties in the line-up are formulated specifically for the four different regions of Japan. The variety for the north of the country (Hokkaido) contains more sugar than the other three, to 'combat cold and energise the body'. The Kansai version (for the Osaka and Kyoto areas) has the highest milk content, at 17 per cent, to cater to the local preference towards milky coffee. In the Tokyo metropolitan area, the Kant version has a moderate combination of sweetness and milk to give a refreshing taste. Finally, the Nangoku variety for the south of the country contains more coffee than the others, to give a bitter flavour suited to the more temperate climate.

The Magnum ice cream brand is set to innovate the chocolate confectionery market with the Italian introduction of Magnum branded milk chocolates (made with select ingredients and 60 per cent pure chocolate). It is a surprising, yet logical, entrant, considering the many chocolate brands that have entered the ice cream market, and also considering the diverse interests from the leading players involved in both markets. The new Magnum chocolates have been introduced by Unilever subsidiary Sagit and comprise Magnum Praline drops, Magnum Essence tablet and Magnum Infinity bar.

Another emerging trend in chocolate confectionery is the development of low-carbohydrate lines to fit in with the popular low-carb diets. The trend is most active in the USA (where low-carbohydrate, pre-packaged foods are appearing in categories including beer and biscuits), but it is slowly making moves into the UK. The latest such UK import is CarboLite's milk chocolate flavour bar. It contains 0.2 g 'net effective carbs' and will be available in Superdrug and Benjy's stores.

ACTIVITY

1 Describe some of the socio-cultural factors that have influenced some of the product trends described in the case study.

2 What role has marketing played in developing these products?

Technological factors

In marketing goods and services, organisations must become aware of new materials as well as developments in manufacturing and business processes. At the same time organisations have to look at the nature of their products and, in particular, their cost-effectiveness as well as their performance in relation to competition. Factors might include:

- new technological processes
- energy-saving techniques
- new materials and substitutes for existing materials
- better equipment
- new product developments.

The technological environment includes the level of advancement in technical knowledge and equipment in society and the rate of their development and application. Technological changes are relevant to the way we make things, and the tools and equipment we use. We live in an age of rapid technological change, and understanding these changes is essential to organisations that want to develop new opportunities: whether in the development of new products or in new technologies that change the way consumers or markets operate. An example is the development of information technology aspects in retailing. The widespread growth of IT capabilities has given marketers instant access to sales trends, cost data, competitive data and statistical analysis.

Marketers need to scan the environments in which their organisation operates in order to understand the key changes that currently face them, as well as to anticipate future changes. If they are going to be able to plan for change, and react to changes effectively, they need to be able to understand the changing environment.

Ecological and ethical factors

Ecological awareness has had a major impact on marketing in recent years. In the late 1980s, the Green movement began to have a major impact first in the United States and then in Europe and beyond. 'Environmentalism' has become a front-line political issue that has been embraced by political parties across the spectrum. Today a very high percentage of consumers make environmental concerns an important factor in purchasing decisions when buying goods as diverse as motor cars, spray cans and organically produced meat and vegetables.

Many companies fall foul of the ethical approach, the problem being that when your marketing strategy incorporates values and ethics, you are expected to be 'squeaky clean', and as soon as you put a foot wrong you instantly become a target for reproach. For example, even the Body Shop has come under fire for exploiting indigenous peoples in the developing world.

Forces external to the organisation are rarely stable, and many of these forces can alter quickly and dramatically. It is important to recognise that while some of these forces will be harmful to marketing efforts, others will create new opportunities.

Micro-environment

The micro-environment is concerned with all the factors that impact upon an organisation and its marketing activities both within the organisation and the markets it serves. In analysing the marketing environment, it is necessary to consider the role of key stakeholders in this environment.

Stakeholders

The notion of stakeholders in an organisation has been a popular one for at least 20 years. The notion of 'stakeholders' was even poached by Tony Blair's New Labour and used to emphasise the idea of a one-nation society in which the views of all relevant groups are taken into account in decision making.

> Stakeholders are individuals, groups or organisations who are affected by, or have some level of involvement in, particular decisions or sets of decisions.

This move towards the notion of stakeholders marks a radical shift from the perspective adopted by many organisations in the past. Traditionally, this country was characterised by top-down command and control organisations. Decisions were made at the top and then passed down to those lower within the organisation. Managers talked about the 'right to manage', that is, the right to make most of the decisions in an organisation. Owners expected to have a major say because, after all, it was 'their organisation'. In marketing terms we associate this period with product orientation.

Reasons for adopting a stakeholder approach

There are a number of reasons for this change in emphasis.

International competition

The growth in international competition means that there is no scope for dinosaur organisations that use out-dated methods. Increasingly, it is being recognised that success is generated by organisations whose operations are based upon the values shared by all the stakeholders in the organisation.

The customer

The growing importance of the customer. Modern organisations are market focused. They recognise that it is customers who ultimately make the choice of whether to spend their money on a particular product. Other important stakeholders are not far behind: employees will be motivated only if they believe in a company that respects them, the local community wants to know that their rights are being respected and so on.

The Japanese example

The Japanese economy flourished following the Second World War until the last few years of the twentieth century. Japanese business practice was based on reducing the division between managers and employees. Their industries were characterised by a more consensual form of practice. They also placed more emphasis upon the customer.

The media

The growing importance of the media has also had a great influence. The media can show an organisation in a good or bad light, which means that organisations need to view the media as important stakeholders

within the environment. In addition, stakeholder groupings are able to use media coverage to provide prominence to their views.

Figure 8.31   Groups of stakeholders

CASE STUDY
Fortum

Fortum is a leading energy company in the Nordic countries and the other parts of the Baltic Rim. Fortum's activities cover the generation, distribution and sale of electricity and heat, the production, refining and marketing of oil, the operation and maintenance of power plants as well as energy-related services. The main products are electricity, heat and steam, traffic fuels and heating oils.

According to its website, 'We give more attention to social responsibility at Fortum. In addition to economic and environmental values, social responsibility has clearly become an important part of business. Social responsibility refers to the good co-operations with the personnel, customers, neighbours of production plants, business partners and investors as well as the media.'

As individuals, groups or organisations are affected by what an organisation does, they are said to have a stake or interest in the decisions it makes. A company's stakeholders, therefore, include not only its customers and owners, but also its workforce, its suppliers (and their families), those living near to its sites, special interest groups and, of course, society as a whole, including the environment.

Types of stakeholder

Stakeholders include the following categories of people.

Employees

Managers and employees at different levels are all employees, but within an organisation managers may have objectives which are quite different from those of other groups of workers. For example, senior managers may have the role of satisfying different groups of stakeholders. This can be difficult, particularly where conflict exists between groups. According to one view, decision makers have neither the time and resources, nor information and cognitive ability, to make maximising decisions. They simply try to provide acceptable levels of satisfaction for everybody. Stakeholders amend their expectations according to how the business is performing, how they see environmental conditions affecting performance, and how well other stakeholders are being treated.

Suppliers

In providing goods and services for an organisation, suppliers hope that by winning contracts they are securing income and profitability for their businesses. The supplier will be concerned about discounts and payment periods. The organisation receiving the supplies may be concerned about other issues, such as the consistency of the quality of supplies and the supplier's ability to keep to delivery dates: both could impact on its operations and ultimately affect its competitive advantage.

Customers

Customers will want something of value from their transaction which provides them with an excess of return over their investment. If organisations are not marketing orientated or do not provide customers with desired levels of satisfaction, the needs, wishes and aspirations of customers will have been ignored and this could affect the success of the organisation.

Intermediaries

There are many indirect and less obvious ways in which an organisation's activities impact upon people in the supply chain. Suppliers will have suppliers and these equally in business-to-business markets will have other suppliers. For example, a fabric manufacturer will have organisations who supply their machines. There are many interdependent relationships within such a chain where shared fortunes are important.

Owners

The traditional view from classical economists such as Adam Smith is that an organisation exists solely for the benefit of its owners and that the sole objective of owners is to maximise their wealth, and this is achieved through the sole aim of profit maximisation. Though this may be true with some small and medium-sized businesses (SMEs), it is unlikely to be the case with larger organisations where often no single shareholder is strong enough to influence the decision making.

Financiers

By providing funds for an organisation, financiers have a clear stake in its fortunes. They do not want the business to do badly or be put in a position where it might default on its debts.

Local community

Organisations provide jobs, create wealth within a local community and may provide some form of corporate support for local schools or other organisations. At the same time, there may be many externalities that impact negatively on the local community such as noise, pollution, radiation and traffic.

Pressure groups

Pressure groups like the Campaign for Real Ale (CamRA) serve to support the interests of their members and influence the actions of others. It is not too sweeping a statement to say that our beer industry today has been transformed because of CamRA, which has had a huge influence upon achieving representation of consumer tastes in the products of the major breweries.

Competitors

Clearly competitors will be affected by the actions of another organisation. Within the competitive environment, there are well-accepted ways of behaving within the context of competition, and organisations are not expected to behave in a way that damages fair competition. Competitors may be direct, such as *The Times* and the *Telegraph*, or indirect where they serve similar needs in different ways, such as a scooter and a motor car.

Media, the government, society, the environment, creditors

Each of these groups will in one way or another be affected by various organisations. The media may want to cover stories to the detriment of some organisations that may behave badly towards other stakeholders. Clearly the government want organisations to contribute to a healthy economy and pay taxes, all of which helps society in general. The environment is increasingly accepted as a stakeholder because of the impact it receives from organisational activities. Creditors are anybody owed money by the organisation, and will therefore, like financiers, be significantly interested in its success.

> **ACTIVITY**
>
> Within your own organisation identify all of the different groups of stakeholders. Briefly explain how each of these groups is affected by the actions of the organisation and describe how the organisation attempts to meet the needs of these groups of stakeholders.

The stakeholder approach

In meeting the needs of its stakeholders, a responsible organisation has a number of distinguishing characteristics:

♦ it meets its marketing objectives by supplying products or services that people want to buy
♦ it contributes to its own and the community's long-term prosperity by making the best possible use of resources
♦ it minimises waste of every kind, and where possible promotes reuse or recycling
♦ it respects the environment locally, nationally and globally
♦ it sets performance standards for its suppliers, and helps in their achievement
♦ it offers its employees worthwhile career prospects, professional training, job satisfaction and a safe working environment
♦ it expects the best from its employees and rewards them accordingly
♦ it acts at all times as a good citizen, aware of its influence on the rest of society, including the communities near its plant and offices.

Modern organisations recognise that marketing orientation involves treating customers as stakeholders and stakeholders as customers. The organisation that simply sets out to maximise its return to shareholders would quickly alienate other stakeholders. For example, recent studies on the change in share price before and after incidents of environmental damage show this clearly. Suppliers and financiers typically have a choice as to whom they do business with, and they are more likely to offer the best terms to organisations with a strongly positive public image.

Porter's competitive forces

One of the most interesting approaches to examining competition in the marketplace was presented by Michael Porter in 1980. Porter argues that the key aspect of the context in which an organisation operates is the industry or the industries in which it competes. He refers to five basic forces which he calls 'the structural determinants of the intensity of competition'. These, he feels, determine the profit potential of any given industry (and of companies working within it).

The five forces are as follows.

Rivalry among existing competitors

This is the most obvious form of competition: the head-to-head rivalry between firms making similar products and selling them in the same market. Rivalry can be intense and cut-throat, or it may be governed by unwritten agreements that help the industry to avoid the damage that excessive price-cutting, advertising and promotion expenses can inflict upon profits. Competition may be over prices or over a range of factors such as advertising, service, quality, outlets, and so on. This element is exemplified by the rivalry between Coca-Cola and Pepsi or Ford and General Motors.

Threat of entry

If it is easy to start up in an industry then, as soon as profits look attractive, new firms will enter. Industries are relatively easy to enter if there are no heavy capital costs at the outset, or restrictive patents and copyrights. For example, it would be very difficult for organisations to compete with Microsoft given its pre-eminence within the software market.

Threat of substitutes

A substitute is something that meets the same needs as the industry's product. The substitute may be quite different in some respects, but provides the same benefits to consumers. If the substitute becomes more attractive in terms of price, performance or both, then buyers will be tempted to move their custom. For example, a wide range of synthetic fibres have replaced silk, cotton, and wool in many furnishings and clothing.

Power of buyers

Powerful buyers can bargain away potential profits. They can cause organisations to undercut each other in order to get the buyer's business, and they can use their power to extract other benefits such as quality improvements and credit. Buyers tend to be powerful when there are relatively few of them buying a large proportion of total output, and often where there are too many small sellers. Supermarkets within the UK have been criticised for the power they exert over farmers and other producers.

Power of suppliers

In a similar way, suppliers of vital resources to an industry can exact high prices, leading to a squeeze on profits through higher input costs. Such suppliers would include suppliers of raw materials, power, skilled labour and components.

Porter identifies a number of strategies that business organisations can choose to pursue on the basis of these five forces. He argues that they can seek:

◆ Marketing advantage: by offering superior products or services that do a better job than competitive offerings; differentiation involves making your product better than that of rivals while at the same time making sure that it is bought by customers.

♦ Cost advantage: by reducing marketing and/or production costs below those of rivals, enabling the company to cut prices or to channel its savings into advertising and other promotional activities. A business can become the lowest-cost producer by making goods in an efficient way using the latest technology. It can also be done by producing and selling very large quantities of products.

Buyer behaviour

The process of buying a good or service is not quite as simple as it might seem. People or organisations rarely go to their supplier without first thinking carefully about what they want. Wherever there is a choice, decisions have to be made and such decisions may be influenced by complex motives which reflect on consumer characteristics and personality. This analysis of the decision-making process is known as **buyer behaviour** and the need to understand such behaviour is a crucial issue in marketing.

Dimensions of buyer behaviour

One of the initial problems associated with examining buyer behaviour is identifying who the buyer actually is. First, a distinction should be made between the customers for a product or service and the consumers of the product. It is traditional to think of the person who buys something as a consumer, but the person who buys is not always the same person who uses the product. Underwear is a good example. A lot of men's underwear is bought by women for partners and sons. This is very significant for the marketer, of course, as the manufacturer is likely to have more success with advertising targeted at women than men.

We also tend to think of a customer as an individual person, but it is commonly accepted today that purchases often involve two or more people. The group who all contribute to the final buying decision are known as the decision-making unit (DMU).

Members of the DMU will have one or more of the following roles:

♦ **users** are those people who will actually use the product
♦ **influencers** are those with technical expertise who set out the specifications for purchasing the product and evaluate the different products
♦ **indicators** or initiators are those who first suggest the idea
♦ **gatekeepers** have the crucial role of controlling the flow of information about the product
♦ **deciders** make the ultimate buying decision about product and supplier
♦ **buyers** select suppliers and negotiate the terms of the sale; often the buyer will be the decider.

In order to promote a product successfully it is necessary to gain access to all the members of the DMU, and it is likely to take a carefully planned activity to achieve this. Similarly, if we wish to understand buyer behaviour we will have to consider all members of the DMU if our conclusions are to be valid.

Environmental influences

Consumers want to make purchases in order to satisfy their needs and wants both today and for the future, and this may depend both upon where and how they live, as well as their own personal circumstances. For example, we all regularly make decisions about our purchases. Sometimes these decisions are made quickly, while in other circumstances we may spend a lot of time weighing up the alternatives. These alternatives can be broken down into three different categories.

Routine response behaviour

This describes what happens when we frequently buy items of low value that requires little thought. For example, we might go into the newsagent to buy a newspaper.

Limited decision making

Some thought might be necessary if an unfamiliar brand comes to the market. For example, if a new chocolate brand is launched in competition to a well-known brand, the consumer might try to find out more information before making a purchase.

Extensive decision making

Some products are durables purchased less frequently. The buyer will need to think about the benefits of different products and will require further information.

Nearly all purchases involve an element of risk. Whenever we make a purchase we hope to obtain something that provides us with value for money as well as a certain degree of satisfaction. However, this does not always happen. For example, if goods are faulty or flawed they will not live up to our expectations or provide us with the satisfaction we require. The supplier can reduce this risk factor by providing reliable goods which persist in providing high levels of satisfaction. This helps to create customer loyalty. Customer loyalty will:

◆ create a customer base which provides regular income and turnover
◆ mean that customers will support their supplier when faced with new competition and products
◆ provide goodwill which will help to develop and strengthen the supplier's market position.

The opposite to customer loyalty is customer dissatisfaction. Too much customer dissatisfaction will reduce customer loyalty and this may harm an organisation.

Impulse buying contrasts with many patterns of behaviour. It occurs when we get a powerful urge to buy something immediately, and it may involve strong or irrational emotions. For some consumers, impulse buying may be regular behaviour. Marketers often try to encourage impulse buying: for example, when placing confectionery close to supermarket checkouts.

CASE STUDY

Buyer behaviour in property markets

Cautious buyer behaviour is masking increased activity in the property market, according to the latest Home Report from Bradford & Bingley.

Throughout 2000 there were an average of six potential purchasers competing to get their foot in the door of every property ahead of the competition, but now every property which comes on the market is being chased by eight hopeful homebuyers.

Increased demand is especially evident in Scotland, where the ratio of buyers to homes has doubled from 4:1 to 8:1. In the south-east, meanwhile, demand has risen by 35 per cent and now stands at 11:1.

But while demand is on the up, buyers are proceeding with caution and are refusing to be rushed into a decision. This has led to an increase in the time taken to sell a property (up one week to an average of ten weeks) and has also had an impact on prices.

Nationally, the percentage of properties selling at the original asking price has dropped from 97 per cent in October 2000 to the current figure of 96 per cent. This trend is slightly more evident in the south-east, where the percentage has fallen to 95 per cent from a September 2000 figure of 97 per cent.

This stand-off threatens to create a bottleneck, says the report, as the supply of properties available fails to match demand. People are therefore advised to put their home on the market as soon as they think about making a move, and realistic pricing is now essential if sellers are serious about packing their bags.

Related figures make clear that the rise of the single household continues unabated. One-third of all properties are now bought by singletons, a figure which shows only slight regional variations.

Overall, the report concludes, the market is in a healthy state. Low unemployment and high consumer confidence should continue to drive prices up, but at a relatively modest rate. The average price of a house, currently £105,956, is not expected to rise by much more than 5 per cent over the course of 2001.

ACTIVITY

1   Describe the buyer behaviour from the report.

2   What factors might be influencing such behaviour?

Personal variables

Situational factors are another type of personal influence. These are the conditions that exist when a customer has to make a purchase. For example, a queue may deter a customer from entering a shop, bad weather or the prospect of shortages may cause consumers to 'stock up', or uncertainty may cause them to delay making large purchases. Time is another situational factor: if a consumer is in a rush, for example, he or she may not process information thoroughly.

The **level of involvement** is an important personal factor. How much interest and attention should a customer spend searching for each product? The whole consumer buying process will depend on the consumer's willingness to be involved with purchasing decisions. Low-involvement buyers engage in limited decision making, and may evaluate a product after they have bought it. With high-involvement buyers, extensive decision making involves time and effort before a choice is made.

There are a number of personal variable models that attempt to examine some of the internal factors that influence buyer behaviour: factors such as perceptions, motives, attitudes and beliefs. Such models recognise that consumers observe certain rules when choosing between alternatives. Four such models are used.

Compensatory or trade-off models

If you were buying a new hi-fi, what features would you look for when choosing the model to buy? Your 'ideal' house will clearly contain all the features you value, but would you always buy one that had all of the features you demand? You may be prepared to compromise on certain features if you only have a limited amount of money to spend. For example, you may sacrifice having a big garden or a fourth bedroom. When choosing between various makes of product, the customer will have in mind an 'ideal' product, but will normally trade off benefits to get the combination of features that offer the best value. The consumer will normally rank preferred features in order of importance and will be prepared to sacrifice those lower down the list. Knowledge of this list of priorities can inform an organisation when designing the features of products and deciding on positioning strategies.

Threshold models

When you are choosing your house there will probably be a level of property that you would not drop below. Thus you might not accept a house without a garage or a kitchen-dining room. Threshold models assume that you can discount certain models because of one feature. Knowledge of such features can inform product design.

Lexicographical or linear additive models

Perhaps when choosing your house, you will have only a few characteristics to consider in a specific order. Once they are satisfied, no other attributes will be considered. Again such models may inform product design.

Disjunctive rules

Perhaps you would choose your house because of one outstanding feature, such as the quality of the kitchen units.

As you can see, while such models are interesting to product designers, they do not attempt to predict buyer behaviour fully. They do, however, form useful components to more complex consumer models.

Complex models

Complex or grand models of consumer behaviour attempt to explain the whole of the buying process in detail and consequently they are long and involved. There are three most commonly used complex models.

The Nicosia model

This model examines how the supplier and the consumer interact and influence one another.

The Howard-Sheth model

This is similar to the black box models (see p. 549) except that it goes on to consider the variables internal to the customer.

The Engel, Blackwell and Miniard model

This model sees the buying process as a series of problems to be solved and goes through the five stages of need recognition, search, alternative evaluation, purchase and outcome.

Demographic variables

One important factor influencing buyers is **demographic characteristics**. Demographic factors may influence family purchasing decisions or form the basis for marketers to target specific groups of consumers with a range of benefits. The study of demography involves examining the characteristics of people who live in certain areas. It covers features such as class or status, occupation, age, gender, race, education, culture, nationality, religion, family size and family lifecycle.

Demographic variables fit alongside processes of socio-economic segmentation: a way of relating demographic information to income categories and lifestyle. Later in this chapter we look at how organisations identify groups of customers according to demographic and socio-economic variables. Such variables are key elements in examining consumer behaviour. Certain assumptions can be made about lifestyles based upon age, gender, where people live and their culture.

Sociological variables

We are quick to make judgements about the status of individuals by examining their possessions or surroundings. We find out that someone has a big house and a smart car and we assume that they are an individual of high status. At work, we see someone with a private office, powerful computer and personal assistant and assume again that this is a high status individual. Someone with an old car, small house, who works in a manual job, is assumed to be of relatively low status.

Status is conferred upon us from a wide variety of sources, some of which are shown in Figure 8.32.

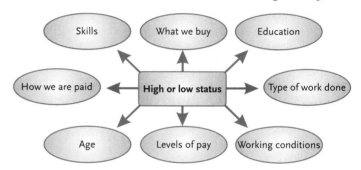

Figure 8.32   The sources of status

Status is an intangible quality that we may ascribe to someone on the basis of how we perceive them, but it is also something that people strive hard to achieve. Although status is conferred in many different ways, we often judge an individual's status by their 'status symbols' such as car, house, clothes, and so on. Consequently items or services that are perceived to be associated with high-status individuals can become sought after. Mobile phones, for example, used to be the exclusive province of young successful business people, and were a sign of success. They became so sought after that they are now owned by vast numbers of people. This particular item has lost its position as a 'status symbol': in fact users are now sometimes ridiculed by others for being pretentious. The moral is, beware the shifting nature of status symbols, if you care about looking silly if you do not keep up with the trends.

Despite these dangers, status is a powerful motivator in people and it works in two important ways for the marketer:

♦ people will work hard to achieve status, and this may involve the purchase of items that confer it
♦ people will also work hard to maintain their relative status with regard to others around them.

Convincing your target market that what you are selling confers status upon the owner can encourage sales. An advertising campaign that portrays the item or service being used by successful, privileged people may appeal to social climbers.

If such people feel that others whom they regard as being below them in status are beginning to catch them up on the social ladder, they will seek out new symbols to reinforce their superior position. Someone might have bought a multimedia computer two or three years ago with a particular processor and considered that to be superior. Nowadays most families have home computers. The new status symbol might be a wireless network of computers across the house.

CASE STUDY

Status effects explain the stagnation of happiness

The stagnation, or decline, of people's reported levels of happiness in the developed world is caused, in part at least, by the presence and innovation of 'status goods' in the economy. That is the contention of Ben Cooper, Cecilia Garcia-Penalosa and Peter Funk (2001), writing in the latest issue of the *Economic Journal*. Status goods are those that confer happiness only at the expense of others who consume less of the good. The result is consumer frustration

as people compete for the fixed supply of goods, and 'excessive' innovation of new kinds of status good at the expense of normal goods.

If we can take such data seriously, then the picture it paints of economic performance over the last 30 years is not a rosy one. There seems to be no trend in happiness levels in the United States, a decline in the UK, Italy and Germany, and an increase in France. Yet real incomes and consumption have more than tripled over this period. If happiness corresponds to 'utility', then happiness stagnation in the face of increasing affluence simply cannot be explained by conventional models of growth.

There are many potential explanations of happiness stagnation. Tibor Scitovsky, for example, suggests that we respond dynamically to consumption. Pleasure, he argues, is related to increases in stimulation and, hence, to the rate of growth of consumption.

An alternative approach is to examine the implications of consumers' desire for status and of the associated 'conspicuous consumption'. Cooper and his colleagues follow Fred Hirsch's distinction between material goods and goods that confer status, which he calls 'positional goods'. In Hirsch's formulation, material goods are reproducible, but positional goods – such as works of art, access to the countryside or employment in leadership roles – are not. The result is consumer frustration as people compete for a fixed supply of positional goods.

Cooper *et al.*'s explanation is based on the ability of capitalist economies to invent new products able to confer status. Their suggestion is that the stagnation or decline observed in average utility levels is caused, in part at least, by the presence and innovation of status goods in the economy. Like Hirsch's positional goods, status goods confer utility only at the expense of someone who consumes less of the good. The utility gains to one individual are cancelled out by the utility losses to another.

ACTIVITY

1   Comment upon the relationship between happiness and consumption.

2   Use an example to describe the ways that marketers use 'status' as part of their positioning strategies.

3   Evaluate the importance of status or high value-added goods within an economy.

Psychological variables

A person may have positive, negative or neutral feelings towards an organisation and its products. One of the objectives of an organisation is to encourage positive attitudes, and once achieved they need to be maintained. The marketer's job is to gain an understanding of the customer's attitude towards the organisation and its products and to alter them to positive where they can translate positive attitudes into a sale.

Psychological factors operate within consumers and are responsible for determining their behaviour patterns. Though psychological factors operate internally, they may also be influenced by social factors.

Motivation

The starting point in the consumer's purchasing decision is a felt need. This reflects the difference between the actual and desired state of affairs. Motives are a form of inner energy which drive a person towards the satisfaction of a felt need. The individual is thus drawn to take action to satisfy a need, in order to reach a condition of equilibrium. Motives, therefore, are situated between individual needs and a form of action. In doing so they:

♦ activate behaviour (when we are hungry this need for food motivates us into action)

♦ are directional in that they determine a particular type of action

♦ reduce tension in order to create the equilibrium condition.

Maslow's hierarchy of needs

One of the best-known theories influencing customer purchasing patterns is that of Abraham Maslow (1970). He suggested that, although it is difficult to analyse individual needs, it is possible to develop a hierarchical picture that can be split into five broad categories.

Basic needs are concerned with acquiring food, shelter and clothing.

Security needs are concerned with physical well-being and the need to provide protection, perhaps with a house in a safe trouble-free environment, with protected and reliable items within it.

Group needs centre on the desire for acceptance, the need for affiliation, and purchases associated with belonging to a community.

Self-esteem needs stem from one's desire for status, for a sense of achievement and for respect for one's accomplishments. This might lead to the possession of prestigious items, through living a more lavish lifestyle, or self-esteem generated, for example, through making donations to charities.

Self-fulfilment is concerned with full personal development and individual creativity. To achieve this level, individuals try to ensure that their individual skills and capacities are being fully utilised.

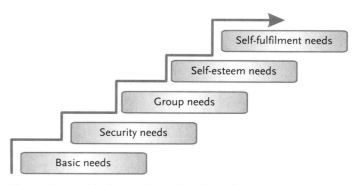

Figure 8.33   Maslow's hierarchy of needs

The implications of Maslow's theory are easy to perceive as different products and services are related to different needs. For example, assurance is rooted in a desire for safety; a Lexus is related to esteem needs and so on. It is noticeable in Western societies that there are far more products related to self-fulfilment needs than in developing countries. Such a theory helps an organisation to bear the consumer more closely in mind.

Perceptions and learning

Another psychologically based area that helps us to understand consumer behaviour is that of perception. Perception is the process by which an individual selects, organises and interprets inputs in order to develop a more meaningful view of reality. These inputs may be received through the five senses of sight, hearing, touch, smell and taste. Different people may perceive inputs in different ways and some may perceive the same inputs in different ways at different times. You can read more about perception in Unit 4: Foundations of organisations and behaviour, p. 69.

Selectivity limits our perceptions and we ignore many of the stimuli from our environment. There are three steps in the perception process.

Step 1: Receiving information

We do not have the ability to take into account all the information inputs in our environment. Studies show that on average we perceive more than 500 advertisements daily, but only a few of them ever break through our 'perceptual screen'. Selective exposure is the process by which individuals select inputs to be exposed to their awareness. Selective distortion occurs where an individual distorts information with his or her own views. Selective retention enables an individual to remember information inputs which support beliefs and forget inputs that do not.

Step 2: Organise and integrate information

New information needs to be organised and integrated with the information that is already stored in the memory.

Step 3: The perceptual process

The individual will then try to create meaning from the information inputs. This might be based on the fact that the information seems familiar or that it appeals to a hidden part of the individual's identity.

Marketers will try to make their message stand out so that it catches the consumer's attention. The psychological concept of closure helps to make a message stand out. **Closure** refers to how an individual creates a complete picture from fragments of a picture:

advertisements that help consumers to do this may break through perceptual screens.

Individuals have self-perceptions or self-images. The 'self' is an individual's perception of himself or herself. Within this 'self' there are various ways to maintain and enhance this image. The individual will make choices – of car, music, clothing, places to shop – which fit his or her perception of 'self'. By discovering how customers wish themselves to be perceived in terms of an image, organisations can design, promote and retail goods that are consistent with those sought by prospective purchasers.

We all as individuals learn as we go through life, and this learning changes our behaviour based upon our experience. According to Kotler and Armstrong (1996), 'Learning theorists say that most human behaviour is learned. Learning occurs through the interplay of drives, stimuli, cues, responses and reinforcement.' The significance of this for marketers is clear. By understanding how people learn, and by using cues and then reinforcing these to help people learn, it is possible to create positive reinforcement that enables people to respond in an appropriate and learned way.

Social factors

Social factors are the forces which other people exert on our buying behaviour. They include:

- culture and sub-cultures
- role and status
- group and reference group influences
- family influences
- social class.

Culture

Culture encompasses standard patterns of behaviour and plays an important role in shaping our purchasing patterns. It stems from traditions, beliefs and values of the community in which we live. It can be defined as 'the complex of values, ideas, attitudes and other meaningful symbols that serve humans to communicate, interpret, and evaluate as members of society'. For example, although alcohol is an ingrained feature of Western life, it is forbidden in Muslim communities. Culture is handed down from one generation to another and provides each society with a unique series of values.

The symbols of culture may be tangible products such as forms of housing, tool and clothing, or intangible concepts such as values, attitudes, beliefs and laws. Culture will have an important influence on the lives of everybody within each community, and so will determine their buying needs. For example, tastes for different types of alcoholic drinks differ widely, not just in various parts of the world but also in different regions in the UK.

Culture will determine how, why, when and for whom products are purchased. It is not a static concept and cultures are continually changing over time. For example, in recent years we have seen greater concern for environmentally friendly products, increased emphasis on health and fitness, as well as increased dependence on convenience products. Marketers must constantly monitor cultural changes in order to adapt their marketing activities, because strategies that are successful for one culture may not be successful for another.

CASE STUDY

Changing culture towards health and fitness

It is not so long ago that we took health and fitness for granted. It was not considered to be 'trendy' either to go running in the morning or to keep stunningly fit. Since the 1970s, however, there has been a steady trend which has seen the development of private sports centres and gyms around the country, many of which are owned and run by chains such as Fitness Exchange.

Started in London Bridge, Fitness Exchange was one of London's first private health clubs in 1974. As the Mike Corby Group, there are now clubs across the city. Each club offers the best facilities and the widest range of fitness classes and complementary therapies available under one roof. These are mainly aimed at the affluent corporate market, mostly being situated within central London, but welcome family and individual members.

The roomy, air-conditioned gyms offer machines and equipment in large training areas. There is a social scene with the younger members. The aerobics studios offer almost every kind of class, including step, aerobics, body conditioning, circuit training and the increasingly popular boxercise. The clubs also have health suites with saunas, steam rooms and sunbeds, as well as beauty treatments, massage and physiotherapy and reflexology.

The clubs sited away from the city offer excellent facilities ranging from swimming pools to racquet sports which are more focused on the family users.

ACTIVITY

1 What does this movement towards health and fitness tell us about our culture?

2 How might this create opportunities and avenues for alternative product concepts?

3 Evaluate the implications for this trend upon organisations such as large sports clubs, and the mix of products and services they provide for their customers.

Sub-cultures

Though a nation might be characterised by one culture, there may be a series of sub-cultures existing within it. A sub-culture is a sub-group with its own distinctive behaviour. Within the UK, sub-cultures are based on race, religion, age, rural as opposed to suburban, and so on. Sub-cultures are important for organisations who wish to target their brands to those who share the values of that particular sub-culture.

547

These groups may in themselves be important market segments for marketers.

Role and status

Status is the relative position that any individual member has in a group, whether the group be formal or informal. We all have a certain status in any situation. Roles are what other members of each group expect from people with certain status. For example, teachers have a certain status within society and we would expect certain roles to be fulfilled by teachers. Where status and roles can be recognised, it may be appropriate to target products at such individuals.

Groups and reference group influences

An individual's buying behaviour may be influenced by many groups. Although we generally like to view ourselves as individuals, it is very likely that many of our purchasing decisions are based on the groups to which we belong. A group becomes a **reference group** when it influences a person's attitudes, values and behaviour. We may all belong to a series of reference groups such as professional groups, families, cricket teams, church, and so on. A reference group may serve an individual by being a source of information and comparisons. Advice, word-of-mouth help, common values may all influence purchasing behaviour. Consumers tend to keep their purchasing behaviour in line with members of their reference group.

People are affected in different ways by reference groups. How strongly an individual is influenced will depend on his or her level of involvement within the group and susceptibility to its influences. Marketers may use reference group influence in their promotions. Within each small group there are **opinion leaders**. These individuals may adopt products before other members of the group and then serve as an information source for others. Opinion leaders can play a crucial role in interpersonal communications within groups.

Family influences

Of all the groups to which we belong, our family probably exerts the most influence on our buying behaviour. Many of us will be members of two families during our lifetime: the family into which we are born (the family of orientation) and the family into which we marry (the family of marriage and procreation). The role that we have within a family directly affects our purchasing decisions. There is an infinite variety of family roles, and these constantly change. For example, it is possible to have a family where the husband is dominant or alternatively one where a wife is dominant.

ACTIVITY

In your group, discuss your buying role within the context of your family. To what extent does that role influence the purchasing patterns the family develops?

A number of factors have affected family roles over recent years: the growing number of women who work outside the home, the impact of two wage-earners, the increasing number of single-parent families and so on. Marketers need to be aware of these changes and their consequences for buyer behaviour.

Social class

Social class represents a ranking of people into 'higher' or 'lower' positions. A class may also be called 'open' because people have the freedom either to move into it or out of it. Within different societies the criteria for determining social classes vary widely. Social class may help to determine housing, cars, types of occupation, and so on. Social class is a major determinant of consumer behaviour.

Physiological stimuli

We only have to look at what Maslow terms 'basic needs' to appreciate the things that in a physiological sense we all need in order to survive, such as food, shelter and clothing. At a very basic level it is possible to appreciate human behaviour in terms of our needs, and how individuals might develop strategies to satisfy such needs. Clearly, these needs might vary according to each individual's different circumstances, but provide us with an elemental understanding of what people need rather than want.

At the same time marketers work upon understanding what it is that makes consumers realise that they have a need, particularly physiological ones, and how to identify a pathway to satisfy them. One way of doing this is to identify a number of influences that might make the consumer behave in a particular way. These are **stimulus response models**.

A stimulus prompts certain behaviour and might include advertising, the influence of peers and physiological factors.

An **endogenous** stimulus is one that has a clearly identifiable effect, such as a well-targeted advertisement. An **exogenous** variable has an effect that is much harder to define and quantify, such as a person's expectations for the future or the results of decisions taken in the past.

Internal variables concern the customer's attitudes, desires and motivations, whilst external variables are factors out of the control of the customer, such as the strength of the economy or the weather.

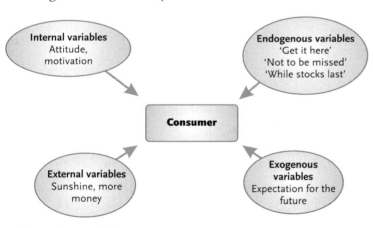

Figure 8.34   Influences on a consumer

All of these factors may combine to produce a response from the consumer: sometimes the response may be the result of many of these factors, and sometimes it may result from one specific stimulus.

It is common to classify consumer models under two groupings: simple and complex models. As the names suggest, simple models attempt to analyse only certain key influences on demand, while complex models use a more comprehensive approach in an attempt to include all aspects of the buying process. Simple models include:

- black box models
- decision process models
- personal variable models
- the PV/PPS model.

The black box model

Black box models are the classic example of a stimulus–response model. If I stick a pin into my hand then feel pain, that is an example of a stimulus–response mechanism. The stimulus is the pin, the response is the pain. Such models assume that consumers react in a predictable way to set stimuli, and they ignore any internal variables such as psychological factors. A typical back box model might look like Figure 8.35.

Figure 8.35   Simple 'black box' model

Other models might consider more stimuli and might concern more than one consumer. Kotler (1988) refers to a more detailed approach containing a comprehensive list of stimuli and a variety of responses (see Figure 8.36).

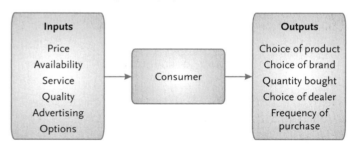

Figure 8.36   Kotler's black box model

ACTIVITY

Remember the last important item you bought. Draw up a black box model based upon Kotler's model to examine the inputs and outputs surrounding the buying decision. If you were promoting this product, what conclusions could you draw from the model you have constructed?

549

Black box models are popular because they are easy to understand. They involve variables that are easy to quantify through observation and they also involve inputs that are easily altered if the model suggests they should be.

Decision process models

Another type of model examines the steps that the buyer goes through when making a buying decision. A specific model can be designed to represent the steps and decisions involved in making a particular purchase. Such a model will contain the steps show in Figure 8.37.

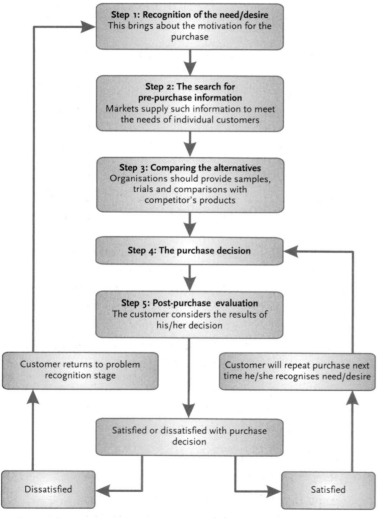

Figure 8.37   Decision process model

This model is useful to the marketer as it identifies the stages that the marketer can influence and should indicate what can be done to encourage purchase. It is

not very predictive, however, as it does not take account of many internal and external factors.

Personal variable models

These attempt to examine some of the internal factors that influence buyer behaviour: factors such as perceptions, motives, attitudes and beliefs. Four such models are used, and are described earlier in this chapter, under Buyer behaviour, p. 540.

The PV/PPS model

Chris Rice (1997) suggests a further model that attempts to combine the key aspects of the personal variable model and the decision process model. His model owes much to the Vroom Valence Expectancy Theory of motivation. He emphasises, as does Victor Vroom, that behaviour is determined by two factors: the perceived value of an outcome, PV (or Valance to use Vroom's terminology) and the perceived probability that the option will satisfy PPS (or Expectancy according to Vroom). If we give a numerical value to each of these we can calculate the subjective utility (SU), meaning the likelihood of the outcome taking place. We do this using the formula:

$$PV \times PPS = SU$$

If we were to use a scale of, say, one to ten to rate PV and PPS, we might get the following situation. I am trying to decide whether to buy a new CD or some new socks. I really want the CD as it is my favourite group, and I know I need the socks but I am not too excited about them. However, while I always buy my socks from a particular shop and am therefore almost certain that they will meet my needs, there have been numerous occasions when I have looked forward to a new CD only to be disappointed by it when it is released, so I cannot be sure that I will enjoy it as much as I think I will. These feelings might translate into the following scores:

Perceived value:	**CD**	8	**Socks**	3
Perceived probability of satisfaction:	**CD**	5	**Socks**	9
Subjective utility:	**CD**	40	**Socks**	27

According to the PV/PPS model, I will choose the option with the highest SU value, which in this instance is the CD.

The PV/PPS model suggests that we are most likely to buy when we not only place a high value on the projected purchase but also have a high expectation that the purchase will satisfy us. Chris Rice (1997) illustrated this using the four quadrants shown in Figure 8.38.

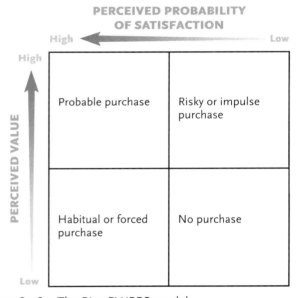

Figure 8.38   The Rice PV/PPS model

The top left quadrant is entitled 'probable purchase' and this is the ideal situation from the marketer's point of view. The customer places a high value on the item and is confident it will satisfy and consequently will probably buy. All of the other quadrants fall below this ideal in one way or another, and it is the marketer's job to address the problems and push the item towards that top left quadrant.

The top right is entitled 'risky or impulse purchase'. Here the buyer acknowledges that there is no guarantee that buying will satisfy him or her, but does place great value on the possibility that it might; consequently,

there is some risk to the purchase but the buyer may not be prepared to take that risk. This might explain our anguish when we are considering buying a cheap alternative product. We know that there is a risk that the quality may be poor, but we very much hope that it will do what we want it to. The marketer's job is to convince the buyer that there is less risk and the increased probability of satisfaction by making these decisions.

The bottom left quadrant is entitled 'habitual or forced purchase' and describes an item that we have to buy and buy regularly, such as bin liners or light bulbs. We place little emphasis on the purchase because we do it all the time, but we have a high expectation that it will satisfy our needs. In such cases we do not bother about which brand we buy, as we are confident that they will meet our needs. The problem for the marketer here is in trying to increase the perceived value of a particular brand and thereby encourage the purchase of it.

The final quadrant is entitled 'no purchase'. The product that falls into this quadrant is seen to be of little value and unlikely to satisfy. The marketer has a very hard, if not impossible, job to change the buyer's mind in these circumstances.

The PV/PPS model suggests that to encourage the prospective buyer we should either:

♦ increase the perceived value of the purchase, or
♦ increase the perceived possibility of satisfaction resulting from the purchase.

Complex or grand models of consumer behaviour

Complex models attempt to explain the whole of the buying process in some detail, and consequently they are long and involved. The most common complex models are the Nicosia model, the Howard-Sheth model and the Engel, Blackwell and Miniard model, which are described under Buyer behaviour on p. 543.

Attitudes

The cognitive dissonance theory was put forward by L. Festinger in 1964. It is concerned with the effects of purchasing decisions made by individuals. Occasionally you buy something and shortly afterwards have pangs of doubt about whether you have made the right purchase. This often happens with cheap alternative products, but it also happens at the other end of the scale with a very large item such as a new computer, car or home. The mental discomfort felt after having made a purchase is called 'dissonance', and it is the marketer's job to reduce the amount of dissonance felt by customers so that they are as happy as possible with the purchase they have made. Happy customers become repeat purchasers and may recommend products to others.

Many people may seek to reduce uncertainty about decisions they have made by trying to eliminate dissonance so that they can achieve consistency or consonance. They may do this in these ways:

♦ By looking for information to support the decision they have taken. This is known as **selective exposure**. Someone having bought a new computer from a manufacturer specialising in cheap PCs may try to convince others that their decision was right. They flick through brochures avoiding information that indicates that another decision would have been preferable; they are undertaking **selective avoidance**.

♦ Customers may try and devalue the source of dissonance. If a magazine report implies that a different decision would have been preferable, a person may shed doubt on the independence of that report. This is known as **selective interpretation**.

♦ Customers may change their attitudes to fit in with the decision they have made. 'I know this computer is a cheaper alternative, but I never really believed in paying just for a brand name.'

♦ Ultimately customers may actually reverse the decision if the dissonance becomes unbearable: they may take it back and buy a different model.

Some people will only make a purchase if their attitude is positive. Marketers try to persuade customers to change their approach to develop positive perceptions.

Perceptions

Six factors contribute to a change in perceptions and attitudes:

Source factors

The source of our information helps to form our attitude. This is why organisations use personalities in advertising. The endorsement of personalities such as David Beckham helps to influence consumers.

Existing attitudes

Our experience of products will carry great weight, but we may seek the opinions of others to get secondary experience. If we cannot find anybody else, advertising may help to reinforce our attitudes.

Message features

A strong message encourages positive attitudes, and a message will be strong if it presents objective facts. The element of objectivity may stem from using strong positive statements, or the endorsements of satisfied customers.

Communication channel

Some routes by which a message arrives may carry more credence than others. An advertisement in a broadsheet newspaper may carry more weight than one in a tabloid.

Attributes of the receiver

Some people are more susceptible to influencing factors than others. Their knowledge, mood and personality may indicate how receptive they are to having their attitudes influenced.

Product features

The stage the product has reached in the product lifecycle and how it compares in performance to its competitors will also contribute to customer perceptions.

Lifestyle variables

As people move through their lives their needs change, so their buying behaviour changes as well. Many models have been put forward to describe these changes, but each recognises a familiar pattern. For example:

♦ Young people up to the age where they settle down with a partner now have significantly more spending power than ever before and, since they have no commitments other than to please themselves, they spend money freely on such things as holidays, entertainment and eating out.

♦ Those in their twenties to thirties are setting up home, buying cars and having children, so this is the period when they borrow the most.

♦ Middle-aged people repay the debts incurred in previous years and start to put money aside for retirement.

♦ Older people draw on their savings or pensions and spend.

The Sagacity Life Cycle Groupings (2003) has four main lifecycle groups. These are:

♦ dependent: mainly under 24s, living at home or full-time students

♦ pre-family: under 35s, who have established their own household but have no children

♦ family: main shoppers and chief income earners, under 65, with one or more children in the household

♦ late: includes all adults whose children have left home or who are over 35 and childless.

ACTIVITY

Comment upon where you feel that you are within a lifecycle. How would you expect your spending, saving and consumption to change over the next few years? What implications might this have for the choice of products and services you buy?

Organisational spending

So far our analysis of consumer behaviour has been focused on consumer markets. Every day in towns and cities across the UK, car dealers hand the keys of new cars to their customers. A complex manufactured product like this will be made up of numerous parts and materials from many suppliers. Whereas it may be easy to think about the sale of a car from a showroom, we tend not to think of the vast number of sales transactions which have taken place beforehand to bring together the components used in the manufacture of the car.

An **organisational market** is one where organisations buy products and services which are used directly or indirectly in the production of other goods and services or are to be resold.

Many people are unaware of the significance of the organisational market. Consider again the number of transactions required to manufacture a car. Iron ore is mined and transported to a plant to be made into steel. The steel is bought and formed into the chassis and body. In order to construct a car with about 12,000 different parts, a manufacturer will probably produce about 6000 parts and then buy the other 6000 from other companies. Many of these companies will only supply one part, so the car manufacturer will have to buy components from several thousand companies. The companies supplying these parts will also have suppliers from whom they buy raw materials and components.

When a company is selling to other organisations it still needs to understand the behaviour of its customers. But whereas a consumer product might have a potential market of 57 million users, there are fewer than 3 million organisations within the UK and the likelihood is that the product on offer will appeal to only a very small number of them.

The demand for organisational products and services is called **derived demand** because the amount purchased is determined by the demand for related goods and services. For example, the number of tyres purchased by a motor manufacturer will depend on the demand for vehicles.

Depending on derived demand can have serious limitations. Organisational markets are subject to business cycles and the demand for industrial products and services may fluctuate unpredictably when the pace of business activity changes. Recessionary economic conditions can therefore lead to severe cutbacks in derived demand for inputs and cause a business to close down plants and lay off workers.

Companies supplying goods in organisational markets face constantly changing circumstances which are often called **contingency factors**. Marketers need to be constantly aware of information relating to such specific conditions. For example:

- the average value of an order follows a lengthy negotiation period and credit facilities will be important
- there is a risk of takeover by the customer
- buyers often deliberately exercise buying power to influence conditions of supply such as terms and prices
- large companies often seek out smaller companies so that they can exercise their buying power more easily
- large buyers may pursue a deliberate policy of delaying payment for goods and services received
- there is a risk of supplier dependency on the customer.

Segmentation

The most appropriate strategy for an organisation will depend upon the nature of the organisation, the type of market in which it competes and the actions of its competitors, and upon what sorts of risks an organisation is willing to undertake. This will depend upon an analysis of the opportunities within the marketplace as well as the uncertainty in the environment in which the organisation is operating.

Remember that the simplest and most important principle of marketing is that marketing and its related activities should be designed to serve the customers. Serving customers' needs with goods and services that do so more precisely than those of competitors in market-orientated society has today become more important than ever. Whereas in the past, in many markets, all customers were treated to a similar diet of goods and services, organisations now recognise that groups of consumers have different needs, wants and tastes.

Process of market selection

Customers have different needs, wants, likes and dislikes. Not every person likes the same make of motor car or has the same taste in clothes. Equally, if cost and production time were of no importance, manufacturers would make products to the exact specifications of each buyer. On the other hand, neither can it serve all customers successfully if it groups all of their needs and wants together.

Instead of trying to serve all customers equally, an organisation may focus its efforts on different parts of the total marketplace. Within the total marketplace it is possible to group customers with similar characteristics and divide the market into parts. This is known as **market segmentation**. Market segments are groups of customers with similar needs and characteristics. The task is to produce and supply different products to suit these segments.

> Market segmentation is therefore a process of separating a total market into parts so that different strategies can be used for different sets of customers.

According to Tom Cannon (1997) market segmentation is, 'the strategy whereby an organisation partitions the market into sub-markets (segments) which will respond in similar ways to marketing inputs'. Cannon then makes the point that:

- segments or parts of the market are more homogeneous (similar) than the market as a whole
- each of these parts can be reached with a specific marketing mix.

ACTIVITY

Does any market today exist where segmentation does not take place?

When it is not possible to satisfy all of its customers' needs with a uniform product, an organisation will use market segmentation to divide consumers into smaller segments consisting of buyers with similar needs or characteristics so that marketing becomes like firing a rifle instead of a blunderbuss.

Market segmentation uses **differentiated marketing strategies** because it tailors separate product and market strategies to different sectors of the market. For example, the market for cars has many segments such as economy, off-road, MPV, luxury, high performance, and so on. This approach recognises that in order to be successful and hit consumer needs, it is necessary to recognise the needs of different groups of consumers and meet them in different ways.

In fact some organisations exist simply to serve highly specialised market segments. They deliberately choose to compete in one segment and develop the most effective mix for that market. This is known as **concentrated marketing.** For example, Morgan serves the specific and highly esoteric needs of customers who like a car from the past. Jaguar cars are associated with luxury market segments. Similarly, quality fashion retailers today increasingly use brand names to position themselves in particular parts of a market. This is sometimes called **niche marketing.** A disadvantage is that if sales of a product decline in that segment, the lack of diversification means that this may affect the performance of the organisation.

Elements of segmentation

There are three elements to segmentation:

Market segments

Market segments are groups of customers with similar needs and characteristics. The task is to produce and supply different products to suit these segments.

Targeting

Once segments have been identified, organisations have to identify one or more segments with a need which can best be met by the organisation. This is known as targeting and may involve mass, undifferentiated marketing or concentrated marketing.

Positioning

Even though parts of the market are divided into segments, and organisations have worked out which ones to target, buyers within each segment will not have identical needs. Positioning involves developing a market strategy through the marketing mix that takes into account the thoughts and perceptions of customers about a product relative to other products and brands. The position is how the product is perceived in the minds of customers. Repositioning involves moving the product away from its current position in the market to another part of the market, where it might compete more effectively. Perhaps the most famous repositioning strategy in recent years is Skoda, who have moved away from a low cost, low reliability position in the market to become a well-respected high value brand.

Macro and micro segmentation

The principle of mass marketing was simply to identify a number of large segments and then, using mass marketing principles, target those segments with goods and services. Nobody could argue that it did not work. A mass marketing macro segment might be baked beans; another could be baked beans with sausages and so on. However, as marketing has evolved and become much more scientifically based, we have seen a movement away from macro segmentation towards micro segmentation, where more specific marketing mixes and strategies are developed and tailored for specific groups of consumers, using a number of different bases for segmentation.

There are a number of reasons for this. Increasingly mass markets have broken down into a whole range of

CASE STUDY

Aiming at the youth market

The Boots 17 brand comprises a range of cosmetics targeted at the youth market. This market is not an easy one in which to compete successfully. It is notoriously fickle and changes constantly as trends and fashions alter. In order for Boots to provide a range of cosmetics for this market, the company has to monitor the profile of the brand and the marketing mix continually to ensure that its values and meanings are relevant for young people.

'Girl power' and the increasing independence of teenagers have changed the way they think about the things they buy. As a result of the changing perceptions of young people, the Boots 17 brand has recently been repositioned from a low-cost budget brand to a cosmetic brand for girls 'with attitude'. The objective of the repositioning process for Boots was to match the further development of the brand with the changing requirements of the users: to provide 17 with a new personality.

ACTIVITY

1   What are the characteristics of the market segment in which the Boots 17 brand appears?

2   Why do consumer requirements and perceptions of a brand constantly change?

3   Examine and comment upon how another product in another market has changed through similar strategies.

smaller micromarkets and segments. In recent years it has become very difficult to develop an appropriate marketing mix for mass marketed products, as consumers almost expect to be served with a tailored marketing mix. At the same time marketing and the development of marketing as a science has become more specific and focused. Electronic technology has provided significantly more information that marketers can use to find out about customers.

Micro marketing today involves a significant amount of regionalisation, with brands tailored to specific areas and ethnic groups. In its most extreme form, it may lead to some form of mass customisation, where everybody within a market has their needs met individually.

Bases for segmenting markets

Geographic segmentation

This form of segmentation assumes that consumers in different regions may be affected by similar climate, natural factors, population density and levels of income. By dividing markets into regions it is possible to recognise and cater for the needs of customers in the regions. For example, people living in certain countries are assumed to have common characteristics that influence buying attitudes.

Demographic segmentation

Demographic factors, which can be measured with relative precision, have helped many organisations to define a basis on which to segment their market. Because demographic variables can be closely related to customer needs and purchasing behaviour, this helps producers to target their products more

ACTIVITY

Look at the data in Figure 8.39 showing demographic trends for males within the UK between 1981 and 2002. Comment upon the different sort of products that might follow some of these trends.

	Under 4	5–14	15–24	25–34	35–44	45–59	60–64	65–74	75+	All
1981	1706	4039	4455	3933	3322	4603	1345	2214	1038	26,655
1982	1737	3887	4514	3826	3462	4554	1401	2179	1073	26,633
1983	1769	3759	4560	3793	3559	4532	1463	2117	1108	26,660
1984	1773	3667	4590	3818	3640	4514	1515	2067	1145	26,729
1985	1781	3608	4594	3866	3705	4501	1462	2117	1176	26,810
1986	1797	3542	4580	3935	3778	4467	1426	2152	1201	26,878
1987	1818	3494	4532	4025	3820	4459	1395	2175	1245	26,963
1988	1849	3468	4443	4113	3838	4490	1379	2180	1277	27,037
1989	1882	3477	4347	4257	3854	4530	1372	2193	1301	27,213
1990	1901	3508	4227	4379	3868	4571	1365	2199	1321	27,339
1991	1928	3555	4095	4473	3887	4614	1358	2219	1337	27,466
1992	1939	3609	3954	4548	3816	4769	1352	2243	1340	27,570
1993	1926	3673	3836	4599	3801	4893	1341	2279	1330	27,678
1994	1920	3704	3749	4642	3825	4992	1331	2309	1319	27,791
1995	1900	3726	3694	4668	3879	5073	1325	2276	1381	27,922
1996	1866	3761	3630	4677	3965	5139	1322	2257	1427	28,044
1997	1841	3796	3582	4650	4070	5193	1327	2244	1466	28,169
1998	1820	3817	3561	4589	4181	5252	1346	2236	1500	28,302
1999	1796	3844	3571	4512	4309	5316	1366	2230	1526	28,470
2000	1771	3838	3598	4435	4444	5379	1376	2233	1552	28,627
2001	1727	3771	3516	3976	4214	5362	1374	2245	1574	27,760
2002	1686	3756	3606	4004	4314	5448	1376	2267	1614	28,072

Figure 8.39   Demographic data on UK males, 1981–2002 (000s)

effectively. Demographic segmentation may involve dividing the population into discrete segments: for example, by age for clothes retailing, by sex for cosmetics, by family size for different sized packages of breakfast cereals.

Segmentation by age

This is widely applied. A good example is the way in which banks and building societies develop products for students, young children, elderly customers, and so on. Many products are also segmented by gender: clothing, alcohol, cosmetics and cars are segmented in such a way.

Marketers may also segment according to ethnic background, particularly for clothes, food and music.

Levels of education can be a segmentation variable: some products clearly appeal to people of higher intellectual ability, such as those who read the *New Scientist* or *The Economist*.

Geo-demographic segmentation

The newest methods of segmentation combine geographic and demographic segmentation principles. These are based on the belief that similar households in a particular locality exhibit similar purchasing behaviour. The best-known geo-demographic method is provided by CACI ACORN in their profile of Great Britain. ACORN stands for A Classification Of Residential Neighbourhoods.

ACORN Category A: Thriving	Pop Proj 2004 19.9%
1.1 Wealthy suburbs, large detached houses	2.9
1.2 Villages with wealthy commuters	2.7
1.3 Mature affluent home-owning areas	2.8
1.4 Affluent suburbs, older families	3.8
1.5 Mature well-off suburbs	2.7
2.6 Agricultural villages, home-based workers	1.6
2.7 Holiday retreats, older people, home-based workers	0.7
3.8 Home-owning areas, well-off older residents	1.4
3.9 Private flats, elderly people	1.2

Figure 8.40   Example of ACORN thriving category

Social grade	Social status	Occupation
A	Upper middle class	Higher managerial, administrative or professional
B	Middle class	Intermediate managerial, administrative or professional
C1	Lower middle class	Supervisory or clerical, and junior managerial or professional
C2	Skilled working class	Skilled manual workers
D	Working class	Semi-skilled and unskilled workers
E	Those at the lowest level of subsistence	State pensioners or widows (no other earner), casual or low-grade worker

Figure 8.41   One form of socio-economic grouping

Psychographic and behavioural segmentation

This form of segmentation divides different groups up on the basis of social class, lifestyle or personality.

Social class

Social class is a socio-economic way of dividing a market according to people's purchasing power and habits. The socio-economic grouping is sometimes called **social stratification** and each class roughly indicates a pattern of behaviour or consumption habits. One of the best-known classifications is the NRS Social Grade Definitions, shown in Figure 8.41.

Lifestyle

Lifestyle influences many of the goods or services that we purchase. Increasingly many make purchases that reflect their various lifestyles. For example, the lifestyle of this author includes healthfood, a love for a particular type of motor car and the occasional glass of Chardonnay.

Personality

Personality is something that we all have. All marketers have to do is to develop goods and services that match the personalities of their consumers. For example, what does it say about someone if they drive an Astra convertible, wear colourful clothes and lots of make-up?

Behavioural segmentation

This method looks at behaviour patterns such as frequency of purchase and loyalty to a product. For example, one segment of the market may always purchase a certain product while another may be made up of people who frequently switch between brands. An experienced drinker may stick with Guinness, while an inexperienced one may try out a range of stouts and beers.

Multivariable segmentation

Given the number and range of bases for segmentation, it is possible to develop the process on a multi-variable basis.

Using the single base involves segmentation by just one variable: for example, dividing a market geographically or according to age. Though this is fairly straightforward, it often only has limited value because it lacks precision.

On the other hand, multi-variable segmentation uses more than one basis to divide a market. This helps to target customer segments with greater precision. In Figure 8.42, the market is segmented according to three variables: socio-economic grouping, usage and region. In the boxes highlighted you will find Bs from the South who are heavy users. As different bases for segmentation are added to this process, a larger number of segments is identified and this helps an organisation to create a more appropriate marketing mix for each.

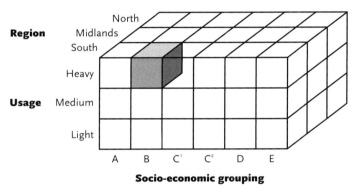

Figure 8.42   Multi-variable segmentation

ACTIVITY

Identify a product market. Show on what basis such a market may be segmented, and explain why you think it has been segmented in such a way.

Benefits of segmentation

Market segmentation helps to turn marketing into a science. Instead of focusing upon an amorphous mass of consumers all of whom may have different characteristics, segmentation adds precision to the ways in which organisations reach their consumers. In an ever-changing marketplace, where competition may be fierce, the process of segmentation enables organisations to focus their competitive efforts upon satisfying the needs of consumers better than their rivals.

Segmentation helps an organisation to understand the market and break it up into segments which match customer needs and requirements. The next step is to identify one or more segments which has a need that can be met by the organisation. This process is known as targeting.

Targeting

As we saw earlier, 'Once segments have been identified, organisations have to identify one or more segments which has a need which can best be met by the organisation.' There are a number of different targeting strategies that organisations can adopt.

Concentration strategy

This involves targeting a single segment with a single product. The organisation's resources are thus concentrated on a very small part of the overall market (see Figure 8.43).

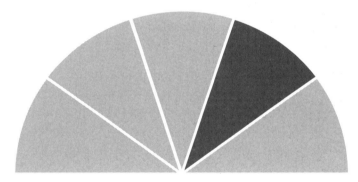

Figure 8.43   Concentration on one segment

This is sometimes called **niche marketing**. For example, until recently Porsche targeted a very exclusive segment of the market for cars. It is now also manufacturing luxury 4 × 4s. The main benefit of this targeting strategy is that it allows for a high degree of specialisation and the development of a marketing mix focused specifically on the needs of a distinctive group of customers. Another benefit is that it allows a small organisation to compete with large organisations in an identified segment. A disadvantage is that if sales of a product decline in that segment, the lack of diversification means that this may affect the performance of the organisation.

If a single product is targeted at the whole market, this is known as **mass** or **undifferentiated marketing** (see Figure 8.44).

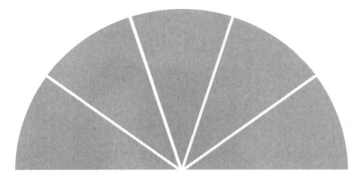

Figure 8.44   Mass-marketing strategy

The great benefit of mass marketing is that economies of scale can be achieved through large-scale production. However, as this approach focuses on customer similarities rather than differences, there are few examples in the private sector of mass marketing taking place today.

Selective marketing

This involves the use of a differentiated approach to target a number of products at a number of segments in the market by tailoring a separate marketing mix for each segment (see Figure 8.45). A good example of selective marketing is the market for cars, where the larger manufacturers target products at a whole range of segments.

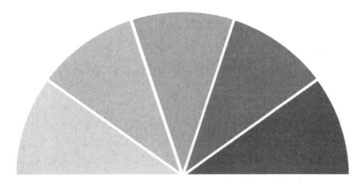

Figure 8.45   Tailoring a separate mix for each segment

Positioning

Even though parts of the market can be divided into segments, within each segment buyers will not have identical needs. Positioning takes into account the thoughts and perceptions of customers about a product, relative to other products and brands. The position is how the product is perceived in the minds of customers.

Positioning a product involves identifying the key variables considered to be important by customers. These are then used to develop and highlight the product's image. For example, price is a key variable for groceries, while for furniture, quality is a key element, and for wine, taste. Market research is important in order to understand a customer's motivations for product purchase.

Repositioning involves moving the product away from its current market position, for example to another part of the market which emphasises attributes where it is superior to its nearest competitors.

The various stages in a positioning plan would be as follows:

♦ research the perceptions of targeted customers
♦ develop a product that caters for their needs
♦ use customers' perceptions to identify the market position
♦ use the marketing mix to develop attributes and image for the chosen market position
♦ communicate attributes and image to customers.

ACTIVITY

Construct a survey to find out how a number of competing businesses are perceived by customers and how they are positioned in relation to each other.

Evaluation of segmentation strategies

Using an inappropriate base for segmentation can lead to missed business opportunities and an inability of an organisation to focus appropriately upon their customers. Kotler (1996) discusses various ways in which segmentation strategies can be evaluated. He identifies three factors.

Segment size and growth

He feels that segments must have the right size and growth characteristics so that they can forecast or predict the profitability of contributing to each segment.

Segment structural attractiveness

Over a period of time Kotler feels that it is important to evaluate the structure of the segment in order to understand 'segment attractiveness'. For example, a segment would be less attractive if it contained 'strong and aggressive competitors'. Other factors might include substitutes, the power of buyers and powerful suppliers.

Company objectives and resources

Organisations need to consider their own resources and objectives in relation to a particular segment. This means that some segments may be ignored because they do not fit in with corporate objectives.

There may be many other bases for evaluating successful segments. Clearly segments need to be stable and capable of being analysed. They also need to be accessible and capable of being entered.

Segmenting industrial or B2B markets

Business markets may use many of the same techniques to segment markets as those used by consumer marketers. Business buyers, for instance, might segment a market geographically or by size, value or quality of service or standards. Within a particular industry, an organisation may set up or develop a series of systems for dealing with customers which suit their methods of segmentation. For example, representatives may be geographically based to reflect the particular areas upon which an organisation wishes to focus.

There are also some different ways in which segmentation takes place in such markets. For example, an organisation may focus upon a particular company size that they wish to deal with. They may also focus upon a range of honed purchasing criteria. For example, a firm dealing in chemicals would only wish to deal with a specified number of particular organisations.

Industrial classification

According to National Statistics Online, 'A Standard Industrial Classification (SIC) was first introduced into the United Kingdom in 1948 for use in classifying business establishments and other statistical units by the

Section	Subsection	Description
A		Agriculture, hunting and forestry
B		Fishing
C		Mining and quarrying
	CA	Mining and quarrying of energy-producing materials
	CB	Mining and quarrying except energy-producing materials
D		Manufacturing
	DA	Manufacture of food products, beverages and tobacco
	DB	Manufacture of textiles and textile products
	DC	Manufacture of leather and leather products
	DD	Manufacture of wood and wood products
	DE	Manufacture of pulp, paper and paper products; publishing and printing
	DF	Manufacture of coke, refined petroleum products and nuclear fuel

Figure 8.46   SIC groupings

561

Section	Subsection	Description
	DG	Manufacture of chemicals, chemical products and man-made fibres
	DH	Manufacture of rubber and plastic products
	DI	Manufacture of other non-metallic mineral products
	DJ	Manufacture of basic metals and fabricated metal products
	DK	Manufacture of machinery and equipment not elsewhere classified
	DL	Manufacture of electrical and optical equipment
	DM	Manufacture of transport equipment
	DN	Manufacturing not elsewhere classified
E		Electricity, gas and water supply
F		Construction
G		Wholesale and retail trade; repair of motor vehicles, motorcycles and personal and household goods
H		Hotels and restaurants
I		Transport, storage and communication
J		Financial intermediation
K		Real estate, renting and business activities
L		Public administration and defence; compulsory social security
M		Education
N		Health and social work
O		Other community, social and personal service activities
P		Private households with employed persons
Q		Extra-territorial organisations and bodies

Figure 8.46   SIC groupings (continued)

type of economic activity in which they are engaged. The classification provides a framework for the collection, tabulation, presentation and analysis of data and its use promotes uniformity. In addition, it can be used for administrative purposes and by non-government bodies as a convenient way of classifying industrial activities into a common structure.' The SIC index, therefore, is the government's way of classifying organisations and dividing markets, and provides a base or structure for other organisations to base their segmentation strategies.

Research and topical articles

This chapter has, in a very broad way, discussed a range of issues related to markets and consumers within these markets. If anything, it has probably emphasised the sheer diversity of human needs and market characteristics and the need to focus upon customers in order to understand what their requirements are as well as into what segment they fall. A considerable amount of research has taken place in this area.

Segmentation strategies

JOURNAL ARTICLE

Sally Dibb (1998) argues that, 'Despite the well-documented benefits which segmentation offers, businesses continue to encounter implementation difficulties. This raises concerns about the cause of these problems and how they might be overcome. These concerns are addressed in this paper in the form of three questions: Is segmentation a good idea? If segmentation is such a good idea, why does it sometimes fail? What can be done to reduce the chance of failure?'

Her paper concludes by suggesting that if marketers are to overcome their segmentation implementation difficulties, they need practical guidance at three stages in the segmentation process. Before the project begins they must understand the role of success factors contributing to a successful result. During the segmentation project the qualities of the emerging segments must be clarified. After segmentation is complete the question of segment attractiveness must be considered. She argues that there is currently a gulf between the priorities of academics and practitioners carrying out segmentation. If this is to be bridged, further research is needed to provide guidance on segmentation success factors.

Dibb, S. 'Market segmentation: strategies for success', *Marketing Intelligence and Planning*, 1998, Vol. 16, No. 7, pp 394–406.

JOURNAL ARTICLE

A particularly interesting article by Goller *et al.* (2002) argues that, 'Since its conception over 60 years ago by Frederick in 1934, the concept of segmentation has gained increasing importance, in both the consumer and the business domains. Examination of research within the latter domain indicates that, although considerable amounts of research have been carried out, these efforts appear to focus on sub-areas of segmentation such as the development of segmentation bases and models, at the expense of a more strategic view. This not only has resulted in a diffused understanding of the subject-matter but also is posited to have slowed the progress of theory development and research in business segmentation.' Their article poses some interesting questions that enables us to understand processes of segmentation more.

Goller, S., Hogg, A., Stavros, P. and Kalafatis, P. 'A new research agenda for business segmentation', *European Journal of Marketing*, 2002, Vol. 36, No. 1, pp 252–71.

Chapter 3
Marketing mix

The marketing mix provides us with a useful way of looking at the marketing of products. Organisations need to create a successful mix of:

♦ the right product (or service)
♦ sold in the right place
♦ at the right price
♦ using the most suitable form of promotion.

Figure 8.47   The marketing mix

Kotler (1988) describes this mix as 'a set of controllable variables that the firm can use to influence the buyer's response'. 'Mix' is an appropriate word to use in this instance. A mix is a composition of ingredients blended together to fulfil a common purpose. Every ingredient is vitally important and each depends upon the others for its contribution. Just as with a cake, each ingredient is not sufficient on its own but with all blended together it is possible to produce something very special. In the same way that there are a variety of cakes to suit various tastes, a marketing mix can be designed to suit the precise requirements of a market.

> The marketing mix is therefore a series of controllable variables that an organisation can use in order to best meet customer needs and ensure that an organisation is successful in the markets in which it serves.

As a result the marketing mix must have:

♦ A **timescale**: an organisation must have a plan which indicates when it expects to achieve its objectives. Some objectives will be set to be attained in the near future. Others might be medium term (one to five years) and others might be visionary strategic objectives for attainment in the longer term.
♦ **Strategic elements**: these will involve the overall strategy of the organisation. They require considerable use of judgement and expertise and are only decided by senior managers. Such decisions involve the development of a new product or a new marketing strategy.
♦ **Tactical or medium-term elements**: the business environment has to be constantly monitored and decisions have to be taken according to the changes taking place. External events affect pricing strategies, product modifications or amendments to marketing plans.
♦ **Short-term operational decisions**: these involve predictable everyday decisions such as contracts with customers, analysis of advertising and less important factors.

Four Ps or seven Ps

This simple mix is often referred to as the 'four Ps' of product, price, place and promotion. This rather straightforward way of looking at what has become an increasingly complex business environment has at times been felt to be a little simplistic and limiting in terms of the real mix and the fullness of our understanding. There are many who might also argue that the mix includes absolutely everything an organisation does to satisfy its customers, and it could be wrong to try to group these factors artificially under headings. However, in recent times, and in order to meet such criticisms, the mix has been expanded to become a seven P mix with the addition of three more Ps.

People

People are widely recognised to be the greatest asset of the modern organisation. The governing principle, whether recognised or not, is that everybody who works for an organisation is a customer, either inside (the internal customer) or outside (the 'traditional customer') the company. Both kinds of customer expect to be supplied with the product or service they need, on time and as specified. This principle holds good for everyone in the company, whatever their level of skill and experience, whether their 'product' is answering a telephone or masterminding a major new project. It works to everyone's benefit. In doing so it provides the individual with genuine responsibility and scope for initiative, and it virtually guarantees that the organisation's performance will be improved.

Provision of customer service

Customer service has become increasingly important in a rapidly changing marketplace. It has become more closely linked with the core product. Customer service is associated with developing bonds with customers in order to create long-term relationships that lead to advantages for all groups. It does not just happen.

It is a process which involves pre-transaction, transaction and post-transaction considerations. Emphasis upon customer service will change from one product to another. For example, when manufacturing goods such as bread or shampoo, customer service may involve developing strong customer relationships with many of the large retailers. In a pure service industry such as hairdressing or insurance, there are no tangible goods, and so customers will view nearly all of the benefits they get on the basis of the service they receive.

Process management

This involves all of the procedures, tasks, mechanisms and activities through which a product or service is delivered to a customer. It is clear that in a modern organisation processes are a key part of the marketing mix, involving developing priorities and ways of meeting customer needs. Processes might involve key

decisions about customer involvement and employee discretion. In today's rapidly changing business environment, in order to meet consumer needs more closely, it is marketing that should determine the processes that link manufacturing with the customer.

CASE STUDY

Creating products, the importance of branding for your customers

Apple Computer's sales of its iPod were up 140 per cent in the fourth quarter of 2003, giving it a 50 per cent share of the digital music player market. Many might ask, how did the company do it? It was achieved with a typical Apple design linking style with high technology, alongside extensive promotions including an ad campaign that Marian Salzman of ad agency Euro RSCG said, 'is about an Apple state of mind'.

The Apple state of mind is a mental image of the brand that consumers have, based on experiences with the company and its products. Apple connects with consumers on an emotional level, much as do Nike and Starbucks.

Branding is a hot topic today, filled with clichés and buzzwords that can sometimes trivialise the real advantage of having a good brand. But what is a brand, and what makes a brand strong? It is not just hype: a logo and graphics communicated with heavy spending on advertising and promotion. That just creates awareness, and being well known is not enough. Strong brands turn need into desire. With strong brands, customers don't just want to buy from an organisation, it is argued that they want to have a relationship with them. A brand therefore involves a focused strategy requiring action. In fact it is argued that it is more than that and that all of the elements of the marketing mix that go to satisfy customer requirements such as the product, price, delivery and customer service are all represented and unified through the brand. Strong brands help simplify customer choice and guide prospects (prospective buyers) to your products, differentiate the company or products, and build strong relationships with ever more demanding customers. This is more critical in today's customer-driven market, and in an economy predicated more on customer needs than manufacturing capabilities.

ACTIVITY

1 Use an example of a brand you use to describe the branding process.

2 What values do you associate with that brand?

3 Which elements of the marketing mix do you associate with the brand?

4 Evaluate how much the brand goes alongside the product.

The product

The product is the most important element in an organisation's marketing mix. According to Sally Dibb *et al.* (1994), 'A product is everything, both favourable and unfavourable, that is received in an exchange.' Dibb implies, and we shall see later that this is supported through the total product concept, that the product is the organisation itself, the brand and everything it does to satisfy customer needs. It includes the very tangible item, if there is one, as well as all of the accompanying intangible benefits that are sometimes less obvious and more difficult to identify.

Products and brands

A **brand** is a part of a particular product and includes characteristics that identify it with a particular producer.

Many mass-produced products are almost identical. For example, most washing powders are similar, as are different types of margarine. These goods tend to be produced by two or three large companies who encourage sales by creating brands which differentiate the products in the minds of consumers.

A brand can be a name, a symbol or a design used to identify a specific product and differentiate it from its competitors. Brand names, designs, trademarks, symbols, slogans and even music can be used to distinguish one product from another and allow an organisation to distinguish its products from competing ones.

The business of creating a brand is a particularly important function of marketing. Often people will buy the brand name as much as the product itself. You will see people in supermarkets pick up an item (which they have not seen before) and say, 'this must be a good one because it is made by ...'

Large organisations swear by the power of the brand. They will fight tooth and nail to raise the status of their brands, and be determined that nothing should affect the power of their brands.

Types of brand

There are three different types of brand.

Manufacturer brands

Examples of these include Kellogg's cornflakes, Nescafé coffee and Heinz baked beans. These manufacturer brands associate the producer with the specific product, and the producer will be heavily involved with the promotion of the product.

Own-label brands

Examples of these include Tesco, St Michael (Marks & Spencer), Farm Foods (Asda), Sainsbury's own label, and so on. These brands are owned and controlled by retailers, and therefore the producers or manufacturers are not associated with the products involved in their promotion.

Generic brands

Such products are extremely rare in the modern competitive market, and those that exist are usually at the lower end of the market with respect to price and quality. These products have no identifiable name or logo. Examples may include plain T-shirts or bin-liners if they have no branded packaging or labels attached that identify the originator.

Organisations seek to create a portfolio of individual products which support the image of a brand. Well-known brand names will therefore emphasise quality throughout the organisation.

A brand which is held in high esteem is worth a lot of money to an organisation. There is a well-known saying in business that, 'an organisation can afford to get rid of its other assets, but not its brand image!'

ACTIVITY

Identify two or three brands of products in a particular market. To what extent could these brands be further developed in a way that exemplifies the attributes of each brand?

Product features, advantages and benefits

Customers as a rule do not buy features, they buy what those features can do for them: the problems they solve, the money or the time they save, and so on. A product is really a bundle of benefits. A key aspect of marketing is to make sure that products create the benefits that a consumer desires in a particular product and that the product offering is better than those of competitors. Associated with this is the need

to make sure that the market fully understands the range of benefits on offer, through strong communications.

When we understand the benefits that customers are looking for in a product, we are best placed to know why they will buy it – and hence focus our marketing accordingly. For example, in buying toothpaste the benefits that customers may be looking for include:

♦ flavour and product appearance
♦ brightness of teeth
♦ decay prevention
♦ price: value for money
♦ appealing brand name and confidence in brand.

Knowing that these are the benefits the consumer requires enables the organisation to focus its efforts on creating products that will produce one or more of them, and then promotion can be used to highlight the organisation's ability to create these benefits.

There are often clear and **tangible features** (things you can touch and see) associated with a product. Tangible features might include shape, design, colour, packaging and size.

Intangible features are not so obvious. These include the reputation of an organisation, the brand image, after sales service, availability of spare parts, service centres, and so on.

It is also argued that products provide advantages for customers through three different dimensions.

Generic dimensions

These are the key benefits of a particular item. For example, shoe polish should, we hope, clean shoes. Freezers should store frozen food. Hairdressers should be able to cut and style hair.

Sensual dimensions

These have an impact upon the senses. They might include design, colour, taste, smell and texture. The sensual benefits are frequently highlighted by advertisers. This is clearly the case when advertising food and drinks: 'smooth and creamy', 'the amber nectar', and so on.

Extended dimensions

A wide range of additional benefits are included here. Examples are servicing agreements, credit facilities, guarantees, maintenance contracts, and so on.

All of these are each in their own way important. However in creating the product we must always focus on those features that best meet customers' requirements for benefits. Concentrating on products themselves rather than on meeting customer needs can lead a business into what Theodore Levitt (1975) calls 'marketing myopia'. It is a mistake if an oil company simply views itself as a producer of petrol instead of a provider of high-quality fuel that helps customers get the most from their vehicles, or if McDonald's saw itself as a producer of fast food rather than as a provider of relatively cheap meals that busy customers can enjoy in clean surroundings without having to wait to be served.

Benefits clearly only last a limited period of time. The classic example is if a marketer stresses the importance of an electric drill. When someone buys a drill, he or she is really buying the benefits from a tool that makes a small hole. If someone comes up with a better way of making a small hole, the drill would be redundant.

The total product concept

A product has a bundle of benefits. For example, digital satellite TV offers a wide range of entertainment in your own home (via lots of channels), convenience (for example, the facility for home shopping, an easy-to-read menu of programmes), a very clear picture (through high definition), and so on.

Products can be viewed in terms of a number of layers beyond the satisfaction of a simple consumer need. At a simple level, a person buys an overcoat to keep warm and dry, buys sunglasses to shade her eyes from the sun, and buys a watch to tell the time. However, buying behaviour is far more complex than this. It is not uncommon to hear someone say, ' I wouldn't be seen dead in one of those', or 'these sunglasses make me look absolutely dreadful'. An item needs to fit in with our particular perceptions of self-image. Products are not usually purchased to meet a single need; the ownership and use

of a product involve a whole range of factors that make up the product concept.

Christine Ennew (1993) argues that we can look at the total product concept at four main levels.

Core product

The core product has certain basic features that are likely to be identical across all products, for example a lawn mower would be expected to cut grass. All products in this category would be able to perform this function.

Tangible product

Differentiation begins to occur at the next level, often described as the tangible or **expected product**. At this level additional features may provide a competitive advantage, for example a brand name and quality differences such as a grass collector box, an engine made from quality castings, a wider range of gear speeds, and so on. It is typically at the level of the tangible product that the greatest level of competition occurs.

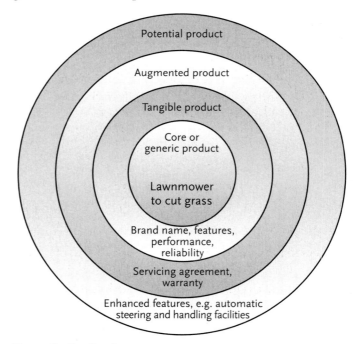

Figure 8.48 Product concept

Augmented product

The third layer is what we call the augmented product. This includes additional aspects of the product which go beyond what the consumer might generally expect and therefore give further competitive advantages, for example customer servicing arrangements. Today, there is ever more pressure on companies to augment their product. Augmenting a product simply means adding to it in order to improve the distinctiveness of the product and thus to increase its competitive advantage.

Potential product

The final level is the potential product, which covers aspects that may become part of the offer in the future.

> ### ACTIVITY
>
> Identify a product, and then list each element it provides that meets customer needs through the four layers.

Product (or service) mix

A **product item** is a specific model, brand or size of a product that an organisation sells, for example a 2 kg box of Uncle Ben's long grain rice.

A **product line** is a group of closely related product items with similar characteristics and/or applications, for example a line of Uncle Ben's rice items, including short grain, long grain and pudding rice.

A **product mix** is all of an organisation's product lines, for example rice, flour, sugar, pickles and other lines. Any product mix can be described according to its width, length, depth and consistency.

Width

Width is the number of different product lines on offer. For example, Coca-Cola has 'stuck to the knitting' and produces quite a narrow range of soft drinks including Sprite, Fanta and Coca-Cola. In contrast, a company like Unilever has a wide range of products from Walls ice-cream and Birds Eye frozen foods to many different types of soap powders and cleaning agents. Having a narrow range of products enables you to benefit from economies of large-scale production whereas breadth enables an organisation to benefit from diversification. Broadening a line to create breadth means extending it beyond its current range.

Length

Length is the total number of items on offer. The decision on the number of lines to offer is very important. Too many lines and you may overstretch yourself, and even start to compete against your own lines. Line stretching involves increasing the product line, either by moving into higher-quality items or moving downmarket.

When the car manufacturer Volkswagen bought a 31 per cent share in Skoda in 1991, the leading Skoda model was the downmarket Favorit. Not only were substantial changes made to the Favorit, but in 1995 a new, more upmarket Felicia was added to Skoda's lines with great success. The process of line filling involves filling in gaps in product lines. For example, confectionery manufacturers regularly develop new chocolate bars to fill perceived gaps in their range of products. Line rationalisation involves cutting out lines that are not central to the organisation's major focus of interest, or those that have lost popularity.

Depth

Depth is the number of variants of each brand, for example the number of different sizes, models or flavours within a product line. Detergent companies like Procter & Gamble or Unilever offer many different sizes of soap powder boxes as well as lots of different kinds of soap powder, all targeted at slightly different groups of customers. It makes sense for a large company to offer a product for all occasions in order to aim for a position of leadership. However, it is important not to cannibalise the sales of your own products. Deepening a product would mean adding more lines within your existing range. Line pruning means cutting the depth of a product line by reducing the number of alternative sizes, models or flavours in the line.

Consistency

Consistency is the closeness of the relationship between each product line.

Creating the optimum product mix means having the right balance in terms of width, depth, length and consistency. An effective product mix should yield a balanced profit contribution from a number of lines – although there will always be some products that are the highest yielders.

Organisations need to decide whether they have the right mix at any one point in time while having an eye on future changes. Key concerns are: Should we stick to the narrow range of lines in which we are successful? What are our current strengths and weaknesses? What are the opportunities and threats of diversifying? How can we avoid competing with ourselves?

The product lifecycle

The life of a product is the period over which it appeals to customers. We can all think of goods that everyone wanted at one time but which have now gone out of fashion. Famous fashion examples from the 1960s include hot-pants and beehive hairstyles.

The sales performance of any product rises from nought when the product is introduced to the market, reaches a peak and then goes into decline (see Figure 8.49). Most products are faced by a limited lifecycle. Initially the product may flourish and grow, eventually the market will mature and finally the product will move towards decline and petrification. At each stage in the product lifecycle there is a close relationship between sales and profits so that as organisations or brands go into decline their profitability decreases.

The lifecycle can be broken down into distinct stages. In the **introductory phase**, growth is slow and volume is low because of limited awareness of the product's existence. Sales then rise rapidly during the period of **growth**. It is during this phase that the profit per unit sold usually reaches a maximum. Towards the end of this phase, competitors enter the market to promote their own products, which reduces the rate of growth of sales of the first product.

This period is known as **maturity**. Competitive jockeying – such as product differentiation in the form of new flavours, colours, sizes, and so on – will sift out the weaker brands. During **saturation**, some brands will drop out of the market. The product market may eventually **decline** and reach a stage when it becomes unprofitable.

Product lifecycle and other areas of the marketing mix

The lifecycle may last for a few months or for hundreds of years. To prolong the lifecycle of a brand or a product, an organisation needs to readjust the ingredients of the marketing mix. Periodic injections of new ideas are needed: product improvements, line extensions or improved promotions. Figure 8.50 illustrates the process of injecting new life into a product.

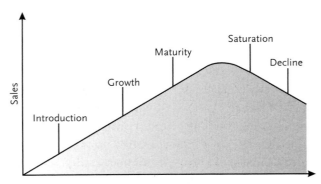

Figure 8.49   The life cycle of a product

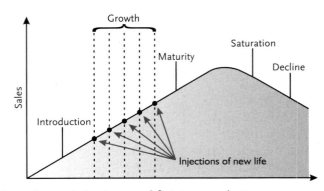

Figure 8.50   Injecting new life into a product

A readjustment of the marketing mix might include:

♦ changing or modifying the product, to keep up with or ahead of the competition
♦ altering distribution patterns, to provide a more suitable place for the consumer to make purchases
♦ changing prices to reflect competitive activities
♦ considering carefully the style of promotion.

Most large organisations produce a range of products each with its own unique lifecycle. By using lifecycles, marketers can plan when to introduce new lines as old products go into decline. The collection of products that an organisation produces is known as its **product portfolio** (see Figure 8.51).

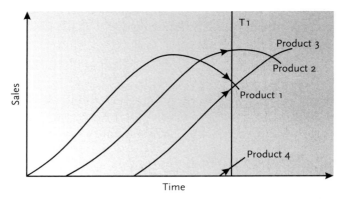

Figure 8.51   A product portfolio

In Figure 8.51, T1 represents a point in time. At that point product 1 is in decline, product 2 is in maturity, product 3 is in growth and product 4 has recently been introduced.

If an organisation's products are increasingly more appealing and are launched at just the right time, the organisation will find it benefits from a continuous period of steady growth.

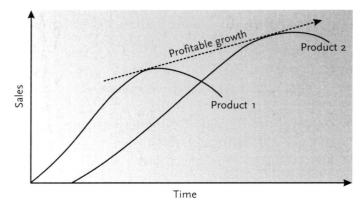

Figure 8.52   Profit growth through multiple products

Product strategy

Examining the lifecycle of a product helps us to appreciate that products go through various phases from infancy to decline. Markets and their structures are changing all of the time. In recent years 'niche marketing' has been popular, particularly with the emergence of branding. Today many organisations have spotted opportunities through the use of the Internet and other technologies to develop their markets.

Market share is important for business organisations. The Boston Consultancy Group (BCG) have argued that the faster the growth of a particular market the greater the cost necessary to maintain position. In a rapidly

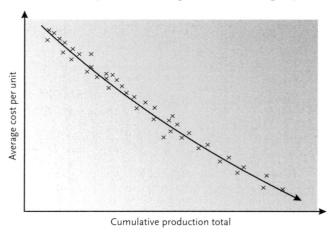

Figure 8.53   The experience curve

571

growing market, considerable expenditure will be required on investment in product lines, and to combat the threat posed by new firms and brands.

Gains in efficiency stem from greater experience. The BCG argued that, as a rough guide, average cost per unit fell by 20–30 per cent with each doubling of experience. Greater experience stems from:

♦ economies of scale
♦ the elimination of less efficient factors of production
♦ increased productivity stemming from technical changes and learning effects
♦ improvements in product design.

The Boston matrix

The Boston Group developed 'The Boston Box' or matrix, which relates closely to product lifecycles. They identify four types of products in an organisation's portfolio (Figure 8.54).

Problem children are products that have just been launched. This is an appropriate name because many products fail to move beyond this phase. Such products are often referred to as **question mark**s. Is it possible to develop these products and turn them into the **stars** and **cash cows** of the future? It might be, but first they will require a lot of financial support and this will represent a heavy financial commitment.

Stars are products that have successfully reached the growth stage in the lifecycle. Although these products too will require a lot of financial support, they will also provide high cash returns. On balance they will provide a neutral cash flow and are good prospects for the future.

Cash cows have reached the maturity stage in their product lifecycle and are now 'yielders'. They have a high market share in markets that are no longer rapidly expanding. Because the market is relatively static, they require few fresh injections of capital; for example, advertising and promotion may be required to inject a little fresh life from time to time. However, the net effect is of a positive cash flow. Cash generated by the cash cows may be used to help the question marks.

Dogs are products in decline. These have a low market share in low-growing or a declining market. As they generate a negative cash flow, they will usually be disposed of.

ACTIVITY

Using your own experience of a product portfolio from an organisation, identify its:

♦ Question marks
♦ Stars
♦ Cash cows
♦ Dogs.

In each case explain what evidence you have for drawing the conclusions you make.

Market growth \ Relative market share	High	Low
High	Stars	Question marks
Low	Cash cows	Dogs

Figure 8.54   The Boston matrix

In order to maintain an effective portfolio development, it is important to have a balance of products at any one time. An organisation will require a number of cash cows to provide its 'bread and butter'. At the same time, it is important to develop the cash cows of the future by investing in the question marks. Fortunately the stars should pay their own way. It is also important to identify the dogs and cut them out.

Products in the top half of the Boston matrix are in the earlier stage of their product lifecycle and so are in high-growth markets. Those in the lower half of the box are in the later stages and so are in markets where growth will have slowed down or stopped.

Ansoff's matrix

Igor Ansoff (1965) developed this theory further by outlining a product–market mix. This looks not just at the management of a product portfolio but also more widely at market developments and opportunities. Ansoff's matrix matches existing and new product strategies with existing and new markets (Figure 8.55).

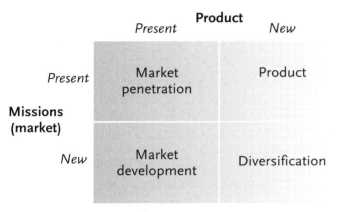

Figure 8.55   The Ansoff matrix

In this way, this matrix suggests four alternative marketing strategies which hinge upon whether the product is new or existing and whether the market is new or existing.

Market penetration

This suggests a further penetration of existing markets with existing products. This will involve a strategy of increasing market share within existing segments and markets. This can be achieved either by selling more to established customers or by finding new customers in the existing markets.

Product development

This involves developing new products for existing markets. To be effective, such a strategy should move the product into new segments.

Market development

This strategy entails using existing products and finding new markets for them. Better targeting, market research and further segmentation will identify these new markets. In recent years companies like Cadbury have developed new markets in Eastern Europe.

Diversification

This will lead to a move away from core activities. This might involve some form of integration of production into related activities. Diversification involves moving into new products and new markets at the same time.

In developing a product strategy it is important to remember that the element of risk increases the further an organisation moves away from known quantities – their existing markets and existing products.

Ansoff's (1965) original article stated that, 'The diversification strategy stands apart from the other

CASE STUDY

Making the coconut market stable through product diversification

Product diversification is one of the answers to the question of bringing stability to the coconut industry according to Dr P. Rethinam.

He feels that the daily variation of the price of coconut oil was because of the availability and low prices of substitute oils in the market. As a result he felt that this called for switching over to other value-added products to keep the market for coconut oil stable.

More than 50 per cent of coconut production was used for culinary purposes. But, there was excellent scope for production of coconut-based items such as dessicated coconut, coconut cream and coconut milk powder.

Dr Rethinam advocates the development of a technology development programme by setting up pilot plants for integrated coconut processing and other activities. Under the programme, aid to technological research projects, especially in the areas of product diversification and by-product utilisation, could be given through recognised research institutions.

three. While the latter are usually followed with the same technical, financial, and merchandising resources which are used for the original product line, diversification usually requires new skills, new techniques, and new facilities. As a result it almost invariably leads to physical and organisational changes in the structure of the business which represent a distinct break with past business experience.'

New product development

A new product may be one which:

♦ replaces an old product
♦ opens up a new market
♦ broadens an existing market.

It may involve an innovation, a technological breakthrough or simply be a line extension based upon a modification. It is often said that only about 10 per cent of new products are really new. In fact, it is often possible to turn old products into new products simply by finding a new market for them.

There are six distinct stages in the development process for new products. These are:

♦ Step 1: Ideas
♦ Step 2: Screening of ideas
♦ Step 3: Marketing analysis
♦ Step 4: Product development
♦ Step 5: Testing
♦ Step 6: Launch and commercialisation

As new products go through each of these stages there is a **mortality rate** (see Figure 8.56).

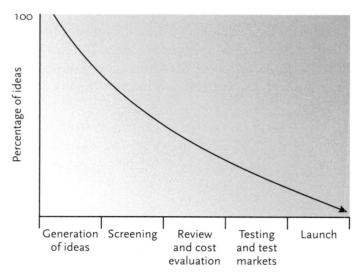

Figure 8.56   Stages in launching a new product

Step 1: Ideas

All new products start from ideas. These ideas may be completely new or simply be an update of an existing product. Ideas may come from:

♦ Research and development: product development and market research working together. Technological breakthroughs and innovations from research are very important.
♦ Mindstorming: involving a few people developing ideas from words and concepts.
♦ Suggestions box: incentives may encourage employees to contribute their own ideas.
♦ Sales force: working close to customers, the sales force understands their needs and requirements.
♦ Forced relationships: sometimes one or more products can be joined together to form new product concepts. For example, combined shampoo and conditioner.
♦ Competitors: monitoring the actions of competitors may provide a rich source of new ideas.

The most common source of ideas for new products is within a company itself. Dalrymple and Parsons (1995) state that surveys indicate that 60 per cent of industrial and 46 per cent of consumer new products came from research staff, engineers, salespeople, marketing research personnel and other employees and executives. Another 25 per cent of industrial new product ideas and 30 per cent of consumer ideas come from new users. Lead users are an especially good source.

Step 2: Screening of ideas

Once ideas have been generated it is important to screen for the ideas likely to be successful and reject the rest. Considerations may include how well the product fits in with others in the product range, the unique elements of any idea that make it competitive, the likely demand for the product and whether or not it could be manufactured economically.

Step 3: Marketing analysis

Once the ideas have been screened, further marketing analysis begins. This involves a thorough analysis of the product's market potential. This type of research helps to identify the market volume (units that could be sold) as well as the value of sales expected. It may also help to identify market potential.

Step 4: Product development

Having come through the test of marketing analysis it is now time to translate the idea or product concept into a product. Design, innovation and the uses of technology are very important in product development. An assessment of packaging and branding may also be involved.

Step 5: Testing

Testing is a vital stage in the product development process. It may involve identifying valuable information through further market research which helps to fine-tune the venture. Test marketing may comprise testing on part of a consumer market or trialling the product to ensure that it meets the required standards.

Step 6: Launch and commercialisation

The launch is the most important day in the life of a product, when it is finally revealed to customers. It may involve rolling from one TV region to another TV region. Today a common technique is to provide sneak glimpses of new products before they are launched.

Adoption process

For a product to achieve success early in its lifecycle, it is important that a 'head of steam' is built up in terms of consumer interest as quickly as possible. Michael Baker (1971) argues that, 'some form of exponential function (represented graphically by a cumulative S-shaped curve) is typical of the manner in which objects or ideas spread or diffuse through populations of adopters'.

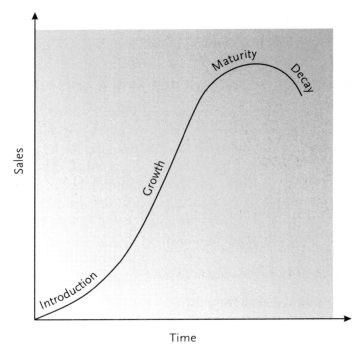

Figure 8.57   Baker's cumulative S-shape

Baker then goes on to argue that, 'the consistent and pervasive nature of the diffusion process approximates a law of nature and reflects an underlying process such that if one can initiate diffusion it will proceed to some extent automatically thereafter due to the "bandwagon" or "contagion" effect'. In terms of the product lifecycle, he feels that it is imperative to hit predetermined sales figures as quickly as possible because proof of a sale adds conviction to the selling process and word-of-mouth recommendation, and the pure visibility of products in the marketplace accelerate the awareness. It is therefore essential to identify the early adopters of products.

Place

The place element within the marketing mix is probably the most underestimated element. In simple terms it provides the basic infrastructure for consumer needs to be satisfied.

> Distribution is the process of the marketing mix that makes goods available for customers where and when they want them.

Customer convenience and availability

The place element of the marketing mix involves making goods available in the most convenient way for the customer. It therefore involves bridging the key gaps in time, place, quantity and variety which exist between the producer and the consumer. Like the other three elements of the mix, effective organisation of place will add value to the product, and getting place right is an important ingredient of competitive advantage.

The two key elements of place are:

♦ **physical distribution** involves getting a product from A to B. Physical distribution management is an important part of the marketing mix. It helps an organisation to meet customer needs profitably and efficiently. In doing so it enables manufacturers and distributors to provide goods for customers at the right time, in the right place and in the condition required. It may also reduce the lead-time, that is, the time measured from when a customer first makes an order until that order is delivered.
♦ **channel management** through which channels can be used to get products to consumers.

Channels and intermediaries

Channels

Channels are the networks of intermediaries linking the producer to the market. Whereas direct selling methods are zero-level channels which do not use an intermediary, indirect selling methods use one or more channels of distribution through which goods are transferred from the producer to the end user. These channels consist of one or more individuals or organisations who help to make the products available for the end user. This movement is not merely of the physical goods, but includes title (ownership), payment, information and promotion.

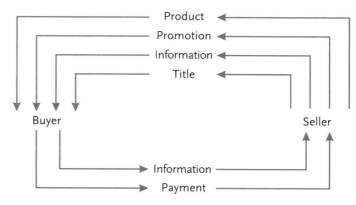

Figure 8.58   Types of channel flows

The seller needs to promote the product to the buyer. Information will need to flow between the buyer and the seller; the seller needs to make clear what the terms of the offer are, and the buyer needs to specify his or her requirements. Invoices, payments and receipts will need to flow between the purchaser and the seller. Nowadays it is common practice to try to integrate these flows; for example, a receipt is frequently complemented by promotional material.

Channel distribution management is the process of developing, organising and managing the distribution system. It is concerned with decisions about whether to sell directly or to use intermediaries, which intermediaries to use, and the contractual arrangements that are negotiated with intermediaries.

Intermediaries

Intermediaries such as wholesalers stock a range of goods from competing manufacturers to sell on to other organisations such as retailers. Most wholesalers take on the title to the goods and so assume many of the associated risks which include the following five actions.

Breaking bulk

Manufacturers produce goods in bulk for sale but they might not want to store the goods themselves. They want to be paid as quickly as possible. A number of wholesalers buy the stock from them and generally payment is prompt. The wholesaler then stocks these goods, along with others bought from other manufacturers, on the premises, ready for purchase by retailers.

Simplifying the distribution process

The chain of distribution without the wholesaler would look something like Figure 8.59. Manufacturer 1 has to carry out four journeys to supply retailers 1, 2, 3 and 4, and has to send out four sets of business documents, and handle four sets of accounts. The same situation applies to each of the manufacturers, so that in total 16 journeys are made and 16 sets of paperwork are required. This is a simplification, because in the real world thousands of different transactions might be involved.

An intermediary can simplify costs and processes of distribution by cutting down on journeys, fuel and other costs as well as cutting down on paperwork such as invoicing and administration.

The chain of distribution with an intermediary such as a wholesaler would look something like Figure 8.60. Clearly everything is simplified.

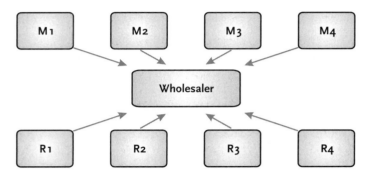

Figure 8.60   Distribution with a wholesaler

Storage

Most retailers have only a limited amount of storage space. The wholesaler can be looked upon as a cupboard for the retailer. Manufacturers are able to unload finished goods on the wholesaler, who then acts as a conduit to the retailers.

Packing and labelling

The wholesaler will in some instances finish off the packaging and labelling of goods, perhaps by putting price tags or brand labels on them.

Offering advice

Being in the middle of a chain of distribution, wholesalers have a lot more information at their fingertips than either the retailer or manufacturer. In particular, wholesalers know which goods are selling well. With this in mind they can advise retailers on what to buy and manufacturers on what to produce.

By contracting out the process of distribution, a company can concentrate on its core functions. Manufacturers may lack the financial resources required to carry out their own direct marketing operation. The expense of direct marketing often requires that several complementary products are sold at the same time.

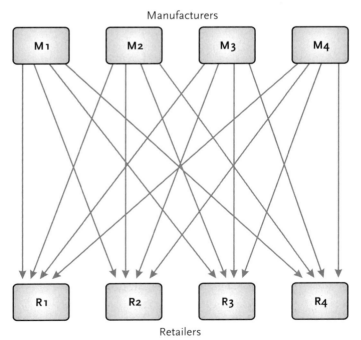

Figure 8.59   Distribution without a wholesaler

ACTIVITY

There are many different aspects to physical distribution, most of which should be designed to work together as a whole. If this book were not available on the shelf of your local bookshop, what processes do you think would be likely to take place once you placed your order?

Channel selection

Kotler (1988) describes the simplest level of distribution, direct selling, as the zero-level channel. A one-level channel involves just one intermediary. The zero-level channel has become increasingly popular within the UK in recent years with organisations looking for new ways of reaching potential customers.

ACTIVITY

In your group, discuss both the advantages and the disadvantages of using the Internet for shopping.

Reasons for using the 'zero-level' channel include:

◆ the need to take control over aspects of the presentation of the final product to the customer
◆ the need to demonstrate a technical product, or provide after-sales service
◆ lack of high-quality intermediaries
◆ inability to persuade existing channels to carry goods
◆ excessive profits demanded by intermediaries
◆ industrial markets, where there may be only a relatively small number of large consumers.

Reasons for not using 'zero-level' channels include:

◆ 'sticking to the knitting': a manufacturer is able to concentrate capital and resources on what it does best: manufacturing of the product
◆ lack of financial resources
◆ lack of know-how and expertise in dealing with customers and managing distribution channels

◆ lack of a wide enough range of products to make it worthwhile retailing them
◆ large numbers of potential customers who are geographically scattered.

A producer may decide to develop a **multi-channel distribution system**. This involves creating a range of different ways of distributing products. For example, a company like Colgate-Palmolive, which manufactures a range of toothpastes, soaps, and so on, will deal with a range of wholesalers, retailers and other outlets.

CASE STUDY

Selling Levi's at Tesco

The supermarket chain Tesco is claiming a victory in a long-running battle to be allowed to sell cut-price designer brands in its stores. The European Court of Justice, considering a test case between the company and clothes manufacturer Levi-Strauss, accepted that traders such as Tesco should have their interests considered.

An EU spokesperson said the legal opinion was 'complex and confusing' and gave no clear indication of how the law on trade marks should be interpreted. 'It's not immediately clear what the implications are going to be', he said.

After the European Court makes its full ruling, the case is due to go back to the UK courts. 'Levi-Strauss & Co welcome this,' Levi's said. Managers from Tesco have added that the retailer would now be looking to other markets, such as the USA, to satisfy the demand from its consumers.

Supermarkets have been keen to branch out beyond their traditional lines; next to the shelves of bread and beans they are now stocking electrical goods, mobile phones and clothes, some from top design names. But the manufacturers of some of those products are not keen to see their brands in supermarket aisles, especially as the prices are often lower than those charged by approved retailers.

Manufacturers can choose whether to create intensive distribution channels where they sell through every available outlet to win sales, or to go for selective distribution where they distribute through a narrow range of outlets. Finally, they may develop an exclusive arrangement whereby only one or a very small number of intermediaries are chosen for distribution.

Integration and distribution systems

Although in many areas of business we have seen the contracting out of non-core business functions, this has not always been the case in the organisation of distribution channels. Many organisations want to have tight control over the distribution process. The term **vertical marketing system** (VMS) has been used to define the vertical integration of distribution. Vertical integration may involve directly owning distributors, or controlling aspects of their operations, or creating very tight contractual arrangements as to how distribution will take place.

The rationale for vertically integrating distribution systems is not concerned only with cutting out the profit margin of the intermediary. More importantly, it is about quality issues, which of course have a key relationship with profitability of operations.

Ennew (1993) makes an important distinction between what she calls corporate VMS and contractual VMS. Corporate VMS is where all aspects of the distribution channel are internalised under the ownership and control of a single organisation, for example Boots, which manufactures, wholesales and retails a large selection of products. Contractual VMS is where the manufacturer imposes strong contractual constraints on distributors, and it is typified by franchising arrangements.

Franchising

Franchising is a particularly effective form of distribution. Research within the UK in the 1980s showed that nine out of ten franchises succeed. It is not surprising, therefore, that we are experiencing a rapid growth in franchising, following in the wake of trail-blazing developments in the USA. By the end of the last century more than 50 per cent of sales within the USA were through franchises.

What is a franchise?

Essentially, a franchise is the permission and contractual right to trade in a product or service in a specified way. The firm that sells a franchise is called a franchisor and the person taking out the franchise is called a franchisee.

At the heart of a successful franchise is the set of relationships that develop between the franchisor and the franchisee, which should constitute a partnership. The franchisee brings to the partnership his or her dreams and skills, which are then combined with the business systems, expertise and experience of the franchisor.

The person taking out the franchise puts up a sum of money as capital and is issued with equipment by the franchising company, to sell or manufacture the product in which the franchising company deals. The franchisee has the exclusive right to operate in a particular area. Franchising is common for fast-food outlets, examples being McDonald's and Pizza Hut.

Physical distribution management and logistics

The physical distribution system that an organisation selects will largely depend upon the scale of operations and the size of an organisation's market. A business handling a lot of international mail, for example, might locate near a large airport. Key decisions about physical distribution may include the following:

♦ Inventory: a business that wants to maximise customer service will have the highest inventory costs, because it needs to hold stock to meet all requests. The key inventory decisions are when and how much to order. The danger of keeping too little in stock is that an organisation could lose custom because of dissatisfaction with the quality of service.
♦ Warehousing: a key decision is where to locate warehouses, and how many to have.
♦ Load size: should units be transported in bulk or broken down into smaller units for delivery? Again, an organisation will have to trade off customer convenience and the cost of distribution.
♦ Communications: it is important to develop an efficient information processing and invoicing system.

Logistics is the process of integrating materials management and physical distribution management, and involves a whole series of activities from moving raw materials through to manufacturing processes and moving finished goods to the final consumer.

Physical distribution must balance the need for customer service against the need to minimise costs. On the one hand, to maximise customer service an organisation may need a lot of stock and warehouse space, efficient staff and rapid transport mechanisms, while on the other, to minimise costs they need low stock levels, limited storage space, few staff and slower transport. Designing a physical distribution system therefore involves trading off costs against service, or inputs against outputs.

Inputs involve all of the distribution costs such as freight costs, inventory costs, warehousing costs and other service costs. It is important to know exactly what each of these costs are and to control them in order to minimise waste. This may involve a detailed analysis of labour time, transport time, and other factors spent on each product.

Outputs can primarily be measured in terms of the value of services provided for customers. Distribution can provide a clear competitive benefit in meeting customer needs, for example by offering a quick and efficient service. Every business must decide how it is going to use distribution and relate this to its competitive advantage. Weaknesses in distribution would clearly need to be compensated for by strengths in other areas of the marketing mix.

Ethical issues

Responsible marketing is based upon having an ethical approach to running an organisation that places the wider community at the heart of marketing. Nowhere is this more evident than within the context of distribution. There are a number of issues that clearly concern the distribution of products or services for markets:

♦ **Environmental issues** are involved with providing consumers with products. To meet environmental targets organisations have to think about local air pollution associated with getting products to consumers and other externalities that may affect communities. This may also involve a series of green plans within an organisation as well as opportunities for re-cycling.
♦ **Consumer rights** are involved in issues such as poor service or damaged goods, products that are advertised unfairly, negligence within the supply chain and any misleading information that could be used by retailers.
♦ **Monopoly control** influencing prices and practices within markets that could undermine and affect consumer rights. Organisations with too much control within the marketplace will have an unfair balance of power.
♦ **Health and safety issues** could stop distributors selling products in certain markets.
♦ **Misleading advertising** creating consumer demand pulling products through the distribution system.
♦ **Use of distribution channels** such as doorstep selling or cold calling, and their impact upon unwitting individuals.

Price

The *Oxford English Dictionary* defines prices as, 'the sum or consideration or sacrifice for which a thing may be bought or attained'. Price is the only element of the marketing mix that directly generates income: other elements of the marketing mix are costs. The importance of price in the marketing mix varies. In low-cost, non-fashion markets price can be critical (for example, in the sale of white emulsion and gloss paint). In fashion markets, such as clothing, it can be one of the least relevant factors. Certain products are designed to suit a particular segment (for example, economy family cars), while others perform a specific function regardless of price (for example, sports cars). For consumers with limited budgets, price is a key purchasing criterion, while for those to whom 'money is no object' price is less important.

Perceived value

Most customers compare prices with the perceived quality of goods and services: they are concerned with making sure that they get value for money. Some customers are value orientated and want to pay low prices for acceptable quality; some buyers want high quality and are willing to pay more for it. It is therefore important to price according to the nature of the customers in the marketplace. On the one hand an organisation may lose customers by charging too high a price, if customers feel they are not getting value for money. On the other hand they may lose custom from charging too low a price: potential customers may feel that the low price indicates lower quality than they are seeking.

Delivery of value is an important ingredient of an exchange. If the seller does not provide customers with a significant value proposition, whatever the price, goods may be returned or customers will not come back.

In the longer term, the success of business organisations (and individuals) will depend on their ability to provide customers with value for money through the exchange process.

Many of today's retailers are using emphasis upon 'value' as a form of competition. Instead of focusing simply upon price, they provide customers with a better value package – more for the same price – than other competitors in that segment of the market.

ACTIVITY

Compare two products or services for which roughly similar prices are charged. Explain which product or service represents a better value proposition.

Pricing context and process

A number of situations can be identified in which pricing decisions have to be made. The most important of these are:

♦ when a price needs to be set for the first time: for example, when a new product is launched on the market, when new outlets are used, or when new contracts are made
♦ when it becomes necessary to make a change in pricing structure: this may be because of the development of competition, a movement along the product lifecycle, a change in demand or changing cost conditions.

Whatever pricing proposition is used, it must fit in with the organisational context and business strategy. Pricing goals have therefore to fit with marketing and business objectives. Such objectives might be any of the following.

Targeted profits

For most organisations the shareholder is the most influential stakeholder. It is often assumed that organisations will attempt to maximise profits by producing at a point where there is the greatest difference between total revenue and total cost. However, the reality is that while organisations seek to make large profits, particularly in the longer term, there are many reasons why they hold back.

Revenue maximisation

As an alternative to profit maximisation, this involves pursuing the marketing objective of sales in order to increase market share. The advantage of driving up market share is that it takes sales away from competitors.

Return on investment

Investors usually have an expectation of what they regard to be an appropriate return on investment. Yield will be an important factor influencing pricing decisions.

'Satisficing'

Herbert Simon (1977) put forward the view that businesses might want to 'satisfice', that is, to achieve given targets for market share and profits from sales which might not maximise profits but would instead inflate boardroom egos. This can arise when the managers of a company are clearly separate from the owners.

Quality leadership

Another pricing strategy is to help the organisation create quality leadership in the market. Price is often regarded by customers as a good indicator of quality. You can therefore help to create a quality feel by charging a high price: although the reverse is also true.

D. Shipley (1981) noted the principal set of pricing objectives of firms shown in Figure 8.61.

Pricing objectives	Percentage of firms
Target profit or return on capital employed	67
Prices fair to firm and customers	13
Prices similar to those of competitors	8
Target sales volume	7
Stable sales volume	5
Target market share	2
Stable prices	2
Other	1

Figure 8.61   Pricing objectives

Demand elasticity

The prices charged for a product are associated with a given level of sales. We can illustrate this relationship by means of a demand curve (see Figure 8.62).

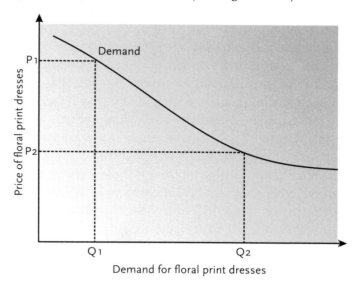

Figure 8.62   Demand curve

The curve in Figure 8.62 shows the levels of demand for a floral print dress sold at different market prices. As with most products, customers for floral dresses would be prepared to make more purchases at a lower than a higher price. The normal way to express customer sensitivity to price changes is through a measure known as **price elasticity of demand.** This is the measure of how much quantities purchased will alter in response to given price changes. Demand is said to be **elastic** if the change in quantity demanded is of a greater proportion than the change in price that initiated it. For example, if the price of a particular brand of washing powder fell by 10 per cent and there was an increase in sales of 20 per cent, the demand for the product would be said to be elastic; the change in price led to a more than proportionate response in quantity demanded.

$$\text{Price elasticity of demand} = \frac{\% \text{ change in quantity demanded}}{\% \text{ change in price}}$$

When a relative change in the quantity sold is less than the relative change in price, demand is said to be inelastic. For example, if a price increase of 10 per cent results in a 5 per cent fall in sales, price elasticity will be –0.5.

Price elasticities vary with the level of competition. The more competition there is in the market, the more likely it is that demand for a particular product line will be elastic. Price elasticity also varies during the product lifecycle. In the early days, when there is little competition, price inelasticity will be the rule within a sensible price range. However, as products mature, elasticity will increase in the competitive price range.

Once pricing objectives have been established, organisations need to establish an appropriate pricing strategy.

Pricing strategies

There are four main types of pricing strategy.

Competition-based pricing

In extremely competitive situations, costs have to be treated as a secondary consideration in short-term price determination. This is particularly true when competing products are almost identical, customers are well informed and where there are few suppliers.

The nature and extent of competition is frequently an important influence upon price. If a product is faced by direct competition, then it will compete against other very similar products in the marketplace. This will constrain pricing decisions so that price setting will need to be kept closely in line with rivals' actions. In contrast, when a product is faced by indirect competition (competition with products in different sectors of the market) then there will be more scope to vary price. This opens up the possibility for a number of strategies. For example, a firm might choose a high-price strategy to give a product a quality feel. In contrast, it might charge a low price so that consumers see the product as a bargain.

An individual organisation might try to insulate itself against price sensitivity by differentiating its products from those of rivals. Markets are sometimes classified according to the level of competition that applies. For example, an extreme level of competition is termed **perfect competition** (which exists in theory rather than in practice). The

other extreme is **monopoly** where a single firm dominates a market. In the real world, most markets lie between these extremes and involve some level of imperfection.

If a perfect market could exist there would be no limitations to new firms entering the market, and buyers would know exactly what was on offer and would incur no costs in buying from one seller rather than another. Products would be almost identical. In a monopoly situation, only one firm exists and barriers prevent new firms from entering the market. The seller has considerable power to control the market.

In imperfect competition, there may be few or many sellers. Products are usually **differentiated** and consumers do not have perfect information about the differences between products.

Where organisations seek to reduce competition and make their products better than those of their rivals, the development of monopolistic powers enables them to push up prices and make larger profits. The level of competition is thus a key determinant of price. Where there are many close competitors, there is little scope to charge a price which is above the market price. Organisations in such markets are **price takers**. In a situation where there is no competition, the seller can often charge a relatively high price. In other words they are a **price maker**. However, the seller cannot charge more than the consumer is prepared to pay. At the end of the day consumers can spend their income on alternative products. Between these two extremes, we find hundreds of different markets. In some the consumer has more power, in others it is the seller.

Skimming

At the launch of a new product, there will frequently be little competition in the market, so that demand for the product may be relatively inelastic. Consumers will probably have little knowledge of the product. Skimming involves setting a reasonably high initial price in order to yield high initial returns from those consumers willing to buy the new product. Once the first group of customers has been satisfied, the seller can then lower prices in order to make sales to new groups of customers. This process can be continued until a larger section of the total market has been catered for. By operating in this way, the business removes the risk of underpricing the product. The name 'skimming' comes from the process of skimming the cream from the top of a milk product.

Expansion pricing

This method involves reducing prices in order to expand market share. The firm will need to seek answers to questions such as, 'If we want to increase market share by 10 per cent, what are the implications for our pricing?' Clearly the benefits of increasing market share will include lower unit costs of production. Expansion pricing is appropriate when economies of scale enable a firm to reduce its price.

Penetration pricing

Penetration pricing is appropriate when the seller knows that demand is likely to be elastic. A low price is therefore required to attract consumers to the product. Penetration pricing is normally associated with the launch of a new product for which the market needs to be penetrated.

Because a price starts low, even though a product will be developing market share, the product may initially make a loss until consumer awareness is increased.

A typical example would be that of a new breakfast cereal or a product being launched in a new overseas market. Initially it would be launched with a relatively low price, coupled with discounts and special offers. As the product penetrates the market, sales and profitability increase. Prices then creep upwards.

Penetration pricing is particularly appropriate for products where economies of scale can be employed to produce large volumes at low unit costs. Products which are produced on a large scale are initially burdened by high fixed costs for research, development and purchases of plant and equipment. It is important to spread these fixed costs quickly over a large volume of output. Penetration pricing is also

common when there is a strong possibility of competition from rival pricing.

Destruction pricing

A policy of destruction pricing can be used to undermine the sales of competitors or to warn potential new rivals not to enter a particular market. Destruction pricing involves reducing the price of an existing product or selling a new product at an artificially low price in order to destroy competitors' sales. This type of policy is based on long-term considerations and is likely to lead to short-term losses. The policy is most likely to be successful when the organisation that initiates it has lower costs than its competitors or potential rivals, or when it is able to draw on profits from other business lines or markets.

Loss leaders

Prices can be lowered from time to time to promote a product. Promotional pricing can be used to inject fresh life into an existing product or to create interest in a new product. It can also be employed to increase the rate at which a product turns over, in order to reduce levels of stock or to increase the rate of activity of a business.

Price wars

A price war occurs when organisations use price as an aggressive means of fighting competitors, usually for market share. Businesses will engage in price wars when they can see a weakness in a rival: perhaps cash flow problems or a loss in market share. Price wars can be a short-term activity or may be a regular feature of market activity.

Costs: full-cost or cost-plus pricing

Any study of organisations in the real world shows that many businesses use no other basis for final cost than a **mark-up** on the cost of providing the product or service concerned. Information about costs is usually easier to piece together than information about other variables such as likely revenue. Firms will often therefore simply add a margin to the **unit cost**.

The unit cost is the average cost of producing each item. For example, if an organisation produces 800 units at a total cost of £24,000, the unit cost will be £30. Talk to many owners of small businesses and they will tell you that they 'cost out' each hour worked and then add a margin for profit; or they will simply mark-up each item sold by a certain percentage. For example, fashion items are frequently marked up by between 100 and 200 per cent.

The process of **cost-plus pricing** can best be illustrated in relation to large organisations where economies of scale can be spread over a considerable range of output.

For a large organisation, unit costs will fall rapidly at first as the overheads are spread over a larger output. It is therefore a relatively simple calculation to add a fixed margin (for example, 20 per cent) to the unit cost. The organisation is able to select an output to produce and to set a price that will be 20 per cent higher than the unit cost of production (see Figure 8.63).

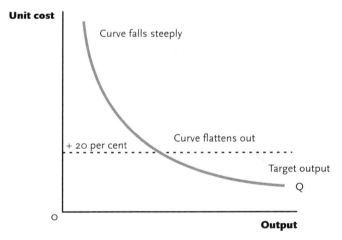

Figure 8.63   Select a target output OQ and then add 20 per cent to the unit cost to get price

Whilst cost-plus pricing is very popular, there are many dangers associated with it. If the price is set too high, sales may fall short of expectations; if the price is set too low, then potential revenue is sacrificed. However, the greatest danger of cost-based pricing is that it indicates a production-orientated approach to the market. Emphasis on costs leads to tunnel vision that looks inwards at the company's product rather than outwards at the customers' perception of it.

> **ACTIVITY**
>
> Why is the margin for luxury goods such as designer goods and fashion accessories likely to be higher than for cigarettes or newspapers?

Psychological pricing

Research itself indicates that there is more to pricing than pure cost. In other words, we need to take into account the customer's perception of price as well as the figure itself. Henry Simon (1989) set out a range of variables which influence price perceptions (see Figure 8.64).

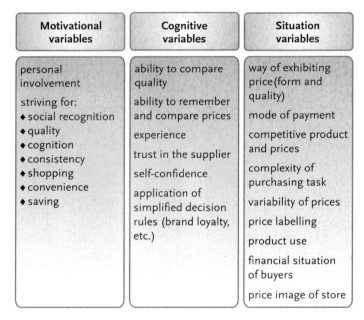

Figure 8.64   Influences on price perception

Many factors can influence perception of price, so this perception is a selective process. In developing a pricing policy, therefore, it makes sense to find out as much as possible about how consumers perceive price in different contexts. How and why do consumers make decisions about what sort of price is appropriate? How can the producer or seller capitalise on these perceptions in order to make the best offer?

Customers develop expectations regarding price levels. They judge prices as being too high or too low on the basis of these expectations and frequently regard price as an indicator of quality. Managers must therefore know as much as possible about consumers' pricing expectations and the associations they make between price and quality. Most consumers develop an acceptable price range for a product category. They will not buy at prices above this range, but nor are they likely to buy at prices below it.

In the marketplace there will be **premium prices** which a seller of a differentiated (branded) product is able to charge over and above the price charged for a product in its raw commodity state (see Figure 8.65). Brand leaders will be those organisations best able to charge prices above the basic commodity level because they are able to focus customer attention on aspects of image, quality, and so on.

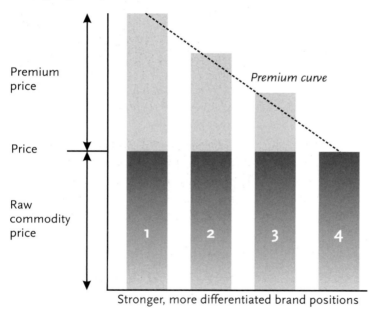

Figure 8.65   The premium curve

Evidence indicates that buying choices are influenced by the levels of risk involved. Where the customer considers that there is a considerable element of risk, for example in buying an electrical product of which they may have little experience, the customer may opt for a higher-priced item if they feel they can reduce the risk.

Discriminatory pricing

Price bundling is the practice of offering combinations of products at a single price. **Price discrimination** involves charging different prices to different customers. It may be carried out in a number of situations.

Customer-orientated discrimination

Some customers may show high demand for a product, while others have weak demand. Discrimination would involve selling the same type of product to the first group of customers at a high price and to the second at a lower price. This can only be done if the market can be physically divided so that the customer with high demand cannot get hold of the item at the lower price.

Product-orientated discrimination

Slight modifications can be made to a product to allow high and low price strategies. For example, many car models offer extras, such as air conditioning or alloy wheels. Customers have the choice of the cheaper or the more expensive version.

Time-orientated discrimination

Sellers are able to discriminate when demand varies by season or by time of day. In high season, a product can be sold at a high price. At other times, prices will need to be reduced. This applies to a wide range of items from hotel rooms to river cruises.

Situation-orientated discrimination

This applies to houses: the same type of house may sell for one price in the centre of a town and another price in a quiet suburban area. House prices vary widely from one area to another. Theatre seats are also priced according to their proximity to the stage. Although production costs are similar, demand varies with the situation. Price discrimination frequently takes place between countries: different countries have different average incomes and other factors that influence demand. Products will therefore be sold at different prices according to elasticities of demand in different countries, and regions within a country.

Ethical issues

Although the other elements of the marketing mix clearly have an influence upon consumer decisions, price remains a key element within the marketing mix. A number of ethical issues surround price. For example:

♦ Pricing is a form of allocation. If somebody can afford something they can have it. Although it can be argued that inequality is a fact of life, in areas such as medicine or education, some might argue that it is unethical for some to have privileged treatment. Pricing may also shut those on low incomes completely out of some markets.

♦ It can be argued that price discrimination is simply a way in which manufacturers manipulate the marketplace using demand elasticities. Why should, for example, buyers on the continent be able to buy cars more cheaply than buyers within the UK?

♦ Prices may be used to distort competition within a marketplace. For example, penetration or destroyer pricing may significantly damage existing competitors within an industry.

Promotion

Awareness and image

Promotion is one of the key elements of the marketing mix. Its purpose is to create an awareness and positive image of an organisation and its products. Promotion involves channelling money and effort into successfully managing what people think and feel, consciously and subconsciously, about a company or product.

CASE STUDY

£1 for using Harrods toilets

Some people go to Harrods because it is the most famous department store in the world, others because there are no other public lavatories between South Kensington and Hyde Park Corner.

Harrods recently introduced a £1 charge for their toilets. The situation was becoming untenable, with queues of people waiting to use the toilets. Although there are no fewer users, many people welcome the new pay lavatories because of the exclusivity they create.

Harrods have invested £1 million in a facelift for all their 13 lavatories, commenting 'We are adamant that there's nothing quite like them as far as the level of service is concerned. The refurbished toilets have marble floors, mahogany fittings and brass fitments. There are hairdryers for those who get caught in a shower.'

ACTIVITY

1 Why has Harrods decided to charge people to use its toilets?

2 What sort of considerations do you think were taken into account before deciding what price to charge?

If the consumer is not aware of a brand it will not be on the shopping list. Promotion covers a range of activities which combine to form the promotional mix: the combination of communications strategies used to convey benefits to customers and influence them to buy.

Effective communication

Wilbur Schramm (1955) defined communication as, 'the process of establishing a commonness or oneness of thought between a sender and a receiver'. Today, the exchange of information takes place through sophisticated media such as networks of computers, fax machines, telephones, and so on. An effective network of communications is essential for promotional activity; it enables an organisation not only to communicate with its customers but also to build up an image in the world at large. Such an image helps people to form a judgement about what the organisation stands for and will influence their dealings with it.

For marketing purposes, communication about products and services contributes to the persuasion process that encourages consumers to buy what is on offer. As all promotion activities involve an element of communication, an understanding of communication theory helps an organisation to make the most of its investments.

Integrated communication process

Organisations are the senders in the communication process and consumers are the receivers. A sender will put information in the form that a receiver can understand. This might involve oral, visual, verbal or written messages to transmit the ideas. This process is called **encoding**. The sender will also choose a particular medium to use to send the message to the receiver (for example, television, radio, newspapers). If the consumer interprets the message as required, it should have the impact that the seller wished for.

Though the message flows through to the receiver there is no guarantee that the receiver will either receive the full message or understand it. This is because the process may be subject to some form of interference, which affects the flow of information. This is known as **noise** and may lead to the downfall of the message. It will take the form of any barrier which acts as an impediment to the smooth flow of information, and may include linguistic and cultural differences between the sender and the receiver. For example, one leaflet put through your door may be lost amongst a sea of direct mail from other organisations.

To increase the chances of a message getting across, an organisation needs to think carefully about the target audience. For example, it is important to channel the

message through the most appropriate media. It might also be necessary to repeat the message several times rather than rely on one transmission.

Once the audience has been identified, the communicator also needs to think about the sort of response required. If, for example, the final response required through the communication process is purchase, there may be six phases to the buyer-readiness process (see Figure 8.67).

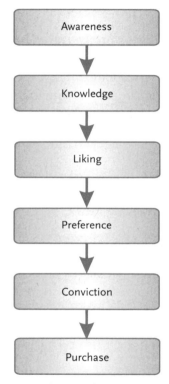

Figure 8.67   Buyer-readiness phases

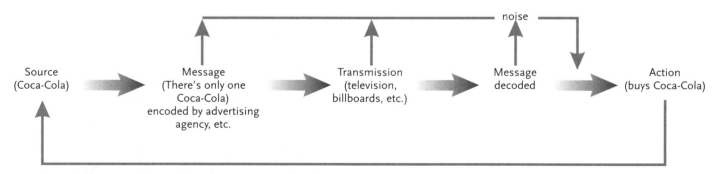

Figure 8.66   The communication process

It is important, therefore, that the promotion mix takes into account each of these stages with different types of promotional activities.

The six Ms

Another way of thinking about effective communications is a model based upon the 'six Ms'. In creating effective

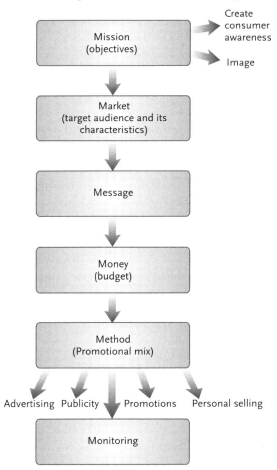

Figure 8.68   The six Ms of effective communication

communications it is necessary to have a clear **mission**, that is, an understanding of goals and objectives. What are you trying to achieve? If a brand is being introduced, the first objective is to establish brand awareness. The next is to create a positive attitude towards the brand. A third objective is to encourage trial of the product, and a fourth is to induce existing users to repeat their purchases so as to create brand loyalty.

You must be clear about the **market** at which you are targeting your communications and the best way of reaching this audience. The **message** is what you want to get across to the audience, and it will be concerned with developing awareness of the product and a positive image of the company or brand.

It is vital to decide upon how much **money** to spend on communications, i.e. there will be budget constraints. Money must be spent in the way that achieves the best possible results. The **method** employed will depend on the money available, the target market and the message that the advertiser wants to get across. The characteristics of various media will involve creative areas such as sound, vision and scripts, and the success of an advertising campaign will depend upon using creative skills effectively within the correct choice of media.

Monitoring is an essential part of the process and the one that completes the circle. Detailed evaluation is possible to identify possible improvements and to check on the effectiveness of existing approaches.

SOSTT + four Ms

Marketers are famous for acronyms that describe a process or exist as a checklist for some form of communication. SOSTT + four Ms is a strategic tool with a purpose of providing a checklist for strategic and tactical communications. The acronym refers to the following:

◆ Situation: this is the current position of the organisation and its relationship to markets. This involves an analysis of the product range and the organisation's resources.
◆ Objectives: these relate to the future. An organisation needs to think about what it hopes to achieve, both in the short and long term.

- Strategy: this is usually long term and envelops the whole organisation. Strategies have to fit objectives.
- Tactics: these are shorter term and are undertaken in order to match strategies.
- Targets: wherever there are objectives it is important to identify what they are. Targets are specific quantitatively based numbers that fit the objectives.
- Men (and women): people are important in the marketing process. The marketing strategy will influence people and it is necessary to identify people for different tasks.
- Money: in order to meet promotional objectives, there has to be a budget and this must be used effectively.
- Minutes: all promotional strategies must have a timescale as well as a series of deadlines. Planning and booking space in the media is important.
- Measurement: monitoring and evaluating the results helps to provide a base for understanding the effectiveness of a promotional campaign. It also provides useful feedback for future campaigns.

AIDA

Another acronym that helps to decide how an organisation meets its objectives is AIDA. With this method:

A a customer's **attention** is captured and they are made aware of the product

I an impact stimulates their **interest**

D they are persuaded that they are **deprived** because they do not have the product, and this helps to stimulate a desire or demand for it

A **action** involves the purchase of the product.

Promotional mix elements

The promotional mix comprises all of the marketing and promotional communication methods used to achieve the objectives of the marketing mix. These methods can be broken down into two distinct areas.

Non-controllable methods

These are marketing messages communicated by word of mouth, personal recommendations and a consumer's overall perception of a particular product or service. Consumer opinions are influenced by a number of factors such as whether their family has regularly used the product. A brand's heritage, character, colour and image will also have helped to create brand loyalty and influenced regular purchasing patterns. Perhaps the most famous brand heritage is that of Rolls-Royce. The term 'a Rolls-Royce company' is applied to organisations that build a strong reputation for their goods and services. On the other hand, public displeasure with a particular organisation may influence purchases, for example if there is criticism of an organisation's employment practices, this could influence consumer perceptions.

Controllable methods

These are marketing methods that are carefully directed to achieve the objectives of an organisation. They include four main areas:

- **Advertisements** are paid, ongoing, non-personal communications from a commercial source such as a manufacturer or retailer.
- **Sales promotions** are of two main types. Consumer promotions are short-term inducements of value to consumers to encourage them to buy a product or service, for example money-off coupons, free samples and competitions. Trade promotions and promotions to retailers may also be used to encourage them to stock a particular brand.
- **Personal selling** is face-to-face communication between sales representatives and customers, and is designed to influence the customer to buy the company's products or services.
- **Publicity** is unpaid communication about the company or its product or service through the mass media.

Push versus pull strategies

It is possible to divide promotional strategies into two clear areas, one of which involves a 'push' strategy, while the other creates a 'pull' strategy. A **push strategy** focuses upon the channel of distribution. This might involve wholesalers or retailers. The aim is to push products into markets through the distribution channel. To do so, sales promotions and various offers may be issued to distributors in the hope that they will equally promote products to eventual customers. This method involves pushing products into markets and this creates a heavy emphasis upon personal selling.

A **pull strategy** focuses upon the consumer. By promoting to the end user advertisers are creating a demand for the product amongst consumers, who will ask for and demand products from retailers. Whereas push strategies are focused upon distribution and involve personal selling, pull strategies focus upon consumers. Most campaigns will contain both push and pull elements.

Advertising above and below the line

Advertising is a method of communicating with groups in the marketplace in order to achieve certain objectives. Advertisements are messages sent through the media which are intended to inform or influence the people who receive them.

What is advertising?

Advertising can be defined as a paid-for type of marketing communication that is non-personal, but aimed at a specific target audience through a mass media channel.

According to the American Marketing Association advertising is 'any paid form of non-personal presentation and promotion of ideas, goods or services by an identifiable sponsor'.

Advertising must be a communication directed at a targeted market, and should draw attention to the characteristics of a product, which will appeal to the buying motives of potential customers. The ultimate purpose of advertising for organisations is to enhance buyers' responses to its products by channelling their desires and preferences to their products ahead of those of their competitors.

Advertising objectives

Within this purpose there may be a range of advertising objectives.

Promoting goods and services

- to assist with selling
- to increase sales
- to develop awareness of new products, or developments to existing products
- to provide information that may assist with selling decisions
- to encourage a desire to own a product
- to generate enquiries.

Developing the image of the organisation

- to provide information for a target audience
- to soften attitudes
- to assist with public relations activities
- to change views
- to provide a better external environment
- to develop support from a community.

Types of advertising

Advertising is often classified under one of three headings.

Informative advertising

This conveys information and raises consumer awareness of the features and benefits of a product. It is often used in the introductory phase of the product lifecycle, or after modification.

Persuasive advertising

This is concerned with creating a desire for the product and stimulating purchase. It is used with established and more mature products.

Reinforcement advertising

This is concerned with reminding consumers about the product, and is used to reinforce the knowledge held by potential consumers about the benefits to be gained from purchase.

Advertising campaign

The starting point for an advertising campaign is to produce an **advertising plan**. This will involve allocating a budget to a range of activities designed to meet advertising objectives. There are seven steps in an advertising campaign. These are:

1 identify the target market
2 define advertising objectives
3 decide on and create the advertising message
4 allocate the budget
5 develop the media plan
6 execute the campaign
7 evaluate the effectiveness of the campaign.

Advertising messages may be sent through a variety of media forms such as TV, radio, cinema, posters, billboards, flyers, transport advertising and the press. For more information about advertising look at the World Advertising Research Center website on www.warc.com.

ACTIVITY

Compare and contrast two advertising campaigns, where one is clearly trying to promote goods and services and the other is trying to improve an image by developing public support for its activities. Comment upon how their approaches to advertising are:

♦ similar
♦ different.

Measuring advertising results

The controllable methods of promotion are often categorised as **above-the-line** or **below-the-line**. While changes in the law have now extinguished the origins of this system, the terms are still often used. 'Above-the-line' refers to the media such as TV, radio and press, for which commission is paid to an advertising agency. Below-the-line comprises all media and promotional techniques for which fees are paid in preference to commissions: these might include exhibitions, sales literature and direct mail.

At all stages in the advertising process it is important to assess how effectively advertisements have contributed to the communication process.

In order to measure objectives DAGMAR has become a fundamental part of good advertising practice. This stands for: Defining Advertising Goals for Measured Advertising Results.

In other words, before any advertising campaign is started, an organisation must define its communication objectives so that achievements can be measured both during and after the campaign.

CASE STUDY

The top six advertisers in 2002

Look at Figure 8.69, showing the top six advertisers, and then use the data as a basis for answering the questions in the Activity.

Rank	Company	Total £000s	TV %	Radio %	Press %	Other %
1	Procter & Gamble	161,890	82.3	3.3	11.1	3.3
2	COI Communications	119,765	47.6	16.4	23.9	12.1
3	British Telecom	96,664	52.1	9.1	26.7	12.1
4	Ford Motor	94,918	53.9	4.7	28.2	13.2
5	L'Oreal Golden	70,845	65.1	0.8	26.5	7.5
6	Nestlé	69,198	74.5	5.2	6.6	13.8

Figure 8.69   The top six advertisers

ACTIVITY

1 What do the allocations of expenditure tell you about the nature and type of advertising undertaken by each of these advertisers? For example, how does each form of media enable them to target appropriate audiences and make maximum use of their advertising budgets?

2 What forms of advertising might fall into the 'other' bracket?

3 Why do you think that the six companies above have such a large advertising spend?

4 If you were working for one of these companies, how would you evaluate the effectiveness of such a spend?

Printed media

Printed media make up by far the largest group of media in the UK. The group includes all newspapers and magazines, both local and national, as well as trade press, periodicals and professional journals. There are about 9000 regular publications in the UK which can be used by the advertiser. They allow the advertiser to send a message to several million people through the press or to target magazines of special interest. For instance, the *Times Educational Supplement* allows the advertiser to communicate with people in the teaching profession. As a result the media allows for accurate targeting and positioning.

Types of customers are identified by analysing *readership profiles*. For example, the *Sun* has a circulation of 3,519,000 papers per day. Its readership is 57 per cent male. Of all the readers, 32 per cent are between the ages of 15 and 34 years, with 33 per cent of readers aged over 55 years. Of these readers 54 per cent fall into the ABC1 category and 46 per cent into the C2DE group.

The benefit of printed media is that long or complex messages can be sent and, as the message is durable, may be read repeatedly. If an advertisement appears in a prestige magazine it may take on the prestige of that particular publication.

Broadcast media include commercial television and commercial radio. Television is the most powerful medium, reaching 98 per cent of households; viewing figures for some programmes can exceed 20 million. Television advertisements are, however, high cost and advertising messages are short-lived.

Packaging

Packaging plays an important part in the promotional mix, although its importance is often neglected under the assumption that it is merely a production cost. In recent years packaging has accounted for an increasing proportion of the total cost of convenience goods.

The basic function of any pack is to protect its contents in transit, in storage and in use, and this plays a major part in determining its shape, size and the materials used. However, consumers increasingly see attractive packaging as adding value to products.

The packaging of consumer goods was originally carried out by retailers. Today manufacturers play the major part in packaging, enabling them to control the image and presentation of the product. Packaging performs the following functions:

♦ it identifies and promotes a brand: for example, the distinctive Coca-Cola bottle and can design
♦ when distinctive it catches the eye of the consumer
♦ it identifies a line of related products
♦ it communicates information on ingredients, quantity and product uses
♦ it helps with the preservation, storage and safety of products.

Public relations

The forces in an organisation's external environment are capable of affecting it in a variety of ways. The forces may be social, economic, political, local or environmental and might be represented by a variety of groups such as customers, shareholders, employees and special interest groups. Reacting positively to such forces and influences is very important.

What is public relations?

Public relations is the planned and sustained effort an organisation makes to establish, develop and build relationships with its many publics.

The purpose of public relations (PR) is therefore to provide an external environment for an organisation in which it is popular and can prosper. Building goodwill in such a way requires behaviour by the organisation which takes into account the attitudes of the many people who come across it and its products.

Whereas many of the other promotional methods are short term, public relations is long term, as it may take a long time for an organisation to improve the way people think more positively about its products and activities. For example, just think about the sort of public relations problems that chemical and oil companies have in a world where consumers have become increasingly environmentally conscious.

The launch of the Millennium Dome in Greenwich in 2000 instantly saw many of the newspapers launch an offensive against some of the activities, as they sought to investigate whether the cost of the Dome was money well spent. This was a typical public relations problem for those operating the Dome, who then had to emphasise its positive attributes. In the political arena, talking positively about activities is sometimes known as 'spin'.

According to Frank Jefkins (1974), PR involves a transfer process which helps to convert the negative feelings of an organisation's many publics into positive ones (see Figure 8.70).

Negative		Positive
Hostility	→	Sympathy
Prejudice	→	Acceptance
Apathy	→	Interest
Ignorance	→	Knowledge

Figure 8.70   The PR transfer process

There are many different types of public relations activities:

♦ Charitable donations and community relations are good for an organisation's image, often provide lots of good publicity and also help to promote and provide for a good cause.

♦ Hospitality at top sporting events is a popular method used by organisations to develop their customer relations. For example, there are opportunities to entertain customers at events such as the FA Cup Final, Wimbledon and the Grand National.

♦ Press releases covering events affecting the organisation, such as news stories, export achievements, policy changes, technical developments and anything which enhances the organisation's image.

♦ Visits and open days are a popular method of inviting people to various events to improve their understanding of what the organisation stands for.

♦ Sponsorship of sporting and cultural events is viewed as a useful opportunity to associate an image with a particular type of function, for example the NatWest Trophy and the Embassy World Snooker Championship.

♦ Lobbying of ministers, officials and important people from outside interest groups, so that an accurate portrayal can be made of a problem or a case, may help to influence their views of the organisation.

♦ Corporate videotapes have become an increasingly popular way of providing interested parties with a 'view' of an organisation's activities.

♦ Minor product changes, such as no testing on animals or environmentally-friendly products, may provide considerable PR benefits.

Sponsorship

Sponsorship is a form of PR activity which has particularly taken off in recent years, becoming increasingly common in connection with the arts and theatre, music festivals and sporting leagues and competitions. Sponsorship is cost effective and tends to be viewed by the public less cynically than other forms of PR activity. A weakness of sponsorship is that the company name becomes associated with an event or performance, rather than with the product itself.

Sponsorship is a good way of increasing brand awareness which, in turn, helps to generate preference and foster brand loyalty. Sponsorship is the material support of an event, activity or organisation by an unrelated donor. It reinforces awareness through the appropriate event whose target market and appeal are similar to that of the customer.

Sponsorship involves an arrangement between a sponsor and a sponsee to provide support, either by supplying a product or service or through financial support, to an event or activity of which the sponsee is at the centre. Sponsorship is not an act of charity as far as the sponsor is concerned, and it must show some form of return. Since sponsorship is a business arrangement, standard evaluative criteria should be used to establish the suitability of a proposed event in relation to the image of the sponsor and its products.

Sponsorship can offer a wide range of benefits for the sponsor. For example, it can be used to raise the image of the organisation as a whole, to promote the virtues of a specific range of products, or even as part of a sales promotion campaign. It can be used as an exercise in corporate hospitality or even, at a local level, can simply be seen as a good community relations initiative.

Before sponsoring an activity, the sponsor must be sure that the event will be successful. It is clearly much easier to sponsor an event with a proven track record. Sports sponsorship is the most common form of sponsorship, and can range in scale from international and national down to regional and local events.

ACTIVITY

Search the press for a PR problem. Having found the problem, discuss in your group how you would attempt to solve this problem and the sort of activities which would help to do so.

CASE STUDY

Students' Union sponsorship deal

Many students at the University of Calgary were 'fuming' to learn their own association, their students' union, has struck a confidential sponsorship deal with a cigarette company, calling it a sell-out to the corporate interests of the tobacco industry.

The students' union defended the deal with Rothmans that sees the organisation receive an unspecified amount of money in return for the Toronto-based company sponsoring entertainment events, such as music concerts. Union officials said that it was a necessary move to raise money in tough budget times. But on the university campus many students were upset about the principle of doing business with a tobacco giant.

ACTIVITY

1 Why would Rothmans want to sponsor student events?

2 What issues might arise within the student union regarding such sponsorship?

3 Who would gain, and who might be damaged through such sponsorship?

Sales promotion

Sales promotion describes a category of techniques which are used to encourage customers to make a purchase. These activities are effectively short term and may be used:

♦ to increase sales
♦ to help with personal selling

- to respond to the actions of competitors
- as an effective alternative to advertising.

What is sales promotion?

The Institute of Sales Promotion defines sales promotion as follows: 'Sales promotion is the function of marketing which seeks to achieve given objectives by the adding of intrinsic, tangible value to a product or service.' The essential feature of a sales promotion is that it is a short-term inducement to encourage customers to react quickly, whereas advertising is usually a process that develops the whole product or brand.

As you walk down a town high street or through a shopping mall, you will see many different examples of sales promotions. Such promotions may serve many different purposes. For example, competitions, vouchers or coupons and trading stamps may be designed to build customer loyalty and perhaps increase the volume purchased by existing customers. **Product sampling** is a strategy that is often used to introduce new products into the marketplace. **Clearance sales** of overstocked goods will increase turnover during part of the year in which business might otherwise be slack. Many sales promotions are undertaken in response to the activities of competitors to ensure that an organisation remains competitive. Sales promotions can be divided into two broad areas:

- promotions assisting with the sale of products to the trade
- promotions assisting the trade in selling products to the final consumer.

'Selling into the pipeline' is an expression used to describe promotions which move products from the manufacturer into the distribution system.

'Selling out of the pipeline' describes promotions which trigger the end user to make a purchase.

There are many different types of sales promotion:

- **Dealer loaders** are among the inducements to attract orders from retailers and wholesalers. They may include a free case with so many cases bought.

- **Competitions** may interest dealers and consumers. For dealers they may be linked to sales with attractive prizes for the most successful dealer. Scratch cards, free draws and bingo cards are popular promotional methods for consumers.
- **Promotional gifts** such as bottles of spirits, clocks, watches or diaries are considered useful bounty for dealers.
- **Price reductions** and **special offers** are usually popular with consumers. They can, however, prove expensive as many consumers would otherwise have been prepared to pay the full price.
- **Premium offers** may offer extra product for the same price. Coupons which offer money off or money back may also be attractive incentives for consumers. These may appear in magazines, be distributed door to door or appear on the side of a pack.
- **Charity promotions** can be popular with younger consumers, who collect box tops or coupons and send them to a manufacturer, which then makes a donation to charity.
- **Loyalty incentives** are today an increasingly used form of sales promotion. Dealer's loyalty might be rewarded with bigger discounts, competitions and prizes or even have their names published as stockists in advertisements. For consumers, loyalty incentives such as loyalty cards and points may provide cash back, free gifts or a variety of other tangible benefits.

Direct marketing and personal selling

Most days of your life you are involved in some form of selling activity. It might be persuading a friend to come with you to the pictures, or asking a relative to buy something for you. What you are doing is using your relationship to sell your ideas to someone else.

Personal or direct selling involves interaction between individuals or groups of individuals.

The objective of personal selling is to make a sale, and it is the culmination of all of the marketing activities that have taken place beforehand. It involves matching a customer's requirements with the goods or services on offer. The better the match, the more lasting the relationship between the seller and the buyer.

ACTIVITY

Make a list of situations in which you have recently been involved in some form of personal selling. Explain how the selling process took place in each instance. Did you have any responsibilities to the other person(s) involved in the exchange process?

The role of personal selling will vary from business to business. It is a two-way process which can be one of the most expensive areas of the promotional mix. This personal communication element can be very important as the final sale might come only as a result of protracted negotiations.

The main benefit of personal selling is the ability to communicate with and focus on customers individually and with precision. For example, if you go into a travel agency and ask for details about a holiday, the sales assistant may explain and point out the features of various packages and any discounts or promotions they might offer. All of the other areas of the promotional mix are targeted at groups of people.

Sales staff

Although we have mental stereotypes of the typical salesperson, selling involves special skills. Whereas there is a tendency to downgrade this role in the UK, in many countries (Germany for example) sales staff require a high degree of technical competence and are generally accepted to be part of the corporate elite. Salespeople are key intermediaries who present information to customers and then provide feedback on customer needs.

Sales staff are representing an organisation and so need to reflect a positive image from that organisation. It is important that they do not offend customers by their appearance: the mode of dress should match the nature of the products and the organisation. For example, a sales assistant in a fashion store should wear something up-to-date, whereas an insurance salesperson should wear more formal clothes. It is often said that the way we look determines the way others look at us.

Similarly, effective speaking will help to create the appropriate image and situation for the sale to take place. Good grammar, vocabulary, diction and voice tone may help to reflect the degree of professionalism required for the sale to take place.

Many organisations spend more on personal selling than on any other area of the promotional mix, and within organisations large numbers of individuals may find that personal selling forms part of their role. Personal selling may involve individuals developing special skills and using them in many different operational situations. To do so, sales staff need to know their products and be well trained in selling techniques.

The selling role

Selling in a highly competitive world means that preparation has never been so important. Though it has been said that salespeople are born and not made, nevertheless skills, knowledge and training can improve performance. Training is designed to build on people's selling skills and to use their personal abilities and understanding to follow the psychological stages of the sales process. Product knowledge is vital, as it allows for feedback from the prospective customer's questions about the product's technical specifications, benefits and functions.

Knowing their customers may help to determine how sales staff communicate with them. For example, some customers may prefer to be addressed with the more formal Mr or Mrs while others like to be called by their first name.

Probing is important in the early stage of a sales presentation, in order to find out the prospect's needs and where his or her priorities might lie. The salesperson can then try to match the product or service with the prospect's requirements. This may involve elaborating on the product's advantages, concentrating on aspects such as savings in costs, design ingredients, performance specifications, after-sales service, and so on.

During the presentation, the salesperson must constantly evaluate whether the product is appropriate to the needs of the prospect. Although it often happens, it is unethical to sell something that is not needed. The large and more complex the order, the more complex the negotiations over supply. In many different situations it is important to provide a number of services to help with the process. For example, these might include:

- ◆ product demonstrations
- ◆ performance specifications
- ◆ sales literature
- ◆ samples
- ◆ a meeting to discuss details
- ◆ credit facilities
- ◆ sales promotions.

The prospective customer may have a variety of objections to the purchase. These objections may be genuine, or as a result of a misunderstanding. There might be reluctance to make a commitment at this stage. Logical, well-presented arguments and incentives may overcome such objections.

Timing is crucial to the sale. A salesperson must look for buying signals which indicate that the prospect is close to a decision, and the customer is almost ready to put a signature on an order form and discuss the contractual arrangements.

It is always important to follow up the sale with post-sale support. Promises that might have been made during the negotiations will have to be fulfilled. If the salesperson guarantees delivery by a certain date, that date must be held. Servicing arrangements must be efficiently carried out, and any problems dealt with. Contacting customers to see if they are happy with the product will encourage repeat buying and improve the supplier's concern for its customers.

Sales staff may also have a number of other related functions. Communication, for example, is an important role. Sales staff act as an information link between suppliers and their customers. As a result, personal selling involves a boundary role: being at the boundary of a supplying organisation and also in direct and close contact with customers. The role is often not only one of selling but also one of interpreting the activities and policies of other organisations. A considerable amount of administration may also therefore accompany the selling role. For example, reports, schedules and computerised information such

as inventory details are part of daily life for a salesperson.

Comprehensive records on customers should be kept and updated after each visit. Keeping sales records enables the salesperson to respond exactly to each customer's individual needs. Knowledge of competitors and their products enables the seller to respond to queries about the relative merits and demerits of products.

Branding

Branding, as we have seen, involves giving a product a character or image. The brand is built around the name but also includes the advertising, packaging and presentation of the product. Today branding is a key ingredient of the promotional mix.

Chernatony and McDonald (1988) argue that today we live in an era of brand power, with strong emotions and imagery attached to products and services. When, for example, Lexus drivers turn the ignition key of their car, they are taking ownership of a symbol with core values of exclusivity and performance.

Perrier is a classic example of shrewd brand management. Through packaging and promotion, an international brand has been created with high brand loyalty and consequently it sells for a price far in excess of the cost of the ingredients. The emotional impact of a brand can differentiate a product and be the difference between success or failure. The psychological aspect is now increasingly evident on the balance sheets of major companies. Branding has thus taken on a key role in the promotional mix, which explains why labels and names have become so important in marketing.

Internet and on-line marketing

Organisations are always looking for alternative ways of meeting their business objectives. The Internet provides a useful and different source not just for secondary and sometimes primary market research, but also different ways of reaching groups of clients and customers. Having said this, many companies invested quickly in Internet technology, expecting that alongside the huge growth in the number of users, that business opportunities would abound, only to have their fingers burned with many users wary about buying on-line. However, there have been some big success stories, and Amazon and eBay are today well-known e-business operators, both of whom operate in widely different ways.

Of course, marketers are famous for their acronyms and the Internet has provided many opportunities to develop new ones including AJ: Ask Jeeves, AOL: America Online, ASP: Application Service Provider, AV: AltaVista, CPA: Cost Per Action, CPC: Cost Per Click, CPS: Cost Per Sale, CTR: Click-Through Rate and DH: Direct Hit.

The evolution of the Internet has:

♦ provided many organisations with opportunities to reach different markets, and in many cases export overseas
♦ enabled organisations to build better relationships with customers through relationship marketing
♦ become a valuable opportunity to undertake secondary market research; it has also enabled organisations to use on-line questionnaires with customers and potential customers
♦ provided a way in which the Internet can be linked with off-line tools such as direct mail
♦ created a steep but evolving learning curve that now has become significantly more scientific as a marketing tool.

From four Ps to seven Ps

Many marketing professionals today have moved beyond the four Ps originally suggested by Jerome McCarthy in 1960. The three new Ps stand for people, provision of customer service and process management.

People

People are widely recognised to be the greatest asset of the modern organisation. The governing principle, whether recognised or not, is that everybody who works for an organisation has a customer, either outside the company (the traditional customer) or inside the organisation (the internal customer). Both kinds of customer expect to be supplied with the product or service they need, on time and as specified.

This principle holds good for everyone in the company, whatever their level of skill and experience, whether their 'product' is answering a telephone or masterminding a major new project. It works to everyone's benefit. It gives the individual genuine responsibility and scope for initiative, and it virtually guarantees that the organisation's performance will be improved.

Attempts have been made to categorise employees according to the frequency of their customer contact, and their involvement in marketing activities.

Contractors

Contractors are heavily involved in marketing activities and have frequent or periodic customer contact. Their roles in the organisation may be advertising, selling or customer service. They need to have an excellent understanding of the organisation's marketing strategy and be extensively trained in all aspects of customer service.

Modifiers

Modifiers are employees who have frequent customer contact without formal involvement in traditional marketing activities. These will include receptionists, switchboard operators, railway porters, the credit department of a company, and so on. Modifiers need to have excellent customer service skills and a good understanding of the objectives of the company's marketing strategy. They will need detailed training in working with customers.

Influencers

Influencers may have relatively little contact with external customers, while being involved with elements of the four Ps. They may, for example, be involved in market research, research and development, despatch of goods, and so on. These staff will need to develop customer service skills as part of their training and development.

Isolateds

Isolateds are people who have few dealings with external customers. Clearly, this group of people is much smaller in modern organisations. They will need to have an understanding of marketing objectives and particularly of how their work contributes to the quality of the organisation and its products.

Provision of customer service

Customers are the most important people for any organisation. They are simply the natural resource upon which the success of any organisation depends. When thinking about the importance of customers it is useful to remember the following points:

- Repeat business is at the backbone of selling. It helps to provide security and certainty.
- Organisations are dependent upon their customers. If they do not develop customer loyalty and satisfaction they could lose their customers.
- Without customers the organisation would simply not exist.
- The purpose of the organisation is to fulfil the needs of customers.
- The customer makes it possible to achieve everything the business aims for.

Attitudes to customer service were discussed under Customer retention, p. 522.

Process management

It is clear that in a modern organisation processes are a key part of the marketing mix, because priorities revolve around meeting customer needs. There has been a substantial change from the days when the producer dominated the business. Today, it is marketing that determines the production process. Organisations must seek to deliver quality products – where quality means 'fitness for purpose', and it is customers who dictate what that purpose will be.

Process management in an organisation must be of the highest standard in meeting customer needs. If good standards are not achieved, customers will not be happy, and there is no way to retain unsatisfied customers in the long term.

Research and topical articles

The marketing mix is the centrepiece of marketing actions as it is about getting things done in order to meet customer needs. As a term, and whether or not it includes four, seven or more Ps, it involves an analysis of the actions that an organisation takes to gain a competitive advantage within a marketing environment.

Direct marketing **JOURNAL ARTICLE**

Martin Evans shows that direct marketing has developed rapidly over the last 15 years owing to technological change and developments in markets and marketing. In 1086 William the Conqueror created the Domesday Book as a record of what each individual owned. The concept developed by George Orwell in his novel *1984* was one of more sinister surveillance by 'Big Brother'. Although marketing might not be seen in either light, it is certainly being manifested in at least a parallel manner. Personalised data are increasingly being integrated via data-fusion to form the next phase of database provision: biographic information. His paper provides a perspective on these developments and raises a variety of marketing and social responsibility issues that are likely to become salient.

Evans, M. 'From 1086 and 1984: direct marketing into the millennium', *Marketing Intelligence and Planning*, 1998, Vol. 16, No. 1, pp 56–67.

New media in marketing

JOURNAL ARTICLE

Lynn *et al.* argue that large firms have traditionally commanded a competitive advantage in the marketplace over small firms by being able to use their financial strength to perform large-scale market research studies, to design and implement wide-reaching advertising campaigns, and to establish computer and information systems to communicate with their staff and suppliers. Their empirical study of 192 large and small companies indicates that small firms are using new media technologies to level the competitive playing field. Cost-effective new media technologies are making it easier for small firms to enjoy some of the benefits that previously were only available to large companies. Little relevant research currently exists on the marketing uses of new media technologies for small firms and their potential for altering the competitive advantages long enjoyed by larger firms. This article identifies some key changes in markets.

Lynn, G., Maltz, A., Jurkat, M. and Hammer, M. 'New media in marketing redefine competitive advantage: a comparison of small and large firms', *Journal of Services Marketing*, 1999, Vol.13, No.199, pp 9–20.

Chapter 4

Different marketing segments and contexts

The word 'market' may mean a number of things to different people. One idea is that markets are places where goods or services are physically bought or sold. Economists argue that a marketplace exists whenever buyers and sellers come into contact to make an exchange, and they relate their definition to the matching of demand from buyers to the supply from sellers. Marketers, however, tend to limit their definition of the market to buyers of a service or a product. Therefore, for the purposes of this text, buyers are either individuals or people from within organisations who have needs for a group of products or for services, and have either the ability to buy something they can pay for themselves, or the authority to buy something on behalf of their organisation.

The marketplace communicates the wishes of buyers and sellers most effectively when these two groups are well informed and there is no interference from outside sources. In some markets the buyer and seller may meet face-to-face every day. In other markets they may rarely meet and simply contact each other by letter, fax or messenger. One of the fastest growing marketplaces is that of maintenance and other recreation variables, reflecting the huge interest that many people have in DIY.

When a buyer and a seller decide to undertake a transaction, the sale will involve:

♦ communication
♦ an offer for sale
♦ an exchange (usually in the form of goods or services for money or credit).

All organisations, whether in the public sector or the private sector, have **customers** who may also be called users or clients. A customer may be a private individual or a buyer from an organisation. A

		1994–2002
1	Maintenance and other recreation durables	183.2
2	Wine, cider and perry	182.5
3	Information processing equipment	138.4
4	Major outdoor recreation variables	112.2
5	Other insurance	108.4
6	Games, toys and hobbies	86.5
7	Motor cycles	85.4
8	Photographic and optical equipment	85.0
9	Refuse collection	79.5

Figure 8.71 The UK's fastest growing markets (percentage change)

ACTIVITY

Comment upon the extent to which the fastest growing markets reflect the changing lifestyles of consumers.

Figure 8.72 A marketplace transaction

customer in a newsagent's shop is clearly a person buying goods on offer. In the public sector, a customer might be an organisation asking for advice from a government department. In your capacity as a student, you may be a customer of a college, university or other educational institution. Customers must:

♦ have a need for a product or service
♦ have the ability to purchase and pay for a product or service
♦ want a particular product or service and be willing to use their buying power
♦ if they work for an organisation, have the authority to buy products and services.

Based upon the characteristics of the customer groups making up each market, markets may be divided into four main categories. These are consumer markets, organisational markets, the market for services and international markets.

Consumer markets

According to Loudon and Bitta (1988), consumer behaviour may be defined as, 'the decision process and physical activity individuals engage in when evaluating, acquiring, using, or disposing of goods and services'. They show that the term 'customer' is typically used to refer to someone who purchases from a shop or a company. However, though a customer may be defined in terms of a business in an organisational market, consumers are people who simply buy for the purpose of household or personal consumption.

Consumer markets are made up of individuals who purchase for personal or domestic consumption, typically from retailers. The needs and wants of consumers will affect their purchasing decisions. Businesses must determine what products or services consumers need and want and make sure that these items are available. To do so, they require detailed knowledge about the age, sex, occupation and social grouping of consumers. Such detail enables them to match the needs of each group of consumers with an appropriate product.

Fast-moving consumer goods (FMCG)

Fast-moving consumer goods are tangible, non-durable goods that have a short shelf life; they are for immediate consumption. Examples are food and confectionery.

Market research and analysis is critical in these markets where changes may be frequent. Such research needs to constantly monitor features such as:

♦ market characteristics, including the way in which competition takes place within the market
♦ measurement of market potential and size
♦ market share analysis of the key players within the market
♦ competitive products, both direct and indirect
♦ new products acceptance and product preference
♦ sales analysis (by region, by consumer, and so on)
♦ short- and long-term sales forecasting
♦ advertisement effectiveness as well as the effectiveness of other elements of the promotional mix
♦ retail stores audit from point of sales data.

CASE STUDY

GfK's market research into consumer markets within Russia

The FMCG department within GfK specialises in carrying out market research in the sector of everyday products and services. Without exception, the experience of all countries has highlighted the importance of marketing information about consumer goods markets. At the present time, over 100 of the biggest international and Russian companies are the department's clients. The department makes use of GfK Group's many years of international research experience, which allows the optimal combination of qualitative and quantitative methods to be found. At the core of every project lie the most up-to-date methods of data collection and means of statistical analysis. The geographical scope of research into the consumer goods market is practically limitless. The department is able to carry out research in any region of Russia and conduct nationwide, representative surveys in any segment of the consumer goods market, with the help of its partners in the CIS, Europe or North America.

For every different type of product, consultants in the department are able to undertake the following tasks: research into market segmentation and recommendations on market positioning; optimal pricing strategy; an examination of advertising efficacy; research into product image; analysis of client satisfaction. The consultants know from their own considerable experience that there is never one single answer to a question: specially designed research is the best aid to getting to grips with any concrete marketing situation.

CASE STUDY

The UK mobile phone market

According to the Oftel Residential Survey, 75 per cent of all adults within the UK either owned or used a mobile phone in May 2003. For 21 per cent this was their main method of telephoning, with 8 per cent of homes now only having a mobile and no fixed line phone.

Not surprisingly, the ownership of mobile phones varies with age. Nearly 90 per cent of people between the ages of 15 and 34 years owned or used a mobile phone during February 2003. However, during the two years between 2001 and 2003 the largest increases occurred among the older age groups, with the proportion of people aged 75 years and over owning a mobile phone doubling.

ACTIVITY

1   How important is market research for FMCG markets?

2   Describe the sort of decisions that might depend upon such research.

ACTIVITY

1   Briefly describe some of the possible reasons for the changes taking place in the market for mobile phones.

2   Over what sort of period would individuals in different demographic groups own a mobile phone?

3   How would phone retailers and manufacturers use this information and what sort of marketing mix might they develop for a particular age group?

Consumer durable goods

Consumer durable goods have a longer life, are not instantly consumed and are expected to last for a relatively long period of time. Examples include cars, washing machines and video recorders.

Using the marketing mix to achieve objectives

The effective use of the marketing mix is essential within both FMCG markets and the market for consumer durables. The starting point for developing a mix for such markets is for an organisation to assess its capability. David Mercer (1996) sets out the following list of key points of information that needs to be collected for auditing an organisation's capability before a marketing mix can be developed:

♦ Who are the customers? It is necessary to find out their key characteristics, and what differentiates them from other members of the population.
♦ What are their needs and wants? What do they expect the product to do and what are their special requirements and perceptions?
♦ What do they think of the organisation and its products and services? What are their attitudes, and what are their buying intentions?

Within the context of the market and the appropriateness of the marketing mix this analysis of information may focus upon:

♦ total market size growth and trends (value/volume)
♦ market characteristics, developments and trends
♦ products and prices
♦ physical distribution channels
♦ customers or consumers
♦ communication industry practices
♦ competition
♦ major competitors
♦ size
♦ market shares
♦ market standing and reputation
♦ production capabilities
♦ distribution policies
♦ marketing methods
♦ extent of diversification
♦ personnel issues
♦ international links
♦ profitability
♦ key strengths and weaknesses.

This process of internal marketing auditing will enable the organisation to review marketing activity in detail, including an existing evaluation of the marketing mix within the context of the seven Ps. It is essential that when operating within consumer markets they ensure that the best possible marketing mix is offered in each product segment. Decisions might include how well product lines fit with the segments in which they operate, how effectively the various forms of distribution work, the competitiveness of pricing policy and the effectiveness of promotions.

Organisational markets

Organisational markets, or industrial markets as they used to be known, consist of buyers who purchase goods and services to be used in the production of other goods or services or to be resold. They include:

♦ industrial consumption goods which have a frequent purchase pattern but a limited life, such as chemicals and lubricants
♦ industrial durable goods which have a longer life, such as machinery and equipment.

Some organisations sell products in both the consumer and industrial markets. For example, a motor manufacturer may produce cars for individuals to buy as well as commercial vehicles for manufacturers to use.

Differences from consumer markets

When a company is selling to other organisations it still needs to understand the behaviour of its customers. But, whereas a consumer product in the UK may have 56 million potential users, there are fewer than 3 million organisations in the UK and the likelihood is that the product on offer will appeal to only a very small number of them.

The demand for organisational products and services is called **derived demand** because the amount purchased is determined by the demand for related goods and services. For example, the number of tyres

605

ACTIVITY

In your group, discuss whether the fluctuating economic conditions for organisations in business-to-business (B2B) markets might encourage them to diversify into other markets.

produced by a motor manufacturer will depend on the demand for vehicles. Depending on derived demand can have serious limitations. Organisational markets are subject to business cycles and the demand for industrial products and services may fluctuate violently as the pace of business activity changes. Recessionary economic conditions can lead to severe cutbacks in derived demand and cause a business to close down plants and lay off workers.

Although there is a body of marketing theory that can be applied to all types of markets, there are substantial differences between organisational and consumer markets. It is often thought that there are four key dimensions in applying the marketing concept to organisational marketing:

♦ aiming for improved profit performance, with sales volume and market share not as important as in consumer marketing
♦ identifying customer needs, which requires understanding the economics of customers' operations, the structure of the industry within which they operate, and how they compete
♦ selecting customer groups for emphasis; this is the classic problem of market segmentation, which takes on special meaning in industrial markets because of the high degree of buyer–seller independence after the sale
♦ designing the product or service package; there is seldom a standard product and the accompanying bundle of services is frequently more important than the product itself: the product must be 'invented'.

A key feature of organisational markets is that of product complexity, with products often requiring a high level of engineered input. Business strategies for industrial companies often call for a high degree of technical inventiveness as well as the ability to take risks, with related high expenditures for research and development. For these organisations the temptation may be to love the product rather than the customer, and thus to lose customer focus.

CASE STUDY

Marks & Spencer

Marks & Spencer (M&S) owns no factories, nor does it make any of the products that it sells in its stores. The company works with manufacturers who supply to its own specifications. M&S set up this practice of dealing directly with suppliers in the 1920s. It is openly proud of the 'personal and friendly' relations it has with its suppliers.

M&S's relationship with suppliers spans the whole supply chain to include raw material suppliers as well as producers. Many suppliers have seen their businesses grow alongside M&S. Their relationship is thus symbiotic: if the stores do well, then suppliers do well. M&S co-ordinates the activities of its suppliers by fitting the business plans of suppliers with its own business strategy.

Sales of clothing account for almost half the turnover at M&S. To maintain a leading market position numerous suppliers are used to create new lines and ranges. Highly experienced buying teams determine the specifications for new lines, assess suppliers' ability to produce the manufactured goods and negotiate price, quantity and delivery.

ACTIVITY

1 What are:

   ♦ the advantages
   ♦ the disadvantages

   of a clothing manufacturer working closely with a large organisation like Marks & Spencer?

2 In what ways would the activities of an organisation in a B2B market dealing with M&S differ from a business dealing with consumer markets?

Adding value through service

One characteristic of organisational marketing is the interdependent relationship between the buyer and the seller. Their relationships are often close and complex and, as the M&S case study shows, usually long term. An important reason for these close relationships is that the supplying business adapts its activities and services to the buyer so as to provide strong elements of added value through the service provided.

The strength of the existing relationships, particularly where there is a powerful value-added element, between buying and selling organisations in industrial markets acts as a barrier to the entry of other organisations. Often, individual contacts between companies become particularly strong, with managers appointed to supervise the relationship. In many circumstances the value generated through the relationship affects many different functions of each business, such as product development, production, quality control and electronic data interchange (EDI).

Another element of added value is the degree to which the seller in organisational markets can solve problems for buyers. In order to help the buyer to be successful, sellers have to satisfy a broad range of needs, some of which might involve building in a range of functions and qualities of the product which provide solutions to problems for the buyer.

There is no single way in which supplying businesses provide added value for their customers. It may include technical adaptations, exchange of information, the benefits of transport economies or help with their logistics of stocking. Because every customer in an industrial market is unique, the relationship between each supplier and its customer and the added value provided will differ in each circumstance.

Types of organisations in B2B markets

Figure 8.73   Organisations in B2B markets

According to Sally Dibb (1994), 'individuals and business organisations that purchase products for the purpose of making a profit by using them to produce other products or by using them in their own operations are classified as producer markets'.

Industrial organisations

Industrial organisations working in producer markets will be involved in the buying of raw materials, semi-finished goods or manufactured items which they then go on to use to produce other products.

Non-profit-making organisations

Non-profit-making organisations such as charities, schools, churches, museums, hospitals or other community-based organisations also trade in B2B markets. It is easy to take such organisations for granted, but their needs are vast, and their spending power great.

Government markets

Both **local authorities** and **government departments** make up government markets. This sector is large, and in order to provide the public with education, defence, health systems and a police force, their spending is considerable. The goods or services bought through these markets will change from time to time, reflecting different political and social priorities. Contractual agreements are also usually different and often dependent upon bids and tenders.

Resellers

Resellers are intermediaries such as wholesalers and retailers who buy finished goods and then sell them on to others, both in B2B markets and consumer markets. Generally speaking, organisations in reseller markets do not change goods very much, and simply add value through the service they provide.

Services

The word 'product' can be used to cover both goods and services. Services are viewed as a product partly because of the tendency for service industries to market themselves using the marketing strategies and techniques used by organisations providing goods. In fact, irrespective of the industry, 'product' is a word widely used to describe output.

Nature and characteristics of service products

A physical product is something tangible that can be used and handled. Though some service industries have products that can be seen and handled – for example, banks supply cheque books and train companies issue tickets and timetables – these do not constitute the service, but complement it in some way. A service is an intangible activity that provides customers with some benefit or element of satisfaction.

Services differ from products in that they are intangible, their **ownership** resides with the seller, there is **inseparability** from the seller, and **heterogeneity**, and varying levels of demand. Though the marketing of services presents many challenges that differ from those involved in marketing goods, increasingly the providers of goods are seeking to add value to their products by providing services to accompany them. For example, if you buy a computer from PC World, you can take advantage of Mastercare service cover for the computer if anything goes wrong.

Since a service cannot be felt, touched or tasted, the intangible benefits provided take on more significance. The image and expertise of the service provider may be of prime importance. Because services have benefits that provide customers with some level of satisfaction, it is important that they are fully explained to customers. Services involve the seller providing expertise to the buyer; for example, a doctor has expertise to supply to a patient, and a teacher has expertise to be used in a classroom: the service is thus inseparable from its supplier.

Another feature of services is heterogeneity: services are not uniform between suppliers. As a result, levels of benefit and satisfaction resulting from a service vary. Some hairdressers provide a better service than others and banks provide different levels of service, as do teachers and doctors.

Some services have a perishability which is not experienced in quite the same way in markets for tangible products. For example, although there is always a demand for some types of banking services, such as cheque books and transfer facilities, levels of demand may vary for other banking services such as loans for cars or currency exchange transactions.

The marketing mix for services

In the last chapter we saw that the seven Ps of the mix include product, place, price, promotion, people, provision of customer service and process management. Although there are many similarities between marketing services and marketing goods, services often present many challenges that may not be inherent in the selling of goods. For example, there are many more internal and external influences affecting service policies and strategies. There is a need to ensure that services develop logically so that the existing service range provides stability. Communicating with customers about something intangible is also more difficult: providers of financial services, for example, have the problem of communicating a range of product benefits to potential customers where some of the benefits provided are complex and difficult to understand.

Many service providers emphasise the quality of the service they provide in their marketing mix. Nearly all services will at some point be modified or superseded by newer, more relevant or perhaps more sophisticated services.

Product

The benefits required by customers can be translated into service features (the product). Any marketing strategy will depend upon how these features are viewed by customers: some services may seem to be more apparent than real. New services will have to fit in with existing services and fit the organisation's image for service provision.

Place

Distribution strategies will vary according to the nature of the service, but place – the convenience, proximity and degree of availability of a service – has to fit the needs of customers. It is important with any service constantly to evaluate new types of distribution. Increasingly, services are being brought to the home: for example, hairdressing and financial services.

Price

As the price for services generates income, pricing policy has to fit with the various elements of service provision. Some organisations discriminate by providing different levels of service at different prices: for example, rail fares vary according to the class of comfort required by customers.

Promotion

Promotional strategies for services need to consider the increasingly complex ways of communicating with customers and providing them with suitable materials. Leaflets and direct mail shots, point-of-sale materials, posters, sales promotions and merchandising are often targeted at narrowly defined customer groups. Services provided by groups such as solicitors and accountants are now being openly promoted for the first time.

People

People and their individual skills are inextricably linked to the quality of service. Customers may visit a restaurant because of the quality of cooking provided by a particular chef. A good teacher who knows what to do to get the best out of his or her students will be sought after.

Provision of customer service

Provision of customer service has become increasingly important in the service environment as a way of winning customers and differentiating the activities of some organisations. For example, financial institutions and airlines try to adopt a quality service approach that distinguishes them from their competitors. There may be a conflict between customer service and productivity because, for example, customer service requires attention to detail. Productivity measures the output achieved from using an organisation's resources. A hairdresser may seem to be productive if he or she cuts the hair of many customers in a short time. From the organisation's point of view this appears to be effective use of time. However, extra service to each customer may result in extra revenue: the hairdresser who spends time cutting two people's hair in an hour may generate £50 or more while the hairdresser who rushes through six may be paid as little as £18.

ACTIVITY

In your group, discuss the different types of service elements provided by one of your service suppliers. How does such an element differentiate it within the context of its marketplace?

Process management is concerned with the ways in which a service is delivered to a customer. There are increasingly sophisticated ways of delivering many different services to customers. Some depend upon technology, such as home entertainment and home banking.

Marketing tangible and intangible benefits

Services go through the same lifecycle states as other products. The behavioural version of the product lifecycle depicted in Figure 8.74 looks at issues similar to those in the more traditional lifecycle, but uses a different approach.

Services are much easier to adapt to changing circumstances than tangible goods and this helps organisations to inject life into services and retain their

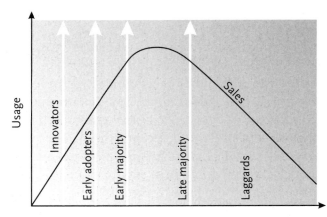

Figure 8.74 Service lifecycle

market position for longer. There are many different alternative strategies for doing this, including:

♦ expanding the range of some services for selected market segments
♦ reducing the range of some services for selected market segments
♦ analysing how services can be modified (instead of introducing new ones)
♦ re-positioning services in chosen market segments in order to provide them with a fresh image
♦ using various elements of the marketing mix to widen the markets to which services are sold
♦ further differentiating services from those of competitors in order to make them more appealing
♦ finding new, untapped markets for services.

Service modification

Modifying services is often preferable, as it does not involve as much risk as introducing new services. Modifications may include the following three types.

Quality modifications

The objective of any quality modification would be to improve the quality, reliability and durability of any service. A quality modification might be used to warn off competitors who seem keen to enter a market segment.

Feature modifications

In a competitive marketplace, adding new features is the cheapest way of keeping ahead of competitors. This may involve simply improving the benefits provided with a service. The advantage of doing this is that they

can be adopted or abandoned quickly, depending on their success.

Style modifications

Many customers are wary of sudden changes in the nature and type of service they receive, particularly in industries where customers are used to long-established kinds of service, such as standard financial services. Adopting style modifications may be more acceptable than making more radical changes.

New services

New services carry the biggest business risk. A service may be new to the service provider but not necessarily new to the customer, or it may be new for everyone. Factors indicating the need for new services may include:

♦ falling sales and profits
♦ competitive factors such as new entrants who may threaten market share
♦ new policies for the marketplace: for example, whether the organisation wishes to be more aggressive in the way it develops its strategies
♦ new profitable markets identified through research.

CASE STUDY

Matching service with workplace experience

This case study is intended to relate to your own experience of working within a service environment. The following range of different areas were described at a recent seminar on customer service.

SERVICE AND/OR QUALITY GAPS

♦ The service reality
♦ Assess your service and/or quality gaps
♦ Framework for closing the gaps

UNDERSTANDING CUSTOMERS' REQUIREMENTS

♦ Segmenting your customer base
♦ What customers want

♦ What customers really need

DEVELOPING A CUSTOMER VALUE PROPOSITION

♦ Defining your business
♦ Developing a customer value proposition and customer-defined measures
♦ Customer value analysis

PROCESSES TO DELIVER YOUR CUSTOMER VALUE PROPOSITION

♦ Identify your high impact processes
♦ Correlate them with your customer value proposition
♦ Align your critical processes

PROCESS MANAGEMENT

♦ Assess priority for improvement
♦ Benchmarking
♦ Techniques for improving your processes

ROLE OF STRUCTURE AND PEOPLE

♦ Considerations for organisational structure and systems
♦ Leadership practices and behaviours
♦ Importance of teamwork

IMPROVING COMMUNICATIONS WITH CUSTOMERS

♦ Nature and impact of external communications
♦ Barriers to internal communications
♦ Strategies and tactics to improve communications

MANAGING YOUR CUSTOMERS' MOMENTS OF TRUTH

♦ Determine your critical cycles of service
♦ Identify your customers' key moments of truth in a cycle of service
♦ Assess customers' base expectations and the opportunities to add value

COMPLAINT MANAGEMENT

♦ Cost of poor service
♦ Guidelines for managing complaints
♦ Action steps for recovery

ACTIVITY

1   What are the problems and issues that arise when working in an environment where customer service is important?

2   Use your own experience of working in an environment where customer service was important to comment upon at least two of the areas identified as necessary for training.

3   Discuss some of the issues that have to be discussed before making any modifications to customer service.

International markets

As a universal activity, marketing transcends geographic, cultural and political borders to serve markets wherever they exist. International marketing involves the marketing of products in two or more countries. In some circumstances it will involve trade between a business organisation and customers in just one other country, but a company may sell in many countries and manufacture in many others.

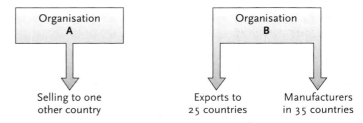

Figure 8.75   International marketing

Reasons to trade internationally

Standard of living

In an increasingly interdependent world, international trade is an economic necessity. We are not self-sufficient and we therefore depend on the import of raw materials and products from other countries. Exporting overseas helps to pay for the imports that make our standard of living possible.

ACTIVITY

Identify the products or services that you buy that are:

♦ exclusively domestically produced
♦ provided by an overseas supplier.

Growth and economies of scale

Many organisations first enter overseas markets by chance: they may receive an unsolicited overseas order and decide to follow it up. Trading overseas may then help them to achieve growth, particularly if the domestic market is static or mature. It may also allow them to use surplus capacity or to reduce dependence upon a single market and so allow them to spread risks. Expanding into overseas markets enables organisations to benefit from greater economies of scale. This means that over a larger output, costs per unit are reduced and provide the supplier with a competitive advantage.

Response to competition

Another reason for trading internationally is in response to competitor activities. For example, intense competition in home markets may encourage an organisation to seek outlets overseas. Alternatively, where markets are dominated by companies who trade on an international basis, the only way to compete with them is also to trade internationally.

Economic benefits in developing countries

Opportunities overseas might arise in developing countries where goods or services produced in more developed countries are in demand. Sometimes a number of economic benefits, such as cheaper labour costs, may exist in other countries, and make it worthwhile producing there. Many companies trade overseas so that they can sell discontinued products or seconds without having to sell them cheaply in the home market. Often the rules, regulations and economic conditions such as taxation and currency values within another country may provide organisations with useful opportunities.

Globalisation

McDonald (1996) argues that, 'national markets are becoming merely niches of global markets. In our view, companies that are not able to make the leap to global status will find themselves increasingly on the sidelines and targets for acquisition by the global giants.' There is no doubt that there is an increasing trend for organisations to broaden their perspectives beyond national boundaries. Overcrowded or saturated home markets encourage organisations to seek new customers overseas.

One result of this increasing globalisation of markets is an increasing interdependence among markets and a continuing growth in opportunities for businesses looking to develop an international orientation. For example, one in seven US manufacturing jobs and one out of every four acres under cultivation in the USA depend on export markets for their existence. Similarly, if foreign institutions decide to pull their investments out of a country many jobs are lost. The recession in south-east Asia in the late 1990s affected many parts of the UK, particularly those with organisations manufacturing semi-conductors, an industry in which many jobs were lost.

McDonald also argues that as customers become more global, they expect to be served not only at a local level but also at a global level. He suggests that the challenge for internationalism is a more pressing one for industrial companies than others, as the pace of change is governed externally by their customers.

Globalisation means that organisations looking for growth in the long term must turn to international markets for new opportunities. Organisations that simply look at the domestic market will at some stage run out of business opportunities, even where the domestic market is large. We have only to look at the high street to appreciate how large some of the retailing chains are, but for many of the UK retail chains the opportunities offered by the European Single Market have meant developing footholds in continental markets.

A key feature of change is that as competition increases, even small and medium-sized organisations will have to look to overseas markets for business opportunities. Growth opportunities exist in international markets for organisations seeking to develop quickly, for new competitors from developing countries and for producers of high-technology products.

CASE STUDY

Globalisation: good or bad?

It is argued that today globalisation is an 'overarching international system shaping the domestic politics and foreign relations of virtually every country'. It has also been said that 'globalisation is much like fire. Fire itself is neither good nor bad. Used properly, it can cook food, sterilise equipment, form iron, and heat our homes. Used carelessly, fire can destroy lives, towns and forests in an instant.' As Friedman says, '[Globalisation] can be incredibly empowering and incredibly coercive. It can democratise opportunity and democratise panic. It makes the whales bigger and the minnows stronger. It leaves you behind faster and faster, and it catches up to you faster and faster. While it is homogenising cultures, it is also enabling people to share their unique individuality farther and wider.'

As a result globalisation has dangers and an ugly dark side. But it can also bring tremendous opportunities and benefits. Just as capitalism requires a network of governing systems to keep it from devouring societies, globalisation requires vigilance and the rule of law.

Globalisation will always have cheerleaders who are blind to the destruction it can cause. And it will always have strident opponents blind to the way globalisation gives some people their first opportunity to fulfil basic aspirations.

As with most issues, the majority of people will be in the middle. They will see globalisation not as something to worship or demonise. Instead, they will see it as something to mould, shape and manage for the betterment of everyone.

ACTIVITY

1 Why might some people consider globalisation as potentially controversial?

2 What are the dangers associated with globalisation?

3 Evaluate how it might be possible to deal with some of these issues.

Standardisation versus adaptation

Two key questions in international marketing are:

♦ Is there a market for the product?
♦ How far will it need to be adapted?

The product must possess characteristics that make it acceptable for the market; these might include features such as size, shape, colour and design. Organisations also have to consider different languages, customers and health and safety regulations.

A business may wish to offer the product in an undifferentiated, standardised form. The great benefit of standardisation is the competitive advantage of low costs spread over a large output. However, others would argue that the success of many products in international markets has come about because marketers have successfully adapted their marketing mix to meet local needs.

In most markets there are barriers to standardisation. The marketing mix for a product might differ markedly from one country to another. For example:

♦ **product**: tastes and habits differ between markets
♦ **place**: systems of distribution vary widely
♦ **price**: consumers have different incomes
♦ **promotion**: consumers' media habits vary widely, as do languages and levels of literacy.

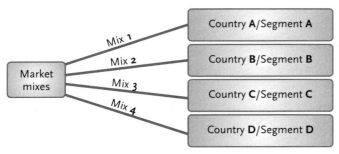

Figure 8.76   Adapting the marketing mix to meet the needs of each market

With differentiated marketing, on the other hand, an organisation will segment its overseas markets and offer a marketing mix to meet the needs of each.

The answer to the standardisation versus adaptation dilemma depends upon an organisation's view of its overseas markets and the degree to which it is prepared to commit itself to meeting the needs of overseas customers. Three different types of approach are usually quoted.

Polycentrism

With this approach to markets, organisations usually establish subsidiaries with their own objectives and marketing policies, which are decentralised from the parent company. Adaptation takes place in every market using different mixes to satisfy customer requirements.

Ethnocentrism

Here, overseas operations are considered to be of little importance, and plans for overseas markets are developed at home. There is little research, the marketing mix is standardised and there is no real attention to different customer needs and requirements in each market.

Geocentrism

With this approach, standardisation takes place wherever possible and adaptation only where necessary.

The European Union

Today, world trading patterns are dominated by huge internal markets such as:

♦ The Single European Market (within the European Union)

♦ The North American Free Trade Area (NAFTA)
♦ The Association of South East Asian Nations (ASEAN).

Creation of the community

The first step towards European integration was the creation of the European Coal and Steel Community (ECSC) in 1951. Jean Monnet (Planning Commissioner responsible for plans for the modernisation of France) and Robert Schumann (French Foreign Affairs minister) were the founding fathers of this scheme which aimed to 'pool' German and French coal and steel resources. The French and Germans were to give up their sovereignty on policy issues relating to their respective coal and steel operations to an independent high authority – a supranational body which would manage and co-ordinate policies in this field – thus linking two of their essential resources. Italy, Belgium, Luxembourg and the Netherlands also joined in the venture.

The next step towards integration came in 1956 when the six countries of the ECSC agreed plans to form a European Economic Community. For a number of years after the war, the countries of Western Europe had debated the benefits of adopting a Free Trade Area (FTA), and it was thought that an FTA would promote trade, increase prosperity and help the countries' economies in the processes of reconstruction and redevelopment. However, the European countries were divided as to the method by which this was to be achieved.

The six members of the ECSC felt that an FTA would not be sufficiently binding to deliver the security and economic benefits to which they aspired. They favoured a supranational model of organisation, in which countries would give up a portion of their decision-making powers to a higher authority (as in the ECSC). This was to be reinforced by the adoption of a common customs union and tariffs barrier.

Britain and another group of European countries (Denmark, Portugal, Switzerland, Norway, Austria and Sweden) preferred an FTA based on intergovernmental co-operation: they objected to the idea of giving up a portion of their sovereignty (their ability as separate nations to control policymaking in every policy area).

In 1957, the ECSC six signed the Treaty of Rome. The Rome Treaty effectively created both the EEC and EURATOM (The European Atomic Community). Together with the ECSC, these three organisations became known as the 'three communities'. Because of the objections outlined above, the other Western European countries declined to join the organisation, although most of them became members later.

Development of the community

Since its creation, the EEC has progressed and developed enormously. The organisation has been enlarged five times and there are now fifteen member states.

The original nations in 1957 were France, Germany, Italy, Belgium, the Netherlands and Luxembourg.

1 Britain, Ireland and Denmark joined in 1973.
2 Greece joined in 1981.
3 Spain and Portugal joined in 1986.
4 East Germany joined in 1990 (on reunification with West Germany).
5 Sweden, Finland and Austria joined in 1995.

The Single European Act was signed by the twelve members of the EC in 1986. Its aim was to kick-start the flagging process of European integration and with this purpose in mind, a deadline was set for the completion of the Single Market by 1992.

The EEC created a European common market protected by a customs union and an external tariffs barrier.

What is a common market?

A common market involves the free movement of goods, trade, labour, services, capital and people between a group of countries.

The problem was that although the Treaties of Rome had removed the most obvious barriers to trade (customs duties and tariff barriers between the member states), the member states found other ways of protecting their home markets against their internal trading partners. Although they had promised to remove all barriers to trade, in practice, they used 'non-tarrif barriers' to give their home markets unfair advantage. Examples of non-tariff barriers include:

♦ state aids such as production subsidies
♦ market-sharing cartels
♦ use of different technical rules and standards (such as different specifications on packaging design or composition)
♦ refusal mutually to recognise professional or educational qualifications.

Non-tariff barriers are generally harder to detect and the Community's practice of unanimous voting to make decisions meant that removing them was a slow process.

The intention of the Single European Market, therefore, was to create an internal European trading space, free from any national trading barriers. The aim of the Single European Act was to remove the hidden, non-tarrif barriers to trade: to harmonise inequalities in national law, such as environmental law, or technical laws, which might otherwise prevent member states from trading with each other on an equal basis.

The European Commission's Strategic Report of 9 October 2002 recommended a further process of enlargement to include Estonia, Latvia, Lithuania, Poland, the Czech Republic, Hungary, Slovakia, Slovenia, Malta and Cyprus by 2004.

Country	Pop (m)	Area (km²)	GDP	GDP per capita
Estonia	1.4	45,226	15.5	11,000
Latvia	2.3	64,589	21.0	8900
Lithuania	3.5	65,200	30.0	8400
Poland	38.6	312,685	373.2	9700
Czech Rep	10.2	78,866	157.1	15,300
Hungary	10.0	93,030	134.0	13,300
Slovakia	5.4	48,845	67.3	12,400
Slovenia	1.9	20,253	37.1	19,200
Malta	0.4	316	6.8	17,200
Cyprus	0.8	9250	9.4	15,000
Subtotal	74.6	738,260	851.4	11,413
EU–15	380.3	3,238,692	9570.8	25,166
EU–25	454.9	3,976,952	10,422.2	22,911

Figure 8.77   Enlargement of the EC, 2004

615

Bulgaria and Romania have been recommended to join the EU on 1 January 2007. There are also plans for further enlargement.

Country	Pop (m)	Area (km²)	GDP	GDP per capita
Turkey	68.1	780,580	489.7	7300
Croatia	4.4	56,542	43.1	9800
Macedonia	2.0	25,333	10.6	5100
Subtotal	74.5	862,455	543.4	7294
Total	178.9	1,950,016	1613.0	9016
EU–30	559.2	5,188,788	11,184.1	20,000

Figure 8.78   Possible EU enlargement after 2007

Benefits and risks

There are many different benefits of trading overseas. We have already mentioned that one key benefit is that organisations may benefit from greater economies of scale. However, there are a number of other economic benefits that result from such trade. For example, cheaper costs may exist in other countries, which may make it worthwhile to produce there. Hong Kong and Taiwan have proved to be attractive places for overseas investment. Similarly, and as stated earlier, many companies trade overseas so that they can sell on discontinued products and seconds, without having to sell them cheaply in home markets.

It may not just be overseas marketing opportunities that provide the base for international trade. Often the rules, regulations and economic conditions such as tax benefits and changing currency values within a country may provide organisations with useful opportunities to prosper from trading links.

However, catering for different markets can involve considerable risk. Developing products for different overseas markets and also being aware of the changes in currency prices requires careful planning and research. Difficulties are also likely to be encountered when competing with another nation's domestic producers in their own home territory as well as other organisations internationally marketing their products and services.

Trading overseas is not easy. It is necessary to be clear about trade barriers, such as tariffs and quotas which might restrict the flow of products across borders, and the extent to which home manufacturers are protected against foreign competition. There may also be problems with marketing and distribution structures that may make it difficult for overseas organisations to enter markets.

Another potential problem is in understanding consumer behaviour, culture and customs. Patterns of demand will be determined by lifestyles, incomes, use of credit and religion. For example, exporting alcohol-based products to Islamic countries would be totally inappropriate.

Communication systems also vary widely in different parts of the world. Business activities require written and spoken communications which influence promotional strategies, for instance where there is a low level of literacy television may be an important form of media. Language difficulties may also be a problem, particularly if several languages are spoken in the same country.

Other risks may include:

- the security associated with guarantees of payment
- variations in currency and their influence upon the profitability of individual contracts
- political risks and events influencing stability levels
- unfamiliar protocols such as diplomatic and other channels.

Market attractiveness

Planning for international markets is a much more complex process than for domestic markets. International marketing involves:

- constantly analysing developments in the international marketing environment
- reviewing the organisation's overseas performance by market, parts of the world, parts of the market and by region
- analysing how strengths have been utilised and opportunities developed, as well as how threats have been minimised and weaknesses corrected
- relating decisions to overseas marketing objectives

◆ indicating how international marketing programmes have been co-ordinated and costs budgeted.

The screening process helps an organisation to analyse how it can benefit from entry into each market. It will use screening criteria against which to measure the returns expected from each market. This will help it to:

◆ identify the best overseas opportunity
◆ assess the potential of each market
◆ determine the extent of research required
◆ decide how the marketing mix should be adapted.

According to Mooii and Keegan (1991), if a decision is made to conduct the total business on an international basis, a number of different approaches are available. They suggest that these five strategies would be:

◆ same product, same message worldwide
◆ same product, different communications
◆ different product, same communications
◆ dual adaptation
◆ product invention.

Majaro (1982) suggests a global segmentation approach to international marketing, which involves choosing segments of the global market in which to operate. By comparing information country to country, it is possible to identify those where some degree of standardisation is possible.

International marketing mix strategies

We have shown within this chapter that organisations operating in overseas markets must decide upon the extent to which they need to adapt their marketing mixes. At the one end of the extreme is the adapted marketing mix where each element is changed to serve the needs of the target market, while at the other end organisations use a standardised marketing mix worldwide.

There are a number of strategies in which products can be adapted for overseas markets.

Straight product extension

This means that a product is sold within an overseas market without any form of change. For example, Black & Decker tools are sold around the world with very few changes.

Product adaptation

This involves changing the product to meet the needs of local markets. Fast-moving consumer goods (FMCGs) are often developed to meet the needs of local markets.

Product invention

This involves developing something new for overseas markets. This might involve reintroducing an earlier product, or it could involve developing a new product to meet a special need in a particular country.

It is not easy to set international prices. For example, setting the same price in all markets would make it difficult for consumers in poorer and less well-developed countries. At the same time the organisation will want prices to reflect transportation costs, tariffs and all of the other costs involved in entering overseas markets and getting products to consumers. Some companies use **dumping** to get rid of surplus goods and this can lead to artificially low prices.

Distributing to organisations in overseas markets can be a major problem for distributors. Channels of distribution vary considerably between countries, with different numbers of distribution services encapsulating a range of wholesalers and retailers. Working around this may not be easy. For example, in some countries retailing is dominated by small independent units rather than large chains.

Although some companies use a standardised marketing message for their consumers in international markets most organisations follow a process of **communication adaptation** so that advertising messages are developed to cater for local needs. Media choice is always a consideration. TV advertising time and habits vary from country to country, as do those for magazines and newspapers.

Research and topical articles

Marketing in emerging countries

The context in which marketing takes place has an important influence upon subsequent decisions that have to be made about products and services. For example, Kwaku Appiah-Adu (1998) discusses Ghana, which has been hailed as a successful bright star of the developing world. In the context of developing countries, his research 'highlights the relevance of marketing and follows this by identifying a number of areas in which effective marketing strategies are gaining increasing importance in Ghana's evolving marketplace, and in this context, discusses case studies of three companies which have achieved superior performance as a result of improved marketing practice'. It is clear that this type of research has not just academic value, but has also, within itself, commercial value in helping organisations understand how to market within different environments.

Kwaku, A. 'Marketing in emerging countries: evidence from a liberalised economy', *Journal of Marketing Practice: Applied Marketing Science*, 1998, Vol. 4, No. 4, pp 118–29.

Internet and international marketing

The use of the Internet has significant ramifications for marketing products and services, particularly within the context of international markets. Hamill (1997) notes that, 'the recent explosion of international business activity on the World Wide Web will have a profound impact on the study and practice of international marketing as we move towards the new millennium'. He examines the implications of such developments for international marketing educators and for the mainstream literature on international marketing and argues that the rapid commercialisation of the Internet calls into question many of the fundamental tenets on which most international marketing research and teaching is based, especially the incremental, evolutionary school of internationalisation. He thinks that the Internet presents a fundamentally different environment for international marketing and new paradigms will have to be developed to take account of internationalision processes in an electronic age. This will require the launch of a major new research initiative to improve our understanding of Internet-enabled international marketing, especially the extent to which the 'Net' provides a low cost 'gateway' to global markets for small and medium-sized enterprises.

Hamill, J. 'The Internet and international marketing', *International Marketing Review*, 1997, Vol. 14, No. 5, pp 300–23.

References

Ansoff, H. (1965) *Corporate Strategy*, New York: McGraw-Hill.

Assael, H. (1993) *Marketing Principles and Strategy*, London: The Dryden Press.

Baker, M. (1971) *Marketing: An Introductory Text*, London: Macmillan.

Cannon, T. (1997) *Basic Marketing: Principles and Practice*, London: Cassell.

Chernatony, L. and McDonald, M. (1998) *Creating Powerful Brands in Consumer Service and Industrial Markets*, Chartered Institute of Marketing, Oxford: Butterworth-Heinemann.

Cook, S. (2002) *Customer Care Excellence: How to Create an Effective Customer Focus*, London: Kogan Page.

Cooper, B., Garcia-Penalosa, C. and Funk, P. (2001) *Status Effects and Negative Utility Growth*, Oxford: Blackwell.

Dalrymple, D. and Parsons, L. (1995) *Basic Marketing Management*, Chichester: Wiley.

Dibb, S. (1998) 'Market segmentation: strategies for success', *Marketing Intelligence and Planning*, Vol. 16, No. 7, pp 394–406.

Dibb, S., Simkin, L., Pride, W. and Ferrell, O. (1994) *Marketing Concepts and Strategies*, London: Houghton Mifflin Company.

Drucker, P. (1970) *Drucker on Management*, London: British Institute of Management.

Ennew, C. (1993) *The Marketing Blueprint*, Oxford: Blackwell.

Evans, M. (1998) 'From 1086 and 1984: direct marketing into the millennium', *Marketing Intelligence and Planning*, No. 16, Vol. 1, pp 56–67.

Festinger, L. (1964) *Conflict, Decision and Dissonance*, London: Tavistock.

Goller, S., Hogg, A., Stavros, P. and Kalafatis, P. (2002) 'A new research agenda for business segmentation', *European Journal of Marketing*, Vol. 36, No. 1, pp 252–71.

Hamill, J. (1997) 'The internet and international marketing', *International Marketing Review*, Vol. 14, No. 5 pp 300–323.

Handy, C. (1994) *The Empty Raincoat: Making Sense of the Future*, London: Arrow.

Jefkins, F. (1974) *Marketing and PR Media Planning*, Oxford: Pergamon.

Johnson, G. and Scholes, K. (1997) *Exploring Corporate Strategy*, London: Prentice Hall.

Kotler, P. (1988) *Marketing Management: Analysis, Planning and Control*, Eaglewood Cliffs, NJ: Prentice Hall.

Kotler, P. and Armstrong, G. (1996) *Principles of Marketing*, Englewood Cliffs, NJ: Prentice Hall.

Kwaku, A. (1998) 'Marketing in emerging countries: evidence from a liberalised economy', *Journal of Marketing Practice: Applied Marketing Science*, Vol. 4 No. 4, pp 118–29.

Levitt, T. (1975) *Marketing Myopia*, Harvard Business Review (Sept), Boston, MA: Harvard Business School.

Loudon, D. and Della Bitta, A. (1988) *Consumer Behaviour*, London: McGraw-Hill.

Lynn, G., Maltz, A., Jurkat, M. and Hammer, M. (1999) 'New media in marketing redefine competitive advantage: a comparison of small and large firms', *Journal of Services Marketing*, Vol. 13, No. 199, pp 9–20.

Majaro, S. (1982) *International Marketing: a Strategic Approach to World Markets*, London: Allen & Unwin.

Maslow, A. (1970) *Motivation and Personality*, New York: Harper and Row.

McCarthy, J. (1960) *Basic Marketing: A Managerial Approach*, New York: Irwin.

McDonald, M. (1996) *Strategic Marketing Planning*, London: Kogan Page.

McNealy, R. (1993) *Making Quality Happen: Step-by-Step Guide to Winning the Quality*, London: Chapman and Hall.

Mercer, D. (1996) *Marketing*, Oxford: Blackwell.

Mooii, M. and Keegan, W. (1991) *Advertising Worldwide: Concepts, Theories and Practice of International, Multinationals and Global Advertising*, London: Prentice Hall.

Needham, D. *et al.* (1999) *Marketing for Higher Awards*, Oxford: Heinemann.

O'Cass, A. (1996) 'Political marketing and the marketing concept', European Journal of Marketing, Vol. 30, No. 10, pp 37–53.

Peppers, D. and Rogers, M. (2000) *The One To One Manager: Real-World Lessons in Customer Relationship Management*, Oxford: Capstone.

Popcorn, F. (1992) *The Popcorn Report*, New York: Harper Business.

Porter, M. (1980) *Competitive Strategy: Techniques for Analysing Industries and Competitors*, New York: Free Press.

Rice, C. (1997) *Understanding Customers*, Oxford: Butterworth-Heinemann.

(2003) Sagacity Life Cycle Groupings, *National Readership Survey*, London: NRS Ltd.

Schramm, W. (1955) *Mass Communication: A Book of Readings*, Urbana: University of Illinois Press.

Shipley, D. (1981) 'Pricing objectives in British manufacturing industry', *Journal of Industrial Economics*, Vol. 29, No. 4 pp 429–43.

Simon, H. (1977) *The New Science of Management Decision*, Eaglewood Cliffs, NJ: Prentice Hall.

Svensson, G. (2001) 'Re-evaluating the marketing concept', *European Business Review*, Vol. 13, No. 2, pp 95–101.

Useful websites

World Advertising Research Center website on www.warc.com.

www.lexus.co.uk/references

Unit 9

Foundations of business decision making

In business, good decision making requires the effective use of information. This unit gives the learner the opportunity to examine a variety of sources and develop techniques for four aspects of information: data gathering, data storage, and the tools available to create useful information and present it.

Computers are used in business for much of this and thus the appreciation and use of appropriate IT software is central to the completion of this unit. Specifically, the learner will use spreadsheets and other software for data analysis and the preparation of information. The results are seen as more important than the mathematical derivations of formulae used. They will also gain an appreciation of information systems currently used at all levels in an organisation as aids to decision making.

Summary of learning outcomes

On completion of this unit you will be able to:
- use a variety of sources for the collection of data, both primary and secondary
- apply a range of techniques to analyse data effectively for business purposes
- produce information in appropriate formats for decision making in an organisational context
- use software-generated information to make decisions at operational, tactical and strategic levels in an organisation.

Chapter 1

Sources for the collection of data

Primary sources

There is an important distinction between primary and secondary sources of information. **Primary sources** are ones where the investigator collects original information direct from 'the source', for example by interviewing people in the street or conducting a postal questionnaire. The information is therefore new, original and first hand. In contrast, the use of **secondary sources** involves researching existing sources of information, for example information previously collected by a market research company, in a report on the Internet, in a book, in a set of government statistics, and so on.

Survey methodology

In carrying out a survey it is essential to consider the methodology to be employed beforehand.

There are two key issues to consider.

Questionnaire design

In creating a questionnaire it is necessary to consider details such as:

♦ the number of questions to be asked (not too many or too few)
♦ clarity of language, to avoid ambiguity
♦ the type of answers expected: will you use closed questions to elicit simple answers, or open-ended questions where the answers will require a lot of recording
♦ avoiding leading the interviewee into giving certain answers.

The size of the sample

How large a sample will be required to make the results of the survey meaningful?

An important consideration will be whether the survey will involve a qualitative or quantitative approach.

A **qualitative approach** involves in-depth work with a relatively small sample. This approach is often used in market research. An interviewer may work with a small group of potential users of a product to discuss in depth their thoughts and feelings about a new product.

In contrast a **quantitative approach** involves less in-depth studies involving larger numbers of subjects. Questionnaires are frequently used in qualitative research, often with closed-ended questions which can then be analysed by using computers and other calculating devices.

When collecting primary data, it is important from the outset to consider the purpose of the survey, as this will not only influence the questions asked but also determine the methods used for the survey. The starting point is always to consider precisely what you want to know. For example, do you need to know totals such as the market for a particular product, or do you require more precise information broken down into key areas for analysis? There is no point collecting too much data or data which is too detailed, if some of that data is unlikely to be used. Similarly, it is pointless collecting data if it is not going to provide the answers to the questions posed. A survey takes time and is a costly exercise. Therefore, in order to maximise the use of resources, it is also important to match the target dates and budget requirements to the nature and purposes of the research.

As surveys generate considerable data, it is important to think about what you are going to do with that data and how the results of the surveys are to be analysed. Planning the analysis may provide the basis for the testing of a hypothesis or answering the questions related to the survey. It may also provide the basis for further and more detailed research.

There are five main methods of collecting information in the field.

Sampling and sample surveys

This is the most common way to gather field data. It involves taking a census of a small sector of the population which represents all of a particular group, for example married working women in Bristol aged 30–45 are taken to represent all urban, married working women in the UK. **Convenience sampling** is taking information from any group which happens to be handy: walking down a high street, for example. **Judgement sampling** is slightly more refined: the interviewer would select high street respondents on the basis of whether or not they appear to belong to a particular segment of the population, say, middle-class business people. **Quota sampling** deals with specific types of respondents: working-class male Asian youths aged 14–19, for example.

Questionnaires

This is the most popular method of extracting information from people. They are usually conducted by post, telephone or in person. Questionnaires are easy to administer and easy for respondents to deal with. They simplify the analysis of results, and can provide surprisingly detailed information. However, they are easy to 'cheat' on and you should include 'control questions' in your questionnaire to check that the questions have been answered in a suitable fashion.

Postal questionnaires

These are easy to administer but unfortunately they yield a poor response. They are rarely used on their own: more often they are used to support a programme of telephone or personal interviews. Benefits include relatively low cost, no interviewer bias, and reaching people who are otherwise inaccessible. Disadvantages are the 'hidden' costs – paper, envelopes, printing, postage, clerical and researcher time, design and collation of the results – which are all are expensive.

Telephone interviews

These are ideal when specific information is required quickly. However as a survey technique they are flawed because the sample will be limited to those people who are most inclined to respond favourably to such approaches, often people with more time on their hands. The benefits are that it is easy to set up and the response is quick. The disadvantages are that a trained tele-interviewer is necessary, it is not possible to get a spread of the total population, and the interview can come to a quick end by someone putting down the receiver.

Personal interviews

In a structured interview, the interviewer has to follow a set pattern of questions and response methods (for example, ticking boxes). In semi-structured interviews the order and wording of the questions are laid out in an interview guide but the response is open ended, and the interviewee is allowed to reply in his or her own words. Unstructured interviews are what they sound like: certain topics are covered in a relaxed fashion. The benefits of personal interviews are that by using trained interviewers, one is able to get a high percentage of usable interviews. It is the most popular and widely used form of gathering information. The disadvantages are the high costs and difficulty of getting trained interviewers. This method also takes a long time and semi-structured and unstructured interviews are difficult to analyse for hard facts.

Questionnaire design

Though it is relatively easy to design questions, it is remarkably difficult to produce a good questionnaire. You must make your introduction simple, your layout clear and try to anticipate any misunderstandings. You want the questionnaire to provide you with the information you need. A question should only be included if it relates to your needs.

Questions can be open or closed. **Open questions** are those which allow the person answering to give an opinion and which encourage him or her to talk at length. **Closed questions** usually require only a 'yes or no' answer or one picked from a range of options. Questionnaires nearly always use closed questions. This tends to mean that the questions can be answered more quickly and more efficiently. It also means that, because the information is much more structured, the answers are easier to analyse. For example:

Do you find the new supermarket layout:

a   Very good   Good   Satisfactory   Poor   Very poor

(tick)   ☐   ☐   ☐   ☐   ☐

or

b   Very good   Very poor

           tendency to   (tick)

The purpose of this type of question should be to try to get people to commit themselves to a definite opinion: in this example, their feelings about the new layout of a supermarket. If instead you had used an open question (for example, 'What is your impression of the new layout?') the likelihood is that you would have got a variety of different answers. Closed questions tie respondents down so that they have to make a decision within a range of choices (in this case a range from very good to very poor).

Closed questions, in which you suggest a range of answers, can make it easy to sort your answers for analysis. For example:

Which of the following supermarkets in our town do you use most regularly? (Tick the relevant box)

ASDA   ☐

Netto   ☐

Sainsbury's   ☐

Tesco   ☐

Others   ☐

To help you to operate the questionnaire, you may like to use a prompt card. This means that if several, or all of the questions in your questionnaire have the same range of set answers, you can number the possible answers, and then record the respondents' answers as numbers:

Example of a prompt card:

ASDA	01
Netto	02
Sainsbury's	03
Tesco	04
Others	05

Sometimes, you will need to ask open questions. For example, if you wanted to find out why people are unhappy or happy with the new layout of a supermarket, the range of answers you would have to provide might be too broad to be practical within a closed question. An open question will help you to discover people's real views on the new layout, and to communicate these views more effectively.

When designing your questionnaire you will need to give careful thought to how you can make sure that respondents concentrate on questions which are relevant to them, and skip over questions which do not relate to them. This will be important, for example, with questions which provide two possible answers. For example:

Question 1   Do you shop at ASDA?

Yes   ☐

No   ☐

If your answer is No, skip to question 20.

Questions 2–19 would then be filled in only by those respondents who shop at ASDA.

Make sure that your follow-up question relates to the objectives of the survey. For example, this questionnaire could have been designed to find out why people used different supermarkets in a town.

The follow-up question (20) could be used to find out why some people do not use particular supermarkets.

Question 20	Why do you not shop at ASDA?
Poor range of goods	☐
Not happy with prices	☐
Inconvenient location	☐
Loyalty to existing store	☐
Other reasons	☐

ACTIVITY

Set out a simple questionnaire to find out one of the following:

♦ What improvements people that you work with would like to see in work arrangements.
♦ Whether people that you work with would like to work more flexible work arrangements.
♦ What improvements people that you work with would like to see in production and/or service provision techniques.

Use the following checklist:

♦ Your questions should be simple and easy to understand.
♦ Make sure that whatever you ask relates to your information needs.
♦ Do not include too many questions.
♦ Make sure that your questions are logical and fit into an ordered sequence.
♦ Do not ask personal questions. You do not want to offend people.
♦ Try to make your questions unambiguous. Make the meaning of your questions clear.
♦ Before you start to construct a questionnaire, consider what you need to know. When you have finished it test it. Trial interviews are essential.
♦ Thank people for giving up their time to help you.

Sample frame

The term **sample frame** means the total population from which a sample is taken. For example, if you wanted to find out why people buy shares in Manchester United you might use all the existing shareholders in Manchester United as the sample frame from which you take a sample.

In business investigations, researchers will usually use samples rather than the entire population.

For example:

♦ in market research, several hundred people may be selected from a total population which may contain millions
♦ in quality control checking and inspection, it is also usual to examine a sample of items for possible faults or imperfections.

However, remember that the larger the size of the sample, the more representative it becomes of the total population.

Information collected by surveying every individual in a population, such as that obtained in the ten-yearly Population Census, comes as close to 100 per cent reliability as possible. However, complete coverage is out of the question in most investigations because of the cost and effort involved.

In most cases – and this includes the collection of statistics by government departments – only a sample of individuals from a population are selected.

For example, the annual Family Expenditure Survey aims to obtain reliable data on household expenditure, income and other aspects of household finances for the whole UK population of 24 million households. However, only some 10,000 households take part in the survey, and of these, only about 7000 actually co-operate in providing the information requested.

Sampling methods

A number of sampling methods are acceptable in different situations.

Simple random sampling

This is a straightforward approach as described on p. 624. It is the preferred method where the whole population can be included in the sampling frame. One approach is to assign a data number to each sample unit and then random numbers are generated to choose the sample. Each item has an equal chance of being selected for the sample. Random numbers can be selected from a spreadsheet by using the random number function.

that the average of this population is 499.5. The average of a truly random sample of 10 numbers will have a value lying within plus or minus 100 from the population average with a high degree of probability: about 99 per cent. If we take several sample averages and these fall outside these limits, we can be pretty certain that the random number function on our calculator is not working correctly.

CASE STUDY

The National Lottery (Lotto)

Figure 9.1   The national lottery logo

A good example of random selection is the National Lottery (Lotto), where numbers are selected in a random order from balls bouncing down a chute. This gives a known probability of any particular number selection being drawn. The winning numbers are thus a random sample from all the possible number combinations.

To ensure that the Lottery draw is fair, it is regularly put to a number of statistical tests to check that the draw is random and unbiased. These are similar to the type of check that can be carried out to ensure that a calculator's 'random number' function is working accurately.

To check whether the 1000 numbers between 000 and 999 are being generated randomly using the random number function, we can proceed by drawing samples of ten numbers and finding their average. We know

ACTIVITY

1   Why do you think that the National Lottery is drawn by using random numbers?

2   Why are regular statistical checks made to ensure that the Lottery is working in this way?

3   In what business situations would it be relevant to use random sampling?

4   Try this. Tap out ten numbers between 000 and 999 using the random number function on your calculator. Average out the numbers. Repeat the exercise five times.

Each time, work out the average of the combined samples: 1 sample's average, 2 samples' combined average, 3 samples' combined average, 4 samples' combined average, 5 samples' combined average. You are likely to find that the average of your combined samples moves closer to the mean of the population (499.5).

You should now be able to understand why a sample size of 7000 used in the Family Expenditure Survey gives a very close estimate of the population's mean household expenditure.

Stratified sampling

One criticism of simple random sampling is that it may not accurately reflect the weighting of different groups within the population. Stratified sampling ensures that the different groups are properly represented and allows the random selection of items within each group.

An example of where stratified sampling may be helpful is when manufacturers of complex engineering products monitor the cost of materials by constructing their own index of material costs. Materials used may fall into distinct groups whose costs are subject to different market conditions. Groups could be steel, wiring, mechanical components, electrical components, computer chips, paints and packaging materials. Once each group has been weighted according to the latest purchase value, individual items within each stock group can be selected using random numbers.

As stratified sampling is used for large populations where there are distinct groups of items; it can result in valuable information about each group in the population. For example, for a particular year, it may be found that packaging costs are up 20 per cent and the cost of computer chips is down 50 per cent.

Systematic sampling

This can be used where the sample must represent a certain percentage of the population, even if the population size is unknown at the outset. It is often used for quality control checks, with items chosen at regular intervals having taken the first item on a random basis. For example, if it is decided that 1 per cent of items are to be checked and the first item chosen was the 46th item, subsequent items would be the 146th, 246th, 346th and so on.

It is important that the interval between selections does not coincide with a regular pattern in the data set. For example, a quality check sample based on an interval of 100 may not be appropriate for a business that produces 100 items a day. The result will be that the sample is taken at the same time every day, when in fact the quality of work may not be uniform throughout the day.

ACTIVITY

To ensure material usage is being properly controlled, it has been decided to obtain a sample of 30 stock-issue notes to check authorisation signatures. The total number of stock issues during the period under review was 695 and each stock-issue note had been referenced from 1 to 695 accordingly. Using a spreadsheet, generate a random number table and starting from column 1, identify the 30 issue notes to be investigated.

Quota sampling

The sampling methods described so far have resulted in the random selection of items. In the case of quota sampling, items are not pre-selected but are chosen by the person collecting the data. The only stipulation is that there should be a fixed quota, either in total or for known groups in the population.

For example, when investigating reasons for job cost overruns, it may be decided that ten jobs should be reviewed in each of three production departments. The method introduces bias in the sampling process as matters of convenience may decide the selection of specific jobs. Despite this, the method is widely used in practice because it is simple to carry out and it minimises the time spent on investigative exercises.

ACTIVITY

1   Describe two situations in which sampling could be used for investigative work.

2   Justify the type of sampling method that would be most appropriate in these situations.

Sample error

Any sample chosen must be as representative of the total population as possible. It must also be chosen in such a way as to minimise the risk of sampling error.

The sampling error of a statistic such as 'average income of managers in the UK' is the difference between the average income of the sample of managers and the average income for the whole population. Some samples will only have a small sampling error. They will produce an estimate close to the population average. Other samples will show a larger sampling error.

Sampling error can occur where:

♦ by chance the sample chosen is unrepresentative of a typical population
♦ the sampling frame is incomplete; for example, some records have not been included in the sample because of the inconvenience and time required to collect them
♦ there is subjective choice in which items will be sampled
♦ the sample frame for systematic sampling is not randomly organised.

Despite these problems, samples are widely used to estimate population characteristics such as mean and standard deviation. It is therefore important to recognise that even when you are using a sampling method that results in true random selection, there will always be the potential for error. The calculation of the sample mean will therefore only be an approximation of the population mean.

ACTIVITY

You are conducting a sample survey of students at your college or university. The sample needs to be representative of the student population, for example in terms of gender, ethnic mix and different courses studied.

1 How will you collect your sample?

2 What do you think will be the main factors that are likely to cause sampling error?

Secondary sources

Secondary data, collected by others, often represents a quicker way of gaining access to information than the painstaking task of collecting primary data. However, in using secondary data it is important to recognise that you are making an important trade-off, as shown in Figure 9.2.

| The more emphasis you place on secondary data, the quicker and more time efficient is your collecting of the data | The more emphasis you place on secondary data the less likely is the data to be precisely tailored to your needs |

Figure 9.2   Pros and cons of secondary data

However, in spite of this trade-off it frequently makes sense to use secondary data, because in the post-Internet world there is so much of it to be accessed quickly and cheaply.

Internet research

A useful starting point to research any topic that requires quantitative information is to access websites on the Internet. It is often surprising how much high-quality up-to-date sources of data can be accessed.

However, in accessing research information that is produced by a private sector organisation the dangers are that:

♦ you might be expected to pay to access the data; this is often the case with market research information, where research organisations make a living by collecting, analysing and selling data to businesses
♦ the data you access may be biased; for example, it may be collected on behalf of a particular trade group or commercial organisation in order to further a particular case or promote their point of view.

To find suitable data for your investigation you need to use a web browser such as Microsoft's Internet Explorer. Internet Explorer is fast and efficient, and it comes pre-installed on all new Windows and Mac OS machines.

In order to carry out a web search open your browser (for example, Internet Explorer). To enter a website you must enter its address to your browser, by clicking on a link or keying in the address. It is easy to find the address bar because it is at the top of the page and says 'Address' on the left-hand side. Once you have entered a legitimate address, your browser will contact the website's server and request the page you require.

Remember that you do not need to add the http:// of the address, but you do need to include the rest, for example www.tt100.biz will connect you to the Business Education site for *The Times 100*. One problem with entering web addresses is that they are case sensitive so make sure that you use the right case (that is, UPPER or lower case).

To move around the web it is usually much quicker to click on links rather than bother with addresses. Web pages are written in a simple language called HyperText Markup Language (HTML) which enables documents to be linked up with other documents. Links work in a one-way direction, so you may not find a link back, but all you need to do is click on the back button at the top of your page to return.

Because we are looking at collecting secondary data from the Internet for analysis, it is helpful to keep a record of where you collected the data. The best way to do this is to file important pages into your 'Favorites' – which you can do by using the Favorites menu.

Favorites can be organised in a systematic way by using folders which can be obtained by selecting 'Organise Favorites' from the Favorites menu.

In collecting and using data there are a number of sites that you will visit regularly, for example your favourite search engine (for example, Yahoo) and certain government sites such as National Statistics Online. Instead of clicking on Favorites each time you access this data or clicking through your favorites it is quicker to put a link to them in your Links bar which is usually found below the address bar, as shown in Figure 9.3.

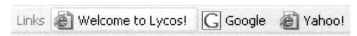

Figure 9.3   Links bar

Search engines

Google	http://www.google.com
Lycos	http://www.lycos.com
Yahoo	http://www.yahoo.com

Search engines such as those listed above enable you quickly to find out information that you are seeking by entering key words, phrases or subject matter: for example, 'market research data confectionery' or 'labour market data'. The search engine will then look for sites containing this combination of words, and often will list thousands of available sites. A good search engine like Google will prioritise the sites so the first ones listed are the ones that are most regularly visited and which are likely to contain the information that is most relevant to your search.

The Internet will provide you with a wealth of relevant information, for example company reports which can be ordered on-line at sites such as:

www.hemscott.net or
www.annualreports.fit.com/

Economic forecasts and changes in the market can be found on sites such as:

Investors Chronicle www.investorschronicle.com.uk
Bloomberg Money   www.bloomberg.com/uk

Newspapers and journals are always helpful such as:

www.economist.com/ and
www.independent.co.uk/

Government and other published data: by product data

The government regularly analyses business activity and publishes the results in collections of statistics. These are large reference books that are often available in college or university libraries or learning centres. Increasingly this information is available through government reports that can be downloaded from the Internet.

ACTIVITY

Carry out an Internet search looking at National Statistics Online. Access the part of this site for *Social Trends*. Look at the introductory material to *Social Trends*. What does it tell you about the categories or headings of social trends which are covered in the survey?

Useful government statistics

Social Trends

This publication draws together social and economic data from a wide range of government departments and other organisations; it paints a broad picture of British society and how it is changing. It covers 13 main areas which you will find out about from your research.

Monthly Digest of Statistics

This summarises information on monthly economic trends.

Expenditure and Food Survey

This provides information on spending patterns on these areas in the UK.

Regional Trends

This covers regional profiles, households, labour, living standards, and so on.

Labour Market Trends

This provides detailed statistics showing employment in different industries, levels of unemployment, wages, and many other useful figures.

Annual Abstract of Statistics

This covers population, social conditions, production, prices and employment.

Census of Production

This provides data about production by organisations in all industries.

Business Monitors

This gives statistics concerning output in different business sectors. The *Retailing Monitor* covers what is being bought by region.

Government statistics by product

To examine government statistics by product classification all you need to do is carry out a web search for 'government statistics by product' (see Figure 9.4).

Web

National **Statistics** Online - **Product** - Experimental **Statistics** ...
... Title: Experimental **Statistics** - Sub Regional **Government** Accounts. National **Statistics** **product**: Yes. Organisation (Sponsor): Type ...
www.**statistics**.gov.uk/statbase/ Product.asp?vlnk=9580&More=Y - 26k -
Cached - Similar pages

   National **Statistics** Online - **Product** - Experimental **Statistics** ...
   ... Experimental **Statistics** - Sub Regional **Government** Accounts, **Product**, Experimental **Statistics** - Sub Regional **Government Statistics**: Sub ...
   www.**statistics**.gov.uk/Product.asp?vlnk=9580 - 22k - 18 Jul 2004 -
   Cached - Similar pages
   [More results from www.statistics.gov.uk]

ESBR: Output
Home > **Government** > Federal **Government Statistics** > Output ... CHART: Gross Domestic **Product** CHART: Gross Domestic **Product**, Gross Domestic **Product** ...
www.whitehouse.gov/fsbr/output.html - 38k - Cached - Similar pages

Foreign Governments/**Statistics**
... Indicators, Historical Indicators, and National Income and **Product** Accounts appear ...
UMich Only): Indexes and abstracts federal **government statistics** since 1974 ...
www.lib.umich.edu/govdocs/forstats.html - 34k - Cached - Similar pages

   Statistical Resources on the Web/Economics
   ... US exporters by name and **product** and US ... state, national, and international energy **statistics**); Federal Acqusitions Jump Station (**government** contracts); Federal ...
   www.lib.umich.edu/govdocs/stecon.html - 43k - 18 Jul 2004 - Cached - Similar pages
   [More results from www.lib.umich.edu]

Figure 9.4   Searching for government statistics by product

ACTIVITY

If you carry out a web search using the key words 'government statistics by product' you will find a detailed list of the different products that you will be able to access on the Internet. Carry out this search and look for data that interests you.

Chapter 2

Techniques to analyse data

Representative values

Statistical information is very important to business organisations and to business analysts because it helps to provide a better picture of what is going on outside the business, as well as inside the business, and to provide a picture of important trends.

It is very important when we look at figures, for example for sales, output, and so on, to identify representative or typical values: ones that give an accurate picture.

For example, if we wanted to measure the performance of a salesperson on a typical day, which of the following figures would we take as being representative? (This salesman works five days a week.)

Sales made by Prakesh Patel

	Number of sales
Monday	20
Tuesday	120
Wednesday	5
Thursday	25
Friday	0

You can see that the sales made varied between 5 on Wednesday and 120 on Tuesday. These were the extreme values. What would a representative value be? Clearly we need to have some form of averaging to give us an accurate picture.

The process of statistical analysis

Statistics begins with the collection of raw data. This is obtained by collecting observations or measurements.

Data can consist of non-numerical qualities such as shapes and colours of different products, or it may be made up of numerical quantities such as costs and sales figures.

All data must be stored in a databank or catalogued as a list. An **inventory** is a document setting out a basic set of data from which different types of inferences can be made.

In most situations the first step of analysis is to determine the **frequency distribution** of the collected data. This can refer to either:

♦ the frequency of occurrence of each listed value or quality
♦ the frequency of occurrence of values or numbers which are in a certain **interval** (also termed a **class** or **fraction**).

Once data have been collected, there are three important steps in making sense of statistical information. These are:

♦ interpreting: establishing what the information means
♦ presenting: choosing the best way of showing the information
♦ organising: assembling the information in a structured way.

If the number of observations collected is small (for example, the sales figures for a new book in the first ten days after publication), the data can be set out in the following way:

50 60 74 120 180 82 75 51 123 96

The same data could be arranged in ascending or descending magnitude:

50 51 60 62 74 75 96 120 123 180

Because there are so few observations in this example, there is very little statistical value to it.

However, it is possible to identify the range of the observations, that is, the difference between the highest and lowest values. This is worked out by subtracting 50 (the lowest number) from 180 (the highest number). The range is therefore 130.

Frequency tables

So far, the examples we have looked at have been relatively simple. But as the number of observations increases, we find we need to arrange the data in a more manageable form.

For example, in an office where employees work flexitime, 100 members of staff work the following daily hours.

5	8	7	9	2	5	6	8	9	6
7	5	8	6	4	5	9	9	9	9
6	4	8	8	9	9	9	8	7	2
5	8	8	9	9	7	9	8	8	6
3	7	7	7	4	9	4	7	4	8
8	9	9	9	7	6	4	9	9	9
8	9	9	8	8	4	6	5	8	8
9	8	9	2	5	5	5	7	8	7
8	9	9	7	7	5	5	6	6	6
9	8	8	8	7	7	9	7	9	9

In this form, the data is of little use. It would be much more useful to display it in what is known as a **frequency table**.

In Figure 9.5, the top line shows all the values of the variable (the number of hours worked per employee). On the bottom line is the number of times that each value of the variable was observed (that is, the frequency).

Frequency table showing number of hours worked by employees

Number of hours worked	2	3	4	5	6	7	8	9
Frequency of observation	3	1	7	11	10	16	23	29

Figure 9.5 Frequency table

Reading from the table, it is easy to see that 3 employees worked 2 hours, 1 employee worked 3 hours, and so on.

You can also calculate the total number of employees who were observed. This is done by adding together all the frequencies:

$$3 + 1 + 7 + 11 + 10 + 16 + 23 + 29 = 100$$

Relative frequency

In the frequency table (Figure 9.5) we can see that 10 employees worked for 6 hours. But is that a large number or not? In order to answer that question we need to set out a relative frequency table.

The formula for relative frequency is:

$$\text{Relative frequency} = \frac{\text{Actual frequency}}{\text{Sum of all the frequencies}}$$

Thus the relative frequency of employees working 6 hours is:

$$\frac{10}{100} = 10\%$$

The complete set of data for relative frequencies can be set out as shown in Figure 9.6.

Relative frequency table showing number of hours worked per employee

Number of hours worked	Relative frequency	%
2	0.3	3
3	0.1	1
4	0.7	7
5	1.1	11
6	1.0	10
7	1.6	16
8	2.3	23
9	2.9	29

Figure 9.6 Relative frequency table

The table shows us that the most frequently observed numbers of hours for employees are 8 (23 per cent) and 9 (29 per cent).

The mean

We are all familiar with the concept of the average; we talk about the 'average' person, the 'average' score, and so on. However, it is important to realise that there are different ways of calculating an average, and that they yield different values. The 'representative' value thus will be slightly different according to the type of averaging technique that we use.

The three most commonly known ways of working out an average are:

♦ the mean
♦ the median
♦ the mode.

Calculating the arithmetical mean

When explaining the difference between the mean, median and mode, it is helpful to use the same set of figures. Here is an array of figures showing the number of packets of photocopying paper ordered by a firm during the first ten months of the year:

Month of the year									
Jan	Feb	Mar	Apr	May	Jun	Jul	Aug	Sept	Oct
Packets ordered 120	110	140	140	150	160	170	180	160	150

If we add together the total number of packets ordered the sum is 1480.

The arithmetic mean is the sum of observations divided by the number of observations:

$$\text{Arithmetic mean} = \frac{\text{Sum of observations}}{\text{Number of observations (months)}}$$

$$= \frac{1480}{10}$$

= 148 packets of paper per month.

Unlike the median and the mode, the **mean** takes into account all items in the data set. Where there are no extreme values, it is a very useful method of averaging. It is widely understood and can be quickly calculated on a computer or calculator.

The disadvantage of the mean is that it is distorted by extreme values in the data set. It does not lend itself to graphical display, and it may not correspond to any of the actual values in the data set. For example, in none of the months were there exactly 148 packets ordered.

Typical uses of the mean as an average in business and economics include calculations of:

♦ average hourly output per unit of input (for example, machinery or labour)
♦ average sales per period of time
♦ average sales per salesperson
♦ average number of customer complaints per day
♦ average price increases (as measured by, for example, the Retail Price Index)
♦ average changes in stock market prices.

The example below explains the process of working out a business's average output over a 50-week period. In the past, this task was time-consuming, tedious and prone to error. Nowadays, figures are continuously updated on computer and averages can be calculated automatically.

Over a 50-week period a business's output figures are as follows:

Output (000s)									
5	6	4	6	2	5	6	2	6	5
5	6	5	6	6	5	3	5	4	5
5	3	2	3	3	4	2	3	6	5
4	1	5	2	4	1	2	5	3	4
5	4	2	5	3	5	4	4	4	5

These figures can be set out in a frequency distribution table as shown in Figure 9.7. The Greek letter sigma (Σ) means 'sum of'.

Weekly output level (000s) x	Frequency of occurrence f	Output level frequency fx
1	2	2
2	7	14
3	7	21
4	10	40
5	16	80
6	8	48
	$\Sigma f = 50$	$\Sigma fx = 205$

Figure 9.7   Frequency distribution table

Calculating the mean

To work out the arithmetic mean – in this case, average weekly output – simply multiply the weekly output figures by the frequency with which they occur, and then divide by the total number of weeks (50).

$$\frac{205,000 \text{ units}}{50 \text{ weeks}} = 4100 \text{ units per day}$$

The formula for the arithmetic mean using a frequency distribution table is therefore:

$$\text{Arithmetic mean} = \frac{\Sigma fx}{\Sigma f}$$

ACTIVITY

The following table shows the annual sales of the major antidepressant drugs in 2002.

Sales of leading antidepressants (source company sales figures)

Drug	Company	2002 sales (US$m)
Seroxat	GlaxoSmithKline	3083
Zoloft	Pfizer	2742
Cipramil	Lundbeck/Forest	2120
Effexor	Wyeth	2072
Wellbutrin	GlaxoSmithKline	1323
Prozac	Eli Lilly	734
Romeron	Akzo Nobel	678

1   Work out the mean annual sale for the seven drugs shown.

2   Do the figures for the mean give a typical picture of average sales of a large company operating in this market?

The median (middle value)

The median is the middle value in a data set.

For example, take the following data set:

2   6   4   3   5   6   3   4   3   2

In order to calculate the median, we must first rearrange the data into order of value:

2   2   3   3   3   4   4   5   6   6

As this is a data set with an even number of items (10), there are two middle values, so it is necessary to take a simple average of the two values:

2   2   3   3   **3**   **4**   4   5   6   6

$$\text{Average} = \frac{3 + 4}{2} = 3.5$$

Where many numbers are involved, we can use a frequency distribution table to calculate the median.

Let us go back to the example (Figure 9.7) of weekly output figures. These were set out in a frequency distribution table as follows:

Weekly output (000s)	Frequency of occurrence (f)
1	2
2	7
3	7
4	10
5	16
6	8
	$\Sigma f = 50$

We use the letter n for the total number of frequencies.

In this case $n = \Sigma f = 50$.

The middle (median) value is thus:

$$\frac{50}{2} = 25$$

In other words the 25th number in the series, which in this case is 4000 units of output.

When calculating the median with an uneven total frequency, for example 51 weeks rather than 50, we use the formula:

$$\text{Median} = \frac{(n+1)}{2}$$

The median is useful for measuring:

♦ average incomes and earnings
♦ average hours worked by employees
♦ average sales made by employees.

It is a useful way of averaging because it avoids the problem of distortion associated with the arithmetic mean. The median is also an actual value which is readily obtained, even if not all the values of the items are known.

A disadvantage is that, although the median gives the value of only one item (the middle), a number of the surrounding items may have the same value. If these items are spread erratically above or below it, the median may lose its value as a representative central figure.

636

ACTIVITY

In a customer satisfaction survey, shoppers were asked to rank the service in a café as follows:

a excellent
b very good
c good
d average
e poor

The results of a sample of 50 customers were as follows:

Customer	Reply	Customer	Reply	Customer	Reply
1	c	18	a	35	a
2	c	19	a	36	a
3	c	20	a	37	b
4	a	21	a	38	a
5	b	22	a	39	b
6	d	23	b	40	a
7	b	24	a	41	a
8	e	25	b	42	a
9	a	26	b	43	b
10	a	27	b	44	b
11	b	28	e	45	b
12	b	29	a	46	a
13	e	30	a	47	c
14	d	31	a	48	b
15	b	32	b	49	a
16	a	33	b	50	a
17	a	34	b		

1 What is the median response given by customers? Show your working.

2 What advantages are there to using the median as a way of averaging figures?

3 Why might the median earnings of employees provide a better average than the mean?

The mode (popular values)

The mode is the value that appears most frequently in a distribution. Because it is the most 'popular' value, it can be seen as another way of indicating a typical or representative value among those recorded.

Take the data set:

2   6   4   3   5   6   3   4   3   2

You can immediately see that 3 is the most popular value, appearing three times in the data set.

The mode is often most useful when the sample being studied concerns categories rather than quantity variables. For example, if market research into soft drinks reveals that there are more consumers of soft drinks in the Midlands than in the South, North, or in London, then 'Midlands' would be the modal category. (It is not possible to calculate a mean or median with category variables.)

Multi-modal distributions

If two or more values are equal first in order of frequency, then the distribution is said to be **multi-modal**. For example, a survey to find out to whom consumers would respond most positively in advertisements for a sports drink, yielded the following results:

Anna Kournikova	36
Tim Henman	10
David Beckham	36
Michael Vaughan	12
Paula Radcliffe	25

Here we have a bi-modal result with two favourite categories, Beckham and Kournikova, each scoring 36.

Uses of the mode

The mode can be very useful in forecasting. For example, by identifying the most popular value for monthly sales, it is possible to forecast likely future sales. However, using the mode as a predictor is more likely to be effective in static situations, that is, those where sales do not change much from month to month, rather than in dynamic situations where there is fluctuation.

Further advantages of using the mode are that it represents an actual recorded value and is not distorted by extreme values. Modes are also easy to understand and can be shown graphically.

In multi-modal situations with a widespread distribution, the mode loses its value as an average. For example, take the case of a survey in which 100 viewers are asked to rate a new film from 10 (excellent) to 1 (very poor). If the results are bi-modal, with 30 rating the film 9 and 30 rating it 2, the results will prove very little, except that it is a film you either love or hate.

ACTIVITY

In April 2000 a Sheffield United supporter claimed that Sheffield Wednesday's 'average' number of goals scored during the season at home was 'a big fat zero'. He made this assertion on the basis of the evidence below. (All the matches shown are home matches. Sheffield Wednesday goals for home matches appear first.)

v. Arsenal	1-1
v. Bradford	2-0
v. Coventry	0-0
v. Derby	0-2
v. Everton	0-2
v. Liverpool	1-2
v. Man United	0-1
v. Middlesborough	1-0
v. Newcastle	0-2
v. Southampton	0-1
v. Tottenham	1-2
v. Watford	2-2
v. West Ham	3-1
v. Wimbledon	5-1

1   What was the basis for the Sheffield United fan's 'average'?

2   How else might the 'average' have been interpreted?

3   What do you think would have been the best way of calculating the average, and why?

Measures of dispersion

As we have seen, while the average of a set of data gives a central value, additional measures are required to determine how values are spread around this central value; in other words we need to measure the extent of dispersion. For example, we may know that in ten games two football strikers, Ron Knut and Ruud van Niestelroy, both score ten goals giving a mean score of 1 goal a game. The central value is 1. However, Ruud scores a goal a game, so that his score in each match is close to the central value. In contrast, Ron scores 5 goals in two games and fails to score in the others. His goal scoring is thus much more widely dispersed around the central value of 1.

In order to measure dispersion we need to get a picture of maximums and minimums and the difference (range) between the two, and deviations from the average (for example, mean).

The range

The range is the difference between the highest and the lowest values in a data set. It is useful because it gives a picture of variation.

For example, take the case of sales made by a group of sales staff. The best salesperson makes 95 sales in a week and the weakest only 15.

The range is therefore:

95 sales − 15 sales = 80 sales

In this case there is a broad range, which shows that there is a considerable difference in success at selling between the strongest and weakest members of the sales team.

In contrast, if the results of the sales made by sales staff were all bunched between 60 and 65 sales per week, the range would only be 5, showing little difference in performance between one seller and another.

The range is thus: Highest value − lowest value.

Dispersion

In business there are many situations in which it is important to be able to measure the extent of variation or dispersion around a 'normal' or 'average' value.

For example, take the stock market trading figures published in the financial pages of the daily press. On Friday 17 October 2003, share price fluctuations over the previous 12 months for some leading food retailers were as follows:

	High	Low	Current price
Safeway	328	197	288.5
Sainsbury's	300	220	266.0
Tesco	244	159	234.8

Looking at these figures, we can see that each had the following range:

Safeway   328−197 = 131
Sainsbury's   300−220 = 80
Tesco   244−159 = 89

Examining the range makes it possible to identify the extent of dispersion from an average figure. In each of the cases above there is extensive dispersion, indicating the relative volatility of share prices during the period in question. The share with the greatest dispersion is Safeway: because during the period in question there had been a number of takeover bids for the company.

ACTIVITY

Examine the Stock Exchange page of a quality paper. Examine the range of share prices during the last 12 months for Safeway, Sainsbury's and Tesco. Does this differ markedly from the figures quoted in the text? How would you explain this?

Advantages and disadvantages of the range as a measure of dispersion

The main advantages of using the range is that it is a simple, cheap and easy way to collect and compare data.

For example, take the case of a bottling company using automatic equipment to fill bottled drinks. Too large a dispersion in the amount of liquid in the bottles has economic consequences. Too large a spread can result in some bottles being too full, resulting in leakage and waste; under-filling can lead to complaints and possible prosecution.

Every hour the company examines a sample of bottles and checks the dispersion of the filling process. The results have to fall between a minimum and a maximum level. The range must be as small as possible.

Disadvantages of the range are that:

♦ While it is good for measuring dispersion in a small sample, it is less useful for larger samples.
♦ It gives the same result from different starting points. For example, if in an exam, one class of students may achieve marks ranging between 70 and 50, and another between 50 and 30. The range is the same (20) but there is a clear difference between the average performance of each set of students.
♦ The range can also be distorted by extreme values. For example, a firm carries out a survey to find out what price to charge for a new novelty product. Of people questioned, 98 out of 100 give values ranging from between £12 and £15. However, one interviewee suggests a price of £1 and another £350. Here the range appears to be £349. (It therefore makes sense to ignore some extreme values when calculating the range in some instances.)

Deviation: a measure of dispersion

Standard deviation is the most commonly used measure of dispersion. Like the mean, it takes into account every observation in a data set.

The table shows the sales revenue of a business over a period of five weeks.

	Week 1	Week 2	Week 3	Week 4	Week 5
Sales Rev (£)	100,000	100,000	100,000	100,000	100,000

In this case, the mean revenue is clearly £100,000, and there is no deviation from this figure. However, in most situations there will be some deviation from the mean.

We use the term **standard deviation** to describe the 'average' deviation from the mean.

The greater the dispersion of observations from the mean, the bigger will be the deviations and thus the greater the standard ('average') deviation.

The following table shows the number of faults reported on two production lines in a factory over a weekly period.

	Mon	Tue	Wed	Thu	Fri	Sat
Line 1	20	22	24	22	24	20
Line 2	15	30	60	15	20	40

It is immediately obvious that the figures for Line 2 are more dispersed than for Line 1, so we can expect the standard deviation to be larger. First look at the deviation for Line 1. The mean for Line 1 is:

$$20 + 22 + 24 + 22 + 24 + 20 = 132/6 = 22$$

The deviations from the mean are therefore:

	Mon	Tue	Wed	Thu	Fri	Sat
Value	20	22	24	22	24	20
Deviation	−2	0	+2	0	+2	−2

The next step is to calculate the standard deviation. There would be no point in taking an arithmetic mean of the deviations as these would always add up to zero (the positive deviations will exactly cancel out the negative ones). What we need to do is to square the deviations in order to get rid of the minus signs:

	Value	20	22	24	22	24	20
Deviation From 22		4	0	4	0	4	4

We use the term **variance** to describe the mean of the squared deviations. In this case the variance is:

$$\frac{4 + 0 + 4 + 0 + 4 + 4}{6} = \frac{16}{6} = 2.66$$

The problem of using variances is that they are set out in the form of the square of an observation. Often this has very little practical use. For example, if we are measuring the level of absenteeism in a factory, this might be set out in terms of days per week or per month. When we examine the variance this would appear as 'squared days per week', a difficult concept to understand.

We therefore need to convert our figures back into more meaningful terms, that is, the original observed values. This involves calculating the square root of the variance. The standard deviation for line 1 is thus
$\sqrt{2.66} = 1.63$

Now to work out the standard deviation for Line 2. Referring back to the table, we can see that the mean value for Line 2 is:

$15 + 30 + 60 + 15 + 20 + 40 = 180/6 = 30$

Value	15	30	60	15	20	40
Deviation from mean (30)	−15	0	+30	−15	−10	+10
Squared deviation	225	0	900	225	100	100

Variance $= \dfrac{225 + 0 + 900 + 225 + 100 + 100}{6} = \dfrac{1550}{6}$
$= 258.33$

Standard deviation for Line 2 is therefore
$\sqrt{258.33} = 16.07$

It can be seen therefore that the standard deviation for Line 2 is substantially greater than for Line 1.

Standard deviation takes into account all the observations in a population or sample and is a useful measure of dispersion. It can be used for:

♦ quality control or checking variations against a standard or average
♦ identifying variations in sales or production figures
♦ establishing acceptable standard deviations for use as bench marks. Where figures exceed the acceptable standard deviation, controlling action can be taken to remedy the situation.

However, when data is skewed, that is, when the mean is towards one or other end of the range, perhaps as a result of some exceptional observations, it is better to use the interquartile range (see p. 642).

ACTIVITY

Two production lines have been set up to package 34 bite-size sweets into bags. Regular quality checks are made to identify the number of sweets in each finished bag. The results of the most recent sample checking are:

Line 1 34 34 35 38 32 33 33 34 33 34
37 32 34 34 34 32 33 34 30 23
34 34 34 33 33 31 30 32 32 24
32 49 32 32 30 30 30 34 34 34

Line 2 34 33 34 35 35 33 34 33 33 33
52 34 34 34 34 34 32 34 34 34
34 33 33 34 34 34 35 35 35 32
33 34 34 35 35 32 34 34 34 34

1 Calculate the range for each of the two production lines.

2 Calculate the standard deviation for each of the two production lines.

3 What are the main advantages and disadvantages of standard deviation as a measure of dispersion?

Statistical process control

A good example of the use of statistics in applied business is that of statistical process control. An important aspect of production is that of continually checking quality standards.

For example, in setting a machine in a factory it is inevitable that there will be some minor differences in the products coming off the machine or down a production line. Typically, production managers will allow an acceptable **tolerance level**, that is, parts being fractionally over or under the norm. By using measures such as standard deviation it is possible to establish statistically acceptable tolerances. However, should the standard deviation go over these acceptable variations then it will be necessary to identify the cause of the unacceptable deviations and to make changes to production techniques, for example to overhaul a machine or production line, to check on the performance of production line workers, and so on.

Using statistical methods to check on processes gives managers greater control.

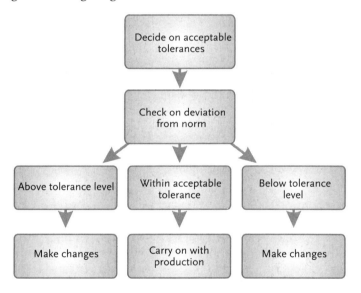

Buffer stock levels

Stock control is another important area where statistical techniques can be used, particularly to drive down costs.

Efficient stock holding is based on establishing the **optimum stock level**: that which will provide a steady flow of the product or service to the customer with the minimum level required to do this.

The **buffer stock** is the level below which stocks must not fall. It is a protection against stocks running out due to unexpected variations in demand.

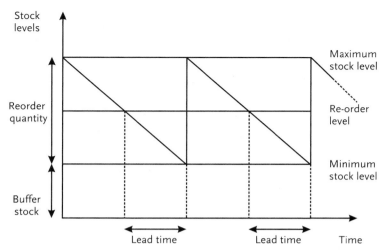

Figure 9.8 Stock control

Figure 9.8 shows the maximum and minimum stock levels, the re-order level and the level of buffer stock.

The lead time represents the length of time between re-order and delivery and administration of stocks. The diagram is based on the assumption that stocks are constantly being used up and that re-ordered stock is delivered on time.

Average stock level represents the average stock held throughout the period of time. For half the time the stocks will be above this level and for half it will be below.

The buffer stock acts as a 'safety net' (that is, a minimum quantity) in case stocks arrive late, or are not of the required quality or if production levels increase unexpectedly.

Statistical techniques are used to calculate appropriate levels of buffer stocks based on standard deviation, for example of changes in production levels over time, observations of errors in production, and so on.

Quartiles, percentiles and the correlation coefficient

In order to use statistics accurately, it is important to avoid distortion. Sometimes when measuring dispersion around an average, it is necessary to concentrate on figures which lie close to the average and exclude extreme or exceptional values. This can be done by eliminating the lower and upper quartiles in the distribution.

As we saw earlier, the median is the middle value in a distribution. Therefore, half the figures are distributed above the median and half below it.

All about quartiles

A **quartile** represents the middle value between two quarters of a distribution.

The **lower quartile** is the value between the first and second quarter of the distribution.

The **upper quartile** is the value between the third and fourth quarter of the distribution.

The **interquartile range** is the difference between the upper and lower quartiles.

Interquartile range = Upper quartile – lower quartile

The interquartile range is a measure which indicates the extent to which the central 50 per cent of values are dispersed.

The interquartile range often provides a better measure of dispersion than the full range. This is because it eliminates extreme values which can distort the overall picture.

The figures below show an array of 40 prices which different booksellers are charging for the same book, some over the Internet and others through *wholesale outlets*.

£

18	20	20	23	24	24	25	25	26	26
27	27	27	28	28	28	28	29	29	29
30	30	30	30	30	31	31	31	31	32
32	35	35	35	36	39	39	39	40	42

The total number of observations (n) is 40.

Calculating quartiles

The lower quartile can be calculated by taking away the bottom quarter of observations, that is, the first ten numbers. The lower quartile will therefore be the number between 26 (the tenth number) and 27 (the eleventh number) = 26.5.

The median lies between the lower 50 per cent of numbers and the top 50 per cent. As the tenth number is 29, and the 30th is 30, the median is 29.5.

The upper quartile can be calculated by taking away the top quarter of observations, that is, the last ten numbers. The upper quartile will therefore be a number that lies between 32 (the 30th number) and 32 (the 31st number), that is, 32.

The interquartile range is therefore 32–26.5.

Further calculations

In addition to breaking down figures into quartiles, it is possible to break them down further into deciles (tenths) and percentiles (hundredths).

For example, in comparisons of income and earnings, the population is often broken down into percentiles and deciles. This allows economists to compare the earnings of, for example, the top and bottom 10 per cent of the population.

ACTIVITY

1   Explain in one sentence what is meant by each of the following:

♦ upper quartile
♦ lower quartile
♦ interquartile range
♦ decile
♦ percentile.

2   Why does the interquartile range not give a better picture of dispersion than a simple range?

Correlation analysis

We use the term correlation to describe the relationship between two variables.

If points in a scatter graph (Figure 9.9) cluster close to the line of best fit, they are said to show a strong correlation; if they are more widely scattered, the correlation is weak.

All about correlation

Correlation refers to situations in which there is an association between the behaviour of two variables.

When both variables are moving consistently in the same direction – for example, consumption increases as income increases – we say there is a **positive correlation**.

When one variable moves consistently in the opposite direction to the other variable (for example, one falls while the other rises), we say there is a **negative correlation**. For example, as my bank withdrawals increase, the amount of money left in my bank account falls.

When there is no pattern to the relationship between two variables we say that there is **no correlation**.

Correlation coefficient

The correlation coefficient is a numerical measure of the strength of a correlation. It is represented by the letter *r*. It measures the closeness to which a sample of paired values fit a straight line.

The most common form of correlation coefficient is the **Pearson correlation coefficient**, which measures the extent to which each value differs from the mean of its own distribution, the standard deviation of the two distributions, and the number of pairs of values.

Most computers and calculators include a function for calculating Pearson's coefficient. The formula is shown below:

The Pearson correlation coefficient is:

$$r = \frac{xy - n\overline{xy}}{\sqrt{\left(\left(\Sigma x^2 - n\bar{x}^2\right)\left(\Sigma y^2 - n\bar{y}^2\right)\right)}}$$

Where *x* and *y* represent each observation of the two variables involved.

The value of *r* varies from +1 for perfect positive correlation to −1 for perfect negative correlation.

In both cases of perfect correlation, all the points would lie on the imaginary straight line. A zero value of *r* indicates that *x* and *y* are independent of each other.

The following illustration, which is widely used in statistics, provides a good way of visualising different strengths of correlation.

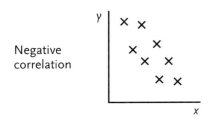

Positive correlation

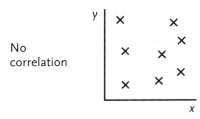

Negative correlation

No correlation

Figure 9.9   Scatter graphs illustrate correlation

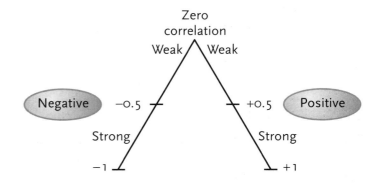

A rough guide to the strength of correlation (both positive and negative) is sometimes given as:

0.0–0.2 very weak
0.2–0.4 weak
0.4–0.7 moderate
0.7–0.9 strong
0.9–1.0 very strong

Uses of correlation analysis

The purpose of correlation analysis is to show the association between data; for example, to show the association between the increase in sales of two separate products.

Very often decision makers need to identify the causal relationship between one variable and another, for example the relationship between interest rates and consumer expenditure, income and consumption or between advertising expenditure and sales of a product.

There is an important distinction between:

♦ the **dependent variable** which responds to the change in the other variable, and
♦ the **independent variable** which causes the change in the other variable.

For example, the Chancellor of the Exchequer may want to analyse the relationship between an increase in taxes on spending (independent variable) and consumer spending patterns (dependent variable).

However, we need to be careful in interpreting the relationship between variables. Often, further probing shows that the 'independent' variable is also dependent on the other variable. In some cases there may be other additional variables that affect the other two.

ACTIVITY

Which of the following would you expect to have a positive and which a negative correlation?

♦ the relationship between the demand for a product and its price
♦ the relationship between the profits of a business and turnover
♦ the relationship between the value of the euro and sales by European companies to the USA
♦ the relationship between the number of hours worked by employees in a factory and the total level of output
♦ the relationship between money spent on training in a factory and the level of reported faults in production work.

Chapter 3

Producing information in appropriate formats

To aid the decision-making process it is important to be able to present information in an appropriate format. **Graphical illustrations** (for example, bar and line charts) may be used to present a key point in an easy to understand way for a relevant audience. At other times it will be helpful to illustrate **trends and patterns**, in order to set out likely forecasts of expected business performance and changes in the external environment. At other times you will need to **make a presentation** or **create a report** using appropriate presentation software and report writing techniques.

Creation and interpretation of graphs using spreadsheets

A spreadsheet is a table of numbers which can be organised and altered on a computer according to preset formulae. The most common spreadsheet package that the student is likely to come across is Microsoft Excel. Spreadsheets are particularly useful for forecasting and financial modelling, as they can show the effects of financial decisions without the need to repeat calculations manually.

Spreadsheets can be likened to a sheet of electronic analysis paper, organised into hundreds of columns and thousands of rows. They allow the user to manipulate and analyse both text and numerical data. Packages like Microsoft Excel include sophisticated features that facilitate the construction of multi-dimensional spreadsheets where a value can be analysed in more than two dimensions. For example, an expenses budget may be analysed by type of expense, by department, by location and into 12 monthly periods.

When constructing models, such as for budgets or project appraisal, the spreadsheet automatically updates calculated cells each time numerical data is put in.

Regularly performed procedures can be automated with a simple programming routine called a 'macro'.

For example, an organisation will make a forecast of all the money coming in and going out over a 12-month period. The spreadsheet can alter the inputs to calculate the effect of, say, lowering a heating bill by a certain amount each month. The computer will automatically recalculate the columns to change the heating figures, total cost figures and profits for each month.

In this way a manager, accountant, or any other user of a spreadsheet can quickly carry out business calculations such as introducing and finding out the effect of minor changes or variables. Spreadsheets not only provide support for simple data storage and retrieval, they can also be used to communicate results, by offering powerful presentation graphics in the forms of charts and graphs, formed on the basis of the numerical information contained within highlighted cells.

A spreadsheet package like Excel can be used to create pie charts, bar charts, line charts and histograms.

Pie charts and bar charts

CASE STUDY

Presenting information about the market share of different supermarket groups

Microsoft Excel enables the student or manager to quickly create useful graphical information to explain business trends. For example, supposing that we want to make a comparison between the market share of different supermarket chains using pie charts and bar charts that we present graphically.

Pie charts

In a pie chart each slice of the pie represents a component's contribution to the total amount. The 360° of the circle is divided up in proportion to the figures obtained. The area of each segment of the pie is in proportion to the values or frequencies of each class. For example, if two firms had 50 per cent of the market each, this would be represented in a pie chart by each firm's market share being allocated 180°.

Bar charts

These are an easily understood way of presenting information that can be used to good effect in business. Bar charts are drawn against a horizontal axis describing the variables, and a vertical axis showing value. The height of each bar corresponds to the frequency for each variable.

We can set out pie and bar charts for the share of the market of the key supermarket chains in this country at any one time. The figures shown below relate to 2003.

1 Find Microsoft Excel in the programme menu of your computer, and click on.
2 You are now presented with a series of rows and columns.
3 Put the heading for the chart, starting in cell 1A – process in per cent of market share of each of the key supermarket chains at the end of 2003.
4 Fill in the name of the supermarkets in the first column, as shown in the illustration: ASDA, TESCO, SAINSBURY'S, SAFEWAY, MORRISONS, OTHER.
5 In the second column enter these figures:

ASDA	16.9
TESCO	27.1
SAINSBURY'S	16.9
SAFEWAY	6.2
MORRISONS	3.2
OTHER	29.7

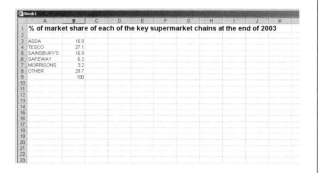

Figure 9.10   Microsoft Excel spreadsheet

6 When you have finished setting out the table, highlight the relevant area.
7 Using the mouse, go to the top of your window where you can see in the middle an icon that looks like a bar chart. If you click on this it will give you a list of options of different chart types. Let us suppose that you want to present your information in the form of a pie chart: click on pie.

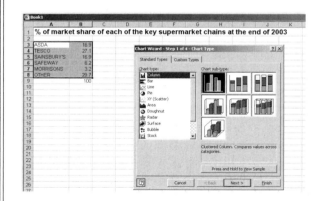

Figure 9.11   Chart type options

8 Select pie chart and the type of pie chart that you want to illustrate. Print off your chart (see Figure 9.12).
9 Repeat the process, selecting bar chart and the type of bar chart that you want. (On Excel horizontal bar charts are referred to as 'bar charts'. You can find a vertical bar,

by choosing the option 'columns'. Then print the bar chart (see Figure 9.13).

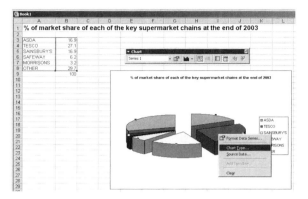

Figure 9.12   Pie chart

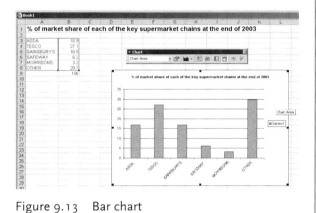

Figure 9.13   Bar chart

Histograms and line graphs

Other ways of representing information graphically include histograms and line graphs. **Histograms** are a special form of bar chart where the data represent continuous rather than discrete categories. For example, a histogram could be used to present details of time spent in leisure centres by people of different ages, because age is a continuous rather than a discrete category.

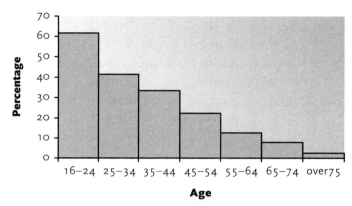

Figure 9.14   Percentage of people spending at least one hour in a leisure centre per week by age

However, because a continuous category may have a large number of possible values, the data is often grouped to reduce the number of data points. For example, instead of drawing a bar for each individual aged between 0 and 65, the data could be grouped into a series of continuous age ranges such as 16–24, 25–34, 35–44, and so on. Unlike a bar chart, in a histogram both the x and y axes have a scale. This means that it is the area of the bar that is proportional to the size of the category represented and not just its height.

Line graphs are particularly useful in showing how values or quantities rise and fall over a period of time. On a line graph it is normal to show time along the horizontal axis and the variables (that is, items whose value changes) on the vertical axis.

Graphs showing changes in the value of variables over time are also called **time series charts**. These types of chart are often used to present information in business reports, especially financial statements and company reports.

Time series charts can be used for showing a wide range of economic variables:

♦ interest rates
♦ unemployment rates
♦ inflation rates
♦ exchange rates
♦ rate of growth of the economy
♦ changes in population
♦ fluctuations in share prices.

For example, Figure 9.15 shows the share price of Wal-Mart, America's biggest retailer and the owner of ASDA, on each day between 3 May and 7 May 2004, following a slowing down of consumer spending in the United States.

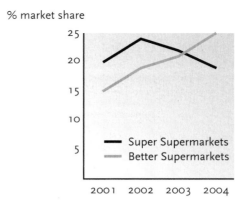

% market share

Figure 9.16   Line graph showing market share change

Line graphs are particularly useful for identifying patterns and trends in the data such as seasonal effects, large changes and turning points.

Scatter (xy) graphs

The simplest way of studying the relationship between two variables is to use a scatter graph. Creating a scatter graph simply involves plotting a series of points for x and y values. Once the points have been plotted, the graph will show whether a relationship can be identified between the two.

The data for a scatter graph is drawn from a single sample of subjects (for example, individuals or business units), with two measurements being made for each subject. Each individual's measurements are plotted at a single point, with the x measurement plotted on the horizontal axis and the y measurement plotted on the vertical axis.

One of the best-known scatter graphs was produced by the Boston Consultancy Group. The group examined two variables in relation to business in America:

♦ the total output produced by firms
♦ the cost of producing units of output.

The group noticed that over time, the cost of producing units of output decreased as a result of the 'experience' that large firms acquired. They developed the hypothesis that with each doubling of experience, average costs per unit tend to fall by 20–30 per cent.

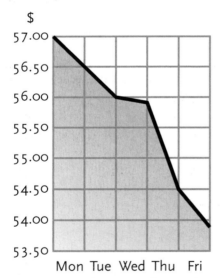

Figure 9.15   Time series chart on Wal-Mart share prices

Line graphs can also be used to make comparisons between two or more sets of observations. A graph like that shown in Figure 9.16 is often used in the financial press to make a comparison between companies.

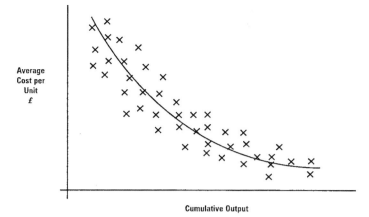

Average Cost per Unit £

Cumulative Output

Figure 9.17   Scatter graph on unit costs and output

The research carried out by the Boston Group showed that profits of a company are related to market share, as shown in Figure 9.18.

Market share %	Profitability %
Under 7	9.6
7–14	12.0
14–22	13.5
22–36	17.9
Over 30	30.2

Figure 9.18   Profits and market share

CASE STUDY

Premiership football success

In order to examine the success of Premier League football businesses in the first ten years of the Premier League, we might want to examine the record of the six most successful football clubs. We could start with the raw data set out in the table below (Figure 9.19).

The first decade of the premiership (1992–2002)

	Played	Won	Drawn	Lost	Goals for	Goals against	Points
1 Manchester United	392	244	93	55	789	360	825
2 Arsenal	392	195	110	87	598	346	695
3 Liverpool	392	189	100	103	643	408	667
4 Leeds	392	167	111	114	543	437	612
5 Chelsea	392	160	118	114	589	451	598
6 Aston Villa	392	154	115	123	491	434	577

Figure 9.19   Premiership records

We could then set out a scatter graph showing the relationship between goals scored and number of matches won, as shown in Figure 9.20.

The scatter graph suggests that there is a relationship between the number of goals scored and the number of games won: as represented by the straight line.

But it is also clear that 'number of goals scored' does not tell the whole story. For example, Arsenal have won more matches than Liverpool because the evidence shows that they have a better defensive record.

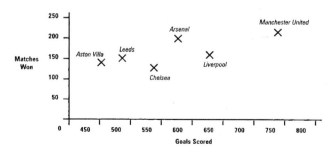

Figure 9.20   Scatter graph showing relationship between goals scored and matches won

The cost of producing each unit falls as total output increases over time. This makes sense: the more you do something, the more experience you have of doing it, and the more likely you are to do it better because you can identify faults and take steps to correct them. Gains from efficiency stem from greater experience. Large firms can also benefit from a range of economies of scale such as bulk buying.

Linear trend lines

A trend is a general direction or tendency whereby a variable appears to rise, fall or fluctuate over a period of time. For example, if you study Figure 9.21 you can see that the price of BT shares fell between 1999 and the end of 2002 when they bottomed out.

Figure 9.21   A trend in BT share prices

Illustrating a trend is helpful. This involves smoothing out some of the short-term fluctuations in order to show a more general tendency.

One way of illustrating an underlying trend that is simple to calculate is to use an approach known as **semi-averages**. For example, if we know that there is a general increase in the demand for a product over time, and that this is not affected by seasonal variations, we can use the semi-averaging approach. We can illustrate the trend line over a 12-month period in the following way. First we examine the data.

We can plot the data onto a graph. We can also show a trend line by means of a semi-average, that is, by creating an average for the first six-month period, and an average for the second six-month period. We then join these two averages together in a straight line.

Month	Quantity of product demanded
January	100
February	90
March	110
April	120
May	130
June	150
July	140
August	160
September	170
October	170
November	190
December	170

The average for the first six months is 700/6 = 116.66.

The average for the second six months is 1000/6 = 166.66.

The straight line in the graph (Figure 9.22) shows the trend line using a semi-averaging approach.

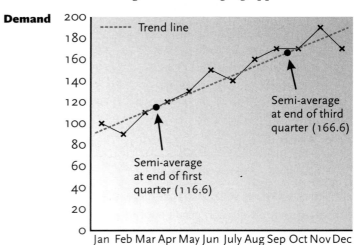

Figure 9.22   The trend in demand for a product

If there is an uneven set of numbers, for example 11 in the sequence rather than 12:

♦ include the middle value (that is, the sixth number) twice
♦ ignore the sixth number.

ACTIVITY

1 Illustrate the trend using the following set of figures which shows the number of employees who worked overtime in a factory over the previous 11 days.

Mon	4
Tue	6
Wed	8
Thu	7
Fri	10
Sat	9
Sun	10
Mon	14
Tue	15
Wed	16
Thu	18

2 Suppose 30 workers had worked overtime on the Saturday. Which approach would be more sensible for working out the semi-average:

♦ to miss out the Saturday
♦ to include Saturday in both the first half and the second half?

Setting out a moving average

Figures that we use in business decision making are influenced by a seasonal factor. For example, demand patterns for clothes change depending on whether the season is winter, spring, summer or autumn.

We can illustrate seasonal trends by taking an example. This helps to illustrate how we can use a **moving average** to smooth out seasonal variations to see what is really happening to the trend over time.

CASE STUDY
Supplying heating oil

A firm supplying oil for central heating faces high demand in autumn and winter and lower demand in spring and summer. In order to find out the long-term trend in demand for its product, the business needs to eliminate the seasonal variation from its demand picture. It does this by creating a moving average which smooths out demand for the four seasons of the year.

The first step is to calculate the average for the first group of four seasons. Then an average is taken for a second group of four seasons, starting with spring, and so on. The demand patterns and resulting moving averages are shown in Figure 9.23.

		Demand for heating oil (000 litres)	Moving average (000 litres)
2004	Winter	100	
	Spring	80	
			85
	Summer	70	
			87.5
	Autumn	90	
			90
2005	Winter	110	
			92.5
	Spring	90	
			95
	Summer	80	
	Autumn	100	

Figure 9.23   Calculating the moving average

You can see from this that in each of the seasons in 2005, values have risen by 10 from 2004. Having removed the seasonal variation, it is therefore possible to identify a steady upward movement.

Plotting a trend simply involves finding moving averages which are relevant to the sequence of quantities that you are studying. If you are studying figures where there are four seasons, then you take moving averages covering every four sets of figures.

In plotting the moving average we do so at a point half-way down the set of values. However, as this does not correspond to any of the actual values, it is helpful to create a **centred value**: half-way between the moving average of the first four values and the moving average of the second, third, fourth and fifth values as shown in Figure 9.24.

		Demand for heating oil (000 litres)	Moving average (000 litres)	Trend (centre of moving averages)
2004	Winter	100		
	Spring	80		
			85	
	Summer	70		86.25
			87.5	
	Autumn	90		88.75
			90	
2005	Winter	110		91.25
			92.5	
	Spring	90		93.75
			95	
	Summer	80		
	Autumn	100		

Figure 9.24   Calculating the centred value

Extrapolation for forecasting

Business forecasting involves looking into the future and is very important if a business is to prepare itself for possible eventualities. Extrapolation involves building a forecast based on what has happened in the past.

In the example above, for the demand for heating oil you can see that demand was increasing by 2.5 (000) litres per period, or 10,000 litres per year. Using this as a basis the heating oil supplier would be able to calculate by how much it will need to increase supplies in coming years. If the trend is a straight line, we could forecast:

Sales rise	
2004	10,000 litres
2005	10,000 litres
2006	10,000 litres, and so on.

What is referred to as **regression analysis** is often used to fit a curve to a scatter diagram so as to be able to make forecast predictions where there is a linear relationship between variables.

The formula for a straight line is:

$$y = a + bx$$

Where a is the point at which the line intercepts the vertical axis and b represents the gradient of the line, that is, the changes in y relative to x.

If the values of a and b are known, then the line can be drawn by inserting values of x into the formula and calculating the corresponding value of y. The values of x used should be within the range of values contained in the data set.

For a scatter graph it is possible to draw a 'line of best fit' by eye. The process requires a line to be drawn that is as near as possible to each of the points plotted. Where there is a cluster of points, the resulting line will tend to pass between them.

Given the equation $y = 10 + 1/20 \times x$ the corresponding straight line can be drawn as follows:

When $x = 0$, then $y = 10$.
When $x = 400$, then $y = 30$
The line can then be drawn.

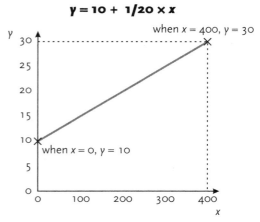

Figure 9.25   Straight line graph

However, the values of a and b can be calculated where an accurate line is required for *n* pairs of observations. The values calculated are least-squares estimates because the resulting line minimises the sum of the squared distances away from each point.

$$a = \frac{\Sigma y - \Sigma x}{n}$$

$$b = \frac{\Sigma xy - \left(\Sigma x \times \Sigma y\right)/n}{\Sigma x^2 - \left(\Sigma x\right)^2/n}$$

Reliability

The real problem with using a range of statistical techniques for forecasting and planning for the future is that there are too many variables which need to be taken into account. Though some are quantifiable and clearly predictable, some are not. The projection of past experience to an uncertain future is always likely to be speculative and hazardous, but there are always likely to be occasions when decisions have to be made upon estimates and incomplete knowledge.

At the end of the day statisticians are forced in many cases to present a range of scenarios which try to predict the impact of changes in a range of variables. For example, the following illustration shows predictions by the Bank of England in 2004 of how people's mortgage bills were likely to rise in 2005 depending on whether such factors as interest rates, consumer spending, house buyer's expectations, and so on rose or fell by varying amounts. You can clearly see that there were a lot of possibilities, although the average trend was for an expected rise in mortgage bills.

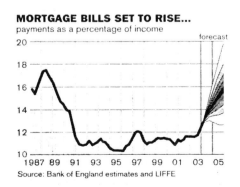

Figure 9.26   Bank of England predictions

You are part of the management team for a clothing retailer. What sort of things will the management team need to make forecasts about for business decision making? For which of these areas will it be easiest to create reliable forecasts?

Use of presentation software and techniques

In Unit 1 we outlined ways in which you can create an effective presentation. Typically, in modern business practice you will frequently be expected to use presentation software to support your presentation. Every year we see the development of new presentation software packages enabling the use of sophisticated multi-media presentations. For example, if you carry out an Internet search by entering the term 'presentation software' you will immediately find offers for exciting packages involving video clips, animation, and many other approaches.

Here we consider the use of PowerPoint, because this is a widely available package that is useful for starting out with. Many students will be already familiar with PowerPoint.

However, before using PowerPoint it is important to stress that the package can be used very badly. Simply talking through a set of PowerPoint slides does not make a good presentation. The term 'death by PowerPoint' has been used to refer to situations where a speaker uses too many slides, while providing a boring and uninspiring presentation.

Important lessons are:

♦ do not use too many slides
♦ make sure that the ones you use are pleasing to the eye, and easy to read
♦ only use graphics if they are relevant and interesting
♦ do not read out what is on the slide; rather explain what is on the slide by using examples, and put over ideas in your own words.

653

CASE STUDY

Making a PowerPoint presentation about training in a local company

1   Select PowerPoint from the program bar on your computer.

2   This will give you the following outline (Figure 9.27). You can now select **Blank Presentation**.

Figure 9.27   Selecting Blank Presentation

3   The **New Slide** dialogue box will appear (Figure 9.28). There are a range of slides to choose from. To start with select the one that appears in the top left-hand corner. A thick blue border indicates the slide that has been selected. Key in the title of your presentation and your name (Figure 9.29).

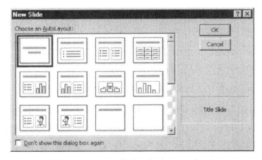

Figure 9.28   New slide dialogue box

Figure 9.29   Enter the title and your name

4   To change the colour of the background of your slide. Choose **Background** from the **Format** menu. This gives you a range of options on a drop-down menu. You can either choose from the most recently used colours, or from the PowerPoint palette. Select the colour you want and then click OK. You can also make the background more interesting by creating fill effects using the options Gradient, Texture and Pattern. Gradient allows you to create a gradual flow between two colours. Texture enables you to choose from different textured backgrounds. Patterns enables you to select a pattern.

5   You can now select from the menu the slide outlines that you want to use in your presentation. For example, the format shown in Figure 9.30 enables you to introduce in your second slide the people involved in training in the company you are discussing. At the bottom of the page you have a note to make a brief comment about the size of the training budget.

Figure 9.30   Entering information

6   You can copy and paste text into your presentation from another source, for

example Web browser (from the Internet). This is done by using the **Outline View** option icon which appears at the bottom of the screen. Draw a text box on your slide then copy the text you require by using the **Edit** menu. Then open your presentation in PowerPoint and switch to **Outline View**. If you click on **Paste** in the **Edit** menu the text will be pasted to your presentation.

7   It is always important to spell-check your presentation because a spelling error has a distracting effect on the audience: they will immediately start to question in their minds the accuracy of other parts of the presentation. You can carry out the spell-check by selecting **Spelling** from the **Tools** menu. The spell checker will automatically take you through your presentation, highlighting any words that may be misspelled.

8   Earlier in the chapter we looked at the importance of using graphics. You can either import these from a Microsoft Excel document that you have prepared using the same processes as outlined for importing text, or by using the graphics options that come with PowerPoint. You can choose a Chart slide from the **AutoLayout** screen. To create an appropriate chart or graph, select **Chart** from the **Insert** menu. You are then presented with a default chart and a table in which you can enter the information to be charted. As you enter information into the table the default chart will automatically change. When you have completed entering the data into the table, click outside the area of the chart and only your chart will appear in the slide. You can change the chart colours and fonts, by selecting the chart and then double-clicking it. This will provide you with a **Format Chart Area** dialogue box. You can now change the patterns and colours of the chart. Figure 9.31 shows a columnar chart

illustrating training done by a business in different regions of the UK.

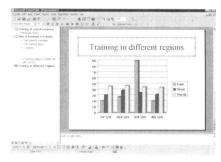

Figure 9.31   Inserting a chart

9   You can also include sound and animated objects into your presentation by going to the **Insert** menu and choosing **Movies and Sounds**. There are a range of options here. For example, you can add a moving image or sound from the PowerPoint gallery. You can also incorporate a file that you have already saved.

10 Having completed your presentation, you will probably want to produce a hard copy of it. You may want to hand this out to your audience or keep it as a guide to help you talk through the presentation.
To print the whole of the presentation go to the **File** menu and choose **Print**. You can then print off all the slides. A common practice is to print off slides leaving space on the page for your audience to add their own notes while you talk it through with them.

11 Finally, to view the presentation, click on **View** at the top of the screen. You can then look at the whole of your slide show by clicking on the **Slide Sorter View** option. This shows you all your slides. Alternatively, to run the presentation simply click on **View Show**. This will take you through your slide show.

12 If you practise running through your show, this will help you when you come to stand in front of an audience, because automatically you will remember the words and phrases that you used during your practice session.

ACTIVITY

Create a PowerPoint presentation comparing two types of graphical presentation, for example pie charts and bar charts, and setting out the advantages and disadvantages of each method. Use practical examples from real businesses to highlight the strengths and weaknesses of these methods.

Report writing

In business it is important to use the appropriate format for presenting information for decision-making purposes. A common form of communication for decision making is the report format (see Chapter 1). It is essential in creating a report to make it as brief as possible and to the point. Set out in the introductory section who the report is for and what it is concerned with. Typically the report will involve some form of investigation, often related to making a decision. Therefore the findings and recommendations sections are important ingredients of the report. A supporting appendix can be used to include statistical and other forms of evidence. The appendix should be easy to access, and clearly laid out. Using IT packages makes it easy to create well-structured reports that can be communicated by a range of means, for example by email.

Chapter 4

Software-generated information

Computers, with their ability to process, organise and communicate information, have become an invaluable tool for decision making. The nature of computers and their associated software is that they can carry out standardised operations such as making calculations very rapidly, and at a very low cost. Modern efficient businesses therefore use computer hardware and software to simplify their business processes throughout the organisation. Key uses of software to generate information include:

♦ management information systems
♦ inventory control
♦ project management
♦ financial tools.

Management information systems

Management information systems are systems designed to provide managers with a range of information that enables them to run a business efficiently and effectively. This information is typically stored on a computer or intranet system which can be accessed by managers and other employees on a 'need to know' basis.

Managing information is about designing and using a management information system (MIS) that turns raw data into something useful: information. Whereas data is facts that have been recorded and which relate to the vast number of activities and transactions carried out by the business, information is something that is useful to the person receiving it.

There are three fundamental operations that need to be included in a management information system.

♦ **Data capture** This is the recording of events that are significant to managers within the business, for

example records of financial transactions, market research information about customers, and so on.
♦ **Processing and storing information** The processes of the MIS need to maintain structured data stores than can be accessed to produce management information. The production of information often requires data to be searched, sorted, and for calculations to be made.
♦ **Communicating information** Management information systems should enable communication to end users using an appropriate medium.

Small businesses have the advantage that the manager is involved in the day-to-day activities of the business. The manager knows about and is able to decipher information from the numerous daily events. But for management to function as the business grows and becomes more complex, a formalised MIS is required that will provide information reliably and consistently.

Managers need to make timely and effective decisions in the execution of their duties. With this aim in mind, information is increasingly being viewed as a strategic resource to achieve corporate objectives.

The ideal MIS will convert data (from internal and external sources) into information that is relevant to the needs of individual managers. The system will enable managers to make informed decisions.

Figure 9.32   Extracting relevant information from data sources

657

Although computer networks provide an important means of communicating information for decision making it is important to remember that both computers and minds are required to create information required for decision making.

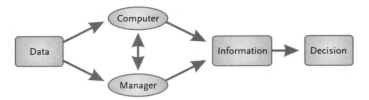

Figure 9.33 Combining computers and managers to make better decisions

CASE STUDY

Insurance

Insurance is about managing risk. For a motor insurer, the risk of a policy can be viewed in terms of claims history, age and occupation of the insured. A forty-year-old vicar who has never been caught speeding is a better bet than a twenty-year-old student who crashed Dad's car last month.

But as all insurers have used the same formula this has resulted in tighter margins and little room for error. The cleverer firms are now using more sophisticated methods of sourcing and analysing information. The ability to search vast banks of data to find a link between a policyholder's risk and some other variable can be just the head start they need. For example, it has been found that people who install smoke detectors in their homes tend to have fewer motor accidents.

One problem is getting hold of all this information without the applicant having to fill in a questionnaire running into reams of paper.

Although this is not a perfect method, the smoke detector question can be partly answered by looking at stored data sorted according to postcode, as there are only about six homes to a postcode. It may not be ideal, but knowing that the applicant lives in a house that has a 3 in 6 chance of having a smoke detector makes him or her a better risk than someone with a 1 in 6 chance. Success in insurance is about managing information effectively.

ACTIVITY

Managing an airline is as much about filling seats as it is about flying planes. Describe how managing information is essential to success in the airline business.

The primary function of management is to make decisions to affect the future and achieve organisational objectives. Information, either historical or applying to the future, is a vital ingredient to help management fulfil their responsibilities. Both types of information are important:

♦ information about the future: to plan, co-ordinate, lead and motivate
♦ historical information: to monitor performance against a benchmark as a basis for controlling future activities.

Decision-making functions are performed by a large number of employees at all levels of the organisational structure. Therefore managers need information that is appropriate to their responsibilities, which must be:

♦ relevant
♦ timely
♦ reliable
♦ complete
♦ accurate enough for the task at hand.

Strategic, tactical and operational decisions

Senior management

Senior managers make **strategic decisions** concerning marketing, procurement of resources and the financing of the business. They need to take a holistic view of the business within its environment over a number of years. The issues they have to address tend to be unpredictable, and are difficult to quantify. They are concerned with the future. Senior managers need to be provided with information through their computer networks about the external environment of the business (for example, indicators such as likely changes in interest rates, social trends, and so on), as well as information about the internal strengths, weaknesses, and policies of the business. Typical programmes that senior managers will use include:

♦ spreadsheets providing financial and marketing data
♦ databases providing information about such things as changes in the external environment over time
♦ presentation software to make presentations
♦ reports and summaries provided for them by others in the organisation.

Middle management

Middle managers are more concerned with **tactical decisions** as well as contributing to strategic ones. They will have functional and project-based responsibilities. Tasks are split between those that are routine and others that are irregular but are sufficiently structured to be solved by a clearly defined decision-making process. For example, for a management accountant, a routine task would be to review the latest job cost report (available through the company intranet) but *ad hoc* requests will occur, such as to evaluate a proposed investment in new plant.

For middle managers, a major responsibility is the control of current operations. Information is needed to highlight variances to the plan, so that time is concentrated on the management of exceptions rather than being wasted on the interpretation of large volumes of data. A spreadsheet is an ideal tool for budget monitoring. In addition, by contributing to the formal budgeting process, middle managers also have a planning horizon of between one and three years. Information for control purposes is derived from internal sources, but information for planning will require greater information from outside the business, depending on the responsibilities of the individual manager.

Typical software programs used by middle managers include:

♦ spreadsheets providing budgeting information
♦ planning software, for example for the construction of Gantt charts (see below)
♦ planning software for project management
♦ databases containing marketing information.

ACTIVITY

1 Identify a middle manager in an organisation with which you are familiar, for example your workplace, college, university.

2 What sort of information does this manager use for carrying out their day-to-day work?

3 What information does this manager generate for use by others in the organisation?

4 How does the middle manager use computer-based systems to generate and use information for management purposes?

Junior management

Junior managers supervise the day-to-day activities of the business by making **operational decisions**. They work within the constraints of operational policy so conditions tend to be relatively stable. Information needs are pre-determined and this facilitates the use of standard forms and, for computer systems, the use of data input screens. Information is frequently historical, relating to individual transactions, and typically comes from internal sources.

Typical software programs used by junior managers include:

♦ production and labour hour schedules set out on a spreadsheet
♦ stock control systems
♦ databases of customer accounts and details.

Level of decision making	Type of information
Strategic	Concerning the whole organisation
	Dealing with issues and decisions that are unpredictable
	Relates to external conditions as well as internal resources
	Has future implications
	Is of a complex nature
Tactical	Concerning departments or projects
	Is more predictable in nature
	Predominantly about internal issues
	Is concerned with future as well as
	historical information
	Is less complex than strategic information
Operational	Concerned with day-to-day activities
	About routine operations
	Largely concerns internal issues
	Is typically of a historical nature

Figure 9.34 Levels of decision making

Reports

Managers will frequently be expected to produce reports and computers are an essential part of this process, enabling:

♦ data input: for example, inputs into a spreadsheet or database
♦ data processing: using computer-based operations
♦ information output
♦ creation of management report.

At each stage human (managers) and physical (computers coupled with relevant software) resources will be used to generate the final end report.

Senior managers will need to have access to an up-to-date, easy-to-access and relevant management system enabling them to make appropriate decisions.

At the same time the efficient organisation will create a range of other software-based systems for handling the day-to-day activities of the organisation.

Typical systems for processing information

Accounting systems allow for the rapid inputting of company sales and purchases and the generation of relevant accounts. Profit and loss and balance sheet figures can then be made available for middle and senior managers.

Payroll processing is used for the generation of wage information for employees, the Inland Revenue, and so on. Senior managers will need to be kept up-to-date with total figures for wages paid so these can be compared with budgeted figures.

Sales order systems are essential to the regular purchase of supplies by the organisation.

Purchase ordering and stock control allow orders typically to be transmitted electronically to suppliers using electronic data interchange (EDI). Stock control software depends on being able to identify all the items that are stocked, for example by using a barcode and light pen.

Airline and other forms of booking have transformed the way that organisations such as airlines and sellers of last minute holidays have been able to communicate and transact with their customers.

Most large businesses today will have management systems designed for them to enable the smooth management of information within the organisation.

Specialist software development

This is often carried out for an organisation by specialist software development companies, using the following six stages.

1   Identify the information needs of the organisation by working closely with the organisation to find out the needs of users.

2   Carry out a feasibility study to see whether it is worth introducing change. Compare possible new solutions with the existing way of doing things within the organisation. Identify the costs and benefits showing how the management of information within the organisation might be improved. Once it has been agreed that the benefits of introducing a new system are greater than the costs, it is possible to move forward.

3   Carry out a detailed investigation of the existing system, identifying what it is expected to achieve, how and when tasks are currently being carried out. This makes it possible to create a system specification setting out what a new management information system will be expected to achieve.

4   Design a new system for the organisation using technical experts who have experience of developing appropriate systems in other organisations.

5   Create the software necessary to introduce the new management information system. This software will need to be tested to make sure that it is effective.

6   Once the new system is in place it can be reviewed and evaluated to identify possible further improvements.

ACTIVITY

Examine the management information system in an organisation with which you are familiar.

1   Who are the main users and generators of information at:

  ♦ strategic level
  ♦ tactical level
  ♦ operational level?

2   What are the main types of information used and generated by managers at each of these levels?

3   How is information technology used within the organisation to enhance the creation of management information?

4   How could the management information system be improved?

Inventory control

The term inventory simply refers to stocks (that is, stock control). Manufacturing companies will hold a number of different types of stock. This can be stock of parts which are then built into final products, or stocks of finished goods. Having the right amount of stock at the right time is essential for the efficient and cost-effective running of the company. This is particularly true in the modern age where more and more companies engage in 'just-in-time' manufacturing and delivery. A stock management system needs to be devised to make sure that stocks arrive just when they are needed and finished goods are delivered just in time.

Computers and relevant software are therefore particularly important for stock control, enabling much higher levels of control than would be possible with manual systems. Stock control software works best when it is possible to identify every type of item in stock, for example by using barcodes that can be read with a light pen or scanner. Barcodes uniquely identify each type of item by a product or item code. This information is then processed by computer stock control systems. The software ensures that when items in stock drop below a pre-determined figure (the **re-order level**) a request will be made for more stock. Computerised systems make it possible to move goods and parts round a factory, and on to distributors at exactly the right times.

Continuous and periodic review

Organisations establish clear re-order policies that can be fed into a computer program. Orders for replenishment are usually placed when stock in hand equals or falls below a fixed value M, which is the re-order level. With a re-order level policy, therefore, the amount of inventory is reviewed continuously. A replenishment order placed within a re-order-level policy is for a fixed quantity. The solid line in Figure 9.35 represents the actual inventory where a finite lead time exists. The **lead time** is the time delay between placing a replenishment order and its delivery. The broken line indicates the inventory that would be held if no lead time existed.

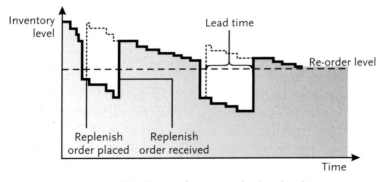

Figure 9.35   Stock balances for a re-order-level policy

The re-order quantity control policy assumes that the stock level is known exactly at every point in time; this is the only way in which we can tell that the re-order level M is reached, when a replacement order for Q is made (M,Q). This is referred to as a **perpetual inventory control system**.

It is possible to think of situations when re-order or continuous review systems are not a good choice.

For example, if a supplier accepts orders once a week, there is no reason to review the stock of those items more often. Instead of using a continuous review system, periodic reviews can be adopted. The time between the two reviews would be the review period spanning R periods of time.

When the review costs are small so that the cost of processing transactions are small compared with ordering costs, a continuous review system can lead to lower overall inventories than a periodic system. Using an MQ policy offers protection over the l-period replenishment lead time.

Under a periodic review period, the situation is different because replenishment decisions are made R periods apart. If the current decision time is t, the next replenishment period will be $t + R$, and with delivery time this will be $t + R + l$. It thus follows that under a periodic review system the safety stock must be large enough to provide protection against the length of time $l + R$.

Therefore, under:

- a re-order system, an organisation will adopt an MQ policy; when the inventory reaches M units, Q is ordered
- a periodic review system, if at a review time, the inventory is less or equal to M, an amount nQ is ordered ($n = 1, 2, 3, ...$); multiple n would ensure that after the order is placed the available inventory reaches a level in the interval of $MM + Q$; if the available inventory is greater than M, no order is placed.

Economic order quantity

The **economic order quantity** (EOQ) approach has been in use for nearly 100 years and involves the application of mathematical modelling to inventory planning. It therefore lends itself to computer programming. EOQ seeks to calculate the most cost-effective quantity of stock to order from a supplier. The calculation seeks to find a compromise between the cost saving resulting from buying in bulk and the extra costs involved in holding large stocks.

The EOQ model makes some simplifying assumptions:

- that the demand for the item of stock is constant
- the lead time is constant (that is, the time between order and delivery)
- there are no items out of stock
- order costs are constant – for example, there are no discounts for large orders
- the costs of holding stock vary proportionately with the amount held.

The formula for EOQ is therefore:

$$EOQ = \sqrt{\frac{2od}{h}}$$

Where o = the ordering cost for the item
d = the annual demand for the item
h = the holding cost of one unit per annum.

ACTIVITY

If 8000 units of an item are demanded each year, and ordering costs are £90 and the cost of holding an item in store is £4 per year, what is the EOQ?

Pareto analysis

The Pareto principle is particulary apt in relation to stock control and is also referred to as the 80:20 principle. It states, for example, that 80 per cent of your value will come from 20 per cent of your stocks, and that 80 per cent of your problems will come from another 20 per cent of your stocks. Using computer modelling to track stock enables managers to identify types of stock that create the greatest value, and stock that creates the greatest problems. Using this approach enables the manager to concentrate resources where there is the greatest impact and to cut out activities where there are the greatest problems.

Computer modelling can also be used to identify material requirements for different processes within the organisation; for example, when the materials will be needed, in what quantities, and so on. Inventory management is also essential in planning manufacturing processes. Inventories need to be in the

right place just in time for their use. The Japanese have developed what is referred to as a *kanban* system for pulling inventories, and semi-manufactured items through a manufacturing system. A *kanban* is simply a sign or symbol which indicates that a user of inventories requires more materials and parts to carry on the production process. The *kanban* might be a buzzer, or other form of signal, a coloured card or simply a basket or tray waiting to be filled.

Project management

Project work lies at the heart of many organisations. A project can be defined as 'a non-routine set of activities culminating in a specific objective'. It generally has a specific start date and finish date. Typically projects involve:

- a task to be completed
- a team of people assigned to the project
- a time sequence, and deadline date for completion.

For example, making sure that this book is completed on time requires careful project management so that the book is of the right quality and appears in time to be taken up on relevant degree-level courses.

A project manager has the responsibility for seeing the project through. Useful tools to help the project manager are networking diagrams and critical path analysis tools, as well as Gantt and PERT charts. Today, these project management tools are typically employed using computer software, because once a particular package has been learned the user is able to generate a project plan much more quickly and with less risk of making a mistake. Accuracy is particularly important when designing a highly complex project, for example the construction of a new road bridge, or the product launch of a new car.

Networking

When co-ordinating a project, it is essential to map out the sequence of events that must be carried out. Activities need to be performed in a planned sequence, for example in building a house the walls are normally assembled before the roof is put on; the layers of a sponge cake are made before the icing is put on, and

663

so on. These events can be linked in a diagrammatic form as shown in Figure 9.36 where before B can be started, A must be completed.

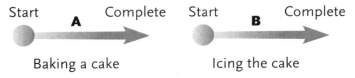

Figure 9.36   Serial events in network analysis

Some activities do not have to take place in sequence; they can be carried out simultaneously. For example, the icing could be prepared at the same time as the cake is being baked. This is illustrated in Figure 9.37, showing that before you bake the cake and/or prepare the icing, you need to mix the ingredients for each, but the later stages of production can be carried out simultaneously.

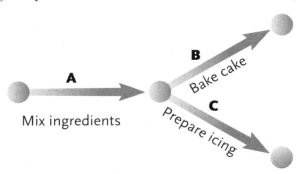

Figure 9.37   Simultaneous activities in network analysis

Network analysis can be used to map out programmes of activities in a way that creates the most effective planning. A further important ingredient in constructing a network is time, which is a crucial element in project planning. Time needs to be incorporated into the diagram (see Figure 9.38).

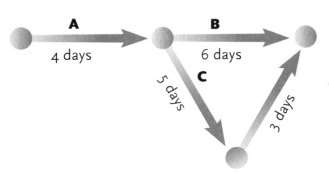

Figure 9.38   Introducing time to a network analysis

ACTIVITY

The organisation you work for is trying to design a network of activities for a new administrative procedure. You have been asked to map out programmes of activities in such a way as to create the most efficient process of planning. Set out a network diagram to indicate the performance of the following activities and their relation to other activities.

♦ Activity A: Must be done first
♦ Activity B: Can be started only when A is finished
♦ Activity C: Can be started only when A is finished
♦ Activity D: Requires completion of B
♦ Activity E: Requires completion of C and D
♦ Activity F: Completes project and must await completion of all other activities.

It now becomes easy to calculate the minimum time required to carry out a particular project. Those activities that take the longest to complete in moving from one state to the next in a project are described as **critical activities**. It is essential that the activities are done well and that they are given priority because delays to them will delay the completion of the project as a whole. This too can be illustrated by a simple diagram (Figure 9.39).

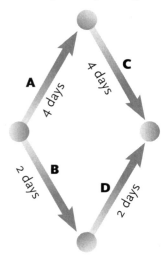

Figure 9.39   Establishing priorities in a network analysis

In Figure 9.39, activities A and B can be carried out simultaneously, as can C and D. However, activities A and C are critical activities in that, if they fall behind in their execution, the whole project will suffer.

Critical path analysis

As we have already seen, the **critical path** is the sequence of key activities that determine the time needed to complete a project.

A **network** is a series of activities and nodes showing the sequence of activities and the time scale involved. We can break down each of the circles (nodes) into three components: the top half of the circle gives the number of the activity and the bottom half can be used to show the earliest and latest times for finishing the activity. For example, in the set of activities shown in Figure 9.40, the earliest time to complete activity C is 16 days. This is because although activities A and C can be completed in 10 days, it takes 16 days to complete activity B and so the earliest time to arrive at node 3 is 16 days. The latest time to finish an activity is calculated by working backwards from the end of the project.

Figure 9.40 shows the number of days required to finish a project with 12 nodes in it. Latest times are calculated by working backwards from right to left across the diagram. (Note that the two activities drawn in dotted lines are 'dummy activities', ones which do not use up time or resources.) The pathway that is the most urgent, that is, the critical path – the one where, if tasks are held up, the whole

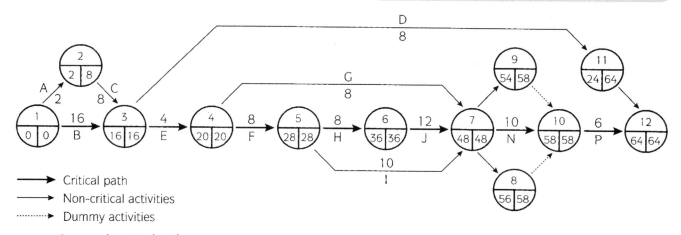

→ Critical path
→ Non-critical activities
┈┈▸ Dummy activities

Figure 9.40   A 12-node critical path

project will be pushed behind schedule – can be highlighted with a thicker line or colour. The critical path is B to E to F to H to J to N to P. The critical path will be the one for which both the earliest and latest times are equal to each and all of the networked nodes. In other words, every activity will need to start and finish on time or delay will take place.

Planning and control in project management involve putting the emphasis on activities along the critical path to ensure the success of a project. If performance of these activities falls below standards, then extra resources will need to be channeled into them immediately or new techniques and plans devised to put the process back on course.

Activities which do not lie on the critical path will not be so urgent (which is not the same as saying that they are not 'critical' in the ordinary sense). The term **total float** is applied to the period by which a non-critical activity can, if necessary, be extended without increasing the total project time. Clearly, an activity should not extend beyond its total float time.

CASE STUDY

Program Evaluation and Review Techniques (PERT)

PERT was first developed by the US navy and was used successfully in the development of the Polaris Weapon System in the late 1950s. In the 1960s and 1970s it became particularly popular as a management technique. Today the principles of PERT are still widely used under different names (for example, **process re-engineering**).

PERT uses time–event network analysis. For example, Figure 9.41 might represent the major milestones of progress in the development and assembly of a passenger airline. Some of the steps may be as follows:

1   Take decision that project will go ahead.
2   Set out and procure engines for aircraft.
3   Complete plans and specification for the aircraft.
4   Complete drawings of main body of aircraft.
5   Award contract for tail section.
6   Award contract for construction of wings.
7   Finish manufacture of main body of plane, including internal fittings.
8   Complete assembly of engine.
9   Receive wings from subcontractor.
10   Receive tail from subcontractor.
11   Assemble various components of aircraft and deliver to airline.

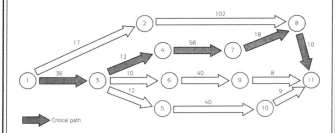

Figure 9.41   Planning aircraft assembly

In Figure 9.41 only one time is shown for each of the activities. In the original PERT programmes three separate times were shown:

1   The optimistic time: the best-case scenario; the time that will be taken if everything goes to plan.
2   The most likely time: the project engineer's realistic estimate of what is most likely to happen.
3   The pessimistic time: a worst-case scenario; the time that will be taken if each set of activities falls behind schedule.

Slack time and crashing activities

Many projects are of such complexity that it is extremely difficult to predict the various outcomes, even though considerable planning has taken place beforehand. In today's world an organisation needs to plan for almost every eventuality. For example, when activities do not take place according to schedule, then **slack time** for other resources might occur where they are waiting for other events or stages to be completed. Similarly, if planning does not run smoothly, more than one stage might require the use of the same resources and so activities may be **crashed**.

Network analysis is inappropriate when activities cannot be clearly identified and broken down into discrete sections. It is also inappropriate for routine mass production operations, though it could be used in the first instance to make plans for such operations. Its prime focus is upon time rather than upon costs. Costs, however, are an extremely important part of any planning process and an organisation ignores costs at its peril. For example, a weakness of central planning in the former Soviet Union was that resources were wasted in trying to meet time deadlines at any cost.

There are, however, a number of key benefits of network and critical path analysis:

♦ it forces managers to plan projects properly
♦ the use of computer software add to the accuracy of the planning process
♦ planning has to work down the line from managers to subordinates; each person involved in the plan will need to take responsibility for part of the sequence
♦ emphasis is placed on the critical path
♦ there can be forward-thinking control because time plans are made in advance of activities taking place; it is possible to measure performance against predetermined standards
♦ because the network of activities is broken down into discrete sections, it becomes possible for managers to target their reports and recommendations to the correct point in the organisation.

Gantt charts

Gantt charts are a form of bar chart developed by the management planner Henry Gantt (1861–1919). They are especially useful as a visual tool for project planning and performance monitoring. Gantt charts are designed to show the relationship between different tasks. Using Gantt charts, managers can check actual progress and spot when hold-ups in a particular task are likely to slow down the completion of the project as a whole. Gantt charts can be drawn manually or produced easily using a graphing package such as Microsoft Project.

To draw a Gantt chart for a project, start by breaking it down into distinct tasks or activities and estimating the time needed to carry out each one. Next identify the relationship between the tasks.

Some activities must be carried out in a serial relationship, that is, C can only be carried out once B is completed, and B can only be completed after A:

A ⇒ B ⇒ C

Activities that can be carried out at the same time because they are independent of one another, are said to have a parallel relationship:

A ⇒
B ⇒
C ⇒

There are some special terms used in Gantt chart design.

The **earliest start time** of an activity means the earliest time that it can commence. This will usually depend on the earliest finish of the preceding activity.

The **earliest finish time** for an activity is the earliest start + the duration of the activity.

Slack is the surplus time that is available between the earliest time that an activity can be completed and the latest time that it can be completed if the project is to run on schedule. If there is no slack time available for an activity, it must be given priority and special care must be taken to ensure that it runs to time. If slack time is available, it is important to check that it is not wasted: even activities with slack time need to be monitored closely.

Constructing a Gantt chart

The following illustrates how a Gantt chart can be constructed manually. Alternatively, use the same figures and construct a chart using Microsoft Project.

1   Draw a grid. Plot the tasks along the vertical axis, and the timescale (up to the end of the project) along the horizontal axis.

2   Draw a horizontal bar from the description of the task on the left of the chart, starting at the earliest start time and ending at the earliest finish time.

3   Show the slack amount by drawing a line from the earliest finish time to the latest finish time.

4   Repeat steps 2 and 3 for each task.

Take the example of a project consisting of eight main tasks (see Figure 9.42).

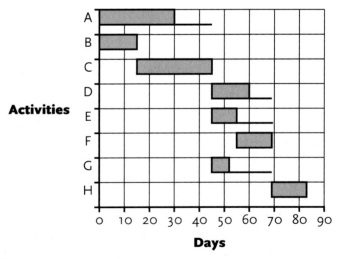

Figure 9.42   Gantt chart for project planning

Task A must be carried out at the start of the project and is expected to take 30 days.
Task B must also be carried out at the start of the project and is expected to take 15 days.
Task C follows B. Duration: 30 days.
Task D follows A and C. Duration: 15 days.
Task E follows C. Duration: 10 days.
Task F follows E. Duration: 14 days.
Task G follows both A and C. Duration: 7 days.
Task H follows D, F and G. Duration: 14 days.
Once H is completed the project is finished.
It is calculated that the project can be carried out in 83 days.

Note that the earliest start and finish times for each activity are drawn in a horizontal bar. The slack times are shown for relevant activities with a line extending to the latest finish time that would be acceptable if the project is to finish on time, that is, 83 days. (You can see, for example, that A does not necessarily have to be completed until the time when D must start.)

ACTIVITY

Using Microsoft Project design a Gantt chart for a simple work-based or study-based project setting out sequences of activities and times required to complete them.

Financial tools

Software-generated information also speeds up and makes more accurate the presentation of complex financial information through the use of simple tables and formulae that are built into the program.

Index numbers are a convenient way to make comparisons of changes in quantities over time. Instead of measuring changes in a variable in terms of units such as '£s of sales' or 'tonnes of output', values are expressed in abstract numbers or ratios, rather like percentages. Most medium and large businesses today use off-the-peg and custom-made accounts packages that will rapidly calculate financial indices in seconds. For example, indicators such as solvency and gearing ratios can be calculated by a modern accountancy package at the press of a button. This has made financial reporting much simpler today.

For example, accounting reports that at one time were tedious and time-consuming to prepare can now be produced very simply.

The main advantages of a computerised system are:

♦ it is relatively cheap to run
♦ it speeds up the process of data capture, analysis and reporting
♦ it improves the accuracy and presentation of reports
♦ financial indicators such as liquidity ratios, profitability ratios, and so on can be worked out automatically by the computer
♦ it allows information to be shared throughout the business for multiple use
♦ it offers a fast, easy-to-access and compact facility for the storage of information.

Monthly financial reporting combines the integrity and discipline of highly structured accounting packages for data stores, with the flexibility of spreadsheets for generating management reports on financial indices.

Computer software is also particularly useful in investment appraisal that typically involves complex calculations. In Unit 6 of this book we examined discounted cash flow techniques and the calculation of the internal rate of return (IRR function).

Cash flows from an investment project accrue at different times over the life of a business project. By reducing all future cash flows to a common measure, comparisons can be made between projects. The total of all cash flows restated in today's money terms is called the **net present value**. The NPV of a future cash flow is found by multiplying it by a discount factor. The size of the factor depends on the discount rate used and the number of years that it is discounted for. The easiest way of finding a discount factor is to look it up in an NPV table, or more simply, use an accounts package to do the work for you. Software-generated information thus takes much of the slog out of accountancy work enabling modern-day accountants to use their time much more effectively by using information technology as a tool.

ACTIVITY

Interview the accountant at a medium or large company to find out how they use software packages to calculate financial indicators, and for investment appraisal.

Research and topical articles

Students can carry out research into decision-making approaches in a number of ways. For example, in seeking secondary information for research purposes it is helpful to carry out an on-line search, for example by accessing *National Statistics for Examining Social Trends*, or by looking at market research information, such as that provided by a research organisation such as MINTEL. To keep up to date with computer- and software-based decision-making tools refer to magazines such as:

♦ *Internet*
♦ *E-business Review*
♦ *Net Profit*
♦ *Computer Weekly*.

The publication *Student Accountant* provides a range of useful summary articles about statistical and other decision-making tools used in business.

Another good source of information is a publication called *Managing Information*, which is designed 'for everyone who uses information'. An extract from an article that recently appeared in the magazine is given here.

Intranets and extranets
JOURNAL ARTICLE

Behind the buzzwords, what exactly are intranets and extranets? Put simply, they are websites that are accessible only to specific groups of users. Intranets are more likely to be restricted to people within one organisation or company; extranets may be open to a wider audience from a number of organisations and companies.

The big benefit is that users (staff, business partners, suppliers and so on) can store, exchange, manage and process information securely from wherever they are. There was a time in the late 1990s when intranets and extranets attracted much publicity because of the amount of money lavished on them and the savings they could achieve through not having to print and post large quantities of literature. They also made the headlines because the concept of intrantets and extranets was still a relatively new one. Today, the situation is very different. They are now accepted as just another IT offering that can improve efficiencies and save money, while still attracting interest because of how they have revolutionised business processes. Oh, and they have come down in price in tandem with the market expanding and creating opportunities for a wave of intranet and extranet designers and builders.

What can you use them for?

Any information management. Trinity College London is one example that focuses on the functional side. For Imperial Tobacco, its extranet is a relationship management and relationship building tool: similar for the Helly Hansen extranet/intranet, which is also used for quality control and internal communications.

Trinity College London, an international examinations board in the performance and communicative arts, runs its multinational, multilingual organisation purely through an extranet; the entire exam process from application, invoicing, examination, marking, and all related staff management is conducted on-line.

Helly Hansen, the sportswear company, runs a combined intranet/extranet to allow their designers around the world to discuss designs and projects, and allow sales and marketing personnel to access product information. The intranet part is for Helly Hansen's own use; the extranet kicks in when external sales and other personnel access information that is intended for them. Helly Hansen also runs a consumer website.

Imperial Tobacco's project is another example of an intranet/extranet combination. The intranet is used by the 500-strong sales force, the extranet by 70,000 retailers and 100 of the supermarkets and store chains. The prime application is delivery of industry reports, product news and other relevant information. The savings in print runs and other efficiencies are considerable.

Cook, A. 'Intranets and extranets', *Managing Information* 2003, July/August

ACTIVITY

1 How does developing an intranet support decision-making processes within an organisation?

2 Give examples of the types of decision that an organisation may be able to carry out more effectively with the support of an intranet system.

3 With reference to an organisation with which you are familiar, give examples of the sort of information that could be put into the intranet communication system to enhance management decision making.

4 What extra benefits does an extranet have in relation to an intranet?

5 What sort of information should go on an intranet but not on an extranet?

Today the Internet is an essential tool for gathering information to enable decision making. However, time is money and it is always essential to reduce time taken to access information on the Internet. The following extract provides the top ten tips for speeding up searching on the Internet. (The original article actually sets out fifty very useful tips.)

Ten tips for Internet searching

JOURNAL ARTICLE

1   No singing, no dancing. Our number one tip! All our experts agreed that turning off images and sound while browsing makes the biggest difference, although many people still don't know how to do it. Without images, you'll get to the information you need much quicker. Good sites will always give a text description of images so you know what's going on. It will also dispense of those annoying banner ads. To do this in Internet Explorer, select Tools: Internet Options: Advanced. In Nestscape you can get this in Edit: Preferences: Advanced.

2   DIY front page. Creating a dedicated web page with all the links and tools that you use regularly is time well spent. It's more flexible than using Favorites, and you can add your own notes on sites.

3   Say no to JavaScript. Switching off JavaScript in your browsers can save huge amounts of time, and was extremely popular with our experts.

4   Bookmark wisely. Don't just bookmark the front page of the websites you look at regularly. You can usually bookmark the individual sections of sites you look at regularly too.

5   Double up. Having two browser windows open simultaneously was universally agreed to be a good thing. When a page downloads on one, don't read it straight away. Get a page download started on the second window and then go back and read the first one.

6   Add the Google search bar. Most people rate Google as a search engine. If you're a fan, why not add Google to your search bar? It lets you search instantly without having to go into the search engine page first.

7   Guess the address. It's possible to guess the addresses of some sites without bothering with search engines at all. It works particularly well with large corporates. For example, you'd get the Tesco site if you guessed www.tesco.co.uk. With multinationals such as Sony, the UK site is easy to guess too: it's www.sony.co.uk.

8   Stay away from the slow. MSN.co.uk is a very popular website. This is partly because it's the default page in Internet Explorer and many people don't know how to change it. When we tested the site, it took 35 seconds to appear over a 56k line. The UK average is 15. Rival website Netscape was 28 seconds. Speedy sites should be a whole lot quicker: Google takes just two second to load. The *Internet Magazine* website, in association with Site Confidence, has a useful website speed tester. See www.internet-magazine.co.uk.

9   Make links. Know about the Links button in Internet Explorer? By default it's hidden by the Go button, but you can click and drag it below the Address bar. To get quicker access to the favourites you use most, try putting them on the Links bar. Drag the sites from your Favorites menu to the Links bar. To rename the new link to something snappy, right-click on the new link and select Rename. Or just drag the Explorer icon in the Address window to the Links bar.

10 Get some wheels. Still using a mouse without a wheel? Shame on you. Splash out on a new one and you can then roll the wheel forward or backward to scroll without using the traditional scroll bars or arrows.

'Scream if you want to go faster', *Internet*, 2001, December.

ACTIVITY

1 Having tried out the tips outlined in the article, which ones do you find particularly useful, and why?

2 Why is it particularly important in research and decision making to be able to use the Internet as a fast an efficient tool?

3 What further tips would you suggest for speeding up Internet searching?

4 What other tips would you suggest for speeding up other methods of carrying out primary research without adversely affecting the quality of the information collected?

End of unit assignment

The assignment for this unit is based on the use of a spreadsheet.

Crash course on spreadsheets

Using a spreadsheet provides you with a worksheet consisting of rows and column. Columns are named with letters of the alphabet and rows are numbered. The box where a row and a column meet is called a cell and the cell reference or address is made up of its column letter and row number, such as E_1 or A_3. The most widely used spreadsheet package is Microsoft Excel, which enables you to create files containing combinations of text and figures. You can also carry

out calculations on those figures. Excel comprises three types of cell:

♦ text cells: for entering 'labels', that is, headings for charts and headings for columns and rows
♦ value cells: for entering numbers; Excel can only carry out calculations using these value cells
♦ formula cells: can be used to input formulas.

When you type '=' Excel immediately recognises that you are creating a formula.

Formulas

When you have inputted the formula the results appear in the appropriate cell, but the formula appears on the formula bar. It is the ability to use formulas that makes spreadsheets a particularly powerful business tool because they enable rapid calculations, and alterations to a single figure in a spreadsheet will lead to an automatic accurate recalculation.

Formulas allow both the calculation of a fixed value and by reference to a cell address. For example, $=C_1+C_2$ will add together the values found in cell addresses C_1 and C_2. Alternatively, another spreadsheet facility, called a function, can be used. The SUM function adds up all the values between two cells, so $=SUM(C_1:C_5)$ has the same effect as $C_1+C_2+C_3+C_4+C_5$.

Creating information from data

Microsoft Excel carries out three activities to help you create relevant information:

♦ data input: the data that you enter into the spreadsheet
♦ data output: the data generated from the spreadsheet (from calculations that you carry out there)
♦ data processing: entering and outputting data.

When using Excel you can quickly navigate around your spreadsheet by using shortcut keys:
Enter Moves you down to the next cell
Shift and **Enter** Moves you up to the previous cell
Alt and **Enter** Starts a new line in the cell
Tab Moves you right to the next cell
Shift and **Tab** Moves you back to the previous cell.

Assignment tasks

For the assignment you will need to:

1 Generate business data using primary and or secondary research.

2 Use some form of averaging process to make sense of some of that data, for example by using a combination of the mean, median and mode.

3 Create a short business report outlining the nature of your investigation, findings and an evaluation.

4 Include in that report relevant charts, such as bar charts, line charts, pie charts.

5 Use presentation software, such as Microsoft PowerPoint, to make a presentation of the findings of your report.

6 Produce a Gantt chart using Microsoft Project to show how you planned out the work for your assignment.

Examples of work that you could do to generate the evidence listed above would include:

♦ An investigation into the market share of different companies in a particular market, indicating how one company might be able to increase market share at the expense of rivals.

♦ A study of the profit and loss accounts of similar firms, to identify differences in profit percentages. You could look at average profit percentage, and try and explain why some firms are making more profit than others. You could then show how a particular firm might be able to make changes to increase its profit margins.

Football revenue

As an alternative, the following asssignment may appeal to students interested in football.

Premier League clubs' earnings in 2003/04 season (£m)

Club	League	European Cup	Cup	Total
Arsenal	35.2	19.4	2.0	56.6
Chelsea	32.8	19.8	1.1	53.7
Man Utd	33.7	19.2	3.5	56.4
Liverpool	29.1	2.0	1.0	32.1
Newcastle	29.4	2.0	0.6	32.0

1 Send for the company report of two of these clubs for the period 2003–2004 to find out what additional revenues they received from merchandising activity.

2 Produce a report comparing the revenues earned by two of these clubs in 2003–2004 and suggesting ways in which they could increase revenues.

3 Find out the average revenues of the five clubs listed above from their three main sources of revenue.

4 In your report generate charts to illustrate sources of revenue and comparisons of revenue between different clubs.

5 Analyse the success of two of the clubs in financial terms and recommend ways in which they could increase their revenues.

6 Set out a Gantt chart to illustrate how you plan to manage your project to complete it by a given deadline date.

Further reading

Bedward, D. (2003) *Quantitative Methods: A Business Perspective* 2nd edn, Oxford: Butterworth-Heinemann.

Coles, M. (1997) *Financial Management for Higher Awards*, Chapter 19, Oxford: Heinemann.

Curwin, D. *et al.* (2004) *Quantitative Methods for Business Decisions* 6th edn, London: Chapman and Hall.

Dransfield, R. (2003) *Statistics Made Easy*, Cheltenham: Nelson Thornes.

Lawson, J. *et al.* (2003) *BTEC National IT Practitioners*, Oxford: Heinemann.

Schultheiis, R. (2003) *Management Information Systems* 6th edn, Maidenhead: McGraw Hill.

Unit 10

Carrying out a research project

Learning about business organisations should allow students the opportunity to identify, set and answer any questions or hypotheses they have thought about in relation to their understanding of key issues. It should also provide an opportunity for students to become empowered in their own process of learning, so that they can develop an area of specialism, interest or expertise to add to their curriculum vitae and which helps in professional development.

The research project is designed to introduce various techniques and methods of research. It requires students to produce a report based upon research into an area of business practice related to a major issue. This study builds upon other knowledge, skills and understanding experienced in other units.

Summary of learning outcomes

On completion of this unit you will be able to:
♦ prepare a research proposal relating to a specified area of business
♦ conduct research using primary and secondary sources of information
♦ carry out the research project into a specified area of business
♦ present and evaluate the findings with regard to the initial proposal.

Chapter 1

Research proposal

Student research

Nearly all undergraduate courses today require learners to produce an extended study or some form of thesis, dissertation or project. This reflects the notion that at least one element of personal research within a course provides the learner with a genuine opportunity to become engrossed in a project with the potential to extend their own interests. For example, this is the time within a course where, to a certain extent, students are 'let off the leash' in a way that enables them not just to take control of their own learning but also the direction it takes. This is particularly useful in helping them to develop a bridge over the gap between being a student and any course that they may want to pursue professionally. They may undertake a piece of research or an extended study related to an area of employment or further professional qualifications that they may like to take.

Extended studies independently undertaken are a real opportunity for students to take theories and concepts learnt in a more formal way within the classroom, and use them for an area of research that they direct, creatively design and manage themselves. In many, but not all, circumstances the research can be applied to a context, or organisational environment where theories can be related to some form of practice.

What is research?

According to Charles (1994), 'the word *research* comes from the French *rechercher* (to travel through or survey) or establish facts and relationships'. This is probably a good appropriation if we think about how as we travel through and survey we often try and find things out. We ask, for example, 'Why does that happen?', 'Isn't that interesting?', 'I wonder why they do it that way?' From the very outset, it is clear that research is not like being in a classroom or lecture hall where we listen, read or take notes and are very much on the receiving end of the educational process. Important though the lecture hall is in acquiring knowledge and understanding, that knowledge and understanding might not be answering many of the questions we may have or in fact going some way but not all of the way in doing so. It is generally argued that research extends knowledge (Brown, 1990) so that instead of having a title and describing, evaluating and interpreting something, a disciplined enquiry is undertaken to find something out so that the conclusions, inferences and implications can be discussed in a way that create findings that are potentially generalisable, that is, having found something out through research, the findings may have applicability to different situations, organisations and contexts.

It could be argued that research is going on around us all of the time. We have all probably participated in some form of questionnaire enquiry which asked us about some form of fast-moving consumer durable. According to Mouly (1978), 'Research is best conceived as the process of arriving at dependable solutions to problems through the planned and systematic collection, analysis, and interpretation of data. It is a most important tool for advancing knowledge, for promoting progress, and for enabling man to relate more effectively to his environment, to accomplish his purposes, and to resolve his conflicts.'

Thinking about the topic to identify is not always easy. The starting point should be, but is not always, the library. By looking through texts, finding out about what interests them, analysing other research that has been undertaken, perhaps by using paper journals or an electronic gateway like Emerald Fulltext, it is possible for students to find out about research that

677

has been undertaken and generate some ideas. Blaxter (1996) suggests ten ways in which to think of a research topic. These are:

♦ ask your supervisor, manager, friends, colleagues, customers, clients or mother
♦ look at previous research
♦ develop some of your previous research, or your practice at work
♦ relate it to your other interests
♦ think of a title
♦ start from a quote that engages you
♦ follow your hunches
♦ draw yourself a picture or a diagram
♦ just start anywhere
♦ but be prepared to change direction.

ACTIVITY

Working in a small group, and using Post-It notes, identify ten possible topics that would make a good business research project. Discuss each of the proposals you identify. Then, starting with what the group feels would make the best project first, stick the Post-Its on a wall in order of priority and present your ideas to the rest of your group.

Research methodologies

The case study

An increasingly popular research method for individuals is that of the case study. Case studies have been widely used as a teaching and learning methodology in areas such as law and medicine for many years. Lawyers and physicians use the case method to identify precedents and cases have been used to represent groups of similar events or symptoms. Future practice has been informed by past history and the case method has become so authoritative, that training within these professions has become heavily based on the case method.

It has, however, been widely observed that it can be difficult to get agreement on what constitutes a case study (Needham, 2001): 'While the literature is replete with references to case studies and with examples of case study reports, there seems to be little agreement about what a case study is.' Since then there has been some progress towards identifying the factors which define a case study. There is widespread agreement that a case study is of 'real life', that it is holistic and it enables the investigation of the relationships between the component parts of the case. In his classic book on case study, Yin (1994) points out that a case study is an empirical enquiry which 'allows investigation into a contemporary phenomenon within its real-life context, especially when the boundaries between the phenomenon and context are not clearly evident'. So does Stake (1995), who describes doing case study research as, 'coming to understand the activity [of a single case] within important circumstances'.

To some extent 'case study' is an overarching term used for a range of research methods. It is not just about a description of an event. The evidence has to be systematically gathered and the interaction of the variables needs to be analysed.

Ethnographic fieldwork

Ethnographic fieldwork was originally developed in order to study a culture or some form of group in detail (Bell, 1999). It is an approach that depends upon observation skills and some form of integration into the situation being examined. As a **participant observer**, this form of research enables the researcher to share the same experiences as the subjects, and by doing so, the researcher is better able to appreciate some of the issues and so develop a better understanding of why individuals act in a particular way. This can be a difficult area to research as the researcher has to be well accepted by the individuals he or she is researching and can involve them being with others for a prolonged period of time.

Surveys

When we first think of research we instantly think of surveys and the way in which many market researchers try to elicit information. Surveys obtain information so that it can analysed. There are generally two forms of survey.

The census

The census uses the survey to ask the same questions of all respondents within a targeted audience. In some instances in business research there might be opportunities for this, particularly if there are just a few types of organisations within an industry.

The sample

In most instances, instead of using a census, organisations will **sample** a representative section of a population, so that findings from the sample will then be representative of the population. There is a problem with surveys, particularly in making sure that they are representative of the target group being surveyed. Questions are also not always easy to word, and they frequently require some careful piloting to ensure that the questions are not ambiguous. According to Bell (1999), 'Surveys can provide answers to the questions What? Where? When? and How?, but it is not so easy to find out Why.'

Experiments (intervention and non-intervention)

The key feature of using experiments within research is that the researcher deliberately controls and manipulates the conditions which determine the events they are analysing. An experiment is any situation in which a change in the value of one variable, the **independent variable**, is observed for its effect upon the change in another variable, the **dependent variable**. For example, and in business terms at a very simple level, what might some form of change in staff communications (the independent variable) have upon staff morale in an office (dependent variable). This is a **research intervention**. Sometimes as part of the research it is necessary to have a control group against which the results of the experiment can be compared. Although the control group is being monitored there is no intervention into the group.

The experimental method allows relationships to be identified. It allows the researcher to manipulate the independent variable, such as heating in a room, in order to observe its impact upon the dependent variable, such as worker productivity. The problem with this sort of research is that the effects may be damaged by a **confounding variable** which obscures the effects of one variable over another.

Longitudinal studies

A longitudinal study is a study over a period of time focused upon a group of subjects or a range of variables. A study is longitudinal because it researches the dynamics of a problem or an issue, by investigating the same situation or people several times, or continuously over the period during which the study runs. For a student project this may be unrealistic, although if a research module takes place over a six-month period, it may be possible to use a longitudinal approach. As long as repeated observations can be made, the researcher can make judgements about the context and its impact upon the subjects or variables being observed.

Narrative enquiry

Narratives or stories have been used for many years as part of a research process, for example by management consultants to discuss examples of successful or unsuccessful events in order to develop an understanding of how to make key decisions. The key to narrative enquiry is trying to think how to structure a story so that it can be analysed effectively, and on the basis of appropriate literature. It is important to think of themes and structures and where these can be identified from the narrative. A narrative should have a beginning, middle and end.

Triangulation

It is quite possible for researchers to use more than one response or method to answer a research question or hypothesis. This process is known as triangulation. As triangulation uses more than one method it overcomes some of the problems and issues of using a single method of research, and also helps to produce results that are more reliable and valid. Denzin (1970) defines triangulation as, 'the combination of methodologies in the study of the same phenomenon'. There is a danger with triangulation, however, that you are using two methods to collect the same data, and that the analysis is then time-consuming and expensive.

Action research

It can be argued that action research is quite different from other forms of research because in action research the researcher tries to identify their own solution to a problem or issue while working as a practitioner or employee. For example, and in simple terms, working as an action researcher you might go into a situation where there is a particular problem. Having diagnosed the problem, you would then come up with a solution which you would then implement and reflect upon.

According to Cohen and Manion (1994) action research is, 'essentially an on-the-spot procedure designed to deal with a concrete problem located in an immediate situation. This means that ideally, the step-by-step process is constantly monitored over varying periods of time and by a variety of mechanisms (questionnaires, diaries, interviews and case studies, for example) so that the ensuing feedback may be translated into modifications, adjustments, directional changes, redefinitions, as necessary, so as to bring about lasting benefit to the ongoing process itself rather than to some future occasion.'

All people in all contexts, almost irrespective of their position, can become action researchers, where they could alter or change what they are doing in order to solve a problem or to improve a situation. The researcher could then write up the situation to emphasise the learning that they benefited from in that particular instance. Action research is thus about identifying a problem or issue, acting upon it by making some changes, and then modifying practice in the light of what has been learnt. Many people would argue that it is simply what people do anyway through their own professional practice.

For example, a research question for an action researcher might be, 'How do I get on better with my customers and will this help to generate more sales?' So, the researcher might then use a range of techniques to build better relationships. Reflecting upon these, they might see what works and what does not work, and again make changes accordingly.

Research questions or hypotheses?

Once you have identified a topic or area to research, you then need to think about whether you need research questions or hypotheses.

The purpose of research questions and hypotheses is to orientate the research. Whereas research questions are a good way to provide focus in order to answer questions, it is difficult to state them in a way that enables issues to be analysed statistically. Hypotheses, on the other hand, are declarations that can be tested statistically as long as it is possible to identify data to do so.

Research question

Research is about using one's mind creatively to ask questions which students then find out the answers to. This notion of 'questioning' or 'questions' is at the very heart of the research process. As someone who actively researches, this author constantly goes back and back again to the research questions he has asked wherever and whenever writing articles. At the back of his mind, he asks how well he is answering his research questions. The research question and any sub-research questions structure his dialogue, how he thinks, how he writes and how he works on the analysis. In fact every part of his research project is concerned with the efficacy of the research questions and the degree to which the thesis answers them. Lewis (1991) showed the crucial part that questions play in the decisions that researchers undertake and how that relates to the sorts of claims that researchers make about the research process.

Functions of research questions

The function of research questions is to:

♦ clarify the area of concern
♦ identify the sort of information that needs to be collected
♦ guide the researcher on how to collect information
♦ provide a framework for developing the project
♦ enable the reader to make judgements about the project.

Research questions add focus to the project. They help students as researchers to think about their aims and objectives as well as about the implications of the findings from the area that they explore.

ACTIVITY

Working in small groups, identify a main research question. Try to break down the research question into smaller questions that would help to provide structure for your project.

Identifying a research question

Trying to identify research questions is not always easy. Students need to think about their area of research interest and of the information that is available to use. Frequently, students come up with research questions without having done any preparatory reading beforehand, and then complain frequently to their tutor that nobody has written about this before and they cannot find anything. If they had done some reading beforehand, identified an issue, and then used their evolving understanding to identify the main and subsidiary research questions, then this would not have happened.

The research question should not only identify the issue or area of interest, but should also suggest the approach that is being taken to a project. For example, how is the appraisal process used to motivate staff at [name of college]? Clearly in this instance, although the theoretical area is highlighted, the student would have to work closely with the chosen organisation, undertaking some element of primary research in

order to answer the question. Alternatively, the researcher might be trying to answer the question: What makes some brands succeed where others fail?' In this instance, the researcher would be looking at the literature, thinking perhaps about a case study of a brand that had been successful.

It is important that a research question is neither too broad nor too narrow. For example, if we choose the topic of accounting, we could ask the following questions:

1 What is a balance sheet?

2 What can be done to reduce the burden of presenting financial information upon companies?

3 Do audited company accounts provide a true and fair record of their activities?

Question one is clearly too narrow, and would simply involve showing what a balance sheet is. Question two is a good question, but a very difficult one to answer, and is very broad, requiring a really good knowledge not just of financial information requirements, but also of what companies might want. The third question is clearly focused, with myriad ways of answering it, and very theoretical. It would be a good one to answer.

Developing a research question

As students develop their research question they need to think about:

♦ all of the other research that has taken place in their area of interest
♦ the resources, including time, available for the research
♦ the strategies that they intend to use to answer the research question.

The research question should relate to the theories required for the study. No enquiry can take place unless it is grounded in theory.

As students develop their research question they may want to ask the following questions to help to evaluate it:

♦ Is the question focused upon a topic or area that is interesting and helps to extend the student's knowledge and understanding of an issue?

- How well is it possible to answer the question?
- What sort of information is required to answer the question?
- Is the question too broad or too narrow?
- What resources will be needed to answer the question?
- Do they have a question that can really be answered by undertaking some research?

Hypotheses

Unlike research questions hypotheses are statements that researchers make which are then tested. The hypothesis guides the researcher into developing tests and experiments that help to test the variables within the hypothesis they have made. For example, we could make the hypothesis that 'low-paid staff are not motivated when their role is enlarged'. Low-paid staff would be one variable, motivation is another and the other would be job enlargement. It would be up to the researcher to use research tools to test the hypothesis that they had made.

According to Verma and Beard (1981) a statement of hypothesis is, 'a tentative proposition which is subject to verification through subsequent investigation. It may also be seen as the guide to the researcher in that it depicts and describes the method to be followed in studying the problem. In many cases hypotheses are hunches that the researcher has about the existence of relationships between variables.'

Having had this hunch it is then up to the researcher to test the variables.

Hypotheses are more typical in scientific or experimental research, more so because this sort of research can be structured to test the hypotheses.

ACTIVITY

In the context of a situation known to you, identify some form of hypothesis. Discuss how you could test this hypothesis, and think of the methods that you might use in order to do so.

Objectives

In some circumstances, instead of identifying a range of hypotheses that can be tested, it can be just as useful to develop a precise list of objectives that can be used to structure the piece of research. Examining the objectives for the research project enables the researcher to identify and structure the purpose of the project so that:

- the concepts that are to be studied can be broken down
- the different elements of the business environment can be identified
- personal learning objectives can be identified
- planning for the project can be developed.

Terms of reference

It is important that before the researcher starts the research project that they fully understand the terms of reference. These will vary by each course and within each institution, but are fundamental in ensuring that the project is delivered in an appropriate format.

Word count is always of importance in this sort of project. A friend of mine recently delivered the thesis for his doctorate, which turned out at more than 400,000 words rather than the 80,000 he was asked to deliver. Before it could be read, he was asked to cut it down, and it is not difficult to imagine how he felt about losing so much that he had put into the project.

The report may have to be presented and structured in a particular way. For example, one method might be to have it presented with the following structure.

Title: identifying what the research is trying to do. Although this should reflect the contents of the study, it should also be kept brief.

Abstract: summarising the research in a certain number of words, perhaps 250 or 300. It may provide an idea of the broad aims and conclusions.

List of contents: this would list the sections and chapters included within the report, providing page numbers so that sections can be accessed.

List of figures and tables: this may be exhaustive in some instances, but is useful. Remember that where figures and tables have been accessed from other sources, they must be acknowledged.

Acknowledgements: it is usual to acknowledge the people who have helped with the research, including appropriate contacts, and, of course, the supervisor.

Objectives or Introduction: this would include discussion of the objectives or the hypotheses or research questions used. It would also provide the reader with an understanding of the study and the scope of the project.

Context: this might explain what the research is doing, and the background to the piece of research.

Literature review: this should cover the theory, knowledge and concepts which are analysed from the various forms of literature. It is important to be selective and for the writer to orientate the dissemination of literature towards the aims, hypotheses or research questions.

Methods: this discusses the various research methods and how they attempt to provide answers to the focus of the project. The researcher needs to think how to justify the design of the project and the research methods that they use. This is often an area that students feel uncomfortable with, but in many ways is the most important part of a research project. Learning about how to undertake a research project should be based upon a developing understanding of how to use research methods to find answers to questions.

Results: discussing the methods and the findings should be set out in an organised way.

Analysis and discussion: through this, the raw data is turned into evidence. It is important that this rigorous process of research produces valid results. This part of the project should draw together and synthesise both the literature and the results from the primary research.

Conclusion and recommendations: it is at this stage that the researcher needs to think about how well the original goals and ambitions of the study have been met.

References: references are important not just within a research project but for everything that you do. The list should be alphabetical and relate to everything that you have referred to within the text.

Appendices: in some circumstances, it is better to put something which affects the flow of the dialogue, or which can be referred to out of context of the text, in an appendix. Often materials that are too detailed are included within an appendix.

You may find that your course team provide guidelines for how your research project should be handed in. For example, it might have to be bound or you may have to present more than one copy.

The guidelines for your research project may also have specific requirements about duration, supervisory guidelines and attendance. For example, there may be a number of lectures or seminars to attend on research methods. There may then be a requirement to submit a work plan or project proposal by a particular date so that it can be approved. Sometimes, a course is sorted into small seminar-style groups of critical friends who meet regularly to share ideas and provide each other with formative and supportive feedback. In some courses it is expected that students will provide a presentation of the results of their research to their peers in a more formal and traditional setting, and this forms part of the assessment process.

It is usual that when students undertake a research project they are allocated a supervisor who will provide support for particular projects. It is particularly important that students regularly maintain contact with supervisors, and either email or constantly provide copies of their work for supervisor approval.

Ethical issues

It is one thing to have an idea about what to research, but at the same time it is necessary to think more widely about some of the attendant issues associated with the research that need to be dealt with, particularly where there are obligations to meet the needs of those involved in or affected by the research. As a result there are a number of moral obligations that may impact upon your research or ethical issues that you may need to consider.

Having chosen an issue, one of the main problems with any form of business research is to know how or if those within an institution might be able to provide help. The starting point would be to apply for permission to carry out a form of investigation. As soon as you know what your topic might be, or have put together some ideas, it is useful to make a written approach either to an organisation or to anybody that you wish to include within the study. You may not find that every organisation or that people want to contribute to the study and so may have to refine your ideas and proposals. This notion of asking individuals is sometimes called **informed consent**, which is in itself, and quite rightly, recognition that individuals have a right to determine whether or not to contribute to a project as well as the right to withdraw if they are unhappy with how it is developing. Informed consent thus provides access to an institution where the research is being conducted and acceptance by those whose permission you require in order to undertake the research process.

There may be some ethical protocols or guidelines that you need to set before you start your research project. For example, the nature of the agreement that you have engaged in with your research subjects or contacts should be made clear. By setting up some form of code or protocol you are identifying in the early phases of your work areas which are acceptable to research and those that are not. For example, you may come up with the following:

◆ all participants will remain anonymous
◆ information will be treated with the strictest confidentiality
◆ interviewees will have the opportunity to verify statements and quotations when the report is in a draft stage
◆ anybody participating in the research will receive a copy of the final report
◆ although the research is being prepared for your work at college, if you wish to use it again at a later stage, permission will be sought to do so.

Remember that the research process can be complex, and as a researcher you may be put in an uncomfortable boundary situation between yourself and the organisation or individuals you are researching. If you are ever in a situation where you have doubts about the ethics of your research, or are concerned about the information and its impact upon people you are investigating, always consult your supervisor.

ACTIVITY

Imagine that you are investigating the impact of leadership upon motivation within the workplace in SMEs and that you are constructing a case study of an SME. What guarantees would you put within your ethical guidelines?

Action plan

The starting point for any project or extended study usually begins when you are allocated a supervisor. The relationship you have with your supervisor is extremely important, and it is useful to know about simple things like telephone numbers, email addresses and availability. Your supervisor may have a number of tutees and may want either individual or group tutorials where participants act as critical friends.

It is important to bounce ideas off your tutor from the outset, to ensure that your thinking is on the right lines. The supervisor–student relationship is particularly important during the early formative stages of your project as you begin to translate your early ideas into some form of project plan.

It is easy to get carried away with an idea that might later turn out to be unrealistic. Having decided upon the area you wish to research it is useful to exchange ideas with your supervisor. In many ways generating ideas cold without referring to reading first is a bit like putting the cart before the horse. The more you read, the more likely it is that the reading will help you not just to clarify but also to refine and fine-tune your thoughts.

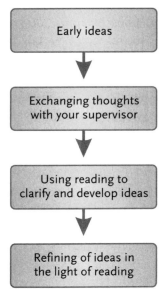

Figure 10.1   Refining early ideas

Rationale for research question or hypothesis

Generating an idea for the research project is not easy, and it may become a time-consuming process. As the researcher looks for a suitable research question or starts to develop hypotheses upon which to base the research, many questions may be generated and issues highlighted. It may be helpful to identify a series of criteria for choosing a problem.

Interest

Is the topic or area that you are going to research one that interests you? A research project is one that you are going to spend a lot of time upon, and if it interests you you may be more motivated to do it well. You may feel that you want to relate it to areas of work or employment that interests you, particularly if you want to emphasise the nature and type of study you have undertaken on your CV.

Importance

Is the area of research important? Perhaps one test for the research is the degree to which it is generalisable. In other words if you are looking at motivation and small businesses, would what is likely to be learned in terms of new knowledge have value for other or similar situations?

Context

Does the topic build upon other research? The bane of any supervisor is to have five or six students undertaking similar research projects with similar research questions, in many instances because they have not put in enough time and effort to read something that creates an exciting proposition or research opportunity. A good topic would build upon and complement other things that have been written.

Practicalities

Are there sufficient resources to research the topic? In an ideal world it should not be necessary to pose this question, and with the emergence of electronic research gateways to on-line journals such as Emerald Fulltext, we should not be asking this. However, resources are important. Students do need access to journals, on-line resources and good library facilities.

It is always useful to take something to your supervisor whenever you meet, so that there is something concrete upon which to base your dialogue. You may want to structure it around the following headings:

> Research questions/hypotheses or area of analysis
>
> Rationale for choosing research topic area
>
> Aims and objectives of research
>
> Areas where background reading can be undertaken
>
> Possible research methods
>
> Problems, issues and pitfalls of choosing this area

Task and review dates

The worst situation for someone to fall into is if when left to their own devises they fall behind and then realise that they only have a couple of weeks to complete the project. This does happen. It is important to set a timetable for your research investigations. Sometimes a lot of this planning may be done for you through your course booklet. For example, there may be dates for:

♦ meetings with supervisors
♦ the presentation of project proposals
♦ presenting findings to other cohort members.

Setting a timetable might include identifying timings for key parts of the project, such as to review the literature or conducting the analysis. In some circumstances, and if a student is familiar with the software, it may be possible to use Microsoft Project or some other form of software to help with the timetabling and planning process.

Making the proposal

As soon as the researcher starts to develop an idea of what they are studying, they need to think about how to make a proposal.

A **statement of the problem** can be used to discuss the questions and issues that students wish to discuss within their research. Again, this sense of rationale is quite important as it helps to get behind many issues to encourage the student to think about the purposes of the research.

The **research questions** or **hypotheses** are fundamental in helping to identify the outcomes of the study. It may be possible to have one major research question or hypothesis, and then follow this up with a series of other research questions or hypotheses.

A summary of the **literature review** may be helpful in clarifying the areas of theory that fall within the context of the research. Although not exhaustive, clearly a literature review may be organic during the process of the project, with the student returning to the literature at any stage as they progress towards completion.

A **procedure** or **methodology** identifies how the student is going to answer the research questions or meet the hypotheses. This is often an area that many students struggle with, and yet it is frequently one of the most important elements of the study. For example, they may try to justify why they are using a case study as research method, or a

particular type of questionnaire, or describing how it was piloted, and so on.

Monitoring and reviewing progress

Analysing and drawing conclusions from the data is not always easy, but is really everything that a project is about. It is important for the student to understand how well they are answering the research questions or hypotheses. They also need to think about the sort of conclusions that can be drawn from the analysis of data.

At the same time it is important to try to evaluate the research process in a way that enables the student to understand how it builds upon or complements theory and reading and the extent to which it uses efficacious research methods.

Research and topical articles

Case studies in business education   JOURNAL ARTICLE

There are many articles that examine research methods of one kind or another. For example, one such article was written by this author for an Australian electronic journal (Needham, 2001). The article argues that teaching and learning about business organisations and the environment in which they operate is contained within a curriculum, but context and events in which they operate is constantly changing. In responding to this context one solution is to construct and use case studies, but these are time-consuming and expensive to produce, need constant up-dating, and may be unsuited for classrooms.

This paper shows how these problems have been overcome by using an innovative methodology based in a continuing public–private partnership (1994–present) between higher education (HE), schools and business organisations. The organisations pay to contribute – and distribute – the case studies which must conform to requirements which ensure classroom materials are relevant, rigorous, up-to-date, and unbiased: cross-referenced to the curriculum; both practical and theoretical; designed to enrich classroom experiences; ethically-based, taking into account the advice of teachers. The paper argues for a way of producing curriculum materials which itself constitutes a methodological contribution to the uses of case study in research-based learning. Whenever students come to see this author about their research methods, particularly where they want to use case study, they are often given a copy of the article, and then asked how they would use it to identify further reading through the references of the article, as well as to consider how it justifies the processes it, as a piece of research, undertook.

Needham, D. 'A case study of case studies: producing real world learning within the business classroom', *Ultibase Journal* 2001, Melbourne: RMIT.

Constructing a survey

JOURNAL ARTICLE

Joseph Janes (1999) in an article simply entitled 'Survey Construction' discusses the idea that, 'A survey is a good way, often the only way, of getting a picture of the current state of a group: a community, an organisation, an electorate, a set of corporations, a profession. We might think of surveying doctors about their opinions about a new therapy, voters about their preference for President in the next election, librarians about how often they use the Web in reference interactions. In many cases, these surveys are snapshots, pictures of a particular

point or period in time, although there are longitudinal surveys which take place over longer periods.

'There are several major steps in building a good survey. We shall talk about two: writing good questions and designing good questionnaires.

'These steps do not happen in a vacuum, though. Before beginning the hard work of developing a survey and asking for people's valuable time in responding, ask yourself some hard questions. Is this survey worth it? Is what I will learn from this valuable enough to justify my time in building it and other people's time in answering? Can I carry it out well? Do I have the necessary skills and resources to make it successful? What do I want to be able to do with the results when it is over?

'If, after all of that soul-searching, you still want to proceed, the whole process goes something like this:

♦ get an idea
♦ see if anybody else has done a similar survey
♦ decide what you want to know
♦ decide on your population of interest (citizens, librarians, high-school students)
♦ write a bunch of possible questions
♦ design a questionnaire
♦ pre-test the questionnaire
♦ modify the questionnaire based on the pre-test
♦ draw a good sample from your population to survey
♦ administer the questionnaire
♦ analyse the data
♦ draw conclusions.'

Janes, J. 'Survey construction', *Library Hi Tech*, 1999, Vol. 19, No.3, pp 321–5.

Chapter 2

Primary and secondary sources

Any form of research project relies on two main sources of information, which can be roughly divided into primary and secondary. Primary sources of data are sometimes referred to as 'from the horse's mouth' because it is first-hand project specific research, empirical in nature for the purpose of bringing new data to answer and respond to the issues identified within your research question or hypothesis. Secondary data consists of data that has been collected beforehand, such as in books, journals, reports and interpretations of primary data, electronic journals, and so on. Secondary data is not project specific as it has been collected by someone else.

Validity and reliability

Data is accurate and of value if it is valid and reliable. Data is **valid** if it depicts or deals directly with a topic or research issue being analysed. According to Hussey (1997), 'Validity is the extent to which the research findings accurately represent what is really happening in the situation.' In other words, validity happens when the data collected actually measures what the research claims that the data will measure.

Reliability is concerned with the findings of the research, that is, if the piece of research were to be repeated and the same results were achieved, it would then be reliable. So, in essence, reliability is a measure of consistency. For example, a computer that runs a program on one particular day and not on another is not reliable.

Qualitative and quantitative approaches

Data variables may either be qualitative or quantitative. **Qualitative** data does not have numbers, although it may, in one way or another, divide people by social class, background or groups. Qualitative data is more likely to come from more open or semi-structured questions. In doing so, qualitative data will help the researcher to:

♦ understand more about the respondents
♦ provide a broader view of a situation
♦ give the respondent the opportunity to provide detailed feedback
♦ provide the respondent with the flexibility to think about and structure their response.

Quantitative data is dependent upon numerical elements. The use of figures, numbers and measurements enables the researcher to understand the scale of the problem, and allows the researcher to use number-crunching techniques to analyse the meaning of the data. For example, this may mean using averages or some measure of dispersion.

Independent and dependent variables

If the researcher is carrying out a positivist study, such as an experiment, before undertaking the study they have to identify the independent and dependent variables relevant for their hypotheses. The independent variable will be the variable manipulated to predict the values of the dependent variable.

ACTIVITY

Make up three different hypotheses and then identify the dependent and independent variables that would be tested in meeting the challenge of these hypotheses. Discuss what sort of data, whether primary or secondary, you might need to test your hypotheses.

Primary sources

Surveys are the most common method used to collect primary data. They involve asking respondents to find out how they react to a range of issues contained in a questionnaire. There are two types of survey, a census and a sample. A **census** involves questioning everybody within a sampling frame, but in most cases this is not likely to be practical except perhaps if you are interviewing everybody within a very small company or just within one department.

According to Jankowicz (1995), 'Sampling can be defined as the deliberate choice of a number of people, the sample, who are to provide you with data from which you can draw conclusions about some larger group, the population, whom these people represent.' Taking a sample involves questioning a selection of respondents from a **sampling frame**. There is usually a temptation to pick as large a sample as possible. Identifying the right number of people to ask questions to is not easy. According to Clegg (1990), there are three main considerations to bear in mind. These are:

- the kind of statistical analysis which is planned
- the expected variability within the samples and the results, based on experience (the greater the expected variation, the larger the sample)
- the traditions in your particular research area regarding appropriate sample size.

Sampling

If the selection of the sample is fair and accurate, then the responses are more likely to produce data that is statistically reliable. If the sample is incomplete and does not accurately represent a group of consumers, misleading data is obtained, and the sample is said to be **biased**.

When choosing a sample, it might fall into one of two categories.

Probability samples are constructed so that every respondent has a known probability or chance of selection and the limits of possible error are known in advance. Included in this category are simple random sampling, systematic sampling, stratified random sampling, cluster sampling and multistage sampling.

Non-probability samples are based simply on the choice of the selector and may be subject to error in sample selection. These include quota sampling, convenience sampling and judgement sampling.

Simple random sampling

With this method the researcher chooses the size of the sample required and then picks the sample on a random basis. The sample must be selected in such a way that every item in the sampling frame has an equal chance of being selected. One way of doing this is to use a computer to draw names or numbers from the list at random.

Systematic sampling

Another way is to use systematic sampling, which involves selecting items from the list at regular intervals after choosing a random starting point. For example, if it is decided to select a sample of 20 names or numbers from 1000, then every 50th name (1000 divided by 20) should be selected, after a random start anywhere in the first 50. If 18 is chosen as the starting point (possibly using a table of random numbers), then the series would start: 18, 68, 118, 168, and so on.

Stratified random sampling

If some respondents are more important than others, then simple random sampling could distort the results. Stratified random sampling therefore weights the sample on the basis of the importance of each group of respondents.

Cluster sampling

With cluster sampling the respondents are divided up into small areas, but instead of sampling from a random selection of these areas, sampling is carried out in areas that are more typical in order to improve the reliability of the results.

Multistage sampling

Multistage sampling cuts the field to be sampled down into smaller units or segments in much the same way as cluster sampling. The purpose of multistage sampling is simply to cut down sampling and research costs.

Quota sampling

Although random sampling, if properly conducted, produces the best results, it can be expensive and time-consuming, and in some situations it is not possible to identify a random sample. In these situations quota sampling is more commonly used. Interviews may be based upon the number of people to interview with a range of characteristics such as sex, age, socio-economic group or other demographic details.

Convenience and judgement sampling

Convenience sampling involves gathering information from anybody available for the interviewer to survey, no matter what their background. Judgement sampling involves selection of respondents by the interviewer based upon his or her judgement that they seem to be representative of the group of respondents in the area being researched.

Questionnaires

The research instrument that we probably all instantly associate with the collection of data is the questionnaire. In the simplest of terms they are simply 'useful tools for collecting data from a large number of respondents' (Wilkinson, 2000). So, once you understand what sort of sample you intend to use, the next step, assuming you are going to use one, is to construct the questionnaire.

Questionnaires can be associated with positivistic methodologies, or those which are phenomenological (Hussey, 1997). This essentially means that very structured or closed questions may be used to create some understanding of numbers within a range of different categories. In this way the more structured questions are much easier to analyse in terms of raw data. On the other hand, more open-ended questions suit the phenomenological approach where the answers have to be interpreted within a qualitative frame.

There are a number of issues that have to be dealt with when constructing questionnaires. First, the notion of **confidentiality** is important when administering the questionnaire. In the last chapter we looked at the need to have some form of ethical guidelines, and it may be necessary for your respondent to be anonymous. Remember that you need permission in order to administer a questionnaire.

In order for a questionnaire to be valid and reliable it is important to design it well. The design is probably the most crucial part of any survey. Although many feel that it is easy to make up some good questions, it is very difficult to produce a good questionnaire, and this may lead to biased results.

Presentation of the questionnaire is another key issue. It is important to think about how it is to be structured and how it will look. If it looks good it will encourage respondents to answer the questions. It is usual to try and win respondents over by providing them with an understanding of the purpose of the research, together with a description of the objectives for the questionnaire. If the questionnaire is ambiguous and it is not immediately obvious how to fill it in, respondents may fill it in incorrectly and ruin the data they could provide or not fill it in at all. According to Syndinos (2002), 'The questionnaire should have a professional appearance and its formatting should make it easy for the respondent to complete or for the interviewer to administer. Instructions should be clear in terms of content and should be distinguishable stylistically from questions. Branching instructions must be user-friendly and as unambiguous as possible. The questionnaire should be constructed to facilitate coding and data entry, bearing in mind the available resources and the intended analyses.'

A good questionnaire will:

- ask questions that relate directly to information needs and requirements
- not ask too many questions
- keep the questions as simple as possible
- not ask leading or intimate questions
- avoid negative questions
- fit questions into a logical sequence

- use the language of the targeted respondent and try to avoid technical language that some might not understand
- only ask one question at a time
- avoid asking respondents questions that are simply a memory test
- avoid questions that encourage respondents to think back to the past, or involve them with any form of calculations
- not use questions that may be perceived as ambiguous
- avoid questions on sexuality, politics and religion unless these are highly relevant.

According to Wilkinson (2000), the key questions to consider when designing questionnaires are:

- To whom is the questionnaire directed?
- Are you sure the instrument will be received and acted upon by that person?
- How will you structure your questions?
- How will you process the returns?
- How will you analyse the responses?
- How can you design your questionnaire to enhance the response rate?

You may want to start the questionnaire with some classification questions which find out more about the respondent, for example questions about their age and occupation, as well as their employment background. These questions help you to understand more about your sample, and this may be useful if you want to undertake some form of cross-tabulation or statistical analysis.

ACTIVITY

Working in groups, create three questions for a questionnaire designed to find out about staff communications.

Remember that words that might mean one thing to the researcher might have a completely different meaning for the respondent. For example, asking somebody at the operations level within an organisation about its corporate strategy might be misleading. The danger is that if you confuse your respondents, they may move on to the next question without answering the previous question.

Leading questions should always be avoided. For example, a question like 'Do you not agree that changes in your workplace will improve the profits of the organisation and the consequent benefits that you will feel?' would be difficult not to agree with, but many of those changes could clearly create a lot of uncertainty about which employees may not feel comfortable.

Types of question

There are a number of different types of question that might appear on a questionnaire. These are:

Open questions

With open questions the anticipated response would be a word or several sentences in which respondents can express their own views. The real problem with open questions is thinking about how to structure the analysis. For example:

> Describe what motivates you while at work.

Instead of just listing things that motivate an employee, the employee might talk about staff relations or something complex like various facets of the working environment. In analysing these types of responses, particularly as they are likely to be varied, it would be necessary to identify a series of themes into which they may fall.

Closed questions

With these questions the respondent has to choose from a variety of categories, which may have been pre-coded to speed up the analysis. Respondents will be required to choose from a variety of options, and these may be limited to two options such as Yes or No. For example:

Do you buy Dopey's Doggy Drops? (Please tick)

Yes	☐	0	(Code)
No	☐	1	(Code)

List

A list of items may be offered to the respondent, for example a list of areas in which the respondent shops, and the respondent would simply tick the areas which reflected their buying habits.

Category

Sometimes questions refer to particular categories and respondents are advised simply to identify the category to which they belong. For example, this might relate to ages, and they would have to identify whether they fell into 19–28 years, 29–38 years, and so on.

Ranking

With ranking questions the respondent is asked to identify their preferences and place a number of items into rank order. For example, if they were identifying elements of customer service, they might point to response times, politeness, pleasant manner, and so on.

Scale

There are a number of scales which can be used with questionnaires. For example, a Likert scale shows how strongly the respondent agrees or disagrees with a range of statements.

Similarly, another question using a scale might ask how strongly the respondent agrees with a statement. For example, they might be asked to circle the appropriate response on the scale following a statement:

I feel that our customer service procedures are better than any of our competitors'

Strongly agree	Agree	Neither agree nor disagree	Disagree	Strongly disagree

Rank order scale questions ask the respondent to put a number beside various items so as to put them in some sort of order or preference, as in the following example:

These are the considerations when choosing where to buy a new computer. Put them in rank order with 1 by the most important, 2 by the second most important, and so on down to 5 against the least important.

Wide choice	_____
Helpful sales staff	_____
Value for money	_____
After-sales service	_____
Quick delivery	_____

	Strongly agree	Agree	Neither agree nor disagree	Disagree	Strongly disagree
The computer network runs smoothly	☐	☐	☐	☐	☐
There are enough work-stations within the office	☐	☐	☐	☐	☐
Computer and IT support is helpful and prompt	☐	☐	☐	☐	☐
We are all well aware of the Data Protection Act	☐	☐	☐	☐	☐

Quantity

Some questions might simply want a response providing an exact or approximate amount or characteristic.

Grid

Some questions provide a grid in which to record answers to two or more questions at the same time. For example:

How many years have you worked at the following types of organisation?

	1 or 2 years	3 or 4 years	5 or 6 years	More than 6 years
SME				
Large private sector organisation				
Multinational organisation				
Local authority				
Government department				

A crucial element in a survey is recording information as the survey takes place and this involves keeping a record of the questionnaires that have been distributed and those that have been returned. There may be a good response initially, with returns then slowing down, and inevitably not all will be returned by the appropriate date. The researcher may follow up non-returned questionnaires, perhaps with a second questionnaire and letter. If names are not given on the questionnaire, then it is possible to develop some form of coding to indicate who has not responded, although it is not appropriate to do this if the anonymity of respondents is promised. Wallace and Mellor (1988) describe three methods for dealing with the non-response from questionnaires. These are:

♦ Analyse and compare responses by date of reply. One method is to send a follow-up letter to those who do not respond to the first enquiry. The questionnaires which result from the follow-up letter are then compared with those from the first request.

♦ Compare the characteristics of those who responded with those of the population, assuming you know them.

♦ Compare the characteristics of the respondents with non-respondents from the sample, assuming you have the relevant data such as age, occupation, and so on.

Piloting process

It may be the case that having produced your questionnaire you have too many questions. It is at this stage that you may think again about your data requirements and perhaps trim one or two questions. It is also important at this stage to pilot your questionnaire. Ideally, it should be sent to groups of people who are roughly similar in nature to your sample. According to Anderson (1998), 'pilot studies are used to test questionnaires and other instruments to see whether there is any possibility that worthwhile results will be found. If promising results do not appear in a pilot study, researchers sometimes reconsider the rationale, design, or viability of their study.' In other words, everything in design, construction and other terms is up for grabs until the questionnaire has been properly piloted and tested. A key role for the researcher is to be prepared to change and refine the questionnaire after the pilot study. For example, if the pilot took the guinea pigs too long to fill in, then it is important to refine the questionnaire and reduce its length.

Questionnaire checklist

1 Think about the sort of information you need to support your hypothesis or to answer your research question.

2 Consider whether a questionnaire is the best type of research instrument to obtain this information.

3 Begin to think about types of information you require and the types of questions you could use within your questionnaire.

4 Consider questionnaire design, that is, how do you want it to look?

5 Construct the questions, and check the wording, using some of the criteria discussed above.

6 Make sure your questions are in an appropriate order.

7 Produce your questionnaire, perhaps seeking guidance and support from tutors or from critical friends or peers.

8 Pilot the questionnaire.

9 Adjust the questionnaire in the light of the pilot.

10 Think about how the questionnaire will be distributed.

11 Construct a covering letter for the questionnaire.

12 Think about how to record those that have been returned, as well as any follow-up questionnaires that you may wish to send.

A key element in any survey is data analysis. In the next chapter we discuss both qualitative and quantitative types of data analysis, which can be undertaken from a questionnaire.

Distribution

Respondents should be informed about the purpose of the research and why they have been selected. This information may be included on the questionnaire or in a covering letter. There are a number of ways in which a questionnaire can be administered.

Face to face

This tends to be the best form of contact. It allows two-way communication between the researcher and the respondent and may allow an experienced researcher to glean more detailed information. It is also flexible, and so gestures, facial expressions and other signs may be noted. With this method response rates are high and it may be possible to deliver a lengthy questionnaire.

Telephone interviewing

This is usually more appropriate when the sample is small. However, this method can be regarded as intrusive and often busy people may not be available for discussion. It is a cost-effective way of reaching people.

Postal questionnaire

The levels of response to a postal questionnaire will vary enormously, depending upon their relevance to the reader and his or her interest. Response rates can be lower than 10 per cent, so answers are less likely to be representative. The way to avoid this outcome is to keep the questionnaire as brief and succinct as possible, and by sending it only to those for whom it is directly relevant. Include a stamped, addressed envelope.

Group distribution

This would involve delivering the survey to one group or a number of sub-groups at the same time. The researcher can explain the purpose of the questionnaire to the respondents who will then be given time to provide their responses.

With some questionnaires it may be possible to distribute them individually and then provide any support or queries that the respondents might have with the questionnaires at that point in time.

The problem of bias

Although it is sometimes difficult to do so, the purpose of the interview is to record feedback from respondents and not prompted feedback that you have encouraged them to make. **Interviewer bias** can sometimes be a problem, particularly where interviewees are not developing their answers in the way in which the interviewer would like. Because interviewers are human beings and not machines, there is always the likelihood of some kind of bias. For example:

♦ the interviewer may antagonise the respondent
♦ the interviewee may not particularly want to be interviewed
♦ the respondent may try too hard to please the interviewer by giving him or her the responses he or she thinks they want

♦ the interviewer may seek answers that just reinforce preconceived notions

If the interviewer holds strong views about the research, this may make the process all the more difficult.

Verification of data

It is not always easy either to analyse the data or to verify the process. At least with a structured set of responses they are far easier to analyse; however, as we have pointed out, with a less structured questionnaire, there must be some way of recording and then analysing the responses. It can take a lot longer to transcribe than deliver interviews, and if you have collected a lot of data, this can be really time-consuming.

It goes without saying that the best way to conduct an interview is to make the respondent feel comfortable, and by thanking them for co-operating with your work. It is not always possible to pick the right environment. Noise from outside can be a real problem as can the sun or other factors. Body or eye language may be a factor, and you may want to record some of your observations. For example, this interviewer conducted a series of interviews a few years ago when the respondents got aggressive, as they thought that by asking certain questions I was questioning their capabilities.

If taping an interview, it is usual to ask the respondent's permission beforehand. The interviewer may wish to take notes as well, particularly if it is semi-structured, and it is always useful to transcribe the interview as soon as possible afterwards when the details can be remembered.

Wherever interview transcripts include statements as direct quotations in the research, it is usual to verify this with the respondent. Otherwise, the respondent may challenge the final copy of the report you supply.

Other research instruments

Although we think about primary research in terms of interviews and questionnaires, there are other usable research instruments.

Focus group interviews

These usually include between six and ten respondents at a time. These are often used by political groups and consumer panels as a form of research, and have been widely used in a variety of ways for business research. The process involves trying to get individuals to contribute in a convivial small group atmosphere within a comfortable environment. Kreuger (1994) suggests that two people should conduct the focus group, one of whom is the moderator who deals with the questions, while the other is the recorder who makes a note of all of the interactions, both verbal and non-verbal, noting behaviour, responses and the sense of consensus. The moderator shapes and steers the thread of conversation, encouraging a range of types of comments.

Ethnography

This puts the researcher in a position where they may observe the activities of a particular group in order to provide a description of their activities. Within ethnography there can be **participant** and **non-participant observation**. The participant observer is part of the situation they are observing, such as in a meeting, whereas a non-participant is detached from the role. The advantage of this method of research, particularly if it is based upon the workplace in which the researcher works, is that it is possible to identify direct evidence from observation, with data providing startling insights into an issue or problem. The problem is that this process is not easy and access to particular situations might be denied. There is also the danger of interviewer bias.

Diary

Another useful research instrument is that of a diary. A diary is a good way of monitoring a research process within a time frame, particularly a small-scale piece of research for a unit like this. It enables the researcher to set targets, sustain and develop reflections and to perform tasks on time. The diary may help to provide some clear frame for analysis as well as a wealth of information. In many ways the diary is a form of self-completed questionnaire, and is really useful for anybody undertaking a project of this kind. As with all diaries, keeping them up to date is not always easy. However, there are a variety of electronic forms of diary that can be used, from the simple use of Microsoft software to some of the more sophisticated uses of modern mobile phones.

Secondary sources

Reading is usually, or should usually be, the starting point for any research topic. Students frequently come up with ideas about areas to research and subjects of interest to them, but to develop focus for these ideas and to make sure that the research questions or hypotheses are appropriate, it is really important to do some preliminary and formative reading behind the topic.

It is not so far in the past that the main sources of secondary data were books and journals. Today, with the development of the Internet and the huge impact of electronic resources that are available to us, the range of sources of secondary data can be extended to include:

♦ books
♦ journals
♦ conference papers
♦ academic websites
♦ statistics from a variety of different sources
♦ corporate sites, reports and accounts
♦ company or organisational websites
♦ magazines, newspapers and specialist publications and their archives
♦ the Internet
♦ portals that lead to fulltext articles and abstracts
♦ electronic databases
♦ videos, CD-ROMs and other forms of media.

In this sense the list is almost endless, and the range, types and emphasis upon different forms of media changes from year to year. The real problem today is often not finding the right data, but actually making sure that you are reading the best data available. With new information constantly appearing alongside an ever-changing media, it is almost impossible to research everything related to a particular project.

Secondary sources in research

There are various phases of the research process.

Familiarisation

Before doing anything it is useful for the researcher to familiarise themself with the range and sources of literature that are available. This may involve talking to a librarian, and many courses where dissertations or projects are a requirement provide a session of some description with the librarian. Finding out about the avenues of research is really helpful as you are likely to find out about access to different gateways of information such as portals to journals, and also learn about the sort of hierarchy within which much of the secondary data that you collect might fall. At the top of the hierarchy would perhaps be academic journals, while towards the bottom would be too much emphasis upon corporate information.

Searching by key word

Having come up with the research question or hypothesis, what areas does the researcher research? There are a number of different ways of doing this. For example, one is to identify a range of key words associated with your research topic and to use the various search engines on the internet to look for data associated with these key words. Sometimes a thesaurus can help in identifying different related words. Sometimes databases have their own form of thesaurus that allows you to develop your search.

Another way to develop key words is to use relevance trees. Starting with one word or concept, a number of branches may be developed from that word or concept. For example, if you started with customer service, you might have a branch moving towards advocates, another to value added, another to quality management, and so on. As the researcher ploughs through the research, and reads or looks at the various sources that are bubbling up, they may wish to get rid of some key words, or through further reading add more. A literature search is an organic evolving process that never finishes during the lifetime of a research project.

Selecting the search tools

Using a range of electronic research tools, the next thing to do is simply search, search and search again, using the key words for library catalogues, archives and electronic portals.

Locating the information

As we have seen, information and data may come from various sources, from databases to libraries, and even corporate websites. The search can take a considerable time.

Information hierarchy

There is a sort of information pecking order. Journal articles would be at the top of the order, particularly if the articles were seminal and of huge value. Books are, of course, important, but when you get to the realms of magazines and newspapers the data loses some of its value. But again, this is something that the researcher should emphasise within their dialogue.

Keeping records

Having got copies of articles, or borrowed books from libraries, what do you do as you read through the data? Different researchers have different learning styles and ways of working with information. Some like to take photocopies of articles and chapters and then use a coloured highlighter to identify the main points as they read through the data. Others might simply read through a chapter making a list of key quotations and points, alongside a reference that can be used later.

Managing information

It is possible to get too much information, and then when you have got it you have to decide what to do with it. Having too much data can be a real problem. A student recently came to me and said that what he looked for were ostensible differences between what he had read in one book and what he had read in another. He felt that by looking for the differences, it gave him something tangible to talk about within his dialogue.

Keeping records

As you manage the information you need to keep records of your articles and the reading you have undertaken, and also think about how the information you have collected can be used to match and develop your research questions and hypotheses.

The secret is never to delay the literature search. It really is the most important part of any project. For example, if you are short of ideas it is often the literature search that puts you on track. And, if you have lots of ideas, the literature review process is the one that puts everything that you do into context.

Referencing

At this stage it is worth briefly mentioning your references. Students may want to support something they have said with one or more references that provides that point with elements of authority. In other circumstances, students may wish to make direct quotations. These are **citations** which represent an acknowledgement within the student text that their dialogue is based upon reading from a source from which information has been obtained. The reference itself is the detailed list of sources that may either appear at the end of the document or as a footnote on each page.

You will probably find that every university or college library will have a booklet on referencing, or their policies may be on a website. It is not the purpose of this chapter to discuss all of the different systems of referencing. However, many organisations encourage their students to use the **Harvard** referencing system when they reference reading they have undertaken and wish to cite it in their written work, although it is not uncommon for some organisations to encourage their students to use the **Vancouver** system. For example, Harvard references should be cited as follows:

Author (Date) *Title*, Edition, Place: Publisher.

An example would be:

Clever, C. (2002) *A History of Referencing*, 3rd Edition, London: Sage.

There are clear and different rules for journals, for extracts from books, for websites and so on, and all of these need to be referenced properly depending upon the particular system your college or university is using.

Here is an example of how citations and references should be set out in the Harvard style.

Citations and List of references

Dow (1964) has produced a book of great value. However, the text could now do with updating to include recent events as described by Watt (2003). I would also suggest that the work of Albers (1994) and Greenfield (1990) is given careful consideration. Blasberg and Vishwanath (2003, p. 20) make a good point when stating that 'conventional wisdom holds that performance hinges on a brand's size, maturity, category, or leadership within a category'. Take a look at Tesco PLC (2002) for further information ...

References

Albers, J. (1994) *Interaction of Color* [CD-ROM], New Haven: Yale University Press.

Blasberg, J. and Vishwanath, V. (2003) 'Making cool brands hot', *Harvard Business Review* [on-line], 81(6), 20. Available at: Business Source Premier [Accessed 23 July 2003].

Dow, D. (1964) *A History of the World*, 3rd edn London: Greenfield.

Greenfield, J. (1990) 'The Sevso Treasure: the legal case', *Apollo*, 132(341), 14–16.

Tesco PLC (2002) *Annual Report and Financial Statements 2002* [on-line]. Tesco PLC. Available at: http://81.201.142.254/presentResults/results2001_02/Prelims/Report/pdfs/Tesco_Report2002.pdf [Accessed 30 June 2003].

Watt, N. (2003) 'Will you still be sending me a valentine? Cherie's lead vocal rescues Blair in China', *Guardian* [on-line], 23 July, 4. Available at: LexisNexis Executive [Accessed 24 July 2003].

To find out more about these systems of referencing, you can obtain help from the following academic websites.

Harvard sites are as follows:
http://lisweb.curtin.edu.au/referencing/harvard.html
http://www.shef.ac.uk/library/libdocs/hsl-dvcl.html
http://www.lmu.ac.uk/lss/ls/docs/harvfron.htm

Vancouver sites are as follows:
http://www.library.soton.ac.uk/infoskills/vancourver.shtml
http://www.library.uq.edu.au/training/citation/vancouv.html
http://www.lib.monash.edu.au/vl/cite/cite07vl.htm

Although referencing and citations are not easy to use, they are fundamental and become more important as you move towards the end of your course. A student who achieved a good degree said, 'I look for reading initially that clarifies my thoughts and supports the direction of my thesis. However, at the same time, I look for reading that has a slightly different view and which I can use to introduce discussion within the context of my dialogue. Doing this helps and supports my analysis.'

Books

As you clarify your topic area and start your reading, the first thing that most researchers look for are related books or chapters that touch in some way upon the research project. It is unlikely that there will be much published that completely matches your focus through your hypothesis or research question, so most of your search involves using key or related words that help you to draw literature together. So, books are really the starting point for what you will probably find will become a much wider search from much more literature.

Sometimes, to clarify terms and just make sure that you understand concepts, you may wish to use a range of generalised or specialist dictionaries or even encyclopaedias. For example, some of the books listed below might make a good starting point as you clarify the context of your study.

Botto, F. (2003) *Dictionary of E-business: a Definitive Guide to Technology and Business Terms*, Chichester: John Wiley.

Capela, J. (1996) *Dictionary of International Business Terms*, New York: Barron's.

Chambers, R. (1995) *An Accounting Thesaurus, 500 Years of Accounting*, Oxford, Pergamon.

Collins Concise Thesaurus (1997) Glasgow: HarperCollins.

Greener, M. (1994) *The Penguin Business Dictionary*, London: Penguin Books.

Pass, C. (1995) *Collins Dictionary of Business*, Glasgow: HarperCollins.

Roget, P. (2002) *Roget's Thesaurus*, Harlow: Longman.

Rosenberg, J. (1994) *Dictionary of International Trade*, New York: Wiley.

Towell, J. (1988) *Business Acronyms*, Detroit, Mich: Gale Research.

Warner, M. (2002) *The International Encyclopedia of Business and Management*, London: Thomson Learning.

Even if these books are not in your library, there will be both general and specialised dictionaries of various types which you might find useful.

Using your library information system you may wish to use a range of key words to access various books that you might require. It is easy to get frustrated at this stage and be in a situation where you just cannot find anything that you require. If there is nothing that pops up, you may want to start looking in broader related texts, and then try to find the information by looking at the contexts and indexes of such books. When you find something, look at the references which are either at the end of each chapter or at the end of the book, and then use those references as a base for your own search and your own reading.

As you find entries from the library information system, remember to make a note of the class numbers. You will come across entries like this:

Title Research methods for business students / Mark N.K. Saunders, Philip Lewis, Adrian Thornhill
Author Saunders, Mark N. K.
Publisher London:Pitman, 1996
Description (xiv,429p)ill, 25cm
ISBN 0273620177
Subjects Business - Research - Methodology
Management - Research - Methodology
Business - Research - Data processing
Other Authors Thornhill, Adrian
Lewis, Philip

Library Holdings		
Location	**Classmark**	**Status**
NTU Boots	658.001.5 SAU	Available [3 WEEK LOAN]
NTU Boots	658.001.5 SAU	DUE BACK: 21 MAY 2004 23:59 [3 WEEK LOAN]
NTU Boots	658.001.5 SAU	Available [ONE WEEK LOAN]
NTU Boots	658.001.5 SAU	DUE BACK: 24 MAY 2004 23:59 [ONE WEEK LOAN]
NTU Boots	658.001.5 SAU	Available [REFERENCE]
NTU Boots	658.001.5 SAU	Available [ONE WEEK LOAN]
NTU Boots	658.001.5 SAU	DUE BACK: 24 MAY 2004 23:59 [ONE WEEK LOAN]
NTU Boots	658.001.5 SAU	Available [ONE WEEK LOAN]
NTU Boots	658.001.5 SAU	Available [3 WEEK LOAN]
NTU Boots	658.001.5 SAU	Missing [3 WEEK LOAN]
NTU Boots	658.001.5 SAU	Available [ONE WEEK LOAN]
NTU Boots	658.001.5 SAU	Available [ONE WEEK LOAN]
NTU Boots	658.001.5 SAU	Missing [ONE WEEK LOAN]
NTU Boots	658.001.5 SAU	Available [3 WEEK LOAN]
NTU Boots	658.001.5 SAU	Available [3 WEEK LOAN]
NTU Boots	658.001.5 SAU	Available [3 WEEK LOAN]

Books for business and management usually start with 658. This book is clearly a popular one in the library at Nottingham Trent University. The system indicates the class number (658.001.5), those that are due back as well as those that are available for loan.

ACTIVITY

See if your library has the text above. If it has not, look for other business research texts using the same class number.

You may well need to broaden your search beyond your own library. To do this there are some general bibliographies that you can use, and you may need to ask your librarian or even search for titles on the Internet. For example, to search The British Library archives you can go on-line through http://blpc.bl.uk/ which gives you access to more than 8.5 million records of material held by the British Library. Alternatively, you may go to the Internet bookshop on www.bookshop.co.uk to find what you need. Once you have a reference for the book you require, you may ask your librarian to place a request for an inter-library loan.

Journals and other business and management information

Having clarified issues and developed your reading through texts, the next step is usually to look for more specialised and focused information available in academic journals. In many instances journals provide much richer information than do books, mainly because in most instances the journal articles are themselves a piece of research. Journals often have volumes which come out yearly, and then several editions that are usually numbered coming out during the year, perhaps quarterly, and so are clearly much more up-to-date and focused than books. And, as they often reflect the views of different academics, some of whom will have different ways of researching and working, they are a great exemplar for students undertaking for the first time their own piece of extended writing and research.

Often the starting point for a journal article may be to look at any references either at the back of a chapter or at the back of a book you are reading. Then see if that article from the journal selected is in the archives within your university or college library. The best way to look for a journal is through indexes and abstracts. Indexes and abstracts enable you to use key words to search for articles that are specially related to your chosen topic, and most come both in CD-ROM, paper form and may also be available on-line to library users. For example, for business and management you may wish to use the following:

- ◆ British Humanities Index: this provides access to indexes and abstracts for over 320 journals.
- ◆ Business Periodicals Index: this covers a range of different business-related areas such as information about business, companies, industry and management information.
- ◆ Employee Relations International: as a bibliographical and abstracts journal this provides information about employee and industrial relations.
- ◆ Personnel Management Abstracts: subjects include organisational behaviour and the management of people.

The nature and type of indexes and abstracts available will inevitably depend upon your university library. Sometimes the starting point for a search of this kind is to look at the specialist help and advice provided by the home page of the particular library within each institution.

Within the university at which this author works, the library has various avenues to access up-to-date business and management information. Looking through the business and management electronic resources, there are a number of on-line guides. For example, one link provides a lead to accounting, finance and taxation journals where there is a series of advice about how to search and use journals in these areas. The following extract is the sort of library information most academic libraries will have.

Listed below are journals held in The Boots Library. They are all available in print and in some cases electronic format (electronic versions are indicated on the list).

Printed versions:

Printed versions of journals are filed on the Lower Ground Floor of Boots Library. Current issues are in subject groups at the following shelf locations:

    657 Accounting   332 Finance   657.9 Taxation

Back copies are filed by alphabetical order of title, in one sequence with journals on other subjects.

All of the journals are listed on the Library catalogue (http://opac.ntu.ac.uk:8000), together with information about years and parts held. To search for a journal on the catalogue, select the Journal Titles option within the catalogue, and enter some keywords from the journal name.

Electronic versions:

You can access electronic versions of our print journals via the A-Z list of electronic journals (http://www.ntu.ac.uk/llr/ejlist1.htm) on the LLR website. Access to electronic journals is constantly developing, and you should check the A-Z list for the latest information.

The A-Z list is not an exhaustive list. Further electronic journals for accounting, finance and taxation, together with other business related topics, can be found in the following databases:

Business Source Premier
Emerald
European Business ASAP

These databases are recommended for literature searching. Access to all electronic databases is via the A-Z list of Databases (http://www.ntu.ac.uk/llr/dblist.asp) on the LLR website.

Accounting journals by title

ACCA Students Newsletter (later title - Student Accountant)

Accountancy (ICAEW)

Accountancy Age

Accountant

Accounting and Business

Accounting and Business Research

Accounting and Finance (plus electronic)

Accounting, Auditing and Accountability (plus electronic)

Accounting, Business and Financial History (plus electronic)

Accounting Education (plus electronic)

Accounting, Organizations and Society (plus electronic)

Accounting Review

Accounting World : the Journal of the Institute of Financial Accountants (later title - Financial Accountant)

Australian Accountant (later title - Australian CPA)

Australian CPA (earlier title - Australian Accountant)

British Accounting Review (British Accounting Association)

British Actuarial Journal

CA: the Accountants Magazine (Institute of Chartered Accountants of Scotland)

CA Charter (earlier title - Charter)

Charter (later title - CA Charter)

CMA Magazine

Company Accountant (Institute of Company Accountants)

Contemporary Accounting Research

Critical Perspectives on Accounting (plus electronic)

European Accounting Review (plus electronic)

Executive Accountant

Financial Accountant (earlier title - Accounting World. Institute of Financial Accountants)

Financial Management (earlier title - Management Accounting. Chartered Institute of Management Accountants)

Financial Management (Financial Management Association)

International Journal of Accounting (plus electronic)

International Journal of Government Auditing

International Journal of Intelligent Systems in Accounting, Finance and Management (plus electronic)

Issues in Accounting Education

Journal of Accountancy

Journal of Accounting and Economics (plus electronic)

Journal of Accounting and Public Policy (plus electronic)

Journal of Accounting, Auditing and Finance

Journal of Accounting Education (plus electronic)

Journal of Accounting Research (plus electronic)

Journal of Business, Finance and Accounting (plus electronic)

Journal of Forensic Accounting

Journal of International Financial Management and Accounting (plus electronic)

Management Accounting (later title - Financial Management. Chartered Institute of Management Accountants)

Management Accounting (American edition)

Management Accounting Research (plus electronic)

Managerial Auditing Journal (plus electronic)

Strategic Finance

Student Accountant (earlier title - ACCA Students Newsletter)

Student Digest (Institute of Company Accountants)

Finance journals by title

Banker

Business Economist (Society of Business Economists)

Corporate Finance

Credit Management (Institute of Credit Management)

Economist

Euromoney

European Investment Bank

Finance and Development (International Monetary Fund)

Financial Accountability and Management (Chartered Association of Certified Accountants. Plus electronic)

Financial Adviser

Financial Analysts Journal (Association for Investment Management and Research - USA)

Financial World (Chartered Institute of Bankers)

Fiscal Studies (Institute for Fiscal Studies. Plus electronic)

FX and MM: the Journal of Foreign Exchange and Money Markets

IMF Survey

Investors Chronicle

Journal of Applied Corporate Finance

Journal of Banking and Finance (plus electronic)

Journal of Cost Management

Journal of Financial Research (Southern/SW Finance Association - USA)

Journal of Money, Credit and Banking

Journal of Portfolio Management

Journal of Risk and Insurance (American Risk and Insurance Association. Plus electronic)

Lloyds Bank Economic Bulletin

Managerial Finance (plus electronic)

Money Management

Mortgage Finance Gazette

Pensions Management

Planned Savings

Post Magazine

Professional Investor (Institute of Investment Management and Research)

Public Finance

Public Money and Management (plus electronic)

Treasurer (Association of Corporate Treasurers)

Taxation journals by title

British Tax Review

Tax Adviser (earlier title - Taxation Practitioner. Chartered Institute of Taxation)

Tax Journal

Taxation

Taxation Practitioner (later title - Tax Adviser)

World Tax Report: Monthly Survey of World Developments in Taxation

Journals by professional organisation

Below is a list of professional bodies from the world of accounting, finance and taxation, together with their key journals.

Association of Chartered Certified Accountants
Accounting and Business

Australian Society of Certified Practising Accountants
Australian Accountant (later title - Australian CPA)
Australian CPA (earlier title - Australian Accountant)

Chartered Institute of Management Accountants
Management Accounting (later title - Financial Management)
Financial Management (earlier title - Management Accounting)

Chartered Institute of Taxation
Taxation Practitioner (later title - Tax Advisor)
Tax Advisor (earlier title - Taxation Practitioner)

Institute of Actuaries and the Faculty of Actuaries (UK)
British Actuarial Journal

Institute of Chartered Accountants in Australia
Charter (later title - CA Charter)
CA Charter (earlier title - Charter)

Institute of Chartered Accountants in England and Wales (ICAEW)
Accountancy

Institute of Chartered Accountants of Scotland
CA: the Accountants Magazine

Institute of Company Accountants (UK)
Company Accountant

Institute of Cost and Executive Accountants (UK)
Executive Accountant

Institute of Credit Management
Credit Management

Institute of Financial Accountants
Accounting World (later title - Financial Accountant)

Financial Accountant (earlier title - Accounting World)

Society of Business Economists
Business Economist

There are a number of databases that can be accessed that may provide information useful for a business and management context. For example, specific databases may refer to:

♦ Accountancy
♦ Business source premier
♦ Emerald Fulltext
♦ European business
♦ GMID (Global Market Information Database)
♦ Harvard Business Review
♦ LEXIS/NEXIS
♦ MINTEL
♦ Social Science Citation Index
♦ WARC Market Research Abstracts
♦ World Market Research Centre

These databases may also provide access to what are known as 'fulltext' or complete journal articles. One such portal, providing access to a huge range of fulltext journal articles is known as Emerald.

According to their website (http://www.emeraldinsight.com/), 'Emerald publishes the world's widest range of management and library and information services journals, as well as a strong specialist range of engineering, applied science and technology journals.

'Our electronic databases allow instant access to the latest research and global thinking. We provide the information, ideas and the opportunity to gain insight into your key management topics.'

By accessing the Fulltext icon, and assuming that your institution subscribes to this electronic portal, you can access Emerald journals from in-house computers or via your learning portal.

Internet and media

Although it is important not to be dependent upon it, and, of course, careful about the sort of sources students use, there are a huge number of sources available on the Internet. Selected sources might include:

http://www.statistics.gov.uk (UK national statistics online)

http://www.marks and spencer.com/ (corporate sites like M&S)

http://education.ntu.ac.uk/resources/BusEd.html (page prepared by a Nottingham Trent University student with of plenty of links to business-related sites)

http://www.bized.ac.uk (bized site full of business information)

http://www.thetimes100.couk/home.asp (The Times 100 case studies and other materials)

http://europa.eu.int/comm/index_en.htm (the European Commission homepage)

The list of such sites is almost endless. You may wish to access press release pages of professional bodies, look at trade union sites, refer to articles in specific publications such as *The Economist*, various newspapers or simply look at archives from various organisations.

Research and topical articles

Literature evolves over a period of time so that if you started a literature review today, it would never finish if you did not put a stop to it.

Primary research methods

JOURNAL ARTICLE

In contrast Marshall (1995), 'offers an introduction to using market research methods and provides an illustrative example of their application to the study of Scottish eating habits'. Marshall then 'examines the pros and cons of several primary research methods commonly used in market(ing) research'. This is typical of many articles that focus upon their own research methods. By doing so, and particularly in this instance where so many primary research techniques in market research are similar to those used in business research, it is a good opportunity to read this sort of evaluation.

Marshall, D. 'Market research methods and Scottish eating habits', *British Food Journal*, 1995, Vol. 7, No. 7, pp 28–31.

Organisational culture literature

JOURNAL ARTICLE

Diane Lewis (1996), 'traces the saga of the organisational culture literature from the organisation development model through to the recent interest in total quality management (TQM), forming a link between the three concepts. It is argued that, while TQM has separate origins from the culture movement, the two fields have recently converged with the idea that to achieve "excellence" and "quality", it is necessary either to change or work with the culture of an organisation. Following on from the first article which dealt with literature that was mainly of academic interest, such as concepts and methods of study, diagnosis and measurement, reviews the literature that heralds and then reflects the growing interest in utilitarianism. This literature is concerned with attempts to study, implement and measure culture change, and with the emerging relationship between culture and TQM.'

As you can see, Lewis's study is completely literature-based, not only with an analysis of literature over a period of time, but also an attempt to understand it within different paradigms and contexts.

Lewis, D. 'The organizational culture saga: from OD to TQM, a critical review of the literature', *Leadership and Organization Development Journal*, 1996, Vol. 17, No. 2, pp 9–17.

Chapter 3

Research project

In Chapter 1 we touched briefly upon how to identify a research problem or issue, and the chapter also looked closely at the nature of selecting either research questions or hypotheses upon which to focus the research project. For many students, the early phases of the research project are some of the most difficult. Simply identifying the right topic is so important if they are to pursue their proposal in a way that leads to worthwhile, and yet also theoretically interesting and valuable results. It is so easy for students to have a general idea of what they want to do. The idea may relate to a career they may be seeking, or be something that they want to put on their curriculum vitae. However, not all ideas make good projects. In fact it is easy to choose an inappropriate topic or one that does not relate to a sufficiently theoretical paradigm capable of being researched. To make this whole process interesting and worthwhile, it is important that assumptions are not made in the early stages and that the initial reading around the topic is used to clarify and develop the research questions or hypotheses.

Preparation: dos and don'ts

At the very early stage of your project, *do not*:

♦ come up with an idea, and then assume all will be well
♦ fail to get grips with the parameters of the issue by not doing any background reading
♦ forget that this is a business research project that requires substantive analysis of a business research issue
♦ allow your focus to be too broad, otherwise it may be difficult either to touch upon or analyse the data
♦ allow your focus to be too narrow, otherwise you may be searching for literature to support your analysis

♦ assume that the project is not going to be organic, and grow, develop and change as you work through it over the year
♦ fail to be flexible or fail to listen to advice
♦ think of something that simply describes theory rather than develops a project for analysis
♦ forget that the project should be focused upon theory with supporting exemplification through research methods such as a case study, rather than the other way around. Some of the worst projects that this author has marked have simply focused upon actions within organisations rather than theory itself.

At this very early stage of your project make sure that you *do*:

♦ put your ideas down on paper
♦ discuss your ideas with other students
♦ use literature to identify, clarify and develop your ideas
♦ make sure that the literature you peruse is not just books and also includes journal articles and the results of other research projects
♦ find out what sort of projects students have undertaken in the past
♦ try and find out what areas make good projects and what areas lead to poor projects
♦ think about your own needs, such as what you feel might be useful for your own CV, or areas that you are genuinely interested in, or perhaps even areas that you might not feel you are strong in and want to learn more about
♦ remember that, even after you have selected a topic or area of research, this might change or have to be fine-tuned as you read the literature
♦ think about planning your project and the timings you need for different elements

- not forget that an important part of the project is your methodology and that it is necessary to refer to dialogue within these chapters as well as in other business research texts
- listen to the advice of your supervisor.

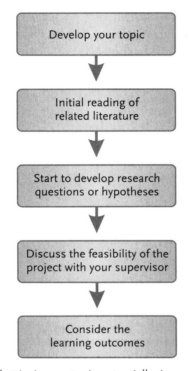

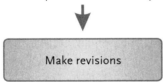

Figure 10.2   Developing the topic idea

Scope and feasibility of research question or hypothesis

At this very early and tentative stage the student may develop a number of different ideas, each of which may need some further research. It is in fact always useful not to put all of the irons in a single fire. The whole purpose of research is to test the feasibility of each proposal and eliminate some of the less realistic propositions.

Remember some projects lend themselves to research at this level, while others may be too difficult and stressful to complete either realistically or properly. In the past, this author has supervised students who have attempted to use quantitative elements within economics, or have wanted to find out more about research issues related to developing nations, both of which have been commendable in themselves, but also extremely difficult to complete. On the other hand, some of the poorer projects have been related to how effective a particular football club is in using its business activities to generate success on the playing field, or finding out how motivation theory in general (encompassing many different theories) is used by business managers. The football club topic invariably focuses too much upon the organisation in question, fails to discuss it within a case study context, but is generally constructed with a sufficient understanding of the club and its activities, while the motivation topic, although commendable in principle, often simply describes all of the different theories of motivation and tries to relate them to all of the different theories of leadership in a rather tenuous way.

It is important for the student, however, to identify a research question related to something they are either interested in or care about. For example, finding out about how small business entrepreneurs deal with stress caused by excessive bureaucracy and paperwork could be interesting and is certainly a project that is feasible. On the other hand, finding out how small business managers manage, would be very broad, and would have to be narrowed down. It may be possible for the student to develop their research question or hypothesis on the basis of experience they already have, particularly if they are either mature students or have some part-time work experience. It may be useful to evaluate or test the research question beforehand, to see if the project is feasible.

Mason (1988) suggests a number of ideas for getting started on small-scale research projects. For example:

- One technique is to keep a **notebook** into which the student could jot any ideas during the course of a week. The student would follow up the ideas by looking at electronic and other sources in the university library.
- Another technique is to develop a **relevance tree**. This is a graph with a general title of the topic area which then branches into other areas related to the topic.
- A way to bubble up ideas may be **morphological analysis**. This is a study of form which involves mixing and matching words within a table. It simply involves identifying a list of adjectives, with two other columns of nouns. The reader would simply link one adjective with two nouns and then use these to try to identify a possible topic for analysis.

For example:

Qualitative	Case study	SME
Quantitative	Survey	Motivation
Analysis	Action research	Leadership
Exploratory	Ethnography	Millennium

At the end of the day, if the student is completely stuck for a topic or an issue, then it may be useful for them to try to brainstorm ideas alongside friends. Diagrams can be helpful for doing this. For example, Hussey (1997) talks about using mind maps as a way to 'show relationships in space or time'. A mind map is simply a creative form of diagram which involves jotting down various elements in a relational way to each other. It was Tony Buzan (1993) who developed mind maps as an efficient way of using the brain's ability for association. This notion of association plays a role in mental functions, and words themselves are no exception. The mind map uses every single word and idea with numerous links attaching it to other ideas and concepts.

To make a mind map, the starting point is in the centre of the page and the creator then works outwards in all directions like the roots of a tree to produce an organised list. The mind map can be enhanced

through the use of images, colour, outlining or emphasis, shapes, icons, codes, patterns, and links. This large amount of information together with their associations can stimulate the user to generate new ideas and associations that have not previously been thought of. They can also be used to organise and structure notes and ideas of the user.

A relevance tree is similar to this. It may be used for generating ideas, or to develop clusters of points from a broad starting point.

ACTIVITY

Use some form of mind map or relevance tree to identify areas of reading for your business research project.

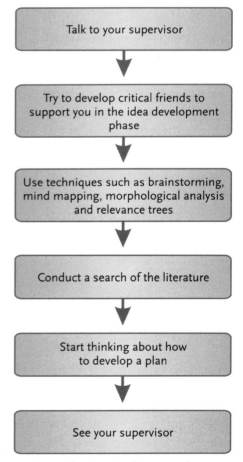

Figure 10.3   The early phases of a research project

According to Torrance (1992), the strategies adopted by students as they developed their projects were as follows:

80%   Brainstorming or writing down a checklist of ideas

78%   Taking verbatim notes from relevant literature

63%   Putting notes in some form of order

54%   Constructing a mind map to provide a spatial representation

84%   Constructing a plan on the content and order of the document

94%   Writing out full drafts not necessarily in polished English

94%   Revising full drafts.

Literature search

Having played with an idea, perhaps through using mind or concept maps, the next stage is to conduct some form of literature search. The concept map, or the initial brainstorming process, should identify a range of areas of literature that relate to the topic. It is important for the student to identify key words and terms that will help to focus the search. By looking at the relevant literature, it should be helpful to use the references at the end of each chapter, text or article to search for other relevant materials, a little bit like a paper chase. If the student finds little material on a particular area either in a well-stocked library or through searching electronic sources, and particularly, electronic journals, then it is probably better not to undertake that project. Conversely, if there is too much, it is probably worth refining the topic and narrowing down the research questions or hypotheses.

Planning the process

After having drawn up a short list of topics the student should undertake some reading before deciding upon an area of investigation. Once the investigation or focus of the study has been decided upon, the student needs to think about their research ques' hypotheses (see Chapter 1).

Structure

At this stage it may be useful to say something about the structure of the project as it is the structure that helps the student to identify how much time they might need to spend upon each section. There may be plenty of flexibility, and the structure suggested is certainly not set in tablets of stone, however it is one that students might want either to use or to adapt.

Title

This should reflect the contents of the report as well as how the research has been undertaken. It should not be too long, and should not simply be the main research question or hypothesis.

Abstract

This is simply a summary of 250–300 words, describing the broad aims of the work and the conclusions.

List of contents

This can be used to list both the chapters and the sectors within the chapters. It helps the marker to understand a little more about the structure of the project.

List of figures and tables

These should be listed, alongside any sources for them.

Preface

This is usually not necessary, but tends to be a personal statement from the author about the rationale for the study.

Acknowledgements

This is to acknowledge the people who have helped the student with the research. It is amazing how many people acknowledge everyone, including their pets, and then forget their supervisor.

Introduction

This should outline the background and purpose of the study, setting out the aims, objectives, questions or hypotheses in a way that provides the reader with an understanding about how the project is contributing to the development of knowledge.

Literature review

As we will see this should deal with the knowledge and concepts that underpin the study. It is necessary to be selective and also useful to orientate the dialogue around the questions or hypotheses underpinning the study.

Methodology

This should discuss the various research methods used within the study, and illustrate how such methods are meeting the questions or hypotheses. It is important to explain and justify why each of the methods was chosen, and also to describe how the data has been analysed, while accepting some of the limitations of the research.

Results

In this section the results should be set out, perhaps in a fairly structured way, in response to a theme, aim or issue.

Analysis and discussion

This is usually one of the more difficult areas of a research project and requires a lot of time. In this section everything should be brought together and synthesised, so that the results and literature can be discussed and related to the original aims of the project.

Conclusions and recommendations

In this section the researcher needs to decide how well the research aims and objectives have been achieved through summarising the research. The report may make recommendations for further research, and draw some key conclusions.

References

This should be an alphabetical list of authors cited or used within the report, using the system specified by the particular establishment.

Appendices

Appendices are useful for inserting related information, often too detailed to include in the main report. This might also include interviews and other method-related data.

Targets, milestones, and action plan

The project structure cited above is how the project could look once it is finished. The real issue for the students is what they have to do to reach that stage. There are a number of ways to do this, but clearly timing is fundamental. You will know the date for submission of the thesis and other deadlines that might be set, for example the completion of a project plan. Once you know this, you can work out the number of weeks required to complete the project. For example, the plan may appear as follows:

	Weeks
Project proposal	6
Introduction	2
Literature review	8
Methodology	2
Results	2
Analysis/discussion	2
Conclusions/recommendations	2
Title, abstract and other	2
	26 weeks

Figure 10.4   Action plan

The timetable should check that all stages and processes in the project are covered, with sufficient time allowed for each element. It should help the student to move on from one stage or phase to another. It is also useful for the student to allow timing for editing once the thesis is near completion. They may also want someone to help them by proofreading the thesis.

The student may in fact add another column to the action plan specifying the word count. Although the word count may be flexible, it will help to ensure that one or more stages is not unbalanced.

Wilkinson (2000) emphasises the need to organise information. He makes the point that the first thing to do is to draft a contents list which is then broken down into chapters and sections. From this he points out that it is useful to identify linkages, and then develop themes and draw links between the themes. These linkages can be expressed diagrammatically, and help the student to identify how the work 'fits' the objectives when the project is viewed as a whole. This notion of fit is important, and helps the report to be much more cohesive and logical, moving with distinct links from one step to another.

Writing up a project is not easy, and it is important for the student to work in a situation where distractions can be avoided and where quality time can be utilised to work in a focused way upon the outcomes. It is accepted that we all have different times of the day when we work better than at other times. For example, if the student is good at working in the evenings, then this is the time of day to build in any action plan.

Monitoring and revision: the role of the supervisor

For an undergraduate project a supervisor will typically have responsibility for a number of students and may make various arrangements for meeting them. For example, he or she might meet students independently, based upon timetabled sessions over a period of a number of weeks. This, perhaps, is the traditional image of supervisory sessions. Alternatively, they may allocate students to a group and then have group tutorial sessions in which group members act as critical friends to each other. In other words, they all contribute to the discussion as individuals within these small groups (no larger than ten), discuss their various proposals and seek advice.

The real problem is matching student expectations with the experiences provided by supervisors. For example, students need to know when they can see their supervisors, and what their policies are in

relation to forms of communication such as phone calls and emails. At the same time tutors will have expectations of their students in terms of completing work and meeting deadlines.

It is usual, even with a self-managed project, for there to be a number of taught sessions focusing upon research methods. These may be followed up with periodic meetings with students to discuss:

♦ their research proposals
♦ the literature reviews
♦ findings
♦ data analysis issues
♦ methodological concerns.

For each of these meetings it is important that students bring materials, so that advice and support can be focused upon work in progress.

Pre-flight research project checklist

☐ Do some preparatory reading.

☐ Talk through your ideas with other people or your study group.

☐ Construct a project proposal and an action plan. Remember your project proposal is not a tablet of stone. It is not intended to be a straitjacket. It is quite likely that your ideas will develop during the project as your study grows.

☐ Identify the names of people who may be able to help you with your project.

☐ Make sure you know what is required.

☐ Meet regularly with your supervisor to elicit feedback.

☐ Make sure you are familiar with the literature for your chosen area.

☐ Construct your research questions/hypotheses as well as some aims and objectives.

☐ Think about the implications of data collection (do not promise too much).

- [ ] Decide upon your research methods and data collection techniques.

- [ ] Think about how you are going to interpret information (qualitative or quantitative?).

- [ ] Read and talk to people; make notes to collect your ideas.

- [ ] Keep a research diary and use it to reflect upon the processes in which you are engaged as well as to support the data collection.

- [ ] Think about how you can develop the project to match the proposed structure and timings.

- [ ] Do some initial piloting of work for data collection and make revisions if necessary.

- [ ] Try to identify any potential bottlenecks, particularly the ones related to the collection of primary data.

- [ ] Consider how you intend to justify your research methods and check the robustness of your project.

- [ ] Think about how you can fit your research project in with other commitments you have.

- [ ] Identify how long you need for reading, note taking and for data collection.

- [ ] Identify your sampling methods.

- [ ] Add time-lags in case of emergency or delays in collecting data.

- [ ] Remember that analysis and interpretation is a key stage in the project. Make sure you leave sufficient time to write your project up. This must not be rushed as this is the time when you make key observations and bring everything together to support and develop your analysis.

- [ ] Think about how you intend to present the project.

Methodology

A research project is an exercise in which you construct some form of argument to support a hypothesis or to answer a research question. In doing so the student uses their ideas and experiences. His or her project is, however, a disciplined enquiry and not:

- mere speculation
- just observation
- about rhetoric
- dependent upon eloquence.

The research project needs to be ordered and relate closely to theoretical principles and business practices. It must also, as it is to be assessed, withstand scrutiny from tutors and external examiners. At the same time, good projects are sometimes:

- free ranging
- exciting
- insightful, illustrating and enabling students to develop skills of analysis and synthesis
- interesting.

A project is not just about 'finding out' using primary research. In fact some of the best projects this tutor has marked have not used primary research at all and have been entirely based upon secondary research. So, the key element within the project is to review the literature to find out what has been written about a chosen topic. At the heart of every research project is theory. Theory is grounded in practice and represents scholarship and knowledge. It has been argued that on the one hand the research seeks the explanations, and on the other hand theory provides the explanations.

Organising the literature

In the last chapter we looked at the nature of secondary research and the avenues available for searching for literature. At the heart of any project is the need to use theory. From the outset, remember that:

- theory is essential, not just for the literature review but also to analyse and develop results and findings

- theory provides an understanding of the parameters of the project
- theory underpins the problems within the project and deals with the practice related to the context
- theories also underlie the assumptions that are made.

As we have seen in the early phases of the project the student needs to review the literature. The student must make sure that they have enough library time. It has been said that 'knowledge does not exist in a vacuum'. The work undertaken has to be seen in relation to work undertaken by other people. The result of a detailed literature review is twofold:

- the student becomes better informed
- they then put themselves in a better position to relate literature to the project.

A key element in an ongoing literature review is the process of referencing. **References** help the user to justify and develop statements in relation to the context of their research in a way that shows an ability to create new knowledge on the basis of existing knowledge. The researcher must think about how they intend to use the references. For example, are they relevant to the research question or hypothesis? Do they complement arguments or help to justify and develop points? Using reading is undoubtedly a skill, and it is important for the student to develop their dialogue around their reading in a way that not only shows that they understand it, but also shows that they can use knowledge and literature to deal with issues relevant to the research question or hypothesis.

Knowing what to look for is always a major problem when searching for literature to support a project. There are often two problems:

- identifying subject matter relevant to the topic
- actually obtaining the publication.

Exploring the literature is undoubtedly just the first stage in a research project as the student clarifies and develops his or her ideas. From the outset they need to:

- Use the literature to provide relevance and focus.
- Identify key words that can be used in search engines as they seek the literature. This can be

difficult and frequently requires brainstorming, but it is very important. Another way to do this is to use some form of mind map. Simply put the research question, topic or issue in the middle of a piece of paper, and then use the map, together with some reading from preliminary texts, to identify a range of relevant concepts.

- Collect articles, books and papers that are relevant to the project, including texts that help the student to understand their methodology.
- Look for further references to reading from the referencing section of the books and articles that are read.
- Understand that a literature search is organic. For the duration of a project it never stops.

How not to use literature

According to Stark (1998), who provides sound advice, the three ways *not* to use literature are as follows:

The magpie approach

This is collecting articles and books which have catchy or interesting titles, in a somewhat haphazard manner. While this may produce an array of colourful and occasionally valuable material, do not be seduced by interesting issues which are tangential to your original purposes.

The diamond necklace approach

This is stringing together 'gems' of quotations from well-known authoritative authors, interspersed with a few words of your own. Restrict the use of quotations to a very few and only where the author captures the essence so brilliantly that you could not better it. Try to summarise or paraphrase what others say: it shows that you have read it and understood it.

The 'dressed to impress' approach

This is a long list of titles, usually presented as a bibliography, which is rarely referred to in the body of the text. It looks good but it is much better to stick to a shorter list of titles, as 'references' which are used to support and develop the arguments in the text.

Writing the literature review

It is important that in undertaking the literature review the student is systematic and well organised. A research diary or log can help with this. As the student reads through different materials, he or she should:

♦ Select relevant materials only.
♦ Make summarised notes of key points.
♦ Wherever they come across a quotation that they feel sums up a point well, or which they feel has a particular relevance to their issue, they should write the reference down in full, in a way that enables it to be used in their own text.
♦ Be critical of what they read. Most writers have a particular view of an issue, and so it is important to get to grips with that view, so that fine distinctions can be made between the views of one author and another.
♦ Consider who the authors are pitching their materials for, as this may well influence their style. For example, in the business field, are the articles being read focused upon managers, academics or researchers?
♦ Think about the issues raised by the materials.
♦ Consider the plausibility of the points being made.
♦ Create a theme or structure for the literature review, which make certain categories and provide a logical structure for the review.

Writing the methodology

For some reason this is often an area that students find difficult to justify. All projects require some kind of methodology that highlights the strengths or limitations of different processes of research. There are a number of business research method texts usually found under the 658.001.5 classmark in libraries. These texts, and the supporting dialogue in this section of this book, are part of the cornerstone of a research project. The methodology identifies the techniques and methods used to answer the research question or hypothesis. It should include:

♦ some form of description of the study
♦ a reflective analysis of what the study is trying to achieve

♦ the use of methodologically sound terms and phrases
♦ an explanation of the methods and research instruments that are then justified through the reading
♦ a description of the data analysis as well as an explanation of how the conclusions were reached.

Categories of research

There are a number of categories of research. They include the following.

Exploratory research

This takes place where there are very few, if any, similar studies related to the issue or problem. With these studies it is difficult to test a hypothesis, but instead the researcher looks for a pattern from which conclusions can be made. Often case studies, observation and historical analysis provide data for this.

Descriptive research

This describes things that exist. For example, the research question might be 'how many days off does the average worker in Nottingham take each year?' The data collected for this research is often statistical.

Analytical research

Also called explanatory research, this takes descriptive research a stage further and is constructive. For example, 'How could the number of sick days be reduced?'

Predictive research

This goes one stage further by trying to forecast the likelihood of a similar situation occurring elsewhere or in another situation. For example, 'Would employee bonus schemes reduce the number of days workers take off sick in Nottingham?'

Quantitative and qualitative research

These are two broad and very different methods of research as we will see later in this chapter. Quantitative research involves focusing upon objective elements based upon analysing numerical data using statistics. Qualitative research is more subjective in nature and involves an analysis of human and organisational activities.

Applied and basic or pure research

These are two other very different forms of research. Applied research applies to a specific problem or issue, whereas pure research is used to improve understanding about particular issues.

Longitudinal studies

These are studies conducted over a time period, by focusing upon a small number of variables such as subjects. They will involve repeated observations allowing the researcher to analyse changes to the context.

Survey data

These are collected through a variety of situations by asking questions or through making observations as well as through experimental data.

Case studies

As we have seen, these are research studies that focus upon an issue, organisation or even a person within a single setting.

Validity and reliability

Within any research project measurement takes place in a situation in which the researcher has some control. It is important that such measurements are valid. In other words, the research accurately represents what is actually happening in a particular situation. On the other hand, results should also be reliable. If the research finding can be repeated and the same results are found, then the research process has been reliable.

Quantitative and qualitative data analysis

Nearly all forms of research relate to the two main research paradigms or systems. These are sometimes called positivist (quantitative) and phenomenological (qualitative).

Quantitative and qualitative research

Quantitative research is based upon the assumption that the research report can be represented through the collection, analysis and dissemination of facts relating to numerical data. The positivist approach to collecting data assumes that because something is happening it can be numerically measured.

Qualitative research is very different from this, and assumes that behaviour can be interpreted and discussed using descriptions or some qualitative method as a base for analysis. Qualitative analysis involves real-life situations and involves the researcher looking for themes from various sources. In some circumstances it involves the researcher finding out about people within the situation under investigation.

According to Jankowicz (1995), 'Neither approach is best. The "best" method is the one that is most appropriate to the kinds of questions you wish to ask at the time, in the sort of environment and with the sort of thesis which you're advocating.' It is possible to have both quantitative and qualitative elements to a study. For example, the quantitative element might identify the extent of the problem or issue and then the qualitative might seek to find the reasons for the problem or the solutions.

Quantitative	Qualitative
objective	subjective
measurable	provide discovery, description and understanding
statistical analysis	rich narrative
researcher separate from process	researcher part of process

Figure 10.5   Quantitative and qualitative elements

Qualitative data analysis

Analysing qualitative data is not easy. The researcher may develop huge amounts of dialogue for analysis which may be disorganised or chaotic, and summarising it and developing conclusions can be extremely complex. The data may comprise:

♦ questionnaires
♦ interviews
♦ diaries
♦ copies of notes
♦ video tapes or other observations
♦ charts, maps and audio tapes.

It is very important with qualitative data to ask what all of the words mean. When analysing documents it is important to think about:

♦ each author
♦ their biases
♦ the data upon which the document was produced
♦ the main points made and any assumptions relating to these points
♦ the strength of the arguments.

Coding

When analysing interviews the researcher needs to identify and summarise the key points and think about what has been left out from the surveys. They also need to think about how the data from the interviews relates to other data collected through using other research methods. If analysing questionnaires, the researcher has to try and get their head around what appears to be a lot of unstructured information. Coding may be important at this stage.

One of the first challenges is to put the qualitative data into some form of manageable group. This may involve reducing the data to make it manageable. According to Miles (1994) data reduction, 'is a form of analysis that sharpens, sorts, focuses, discards and reorganises the data in such a way that "final" conclusions can be drawn and verified'. This is a way of summarising the data and can involve an element of coding. Codes are labels that enable the qualitative data to be separated, compiled and organised.

Open coding

This method helps to categorise and sort the data. The researcher breaks down the different elements of information/data, making it more recognisable and easier to manage. Codes are attached to a range of concepts and categories. The labels or codes chosen by the researcher are their own choice and are entirely subjective and reflect their content.

Axial coding

This is a more extended form of coding involving the researching to connect categories and sub-categories. It involves the restructuring of data to build up particular patterns based upon a range of relationships.

Content analysis

This is considered to be a formal way of analysing qualitative data and is a systematic way of converting text to numbers so that it can be analysed quantitatively. For example, it may be possible to identify a number of key words or phrases that have appeared within dialogue or to identify the number of times particular themes crop up during interviews.

Cognitive mapping

Another method of interpreting data is through cognitive mapping. It can be used to make sense of dialogue and may be complex. It involves:

♦ analysing data collected from an interview by breaking down the interview into a number of phrases that retain the language of the interviewee
♦ comparing these phrases with each other, linking one concept to another
♦ developing a hierarchy within one concept so that explanations can be linked to consequences.

As the researcher starts to organise the data, he or she needs to think about:

♦ what the data means
♦ how the data compares to other research identified through the literature review
♦ any significant elements coming from the data

- aspects of the data that do not fit the research question or hypothesis
- the need to collect more data to corroborate or strengthen the findings.

Although the qualitative data will have been collected through dialogue, this may not be the best way of presenting it within the research report, so it may be appropriate to convert it into diagrams and other means by which it can be viewed and used for analysis.

Quantitative data analysis

Once the quantitative data have been collected, the next stage is to analyse it. Quantitative data is positivist and involves figures, so the first stage is to think of some way of analysing the statistics that you have collected. There are two broad areas of statistics. Some statistics are just for display because they have meaning in themselves. This data is known as **descriptive statistics** and it is simply displayed or summarised. From other statistics it is possible to undertake some serious data analysis. Some of this data analysis may be **exploratory data analysis** which summarises, displays or describes the data, while other data may be taken through a process of **confirmatory data analysis** from which inferences and trends can be identified and drawn.

There are a number of specialist computer statistical packages that can be used to analyse quantitative data including:

- Minitab
- Statistical Package for the Social Sciences (SPSS)
- Excel or any other form of spreadsheet.

There are a number of different ways of presenting findings from data analysis.

Arranging data

Even where only small amounts of data has been collected, it will need to be arranged and the first step is to examine the frequency distribution for each variable. The **frequency** is a numerical value representing the total number of observations undertaken within the survey. For example, you may have talked to a certain number of people at each level within an organisation. If the frequencies are then arranged in size order they become an **array** and this may then be used to construct tables, charts or graphs.

Frequency distribution

A frequency distribution table presents the frequency data in size order. For example, assume that a business's sales figures (in units) over 50 days are as follows:

Output (000s)									
5	6	4	6	2	5	6	2	6	5
5	6	5	6	6	5	3	5	4	5
5	3	2	3	3	4	2	3	6	5
4	1	5	2	4	1	2	5	3	4
5	4	2	5	3	5	4	4	4	5

These figures can be set out in a frequency distribution table as shown below. The Greek letter sigma (Σ) means 'sum of'.

Weekly output level (000s)	Frequency of occurrence	Output level frequency
x	f	fx
1	2	2
2	7	14
3	7	21
4	10	40
5	16	80
6	8	48
	$\Sigma f = 50$	$\Sigma fx = 205$

On multiplying each value or daily sales figure x by the frequency with which it occurs (f), a total is achieved: $\Sigma(fx)$. This can then be divided by the number of days to derive the arithmetic mean.

Bar charts

A bar chart is a way in which numerical information can be represented by bars and blocks and these can be drawn either vertically or horizontally. They enable results to be shown quickly and clearly.

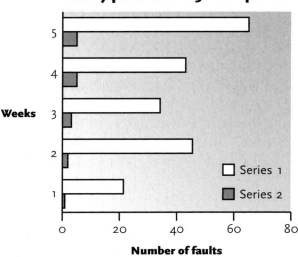

Line graphs

Line graphs are the most common form of graph. The axes on a line graph represent scales, with the independent variable on the horizontal axis and the dependent variable on the vertical axis.

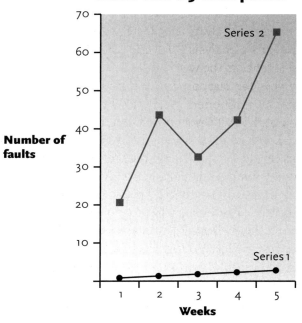

As shown above, one of the advantages that line graphs have over other forms of graphical display is that a number of lines/graphs can be put on the same axis allowing comparisons to be made.

Trends and forecasts

The use of basic statistics enables trends and forecasts to be identified within the context of the research project. These may also provide a focus for the follow-up qualitative research which may draw upon the findings of the quantitative research.

Pie charts

In pie charts the total amount of data is represented by a circle, divided into a number of different segments. To find out the value of each part the formula below is used:

$$\frac{\text{Value of part} \times 360 \text{ degrees}}{\text{Total}}$$

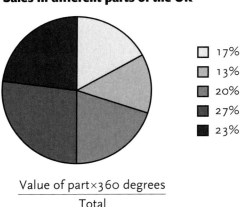

$$\frac{\text{Value of part} \times 360 \text{ degrees}}{\text{Total}}$$

Research and topical articles

Analysing qualitative data

JOURNAL ARTICLE

As qualitative data analysis is very complex, researchers are always looking for ways to simplify data analysis. Maclaran and Catterall (2002) discuss the ways that 'software programs can support qualitative market research practitioners in data analysis and interpretation'. They conducted a survey to identify how the academic and practitioner research communities might work together for mutual benefit. Their survey 'pinpointed analysis methods and interpretation as a significant area where this could be achieved. Commercial practitioners indicated that this was one of the areas where they saw potential for learning from academics, and one where they would like to develop their knowledge of theory as well as practical skills. In this respect the computer analysis of qualitative data was also emphasised by around one-third of the survey respondents. In response to these issues, then, this paper is targeted at qualitative market researchers who have not yet used a CAQDAS (computer-assisted qualitative data analysis software) program and are interested in finding out more about them before they do so.'

Maclaran, P. and Catterall, M. 'Analysing qualitative data: computer software and the market research practitioner', *Qualitative Market Research*, 2002, Vol. 5, No. 1, pp 28–38.

Statistics in practice

JOURNAL ARTICLE

The constructive use of statistics was shown by Smith (1996). His paper discussed the use of library statistics to justify budget increases for public library programmes. It focuses on three major budget areas: staff, collection, and facilities. His paper 'provides guidance on deciding which data are relevant to a specific argument, and identifies internal and external sources of data'. It also 'describes methods of using data to create an effective budget presentation including simple data use techniques and tips for creating more straightforward and effective graphical displays of data'. He shows the various forms of display used.

Smith, M. 'Using statistics to increase library budgets', *The Bottom Line: Managing Library Finances*, 1996, Vol. 9, No.3

Chapter 4

Present and evaluate

Many people who undertake research reports find the prospect of writing it up daunting. They know that as the research project has a major impact upon their marks and their final outcome, it is important to get it right, if they can! It is very easy to talk a good research project, without doing the necessary work to get it completed on time.

According to Bogdan (1982), 'writing is something you must make a conscious decision to do and then discipline yourself to follow through'.

Writing, as we saw in Chapter 3, is and should be part of or built in to the planning process with time allowed for the writing of each part. In fact the writing for a research project should start almost immediately as the project begins. As soon as the student starts reading the literature, he or she should take notes and then write that up in a way that allows it to be edited and themed into some form of literature review.

Writing up a project is so much easier if the student focuses upon the writing process from day 1 of the start of the project. As soon as the student has something tangible on paper, they have materials which can be used for tutorials and from which they can get feedback from their supervisor. It is really helpful for the student if the supervisor contributes to the process by setting them targets and deadlines, for example a timetable of deadlines during the course of the year, when students can bring work to their supervisor for discussion.

Writing the report

Here is a list of helpful ideas to remember when writing up your work.

♦ Begin the writing as soon as the project starts, usually by making notes about the project proposal and justifying the choice and then by looking and reading the literature. As each part of the literature is read it should be written up.

♦ Writing regularly, sometimes weekly, is a good way of making sure the student is on target with deadlines. Even if this means the student goes beyond the word count, it can be trimmed at a later stage.

♦ Continuous consultation with a supervisor, so that work can be seen as and when it is written up, enables the supervisor to provide constant and ongoing feedback that improves the overall outcome. The evidence is that students who regularly consult their supervisors, particularly in the final year of their studies, perform better.

♦ Using the structure suggested on pp 707–8, students should keep writing up and contributing to sections. As the research evolves, it is perfectly possible to come back and make some revisions, particularly if the student has come across some new literature.

♦ Students should write at a time of the day when they feel 'inspired'. This may seem like a strange comment, but some people work better in the morning, while others work better in the evening and some burn the midnight oil and work through the night.

♦ Writing to a routine is important, and it is helpful that others know when the student is working, and so are less likely to be a distraction. One method of working which is often undertaken by final year undergraduates is that of study groups. Often students arrange to meet regularly, perhaps three or four mornings a week, where they work together in the same part of a resource centre. The aim of the study group is not just to provide a regular way of working, but it is also a mechanism that provides students with the ability to support and proofread each other's work.

♦ It is always useful for students to work in a place where distractions are minimised. This can be difficult. In larger universities some students simply just look for the resource rooms that are quieter or more isolated, or places where friends do not go.

♦ Once something is written up it is not finished. In fact this is far from the truth. The materials need to be shown to a tutor so that feedback can be received, and they also need to be evaluated so that they fit in with other materials that have been written.

♦ It is really important for students to think about the audience they are addressing. Denscombe (1998) points out that 'there is no single set of rules and guidelines for writing up research which covers all situations and provides a universally accepted convention'. However, a student's tutors as well as the external examiner will have expectations, and it is important for the student to find out what these are. Something which concerns many individuals is their writing style, and if they have had the same tutors for previous modules, it may be possible to get feedback about their style and find out what are the expectations of their tutors. As students work through higher education the emphasis is more usually on 'how they use their reading', and the extent to which they interpret and discuss their references and use this successfully as a base for analysis and discussion.

♦ Looking at other business research projects is always going to be useful. Even if the projects are not necessarily for foundation degrees, but for undergraduate awards, or even post-graduate awards, looking at previously completed pieces of work can provide the student with a sense of what is required.

Presentation

Often the written format will depend upon the requirements of individual tutors. In the previous chapter we looked at a suggested structure for a report. There is no definitive way of producing such a report and clearly some tutors may have different requirements. For example, some tutors may insist that students put references at the end of every chapter rather than at the end of the work, or that they submit two final versions.

Written format

From the start of your project you will have been told the word count or length of your piece of work. It is important to try to keep to this, and different tutors will have different policies upon the length of research reports. Longer is not necessarily better. It is the quality that counts. However, from the outset, if you have a word limit, it is best to divide up the word count between various parts of the report. For example, if you have been allocated 6000 words, you may allocate 1500 words to the literature review, 600 to the methodology, 1500 to the analysis and so on.

It is important that the student thinks about what they want to get from their research report. In the early stages it is worth thinking about:

♦ what their aims are
♦ how these aims are dealt with in the context of the research question/hypothesis
♦ who is likely to read the report and be doing the marking
♦ what instructions they have been given
♦ what sort of feedback they have been given on previous occasions
♦ what the marker's preferences are and what they consider to be a good research report.

The student should not forget to:

♦ discuss the research question or hypothesis as well as the aims and objectives
♦ link the literature review with the research question or hypothesis in a way that provides a sense of relevance and seamlessness within the context of the report
♦ justify the methodology and show that the methods used are the most appropriate for answering the hypothesis or research question in the chosen context
♦ develop a critical argument that uses both the findings and the literature to support the analysis; this involves bringing everything together for the analysis, in a way that links the primary evidence with the literature
♦ justify the conclusions that are made, again with reference to the literature and the primary research evidence.

The writing style of a student is an extremely important part of a small-scale research project, and is often the most difficult thing for some students to develop. Writing style involves the use of language, the amount of detail that the student goes into, the use and discussion of references and the way in which language is used for analysis. It may also include the quality of analysis, the length of sentences, paragraphs and anything that makes the research report interesting and distinctive to read.

One way for students to think about and try to improve their level of analysis is to look at Bloom's Taxonomy. In 1956 Benjamin Bloom and some colleagues at the University of Chicago identified what became known as Bloom's Taxonomy. The taxonomy is helpful in creating a lens that provides a more precise focus on the 'cogs' that students need to perform at the highest levels. These 'cogs' appear in examination literature and assessment schemes, in a way that illustrates how they have been adapted.

The 'cogs'	Forms of response/cues
Knowledge rote memory, for example of facts, terms, procedures	Making observations, recall, mastery of subject matter, knowledge of all major ideas. **Cues:** list, define, describe, identify, collect, show, label, tabulate, name, quote ...
Comprehension an ability to translate, paraphrase, interpolate, extrapolate	Understanding information, interpretation, translating knowledge into new context, prediction, ordering, grouping, comparing, contrasting. **Cues:** describe, summarise, interpret, predict, distinguish, discuss ...
Application a capacity to transfer and apply knowledge in unfamiliar settings	Use information, methods, concepts, solve problems using knowledge and skills. **Cues:** apply, demonstrate, calculate, illustrate, examine, discover, solve, modify, complete ...
Analysis the ability to break down information into its integral parts and to identify the relationship of each part within a *structure*	Seeing patterns, identification and organisation of parts, recognising hidden meanings. **Cues:** analyse, separate, order, explain, connect, classify, compare, arrange ...
Synthesis the ability to combine existing elements together to create something new	Using old ideas to create new ones, for example business planning, generalising, making connections between knowledge gained from different domains of business. **Cues:** combine, integrate, rearrange, design, plan, formulate, prepare, generalise ...
Evaluation the ability to make judgement about the value of something by comparison with a standard	*Compare and discriminate between ideas* – what the similarities/ differences are *and the basis for such discrimination.* *Assess value of theories and presentations* – desirable, appropriate, good/bad *on the basis of who, what, where, how, why.* *Make choices based on reasoned argument* – What are your premises? What is the precise subject (theme, form of thinking, feeling) of your argument? What is the precise object (thing to which actions, feelings are directed)? Identify strengths/weaknesses of theoretical positions. Recognise sources of opinion/anecdotes and so on. *Verify the value of evidence* – sources of triangulation, authority/ legitimacy of the sources used. **Cues:** assess, decide, rank, grade, convince, judge, explain, recommend ...

Figure 10.6 The cogs of cognition adapted from *Bloom's Taxonomy* (Needham 2003) from Bloom.

The role of the cues in Figure 10.6 is to provide the student with tips about how to improve their level of analysis, so that much of it provides evidence of higher level intellectual skills such as those involved with evaluation.

Developing these higher level skills should not simply involve using long sentences and long words. In fact it is not good practice to use lots of long sentences. Varying sentence length to provide a coherent writing style is instead important. Sentences that are too long can be difficult to understand, and may not make appropriate points. Similarly, long and convoluted words may be misinterpreted and are not always a good indicator of the academic abilities of a candidate. It is more important to make sure that a project is focused upon the research question and hypothesis, and the dialogue is supportive and clearly understood.

Punctuation and spelling are important. There is nothing more annoying than marking a project that has clearly not been spell-checked, or simply comprises what seems to be an endless paragraph.

There are likely to be times during the course of a report when a student has to accept feedback that might not always be complimentary. This might be difficult, but whether formally written or informally provided, sometimes students have to take the criticism and use it to improve their own learning outcomes. Feedback from tutors is really important during the writing process, and the more feedback it is possible to get, the better the potential learning outcomes.

How not to write a research report

There are several pitfalls to avoid in writing up research reports.

Disjointedness

Avoid writing a report that is not seamless. Students should remember that they are answering a question or meeting a hypothesis and so there should be a notion of 'fit' running throughout the report.

Contradiction

Again this relates to the notion of 'fit'. While it is acceptable for the student to identify references that contradict, they can then make fine distinctions about them in relation to the context. However, it is important that the argument that the student puts together does not contradict itself, particularly in a way that shows a limited understanding of the issues.

Generalisation

It is easy to make broad comments, particularly when setting the context, but these have to be justified on the basis of the student's reading.

Unsubstantiation

This is the problem of reaching conclusions without the evidence. Some students seem to know what their report is trying to achieve and what the results are even before the research takes place. They have to remember that this process is investigative, and that surprising results might occur.

Plagiarism and cheating

At this point it is worth saying something about plagiarism. Plagiarism and cheating are serious matters. Students should not submit work which has been copied from others: whether from students, texts or the Internet. The coursework should be their own original work, with attributions for references. Plagiarism panels meet in all colleges, because students, sometimes in desperation, use the Internet to cut and paste parts of articles which are then submitted for marking. Different institutions have different policies about this form of cheating. It has meant that students have been referred, and in some instances are unable to graduate. It is essential that students are aware of the university regulations and guidelines on plagiarism and know how to reference properly so that no inadvertent problems or issues materialise.

Diagrammatic or graphical figures

When presenting diagrams or graphs it is important to present the information in a way that is clear and can be easily understood. If a table is difficult to interpret, then it is important to refer to it within the dialogue in a way that provides the reader with an understanding of what the student is trying to do by using the table figure. It is for this reason that figures and tables or any other diagrammatic form should be given a number and a title.

Viva voce or oral presentation

There are some situations in which students are either asked to give an oral presentation of a project or be asked to attend a viva. A viva, or *viva voce* as it is sometimes known, is an individual oral examination.

Some tutors may, at the end of the research period, ask students to come back and present their findings to other members of their student cohort in a formal way. This is quite common. Other tutors may do this within an informal setting, with students coming back to present their ideas, not using PowerPoint or electronic wizardry, but simply to discuss their findings with the small group of critical friends with whom they have been working.

When presenting research findings formally to students, it helps if the presenter is confident and knows the subject matter so well that they do not have continuously to look down at their notes. PowerPoint does help and can be used as a way of structuring information. Reading from notes is not usually recommended, and is not interesting for those listening. An audience in this context will want to know about the rationale for the project as well as its aims. They may also respond to the motivations that the student has for the project. Being interesting or occasionally showing humour can help and it is important to use eye and body language to help the process go smoothly.

With this sort of project, informal presentations are often best. In an informal setting students can get to grips with the issue and may be asked a series of questions to provide a learning experience for all participants to the process.

The viva can be a nerve-racking experience. If not built into a course, it may simply be used as a random process of checking students' experiences by interviewing a small number through the *viva voce* method. It will usually consist of the supervisor and the external examiner, and sometimes an internal examiner. They will each have a copy of the thesis, and will ask the student-participant to go through various key elements as a way of testing their knowledge and understanding of the processes they have been through.

A few tips for students are:

♦ Run a mock viva beforehand, possibly with family and friends.
♦ Make sure you understand the research project.
♦ Try to understand where the weaknesses and strengths of the study lie, and think about how to respond to any questions about these.
♦ Be measured about providing responses and do not argue with examiners.

Methodology

Working on a research project on their own does not suit all students and some may find it difficult. It is important not just to be organised, but also to be committed to the process of working with a supervisory tutor. Tutors may expect their students to:

♦ bring work to tutorials
♦ look for times of meetings
♦ produce work for meetings, including the submission of a plan
♦ attend meetings regularly
♦ report on their progress.

With any relationship there is a two-way commitment. So, students will also have expectations of their tutors. For example, they will want to know when and where they are available and if meetings are not scheduled, when they can meet. Many tutors provide information about the times of their availability on their office doors, while others may spend a lot of time in their offices, and may always be receptive to an unsolicited knock.

Using technology

There are many different uses of technology within a research project and IT is fundamental to its success. It can also present various problems and create issues that need to be dealt with.

During the course of the research process, by using information and communications technology, the student may collect significant data. Although this can be positive, it can also be problematic as such data might require a significant amount of time transcribing. For example, a 45-minute interview might take several hours to listen to and type up. And this is all before the student has decided how to use the data.

There may be other problems. For example, data may be collected and then saved onto a floppy disk which could become corrupted. This may be a significant issue. There are many examples of students who have lost their work because of corruption or the crashing of a hard disk. It is important to save information in a variety of places, and also to protect themselves; keeping a hard paper copy is essential at all times.

A variety of other technological and visual aids may be used within the data collecting process. These may include voice recorders, cameras and even video cameras, depending upon the various research methods used. Familiarisation and confidence with such technology is essential to ensure that technical issues do not materialise.

Many supervisors today feel hounded by some of the technologies they use. Students frequently send drafts of sections of projects to their tutors or leave messages on voicemail systems. We live in a world that has become increasingly dependent upon technologies, and many tutors may feel that providing on-line help through email is a good way of giving their students formative feedback, which takes away the necessity for students to knock on the doors of their tutors as regularly as they might otherwise.

Recommendations and areas for future research

The key element in any project is how well the project met the research question or hypothesis. Within the conclusions of the project, the researcher should not only comment upon how well the project met the original goals, but also take the opportunity to reflect upon and discuss the effectiveness of the various research methods that have been used.

Processes of research are by their very nature cyclical. As one project finishes, it opens up avenues for other research projects and developments. It is quite possible that the recommendations from one project suggest further research on one or more complementary areas identified within the original study.

Evaluation

In the modern workplace most people at one time or another have to evaluate the work they have undertaken. Evaluation is an important process for any project. In many ways, and in research terms evaluation enables you to ask questions such as:

♦ How good is the piece of work?
♦ What were the issues that influenced its outcome?
♦ Are the research questions or hypotheses being dealth with?

Evaluation in this sense involves asking a series of questions that help you to make judgements about your project based upon your research question or hypothesis and aims for the project. In other words, the process of evaluation involves the student in making judgements about their own learning on a project based upon the thinking about the assumptions made at the start of the project.

In making the evaluation students need to make judgements about the outcomes, the ability to meet their programme of work and the barriers to doing so, the expectations they had for the project and, of course, their own criteria and brief for assessment.

Evaluation also involves students thinking about the advice and help they have had from their tutors and the process of evaluation may involve getting some feedback from others who may be able to comment upon what the student has done.

If a student needs to make an evaluation, perhaps the first thing to do is to read about evaluation as a process. They have to think about what the purpose of the evaluation is and how the evaluation is to be used in relation to their own learning. There are many different types of evaluation and a lot has been written about evaluation within recent years.

A starting point for an evaluation for a student might be to discuss their own motivations for the project and the relationship of their motivations to the outcomes from the project. A key part of the evaluation is, therefore, an understanding of what they have learned from the research process and how that has contributed to their own development.

As you develop your evaluation you will want to discuss any problems, contingencies, issues and other extraneous elements within the project. For example, does the student feel that they had the right title for the study and did the research question or hypothesis provide an appropriate focus? As we have discussed in the research section, getting the right topic for the project is paramount. It is easy for students to come up with ideas before they read the literature and then find it difficult to broach the area.

One area which needs to be evaluated is the use of English. Writing at this level can be difficult and challenging, and part of the process of evaluation would have to consider how well written the research project report is. This may include focusing upon:

- use of grammar
- tenses
- punctuation
- spelling
- the use of referencing
- the structure of the report itself.

Another key element in the evaluation is to think about whether the research question or hypothesis is proved, as well as whether the aims of the report have been met. This may lead to a number of related issues. For example:

- Was the literature supportive?
- Were there gaps in some areas of reading?
- How difficult was it to structure the literature review?
- What range of literature was available?
- What research methods were used?
- Were such methods the most appropriate for this type of project?

- What issues of data collection arose?
- How well was information presented?
- Were the appropriate statistical techniques used?
- Is there any evidence of bias in the report?
- Is the data reliable?
- How good or appropriate were the sampling techniques?
- Are there any limitations to the study as a result of the research methods chosen?

There may be problems, contingencies, issues and other extraneous elements to the project. This may include looking back at the process to think about what might need to be improved if the student was asked to complete the process again. For example, they may look at their action plan and project timings to comment upon whether they were realistic. They may also look at any personal difficulties they had when constructing the project report, and discuss them within the context of their own strengths and weaknesses.

As part of the evaluation it may be possible to test the findings and recommendations upon other people as part of the evaluation process. The person could be a relative, a local business person or even another tutor. Their feedback could be used to help with the evaluation process.

Evaluation also includes evaluating the literature. Within the evaluation the student should use the literature and discuss the effectiveness of the literature as an evaluation base.

And finally, it is important for the student to use the evaluation process to comment upon what effect constructing a research project has had on their own learning.

Criteria

The purpose of a research project is to bring everything that you have learned together, in a way that enables you to apply learning to something that involves your own ideas. It is one of the few occasions within education when you take control of the project yourself. It is both exciting and also potentially very challenging.

The research project should have:

♦ provided the student with the opportunity to test concepts and techniques that the student has learned about within other parts of their programme

♦ linked the student's own knowledge and ideas with existing literature

♦ provided the student with the opportunity to undertake a process of learning of their own choice, possibly focused upon their own career preferences.

Throughout the research process the student has gone through a personal learning experience in which they have been able to develop their own skills, possibly in relation to an organisational context.

Editing and format

As the project draws to a close it is important to trim your project in a way that enables it to meet the course requirements. Your college or university will probably have a series of guidelines and expectations to help you with this. After proofreading the project, the next thing is to think about how it is presented. Again there might be some requirements. For example:

♦ Will it have to be presented in single-line spacing or double-line spacing?

♦ Are there any requirements about margins?

♦ How many copies should be submitted?

♦ How should the project be bound?

♦ What are the other requirements?

Discussion of evidence and findings

As part of the final process and as the student hands the project in and 'puts it to bed', there may be, as suggested earlier in this chapter, an opportunity to discuss the evidence and findings.

References

Anderson, G. and Arsenault, N. (1998) *Fundamentals of Educational Research*, London: Falmer Press.

Bell, J. (1999) *Doing Your Research Project: A guide for first-time researchers in education and social science*, Buckingham: Open University Press.

Blaxter, L., Hughes, C. and Tight, M. (1996) *How to Research*, Buckingham: Open University Press.

Bogdan, R. and Biklen, S. (1982) *Qualitative Research for Education: An Introduction to Theory and Methods*, Boston, MA: Allyn & Bacon.

Brown, S. (1990) *Planning Small-Scale Research*, Edinburgh: SCRE.

Buzan, T. (1993). *The Mind Map Book*, London: Penguin.

Charles, C. (1994) *Introduction to Educational Research*, London: Longman.

Clegg, F. (1990) *Simple Statistics*, Cambridge: Cambridge University Press.

Cohen, L. and Manion, L. (1994) *Research Methods in Education*, London: Routledge.

Denscombe, M. (1998) *The Good Researcher Guide for Small-Scale Social Research Projects*, Buckingham: Open University Press.

Denzin, N. (1970) *The Research Act: A Theoretical Introduction to Sociological Methods*, Thousand Oaks: Sage.

Hussey, J. and Hussey, R. (1997) *Business Research: A Practical Guide for Undergraduate and Postgraduate Students*, Basingstoke: Palgrave.

Jaconowicz, A. (1995) *Business Research Projects*, London: International Thomson Business Press.

Janes, J. (1999) 'Survey construction', *Library Hi Tech*, Vol. 17, No. 3, pp 321–325, London: Emerald Fulltext.

Krueger, R. (1994) *Focus Groups: A Practical Guide for Applied Research*, London: Sage.

Lewis, I. and Munn, A. (1991) *So you Want to do Research? A Guide for Teachers on How to Formulate Research Questions*, Edinburgh: SCRE.

Lewis, D. (1996) 'The organizational culture saga, from OD to TQM: a critical review of the literature', *Leadership and Organization Development Journal*, Vol. 17, No. 2, pp 9–17.

Maclaran, P. and Catterall, M. (2002) 'Analysing qualitative data: computer software and the market research practitioner', *Qualitative Market Research*, Vol. 5, No. 1, pp 28–38.

Marshall, D. (1995) 'Market research methods and Scottish eating habits', *British Food Journal*, Vol. 7, No. 7, pp 28–31.

Mason, D. (1988) 'Gissa project!' *Times Higher Educational Supplement*, 18 March, London: Times Newspapers.

Miles, M. and Huberman, M. (1994) *Qualitative Data Analysis*, Thousand Oaks: Sage.

Mouly, G. (1978) *Education Research: The Art and Science of Investigation*, Boston, MA: Allyn & Bacon.

Needham, D. and Flint, K. (2003) 'Uncovering the truth behind Vygotsky's cognitive apprenticeship: engaging reflective practitioners in the "master–apprentice" relationship', *International Journal of Learning*, Vol. 10.

Needham, D. (2001) 'A case study of case studies: producing real world learning within the business classroom', *Ultibase Journal*, Nov., Melbourne: RMIT.

Smith, M. (1996) 'Using statistics to increase library budgets', *The Bottom Line: Managing Library Finances*, Vol. 9, No. 3, pp 4–13, New York: MCB University Press.

Stake, R. E. (1995) *The Art of Case Study Research*, London: Sage.

Stark, R. (1998) *Practitioner Research: The Purposes of Reviewing the Literature Within an Enquiry*, Edinburgh: SCRE.

Synodinos, N. (2002) 'The "art" of questionnaire construction: some important considerations for manufacturing studies', *Integrated Manufacturing Systems*, Vol. 14, No. 3, pp 221–37.

Torrance, M., Thomas, G. and Robinson, E. (1992) 'The writing experiences of social science research students', *Studies in Higher Education*, Vol. 17, No. 2, pp 155–67.

Verma, G. and Beard, R. (1981) *What is Educational Research? Perspectives on Techniques of Research*, Aldershot: Gower.

Wallace, R. and Mellor, C. (1988) 'Non-response bias in mail accounting surveys: a pedagogical note', *British Accounting Review*, No. 20, pp 131–9.

Wilkinson, D. (2000) *The Researcher's Toolkit: The Complete Guide to Practitioner Research*, London: RoutledgeFalmer.

Yin, R. K. (1994) *Case Study Research: Design and Methods*, London: Sage.

Unit
11

Foundations of law

The aim of this unit is to provide an introduction to the law of contract, with a particular focus on the formation and operation of a business contract. The learner is encouraged to explore the contents of such an agreement and in particular to appreciate the practical application of standard form business contracts. Additionally, the unit enables the learner to understand how the law of tort differs from the law of contract and examines the tort of negligence and issues of liability pertinent to business.

Summary of learning outcomes

On completion of this unit you will be able to:
♦ understand the essential elements of a valid and legally binding contract and its role in a business context
♦ explore the significance of specific terms in a business contract
♦ examine the role of the law of tort in business activities assessing particular forms of tortious liability
♦ understand and apply the elements of the tort of negligence.

Chapter 1

Essential elements of a valid contract and its role in business

Contractual agreements and business

Business activities will only be efficient when business people feel secure that their activity is taking place in an orderly environment in which they have legal protection. For example, a supplier of goods needs to feel secure that they will receive payment, and a buyer of goods needs to rest assured that they will receive some form of compensation if the goods are not of the standard specified. Hence the importance of contracts which are binding on the parties involved and which are enforceable by the courts.

> A **contract** is an agreement between two or more parties (for example, a business and its trading partners in the case of a supply contract), who promise to give and receive something from each other (consideration) and who intend the contract to be legally binding.

Businesses are continually dealing with outsiders, and in doing so enter into relationships which are regarded as contracts in law. For example, in the process of setting up, a business may borrow money from outsiders, and buy buildings, plant and equipment. It will then employ labour and purchase stocks for resale. In the course of time it will make sales and in doing so enter into contracts with customers. Already we have several groups of people with whom contracts have been formed, as shown in Figure 11.1.

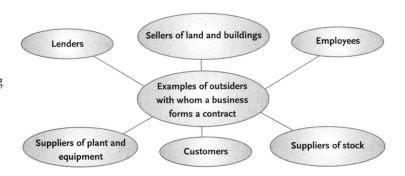

Figure 11.1   Contracts with outsiders

CASE STUDY

Figure 11.2   Manchester United supporters

In the first few years of the twenty-first century Manchester United PLC engaged in an expansion programme designed to establish itself as the premier global football brand. This involved organising a range of business deals. Foremost among these were ground improvement projects including the building of a new training ground. The club also agreed to extend the period during which it was managed by Sir Alex Ferguson. A number of high profile transfer transactions took place, including the sale of David Beckham to Real Madrid, and the purchase of Ruud van Nistelroy. At the same time the club developed links between the brand and a range of other products such as Vodafone which produced a range of Manchester United oriented mobile phones. Major sources of income for the club in the period included revenues from the European Champions League, as well as television rights and sponsorship deals.

ACTIVITY

Using the information provided in the case study, identify eight different individuals or groups with whom Manchester United would have formed contracts during this period, and explain why the forming of contracts is so important to the club.

The legal term **consideration** is used to refer to the promise to give and receive something which is made between the two parties.

Typical business contracts

Business contracts are typically concerned with the following areas.

The supply of goods

The most common form of contract relates to the Sale of Goods. The Sale of Goods Act defines a contract for the sale of goods as, 'A contract by which the seller transfers or agrees to transfer the property in goods to the buyer for a money consideration called the price.' The handing over of money is thus part of the contract.

The supply of work and materials

Another form of contract is for the supply of work and materials, for example when a contractor refits a shop.

The supply of goods on credit

Because today we live in a credit-based economy, there are detailed contractual requirements covering this area.

Contracts of bailment

These relate to situations where the owner of goods (the bailor) entrusts the possession of them to another (the bailee), for example when a solicitor or bank holds important documents for a business.

Employment contracts

Contracts of agency

These are contracts where an organisation or individual employs an agent to work on their behalf when dealing with third parties, for example a sports or pop star may employ an agent.

Contracts concerning land

Financial services contracts

A business uses a range of financial services, for example bank loans and insurance. These all involve contracts such as those relating to details of what might be lawfully claimed from an insurance company in relation to the liability of a company to its employees and customers.

Main types of contract

There are two main types of contract.

Speciality contracts

These are also known as contracts by deed or under seal. Here the contract must be in writing and must be 'signed, sealed and delivered'. Since 1989, the Law of Property Act has done away with the need to 'seal' contracts, and as this form of contract has little relevance to us simply needs to be noted.

Simple contracts

These are far more important and therefore the outlines that follow relate to these contracts. These are informal contracts and can be made in any way: by word of mouth, in writing, or simply implied by a person's conduct. For example, if you bought this book from a bookstore you entered into a contract with the seller, giving you certain rights. For example, if some of the pages are missing you could ask for a replacement.

Legal requirements for contracts

The essential ingredients required for an effective agreement are:

♦ the making of a valid offer and its unconditional acceptance
♦ the existence of a clear and unambiguous intention supported by sufficient consideration
♦ the parties to the agreement possessing the necessary capacity and being privy to the agreement.

Each of these points can now be explained in more detail.

An agreement exists in law when one party accepts another's offer. For example, an offer to sell David Beckham to Real Madrid for a stipulated price, for example £25m.

Figure 11.3   David Beckham signs for Real Madrid

Consideration involves the two parties showing that their agreement is part of a bargain, that is, they each promise to give or do something for the other. For example, Real Madrid make a payment and Real Madrid have Beckham on their playing staff.

The two parties need to **intend** their contract to have legal status. For example, if I promise my wife to cut the grass this morning, we would not see that as a legal contract. However, when Real Madrid promise to pay a set sum for Beckham under agreed terms the intention is to form a legal contract.

In many cases various **formalities (form)** are required such as the completion of legal documents, for the transfer of a football player.

The two parties must be legally **capable (capacity)** of making an agreement. Certain individuals are not regarded to be legally capable because they are too young, too old, too ill, and so on. For example, some football clubs today are seeking to secure the services of footballers as young as 11 years of age – when clearly they are too young to form a legally binding contract.

The agreement has to be entered into freely and involve a meeting of minds rather than being a forced agreement. There has to be **genuineness of consent**. For example, where an individual is threatened or misled about the terms of an agreement then they would not have genuinely consented to the agreement.

The agreement must be a lawful one. There must be **legality**. For example, an agreement made by a laundry worker for Manchester United to sell off a set of club shirts without permission would also be unlawful.

If the above requirements are present then a contract is said to be **valid**. Should essential elements be missing the contract will then be considered void, voidable or unenforceable.

Void, voidable and unenforceable contracts

The notion of a void contract is a contradiction, because if it is void it is not actually a contract. A contract is considered to be **void** if it turns out to be invalid because a mistake has been made and the requirements set out above have not been met. When a contract is declared void then the parties must return (wherever possible) what they have taken from each other, for example goods, money, and so on.

A **voidable** contract is one that can be made void because there has been some form of misrepresentation or because the contract has been made by someone who does not have the capacity to make one (for example, someone who is too ill to make a rational decision). Once again measures should be taken to return goods, money, or whatever to parties who have mistakenly handed them over to someone else.

An **unenforceable** contract is one which is valid but which cannot be enforced in the court because one of the parties refuses to carry out the terms of the contract.

Forming an agreement

An **offer** is a statement of the terms by which the offeror is prepared to be bound. There are three components to an agreement.

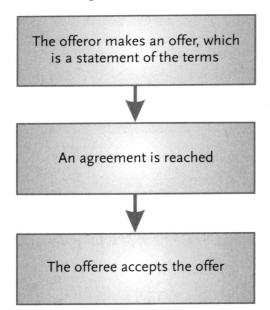

Once these three ingredients come together in an agreement we have a firm basis for a contract.

CASE STUDY

The importance of case law

Much of contract law is based on past case laws, that is, on judgements that have been made over time. It is therefore important to examine relevant case examples.

Making an offer is both a proposal and a promise to comply with the stated terms. One of the best-known early cases in contract law which is relevant to many business agreements is Carlill *v* Carbolic Smoke Ball Co. (1893).

The defendants, the Carbolic Smoke Ball Company, placed advertisements in newspapers stating that they would pay £100 to anybody who caught flu after using one of their smoke balls in the way directed for 14 days. In the adverts they also stated that they had deposited £1000 with the Alliance Bank to meet any possible claims.

A Mrs Carlill bought one of the smoke balls and used it in the way outlined but still caught the flu. When she tried to claim the £100 she was turned down, and therefore sued the company.

In the court case the defendants claimed that they had attempted to contract with the whole world and that would be impossible. However, the judge held that they had indeed made an offer to the whole world and therefore should be liable to anyone who caught the flu after using their product as set out. Mrs Carlill was able to recover £100. The case highlights the way in which the law recognises offers that have been made to individuals, groups or to the whole world.

ACTIVITY

1 Why had the Carbolic Smoke Bomb Company formed a contract with Mrs Carlill?

2 Do you agree with the judgement?

'Invitation to treat'

When a business organisation makes an offer to sell something it is not always bound in law to accept the first offer made. We use the term **invitation to treat** to describe a situation where an individual or organisation holds themselves open to offers which they can then accept or reject.

For example, when a company publishes a prospectus inviting people to apply for shares, this is an offer to treat: it can choose to whom it allocates shares. Similarly, when a mail order company publishes a catalogue advertising goods and stating the terms this is an offer to treat. In advertising goods it is very important for a company to get the wording right so that it is clear which is the case.

In an important case, Pharmaceutical Society of Great Britain *v* Boots Cash Chemists Ltd (1953), the Court of Appeal decided that a customer makes an offer when goods are presented for payment at the cash till, and acceptance takes place when the cashier accepts the money (the implication is that the cashier could reject the offer).

What constitutes acceptance of an offer?

Acceptance must take place while an offer is still open, and involve full acceptance.

Case law has established the following rules of acceptance. (Note that the term case law refers to what is termed **judicial precedent**: that is, previous judgements that have been made in the law courts.)

1   Acceptance can only be made by the person to whom the offer is made. For example, if a mail order company offers a discount to a regular customer, then this offer is not being made to other non-regular customers.

2   Acceptance must be absolute and unqualified. The offeree can not add extra terms and conditions (that requires a new offer). Altering the terms and conditions is referred to as a counter offer. It would then be up to the offeror to make a new offer and have it accepted for acceptance to be absolute and unqualified.

3   Acceptance has to be communicated to the offeror. Typically this will be through word of mouth or written communication (including electronic means). However, the court may deem that the acceptance is implied by the conduct of the acceptor.

4   Acceptance must be in the mode set out in the offer. For example, an advertisement might ask for an order to be made in writing.

Capacity to contract

The law places restrictions on who is able to make contracts. The purpose of restricting the ability to contract is to protect the individuals concerned. For example, there are restrictions on the ability of minors (people aged under 18) and those suffering a mental disorder from entering into contracts. Mental disorders relate both to those who are mentally ill and those temporarily disordered through drink or drugs, who can avoid contracts entered into while they were unaware of events if it can be shown that the other party knew of the incapacity.

Minors

Of course, minors enter into contracts every day of the week, for example buying sweets, DVDs and traveling on the bus. They are allowed to enter into contracts but are protected from certain types of contract. For example, a minor can be bound in a contract for necessaries (that is, food, shelter, clothing and education).

> Necessaries are defined as 'goods suitable to the condition in life of such a minor, and his actual requirements at the time of sale and delivery'.

It must be shown that the goods are necessaries. In a famous case, Nash *v* Inman (1908), where an undergraduate student built up a debt for clothing, the court held that the contract was not binding in a contract for clothing. The undergraduate had bought among other things 11 fancy waistcoats which were deemed not to be necessaries.

Contracts concerning minors can therefore be judged as:

◆ binding contracts: where the minor must comply with the contract
◆ voidable contracts: where the minor is not bound but the other party is.

In the case of Nash *v* Inman the undergraduate was expected to return the waistcoats.

People with mental disorders

In the case of mental patients, contracts made during periods in which they are lucid are regarded as binding.

Intention to be legally bound

In addition to individuals engaging in contracts having the capacity to contract, it is also a necessary requirement for a contract for the parties to have the intention of being legally bound.

Commercial agreements are regarded to be legally binding and are assumed to be intended to create legal relations. However, if in the wording to such an agreement it is stated 'this is not intended to be a legal agreement' then in law this is not regarded as being intended to create legal arrangements.

What is meant by consideration?

Consideration is the process of exchange in a bargain: one party agrees to do one thing for the other and this benefit is reciprocated. An example of a simple exchange involves paying money to a shopkeeper to receive goods.

A good way of thinking about consideration from the point of view of the parties concerned is that it is what they expect to get out of a bargain that they have entered into. If they do not get this consideration then they might want to take the case to the courts.

Chapter 2

Specific terms in a business contract

Contents of a valid contract

We have seen that there are a number of ingredients of a valid contract, that is:

♦ agreement
♦ consideration
♦ intention
♦ capacity
♦ legality
♦ genuineness of consent
♦ form.

In law a court action cannot arise from an illegal act. So if a contract requires one or both parties to do something illegal then it is not a lawful contract.

Illegal contracts

A contract is considered to be illegal if:

♦ it involves an act that directly breaks the law; for example, I make a contract with you to buy stolen property from you
♦ it involves an act that is harmful to public policy.

Where a contract is illegal it will be considered void right from the start and will thus be unenforceable.

Regular contracts lacking consent

A contract which is regular in all ways may still not be regarded to be valid because there is no real consent to it by one or both of the parties. There is no *consensus ad idem* or meeting of the minds. Consent may be rendered unreal by mistake, misrepresentation, or duress and undue influence.

Mistake

Mistake does not generally make a contract unavoidable unless a real agreement between the parties was never formed. In an interesting case, Raffles *v* Wichelhaus (1864), the buyer had agreed to purchase cotton sailing on the *SS Peerless* from Bombay. However, what neither of the parties to the contract knew was that there were two ships called *SS Peerless* sailing in different months. The buyer thought that he had bought cotton sailing on the first ship, whereas the seller thought he had sold cotton on the second ship. Because of this mistake the contract was not upheld.

If a party to a contract knows all the relevant facts then his or her bad judgement is not considered to be a mistake.

Misrepresentation

The term misrepresentation is used to describe a situation in which there is no genuineness of consent to a contract by one of the parties. A misrepresentation is a false statement of facts or past events. The effect on the contract is less serious because the contract becomes voidable rather than void. The injured party can then ask the court to put them back in the position they were in before the contract was made.

In law, misrepresentation must be distinguished from manufacturers' and sellers' boasts or 'puffs'. Today we use the term 'hype' to describe what is quaintly termed a 'puff'. There are three main types of misrepresentation.

Fraud

This is where a false statement is made:

♦ knowingly
♦ without belief in its truth
♦ recklessly, not caring whether true or false.

Innocent

This is where a false statement was made unknowingly.

Negligent

This is where a false statement is made where the maker did not have reasonable grounds for believing the statement to be true.

The legal concept of **duress** means actual violence or threats of violence to the person or the contracting party or those near and dear to him or her. In some cases the courts judge that duress makes a contract voidable whereas in others that it makes a contract void.

The legal concept of **undue influence** deals with contracts or gifts obtained without free consent by the influence of one mind over another.

Standard form business contracts

Businesses set out precisely and in detail the terms applying to a contract. This is typically done in a standard form contract. This is a printed document made up of a uniform set of terms for use by an organisation as the basis on which it trades. Using one:

♦ saves a great deal of time in the preparation of contracts
♦ advantages the organisation, by being set out in terms that favour the organisation.

The law seeks to make sure that standard form contracts do not unduly disadvantage one of the parties. For example, there are restrictions on the sort of standard form contract with which you will be familiar in taking out a credit agreement.

ACTIVITY

Study the section of a credit agreement below.

1   What benefits are there to the store in setting out standard terms?

2   How is the store likely to skew these terms in its favour?

3   What is the importance of the Consumer Credit Act in this context?

4   Study a standard form contract for the Sale of Goods and indicate ways in which it favours the seller.

Here is your Clothing Store Account Card, you can use it at any or our branches.

This credit agreement is regulated by the Consumer Credit Act, 1974.

This is a copy of your agreement for you to keep. It includes a notice about your cancellation rights which you should read.

We will determine your credit limit from time to time and give you notice of it.

Interest will be charged on the account at the rate of x% per month.

The minimum payment due from you each month will be the greater of £4 or 4 per cent of the outstanding balance of the account.

(There then follows a list of standard terms such as the credit limit and repayment conditions.)

Express and implied terms

In cases involving contracts it is necessary to consider what was said by the parties concerned and the extent to which this can be considered a contract.

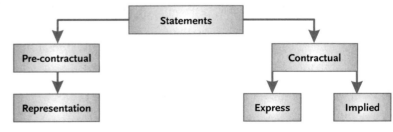

Figure 11.4   The status of different types of statements

Prior to a contract being made, **representations** will be made of various facts and information that are relevant to a contract. If these are false then misrepresentation will have occurred as discussed earlier. In the creation of the contract itself various terms will be specified and these can be broken down into two main types: express and implied terms.

The courts will seek to implement the intentions of the contracting parties as they appear from the statements that they make.

When the statement is such that a party to the contract would not have made the contract without it, then it should be considered a **term** of the statement.

The **express terms** of a contract involve what was said or written in relation to what each of the parties to a contract intend to do in order to undertake their part of the contact.

In any contract, some of the terms are going to be more important to the overall contract than others. The law therefore distinguishes several kinds of terms.

Conditions

Conditions are the fundamental obligations set out in the contract.

Warranties

Warranties are less important (subsidiary) obligations. A failure to perform these does not undermine the roots of the contract. Note that this use of the term warranty is different from the more familiar one of a guarantee.

Innominate terms

Innominate terms (the term with no names) is a category that was invented in 1962 to refer to terms which lie somewhere between conditions and warranties in some contracts; that is, their significance depends on interpretation. In deciding whether or not a breach of an innominate term enables the injured party to terminate the contract, the court look at the effect of the breach. If the injured party substantially loses the benefit of the contract, he or she can treat the contract as repudiated and claim damages.

If they do not substantially lose the contract's benefit then they can only claim damages.

In addition to the express terms set out by the parties, a contract may also contain and be subject to **implied terms**. These terms arise from custom or legal statute, and in addition implied terms may be implied by the court to achieve what the court views as the original intentions of the parties. For example, if by custom and practice a firm has typically received goods of a given quality standard from its supplier, it would be assumed that a new contract to supply, say, football shirts would also imply a similar level of quality.

In addition to customary terms, a judge may also imply a term into a contract because he or she sees it as enabling the express terms of the contract to meet the original intentions of the parties.

Finally, the implied terms of a contract are assumed to be those that comply with the law even though these may not be stated in a written or oral contract.

To take the example of contracts of employment, the courts apply a number of tests in deciding whether a term is implied in a contract. They ask whether it is:

♦ necessary to the functioning of the contract
♦ reflecting the obvious intention of the parties at the time the contract was concluded
♦ an inevitable incidence of the employment relationship.

The breach of a condition, warranty or an implied (innominate) term

The breach of a condition allows an injured party to treat a contract as repudiated and claim damages, whereas this is not the case for warranties. Typically the court looks back at the time when the contract was made and considers whether the parties would consider a term to be a condition or a warranty.

There are four main ways in which a contract can be discharged (terminated), shown in Figure 11.5.

Figure 11.5   Ways of discharging a contract

By agreement

In creating an agreement the parties may agree a point at which it will be terminated. For example, a Premier League player is contracted to play for a club for a two-year period. Generally, in such a contract there would be terms allowing termination by notice. There are usually statutory requirements relating to the amount of notice that should be given.

A contract can also be terminated by the creation of a new agreement, which must include consideration. If neither party has yet kept their side of the original agreement then this is easy, because the consideration is the fact that each of the parties waives their rights. However, if only one party has not kept their side of the agreement, then typically they will have to provide fresh consideration.

By performance

Performance involves parties to the contract performing their part of the bargain, for example to supply materials and be paid for them.

There are varying levels of performance that are acceptable to the court:

♦ Complete performance: where every term and warranty has been discharged.

♦ Substantial performance: where the court is of the opinion that the contract is substantially performed it may allow one or both parties to make recovery for minor details not fully completed. For substantial performance to be discharged the court would make a distinction between conditions and warranties, with the conditions needing to be discharged for substantial performance.

♦ Acceptance of partial performance: if a party accepts an element of partial performance, for example paying for 100 books when 200 have been ordered, they will only be able to make a claim on the further 100 undelivered books.

Frustration

If it is impossible to perform a contract from the outset then it is void; for example, if a bookseller agreed to supply a book but then found that it was no longer available from the publisher, or if a farmer agreed to sell a crop that was destroyed by weather conditions.

Breach of contract

Breach occurs when a party to the contract fails to discharge their part of the contract lawfully. Breach typically fits into two categories: anticipatory and actual breach.

Anticipatory breach takes place when breach occurs before the time for performance to arrive. The wronged party can immediately sue for damages or wait until the time when the performance is expected to occur.

Actual breach involves breach in the performance of the contractual terms. It is necessary for an innocent party to show that the breach affects a vital part of the contract, that is, a condition rather than a warranty.

Exclusion clauses

We now look at the legal effect on the agreement of the incorporation of an exclusion clause.

Exclusion clauses often present one of the nastier sides of contract law and are usually presented in the small print of a contract. They come into play when someone who believes that they have a contract of a certain nature suddenly finds there are various exclusion clauses that appear to exclude the other party from meeting the contract in the way expected.

Although exclusion clauses are allowed, both the courts and parliament are reluctant to allow exclusion clauses to operate where they are imposed on a weaker party such as an ordinary consumer, by a stronger party such as a large high street discount store.

Typically the courts will protect the consumer by:

◆ stating that the exclusion clauses were not part of the contract
◆ interpreting the contract so as to prevent the application of the exclusion clause or clauses.

CASE STUDY

Andrews Bros Ltd *v* Singer and Co. Ltd (1934)

The claimants in this case had agreed to buy supposedly new Singer cars. The cars they received were not new. The Sale of Goods Act states that goods must meet the descriptions given. On the basis of this the claimants sought compensation. However, the defendants pointed to an exclusion clause which stated 'All conditions, warranties and liabilities implied by statute, common law or otherwise are excluded.'

The court held that the exclusion clause did not apply. It was an express term that the cars should be new.

ACTIVITY

1 What is your view of the decision made by the court?

2 Can you think of parallel situations where organisations seek to use exclusion clauses?

3 How are these exclusion clauses likely to be viewed by the courts?

Key features of the law relating to exclusion clauses

1 The party seeking to enforce the exclusion clause will need to show that the other party agreed to the clause when the contract was made.

2 If the clause is part of a written document, then the signer is usually bound to what they have signed even if they have not read it, unless misrepresentation took place.

3 If the clause is not part of a written document then the person seeking to rely on the exclusion clause will need to be able to show that attention had been drawn to the clause.

4 Any attempt to introduce an exclusion clause after a contract has been made is ineffective because the consideration for the clause is in the past.

5 An exclusion clause may be made ineffective by an inconsistent oral promise. For example, if one thing is written in the small print of a contract, and another understanding is communicated orally then the small print is not held as being an acceptable exclusion.

6 If there is ambiguity or reason for doubt about the meaning of an exclusion clause, the courts will view it in a way that is unfavourable to the party that drew up the exclusion clause.

7 What is known as the 'repugnancy rule' sets out that if the exclusion clause is in direct contradiction to the purposes of the contract then the clause can be struck out.

8 If a party to a contract does something which is fundamentally against what they have been contracted to do then an exclusion clause will not protect them.

Chapter 3

The law of tort and business

This chapter deals with the law of tort as it relates to business activities, and with particular forms of tortious liability.

Fundamental aspects of tort

The two main branches of law in this country are:

♦ criminal law: dealing with cases where the law of the land has been broken, that is, criminal offences
♦ civil law: dealing with disputes between individuals and groups, for example between one business and another.

Criminal cases are tried in the criminal courts whereas civil disputes are dealt with by the civil courts such as the small claims and county courts.

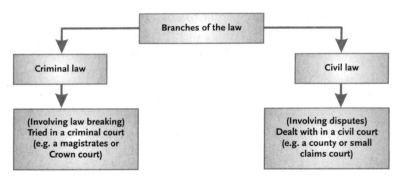

Figure 11.6   Branches of the law

In practice it is difficult to define a tort but a good way of thinking about a tort is that it involves a civil wrong other than a breach of contract. A tort is a duty fixed by law which affects everyone. There are all sorts of torts, including wrongs such as trespassing on someone's land, defamation of character and nuisance. The purpose of **taking action in tort** is to obtain compensation.

The most common form of civil case involving businesses and the law of tort is **negligence**, which is dealt with in Chapter 4 of this unit. Other types

of tort with a significant impact for business are those relating to the Consumer Protection Act of 1987 and private nuisance, where liability arises under the Occupier's Liability Acts of 1957 and 1984.

In examining a tort the law courts are concerned with what was done rather than why it was done. The key is that if someone's rights are infringed then they may be entitled to compensation. It should be obvious that a particular event or action might involve a crime, a breach of contract and a tort. For example, I have a contract with a supplier to supply me with new components. The supplier breaks into my premises to steal used components which they then sell on to me as new. They have:

♦ broken the contract
♦ trespassed on my property
♦ stolen from my company.

Tortious liability and business operations

Whereas contracts are entered into voluntarily by the two parties concerned, in the case of a tort responsibility is not voluntary. For example, a company has a responsibility to ensure that its premises are safe. This is a responsibility of the company. Failure to keep safe premises which causes injury is likely to result in the injured party seeking compensation.

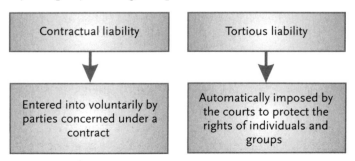

Figure 11.7   Contractual and tortious liability

740

In a similar way, if I injure a pedestrian when driving my car, then the pedestrian will seek compensation by taking legal action. I have no choice about accepting liability because the courts will automatically impose it on me.

The remedy for breaking a contract or for tortious liability are the same, that is, both involve liability for damages. However, the purpose of **contractual damages** is to put the injured party back into the position which would arise if the contract had been successfully fulfilled. In contrast, the purpose of **damages under tort** is to put the injured party back in the position that they were in before the tort was committed.

A person affected by a tort will often also seek an injunction against the person committing the tort. The purpose of the injunction is to prevent or restrain the other party from committing the tort, or receive a penalty of a fine or an imprisonment.

Advantages of using tortious remedies

Although many civil disputes involving businesses are of a contractual nature, more and more cases are going through the English courts which involve tortious liability. By pursuing the torts route business organisations are able to insist on their rights being met, with the advantage that the emphasis is on putting them back in the position they would have been in before the tort was committed.

Taking the contractual route to receive remedies involves studying the fine print of a contract, involving a lot of legal work, particularly when important aspects have not been clearly set out in the contract; whereas tortious remedies are based on elaborate case law involving similar cases over time.

Types of tortious liability

There are a number of types of tortious liability that are particularly important in business law.

The tortious liability of occupiers

Occupiers of business property have a responsibility under the Occupiers Liability Act 1957 to make sure of the safety of lawful entrants to business premises and under the Occupiers Liability Act 1984 to apply the same principle of taking reasonable care for uninvited visitors.

The occupier has the common duty of care to these visitors which involves taking care in all circumstances where it is reasonable to provide for their safety.

The duty is owed by the occupier, that is, the person in control of the premises at the time who may be a tenant or licencee. However, frequently there is a joint responsibility between the landlord and the tenants for premises, for example in a block of offices the landlord may have responsibility for common areas such as the lifts, stairs, forecourt, and so on.

CASE STUDY

O'Connor v Swan & Edgar (1963)

In this case the plaintiff (the party seeking compensation) was injured by plaster which fell on her while she was working as a demonstrator on the first defendants' premises. However, the tort occurred because of the work carried out by the second defendants who were contractors working on the premises at the time. The court decided that the first defendant had performed their reasonable duty of care by making sure that they employed reputable contractors. The court placed the liability for the damages on the second defendants.

ACTIVITY

1   Why do you think that the first defendants were not held liable for this tort?

2   Under what circumstances in your view might a business premises owner be held liable for a similar accident?

The 1957 Act sets out that children are likely to be less careful on business premises so that the duty of reasonable care is more extensive with regard to children, so premises need to be more carefully 'child proofed'.

Organisations must also take care to protect unwanted visitors such as trespassers against harm. For example, in the case of Adams *v* Southern Electricity Board, the court ruled that the Board owed a duty of care to a fifteen-year-old who had climbed a pole-mounted high voltage electrical installation. The Board had fitted an anti-climbing device but it was not properly operational at the time.

Employer's liability

The Employer's Liability (Compulsory Insurance) Act 1969 makes it compulsory for every employer to insure against liability for injury or disease incurred by their employees and arising in the course of their employment.

Employers have a general duty to take care of their employees. People employed under a contract of employment, or a 'contract of service', are employees. (Note that employers are typically not responsible for the torts of contractors.)

Over the years the courts have developed a number of tests to ascertain whether an individual can be regarded to be an employee or a contractor. One of the early tests used was the 'control test', that is, whether an individual could be told what to do and how to do it. This did not work particularly well so in the 1950s an 'integration test' was applied, whereby an employee was seen as someone whose work could be regarded as an 'integral part of the business'.

In 1968 the 'economic reality test' was applied which held that someone would be an employee if three conditions are satisfied:

♦ the employee provides their work and skill in return for a wage or other payment
♦ the worker must agree that he or she is under the control of the person providing the employment
♦ the contract must be consistent with a contract of employment.

Discussion about the nature of the term 'employee' has continued and has been clouded by the development of new types of flexible, casual and part-time employees in the modern economy.

The term **vicarious liability** is used when a person is liable for the torts of another and is most commonly found in relation to employer's liability.

The thinking behind vicarious liability is:

♦ to make sure that employers develop safe working systems
♦ to prevent employers taking on employees to commit torts on their behalf, and
♦ because employers will be better placed to pay compensation than their employees.

Vicarious liability exists even when the employee carries out an action that they have been expressly told not to do by their employer. However, if the employee leaves his or her duty and carries out a 'frolic on his own' then the employer is not liable; for example, a sales rep who is supposed to be visiting customers in Luton, who crashes his company car on a trip to a pop concert in Paris.

All that must be proved for vicarious liability is that:

♦ an actionable wrong was committed by the employee
♦ the worker is an employee
♦ the wrongful act occurred during the course of the employee's employment.

ACTIVITY

In which of the following situations would vicarious liability apply?

1   An employee of a boat-building firm takes a company boat at the weekend for a harbour trip causing damage to another vessel.

2   A friend of a car salesman steals a set of car keys belonging to the salesman and knocks down a pedestrian in one of the company's cars.

3   A night porter of a hotel inadvertently backs a customer's car that he has been asked to park into another vehicle.

4 While driving a lorry between Blackpool and Manchester one of the company's lorry drivers causes an accident involving another vehicle.

5 An individual is due to start work for a company on 13 August. He decides to have a look round the premises on 12 August and gives instructions to a customer which leads to the customer having a fall.

Health and safety issues

Health and safety is an important area of employer (and employee) responsibility. Health and safety regulations were set out in 1992 in a series of measures known as the 'six pack'. These regulations set out the general duties that employers have to their employees and members of the public, as well as obligations that employees have to each other.

The Management of Health and Safety Regulations 1997 set out clearly what managers have to do in relation to every work activity.

The main requirements of health and safety regulations in this country are that:

- every employer with five or more employees must carry out a risk assessment
- the employer must then take health and safety measures in line with the risk assessment
- the employer must appoint competent people to help carry out the health and safety arrangements
- employers must set up emergency procedures
- employers must provide clear information and training to employees.

The safety policy must be in writing and set out who is responsible for workplace health and safety and the arrangements that have been made for health and safety. This policy must also be communicated to everyone in the workplace.

Safety in the workplace is not just a management responsibility. It is also up to employees to take steps to ensure their own – and other people's – health and safety. In particular, employees must:

- comply with company arrangements and procedures for securing a safe workplace
- report incidents to management that have led, or may lead, to injury
- co-operate in the investigation of accidents in order to prevent them happening again.

Strict liability and its application

Business organisations (and individuals) are typically liable in tort when they carry out an intentional act (such as trespass) or behave negligently. However, there are other cases where the business acts neither intentionally nor negligently. In these situations the law has imposed a strict limit on the organisation's or person's activities. If this limit is exceeded the defendant is **strictly** or **absolutely liable**. A good example of a law involving strict liability is the Consumer Protection Act 1987 which creates strict liability for producers of defective goods which cause damage to an individual or to property.

Business organisations are liable if they can be shown to have committed a crime. This principle applies to a range of torts ranging from failure to apply health and safety regulations to failure to provide safe goods under the Consumer Protection Act.

To get a better understanding of how tortious liability operates in relation to the Consumer Protection Act, it is helpful first to develop a picture of the nature of criminal liability in relation to consumer protection. However, remember that while this next section outlines the nature of criminal offences such as false trade descriptions, our overall concern is with developing an understanding of the nature of torts.

Tortious liability and consumer protection

Criminal offences are made up of two elements:

> - an *actus rea* or guilty act
> - *mens rea* or guilty mind. The *mens rea* element is concerned with an individual deliberately seeking or intending to carry out the act. In a law court the prosecution needs to prove both the *actus rea* and the *mens rea* beyond a reasonable doubt. The *actus rea* of the crime and the *mens rea* must be proved to have taken place at the same time.

In recent years we have seen the development of detailed sets of laws and regulations designed to protect buyers, including consumers. This is not surprising because trading is such an essential part of business activity.

Trading law

Law relating to trading activity has created a range of legal devices including:

- the regulation of trading activity such as the licensing of consumer credit provision and registration under the Data Protection Act
- creating legal remedies which are available through legal action through the courts, for example under the Sale of Goods Act
- establishing criminal liability for certain unacceptable trading activities, for example under the Consumer Protection Act and the Trades Descriptions Act.

The Sale of Goods Act 1979 (amended by the Sale and Supply of Goods Act 1994) illustrates the principle of tortious liability. These two Acts provide an important framework of protection for consumers of goods and services. These requirements relate to any sort of trader (shop, street market, mail order, or door-to-door salesperson) and any goods you buy from these traders should meet three basic requirements:

- 'of satisfactory quality': that is, free from significant faults

- 'fit for the purpose': including any particular purpose mentioned by the customer to the seller
- 'as described': that is, on the package or sales literature, or verbally by the seller.

If there is something wrong with a good or service the buyer should tell the seller as soon as possible. Taking faulty goods back straight away should entitle the buyer to getting their money back. They have not legally 'accepted' the goods, and this means they can 'reject' them.

The Sale of Goods Act is based on the assumption that there are a number of implied terms involved 'where the seller sells goods in the course of their business'. For example, there is an implied condition that the goods supplied under the contract are of a satisfactory quality and are fit for the purpose.

CASE STUDY

Fitness of purpose in terms of Jewson Ltd *v* Kelly (2002)

In this case, the claimant ('Jewson') brought an action for £55,322.43 for the sale and delivery of 12 electric boilers supplied to the defendant. The defendant argued that the boilers were not fit for the particular purpose for which Jewson knew that they were required and counterclaimed for the substantial losses he claimed to have suffered as a result.

Kelly argued that the boilers had a very low SAP rating (a rating which gives guidance on the energy efficiency of the heating system in a domestic property).

The court concluded that an unacceptable SAP rating would substantially increase the risk that a proposed sale of a property would be delayed significantly or even abandoned. Although there was no intrinsic defect in the boilers, the Court concluded that they were not of satisfactory quality.

A new piece of consumer legislation took effect from March 2003 (The Sale and Supply of Goods to Consumers Regulations). This sets out that for the first six months after purchase or delivery, the burden of proof when reporting faulty goods is reversed in the consumer's favour. The regulations therefore insert a new rule into the Sale of Goods Act. This states that where goods sold to a consumer do not conform to the contract of sale 'at any time within the period of six months starting with the date on which the goods were delivered to the buyer', they must be taken not to have so conformed at that date.

The Consumer Protection Act 1987 protects consumers against defective goods, including goods within the Sale of Goods Act, and a range of other goods such as crops and intangible goods such as electricity supply as well as components. The Act provides for liability for damage if goods do not meet the required standards and cause harm to people.

The Act is designed to encourage producers to supply safe goods which are free from defects and gives consumers the right to seek remedies when producers fail in this duty.

The case that the plaintiff must present is that:

♦ the product contained the stated defect
♦ the plaintiff suffered damage as a result
♦ the product caused the damage
♦ the defendant was the producer of the good.

Parliament has created a number of crimes of strict liability in which the prosecution do not need to prove the *mens rea* in relation to one or more elements of the *actus rea*.

An example of strict liability relates to elements of the Trades Descriptions Act 1968. Here it is an offence to apply a false trade description to goods (and services). It is also an offence to supply goods to which a false description has been applied. Both of these offences are crimes of strict liability. They can only be carried out by people acting in the course of a trade or business, for example someone who sells used cars for a living, and adjusts the milometer on these vehicles to make them appear newer than they are.

In cases like these it is possible to defend by arguing that, for example, it is a one-off mistake, or that the activity carried out by the business for which the description is applied is not typically part of normal business activities for that company.

Chapter 4

Elements of negligence

Negligence

Negligence takes place when a person or organisation fails to live up to the standard of care expected of them in law, and someone else is injured as a result.

There are three aspects which typically the plaintiff must prove:

♦ the defendant owed him or her a duty of care
♦ that the defendant acted in breach of that duty, and
♦ as a result the plaintiff suffered.

Liability in relation to the **tort of negligence** arises when foreseeable damage to the plaintiff is caused by the defendant failing to uphold their legal duty to take care. Negligence applies to all sorts of situations, including losses as a result of injuries at work, in dangerous premises, defective products and professional malpractice.

The nature and scope of the duty of care

Liability in negligence cases is fault based, that is, it is dependant on the plaintiff showing that the defendant failed to take proper care.

One of the groundbreaking cases in developing case law about the duty of care was Donoghue *v* Stevenson (1932). Mrs May Donoghue drank some ginger beer, purchased for her by a friend in an ice-cream parlour. The bottle was opaque so that she could not see inside it. In the bottle was a decomposing snail. As she had not bought the bottle herself she had not entered into a contract with the seller. So she sued the manufacturer for negligence.

The case was eventually tried in the House of Lords, which at the time was the highest court. The judgement was in terms of the responsibility to look after our neighbours: we have a duty of care for them. In this case neighbours does not relate to the person who lives next door but more generally to the person or people who the defendant should have been concerned with protecting. Lord Atkin decreed, 'The rule that you are to love your neighbour becomes in law, you must not injure your neighbour, and the lawyers' question, "Who is my neighbour?" receives a restricted reply. You must take reasonable care to avoid acts or omissions which you can reasonably foresee would be likely to injure your neighbour. Who, then in law, is my neighbour? The answer seems to be: persons who are so closely and directly affected by my act that I ought reasonably to have them in contemplation as being so affected when I am directing my mind to the acts or omissions which are called in question.'

CASE STUDY

Duty of care

In another case, Home Office *v* Dorset Yacht Co. (1970), the plaintiff's yacht was damaged by a group of youth offenders who escaped from their guards on a training exercise. It was shown that they were carelessly supervised by their guards, and that the offenders might reasonably be expected to steal the yacht as a means of escape from an island to the mainland. The defendant (the Home Office) was held to be vicariously liable for its employees' responsibility to supervise the young offenders. In the judgement on this case it was stated that 'I think that the time has come when we can and should say that it (the statement of principle in the Donoghue *v* Stevenson case) ought to apply unless there is some justification or valid explanation for its exclusion.'

Establishing a duty of care

More recently the concept of 'duty of care' has been refined. There is now a three-stage approach to establishing a duty of care:

♦ Was the harm caused reasonably foreseeable?
♦ Was there a relationship of proximity between the defendant and the plaintiff?
♦ In all the circumstances is it just, fair and reasonable to impose a duty of care?

Breach of duty and standard of care

The **duty of care** is broken when a person or organisation fails to do what a reasonable person would do in the same situation.

This is clearly set out in the judgement in Blyth *v* Birmingham Waterworks Co. (1856). 'Negligence (in the sense of a breach of duty) is the omission to do something which a reasonable man, guided upon those considerations which ordinarily regulate the conduct of human affairs, would do, or something which a reasonable and prudent man would not do.'

Of course, breach of duty depends on the 'standard of care' that would be expected in a given situation. For example, we would expect a trained teacher to employ a much higher and more professional standard of care in the classroom than a novice on their first day of teaching practice. A brain surgeon would be expected to employ the skills and expertise that results from years of training, whereas a hospital porter would not be expected to have more than basic skills.

However, individuals are expected to display the standard of care required to meet the standard of care expected of them in a specific context, for example, a hospital porter would be expected to handle with extreme care any patient who had recently undergone an operation.

In judging whether the duty of care has been met the courts must decide whether the behaviour of the individual concerned is reasonable or unreasonable. Key considerations in judging whether breach has taken place or not are:

♦ the extent of the risk resulting from the defendant's behaviour: whether the risk is obvious and serious
♦ the nature of harm caused to the plaintiff
♦ the ease and expense of taking steps to minimise the risk
♦ the individual circumstances of the case.

In a well-known case, Bolton *v* Stone (1951), the plaintiff was struck by a cricket ball that had been knocked out of a cricket ground. The ground was surrounded by a 17-foot-high perimeter fence. There was very little history of a ball being hit out of the ground before. The judgement was that, 'The standard of care in the law of negligence is the standard of an ordinarily careful man, but in my opinion an ordinarily careful man does not take precautions against every foreseeable risk. He can, of course, foresee the possibility of many risks, but life would be almost impossible if he were to attempt to take precautions against every risk which he can foresee. He takes precautions against risks which are reasonably likely to happen.'

In this case it was judged that the cricket club had not breached its duty of care.

In order to prove that a defendant has breached their duty of care, as in other civil cases, the plaintiff must show enough evidence to prove the case on the balance of probabilities. In relation to negligence this involves showing that a defendant did not act in a reasonable way.

Evidence for breach of duty

It is not always easy to gather sufficient evidence of breach of duty. This is illustrated by the fact that cases involving damages to unborn children resulting from the drug thalidomide were never taken to court. The reasons for this included lack of clarity of whether a duty of care could be allowed to an unborn child (this situation has now changed), and also because it was unlikely that the plaintiffs would be able to show that reasonable care had not been taken: the new drug had been extensively tested. In the event compensation was agreed on out of court.

Resulting damage: causation and remoteness

So far we have examined the legal duty of care and breach of that duty. The third ingredient of liability in cases of negligence is whether the breach of duty resulted in foreseeable loss or damage. This involves two issues:

♦ causation
♦ remoteness of damage.

Causation

The plaintiff needs to be able to show that it was the defendant's actions that caused the loss. It is thus a matter of proving a link between cause and effect. In many cases it is easy to prove this cause–effect link, as for example in Walton v British Leyland Ltd (1978) it was shown that the effect of a defect in wheel bearings was that accidents would occur.

CASE STUDY

In Barnett v Chelsea and Kensington Hospital Management Committee (1969) the plaintiff's husband called in at the hospital early in the morning complaining of a stomach ache and vomiting. The hospital sent the patient home telling him to visit his doctor later that day. The patient was suffering from arsenic poisoning and died later in the day.

ACTIVITY

1 What do you think the court's verdict would have been?

2 Had the hospital maintained its duty of care? Was the hospital negligent?

Remoteness of damage

If a plaintiff can prove breach of care then they may be able to claim damages provided the injuries sustained are not too remote from the cause of the breach. Some damage resulting from breach of care may be deemed to be too remote to warrant compensation.

The defendant will only be expected to pay for the damage which is of a kind that the reasonable man should have foreseen. Liability is thus not limited by the extent of the loss. This ruling comes from an Australian case, *The Wagon Mound* (1961). In this case the defendants spilt oil on to seawater. Sparks from welding which was taking place nearby set the oil on fire destroying the plaintiff's wharf. Clearly the defendant had caused the spillage but the sort of damages that resulted could not reasonably have been foreseen.

In contrast, if it can be shown that the type of injury a plaintiff suffers had been foreseeable then the defendant can be liable for all the injury of that type which results.

Defence against liability in negligence

There are a number of defences that can be put forward in a negligence case.

Contributory negligence

In contributory negligence the defendant contributed to their own injury by negligence on their part. The damages received by the plaintiff are likely to be reduced in proportion to the contribution that they make to the negligence. For example, in Froome v Butcher (1976) it was held that failing to wear a seat belt contributed to the negligence and that an appropriate reduction in damages was 25 per cent if the seat belt would have prevented the injury completely, and 15 per cent if it would have reduced the extent of the injury.

Volenti non fit injuria

This means that the plaintiff had voluntarily taken responsibility for the risk of their own injury. For example, in Cutler *v* United Dairies, the plaintiff stopped a runaway horse in a field that posed no danger to anyone. He was injured in the process. Because he was deemed to have voluntarily engaged in the action he could not claim compensation.

Late claim

This defence is that the plaintiff's claim has been made too late, that is, outside of the normal time period for making a claim.

Students claim for damages

JOURNAL ARTICLE

This article followed widespread public interest concerning claims that the examination boards had been encouraged by the Qualifications and Curriculum Authority to lower some of the marks given to A-level candidates in some subjects to counteract 'grade inflation'.

It is possible that some of the individuals concerned could take their cases to the courts basing their claims on contract law and the tort of negligence.

A starting point is Donoghue *v* Stevenson. Clearly exam boards owe a duty of care to candidates given the close relationship between a candidate and the exam board coupled with the evidence provided by upgrading.

The exam board is an obvious choice for the role of defendant. However the boards may claim that their actions were determined by the Qualifications and Curriculum Authority whose code of practice gave unclear guidance to the boards.

Claimants will then have to go on to prove foreseeable damage and by far the most straightforward claim will be that of the student who can demonstrate that, as a result of the award of an erroneously low grade, he has failed to get into his first choice university, has had to take a gap year whilst waiting for the mess to be sorted out, and has therefore lost a year's earnings as a result. If he can demonstrate any other disadvantage in the job market – for example, an unusual shortage of job vacancies in graduation year – so much the better.

In terms of contract law the first issue which arises is whether the aggrieved student has a right to sue at all. It is relatively rare for students to enter into a direct contract with the exam board: examination entries are usually made by the school or college concerned, with fees being borne either by the school or the candidates' parents or guardians. However, candidates will now almost certainly be able to take advantage of the Contracts (Right of Third Parties) Act 1999 which provides that a person who is not a party of a contract may enforce it in his own right if the relevant contract term purports to confer a benefit on him.

Wright, E. A. 'A-level regrading claims', *New Law Journal*, 2002, 1 November, Vol. 152, No. 7054, pp 161–64.

ACTIVITY

Discuss the following questions in your group.

1 Why might candidates wrongly graded make a claim for compensation?

2 How is the Donoghue *v* Stevenson case relevant in this instance?

3 How could the exam boards claim that they are not liable in this case?

4 Do aggrieved candidates have a right to sue?

Harassment outside the workplace JOURNAL ARTICLE

This article provides an overview of an employer's (and employees') potential liability for sexual and racial harassment arising out of behaviour which occurs away from the work environment.

In general the employer has a duty to protect its employees from harassment on grounds of sex and race and may be vicariously liable unless the employer is able to demonstrate that reasonable and practicable steps have been taken to prevent harassment.

An employer will be vicariously liable for the acts of employees done in the course of their employment irrespective of whether the employer knew or approved of the offending conduct.

Sexual harassment is defined as 'words or conduct which are unwelcome to the recipient and which undermine the victim's dignity at work (Reed v Steadman, 1999)'. Moreover, it is for the recipient to decide what is acceptable words or conduct or what is unwelcome or offensive. The same applies to racial harassment.

The term 'in the course of employment' has been expanded by the courts in relation to statutory rights of individuals not to be discriminated against in terms of sex or race. For example, in the case of Chief Constable of Lincolnshire Police v Stubbs (1999), Deborah Stubbs was a police officer seconded to the Regional Crime Squad. She complained of two incidents of inappropriate sexual behaviour to an employment tribunal.

In the first incident she attended a pub where she met other police officers, including the officer complained of. On this occasion in full public view he conducted himself as if he was in a relationship with her.

In the second incident she was leaving a party with her partner when the officer complained of made an extremely offensive sexual remark.

The tribunal set out that acting in the 'course of employment' could be applied to situations even though they are a social event. However, it excluded purely social functions, or where an incident took place after work hours, and in chance meetings.

An employer may resist a harassment claim if it can be demonstrated that the employer 'took such steps as were reasonably practicable to prevent' the harassment 'or from doing, in the course of his employment acts of that description'.

The article concluded by saying that employers should ensure that they implement appropriate harassment policies, which should provide examples of the type of conduct that is prohibited and every employee's right to be treated with dignity at work. It is sensible to reiterate and to stress this information in the run up to office-related events.

Tyme, D. 'Fancy a drink after work? Can an employer be liable for sex and racial harassment outside the workplace?', *New Law Journal*, 2003, 7 February, Vol. 153, No. 7066, pp 157–62.

ACTIVITY

Discuss the following questions in your group.

1 How is vicarious liability relevant to the discussion above?

2 Why was the defendant in the case the Chief Constable of Lincolnshire rather than the officer concerned with the harassment case?

3 What is the duty of care relevant to this case?

4 How does the case involve an extension of the concept of 'in the course of employment'?

5 Are you in favour of this wider view of 'in the course of employment'?

Legal liability of the fire service

JOURNAL ARTICLE

This article was written against the background of the firefighters' dispute. It asks whether we have a legal right to be protected from fire, so that the fire service would be liable for damages for failure to put out fires effectively.

'Twenty-nine people died during the two national firefighters' strikes. What is the legal liability of the fire service? Should litigation take place?'

The traditional position of firefighters and their employers was set out in Capital & Counties PLC *v* Hampshire CC (1997).

'The fire brigade are not under a common law duty to answer the call for help, and are not under a duty of care to do so. If therefore they fail to turn up, or fail to turn up on time, because they have carelessly misunderstood the message, got lost on the way or run into a tree, they are not liable'.

In addition they are not liable if they turn up and incompetently or apathetically fail to improve the situation.

However, this judgement has been thrown out by the Court of Appeal in the decision Kent *v* Griffiths (2000). In that case it was stated that the ambulance service does owe a legal duty to take care in answering emergency calls, so long as they have been accepted.

Hickman, T. 'Watching Britain burn, can we demand protection from fire?' *New Law Journal*, 2002, 6 December, Vol. 152, No. 7059, pp 1863–5.

ACTIVITY

Discuss the following questions in your group.

1   What do you understand by the term 'duty of care'?

2   How does the 'duty of care' vary between different employees?

3   What do you see as being a reasonable 'duty of care' for firefighters and ambulance workers?

4   How does this affect the right to strike of these groups?

End of unit assignment

Completing the assignment will show that you can successfully meet the outcomes for this unit.

Outcome 1

Understand the essential elements of a valid and legally binding contract and its role in a business context

1   Explain the different types of business agreement and the importance of the key elements required for the formation of a valid contract. (You will need briefly to explain different types of business agreement, and by reference to a specific contract, for example for the sale of goods, be able to exemplify what the essential elements are.)

2   Apply the rules of offer and acceptance in a given scenario, also considering any impact of new technology. (Examine a specific business transaction, for example the offer to sell, order and subsequent payment for goods, to highlight the nature of offer and acceptance. Briefly explain how new technologies are involved in such transactions, for example e-tailing and the implications for offer and acceptance.)

3   Assess the importance of the rules of intention and consideration of the parties to the agreement. (Use the same scenario as in No. 2 to outline these aspects in practice.)

4   Explain the importance of the contracting parties having the appropriate legal capacity to enter into a binding agreement. (For example, you could explore the implications of minors making purchases that they do not need over the Internet, and difficulties arising when individuals are not of sound mind who enter into contractual arrangements.)

Outcome 2

Analyse the significance of specific terms in a business contract

1   Analyse specific contract terms with reference to their importance and impact if these terms are broken. (Examine a specific contract between two companies, identifying key terms, and potential problems when these terms are broken. A useful starting point is to examine an issue in the press where one firm is seeking legal redress from another for failure to meet contract terms.)

2   Apply and analyse the law on standard form contracts. (Examine a standard form contract involving consumer credit to outline key aspects of standard form contracts.)

3   Discuss the effect of exclusion clauses in attempting to exclude contractual liability. (Try to identify the exclusion clauses in a specific standard form contract for consumer credit. Discuss the validity of these clauses.)

Outcome 3

Examine the role of the law of tort in business activities, assessing particular form of tortious liability

1   Describe the nature of general tortious liability, comparing and contrasting to contractual liability. (Give a broad description of these two types of liability, picking out key points of difference.)

2   Explain the liability applicable to an occupier of premises. (Interview an owner of a business premises to identify the extent to which they are familiar with their liability. Briefly outline relevant liability.)

3   Discuss the nature of an employer's liability with reference to vicarious liability and health and safety implications. (Explain what is meant by vicarious liability in the context of employer's liability and health and safety.)

4   Distinguish strict liability from general tortious liability. (Give an example which highlights the difference.)

Outcome 4

Understand and apply the elements of the tort of negligence.

1   Explain and understand the application of the elements of the tort of negligence. (Give a brief summary of the tort of negligence and how this can be applied in business cases.)

2   Analyse the practical applications of particular elements of the tort of negligence. (Take a recent example of a case that has appeared in the newspapers relating to the tort of negligence – outline how the aspects of this tort have been applied in this specific case.)

Further reading

Atiyah, P. S. (1995) *Introduction to the Law of Contract*, Oxford: Clarendon Press.

Beale, H., Bishop, W. and Furmston, M. (2001) *Contract: Cases and Materials*, Oxford: Butterworth.

Cheshire, G., Fitfoot, C. and Furmston, M. (2001) *Law of Contract*, Oxford: Butterworth.

Cooke, J. (1997) *Law of Tort*, London: Prentice Hall.

Dransfield, R. (2003) *Business Law Made Easy*, Cheltenham: Nelson Thornes.

Elliott, C. and Quinn, F. (2002) *Contract Law*, London: Longman.

Elliot, C. and Quinn, F. (1997) *Tort Law*, London: Longman.

Harvey, B. and Marston, J. (1998) *Cases and Commentary on Tort*, London: Prentice Hall.

Hodgson, J. and Lewthwaite, J. (2001) *Law of Torts*, London: Blackstone.

Jones, M. (2002) *Textbook on Torts*, Oxford: Oxford University Press.

Pannett, A. (1997) *Law of Torts*, London: Prentice Hall.

Treitel, G. (2003) *Law of Contract*, London: Sweet and Maxwell.

Young, M. (1997) *Cases and Commentary in Contract Law*, London: Prentice Hall.

Journals

New Law Journal

Law Society Gazette

Index